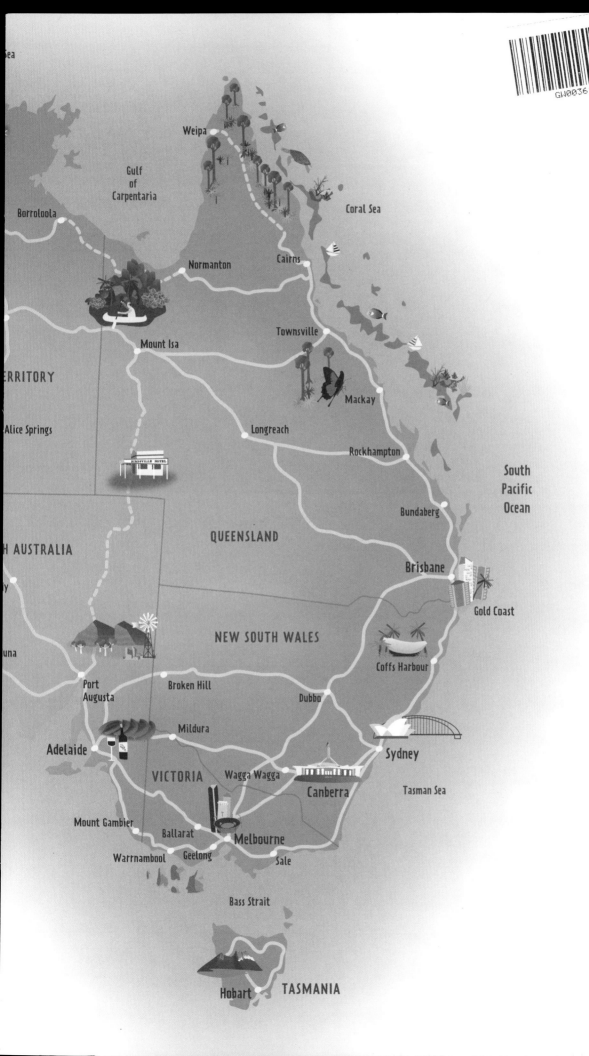

Amanda

Happy 40th !

with love from
Garry, Fliss, Shirley, Nick,
Conrad, Graham, Angie,
Brad + Annette

x x x x x x x x x

EXPLORE
AUSTRALIA

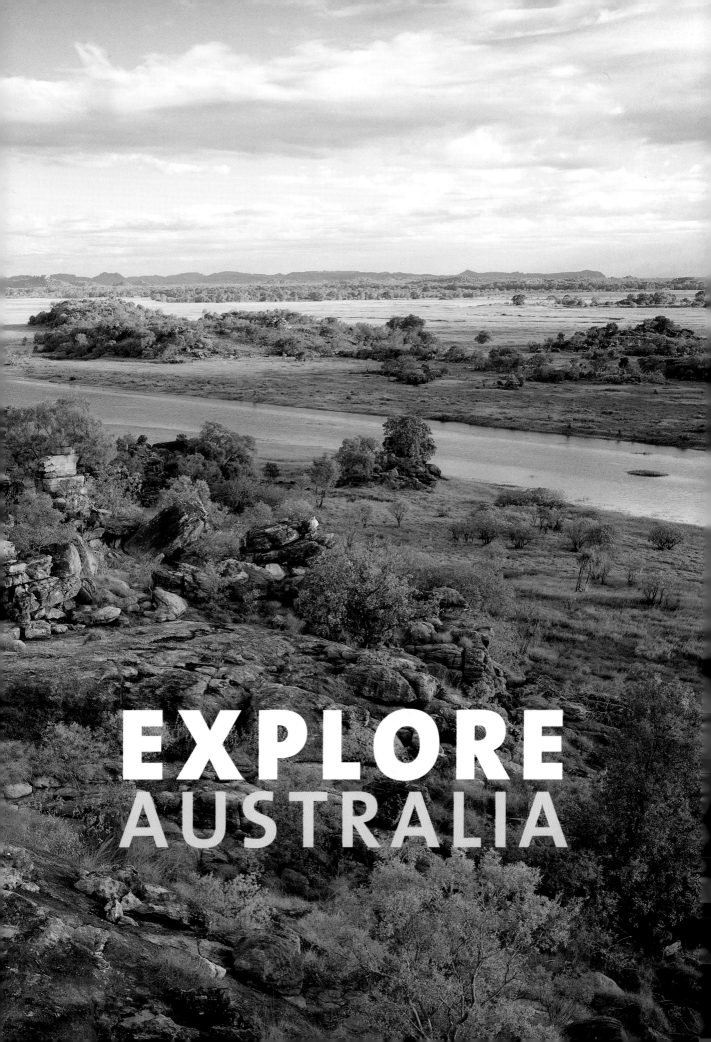

EXPLORE
AUSTRALIA

CONTENTS

JOURNEY THROUGH AUSTRALIA

Australia is a small, modern nation in a vast, ancient land. Covering an area the size of Europe, Australia is the world's largest island continent. It is also the oldest, flattest and – with the exception of Antarctica – the driest place on earth.

For about 70 000 years the continent was the preserve of around 600 groups of Aboriginal people. Theirs was the longest continuous occupation in human history. The British settled the east coast in 1788. Over the past two hundred years their colonial prison outpost has been transformed into a nation of 20 million people.

FACT FILE

Total land area 7 692 030 sq km
Length of coastline including islands 59 736 km
Number of islands 8222
Number of beaches 7000
Longest river Murray River (2520 km)
Highest mountain Mt Kosciuszko (2228 m)
Largest lake Lake Eyre (9500 sq km)
Hottest town Marble Bar, Western Australia (average summer maximum 41°C)
Coldest place Liawenee, Tasmania (average winter minimum -1.5°C)
Wettest place Tully, Queensland (average rainfall 4300 mm per year)
Population 20 008 700
Indigenous population 458 500
Population born overseas 21 percent
Population residing in capital cities 64 percent

INDIGENOUS AUSTRALIA

Australia's indigenous people have the longest continuous history of any people in the world – between 50 000 and 70 000 years. There are two racially distinct groups: the Aboriginal people, who occupied the mainland and Tasmania, and the Torres Strait Islanders, from the islands off the tip of Cape York. At the time of white settlement the estimated 300 000 Aboriginal people comprised around 600 distinct societies. Today the history of our indigenous people is central to any understanding of what we are as a nation. Increasingly, Aboriginal tourism is the most tangible bridge between Australian indigenous culture and the non-indigenous culture of locals and overseas visitors. Experiences of indigenous culture might include a bush-tucker tour, travelling to a rock-art site, attendance at a dance performance or a visit to a cultural centre.

◄ TROPICAL NORTH QUEENSLAND
The distinctive art of the East Cape peoples in tropical north Queensland survives in the spectacular rock-art galleries near Laura. Near Cairns is the Tjapukai Aboriginal Cultural Park, an excellent centre featuring performance, demonstrations and art. There are flights from Cairns to the Torres Strait Islands; the best time to visit is July for the Coming of the Light Festival. *See also Cairns & The Tropics p. 391 and Cape York p. 392.*

KAKADU, NT ▶
The name Kakadu is derived from Gagudju, one of the three traditional owners and now managers of this World Heritage area. The area – one of the most intensely populated before white settlement – has over 5000 rock-art sites, the largest collection in the world. There are numerous ways to explore the magnificent Aboriginal heritage of this area: start at the Bowali Visitor Centre, with its many historic displays and general tour information. *See also Kakadu & Arnhem Land p. 344.*

Tasmania's Aboriginal people

Tasmania's indigenous population, known as Palawa, migrated to the island about 35 000 years ago. On the eve of white settlement their population of over 4000 was divided between nine groups. White settlers drove the Palawa from their hunting grounds by use of violence and the spread of disease. The Black War, as it became known, culminated in the 1830s with the colonial government rounding up the 160 remaining survivors and banishing them to Flinders Island (see Bass Strait Islands p. 459). Many of Tasmania's traditional sites, from middens to rock art, lie in protected areas and are not easily accessible. The rich repository of sites in the Tasmanian wilderness played a significant part in the area's World Heritage listing. Kutikina Cave, with evidence of 20 000 years of occupation, can be reached via a rafting tour of the Franklin River.

▼ THE OUTBACK, NSW

Lake Mungo is Australia's most significant archaeological site. Burial sites, cooking hearths and campfires, preserved in lunar-like dunes, provide evidence of a period of human occupation dating back to at least 40 000 years. Cultural tours operate from Mildura. Superb rock art is to be found at Mount Grenfell Historic Site (near Cobar), home of the Ngiyambaa, and in Mutawintji National Park, Wiljali country, where the traditional owners conduct regular tours of some of the sites. See also Outback p. 51.

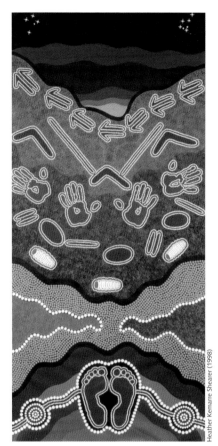

Heather Kemarre Shearer (1998)

▲ ADELAIDE, SA

Adelaide is home to two major centres dealing with Aboriginal culture. The Aboriginal-owned-and-operated Tandanya houses a permanent collection of art, hosts contemporary art exhibitions and stages performance events. The South Australian Museum is home to the largest collection of Aboriginal cultural materials in the world. These items are presented in a series of sensitive and provocative displays in the Aboriginal Cultures Gallery. See also Adelaide p. 208.

◄ RED CENTRE, NT

The World Heritage Uluru–Kata Tjuta National Park is the traditional land of the Anangu, who co-manage tours to art sites and other places of cultural and spiritual significance. To the north, in Alice Springs, which is Arrernte country, are a number of galleries and centres including the award-winning Aboriginal Australia Art and Cultural Centre. See also Red Centre p. 348.

TIMELINE

70 000–50 000 BC The first indigenous people cross from Indonesia to the New Guinea–Australia landmass

35 000 BC Aboriginal people reach Tasmania

10 000 BC Rising sea levels after the last Ice Age isolate Aboriginal people in Australia from Asia, and those in Tasmania from the mainland

6000 BC Distinct tribes and clans occupy the entire continent; economies adapt to different environments; religious beliefs and oral traditions derived from the Dreamtime indicate complex social organisation; extensive rock art appears

1770 The Tharawal of the Botany Bay region make contact with Captain Cook

1778 The Eora are displaced by the establishment of a penal colony at Sydney Cove

1789 A smallpox epidemic kills about half the Aboriginal population living in the vicinity of Sydney's penal colony

1838 Twelve white people massacre 28 Aboriginal people at Myall Creek. While the early 1800s are heavy with the blood of many Aboriginal people, this is the first massacre for which the perpetrators are punished by law and are hanged.

1876 Truganini, the last tribal-born Tasmanian Aboriginal, dies

1860–1900 Protection boards are established across Australia; most Aboriginal people are living on missions or government reserves

1901 The Commonwealth constitution does not allow federal parliament to legislate for Aboriginal people to be counted in the census

1910 Legislation in New South Wales increases government powers to remove Aboriginal children from their parents; similar provisions are enacted in other states

1967 In a referendum, Australians vote with a 90 percent majority to count Aboriginal people in the census

1971 Neville Bonner, the first Aboriginal parliamentarian, is elected to the senate

1972 Aboriginal people erect a tent embassy outside Parliament House, Canberra, marking a new era of political activism

1992 In a decision known as Mabo, the High Court rejects the notion of terra nullius ('land belonging to no one') and affirms that Aboriginal people were in possession of the land before 1788

1996 In the Wik case, the High Court holds that pastoral leases granted by the Queensland Government do not extinguish native title

1997 Bringing Them Home, the report of a government inquiry into the Stolen Generation, is tabled in federal parliament. The Howard government refuses to make a formal apology but the spirit of reconciliation is embraced by many Australians

...INDERS RANGES, SA

...e ancient hills are home to the Adnyamathanha – ...ing 'hills people', a collective term for a number ...guage groups. Highlights of this culturally rich ...piritually significant area include the Yourambulla ...s, where there are rock shelters with charcoal ...ngs and ochre paintings. A number of sites ...und the stunning visual centrepiece of Wilpena ...d ('Wilpena' derives from an Adnyamathanha ...meaning 'cupped hands' or 'bent fingers'). ...lso Flinders Ranges & Outback p. 228.

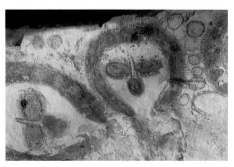

◄ THE KIMBERLEY, WA

At least 50 percent of the total Kimberley population is Aboriginal. This remote area has one of the country's most important collections of rock art, of which there are two main types: the Bradshaw and the more recent Wandjina. Tours of rock-art sites are available from some of the big stations in the area, and a variety of cultural tours operate from the region's community and cultural centres. See also Kimberley p. 290.

NEW ARRIVALS

Since the arrival of the First Fleet in 1788, the pace of
development in Australia has been rapid and far-reaching.
While not all our colonial heritage has been preserved, what does
remain offers a substantial interpretation of the unique and often
remarkable events of Australian history. Convict settlements tell
the story of the grim and unpromising early years; isolated
townships provide evidence of courageous attempts to tame
a harsh environment; and ornate Victorian architecture boasts
of some of the greatest gold rushes in history. A new appreciation
of this unique heritage has resulted in the restoration of many
historic sites over the past couple of decades, with locations now
popular with a large number of visitors.

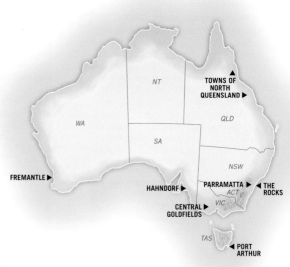

▲ THE ROCKS, NSW
The Rocks marks the site of the first European
settlement in Australia and is probably the
country's most intact historic precinct. A mix
of early buildings – bond stores, churches, pubs,
low-slung cottages and wharves – is crowded
across the peninsula at the heart of Sydney's CBD.
See also Sydney p. 20.

HAHNDORF, SA ▶
This charming village was settled in the 1830s by
Australia's first significant non-British immigrant
group – German Lutheran peasants fleeing
religious persecution. Today much of their culture
is preserved through buildings, produce shops,
restaurants and festivals. The nearby Barossa
Valley, Australia's most famous wine region, was
also established by German settlers. *See also
Adelaide Hills p. 222.*

PORT ARTHUR, TAS ▶
There is no other site in the world like Port
Arthur. Built in the early 1800s by convicts
as a prison for convicts, it is our most graphic
reminder of why and how modern Australia
came into being. The site comprises a clutch
of sandstone buildings – a penitentiary, hospital,
asylum and church among them – set along the
dramatic coast of the Tasman Peninsula. *See
also South-East p. 454.*

▲ FREMANTLE, WA
Fremantle is one of the world's best-preserved 19th-century ports and serves as a fascinating reminder of the significance of the sea in an island nation. Established in 1829, Fremantle contains a range of buildings that includes public offices, warehouses, shipping-company headquarters, shopfronts and houses, many now open to the public as museums and galleries. *See also Perth p. 266.*

▼ PARRAMATTA, NSW
Now an outer suburb of Sydney, Parramatta was originally preferred over Sydney Harbour by European settlers and officials, not least because of its proximity to farmland and distance from the convict population. Parramatta preserves important fragments of the earliest colonial years, including the country's oldest buildings – Elizabeth Farm, home to pastoralists John and Elizabeth Macarthur, and the first Government House. Both are open to the public. *See also Sydney p. 20.*

▲ CENTRAL GOLDFIELDS, VIC
Many areas in Australia experienced a gold rush in the second half of the 19th century, but nowhere were the yields as great and the effects as dramatic as in Victoria. The legacy is a series of towns – particularly Ballarat and Bendigo – boasting significant concentrations of rural Victorian-era architecture. Less conspicuous but also significant are the sites marking the history of the Chinese in Australia. *See also Goldfields p. 150.*

TIMELINE

1606 *The Duyfken, a Dutch ship, explores the western coast of Cape York Peninsula*

1616 *Dirk Hartog on the Eendracht lands on an island off the Western Australian coast*

1770 *James Cook takes possession of the east coast of New Holland for the British Crown*

1788 *The First Fleet establishes a British penal colony at Botany Bay*

1803 *Matthew Flinders completes the first circumnavigation of Australia and establishes it as a continent*

1803 *A British settlement is established on the River Derwent in Van Diemen's Land*

1813 *Wentworth, Blaxland and Lawson find a path across the Blue Mountains*

1824 *The Moreton Bay Penal Settlement is established near what will become Brisbane*

1829 *Western Australia is founded by British emigrants*

1835 *John Batman 'buys' the site of Melbourne from the Kulin people*

1836 *South Australia is proclaimed a British colony*

1840 *The British Government abolishes convict transportation to New South Wales after more than 84 000 convicts have arrived*

1851 *Gold is discovered in New South Wales and Victoria*

1901 *The six Australian colonies federate to form the Commonwealth of Australia*

1908 *Land known as Canberra, at the foothills of the Australian Alps, is chosen as the site of the national capital*

1914–18 *World War I: Australia fights against Germany with the loss of almost 62 000 Australian lives*

1929 *The Great Depression, triggered by the Wall Street crash, spreads to Australia*

1939–45 *World War II: Australia fights in Europe, Asia and the Pacific, with the loss of more than 39 000 Australian lives*

1966 *The government begins dismantling restrictive immigration legislation known as the 'White Australia' policy*

1988 *Australia celebrates 200 years of European settlement*

◄ TOWNS OF NORTH QUEENSLAND
Early settlement in the remote towns of Cooktown, Townsville, Charters Towers and Ravenswood was underpinned by the Australian themes of isolation, hardship and adaptation. Settled for a variety of reasons – to service farming communities or the gold rush, or as ports – they preserve significant recollections of the 19th century. Of particular interest is the architecture, including the grand facades and cool interiors of Charters Towers. *See also The Mid-Tropics p. 390 and Cairns & The Tropics p. 391.*

LIVEABLE CITIES

Although Australia is famed for its natural environment, most of its residents live in cities and large towns. The eight capital cities of the states and territories vary sharply in size and character. Much of this has to do with the considerable distances that separate them, and the geographical conditions and historical circumstances that formed them. Some of the similarities come from a shared sense of what constitutes the good life and – hand-in-hand with this – a willingness to take of and embrace the superb natural landscapes that surround them.

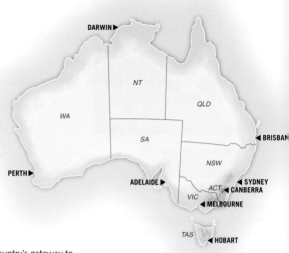

◀ SYDNEY, NSW

Australia's oldest and largest city is the country's gateway to the world. It is loud, lively and bustling with a cosmopolitan mix of people. Set around the incomparable Sydney Harbour, bordered by bushland on three sides and the surf beaches of the Pacific on the fourth, it combines the excitement and facilities of an international city with the best of what the nation is so well known for – lifestyle. *See also Sydney p. 20.*

▼ HOBART, TAS

The sea and a sense of history dominate Hobart. Australia's second oldest city and the capital of the only island state, it preserves an intimate relationship with things maritime. Situated on the banks of the Derwent estuary and in the shadow of the frequently snow-covered Mt Wellington, the city has a pronounced European feel, although the rugged wilderness of the surrounding landscape marks it as distinctly Australian. *See also Hobart p. 442.*

▲ CANBERRA, ACT

The national capital is also the country's most unusual city. Brought into being by an act of parliament, and fully planned around its inland location at the foothills of the Australian Alps, it lacks the urban intensity, history and coastal flavour of the other cities. Yet Canberra makes up for this with a sense of restrained elegance, apparent in its wide boulevards, lakeside public buildings and extensive parklands. *See also Canberra p. 112.*

7

◄ ADELAIDE, SA

This charming, boutique-sized city, with its elegant 19th-century stone buildings, well-planned streets and squares, formal parklands and a European sense of scale, sits within reach of a remote and arid wilderness while enjoying a softer immediate setting of hills, plains and beaches. The city boasts world-class festivals, excellent art and museum collections and an appreciation of top-quality food and wine. *See also Adelaide p. 208.*

▼ MELBOURNE, VIC

Southerly Melbourne with its unpredictable weather is the centre of style and substance. It is the birthplace of Australian art and literature and continues to foster the arts through its institutions and festivals. Melbourne boasts fine contemporary buildings, side by side with Victorian-era architecture that is second to none. It is the country's most educated, cosmopolitan and liberal city and its role as Australia's sporting capital is uncontested. *See also Melbourne p. 126.*

▲ PERTH, WA

This western outpost is closer to the cities of Asia than it is to Australia's population base on the eastern seaboard. Isolated from the mainstream, Perth, along with its home state, has earned itself a reputation for being aggressively individualist and forward-thinking. Perth is a big, bright and overwhelmingly modern city, and its considerable natural advantages include its unique Indian Ocean frontage, the Swan River, which cuts a course through the city, and a Mediterranean-style climate. *See also Perth p. 266.*

▼ DARWIN, NT

Darwin, small and remote, remains a town of the frontier – robust, good humoured and eclectic. It is populated by indigenous Australians who have occupied the region for around 70 000 years; people of European descent (including visitors who have never left); southerners on secondment; and a large number of immigrants from nearby Asian countries. Theirs is a paradise set against a backdrop of the Wet and Dry climate pattern, extreme tides and riotous tropical vegetation. *See also Darwin p. 334.*

CITY FACT FILE

ADELAIDE
Population 1 096 102
Date founded 1836
Signature attraction South Australian Museum
Top event Adelaide Festival of Arts

BRISBANE
Population 1 626 865
Date founded 1825
Signature attraction South Bank
Top event The Ekka (Royal Queensland Show)

CANBERRA
Population 310 521
Date founded 1908
Signature attraction Parliament House
Top event Floriade

DARWIN
Population 90 001
Date founded 1839
Signature attraction Mindil Beach Sunset Markets
Top event Darwin Beer Can Regatta

HOBART
Population 194 228
Date founded 1803
Signature attraction Historic waterfront
Top event Ten Days on the Island

MELBOURNE
Population 3 466 025
Date founded 1835
Signature attraction Federation Square
Top event Melbourne Cup

PERTH
Population 1 381 127
Date founded 1829
Signature attraction Kings Park
Top event Perth International Arts Festival

SYDNEY
Population 4 085 578
Date founded 1788
Signature attraction Sydney Harbour
Top event Gay and Lesbian Mardi Gras

BRISBANE, QLD ▲

This metropolis of the subtropics, Australia's third largest centre, is a city of light. The lazy curves of the Brisbane River, the glass and metal of the modern office towers, the sandstone of the colonial buildings and the lush foliage of the extensive parklands radiate with the sunshine and warmth that soak the city in all seasons. Open-air markets are a way of life here, with the lively Riverside and Eagle Street Pier markets held every Sunday. Needless to say this is a relaxed place: business-like yes, motivated of course, but never willing to ignore the considerable pleasures of its natural environment. *See also Brisbane p. 364.*

NATURAL WONDERS

Australia is renowned for the beauty and diversity of its natural environment. As well as the vast tracts of desert that one would expect in the earth's oldest, driest and flattest continent, it is a place of lush forests, wild rivers, ancient mountains, dramatic alpine peaks, glacial lakes and a magnificent coastline. Two sites, the stunning Great Barrier Reef and the massive monolith of Uluru – both among the most recognised natural features in the world – have contributed greatly to the development of Australia as a major nature-travel destination. Other places, like the remote wilds of Tasmania and the vast expanse of the Kimberley, are valued for their lonely beauty and remarkably unspoiled condition.

▼ AUSTRALIAN ALPS, NSW & VIC

Few people realise that Australia has an alpine area more extensive than the snowfields of Austria and Switzerland combined. Straddling the Great Dividing Range, the Alps are preserved in a series of connecting national parks. A landscape of glacial lakes, mighty rivers and rugged peaks make this one of the world's most spectacular alpine regions. *See also Snowy Mountains p. 48 and High Country p. 156.*

▲ THE DAINTREE, QLD

Part of the Wet Tropics World Heritage Area, the Daintree is popular place for exploring the dense and tangled primeval forests of tropical north Queensland. Phenomenally diverse and spectacularly beautiful, the forests are home to some of the world's most ancient plant species, as well as some of Australia's most brilliant birds and butterflies. *See also Cairns & The Tropics p. 391.*

◄ TWELVE APOSTLES, VIC

These massive limestone obelisks were once part of the cliff-line, but have since become stranded under the constant pressure of sea and wind erosion. Surrounded by swirling waves, and capturing the ever-changing coastal light, the Twelve Apostles are regarded as one of Australia's great scenic experiences. *See also South-West Coast p. 148.*

▲ BUNGLE BUNGLE RANGE, WA

These striped, weathered mounds within Purnululu National Park rise up out of the remote plains of the Kimberley. They were created 350 million years ago and contain sedimentary layers said to be 1600 million years old. Palm-lined gorges and clear pools intersect the ancient domes. Access to the area is by four-wheel drive or scenic flight. *See also Kimberley p. 290.*

The continent up close

The Australian landscape dates back 290 million years to a time when the continent was submerged under a huge ice cap. Since then, the deep valleys and high mountains of a glaciated environment have been eroded away to a fairly uniform flatness (with some exceptions spectacular for their shape – the Bungle Bungles and Uluru among them). The loss of high mountains brought a gradual increase in aridity. The formation of rain clouds slowed and vast tracts of desert began to appear where lush forests had once stood. Today approximately 80 percent of the continent is arid. The figure would probably be more than this except for a dramatic geological episode 80 million years ago – the upthrust of the Great Dividing Range. This feature, stretching from north to south on the east of the continent, is where Australia's tallest peaks, grandest forests and most significant rivers are found.

◄ TASMANIAN WILDERNESS
Covering nearly 20 percent of the
total area of the island, the Tasmanian
wilderness is one of only three temperate
wildernesses remaining in the Southern
Hemisphere. It encompasses Australia's
longest caves, ancient rocks, remote wild
rivers, some of the world's oldest trees,
and the stunning glaciated landscape of
Cradle Mountain–Lake St Clair. *See also
South-West Wilderness p. 456 and North-
West p. 457.*

▲ GREAT BARRIER REEF, QLD
The world's largest reef is an enduring symbol
of the rarity and beauty of Australia's natural
environment. Stretching for 2000 km along the
coast of Queensland, this maze of coral reefs
and cays supports an astonishing diversity of
life, from 1500 species of fish to sea mammals,
turtles, sea grasses and molluscs. Brilliant colours,
forms and textures have made this underwater
landscape one of the world's great diving
destinations. *See also Great Barrier Reef p. 385.*

◄ ULURU–KATA TJUTA, NT
These rock formations sit above an
otherwise flat desert plain at the
geographic heart of the continent. Uluru,
with a height of 348 m and a base
circumference of 9.4 km, is the largest
monolith in the world. Neighbouring Kata
Tjuta comprises 36 steep-sided domes
that are possibly the eroded remains of
a monolith many times the size of Uluru.
See also Red Centre p. 348.

World Heritage sites

**1 Australian Fossil Mammal Sites
(Naracoorte & Riversleigh)**
Two sites that have yielded 20 million-year-old
fossils of extinct Australian species. *See also
South-East p. 227 and Savannah Gulf p. 393.*

**2 Central Eastern Rainforest Reserves
of Australia**
Large discontinuous patches of subtropical,
warm temperate and Antarctic beech cool
temperate rainforest. *See also Holiday Coast
p. 42, Tropical North Coast p. 43, New England
p. 44 and Gold Coast & Hinterland p. 380.*

3 Fraser Island
World's largest sand island, with a complex dune
system, freshwater dune lakes and rainforest.
See also Fraser Island & Coast p. 384.

4 Great Barrier Reef
World's largest reef, with the most diverse reef
fauna. *See also Great Barrier Reef p. 385.*

5 Greater Blue Mountains Area
A deeply incised plateau with dramatic cliffs
and valleys and eucalypt forests. *See also
Blue Mountains p. 38 and Central Coast &
Hawkesbury p. 40.*

6 Heard and McDonald Islands
An active volcano (on Heard), glacial landscapes
and rare sub-Antarctic flora and fauna.

7 Kakadu National Park
Myriad natural environments and the world's
oldest, most extensive rock art. *See also Kakadu
& Arnhem Land p. 344.*

8 Lord Howe Island
Home to a wealth of flora and fauna, many
species unique to this remote volcanic island.
See also Lord Howe Island p. 52.

9 Macquarie Island
An island composed of oceanic crust and mantle
rocks, home to 850 000 penguin pairs.

10 Purnululu National Park
Beehive-shaped rock formations that speak of
20 million years of geological history. *See also
Kimberley p. 290.*

11 Shark Bay
Large population of sea mammals, and
3.5 billion-year-old stromatolites representing
the oldest life on earth. *See also Outback Coast
& Mid-West p. 288.*

12 Tasmanian Wilderness
Forest, rivers, caves, glacial lakes, and 40
Aboriginal sites pointing to at least 30 000 years'
occupation. *See also South-West Wilderness
p. 456 and North-West p. 457.*

13 Uluru–Kata Tjuta National Park
Massive rock formations in the desert, with
numerous Aboriginal sites. *See also Red Centre
p. 348.*

14 Wet Tropics of Queensland
Ancient rainforests containing an almost
complete evolutionary record of earth's plant life.
*See also The Mid-Tropics p. 390 and Cairns &
The Tropics p. 391.*

15 Willandra Lakes
Landscape of ancient lunettes, and site of
excavations that show an Aboriginal presence
dating back at least 40 000 years. *See also
Outback p. 51.*

MAGNIFICENT COASTLINE

The outback may be the place of Australian myth and legend, but most Australians choose to live – and holiday – within reach of a beach. The superb scenery of almost 60 000 kilometres of coastline, which takes in the country's hundreds of offshore islands, ranges from the sultry mangrove inlets of the far north to the white sweeping sands of the Indian Ocean coast and the rugged cliffs and legendary surf of the continent's south. Going to the beach in Australia can mean an afternoon of bodysurfing in the suburbs, a sojourn in a tropical resort, time out in a reclusive fishing community, a drive along dramatic cliff-tops, or an exploration of one of several coastal World Heritage areas of great beauty and environmental significance.

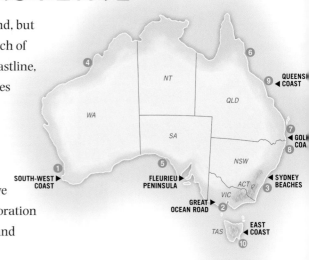

▲ GREAT OCEAN ROAD, VIC
Australia's most scenic coastal road links the many towns and attractions of this popular holiday region. The diverse attractions include breathtaking scenery, top surfing breaks and their attendant communities, thickly forested mountains, family beaches, restaurants to suit everyone, wildlife-watching and some remarkable historic maritime sites. *See also South-West Coast p. 148.*

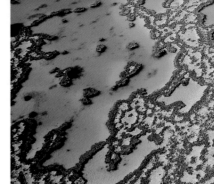

▲ SOUTH-WEST COAST, WA
This wild and rugged coastline stretches from Cape Naturaliste to Cape Leeuwin, where the Indian and Southern oceans meet. There are a couple of small holiday villages and the popular hinterland winegrowing area of Margaret River, but most of the coast – with its cliffs, limestone caves, sand dunes and forests – is untouched by development and preserved within Leeuwin–Naturaliste National Park. The area is renowned for its world-class surfing breaks. *See also The South-West p. 282.*

▲ GOLD COAST, QLD
Australia's largest and best-known resort is centred on an outstanding subtropical coastline featuring 35 beautiful beaches, great surf and year-round sunshine. Once a sleepy holiday backwater, the area is now a major urban centre offering everything from 18-hole golf to designer shopping, deep-sea fishing, fine dining and major theme parks. *See also Gold Coast & Hinterland p. 380.*

Coast safety

Swim between the flags on patrolled beaches; on unpatrolled beaches, take a walk and enjoy the scenery. Most beaches in popular areas, particularly near towns, are patrolled in the high season and some are patrolled year round. Surfers should always check conditions with locals before taking to the water, as should anglers. Between October and May the extremely dangerous box stinger inhabits the coastal waters of Queensland and other parts of northern Australia; beachgoers are advised not to enter the water during this period. Sharks are common in Australian waters and warnings should be heeded. In northern Australia saltwater crocodiles are found in the sea, estuaries and tidal rivers, and on land at the water's edge, and are extremely dangerous. Do not enter the water or remain at the water's edge in known crocodile areas and, if unsure, check with the locals.

◀ **EAST COAST, TAS**
One of Australia's most relaxed, old-fashioned and least hurried coastal regions, the east coast of Tasmania is a haven of tiny fishing villages, bushland, farmland and pristine beaches. Highlights include the history and scenic beauty of Maria Island, superb underwater scenery near Bicheno, and the magnificent Freycinet Peninsula. *See also East Coast p. 453.*

▲ **FLEURIEU PENINSULA, SA**
Just an hour or two from Adelaide, this is South Australia's premier coastal retreat. On the east and south coasts lie surf beaches, conservation parks and the busy resort town of Victor Harbor; on the west coast are the calm, blue waters of Gulf St Vincent, a string of pretty, low-key holiday villages and some stunning coastal scenery. Nudging the coast are some idyllic rural landscapes, incorporating one of Australia's top wine and food districts. *See also Fleurieu Peninsula p. 220.*

Top beaches

1 **The Basin beaches, Rottnest Island, WA**
On the island's north side, reef-protected beaches offer a safe haven for holidaying families. *See also Rottnest Island p. 280.*

2 **Bells Beach, Torquay, VIC**
Australia's top surfing destination and site of the legendary Rip Curl Pro each Easter. *See also South-West Coast p. 148.*

3 **Booderee National Park beaches, Jervis Bay, NSW**
A series of near-deserted beaches, surrounded by native bush and boasting what is claimed to be the whitest sand in the world. *See also South Coast p. 47.*

4 **Cable Beach, Broome, WA**
A luxurious sweep of white sand fronting turquoise waters, forming the scenic centrepiece of Australia's most remote and exotic resort town. *See also Kimberley p. 290.*

5 **Cactus Beach, Penong, SA**
The three famous surfing breaks of this remote destination are strictly for surfers with a frontier spirit and the skill to match. *See also Eyre Peninsula & Nullarbor p. 229.*

6 **Four Mile Beach, Port Douglas, QLD**
A beach so beautiful that it helped turn a sleepy seaside village into an international resort. *See also Cairns & The Tropics p. 391.*

7 **Noosa National Park beaches, QLD**
A subtropical wonderland of peaceful, pandanus-fringed coves providing a retreat from the bustling Sunshine Coast. *See also Sunshine Coast p. 383.*

8 **Watego Beach, Byron Bay, NSW**
Tune out and drop in at this popular north-facing surf beach in one of Australia's less conventional towns. *See also Tropical North Coast p. 43.*

9 **Whitehaven, Whitsunday Island, QLD**
A paradise, 7 km long, on a pristine, uninhabited island. *See also Great Barrier Reef p. 385.*

10 **Wineglass Bay, Freycinet Peninsula, TAS**
Bushland opens up to this magnificently sculpted, crescent-shaped beach. *See also East Coast p. 453.*

▲ **QUEENSLAND COAST**
The hundreds of beautiful islands that crowd the Queensland coast include the islands near Brisbane; the outstanding World Heritage-listed Fraser Island; and about 1000 Great Barrier Reef islands (of which 22 offer accommodation). There is an island to suit everyone's idea of a holiday in paradise, be it a lonely campsite beneath palm trees, a fishing, water-skiing and diving adventure, or a week by a pool with a book. *See also Brisbane Islands p. 379, Fraser Island & Coast p. 384 and Great Barrier Reef p. 385.*

SYDNEY BEACHES, NSW ▶
Sydney's surf beaches are the envy of many a metropolis. Flanking the city to the north and south, generous in length and width, and patrolled for most of the year, they provide an easy escape from the bustle of city life for thousands of residents and holiday-makers. The jewel in the crown is the world-famous Bondi – a cultural institution as much as a patch of sand and surf. *See also Sydney p. 20.*

WILD AUSTRALIA

Australia has some of the world's most distinctive plants and animals. Pouched mammals, prehistoric reptiles, majestic gums and brilliant desert flowers are just a sample of the country's many strange and beautiful living things. Around a quarter of overseas visitors rate the wildlife as a major attraction and at least a couple of our more famous creatures – kangaroos and koalas in particular – are regarded as national icons. Beyond the fascination of individual species, Australia offers a series of exceptionally well-preserved natural environments, from marine waters to deserts and rainforests, where animals and plants can be seen in their natural settings and as part of the complex communities to which they belong.

▼ SHARK BAY, WA

This World Heritage wonderland is best known for its bottlenose dolphins, which glide into the shallow waters of Monkey Mia and approach entranced visitors. Other highlights of this extraordinary area include the 230 bird species and a population of about 10 000 dugongs – the largest population in the world. *See also Outback Coast & Mid-West p. 288.*

▲ THE OUTBACK

Although referred to as the continent's 'dead heart', the vast areas of arid land at the centre of Australia support prolific and varied life including 2000 plant species and the highest concentration of reptiles in the world. Among its mammal species is the mighty red, the largest member of the kangaroo family with the male reaching two metres in height. *See also Outback p. 51, Flinders Ranges & Outback p. 228, Kimberley p. 290, Pilbara p. 289, Red Centre p. 348 and Outback p. 394.*

Isolation and evolution

For 50 million years Australia developed in isolation; the result is a unique set of plants and animals. Marsupials, represented by 180 species, are uncommon elsewhere. Likewise, the curious monotreme (an exclusive club with only platypuses and echidnas as members) is found nowhere else except New Guinea. When it comes to plants, only 15 percent of our 28 000 indigenous species are found beyond Australia's shores. Aridity and poor soil have brought about this uniqueness, with many species developing special characteristics to cope with harsh conditions. These adaptations have led to enormous biodiversity. Western Australia has 12 500 wildflower species, giving the state one of the world's richest floras, while the rainforests of the east coast are among the most biologically complex places on earth.

▲ KAKADU NATIONAL PARK, NT
This large World Heritage-listed park is one of Australia's most biologically diverse and prolific regions. Around 1600 plant species thrive in Kakadu, forming most of the native habitats of northern Australia. The wildlife is no less impressive and includes 280 bird species (one third of all Australian species), 123 reptile species and 52 freshwater fish species. *See also Kakadu & Arnhem Land p. 344.*

◀ PORT STEPHENS, NSW
One of the largest koala colonies in Australia is to be found in the wild here at Tilligerry Habitat. Probably the country's best known native animal, these short, tailless marsupials are usually inactive for 20 hours a day and feed mostly on eucalyptus leaves. The waters of Port Stephens are home to around 160 bottlenose dolphins and, in season, serve as a thoroughfare for migrating humpback whales. *See also Hunter Valley & Coast p. 41.*

▼ KANGAROO ISLAND, SA
Isolation from the mainland has helped Australia's third largest island maintain an unusual concentration of wildlife. Highlights include a large colony of Australian sea lions at Seal Bay, about 600 New Zealand fur seals at Cape du Couedic, 240 bird species and plenty of kangaroos, wallabies and possums as well as koalas and platypuses. *See also Kangaroo Island p. 221.*

◀ HERVEY BAY, QLD
Between July and November each year up to 400 humpback whales visit Hervey Bay, the whale-watching capital of Australia. They pause here for rest and recreation on their 12 000 km journey between their breeding grounds in the Pacific Ocean and their feeding grounds in the Antarctic. Whale-watching cruises operate in the bay. *See also Fraser Island & Coast p. 384.*

▲ PHILLIP ISLAND, VIC
The little penguins of Phillip Island are Victoria's best-known wildlife attraction. Each evening visitors can watch scores of these small creatures, measuring about 33 cm tall, returning to their sand burrows after a day of fishing. Other island residents include the koalas at the Koala Conservation Centre and the seals, which can be seen on a cruise to Seal Rocks. *See also Phillip Island & Gippsland p. 144.*

Floral emblems

Commonwealth of Australia

Golden wattle (*Acacia pycnantha*)

New South Wales

Waratah (*Telopea speciosissima*)

Australian Capital Territory

Royal bluebell (*Wahlenbergia gloriosa*)

Victoria

Common heath (*Epacris impressa*)

South Australia

Sturt's desert pea (*Swainsona formosa*)

Western Australia

Red and green kangaroo paw (*Anigozanthos manglesii*)

Northern Territory

Sturt's desert rose (*Gossypium sturtianum*)

Queensland
Cooktown orchid (*Dendrobium phalaenopsis*)

Tasmania

Tasmanian blue gum (*Eucalyptus globulus*)

ADVENTURE HOLIDAYS

When it comes to adventure holidays and outdoor activities, Australia is a destination without peer. The continent's diverse and well-preserved environment of remote bush, snowfields, rugged cliffs, wild rivers, extensive coastline and underwater reefs is a mecca for the world's walkers, skiers, climbers, rafters, anglers and divers. Many of these activities are offered within the boundaries of national parks and other conservation areas. Australia's regulated and well-organised tourism industry means that there are plenty of experienced operators offering training, tours, charters and equipment.

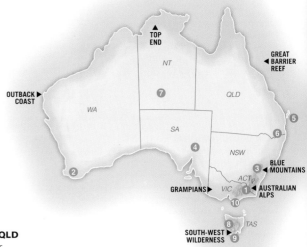

◄ GREAT BARRIER REEF, QLD

Novices and experienced divers alike come from around the world to test their skills in what is the most challenging and fascinating diving environment on earth. From Bundaberg to Cooktown, the facilities are extensive. The reef's islands, particularly the Whitsundays, are also known for their superb sailing opportunities. Most popular is bareboating, which involves hiring a fully equipped yacht (without a crew, but relatively easy to sail) for at least several days' touring. *See also Great Barrier Reef p. 385.*

◄ TOP END, NT

The remote and sparsely populated tropical north attracts adventurers with a frontier spirit. Activities include barramundi fishing in the tidal rivers of the west coast or the crystal clear rivers of the east; deep-sea fishing via Darwin or the Gove Peninsula; canoeing in the gorges of Nitmiluk National Park; and four-wheel driving in Litchfield National Park. *See also Kakadu & Arnhem Land p. 344, Around Darwin p. 346 and Gulf to Gulf p. 347.*

▼ AUSTRALIAN ALPS, NSW & VIC

This region, incorporating the ski slopes of Victoria and New South Wales, is the hallowed ground of winter-sports enthusiasts including downhill and cross-country skiers. Less well known is the range of adventure activities available during the summer months; these include walking, caving, horseriding and whitewater rafting. *See also Snowy Mountains p. 48 and High Country p. 156.*

▲ SOUTH-WEST WILDERNESS, TAS

Tasmania's Southwest National Park protects one of Australia's most untouched environments. Tall peaks form natural amphitheatres to wide bays, while dense forest can suddenly open up to reveal a vast harbour that can only be crossed by boat. Serious bushwalkers delight in the remoteness of this region, and two walking tracks – the South Coast and Port Davey tracks – lead into the heart of the wilderness. *See also South-West Wilderness p. 456.*

Top tracks

1 **Australian Alps Walking Track, ACT, NSW & VIC**
A 680 km track, usually completed in sections, taking in rivers, peaks and valleys. *See also Snowy Mountains p. 48 and High Country p. 156.*

2 **Bibbulmun Track, WA**
A walk that traverses Western Australia's spectacular south-west. It can be done in total (963 km from Kalamunda to Albany) or in part. *See also Darling Range & Swan p. 281, The South-West p. 282 and Great Southern p. 285.*

3 **Blue Mountains, NSW**
Anything from an hour's stroll to a week-long trek through some of Australia's most accessible bush. *See also Blue Mountains p. 38.*

4 **Flinders Ranges, SA**
A range of walks weaves across the ridges, gorges and river valleys of this ancient landscape. *See also Flinders Ranges & Outback p. 228.*

5 **Fraser Island, QLD**
Short walks to extended treks across this massive sand island, taking in lakes, forests and dunes. *See also Fraser Island & Coast p. 384.*

6 **Lamington National Park, QLD**
Around 160 km of walking tracks through primordial subtropical forests. *See also Gold Coast & Hinterland p. 380.*

7 **Larapinta Trail, NT**
A 220 km walking track along the gorges, chasms, pools and arid habitats of the West MacDonnell Ranges. *See also Red Centre p. 348.*

8 **Overland Track, TAS**
Australia's best-known long-distance walk – seven days from Cradle Mountain to Lake St Clair. *See also North-West p. 457.*

9 **South Coast Track, TAS**
A challenging six-to-nine-day hike that explores Tasmania's uninhabited south coast. *See also South-West Wilderness p. 456.*

10 **Wilsons Promontory, VIC**
Pristine beaches and bush accessed along 150 km of tracks in one of Australia's most beautiful coastal parks. *See also Phillip Island & Gippsland p. 144.*

▲ OUTBACK COAST, WA
Way off the beaten track, this remote coastal area has a range of adventure attractions that make the long journey worthwhile. Ningaloo Reef, second only in scale and interest to the Great Barrier Reef, offers superb diving (where possibilities include swimming with whale sharks) and is also emerging as a popular sea-kayaking destination. Further south, Kalbarri National Park has 80 km of deep gorges for canoeing, as well as good walking tracks and top-class fishing off the coast. *See also Outback Coast & Mid-West p. 288.*

◀ GRAMPIANS, VIC
Mt Arapiles, just to the west of the Grampians, is regarded as Australia's best rock-climbing venue. It has 2000 climbing routes across its surface, attracting enthusiasts from around the world. Rock-climbing, abseiling and bushwalking also take place in the Grampians, as well as hot-air ballooning via the town of Stawell. *See also Grampians & Central-West p. 152.*

◀ BLUE MOUNTAINS, NSW
The dense bush, misty valleys, deep canyons and rugged cliffs of this World Heritage area make it a natural adventure-playground for mountaineering enthusiasts. Rock-climbing, abseiling and canyoning are all on offer and the attendant facilities are excellent. Horseriding in the Megalong Valley is a gentler choice of activity, while the bushwalking through the mountains is some of the best in the country. *See also Blue Mountains p. 38.*

Safety and environment

Adventure activities may involve risks that can prove fatal if participants are ill prepared. For the more hazardous sports, such as rock-climbing, cross-country skiing, sport-fishing and diving, training with a professional operator is recommended, and even experienced participants should consider joining a tour or charter. Local visitor information centres and activity-based clubs can make recommendations. For bushwalking, a few rules stand fast. Always tell someone where you are going and when you expect to be back. For walks in national parks, get ranger advice about which walks suit your fitness. Always carry water – no matter how short the walk – and wear sturdy shoes and a hat. Observe fire warnings and fire bans. Walks of more than a day should be attempted only with a tour group or by experienced walkers. The flipside to many adventure activities in Australia is their potential for causing environmental damage. Participants can do their bit by observing the following: take only photographs and stay on designated tracks.

NEW SOUTH WALES

New South Wales is a land of extremes. The harsh temperatures of White Cliffs, where residents escape the heat by living underground, exist in harmony with the best snowfields and highest mountains in Australia. Ancient Aboriginal culture is celebrated, as is cutting-edge art and fashion in Sydney, the country's largest and best-known metropolis.

Lush rainforests, pristine beaches and the rugged beauty of the outback all vie for visitors' attention.

Lush rainforests, pristine beaches and the rugged beauty of the outback all vie for visitors' attention.

Beaches are a clear drawcard in New South Wales, with those at Bondi and Byron Bay among the most popular. Surfing, swimming and whale-watching can be enjoyed almost anywhere along the coast, but in Jervis Bay National Park is Hyams Beach, home to the whitest sand in the world.

The history of the state stretches much further back beyond its establishment as a British penal colony in the 18th century. Mungo Man, the remains of a man over two metres tall discovered at Lake Mungo in 1974, proves that civilisation existed here up to 62 000 years ago. Numerous Aboriginal nations have called the state home, and still do. The well-preserved fish traps of Brewarrina are estimated to be 40 000 years old and are thought by some to be the oldest man-made structures in the world. In ancient times they provided a focal point for seasonal celebrations that were attended by up to 50 000 Aboriginal people from all along the east coast.

After the American War of Independence spelt the end for British penal settlements in America, the recently annexed New South Wales was an obvious solution to the problem of overcrowded prisons. Conditions were harsh; the first inmates of Maitland Gaol, who included many children, were forced to march the six kilometres to the

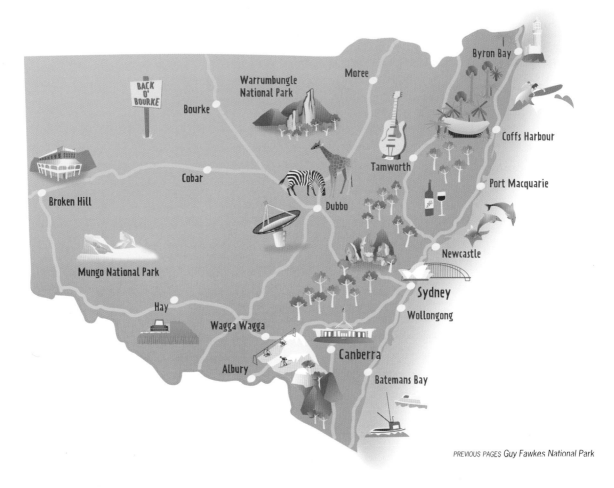

PREVIOUS PAGES *Guy Fawkes National Park*

Mimosa Rocks National Park, on the South Coast

prison in shackles and chains. After almost 150 years of misery, murder and misadventure, the prison is reputedly the most haunted in the country.

Harsh conditions were not limited to the prisons, with the fascinating and often demanding New South Wales outback claiming many lives. In 1845, explorer Charles Sturt lost his second-in-command and was stranded for six months near Milparinka while waiting for enough rain to replenish his party's water supply. Today remote Silverton is the quintessential outback town, with its buildings and stark surrounds featuring in Australian films such as *Mad Max II* and *The Adventures of Priscilla Queen of the Desert*.

In stunning contrast, the bright lights and sophistication of Sydney sit beside the sparkling waters of the largest natural harbour in the world. The iconic images of the Harbour Bridge and the Opera House, along with the successes of the 2000 Olympics and the popular Gay and Lesbian Mardi Gras, have ensured Sydney and New South Wales a place on the world stage.

FACT FILE

Population 6 716 277
Total land area 800 628 sq km
People per square kilometre 8
Sheep per square kilometre 48
Length of coastline 2007 km
Number of islands 109
Longest river Darling River (1390 km)
Largest lake Lake Eucumbene (dam), 145 sq km
Highest mountain Mt Kosciuszko (2228 m)
Highest waterfall Wollomombi Falls (220 m), Oxley Wild Rivers National Park
Highest town Cabramurra (1488 m)
Hottest place Bourke (average 35.6°C in summer)
Coldest place Charlotte Pass (average 2.6°C in winter)
Wettest place Dorrigo (average 2004 mm per year)
Most remote town Tibooburra
Strangest place name Come-by-Chance
Most famous person Nicole Kidman
Quirkiest festival Stroud International Brick and Rolling Pin Throwing Competition
Number of 'big things' 49
Most scenic road Lawrence Hargrave Drive, Royal National Park
Favourite food Sydney rock oysters
Local beer Tooheys
Interesting fact The Stockton Sand Dunes, 32 km long, 2 km wide and up to 30 m high, form the largest moving coastal sand mass in the Southern Hemisphere

TIMELINE

1770
Captain Cook comes ashore at Kurnell in Botany Bay.

1788
Over 1000 people, including 736 convicts, arrive in the First Fleet under the command of Arthur Phillip. Settlements are established at Sydney Cove and Parramatta.

1813
Blaxland, Lawson and Wentworth cross the Blue Mountains, opening up the wide plains of the inland.

1850
Transportation of convicts ceases, though many transportees have still to serve their sentences.

1851
Gold is discovered north of Bathurst, bringing a flood of immigrants, among them many Chinese. It heralds an era of prosperity – some miners even pay for goods in gold dust and nuggets.

1932
The Sydney Harbour Bridge is completed. Thousands cross it on foot on the opening day, with school children ordered not to march in step, in case it should prove too much for the structure.

1949
The Snowy Mountains Hydro-electric Scheme begins, attracting thousands of New Australians.

1973
The Sydney Opera House is finished and declared open by the Queen.

2000
Sydney hosts the Olympic games; they are declared 'the best games ever'.

SYDNEY

SYDNEY IS . . .

Bodysurfing at Bondi

Wandering through the lanes and alleyways of The Rocks

Views from Sydney Tower

A trip on the Manly Ferry

Fish and chips at Watsons Bay

Soaking up the atmosphere of Kings Cross

A picnic at Taronga Zoo

Harbour views from Mrs Macquaries Chair

A performance at the Sydney Opera House

Climbing the Sydney Harbour Bridge

A stroll through Balmain

Bargain hunting at Paddy's Markets

Following the Games Trail at Olympic Park

Visiting Elizabeth Farm in Parramatta

Visitor information

Sydney Visitor Centres
106 George St, The Rocks
(02) 9240 8788

Palm Grove, Darling Harbour
(02) 9240 8788
www.sydneyvisitorcentre.com

Aerial view of Sydney

Radiating from the sparkling waters of Sydney Harbour, Australia's largest city stretches from the shores of the Pacific Ocean to the foot of the Blue Mountains. Along with outstanding natural assets – stunning beaches, extensive parklands and the vast expanse of the harbour – Sydney boasts an impressive list of urban attractions, including world-class shopping venues and a host of superb restaurants and nightclubs. Its cityscape ranges from sandstone buildings of Georgian elegance to skyscrapers of futuristic design.

Sydney began life in 1788 as a penal colony and dumping ground for Britain's unwanted felons, a fact long considered a taint on the city's character. Today however, the convict past is proudly embraced, and echoes of those bygone days remain in areas such as The Rocks, Macquarie Street and the western suburb of Parramatta.

Since those early days, the one-time prison settlement has become internationally the most recognised city in Australia, and one of the world's great cities. Home to two of Australia's most famous icons, the Sydney Harbour Bridge and the Sydney Opera House, Sydney attracts more than two million international visitors a year. In 2000 the Olympic Games attracted record numbers of tourists and provided the city with several world-class sporting venues. For a true Sydney experience, try watching a Rugby League Grand Final at the Olympic Stadium with a crowd of 80 000 cheering fans. Or if good food and fine wine is more your style, sample the waterfront dining at Circular Quay.

Sydney offers a multitude of activities. Surf the breakers at Bondi Beach or jump on a Manly ferry and see the harbour sights. Whatever you do, Sydney is a great place to explore.

Central Sydney

Central Sydney lies between Circular Quay and the town hall, and is bounded by Woolloomooloo to the east and Darling Harbour to the west. Its layout is somewhat confusing between Circular Quay and Hunter Street but the rest of the city streets run north to south or east to west, making it fairly easy to find your way around. The streets between Bridge Street and Martin Place comprise the main business area, with the major shopping precinct located in the block between King, George, Park and Elizabeth streets. Most of the attractions centre around the Macquarie Street/ Hyde Park area and Circular Quay.

CITY CENTRE

Taking in the area between Martin Place, Bathurst Street, Elizabeth Street and George Street, this is primarily a retail district, with Pitt Street Mall, the main shopping precinct, situated between King and Market streets, and the exclusive shops of Castlereagh Street to the east.

Martin Place
The best time to see Martin Place is at about 5am on 25 April each year. This is when the Anzac Day pre-dawn service is held, with crowds of silent people watching wreathes being laid at the **Cenotaph**. If you can't manage this, it's still worth a visit just to see the sweeping vista of buildings in the High Victorian and Art Deco styles that line the plaza all the way to Macquarie Street. Chief among these notable buildings is the old GPO on the corner of Martin Place and George Street, which was designed by colonial architect James Barnet and which has now been gloriously transformed into the **Westin Sydney**, a five-star hotel with stunning interiors. The lower ground floor is also worth a look, as it contains an up-market food hall along with a carefully preserved part of the old **Tank Stream**, which until recently was thought to be irretrievably lost below the streets of Sydney. Once a major source of water for the Eora people, it was also a deciding factor in the choice of Sydney Cove as a settlement site.

Pitt Street Mall
If you head south along Pitt Street from Martin Place you'll come to a busy pedestrian precinct. This is Pitt Street Mall, the heart of the CBD's retail area, which is connected to a network of overhead walkways, small arcades and underground tunnels that lead to places as far away as David Jones and the QVB (the Queen Victoria Building). The mall houses beautiful department stores, stylish boutiques and vast emporiums selling music and books. Here too is the lovely **Strand**, last of the old arcades in what was once a city of arcades. The Strand has three levels of beautiful and unusual shops to explore.

Sydney Tower
A visit to Sydney Tower is a must for any visitor to Sydney. Accessed by way of the Centrepoint shopping complex in Pitt Street Mall, your ticket grants you access to the observation tower. At 250 metres above street level, it commands superb

Getting around

Sydney has an extensive network of rail, bus and ferry services. When negotiating the inner city, buses are probably best, with regular services on George and Elizabeth streets, between Park Street and Circular Quay. The Red Explorer bus covers city attractions, and the Blue Explorer bus focuses on the eastern beach and harbourside suburbs. Trains are another option, with services every two or three minutes on the City Circle line, which runs in a loop between Central Station and Circular Quay.

The Monorail, an elevated ride through the streets of Sydney, is an experience in itself. It runs in a circle that includes the north, west and south sides of Darling Harbour, and Liverpool, Pitt and Market streets.

The Light Rail service runs from Central Station to the inner-west suburb of Lilyfield. As Sydney's only tram service, it is particularly useful for accessing places such as Star City and the Sydney Fish Market.

Ferries are also a great way to travel, with services to many locations on the inner and outer harbour (see Getting around on ferries, p. 25). Enquire about Travel 10, Daytripper and weekly tickets, as these can considerably reduce the cost of your trip.

If you're driving, an updated road map is essential, as Sydney streets can be confusing and many of them are restricted to one-way traffic. There are five tollways in Sydney, including the Harbour Bridge. Tolls can be paid on the spot or by way of E-tag, an electronic device that can be obtained at the RTA.

Public transport Train, bus and ferry information line 13 1500

Specialty trips Monorail and Metro Light Rail (02) 8584 5288

Airport rail service Airport Link 13 1500

Tollway Roads and Traffic Authority (RTA) 13 1865

Motoring organisation NRMA 13 1122

Car rental Avis 13 6333; Budget 13 2727; Hertz 13 3039; Thrifty 1300 367 227

Tourist buses Red Explorer, Blue Explorer 13 1500

Taxis ABC Taxis 13 2522; Legion Cabs 13 1451; Manly Warringah Cabs 13 1668; Premier Cabs 13 1017

Water taxis Yellow Water Taxis (02) 9299 0199; Water Taxis Combined (02) 9555 8888; Dolphin Water Taxis 0413 119 960

Harbour ferries and cruises Sydney Ferries 13 1500; Matilda Cruises (02) 9264 7377

Bicycle hire Bicycles in the City (02) 9281 6977; Centennial Park Cycles (02) 9398 5027

NEW SOUTH WALES

Climate

Sydney is blessed with a warm, sunny climate, often described as Mediterranean, making it possible to enjoy outdoor activities all year round. The driest time of year occurs in spring, with autumn being the wettest season. Summers are hot and humid, with temperatures often in the mid 30s, while winters are cool and mostly dry, with temperatures usually around 15–17°C.

	J	F	M	A	M	J	J	A	S	O	N	D
Max °C	26	26	25	22	19	17	16	18	20	22	24	25
Min °C	19	19	17	15	11	9	8	9	11	13	16	17
Rain mm	104	113	134	126	121	131	101	80	69	79	83	78
Raindays	12	12	13	12	12	12	10	10	11	12	11	12

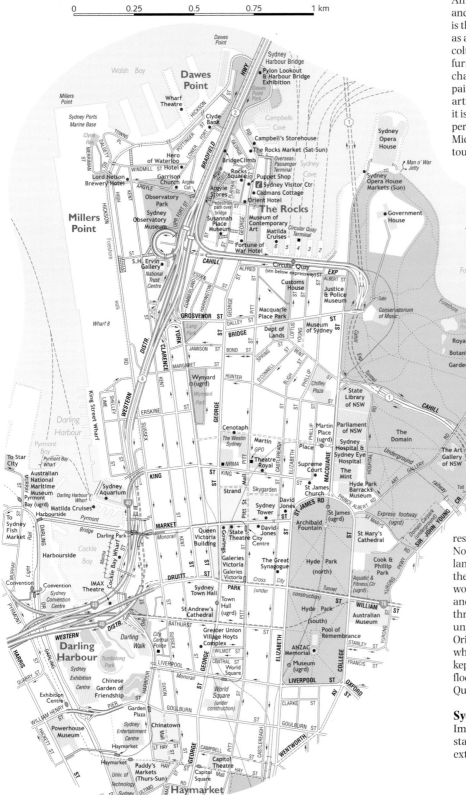

views of Sydney, from the Blue Mountains to the Pacific Ocean. Included in your ticket price is Skytour, a virtual tour of Australia and the Outback. For those who like to live dangerously, there's the new Skywalk (due to open late 2004), a 75-minute ramble over the roof of the Sydney Tower. *100 Market St; open 9.30am–10.30pm daily; admission fee applies.*

State Theatre

An extravagant mix of Art Deco, Italianate and Gothic architecture, the State Theatre is the final word in opulence. Built in 1929 as a 'Palace of Dreams' with marble columns, mosaic floors and plush furnishings, it boasts a beautiful chandelier, the Koh-I-Noor, and several paintings by well-known Australian artists. Classified by the National Trust, it is still a working theatre, and has seen performances by artists such as Bette Midler and Rudolf Nureyev. Self-guide tours of the building are available, but it's best to ring first to check availability. *49 Market St; open 11.30am–3pm Mon–Fri; admission fee applies; (02) 9373 6655.*

Queen Victoria Building

It's astonishing to realise now that the QVB was once in danger of becoming a multistorey car-park, but this was indeed the case. Built in 1898 to replace the old Sydney markets, it was later used for a number of purposes, at various times housing a concert hall and the city library before being restored in 1984 to its former splendour. Now one of Sydney's most cherished landmarks, it is considered by some to be the most beautiful shopping centre in the world, with three levels of stylish shops and cafes. Objects of interest are found throughout the building, including two unusual hanging clocks and a life-sized Oriental coach carved entirely from jade, which stands close to the building's best kept secret: the old ballroom on the third floor, now used as the supremely elegant Queen Victoria Tearooms. *455 George St.*

Sydney Town Hall

Immediately to the south of the QVB stands the Sydney Town Hall, a wildly extravagant piece of Victoriana, now the seat of city government. Begun in 1868, it was built on the site of a convict burial ground – as recently evidenced by the accidental discovery of an old brick tomb. While you're here, slip inside for a look at the Grand Organ, which was built in London by William Hill & Son and installed in the Concert Hall in 1890. Free lunchtime concerts are held once a month. *483 George St; phone (02) 9265 9189 to find out concert dates.*

HYDE PARK AND MACQUARIE STREET

One of the most historically significant areas of Sydney, this district contains one of the oldest parks in the city, Australia's first museum, a Gothic cathedral, and the beautiful old buildings of Macquarie Street, once the heart of Sydney's fashionable society.

Hyde Park

Originally laid out as the city's first racecourse, Hyde Park is now a place of sunny lawns and wide avenues shaded by spreading trees. At the quiet end of the park, near Liverpool Street, you'll find the beautiful Art Deco **ANZAC Memorial** and the **Pool of Remembrance**. In the offices below the memorial, there's an excellent ongoing photographic exhibition 'Australians at War'. At the busy end of the park stands the gorgeously kitsch **Archibald Fountain**, which commemorates the association of France and Australia during World War I. This is where all the action is, so find yourself a place in the sun and take in a game of giant chess, or simply watch the world go by.

Australian Museum

On the corner of William Street and College Street, you'll find the excellent Australian Museum. Established in 1827, the present complex is an intriguing mix of Victorian museum and 21st-century educational centre. It houses several unique natural history collections as well as a superb display of indigenous Australian culture, with lots of hands-on activities and weekly sessions of Aboriginal music and dance. *6 College St; open daily; admission fee applies.*

Cook and Phillip Park

For a change of pace, do as the locals do and go for a swim at the **Cook and Phillip Aquatic & Fitness Centre**, which is located across from the Australian Museum at the southern end of the park. The complex offers a full range of swimming and recreational activities, but it's worth visiting just to see the mural that graces the western wall of the Olympic pool. Inspired by the life of Australian swimming champion Annette Kellerman, it consists of eight painted panels depicting scenes from

a long and colourful career. Also worth a look is the **Yurong Water Garden** near the northern end of Cook and Phillip Park.

St Mary's Cathedral

The cathedral is located on the east side of Hyde Park North. Designed by William Wardell in a soaring Gothic Revival style that recalls the cathedrals of medieval Europe, work on the cathedral began in 1868 and finished in 1928, leaving the twin towers in the southern facade without their spires. These spires were completed (to Wardell's original design) and added to the cathedral in 2000 by helicopter – much to the interest and delight of watching Sydneysiders. A particular highlight is the crypt beneath the nave, which features a stunning terrazzo mosaic floor. *College St, facing Hyde Park.*

Hyde Park Barracks Museum

One of the loveliest of Sydney's older buildings, every elegant line and delicate arch of Hyde Park Barracks bears the stamp of its convict architect, Francis Greenway. Built in 1819, the barracks have provided accommodation for a wide range of individuals including convicts, immigrants, and people who were simply down on their luck. Various ongoing exhibitions reveal the many layers of this building's rich social history, with poignant displays of artefacts gleaned from recent excavations. *Cnr College & Macquarie sts; open daily; admission fee applies.*

St James Church

This fine sandstone church, with its elegant tower and copper-sheathed spire, is the oldest ecclesiastical building in the city. The commemorative tablets on the walls read like a page from a history of early Australia. Don't miss the little children's chapel either, which is located in the crypt. The chapel is decorated with an enchanting mural inspired by the Christmas carol 'I saw three ships come sailing in', which depicts the land and seascapes of Sydney Harbour. *Queens Sq, opposite Hyde Park.*

Macquarie Street

Named for one of Sydney's most dynamic and far-seeing governors, Macquarie Street was a thriving centre of upper-class society during the 19th century, evidence of which can still be seen in the magnificent buildings that line the eastern side of the street. In keeping with its old-world character, Macquarie Street is also home to a number of statues. Up near Hyde Park, for example, you'll find **Queen Victoria** and her royal consort, **Prince Albert**. While you're in this part of Macquarie Street, take the lift to the 14th floor of the **Supreme Court** building and visit the **Buena Vista** cafe. You can enjoy a relaxing half-hour, a great cup of coffee, and one of the best harbour views in Sydney, all for the price of a latte. *Open 7am–4pm Mon–Fri.*

Getting around on ferries

Ferries are a great way to get about and see the harbour. Sydney Ferries and private operators run daily services from Circular Quay to more than 30 locations around the harbour and Parramatta River. Timetables, network maps and information about link tickets (combining a ferry fare with admission to various tourist attractions) can be obtained from the Sydney Ferries Information Centre at Circular Quay. Matilda Cruises is the main private operator out of Darling Harbour. It runs the Rocket ferries, which provide express services to various points around Sydney Harbour, including some not serviced by Sydney Ferries. Tickets, including combined tickets (which combine admission to various tourist attractions and full-day Rocket Express passes), can be purchased on board the ferries.

Sydney Ferries from Circular Quay

Manly Ferry Departs Wharf 3

Manly JetCat Express service to Manly, departs Wharf 2

Taronga Zoo Ferry Departs Wharf 2

Watsons Bay Ferry Darling Point (Mon–Fri only), Double Bay, Rose Bay and Watsons Bay, departs Wharf 4

Mosman Ferry Mosman and Cremorne, departs Wharf 4 (Mon–Fri) and Wharf 2 (Sun)

North Sydney Ferry Kirribilli, North Sydney and Neutral Bay, departs Wharf 4

Woolwich Ferry North Shore, Balmain and Hunters Hill, departs Wharf 5 (Mon–Fri) and Wharf 4 (Sun)

Parramatta RiverCat Express service to Parramatta, departs Wharf 5

Rydalmere RiverCat North Sydney, Balmain, Darling Harbour and the Parramatta River to Rydalmere, departs Wharf 5

Birkenhead Point Ferry North Sydney, Balmain and Birkenhead Point, departs Wharf 5

Darling Harbour Ferry North Sydney, Balmain and Darling Harbour, departs Wharf 5

Matilda Cruises from Darling Harbour

Rocket Harbour Express Harbour loop: Circular Quay, Sydney Opera House, Taronga Zoo and Watsons Bay, with the option of getting off and rejoining throughout the day, departs every hour

Manly Rocket Express Harbour loop including Circular Quay, Rose Bay and Manly, with the option of getting off and rejoining throughout the day, departs every hour

Darling Harbour Service Express service from Darling Harbour via Casino Wharf to Circular Quay, departs every 15 min

NEW SOUTH WALES

Top events

The Mint

Once the South Wing of the old Rum Hospital, the site of the colony's first mint is now the headquarters of the Historic Houses Trust. Besides a pleasant reading room there's a good cafe on the upper floor with balcony seating and fine views of Macquarie Street and Hyde Park. The mint artefacts are now housed in the Powerhouse Musuem. *Open Mon–Fri; general admission free.*

Sydney Hospital

Now housing both the Sydney Hospital and the Sydney Eye Hospital, this imposing complex of sandstone buildings occupies the original site of the centre wing of the old Rum Hospital. Tours of the hospital's historic buildings are available, and while bookings are preferred (02) 9382 7111, it is possible to drop in and join an existing group. The little cobbled walkways that lead to the rear of the complex bring you to the courtyard, which is worth visiting just to see the fountain. Here stands the oldest building in the complex, the Nightingale Wing, which houses the **Lucy Osborne–Nightingale Foundation Museum**. Among other items, you can see the sewing basket used by Florence Nightingale in the Crimea. *Museum open 10am–3pm Tues; admission fee applies.*

Before you move on, don't forget to pay a visit to '**Il Porcellino**', a favourite photo opportunity with tourists and a 'collector' of money for the hospital. It is considered lucky to rub the statue's nose, then toss a coin in the fountain and make a wish.

Parliament of New South Wales

Between the Sydney Hospital and the State Library stands the northern wing of the old Rum Hospital, now the seat of the Parliament of New South Wales. Tours of Parliament House begin at 9.30am and every 90 minutes thereafter except on sitting days, when both houses are in session. On sitting days tours commence at 1.30pm, and are followed by attendance at Question Time. Bookings for these days are essential. *Open daily; general admission free; (02) 9230 3444.*

State Library of New South Wales

Facing the Royal Botanic Gardens, on the corner of Macquarie Street and Shakespeare Place, stands the state library. It houses a remarkable collection of Australian books, records, personal papers, drawings, paintings and photographs, most of which are regularly displayed in the library's five public galleries. The magnificent Mitchell Library Reading Room is worth a look, as is the exquisite mosaic on the floor of the lobby, which depicts Abel Tasman's map of Australia in terrazzo, marble and brass. Check out the statues that stand just outside the library. They are of **Matthew Flinders** and his beloved cat **Trim**. Stolen at least four times, Trim now perches on a sandstone ledge, well beyond the reach of souvenir hunters. *Open 11am–5pm daily.*

GARDENS AND THE DOMAIN

One of the loveliest parts of the city, this area largely consists of extensive parkland, much of which was once the domain of the first Government House. It is thanks to the wisdom of Governors Phillip and Macquarie that so much of this land was preserved, saving it from 200 years of ferocious development. Covering this much ground requires a fair bit of walking; however, the attractions are worth it.

Royal Botanic Gardens

A landscaped oasis on the edge of the harbour, the gardens are a wonderful place in which to stroll or relax with

Circular Quay, with the Museum of Contemporary Art on the left

Eora country

In 1788, when Arthur Phillip arrived in Sydney Harbour and established a settlement at what is now Circular Quay, he was settling upon land that was already occupied by the Cadigal people, one of a number of Aboriginal tribes that lived around that part of the coast. When the newcomers asked the Aboriginal people who they were and by what name they referred to the country around them, they received the answer 'Eora', which means 'our place'. Eora country became Sydney Town, and Sydney Town grew into Sydney, a vibrant, cosmopolitan metropolis and one of the great cities of the world. To the descendants of those who watched the tall ships arrive, however, it is still Eora country.

The old campsites and corroboree grounds have long been buried beneath the roads and buildings of Sydney, but Eora country is still recognised in various works of art around the CBD. These include The Edge of Trees, a sculpture which stands in front of the Museum of Sydney; Wuganmagulya, an artwork set in the pathway around Farm Cove; and the Cadi Jam Ora display in the Royal Botanic Gardens, which brings to life the original landscape of Eora Country and highlights its particular significance to the Cadigal people.

While these artworks are monuments to a landscape that has altered almost beyond recognition, Eora Country is far from being a thing of the past. It is a thriving entity still, which finds its expression in the many significant contributions that have been made to the political, economic and cultural life of Sydney by the descendants of those who first called this place 'Eora'.

a picnic. Aside from its sweeping parklands, there are several formal gardens, including the Aboriginal garden, Cadi Jam Ora, and a stunning rose garden. Stock up on bush tucker, take in the botanical drawings at the Red Box Gallery, or see a film by moonlight – you can even adopt a tree. Ask at the Gardens Shop for details. *Mrs Macquaries Rd.*

Government House

Government House is located in the north-west corner of the Botanic Gardens, close to Macquarie's old stables, now the **Conservatorium of Music** (*see Grand old buildings, p. 31*). Built in 1845, Government House is an elaborate example of the Gothic Revival style, with extensive gardens and harbour views. Free guided tours of the state apartments are available, and there are 'Below Stairs' tours of the servants' halls, cellars, kitchens and dairies, though these are run by the Historic Houses Trust and require an admission fee. Contact Trust headquarters at the mint (*see The Mint, facing page*) for details.

The Domain

Separated from the Botanic Gardens by the Cahill Expressway, the Domain falls into two distinct parts. South of the expressway, it's a wide green park where soapbox orators and an attendant crowd of hecklers once gathered each Sunday to debate the issues of the day. Now a place where office workers come to soak up the sun and play some lunchtime soccer, this area comes into its own in January when it hosts popular jazz, opera and symphony concerts. North of the Cahill, the rest of the Domain runs along the promontory to **Mrs Macquaries Chair**, a bench that was carved out of the sandstone bluff specifically so that Elizabeth Macquarie could sit in comfort as she watched for

ships arriving from England with longed-for letters from home.

The Art Gallery of New South Wales

The gallery is situated to the south of the Cahill Expressway, opposite the South Domain. Built in an imposing Classical Revival style with ultra-modern additions, it houses an impressive collection of both Australian and international artworks, including a large permanent collection of Aboriginal art and a superb Asian collection. *Art Gallery Rd, The Domain; open daily; admission free.*

AROUND CIRCULAR QUAY

Bounded by the 19th-century streetscape of Bridge Street and including the promenades of East and West Circular Quay, this area contains one of Sydney's most famous icons. It also houses two must-see museums and boasts one of the few corners of the CBD that has remained unaltered for almost 200 years.

Circular Quay

From the moment that Sydney was declared a settlement, Circular Quay has been where it all happens. With many journeys beginning and ending here, it's a major junction for bus, rail and ferry transport (*see Getting around, p. 23*), and a natural meeting place. There's entertainment on the quay itself in the form of buskers and street performers, while the many excellent cafes and bars offer stunning views of the harbour.

Sydney Opera House

One of the great buildings of the 20th century, the Sydney Opera House stands at the far end of East Circular

Museums

Brett Whiteley Studio *Paintings and sculptures in the former studio and home of this great Australian artist. 2 Raper St, Surry Hills; 10am–4pm weekends; admission fee applies.*

Mary MacKillop Museum *A tribute to this remarkable woman who brought education to the children of the bush and became Australia's first saint. 7 Mount St, North Sydney; 10am–4pm daily; admission fee applies.*

Museum of Fire *History of fire and its effect on the Australian landscape, with memorabilia from two hundred years of firefighting. Castlereagh Rd, Penrith; 10am–3pm daily; admission fee applies.*

Sydney Jewish Museum *A history of the Jewish people in Australia, along with a poignant tribute to the victims of the Holocaust. Cnr Darlinghurst Rd & Burton St, Darlinghurst; closed Sat & Jewish holidays; admission fee applies.*

Justice and Police Museum *Located in the old Water Police Station, with exhibitions on crime and punishment in Sydney, including the city's most notorious cases. Cnr Albert & Phillip sts, Circular Quay; open weekends, daily in January; admission fee applies.*

Victoria Barracks Museum *Military pride in a colonial setting, with a stirring flag-raising ceremony, followed by a guided tour of the barracks and the museum. Oxford St, Paddington; 10am–2pm Thurs; admission free.*

Sydney Tramway Museum *Historic trams from Sydney, Nagasaki, Berlin and San Francisco. Entry fee includes unlimited rides on the trams. Cnr Pitt St & Princes Hwy, Loftus; 10.00am–5.00pm Sun, 9.30am–3.30pm Wed.*

National Artillery Museum *A glimpse into the past of Fortress Australia, coupled with breathtaking views of the harbour. North Fort, North Head Scenic Dr, Manly; 11am–4pm Wed, Sat, Sun; admission fee applies.*

See also Australian Museum, p. 25, Hyde Park Barracks Museum, p. 25, Museum of Sydney, p. 28, Museum of Contemporary Art, p. 29, Susannah Place Museum, p. 29, Australian National Maritime Museum, p. 31, Powerhouse Museum, p. 31, and La Perouse Museum, p. 34

NEW SOUTH WALES

Shopping

Pitt Street Mall, City *Sydney's major shopping area, in the heart of the CBD. See map on p. 24*

Castlereagh Street, City *Sheer indulgence with some of the world's leading designer labels. See map on p. 24*

Galleries Victoria, City *A dazzling array of top-quality fashion and lifestyle brands. See map on p. 24*

The Rocks *The place to go for top-quality Australian art, jewellery and clothing. See map on p. 24*

Oxford Street, Darlinghurst *Up-to-the-minute street fashion and funky alternative clothing. 22 D6*

Oxford Street, Paddington *Home to the most cutting edge designers and a mecca for antique hunters. 22 D6*

Double Bay *Sydney's most exclusive shopping suburb. 22 E6*

Birkenhead Point, Drummoyne *Designer shopping at bargain prices in a historic waterfront venue. 22 A5*

Military Road, Mosman *Classy shopping in a village atmosphere. 22 E3*

Quay, breathtaking in its beauty against the backdrop of Sydney Harbour. Thought by many to echo the sails seen in the harbour, it was in fact the natural fall of a segmented orange that inspired Jørn Utzon's design, although Utzon has never seen the completed building. After resigning in anger over changes made to the interior design, he left, swearing never to return. The recent renovations to the interior were carried out under his direction from a base in the Philippines. With over 1000 rooms that include theatres and concert halls, rehearsal studios and dressing-rooms, a guided tour is well worth the effort. Bookings are essential (02) 9250 7111.

Museum of Sydney

A tiny gem of a museum built of sandstone, steel and glass, the Museum of Sydney is situated on the site of the first Government House, the original foundations of which can still be seen. Through a series of intriguing displays, exhibitions and films, the many layers that have gone into the making of modern Sydney are revealed. A highlight is the 'Lost City' exhibition, which offers a glimpse of Sydney's urban and cultural past as you walk through a scale model of King Street in the 1890s. *Cnr Phillip & Bridge sts; open daily; admission fee applies.*

Macquarie Place Park

Not far from the Museum of Sydney, on the corner of Loftus and Bridge streets, stands a tiny remnant of the old Government House garden, now known as Macquarie Place Park. Hardly changed from the days when Macquarie designated it the city centre, you can find an elegant sandstone obelisk near the south-east corner of the park. This is the place from which all distances in the colony were once measured. The nearby anchor and small gun once belonged to Arthur Phillip's flagship *Sirius*, and until recently were the only known remains of the First Fleet. More of this historic ship has since been recovered, and can be viewed at the Australian National Maritime Museum (*see p. 31*).

THE ROCKS

Once the haunt of a dazzling mix of pickpockets, prostitutes, merchants and sailors, The Rocks contains some of the city's most important historic sites, and one of Sydney's most treasured attractions. Divided into two parts by the approaches to the Harbour Bridge, the area on the eastern side of the Argyle Cut is centred on the streets and lanes around the northern section of George Street, while the area to the west takes in one of Sydney's most beautiful parks and the gracious 19th-century houses of Lower Fort Street.

Sydney Visitor Centre

The old Sailor's Home is where you'll find the excellent Sydney Visitor Centre with all the information you'll need for tours of the area. Make sure you check out the mezzanine level: with its bare walls of painted wood, it's still very much as visiting sailors must have found it when, under the auspices of the Seaman's Chapel next door, they were offered a bed, a meal, and a nice hot bath. There is also a fascinating potted history of The Rocks, which charts its growth from unspoiled possession of the Aboriginal people to the major tourist destination it is today. *106 George St.*

George Street – north

This was where whalers, sailors and 'old hands' hung out, and much of The Rocks' previous character as a notorious seaport rookery can still be glimpsed in the winding streets and tiny lanes that run behind George Street. There are quiet courtyard cafes and some unusual shops to be found here including the enchanting **Puppet Shop**, with hundreds of exquisitely handcrafted marionettes hanging from the ceilings of four rooms. Located in the sandstone cellars of 77 George Street, it's a must-see, and not just for children.

Subterranean Sydney

Deep in The Rocks, on the corner of Lower Fort and Windmill streets, stands the Hero of Waterloo. One of the oldest pubs in Sydney, it serves a great schooner of beer, but perhaps the most intriguing thing about the hotel is the legend of an old tunnel that begins in its cellars and finishes somewhere at the quay. It's said that the tunnel was used for conveying shanghaied sailors to rotting vessels that would almost certainly founder on the high seas, thus enabling the owners to claim the insurance.

Unbelievable as it sounds, it is quite possible that such a tunnel did exist, for Sydney is riddled with such subterranean passages. Busby's Bore is a tunnel that was hand-hewn by convicts to bring water from the Lachlan Swamps to Hyde Park.

Though now no longer in use, it is still there: a watery, echoing space beneath the sunny streets of eastern Sydney. There are also stories of a tunnel from Hyde Park Barracks to St James Church, built for the purpose of keeping the church-going convicts away from the public. While no evidence of this tunnel has ever been found, the rumour persists.

What is certain is that there are a number of disused railway tunnels running beneath Sydney, explorations of which have revealed the presence of a vast underground lake. The Australian Railway Historical Society (02 9749 5280) occasionally runs tours of these tunnels, but they are not for the faint-hearted. Bring your own torch, a pair of gumboots, and a lot of intestinal fortitude.

Susannah Place Museum

Museum of Contemporary Art
The museum occupies the old Maritime Services building – a brooding Art Deco structure that dominates the western side of Circular Quay. With massive rooms forming a stark backdrop to an ever-changing display of innovative sculptures, paintings and photographs, it's the perfect showcase for a fascinating collection of modern art. *Open 10am–5pm daily; admission free.*

Cadmans Cottage
This charming little cottage has the distinction of being Sydney's oldest surviving residence. Built in 1816, for many years it was the home of John Cadman, an ex-convict and boatman to Governor Macquarie. Today it is the Sydney Harbour National Park Information Centre and the starting point for tours of the harbour islands (*see Harbour islands, p. 36*). *110 George St; open daily; (02) 9252 1144.*

Playfair Street
The heart and soul of The Rocks, Playfair Street is the place to be, particularly on the weekends. There's corn-on-the-cob, wandering street performers, endless live entertainment, and a fantastic vibe from the crowd that's constantly on the move. Find a seat in **Rocks Square** and soak it all up. Not far from Rocks Square is **Argyle Stores**, a converted warehouse that now houses a collection of open-plan shops specialising in beautiful and unusual clothes. The main entrance to the stores is on Argyle Street, by way of Mary Reibey's old bond stores. As you pass through the arched gateway, spare a thought for this remarkable woman. Mary arrived is Australia in 1792, at the age of fourteen, having been sentenced to seven years' transportation for horse-stealing. She later married Thomas Reibey, a businessman, and, after his death, assumed control of their numerous business enterprises. Remembered as one of the most successful businesswomen in the colony of New South Wales, today Mary Reibey's portrait appears on the twenty-dollar note.

Foundation Park
This is the sort of place that's easy to miss unless you know it's there. Situated behind a row of souvenir shops in Playfair Street, the quirky and charming Foundation Park occupies the almost vertical site of three former dwellings that were built into the face of the sandstone escarpment. A front door was situated at the top of the cliff, and a back door halfway down. All that remains now is a few scattered foundations among the grassy terraces of the park and a steep stairway or two leading nowhere, but here and there you can find a chair, a fireplace, a clock or a table, recalling those long-vanished homes.

Susannah Place Museum
From the top of Foundation Park, this wonderful museum is just up the Argyle Stairs and around the corner in Gloucester Street. Occupying four terrace houses, it affords a glimpse of what it was like for working-class people living in The Rocks at varying stages in its history. The downstairs toilets-cum-laundry arrangements are particularly interesting. It is extremely people-friendly, with visitors encouraged to linger among the exhibits and try the piano in the parlour of No. 64. Take a moment to look around the little shop before you go – re-created in turn-of-the-century style, it sells toys, sweets, soft drinks and other goods from that era. *Gloucester St; open weekends, daily in January; admission fee applies.*

Markets

Paddy's Markets *Sydney's most famous markets, with superb fresh produce and bargains in clothing, souvenirs, toys and gifts. Haymarket, Thurs–Sun. See map on p. 24*

The Rocks Market *Classic street market with some superb indigenous art, stylish homewares and exquisite jewellery for sale. Sat–Sun. See map on p. 24*

Sydney Opera House Markets *Australian souvenirs, arts and crafts in a glorious harbour setting. Sun. See map on p. 24*

Paddington Markets *Fabulous mix of fashion, artworks, jewellery and collectibles in one of Sydney's trendiest suburbs. Sat. 22 D6*

Sydney Flower Market *Freshly cut flowers at wholesale prices, and breakfast at the market cafes. Flemington, Mon–Sat. 491 E7*

Fox Studios Weekend Market *Plants, giftware, arts, crafts and collectibles and movie memorabilia in the village-like atmosphere of the Showring. Moore Park, Sat–Sun. 22 D7*

Balmain Markets *Jewellery and leather goods, arts and craft in the grounds of an old sandstone church. St Andrews Church, Sat. 22 B5*

Bondi Beach Markets *Clothes, jewellery, a range of new and second-hand collectibles, and a lively beachside atmosphere. Sun. 22 G6*

The Good Living Growers Market *The gourmet's choice, with superb breads, cheeses, fruit and vegetables, close to Darling Harbour. 1st Sat each month. 22 C6*

Glebe Markets *Decorative homewares, arts and crafts, new and second-hand clothing, with a background of live jazz. Sat. 22 B6*

Sydney Swap and Sell Market *Sydney's biggest garage sale where second-hand goods are bought and sold and occasionally even swapped. Flemington, Sat. 491 E7*

See also Sydney Fish Market, p. 31

NEW SOUTH WALES

The monorail is a good way to get around Darling Harbour

Walks and tours

The Rocks Walking Tours *The history of The Rocks and its many colourful characters are brought to life during this 90-minute tour. Bookings (02) 9247 6678.*

BridgeClimb *The ultimate tour of the Harbour Bridge, you can climb to the top of the span clad in protective clothing and secured with a harness. Bookings (02) 8274 7777.*

Aussie Duck Tours *Combine a tour of the city and harbour in this unique amphibious vehicle. Bookings (02) 9211 3192.*

The Rocks Pub Tours *Tales of scandal and intrigue unfold on this pub crawl with a difference, as you knock back a schooner or two at The Rocks' most famous hotels. Bookings (02) 9240 8788.*

Harbour Jet Tours *Tour the harbour in a high-performance V8 Jet Boat, renowned for fishtail turns and thrilling spins. Bookings (02) 9938 2000.*

Destiny Tours *Sex, scandal and the supernatural – explore Sydney's darker side in a classic Cadillac hearse. Bookings (02) 9211 3192.*

Harley Davidson Tours *See Sydney from the back of an East Coast Harley Davidson. Bookings 1300 882 065.*

Darling Harbour to Pyrmont Walk *Self-guided walk along paths from Darling Harbour to Pyrmont Park, past ANZAC Bridge to Blackwattle Bay and the Sydney Fish Market. Brochures detailing this walk and others are available from the visitor centre.*

Sydney Ferry Walkabout Tours *Discover some of Sydney's more out-of-the-way places on foot. Pick up a brochure at the Sydney Ferries Information Centre at Circular Quay, take a ferry to any of the listed destinations, and start walking.*

Sydney Harbour Bridge

With almost every view in The Rocks dominated by its soaring arch, it's hard to ignore the presence of Sydney's magnificent Harbour Bridge. The second longest single-span bridge in the world (New York's Bayonne Bridge beats it by a few centimetres), it was completed and opened to traffic in 1932, and is now a Sydney icon. One of the best views of Sydney can be had from the **Pylon Lookout**, which also contains an excellent exhibition detailing the bridge's history, from the first sketches to Francis de Groot's attempt to sabotage the opening ceremony. *Admission fee applies.*

Access to the bridge is via Cumberland Street, where **BridgeClimb**, an organisation that offers unique and unforgettable tours to the very top of the span, is located (*see Walks and tours, on this page*). *5 Cumberland St; fee applies.*

Argyle Cut

Connecting the eastern and western sides of The Rocks, work on the cut was commenced in 1843 with chained convicts doing most of the hard labour. Initially much narrower than it is now, it was once the haunt of 'pushes': larrikin youths who dressed like Pearlie kings and specialised in gang warfare and rolling the lone passer-by. In the heyday of the pushes, even the police went through the cut in pairs.

Clyde Bank

In the shadow of the Harbour Bridge stands Clyde Bank, a beautifully restored mansion that houses a magnificent collection of colonial art and furniture. See how the rich lived in this lovely house with elegant, high-ceiling rooms and superb views of the harbour. Examine the collection either with a guide, or at your own pace. *43 Lower Fort St; open 10am–6pm Wed–Sat; admission fee applies.*

Observatory Park

High above The Rocks stands what is perhaps the loveliest park in Sydney. It has an old-world ambience and stunning views of the western harbour. For stargazers, there's the **Sydney Observatory Museum**, which boasts exhibitions on astronomy as well as talks, films and viewings of the night sky. *Open daily; admission is free during the day, but a small fee applies for night tours; bookings essential; (02) 9217 0481.*

Not far from the observatory, hidden by a curve of the Cahill Expressway, stands the old Fort Street School for Girls, now the headquarters for the National Trust. This is where you'll find the **S. H. Ervin Gallery**, which is renowned for its innovative and unusual art exhibitions.

DARLING HARBOUR

Located to the immediate west of the CBD and easily accessed by ferry, light rail and monorail, Darling Harbour is Sydney's most prominent leisure centre, and the focus of much of the city's culture and entertainment.

Darling Harbour East

Once very much a working harbour, Darling Harbour's maritime past is reflected in the structures that surround its landscaped promenades and parks. One good example is the National Trust-classified **Pyrmont Bridge**, which spans the harbour from east to west. North-east of the bridge are **King Street Wharf** and **Cockle Bay Wharf**, renowned for exclusive shopping and dining. South-east of Pyrmont Bridge, the ultra-modern **Imax Theatre** boasts the largest cinema screen in the world and offers films in both 2D and 3D format, with sessions every hour on the hour.

Sydney Aquarium

The Sydney Aquarium rates high among aquariums of the world for sheer spectacle-value. Highlights include the fabulous underwater tunnels that enable you to walk with the stingrays and stroll with the sharks, a Great Barrier Reef exhibition that's pure magic, and the Seal Sanctuary, where you can watch the seals flirt and frolic all around you. *Aquarium Pier; open 9am–10pm daily; admission fee applies.*

Chinese Garden of Friendship

Tucked away to the south is the garden – airy pavilions and tiny arched bridges stand reflected in tranquil lakes, surrounded by weeping willows and graceful bamboo. There's an elegant teahouse that serves traditional Chinese teas, as well as a tiny pavilion where for a small fee you can dress up in costumes from the Peking Opera. *Open daily; admission fee applies.*

Australian National Maritime Museum

Not far from the exclusive fashion boutiques and gift shops of **Harbourside**, on the western side of Darling Harbour, the museum is located to the north of Pyrmont Bridge. Several imaginative and awe-inspiring exhibitions highlight Australia's multifaceted relationship with the sea, from the days of convict transports and immigrant ships, up to and including the beach culture of today. While there is a fee for the special exhibitions, which include tours of the museum's fleet, entry to the museum galleries is free. *21 Murray St, Darling Harbour; open daily.*

South of the harbour

At the point where Darling Harbour becomes Haymarket, just past the Sydney Entertainment Centre, you'll find **Paddy's Markets** (*see Markets, p. 29*). Opposite the Thomas Street entrance to the market is Dixon Street, the main thoroughfare of **Chinatown**, and the heart of Sydney's thriving Chinese community. There are colourful shops offering everything from inexpensive souvenirs to beautiful and costly Chinese items, as well as superb Asian cuisine to suit every taste.

Powerhouse Museum

Situated to the south-west of Darling Harbour, the museum is best accessed by monorail. One of Sydney's most fascinating museums, it houses an extraordinary collection of oddments and treasures. Highlights include the Hall of Transport, with its fleet of aeroplanes suspended from the ceiling, and the tiny 1930s-style cinema with its program of old newsreels and documentaries. Free guided tours are available as well as a broad range of daily activities. *500 Harris St, Ultimo; open daily; admission fee applies.*

Star City

Star City, Sydney's only official casino, can be found to the north-west of Darling Harbour, towering high above the Pyrmont wharves. Worth a visit just to see its extraordinary interiors, with glittering lights and dazzling aquatic displays, Star City is also home to two of Sydney's finest theatres as well as several restaurants that offer fine dining with panoramic views of Darling Harbour. *80 Pyrmont St, Pyrmont; open 24 hours.*

Sydney Fish Market

Lying a little further to the west on the edge of Blackwattle Bay, the Sydney Fish Market is still within walking distance of Darling Harbour, but is probably best accessed by light rail. Fast-paced and vibrant, with a good bakery, an excellent deli and some of the best and freshest seafood you're ever likely to find, the market is a great place to visit. There are guided tours that enable you to watch a Dutch auction (where the price actually *drops* every minute), but only for the early risers. Phone the Fish Line for details. *Bank St, Pyrmont; open 7am–4pm daily; (02) 9004 1122.*

Inner eastern suburbs

The inner eastern suburbs begin just beyond the eastern side of the Domain and include Kings Cross, the old maritime suburb of Woolloomooloo, and **Darlinghurst**, once the haunt of some of the city's most notorious gangsters, now home to some very trendy cafes and restaurants.

Woolloomooloo 22 D5

While there are buses that service this area, the best way to get to Woolloomooloo is to take the stairs that are located next to the art gallery in Mrs Macquaries Road. These will bring you down close to the **Andrew (Boy) Charlton Pool**, which is a sensational place for a quick dip; and Woolloomooloo's most recent and controversial development, the **Finger Wharf**. A remnant of the days when the 'Loo had a reputation for toughness and lawlessness, the Finger Wharf is now one of Sydney's most exclusive addresses. For a traditional Sydney culinary experience, try **Harry's Cafe de Wheels**, a pie-wagon and long-time Sydney icon that stands on the eastern side of the bay.

Kings Cross 22 D6

Located south-east of Woolloomooloo, there are many ways to reach Kings Cross. You could use the **McElhone Stairs,** not far from Harry's Cafe de Wheels, or arrive by train or bus. If driving up William Street, head towards the Coca Cola sign – a landmark since the days of the Vietnam

Grand old buildings

Customs House *Elegant sandstone building designed by colonial architect James Barnet in the Classical Revival style. Alfred St, Circular Quay.*

Department of Lands *This building is particularly noteworthy for the statues of famous explorers and legislators that grace the exterior. 22–33 Bridge St, City.*

Conservatorium of Music *Much altered, but the castellated facade still recalls Macquarie's fancy Government House Stables. Macquarie St, City.*

Cadmans Cottage *Sydney's oldest surviving residence, now a NPWS office. 110 George St, The Rocks.*

Campbell's Storehouse *Built from bricks made by convicts, its serried roof has long been a Sydney landmark. Hickson Rd, The Rocks.*

Garrison Church *View the red-cedar pulpit and the beautiful stained-glass window. Lower Fort St, Millers Point.*

The Great Synagogue *Exotic and remarkable in its originality, with a gorgeous mix of Byzantine and Gothic architecture, and sumptuous interiors. Elizabeth St, City.*

St Andrew's Cathedral *With twin towers that recall York Minster, it is best seen in November through a cloud of purple jacaranda. Cnr Bathurst & George sts, City.*

Old Darlinghurst Gaol *A sandstone wall of beautiful proportions, an imposing entrance and glimpses of early Victorian prison architecture. It now houses the Sydney Institute of Technology. Cnr Forbes & Burton sts, Darlinghurst.*

The University of Sydney *Landscaped grounds and historic sandstone buildings. Parramatta Rd, Broadway.*

See also Queen Victoria Building, p. 24, Sydney Town Hall, p. 24, Hyde Park Barracks Museum, p. 25, and Government House, p. 27

NEW SOUTH WALES

The walking track from Bondi to Coogee, with Bondi Beach in the background

Sport

Sydneysiders have always been passionate about their sport. As a city that has recently hosted the Olympic Games, Sydney is now home to some of the best sporting facilities in the world.

*Football, cricket and racing dominate the sporting scene. Although Sydney does have an **AFL** team – the Sydney Swans – Rugby League and Rugby Union hold more sway here, with the season for both codes beginning in March. Key games throughout the **Rugby League** season are played at the Aussie Stadium at Moore Park, with the Grand Final taking place in September at Telstra Stadium, in Olympic Park. A particular highlight is the **State of Origin** competition, which showcases the cream of Rugby League talent in a series of three matches between Queensland and New South Wales. These take place in the middle of the season, and the New South Wales matches are played at Telstra Stadium.*

*The Waratahs are the New South Wales side in the Super 12's, the **Rugby Union** competition in which local and overseas teams go head to head. These games are played at Aussie Stadium, while the **Bledisloe Cup** games (usually involving the New Zealand All Blacks) are played at Telstra Stadium and attract up to 80 000 spectators.*

*In summer, **cricket** takes centre stage. The highlight is the New Year's Day Test, followed by the One-Day Internationals, all of which are played at the SCG. **Basketball** is another summertime sport with two Sydney teams in the National Basketball League – the Sydney Kings and the West Sydney Razorbacks. Basketball games are played at various venues throughout the city. Check the sports pages of any newspaper for times and locations. Other sporting highlights include the **Spring** and **Autumn Racing Carnivals**, with the world's richest horserace for two-year-olds, the Golden Slipper, being held just before Easter.*

War. With something of a dual personality, the Cross is one of the most fascinating parts of Sydney. At night, when the strip clubs of Macleay Street swing into action, the vibe is raw and edgy. By daylight it retains the charm of its bohemian past, with gracious tree-lined streets and pretty sidewalk cafes. Look for the **El Alamein Fountain**, possibly the most original and certainly the most photographed fountain in Sydney. For something completely different, you could indulge in a dip and massage at the **Korean Bathhouse** in the Crest Hotel (*111 Darlinghurst Rd*).

Elizabeth Bay House 22 D5
Designed by John Verge as a home for Alexander Macleay (whose family history is displayed on the walls of St James Church in Queens Square), the house is particularly famous for the stunning proportions of its elegant oval saloon with a sky-lit dome, and beautiful curving staircase. After spending many years as a shabby boarding house and artists' squat, it is now a Historic Houses Trust museum, and its rooms have been restored to their former 19th-century graciousness. *7 Onslow Ave, Elizabeth Bay; open 10am–4.30pm Tues–Sun; admission fee applies.*

Outer eastern suburbs

Said to contain some of the most expensive real estate in the Southern Hemisphere, the outer eastern suburbs of Sydney begin at Paddington and include the leafy multimillion-dollar suburbs of Rose Bay and Vaucluse and the one-time fishing village of Watsons Bay. The best way to see the mansions is to take the Watsons Bay ferry from Circular Quay. After stopping at Darling Point and Double Bay, it skirts

close to Point Piper and stops at Rose Bay, then rounds the point at Vaucluse. It passes close to Parsley Bay before finally arriving at Watsons Bay. Alternatively, you could take the 325 bus route along New South Head Road. This would enable you to stop and take advantage of the exclusive shopping at **Double Bay** or go for a swim with the rich and famous at the Vaucluse harbour beach of **Nielsen Park**. Around South Head the suburbs are a little more down-to-earth, and encompass Bondi, Tamarama, Bronte and Coogee, and La Perouse.

Paddington 22 D6
Considered an eyesore until quite recently, Paddington is now one of Sydney's most beautiful suburbs. Its back streets are lined with rows of iron-lace-trimmed terraces decked with flowers, and its main thoroughfare, Oxford Street, is home to dozens of boutiques, galleries and cafes. Always busy, it is at its most vibrant on weekends, when the **Paddington Markets** are in full swing (*see Markets, p. 29*). Paddington is easily accessed by bus – you can disembark in Oxford Street and walk around.

Centennial Park 22 E7
Just south of Paddington lies Centennial Park, a massive complex of parklands, playing fields, bridle paths and riding tracks. The park has been popular with horseriders for more than a hundred years, with the five riding schools at the nearby **Equestrian Centre** offering park rides for those who have experience and riding lessons for those who do not. The Equestrian Centre is located on the corner of Lang and Cook roads in Moore Park. If riding a bike is more your style, try one of the bicycle-hire shops in Clovelly Road, located on the south side of the park (*see Getting around, p. 23*). If you feel less

energetic, the park is also a great place to get away from it all and relax with a picnic.

Fox Studios 22 D7

One of Sydney's newer entertainment centres, Fox Studios occupies the site of the old showgrounds and is located next to the **Sydney Cricket Ground** at Moore Park. While film studios and sound sets occupy much of the site, the Showring is now a vast village green, adjacent to a lively pedestrian precinct lined with top-quality fashion and homeware outlets. Fox Studios also boasts a massive cinema complex and more than a dozen cafes, restaurants and bars. Always lively, the village atmosphere is most noticeable when the weekly markets (*see Markets, p. 29*) set up their stalls in the Showring.

Vaucluse House 22 F5

Vaucluse House lies in the heart of Vaucluse, not far from the harbour. It is an early 19th-century house that was once owned by the flamboyant William Charles Wentworth. Now a Historic Houses Trust museum, it is a beautifully preserved example of an early Victorian well-to-do household. The gardens are open to the public daily; guided tours of the house are available on request. *Open Tues–Sun; admission fee applies.*

Watsons Bay 23 G4

All roads in the eastern suburbs lead to Watsons Bay. This is where you'll find **The Gap**, spectacular ocean cliffs, and **Doyles**, a famous seafood restaurant with superb views of the city. Nearby is **Camp Cove**, a popular family beach and the starting point of a 1.5 kilometre walking track, which takes you past Sydney's first nude-bathing beach, **Lady Bay**, to the windswept promontory of **South Head**. South Head boasts magnificent views across the harbour to Manly and a poignant memorial to the crew and passengers of the *Dunbar* who were all lost in 1853 when the ill-fated ship ran aground and sank just outside the heads.

Bondi to Coogee Walk 22 F7

Though all these suburbs are easily accessed by bus, the best way to view them is by a walking track that starts at the southern end of **Bondi Beach**, one of the world's most famous beaches. The suburb houses several cutting edge clothing boutiques, an excellent weekend market (*see Markets, p. 29*) and some very chic sidewalk cafes. From Bondi, the walking track winds south along the cliffs through the tiny boutique beach of **Tamarama** (which is possibly the most dangerous beach in Sydney owing to its wild surf), and finishes at **Bronte**, a lovely beach with a natural-rock swimming pool known as the Bogy Hole, and a large park popular for picnics and barbecues. For those who want to explore further, the walk extends through **Waverley Cemetery** (where you can find the grave of Henry Lawson), past **Clovelly** (a popular swimming place), to **Coogee**, a smaller, more intimate version of Bondi. Along with the shops and cafes of Arden Street, you can visit the **Coogee Bay Hotel**, a lively pub with a sunny, waterfront beer garden, which lies directly opposite the beach.

La Perouse 491 H10

La Perouse is situated on the northern head of Botany Bay. Originally the home of the Muru-ora-dial people, it was named after the Comte de La Perouse, a French navigator who arrived in Botany Bay around the same time as the First Fleet, as part of a competing French contingent. With some beautiful beaches and interesting walks, it also contains a couple of important historic sites as well as an excellent museum (*see entry on p. 34*). If you're there on a weekend, watch the Snake Man in action. A major

(*see entry on p. 34*)

Charles Dickens and Sydney

Most people familiar with the works of Charles Dickens have probably read *Great Expectations*. Not many would be aware of the extraordinary connection that exists between a suburb of Sydney and one of Dickens' most famous novels.

On a morning in the early 1850s, in the then fashionable suburb of Newtown, the cream of Sydney society gathered to witness the wedding of the beautiful young heiress, Eliza Donnithorne. The bride was dressed, the wedding breakfast lay ready, but for reasons that were never discovered, the bridegroom failed to arrive. The embarrassed guests left quietly, and the jilted bride was left alone with the untouched feast. She became a recluse, and Newtown legend has it that she wore her wedding garments and refused to allow the wedding breakfast to be touched until the day she died in 1886.

Those who are familiar with Dickens' novel will recognise Miss Havisham immediately, and although it has never been established that Miss Donnithorne was the model for Miss Havisham, there is some compelling evidence to support the theory. The story of the unhappy affair and its bizarre sequel was well known in Newtown long before the publication of *Great Expectations* in 1860, and though Dickens never came to Australia, stories and anecdotes from this part of the world had been appearing in his periodical *Household Words* since its inception in 1850. It is quite likely that the story came to him from one of these contributors, thus ensuring for Miss Donnithorne eternal fame, albeit under a pseudonym, as one of Dickens' most memorable characters.

Entertainment

Cinema

Located in George Street, between Bathurst and Liverpool streets, the 17-screen Greater Union Village Hoyts Complex is the major cinema centre in the CBD. Arthouse cinemas include the Valhalla in Glebe; the Chauvel at Paddington Town Hall; the Dendy at Martin Place and Circular Quay; and the Cinema Paris at Fox Studios. For a unique cinema experience, try the Hayden Orpheum Picture Palace in Cremorne, famous for its Art Deco interior and Wurlitzer pipe organ. See the newspapers for details of films being shown.

Live music

Sydney has always had a strong live-music scene with some excellent venues in the city. Apart from the larger, more formal places for live bands that include the Enmore Theatre on Enmore Road and The Metro in George Street, the pubs are the main venues for live music. Try the Annandale Hotel or the Hopetoun in Surry Hills (popular venues for local indie bands) or the legendary Bridge Hotel in Rozelle, which specialises in blues and pub rock. For jazz lovers, there's the famous Basement at Circular Quay or the old Soup Kitchen, a basement restaurant in George Street that has been serving up a mixture of soup and jazz for more than 30 years. Check newspaper lift-outs such as the 'Metro' or one of the free magazines such as On the Street or Drum Media for details of what's on.

Classical music and performing arts

The ultimate venue for theatre, dance and classical music, the Sydney Opera House plays host to companies such as the Sydney Symphony Orchestra, the Sydney Theatre Company, Opera Australia and the Australian Ballet Company. It's worth checking out some of the smaller venues, such as the City Recital Hall in Angel Place or the Conservatorium of Music. Other venues for excellent live theatre include the Belvoir Street Theatre in Surry Hills and the Wharf Theatre at The Rocks. If you are interested in dance, you can catch the Sydney Dance Company and the Bangarra Aboriginal dance group between tours at the Wharf Theatre or at the Sydney Opera House. For details, check the Sydney Morning Herald's Friday lift-out, the 'Metro'.

tourist attraction since 1919, the reptile show begins at 1.30pm and still draws big crowds.

Bare Island 491 H10

From the earliest days of European settlement, La Perouse was considered to be crucial to the defence of the colony. Governor Macquarie built the sandstone tower that stands at the highest point of the promontory, and the fortifications at Bare Island were added in 1885. Guided tours are the only way to view these buildings (which movie fans will recognise from *Mission Impossible 2*), and are available on Saturdays and Sundays, hourly on the half-hour, between 12.30 and 3.30pm. *Bare Island is accessed via a footbridge from Anzac Pde; admission fee applies.*

La Perouse Museum 491 H10

This highly recommended museum occupies the old Cable Station, and presents the rich and varied history of La Perouse to visitors – it was once the site of an Aboriginal mission station and a Depression-era shanty town. The real focus of the museum is the life and times of La Perouse himself, with galleries devoted to the history of Pacific exploration, the voyage to Botany Bay and the eventual wreck and loss of the entire expedition. Not far from the museum is a monument to La Perouse near the grave of Father Receveur, the chaplain on the expedition. *Anzac Pde, La Perouse; open 10am–4pm Sat–Sun; admission fee applies.*

Western suburbs

The western suburbs start at the beginning of Parramatta Road, near Sydney University, and stretch all the way to the foot of the Blue Mountains. Encompassing the greater part of the Sydney metropolitan area, they offer many places of interest to explore.

Glebe 22 B6

Once a predominantly working-class suburb, Glebe has become more refined over the years. With Sydney University close by, students form a large part of the suburb's population. You can find excellent bookshops, lively cafes, and some great weekend markets here (*see Markets, p. 29*). With its leafy streets lined with old weatherboard houses, Victorian terraces, and the occasional mansion, it's a fabulous area to explore on foot. At the far end of Glebe Point Road is **Glebe Park**, which features landscaped walks with views of Blackwattle Bay and ANZAC Bridge.

Balmain 22 B5

Tucked away on its own little peninsula, Balmain is another suburb of quaint houses, stepped lanes and harbour views. The main shopping centre is located in Darling Street, a lively area containing several cafes, clothing boutiques and top-quality shops. Quickly and easily reached by ferry, this is another suburb that is best seen on foot.

Sydney Olympic Park 491 E7

The site of the 2000 Olympic Games, the park now hosts Sydney's yearly Royal Easter Show and is home to several other attractions and events. It is located at Homebush Bay and can be accessed by Parramatta Road, by rail or by RiverCat from Circular Quay. Take a lift to the Observation Deck on the 17th floor of the Novotel Hotel to see fantastic views of the entire park. There are various activities available, as well as Bicentennial Park, with its extensive wetlands and bird sanctuaries, and the fabulous Aquatic centre.

Featherdale Wildlife Park 491 B6

This is the place to get up close and personal with Australian wildlife. Over 2000 animals live in a beautiful bushland setting, and there are opportunities to cuddle koalas and handfeed kangaroos. It is also a perfect venue for picnics and barbecues. *217 Kildare Rd, Doonside; open daily; admission fee applies.*

Parramatta

The quickest way to get to Parramatta is probably by train, but the most pleasant and relaxing way to travel is by RiverCat. The area was discovered not long after the arrival of the First Fleet, and Arthur Phillip immediately recognised its farming potential. Parramatta was settled and the colony's first private farm was established in November 1788, making this outer suburb almost as old as Sydney itself. With places of historical interest around every corner and the lively commercial atmosphere of a busy regional centre, Parramatta is a fascinating place to visit.

Eating out

Circular Quay *Superb cuisine with stunning views of the Opera House and the Harbour Bridge. See map on p. 24*

No 1. Martin Place, City *An up-market food hall with some of the CBD's trendiest bars and restaurants. See map on p. 24*

Cockle Bay Wharf, Darling Harbour *Exclusive waterfront dining. See map on p. 24*

Liverpool Street, City *Sangria and tapas are the go in Sydney's Spanish quarter. See map on p. 24*

Dixon Street, Chinatown *Renowned for its yum cha venues and the superb quality of its food halls. See map on p. 24*

Watsons Bay *Fabulous fish and chips on the bay, with stunning city views. 23 G4*

Norton Street, Leichhardt *The place to go for truly authentic foccacia, pizza and pasta. 22 A6*

Victoria Street, Kings Cross *Great atmosphere, some of the best and cheapest coffee in Sydney, and great patisseries. 22 D6*

John Street, Cabramatta *Packed with inexpensive authentic Vietnamese eateries. 491 C8*

Darling Street, Balmain *A famous 'eat street' with an endless selection of restaurant, cafe and pub food. 22 B5*

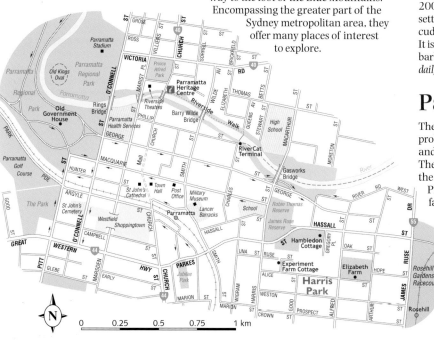

Parramatta Heritage Centre
Once you arrive in Parramatta, your first stop should be the Parramatta Heritage Centre at 346a Church Street, alongside the Parramatta River. With exhibitions that highlight the experiences of those who helped to shape this part of Sydney, it's a fascinating place to start exploring.

Riverside Walk
A stroll by the river takes on a whole new meaning when you follow the painted path of this fascinating artwork, which stretches 800 metres along the banks of the Parramatta River. A combination of paintings, interpretive plaques and native gardens reveal the history of the area and its inhabitants, all from the perspective of the Aboriginal people. Culminating in a moving soundscape of music and spoken words, it's an experience that shouldn't be missed.

Old Government House
Located in the sweeping grounds of Parramatta Regional Park, Old Government House is the oldest public building in Australia. Built between 1799 and 1818, chiefly by Governors Hunter and Macquarie, it is very much Macquarie's house. It has been restored to reflect the life and times of the Macquarie family, and includes a fine collection of their own furniture. Guided tours are available. In addition, there is a Ghost Tour that runs on the first and third Friday of each month, bookings essential. *Open daily; admission fee applies; (02) 9635 8149.*

Elizabeth Farm
Elizabeth Macarthur was one of the more fascinating and unusual characters in early Australian history. With her husband, John, she gave the Australian wool industry a kick-start, running their large merino farm while John was away in England. The lovely sandstone building surrounded by gardens is now a museum run by the Historic Houses Trust. Visitors are encouraged to wander the rooms, touch the furniture, try the featherbeds and generally behave as if they are guests of the family. *Open daily; admission fee applies.*

Hambledon Cottage
Not far from Elizabeth Farm, in Hassall Street, is the charming Hambledon Cottage, built for a Miss Penelope Lucas, governess of the Macarthur children. Small but elegant, it has been restored and furnished in a style that reflects the early reign of Queen Victoria. It is surrounded by trees said to have been planted by John Macarthur himself. *Open 11am–4pm Thurs–Sun; admission fee applies.*

Experiment Farm Cottage
Close to both Elizabeth Farm and Hambledon Cottage, Experiment Farm Cottage is situated in Ruse Street. Built in 1798 and named because it was built on the site of Australia's first private farm, the cottage is now run by the National Trust. It features lovely gardens as well as an excellent collection of 1830s furniture. If you are fortunate, your visit may coincide with one of the National Trust exhibitions that are held there from time to time. *Open 10.30am–3.30pm Tues–Fri, 11am–3.30pm weekends; admission fee applies.*

The north shore
Less densely populated than the suburbs west and south of the bridge, the suburbs north of the harbour conjure images of tree-lined streets and leafy gardens. In the lovely old federation suburbs that lie between North Sydney and the Spit Bridge are attractions such as the beautiful **Kirribilli House**, the Australian prime minister's Sydney residence, along with the house and garden of a famous children's writer, one of the world's finest zoos and an elegant harbour beach.

Nutcote 22 D4
Nutcote is a must-see for anyone who remembers the characters of Snugglepot, Cuddlepie and the Banksia Men. Once home to May Gibbs, one of Australia's best-known authors and illustrators of children's books, Nutcote is situated in the exclusive harbourside suburb of Neutral Bay. It has been restored and furnished as it would have been in the 1930s, when May Gibbs lived there. It is now a centre for children's literature, the arts and the environment. *5 Wallaringa Ave; open 11am–3pm Wed–Sun; admission fee applies.*

Taronga Zoo 22 E4
Located at the end of Bradleys Head Road in Mosman, Taronga Zoo is best accessed by way of a ferry from Circular Quay. A world-class institution, it has an impressive reputation in the fields of conservation and the care and management of rare and endangered species. It houses over 2000 animals, most of which enjoy stunning views of the harbour and city. Visitors can enjoy animal feeding, keeper talks, and displays. There is also a Skyline Safari, which offers panoramic views of the harbour as well as a unique way of observing the animals. The zoo boasts plenty of places for picnics and barbecues. It is also the venue for the ever-popular *Twilight at Taronga* open-air concerts, which take place in February and March. *Open daily; admission fee applies.*

Outer suburbs

Surry Hills *Where old Sydney meets new urban chic. 19th-century streetscapes, trendy cafes and clusters of fashion warehouses close to Central Station. 22 C6*

Newtown *A suburb with a funky, alternative feel, Newtown seems to sleep late and party late. It is best visited in the afternoon and early evening, when the shops and cafes of King Street come alive. 22 A7*

Leichhardt *Sydney's little Italy, with some of the city's best Italian restaurants, superb shopping in Norton Street and the unique shopping and dining precinct of Italian Forum. 22 A6*

Cabramatta *The heart of the Vietnamese community, with a vibrant shopping strip specialising in good-quality fabrics, fresh Asian produce, and fabulous pho (rice noodle soup). 491 C8*

Avalon *Pretty beachside village with a stunning backdrop of bush-clad hills, and a laid-back shopping precinct crammed with delis, cafes and some very up-market clothing and homeware stores. 491 I2*

Penrith *Close to the Nepean River, this is a paradise for watersports enthusiasts with the Cables Waterski Park and the Whitewater Stadium located here. There is a pleasant shopping precinct with some good eateries, and an excellent regional gallery. 493 K7*

Camden *One of Sydney's most far-flung suburbs, with a pleasant rural atmosphere, pretty, old-world streetscapes and good cafes. 493 K10*

Cronulla *With some interesting shops and cafes in the main street and a superb beach close by, this is a good starting point for trips to Royal National Park and the important historical site of Kurnell (Captain Cook's landing site and the birthplace of modern Australia). 491 G11*

NEW SOUTH WALES

Harbour islands

Sydney Harbour is dotted with islands, but currently only five of them are open to the public. These come under the authority of the National Parks and Wildlife Service, who charge a $5.00 landing fee per person. All visits must be prebooked and prepaid, so the information and tour booking office located in Cadmans Cottage, George St, The Rocks, is the starting point for any tour or visit to the islands.

Goat Island *Crammed with historical buildings and relics from its convict past as a prison for repeat offenders, Goat Island is a fascinating place to visit. It is accessed by guided tours only, and these include a heritage tour and the Gruesome Goat Island tour by lamplight. 22 C4*

Fort Denison *Crime, punishment and the defence of Sydney Harbour are all part of Fort Denison's past. Now it plays a vital role in assessing and predicting the movements of the tides, and is the site for the firing of the One O'clock Gun. Access is by guided tour only, with weekend brunch packages offered that combine a tour and breakfast at the island cafe. 22 D5*

Shark Island *Sandy beaches, shaded grassy areas and superb views of the harbour make this the perfect place for a picnic. A ferry service runs from Circular Quay to Shark Island four times a day on Sat & Sun. The fare includes the price of the landing fee. 22 F5*

Clark Island *Named for Ralph Clark, an officer of the First Fleet who once planted a vegetable garden here, Clark Island is now a place of unspoiled bushland and pleasant grassy areas, and is popular with picnicking families. Access by private vessel or water taxi. 22 E5*

Rodd Island *Another favourite picnic place, Rodd Island is particularly noteworthy because of its colonial-style hall, which dates back to 1889, and the 1920s summer houses that shelter long tables, making the island suitable for picnicking in all seasons. Access by private vessel or water taxi. 22 A5*

Balmoral 22 E3
With its curving promenade, shady trees, and the elegant bridge connecting a rocky outcrop to the mainland, some say Balmoral is reminiscent of an Edwardian Sydney. Extremely popular in summer, Balmoral has a lovely beach with a fenced-in pool, pleasant foreshore and some excellent restaurants.

Manly 22 G1
A ferry company once promoted Manly as 'Seven miles from Sydney, and a thousand miles from care'. Today it still retains much of the holiday atmosphere of a seaside village. The Manly ferry, which travels to and from Circular Quay, is an experience in itself, and the most pleasant way of getting there. With two beaches, an aquarium (*see next entry*), the Old Quarantine Station (*see entry on this page*) and the carnival atmosphere of Manly Corso, a visit to Manly is a must.

Oceanworld Manly 22 G1
Situated to the west of the ferry terminal, Oceanworld is an exciting bottom-of-the-sea experience. With colourful displays of marine life that include a touch pool and an underwater tunnel, it also shows some of the scarier aspects of the continent's wildlife. There are shark-feedings daily and exhibitions that involve some of Australia's deadliest snakes and spiders. *West Espl, Manly; open daily, admission fee applies.*

Old Quarantine Station 23 G2
Up the road from Manly, on the west side of North Head, stands the Old Quarantine Station. Built to protect the rest of Sydney from infectious diseases brought by immigrants, it is now a silent memorial to the hundreds who never made it to Australia. There's an extensive collection of heritage buildings as well as some fascinating 19th-century rock carvings that were made by the crew and passengers of the many ships that underwent quarantine here. Access is by guided tour only, and ghost tours of Australia's reputedly most haunted site are particularly recommended, bookings essential. *North Head Scenic Dr, Manly; open Mon, Wed, Fri & weekends; admission fee applies; (02) 9247 5033.*

The northern beaches 491 I4
One of Sydney's loveliest natural assets, the northern beaches stretch from Sydney Harbour to Broken Bay, with Pittwater Road running alongside most of the way. An unbroken journey from Manly to Palm Beach will take you about 45 minutes. Beginning in Manly, the road takes you past some suburbs of light industry, before turning back to the coast and the suburbs of **Dee Why**, **Long Reef**, **Collaroy** and **Narrabeen**. All have cafe strips, and each contains lovely and sweeping beaches. Look out for McCarrs Creek Road (West Head Road) off Mona Vale Road in Terrey Hills. This will take you through Ku-ring-gai Chase National Park (a fee applies here) and up to **West Head** with its sublime views of Pittwater and Broken Bay. (Note that there is nothing but unspoiled bushland up here, so bring your own thermos.) From Mona Vale, the scenery becomes wilder, the beaches smaller, and the suburbs more exclusive until you reach **Whale Beach** and **Palm Beach**, which are very swish indeed. There are several good restaurants in this area, and you can walk to **Barrenjoey Lighthouse**, take a cruise around Pittwater or catch a ferry across to the Central Coast township of Ettalong.

Day tours

Blue Mountains *Only 100 kilometres from Sydney, the brooding sandstone cliffs and deep, tree-lined gorges of the Blue Mountains provide a superb natural retreat. Aboriginal cave art, cool-climate gardens, charming mountain villages, walking trails and adventure activities are among the many attractions. For more details see p. 38*

Southern Highlands *Nestled into the folds and hills of the Great Dividing Range, the Southern Highlands offer pretty rural scenery, historic townships with superb European-style gardens, a variety of festivals, and wonderful guesthouses and restaurants. For more details see p. 39*

Ku-ring-gai Chase and the Hawksbury *North of Sydney, Ku-ring-gai Chase National Park encloses a magnificent stretch of bushland, set around the glittering waters of the Hawksbury River and Broken Bay. Fishing, river cruises and bushwalking are popular activities here. The Upper Hawksbury, north-west of Sydney, encompasses a scenic river landscape dotted with charming Georgian villages. It is Australia's most historic rural area. For more details see p. 40*

South along the coast *Abutting Sydney's southern suburbs, Royal National Park encloses a landscape of sandstone outcrops, wild heathland, rainforest, plunging cliffs and secluded beaches – perfect for walks, fishing, wildlife-watching and camping. Beyond the park you'll find the city of Wollongong and a magnificent stretch of surf coast dotted with pleasant resort towns. For more details see p. 39*

Hunter Valley *Located about 160 kilometres north-west of Sydney, the Lower Hunter area is Australia's oldest winegrowing district, with over 60 wineries radiating from the town of Cessnock. Take a tour of the wineries, starting with a visit to the wine centre in town. Book into one of the many excellent restaurants or pack a picnic and enjoy a rustic landscape of rolling hills and neal rows of vines. For more details see p. 41*

NEW SOUTH WALES'
REGIONS

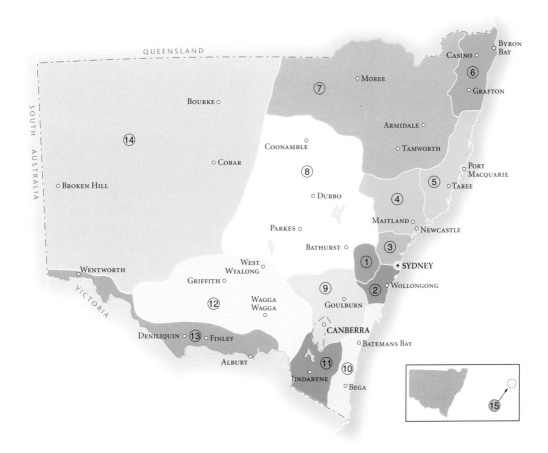

BLUE MOUNTAINS

The misty, bush-clad cliffs and valleys of the Blue Mountains are the eroded remains of a giant plateau that rose up out of a river delta 80 million years ago. Occupied for at least 20 000 years by Aboriginal people, the mountains proved an impenetrable barrier to the European settlers of Sydney until 1813. These days the area provides an accessible and spectacularly beautiful nature retreat for the city's residents, with bushwalking, adventure sports, gourmet retreats and cool-climate gardens among the many attractions.

Blue Mountains National Park, near Wentworth Falls

Top events

Feb/Mar	Blue Mountains Festival of Folk, Roots and Blues (Katoomba)
Mar	Kowmung Music Festival (Oberon)
April	Ironfest (Lithgow)
June	Winter Magic Festival (Katoomba)
June–Aug	Yulefest (throughout region)
Sept–Nov	Spring Gardens Festival (throughout region)
Sept	Daffodil Festival (Oberon)
Oct	Greystanes Spring Gardens (Leura) Village Fair (Leura)
Nov	Rhododendron Festival (Blackheath)

Focus on

Gardens

Volcanic soil and cool-climate conditions have made the Blue Mountains one of the best-known gardening regions in Australia. Visit Everglades near Leura, a 6-hectare classically designed garden that melds with the surrounding bush. Mount Wilson is a tiny village of grand, historic estates, nearly all with large gardens of formal lawns, cool-climate plantings and tall European trees; many properties are open to the public. Mount Tomah Botanic Garden is the cool-climate annexe of Sydney's Royal Botanic Gardens. Here specialist displays bring together thousands of rare species from around the world, with a focus on those from the Southern Hemisphere. One feature is the grove of young Wollemi pines – this species was only discovered in 1994 in Wollemi National Park.

Heritage Centre

The Blue Mountains Heritage Centre east of Blackheath has a wealth of knowledge on the geology, history, flora and fauna of the mountains, and also on the network of walking trails leading into their heart. Nearby Govetts Leap Lookout, high above the Grose Valley, is the starting point for a handful of trails.

Jenolan Caves

Formed 400 million years ago, the Jenolan Caves make up one of the most extensive and complex underground limestone cave systems in the world. Of the 300 or so 'rooms', nine are open to the public – by tour only.

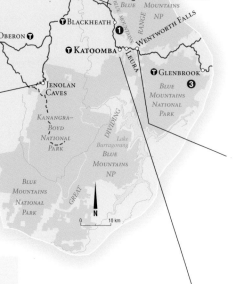

CLIMATE KATOOMBA

	J	F	M	A	M	J	J	A	S	O	N	D
Max °C	23	22	20	17	13	10	9	11	14	18	20	22
Min °C	13	13	11	9	6	4	3	3	5	8	10	12
Rain mm	160	174	170	123	104	117	85	82	73	90	103	124
Raindays	13	13	13	11	10	10	9	9	9	11	11	12

Wentworth Falls

One of the most beautiful towns in the Blue Mountains, Wentworth Falls offers bushwalks with phenomenal views. A corridor of trees leads to picturesque Wentworth Falls Lake, a popular picnic spot, and the massive waterfall after which the town was named.

Experience it!

❶ **Go** *canyoning in the Grand Canyon, southeast of Blackheath*

❷ **Take** *a ride on the Zig Zag Railway from Clarence, east of Lithgow*

❸ **Admire** *the stencils that decorate Red Hands Cave near Glenbrook – they were painted by Aboriginal tribes up to 1600 years ago*

For more detail see maps 492–3, 494–5 & 508–9. For descriptions of ❶ towns see Towns from A–Z (p. 53).

Three Sisters and Echo Point

The lookout at Echo Point is the best vantage point to view the famous Three Sisters. Echo Point and the Sisters were once joined, but over time great blocks of rock broke off and fell away into the Jamison Valley. Visitors can ride on the Scenic Railway, the steepest railway in the world, or enjoy views from the Scenic Skyway.

SOUTHERN HIGHLANDS

View from Bald Hill, Wollongong

This region combines European-style rural scenery with a fine stretch of typically Australian coastline. The highlands are an area of colonial sandstone buildings, colourful gardens, quaint villages, and excellent B&Bs and guesthouses catering for the steady stream of visitors who for well over a century have been arriving from Sydney to seek the peace and clean air of a hillside retreat. Towards the coast, the rural landscape drops away into escarpments, woodlands, rainforests and waterfalls, while on the coastal plains the scene is one of dairy farms, river valleys, surf beaches and rugged sea cliffs.

Morton National Park
The northern reaches of Morton National Park were once known as the Bundanoon Gullies; in autumn, mists roll out and engulf the town, giving it the feeling of Brigadoon. Explore the sandstone cliffs, wooded valleys and waterfalls of the park on one of the various walking tracks from the town.

For more detail see maps 491, 493, 500, 501, 507 & 509. For descriptions of ⊤ towns see Towns from A–Z (p. 53).

Experience it!

❶ Tour the gracious, European-style gardens around Bowral and Mittagong in autumn and spring

❷ Try locally brewed Bavarian-style beer at the George IV Inn in Picton

❸ Go boating at Audley in Royal National Park – rowboats, paddleboats and canoes are for hire

Kangaroo Valley
This valley, known for its lovely combination of rural and native scenery, can be explored on the scenic route leading from the highlands to the coast (from Moss Vale to Nowra). The route takes in the 80 m high Fitzroy Falls, crosses Australia's oldest suspension bridge, and passes through the historic township of Kangaroo Valley.

Top events

Feb	Jazz Festival (Kiama)
Mar	Viva la Gong (Wollongong)
	Southern Highlands Jazz and Ragtime Festival (Bowral)
April	Bundanoon is Brigadoon Highland Gathering
Sept	Illawarra Folk Festival (Jamberoo)
	Festival of the Forest (Shellharbour)
Sept–Oct	Tulip Time Festival (Bowral)
Nov	Festival of Fisher's Ghost (Campbelltown)

Focus on

Towns of the highlands
Bowral, with its historic streetscapes, restaurants and cafes, guesthouses and superb gardens, is the centre of the highlands. Historic Berrima, once the commercial heart of the district, now serves as a timepiece of colonial Australia. Nearby Mittagong boasts lovely gardens as well as good cafes and interesting shopfront architecture. Sutton Forest and Moss Vale are pretty towns with an air of the English countryside, while Bundanoon, further south, is known for its excellent guesthouses, health resort and views across Morton National Park. Away from the main tourist route are Robertson and Burrawang, peaceful settlements steeped in history. Don't miss Burrawang's general store (c. 1875), still with a sign advertising the *Sydney Morning Herald* for a penny. The rolling hills of this district were the backdrop for the Australian film *Babe* (1995). To the south is Berry, set in the dairy country of the Shoalhaven River district and boasting charming heritage buildings, galleries, antique shops and guesthouses.

CLIMATE BOWRAL

	J	F	M	A	M	J	J	A	S	O	N	D
Max °C	25	25	22	19	15	12	12	13	16	19	21	24
Min °C	13	13	11	8	5	3	2	3	5	7	9	11
Rain mm	87	91	97	86	77	82	46	66	59	75	92	71
Raindays	14	13	14	11	13	11	10	10	11	12	13	12

Wollongong
'Australia's most liveable regional city' is set along 17 surf beaches and surrounded by fantastic mountain scenery. Visit the city's boat harbour, fish co-op and restaurants on Flagstaff Point; drive north through the old coalmines for coastal views; and see Nan Tien Temple, the largest Buddhist temple in the Southern Hemisphere.

Minnamurra Falls
Minnamurra Falls, in Budderoo National Park, is one of several waterfalls formed by the massive sandstone escarpment that defines the edge of the Southern Highlands. Nearby is the Minnamurra Rainforest Centre, which incorporates a raised walkway leading into pockets of dense temperate and subtropical rainforest.

NEW SOUTH WALES

CENTRAL COAST & HAWKESBURY

Berowra Waters,
near the
Hawkesbury River

Top events

May	Bridge to Bridge Powerboat Classic (Windsor)
July	Terrigal Beach Food and Wine Festival
Sept	Hawkesbury Waratah Festival (Richmond)
Sept–Nov	Fruits of the Hawkesbury Festival (Windsor and Richmond)
Oct	Gosford City Arts Festival
Dec	Tuggerah Lakes Mardi Gras Festival (The Entrance)

W ithin an hour of Sydney, visitors will discover a vast and largely untouched wilderness, Australia's most historic farming district, and the glittering waters and sandstone cliffs of one of the country's most popular national parks. The great sweep of magnificent coastline supports lively holiday settlements, such as cosmopolitan Terrigal, The Entrance with its family-friendly pace, and exclusive Pearl Beach near Woy Woy. Explore these places as daytrips from the city or take a couple of days, book into a B&B, a caravan park or a luxury resort, and discover the charms and diversity of Sydney's favourite weekend retreats.

Focus on
Fishing
Fishing is one of the area's great attractions. There are plenty of boat ramps and boat-hire outlets, and no shortage of local bait-and-tackle suppliers. The trouble-free waters of the Hawkesbury are good for bream, luderick, mulloway and flathead, with bass in the upper reaches. Bream and whiting are a possibility for anglers in the calm stretches of Brisbane Water and Tuggerah Lake. On the coast, beach-fishing yields bream, tailor and mulloway. There are rock platforms, particularly around Terrigal, where anglers try for some of the big ocean fish, including tuna and kingfish.

Wollemi National Park
This 500 000 ha wilderness includes areas still unmapped. In 1994 the discovery of a new tree species – the Wollemi pine – in a rainforest gully was compared to finding a living dinosaur. Visit Newnes' historic ruins, walk to the Glow Worm Tunnel, or visit the secluded beaches along the Colo River.

CLIMATE GOSFORD

	J	F	M	A	M	J	J	A	S	O	N	D
Max °C	27	27	26	24	20	18	17	19	21	24	25	27
Min °C	17	17	15	12	8	6	5	5	8	11	13	15
Rain mm	139	148	150	136	119	128	79	76	69	83	92	102
Raindays	11	11	11	11	9	10	8	8	8	9	10	10

Macquarie towns
In 1810 Governor Macquarie established a number of towns on fertile river plains north-west of Sydney. The area now preserves some of Australia's oldest buildings and sites. In Windsor is a cemetery containing the graves of some of the pioneers who arrived in the First Fleet, and to the north in Ebenezer is Australia's oldest church, built in 1809.

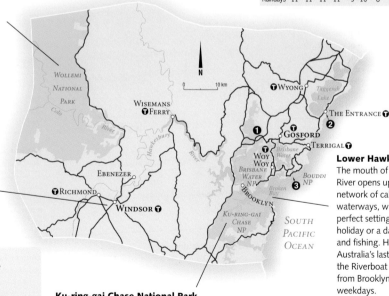

Experience it!

❶ **Explore** the Australian Reptile Park, west of Gosford

❷ **Attend** the daily pelican feeding at Memorial Park, The Entrance

❸ **Investigate** the wreck of PS Maitland while snorkelling in Maitland Bay in Bouddi National Park

Ku-ring-gai Chase National Park
This 15 000 ha bush, river and sandstone landscape forms a scenic border on the edge of Sydney's northern suburbs. Hidden coves, sheltered beaches and scenic lookouts combine with a rich Aboriginal heritage. See the Guringgai rock engravings on the Basin Trail at West Head.

Lower Hawkesbury
The mouth of the Hawkesbury River opens up into a dazzling network of calm, bush-lined waterways, which provide the perfect setting for a houseboat holiday or a day of boating and fishing. Hop aboard Australia's last river postal run: the Riverboat Postman departs from Brooklyn at 9.30am on weekdays.

*For more detail see maps 491, 493, 496 & 509.
For descriptions of ❶ towns see Towns from A–Z (p. 53).*

HUNTER VALLEY & COAST

Vineyards of the
Lower Hunter

The Hunter is one of Australia's top wine-producing regions, but this is
only a small part of its charm for visitors. Rich alluvial plains, historic
towns and tree-lined country avenues create one of the state's most
attractive rural landscapes. In the north-west are the colonial buildings
of Merriwa and the horse-breeding centre of Scone; east of here is the
rainforest wilderness of Barrington Tops National Park. On the coast is the
saltwater paradise of Lake Macquarie, a semi-enclosed body of water four
times the size of Sydney Harbour. Ringed by the white volcanic sands of
idyllic beaches, this is a venue for every kind of watersport. Beyond here
is Australia's second oldest city, Newcastle.

Top events

Feb	Vintage Festival (Lower Hunter)
Mar	Beaumont Street Jazz and Arts Festival (Newcastle)
Mar–April	Harvest Festival (throughout region)
April	Heritage Month (Maitland)
May	Lovedale Long Lunch (Lovedale, near Cessnock)
Sept	Jazz Festival (Morpeth)
Oct	Jazz in the Vines (Cessnock)
	Opera in the Vineyards (Cessnock)
	Festival of Wine and Roses (Singleton)
Dec	King Street Fair (Newcastle)

Focus on

Wines
Over 130 wineries – 90 with cellar doors – have
made the Hunter Valley into Australia's premier
wine-tourism destination. The region built its
reputation on outstanding semillon, shiraz,
chardonnay and verdelho, but exciting new
wines are emerging, including merlot,
chambourcin and pinot noir. The wine industry
here is huge, taking up over 4000 hectares and
making around $200 million worth of wine
each year. The red earth found on the hillsides
produces some of the country's great reds,
including Tyrell's Shiraz, Lake's Folly Cabernet
and McWilliams Rosehill Shiraz. The alluvial
soils of the river flats produce excellent
semillons, many coming from Tyrell's and
McWilliams Lovedale. To complete a day of
tasting, enjoy a night in one of the valley's
gourmet restaurants or boutique hotels.

Barrington Tops National Park
The World Heritage-listed Barrington
Tops are situated on one of the highest
points of the Great Dividing Range
(1600 m). This landscape of rugged
basalt cliffs, rainforests, gorges and
waterfalls, with a touch of snow in
winter, is a mecca for walkers,
campers and climbers.

Lower Hunter
The Lower Hunter is Australia's oldest and
best-known wine-producing district. Around
3000 ha of vines and over 60 wineries sprawl
across the foothills of the Broken Back Range.
A day tour should start at the Wine and
Visitors Centre in Cessnock. Excellent food
and accommodation are available throughout
the region.

Experience it!

1 **Take** an evening ghost tour of Maitland Gaol,
the most haunted gaol in the country

2 **Go** on a sandboarding and whale-watching
safari over the 32 km Stockton Sand Dunes

3 **Shop** for antiques, crafts and curios at
heritage-listed Morpeth, Australia's oldest
river port

For more detail see maps 497,
498, 499 & 509.
For descriptions of **T** towns
see Towns from A–Z (p. 53).

CLIMATE CESSNOCK

	J	F	M	A	M	J	J	A	S	O	N	D
Max °C	30	29	27	25	21	18	18	20	23	25	27	30
Min°C	18	18	15	12	9	6	5	8	11	14	16	
Rain mm	91	100	90	58	57	50	33	38	41	58	69	69
Raindays	10	10	11	9	9	9	7	8	8	9	11	9

Port Stephens
Port Stephens, reached via the township
of Nelson Bay, is a haven of calm blue
waters and sandy beaches, offering
excellent boating, fishing and swimming.
It is also something of a wildlife haven:
about 160 bottlenose dolphins are
permanent residents here;
migrating whales can be
seen in season on a boat
cruise; and koalas can be
spotted at Tilligerry Habitat.

Newcastle
Australia's second oldest city was founded as
a penal colony in 1804. Newcastle rises up
the surrounding hills from a spectacular surf
coastline, its buildings a pleasant chaos of
architectural styles from different periods. The
city boasts a range of attractions including
cosmopolitan restaurants, a premier regional
art gallery and many historic sites.

NEW SOUTH WALES

HOLIDAY COAST

This is classic Australian holiday territory: miles of perfect beaches, friendly seaside towns, areas of pristine wilderness, and a near-perfect subtropical climate. Choose between the tranquillity of a small fishing settlement – Seal Rocks, for example – and the bustle and excitement of somewhere like Coffs Harbour. As you would expect, the accommodation choices in the area are substantial, ranging from campsites in the rainforests to well-serviced caravan parks, guesthouses and luxury resorts.

Crowdy Bay National Park

Top events

Jan	Golden Lure Tournament (Port Macquarie)
Easter	Gaol Break Festival (South West Rocks, near Kempsey)
May	Shakespeare Festival (Gloucester)
June	Non-Conventional Homes Eco Tour and Envirofair (Taree)
July	International Brick and Rolling Pin Throwing Competition (Stroud)
Sept	Country Music Festival (Kempsey)
Oct	Global Carnival (Bellingen)
	Food and Wine Fiesta (Coffs Harbour)
	Oyster Festival (Forster–Tuncurry)

Focus on

Beaches

Just like the towns here, the beaches of this region cover both ends of the scale; you can choose a stretch of sand with a lively social scene, a secluded inlet, or one of the many options in between. Elizabeth Beach (near Forster) is calm, seasonally patrolled and popular with families. Solitude seekers and nature lovers should explore the bays and coves protected by Crowdy Bay National Park. Further north, top spots include Crescent Head (popular with surfers, particularly long-board riders), South West Rocks, the beaches of Hat Head National Park and those around Coffs Harbour.

Coffs Harbour

During the holiday season the population of Coffs quadruples. Attractions include the Big Banana, marking one of the area's largest industries; the Pet Porpoise Pool, which features trained sea mammals; and Muttonbird Island, the breeding ground of thousands of wedge-tailed shearwaters, which you can access via a short walk along the sea wall.

Dorrigo National Park

This World Heritage-listed park preserves rugged escarpment country and the continent's most accessible area of temperate rainforest. There are excellent walking tracks, lookouts and picnic areas, and opportunities to see lyrebirds and brush turkeys. The popular Skywalk is an elevated walkway high above the rainforest canopy.

CLIMATE PORT MACQUARIE

	J	F	M	A	M	J	J	A	S	O	N	D
Max °C	26	26	25	23	21	19	18	19	20	22	23	25
Min °C	18	18	17	14	11	9	7	8	10	13	15	17
Rain mm	153	177	176	170	147	132	98	83	83	94	102	127
Raindays	12	13	14	13	11	10	9	9	9	11	11	11

Experience it!

1. **Take** the Ocean Drive from Kew to Port Macquarie, past golden beaches, rugged cliffs and tranquil lakes

2. **Dine** on oysters and watch the trawlers at Tuncurry's Wallis Lake Fishermen's Co-op

3. **Witness** the dusk flight of thousands of bats as they begin their nightly search for food at Bellingen Bat Island

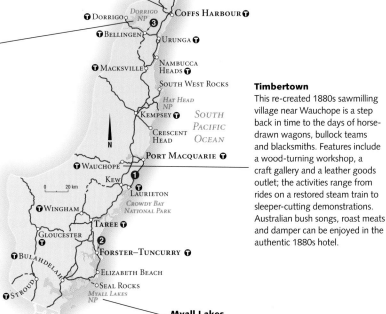

Timbertown

This re-created 1880s sawmilling village near Wauchope is a step back in time to the days of horse-drawn wagons, bullock teams and blacksmiths. Features include a wood-turning workshop, a craft gallery and a leather goods outlet; the activities range from rides on a restored steam train to sleeper-cutting demonstrations. Australian bush songs, roast meats and damper can be enjoyed in the authentic 1880s hotel.

Myall Lakes

The 'Murmuring Myalls' are 10 000 ha of connected lakes protected from the South Pacific by a long line of windswept dunes. Hire a houseboat and explore the calm waters, or enjoy fishing, windsurfing or canoeing. There are 40 km of spectacular beaches and lookouts along the adjoining coast.

For more detail see maps 509, 515 & 516.
For descriptions of ⊕ towns see Towns from A–Z (p. 53).

TROPICAL NORTH COAST

Coastline near
Byron Bay

E xquisite beaches, wide rivers, World Heritage rainforest and
an alternative lifestyle are some of the features of this tropical
paradise in the far north-east of the state. Popular activities include
fishing, whitewater rafting, diving and surfing. And for the more
laid-back traveller there are markets, festivals, scenic drives, excellent
local restaurants, and accommodation offering everything from
rainforest retreats to beachfront B&Bs. The region is a magnet for visitors
world-wide, but avoids the trappings of most large-scale popular resorts.
It remains culturally interesting as well as environmentally 'tuned in'.

Top events

Easter	East Coast Blues and Roots Festival (Byron Bay)
May	Mardi Grass Festival (Nimbin)
June	Wintersun Carnival (Tweed Heads)
July	Fairymount Festival of Fairytales (Kyogle)
Aug	Tweed Valley Banana Festival and Harvest Week (Murwillumbah)
Sept	Chincogan Fiesta (Mullumbimby)
	Rainforest Week (Tweed Heads)
Oct–Nov	Jacaranda Festival (Grafton)

Focus on

Rainforest

The region's tropical heat and humidity create the perfect conditions for lush rainforest – the largest remaining area of rainforest in New South Wales. With rainforest comes abundant wildlife, especially native reptiles and mammals, and tours can be arranged through the National Parks and Wildlife Service. Kyogle is known as the 'gateway to the rainforests' as it is almost completely surrounded by them; nearby Border Ranges National Park is a forest full of gorges, creeks and waterfalls. The stunning swimming hole of Wanganui Gorge, west of Mullumbimby, is surrounded by rainforest and strangler figs, and Rotary Rainforest Reserve is 6 hectares of rainforest in the centre of Lismore.

Mount Warning National Park

The summit of Mt Warning is the first place in Australia to be lit by the morning sun, being the highest point along Australia's eastern ledge. A bushwalking track leads up from the carpark through pockets of subtropical and warm-temperate rainforest. The park is World Heritage-listed and the mountain itself is the plug of one of the world's oldest volcanoes, which stretches as far as Cape Byron.

Nimbin

This quiet farming town took off in 1974 when the Aquarius Festival established it as the alternative-culture capital. Alternative-lifestylers are attracted from all over the world to Nimbin's magnificent valley surrounds and its laid-back and permissive culture. According to Bundjalung Dreamtime legend, Nimbin is the resting place of the rainbow serpent.

Experience it!

1 **Dive** with turtles in the warm waters of Julian Rocks Aquatic Reserve, near Byron Bay

2 **Visit** Tropical Fruit World, north of Murwillumbah, to see 500 varieties of tropical fruit

3 **Stand** at the tip of Cape Byron, the continent's most easterly point. If you're here in the cooler months, watch for migrating humpback whales offshore

CLIMATE BYRON BAY

	J	F	M	A	M	J	J	A	S	O	N	D
Max °C	28	28	27	25	22	20	19	20	22	23	25	26
Min °C	21	21	20	17	15	12	12	13	14	16	18	20
Rain mm	161	192	215	185	188	158	100	92	66	102	118	143
Raindays	15	16	17	15	15	12	10	9	9	11	12	13

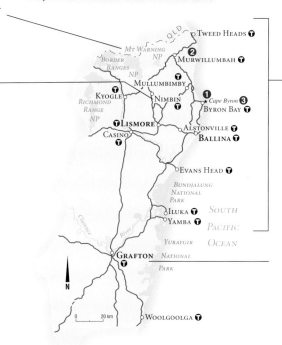

Holiday coast

The combination of excellent weather and pristine beaches makes this region popular with visitors year-round. Visit family-friendly Tweed Heads or the fishing towns of Iluka and Yamba, great for their fresh seafood. Laid-back Byron Bay is perfect for surfers and backpackers, and outstanding camping and caravan facilities in Evans Head and Ballina appeal to those on a budget.

Grafton

This picturesque rural town, with a number of 19th-century buildings, is best known for its beautiful civic landscaping, particularly for the mature jacaranda trees with their vivid purple springtime blossom. Located on the Clarence River, Grafton is also a busy centre for watersports, including whitewater rafting and canoeing.

For more detail see map 515.
For descriptions of ❶ towns see Towns from A–Z (p. 53).

NEW SOUTH WALES

NEW ENGLAND

The New England district, centred around Armidale, lies some 200 kilometres inland and approximately 1000 metres above sea level. Chilly winters, golden autumns, heritage buildings and large stretches of farmland contrast with the tropical scenery of the nearby north coast. From the east to the west, superb tracts of rainforest gradually flatten out into plains, with the occasional dramatic outcrop; here you'll find historic towns and the first red reaches of the outback. The region is also known for its fossicking – for everything from sapphires to rare black opals.

A road through the New England district in autumn

Top events

Jan	Tamworth Country Music Festival
Mar	German Beer Fest (Tenterfield)
Mar–May	Autumn Festival (Armidale)
April	Oracles of the Bush (bush poetry, Tenterfield)
May	Australian Celtic Festival (Glen Innes)
Nov	Golden Grain and Cotton Festival (Moree)
	Land of the Beardies Bush Festival (Glen Innes)
Dec	Great Inland Fishing Festival (Inverell)

Focus on

Fossicking

The New England district is a fossicker's paradise. Quartz, jasper, serpentine and crystal are common finds, while sapphires, diamonds and gold present more of a challenge. Fossickers Way is a well-signposted route that introduces visitors to the district, beginning at Nundle and travelling north as far as Glen Innes. It passes through a number of towns including Inverell, the world's largest producer of sapphires. In the far west of the district, Lightning Ridge is known as a source of the famed black opal.

CLIMATE ARMIDALE

	J	F	M	A	M	J	J	A	S	O	N	D
Max °C	27	26	24	21	16	13	12	14	18	21	24	27
Min°C	13	13	11	8	4	2	0	1	4	7	10	12
Rain mm	105	87	65	46	44	57	49	48	52	68	80	89
Raindays	10	10	10	8	8	10	9	9	8	9	9	10

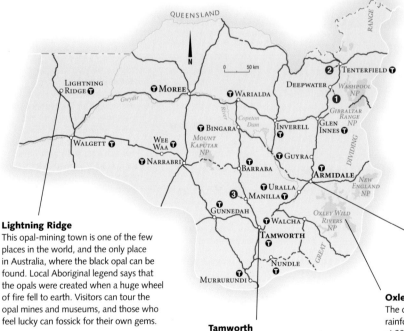

Armidale
Armidale is a sophisticated town with over 30 National Trust-listed buildings, two cathedrals, and the first Australian university established outside a capital city, all set in gracious tree-lined streets. Visit the New England Regional Art Museum, featuring the multimillion-dollar Hinton and Coventry collections, Australia's most significant provincial art holdings.

Lightning Ridge
This opal-mining town is one of the few places in the world, and the only place in Australia, where the black opal can be found. Local Aboriginal legend says that the opals were created when a huge wheel of fire fell to earth. Visitors can tour the opal mines and museums, and those who feel lucky can fossick for their own gems.

Experience it!

❶ **Go** on a fishing safari for trout, perch and cod at Deepwater, north of Glen Innes

❷ **Visit** the Tenterfield Saddler, the shop that inspired Peter Allen's song of the same name

❸ **Sample** traditional mead at Dutton's Meadery in Manilla

Tamworth
Tamworth is Australia's country music capital, hosting the huge Tamworth Country Music Festival each January. Beneath the 12 m Golden Guitar you'll find the Gallery of Stars Wax Museum, with replicas of favourite country artists, and the Country Music Roll of Renown – Australia's highest country music honour. The Hands of Fame Park contains the handprints of over 200 country music stars.

Oxley Wild Rivers National Park
The centrepiece of this World Heritage-listed rainforest is the stunning Wollomombi Falls – at 220 m, they are one of the highest falls in Australia. The ruggedly beautiful Dangars Falls drop 120 m into a spectacular gorge. Activities in the park include camping, canoeing, walking and horseriding.

For more detail see map 514–15.
For descriptions of ❶ towns see Towns from A–Z (p. 53).

CENTRAL WEST

Feeding a giraffe,
Western Plains Zoo

This land of open spaces straddles the western slopes of the Great Dividing Range and the expanse of the Western Plains. Cotton crops, vineyards, and sheep and cattle farms draw on the rich volcanic soil and dominate the landscape, but nature exerts its presence often and, in the case of the Warrumbungles, with great spectacle. The history of the district is well preserved – old goldmining settlements like Hill End have retained their 19th-century streetscapes and inspired the likes of painter Russell Drysdale. Modern attractions include the Western Plains Zoo, and two major observatories built to take advantage of the region's endless stretch of clear sky.

Top events

Easter	Orana Country Music Easter Festival (Dubbo)
April	Red Ochre Corroborree (Dubbo)
	Marti's Balloon Fiesta (Canowindra)
Sept	Mudgee Wine Festival
Oct	Coo-ee Festival (Gilgandra)
	Festival of the Stars (Coonabarabran)
	Sakura Matsuri (cherry blossom festival, Cowra)
	Country Music Spectacular (Parkes)
	V8 Supercars 1000 (Bathurst)

Focus on
Mudgee region wines
German settler Adam Roth planted vines at Mudgee in the 1850s. Thirteen wineries were established by 1890, but just three survived the depression later in the decade. The red-wine boom of the 1960s saw many new vines planted, and today the Mudgee region, stretching from Dunedoo in the north down through Gulgong, Mudgee, Rylstone and Kandos, has around 30 vineyards, most of which offer tastings. Warm summers favour the production of full-bodied shiraz and chardonnay. Try Huntington's shiraz; the organic, preservative-free wines of Botobolar; Craigmoor's chardonnay; or the cabernet sauvignon from Thistle Hill.

NEW SOUTH WALES

Warrumbungle National Park
The Warrumbungles are extraordinary rock formations created by ancient volcanic activity. Best known is The Breadknife, which juts savagely out of the surrounding bushland. The 21 000 ha national park marks the area where the flora and fauna of the Western Plains merge with that of the Great Dividing Range.

Western Plains Zoo
Five kilometres from Dubbo, this excellent open-range zoo covers 300 ha and is home to animals representing five continents. The zoo is renowned throughout the world for its breeding programs, particularly of endangered species. Visitors can use their own cars, hire bikes or walk along the trails to all areas.

Experience it!

1 **Visit** *Siding Springs Observatory, west of Coonabarabran, home to Australia's largest telescope*

2 **Go** *birdwatching at the 20 000 ha wetlands of Macquarie Marshes Nature Reserve*

3 **Drive** *up Cowra's cherry tree-lined Sakura Avenue to the site of the old POW camp*

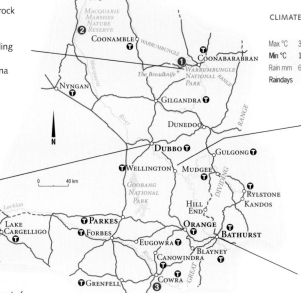

*For more detail see maps 492, 508, 511, 513 & 514.
For descriptions of ❶ towns see Towns from A–Z (p. 53).*

CLIMATE **DUBBO**

	J	F	M	A	M	J	J	A	S	O	N	D
Max °C	33	32	29	25	20	16	15	17	21	25	29	32
Min °C	18	18	15	11	7	4	3	4	6	10	13	16
Rain mm	61	54	48	45	48	49	45	45	44	49	51	50
Raindays	6	5	5	5	6	8	8	8	7	7	6	6

Wellington Caves
One of the largest stalagmites in the world (with a circumference of 32 m) can be viewed in the limestone caves west of Wellington. The caves also contain rare cave coral and for thousands of years have acted as natural animal traps. Fossils of a diprotodon and a giant kangaroo have been found here.

Bathurst
This is Australia's oldest inland settlement. Founded in 1815, Bathurst is noted for its colonial and Victorian architecture, including Miss Traill's House (1845), open to the public. Also of interest are Ben Chifley's Cottage, the excellent regional art gallery and Mount Panorama, venue for the V8 Supercars 1000 (Bathurst 1000).

CAPITAL COUNTRY

This is a rich agricultural region extending north from the borders of the Australian Capital Territory. Set along the tableland of the Great Dividing Range, it is characterised by undulating hills, golden plains and rocky outcrops. It is best known for its colonial history, which – dating back to the 1820s – is recorded in the heritage architecture of the district's towns. Other attractions include boutique cool-climate wineries around Murrumbateman and some beautiful areas of native landscape that have survived early clearing and settlement. Most attractions are an easy daytrip from Canberra.

Tidbinbilla Valley, near Namadgi National Park

Top events

Feb	Australian Blues Music Festival (Goulburn)
	Hilltops Flavours of the Harvest Festival (Young)
Mar	Country Weekend (Crookwell)
	Celebration of Heritage, Jazz and Roses (Goulburn)
April	Heritage Festival (Braidwood)
Oct	Lilac City Festival (Goulburn)
	Days of Wine and Roses (throughout Murrumbateman district)
Nov	Music at the Creek (Braidwood)
	Yass River Festival
Nov/Dec	National Cherry Festival (Young)

Focus on

History
The first inhabitants of the area were the Ngunnawal, whose ancestors may have arrived anywhere from 75 000 to 12 000 years ago according to archaeological evidence from Lake George. Europeans sighted the district in the late 1790s and the Goulburn plains were named in 1818. Settlers arrived between the 1820s and the 1850s, first attracted by the rich grazing land and later by the discovery of gold. Today a number of towns, including Yass, Young, Gunning, Bungendore and Braidwood, showcase heritage buildings and charming streetscapes. The district as a whole provides an evocative glimpse of 19th-century life in rural Australia.

Wombeyan Caves and Wombeyan Gorge
The Wombeyan Caves are one of a handful of caves found on the western edge of the Blue Mountains. They include five show-caves – four that are accessible by guided tour, and one, the Figtree Cave, that is considered Australia's best automated self-guide cave (the lighting turns on once you enter). The adjoining Wombeyan Gorge is naturally lined with marble and provides a cool swimming experience in the warmer months.

CLIMATE GOULBURN

	J	F	M	A	M	J	J	A	S	O	N	D
Max °C	27	26	24	20	16	12	12	13	16	19	22	26
Min °C	13	14	11	8	5	2	1	2	5	7	9	12
Rain mm	61	59	57	53	49	47	45	58	51	56	66	55
Raindays	10	9	9	9	11	11	12	12	11	11	12	9

Namadgi National Park
Namadgi takes in much of the Brindabella Range, covering almost half of the ACT. It boasts significant Aboriginal rock art and a beautiful environment of mountains, valleys and bush, regenerating after the 2003 bushfires. Camping and bushwalking are popular. The excellent Namadgi Visitor Centre is just south of Tharwa.

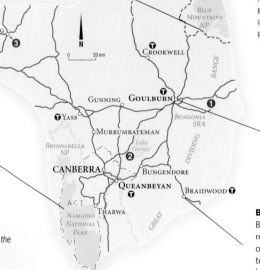

Goulburn
Established in 1833, this town displays elaborate 19th-century architecture, a legacy of early wool-growing wealth. On the town's outskirts, the Big Merino sells wool products, has an educational display on the history of wool, and provides a lookout with sweeping views of Goulburn and surrounds.

Braidwood
Braidwood's elegant Georgian buildings recall early agricultural settlement, while ornate Victorian structures mark the town's goldmining boom. It was once the haunt of bushrangers like Ben Hall, and today it is the haunt of people making movies about bushrangers (and other things). *Ned Kelly* was filmed here in 1969, and *On Our Selection* was filmed here in 1994.

Experience it!

1. **Go** caving, canyoning and canoeing in the wild Bungonia State Recreation Area
2. **Travel** back in time at the Bywong Goldmining Town, a re-creation of an early mining settlement, north-west of Bungendore
3. **Pick** cherries in season in the orchards of Young

For more detail see maps 504, 505, 506, 507 & 508. For descriptions of ☉ towns see Towns from A–Z (p. 53).

SOUTH COAST

Merimbula

T his landscape of sandy beaches, rivers, lakes, fishing villages, rolling hills, rugged escarpments and native forests has proved remarkably resilient to the excesses of coastal development. The region had its beginnings in whaling, but today sustainable tourism and dairying are the mainstays. The cooler climate makes summer the peak period – though even then the area has a laid-back feel. Many people come on weekend trips from Canberra, but visitors from Sydney and Melbourne usually stay for at least a week to soak up the laid-back coastal life.

Top events

Jan	Blue Water Fishing Classic (Bermagui)
Mar	Seaside Fair (Bermagui)
Easter	Tilba Festival (Central Tilba)
Aug	Festival of Food and Wine by the Sea (Ulladulla)
Oct	Eden Whale Festival
	Country Music Festival (Merimbula)
	Jazz Festival (Moruya)
	Great Southern Blues and Rockabilly Festival (Narooma)
Nov	Riverside Festival (Bombala)

Focus on
Aboriginal culture
Before European colonisation, the Yuin occupied the area from Jervis Bay to Twofold Bay, sustained by the produce of coast and rivers. Today the area remains steeped in Yuin history. At Wallaga Lake the Umbarra Cultural Centre offers tours, including one to the summit of Mt Dromedary (Gulaga) where, according to legend, the great creation spirit, Daramulun, ascended to the sky. Booderee National Park, in Jervis Bay Territory, is once again Yuin land after a successful 1995 land claim. Jointly managed by the Wreck Bay Aboriginal Community and Parks Australia, Booderee has middens and other significant sites, and an art and craft centre. The Murramarang Aboriginal Area, near Bawley Point, offers a self-guide interpretive walk.

CLIMATE MERIMBULA

	J	F	M	A	M	J	J	A	S	O	N	D
Max °C	24	25	23	21	19	16	16	17	18	20	21	23
Min °C	15	15	14	11	8	6	4	5	7	9	12	14
Rain mm	77	79	91	83	65	69	41	42	56	69	88	78
Raindays	10	10	10	9	9	9	7	9	11	11	13	11

Central Tilba
Classified by the National Trust as an 'unusual mountain village', picturesque Central Tilba is a showcase for late-19th-century rural architecture, set in a magnificent mountain landscape. New buildings are required to meet National Trust specifications, maintaining the original charm of the streetscapes. Central Tilba was founded in 1895 as a goldmining town, but now caters for tourists with cafes, galleries and art and craft shops.

Jervis Bay
Part of this area is in Jervis Bay Territory (the third and least-known mainland territory of Australia) and includes the national capital's seaport. The bay, partially flanked by NSW Jervis Bay National Park, is known for its dramatic underwater landscapes and its dolphins; diving and dolphin cruises are available.

Mogo
Mogo is an old goldmining town that has been restored and turned into a tourist destination, with several craft shops and a zoo that specialises in raising endangered species. Visitors can pan for gold and take a mine tour at Goldfields Park, visit the reconstructed 19th-century goldmining village of Old Mogo Town or enjoy the sclerophyll forest of the Mogo Bushwalk.

Mimosa Rocks National Park
The park, named after a wrecked paddlesteamer, crosses a landscape of beaches, sea caves, cliffs, forests and wetlands. Rocks tumble across the beaches and form impressive sculptural stacks. There are several secluded campsites, and swimming, walking, diving, fishing and birdwatching are among the activities on offer.

Experience it!

1 Board a charter boat and go deep-sea fishing offshore from Bermagui

2 Take a cruise from Narooma to Montague Island, home to 8000 pairs of little penguins and 600 Australian fur seals

3 Eat fresh Clyde River oysters on the waterfront at Batemans Bay

For more detail see maps 501, 502, 507 & 509. For descriptions of ❶ towns see Towns from A–Z (p. 53).

SNOWY MOUNTAINS

Skiing near Perisher, Kosciuszko National Park

Alpine New South Wales stretches from the ACT to the border of Victoria along the spine of the Great Dividing Range. Kosciuszko National Park lies at the centre, protecting the continent's highest mountain, its only glacial lakes, some of its rarest native species, and the headwaters of legendary rivers. Nestled in the mountains are world-class ski resorts that attract hundreds of thousands of skiers each winter. In spring and summer brilliant wildflowers cover the fields, mountain streams run full with melting snow, and groups of bushwalkers, campers, anglers, whitewater rafters and mountain-bike riders arrive to savour the warm-weather delights of this diverse and spectacular 'roof' of Australia.

Focus on

Ski resorts

The Snowy Mountains resorts are well equipped in terms of lessons, lifts, ski hire, transport, food, accommodation and entertainment. Perisher, Smiggin Holes, Guthega and Mt Blue Cow (near Guthega) are collectively known as Perisher Blue, the largest ski resort in Australia, with 50 lifts and a variety of slopes. A good range of accommodation is available at Perisher and Smiggin Holes, but overnight parking is limited (many visitors leave their cars at Bullocks Flat and take the Skitube). Accommodation is limited at Guthega and not available at Blue Cow. Thredbo, the main village, has excellent skiing and tourist facilities. Charlotte Pass provides access to some of the region's most spectacular runs for experienced skiers. In the north of the park, Mt Selwyn is a good place for families and beginners, and is one of the main centres for cross-country skiing.

Alpine Way

Stretching 111 km from Jindabyne to Khancoban, this spectacular route winds around the Thredbo slopes, passes through Dead Horse Gap, and crosses the valley of the Murray headwaters. It is best driven during spring and summer, although the winter scenery is superb.

Thredbo

This charming alpine village with its peaked European-style lodges makes for an unusual sight in the Australian landscape. Packed and brimming with life during winter, it is also popular in summer with wildflower enthusiasts, anglers, mountain-bike riders and bushwalkers wanting to tackle Mt Kosciuzko. A chairlift drops people at the beginning of a 6 km walk to the summit.

Snowy River power

This once mighty river was dammed and diverted for the Snowy Mountains Scheme. Some 100 000 men from 30 countries worked for 25 years on the largest engineering project of its kind in Australia. Drop in at the Snowy Mountains Authority Information Centre in Cooma, or visit the power stations near Khancoban.

CLIMATE THREDBO

	J	F	M	A	M	J	J	A	S	O	N	D
Max °C	21	21	18	14	10	6	5	6	10	13	16	19
Min °C	7	7	4	2	0	-3	-4	-2	-1	1	4	5
Rain mm	108	87	112	114	165	166	158	192	212	206	155	117
Raindays	11	10	11	13	15	16	17	17	18	16	15	12

Experience it!

1 Explore Yarrangobilly Caves with their underground pools, frozen waterfalls and weird web of limestone formations

2 Relive the adventures of legendary mountain horsemen on a horseriding tour via Adaminaby

3 Take a 24 km return walk from Charlotte Pass (via Jindabyne) along Australia's highest walking track past the glacial Blue Lake

Lake Jindabyne

Created as part of the Snowy Mountains Scheme, this huge lake, along with nearby Lake Eucumbene, has a reputation as one of the best inland fishing destinations in the state, particularly for trout. Sailing, windsurfing and waterskiing are popular in summer.

For more detail see maps 502, 503 & 507.
For descriptions of ⊤ towns see Towns from A–Z (p. 53).

RIVERINA

The Riverina stretches across the flat, fertile plains of south-central New South Wales. It is one of Australia's richest agricultural regions, watered by the Murrumbidgee River through a vast irrigation system. The spacious landscape, brilliant clear skies and warm weather make touring the district a pleasure. The towns of the region are busy, prosperous places, some bearing a strong Southern European character after almost a century of settlement by immigrant farmers. Good restaurants and cafes, heritage buildings and excellent accommodation are easy to find.

Ruins of the One Tree Hotel, near Hay

Top events

Feb	Tumbafest (food and wine, Tumbarumba)
Mar	John O'Brien Bush Festival (Narrandera)
Easter	La Festa (Griffith)
	Yabby Races (Moulamein)
April	Apple Harvest Festival (Batlow)
April–May	Festival of the Falling Leaf (Tumut)
Aug	Wattle Time Festival (Cootamundra)
Sept	Jazz Festival (Wagga Wagga)
Oct	Festival of Gardens (Griffith)
Nov	Dog on the Tuckerbox Festival and Snake Gully Cup (Gundagai)

Focus on

Regional produce

The Riverina produces vast quantities of rice, citrus and stone fruit, grapes, poultry and vegetables. To learn about the rice industry, visit the Sunrice Country Visitors Centre in Leeton. For fruit products, tour the Berri Juice Factory at Leeton and the Catania Fruit Salad Farm at Hanwood (near Griffith). For the gourmet, Mick's Bakehouse in Leeton makes excellent breads and award-winning pies, while the Riverina Cheese Factory sells its produce at the town's fresh-fruit market. Drop in to Tavenders Gourmet Produce in Wagga Wagga for local products.

Hay

Hay lies at the centre of a huge stretch of semi-arid grazing country known as the Hay Plains. Established in 1859, the town boasts an interesting collection of late-19th-century buildings. The POW Internment Camp Interpretive Centre tells the fascinating and sometimes inspirational stories of Hay's role as a prison camp in World War II.

Griffith

The main township of the Riverina, Griffith developed in the early days of irrigation and was designed by Walter Burley Griffin, architect of Canberra. It is surrounded by farms and vineyards, but nearby, in Cocoparra National Park, there is also an opportunity to glimpse the landscape as it once was.

CLIMATE TEMORA

	J	F	M	A	M	J	J	A	S	O	N	D
Max °C	31	31	28	23	18	14	13	15	18	22	26	30
Min °C	16	16	13	9	6	3	2	3	5	8	11	14
Rain mm	48	37	41	43	45	43	47	45	42	54	45	41
Raindays	5	5	5	6	9	10	13	12	9	9	7	6

Riverina wineries

The Riverina is responsible for 60 percent of the grapes grown in New South Wales. There are 14 wineries in the district, mostly around Griffith, including the De Bortoli, Miranda and McWilliams estates. This region is best known for its rich botrytised semillon (semillon improved by flavour-enhancing fungus).

Wagga Wagga

On the banks of the Murrumbidgee, Wagga Wagga is the state's largest inland city and a major centre for commerce, agriculture and education. Visit the Museum of the Riverina (incorporating the Sporting Hall of Fame), the Botanic Gardens and the Regional Art Gallery, home of the National Art Glass Collection. River walks and cruises are also on offer.

Experience it!

1 **Visit** the Dog on the Tuckerbox, 'five miles from Gundagai'

2 **Fish** for trout in the mountain streams around Tumut

3 **Learn** about bush tucker at Green Tree Indigenous Food Gardens, north of Cootamundra

For more detail see maps 507, 508 & 510–1.
For descriptions of ⊤ towns see Towns from A–Z (p. 53).

Map labels

WEST WYALONG · COCOPARRA NP · GRIFFITH · Murrumbidgee · HAY · BALRANALD · LEETON · YANCO · TEMORA · NARRANDERA · COOTAMUNDRA · WAGGA WAGGA · GUNDAGAI · TUMUT · ADELONG · BATLOW · MOULAMEIN · TUMBARUMBA · VIC · River · N · 0   30 km

MURRAY

Murray River scenery near Wentworth

Top events

Jan	Federation Festival (Corowa)
	Sun Festival (Deniliquin)
Feb	Border Vintage Engine Rally (Barham)
Mar	Music Under the Stars (Perry Sandhills)
Mar–April	Albury Gold Cup Racing Carnival
Easter	Stampede (Deniliquin)
Sept/Oct	Play on the Plains Festival and Ute Muster (Deniliquin)
	Food and Wine Festival (Albury)

T he Murray, Australia's most important river, runs for over
2 500 kilometres from the peaks of the Snowy Mountains to the
south-east coast of South Australia. Its path cuts a border between Victoria
and New South Wales, with many towns along its banks. The river was a
great natural resource for indigenous people, who settled here in greater
numbers than anywhere else on the continent. European settlers used
the river as a major trade route, and today continue to use it as a water
source for agriculture. More recently the Murray has developed as a
holiday destination, thanks to magnificent river red gum scenery and quiet
sandy beaches, and the myriad golf courses, vineyards, river cruises and
watersports now associated with it.

Focus on

Along the river

The Murray River provides endless opportunities for swimming, boating, watersports and fishing. Perch, catfish and yabbies are plentiful, and Murray cod is the catch that almost every angler seeks. The parklands of Albury feature pleasant riverside walks and picnic facilities, and at Corowa Yabby Farm visitors can catch and cook their own yabbies. Lake Mulwala was formed by damming the Murray and is now a haven for watersports. The Rocks of Tocumwal, on the banks of the river, change colour according to the weather and, as Aboriginal legend has it, the mysterious Blowhole nearby is the scene of children being eaten by a giant Murray cod. The Barham Lakes consist of four artificial lakes stocked with yabbies and fish, with walking trails through the surrounding bushland.

Corowa

Corowa is the quintessential Australian river town, with wide streets and turn-of-the-century architecture. Federation got a jump-start here in 1893 at the Corowa Federation Conference, now commemorated in the Federation Museum. In 1889 Tom Roberts completed his iconic work *Shearing the Rams* at a sheep station nearby.

CLIMATE **ALBURY**

	J	F	M	A	M	J	J	A	S	O	N	D
Max °C	31	31	27	23	18	14	13	15	18	21	25	29
Min°C	15	15	12	9	6	4	3	4	6	8	11	13
Rain mm	55	36	43	49	64	71	87	89	72	72	53	51
Raindays	6	6	6	7	11	14	16	15	13	11	9	7

For more detail see map 510–11.
For descriptions of ☂ towns see Towns from A–Z (p. 53).

Perry Sandhills

The vast red dunes of Perry Sandhills near Wentworth cover 10 ha and were formed after an ice age around 40 000 years ago. They hold the remains of megafauna such as kangaroos, wombats, emus and lions. Today the dunes are often used as a backdrop in film and television production.

Experience it!

1 **Go** on a camel trek to the wineries around Albury

2 **Play** a game of golf at one of the many renowned courses along the riverbank – the Cobram Barooga Golf Club has one of the best

3 **Learn** to throw a boomerang at Binghi Boomerang Factory in Barooga

Lake Mulwala

The construction of the Yarrawonga Weir in 1939 created this 6000 ha artificial lake, around which the town of Mulwala has grown. The lake is now a premier destination for watersports, offering yachting, sailboarding, swimming, canoeing and fishing, and the largest waterskiing school in the world.

Albury

Once a meeting place for the local Aboriginal tribes, Albury today is a large regional centre familiar to motorists who travel the busy Sydney-to-Melbourne Hume Highway. Attractions include interesting heritage buildings, a large regional art gallery and good restaurants. Nearby Lake Hume, one of Australia's biggest artificial lakes, is another popular spot for watersports.

Map labels: WENTWORTH, MILDURA (Vic.), SA, Murray, River, (Vic.) SWAN HILL, NSW, VIC, BARHAM, DENILIQUIN, FINLEY, JERILDERIE, TOCUMWAL, MULWALA, CULCAIRN, HOLBROOK, COBRAM (Vic.), MOAMA, ECHUCA (Vic.), Lake Mulwala, COROWA, WODONGA (Vic.), ALBURY, Lake Hume, BAROOGA, 0 30 km

OUTBACK

An artist's residence in Silverton

This vast, arid and sparsely populated landscape covers a good two-thirds of the country's most urbanised state. Mining and sheep-farming, the main industries, keep life firmly rooted in a frontier past, although such contemporary touches as the occasional film crew or espresso cafe are evident. One radical change has been the creation of a series of national parks over several decades. These parks preserve the region's stunning landscapes, natural heritage and rich indigenous history. Travelling conditions can be difficult out here, and adequate preparations should be made for any ventures off the beaten track.

Top events

Mar	Outback and All That Jazz (Broken Hill)
July	Tibooburra Festival
Aug	Festival of the Miner's Ghost (Cobar)
	Burke and Wills Fishing Challenge (Menindee)
Sept	Mateship Festival (Bourke)
Sept/Oct	Darling River Outback Surfboat Classic (Brewarrina)
Oct	Country Music Festival (Broken Hill)

Focus on

Rugged reputation

Charles Sturt was marooned north-west of Milparinka for six months while waiting for rain to replenish his party's drinking water in 1845. Although some towns have been successfully established in this harsh but beautiful environment, unpredictable conditions mean that it will never be tamed. The land of Broken Hill has brought forth valuable minerals, which can be viewed at Delprat's Mine (the original home of BHP) and White's Mineral Art and Mining Museum. White Cliffs receives the most solar radiation in New South Wales and so was the natural choice for Australia's first solar-power station. Sturt National Park is home to the red sands and reptiles of the Strzelecki Desert; here day temperatures are often over 40°C and nights are often below freezing.

White Cliffs

The area around White Cliffs has been rendered a moonscape, thanks to 5000 abandoned opal digs. Owing to soaring temperatures in summer much of the town has been built underground, where the temperature remains a steady 27°C. Opals are still mined here, and nearby is spectacular Mutawintji National Park with its sandstone cliffs, river red gums, gorges, rock pools, desert plains and some of the state's best Aboriginal rock art.

Sturt National Park

Occupying 310 000 ha of Corner Country – the point where three states meet – Sturt National Park offers a varied landscape of hills, rocks and plains, congregations of native birds and animals, and wonderful wildflowers after rain. Camping is available; check in at the park office in Tibooburra, and take advantage of their tours.

For more detail see maps 510–11 & 512–13. For descriptions of ⊺ *towns see Towns from A–Z (p. 53).*

Bourke

'If you know Bourke you know Australia,' said Henry Lawson. This Darling River town has become synonymous with the outback and is rich in heritage sites. The Back O' Bourke Exhibition Centre is a fascinating and important modern facility set among river red gums. It tells the story of the river and the outback from the Dreamtime until now.

CLIMATE BROKEN HILL

	J	F	M	A	M	J	J	A	S	O	N	D
Max °C	33	32	29	24	19	16	15	17	21	25	29	31
Min °C	18	18	16	12	9	6	5	6	9	12	15	17
Rain mm	23	25	20	18	23	21	19	19	21	25	20	22
Raindays	3	3	3	3	5	5	6	5	4	5	4	3

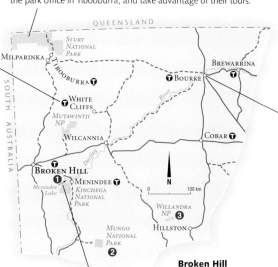

Experience it!

❶ Go *yachting, fishing, swimming or camping at lakes near Menindee*

❷ Take *the 60 km signposted drive through the ancient wonders of Mungo National Park*

❸ Explore *Willandra, once the west's best-known sheep station, now part of Willandra National Park (via Hillston)*

Broken Hill

Broken Hill was established in the 1880s to service the mining of massive deposits of silver, lead and zinc in the Barrier Ranges. With its historic buildings, 20 or so art galleries and decent eating options, it is an oasis of civilisation in a sparse landscape. Nearby Silverton is a quintessential outback town, made famous in films such as *Mad Max II* (1981).

LORD HOWE ISLAND

*Looking across
The Lagoon
towards Mt Gower*

The Lord Howe Group of Islands lies in subtropical waters about 500 kilometres off the northern New South Wales coast. Listed as a World Heritage site, these volcanic remnants have great natural value and beauty, with sandy beaches, coral reefs, imposing forest-covered mountains and some of the rarest flora and fauna on earth. Fly from Sydney, Brisbane or Port Macquarie for wildlife-watching, walking, surfing, cruising, diving and relaxing in one of Australia's most unspoiled holiday environments. The narrow crescent-shaped main island is 11 kilometres long and has a strict tourist capacity of 400, so book well in advance to avoid disappointment.

Top events

Feb	*Discovery Day*
Oct/Nov	*Gosford to Lord Howe Island Yacht Race*
Nov	*Lord Howe Island Golf Open*

Focus on

A world of its own

The Lord Howe Group of Islands comprises a series of seven-million-year-old volcanic formations. Because of its isolation and the absence of humans until recent times, Lord Howe has a unique natural history. Fifty-seven of the islands' 180 flowering plants and 54 fern species are not found anywhere else. At settlement (1834) there were 15 species of land birds, 14 of which were unique. Six species survive today. Hundreds of thousands of seabirds roost on the islands. These include sooty terns, brown noddies, several shearwater species, the world's largest colony of red-tailed tropic birds, and the world's only breeding colony of providence petrels.

CLIMATE LORD HOWE ISLAND

	J	F	M	A	M	J	J	A	S	O	N	D
Max °C	25	26	25	23	21	19	19	19	20	21	22	24
Min °C	20	20	20	18	16	14	13	13	14	15	17	19
Rain mm	108	114	122	149	160	177	178	141	135	127	116	117
Raindays	11	13	15	18	21	22	23	21	17	14	12	12

The Lagoon

A coral reef encloses the crystal waters of this 6 km long lagoon on the western side of the island. Spend the day relaxing and swimming at Old Settlement Beach or snorkel at Escotts Hole, about 1 km out. Glass-bottomed boat and snorkelling tours are available.

Neds Beach

Lush forests of kentia and banyan trees, two of the island's most prolific and distinctive species, fringe this beautiful surf beach. Handfeed the tropical fish, swim, surf, snorkel or take a 45-minute walk up Malabar Hill on the northern headland for superb island views.

Mt Gower

This 875 m mountain is the island's highest point. Take a 9-hour guided walk to the summit through areas of stunted rainforest – a fairytale world of gnarled trees, orchids and moss-covered basalt outcrops. Mists permitting, the view from the summit is spectacular.

Balls Pyramid

This extraordinary cathedral-shaped rock rises 551 m out of the sea 25 km south-east of the main island. Once nearly 6 km wide, the rock's width has been eroded to only 400 m. The island is a major breeding ground for seabirds and can be seen by air charter or boat cruise. Deep-sea fishing in the vicinity is excellent.

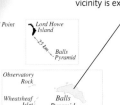

Roach Island
ADMIRALTY ISLANDS ❶
SUGARLOAF PASSAGE
Malabar Hill 208m
Fishy Point
LORD
Neds Beach
Searles Point
North Head
Old Settlement Beach ❸
Clear Place Point
SOUTH PACIFIC OCEAN
Blackburn Island
HOWE
Mutton Bird Island
Blinky Beach
Blinkenthorpe Bay
Mutton Bird Point
THE LAGOON
N
0   1 km
ISLAND ❷
Mt Lidgbird 777m
Boat Harbour Point
East Point
TASMAN SEA
LORD HOWE ISLAND PERMANENT PARK PRESERVE NATURE RESERVE
Red Point
Lord Howe Island
25 km
Balls Pyramid
Mt Gower 875m
South Head
King Point
Gower Island
Observatory Rock
Wheatsheaf Islet
Balls Pyramid

Experience it!

❶ **Take** *a cruise to the Admiralty Islands, a breeding ground for seabirds*

❷ **Tee-off** *at one of the world's most scenic golf courses at the base of Mt Lidgbird*

❸ **Enjoy** *knockout views of The Lagoon along with fine food at the White Gallinule restaurant*

Coolamine Homestead, Kosciuszko National Park, north-west of Adaminaby

Adaminaby Pop. 451

Map ref. 503 H5, 507 D8, 537 L1

Over a hundred buildings were moved in the 1950s to the current town site. The remaining town and surrounding valley were flooded to create Lake Eucumbene as part of the Snowy Mountains Hydro-electric Scheme. Adaminaby is now a haven for anglers and skiers.

IN TOWN The Big Trout The world's largest trout, a fibreglass construction, was erected after a local angler, attempting to drink a gallon of Guinness while fishing, was pulled into the water by a large trout and almost drowned. Legend has it the man then managed to finish the Guinness, but the trout stands as a tribute to 'the one that got away'. Lions Club Park at town entrance.
Historic buildings: several buildings, including two churches that were moved from Adaminaby's original site; contact visitor centre for details.

NEARBY Lake Eucumbene It is said that anyone can catch a trout in Lake Eucumbene, the largest of the Snowy Mountains artificial lakes. Its abundance of rainbow trout, brown trout and Atlantic salmon make it a popular spot for anglers. The Snowy Mountains Trout Festival draws hundreds of anglers every November. Fishing boats can be hired at Old Adaminaby and for fly-fishing tours, contact the visitor centre. Access via Old Adaminaby.

Old Adaminaby Race Track: featured in the film *Phar Lap* (1984); on the road to Rosedale, Cooma side of town. *Kosciuszko National Park:* on the road to Tumut is the Mt Selwyn ski area, the historic goldmining site of Kiandra and the Yarrangobilly Caves. North of the road, via Long Plain Rd, is historic Coolamine Homestead. *For more details see feature on p. 92.* Power stations: tours and interactive displays; details from visitor centre.
ⓘ The Bakehouse, 11 Denison St; (02) 6454 2453; www.snowymountains. com.au

Adelong Pop. 807

Map ref. 507 B5, 508 D13

Adelong, a picturesque tablelands town on the Adelong River, was established and thrived as a goldmining town in the late 19th century. Wilham Williams discovered reef and alluvial gold, and prospectors flocked to Adelong to seek their fortunes. Legend has it that Williams bought a mining claim for £40 000, only to sell it later the same day for £75 000. By World War I, over a million ounces of gold had been extracted from the mines, leaving little behind. The people began to disappear immediately. What is left is a charming rural village with a turn-of-the-century feel.

IN TOWN Historic Adelong Walk Many of the beautifully preserved buildings in Adelong have been classified by the

National Trust. *Welcome to Historic Adelong*, available from the visitor centre, guides visitors through Adelong's streets to discover banks, hotels and churches of the gold-rush era.

NEARBY Adelong Falls Reserve Richie's Gold Battery at Adelong Falls Reserve was one of the foremost gold-processing and quartz-crushing facilities in the country. The ruins of its reefer machine, including water wheels and a red brick chimney, are easily recognisable today. Three clearly signposted walks explore the falls and other ruins. 1 km N.
ⓘ York's Newsagency, 57 Tumut St; (02) 6946 2051

Albury   Pop. 42 005

Map ref. 511 Q13, 536 C1, 539 P4

The twin towns of Albury–Wodonga are seven kilometres apart on opposite sides of the Murray River, which is also the New South Wales–Victoria border. Together they form a significant urban centre in Australia's busiest inland corridor between Canberra, Sydney and Melbourne. Originally inhabited by Aboriginal people, the Albury area was 'discovered' by explorers Hume and Hovell in 1824 where they carved their comments into the trunks of two trees. Hume's tree was destroyed by fire, but Hovell's still stands today in Hovell Tree Park.

IN TOWN Albury Regional Museum Exhibits illustrate the history and cultural diversity of the region and include one on Australia's largest postwar migrant centre, which existed at nearby Bonegilla. Wodonga Pl.
Botanical Gardens: array of native and exotic plants and signposted rainforest and heritage walks; cnr Wodonga Pl and Dean St. *The Parklands:* comprises Hovell Tree Reserve and Noreuil and Australia parks. Enjoy riverside walks, swimming, kiosk and picnic areas. Wodonga Pl. *Monument Hill:* spectacular views of town and alps; Dean St. *PS Cumberoona:* replica of 1886 paddlesteamer departs from Noreuil Park daily in season; call visitor centre for details. *Albury Regional Art Centre:* extensive Russell Drysdale collection; Dean St.
WHAT'S ON *Rotary Community Market:* Townsend St; Sun. *Albury Gold Cup Racing Carnival:* Mar/April. *Food and Wine Festival:* Sept/Oct. *Festival of Sport:* Dec–Feb.
NEARBY Ettamogah A tiny but famous town in Australia, thanks to cartoonist Ken Maynard's Ettamogah Pub. This was the country's original Ettamogah Pub, and as well as being a great place for a drink, you can also arrange camel rides here. 12 km NE. The Ettamogah Wildlife Sanctuary is worth a visit and Cooper's Ettamogah Winery is 3 km further along. *Lake Hume:* watersports, camping and spectacular dam wall; 14 km E. *Hume Weir Trout Farm:* handfeeding and fishing for thousands of rainbow trout; Lake

Hume; 14 km E. *Jindera Pioneer Museum:* originally a German settlement, featuring a traditional general store, a slab hut and a wattle and daub cottage; 14 km NW. *Linbrae Camel Farm:* winery and river treks; off Urana Rd; 16 km N; bookings (02) 6026 3452. *Albury–Wodonga Trail System:* walking trails in the footsteps of Hume and Hovell; maps available from visitor centre. *Hume and Hovell Walking Track:* 23-day, 440 km trek from Albury to Yass. For a kit, including maps, contact Department of Infrastructure, Planning and Natural Resources, Sydney; (02) 9762 8044.
ⓘ Lincoln Causeway, Wodonga; 1300 796 222

Alstonville   Pop. 4747

Map ref. 515 Q3, 607 Q12

Alstonville is nestled in the hinterland hills between Lismore and Ballina where it is surrounded by macadamia and avocado plantations. Visitors will find quirky antique and gift shops in this quaint tourist town, known for its immaculate gardens and purple tibouchina trees that blossom in March.

IN TOWN *Lumley Park:* walk-through reserve of native plants, flying fox colony and open-air pioneer transport museum; Bruxner Hwy. *Budgen Avenue:* several shops and galleries with local art and craft. *Elizabeth Ann Brown Park:* rainforest park with picnic facilities; Main St.
NEARBY Victoria Park Nature Reserve This remarkable rainforest reserve contains 68 species of trees in only 17.5 hectares, 8 hectares of which remain largely untouched. The area is also home to red-legged pademelons, potoroos, water rats and possums. There are clearly marked walking trails and a spectacular lookout taking in the surrounding countryside. 8 km S. *Summerland House With No Steps:* nursery, avocado and macadamia orchard, garden, crafts, fruit-processing plant and Devonshire teas. Completely run by people with disabilities. 3 km S.
ⓘ Ballina Visitor Information Centre, cnr Las Balsas Plaza and River St, Ballina; (02) 6686 3484

Armidale   Pop. 20 068

Map ref. 515 L9

Armidale is the largest town of the New England district of New South Wales's northern tablelands. It is truly a university city, being home to New England University, the first university in Australia established outside a capital city. The transplanted birch, poplar and ash trees that line the streets make Armidale seem like an English village. It is one of those rare towns in Australia that enjoy four distinct seasons, with autumn turning the leaves stunning shades of crimson and gold. National

parks in the area offer breathtaking forests, gorges and waterfalls.

IN TOWN New England Regional Art Museum The museum (closed Mon) accommodates over 40 000 visitors each year and has eight gallery spaces, an audiovisual theatre, artist studio and cafe. The Howard Hinton and Chandler Coventry collections are two of the most important and extensive collections of Australian art in regional Australia. They include works by legendary Australian artists such as Arthur Streeton, Tom Roberts, Margaret Preston and John Coburn. There is also a separate Museum of Printing (open Thurs–Sun) featuring the F. T. Wimble & Co collection. Kentucky St.
Armidale Heritage Tour: includes Railway Museum, St Peter's Anglican Cathedral (built with 'Armidale blues' bricks) and University of New England; departs daily from visitor centre. *Aboriginal Cultural Centre and Keeping Place:* includes museum, education centre and craft displays; Kentucky St. *Armidale Folk Museum:* National Trust-classified building with comprehensive collection of pioneer artefacts from the region including toys and buggies; cnr Faulkner and Rusden sts; open 1pm–4pm daily. *Self-guide Heritage Walk and Heritage Drive:* 3 km walk and 25 km drive provide history and points of interest in and around the town; maps from visitor centre.
WHAT'S ON *Armidale Markets:* Beardy St; last Sun each month (3rd Sun in Dec). *Autumn Festival:* Mar–May.
NEARBY Oxley Wild Rivers National Park World Heritage-listed Oxley Wild Rivers National Park has the largest area of dry rainforest in NSW. Features worth a visit include Dangars Falls (21 km SE), a 120 m waterfall in a spectacular gorge setting, and Wollomombi Falls (40 km E), at 220 m one of the highest falls in the state. *University of New England:* features Booloominbah Homestead, Antiquities Museum, Zoology Museum, and kangaroo and deer park; 5 km NW. *Saumarez Homestead:* National Trust-owned house offering tours (closed mid-June to end Aug); 5 km S. *Dumaresq Dam:* walking trails, boating, swimming and trout fishing (Oct–June); 15 km NE. *Hillgrove:* former mining town with Rural Life and History Museum featuring goldmining equipment (open Fri–Mon) and self-guide walk through old townsite; maps at visitor centre; 31 km E.
ⓘ 82 Marsh St; (02) 6772 4655 or 1800 627 736; www.new-england.org/armidale

Ballina   Pop. 16 517

Map ref. 515 Q3, 607 R12

Ballina sits on an island at the mouth of the Richmond River in northern New South Wales surrounded by the Pacific Ocean and nearby fields of sugarcane.

The sandy white beaches and warm weather make the area popular with visitors. Ballina's name comes from the Aboriginal word 'bullenah', which is said to mean 'place where oysters are plentiful'. This is still the case, with fresh seafood readily available in many seaside restaurants.

IN TOWN Shelly Beach A superb spot for the whole family. Dolphins can be seen frolicking in the waves all year round and awe-inspiring humpback whales migrate through these waters June–July and Sept–Oct. The beach itself has rock pools, a wading pool for toddlers and a beachside cafe. Off Shelly Beach Rd.
Naval and Maritime Museum: features a restored Las Balsas Expedition raft that sailed from South America in 1973; Regatta Ave. *Kerry Saxby Walkway:* from behind the visitor centre to the river mouth with great river and ocean views. *The Big Prawn:* opal and gem museum, as well as art and craft and fresh seafood; Pacific Hwy. *Richmond Princess and Bennelong:* daily river cruises; bookings at information centre. *Shaws Bay:* swimming and picnic area; off Compton Dr. *Ballina Water Slide:* River St.

WHAT'S ON *Ballina Markets:* Outdoor Entertainment Reserve; 3rd Sun each month. *Ballina Cup:* horserace; Sept.

NEARBY Lennox Head A pleasant and relatively undeveloped beachside town with a good market on the 2nd and 5th Sun each month on the shores of Lake Ainsworth (also a popular spot for windsurfing). Pat Morton Lookout affords excellent views along the coast, with whale-watching June–July and Sept–Oct. Below is The Point, a world-renowned surf beach. The outskirts of town offer scenic rainforest walks. 10 km N.
Thursday Plantation: tea tree plantation with product sales and maze; 3 km W. *Whale-watching and diving:* bookings at visitor centre.
ⓘ Cnr Las Balsas Plaza and River St; (02) 6686 3484; www.discoverballina.com

Balranald   Pop. 1282

Map ref. 510 H8, 545 N6

Balranald is the oldest town on the lower part of the Murrumbidgee River. Situated on saltbush and mallee plains, the area has recently expanded its traditional agriculture to embrace viticulture, horticulture and tourism. A string of dry lake beds stretches away to the north of Balranald, the most famous of which are preserved in Mungo National Park (*see feature on this page*).

IN TOWN Heritage Park Well worth a stroll to investigate the old gaol, the Murray pine school house, local history displays and a historical museum (open Wed and Fri mornings). There are also picnic and barbecue facilities. Market St. *Balranald Weir:* barbecues, picnics, fishing. *Memorial Drive:* great views. *Self-guide Town Walk:* stroll through the historically

A section of The Walls of China

Mungo National Park

Mungo National Park is the focal point of the Willandra Lakes World Heritage Area, a 240 000-hectare region of 17 dry Pleistocene lakes over two million years old. The arid landscape, where temperatures in summer can reach up to 50°C, was part of the Mungo sheep station before being declared a national park in 1981. The 19th-century woolshed and station are now open as part of the park.

On the edge of Lake Mungo is the remarkable three-kilometre formation called The Walls of China, so named because its sheer vastness reminded local Chinese workers of the Great Wall. Erosion of the wall has uncovered mega-fauna fossils including giant Tasmanian tigers, echidnas, bats and three-metre kangaroos. Also exposed in the wall are ancient fireplaces, artefacts and tools, proving this region has been the site of continuous human occupation for many thousands of years.

The dry bed of Lake Mungo features a lunette, a semicircular formation of sand and clay layers that is an excellent indicator of climate changes. Prior to the Ice Age, the lake was full of water and teeming with fish, and the banks were rich in trees, plants and animals, including the diprotodon, a wombat the size of a rhinoceros. Here also lived an ancient civilisation thought even to precede Aboriginal people in Australia, although where they came from remains a mystery. In 1969 Mungo Woman was uncovered on the shores of Lake Mungo. She is thought to be around 40 000 years old and is the earliest example of cremation in the world. While she was fine-boned and similar in stature to women of today, Mungo Man, discovered 300 metres away in 1974, was over seven feet (2.1 metres) tall.

Mungo Man's age has caused much debate in the scientific world, with agreement only that he is between 40 000 and 62 000 years old. What is remarkable about Mungo Man, apart from his age, is that he was found with his hands neatly folded over his genital region and his body decorated in red ochre. Red ochre has never been found closer than 150 kilometres away, leading experts to conclude that Mungo Man was prepared for burial. This makes him the oldest example of ceremonial burial in the world or, as Professor Jim Bowler, the man who discovered Mungo Woman, described it, the 'earliest evidence on earth of cultural sophistication'.

significant buildings in the town; maps available at visitor centre.

WHAT'S ON *Balranald Race:* horserace; Sat before Melbourne Cup.

NEARBY Moulamein The oldest town in the Riverina, Moulamein has fascinating historic structures to explore including its restored courthouse (1845) and Old Wharf (1850s). There are picnic areas by the Edward River and Lake Moulamein, and yabby races each Easter. 99 km SE. *Yanga Lake:* fishing and watersports; 7 km SE. *Homebush Hotel:* built in 1878 as a Cobb & Co station, it now provides meals and accommodation; 25 km N. *Kyalite:* home to Australia's largest commercial pistachio nut farm and a popular town with campers and anglers; 36 km S.

Redbank Weir: barbecues and picnics; Homebush–Oxley Rd; 58 km N.
ⓘ Heritage Park, Market St; (03) 5020 1599

Barham   Pop. 1186

Map ref. 510 I12, 538 B1, 543 Q2, 545 Q13

Barham and its twin town, Koondrook, sit astride the Murray River and the New South Wales–Victoria border. Barham is known as the southern gateway to Golden Rivers country and is surrounded by river flats and red hills. The Murray River makes Barham a rewarding place for anglers with Murray cod, golden perch, catfish and yabbies in abundance. Barham Bridge is one of the oldest bridges

Sawn Rocks, Mount Kaputar National Park, west of Barraba

on the Murray and was lifted manually until 1997.

IN TOWN Barham Lakes Complex
The complex is popular with locals and visitors alike. It has four artificial lakes stocked with fish and yabbies, grasslands with hundreds of native plants, a walking track and barbecue facilities. Murray St.

WHAT'S ON *Border Vintage Engine Rally:* Feb. *The Country Music Stampede:* Feb and Aug. *Jazz Festival:* June. *Golden Rivers Produce and Food Festival:* July. *Golden Rivers Red Gum Forest to Furniture Showcase:* Oct.

NEARBY Koondrook State Forest
Koondrook State Forest is 31 000 hectares of native bushland that is perfect for birdwatchers and nature enthusiasts. The forest has over 100 bird species, kangaroos, emus and wild pigs. Forest drives winding through the park are well signposted. 12 km NE.
Koondrook: old sawmilling town and river port with historic buildings and tramway; 5 km SW. *Murrabit:* largest country markets in the region; 1st Sat each month; Murrabit Rd; 24 km NW.
ⓘ Golden Rivers Tourism, 15 Murray St; (03) 5453 3100 or 1800 621 882

Barraba   Pop. 1202

Map ref. 514 I8

The tree-lined streets of Barraba lie in the valley of the Manilla River. Surrounded by the Nandewar Ranges, Horton Valley and undulating tablelands, Barraba is a quiet and idyllic town. The area was once busy with mining and, although some mines still operate, the main industries today centre around sheep and wool.

IN TOWN Heritage walk Guides are available from the visitor centre or the website that lead the visitor through historic Barraba. The walk takes in a heritage-listed organ and historic buildings such as the courthouse,

church, clock tower, and the visitor centre itself. The Commercial Hotel on Queen St was once a Cobb & Co changing station. *Clay Pan and Fuller Gallery:* exhibits art, craft and pottery; Queen St.

WHAT'S ON *Australia's Smallest Country Music Festival:* Jan. *Barraba Agricultural Show and Rodeo:* Feb/Mar. *Australia's Smallest Jazz and Blues Festival:* Easter Sat. *BarrArbor Cultural Festival:* celebration of trees and culture; Nov. *Horton Valley Rodeo:* Dec.

NEARBY Mount Kaputar National Park
This park is excellent for hiking, rises as high as 1200 m and is the site of the now extinct Nandewar Volcano. The diverse vegetation ranges from semi-arid woodland to wet sclerophyll forest and alpine growth. Wildlife is abundant, especially bats, birds and quolls. Access to the park is by foot only, although special permission for 4WD access may be granted by the visitor centre for those with problems walking. 48 km W.
Adam's Lookout: panoramic views of the town and countryside; 4 km N. *Millie Park Vineyard:* organic wine cellar-door tastings and sales; 4 km N. *Glen Riddle Recreation Reserve:* on Manilla River north of Split Rock Dam, for boating, fishing and picnicking; 15 km SE. *Ironbark Creek:* gold and mineral fossicking; 18 km E. *Horton River Falls:* 83 m waterfall, swimming and bushwalking; 38 km W. *Birdwatching trails:* the 165 species in the area include the rare regent honeyeater. Guides are available from the visitor centre or website.
ⓘ 116 Queen St; (02) 6782 1255; www.barraba.org

Batemans Bay   Pop. 10 181

Map ref. 507 H7

Batemans Bay is a popular town for holiday-makers at the mouth of the Clyde River. It has something for everyone with

rolling surf beaches, quiet coves and rock pools, and wonderful views upriver to the hinterland mountains and out to sea to the islands on the horizon. Batemans Bay is the home of the famous Clyde River oyster and other excellent fresh seafood.

IN TOWN *Birdland Animal Park:* native wildlife and rainforest trail; Beach Rd. *River cruises:* daily cruises on the *Clyde Princess* or *Merinda* to historic Nelligen depart Ferry Wharf; contact visitor centre for times. *Houseboat hire and fishing charters:* bookings at visitor centre.

WHAT'S ON *Batemans Bay Market:* behind Lobster Pot Arcade, 1st, 2nd and 4th Sat each month; and at high school, 3rd Sun each month.

NEARBY Mogo Alive with a quaint village atmosphere, Old Mogo Town re-creates the 19th-century goldmining town that Mogo once was. Prospectors may still have some luck panning for gold at Mogo Goldfields Park. Wildlife enthusiasts will enjoy Mogo Zoo – it specialises in raising endangered species such as tigers, snow leopards and red pandas. Mogo offers fabulous village-style shopping and cafes. 8 km S.
Eurobodalla Native Botanic Gardens: native plants, walking tracks, nursery and picnic area; 4 km S; open Wed–Sun. *Durras Lake:* fishing and swimming; 8 km NE. *Murramarang National Park:* undisturbed coastline and abundant kangaroos; 10 km NE. *Murramarang Aboriginal Area:* signposted walk through 12 000-year-old Aboriginal sites; just north of Murramarang National Park. *Nelligen:* historic town with country music festival each Jan; 10 km NW. *Calligraphy Gallery:* local art; 12 km SE. *Malua Bay:* excellent surfing; 14 km SE.
ⓘ Cnr Princes Hwy and Beach Rd; (02) 4472 6900 or 1800 802 528; www.naturecoast-tourism.com.au

Bathurst   Pop. 26 920

Map ref. 492 B4, 508 H6

Bathurst, on the western side of the Great Dividing Range, is Australia's oldest inland city. Originally occupied by the Wiradjuri people, it was the site of enormous conflict in 1824 between its original inhabitants and the European settlers. Since then, Bathurst has become known as the birthplace of Ben Chifley, Australian prime minister 1945–49, and for its magnificent Georgian and Victorian architecture. Today it is best known for its motor racing circuit, Mount Panorama.

IN TOWN Miss Traill's House Ida Traill (1889–1976) was a fourth-generation descendant of pioneers William Lee and Thomas Kite who came to Bathurst in 1818. During her lifetime, Miss Traill amassed a significant collection of artefacts from four generations of the Lee family, which reflect Bathurst's pastoral heritage. Her house, a colonial Georgian bungalow bequeathed to the National

Trust, was built in 1845, making it one of the oldest houses in Bathurst. The surrounding formal 19th-century cottage garden is particularly charming in spring, when it is ablaze with colour. The house is open 10am–3pm, Fri–Sun. Russell St. *Historical Society Museum:* features notable local Aboriginal artefacts in the east wing of the Neoclassical Bathurst Courthouse; Russell St. *Bathurst Regional Art Gallery:* focuses on Australian art after 1955, including an impressive Lloyd Rees collection; Keppel St. *Machattie Park:* Victorian-era buildings and gardens with sculptures, a lake, a fernery and a begonia house (in bloom Feb–Easter); Keppel, William and George sts. *Self-guide historical walking tour and Rotary self-drive tour:* takes in Bathurst Gaol and historic homes including Ben Chifley's house; map from visitor centre.
WHAT'S ON *Gold Crown Festival:* harness racing; Mar. *East Coast Classic Rally:* vintage cars; Mar. *Autumn Colours Program:* variety of events celebrating autumn; Mar–May. *Autumn Heritage Festival:* April. *V8 Supercars 1000:* Oct. *Cool Climate Wine Show:* Oct. *Bathurst 24-hour:* car race; Nov.
NEARBY Mount Panorama The inaugural Bathurst 1000 was held here in 1960 and has since become an Australian institution, drawing a crowd of 40 000 annually and viewed by millions around the country. The 6.2 km scenic circuit is open year-round, and while the lap record is 129.7 seconds (over 170 km/h), visitors are limited to 60 km/h. The National Motor Racing Museum at the circuit exhibits race cars, trophies, memorabilia and special exhibits. Also at Mount Panorama are the Bathurst Goldfields, a reconstruction of a historic goldmining area, and McPhillamy Park, which features the Sir Joseph Banks Nature Reserve with outstanding views over Bathurst, especially at sunrise and sunset. 2 km s. *Abercrombie House:* impressive 1870s baronial-style Gothic mansion; Ophir Rd; 6 km w. *Bathurst Sheep and Cattle Drome:* visitors can milk a cow and see shearing and sheepdog demonstrations; Limekilns Rd; 6 km NE. *Bathurst Observatory:* program varies throughout the year. The visitor centre features mineral, fossil and space display. The complex is closed in inclement weather. 12 km NE. *Wallaby Rocks:* wall of rock rising from the Turon River and a popular spot for kangaroos and wallabies. Also an ideal swimming and picnic spot. 40 km N. *Sofala:* historic gold town and the setting for scenes from the films *The Cars That Ate Paris* (1974) and *Sirens* (1994); 42 km N. *Hill End Historic Site:* former goldfield with many original buildings. The area has inspired painters Russell Drysdale, Donald Friend, John Olsen and Brett Whiteley. There is a National Parks and Wildlife visitor

centre in old Hill End Hospital, including a historical display and information on panning and fossicking, with equipment for hire. Old gold towns nearby include Peel, Wattle Flat, Rockley, O'Connell and Trunkey. 86 km NW.
ⓘ Kendall Ave; (02) 6332 1444 or 1800 681 000; www.bathurst.nsw.gov.au

Batlow   Pop. 973
Map ref. 507 B6, 508 D13

In the 19th-century gold rush prospectors quickly converged on nearby Reedy Creek, which sparked a sudden demand for fresh produce. The resulting orchards and farms became the town of Batlow. Set in the low-lying mountains of the state's south-west slopes, Batlow is a picturesque town still surrounded by orchards of delicious apples, pears, berries, cherries and stone fruit.
IN TOWN *Cascade Fuchsia Nursery:* country garden serving morning and afternoon tea; Fosters Rd; open Oct–Apr. *Weemala Lookout:* breathtaking views of town and Snowy Mountains; H. V. Smith Dr.
WHAT'S ON *Apple Harvest Festival:* April. *Daffodil Show:* Sept.
NEARBY *Hume and Hovell Lookout:* spectacular views over Blowering Valley and Blowering Reservoir, with picnic area at site where explorers rested in 1824; 6 km E. *Tumut Rd:* pick your own fruit at farms along the road. Springfield Orchard, 6 km N, grows 16 apple varieties and has picnic and barbecue facilities. *Kosciuszko National Park:* this massive alpine park to the east includes nearby Bowering Reservoir and Buddong Falls; *for more details see feature on p. 92. Hume and Hovell Walking Track:* access to short sections of the 440 km track via Tumut Rd. Maps available from Department of Infrastructure, Planning and Natural Resources, (02) 9762 8044.
ⓘ Old Butter Factory, Adelong Rd, Tumut; (02) 6947 7025; www.tumut.nsw.gov.au

Bega   Pop. 4384
Map ref. 502 F7, 507 G10, 537 Q6

It is possible to ski and surf on the same day from Bega, set as it is in a fertile valley with the awe-inspiring mountains of the Kosciuszko snow resorts to the west and breathtaking coastline to the east. Bega is best known throughout Australia for its dairy production, particularly cheese.
IN TOWN *Bega Family Museum:* houses town memorabilia including silverware, ball gowns and farm machinery; cnr Bega and Auckland sts; closed Sun Sept–May, open Tues and Fri June–Aug.
WHAT'S ON *Bega Valley Art Awards:* Oct.
NEARBY Biamanga National Park Now a popular spot for swimming, bushwalking and picnics, Biamanga National Park has long been a sacred site to the Yuin people.

Mumbulla Mountain was an initiation site for young men and Mumbulla Creek was used to wash off ceremonial ochre. Visitors can now enjoy the rock pools, natural water slides, boardwalks, viewing platforms and picnic sites of this culturally significant area. 19 km NE. *Bega Cheese Heritage Centre:* restored cheese factory with cheese-tasting and displays of cheese-making equipment; 3 km N. *Lookouts:* excellent views over the valley and mountains at Bega Valley Lookout (3 km N) and Dr George Lookout (8 km NE). *Grevillea Estate Winery:* vineyard and farm featuring cellar-door tastings, a wetland and farm walk and a restaurant. See cows being milked at the dairy at 3pm daily. Buckajo Rd; 5 km w. *Candelo:* charming and peaceful village, seemingly untouched by time, with market on 1st Sun each month; 24 km sw. *Brogo Dam:* haven for native birdlife such as sea eagles and azure kingfishers. Also popular for bass fishing, swimming, picnicking, boating and canoeing (canoe hire on site). 30 km NW.
ⓘ Princes Hwy; (02) 6492 2045 or 1800 633 012; www.sapphirecoast.com.au

Bellingen   Pop. 2720
Map ref. 515 P8

Bellingen is an attractive tree-lined town on the banks of the Bellinger River, surrounded by rich pasturelands. Traditionally serving dairy farmers and timber cutters, Bellingen is now a haven for urban folk fleeing the big cities, attracted to the relaxed and alternative lifestyle Bellingen offers. City touches can be found in shops and cafes, but the town retains its laid-back feel. The area is the setting for Peter Carey's *Oscar and Lucinda*.
IN TOWN Bellingen Bat Island This 3 ha island is home to a colony of up to 40 000 grey-headed flying foxes (fruit bats). At dusk the flying foxes set off in search of food, filling the sky to spectacular effect. Visitors arriving at this time are understandably advised to wear hats. The best time to visit is Sept–Mar. Access is via Bellingen Caravan Park, Dowle St. *Bellingen Museum:* features extensive photo collection of early pioneer life and early transportation; Hyde St. *Hammond and Wheatley Emporium:* the first concrete block construction in Australia, the emporium has been magnificently restored – including a grand staircase leading to a mezzanine floor – and is now home to boutiques and homewares retailers; Hyde St. *Local art and craft:* at The Yellow Shed, cnr Hyde and Prince sts, and The Old Butter Factory, Doepel La.
WHAT'S ON *Bellingen Markets:* Bellingen Park, Church St; 3rd Sat each month. *Jazz Festival:* Aug. *Global Carnival:* world music; Oct.
NEARBY *Raleigh Vineyard and Winery:* tastings and barbecue facilities; 11 km E. *Walking, cycling, horseriding and canoeing:*

along the Bellinger River and in forest areas; equipment hire information and maps from visitor centre. *Trout fishing:* in streams on Dorrigo Plateau (between Dorrigo and Urunga); contact visitor centre for locations. *Scenic drive:* north-east through wooded valleys and farmlands, across Never Never Creek to Promised Land; map available from visitor centre. *Gambaarri Aboriginal Cultural Tours:* to same area; bookings (02) 6655 5195. ⓘ Pacific Hwy, Urunga; (02) 6655 5711; www.bellingentourism.com.au

Bermagui   Pop. 1196

Map ref. 502 H4, 507 H9, 537 R4

Bermagui is a charming and sleepy coastal village with a well-earned reputation for being an outstanding fishing spot. The continental shelf is at its closest off Bermagui and this results in excellent fishing for marlin, tuna and shark. Zane Grey was a famous visitor in the 1930s and the town featured in two of his books. Bermagui is also the centre of a mystery involving a geologist, Lamont Young, who was sent to investigate goldfields in 1880. When he decided to head north to investigate further, he and his assistant were offered passage on a small boat with three men. All five disappeared en route. When their boat was discovered, it was found to have five bags of clothing, Young's books and papers, and a bullet in the starboard side. Despite extensive searches and media attention, no trace of the men was ever found.

IN TOWN *Fish Co-op:* freshly caught fish and prawns; Fishermans Wharf, harbourside. *Blue Pool:* large and attractive saltwater rock pool offering an unusual swimming experience; off Scenic Drive. *Horseshoe Bay Beach:* safe swimming spot. *Good surfing beaches:* Beares, Mooreheads, Cuttagee and Haywards beaches; maps from visitor centre. *Gamefishing, deep-sea fishing and reef-fishing:* bookings at visitor centre. *Dolphin- and whale-watching cruises:* Sept–Nov; depart from harbour.

WHAT'S ON *Craft Market:* Dickinson Park; last Sun each month. *Blue Water Fishing Classic:* Jan. *International Dog Show:* Feb. *Seaside Fair:* Mar. *Tag and Release Gamefishing Tournament:* Mar. *Four Winds Easter Concert:* even-numbered years, Easter. *Victorian Gamefishing Tournament:* Easter.

NEARBY Wallaga Lake National Park There is an 8 km coastal walk through wetland flora and fauna reserves and remnants of the Montreal Goldfields north to Wallaga Lake. It passes Camel Rock, an unusual rock formation in the general shape of a camel (squinting may be required). The park is hilly with steep gullies, so it is best explored by boat (available for hire from Regatta Pt and Beauty Pt). But for the energetic there are good walking trails, including one to the summit of Mt Dromedary. The park is

excellent for boating, fishing, swimming, picnicking and bushwalking. The Yuin people run Aboriginal cultural tours from the Umballa Cultural Centre, sharing Dreamtime stories that have never been recorded on paper. Activities include ochre painting, bark-hut building and boomerang throwing. Bookings (02) 4473 7232.
Mimosa Rocks National Park: 17 km s; *see Tathra. Mystery Bay:* the site of the discovery of Lamont Young's abandoned boat and a memorial; 17 km N. *Cobargo:* unspoiled historic working village with art galleries, wood and leather crafts, iron forge, pottery and tearooms. Also home to a country market on 4th Sat each month at RSL hall grounds. 20 km w. ⓘ Lamont St; (02) 6493 3054; www.sapphirecoast.com.au

Berridale   Pop. 1347

Map ref. 503 I10, 507 D9, 537 L4

This charming small town calls itself the 'Crossroads of the Snowy' and is a popular stopover point in winter between Cooma and the snowfields. In the 1860s and 1870s it was known as Gegedzerick, but later changed its name to Berridale, the name of a local property. The main street is lined with poplars that provide a striking show in autumn. The trees were planted about 100 years ago by children from Berridale School.

IN TOWN *Historic buildings:* St Mary's (1860), Mary St; Berridale School (1883), Oliver St; Berridale Inn (1863), Exchange Sq; Berridale Store (1863), Exchange Sq.
WHAT'S ON *Berridale Fair:* Easter.
NEARBY *Snowy River Winery:* wine-tastings and restaurant; Old Dalgety Rd; 3 km N. *Dalgety:* small town featuring historic Buckley's Crossing Hotel, which marks the spot where cattle used to cross the Snowy River; 18 km s. *Eucumbene Trout Farm:* sales, horseriding and tours; 19 km N. *Snowy River Ag Barn and Fibre Centre:* museum, craft and fibre shop, animals and restaurant; 21 km s. ⓘ Berridale Store, 64 Jindabyne Rd; (02) 6456 3206

Berrima   Pop. 876

Map ref. 501 B6, 507 H3, 509 J10

A superbly preserved 1830s village, Berrima is nestled in a valley next to the Wingecarribee River. The National Heritage Council declared the entire village a historic precinct in the 1960s. Many old buildings have been restored as antique shops, restaurants and galleries.

IN TOWN Berrima Courthouse Museum The courthouse was the scene in 1841 of Australia's first trial by jury, in which Lucretia Dunkley and Martin Beech were accused of having an affair and tried for murdering Lucretia's much older husband, Henry, with an axe. They

were both found guilty and hanged. The building, said to be the finest in town, now houses displays on the trial and early Berrima. Cnr Wilshire and Argyle sts. *Berrima District Historical Museum:* displays focus on colonial settlement and the struggles of pioneer days; Market Pl. *Australian Alpaca Centre:* sales of knitwear and toys; Market Pl. *The Surveyor General:* built in 1835, Australia's oldest continually licensed hotel; Old Hume Hwy. *Berrima Gaol:* built in 1839 and still in use; Argyle St.
NEARBY *Amber Park Emu and Ostrich Farm:* tours, animal nursery, feedings, picnic area and kiosk; 11 km NW. *Wineries:* numerous in the area with cellar-door tastings; maps from visitor centre. ⓘ Berrima Courthouse Museum, cnr Wilshire and Argyle sts; (02) 4877 1505; www.highlandsnsw.com.au/bcourt

Berry   Pop. 1591

Map ref. 501 F11, 507 I4, 509 K11

The local Chamber of Commerce named Berry 'The Town of Trees' because of the extensive stands of English oaks, elms and beech trees planted by settlers in the 1800s. Many still stand today, giving the town a distinctly English feel. Berry is a popular weekend destination for Sydneysiders searching for bargains in the antique and craft shops and enjoying the laid-back atmosphere.

IN TOWN *Berry Historical Museum:* records and photographs of early settlement in Berry; Queen St; open 11am–2pm Sat, 11am–3pm Sun, daily during school holidays. *Precinct Galleries:* local contemporary art, craft and design; Alexandra St. *Great Warrior Aboriginal Art Gallery:* contemporary and traditional Aboriginal art, weapons, artefacts and didgeridoos; Queen St. *Antique and craft shops:* contact visitor centre for details.
WHAT'S ON *Country Fair Markets:* showground, cnr Alexandra and Victoria sts, 1st Sun each month; Great Southern Hotel, Queen St, 3rd Sun each month.
NEARBY *Coolangatta:* convict-built cottages, winery (open for tastings) and accommodation on site of first European settlement in area; 11 km SE. *Other wineries in area:* open for tastings and sales; map from visitor centre. *Mild to Wild Tours:* adventure tours including sea-kayaking with dolphins, rockclimbing, moonlight canoeing and mountain-biking; bookings (02) 4464 2211. ⓘ Shoalhaven Visitors Centre, cnr Princes Hwy and Pleasant Way, Nowra; (02) 4421 0778 or 1300 662 808; www.berry.org.au

Bingara   Pop. 1170

Map ref. 514 I6

Located in the centre of an area known as Fossickers Way, Bingara is an old gold-mining and diamond-mining town in the

Gwydir River Valley. Gold was discovered here in 1852. Prospectors have been attracted to the town ever since, drawn by the chance of discovering their own fortunes in gold, tourmaline, sapphires and garnets as well as by the peaceful cypress-covered mountain surrounds.

IN TOWN Orange Tree Memorial A row of orange trees along Finch St and surrounding Gwydir Oval stand as a living memorial to those who have fallen in war. It is a closely followed town tradition that each year during the Orange Festival Bingara's children pick the fruit and present it to hospital patients and the elderly.

All Nations Goldmine: a stamper battery is the only visible remnant; Hill St. *Bingara Historical Museum:* slab building (1860) displays gems and minerals and 19th-century furniture and photographs; Maitland St. *Visitor Information Centre:* set in the beautifully restored 1930s Art Deco Roxy Theatre complex; Maitland St. *Gwydir River Rides:* trail rides; Keera St. *Gwydir River:* walking track along the bank, and reportedly the best Murray cod fishing in NSW. *Self-guide historical/scenic town walk and drive:* contact visitor centre for maps.

WHAT'S ON *Australia Day Race Meeting:* Jan. *Easterfish:* fishing competition; Easter. *Orange Festival:* July/Aug.

NEARBY *Three Creeks Goldmine:* working mine open to the public for gold panning, crystal fossicking and bushwalking; 24 km s. *Myall Creek Memorial:* monument to 28 Aboriginal men, women and children killed in the massacre of 1838; Delungra–Bingara Rd; 27 km NE. *Rocky Creek glacial area:* unusual conglomerate rock formations; 37 km SW. *Birdwatching and fossicking:* contact visitor centre for maps.
ℹ️ Roxy Theatre Building, Maitland St; (02) 6724 0066 or 1300 659 919; www.bingara.nsw.gov.au

Blackheath   Pop. 4046
Map ref. 492 H6, 494 C5, 509 J7

This pretty resort town, the highest in the Blue Mountains, has breathtaking views. Known for its guesthouses, gardens and bushwalks, Blackheath is in an ideal location at the edge of Blue Mountains National Park. It is also known as Rhododendron Town for the myriad varieties around that bloom every November.

IN TOWN National Parks and Wildlife Heritage Centre This is more than just an information centre. It features an interactive display on the geology, wildlife, and Aboriginal and European history of the area and offers historical tours and guided walks. The centre is the starting point for the Fairfax Heritage Walk, a gentle bushwalk with wheelchair access and facilities for the visually impaired. The 4 km return trail goes to Govetts Leap Lookout for views across several waterfalls and the Grose Valley. Govetts Leap Rd.

Rock wall near Hanging Rock, Blue Mountains National Park, near Blackheath

Govett statue: commemorates the bushranger known as Govett, said to have ridden his horse over a cliff rather than be captured by police; centre of town.
WHAT'S ON *Markets:* Community hall, Great Western Hwy; 3rd Sun each month. *Rhododendron Festival:* Nov.
NEARBY Mount Victoria National Trust-classified Mount Victoria is the westernmost township of the Blue Mountains. There are charming buildings from the 1870s, including the Imperial Hotel, St Peter's Church of England and The Manor House. Also in town are craft shops, a museum at the train station and the Mount Vic Flicks historic cinema (open Thurs–Sun and school holidays). Mount Victoria affords wonderful views of the mountains and offers many picnic spots and walking trails. 6 km NW.
Bacchante Gardens: rhododendrons and azaleas; 1.5 km N. *Mermaid Cave:* picturesque rock cave where parts of *Mad Max III* (1985) were filmed; Megalong Rd; 4 km S. *Shipley Gallery:* art exhibitions (open weekends); Shipley Rd; 4.6 km S. *Pulpit Rock Reserve and Lookout:* sweeping views of Mt Banks and Grose Valley; 6 km E. *Hargraves Lookout:* overlooking Megalong Valley; Panorama Point Rd; 7.4 km SW via Shipley Gallery.

Mt Blackheath Lookout: views of Kanimbla Valley; Mount Blackheath Rd; 8.2 km N via Shipley Gallery. *Megalong Australian Heritage Centre:* horseriding, adventure tours and tourist farm; 9 km S. *Blue Mountains National Park:* in the area east of Blackheath are various waterfalls and lookout points, and the much-photographed Hanging Rock (around 9 km N via Ridgewell Rd). *For other parts of the park see Katoomba and Glenbrook, and feature on p. 80. Werriberri Trail Rides:* various trail rides on horseback; bookings (02) 4787 9171.
ℹ️ Heritage Centre, Govetts Leap Rd; (02) 4787 8877; www.bluemountains tourism.org.au

Blayney   Pop. 2608
Map ref. 508 G6

Blayney is a farming town in the central tablelands of New South Wales. National Trust-classified buildings and avenues of deciduous trees add a touch of charm to the town, particularly in autumn.

IN TOWN *Heritage Park:* small wetland area, barbecue facilities and tennis courts; Adelaide St. *Local craft shops:* contact visitor centre for details. *Self-guide heritage walk:* includes churches and the courthouse; brochure from visitor centre.

Outback station, 'back o' Bourke'

NEARBY **Carcoar** The National Trust-classified town of Carcoar, surrounded by oak trees on the banks of the Belubula River, is full of historic buildings. In early settlement days, convicts and bushrangers caused a lot of trouble in the town. Johnny Gilbert and John O'Meally committed Australia's first daylight bank robbery in 1863 at the Commercial Bank on Belubula St (still standing). The hold-up was unsuccessful and the robbers fled when a teller fired a shot into the ceiling to alert the townsfolk. 14 km sw.
Local art and craft: at Taroona Wool Park (5 km NE) and Cottesbrook Gallery (15 km NE), both on Mid Western Hwy. *Millthorpe:* National Trust-classified village with quaint shopfronts, art and craft shops, historic churches and a museum with blacksmith's shop and old-style kitchen; 11 km NW. *Carcoar Dam:* watersports and camping with picnic and barbecue facilities; 12 km sw. *Newbridge:* historic buildings and craft shops; 20 km E. *Abercrombie Caves:* stunning cave system in a 220 ha reserve that features the largest natural limestone arch in the Southern Hemisphere. Carols in the Caves is held here in Dec. 50 km SE.
ⓘ 97 Adelaide St; (02) 6368 3534; www.blayney.nsw.gov.au

Bombala   Pop. 1221

Map ref. 502 A9, 507 E11, 537 N7

The main road from Cooma to the coast does not pass through Bombala, so this charming small town has remained largely untouched by time. It is the centre for the surrounding wool, beef, lamb, vegetable and timber industries. The Bombala River is well known for its platypuses and excellent trout fishing.
IN TOWN **Railway Park** There is much to see at Railway Park, including the historic engine shed (open by appt) and the museum of local artefacts and farm implements. The most unusual, though, is Lavender House, home to the oldest

lavender association in the country. Lavender House has education facilities, displays on distillation and an array of lavender products such as lavender jams, soaps and oils. Monaro Hwy.
Endeavour Reserve: with a 2 km return walking track to a lookout with views over town; Caveat St. *Bicentennial Park:* wetlands and a pleasant river walk; Mahratta St. *Self-guide historical walk:* 1 hr walk includes courthouse (1882) and School of Art (1871); leaflet available from visitor centre.
WHAT'S ON *Markets:* Railway Park; 1st Sat each month. *Wool and Wood Festival:* Jan. *Celebrate Lavender:* Jan. *Celebration of Motorcycles:* Sept. *Riverside Festival:* celebration of diversity of regional crafts and products; Nov.
NEARBY **Platypus Sanctuary** Bombala has one of the densest populations of platypuses in NSW. They can be seen here in their natural environment from the Platypus Reserve Viewing Platform. The sanctuary provides a safe and peaceful setting and the notoriously shy platypus frolics happily here in full sight of visitors. The best times for viewing are at dawn and dusk, when platypuses are at their most active, but they can be seen at any time of day. Off Monaro Hwy on the road to Delegate; 3 km s.
Cathcart: charming township with historical town walk and Cathcart Collectables, a fascinating collection of Monaro history; brochure from visitor centre; 14 km NE. *Myanba Gorge:* boardwalk and bushwalks through old-growth eucalypt forest with spectacular views of waterfalls, granite boulders and Towamba Valley. Enjoy a picnic or barbecue at the gorge. South East Forest National Park; 20 km SE. *Delegate:* scenic town with Early Settlers Hut, believed to be the first dwelling on the Monaro plains, and Platypus Walk and River Walk (leaflets from visitor centre); 36 km sw. *Scenic drive:* gold fossicking en route to Bendoc Mines in Vic; 57 km sw. *Fly-fishing and trout fishing:* maps available from visitor centre.

ⓘ Platypus Country Tourist Information Centre, Railway Park, Monaro Hwy; (02) 6458 4622; www.bombalaregion.com

Bourke   Pop. 2558

Map ref. 513 N5

The saying 'back o' Bourke' has come to mean the middle of nowhere, which is why Bourke is known as the gateway to the real outback. Bourke is a prosperous country town in the centre of thriving wool, cotton and citrus areas on the Darling River. It wasn't always so and the region did not appeal to Charles Sturt, who described it as 'unlikely to become the haunt of civilised man'. In 1835 Sir Thomas Mitchell came to the area and, thinking that the local Aboriginal people were a great threat, built himself a sturdy fort out of logs. He named it Fort Bourke after the governor of New South Wales. The fort provided the idea that permanent settlement of the area was possible. Bourke quickly became a bustling major town, with Henry Lawson describing it as 'the metropolis of great scrubs'.
IN TOWN **Back O' Bourke Exhibition Centre** This fascinating modern facility is set among the river red gums on the Darling River. It tells the story of the river and the outback from the Dreamtime to 100 years into the future. Visitors walk through colourful displays representing paddleboats, early settlers and pastoralists, Afghan cameleers, Cobb & Co coaches, the history of unionism and Aboriginal heritage. The centre also looks at the sustainability of agriculture and the social structures of the outback. Kidman Way.
Old Railway Station: displays of Aboriginal artefacts and local history; Anson St. *Fred Hollows' Grave and Memorial:* the eye surgeon and famous humanitarian is buried in the cemetery; Cobar Rd. *Historic wharf replica:* reminder of days when Bourke was a busy paddlesteamer port. Take a paddlesteamer ride on the river. Sturt St. *Mateship Country Tours:* include historic

buildings of Bourke (such as the Carriers Arms Inn, frequented by Henry Lawson) and surrounding citrus and grape farms; contact visitor centre for bookings.

WHAT'S ON *Outback Fishing Challenge:* Easter. *Mateship Festival:* Sept. *Police and Community Outback Trek:* Oct. *Rodeo:* Oct.

NEARBY Gundabooka National Park The park is a woodland haven for wildlife. There are over 130 species of bird, including the endangered pink cockatoo, pied honeyeater and painted honeyeater. Kangaroos, euros and endangered bats also make their homes here. For the visitor there are rewarding walking tracks up Mt Gundabooka and a spectacular lookout over red cliffs, gorges and hills. The Ngemba people have a history of ceremonial gatherings in the area and their art can be seen in some caves (to book tours, contact National Parks and Wildlife Service (02) 6872 2744). The park also provides excellent camping and barbecue facilities. 74 km s. *Fort Bourke Stockade replica:* memorial to Sir Thomas Mitchell, who built the original fort; 20 km sw. *Mt Oxley:* home to wedge-tailed eagles and with views of plains from the summit; 40 km se.
ⓘ Old Railway Station, Anson St; (02) 6872 2280; www.backobourke.com.au

Bowral   Pop. 10 325

Map ref. 501 C6, 507 I3, 509 J10

Bowral is best known as the home town of 'the boy from Bowral', cricketing legend Sir Donald Bradman. Adoration of Bradman is evident throughout the town with tours, a sporting ground and a museum. An up-market tourist town and the commercial centre of the Southern Highlands, Bowral's close proximity to Sydney meant that it was a popular retreat for the wealthy. This is still evident today in the magnificent mansions and gardens around town.

IN TOWN Bradman Museum A comprehensive history of cricket is on display, including an oak bat from the 1750s. An extensive Don Bradman memorabilia collection includes the bat he used to score 304 at Headingly in 1934. A cinema plays Bradman footage and newsreels. The Bradman Walk through town takes in significant sites including the Don's two family homes. A leaflet is available from the museum. Bradman Oval; St Jude St.
Bong Bong Street: specialty shopping and antiques. *Historic buildings:* mostly in Wingecarribe and Bendooley sts; leaflet available from visitor centre.

WHAT'S ON *Market:* Rudolf Steiner School, Lyall Ave; 3rd Sun each month. *Autumn Gardens in the Southern Highlands:* throughout region; April. *District Art Society Exhibition:* Sept/Oct. *Tulip Time Festival:* Sept–Oct. *Bong Bong Races:* Nov.

NEARBY Mittagong This small and appealing town has interesting historic cemeteries and buildings. Lake Alexandra in Queen St is artificial, and an excellent spot for birdwatching and walking. There is a market at the Uniting Church hall on the 3rd Sat each month. 8 km ne. *Mt Gibraltar:* bushwalking trails and lookout over Bowral and Mittagong; 2 km n. *Box Vale walking track:* begins at the northern end of Welby; 12 km n. *Nattai National Park:* reserved to protect landforms, geological features, catchments and biodiversity in the Sydney basin. Only low-impact activities are encouraged and there is a 3 km exclusion zone around Lake Burragorang. Via Hilltop; 19 km n. *Magnificent private gardens:* include Milton Park, reputedly one of the finest gardens in the world. Open seasonally for tours; details from visitor centre.
ⓘ Southern Highlands Visitor Information Centre, 62–70 Main St, Mittagong; (02) 4871 2888 or 1300 657 559; www.southern-highlands.com.au

Braidwood   Pop. 1003

Map ref. 507 G6, 508 H13

Braidwood is an old gold-rush area that has been declared a historic town by the National Trust. Gold was plentiful here in the 1800s, the largest gold discovery being 170 kg in 1869. With the discovery of gold came bushrangers, such as the Clarke gang and Ben Hall, and Braidwood became one of the most infamous and dangerous towns in the region. The 19th-century buildings have been carefully maintained and restored and are still in use for both commercial and residential purposes. The result is a charming town that appears to be from a bygone era. This has come in handy for film producers, who have found Braidwood a perfect setting for movies such as *Ned Kelly* (1969), *The Year My Voice Broke* (1986) and *On Our Selection* (1994).

IN TOWN Braidwood Museum Built of local granite and originally the Royal Mail Hotel, the museum now houses over 2100 artefacts and 900 photographs. On display are exhibits of Aboriginal history, goldmining, the armour worn by Mick Jagger in *Ned Kelly*, a machinery shed and a library of local records, newspapers and family histories. A particularly unusual feature is the Namchong Collection of items from the Namchong family, who came here from China during the gold rush and became traders in town from the 1870s to the 1990s. Wallace St; open Fri–Mon, daily during school holidays. *Galleries and craft and antique shops:* details from visitor centre. *Tallaganda Heritage Trail and scenic drive:* tours of historic buildings such as the Royal Mail Hotel and St Andrew's Church; leaflet from visitor centre.

WHAT'S ON *Heritage Festival:* April. *Music at the Creek:* Nov. *The Quilt Event:* Nov.

NEARBY The Big Hole and Marble Arch The Big Hole is thought to have formed when overlying sandstone collapsed into a subterranean limestone cavern creating an impressive chasm 96 m deep and 50 m wide. Wildlife in the area includes native birds, echidnas, wallabies, wombats and tiger quolls. Marble Arch is a narrow canyon 3–4 m wide and 25 m deep. It is over 1 km in length and bands of marble are visible along the walls. There are caves along the way, but special permission is required to enter some of them. Some are very dark and require a torch, so it is best to check with the National Parks and Wildlife Service if you intend to explore. Enquiries (02) 4887 7270. Near Gundillion; 45 km s. *Scenic drives:* rugged countryside; brochure from visitor centre.
ⓘ National Theatre, Wallace St; (02) 4842 1144; www.braidwood-tourism.com

Brewarrina fish traps

Australia's Aboriginal history stretches back tens of thousands of years; in Brewarrina, evidence of this lies right on the surface. Around town are sacred sites including burial and ceremonial grounds, pointing to a culture that revolved around the river. But by far the most impressive relics are the ancient stone fish traps of the Barwon River estimated to be 40 000 years old – one of the oldest constructed structures in the world.

The traditional Aboriginal story states that the traps were built by Baiame and his two sons Booma-ooma-nowi and Ghinda-inda-mui when there was a drought. Gurrungga (the water hole at Brewarrina) dried up and the three men used this opportunity to build the traps in the dry bed. The Ngemba people, who were facing famine, were never hungry again. Anthropologists have claimed that the traps are impressive evidence of early engineering, river hydrology and knowledge of fish biology.

Around 500 metres long, these traps relied on the currents to sweep the fish inside, where they would be confined when the water level dropped. Here they would live until it was time for them to be eaten, which meant there was almost always fresh fish on demand.

Thousands of years ago, the traps formed the centrepiece of a seasonal festival, regularly attended by up to 50 000 people from Aboriginal groups along the east coast who travelled for days or weeks to the celebration and feast of fish. At night they held corroborees and shared stories around campfires in a language common to the region. The traps preserve the memory of these ancient times.

NEW SOUTH WALES

Brewarrina   Pop. 1199

Map ref. 513 Q5

This charming outback town on the banks of the Barwon River is affectionately known as Bre. It was developed in the 1860s as a river crossing for stock, but later thrived because of its position on a Cobb & Co route. Brewarrina's Aboriginal heritage stretches back many thousands of years, as a meeting place between tribes and the site of some incredible stone fish traps (*see feature on p. 61*).

IN TOWN *Aboriginal Cultural Museum:* displays on aspects of Aboriginal life, from tales of the Dreamtime to the present; Bathurst St; open Mon–Fri. *Wildlife Park:* native fauna in bush setting; Doyle St. *Self-guide drive:* 19th-century buildings; brochure from visitor centre.

WHAT'S ON *Darling River Outback Surfboat Classic:* Sept/Oct.

NEARBY *Narran Lake Nature Reserve:* wetlands and a breeding ground for native and migratory birds; 40 km NE. *Fishing:* plentiful Murray cod in the Barwon River. *Start of Darling River Run:* self-drive tour; brochure from visitor centre.
ⓘ Bathurst St; (02) 6872 1222

Broken Hill   Pop. 19 753

Map ref. 512 B12

An oasis of green parks and gardens in the vast arid lands of far-western New South Wales, Broken Hill was first an intermittent home for the Willyama people. Its lack of water made it impossible to settle permanently. When Charles Sturt encountered the area while searching for an inland sea, he described it as some of the most barren and desolate land he had ever seen. Enthusiasm was soon generated, however, with the discovery of silver. Prospectors flocked to the harsh land and Broken Hill was born. A syndicate of seven men quickly bought much of the land and in 1885 they discovered the world's largest silver-lead-zinc lodes. Later that same year they decided to form a company and float shares. That company was Broken Hill Proprietary (BHP) and it is now the largest company in Australia. Broken Hill, referred to as the 'silver city', is still a true mining town with streets named after metals, minerals and mine managers. It is also the centre of the 16-million-hectare West Darling pastoral industry, which has 1.75 million merino sheep surrounded by a 600-kilometre dog-proof fence. As you would expect of a hot, arid mining town, Broken Hill has a large number of pubs. Note that Broken Hill operates on Central Standard Time, half an hour behind the rest of New South Wales.

IN TOWN **Delprat's Underground Tourist Mine** Tours are conducted of the original BHP mine. Visitors don miners' hats and lamps and descend over 130 m down the mine shaft in a cage. The tour takes in drives, stopes and mining machinery in working order. Tours are conducted 10.30am weekdays and 2pm Sat and during school holidays. Federation Way. *Railway, Mineral and Train Museum:* displays on old mining and rail services; cnr Blende and Bromide sts. *Albert Kersten Geocentre:* displays of minerals and mining specimens; cnr Crystal and Bromide sts. *White's Mineral Art and Mining Museum:* walk-in mine and mining models; Allendale St. *Joe Keenan's Lookout:* view of town and mining dumps; Marks St. *Thankakali Aboriginal Arts and Crafts:* see works created on the premises, talk to artists and purchase pieces; cnr Buck and Beryl sts. *Muslim Mosque:* built by Afghan community in 1891. Contact visitor centre for opening times; Buck St. *Zinc Twin Lakes:* popular picnic spot at lakes used as a water source for mines; off Wentworth Rd. *Art galleries:* over 20 in town including Pro Hart Gallery and Jack Absalom's Gallery; details from visitor centre. *Heroes, Larrikins and Visionaries of Broken Hill Walk and Silver Trail self-guide historical town drive:* leaflets from visitor centre.

WHAT'S ON *Outback and All That Jazz:* Mar. *St Patrick's Race Day:* horse races; Mar/April. *National 4x4 Challenge:* 4WD rally; May. *Country Music Festival:* Oct.

NEARBY **Silverton** The National Trust-classified town of Silverton was established when silver chloride was found 27 km NW of Broken Hill in 1883. It now has less than 100 inhabitants and is surrounded by stark, arid plains, making it popular with filmmakers wanting an outback setting. Films such as *Mad Max II* (1981), *Razorback* (1983), *Young Einstein* (1988), *The Adventures of Priscilla, Queen of the Desert* (1994) and *Dirty Deeds* (2001) have been filmed here, and the Silverton Hotel displays photographs of the film sets on its walls. Take the Silverton Heritage Walking Trail (leaflet from visitor centre) and visit the Silverton Gaol Museum. Silverton Camel Farm offers 15 min rides around the outskirts of town. Mundi Mundi Plain Lookout, a further 10 km N, affords views of the desolate yet awe-inspiring landscape. Daydream Mine, 13 km NE, operated in the 1880s and is now open for 45 min guided tours, 10am–3.30pm daily. *Living Desert:* magnificent sandstone sculptures on hillside, particularly striking at sunrise and sunset; leaflet available from visitor centre; Nine Mile Rd; 5 km N. *Sundown Nature Trail:* 2.8 km return walking path taking in wildflowers, native plants and fauna. The wildlife is most active and the scenery at its most striking just after sunrise or just before sunset. A leaflet is available from visitor centre; begins Tibooburra Rd; 9 km N. *Royal Flying Doctor Service base and visitor centre:* headquarters, radio room and aircraft hangar open to visitors; at airport; 10 km S.

ⓘ Cnr Blende and Bromide sts; (08) 8087 6077; www.visitbrokenhill.com.au

Bulahdelah   Pop. 1151

Map ref. 509 O3

Bulahdelah is a pretty town at the foot of Bulahdelah Mountain (known to locals as Alum Mountain because of the alunite that was mined here). Surrounded by rainforests and the beautiful Myall Lakes, it is a popular destination for bushwalkers and watersports enthusiasts.

IN TOWN **Bulahdelah Mountain Park** A park of contrasts with meandering walking trails in tall forest passing rare orchids in spring and the remains of alunite mining machinery. The park also features picnic and barbecue facilities and a spectacular lookout over Bulahdelah and the Myall Lakes. Meade St. *Bulahdelah Court House:* restored as a museum with cells out the back; cnr Crawford and Anne sts; open Sat mornings or by appt; bookings (02) 6597 4838.

WHAT'S ON *Market:* beside visitor centre, Crawford St; 1st Sat each month. *The Bass Bash:* fishing festival; Feb. *Junior Rodeo:* July. *Bulahdelah Show:* campdraft and rodeo; Nov. *Bulahdelah Music Festival:* Nov.

NEARBY **Myall Lakes National Park** A largely unspoiled 10 000 ha network of coastal lakes and 40 km of beaches have made this national park one of the most visited in the state. It is also a Ramsar Wetland of International Importance. The year-round pleasant weather conditions make the beaches and rivers an ideal place for all types of watersports and activities. Canoe and houseboat hire is available. Broughton Island, 2 km offshore, is a popular spot for diving. The rainforest, heathlands and eucalypt forest are abundant in native flora and fauna and are perfect for camping and bushwalks. 12 km E. *Bulahdelah State Forest:* with scenic picnic area and walking trails along old mining trolley lines, and one of the tallest trees in NSW – the 76 m flooded gum (*Eucalyptus grandis*); off the Lakes Way; 14 km N. *Wootton:* charming small town with a rainforest walk along a reconstructed timber railway to a historic trestle bridge with picnic and barbecue facilities nearby; 15 km N. *Sugar Creek Toymakers:* fine wooden toys and handpainted dolls; 31 km E. *Seal Rocks:* fishing village with seals sometimes resting on the offshore rocks. Grey nurse sharks breed in underwater caves and whales pass by in June–Aug. Sugarloaf Point Lighthouse (1875) is worth a visit, as are the pleasant beaches and camping areas. 40 km E. *Wallingat National Park:* walking trails and picnic facilities. Stop at Whoota Whoota Lookout for magnificent sweeping views of forest, coast and lakes. 43 km NE.
ⓘ Cnr Pacific Hwy and Crawford St; (02) 4997 4981; www.greatlakes.org.au

Bundanoon   Pop. 1937

Map ref. 501 A9, 507 H3, 509 J10

Bundanoon is a quiet and attractive village with a European feel to it thanks to lush greenery and tree-lined avenues. The first European to investigate the district was ex-convict John Wilson. He was sent by Governor Hunter to collect information on the area that would discourage convicts from trying to escape. It was commonly believed among the prisoners that China lay 150 miles to the south. Today the sleepy town is a popular yet unspoiled tourist destination with many delightful guesthouses and a health resort. The old-world atmosphere makes it popular with honeymooners.

IN TOWN *Craft shops and art galleries:* several in town featuring local work; contact visitor centre for details. *Drive and walk to several lookouts:* map from visitor centre.

WHAT'S ON *Market:* Memorial Hall, Railway Ave; 1st Sun each month. *Bundanoon is Brigadoon:* highland gathering; April. *Village Garden Ramble:* Oct.

NEARBY Morton National Park, Bundanoon section This section of the park has stunning views, lookouts and walking trails. The park consists mainly of rainforest and eucalypts and is home to myriad native fauna including wallabies, potoroos and bush rats. See glow worms at night in the remarkable Glow Worm Glen. 1 km s. *For other sections of the park see Nowra, Robertson and Ulladulla. Exeter:* quaint village with Old English Fayre each Nov; 7 km N.
ⓘ Southern Highlands Visitor Information Centre, 62–70 Main St, Mittagong; (02) 4871 2888 or 1 300 657 559; www.southern-highlands.com.au

Byron Bay   Pop. 5919

Map ref. 515 R2, 607 R12

Byron Bay has excellent beaches, a laid-back feel and great weather, making it a popular destination for surfers, backpackers and alternative-lifestylers. In the 1980s, a number of celebrities bought property in the area and it has since become popular with many holiday-makers. Luckily the town has not changed much – it is just busier, and sprawling a little bit further out. A forward-thinking council moved early to ban all drive-in takeaway food outlets and all buildings more than three storeys high. Now people from all walks of life flock to Byron Bay for the same reasons: whale-watching, surfing and swimming. The town centre has an array of wonderful shops selling discount surfboards, new-age products, handmade jewellery and glass products, timber furniture and interesting clothing.

IN TOWN *Beach Hotel:* beer garden with magnificent ocean views and meals, accommodation and regular entertainment; cnr Jonson and Bay sts.

Aerial view of Cape Byron Lighthouse

Galleries, handmade jewellery, craft shops and natural therapies: see visitor centre for details.

WHAT'S ON *Market:* Buttler St Reserve; 1st Sun each month. *East Coast Blues and Roots Festival:* Easter. *Splendour in the Grass:* music festival; July. *Byron Writers Festival:* Aug. *A Taste of Byron:* food festival; Sept. *Yoga Play Byron Bay:* Oct. *Buzz Film Festival:* Nov.

NEARBY Cape Byron This headland forms part of the world's oldest caldera – the rim of an enormous extinct volcano (the centre is Mt Warning). It is the easternmost point on mainland Australia and provides visitors with breathtaking views up and down the coast. Dolphins can be seen frolicking year-round in the Pacific Ocean and magnificent humpback whales migrate up the coast June–July and back down Sept–Oct. Cape Byron Lighthouse is the most visible attraction – the 22 m structure, completed in 1901, houses a visitor centre with displays of the area's cultural and natural history. 3 km SE. *Julian Rocks Aquatic Reserve:* protects 450 underwater species and is great for diving; 3 km s. *Broken Head Nature Reserve:* rainforest, secluded beaches and dolphin-watching; 9 km s. *Bangalow:* rustic village with magnificent scenery, antique shops, arts and crafts, walking tracks and a popular market on the 4th Sun each month; 10 km SW.
ⓘ 80 Jonson St; (02) 6685 8050; www.visitbyronbay.com

Camden   Pop. 6461

Map ref. 493 K10, 501 F1, 507 I1, 509 K8

Camden, on the Nepean River just south-west of Sydney, was once a hunting ground of the Gundungurra people, who called it 'Benkennie', meaning 'dry land'.

Governor Macquarie sent men to kill or imprison the Aboriginal people in 1816, and although records are poor, the brutal mission had some success. European settlement originated after eight cattle wandered off four months after the First Fleet landed. They were not seen again until 1795 when it was discovered their number had grown to more than 40. The site on which they were found was named Cowpasture Plains, but was later changed to Camden. Camden was home to John and Elizabeth Macarthur, pioneers of the Australian wool industry. They were also the first in Australia to grow tobacco, use mechanical irrigation, produce wine of respectable quality and quantity, and produce brandy. The Macarthurs sent thousands of vines to the Barossa Valley and are thereby credited with helping to start South Australia's wine industry. Today Camden is a town steeped in history in a picturesque rural setting.

IN TOWN *Self-guide walk and scenic drive:* includes historic buildings such as the Macarthur Camden Estate, St John the Evangelist Church and Kirkham Stables; brochure from visitor centre.

WHAT'S ON *Produce Market:* behind Woolworths supermarket; 2nd and 4th Sat each month. *Art and Craft Market:* Onslow Park, Cawdor Rd; 3rd Sat each month. *Heritage Wine and Food Fair:* Feb. *Camden House Open Weekend:* Sept.

NEARBY Camden Museum of Aviation With military aircraft, engines and tanks, this privately owned museum has the largest specialist aircraft collection in Australia. Where possible, the aircraft have been painstakingly restored to a taxiable standard (meaning that they can taxi along a runway but can't necessarily fly), with accurate wartime markings and camouflage colours carefully researched

through service records and photographs. The museum is open, with knowledgeable owners on hand to answer questions, Sun and public holidays. 3 km NE. *Struggletown Fine Arts Complex:* gallery featuring stained glass, pottery and traditional art; 3 km N. *Camden Aerodrome:* ballooning and gliding with vintage aircraft on display; 3 km NW. *Cobbity:* historic rural village with market 1st Sat each month; 11 km NW. *The Oaks:* small town in open countryside featuring the slab-built St Matthew's Church and Wollondilly Heritage Centre, a social history museum; 16 km W. *Burragorang Lookout:* views over Lake Burragorang; 24 km W. *Yerranderie:* this fascinating old silver-mining town can be reached by normal vehicle only in dry conditions, otherwise only by 4WD or plane; 40 km W. *Wineries:* several in the area; contact visitor centre for map. Kirkham Estate (1 km N) has regular jazz evenings and Gledswood (10 km N) features a working colonial farm.
ⓘ John Oxley Cottage, Camden Valley Way; (02) 4658 1370; www.camden. nsw.gov.au

Campbelltown   Pop. 6461

Map ref. 491 A12, 493 L11, 501 G1, 509 K8

Campbelltown was founded in 1820 by Governor Macquarie and named after his wife, Elizabeth Campbell. Campbelltown is in the process of being engulfed by the urban sprawl of Sydney (Sydney's city centre is 53 km NE), but it manages to combine the best of two worlds, enjoying the convenience of city living with the rustic charm of 19th-century buildings. It is also the location of the legend of Fisher's ghost. In 1826 an ex-convict, Frederick Fisher, disappeared. Another ex-convict, George Worrell, claimed that Fisher had left town, leaving him in charge of Fisher's farm. A farmer claimed to have seen the ghost of Fisher pointing at the creek bank where his body was subsequently found. Worrell was tried and hanged for Fisher's murder.
IN TOWN Campbelltown City Bicentennial Art Gallery Visitors can see, explore and participate in art-making at this interactive centre. Exhibitions are diverse and include local, regional, national and international shows of art and craft. Behind the gallery is a sculpture garden established in 2001 as a Centenary of Federation project. New permanent sculptures are being added to the garden on a regular basis. Adjacent to the gallery is the Koshigaya-tei Japanese Teahouse and Garden, a bicentennial gift to the people of Campbelltown from its sister city, Koshigaya. The garden is a peaceful area with a waterfall, koi pond and timber bridge, perfect for picnics and tranquil contemplation. Art Gallery Rd.
Quandong Visitor Information Centre: formerly St Patrick's, the first Catholic

school in Australia, its displays include early world maps, desks, inkwells, canes and curriculums (1840); Art Gallery Rd. *Stables Museum:* display of historic farm equipment and household goods on the 1st, 3rd and 5th Sun each month; Lithgow St. *Self-guide heritage walks:* take in numerous historic buildings including St Peter's Church (1823), Emily Cottage (1840) and Fisher's Ghost restaurant, formerly Kendall's Millhouse (1844); leaflet from visitor centre.
WHAT'S ON *Festival of Fisher's Ghost:* Nov.
NEARBY Mount Annan Botanic Garden A striking 400 ha garden with 20 km of walking trails. Attractions include two ornamental lakes with picnic areas, a nursery, an arboretum and themed gardens such as the woodland conservation area, the rare and endangered plants garden and the banksia garden. The botanic garden is a haven to over 160 bird species and mammals such as the wallaroo and the swamp wallaby. The human sundial allows visitors to tell the time by standing in the middle of it and raising their arms. 3 km W.
Steam and Machinery Museum: several old steam trains running on tracks on the 1st Sun each month; Menangle Rd; 5 km SW. *Menangle:* small town featuring The Store (1904), an old-style country store with everything from antiques to ice-creams, and the Menangle Railway Bridge (1863), the colony's first iron bridge; 9 km SW. *Eschol Park House:* grand colonial home (1820) set in landscaped gardens; 15 km N. *Appin:* historic coalmining town with a monument to Hume and Hovell (who began their 1824 expedition to Port Phillip from this district). Also here are weekend markets in 10 locations (leaflet available from visitor centre) and a celebration of Scottish links through the Highland Gathering and Pioneer Festival each Nov. 16 km S.
ⓘ Quandong Visitor Information Centre, Art Gallery Rd; (02) 4645 4921; www. campbelltown.nsw.gov.au

Canowindra   Pop. 1511

Map ref. 508 E7

Canowindra, meaning 'home' in the Wiradjuri language, is in the Lachlan Valley with sandstone mountains to the west and the old volcano, Mt Candobolas, to the north-east. Ben Hall and his gang struck in the town twice in 1863. During the first visit they robbed two homesteads and then forced residents and local police into Robinson's Inn (now the Royal Hotel) where they held an impromptu and compulsory two-day party. Two weeks later they returned and held a similar three-day party, reportedly at their own expense. Today Canowindra is still a genuine old-style country town with a National Trust-classified main street (Gaskill St) that follows the crooked path of an old bullock track. It is now known

for two things: balloons and fossils. Canowindra calls itself the 'balloon capital of Australia' because there are more hot-air balloon flights here than anywhere else in the country. In 1956, 3500 fish fossils over 360 million years old were found in the area. Another major dig took place in 1993.
IN TOWN Age of Fishes Museum Long before dinosaurs walked the earth bizarre fish populated local rivers, including fish with armoured shells, fish with lungs and fish with jaws like crocodiles. The museum displays many of the fossils from the Devonian era found during the 1956 and 1993 digs along with information about the digs. There are also live aquarium displays and re-creations of life in the Devonian period. Gaskill St.
Historical museum: local history displays and agricultural equipment; Gaskill St; open Sat afternoon and all day Sun. *Hot-air balloon rides:* over picturesque Lachlan Valley; Mar–Nov (weather permitting); details at visitor centre. *Historical tourist drive and riverbank self-guide walks:* include historic buildings of Gaskill St; brochure available from visitor centre.
WHAT'S ON *Marti's Balloon Fiesta:* April. *Model Aircraft Championships:* Easter. *Springfest:* wine and art; Oct.
NEARBY Gondwana Dreaming Historical Fossil Digs Tours of 1–6 days can be arranged for visitors to go on real archaeological digs led by palaeontologists to learn about and possibly find fossils. The tours promote hands-on learning and focus on the area as a whole, including local flora and fauna. This program funds the group's ongoing scientific research. Bookings (02) 6285 1872.
Wineries and vineyards: cellar-door tastings and tours; maps from visitor centre.
ⓘ Age of Fishes Museum, Gaskill St; (02) 6344 1008; www.ageoffishes.org.au

Casino   Pop. 9151

Map ref. 515 P3, 607 P12

Beside the Richmond River in the north-east of the state, Casino is a typical country town of grand old buildings surrounded by magnificent parklands. Casino is named after the beautiful Italian town of Monte Cassino and is known as the beef capital of Australia. More than 12 000 cattle are sold each year at the Casino Livestock Selling Centre.
IN TOWN Jabiru Geneebeinga Wetlands These picturesque parklands have picnic facilities and are home to native bird species and wildlife including the jabiru (black-necked stork), egret and black swan. The park is circled by a mini-railway that operates each Sun. West St.
Casino Folk Museum: locally significant documents and photographs; Walker St; open Wed afternoons and Sun mornings. *Self-guide heritage and scenic walks and drives:* include Bicentennial Mural,

Coffs Harbour jetty, with Muttonbird Island in the distance

St Mark's Church of England and Cecil Hotel; maps from visitor centre.
WHAT'S ON *Beef Week Festival:* May. *Primex:* primary industry exhibition; June. *Gold Cup:* horseracing; Aug.
NEARBY *Fossicking:* gold, labradorite and quartz (smoky and clear types); maps from visitor centre. *Freshwater fishing:* on Cooke's Weir and Richmond River; maps from visitor centre.
ⓘ Centre St; (02) 6662 3566; www.richmondvalley.nsw.gov.au

Cessnock   Pop. 17 790

Map ref. 497 E11, 499 B10, 509 M4

Cessnock was once a coalmining town, but that was before the Hunter Valley, of which Cessnock is at the southern end, began producing some of Australia's best wines. A visit to Cessnock almost guarantees relaxation as it focuses on fresh produce and wine in the spectacular scenery of rainforests and green valleys.
IN TOWN *Galleries and antique and craft shops:* brochures from visitor centre.
WHAT'S ON *Vintage Festival:* throughout region; Feb. *Harvest Festival:* throughout region; Mar–April. *Budfest Festival:* food, wine, street parade; Sept. *Jazz in the Vines:* Oct. *Opera in the Vineyards:* Oct.
NEARBY Watagan National Park This park features several lookout points over mountains and valleys. The lookout at Gap Creek Falls reveals rainforest gullies of magnificent red cedar and Illawarra flame trees, and the Monkey Face Lookout takes in the Martinsville Valley below. There are many scenic rainforest walks along the creek, which is ideal for swimming. Some walks lead to picnic and barbecue facilities at Heaton, Hunter and McLean's lookouts and the serene Boarding House Dam picnic area, which is set among large blackbutt and blue gum trees. 33 km SE.
Rusa Park Zoo: hands-on zoo where most animals (native and introduced) can be patted and fed; 7 km NW. *Lovedale:* home of the Long Lunch (food, wine and music), held at 6 vineyards in May; 10 km N. *Bimbadeen Lookout:* spectacular views over Hunter Valley; 10 km E. *Rothbury:* hot-air ballooning, and a chance to pat an alpaca

and purchase alpaca wool products at Charlicia Alpacas, Talga Rd. Also good picnic and barbecue facilities. 11 km N. *Hunter Valley Cheese Factory:* factory tours, tastings and sales; McGuigan Cellars Complex, McDonalds Rd; 13 km NW. *Richmond Vale Railway Museum:* rail and mining museum with steam-train rides and John Brown's Richmond Main Colliery, once the largest shaft mine in the Southern Hemisphere; 17 km NE. *Wollombi:* picturesque village with a wealth of historic sandstone buildings. Tour the Aboriginal cave paintings (inquire at general store). Visit Undercliff Winery and Studio (for etchings) and in Sept enjoy the folk festival. 29 km SW. *Hunter Valley Wineries, Galleries and Craft shops:* over 60 wineries, most open for cellar-door tastings, and art and crafts by local artists; maps and brochures from visitor centre.
ⓘ Lot 111, Main Rd, Pokolbin; (02) 4990 4477; www.winecountry.com.au

Cobar   Pop. 4103

Map ref. 513 N10

Cobar got its name from the Aboriginal word 'gubar', meaning 'red ochre'. The story goes that a European settler found an Aboriginal man painting himself in bright red paint. When asked what it was, he was told it was 'gubar'. On investigation, it was found that this 'gubar' was actually copper and the Cobar mining industry was born. The mines made Cobar so prosperous that at one point the town had a population of 10 000 and its own stock exchange. The still-operating CSA mine is the largest producer of copper and zinc in New South Wales. Today Cobar is a surprisingly green and picturesque outback town.
IN TOWN Great Cobar Outback Heritage Centre This heritage centre has a full-time curator and is fully interactive, with visitors encouraged to touch and smell displays. There are displays on the local mining of copper, gold and silver-lead-zinc. The pastoral section has an authentic re-creation of a local woolshed, and Aboriginal culture is explored through artefacts and bushfoods. The

tough years of early European occupation are shown with displays on the problem of water shortages and the bush skills that settlers had to quickly acquire to survive in the harsh environment. The Centenary of Federation Walking Track begins here and is a 2 hr scenic walk past mines and a slag dump. Barrier Hwy. *Commonwealth Meteorological Station:* visitors can view the radar tracking process and the launching of weather balloons at 9.15am and 3.15pm daily (Eastern Standard Time). Short tours are conducted after the 9.15am launch. Louth Rd. *Golden Walk:* tour the operating Peak Gold Mine; brochure from visitor centre. *Self-guide heritage walks and heritage bus tours:* historic buildings including the courthouse and the Great Western Hotel (with the longest iron-lace verandah in NSW), and mining and agricultural sites around town; brochure from visitor centre.
WHAT'S ON *Market:* at the railway station; last Sat each month. *Festival of the Miner's Ghost:* Aug.
NEARBY Mount Grenfell Historic Site The 5 km Ngiyambaa Walkabout leads visitors on a scenic tour with breathtaking views of the Cobar area. There are hundreds of Aboriginal stencils and paintings of great cultural significance in spectacular reds, yellows and ochres on rock overhangs along the trail. Picnic and barbecue facilities are available. Off Barrier Hwy; 67 km NW. *The Old Reservoir and Devil's Rock:* Devil's Rock was a site for ceremonial rites for the Ngemba people. Good swimming and watersports at the reservoir; 3 km N. *Glenhope Lavender Farm:* lavender products and gift shop; 6 km E. *Mount Drysdale:* deserted mining town with old shafts and historic Aboriginal sites; permission required (02) 6836 3462; 34 km N.
ⓘ Great Cobar Heritage Centre, Barrier Hwy; (02) 6836 2448; www.cobar. nsw.gov.au

Coffs Harbour   Pop. 25 828

Map ref. 515 P8

Coffs Harbour, a subtropical holiday town on the Holiday Coast, is known for its banana plantations and the iconic

The Breadknife, Warrumbungle National Park, west of Coonabarabran

Big Banana, and for its great fishing. The combination of great weather, stunning hinterland forests, sandy beaches and a growing cosmopolitan centre make Coffs Harbour a popular spot for tourists seeking fun and relaxation.

IN TOWN **Muttonbird Island Nature Reserve** Visitors can get an up-close look at the life cycle of one of Australia's most interesting migratory birds. The wedge-tailed shearwaters (muttonbirds) fly thousands of kilometres from south-east Asia each August, with large numbers settling at Muttonbird Island to breed. The walking trail winds through the burrows of the birds, which can be seen Aug–April. Muttonbird Island is also an excellent vantage point for whale-watching June–Nov and great for fishing and picnics. Access is via a 500 m walk along the sea wall from the harbour. *Loumar Collectables Museum:* vast collection of Royal Doulton crockery, dolls, teddy bears and toys; Victoria St. *Coffs Harbour City Gallery:* varied program of contemporary art exhibitions; cnr Coff and Duke sts. *Coffs Harbour Museum:* pioneer artefacts and photographs, and the original lantern of the lighthouse built on Split Solitary Island in 1880; High St. *The Marina:* departure point for fishing charters, scuba diving and whale-watching trips (June–Nov); High St. *North Coast Regional Botanical Gardens Complex:* rainforest, mangrove boardwalks, herbarium and diverse birdlife; Hardacre St. *Pet Porpoise Pool:* performing dolphins and seals with research and nursery facilities; Orlando St. *Aquajet Waterslide:* fun park with water slide and minigolf; Park Beach Rd. *Self-guide walks:* include Jetty Walk and Coffs Creek Walk; maps from visitor centre.

WHAT'S ON *Growers market:* Harbour Dr; Thurs. *Market:* jetty, High St; Sun. *Uptown Market:* Vernon St; Sun. *Pittwater to Coffs Harbour Yacht Classic:* Jan. *Food and Wine Fiesta:* Oct.

NEARBY **Bindarri National Park** Not for the unseasoned bushwalker, Bindarri National Park is a largely untouched forest without facilities, but amazing views reward those who make the effort. The headwaters of the Urumbilum River form breathtaking waterfalls in a remote and rugged setting. Pockets of old-growth forest are scattered across the plateau and rich rainforest protects the steeper slopes. While there are no campgrounds, backpack camping is allowed and there are bushwalking trails to follow. 20 km w. *Clog Barn:* Dutch village with clog-making; Pacific Hwy; 2 km N. *Big Banana:* large banana-shaped landmark with displays on the banana industry, a skywalk and train rides through a banana plantation, and an Aboriginal Dreamtime cave experience; 4 km N. *Bruxner Park Floral Reserve:* dense tropical jungle area of vines, ferns and orchids with bushwalking trails and picnic area; Korora; 9 km NW. *Coffs Harbour Zoo:* extensive array of native Australian animals and a daily koala show; 14 km N. *George's Goldmine:* rainforest setting with tours of a goldmine shaft, pioneer house and barn, and steam engines. Also has picnic and barbecue facilities. 38 km w. *Gambaarri Aboriginal Cultural Tours:* half- and full-day tours of significant Aboriginal sites; (02) 6655 4195. *Adventure tours:* include whitewater rafting, canoeing, reef-fishing, diving, horseriding through rainforest, Harley rides and 4WD tours; see visitor centre for brochures and bookings.

ⓘ Cnr Pacific Hwy and McLean St; (02) 6652 1522 or 1300 369 070; www.coffscoast.com.au

Cooma   Pop. 6914

Map ref. 502 A2, 507 E9, 537 M3

The main town of the Snowy Mountains, Cooma was once dubbed Australia's most cosmopolitan city, thanks to the thousands of migrants who flocked to the region to work on the Snowy Mountains Hydro-electric Scheme. It is a charming and bustling centre with visitors coming for the snow in winter and the greenery and crisp mountain air in summer. Motorists are advised to stop here to check tyres and stock up on petrol and provisions before heading into alpine country.

IN TOWN **Centennial Park** Originally a swamp, Centennial Park was built in 1890. During WW II slit trenches were dug here in case of air attacks on the town. The International Avenue of Flags was constructed in 1959 to commemorate the 10th anniversary of the Snowy Mountains Hydro-electric Authority with one flag for each of the 27 nationalities of the workers. The Time Walk depicts the district's history in 40 ceramic mosaics laid out throughout the park. There is also a sculpture of The Man from Snowy River. Sharp St. *Southern Cloud Park:* features Southern Cloud Memorial, a display of remains of the aircraft *Southern Cloud*, which crashed here in 1931 and was found in 1958. *Snowy Mountains Hydro-electric Authority Information Centre:* displays and films on the scheme. A memorial next door commemorates the 121 people killed while working on it. Monaro Hwy. *Nanny Goat Hill Lookout:* beautiful views of the town; Massie St. *Bike track:* picturesque path following Cooma Creek between Lambie St and Rotary Oval. *Lambie Town self-guide walk:* includes Lambie St, lined with huge oaks, pines and elms, and St Paul's Church, constructed with local alpine ash and granite and with striking stained-glass windows; brochure from visitor centre. *Art galleries:* several with work by local artists; details from visitor centre. *Historic railcar:* trips from Cooma to Bunyan on weekends; bookings from visitor centre.

WHAT'S ON *Market:* Centennial Park; 3rd Sun each month. *Rodeo:* Jan. *Coomafest:* street fair celebrating Cooma's multicultural society; Nov.

NEARBY **Tuross Falls** Part of Wadbilliga National Park, the stunning Tuross Falls are a drop of 35 m. A picturesque 2 km walk from the camping area at Cascades leads visitors to the lookout platform, which affords views of the falls and the Tuross River Gorge. 30 km E. *Kosciuszko Memorial:* donated in 1988 by the Polish government commemorating Tadeuz Kosciuszko, a champion of the underprivileged, after whom Australia's

highest mountain is named; 2.5 km N. *Mt Gladstone Lookout:* impressive views, mountain-bike trails and Austrian teahouse; 6.5 km W. *Transylvania Winery:* cellar-door tastings of cool-climate organic wines; Monaro Hwy; 14 km N.
ⓘ 119 Sharp St; (02) 6450 1742 or 1800 636 525; www.visitcooma.com.au

Coonabarabran   Pop. 2736

Map ref. 514 F11

Coonabarabran is a modern and friendly town on the Castlereagh River. It is known as the 'Gateway to the Warrumbungles', as the rugged mountains arc around the city to the west, north and east. It is also a haven for astronomy fans with the wide open spaces providing excellent viewing from the two observatories nearby.

IN TOWN Information centre The Australian Museum worked with Coonabarabran Council to produce the unique Diprotodon Display. The diprotodon is the largest marsupial that ever lived and the skeleton on show was found in a creek bed east of town. Also on display is a collection of fossils. The story of the birth of the Warrumbungles is presented, linking the Aboriginal Dreamtime with geological and astronomical history. Newell Hwy. *Crystal Kingdom:* unique collection of minerals, including zeolite crystals and fossils, from the Warrumbungle Range; Newell Hwy. *Newcastle Hats:* hat factory offers tours; Ulan St.

WHAT'S ON *Market:* Neilson Park; last Sun each month. *Carnival:* includes market; Easter. *Festival of the Stars:* includes Coona Cup Racing Carnival; Oct.

NEARBY Warrumbungle National Park The park is a combination of forested ridges, rocky spires and deep gorges. The excellent camping and visitor facilities have made it one of the state's most popular parks. Highlights include the Breadknife, a 90 m high rock wall, and the Grand High Tops walking trail with fabulous views of ancient volcanic remains. The park is an outstanding spot for rockclimbing, but climbing is prohibited on the Breadknife and permits are required for other areas (contact visitor centre). Guided nature walks are conducted during school holidays or by appt. 35 km W.
Skywatch Night and Day Observatory: interactive display, planetarium, night-sky viewing through telescopes and space-themed minigolf; National Park Rd; 2 km NW. *Siding Springs Observatory:* Australia's largest optical telescope, with a hands-on exhibition, 'Exploring the Universe', and science shop and cafe; National Park Rd; 28 km W. *Pilliga Pottery and Bush Cafe:* terracotta pottery, showrooms and tearooms in an attractive bushland setting; off Newell Hwy; 34 km NW. *Sandstone caves:* formed by natural erosion of sandstone, these impressive caves are not signposted, so visitors are advised to seek directions from the visitor centre; 35 km N. *Pilliga Scrub:* 450 000 ha of white cypress and ironbark trees, with plains of dense heath and scrub. It is an excellent habitat for koalas, which can be spotted from signposted viewing areas. Also scenic forest drives and walking trails; maps available from the visitor centre; 44 km NW.
ⓘ Newell Hwy; (02) 6842 1441 or 1800 242 881; www.lisp.com.au/coonabarabran

Coonamble   Pop. 2658

Map ref. 514 C10

This town lost many of its buildings in the great fire of 1929. Castlereagh Street had to be rebuilt, so most constructions are relatively modern. Coonamble is on the Great Inland Way, which provides an alternative to the more commonly taken coastal route between Queensland and the southern states.

IN TOWN Coonamble Historical Museum The museum outlines the rich Aboriginal and pastoral history of Coonamble through photographs, household items and stables. Behind the museum is an authentic Cobb & Co coach and the Zobel Gallery, with works by local artists. Aberford St; open Mon–Fri. *Warrana Creek Weir:* swimming, boating and fishing; southern outskirts of town. *Self-guide town walk:* takes in historic sites; brochure from visitor centre.

WHAT'S ON *Rodeo and Campdraft:* June. *Gold Cup Race Meeting:* Oct.

NEARBY Quambone Locally known as the gateway to Macquarie Marshes, Quambone also has Australia's smallest library. There is much to see and do here throughout the year, including the Marthaguy Picnic Races in July, the Quambone Polocrosse Carnival in July/Aug and the Nature Reserve Open Day in Oct. Camping facilities are available at Quambone Race Track. Bookings (02) 6824 2077. 55 km W.
Gulargambone: a small town with a restored steam train in Memorial Park and Gular Crays, a large yabby hatchery with tours and cooking ideas, in Armitree St; 45 km S. *Macquarie Marshes:* 80 km W; *see Nyngan. Hot-bore baths:* maps available from visitor centre.
ⓘ Council offices, Castlereagh St; (02) 6827 1900; www.coonamble.org

Cootamundra   Pop. 5482

Map ref. 507 B3, 508 D10

This prosperous rural service centre and major junction on the railway line between Sydney and Melbourne prides itself on being the birthplace of cricketing legend Sir Donald Bradman. Much reference is made to him and to cricket around the town (although Bradman's childhood home has been moved to a museum in nearby Temora). Cootamundra also lends its name to the famous Cootamundra wattle (*Acacia baileyana*), which blooms in the area each July and August, and Cootamundra Gold, the locally produced canola oil.

IN TOWN Pioneer Park This natural bushland reserve on the northern outskirts of town has a scenic 1.3 km walking trail, which is an easy uphill stroll to the top of Mt Slippery. At the summit there are panoramic views over the town. The park also has excellent picnic sites. Backbrawlin St. *Memorabilia Cottage:* displays local history memorabilia and bric-a-brac; Adams St. *Captains Walk:* bronze sculptures of Australia's past cricket captains; Jubilee Park, Wallendoon St. *Heritage Centre:* local memorabilia including an Olympic cauldron and war relics; railway station, Hovell St. *Self-guide 'Two Foot Tour':* includes Sir Donald Bradman's birthplace on Adams St and the town's historic buildings; brochure from visitor centre. *Local crafts:* at visitor centre and at Art and Craft Centre, Hovell St.

WHAT'S ON *Markets:* Mackay St; 1st Sun each month. *Wattle Time Festival:* Aug. *Art Show:* Aug. *Christmas Carnival:* Dec.

NEARBY Murrumburrah This small rural community has the Harden–Murrumburrah Historical Museum, which is open weekends and features pioneer artefacts, an old chemist shop exhibit and early Australian kitchenwares. Also in town are local craft shops and outstanding picnic spots. The Picnic Races are held here in Nov. 35 km NE. Stocks Native Nursery in Harden, 2 km E on Simmonds Rd, features 1.5 ha of native bush garden with a scenic walking trail and billabong. *Green Tree Indigenous Food Gardens:* Australian bush garden providing education on how indigenous people survived on bush tucker; 8 km N; open by appt; bookings (02) 6943 2628. *The Milestones:* cast-concrete sculptures representing the importance of wheat to the area; 19 km NE. *Bethungra:* dam ideal for canoeing and sailing. The rail spiral is an unusual engineering feat. 23 km SW. *Kamilaroi Cottage Violets:* violet farm with tours by appt; 25 km N; bookings (02) 6943 2207. *Illabo:* charming town with impressive clock museum; 33 km SW. *Cellar doors:* in the Harden area; winery brochure from visitor centre.
ⓘ Railway station, Hovell St; (02) 6942 4212; www.cootamundra.nsw.gov.au

Corowa   Pop. 5208

Map ref. 511 O13, 539 M3

Corowa has been known for its goldmining, wine-making and timber-milling, but what it is most proud of is its reputation as the 'birthplace of

Federation'. Traders had to pay taxes both in New South Wales and Victoria when taking goods over the border, which caused much agitation. It was argued that free trade would benefit everyone and the Border Federation League was formed in Corowa, which led to the 1893 Corowa Federation Conference. In 1895 the proposals put forth at the conference were acted upon, and on 1 January 1901 the Commowealth of Australia was born.

IN TOWN Federation Museum This museum focuses on the reasons behind Federation and Corowa's involvement in it. Also on display are local Aboriginal artefacts, Tommy McRae sketches, horse-drawn vehicles and saddlery, and antique agricultural implements. There are hosted Federation walks on the 1st Sun each month or by appt (02) 6033 1568 or 1800 814 054. Queen St. Open Sat and Sun afternoons. *Murray Bank Yabby Farm:* catch and cook yabbies, go canoeing and enjoy a picnic or barbecue; Federation Ave. *Self-guide historical town walk:* includes Sanger St, Corowa's wide main street with its century-old verandahed buildings. Guide available for groups; brochure from visitor centre.

WHAT'S ON *Market:* Sanger St; 1st Sun each month. *Federation Festival:* Jan. *Billycart Races:* Easter.

NEARBY All Saints Estate Situated in Victoria's respected Rutherglen district, All Saints is a winery like no other. Behind the impressive hedge fence and imposing set of gates lies an enormous medieval castle built by the original owner, George Smith, based on the Castle of Mey in Scotland. Now owned and operated by Peter Brown (of the famous Brown Brothers), All Saints offers a large cellar-door operation, a renowned restaurant and beautiful gardens. 5 km sw. *Gliding and skydiving:* weekends, weather permitting; off Redlands Rd.
ⓘ 88 Sanger St; (02) 6033 3221; www.corowa.nsw.gov.au

Cowra　　Pop. 8693

Map ref. 508 F8

Cowra is a cosmopolitan and sophisticated spot with many outstanding restaurants and shops. The peaceful air of this pretty town on the Lachlan River belies its dramatic history. The Cowra breakout is an infamous World War II incident in Australia, but while it remains what Cowra is most famous for, the town has tried to move forward.

IN TOWN Australia's World Peace Bell Each country has only one peace bell and it is normally located in the nation's capital, but Cowra was awarded Australia's Peace Bell owing to local efforts for peace. The bell is a replica of the United Nations World Peace Bell in New York City and was made by melting down coins donated from 103 member countries of the United Nations. It is rung each year during the Festival of International Understanding. Darling St. **Japanese Garden** This garden, opened in 1979, is complete with a cultural centre (with a collection of Japanese artwork and artefacts), a traditional tea house, a bonsai house and a pottery. The garden itself represents the landscape of Japan, with mountain, river and sea. From here gracious Sakura Avenue, lined with cherry trees that blossom in spring, leads to the site of the POW camp and to the Australian and Japanese cemeteries. Off Binni Creek Rd. *Olympic Park:* information centre with a fascinating interpretive POW display and theatre. Also here is Cowra Rose Garden with over 1000 rose bushes in over 100 varieties. Mid Western Hwy. *Cowra–Italy Friendship Monument:* in recognition of Italians who died in WW II (Italian POWs interned at Cowra formed a strong friendship with the town); Kendal St. *Parkland Gardens and Bird Farm:* wander through the expansive gardens with exotic and native trees and flowers, a fish pond and fountain, and abundant birdlife such as parrots, finches and ducks. Take a free guided tour. Dawson Dr. *Lachlan Valley Rail and Steam Museum:* displays and train rides; Campbell St. *Coleman's Country Corner:* country music museum with Australian and overseas memorabilia; cnr Mulyan and Cooyal sts. *Cowra Mill Winery:* winery in former flour mill (1861) with cellar-door tastings; Vaux St. *Aboriginal murals:* by local artist Kym Freeman on pylons of bridge over the Lachlan River. *Cowra Heritage Walk:* Federation, colonial and Victorian buildings including the town's first hotel and oldest home; map from visitor centre.

WHAT'S ON *Farmers market:* showgrounds; 3rd Sat each month. *Festival of International Understanding:* Mar. *Picnic Races:* July. *Sakura Matsuri:* cherry blossom festival; Oct. *Chardonnay Festival:* Nov. *Cowra Food and Wine Festival:* Nov.

NEARBY *Cowra museums:* war, rail and rural museums all in one complex; Sydney Rd; 5 km e. *Darby Falls Observatory:* one of the largest telescopes accessible to the public; 25 km se; check opening times (02) 6345 1900 or 0417 461 162. *Conimbla National Park:* known for its wildflowers, rock ledges and waterfalls. Also an excellent spot for bushwalks and picnics. 27 km w. *Lake Wyangala and Grabine Lakeside State Park:* ideal for watersports and fishing; 40 km se. *Self-guide drives:* through surrounding countryside and including a wine-lovers' drive; brochure from visitor centre. *Local wineries:* open for cellar-door tastings; brochure from visitor centre.
ⓘ Olympic Park, Mid Western Hwy; (02) 6342 4333; www.cowratourism.com.au

The Cowra breakout

In 1941 a prisoner-of-war (POW) camp was established on the outskirts of Cowra. It was an overcrowded complex, detaining many Japanese POWs. While a harrowing experience for all POWs, for the Japanese it was seen as a great disgrace to a soldier's family for him to be subservient to the enemy. Prisoners gave false names to avoid the shame, and Japanese authorities reported all those missing in action as dead. There was simply no such thing as a Japanese POW and many died without ever admitting their capture to their families.

At 1.30am on 5 August 1944, the camp became the scene of the largest mass POW escape in British military history. Camp B erupted as a bugle sounded and men rushed at an internal fence armed with knives, baseball bats, chisels, forks and axe handles. These men were a decoy as others threw heavy blankets over the barbed wire of the perimeter fence and hauled themselves over. Even though the authorities had been warned that trouble was brewing, 20 buildings were set alight and 378 Japanese prisoners escaped (although many were also killed).

It took only nine days for authorities and civilians to recapture 334 of the escapees, the most ambitious of whom had travelled to Eugowra, 50 kilometres away. Other escapees were either killed or committed suicide, leaving a total of 234 prisoners dead and 105 injured. The POWs made a pact not to harm civilians, which they adhered to, and some civilians acted to help them. A lady named May Weir refused to hand over two Japanese men to military guards until she had fed them tea and scones, claiming that they were fellow human beings who hadn't eaten for days and at least deserved sustenance. The two Japanese men visited the Weir family 40 years later to thank them for her kindness.

It is this spirit of support and understanding that Cowra has nurtured since the war, not only to repair relations with Japan and other nations whose soldiers were detained here, but to form strong alliances in the name of peace. A student-exchange program between Cowra High School and Seikei High School in Tokyo was established in 1970 and there are several memorials in town honouring the special relationship.

Crookwell　　Pop. 1926

Map ref. 507 F3, 508 H10

This picturesque tree-lined township is a service centre to the local agricultural and pastoral district. At 914 metres above sea level it enjoys a cool climate and lush, colourful gardens. Australia's first grid-connected wind farm was opened here in 1998 and is capable of supplying electricity to 3500 homes. The Country Women's Association was formed here in 1922 and has since spread nationwide.

IN TOWN *Crookwell Wind Farm:* viewing platform and information board; Goulburn Rd.

WHAT'S ON *Market:* Uniting Church, Goulburn St; 1st Sat each month. *Country Weekend:* traditional country festival with music, markets, sports and a parade; Mar. *Open Gardens weekends:* spring and autumn (dates from visitor centre).

NEARBY Wombeyan Caves There are 5 caves open to the public including Figtree Cave, widely regarded as the best self-guide cave in NSW. Junction Cave has a colourful underground river; Wollondilly Cave has 5 main chambers with outstanding formations; Mulwarree Cave is intimate, with delicate formations; and Kooringa Cave is huge and majestic. Wombeyan Gorge is made of marble, providing an unusual swimming experience. There are several campgrounds and walking trails in the area. 60 km E. *Redground Lookout:* excellent views of surrounding area; 8 km NW. *Willow Vale Mill:* restored flour mill with restaurant and accommodation; Laggan; 9 km NE. *Lake Wyangala and Grabine Lakeside State Park:* upper reaches ideal for waterskiing, picnicking, fishing, bushwalking and camping; 65 km NW. *Historic villages:* associated with goldmining, coppermining and bushrangers, these vilages include Tuena, Peelwood, Laggan, Bigga, Binda (all north) and Roslyn (south), which is also known as the birthplace of poet Dame Mary Gilmore; maps from visitor centre. *Historical and scenic drives:* explore significant sites and surrounding countryside frequented by bushrangers such as Ben Hall; brochure from visitor centre.
ⓘ 106 Goulburn St; (02) 4832 1988; www.crookwell.nsw.gov.au

Culcairn   Pop. 1019

Map ref. 511 Q12, 539 Q1

Culcairn is located at the heart of 'Morgan country' where Dan 'Mad Dog' Morgan terrorised the district between 1862 and 1865. Despite its past, the town is peaceful. It owes its tree-lined streets and lush green parks to an underground water supply discovered in 1926.

IN TOWN *National Trust-classified buildings:* include historic Culcairn Hotel (1891), still operating; Railway Pde and Olympic Way.

NEARBY Henty This historic pastoral town has the Headlie Taylor Header Memorial, a tribute to the mechanical header harvester that revolutionised the grain industry. The nearby Sergeant Smith Memorial Stone marks the spot where Morgan fatally wounded a police officer, and the adjacent Doodle Cooma Swamp is 2000 ha of breeding area for waterbirds. 24 km N.

Jumping off a pier into the Edward River, Deniliquin

John McLean's grave: McLean was shot by Mad Dog Morgan; 3 km E. *Round Hill Station:* where Morgan committed his first hold-up in the area; Holbrook Rd; 15 km E. *Walla Walla:* old schoolhouse (1875) and the largest Lutheran church in NSW (1924); 18 km SW. *Morgan's Lookout:* granite outcrop on otherwise flat land, allegedly used by Morgan to look for approaching victims and police; 18 km NW.
ⓘ Post office, 33a Balfour St; (02) 6029 8521

Deniliquin   Pop. 7781

Map ref. 511 L11

Deniliquin, at the centre of the largest irrigation system in Australia, lies on the Edward River, which is part of the Murray River formed by a fault in the earth. As a result of all this water, the town produces many high-water crops, such as rice, and has the largest rice mill in the Southern Hemisphere.

IN TOWN Peppin Heritage Centre This museum is dedicated to George Hall Peppin and his sons' development of the merino sheep industry. Dissatisfied with the quality and yield of the wool from merino sheep, they developed a new breed, the peppin, that was better adapted to Australian conditions. Peppin sheep now predominate among flocks in New Zealand, South Africa and South America. The museum is housed in the National Trust-classified Old George Street Public School (1879), which still has an intact classroom on display. There is also a lock-up gaol from Wanganella and a 1920s thatched ram shed. George St. *Blake Botanic Reserve:* community project to present local flora in its natural environment; cnr Harfleur and Fowler sts. *Island Sanctuary:* features kangaroos and birdlife; off Cressy St footbridge. *River beaches:* excellent spots for swimming, waterskiing, canoeing,

boating and fishing, including McLean and Willoughby's beaches. *Self-guide walks:* historical and nature walks taking in National Trust-classified buildings and striking town gardens; brochure from visitor centre.

WHAT'S ON *Market:* Davidson St; 4th Sat each month. *Sun Festival:* includes gala parade and international food and entertainment; Jan. *RSL Fishing Classic:* Jan. *Stampede:* celebration of Australian outback; Easter. *Play on the Plains Festival and Ute Muster:* celebration of country music and cars; Sept/Oct.

NEARBY Pioneer Tourist Park Now a modern caravan park, Pioneer Tourist Park maintains charming features of the past (open to the public), including an antique steam and pump display and a blacksmith shop. There is also a mini-rural museum, a local art and craft gallery and a nursery. 2 km N. *Irrigation works:* at Lawsons Syphon (7 km E) and Stevens Weir (25 km W). *Country Patch Cottage and Garden:* farm with fresh seasonal produce for sale. Call for produce in season (03) 5881 5417. 8 km W. *Clancy's Winery:* cellar-door tastings and sales; 18 km N. *Conargo Pub:* authentic bush pub with photo gallery depicting history of merino wool in the area; 25 km NE. *Bird Observatory Tower:* excellent vantage point for birdwatching; Mathoura; 34 km S.
ⓘ Peppin Heritage Centre, George St; (03) 5881 2878 or 1800 650 712; www.denitourism.com.au

Dorrigo   Pop. 966

Map ref. 515 O8

Dorrigo is known as 'Australia's national park capital', and rightly so, as it is entirely surrounded by national park. The Dorrigo plateau provides crisp, clean air and wonderful views in all directions. The town is small enough to be friendly

Boyd's Tower, Ben Boyd National Park, near Eden

and intimate, but popular enough to provide excellent facilities for visitors.

IN TOWN *Historical museum:* memorabilia, documents and photographs detailing the history of Dorrigo and surrounding national parks; Cudgery St. *Local crafts:* at Calico Cottage, Hickory St, and The Art Place and Country Crafts, Cudgery St. *Wood-fired bakery:* produces popular products with local produce; Hickory St.

WHAT'S ON *Market:* showground, Armidale Rd; 1st Sat each month. *Arts and Crafts Exhibition:* Easter. *Spring Festival:* Oct.

NEARBY Dorrigo National Park This park takes in World Heritage-listed rainforest with a lot for visitors to see and do. Attractions include spectacular waterfalls and a variety of birds such as bowerbirds and lyrebirds. The Rainforest Centre has picnic facilities, a cafe, a video theatre and exhibitions. There is also the Skywalk, a boardwalk offering views over the canopy of the rainforest, and the Walk with the Birds boardwalk. 3 km E.

Cathedral Rock National Park Giant boulders, sculpted rock, distinctive granite hills and wedge-tailed eagles make Cathedral Rock spectacular viewing and popular among photographers. It is a lovely spot for picnicking, and walks include a 3 hr circuit walk to the summit of Cathedral Rock for amazing 360-degree views of the tableland. 56 km SW. *Dangar Falls:* viewing platform over 30 m waterfall; 2 km N. *Griffiths Lookout:* sweeping views of the mountains; 6 km S. *Guy Fawkes River National Park:* rugged and scenic surrounds with limited facilities, but worth the effort for experienced bushwalkers. Ebor Falls has cliff-top viewing platforms above and there is also good canoeing and fishing. 40 km W. *L. P. Dutton Trout Hatchery:* educational visitor centre and trout feeding; 63 km SW. *Point Lookout:* in New England National Park for spectacular views of Bellinger Valley and across to the ocean; 74 km SW.
ⓘ Hickory St; (02) 6657 2486; www.dorrigo.com

Dubbo   Pop. 30 860

Map ref. 508 E2

One of Australia's fastest growing inland cities, Dubbo is most famous for its world-class open-range zoo. The city, on the banks of the Macquarie River, is thriving and prosperous with more than half a million visitors each year. Dubbo prides itself on having the standards demanded of a city but 'accompanied with a country smile'.

IN TOWN Old Dubbo Gaol Closed as a penal institution in 1966, Old Dubbo Gaol now offers visitors a glimpse at convict life. See the original gallows (where 8 men were hanged for murder) and solitary confinement cells, or walk along the watchtower. An amazing animatronic robot tells historical tales of bushrangers, murders and prison life. Macquarie St.

Shoyoen Sister City Garden: Japanese garden and tea house designed and built with the support of Dubbo's sister city, Minokamo; Coronation Dr East. *Miniland:* dinosaur-themed fun park with craft fair, cafe and picnic and barbecue facilities; Camp Rd. *Jedda Boomerangs:* Aboriginal art and culture displays; Minore Rd; open Mon–Fri. *The Clay Pan Gallery:* exhibits include paintings, pottery, silver jewellery, wood-turning, ceramics and local craft; Depot Rd; closed Mon.

WHAT'S ON *Market:* showgrounds; 2nd Sun each month. *Orana Country Music Easter Festival:* Easter. *Red Ochre Corroboree:* April. *Jazz Festival:* Aug.

NEARBY Western Plains Zoo Australia's first open-range zoo, with over 1000 animals from 5 continents, is set on more than 300 ha of bushland. The zoo is renowned for its successful breeding programs (especially with endangered species), conservation programs and education facilities and exhibits. There is a program of talks by the keepers and early morning walks, as well as accommodation at Zoofari Lodge. The Tracker Riley Cycleway paves

the 5 km from Dubbo to the zoo and bicycles and maps are available from the visitor centre. 5 km S.

Dundullimal Homestead: 1840s restored squatter's slab-style homestead with working saddler and blacksmith, animals and the Woolshed Cafe; 7 km SE. *Macquarie River Cruises:* aboard the 'biggest boat in the outback', departing from Dundullimal; bookings at visitor centre; 7 km SE. *Big M:* open-air hands-on military museum, science expo and observatory; 8 km S. *Narromine:* agricultural centre well known for gliding and an outstanding aviation museum. The Festival of Flight is held here each Nov. 40 km E. *Heritage drives and river cruises:* brochures from visitor centre. *Wineries:* several in region offering cellar-door tastings; brochure from visitor centre.
ⓘ Cnr Newell Hwy and Macquarie St; (02) 6884 1422 or 1800 674 443; www.dubbotourism.com.au

Eden   Pop. 3145

Map ref. 502 F11, 507 G11, 537 Q8

Situated on the far south coast, the aptly named Eden is an idyllic and peaceful town on Twofold Bay. The location is excellent, with national park to the north and south, water to the east and woodland to the west. The beautiful bay is rimmed with mountains. Originally settled by whalers, it is now a fishing port and a popular, but relatively undeveloped, tourist town.

IN TOWN *Aslings Beach:* surf beach with rock pools and excellent platforms for whale-watching Oct–Nov; Showground Rd. *Snug Cove:* protected beach with attractive caves. *Eden Killer Whale Museum:* fascinating displays on the history of the local whaling industry include the skeleton of 'Old Tom' the killer whale; Imlay St.

WHAT'S ON *Amateur Fish Club Competition:* Mar. *Eden Whale Festival:* Oct. *Nautical Picnic on the Wharf:* Dec.

NEARBY Ben Boyd National Park The park extends north and south of Eden with scenery including rugged stretches of coastline, unique rock formations, heaths and banksia forest. The area is excellent for fishing, swimming, wreck diving, bushwalking and camping. Boyd's Tower at Red Point, 32 km SE, was originally built for whale-spotting. The Pinnacles, 8 km N, are an unusual earth formation with red gravel atop white sand cliffs. *Jiggamy Farm:* Aboriginal cultural and bush tucker experience; 9 km N. *Boydtown:* former rival settlement on the shores of Twofold Bay with convict-built Seahorse Inn (still licensed), safe beach and good fishing; 9 km S. *Davidson Whaling Station Historic Site:* provides unique insight into the lives of 19th-century whalers; Kiah Inlet; 30 km SE. *Harris Daishowa Chipmill Visitors Centre:* logging and milling displays; Jews Head; 34 km SE. *Nadgee State Forest:* scenic drive and easy rainforest walk; 35 km SE. *Wonboyn Lake:* scenic area with good fishing and 4WD tracks; 40 km S. *Green Cape Lighthouse:* first cast-concrete lighthouse in Australia and the second tallest in NSW; 45 km SE; tours by appt; bookings (02) 6495 5000. ❶ Eden Gateway Centre, Princes Hwy; (02) 6496 1953 or 1800 633 012; www.sapphirecoast.com.au

Eugowra   Pop. 589

Map ref. 508 E6

Situated on the rich basin of the Lachlan River, Eugowra is a tiny country town known for its crafts. It was nearby on the Orange–Forbes road that the famous Gold Escort Robbery took place in 1862.

IN TOWN *Eugowra Museum:* Aboriginal artefacts, gemstones, early farm equipment and wagons; call for opening hours (02) 6859 2214. *Nangar Gems:* display and sales of sapphires, opals, emeralds and garnets; Norton St. *Local craft shops:* leaflet from visitor centre.

NEARBY Nangar National Park The horseshoe-shaped red cliffs of the Nangar–Murga Range stand out against the central west's plains. Nangar National Park's flowering shrubs and timbered hills provide an important wildlife refuge among mostly cleared land. Rocky slopes and pretty creeks make it a scenic site for bushwalks and popular for rockclimbing. The park does not have facilities, so visitors are advised to take water and provisions with them and to give friends or family their itinerary. 10 km E. *Escort Rock:* where bushranger Frank Gardiner and gang (including Ben Hall) hid before ambushing the Forbes gold escort. A plaque on the road gives details. 3 km E. *Nanami Lane Lavender Farm:* products and plants for sale and workshops on growing lavender; 19 km SE. ❶ Civic Square, Byng St, Orange; (02) 6393 8226; www.orange.nsw.gov.au

Evans Head   Pop. 2608

Map ref. 515 Q4, 607 Q13

Evans Head is located at the mouth of the Evans River. It was the first prawning port in Australia and is still predominantly a fishing village, but with six kilometres of safe and uncrowded surfing beaches, sandy river flats and wonderful coastal scenery, it is also very much a tourist town. There is excellent rock, beach and ocean fishing.

IN TOWN *Goanna Headland:* site of great mythical importance to the Bundjalung people and favourite spot of serious surfers. *Razorback Lookout:* views up and down the coast. On a clear day, Cape Byron Lighthouse can be seen to the north. Ocean Dr.

WHAT'S ON *Market:* cnr Oak and Park sts; 4th Sat each month. *Fishing Classic:* July. *Evans Head Flower Show:* Sept.

NEARBY New Italy A monument and remains are all that are left of this settlement that was the result of the ill-fated Marquis de Rays expedition in 1880. The Marquis tricked 340 Italians into purchasing non-existent property in a Pacific paradise. Disaster struck several times for the emigrants, as they travelled first to Papua New Guinea and then to New Caledonia. Eventually Sir Henry Parkes arranged for their passage to Australia, where the 217 survivors built this village. Also in the New Italy Complex, Guuragai Aboriginal Arts and Crafts offers quality works and information on Aboriginal culture. 23 km SW. *Bundjalung National Park:* Aboriginal relics, fishing, swimming and bushwalking; 2 km S. *Broadwater National Park:* bushwalking, birdwatching, fishing and swimming; 5 km N. *Woodburn:* friendly town on the Richmond River with great spots for picnicking, swimming, fishing and boating; 11 km NW. ❶ The Professionals Real Estate, 9 Oak St; (02) 6682 4611; www.tropicalnsw. com.au

Finley   Pop. 1909

Map ref. 511 M12, 538 I1

This town, on the Newell Highway and close to the Victorian border, is a tidy and peaceful spot. It is the centre of the Berriquin Irrigation Area. The main street spans Mulwala Canal, the largest irrigation channel in Australia.

IN TOWN Mary Lawson Wayside Rest A step back in time, Mary Lawson Wayside Rest features a log cabin that is an authentic replica of a pioneer home. It houses the Finley and District Historical Museum with displays of antique pumping equipment and machinery. Newell Hwy. *Finley Lake:* popular boating, sailboarding and picnic area; Newell Hwy.

WHAT'S ON *Rodeo and Country Music Festival:* Jan.

NEARBY *Berrigan:* charming historic town known for its connections to horseracing; 22 km E. *Sojourn Station Art Studio:* spacious rural property providing accommodation for visiting artists; 25 km SE via Berrigan. *Grassleigh Woodturning:* displays of wood-turning in action and wood products; 37 km NE via Berrigan. ❶ Finley and District Historical Museum, Newell Hwy; (03) 5881 8336 or 1800 650 712

Forbes   Pop. 7094

Map ref. 508 D6

When John Oxley passed through in 1817, he was so unimpressed by the area's clay soil, poor timber and swamps that he claimed 'it is impossible to

Eden's killer whales

There is evidence that killer whales were stalking the waters and terrorising other whales around Twofold Bay even before the whaling industry began in Eden in the early 19th century. Matthew Flinders was offered whale blubber in 1798 by a local Aboriginal man; he swapped it for a biscuit. Flinders wrote that, while 'watching for an opportunity to spit it out when he should not be looking, I perceived him doing the same thing with our biscuit'. It is assumed that the killer whales forced other whales in the area to beach themselves, inadvertently providing a convenient food source for the Aboriginal people.

The success of Eden's whaling station in the 1800s was largely due to a pod of killer whales that returned each year, known to the locals by their markings and named Tom, Hooky, Humpy and Stranger. These killer whales would herd baleen whales into the shallow water of Twofold Bay and alert the whalers by 'flop-tailing' (thrashing the water with their tails) in front of the whaling station. The whalers would harpoon the baleens and the killers would nip at the whales' bodies, throw themselves over their blowholes to stop them breathing and swim beneath them to prevent them from sounding for help. The mutually beneficial relationship resulted in the killers feasting on the whales' lips and tongues, leaving the rest of the carcasses for the whalers to bring ashore.

This association continued until whaling ceased in 1928. The final farewell came when Old Tom, the leader of the pod, was found dead in the bay in 1930. He was brought ashore and his skeleton was cleaned and mounted. This saw the beginning of the Eden Killer Whale Museum, where Old Tom continues to be a popular display.

NEW SOUTH WALES

imagine a worse country'. Today it is hard to see what Oxley meant because Forbes is a pleasant spot bisected by Lake Forbes, a large lagoon in the middle of town. It was the discovery of gold that caused the town to be built and the legends of old bushrangers that keep it buzzing today.

IN TOWN Albion Hotel The first hotel in Forbes, the Albion Hotel was so popular during the gold rush that it allegedly sold more alcohol in the 1860s than any hotel in Australia – not bad for an outback town. The hotel is a former Cobb & Co depot and now houses displays on the history of the gold strikes and the must-see Bushranger Hall of Fame. Lachlan St. *Historical Museum:* features relics associated with Ben Hall, a vintage colonial kitchen and antique farm machinery; Cross St; open 2pm–4pm winter and 3pm–5pm summer. *Cemetery:* graves of Ben Hall, Kate Foster (Ned Kelly's sister), Rebecca Shields (Captain Cook's niece) and French author Paul Wenz; Bogan Gate Rd; *King George V Park:* memorial where 'German Harry' discovered gold in 1861, and a pleasant spot for picnics and barbecues; Lawler St. *Dowling Street Park:* memorial marks the spot where John Oxley first passed through in 1817; Dowling St. *Fossil sites:* on town outskirts; brochure from visitor centre. *Historical town walk:* includes the post office (1862) and the town hall (1861) where Dame Nellie Melba performed in 1909; map from visitor centre. *Local arts and crafts:* brochure from visitor centre.

WHAT'S ON *Jazz Festival:* Jan. *Ben Hall Bike Show:* Mar.

NEARBY Lachlan Vintage Village A village of historic buildings re-creating district life in 1860–1900. There is a sharp contrast in the living standards apparent in the poor gold-seekers' huts and the grand homesteads of the farmers and graziers. Also of interest are Henry Lawson's home, Tichbourne School and a replica of Ben Hall's Sandy Creek homestead. 1 km s. *Gum Swamp Sanctuary:* birdlife and other fauna, best seen at sunrise or sunset; 4 km s. *Sandhills Vineyard:* French wine-maker with cellar-door tastings; off Orange Rd; 5 km e. *Chateau Champsaur:* oldest winery in the area (1886), with cellar-door tastings; 5 km se. *Ben Hall's Place:* marks the site where the bushranger was shot by policemen; 8 km w.
ⓘ Railway station, Union St; (02) 6852 4155; www.forbes.nsw.gov.au

Forster–Tuncurry Pop. 17 939

Map ref. 509 P2

Located in the picturesque Great Lakes district, Forster is connected to its twin town, Tuncurry, by a large concrete bridge across Wallis Lake, forming one large holiday resort town. The area has an excellent reputation for its fishing and seafood, particularly its oysters.

IN TOWN *Forster Arts and Crafts Centre:* the largest working craft centre in NSW; Breese Pde. *Tobwabba Art Studio:* specialises in urban coastal Aboriginal art; cnr Breckenridge and Little sts, Forster. *Pebbly Beach Bicentennial Walk:* gentle and scenic 2 km walk to Bennetts Head, beginning at baths off North St, Forster. *Wallis Lake Fishermen's Co-op:* fresh and cooked oysters and ocean fish; Wharf St, Tuncurry. *Dolphin-spotting and lake cruises:* bookings at visitor centre. Dolphins can also be seen from Tuncurry Breakwall and Bennetts Head. *Launch and boat hire:* for lake and deep-sea fishing; bookings at visitor centre.

WHAT'S ON *Forster Market:* Town Park; 2nd Sun each month. *Tuncurry Market:* John Wright Park; 4th Sat each month. *Australian Ironman Triathlon:* April. *Oyster Festival:* Oct. *Half Ironman Triathlon:* Nov.

NEARBY Booti Booti National Park An ideal spot for water activities, Booti Booti National Park has beautiful beaches including Elizabeth, Boomerang and Blueys beaches, all fabulous for surfing, swimming and fishing. Elizabeth Beach is patrolled by lifesavers in season. The lookout tower on Cape Hawke offers 360-degree views over Booti Booti and Wallingat national parks, the foothills of the Barrington Tops, Seal Rocks, and Crowdy Bay. The park offers a variety of walking trails. 17 km s. *Curtis Collection Museum:* vintage cars and Australian memorabilia including stamps and telephones; 3 km s. *Cape Hawke:* steep 400 m track to summit for views of Wallis Lake, Seal Rocks, and inland to Great Dividing Range; 8 km s. *The Green Cathedral:* open-air church with pews and altar, sheltered by cabbage palm canopy; Tiona, on the shores of Wallis Lake; 13 km s. *Smiths Lake:* sheltered lake for safe swimming; 30 km s. *Tours of Great Lakes area:* kayak, 4WD, nature and eco tours, including bushwalks; brochure from visitor centre.
ⓘ Little St; (02) 6554 8799 or 1800 802 692; www.greatlakes.org.au

Gilgandra Pop. 2717

Map ref. 514 D13

A historic country town at the junction of three highways, 'Gil', as the locals call it, is the centre for the surrounding wool and farming country. It saw the start of the 1915 Coo-ee March in which 35 men, given no support from the army, decided to march the 500 kilometres to Sydney to enlist for World War I. Along the way they recruited over 200 men, announcing their arrival in each town with a call of 'coo-ee!' The march sparked seven other such marches from country towns.

IN TOWN Coo-ee Heritage Centre This museum has memorabilia from the 1915 Coo-ee March, and items relating to the Breelong Massacre, which took place near town after an Aboriginal man was insulted for marrying a white woman, and

on which Thomas Keneally's *The Chant of Jimmy Blacksmith* was based. Coo-ee March Memorial Park, Newell Hwy. *Rural Museum:* antique farm machinery and early-model tractors on display; Newell Hwy. *Hitchen House Museum:* the home of the Hitchen brothers, who initiated the Coo-ee March. The museum has memorabilia from WW I, WW II and Vietnam. Miller St. *Orana Cactus World:* almost 1000 different cacti on display collected over 40 years; Newell Hwy; open most weekends and by appt; bookings (02) 6847 0566. *Gilgandra Observatory and Display Centre:* Newtonian reflector and refractor telescopes, a sundial, and fossil and rock displays; cnr Wamboin and Willie sts; open 7pm–10pm (8.30pm–11pm during daylight saving) Mon–Sat. *Tourist drives:* around town; brochure from visitor centre.

WHAT'S ON *Vintage Farm and Steam Rally:* Easter. *Coo-ee Festival:* Oct.

NEARBY Warren Its location on the Macquarie River makes Warren a popular spot with anglers. For a stroll along the riverbank take the River Red Gum Walk, for birdwatching go to Tiger Bay Wildlife Reserve, and for a lazy day of picnicking and swimming visit Warren Weir. The racecourse south of town is known as the 'Randwick of the west' and hosts some fantastic race days. 85 km w. *Gilgandra Flora Reserve:* 8.5 ha of bushland, perfect for picnics and barbecues. Most plants flower in spring, making the park particularly spectacular Sept–Nov. 14 km ne.
ⓘ Coo-ee Heritage Centre, Coo-ee March Memorial Park, Newell Hwy; (02) 6847 2045; www.gilgandra.nsw.gov.au

Glen Innes Pop. 5706

Map ref. 515 L6

This beautiful town, set among rolling hills on the northern tablelands of New South Wales at an elevation of 1075 metres, is known for its fine parks, which are especially striking in autumn. It was the scene of many bushranging exploits in the 19th century, including some by the infamous Captain Thunderbolt. In 1835 two particularly hairy convict stockmen, Chandler and Duval, were the first white men to work in the area. They advised and guided settlers to new land where they settled stations in the 1830s. Because of Chandler and Duval, people came to know Glen Innes as the 'land of the beardies', a nickname that has stuck to this day. The town is undeniably proud of its Celtic beginnings (the first settlers were predominantly Scots) as illustrated by their attractions and festivals.

IN TOWN Centennial Parklands The site of Celtic monument 'Australian Standing Stones', which was built with 38 giant granite monoliths in recognition of the contribution made in Australia by people of Celtic origin. A full explanation of the stones can be read at Crofters Cottage, which also sells Celtic food and gifts. St Martin's Lookout provides superb views over the town and surrounds. Meade St. *Cooramah Aboriginal Cultural Centre:* Aboriginal art and craft, historic artefacts, restaurant with bush tucker; cnr McKenzie St and New England Hwy. *Land of the Beardies History House:* folk museum in the town's first hospital building. Set in extensive grounds, it has a reconstructed slab hut, period room settings and pioneer relics. Cnr Ferguson St and West Ave. *Self-guide walks:* past historic public buildings, especially on Grey St; brochure from visitor centre.

WHAT'S ON *Market:* Grey St; 2nd Sun each month. *Minerama Gem Festival:* Mar. *Australian Celtic Festival:* May. *Land of the Beardies Bush Festival:* Nov.

NEARBY Gibraltar Range National Park and Washpool National Park These adjoining parks were World Heritage-listed in 1986 because of their ancient and isolated remnants of rainforest and their great variety of plant and animal species. Gibraltar Range is known for its scenic creeks and cascades and its unusual granite formations, The Needles and Anvil Rock. Gibraltar Range also contains over 100 km of excellent walking trails. 70 km NE. Washpool has the largest remaining stand of coachwood rainforest in the world and a unique array of eucalypt woods and rainforest. It has some of the least disturbed forest in NSW. 75 km NE. *Stonehenge:* unusual balancing rock formations; 18 km S. *Emmaville:* the Australian beginnings of St John Ambulance occurred here. This old mining town also offers fossicking for sapphires, topaz and quartz. 39 km NW. *Deepwater:* good fishing for trout, perch and cod with regular fishing safaris; bookings at visitor centre; 40 km N. *The Willows:* farm with fishing, bushwalking and camping. Also here is an Aboriginal tourism centre with traditional activities on offer (permit from Cooramah Centre in town). 45 km NW. *Torrington:* gem fossicking, bushwalks and unusual rock formations; 66 km NW. *Convict-carved tunnel:* road tunnel halfway between Glen Innes and Grafton; Old Grafton Rd; 72 km W. *Horse treks:* accommodation at historic pubs; bookings at visitor centre. 🛈 152 Church St; (02) 6732 2397; www.gleninnestourism.com

Glenbrook   Pop. 5948

Map ref. 493 J7, 495 Q9

Glenbrook is a picturesque village on the edge of the Blue Mountains. It was originally known as Watertank because it was used for the storage of water for local steam trains. Today it is a charming town with a large lagoon, close to the impressive Red Hands Cave that lies in Blue Mountains National Park.

Polblue Swamp, Barrington Tops National Park, west of Gloucester

IN TOWN Lapstone Zig Zag Walking Track The track follows the 3 km path of the original Lapstone Zig Zag Railway. The track includes convict-built Lennox Bridge (the oldest surviving bridge on the mainland), the abandoned Lucasville Station and numerous lookouts with views of Penrith and the Cumberland Plain. Nearby there is a monument to John Whitton, a pioneer in railway development. Starts in Knapsack St. *Glenbrook Lagoon:* filled with ducks, and a perfect picnic spot.

WHAT'S ON *Market:* Community Hall, Great Western Hwy; 1st Sun each month, Feb–Dec.

NEARBY Faulconbridge This scenic town features the Corridor of Oaks, a line of trees, each one planted by an Australian prime minister. There is also the grave of Sir Henry Parkes, 'the father of Federation', in the cemetery that he established, and the stone cottage where Norman Lindsay lived, now a gallery and museum dedicated to his life and work. Lindsay was the author of Australian classics such as *The Magic Pudding* and was the subject of the film *Sirens* (1994). 16 km NW.

Wascoe Siding Miniature Railway: 300 m of steam and motor railway plus picnic and barbecue facilities. Trains operate 1st Sun each month. Off Great Western Hwy; 2.5 km W. *Blue Mountains National Park:* Red Hands Cave is accessed by a 6 km return walk; *for information see feature on p. 80.* Euroka Clearing, 4 km S, is a popular camping spot home to many kangaroos.

For other parts of the park see Katoomba and Blackheath. Springwood: galleries and craft and antique shops. Also home to the Ivy Markets 2nd Sat each month (except Jan) at civic centre, Macquarie Rd, and Blue Gum Market 4th Sat each month at school, Macquarie Rd. 12 km NW. *Linden:* impressive Kings Cave with Caleys Repulse Cairn nearby commemorating early surveyor George Caley; 20 km W. 🛈 Blue Mountains Tourism, Great Western Hwy; 1300 653 408; www.bluemountainstourism.org.au

Gloucester   Pop. 2468

Map ref. 509 N1

At the foot of the impressive monolith hills of the Bucketts Range, Gloucester calls itself the base camp to the Barrington Tops because of its close proximity to the national park. This green and peaceful town was recently named as one of the safest places to live in New South Wales and is known for its top-quality Barrington beef and perch.

IN TOWN *Belbouri Aboriginal Art Centre:* furniture, paintings and jewellery; Hume St. *Folk Museum:* collections include pioneer household relics, toys, and gemstones and rocks; Church St; open 10am–2pm Thurs and Sat. *Town Heritage Walk:* includes Lostrochs Cordial Factory and Gloucester Powerhouse; brochure from visitor centre.

WHAT'S ON *Shakespeare Festival:* May. *Snow Fest:* July. *Mountain Man Triathlon:* kayaking, mountain-biking and running; Sept.

Cottage Point, Ku-ring-gai Chase National Park, near Gosford

NEARBY Barrington Tops National Park
This World Heritage-listed rainforest is
enormous and has a great variety of
landscapes, flora and fauna. Much of it is
wilderness, including alpine plateaus and
gushing rivers, criss-crossed with some
good walking trails. For the less energetic,
there are also beautiful forest drives and
breathtaking views from Mt Allyn,
1100 m above sea level. The Barrington
Tops Forest Drive from Gloucester to
Scone has rainforest walks and picnic
spots en route; brochure from visitor
centre. 60 km w.
The Bucketts Walk: 90 min return with
great views of town; Bucketts Rd; 2 km w.
Aerodrome: offers scenic flights; 4 km s.
Lookouts: amazing views of the national
park, town and surrounding hills at
Kia-ora Lookout (4 km N), Mograni
Lookout (5 km E) and Berrico Trig Station
(14 km w). *Goldtown:* former site of the
Mountain Maid Goldmine (1876), now
mostly covered with rainforest. Also a
historical museum, gold panning and
underground mine tours. 16 km w.
ⓘ 27 Denison St; (02) 6558 1408;
www.gloucester.org.au

Gosford   Pop. 2777

Map ref. 493 P4, 496 F6, 509 M6

Part of the idyllic Central Coast region,
Gosford is surrounded by national parks,
steep hills and valleys, rainforest, lakes
and ocean beaches. Understandably,
Gosford continues to increase in
popularity and has grown into a bustling
city known for its high standard of
tourism and its orchards and seafood.
IN TOWN *Art galleries and craft and
antique shops:* many in town; contact
visitor centre for details.

WHAT'S ON *Springtime Flora Festival:*
Sept. *Mangrove Mountain District Country Fair:*
Oct. *Gosford City Arts Festival:* Oct. *Gosford
to Lord Howe Island Yacht Race:* Oct/Nov.
NEARBY Ku-ring-gai Chase National Park
Here the Hawkesbury River meets the sea
with winding creeks, attractive beaches,
hidden coves and clear water. Highlights
are Resolute Track, with Aboriginal rock
engravings and hand stencils, Bobbin
Head, with a visitor centre and marina,
and West Head Lookout, with panoramic
views over the water. 33 km sw.
Gosford City Arts Centre: local art and craft
and Japanese garden; 3 km E. *Henry Kendall
Cottage:* museum in the poet's sandstone
home. Also picnic and barbecue facilities
in the grounds. 3 km sw. *Central Coast
Winery:* housed in old stables, the winery
offers cellar-door tastings of wines, ports
and sherries; 11 km NE. *Forest of Tranquillity:*
walking trails through peaceful rainforest.
The Firefly Festival is held here Nov–Dec.
14 km NW. *Australian Reptile Park:* snakes,
spiders and Galapagos tortoises. See
shows throughout the day. Somersby
Falls nearby provide an ideal picnic
spot. 15 km sw. *Calga Springs Sanctuary:*
native forest with 2 km of walking trails.
Animals extinct in the area have been
re-introduced with success thanks to
the fence that keeps out feral animals.
20 km NW. *Brooklyn:* access to lower
Hawkesbury for housebarting, fishing and
river cruises. Historic Riverboat Postman
ferry leaves Brooklyn weekdays for cruises
and postal deliveries. 32 km s. *Central Coast
Bushworks:* abseiling, bushwalking and
climbing workshops and trips; by appt;
bookings (02) 4363 2028.
ⓘ 200 Mann St; (02) 4385 4430 or
1300 130 708; www.cctourism.com.au

Goulburn   Pop. 20 846

Map ref. 507 G3, 508 H11

Goulburn is at the junction of the
Wollondilly and Mulwaree rivers, at the
centre of a wealthy farming district.
It was one of Australia's first inland
settlements and is widely known for its
merino wool industry.
IN TOWN The Big Merino Even though
it was only built in 1985, the Big Merino
is an instantly recognisable landmark
associated across Australia with Goulburn
and its thriving merino wool industry.
The 15 m high and 18 m long sculptured
sheep has three floors with a souvenir
shop, an educational display on the
history of wool in the area and a lookout
across Goulburn. There is also a 24 hr
restaurant and a tavern. Hume Hwy.
Regional art gallery: diverse and ever-
changing exhibitions and public
programs; Bourke St. *Marsden Weir:*
attractive parkland with picnic and
barbecue facilities. Waterworks Museum
displays antique waterworks engines. Off
Fitzroy St. *Rocky Hill War Memorial:* erected
in 1925 as a tribute to the Goulburn men
and women who served during WW I,
it offers outstanding views across the
city; Memorial Dr. *Two-foot tour:* historic
buildings include Goulburn Courthouse
and St Saviour's Cathedral; brochure
from visitor centre.
WHAT'S ON *East Goulburn Market:* East
Goulburn Primary School; 3rd Sat each
month. *Australia Day Rodeo:* Jan. *Australian
Blues Music Festival:* Feb. *Celebration of
Heritage, Jazz and Roses:* Mar. *Lilac City
Festival:* Oct.
**NEARBY Bungonia State Conservation
Area** A popular spot for adventure
recreation with perfect terrain for
canyoning, caving and canoeing. For
those less energetic, walking trails offer
fantastic river and canyon views. One
walk passes through the spectacular
Bungonia Gorge. 35 km E.
Pelican Sheep Station: farm tours,
shearing and sheepdog demonstrations
by appt; bookings (02) 4821 4668.
Accommodation is available. 10 km s.
Lake George: 25 km long lake that
regularly fills and empties. It has excellent
picnic sites. 40 km sw.
ⓘ 201 Sloane St; (02) 4823 4492 or
1800 353 646; www.igoulburn.com

Grafton   Pop. 17 380

Map ref. 515 P6

An attractive garden city, Grafton is
known for its riverbank parks and
jacaranda trees. The city has over 6500
trees in 24 parks. Grafton's city centre
adds to the charm with wide streets,
elegant Victorian buildings and the
Clarence River passing through. Water
lovers are spoiled in Grafton as there
are excellent facilities for those seeking
whitewater adventure, a serene spot of

fishing or just about anything in between.
IN TOWN Susan Island This rainforest recreation reserve in the Clarence River is home to a large fruit bat colony. Dusk is the time to visit with the bats flying off in search of food (wearing a hat is advisable if visiting at this time). During the day the island is a pleasant spot for rainforest walks, barbecues and picnics. Access is via hired boat, skippered cruise or Clarence Islander ferry.
Grafton Regional Gallery: rated as one of the most outstanding regional galleries in Australia, the Grafton Regional Gallery inside Prentice House has permanent exhibitions such as the Jacaranda Art Society and Contemporary Australian Drawing collections; Fitzroy St. *National Trust-classified buildings:* include Schaeffer House, home of the Clarence River Historical Society, and Christ Church Cathedral; brochure from visitor centre. *Local art and craft shops:* brochure from visitor centre.
WHAT'S ON *Old Schoolhouse Market:* Lawrence Rd; last Sat each month. *Grafton Cup:* richest horserace in rural Australia; July. *Grafton to Inverell International Cycling Classic:* Sept. *Bridge to Bridge Ski Race:* Oct. *Jacaranda Festival:* Oct–Nov. *Bridge to Bridge Sailing Classic:* Nov.
NEARBY Nymboida Waters pumped by the hydro-electric power station from the Nymboida River into Goolang Creek provide a high-standard canoe course that hosts competitions throughout the year. Canoe hire and lessons are on offer and facilities range from the learners' pond for beginners to grade III rapids for the experienced, thrill-seeking canoeist. The beautiful rainforest surrounds are excellent for bushwalking, abseiling, trail rides and platypus viewing. 47 km SW.
Ulmarra Village: National Trust-classified turn-of-the-century river port with exceptional galleries, craft shops and studios where you can watch artists at work; 12 km NE. *Yuraygir National Park:* highlights include Wooli for unspoiled surf beaches and Minnie Water for walking trails, secluded beaches, camping and abundant wildlife (especially the very friendly wallabies). Minnie Lagoon is a popular swimming, picnicking and boating spot. 50 km SE. *Fishing:* river fishing for saltwater or freshwater fish, depending on time of year and rainfall; details at visitor centre.
ℹ Clarence River Visitor Information Centre, Pacific Hwy, South Grafton; (02) 6642 4677; www.clarencetourism.com

Grenfell   Pop. 1925

Map ref. 507 B1, 508 D8

Nestled at the foot of the Weddin Mountains, Grenfell is best known as the birthplace of great Australian writer Henry Lawson. The wealth appropriated during the heady days of the gold rush is evident in the opulent original buildings on Main Street, but everything seems to move at a more leisurely pace today. Originally named Emu Creek, the town was renamed after Gold Commissioner John Granville Grenfell, who was gunned down by bushrangers.
IN TOWN *Henry Lawson Obelisk:* memorial on the site of the house where the poet is believed to have been born; next to Lawson Park on the road to Young. *Grenfell Museum:* local relics (and the stories behind them) from world wars, the gold rush, Henry Lawson and bushrangers; Camp St; open weekends 2pm–4pm. *O'Brien's Reef Lookout:* views of the town on a gold-discovery site with walkway and picnic facilities. An endemic plant and iris garden is adjacent to the lookout. Access from O'Brien St. *Guide to Historic Buildings of Grenfell and Tour of Grenfell Town:* walk and drive; brochures from visitor centre.
WHAT'S ON *Guinea Pig Races:* Easter. *Henry Lawson Festival of Arts:* June. *Iris Festival:* Oct. *Grenfell Guineas:* horserace; Nov.
NEARBY Weddin Mountains National Park The park is a rugged crescent of cliffs and gullies providing superb bushwalking, camping and picnicking spots. Two of the highlights of the bushwalks are Ben Hall's Cave, where the bushranger hid from the police, and Seaton's Farm, a historic homestead set on beautiful parkland. The bush is also rich with fauna including wedge-tailed eagles, honeyeaters and wallabies. 18 km SW. *Company Dam Nature Reserve:* excellent bushwalking area; 1 km NW. *Lirambenda Riding School and Animal Farm:* scenic trail-rides and accommodation; 20 km S. *Site of Ben Hall's farmhouse and stockyards:* memorial; Sandy Creek Rd, off Mid Western Hwy; 25 km W. *Adelargo Drive:* attractive drive with diversion to Cypress Valley Ostrich Facility on Peaks Creek Rd; 30 km NE; self-guide brochure from visitor centre. *Old Richmond Cottage:* tours of cottage gardens, bush stories, poetry readings and Devonshire teas. By appt through the visitor centre only. Quandialla; 30 km W.
ℹ CWA Wool and Craft Centre, 68 Main St; (02) 6343 1612

Griffith   Pop. 15 937

Map ref. 511 N7

Griffith is in an idyllic position, surrounded by low hills and fragrant citrus orchards in the heart of the Murrumbidgee Irrigation Area. It was designed by Walter Burley Griffin and named after Sir Arthur Griffith, the first Minister for Public Works in New South Wales. The area is one of the largest vegetable-production regions in Australia and produces more than 70 percent of the state's wine.
IN TOWN Hermits Cave and Sir Dudley de Chair's Lookout With beautiful views over orange orchards, vineyards and rice paddies to Cocoparra National Park, Hermits Cave is located down a path below the lookout. The cave is named because it was once home to Valerio Riccett, an Italian miner from Broken Hill. After being jilted, he left his home and job and became a hermit in this cave. He left to serve in WW II, but then returned only to become seriously ill. In return for tending the doctor's garden, he was treated in town, but when his illness became serious, the local citizens collected money and sent him home to Italy where he died three months later. Scenic Drive.
Pioneer Park Museum: 18 ha of bushland featuring drop-log buildings, early 20th-century memorabilia and re-created Bagtown Village; Remembrance Dr. *Riverina Grove:* local produce with tastings; Whybrow St; closed Sat afternoon and Sun. *Griffith Regional Art Gallery:* exhibition program of international and Australian artists that changes monthly; Banna Ave. *Griffith Cottage Gallery:* local and imported paintings, pottery and handicrafts with exhibitions at various times throughout the year; Bridge Rd. *Two Foot Tour and self-drive tour:* feature the city's historic buildings and surrounding pastures; brochure from visitor centre.
WHAT'S ON *Market:* Police and Citizens Youth Club, Olympic St; Sun. *Community Market:* visitor centre; 3rd Sun each month. *La Festa:* food and wine festival celebrating cultural diversity; Easter. *UnWined in the Riverina:* food and wine festival; June. *Festival of Gardens:* Oct.
NEARBY Cocoparra National Park Original Riverina forest full of wattles, orchids and ironbarks, the park is spectacular in spring, when the wildflowers bloom. The site is ideal for bushwalking, camping, birdwatching and picnicking, and the rugged terrain and vivid colours also make it popular with photographers. 25 km NE.
Private gardens: Belle Amour (5 km N) and Casuarina (11 km N); open Sept–May; brochure at visitor centre. *Catania Fruit Salad Farm:* horticultural farm offering demonstrations and tours at 1.30pm daily; Cox Rd, Hanwood; 8 km S. *Lake Wyangan:* good spot for variety of watersports; 10 km NW. *Many wineries:* include Miranda, De Bortoli and McWilliams, open for cellar-door tastings; map from visitor centre.
ℹ Cnr Banna and Jondaryan aves; (02) 6962 4145 or 1800 681 141; www.riverinatourism.com.au

Gulgong   Pop. 2017

Map ref. 508 H2

Gulgong is known as 'the town on the ten dollar note', even though that ten dollar note has long since been replaced. Named by the Wiradjuri people – the name means 'deep waterhole' – Gulgong did not excite European interest until gold was discovered in 1866. By 1872 there were 20 000 people living in the area. By the end of the decade 15 000 kilograms of gold had been unearthed, the prospectors had gone and almost all of the local Aboriginal people had been slaughtered. The town stands today almost unchanged from these times. The narrow, winding streets follow the paths of the original bullock tracks past iron-lace verandahs, horse troughs and hitching rails.

IN TOWN Henry Lawson Centre The collection is housed in the Salvation Army Hall, which was built in 1922, the year Lawson died. The centre has the largest collection of Lawson memorabilia outside Sydney's Mitchell Library and includes original manuscripts, artefacts, photographs, paintings and an extensive collection of rare first editions. 'A Walk Through Lawson's Life' is an exhibition that uses Lawson's words to illustrate the poverty, family disintegration, deafness and alcoholism that shaped his life, as well as the causes he was passionate about such as republicanism, unionism and votes for women. Mayne St. *Pioneers Museum:* illustrates every era of Gulgong's history. Exhibits include a replica of a classroom from the 1880s, period clothing and rare antique crockery; cnr Herbert and Bayly sts. *Red Hill:* site of the town's original gold strike, featuring restored stamper mill, poppet head and memorial to Henry Lawson; off White St. *Town trail:* self-guide walking tour of historic buildings such as Prince of Wales Opera House and Ten Dollar Town Motel; brochure from visitor centre.

WHAT'S ON *Folk Festival:* Jan. *Henry Lawson Festival:* June.

NEARBY Goulburn River National Park The park follows approximately 90 km of the Goulburn River with sandy riverbanks making easy walking trails and beautiful camping sites. Rare and threatened plants abound here, as do wombats, eastern grey kangaroos, emus and birds. Highlights of the area include the Drip, 50 m curtains of water dripping through the rocks alongside the Goulburn River, sandstone cliffs honeycombed with caves, and over 300 significant Aboriginal sites. 30 km NE. *Ulan:* Ulan Coal Mine has viewing areas overlooking a large open-cut mine. Also here is Hands on the Rock, a prime example of Aboriginal rock art. 22 km NE. *Talbragar Fossil Fish Beds:* one of the few Jurassic period fossil deposits in Australia; 35 km NE. *Wineries:* cellar-door tastings; brochure from visitor centre.
🛈 109 Herbert St; (02) 6374 1202; www.mudgee-gulgong.org

Gundagai   Pop. 1990

Map ref. 507 B5, 508 D12

Gundagai is a tiny town on the Murrumbidgee River at the foot of Mt Parnassus. Synonymous with Australiana, Gundagai and the nearby dog on the tuckerbox have been celebrated through song and verse for many years. Banjo Paterson, C. J. Dennis and Henry Lawson all included the town in their works. It was also the scene in 1852 of Australia's worst flood disaster when 89 of the 250 townsfolk died. The count could have been worse but for local Aboriginal man Yarri, who paddled his bark canoe throughout the night to rescue stranded victims. Gundagai was moved to higher ground soon after, and there are several monuments celebrating Yarri's efforts.

IN TOWN Marble Masterpiece In an amazing display of patience and determination, local sculptor Frank Rusconi, who is also responsible for the dog on the tuckerbox, worked to create this original cathedral model. He built it in his spare time over 28 years, hand-turning and polishing the 20 948 individual pieces required to build it. Visitor centre, Sheridan St. *Gabriel Gallery:* outstanding collection of photographs, letters and possessions illustrating Gundagai's unique history; Sheridan St. *Gundagai Museum:* relics include Phar Lap's saddle, Frank Rusconi's tools, and artefacts from the horse and buggy era; Homer St. *Lookouts:* excellent views of the town and surrounding green valleys from the Mt Parnassus Lookout in Hanley St and the Rotary Lookout in Luke St; South Gundagai. *Historical town walk:* includes the National Trust-classified Prince Alfred Bridge and St John's Anglican Church; leaflet from visitor centre.

WHAT'S ON *Spring Flower Show:* Oct. *Dog on the Tuckerbox Festival:* Nov. *Snake Gully Cup:* horserace; Nov. *Rodeo:* Dec.

NEARBY The Dog on the Tuckerbox Originally mentioned in the poem 'Bill the Bullocky' by Bowyang Yorke, this monument to pioneer teamsters and their dogs is recognised throughout the nation as an Australian icon. It was celebrated in the song 'Where the Dog Sits on the Tuckerbox' by Jack O'Hagan (the songwriter responsible for 'Along the Road to Gundagai'). The dog was unveiled in 1932 by Prime Minister Joseph Lyons. Nearby are statues of Dad and Dave (characters from the writings of Steele Rudd), a kiosk, a fernery and the ruins of Five Mile Pub. 8 km N.
🛈 249 Sheridan St; (02) 6944 1341; www.gundagaishire.nsw.gov.au

Gunnedah   Pop. 7855

Map ref. 514 H10

At the heart of the Namoi Valley, Gunnedah is instantly recognisable by the grain silos that tower over the town. The area is abundant with native wildlife, especially koalas, with Gunnedah claiming to be the koala capital of the world. At least 25 koalas are known to live in the town itself. A rather large town, Gunnedah still manages to keep a laid-back atmosphere and has been home to famous Australians such as Dorothea Mackellar and Breaker Morant.

IN TOWN Anzac Park The Water Tower Museum here housed, in the town's main water tower, has a mural and display of early explorers, memorabilia from several wars and schools, and an Aboriginal history display. Views from the top extend across town (open 2pm–5pm Sat). Dorothea Mackellar, the renowned Australian poet responsible for *My Country*, has a memorial statue in the park. Memorabilia of her life and of the annual national school poetry competition in her name can be viewed at the park's visitor centre. South St. *Rural Museum:* early agricultural machinery and the largest privately owned firearm collection in the country; Mullaley Rd. *Red Chief Memorial:* to Aboriginal warrior Cumbo Gunnerah, of the Gunn-e-dar group; State Office building, Abbott St. *Old Bank Gallery:* local art and craft; Conadilly St. *Bicentennial Creative Arts Centre:* art and pottery display and the watercolour series 'My Country' by Jean Isherwood; Chandos St; open 10am–4pm Fri–Sun. *Plains of Plenty:* local craft and produce; South St. *Eighth Division Memorial Avenue:* 45 flowering gums, each with a plaque in memory of men who served in the Eighth Division in WW II; Memorial Ave. *Breaker Morant Drive:* a plaque tells the story of Henry Morant, known as 'the breaker' because of his skill with horses (and some say hearts). A 500 m path shows sites where he jumped horses. Kitchener Park. *Bindea Walking Track and Town Walk:* memorials, koala and kangaroo sites, lookouts and porcupine reserve; brochure from visitor centre.

WHAT'S ON *Market:* Wolseley Park, Conadilly St; 3rd Sat each month. *National Tomato Competition:* search for Australia's biggest tomato, and related celebrations; Jan. *Week of Speed:* races include go-karts, cars, bikes and athletics; Mar. *Gunnedah Bird Expo and Sale:* April. *Ag Quip:* agricultural field days; Aug. *Vintage Car Swap Meet:* Sept.

NEARBY Lake Keepit This lake is great for watersports, fishing and boating, and there is even a children's pool. If you want to stay a while longer, then there is the Keepit Country Campout. City folk will notice that the sky is huge and full of stars out here. The campout provides all the facilities needed to camp without roughing it too much, including tents, a kitchen and showers and toilets, and there is a campfire amphitheatre for evening entertainment. For the daytime, there is all the equipment needed for canoeing, kayaking, rockclimbing, gliding and bushwalking. 34 km NE. *Porcupine Lookout:* views over town and surrounding agricultural area; 3 km SE. *Waterways Wildlife Park:* abundant with native animals such as kangaroos,

koalas, wombats and emus; Mullaley Rd; 7 km w. *150° East Time Meridian:* the basis of Eastern Standard Time, crossing the Oxley Hwy; 28 km w.
ⓘ Anzac Park, South St; (02) 6740 2230; www.infogunnedah.com.au

Guyra   Pop. 1721

Map ref. 515 L8

Guyra is the highest town on the New England tableland at an altitude of 1320 metres on the watershed of the Great Dividing Range. Snow is not unusual in winter and at other times the town is crisp and green.
IN TOWN Mother of Ducks Lagoon The reserve is a rare high-country wetland and home to hundreds of waterbirds. The migratory Japanese snipe is known to stop here and it is a nesting site for swans. There is a viewing platform with an identification board covering dozens of different birds. McKie Pde.
Historical Society Museum: themed room displaying town memorabilia and the story of the Guyra ghost; Bradley St; open by appt; bookings (02) 6779 2132.
Railway Station: large display of antique machinery, rail train rides; Bradley St.
WHAT'S ON *Lamb and Potato Festival:* includes Hydrangea Festival; Jan. *Wine, Food and Music Festival:* April.
NEARBY *Handcraft Hall – The Pink Stop:* hand-knitted garments, paintings, pottery and Devonshire teas; 10 km N. *Thunderbolt's Cave:* picturesque and secluded cave, rumoured to be where the bushranger Captain Thunderbolt hid from police; 10 km s. *Chandler's Peak:* spectacular views of the tablelands from an altitude of 1471 m; 20 km E.
ⓘ Council offices, 158 Bradley St; (02) 6779 1577

Hay   Pop. 2693

Map ref. 511 K8

Located in the heart of the Riverina, the most striking thing about Hay is the incredibly flat plains in which it sits. The saltbush flats afford amazing views across the land, especially at sunrise and sunset, and the terrain makes bicycles a popular and easy mode of transport for residents. American travel writer Bill Bryson described Hay as 'a modest splat' and 'extremely likable'.
IN TOWN POW Internment Camp Interpretive Centre Housed in Hay's magnificent restored railway station, the centre documents the WW II internment in Hay of over 3000 prisoners of war. The first internees were known as the 'Dunera boys', Jewish intellectuals who had fled Germany and Austria. During the war years the camp established a garrison band and a newspaper, and printed camp money. The Dunera boys even ran their own 'university', teaching subjects such as atomic research and classical Greek.

Handpiece display, Shear Outback Centre, Hay

The Dunera boys held a reunion in Hay in 1990 and there is a memorial on Showground Rd. Murray St.
Shear Outback Centre: comprises the Australian Shearers Hall of Fame, historic Murray Downs Woolshed and exhibitions; Sturt Hwy. *Witcombe Fountain:* ornate drinking fountain presented to the people of Hay by mayor John Witcombe in 1883; Lachlan St. *Coach house:* features an 1886 Cobb & Co coach, which travelled the Deniliquin–Hay–Wilcannia route until 1901; Lachlan St. *Hay Gaol Museum:* contains memorabilia and photographs of the town, and the building's history from 1878 as a gaol, maternity hospital, lock hospital for the insane and POW compound; Church St. *War Memorial High School Museum:* built in recognition of those who served in WW I, with war memorabilia and an honour roll. The building still operates as a school, so call for opening times (02) 6993 1408. Pine St. *Bishop's Lodge:* restored 1888 iron house, now a museum and gallery with a unique and remarkable collection of heritage roses. Holds a market 3rd Sun in Oct. Cnr Roset St and Sturt Hwy; open 10am–12.30pm in summer and 2pm–4.30pm in winter. *Ruberto's Winery:* cellar-door tastings; Sturt Hwy. *Hay Wetlands:* especially spectacular in spring, the land is a breeding ground for over 60 inland bird species with a breeding island and tree plantation; north-western edge of town; brochure from visitor centre. *Hay Park:* pleasant picnic spot with a nature walk along the banks of the

river; off Brunker St. *Murrumbidgee River:* excellent sandy river beaches and calm water, perfect for waterskiing, canoeing, swimming and picnics. Enjoy excellent freshwater fishing for Murray cod, yellow-belly perch and redfin. A licence is required; available from outlets in town, including visitor centre. *Heritage walk and scenic drive:* walk includes city structures built for the harsh outback such as the beautifully restored courthouse (1892) on Moppett St and the shire office (1877) on Lachlan St. The drive takes in the parklands, river and surrounding saltbush plains; brochure from visitor centre.
WHAT'S ON *Surf Carnival:* Jan. *Sheep Show:* June. *Rodeo:* Oct. *Hay Races:* Nov.
NEARBY Booligal Situated in an area known as the 'devil's claypan', this hot and dusty sheep- and cattle-town is mentioned in Banjo Paterson's poem 'Hay and Hell and Booligal'. The poem says that a visit to Booligal is a fate worse than hell, which is a matter for the visitor to decide, but topics of complaint include heat, flies, dust, rabbits, mosquitoes and snakes. On the plus side, the atmosphere is relaxed and friendly. It is off the beaten tourist track and there is an interesting memorial to John Oxley, the first European in the area, in the shape of a giant theodolite (surveyor's tool). 78 km N. Halfway to Booligal, look out for the lonely ruins of One Tree Hotel. *Hay Weir:* on the Murrumbidgee River, excellent for picnics, barbecues and Murray cod fishing; 12 km w. *Sunset viewing area:* the vast plains provide amazingly broad and spectacular sunsets; Booligal Rd; 16 km N. *Maude Weir:* surprisingly green and lush oasis, perfect for picnics and barbecues; 53 km w. *Goonawarra Nature Reserve:* no facilities for visitors, but the flood plains with river red gum forests and black box woodlands are still worth a visit – waterfowl in the billabongs, plenty of Murray cod in the Lachlan River and kangaroos and emus on the plains; 59 km N. *Oxley:* tiny town with river red gums and prolific wildlife (best seen at dusk); 87 km NW.
ⓘ 407 Moppett St; (02) 6993 4045; www.visithay.com.au

Holbrook   Pop. 1272

Map ref. 511 R12, 539 R1

Holbrook is a well-known stock-breeding centre rich with history. Originally called The Germans because of its first European settlers, the name was later changed to Germanton. During World War I, when the allies were fighting the Germans, even this name became unacceptable and a new name had to be found. British Commander Norman Holbrook was in the news a great deal as a war hero and had been awarded the Victoria Cross and the French Legion of Honour, so it was decided the town would be named after him.

IN TOWN Otway Submarine The 30 m vessel, once under the command of Norman Holbrook, was decommissioned in 1995. The town was given the fin of the submarine by the Royal Australian Navy and was busily trying to raise funds to purchase the full piece of history, when a gift of $100 000 from Commander Holbrook's widow (his second wife) made the purchase possible. Mrs Holbrook was the guest of honour at the unveiling in 1996. Hume Hwy.
Bronze statue: Commander Holbrook and his submarine, a scale model of the one in which Holbrook won the VC in WW I; Holbrook Park, Hume Hwy. *Woolpack Inn Museum:* 20 rooms furnished in turn-of-the-century style, bakery, horse-drawn vehicles and farm equipment; Hume Hwy. *Ten Mile Creek:* attractive gardens, excellent for picnics; behind museum.
WHAT'S ON *Beef Fest:* even-numbered years, April.
NEARBY *Ultralight Centre:* flights over town and surrounds available; 3 km N. *Hume and Hovell Walking Track:* access to short sections of the 440 km track from Albury to Yass via Woomargama; 15 km S; brochure from Department of Infrastructure, Planning and Natural Resources, Sydney; (02) 9762 8044.
ⓘ Woolpack Inn Museum, Hume Hwy; (02) 6036 2131

Huskisson   Pop. 3289

Map ref. 507 I4, 509 K12

Huskisson is a sleepy holiday resort and fishing port on Jervis (pronounced 'Jarvis') Bay. It was named after British politician William Huskisson, secretary for the colonies and leader of the House of Commons, who was run over and killed by a train in 1830 while talking to the Duke of Wellington at a railway opening. The idyllic bay is renowned for its white sand and clear water, which is why it is often used for underwater filming. There are usually several pods of dolphins living in the bay, making the area ideal for cruises and diving.
IN TOWN Lady Denman Heritage Complex The centre features displays on the history of wooden shipbuilding at Huskisson. There is also Laddie Timbery's Aboriginal Art and Craft Centre, with bush tucker demonstrations and talks on request, and the Museum of Jervis Bay Science and the Sea with fine maritime and surveying collections. Woollamia Rd.
WHAT'S ON *Market:* White Sands Park; 2nd Sun each month. *White Sands Carnival:* stalls, music and entertainment; Easter.
NEARBY Booderee National Park This magnificent park is jointly managed by the Wreck Bay Aboriginal Community and Environment Australia. Highlights include Aboriginal sites, the Cape George Lighthouse, Booderee Botanic Gardens and magnificent beaches. Barry's Bush Tucker Tours offers guided walks drawing on Aboriginal food and culture. Bookings (02) 4442 1168. 11 km S.
NSW Jervis Bay National Park: walking tracks, mangrove boardwalk and amazing beaches (Hyams Beach claims the whitest sand in the world); north and south of town. *Jervis Bay Marine Park:* the clear waters, reefs and deep-water cliffs with caves offer superb diving. Also boating with dolphins. Bookings are taken at the visitor centre for diving and dolphin-watching cruises.
ⓘ Shoalhaven Visitors Centre, cnr Princes Hwy and Pleasant Way, Nowra; (02) 4421 0778 or 1800 024 261; www.shoalhaven.nsw.gov.au

Iluka   Pop. 1852

Map ref. 515 Q5

Located at the mouth of the Clarence River on the north coast, Iluka is a relatively uncommercial fishing and holiday village. Its attractiveness is evident in the long stretches of sandy white beaches and rare and accessible rainforest. Iluka Nature Reserve has the largest remnant of littoral rainforest (trees obtaining water via filtration through coastal sand and nutrients from airborne particles) in New South Wales.
IN TOWN *River cruises:* day cruises and evening barbecue cruises (Wed only); Wed, Fri and Sun; from the Boatshed. *Passenger ferry:* travelling daily to Yamba; from the Boatshed. *Iluka Fish Co-op:* fresh catches on sale from 9am; adjacent to the Boatshed. *Walking track:* picturesque coastline walk; access via Iluka Bluff to the north and Long St to the south.
NEARBY Iluka Nature Reserve This area, nestled on the narrow peninsula where the Clarence River meets the ocean, was World Heritage-listed in 1986 as a valuable remnant of extensive coastal forest. It happens to be the largest remaining coastal rainforest in NSW.
It is rich with birdlife and is a beautiful spot for activities such as fishing, swimming, surfing, canoeing, walking and camping. 1 km N.
Iluka Bluff Beach: safe swimming beach; 1 km N. *Bundjalung National Park:* with ancient rainforest and the Esk River, the largest untouched coastal river system on the north coast. Woody Head has rare rainforest with campground, fishing and swimming. 4 km N. *Woombah Coffee Plantation:* world's southern-most coffee plantation; 12 km NW; tours by appt; bookings (02) 6646 4121.
ⓘ Lower Clarence Visitor Centre, Ferry Park, Pacific Hwy, Maclean; (02) 6645 4121

Inverell   Pop. 9525

Map ref. 515 K6

This town on the Macintyre River at the centre of the New England tablelands is known as 'sapphire city' because it has long been a source of sapphires for much of the world. It is also rich in other mineral deposits, including zircons, industrial diamonds and tin. The country here has lush farm and grazing land and excellent weather conditions with cool nights and warm sunny days.
IN TOWN Pioneer Village This collection of homes and buildings dating from 1840 was moved from its original site to form a 'village of yesteryear'. Attractions include Grove homestead, Paddy's Pub and Mount Drummond Woolshed. Gooda Cottage has an impressive collection of gems and minerals. Tea and damper are served Sun afternoons. Tingha Rd.
Visitor Centre and Mining Museum: local and imported gems, a static display on the local mining industry, photographs and a video of local mines, and a working scale model of a sapphire plant; Water Towers Complex, Campbell St. *Art Society Gallery:* paintings, pottery and craft; Evans St.

Bundjalung National Park, near Iluka

Gem Centre: visitors can see local stones being processed; Byron St. *Transport Museum:* over 200 vehicles on display with an impressive collection of rarities; Taylor Ave. *Town Stroll:* includes sites such as the National Trust-classified courthouse and the CBC Bank building with stables at the rear; brochure from visitor centre. *Town and Country Drive:* historic town buildings, surrounding parks and lookouts; brochure from visitor centre. *Arts, crafts and wood-turning:* work by local artists; brochure from visitor centre.

WHAT'S ON *Hobby Market:* Campbell Park; 1st Sun each month. *Inverell Jockey Club Cup Race Day:* Jan. *Art Exhibition:* Mar. *Grafton to Inverell International Cycling Classic:* Sept. *Sapphire City Festival:* Oct. *Great Inland Fishing Festival:* Dec. *Inverell Jockey Club Boxing Day Meeting:* Dec. *Venetian Carnival:* food and entertainment; Dec.

NEARBY Kwiambal National Park The Macintyre River flows through granite gorges and plunge pools to the stunning Macintyre Falls and then leads into the Severn River. The park is rich with protected woodlands of white cypress pine, box and ironbark. Bat nurseries can be viewed with a torch in the remarkable Ashford Caves, which until the 1960s were mined for guano (bat droppings) to be used as fertiliser on local farms. The park makes a serene site for swimming, bushwalking and camping. Encounters with kangaroos, emus and koalas are common. 90 km N. *McIlveen Lookout:* excellent views of town and surrounding pastures and nature reserve; 2 km W. *Lake Inverell Reserve:* 100 ha of unique aquatic sanctuary for birds and wildlife. Also an excellent site for picnics, bushwalking, birdwatching and fishing. 3 km E. *Draught Horse Centre:* 6 breeds of horse and displays of harnesses and memorabilia; Fishers Rd; 4 km E. *Goonoowigall Bushland Reserve:* rough granite country rich with birdlife and marsupials, it offers superb birdwatching, bushwalking and picnic areas; 5 km S. *Morris' Honey Farm:* visitors can see working bees, taste honey and learn how it is produced. Ride the miniature train and explore the animal park and bottle museum. 8 km SW. *Copeton Dam State Recreation Area:* perfect for boating, waterskiing, swimming, fishing, bushwalking and rockclimbing. It also has adventure playgrounds, water slides, and picnic and barbecue facilities. Kangaroos graze on the golf course at dusk. 17 km S. *DeJon Sapphire Centre:* working sapphire mine with tours and sales; Glen Innes Rd; 19 km E. *Gwydir Ranch 4WD Park:* rugged and colourful gorge country ideal for camping, fishing, bushwalking and swimming. Also popular with photographers and artists. 28 km W. *Green Valley Farm:* working sheep property with zoo, extensive gardens, playground and picnic and barbecue facilities. The highlight is Smith's Mining

and Natural History Museum, which houses a rare collection of gems and minerals from all over the world, local Aboriginal artefacts, antiques and period clothing. 36 km SE; open weekends, public holidays and Qld and NSW school holidays. *Pindari Dam:* fishing, swimming, camping and picnic and barbecue facilities; 58 km N. *Gwydir River:* one of the best whitewater rafting locations in the country during the summer months; brochure from visitor centre. *Warm-weather wineries:* cellar-door tastings; brochure from visitor centre. *Fossicking sites:* great spots for searching for tin, sapphires, quartz or even diamonds; maps at visitor centre.
ⓘ Campbell St; (02) 6722 1693; www.inverell-online.com.au

Jamberoo — Pop. 940

Map ref. 501 G9, 509 K10

One of the most picturesque areas of the New South Wales coast, Jamberoo was once tropical forest but is now a town of rolling hills in the Jamberoo Valley. The town is still surrounded by nature reserves and national parks, but is now situated on the lush green dairy pastures that have made Jamberoo prosperous as a dairy farming region. The surrounding forests are popular with bushwalkers and birdwatchers.

IN TOWN *Jamberoo Hotel:* charming 1857 building with meals and Sun afternoon entertainment; Allowrie St.

WHAT'S ON *Market:* Kevin Walsh Oval, last Sun each month. *Illawarra Folk Festival:* Sept.

NEARBY Budderoo National Park With views from a plateau across sandstone country, heathlands and rainforest. There are excellent walking trails, including one that is accessible by wheelchair, and there are 3 lookouts with views of Carrington Falls. The Minnamurra Rainforest Centre is the highlight with an elevated boardwalk through rainforest and a steep paved walkway to Minnamurra Falls. 4 km W. *Jamberoo Recreation Park:* family fun park with water slides, speed boats, racing cars and bobsleds; 3 km N; open weekends, public holidays and school holidays. *Saddleback Lookout:* 180-degree views of the coast and the starting point for Hoddles Trail, a 1 hr walk with beautiful views to Barren Grounds escarpment; 7 km S. *Barren Grounds Bird Observatory and Nature Reserve:* this 1750 ha of heathland on Hawkesbury sandstone plateau protects over 450 species of plant and 150 species of bird, including the rare ground parrot and eastern bristlebird. It has fabulous bushwalking and birdwatching and also provides educational courses. 10 km SW.
ⓘ Blowhole Point Rd, Kiama; (02) 4232 3322 or 1300 654 262; www.kiama.com.au

Jerilderie — Pop. 797

Map ref. 511 M11

Jerilderie is an important merino stud area, but is better known for its links with the Kelly gang. In 1879 they captured the police, held the townspeople hostage for two days, cut the telegraph wires and robbed the bank. It was here that Kelly handed over the famous Jerilderie Letter, justifying his actions and voicing his disrespect for police, whom he called 'a parcel of big ugly fat-necked wombat-headed, big-bellied, magpie-legged, narrow-hipped, splay-footed sons of Irish bailiffs or English landlords'.

IN TOWN Telegraph Office and The Willows Museum The well-preserved Telegraph Office is where the Kelly Gang cut the telegraph wires in 1879 and The Willows Museum next door stands on the site of a former stone-grind flour mill. It houses photographs, including some of the Kelly gang, documents of local historical significance and the cell door from the old police station. Samples of local craft are also on display and Devonshire teas are available. Powell St. *St Luke Park:* features Steel Wings, one of the largest windmills in the Southern Hemisphere. The park runs along the bank of Lake Jerilderie, which is popular for all watersports, especially waterskiing. *Mini Heritage Steam Rail:* runs along charming Billabong Creek, which also features the 1.8 km Horgans Walk. Entry via The Willows Museum; runs 2nd and 5th Sun each month.

NEARBY Coleambally Officially opened in 1968, Coleambally is NSW's newest town and is at the centre of the Coleambally Irrigation Area. It features the Wineglass Water Tower and a dragline excavator used in the irrigation scheme. The excavator is still in working order and can be viewed in the Lions Park at the town's entrance. The area is a haven for birdlife and kangaroos. 62 km N.
ⓘ The Willows Museum, 11 Powell St; (03) 5886 1666

Jindabyne — Pop. 4254

Map ref. 503 G11, 507 D9, 537 K4

Jindabyne, just below the snowline next to Kosciuszko National Park (*see feature on p. 92*), was moved from its original site on the banks of the Snowy River to make way for the Snowy Mountains Hydro-electric Scheme. The original town was flooded, but a few of the buildings were moved to their current site beside Lake Jindabyne. The area is popular with skiers in the winter and with anglers, bushwalkers and whitewater rafters in the summer.

IN TOWN *Walkway and cycleway:* around Lake Jindabyne's foreshore, from Banjo Paterson Park on Kosciuszko Rd to Snowline Caravan Park. *Winter shuttle bus service:* departs from various spots

NEW SOUTH WALES

in town to Bullocks Flat and Thredbo; bookings at visitor centre.

WHAT'S ON *Easter Fun Festival:* Easter. *Snowy Mountains Trout Festival:* fishing competition throughout region; Nov. *Man From Snowy River Rodeo:* Dec. *Lake Jindabyne Sailing Club Hobie Cat Races:* Dec.

NEARBY Perisher Blue The largest ski resort in Australia with an impressive 1250 ha of skiable terrain, Perisher Blue caters for all levels of skier and snowboarder. State-of-the-art equipment includes many high-quality snow guns and Australia's first 8-seater chairlifts. The resort consists of slopes, accommodation, restaurants, bars and all the facilities and equipment hire needed to enjoy winter sports at Perisher and the nearby skiing areas of Smiggin Holes, Mt Blue Cow and Guthega. Xtreme Winter Games are held each Sept. 30 km w. *Lake Jindabyne:* well-stocked with rainbow trout and ideal for boating, waterskiing and other watersports. Take a lake cruise in summer. Western edge of town. *Kunama Gallery:* over 200 paintings with emphasis on local artists and work by internationally acclaimed water colourist Alan Grosvenor. Also panoramic views of Lake Jindabyne. 7 km NE. *Snowy Valley Lookout:* stunning views of Lake Jindabyne; 8 km N. *Gaden Trout Hatchery:* daily tours and barbecues along Thredbo River; 10 km NW. *Crackenback Cottage:* local craft, maze and restaurant; 12 km SW. *Sawpit Creek:* the Kosciuszko Education Centre can be found here, with interactive displays and children's environment programs. The start of the Palliabo (walking) Track is at the Sawpit Creek picnic area. 14 km NW. *Bullocks Flat:* terminal for Skitube, a European-style alpine train to Perisher Blue ski resort; 20 km SW; operates daily during ski season. *Wallace Craigie Lookout:* views of Snowy River Valley; 40 km SW. *Charlotte Pass:* highest ski resort in Australia with challenging slopes for experienced skiers. Magnificent 24 km walking track past Blue Lake in summer. 45 km W. *Scenic walks:* varying lengths; brochures from visitor centre. *Alpine Way:* 111 km road through mountains to Khancoban with superb scenic touring in summer. ⓘ Snowy Region Visitor Centre, Kosciuszko Rd; (02) 6450 5600; www. snowymountains.com.au

Katoomba   Pop. 17 999

Map ref. 492 H7, 494 E9, 509 J7

Originally named Crushers but renamed a year later, Katoomba stands at an elevation of 1017 metres in the World Heritage-listed Blue Mountains. It is the principal tourist destination and residential area in the region and has excellent accommodation and facilities. Blue Mountains National Park lies to the north and south of town. The explanation why these mountains look

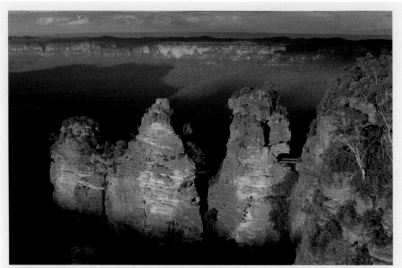

The Three Sisters

Aboriginal heritage in the Blue Mountains

The Blue Mountains have been home to Aboriginal people for at least 22 000 years – the Gundungurra people in the north and the Dharug people in the south. As a result, it is an area rich not only with Dreamtime stories but also with over 700 significant Aboriginal heritage sites that descendants of these original inhabitants continue to protect today.

Red Hands Cave, near Glenbrook, features hand stencils (mostly red, although some are white or orange) that were created between 500 and 1600 years ago. The artists created the stencils by placing their hands against the cave wall and blowing a mixture of ochre and water from their mouths. Lyrebird Dell, near Leura, is an Aboriginal campsite that has been estimated to be 12 000 years old. Relics can be found throughout the area, including rock engravings, axe-grinding grooves and cave paintings. All Aboriginal sites, discovered or undiscovered, are protected and are not to be altered by visitors.

Perhaps the most recognisable Aboriginal site in the park is the mountain formation of the Three Sisters. Aboriginal Dreamtime legend tells of three beautiful sisters, Meehni, Wimlah and Gunnedoo, who lived in the Jamison Valley with the Katoomba tribe. The girls fell in love with three brothers from the Nepean tribe, but tribal law forbade their marriage. The brothers would not accept this law and they attempted to capture the sisters by force, causing a major battle between the two tribes.

A witchdoctor from the Katoomba tribe feared that the girls were in danger, so he turned them to stone to protect them, intending to return them to their true forms when the battle was over. This was not to be, however, as the witchdoctor was killed in battle. Nobody else knew how to reverse the spell and the three sisters, at 922 metres, 918 metres and 906 metres, remain trapped as a magnificent rock formation. Nearby Orphan Rock is thought to be the witchdoctor.

blue lies in the eucalyptus trees that cover them; they disperse eucalyptus oil into the atmosphere, which makes the blue light-rays of the sun more effective.

IN TOWN *The Edge Cinema:* daily screenings of *The Edge* (images of Blue Mountains) on a 6-storey screen; Great Western Hwy (access through Civic Pl); programs (02) 4782 8900. *The Carrington Hotel:* opulent hotel providing tours and history of the area; Katoomba St. *Paragon Cafe:* National Trust-listed 1930s Art Deco milk bar retaining old-style ambience; Katoomba St.

WHAT'S ON *Blue Mountains Festival of Folk, Roots and Blues:* Feb/Mar. *Winter Magic Festival:* June. *Yulefest:* throughout region; June–Aug. *Spring Gardens Festival:* throughout region; Sept–Nov.

NEARBY Leura Considered the most urbane and sophisticated village in

the Blue Mountains, Leura has a beautiful tree-lined main street with impressive gardens, specialty shops, galleries and restaurants. Everglades Gardens (Everglades Ave) is a celebrated 1930s garden with a gallery devoted to its creator, Paul Sorensen. Leuralla (Olympian Pde) is a historic Art Deco mansion with a major collection of toys, dolls, trains and railway memorabilia. There are spectacular mountain views from Sublime Point and Cliff Drive. Markets are on the 1st Sun each month at the public school on the Great Western Hwy. The Legacy Gardens Festival runs Sept– Oct and the Village Fair and Greystanes Spring Gardens are in Oct. 3 km E.

Blue Mountains Scenic World Located near Katoomba Falls, the Three Sisters and Echo Point, Blue Mountains Scenic World takes in some of the best scenery in the national

park. Take a ride on the Scenic Railway, which was originally built to transport coal and miners and is the world's steepest railway, or on the Scenic Skyway, a 7 km ride in a cable car high up over the Jamison Valley. There is also Sceniscender, which descends into the heart of the valley, and plenty of other attractions to explore on foot. South of town.
Explorers Tree: blackbutt tree reportedly carved with initials of Blaxland, Wentworth and Lawson (there is some question about whether this was done by the explorers or by early tourism operators); west of town, off hwy. *Hazelbrook:* small village with Selwood Science and Puzzles featuring a puzzle room, science kits, bookshop and local artwork. Hazelbrook hosts Regatta Day in Feb on Wentworth Falls Lake. 17 km E. *Blue Mountains National Park:* Echo Point is the best place to view the Three Sisters, which are floodlit at night. Near Wentworth Falls, 7 km E, is an eco-designed cafe with great views, and the Valley of the Waters picnic area. *For other parts of the park see Blackheath and Glenbrook, and feature on facing page.*
ℹ Echo Point Rd; 1300 653 408; www.bluemountainstourism.org.au

Kempsey   Pop. 8444

Map ref. 515 O11, 516 G3

Kempsey is an attractive town in the Macleay River Valley on the mid-north coast, with white sandy beaches and an unspoiled hinterland. It claims two quintessential Aussies as its own: singer Slim Dusty was born here in 1927 (while he died in 2003, he remains one of the country's best-loved country singers) and the Akubra hat has been made here since 1974.
IN TOWN *Wigay Aboriginal Cultural Park:* Aboriginal cultural experience, including introduction to bush tucker, learning about the use of plants and throwing a boomerang; Sea St. *Cultural Centre:* incorporates the Macleay River Historical Society Museum, a settlers cottage, displays on Akubra hats and Slim Dusty, and a working model of a timber mill; Pacific Hwy, South Kempsey. *Historical walks:* carefully restored historic buildings include the courthouse, post office and West Kempsey Hotel; brochure from visitor centre.
WHAT'S ON *Market:* showground, 1st Sat each month; and South West Rocks, 2nd Sat each month. *South West Rocks Fishing Classic:* May. *Kempsey Cup:* horserace; May. *Off-road Race:* July. *Country Music Festival:* Sept. *Food and Wine Festival:* Sept. *Natureland Motorcycle Rally:* Nov.
NEARBY Limeburners Creek Nature Reserve This peaceful area showcases a beautiful coastline of heathlands, banksia and blackbutt forests. The rare rainforest of Big Hill is home to the threatened ground parrot. The beach is popular for

swimming, surfing and fishing and there are camping areas with varying levels of facilities. 33 km SE.
South West Rocks Attractions include a pristine white beach, a maritime history display at the restored Boatmans Cottage and the opportunity to handfeed fish at the Everglades Aquarium. The area is excellent for watersports, diving, camping and boating. The nearby Trial Bay Gaol (1886) was a public works prison until 1903 and reopened to hold 'enemy aliens' in WW I. Smoky Cape has a lighthouse offering tours and accommodation and clear views up and down the coast. Fish Rock Cave, just off the cape, is well known for its excellent diving. The Gaol Break Festival is held here each Easter. 37 km NE. *Frederickton:* 'Fredo' has beautiful views of river flats, and its award-winning pie shop boasts 148 varieties. Also home to a Blues Festival each Jan. 8 km NE. *Kundabung:* tiny village with Pioneer Weather Stone, never known to be wrong, and Australasian bull-riding titles in Oct; 12 km S. *Gladstone:* fishing, antiques and crafts, and Pumpkin Festival each Apr; 15 km NE. *Crescent Head:* this popular seaside holiday town has good surfing. There is an Aboriginal bora ring (ceremonial ground) just north. The Sky Show with kites, flying displays and fireworks is held each June. 20 km SE. *Brandybrook Lavender Farm:* offers lavender products such as lavender scones, jam, biscuits, ice-cream, honey and tea; Clybucca; 23 km N. *Barnett's Rainbow Beach Oyster Barn:* direct purchases and viewing of oyster processing; 31 km NE. *Hat Head National Park:* coastal park with magnificent dunes and unspoiled beaches, popular for birdwatching, snorkelling, swimming and walking. Korogoro Point is a fabulous spot for whale-watching May–July and Sept–Oct. 32 km E. *Bellbrook:* classified by the National Trust as a significant example of a turn-of-the-century hamlet; 47 km NW. *Walks and self-guide drives:* nature-reserve walks and historical and scenic drives; details from visitor centre.
ℹ Cultural Centre, Pacific Hwy, South Kempsey; (02) 6563 1555 or 1800 642 480; www.kempsey.midcoast.com.au

Kiama   Pop. 12 241

Map ref. 501 H9, 509 K10

This popular holiday town, hosting one million visitors each year, is best known as the home of the Kiama Blowhole. The rocky coastline, sandy beaches and appealing harbour provide an attractive contrast to the rolling hills of the lush dairy pastures of the hinterland.
IN TOWN Kiama Blowhole The spectacular blowhole sprays to heights of 60 m and is dramatically floodlit at night. Beside the blowhole is a constructed rock pool and a cafe. Pilots Cottage Historical Museum has displays on the blowhole,

early settlement, the dairy industry and shipping. It is open 11am–3pm, Mon–Fri. Blowhole Point.
Family History Centre: world-wide collection of records for tracing family history; Railway Pde. *Heritage walk:* includes terraced houses in Collins St and Pilots Cottage; leaflet from visitor centre. *Specialty and craft shops:* several in town showcasing local work; leaflet from visitor centre. *Beaches:* perfect for surfing, swimming and fishing.
WHAT'S ON *Craft market:* Hindmarsh Park and Black Beach; 3rd Sun each month. *Produce market:* Black Beach; 4th Sat each month. *Rotary Antique Show:* Jan. *Jazz Festival:* Feb. *Rugby Seven-a-Side Competition:* Feb. *Big Fish Classic:* game-fishing competition; April. *Folk Music Festival:* June. *Seaside Festival:* Oct.
NEARBY Gerringong This is a picturesque coastal town with a renowned heritage museum featuring remarkable scale models of the Illawarra coast. Gerringong's name comes from the Wodi Wodi language and is said to mean 'place of peril'. It is unclear where the peril lies, however, with safe beaches ideal for surfing, swimming and fishing. Unusually heavy rainfall means the hinterland is lush and green. 10 km S. *Little Blowhole:* smaller but more active than the Kiama Blowhole; off Tingira Cres; 2 km S. *Bombo Headland:* blue-metal quarrying in the 1880s left an eerie 'moonscape' of basalt walls and columns, which have been popular for use in commercials and video clips; 2.5 km N. *Cathedral Rocks:* scenic rocky outcrop best viewed at dawn; Jones Beach; 3 km N. *Kingsford Smith Memorial and Lookout:* site of Charles Kingsford Smith's 1933 take-off in the *Southern Cross*, with panoramic ocean views; 14 km S. *Seven Mile Beach National Park:* surrounded by sand dunes, this low forest is inhabited by birds and small marsupials. It makes a pretty spot for picnics and barbecues, beach fishing and swimming. 17 km S. *Scenic drives:* in all directions to visit beaches, rock formations, cemeteries and craft shops; brochure from visitor centre.
ℹ Blowhole Point Rd, Kiama; (02) 4232 3322 or 1300 654 262; www.kiama.com.au

Kyogle   Pop. 2733

Map ref. 515 P2, 607 P12

Located at the upper reaches of the Richmond River and the base of the charmingly named Fairy Mountain, Kyogle is known as the 'gateway to the rainforests'. It is almost completely surrounded by the largest remaining areas of rainforest in New South Wales.
IN TOWN *Captain Cook Memorial Lookout:* at the top of Mt Fairy, the lookout provides stunning views of the town and surrounding countryside; Fairy St. *Botanical Gardens:* combination of

NEW SOUTH WALES

formal gardens and revegetated creek environments on the banks of Fawcetts Creek; Summerland Way.

WHAT'S ON *Fairymount Festival of Fairytales:* celebration of Fairy Mountain; July.

NEARBY Border Ranges National Park World Heritage-listed, this 30 000 ha park has walking tracks, camping, swimming, rockclimbing and fantastic views of Mt Warning and the Tweed Valley. Sheepstation Creek is an attractive picnic spot. The Tweed Range Scenic Drive (64 km) leads visitors on a breathtaking path of pristine rainforest, deep gorges and waterfalls. Brochure from visitor centre. 27 km N.

Wiangaree: rural community with rodeo in Mar; 15 km N. *Roseberry Forest Park:* picturesque picnic spot; 23 km N. *Moore Park Nature Reserve:* tiny reserve with the most important example of black bean rainforest in NSW; 26 km NW. *Toonumbar Dam:* built from earth and rocks, it offers scenic bushwalking with picnic and barbecue facilities. Nearby Bells Bay is known for its bass fishing and has a campsite. 31 km W. *Toonumbar National Park:* contains 2 World Heritage-listed rainforests and the volcanic remnants of Edinburgh Castle, Dome Mountain and Mt Lindesay; 35 km W. *Richmond Range National Park:* protected rainforest perfect for camping, birdwatching, picnics and barbecues, with good bushwalking on a 2 km or 6 km track; 40 km W. *Scenic forest drive:* via Mt Lindesay (45 km NW), offers magnificent views of rainforest and countryside; brochure from visitor centre.
ⓘ Council offices, Stratheden St; (02) 6632 1611; www.tropicalnsw.com.au

Lake Cargelligo   Pop. 1203

Map ref. 511 O4

Lake Cargelligo is a surprisingly attractive small town in the heart of wide brown Riverina plains. Built beside the lake of the same name, the town's activities seem to revolve around the water with fishing and regular lake festivals.

IN TOWN Lake Cargelligo The lake dominates the town and is popular for fishing (silver perch, golden perch and redfin), boating, sailing, waterskiing and swimming. It is also appealing to birdwatchers, being home to many bird species including the rare black cockatoo. *Information centre:* houses a large gem collection; Foster St.

WHAT'S ON *Lake Show:* Sept. *Rodeo:* Oct. *Lake Festivale:* Dec.

NEARBY Willandra National Park Once one-eighth of a huge merino sheep station, the 20 000 ha park features a restored homestead, stables, a shearing complex and men's quarters. The buildings house a display of pastoral and natural history of the area. Plains, wetlands and Willandra Creek make up the rest of the park, with a walking track

that is best at dawn or dusk to see the myriad waterbirds, kangaroos and emus. The creek is popular for canoeing and fishing. 163 km W.
Lake Brewster: 1500 ha birdwatcher's paradise with fishing and picnic area. No guns, dogs or boats; 41 km W. *Nombinnie Nature Reserve:* birdwatching, bushwalking and abundant spring wildflowers Sept–Dec; 45 km N. *Hillston:* surprisingly green town with a main street lined with palms, thanks to its situation on top of a large artesian basin. Hillston Lake is popular for watersports and picnics, and a swinging bridge provides access to a nature reserve and walking trail. 93 km SW.
ⓘ 1 Foster St; (02) 6898 1501

Laurieton   Pop. 1818

Map ref. 515 O13, 516 F10

Laurieton is on an attractive tidal inlet at the base of North Brother Mountain, home to the Gadang people for tens of thousands of years. The mountain, which was named by Captain Cook in 1770, provides Laurieton with shelter from the wind, so the weather is mild all year round. There is a peaceful air to the region, surrounded as it is by ocean, lakes and national parks and reserves. There are spectacular views and bushwalks on the mountain and the inlet is popular for estuary fishing.

IN TOWN *Historical museum:* documents history of the town in old post office; Laurie St; open by appt; bookings (02) 6559 9096. *High Adventure:* learn to hang-glide and paraglide; inquiries 1800 063 648; Bold St.

WHAT'S ON *Riverwalk Market:* cnr Tunis and Short sts; 3rd Sun each month.

NEARBY Crowdy Bay National Park The park is known for its prolific birdlife and magnificent ocean beach. Diamond Head is an interesting sculpted rock formation and the hut beneath is where Kylie Tennant wrote *The Man and the Headland.* A headland walking track offers stunning ocean views and the area is also popular for fishing, birdwatching and the abundant wildlife. Campsites are at Diamond Head, Indian Head and Kylies Beach. 5 km S.
Kattang Nature Reserve: in spring the Flower Bowl Circuit leads through stunning wildflowers. Enjoy good coastal views all year round from sharp cliffs jutting into the ocean. 5 km E. *Dooragan National Park:* according to local Aboriginal legend, Dooragan (North Brother Mountain) was the youngest of three brothers who avenged his brothers' deaths at the hands of a witch by killing the witch and then killing himself. Blackbutt and subtropical forest is home to gliders, bats and koalas. Viewing platforms on North Brother Mountain provide some of the best views anywhere on the NSW coast. 6 km W.
Kendall: art and craft galleries, including

Craft Co-op, are at the railway station. Also markets 1st Sun each month on Logans Crossing Rd. 10 km W. *Big Fella Gum Tree:* 67 m flooded gum tree in Middle Brother State Forest; 18 km SW. *Norfolk Punch Factory:* traditional English punch made on premises with tastings and a display of historic kitchen appliances; 20 km W. *Lorne Valley Macadamia Farm:* tours at 11am and 2pm, products for sale and cafe; 23 km W; open Sat–Thurs.
ⓘ Pacific Hwy, Kew; (02) 6559 4400 or 1300 303 154; www.camdenhaven info.org.au

Leeton   Pop. 6900

Map ref. 511 O8

Leeton was designed by Walter Burley Griffin, the American architect who designed Canberra. Like Canberra, the town is built in a circular fashion with streets radiating from the centre. The Murrumbidgee Irrigation Area brought fertility to the dry plains of the Riverina and now Leeton has 102 hectares of public parks and reserves and a thriving primary industry.

IN TOWN *Visitor centre:* beautifully restored building with photographic displays, local artwork and a heritage garden; Yanco Ave. *Sunrice Country Visitors Centre:* rice-milling demonstrations, product displays and tastings, with presentations 9.30am and 2.45pm on weekdays; Calrose St. *Berri Juice Factory:* one of the largest citrus-processing plants in the country, with weekday tours including processing and packaging; Brady Way. *Mick's Bakehouse:* won 19 gold and 1 silver out of a possible 20 medals at the Great Aussie Meat Pie Competition; Pine Ave. *Riverina Cheese Factory:* viewing window for visitors to see the cheese-making process; Massey Ave. *Art Deco streetscape:* includes Roxy Theatre and historic Hydro Hotel; Chelmsford Pl.

WHAT'S ON *Boot Sale:* all manner of things for sale from car boots; Brobenah Park; 2nd Sun each month. *Bidgee Fishing Classic:* Feb/Mar. *Rodeo:* Mar. *Sunrice Festival:* even-numbered years, Easter. *Picnic Races:* May.

NEARBY Yanco This town is the site where Sir Samuel McCaughey developed the irrigation scheme that led to the establishment of the Murrumbidgee Irrigation Area. Attractions in town include McCaughey Aquatic Park, and the Powerhouse Museum with local history displays and a miniature train that runs on market days. Village Markets are held at Yanco Hall on the last Sun each month. 8 km S.
Fivebough Swamp: 400 ha home to over 150 species of waterbird with interpretive centre, walking trails and viewing hides; 2 km N. *Yanco Weir:* fishing, boating and picnics; 7 km S. *Brobenah Airfield:* gliding and hot-air ballooning; 9 km N. *McCaughey's Mansion:* 1899 mansion with

Sunrise at Diamond Head, Crowdy Bay National Park, near Laurieton

stained-glass windows and attractive gardens, now an agricultural high school, but drive-through inspections welcome. Yanco Agricultural Institute nearby is open to the public and provides farmer-training facilities and research and advisory services. 11 km s. *Murrumbidgee State Forest:* scenic drives; brochure from visitor centre; 12 km s. *Whitton Historical Museum:* housed in old courthouse and gaol with photographs, documents and early farming equipment; 23 km w. *Gogeldrie Weir:* pleasant spot for fishing, picnics and barbecues; 23 km sw. *Wineries:* cellar-door tastings and tours at Toorak and Lillypilly Estate; brochure at visitor centre.

ⓘ 10 Yanco Ave; (02) 6953 6481; www.leeton.nsw.gov.au

Lightning Ridge   Pop. 1826

Map ref. 514 B5

This famous opal-mining town is the only place in Australia and one of the few in the world where black opals are found. The otherwise desolate area receives 80 000 visitors each year, which has prompted modern facilities to be built in an otherwise minimalist town. Famous finds in the region include Big Ben and the Flame Queen, which was sold for £80 because the miner who found it had not eaten properly in three weeks. Local Aboriginal legend explains the opals by saying that a huge wheel of fire fell to earth, spraying the land with brilliant stones. Lightning Ridge is notoriously hot in summer but boasts ideal weather in winter. It is a good place for spotting native marsupials and birdlife.

IN TOWN *Big Opal:* opal-cutting demonstrations and daily underground working-mine tours; Three Mile Rd. *Bottle House Museum:* collection of bottles, minerals and mining relics; Opal St. *John Murray Art:* exclusive outlet for original paintings, limited edition prints, postcards and posters; Opal St. *Goondee Aboriginal Keeping Place:* Aboriginal

artefacts and educational tours of the premises; Pandora St. *Displays of art and craft:* including opal jewellery; several locations; leaflet from visitor centre.

WHAT'S ON *Local craft market:* Morilla St; Fri. *Great Boat Race:* Easter. *Rodeo:* Easter. *Opal Open Pistol Shoot:* June. *Opal and Gem Festival:* July.

NEARBY *Walk-In Mine:* working mine with easy access and tours on demand. Also a cactus nursery nearby. Off Bald Hill Rd; 2 km n. *Hot artesian bore baths:* open baths with average temperature 42°C; 2 km nᴇ. *Kangaroo Hill Tourist Complex:* displays of antiques, bottles, shells, rocks and minerals, and mining memorabilia with a fossicking area outside; 3 km s. *Opal fields:* Grawin (65 km w) and Sheepyards (76 km w); brochure from visitor centre. *Designated fossicking areas:* maps from visitor centre.

ⓘ Bill O'Brien Way; (02) 6829 0565

Lismore   Pop. 27 193

Map ref. 515 Q3, 607 Q12

This regional centre of the Northern Rivers district is on the banks of Wilsons River. European settlement came in 1840 when John Brown broke an axle near a small chain of ponds and stopped to have a look around. He liked what he saw and decided to settle. Called Browns Water Hole until 1853, it was changed to Lismore after a town in Ireland.

IN TOWN **Rotary Rainforest Reserve** There are 6 ha of original tropical rainforest in the middle of the city, but this is only a small remnant of the original 'Big Scrub' that stood here before European settlement. Over 3 km of paths, including a boardwalk, lead visitors past hoop pines and giant figs, with rare species of rainforest plants labelled. Rotary Dr.
Visitor centre: indoor rainforest walk and local art and craft displays. The surrounding Heritage Park has pleasant picnic areas and a mini steam train offering rides (10am–2pm Thurs–Sun

and school holidays). Cnr Ballina and Molesworth sts. *Cedar Log Memorial:* giant cedar log in memory of the first cedar-getters of the Richmond Valley; Ballina St. *Richmond River Historical Museum:* geological specimens, Aboriginal artefacts and pioneer clothing, implements, furniture and handiwork; Molesworth St. *Lismore Regional Art Gallery:* permanent collection of paintings, pottery and ceramics with changing exhibitions by local and touring artists; Molesworth St. *Robinson's Lookout:* views south across the river to South Lismore and north to the mountains; Robinson Ave. *Claude Riley Memorial Lookout:* views over Lismore city; New Ballina Rd. *Wilsons Park:* park contains original rainforest with trees labelled; Wyrallah St, East Lismore. *Heritage walk:* historic buildings and churches; brochure from visitor centre.

WHAT'S ON *Car Boot Markets:* Shopping Square, Uralba St; 1st and 3rd Sun each month. *Lantern Parade:* June. *Northern Rivers Herb Festival:* Aug. *Cup Day:* horserace; Sept.

NEARBY *Lismore Lake:* good lagoon for swimming with picnic and barbecue facilities and an adventure park; 3 km s. *Boatharbour Reserve:* 17 ha of rainforest, wildlife sanctuary, picnic area and walking tracks; maps from visitor centre; 6 km ᴇ. *Tucki Tucki Koala Reserve:* woodland planted by local residents to protect the diminishing koala population, with walking track and Aboriginal bora ring nearby; 15 km s.

ⓘ Cnr Ballina and Molesworth sts; (02) 6622 0122 or 1300 369 795; www.liscity.nsw.gov.au

Lithgow   Pop. 11 023

Map ref. 492 G5, 508 I6

Lithgow promotes itself as being 'surrounded by nature'. Easy access to several of the state's finest national parks and the charm of the city itself make it worth the effort of visiting this isolated but staggeringly beautiful region. It was

NEW SOUTH WALES

Shearing sheds, Kinchega National Park, near Menindee

isolated from the coastal cities until the revolutionary Zig Zag Railway, built with gently sloping ramps to cut through the mountains, opened it up in 1869.

IN TOWN Eskbank House Museum Built in 1842, this sandstone Georgian mansion now houses an extensive collection of Lithgow pottery and memorabilia and photographs of early Lithgow. The front four rooms are authentically furnished with regency and Victorian furniture. In the attractive gardens are a stone stable, coach house and picnic area. Bennett St. Open Wed–Sun.
Blast Furnace Park: ruins of Australia's first blast furnace complex (1886) with a pleasant walk around adjacent Lake Pillans Wetland; off Inch St. *State Mine Railway Heritage Park:* mining and railway equipment and historic mining buildings; State Mine Gully Rd. *Small Arms Museum:* established in 1912, some argue that this is the birthplace of modern manufacturing in Australia. Displays range from firearms to sewing machines. Methven St; open 10am–2pm Tue, Thurs, public and school holidays.
WHAT'S ON *Ironfest:* cultural festival celebrating metal; April. *Yulefest:* across region; June–Aug. *National Go-Kart Championships:* Oct. *Celebrate Lithgow:* Nov.
NEARBY Wollemi National Park This is the largest wilderness area in NSW and is a breathtaking display of canyons, cliffs and undisturbed forest. Highlights include historic ruins at Newnes, the beaches of the Colo Gorge and the glow worms in a disused rail tunnel. Mount Wilson, surrounded by the park, is a 19th-century village with large homes and superb gardens, many open to the public. Via the town is the Cathedral of Ferns. Begins 16 km E.
Hassans Walls Lookout: spectacular views of the Blue Mountains and Hartley Valley; via Hassans Walls Rd; 5 km S. *Archvale Rainbow Trout Farm:* fishing and sales; 7 km W. *Lake Lyell:* stunning lake in mountain setting, popular for activities

such as powerboating, waterskiing, trout fishing and picnics. Also canoe and boat hire available on-site. 9 km W. *Zig Zag Railway:* built in 1869, and later restored, it offers train trips 1 hr 40 min return, departing 11am, 1pm and 3pm daily; via Bells Line of Road, Clarence; 10 km E. *Lake Wallace:* sailing and trout fishing; 11 km NW. *Jannei Goat Dairy:* produces cheeses, yoghurt and milk and is open to visitors, with free cheese tastings; 11 km NW. *Hartley:* became obsolete after the construction of the Great Western Railway in 1887. Explore 17 buildings of historical significance administered by the National Parks and Wildlife Service. 14 km SE. *Portland:* charming rural town with a power station offering tours and interactive exhibits, a museum with a vast amount of Australian memorabilia and several pleasant picnic areas; 17 km NW. *Mt Piper Power Station:* hands-on exhibits in the information centre and daily tours at 11am; 21 km NW. *Gardens of Stone National Park:* fascinating pagoda rock formations, sandstone escarpments and beehive-shaped domes caused by erosion. This is a great spot for rockclimbing and picnics. 30 km N. *Mount Tomah Botanic Garden:* 5000 species of cool-climate plants over 1000 m above sea level. Also award-winning restaurant. 35 km E.
ⓘ 1 Cooerwull Rd; (02) 6353 1859; www.lithgow-tourism.com

Macksville   Pop. 2658
Map ref. 515 P9

Macksville is a fishing and oyster-farming town on the banks of the Nambucca River. There is an abundance of water-based activities, with picnic areas and riverside parks from which dolphins can often be observed. The town bustles with activities and festivals including the country's second oldest footrace, the Macksville Gift, each November.

IN TOWN *Mary Boulton Pioneer Cottage:* replica of a pioneer home with horse-

drawn vehicles; River St. *Star Hotel:* meeting place in Macksville since 1885, it still has original features and offers meals and accommodation; River St.
WHAT'S ON *Craft market:* Scout Hall, Partridge St; 4th Sat each month. *Patchwork and Quilt Display:* Easter. *Egg-throwing Championships:* May. *Trek to the Pub With No Beer:* June. *Rusty Iron Rally:* heritage machinery show; Sept. *Macksville Gift:* Nov.
NEARBY Bowraville This unspoiled town has much to see with a National Trust-classified main street, the Joseph and Eliza Newman Folk Museum, Red Cedars Gallery and Bawrrung Cultural Centre. There are markets each Sat, regular races at the racecourse and the Back to Bowra festival each Oct. 16 km NW.
Mt Yarahappini Lookout: the highest point in Nambucca Valley with fabulous 360-degree views; 10 km S. *Ingalba Saddle Trails:* horseriding excursions through picturesque Ingalba State Forest; bookings (02) 6569 9341; 10 km SE. *Scotts Head:* coastal town with good beaches for surfing, swimming, fishing and dolphin-watching; 18 km SE. *Cosmopolitan Hotel:* built in 1896, this is the hotel that was made famous in Slim Dusty's song 'The Pub With No Beer', so named because it would often run out of beer before the next quota arrived. It is still largely in its original form and offers meals. 26 km SW. *Bakers Creek Station:* old cattle station, now an impressive resort offering horseriding, fishing, rainforest walking, canoeing and picnicking as well as accommodation; 30 km W. *Local craft:* featured in several shops and galleries in the area; leaflet from visitor centre. *Scenic drives:* through local forests; brochure from visitor centre.
ⓘ Cnr Pacific Hwy and Riverside Dr, Nambucca Heads; 1800 646 587 or (02) 6568 6954; www.nambucca tourism.com

Maitland   Pop. 53 391
Map ref. 499 C7, 509 M4

Maitland is in the heart of the world-class Hunter Valley wine region, on the Hunter River. Built on flood plains, it has suffered 15 major floods since settlement. The city has a significant Polish contingent as a result of immigration after World War II.
IN TOWN Maitland Gaol The gaol was built in 1844 and served as a maximum security prison for 154 years. The first inmates were convicts, including some children, forced to march 6 km in shackles and chains. Since then it has been 'home' to some of Australia's most notorious and dangerous criminals. It is now said to be the most haunted gaol in the country. Self-guide tours are available or there are guided tours with ex-inmates and ex-officers. For the extremely brave, there are also overnight stays. Bookings (02) 4936 6610. John St, East Maitland.
Grossman House: National Trust-classified Georgian-style house, now a

folk museum with pioneer silverware, porcelain and handmade clothing; Church St. *Maitland Regional Gallery:* city's art collection specialising in local works; High St. *Self-guide heritage walks:* include one for children showcasing Maitland's National Trust-classified High St and city buildings; brochures from visitor centre.
WHAT'S ON *Market:* showground; 1st Sun each month (not Jan). *Craft-a-Fair:* Mar. *Heritage Month:* April. *Hunter Valley Steamfest:* celebration of steam trains; April. *Garden Ramble:* Sept.
NEARBY Morpeth This tiny riverside village has been classified by the National Trust. The entire town is walkable and features magnificent old sandstone buildings such as St James Church (1830s), and several antique and craft shops. There is the Weird and Wonderful Novelty Teapot Exhibition in Aug and a Jazz Festival in Sept. A self-guide heritage walk brochure is available from the visitor centre. 5 km NE. *Walka Waterworks:* it is a scenic drive from Maitland to this former pumping station, now an excellent recreation area, popular for picnics and bushwalks; 3 km N. *Tocal Homestead:* historic Georgian homestead; 14 km N; open by appt; bookings (02) 4939 8939. *Paterson:* signposted scenic drive leads to this charming hamlet on the Paterson River; 16 km N. *Hunter Valley Wine Trail:* tour of vineyards and cellar doors; brochure from visitor centre.
🛈 Ministers Park, cnr New England Hwy and High St; (02) 4933 2611; www.hunterrivercountry.com.au

Manilla
Pop. 2037

Map ref. 515 J9

This rural town is located at the junction of the Manilla and Namoi rivers and surrounded by attractive rural countryside. Its location between Lake Keepit and Split Rock Dam has made it a popular setting for myriad outdoor activities and it hosts the state's hang-gliding championships each year. Manilla is also known for its production of mead (an alcoholic drink made from fermented honey and water). It is home to one of only two meaderies in the country.
IN TOWN *Dutton's Meadery:* tastings and sales of honey and mead; Barraba St. *Manilla St:* antique and coffee shops. Royce Cottage Historical Museum exhibits pioneer relics such as clothing, furniture and documents.
WHAT'S ON *NSW Hang-gliding Championships:* Mar. *Festival of Spring Flowers:* Oct.
NEARBY Warrabah National Park At this peaceful riverside retreat you'll find enormous granite boulders sitting above still valley pools, and there are rapids suitable for experienced canoeists. Activities in the park include swimming and fishing in the Namoi and Manilla rivers and rockclimbing on the cliffs. 40 km NE.

Split Rock Dam: watersports, boating and fishing for species such as Murray cod and golden perch; turn-off 15 km N. *Manilla Ski Gardens:* recreation area at the northern end of Lake Keepit with waterskiing, fishing and swimming; 20 km SW. *For more details on Lake Keepit see Gunnedah.*
🛈 79 Arthur St; (02) 6785 1113; www.manilla-info.net

Menindee
Pop. 391

Map ref. 510 E1, 512 E13

Menindee is like an oasis in the middle of a desert. Although located in the state's arid inland plains, it is immediately surrounded by fertile land thanks to the 20 lakes in the area fed by the Darling River. The fragrant orchards and vegetable farms provide a stark contrast to the saltbush and red soil on the way into this tiny settlement.
IN TOWN *Maiden's Hotel:* Burke and Wills lodged here in 1860. Meals and accommodation are available; Yartla St. *Ah Chung's Bakehouse Gallery:* William Ah Chung established one of the first market gardens in town. His bakery (c. 1880) now houses a gallery featuring local artists. Menindee St.
WHAT'S ON *Inland Speedboat Championships:* May. *Burke and Wills Fishing Challenge:* Aug.
NEARBY Kinchega National Park The park contrasts dry landscape with healthy lakes supporting waterbirds and numerous other wildlife. There are giant river red gums growing along the banks of the Darling River. Facilities and attractions are excellent and include a visitor centre, the wreck of paddlesteamer *Providence,* and restored shearers' quarters offering accommodation. Activities include swimming, fishing, camping and canoeing. 1 km W. *Menindee Lake:* the largest lake in the area and part of the water-storage scheme for Broken Hill, it has good fishing for Murray cod; 1 km NW. *Menindee Lake Lookout:* good views of the lake; 10 km N. *Copi Hollow:* great spot for waterskiers, swimmers and powerboat enthusiasts; 18 km N. *Local lakes:* several good for yachting, fishing, swimming, watersports and camping; map at visitor centre.
🛈 Railway station, Maiden St; (08) 8091 4274

Merimbula
Pop. 4864

Map ref. 502 F9, 507 G11

Merimbula is a modern seaside town known for its surfing, fishing and oyster-farming. Middens can still be found in the area, which indicates that oysters were caught here by Aboriginal people well before the arrival of Europeans. The town began as a private village belonging to Twofold Bay Pastoral Association, who opened it as a port in 1855.

IN TOWN Merimbula Aquarium Twenty-seven tanks present an extensive range of sea life. Exhibits range from bottom-dwelling species or venomous fish to tropical or tidal pools. For those who can disassociate what they have just seen from their lunch, there is an excellent seafood restaurant on-site. Merimbula Wharf, Lake St.
Old School Museum: town history displayed in excellent collection of photos, documents and memorabilia; Main St.
WHAT'S ON *Jazz Festival:* June. *Country Music Festival:* Oct.
NEARBY Pambula This historic sister village of Merimbula has excellent fishing on the Pambula River and a market 2nd Sun each month. Pambula Beach has a scenic walking track and lookout, with kangaroos and wallabies gathering on the foreshore at dawn and dusk. 7 km SW. *Magic Mountain Family Recreation Park:* rollercoaster, water slides, minigolf and picnic area; Sapphire Coast Drive; 5 km N. *Tura Beach:* modern resort town with excellent beach for surfing and swimming; 5 km NE. *Yellow Pinch Wildlife Park:* peaceful bushland setting with array of native animals, birds and reptiles; 5 km E. *Scenic flights, whale-watching (Oct–Nov), boat cruises and boat hire:* bookings at visitor centre.
🛈 Beach St; (02) 6495 1129; www.sapphirecoast.com.au

Merriwa
Pop. 987

Map ref. 509 J2

This small town in the western Hunter region beside the Merriwa River is known for its majestic early colonial buildings. It is the centre of a vast farming district of cattle, sheep, horses, wheat and olive trees. People converge on the town each year for the Festival of the Fleeces, which includes shearing competitions, yard dog trials and a woolshed dance.
IN TOWN *Historical Museum:* in stone cottage (1857) with documented history of the region and the belongings of European pioneers; Bettington St. *Bottle Museum:* over 5000 bottles of all shapes and sizes; visitor centre, Vennacher St; open Mon–Fri. *Self-guide historical walk:* early school buildings, Holy Trinity Anglican Church (1875) and the Fitzroy Hotel (1892); brochure from visitor centre.
WHAT'S ON *Polocrosse Carnival:* May. *Festival of the Fleeces:* June.
NEARBY Coolah Tops National Park The plateaus at high altitude in this park provide wonderful lookouts over the Liverpool plains and spectacular waterfalls. Vegetation consists of giant grass trees and tall open forests of snow gums, providing a home for wallabies, gliders, eagles and rare owls. There are superb campsites, walking trails and picnic spots. 107 km NW. *Cassilis:* tiny village with historic sandstone buildings including St Columba's Anglican Church (1899)

and the courthouse/police station (1858). The main streets have been declared an urban conservation area. 25 km NW. *Flags Rd:* old convict-built road leading to Gungal; 25 km SW. *Gem-fossicking area:* open to the public; 27 km SW.
ℹ Council offices, Vennacher St; (02) 6548 2109

Moree   Pop. 9247

Map ref. 514 G5

Moree sits at the junction of the Mehi and Gwydir rivers and is the centre of the local farming district. It is an affluent area, thanks to its rich black-soil plains. One local claimed the soil is so fertile, 'You could put a matchstick in the ground overnight and get a walking stick in the morning'. The town is also known for its artesian spas, with therapeutic qualities said to cure arthritis and rheumatism.

IN TOWN Spa complex These spas were discovered accidentally when settlers were searching for reliable irrigation water. A bore was sunk into the Great Artesian Basin and the water that emerged was 41°C. The complex also has an outdoor heated pool and an array of leisure activities that attract 300 000 visitors each year. Cnr Anne and Gosport sts. *Moree Plains Regional Gallery:* contemporary Aboriginal art and artefacts and changing exhibitions; Frome St. *Yurundiali Aboriginal Corporation:* screen-printers specialising in wall hangings, materials and paper and clothing; Endeavour La; tours by appt; bookings (02) 6757 3350. *The Big Plane:* DC3 transport plane with tours available at Amaroo Tavern; Amaroo Dr. *Barry Roberts Historical Walk:* self-guide tour includes the courthouse and the Moree Lands Office, which was restored after a fire in 1982; brochure from visitor centre.
WHAT'S ON *Market:* Jellicoe Park; 1st Sun each month. *Carnival of Sport:* Easter. *Golden Grain and Cotton Festival:* Nov.
NEARBY *Trewalla Pecan Farm:* largest orchard in the Southern Hemisphere yielding 95 percent of Australia's pecans; tour bookings at visitor centre; 35 km E. *Cotton Gins:* inspections during harvest, April–July; details at visitor centre. *Birdwatching:* several excellent sites in the area; brochure from visitor centre.
ℹ Lyle Houlihan Park, cnr Newell and Gwydir hwys; (02) 6757 3350; www.moreeonline.net.au

Moruya   Pop. 2543

Map ref. 507 H7

This town on the Moruya River was once a gateway to local goldfields, but is now a dairying and oyster-farming centre. It is also known for its granite, which can be seen in some of the older buildings in town and was also used to build the pylons of the Sydney Harbour Bridge.

IN TOWN *Eurobodalla Historic Museum:* depicts gold discovery at Mogo and the district history of shipping, dairying and goldmining; town centre. *South Head:* beautiful views across the river mouth. *Historical town walk:* includes courthouse (1880) and St Mary's Catholic Church (1889); leaflet from visitor centre. *Antique and second-hand shops:* several in town; leaflet from visitor centre.
WHAT'S ON *Market:* Main St; Sat. *Deua River Bush Races:* June. *Jazz Festival:* Oct.
NEARBY Deua National Park The park is a wilderness of rugged mountain ranges, plateaus, gentle and wild rivers and a magnificent limestone belt, which makes the area popular for canyoning and caving. The rivers are a base for most water activities, including swimming, fishing and canoeing. There are scenic walking and 4WD tracks and 4 main campsites to choose from. 20 km W. *Bodalla:* town well known in Australia for its cheese-making. The Big Cheese complex is at the northern end of town. Also here is Coomerang House, the home of 19th-century industrialist and dairy farmer Thomas Sutcliffe Mort, open to visitors. The Mort Memorial Church and cemetery are nearby. 24 km S. *Nerrigundah:* former goldmining town with a monument to Miles O'Grady, who was killed in battle with the Clarke bushranging gang in town; 44 km SW.
ℹ Cnr Princes Hwy and Beach Rd, Batemans Bay; (02) 4472 6900 or 1800 240 003; www.naturecoast-tourism.com.au

Moss Vale   Pop. 6601

Map ref. 501 B7, 507 I3, 509 J10

Moss Vale is the industrial and agricultural centre of Wingecarribee Shire and the Southern Highlands. Once it was home to the Dharawal people, but by the 1870s they had all been driven off or killed. The town stands on part of the one thousand acres (approximately 400 hectares) of land granted to explorer Charles Throsby by Governor Macquarie in 1819.

IN TOWN *Leighton Gardens:* picturesque area popular for picnics; Main St. *Historical walk:* includes Aurora College (formerly Dominican Convent) and Kalourgan, believed to have been a residence of Mary MacKillop for a short time; brochure from visitor centre.
WHAT'S ON *Southern Highlands Country Fair:* showgrounds; 4th Sun each month. *Autumn Gardens in the Southern Highlands:* throughout region; April. *Tulip Time Festival:* throughout region; Sept–Oct.
NEARBY Sutton Forest This tiny settlement is set among green hills, with a shop called A Little Piece of Scotland (in the town's old butcher shop) for all things Scottish, and Sutton Forest Village Market 3rd Sun each month. Hillview House, just north, was the official residence of NSW governors 1882–1958. 6 km SW.

Throsby Park Historic Site: owned for 150 years by the Throsby family. Buildings that depict early settlement life include original stables, former barn, flour mill, Gundagai Cottage and Christ Church. 1.5 km E. Access is by tour only; bookings (02) 4887 7270. *Cecil Hoskins Nature Reserve:* tranquil wetland with over 90 different bird species, one-third of which are waterfowl; 3 km NE.
ℹ Southern Highlands Visitor Centre, 62–70 Main St, Mittagong; (02) 4871 2888 or 1300 657 559; www.southern-highlands.com.au

Mudgee   Pop. 8603

Map ref. 508 H3

Mudgee derives its name from the Wiradjuri word 'moothi', meaning 'nest in the hills'. The name is apt as the town is situated among green and blue hills in the Cudgegong River Valley. Mudgee is full of wide streets and historic Victorian buildings and is the centre of the Mudgee Wine Region, one of the largest winegrowing regions in Australia. Local produce features heavily in town with visitors able to try wonderfully fresh silver perch, yabbies, venison, lamb, asparagus, summer berries, peaches and hazelnuts.

IN TOWN *Colonial Inn Museum:* local history in photographs, documents, machinery, dolls and agricultural implements; Market St. *Honey Hive:* honey, jam and mustard tastings, and bees under glass; cnr Hill End and Gulgong rds. *Heart of Mudgee:* local produce, tastings, local art and craft; Court St. *Lawson Park:* home to possums, water rats and tortoises. Includes a playground, barbecues and duck pond. Short St. *Mandurah at the Railway:* local art and craft cooperative at the historic railway station; cnr Inglis and Church sts. *Roth's Wine Bar:* oldest wine bar in NSW with displays of wine history in the region and a wide selection of local wines; Market St. *Melrose Park Venison:* deer park in parkland setting with venison tastings and sales; Melrose Rd. *Town trail:* self-guide walk taking in National Trust-classified buildings including St John's Church of England (1860) and the Regent Theatre; brochure from visitor centre.
WHAT'S ON *Market:* St John's Anglican Church, 1st Sat each month; Lawson Park, 2nd Sat each month. *Small Farm Field Days:* July. *Mudgee Wine Festival:* Sept.
NEARBY Munghorn Gap Nature Reserve Over 160 bird species have been identified here, including the rare regent honeyeater. For bushwalkers, the Castle Rock walking trail is an 8 km journey with stunning views from sandstone outcrops. Camping, barbecue and picnic facilities are available. 34 km NE. *Mount Vincent Mead:* one of the few places in the country producing mead (an alcoholic drink made from fermented honey and water). Tastings and sales available. 4 km SW. *Site of Old Bark School:* attended by Henry Lawson and made famous in several

of his poems. *Eurunderee Provisional School* is nearby with historical displays of school life. 6 km N. *Fragrant Farm:* garden and craft shop with doll museum; 8 km SW. *Pick Your Own Farm:* variety of fruit and vegetables; 12 km S; open Oct–May. *Windermere Dam:* watersports, trout fishing and camping facilities; 24 km SE. *Hargraves:* old goldmining town where Kerr's Hundredweight was discovered in 1851, yielding 1272 ounces of gold. Ask at general store for gold-panning tours. 39 km SW. *Wineries:* over 100 in the area (many offering cellar-door tastings) including Poet's Corner, Huntington Estate and Botobolar; self-guide drives brochure from visitor centre.
ⓘ 84 Market St; (02) 6372 1020; www.mudgee-gulgong.org

Mullumbimby   Pop. 2992

Map ref. 515 Q2, 607 Q12

When Mullumbimby's economy, based on local agriculture, started to flag in the late 1960s, the town was saved by becoming one of the country's great alternative lifestyle centres. Drawn by lush subtropical countryside and excellent weather conditions, people settled at the foot of Mt Chincogan. The town still has a delightful laid-back feel today with all the facilities of a mature tourist town.

IN TOWN Brunswick Valley Historical Museum The museum covers local history in detail, including timber-getters, dairy farmers, pioneers and local government. It is in a pleasant park on the banks of Saltwater Creek. Outdoor displays include horse-drawn agricultural equipment and a pioneer slab cottage. Stuart St. Check opening times (02) 6685 1385. *Mullumbimby Art Gallery:* changing exhibitions of paintings, sculptures and prints; cnr Burringbar and Stuart sts. *Cedar House:* National Trust-classified building housing an antiques gallery; Dalley St. *Brunswick Valley Heritage Park:* over 200 rainforest plants, including palms, and a 2 km park and river walk; Tyagarah St.

WHAT'S ON *Market:* Stuart St; 3rd Sat each month. *Chincogan Fiesta:* stalls, parade and mountain footrace; Sept.

NEARBY Brunswick Heads This town on the Brunswick River estuary is a charming mix of quiet holiday retreat and large commercial fishing town. Despite having some truly beautiful beaches, Brunswick Heads has managed to remain remarkably serene and unassuming. Enjoy the excellent seafood in town. Highlights during the year include a wood-chopping festival in Jan and the Kite and Bike Festival in Mar. 7 km W. *Crystal Castle:* spectacular natural crystal display, jewellery and gifts; 7 km SW. *Tyagarah Airstrip:* skydiving and paragliding; Pacific Hwy; 13 km SW. *Wanganui Gorge:* scenic 4 km bushwalk through the gorge with rainforest trees, enormous strangler figs and a pretty swimming hole; 20 km W.

ⓘ 80 Jonson St, Byron Bay; (02) 6685 8050; www.tropicalnsw.com.au

Mulwala   Pop. 1677

Map ref. 511 N13, 539 L3

Mulwala and Yarrawonga (in Victoria) are twin towns sitting astride the Murray River. Mulwala prides itself on being an 'inland aquatic paradise', with plenty of water-based activities for visitors to enjoy. It is surrounded by forests and vineyards.

IN TOWN Lake Mulwala This artificial lake was formed by the 1939 damming of the Murray River at Yarrawonga Weir and is now home to myriad birdlife. The north end has ghost gums up to 6000 years old. The lake is popular for yachting, sailboarding, canoeing, swimming and fishing (especially for Murray cod). The waterskiing school is the largest in the world with 4000 members; it offers lessons and equipment hire for skiing, wakeboarding, and banana and tube rides. Day and evening cruises can be booked at the visitor centre.
Linley Park Animal Farm: working farm with horse and pony rides, and opportunity to handfeed native and exotic animals; Corowa Rd; open long weekends and school holidays. *Pioneer Museum:* historic farming exhibits, photographs and local artefacts; Melbourne St; open Wed–Sun. *Tunzafun Amusement Park:* minigolf, mini-train and dodgem cars; Melbourne St.

NEARBY *Savenake Station Woolshed:* 1930s-style woolshed in working order producing merino wool; 28 km N; open by appt; bookings (02) 6035 9415. *Everglade and swamp tours:* to waterbird rookeries and native animal habitats; bookings at visitor centre. *Local wineries:* several in area offering cellar-door tastings; brochure from visitor centre.
ⓘ Irvine Pd, Yarrawonga; (03) 5744 1989 or 1800 062 260; www.yarrawongamulwala.com.au

Murrurundi   Pop. 791

Map ref. 515 J13

Murrurundi (pronounced 'Murrurund-eye') is a rural town set in the lush Pages River Valley at the foot of the Liverpool Ranges. It is a well-preserved, quiet town and any changes have been gradual, thanks to the lack of heavy industry in the region. The main street has been declared an urban conservation area.

IN TOWN Paradise Park This horseshoe-shaped park is surrounded by mountains. Behind the park is the difficult 'Through the Eye of the Needle' walk, which involves fitting through a small gap in the rocks but offers a fantastic view from the top of the rock formation. Paradise Rd. *St Joseph's Catholic Church:* 1000-piece Italian marble altar; Polding St.

WHAT'S ON *Australia Day Carnival:* markets, parade and activities; Jan. *Sheepdog trials:* April. *Billycart competition:* Sept. *Bushmans Carnival:* Oct.

NEARBY Wallabadah Rock The second largest monolith in the Southern Hemisphere, the rock is a large plug (959 m high) of an extinct volcano. There are spectacular flowering orchids in Oct. It is on private property, but there is a good view from the road. Access is possible with the owner's permission (02) 6543 7521. 26 km NE. *Chilcotts Creek:* huge diprotodon remains were found here (now in Australian Museum, Sydney); 15 km N. *Burning Mountain:* deep coal seam that has been smouldering for at least 5000 years; 20 km S.
ⓘ 113 Mayne St; (02) 6546 6446

Murwillumbah   Pop. 7543

Map ref. 515 Q1, 607 Q11

Murwillumbah is located on the banks of the Tweed River near the Queensland border. It is a centre for sugarcane, banana and cattle farms with the town

Lisnagar homestead, Murwillumbah

virtually surrounded by sugarcane fields. In 1907 Murwillumbah was almost completely wiped out by fire. The town was rebuilt and many of those buildings can still be seen on the main street today.

IN TOWN Tweed River Regional Art Gallery This gallery displays a variety of paintings, portraits, glasswork, pottery, ceramics and photography. It is home to the Doug Moran National Portrait Prize, the richest portrait prize in the world. Past winners are on display along with changing exhibitions. Mistral Rd. *World Heritage Rainforest Centre:* visitor centre with displays on local vegetation and wildlife; cnr Pacific Hwy and Alma St. *Tweed River Historical Society Museum:* war memorabilia, genealogy documents, and domestic items and clothing through the ages; cnr Queensland Rd and Bent St; open Wed, Fri and 4th Sun each month.

WHAT'S ON *Market:* Knox Park, 2nd Sun each month; showground, 4th Sun each month. *Tweed Valley Banana Festival and Harvest Week:* Aug.

NEARBY Mount Warning National Park World Heritage-listed Mt Warning is the rhyolite plug of a massive ancient volcano left behind after surrounding basalt eroded away. The local Bundjalung nation calls the mountain Wollumbin. It is a traditional place of cultural law, initiation and spiritual education, so visitors are requested to consider not climbing the mountain. For those who do decide to climb, it is steep in places and the return trip takes 4–5 hours, so take plenty of water and make sure there is enough time to return before sunset. The National Parks and Wildlife Service conducts regular tours in the park including a rock-pool ramble, searches for threatened shorebirds and canoe tours. Bookings (02) 6627 0200. 17 km sw. *Lisnagar:* historic homestead in lush surrounds; northern edge of town just past showgrounds; open Sun. *Condong Sugar Mill:* over 100 years old and still operating, with tours, videos and educational displays; 5 km N; open Mon–Fri July–Nov. *Treetops Environment Centre:* furniture crafted from salvaged timber; 8 km NE. *Madura Tea Estates:* tea plantation with tastings and tours by appt; bookings (02) 6677 7215; 12 km NE. *Banana Cabana:* garden and shop with over 20 bush tucker species and exotic fruits; 12 km NW. *Mooball:* small town that has embraced the cow theme suggested by its name by painting almost anything that stands still in the style of a black and white cow, including buildings, cars and electricity poles. The local Pioneer Plantation is a working banana plantation with farm animals, native gardens, nectar-feeding birds and tours including a 6WD trip to the top of Banana Mountain. 19 km SE.
ⓘ World Heritage Rainforest Centre, cnr Pacific Hwy and Alma St; (02) 6672 1340; www.tropicalnsw.com.au

Muswellbrook   Pop. 10 010

Map ref. 509 K2

Muswellbrook (the 'w' is silent) is in the Upper Hunter Valley and prides itself on being 'blue heeler country'. It is in this region that cattle farmers developed the blue heeler dog by crossing dingoes with Northumberland Blue Merles to produce an outstanding working dog that thrives in Australia's harsh conditions. The blue heeler is now in demand all over the world. There are several open-cut coal mines in the local area and the Upper Hunter Valley has many fine wineries.

IN TOWN *Muswellbrook Art Gallery:* in the restored town hall and School of the Arts building, its centrepiece is the Max Watters collection, which displays signature pieces from renowned Australian artists in paintings, drawings, ceramics and sculptures; Bridge St. *Upper Hunter Wine Centre:* displays on the local wine industry and information on Upper Hunter wineries; Loxton House, Bridge St. *Historical town walk:* 4.5 km walk featuring St Alban's Church, the police station and the town hall; map from visitor centre.

WHAT'S ON *Spring Festival:* Aug–Nov.

NEARBY Aberdeen This small town is famous for its prize-winning beef cattle. There are markets at St Joseph's High School on the 3rd Sun each month and the famous Aberdeen Highland Games are held here each July. This is a week of Scottish festivities including Scottish food and music, Highland dancing, caber tossing, a jousting tournament, a warriors competition and a kilted dash. 12 km N. *Bayswater Power Station:* massive electricity source with coal-fired boilers and cooling towers; 16 km S; tours Tues and Fri. *Sandy Hollow:* picturesque village surrounded by horse studs and vineyards, with Bush Ride in April; 36 km SW. *Local wineries:* those open for cellar-door tastings include Arrowfield Wines (28 km S) and Rosemount Estate (35 km SW); brochure from visitor centre.
ⓘ 87 Hill St; (02) 6541 4050; www.muswellbrook.org.au

Nambucca Heads   Pop. 6121

Map ref. 515 P9

Located at the mouth of the Nambucca River, Nambucca Heads is a beautiful coastal holiday town. The stunning long, white beaches offer perfect conditions for fishing, swimming, boating and surfing.

IN TOWN V-Wall Breakwater Also known as the Graffiti Gallery, this unique rock wall gives visitors the opportunity to paint their own postcards on a rock. Mementos by visitors from all over the world are on display, including cartoons, paintings and poetry. Wellington Dr. *Headland Historical Museum:* photographic history of the town and its residents, historic documents, antique farming

implements and household tools; Headland Reserve. *Model Train Museum:* miniature display models, including the Ghan and the Indian Pacific; Pelican Cres. *Stringer Art Gallery:* showcases local art and craft; Ridge St. *Valley Community Art:* cooperative of local artists and crafters with work for sale; Bowra St. *Mosaic sculpture:* the history of the town portrayed in a mosaic wrapped around a corner of the police station; Bowra St. *Gordon Park Rainforest:* unique walking trails through rainforest in the middle of urban development; between town centre and Inner Harbour. *Copenhagen Mill and Shipyard Foreshore Walk:* historical walk with shipbuilding yard and maritime tales; brochure from visitor centre.

WHAT'S ON *Market:* Nambucca Plaza; 2nd Sun each month. *Country Music Jamboree:* Easter. *VW Spectacular:* odd-numbered years, Aug. *Show 'n' Shine Hot Rod Exhibition:* Oct.

NEARBY Valla Beach Apart from beautiful secluded beaches and rainforest surrounds, the town of Valla Beach is a hive of activity. Attractions include an art and craft gallery, the Valla Smokehouse (specialising in gourmet smoked products), the Australiana Workshop and the Gallery of Hidden Treasures. The Valla Beach Fair is held each Jan. 10 km N. *Swiss Toymaker:* visitors can view wooden toys being crafted; 5 km N; closed Sun.
ⓘ Cnr Pacific Hwy and Riverside Dr; (02) 6568 6954 or 1800 646 587; www.nambuccatourism.com

Narooma   Pop. 3391

Map ref. 502 I2, 507 H9, 537 R2

Narooma is a tranquil resort and fishing town at the mouth of Wagonga Inlet, well known for its natural beauty. The stunning beaches and waterways continue to draw people back to enjoy the excellent boating, aquatic sports and big-game fishing. Excellent fresh local seafood is a specialty in many of the restaurants.

IN TOWN Wagonga Princess This environmentally friendly, electronically powered boat is a converted huon pine ferry offering scenic cruises most days, taking in mangroves, forests and birdlife. The tour includes Devonshire tea. Commentary and tales (both tall and true) of local history, flora and fauna are provided by a third-generation local. Bookings (02) 4476 2665. *Whale-watching cruises:* humpback and killer whales can be seen migrating, often with calves, Sept–Nov; bookings at visitor centre. *Scuba diving cruises:* to shipwrecks; bookings at visitor centre.

WHAT'S ON *Great Southern Blues and Rockabilly Festival:* Oct.

NEARBY Montague Island Nature Reserve This isolated island, with access only by guided tours (bookings at visitor centre), is a major shearwater breeding site and home to little penguins and Australian and New Zealand fur seals. Whales can be viewed off the coast Sept–Nov. The tour includes historic buildings such as the Montague Lighthouse, which was first lit in 1881, but is now fully automated. Guides also explain the history of the island (known as Barunguba) as a fertile hunting ground for the Walbanga and Djiringanj tribes. 9 km SE.

Central Tilba Classified as an 'unusual mountain village' by the National Trust, Central Tilba was founded in 1895 and is now home to many shops selling quality arts and crafts. It has several old buildings worth a visit, including the ABC Cheese Factory in original 19th-century condition. The Tilba Festival is held here each Easter. 17 km SW. Tilba Tilba, a further 2 km S, features Foxglove Spires, a historic cottage surrounded by a beautiful 3.5 ha garden.

Mystery Bay: popular spot with lapidary enthusiasts, with strange stones and rock formations; 17 km S.

ⓘ Princes Hwy; (02) 4476 2881 or 1800 240 003; www.naturecoast-tourism.com.au

Narrabri   Pop. 6235

Map ref. 514 G8

The fledgling town of Narrabri was devastated by a flood in 1864, but was rebuilt and grew in regional importance from 1865 when the newly constructed courthouse took over local services from Wee Waa. Cotton was introduced to the area in 1962 and the region now enjoys one of Australia's largest yields. This success has brought prosperity to Narrabri and surrounding towns. The town is located between the Nandewar Range and Pilliga scrub country in the Namoi River Valley.

IN TOWN *Riverside park:* pleasant surroundings next to the Namoi River with barbecue and picnic facilities; Tibbereena St. *Self-guide town walk:* historic buildings including the original courthouse (1865) and police residence (1879); leaflet from visitor centre.

WHAT'S ON *Nosh on the Namoi:* food and wine festival; Mar. *Pro Rodeo:* Mar. *Farm-craft:* June. *Spring Festival:* Oct.

NEARBY Park Wild Observatory Here you'll find an impressive line of five 22-m-diametre antennas all facing the sky. They are connected on a rail track and are moved around to different locations to get full coverage. A sixth antenna lies 3 km away, and all six are sometimes connected with telescopes at Coonabarabran and Parkes. The visitor centre features a video, displays and an opportunity to view the telescope. 25 km W. Open Mon–Fri (weekends during school holidays).

Yarrie Lake: birdwatching, waterskiing and windsurfing; 32 km W. *Cotton fields and gin-processing plants:* tours available, bookings at visitor centre; open April–June. *Scenic*

drive: includes Mount Kaputar National Park (*see Barraba*) and cotton fields; leaflet from visitor centre.

ⓘ Newell Hwy; (02) 6799 6760

Narrandera   Pop. 4114

Map ref. 511 P9

This historic town on the Murrumbidgee River in the Riverina district is an urban conservation area with several National Trust-classified buildings. It has been home to two Australian writers. Local magistrate Thomas Alexander Browne used the nom de plume Rolf Boldrewood to write early Australian novels such as *Robbery Under Arms.* Father Patrick Hartigan, parish priest of St Mel's Catholic Church, was better known as poet John O'Brien.

IN TOWN Parkside Cottage Museum Displays include the scarlet Macarthur Opera Cloak, made from the first bale of merino wool the Macarthur family sent to England in 1816. Also on display are a snow shoe and ski from Scott's Antarctic expedition, a valuable collection of shells from around the world and a set of silver ingots commemorating 1000 years of the British monarchy. Newell Hwy. Open 2pm–5pm daily.

Lake Talbot: boating, waterskiing, fishing and canoeing. Also scenic walking trails around the lake. Lake Dr. *Lake Talbot Aquatic Playground:* water slides, swimming and barbecue facilities; Lake Dr; open Nov–Mar. *NSW Forestry Tree Nursery:* seedlings of a huge range of native trees for sale; Broad St; open Mon–Fri. *Tiger Moth Memorial:* restored DN82 Tiger Moth commemorating the WW II pilots who trained in the district; Newell Hwy. *Visitor Centre:* features a 5.8 m playable guitar; Narrandera Park. *Lavender Farm:* tours and product sales; Bells Rd. *Two-foot town heritage tour:* sights include the Royal Mail Hotel (1868) and the former police station (c. 1870); leaflet from visitor centre. *Bundidgerry Walking Track:* through nature reserve with koalas and

kangaroos. Best viewing time is at dawn; leaflet from visitor centre. *Blue Arrow Scenic Drive:* historic sites, cemetery and lake; brochure from visitor centre.

WHAT'S ON *John O'Brien Bush Festival:* Mar. *Hot Rod Easter Rally:* Easter. *National Cavy Show:* guinea pig show; Aug. *Camellia Show:* Aug. *Tree-mendous Festival:* Oct.

NEARBY *Inland Fisheries Research Station:* visitor centre with live exhibits, audio visual presentations and guided tours; 6 km SE; open Mon–Fri. *Craigtop Deer Farm:* deer raised for venison and velvet with presentation on deer-farming and a tour of the deer-handling facility; 8 km NW. *Berembed Weir:* picnicking, fishing and boating; 40 km SE.

ⓘ Narrandera Park, Newell Hwy; (02) 6959 1766 or 1800 672 392; www.riverinatourism.com.au

Nelson Bay   Pop. 7968

Map ref. 499 H2, 509 O4

Nelson Bay is a coastal tourist centre that has remained small enough to maintain its charm. With outstanding white beaches and gentle waters, it is a superb spot for all aquatic activities and enjoys close proximity to Tomaree National Park. The attractive bay is the main anchorage of Port Stephens.

IN TOWN Inner Lighthouse This 1872 lighthouse, originally lit with 4 kerosene lamps, has been restored by the National Trust and is now completely automated. The adjacent museum features a display of the area's early history, souvenirs and a teahouse. Views of Nelson Bay are stunning. Nelson Head.

Self-guide heritage walk: from Dutchmans Bay to Little Beach; brochure from visitor centre. *Cruises:* dolphin-watching (all year round) and whale-watching (May–July and Sept–Nov); on the harbour, Myall River and to Broughton Island. Also dive charters. Bookings at visitor centre.

4WD tours: along coastal dunes; bookings at visitor centre.

Graffiti Gallery, Nambucca Heads

NEW SOUTH WALES

WHAT'S ON *Craft markets:* Neil Carroll Park, Shoal Bay Rd; 1st and 3rd Sun each month; and Lutheran Church grounds, Anna Bay; 1st Sat each month. *Tomaree Markets:* Tomaree Sports Complex, Nelson Bay Rd, Salamander Bay; 2nd and 4th Sun each month. *Blessing of the Fleet:* Jan.

NEARBY Tomaree National Park This park consists of bushland, sand dunes, heathland, native forest and over 20 km of rocky coastline and beaches. There is a signposted walk around the headland and another up to Fort Tomaree Lookout for breathtaking 360-degree views. Yacaaba Lookout across the bay (70 km by road) also offers great views. The park is a popular spot for bushwalking, swimming, surfing, snorkelling, fishing and picnicking. The park stretches from Shoal Bay (3 km NE) to Anna Bay (10 km SW).
Little Beach: white beach with native flora reserve behind; 1 km E. *Gan Gan Lookout:* spectacular views south to Newcastle and north to Myall Lakes; Nelson Bay Rd; 2 km S. *Shoal Bay:* popular and protected bay with spa resort and Jazz, Wine and Food Fair in June; 3 km NE. *Shell Museum:* diverse display of shells, some rare; Sandy Point Rd; 3 km SW. *Toboggan Hill Park:* toboggan runs, minigolf and indoor wall-climbing; 5 km SW. *Oakvale Farm and Fauna World:* 150 species of native and farm animals, with visitor activities and feeding shows; 16 km SW. *Tomago House:* 1843 sandstone villa with family chapel and 19th-century gardens; Tomago Rd; 30 km SW; open 11am–3pm Sun. *Stockton Sand Dunes:* huge dune area popular for sand-boarding and whale-watching. Access is from Anna Bay or Williamtown by 4WD or safari (bookings at visitor centre). 38 km SW. *Port Stephens wineries:* several in area, with Stephens Winery featuring Jazz at the Winery in Mar; brochure from visitor centre.
ⓘ Port Stephens Visitor Information Centre, Victoria Pde; (02) 4981 1579 or 1800 808 900; www.portstephens.org.au

Newcastle   Pop. 278 773

Map ref. 498 H6, 499 G7, 509 N4

Newcastle began as a penal settlement and coalmining town, with a shipment of coal to Bengal in 1799 noted as Australia's first export. It soon became an industrial city, known for its steelworks and port. As the steel industry is phased out, Newcastle is developing a reputation for being an elegant and cosmopolitan seaside city. The spectacular harbour is the largest export harbour in the Commonwealth and the town is bordered by some of the world's finest surfing beaches.

IN TOWN Fort Scratchley This fascinating fort was built in 1882 amid fears of Russian attack. Soldiers' barracks and officers' residences were built in 1886. It is one of the few gun installations to have fired on the Japanese

in WW II and it remains in excellent condition. Explore networks of tunnels, gun emplacements and fascinating military and maritime museums, all perched high above Newcastle Harbour. Nobbys Rd.
Queens Wharf: centre point of foreshore redevelopment with restaurants, boutique brewery and observation tower linked by a walkway to City Mall; Hunter St. *Newcastle Regional Museum:* the largest regional museum in the country, featuring permanent displays ranging from ceramics to war memorabilia as well as visiting exhibitions. The incorporated Supernova Museum has over 80 interactive displays for children; Hunter St. *Newcastle Regional Art Gallery:* broad collection of Australian art including works by Arthur Streeton, Brett Whiteley, William Dobell, Sidney Nolan and Russell Drysdale, as well as changing exhibitions; Laman St. *King Edward Park:* waterfront recreation reserve since 1863 featuring sunken gardens, ocean views, band rotunda (1898), Soldiers Baths (public pool) and Bogey Hole, a hole cut in rocks by convicts; Shortland Esp. *Merewether Baths:* largest ocean baths in the Southern Hemisphere; Scenic Dr. *Blackbutt Reserve:* 182 ha of bushland with duck ponds, native animal enclosures, walking trails, and picnic and barbecue facilities; New Lambton; off Carnley Ave. *Self-guide walks:* include Town Walk and Shipwreck Walk; maps from visitor centre. *Cruises:* on the river and harbour; bookings at visitor centre.
WHAT'S ON *Maritime Festival:* Jan. *Surfest:* Mar. *Beaumont Street Jazz and Arts Festival:* April. *Cathedral Flower Festival:* Aug/Sept. *Hamilton Fiesta:* Sept. *Cathedral Music Festival:* Sept. *Mattara Festival:* celebration of the culture and beauty of Newcastle; Oct. *King Street Fair:* Dec.
NEARBY Lake Macquarie The enormous saltwater lake provides a huge aquatic playground with secluded bays and coves, sandy beaches and well-maintained parks lining its foreshore. Lake cruises leave from Toronto Wharf and Belmont Public Wharf. Dobell House, on the shore at Wangi Wangi, was the home of artist Sir William Dobell and has a collection of his work and memorabilia open to the public on Sun. The Lake Macquarie Heritage Afloat Festival is held here every Apr. 20 km S.
Munmorah State Recreation Area: coastal wilderness area including Shortland Wetlands, a bird and reptile habitat with walking, cycling and canoeing trails; 15 km W. *Eraring Power Station:* regular tours include access to cooling towers and a simulator used to train operators; 22 km S; bookings essential, phone (02) 4973 2933. *Swansea:* modern resort town enjoying both lake and ocean exposure. It is popular with anglers and has excellent surf beaches. 24 km S. *Surf beaches:* many with world-class breaks, including

Newcastle, Merewether and Nobbys; details from visitor centre.
ⓘ Wheeler Place, 363 Hunter St; (02) 4974 2999 or 1800 654 558; www.newcastletourism.com

Nimbin   Pop. 329

Map ref. 515 Q2, 607 Q12

Situated in a beautiful valley, Nimbin is a place of healing and initiation for the Bundjalung people and the resting place of Warrajum, the Rainbow Serpent. When its original industry of timber faltered, the cleared land was put to use for dairy and banana farming, but Nimbin hit a depression in the late 1960s when the dairy industry collapsed. It took the 1973 Aquarius Festival to establish Nimbin as the alternative-culture capital of Australia and resurrect its fortunes. Today the friendly atmosphere attracts alternative-lifestylers from all over.

IN TOWN *Nimbin Museum:* dedicated to hippy culture and Aboriginal heritage, including the Rainbow Serpent; Cullen St. *Town Hall:* features mural of Aboriginal art; Cullen St. *Rainbow Power Company:* take a tour of this alternative-power supplier, now exporting power products such as solar water pumps and hydro-generators to over 20 countries; Alternative Way. *Local art, craft and psychedelia:* brochure from visitor centre.
WHAT'S ON *Market:* Alternative Way; Sat. *Aquarius Fair:* local craft; Nimbin Community Centre; 3rd Sun each month. *Mardi Grass Festival:* organised by the Nimbin HEMP (Help End Marijuana Prohibition) Embassy; May.
NEARBY Nightcap National Park This lush World Heritage-listed forest offers signposted bushwalks from easy to very difficultm, requiring a map and compass. The dramatic Protestors Falls is the site of the 1979 anti-logging protest that led to the area being gazetted as a national park. Rocky Creek Dam has a platypus-viewing platform and views of Mt Warning and surrounding valleys. 5 km NE.
Nimbin Rocks: spectacular remnants of an ancient volcano overlooking the town. This is a sacred initiation site for the Bundjalung people, so viewing is from the road only; Lismore Rd; 3 km S. *The Channon:* town featuring an alternative-craft market 2nd Sun each month, Opera at the Channon in Aug and Music Bowl Live Band Concert in Nov; 15 km SE.
ⓘ Cnr Ballina and Molesworth sts, Lismore; (02) 6622 0122 or 1300 369 795

Nowra   Pop. 23 946

Map ref. 501 E12, 507 I4, 509 K11

Nowra is the principal town in the Shoalhaven district and is popular with tourists for its attractive river and water activities. The racehorse Archer began his famous 550-mile (880-kilometre) walk

Wangi Wangi on the shores of Lake Macquarie, south of Newcastle

from Terara, on the outskirts of Nowra, to compete in the Melbourne Cup. He was led and ridden by his jockey, Dave Power. The two went on to be the first winners of the Melbourne Cup in 1861 and returned for a second win in 1862.

IN TOWN Meroogal Said to be the most intact 19th-century home in NSW, this 1885 property was passed down through 4 generations of women. Furniture, household objects, diaries, letters, scrapbooks, photographs and even clothes have been saved and preserved so that visitors now have an opportunity to sift through relics from each generation of its occupation. Cnr Worrigee and West sts. Open Sat afternoon and Sun. *Shoalhaven Historical Museum:* old police station exhibiting the history of the town in records, photographs, household items and tools; cnr Plunkett and Kinghorne sts. *Shoalhaven River:* fishing, waterskiing, canoeing and sailing. *Shoalhaven River Cruises:* check times (02) 4447 1978; departing from Nowra Wharf, Riverview Rd. *Hanging Rock:* 46.25 m above the river with scenic views; off Junction St. *Nowra Animal Park:* native animals, reptiles and birds plus pony rides and opportunities to pat a koala; Rockhill Rd. *Scenic walks:* include Bens Walk along the river and Bomaderry Creek Walk from Bomaderry; leaflets from visitor centre.

WHAT'S ON *Market:* Stewart Pl; 3rd Sun each month.

NEARBY Kangaroo Valley This charming town of historic buildings has the National Trust-classified Friendly Inn, a Pioneer Settlement Reserve (a reconstruction of an 1880s dairy farm) and the Hampden Bridge, which was built in 1898 and is the oldest suspension bridge in Australia. Kangaroo Valley Fruit World is a working fruit farm open to visitors. Canoeing and kayaking safaris to Kangaroo River and Shoalhaven Gorge can be booked at the visitor centre. There is also beautiful rural scenery along Nowra Rd. 23 km NW.

Australia's Museum of Flight: world-class aviation museum with displays and planes over 6000 sq m; 8 km SW. *Marayong Park Emu Farm:* tours include the emu incubation room, brooder area, chick-rearing shed and breeding pen. Chicks hatch from July to Dec. 11 km S. *Cambewarra Lookout:* spectacular views of the Shoalhaven River and Kangaroo Valley; 12 km NW. *Greenwell Point:* fresh fish and oyster sales; 14 km E. *Bundanon:* National Estate-listed homestead donated to the nation by artist Arthur Boyd and his wife Yvonne. The Bundanon collection and Boyd's studio are open 1st Sun each month (tickets from visitor centre; advance bookings essential). 21 km W. *Culburra:* nearby Lake Wollumboola and coastal beaches are good for surfing, swimming, prawning and fishing. Culburra also holds the Open Fishing Carnival each Jan. 21 km SE. *Morton National Park:* the Nowra section features the Tallowa Dam water-catchment area, a popular spot for picnics; via Kangaroo Valley; 38 km NW. *For other sections of the park see Bundanoon, Robertson and Ulladulla. Beaches:* many beautiful beaches in the vicinity for swimming and surfing; maps at visitor centre. *Wineries:* several in region offering cellar-door tastings; brochure from visitor centre. ⓘ Shoalhaven Visitors Centre, cnr Princes Hwy and Pleasant Way, Nowra; (02) 4421 0778 or 1300 662 808; www.shoalhaven.nsw.gov.au

Nundle   Pop. 261

Map ref. 515 K12

A thriving gold town in the 1850s, Nundle drew prospectors from California, Jamaica, China and Europe. Today Nundle is an attractive and quiet town nestled between the Great Dividing Range and the Peel River, but traces of gold can still be found and it is known as 'the town in the hills of gold'. The Peel River is well known for its fishing, with yellow-belly, trout and catfish being common catches.

IN TOWN *Courthouse Museum:* built in 1880, now housing a history of Nundle concentrating on the gold-rush era; Jenkins St. *Peel Inn:* 1860s pub with meals and accommodation; Jenkins St. *Goldmining display:* in a restored coffin factory; Gill St. *Woollen Mill:* mezzanine viewing platform with views over the working mill; Oakenville St.

WHAT'S ON *Go for Gold Festival:* Easter. *Nundle Dog Race:* May. *Campdrafting:* Dec.

NEARBY Hanging Rock The area is popular for mineral fossicking, with good samples of scheelite and an excellent site for gold panning on the Peel River. Sheba Dams Reserve is home to numerous birds and animals. Activities include picnicking, bushwalking, camping and fishing, with regular stockings of trout and salmon. 11 km W. *Chaffey Reservoir:* enjoy good swimming, fishing, sailing and picnicking. Dulegal Arboretum, an attractive garden of native trees and shrubs, is on the foreshore. 11 km N. *Fossicker's Way tour:* through scenic New England countryside; brochure from visitor centre. ⓘ Country Cafe, Jenkins St; (02) 6769 3158

Nyngan   Pop. 2067

Map ref. 513 R10

Nyngan is a pleasant country town on the Bogan River, on the edge of the outback. It was largely unknown to the rest of the country until 1990, when the worst floods of the century struck here, doing $50 million damage. A helicopter was called in to airlift 2000 people – almost the whole town – to safety. Today the town, at the centre of a sheep, wheat and wool district, is happily less eventful.

IN TOWN *Nyngan Museum:* local memorabilia, photographs, an audio room with local stories, an 1800s kitchen and remnants from the 1990 flood; at railway station, Pangee St; open Mon–Fri. *Cobb & Co Coach Yard:* old coaches, working

Blue Lake, north of Thredbo

Kosciuszko National Park

The state's largest national park encompasses 690 000 hectares of valleys, glacial lakes, woodlands, fields and the highest mountains in the country, protecting rare and unusual species including the pygmy possum, which lives above altitudes of 1400 metres, and the snow gum, the only native tree that can survive above 1800 metres. All of New South Wales' ski fields exist inside the park, including Thredbo and Charlotte Pass in the south and Mt Selwyn in the centre.

The focal point of the park is Mt Kosciuszko, Australia's highest mountain, standing at 2228 metres above sea level. Polish patriot Tadeusz Kosciuszko never knew a significant mountain had been named in his honour in a faraway land. It was named by explorer Paul Edmund de Strzelecki in 1840 because the domed shape of the mountain reminded him of Kosciuszko's tomb and he wanted to celebrate the freedom fighter's efforts in a land where he was 'among a free people who appreciate freedom'. Strzelecki travelled with two Aboriginal guides and James Macarthur, son of renowned wool pioneers John and Elizabeth Macarthur. The summit can be reached easily today via the Kosciuszko Express Chairlift, which drops you at the beginning of a 13-kilometre-return walk. The chairlift operates year-round from Thredbo, but the walk is obviously best attempted in spring and summer when the days are warmer and the wildflowers are in bloom.

Among myriad natural wonders in the park, the Yarrangobilly Caves stand out as a world-class attraction. The string of 70 caves is located at the northern end of the park and is said to be the most lavishly decorated in the country. The limestone that these caves are made of was formed from the shells and skeletons of sea animals laid down before the area rose 1200 metres above sea level around 40 million years ago. The belt of limestone is 14 kilometres long and 1.5 kilometres wide – through it the Yarrangobilly River has forged a valley over 200 metres deep. Six caves are open to the public, with highlights including underground pools, frozen waterfalls and a bizarre web of limestone formations. There is a picturesque picnic area and a naturally formed thermal pool offering year-round swimming in constant 27°C water.

For information on other attractions in the park see Jindabyne and Thredbo.

---

forge and museum; cnr Nymagee St and Monagee Rd. *Mid-state Shearing Shed:* informative displays of the continuing importance of shearing to the region, with work of local artists in murals; Mitchell Hwy; open Mon–Fri. *Historical town drive and Levee Tour:* includes historic buildings in Cobar and Pangee sts, the Bicentennial Mural Wall and the heritage-listed railway overbridge with a lookout over town. The levee was built after the 1990 floods. Brochure from visitor centre.
WHAT'S ON *Anzac Day Race Meeting:* horserace; April. *Dog Trials:* Aug. *Spring into Nyngan:* Sept.

NEARBY **Macquarie Marshes** This mosaic of semi-permanent wetlands includes two major areas: the south marsh and the north marsh. The wetlands expand and contract, depending on recent rainfall, and provide a waterbird sanctuary and breeding ground. It is thought that the Macquarie Marshes contributed to the early myth of an inland sea, which led explorers – most notably Charles Sturt – on many ill-fated journeys. 64 km N. *Cairn:* marking the geographic centre of NSW. It is on private property but visible from the road. 65 km S. *Richard Cunningham's grave:* botanist with explorer

Major Mitchell's party, Cunningham was killed by Aboriginal people in 1835 and buried here; 70 km S.
ⓘ Nyngan Video Parlour, 105 Pangee St; (02) 6832 1155; www.nyngan.com

Oberon   Pop. 2515

Map ref. 492 E7, 508 I7

This picturesque farming town is 1113 metres above sea level, which gives Oberon a mountain climate of cool summers, crisp winters and occasional snow. The town was named after the king in *A Midsummer Night's Dream* at the suggestion of a local Shakespeare enthusiast, after it was decided that the original name Glyndwr was unpleasant to the ear.

IN TOWN **Oberon Museum** Almost 1 ha of displays include over 150 pieces of early farming equipment, an authentic, fully furnished early settlers' house, a blacksmith shop and a functioning forge. A wide collection of artefacts and memorabilia are housed in the town's original 1920s railway station. Lowes Mount Rd.
Lake Oberon: outstanding site for brown and rainbow trout fishing. Boats and swimming are not permitted, but there are barbecue and picnic facilities. Jenolan St. *The Common:* green park with a small lake and picnic facilities; Edith Rd. *Reef Reserve:* natural bushland with access to the lake foreshore; Reef Rd. *Cobweb Craft Shop:* 8 tapestries on show depicting the town's landscape and buildings; Oberon St.
WHAT'S ON *Rodeo:* Feb. *Kowmung Music Festival:* chamber music in caves; Mar. *Daffodil Festival:* Sept. *Oberon Woodcraft Exhibition:* Sept.
NEARBY **Kanangra–Boyd National Park** This is a rugged and dramatic piece of Australia with vast gorges, spectacular lookouts and scenic rivers. Sandstone formations of Thurat Spires, Kanangra Walls and Mt Cloudmaker are breathtaking and the park is excellent for bushwalking, rockclimbing and camping. The Jenolan Caves are just outside the park border and are justifiably the country's best-known cluster of caves. Tours of the majestic caverns feature fascinating flowstone deposits, helictites, columns and lakes. On the south-east edge of the park is Yerranderie, a restored silver-mining town with accommodation and walking trails. Jenolan Caves 30 km SE; Kanangra Walls 52 km SE; Yerranderie 85 km SE.
Evans Crown Nature Reserve: bushwalking area with diverse flora and fauna and granite tors. Crown Rock was an initiation and corroboree site for the Wirradjuri people and is now popular for abseiling. 21 km N. *Abercrombie River National Park:* low eucalypt forest ideal for bushwalks, with kangaroos, wallaroos and wallabies. Abercrombie River, Retreat River and Silent Creek are havens for

platypuses and water rats and great for fishing, swimming and canoeing. 40 km s. *Driving tours:* routes taking in caves, national parks and surrounding towns; brochure from visitor centre. *Wood mushrooms:* delicacies that grow in Jenolan, Vulcan and Gurnang state forests Jan–early May. Mushrooms should be correctly identified before picking. Brochure from visitor centre. ⓘ 137–139 Oberon St; (02) 6336 0666; www.oberonweb.com

Orange   Pop. 31 923

Map ref. 508 G6

Before European occupation this area was home to the Wiradjuri people, who thrived on the plentiful bush tucker resulting from the fertile volcanic soil and the abundant kangaroos and wallabies. The town was named by explorer Sir Thomas Mitchell after the Prince of Orange. Today the prosperous 'colour city' on the slopes of Mt Canobolas enjoys a reputation for excellent food, wines, parks and gardens. It is also known for its goldmining history and as the birthplace of renowned Australian poet A. B. (Banjo) Paterson.

IN TOWN Civic Gardens The gardens are home to the City Library, visitor centre, Civic Theatre and a monument to Banjo Paterson. The Orange Regional Gallery, also in the park, features 3 rooms of diverse and changing exhibitions from local, national and international artists and is one of the busiest regional galleries in the country. Permanent collections focus on jewellery, ceramics, art and clothes. Byng St. Open Tues–Sat, 2pm– 5pm Sun and public holidays. *Cook Park:* colourful in any season with a begonia house (flowers Feb–May), duck pond, fernery, native bird aviary, Cook Park Guildry and picnic area. Brochure available from the guildry or visitor centre for a self-guide walk through the park. Summer St. *Botanic Gardens:* 17 ha parklands with an impressive exotic and native plant collection and a signposted walk through billabongs, rose gardens, orchards and woodlands; Kearneys Dr. *Banjo Paterson Memorial Park:* remains of Narambla Homestead, Paterson's birthplace, and a memorial obelisk; Ophir Rd. *Self-guide historical walk:* 90 min stroll through historic homes and commercial structures; brochure from visitor centre. **WHAT'S ON** *Market:* Kmart carpark; Sun. *Picnic Races:* Jan. *FOOD (Food of Orange District) Week:* April. *Craftalive:* Aug. *Orange Region Winefest:* Oct. *Byng Street Dash:* fun run; Dec. **NEARBY Ophir goldfields** This was the site of the first discovery of payable gold in Australia (1851). The 1850s saw an influx of immigrants from Britain, Germany and China, all hoping to strike it rich. Features today include a fossicking centre, picnic area, walking trails to historic tunnels and tours of a working

goldmine. There is still plenty of gold to be found in the area; the gold medals at the 2000 Sydney Olympic Games were made of Ophir gold. Brochure from visitor centre. 27 km N. *Campbell's Corner:* popular roadside picnic and barbecue spot; Pinnacle Rd; 8 km s. *Lake Canobolas Park:* recreation and camping area with trout fishing in the lake, deer park, children's playground and picnic and barbecue facilities; 8 km sw. *Lucknow:* old goldmining town, site of Australia's second gold discovery, now with historic bluestone buildings and craft shops; 10 km SE. *Mount Canobolas Park:* 1500 ha bird and animal sanctuary; 14 km sw. *Borenore Caves:* undeveloped caves with evidence of fossils. Outside are walking trails, and picnic and barbecue facilities. Torch required if entering the caves; brochure from visitor centre. 17 km w. *Cadia Mines:* largest goldmine and coppermine in NSW; check with visitor centre for open days; 25 km SE. *Mitchell's Monument:* site of Sir Thomas Mitchell's base camp; 31 km w. *Molong:* charming rural town with Yarn Market, Craft Cottage and Coach House Gallery; 35 km NW. Grave of Yuranigh, Mitchell's Aboriginal guide, lies 2 km E of Molong. *Wineries:* several in area with cellar-door tastings; brochure from visitor centre. ⓘ Cnr Byng and Peisley sts; (02) 6393 8226 or 1800 069 466; www.orange. nsw.gov.au

Parkes   Pop. 9789

Map ref. 508 D5

Parkes is most famous in Australia for its huge telescope north of town. It originated as a tent city, which grew into a town named Bushmans, built almost overnight when gold was found in the area in 1862. The name of the town changed after the governor of New South Wales, Henry Parkes, visited in 1873. The main street, Clarinda Street, was named after Mrs Parkes the following year.

IN TOWN Pioneer Park Museum Set in a historic school and church, displays include early farm machinery and transport. The museum incorporates the collection of the previously separate Henry Parkes Historical Museum, which specialises in memorabilia from the gold rush, and includes the fascinating 1000- volume personal library of Sir Henry Parkes. Pioneer St, North Parkes. *Motor Museum:* displays of vintage and veteran vehicles and local art and craft; cnr Bogan and Dalton sts. *Memorial Hill:* excellent views of the town and surrounds; Bushman St, North Parkes. *Kelly Reserve:* playground and picnic and barbecue facilities in bush setting; Newell Hwy, North Parkes. *Bushmans Hill Reserve:* site of one of the town's first goldmines. Take the walking trail to a lookout, passing mining relics and a memorial to those who lost their lives in local mines.

Newell Hwy, North Parkes. *Self-guide historical town walk and drive:* highlights include the police station (1875), post office (c. 1880) and Balmoral, one of the town's oldest homes, noted for its iron lace, Italian marble and stained-glass windows; brochure from visitor centre. **WHAT'S ON** *Elvis Revival:* Jan. *Parkes National Marbles Championships:* Mar. *Antique Machinery Museum Open Day:* Easter. *Art and Craft Exhibition:* June. *Trundle Bush Tucker Day:* Sept. *Country Music Spectacular:* Oct. *Antique Motor Bike Rally:* Oct.

NEARBY CSIRO Parkes Radio Telescope Commissioned in 1961, the telescope is the largest and oldest of the 8 antennae making up the Australian Telescope National Facility. It has been used for globally important work such as identifying the first quasar in 1963, mapping important regions of the Milky Way, and the NASA Apollo moon missions. It was most famously instrumental in transmitting images of Neil Armstrong's first steps on the moon to the world (although there has been some concern over the authenticity of the images). The story of the events on the ground at Parkes is portrayed in the film *The Dish* (2000). The visitor centre explains the uses of the telescope and has 3D displays. 23 km N. **Condobolin** This unassuming country town is where *Australian Idol* runner-up Shannon Noll has his roots. A lookout on Reservoir Hill gives views over the town, which is at the junction of two rivers and surrounded by red-soil plains. Mt Tilga, 8 km N, is said to be the geographical centre of NSW, and Gum Bend Lake, 5 km w, is a good spot for fishing and watersports. 95 km w. *Peak Hill:* working goldmine with lookout offering views of Parkes; 48 km N. ⓘ Kelly Reserve, Newell Hwy; (02) 6862 4365

Picton   Pop. 2921

Map ref. 493 J12, 501 E2, 507 I2, 509 K9

Located in the foothills of the Southern Highlands, Picton was once a thriving town, but since the re-routing of the Hume Highway it has become a peaceful and well-preserved village. The old buildings and quiet hills are reminiscent of an earlier era. Originally gazetted as Stonequarry, the town was renamed after Thomas Picton, one of Wellington's generals at the battle of Waterloo.

IN TOWN George IV Inn and Scharer's Brewery This is one of Australia's oldest operating inns. It only serves beer from its own brewery (one of only a few pub breweries in the country) and has meals and regular entertainment. Beer-maker Geoffrey Scharer was born in a pub and is a fourth-generation publican, so can answer almost any question about beer. He worked for many years to perfect his traditional Bavarian recipe. Argyle St.

NEW SOUTH WALES

Self-guide historical walk: includes the splendid railway viaduct (1862) over Stonequarry Creek, and St Mark's Church (1848). *Ghost tours:* local pioneer ghost tour and tales with supper or 2-course meal. Tamer children's tours are also available. Bookings essential (02) 4677 2044; open Fri and Sat night.

WHAT'S ON *Brush with the Bush:* art festival; Oct. *White Waratah Festival:* Oct.

NEARBY Thirlmere This quiet and attractive town is best known for its NSW Rail Transport Museum. The complex offers steam-train rides to Buxton each Sun (Buxton has craft markets 3rd Sun each month). The Festival of Steam is held here in Mar, and includes a fun run, market stalls and ferret races. 5 km sw. Thirlmere Lakes National Park (a further 3 km sw) protects 5 reed-fringed freshwater lakes that are home to waterbirds. This is a great place for swimming, picnicking and canoeing (no large boats) and there is a scenic drive around the lakes. *Jarvisfield Homestead:* 1865 home of pioneer landowners, now the clubhouse of Antill Park Golf Club; Remembrance Dr; 2 km N. *Wool Away! Woolshed:* 3-course meals, bush dances and regular shows; bookings required (03) 4677 1379; 3 km N. *Sydney Skydiving Centre:* catering for beginners and experienced skydivers with video-viewing facilities and a picnic and barbecue area; 5 km E. *Maldon Suspension Bridge:* bungee jumping; 5 km SE. *Wirrimbirra Sanctuary:* native flora and fauna with regular events and twilight tours. Overnight cabins are available. 13 km sw. *Dingo Sanctuary:* native dogs in native bushland with picnic facilities; 15 km s; open Mon, Thurs, Sat, Sun.
ⓘ Old Post Office, cnr Argyle and Menangle sts; (02) 4677 3962; www.stonequarry.com.au

Port Macquarie   Pop. 37 696

Map ref. 515 P12, 516 G7

Port Macquarie, one of the oldest sites in the state, was established in 1821 as a self-sufficient penal settlement. Convicts chosen for their skills and good behaviour maintained the fledgling town, doing everything from farming, boatbuilding and blacksmithing to teaching, baking and clerical duties. Today the city is a major holiday resort at the mouth of the Hastings River. It provides a fascinating history and historic buildings, nature reserves, excellent surf and fishing beaches, an outstanding museum and scenic coastal walking tracks.

IN TOWN Hastings Historical Museum This award-winning museum has over 20 000 items in its ever-increasing collection. It specialises in letters, photographs and documents covering convict and free settlement and the evolution of the town from penal colony to coastal metropolis. The museum is in

The October rodeo in Bungendore, north-east of Queanbeyan

one of the town's beautifully restored older buildings (c. 1836). Clarence St. *St Thomas' Church:* 3rd oldest surviving church in Australia (1824–28), designed by convict architect Thomas Owen; Hay St. *Port Macquarie Historic Courthouse:* built in 1869, it served the community for 117 years; tours of the restored building daily; cnr Hay and Clarence sts; closed Sun. *Mid-north Coast Maritime Museum:* shipwreck relics, model ships and early photographs; William St. *Kooloonbung Creek Nature Reserve:* 50 ha of bushland with boardwalks. Visit the historic cemetery nearby dating from 1842. Horton St. *Roto House and Macquarie Nature Reserve:* koala hospital and study centre; Lord St. *Port Macquarie Observatory:* planetarium, telescope and solar system display; William St; call for opening times (02) 6583 1933. *Fantasy Glades:* rainforest gardens and picnic and barbecue facilities; Pacific Dr. *Billabong Koala and Aussie Wildlife Park:* farmyard animals and over 50 species of Australian wildlife with talking cockatoos and several kangaroo-feeding and koala photo sessions each day; Billabong Dr. *Kingfisher Park:* rare and threatened native animals kept in natural bushland and landscaped gardens; Kingfisher Rd. *Town beach:* surf at one end and sheltered coves at the other. *Peppermint Park:* water slides, 2 monkey enclosures, minigolf and rollerblading (rollerblades for hire); cnr Pacific Dr and Ocean St. *River cruises:* depart daily; bookings at visitor centre. *Scenic walk:* following coastal headlands

from breakwall to lighthouse (8 km); brochure from visitor centre.

WHAT'S ON *Market:* Findlay Ave; 2nd and 4th Sun each month. *Golden Lure Tournament:* deep-sea fishing; Jan. *Easter Fiesta:* Easter. *Food and Wine Festival:* Oct.

NEARBY Lake Innes Nature Reserve The picturesque reserve is home to koalas, kangaroos and bats, but was once the location of the grand Lake Innes House. Major Innes was an early settler and had fantastic visions of the future of Port Macquarie. He built his stately home and proceeded to invest his money in property in the fledgling town. When he realised he had overstretched himself, he left the house and declared himself bankrupt. It was left to decay, and the ruins are all that remain today. Guided tours are available; brochure at visitor centre. 7 km sw. *Sea Acres Rainforest Centre:* elevated 1.3 km boardwalk through canopy; tours available; 4 km s. *Lighthouse Beach:* 16 km expanse of white sand with camel rides, dolphin-watching from shore and breathtaking views up and down the coast from the grounds of Tacking Point Lighthouse at the northern end of the beach (lighthouse not open to public). 10 km s. *Lake Cathie:* holiday town between surf beach and tidal lake for swimming and fishing; 16 km s. *Wineries:* several in the area offering cellar-door tastings. Cassegrain Winery (13 km w) hosts Discovery Concert under the stars each Oct. Brochure from visitor centre. *Horseriding, Harley Davidson motorbike tours, 4WD tours, watersports, abseiling and skydiving:* brochures at visitor centre.
ⓘ Clarence St; (02) 6581 8000 or 1300 303 155; www.portmacquarie info.com.au

Queanbeyan   Pop. 29 752

Map ref. 505 I6, 506 G4, 507 E5, 508 G13

Queanbeyan is a growing city adjoining Canberra. Even though most of the city is in New South Wales, the outskirts sprawl into the Australian Capital Territory. Queanbeyan takes its name from a squat once held by ex-convict Timothy Beard beside the nearby Molonglo River that he called 'Quinbean' after an Aboriginal word meaning 'clear waters'.

IN TOWN *History Museum:* documented history of the city in restored police sergeant's residence; Farrer Pl; open 2pm–4pm Sun Sept–June. *Queanbeyan Art Society Inc:* exhibits local art and craft; Trinculo Pl. *Railway Historical Society:* steam-train rides depart from station in Henderson St; check times (02) 6284 2790. *Self-guide town walks:* include Byrne's Mill (1883) and Byrne's Mill House, now Queanbeyan Books and Prints; brochure from visitor centre.

WHAT'S ON *Queanbeyan Rotary Cottage market:* Queen Elizabeth Park; 2nd Sun each month (except Jan). *Sporting Weekend Spectacular:* Nov.

NEARBY Bungendore This historic country village is set in a picturesque valley near Lake George and still consists of old stone, brick and timber buildings that have been there since the 19th century. The town square contains charming colonial-style shops selling crafts and antiques, and there are several hobby farms in the area. There is a Country Muster in Feb and a rodeo in Oct. 26 km NE. Lark Hill Winery, 7 km N of Bungendore, has cellar-door tastings and sales.
Molonglo Gorge: scenic drive and 3 km walking trail provide spectacular views of Molonglo River; 2 km N. *Googong Dam:* fishing, bushwalking and picnicking; 10 km S. *London Bridge Woolshed and Shearers' Quarters:* visual history of turn-of-the-century farming and settlement life. Take the easy 1 km walk to a remarkable limestone arch. 24 km S. *Bywong Goldmining Town:* re-creation of early mining settlement; 31 km NE. *Captains Flat:* tiny mining town, ideal for walking around, with historic buildings and Yesteryear Museum; 45 km S.
ⓘ Cnr Farrer Pl and Lowe St; (02) 6298 0241 or 1800 026 192; www.queanbeyan.nsw.gov.au

Raymond Terrace   Pop. 12 482

Map ref. 499 E6, 509 N4

Situated on the banks of the Hunter and William rivers just outside Newcastle, Raymond Terrace was an important wool-shipping area in the 1840s. Many historic buildings from that era remain today. The town is in the middle of a koala corridor thanks to the vast remaining eucalypt forests in the region.
IN TOWN *Sketchley Cottage:* built in 1840 and rebuilt after being destroyed by fire in 1857. Displays include early Australian farming equipment, wine casks, furniture, handcrafts and photography; Pacific Hwy. *Self-guide historical town walk:* includes courthouse (1838) and an 1830s Anglican church built of hand-hewn sandstone; map from visitor centre.
NEARBY Tanilba House Home to the first white settler in Tanilba Bay, Lieutenant Caswell, Tanilba House was convict-built in 1831. Features of the house include half-metre thick walls, decorative quoins defining the building edge and door and window openings, and high ceilings, archways and large rooms. There is said to be a resident ghost, thought to be an 1830s governess. 36 km NE.
Hunter Region Botanic Gardens: over 2000 native plants and several theme gardens; Pacific Hwy; 3 km S. *Grahamstown Lake:* beautiful serene lake with picnic facilities; 12 km N. *Fighter World:* hands-on displays of old fighter planes, engines and equipment; RAAF base, Williamtown; 16 km NE. *Clarence Town:* this historic village was one of the first European

settlements in Australia; 27 km NW. *Tilligerry Habitat:* ecotourism centre with art and craft and guided walks to see koalas; 34 km NE. *Koala Reserve:* boardwalk through koala colony; 40 km N.
ⓘ 240 Pacific Hwy; (02) 4987 1211; www.portstephens.org.au

Richmond   Pop. 4604

Map ref. 493 K6, 509 K7

Richmond provides a peaceful country atmosphere on the Hawkesbury River, but is close enough to Sydney to enjoy the best of both worlds. Many residents commute to the city each day. The township was settled in 1794 because of the rich Hawkesbury river flats. Richmond was soon being used as a granary to supply half of Sydney's grain and is still important agriculturally. There are good views of the Blue Mountains.
IN TOWN *Macquarie Town Art Society:* paintings by accomplished local and national artists; Lennox St; open Thurs and Sat. *Bowman Cottage:* restored c. 1815 cottage, now tearooms; Windsor St. *Pugh's Lagoon:* pleasant picnic spot with plentiful waterbirds; Kurrajong Rd. *Self-guide historical town walks:* include the privately owned Hobarville, St Peter's Church (1841) and adjacent pioneer graves; brochure from visitor centre.
WHAT'S ON *Bellbird Craft Markets:* March St; 1st Sat each month. *Hawkesbury Waratah Festival:* Sept. *Fruits of the Hawkesbury Festival:* throughout region; Sept–Nov.
NEARBY Bilpin This tiny town is known for its apples and apple juice. It was originally named Belpin after Archibald Bell Jnr, who was the first European to cross the mountains from Richmond (Bells Line of Road is also named after him). The fact that he achieved this with the guidance of local Aboriginal people who had been doing it for thousands of years did not seem to detract from the achievement. In keeping with the Australian penchant for 'big' attractions, Bilpin has the Big Bowl of Fruit. There are markets each Sat and the Fruitfest in Apr. 31 km NW.
RAAF base: oldest Air Force establishment in Australia, used for civilian flying from 1915; Windsor–Richmond Rd; 3 km E. *Bellbird Hill Lookout:* clear views across to Sydney skyline; Kurrajong Heights; 13 km NW. *Hawkesbury Lookout:* great views of Sydney over the Cumberland plain; 15 km SW. *Avoca Lookout:* stunning views over Grose Valley; 20 km W. *Mountain Lagoon:* mountain bushland setting with walking trails and cabins; brochure from visitor centre; 40 km NW.
ⓘ Tourism Hawkesbury, Bicentenary Park, Ham Common, Windsor–Richmond Rd, Clarendon; (02) 4588 5895; www.hawkesburyvalley.com

Robertson   Pop. 1019

Map ref. 501 E8, 507 I3, 509 K10

Robertson sits high atop Macquarie Pass with some points in town enjoying spectacular views all the way across to the Pacific Ocean. The region's rich red soil has made Robertson the centre of the largest potato-growing district in New South Wales and there is a 'big potato' on the main street, although it is not signposted and visitors could be forgiven for thinking it is merely a large brown cylinder. The undulating hills of the town and region create a picturesque setting and were featured in the film *Babe* (1996).
IN TOWN Kev Neels Old Time Music Machines This music museum displays antique gramophones (some still in working condition) and music memorabilia from as early as the 1800s. Outside are deer, birds and views of the Illawarra escarpment. Visitors are encouraged to tour the grounds and use the picnic facilities. Illawarra Hwy. *Cockatoo Run Heritage Railway:* steam train (when available) to Port Kembla. Robertson Railway Station. For running times call 1300 653 801. *Art and craft shops:* several in town featuring local work; details from visitor centre.
WHAT'S ON *Market:* Robertson School of Arts; 2nd Sun each month.
NEARBY Morton National Park, Robertson section This section of the park has two attractive features: Belmore Falls (10 km SW) and Fitzroy Falls (15 km SW). Belmore Falls plunges into two separate rock pools, which then cascade down to the valley below. The area also features walking tracks and pleasant picnic facilities. At Fitzroy Falls is the National Parks and Wildlife Service visitor centre, which has maps and information about the entire national park and offers guided tours. The falls drop 80 m over sandstone cliffs onto black rocks and then another 40 m into the valley below. The walking trail around the falls has excellent lookouts. *For other sections of the park see Bundanoon, Nowra and Ulladulla. Robertson Rainforest:* 5 ha portion of what was the 2500 ha Yarrawah Brush. It is home to abundant birdlife and features an attractive bushwalk; 2 km S. *Ranelagh House:* manor-style home (1924) with over 80 rooms and uninterrupted views of the surrounding hills and valley. Deer and peacocks roam the immaculate, landscaped grounds. It is now a guesthouse and function centre. Illawarra Hwy; 3 km E. *Burrawang:* 19th-century village with historic general store; 6 km W. *Macquarie Pass National Park:* preserved section of the Illawarra Escarpment with bushwalks through eucalypt forest and picnic facilities; 10 km E. *Budderoo National Park:* Robertson section features Carrington Falls, a 50 m waterfall with adjacent walking tracks, lookouts and picnic facilities; 10 km SE.

NEW SOUTH WALES

Manning Lookout: views over Kangaroo Valley; 16 km sw.

ⓘ Southern Highlands Visitor Information Centre, 62–70 Main St, Mittagong; (02) 4871 2888 or 1300 657 559; www.southern-highlands.com.au

Rylstone   Pop. 651

Map ref. 508 I4

Visitors are drawn to Rylstone for its rural tranquillity. This old stone village is on the Cudgegong River and is a popular spot for birdwatching and fishing.

IN TOWN Jack Tindale Park This park is a pleasant green reserve, perfect for swimming, picnics and barbecues. Platypuses are sometimes spotted in the

Fitzroy Falls, Morton National Park, south-west of Robertson

water here and in the river below the showground. Cox St.
Self-guide historical walk: includes the Bridge View Inn (restaurant, formerly a bank) and the post office; brochure from visitor centre. *Art and craft outlets:* several featuring local work; details at visitor centre.

NEARBY Glen Davis This fascinating shale oil ghost town is at the eastern end of the Capertee Valley. The valley is almost 30 km across and is surrounded by sheer sandstone cliffs, which makes it the largest enclosed valley in the Southern Hemisphere. The town is a picturesque spot for picnics, barbecues and camping and there is a museum documenting the town's fluctuating fortunes. 56 km SE. Open weekends.
Kandos: industrial town known for its cement. It features the Bicentennial Industrial Museum (open weekends) and holds the Kandos Street Machine and Hot Rod Show each Jan. 3 km s. *Fern Tree Gully:* tree ferns in picturesque subtropical forest with walking trails and lookouts; 16 km N. *Dunn's Swamp:* camping, fishing, bushwalking; 18 km E. *Windermere Dam:* watersports, fishing, camping, picnic and barbecue facilities. Also home of fishing competition each Easter. 19 km W. *Military Vehicle Museum:* vehicles from WW II and the Korean and Vietnam wars; 20 km N. *Turon Technology Museum:* power museum with restored steam engines; 20 km s. *Wineries:* several in the area; brochure from visitor centre.
ⓘ Council offices, Louee St; (02) 6379 1132; www.rylstone.com

Scone   Pop. 4555

Map ref. 509 K1

Set among rolling green hills in the Hunter Valley, Scone (rhymes with stone) is a pleasant rural town with tree-lined streets. It is known as the 'horse capital of Australia' and is actually the world's second largest thoroughbred and horse-breeding centre.

IN TOWN *Australian Stock Horse Museum:* photographs and displays on the history of stockhorses in Australia and the headquarters of the Australian Stock Horse Society; Kelly St; open Mon–Fri. *Mare and Foal:* life-size sculpture by Gabriel Sterk; Kelly St. *Historical Society Museum:* large collection of local photographs and household furniture and appliances in an old lock-up (1870); Kingdon St; open 9.30am–2.30pm Wed and 2.30pm–4.30pm Sun.

WHAT'S ON *Horse Festival:* May. *Warbirds Over Scone:* air show; odd-numbered years, Oct. *Rodeo:* Nov.

NEARBY Moonan Flat This small town sits at the base of the Barrington Tops. It has a beautiful suspension bridge, a small post office and the Victoria Hotel (1856). The hotel was a Cobb & Co coach stop during the gold-rush era and was reputedly patronised by bushranger

Captain Thunderbolt. It is small but friendly, and has accommodation and an adjoining restaurant. The town hosts Jazz by the River each Oct. 50 km NE.
For Barrington Tops National Park, see Gloucester.
Lake Glenbawn: watersports, bass fishing, lakeside horserides (in summer), picnic, barbecue and camping facilities and a rural life museum; 15 km E. *Burning Mountain:* fascinating deep coal seam that has been smouldering for at least 5000 years; 20 km N. *Wineries:* several in the area offering cellar-door tastings; brochure from visitor centre. *Tours:* thoroughbred stud and sheep station; bookings at visitor centre. *Trail-rides:* throughout area; bookings at visitor centre.
ⓘ Cnr Susan and Kelly sts; (02) 6545 1526; www.horsecapital.com.au

Shellharbour   Pop. 3335

Map ref. 501 H8, 509 K10

Shellharbour was a thriving port in the 1830s when development could not keep up with demand. The first shops did not appear until the 1850s and the courthouse and gaol were erected in 1877. Prior to this the local constable had to tie felons to a tree. Today it is an attractive holiday resort close to Lake Illawarra and one of the oldest settlements on the South Coast.

IN TOWN Illawarra Light Railway Museum The museum offers tram rides, displays of steam trains and vintage carriages and a miniature railway in a bushland setting. The ticket office and kiosk are in an original 1890s rail terminus and the volunteer staff are knowledgeable. Russell St. Open Tues, Thurs and Sat. Steam-train rides 2nd Sun each month and Sun during public holiday weekends.

WHAT'S ON *Festival of the Forest:* Sept.

NEARBY Lake Illawarra This large tidal estuary was once a valuable source of food for the Wadi Wadi people. It is home to waterbirds such as black swans, pelicans and royal spoonbills and has plenty of pleasant picnic and barbecue areas. The lake is excellent for boating, swimming, waterskiing, windsurfing, fishing and prawning. 7 km N.
Blackbutt Forest Reserve: remnant of coastal plain forest in urban area. Walking trails offer views of Lake Illawarra and Illawarra Escarpment; 2 km W. *Killalea Recreation Park:* foreshore picnic area with an ideal beach for surfing, diving, snorkelling and fishing; 3 km s. *Bass Point Aquatic and Marine Reserve:* top spot for scuba diving, snorkelling, fishing and surfing, with a nice picnic area on the shore; 5 km SE.
ⓘ Lamerton House, Lamerton Cres; (02) 4221 6169; www.tourismshell harbour.com.au

Singleton   Pop. 12 495

Map ref. 509 L3

Singleton is a pleasant and sleepy town set next to the Hunter River among beautiful pasturelands, mountains and national parks. It is the geographical heart of the Hunter Valley and is known for its excellent wines, with several famous vineyards in the region.

IN TOWN Singleton Mercy Convent The Sisters of Mercy arrived from Ireland in 1875 and set up this convent. Set in manicured gardens is the prominent convent, a chapel with an impressive marble altar, and the Sisters of Mercy Museum in an old Georgian cottage. Tours are conducted by the sisters at 2pm on weekends. Queen St.
James Cook Park: riverside park with picnic facilities and the largest monolithic sundial in the Southern Hemisphere; Ryan Ave. *Singleton Historical Museum:* memorabilia in Singleton's first courthouse and gaol dating back to the town's pioneer days; Burdekin Park, New England Hwy. *Town walk:* includes a historic Anglican church and lush parklands; brochure from visitor centre.
WHAT'S ON *Market:* Burdekin Park, New England Hwy; 4th Sun each month. *Festival of Wine and Roses:* Oct.

NEARBY Yengo National Park Mt Yengo is of cultural significance to local Aboriginal communities and there are extensive carvings and paintings in the area. The park is a rugged area of steep gorges and rocky ridges with several walking tracks and lookouts. Old Great North Rd, along the south-east boundary, is an intact example of early 19th-century convict roadbuilding. There are picnic and barbecue areas and campsites throughout the park. 15 km s.
Royal Australian Military Corps Museum: traces history of the infantry corps in Australia; 5 km s. *Wollemi National Park:* Singleton section features picturesque walking trails, lookouts and campsites; 15 km sw. *For further details on the park see Lithgow. Hillside Orange Orchard:* pick your own oranges; Windsor–Putty Rd; 25 km sw. *Lake St Clair:* extensive recreational and waterway facilities and you can camp onshore. Nearby lookouts offer magnificent views of Mount Royal Range. 25 km n. *Broke:* tiny township with breathtaking national park views and Village Fair in Sept; 26 km s. *Mount Royal National Park:* rainforest area with scenic walking tracks and lookouts with spectacular 360-degree views from Mt Royal over the entire region; 32 km n. *Local Hunter Valley wineries:* wineries with cellar-door tastings including Wyndham Estate and Cockfighters Ghost; tours available; brochure from visitor centre.
ⓘ 33 George St; (02) 6571 5888 or 1800 449 888; www.singleton.nsw.gov.au

Stroud   Pop. 669

Map ref. 509 N3

This delightful town is nestled in the green Karuah Valley and seems to be from another era. The absence of tourist facilities combined with the plethora of historic buildings gives Stroud an unaffected charm. The annual International Brick and Rolling Pin Throwing Competition sees residents competing against towns called Stroud in the United States, England and Canada.

IN TOWN St John's Anglican Church This convict-built church was made with bricks of local clay in 1833 and features beautiful stained-glass windows and original cedar furnishings. Apart from its lovely humble structure, this church is noted as the place where bushranger Captain Thunderbolt married Mary Ann Bugg. Cowper St.
Underground silo: one of 8 brick-lined silos built in 1841 for grain storage, it can be inspected by descending a steel ladder; Silo Hill Reserve, off Broadway St. *Self-guide town walk:* covers 32 historic sites including Orchard Cottage (1830s) and St Columbanus Catholic Church (1857), which is still in original condition; brochure from visitor centre.
WHAT'S ON *International Brick and Rolling Pin Throwing Competition:* July. *Rodeo:* Sept/Oct.

NEARBY Dungog In 1838 this town, nestled in the Williams River valley, was established as a military outpost to prevent bushranging by local villains such as Captain Thunderbolt. North of Dungog is Chichester Dam, with its blue-gum surrounds, and east of the dam is Chichester State Forest. In the foothills of the Barringtons, the forest has camping, picnic spots, lookouts and walking trails. 22 km w.
ⓘ Stroud Newsagency, Cowper St; (02) 4994 5117; www.greatlakes.org.au

Tamworth   Pop. 32 440

Map ref. 515 J11

Tamworth is a prosperous city and the self-proclaimed country music capital of Australia – an image that has been carefully cultivated since the late 1960s. There is no question that Tamworth has increased country music's credibility and acceptance in Australia with local events helping to launch the international careers of several stars. Thousands of fans flock to the Tamworth Country Music Festival every year.

IN TOWN Walk a Country Mile Interpretive Centre From the air this building is guitar-shaped, and it features various interactive displays including one that cleverly documents the history of country music through lyrics. This is also Tamworth's visitor centre, and the first port of call for information on the festival. Peel St.
Hands of Fame Park: Country Music Hands of Fame cornerstone features handprints of over 200 country music stars; cnr New England Hwy and Kable Ave. *Australian Country Music Foundation:* features the Legends of Australian Country Music exhibition, a display on the Country Music Awards and a theatrette playing films and documentaries; Brisbane St. *Calala Cottage:* National Trust-classified home of Tamworth's first mayor with antique household items and original shepherd's slab hut; Denson St. *Tamworth City Gallery:* houses over 700 works including some by Hans Heysen and Will Ashton, and the National Fibre Collection; Marius St; open 9am–12pm Mon–Fri and 1pm–4pm Sat. *Powerhouse Motorcycle Museum:* collection of immaculate motorbikes from the 1950s through to the 1980s; Armidale Rd. *Oxley Park Wildlife Sanctuary:* parkland for kangaroos and other marsupials, with picnic and barbecue facilities; off Brisbane St. *Oxley Lookout:* views of the city and beautiful Peel Valley. It is also the starting point for the Kamilaroi walking track (6.2 km). Brochure from visitor centre; top of White St. *Power Station Museum:* traces Tamworth's history as the first city in the Southern Hemisphere to have electric street lighting (installed in 1888); cnr Peel and Darling sts. *Joe Maguire's Pub:* features Noses of Fame, nose imprints of country music stars; Peel St. *Anzac Park:* attractive picnic and barbecue spot with playground; bordered by Brisbane, Napier, Fitzroy and Upper sts. *Bicentennial Park:* fountains, granite sculptures and period lighting; Kable Ave. *Regional Botanic Gardens:* 28 ha of native flora and exotic displays; top of Piper St. *Line dancing:* various regular venues; lessons offered; brochure at visitor centre. *Historical town walks:* two available of 90 min each, visiting churches, theatres and hotels; brochure from visitor centre. *Art and craft:* several shops and galleries; brochure at visitor centre.
WHAT'S ON *Country Music Jamboree:* Tamworth RSL; Thurs 8pm. *Stamp and Coin Market:* St Paul's Church; 1st Sat each month. *Market:* Showground Pavilion; 2nd Sun each month. *Main St Market:* Peel St Blvd; 3rd Sun each month. *Tamworth Country Music Festival:* Jan. *National Pro Rodeo:* Jan. *Gold Cup Race Meeting:* horserace; April. *Hats Off to Country Festival:* June. *National Cutting Horse Association Futurity:* competition and entertainment; June.

NEARBY Big Golden Guitar Tourist Centre The 12 m golden guitar, a replica of the country music awards, is instantly recognisable as an Australian icon. Inside the complex is the Gallery of Stars Wax Museum, which features wax models of Australian country music legends alongside current stars. Opposite is the outdoor Country Music Roll of Renown; to have your name inscribed in a plaque here is said to be Australia's highest honour in country music. There are special tributes to, among others, Tex Morton, Smoky Dawson and Slim Dusty. 6 km s.

Oxley anchor: the original anchor from John Oxley's ship marks the point where he crossed the Peel River on his expedition to the coast; 9 km NW.

ⓘ 561 Peel St; (02) 6755 4300; www.visittamworth.com.au

Taree   Pop. 16 621

Map ref. 509 O1, 515 N13, 516 C13

Taree is a big modern town on the Manning River and the commercial hub of the Manning River district. The area is well known for its handicrafts and its beautiful parklands and nature reserves.

IN TOWN Fotheringham Park These pleasant green parklands make an ideal riverside picnic spot where visitors and locals relax and watch the boats go by. To mark the bicentenary in 1988, an unusual herb and sculpture garden was established – the herbs are available to locals for cooking. There are also several memorials throughout the park. Between Pacific Hwy and Manning River.

Taree Craft Centre: huge craft centre featuring local work and picnic facilities; Old Pacific Hwy, Taree North. *Manning Regional Art Gallery:* changing exhibitions always include some local works; Macquarie St. *Organic Edible Landscapes:* nursery with over 100 species of native and edible plants. There are chickens, ducks, pigeons and quails on-site, as well as rabbits 'mowing' the lawn. Denva Rd. *Houseboat and dinghy hire:* long-term or daily hire on the Manning River; Crescent Ave. *Self-guide historical walks:* through eastern and western sections of town, focusing on its rich agricultural history; brochure from visitor centre.

WHAT'S ON *Weekly markets:* at various venues in the region; contact visitor centre for details. *Craftathon:* Jan. *Powerboat racing:* Easter. *Non-conventional Homes Eco Tour and Envirofair:* June.

NEARBY Coorabakh National Park The park features the volcanic plug outcrops of Big Nellie, Flat Nellie and Little Nellie. A 40 min hike (for fit walkers only, and not to be attempted in wet or windy weather) leads to the top of Big Nellie and views of Camboyne Plateau, Hannam Vale and Lansdowne Valley. The Lansdowne escarpment is made up of sandstone cliffs and also has spectacular views. From Newbys Lookout you might see sea-eagles and wedge-tailed eagles. 20 km NE.

Joy-flights: flights over the Manning Valley depart from the airport on the northern outskirts of town; Lansdowne Rd. *Deep Water Shark Gallery:* Aboriginal art and craft; Peverill St; 8 km sw. *The Big Oyster:* bizarre and run-down celebration of the Manning River oyster-farming industry. Worth a look for the views from inside the 'shell' and for the kitsch factor. 14 km s. *The Big Buzz Funpark:* toboggan run, water slides and mountain-boarding; Lakes Way; 15 km s. *Beaches:* excellent surfing conditions; 16 km E. *Hallidays Point:* features a rainforest nature walk; brochure from visitor centre; 25 km SE. *High Adventure Air Park:* light airsports centre; 38 km NE. *Manning River:* 150 km of navigable waterway with beaches, good fishing and holiday spots. *Art and craft galleries:* several in the area; brochure from visitor centre. *Manning Valley tours:* 4WD, mountain-bike, horseriding and self-drive; brochures and bookings at visitor centre. *Nature reserves:* 11 in the area with abundant wildlife in rainforest settings; map from visitor centre.

ⓘ Manning Valley Visitor Information Centre, 21 Manning River Dr, Taree North; (02) 6552 1900 or 1800 801 522; www.manningvalley.info

Tathra   Pop. 1646

Map ref. 502 G8, 507 G10, 537 R6

Tathra is an idyllic family holiday location with a 3-kilometre surf beach, frequented by dolphins, that is safe for swimming and excellent for fishing. There is a scenic national park to the north and south and the South Pacific Ocean to the east. The town started as a small jetty that served as a shipping outlet for a group of local farmers. It is now the only sea wharf on the east coast. The region is abundant with prawns from November to May.

IN TOWN Sea wharf Deterioration of the 1860s wharf led to a demolition order in 1973. Only strenuous local action and the intervention of the National Trust saved the wharf. It has always been a popular fishing platform and there is also a seafood cafe. Above the wharf is the Maritime Museum, which traces the history of the wharf and steam shipping in the area and has replicas of early vessels. Fur seals and little penguins can often be seen.

Tathra Beach: 3 km patrolled beach with excellent surfing conditions. *Fishing spots:* several good spots for salmon and tailor; map at visitor centre.

WHAT'S ON *Amateur Fishing Comp:* Oct.

NEARBY Mimosa Rocks National Park This beautifully rugged coastal park features surf beaches, caves, offshore rock stacks, lagoons, patches of rainforest and incredible volcanic sculptures. It is excellent for snorkelling, surfing, bushwalking, birdwatching and foreshore fossicking. The name of the park comes from the steamship *Mimosa*, which was wrecked on volcanic rock in 1863. 17 km N.

Kianinny Bay: known fossil site with steep cliffs and rugged rocks, and diving and deep-sea fishing charters available. The 9 km Kangarutha track follows the coast with spectacular scenery. 1 km s. *Mogareeka Inlet:* safe swimming ideal for small children; northern end of Tathra Beach; 2 km N. *Bournda National Park:* picturesque conservation area for great camping and bushwalking. Wallagoot Lake has a wetland area with birdwatching, fishing, prawning, swimming, watersports and boat hire. 11 km s.

ⓘ Tathra Wharf; (02) 6494 4062 or 1800 633 012; www.sapphirecoast.com.au

Temora   Pop. 4144

Map ref. 507 A2, 508 C10, 511 R8

In 1879 gold was discovered in the area and in 1880 the townsite was chosen. By 1881 the Temora district was producing half of the state's gold. Of course this could not be maintained, and the population of around 20 000 dwindled quickly. What is left now is a quiet rural Riverina town with several buildings remaining from the late 1800s. It is a harness-racing centre with numerous studs in the district.

IN TOWN Temora Rural Museum This award-winning museum has several impressive displays on rural life. There are fashions from the mid-1800s ranging from baby clothes to wedding dresses, and a replica flour mill and display explains the history of wheat since 3000 BC. Don Bradman's first home, a hardwood slab cottage, has been moved to the grounds from Cootamundra. There is also an impressive rock and mineral collection with an emphasis on the local gold industry. Wagga Rd. Open 2pm–5pm Mon–Sat and 1.30pm–5pm Sun and public holidays.

Skydive Centre: instruction and adventure jumps; weekends; Aerodrome Rd. *Aviation Museum:* displays of military aircraft in working order, including the only operational Gloster Meteor F8 in the world; Menzies St; open Wed–Sun. *Heritage walk and drives:* include Edwardian and Federation buildings around town; brochure from visitor centre.

WHAT'S ON *Quota Markets:* Pale Face Park; last Sat each month. *Golden Gift:* foot race; Feb. *Temora Rural Museum Exhibition Day:* Mar. *Antique Engine Field Day and Swap Meet:* Oct.

NEARBY *Lake Centenary:* boating, swimming and picnicking; 3 km N. *Paragon Goldmine:* working mine until 1996; 15 km N; open by appt through visitor centre. *Ariah Park:* town once known as Wowsers Bowsers, with beautiful historic streetscape lined with peppercorn trees; 35 km w.

ⓘ 294–296 Hoskins St; (02) 6977 1511; www.temora.nsw.gov.au

Tenterfield   Pop. 3175

Map ref. 515 M4, 607 N13

Tenterfield is a town of four seasons with many deciduous trees making it particularly spectacular in autumn. It is

Mimosa Rocks National Park, north of Tathra

perhaps best known from Peter Allen's song 'Tenterfield Saddler', which he wrote about his grandfather, George Woolnough. But Tenterfield is also the self-proclaimed 'birthplace of the nation', as it is where Sir Henry Parkes delivered his famous Federation speech in 1889.

IN TOWN **Sir Henry Parkes Museum** Sir Henry Parkes made his Federation speech in this building when it was the School of Arts. The National Trust-classified building built in 1876 stands today as a monument to Parkes. Memorabilia includes a life-size portrait by Julian Ashton and Parkes' scrimshaw walking stick made of whale ivory and baleen. Guided tours are conducted daily at 11am and 2pm. Cnr Manners and Rouse sts. *Centenary Cottage:* 1871 home with local history collection; Logan St; open Wed–Sun. *Railway Museum:* railway memorabilia in a beautifully restored station; Railway Ave. *Tenterfield Saddler:* handmade saddles at the place that inspired the Peter Allen song; High St. *Clear Creek Gallery:* features work by New England artists including renowned watercolourist Anni Washington; Rouse St; open Tue, Wed, Fri and Sat. *Self-guide historical town walk:* includes early residential buildings in Logan St, St Stephens Presbyterian (now Anglican) Church where Banjo Paterson married Alice Walker in 1903 and the grand National Trust-classified post office; brochure at visitor centre.

WHAT'S ON *Railway Market:* railway station; even-numbered months, 1st Sat. *German Beer Fest:* Mar. *Oracles of the Bush:* Australian culture and bush poetry festival; April. *Federation activities:* Oct.

NEARBY **Bald Rock National Park** There are excellent 360-degree views from the water-streaked summit of Bald Rock, the largest granite monolith in Australia. The park is full of impressve canyons and stone arches, and kangaroos abound. Guided tours are available daily to Bald Rock with information on the park's Aboriginal and European heritage. Bookings at visitor centre. 35 km N. *Mt McKenzie Granite Drive:* 30 km circuit from Molesworth St in town including Ghost Gully and Bluff Rock, an unusual granite outcrop; 10 km s. *Thunderbolt's Hideout:* reputed haunt of bushranger Captain Thunderbolt; 11 km NE. *Drake:* old goldmining town now popular for fossicking and fishing; 31 km NE. *Boonoo Boonoo National Park:* several attractive bushwalks include an easy 30 min stroll to the spectacular 210 m Boonoo Boonoo Falls. Pleasant swimming area above the falls. 32 km NE. *Wineries:* several in the area offering cellar-door tastings; tours available; brochure and bookings at visitor centre.
ⓘ 157 Rouse St; (02) 6736 1082; www.tenterfield.com

Terrigal
Pop. 9462

Map ref. 493 Q4, 496 H5, 509 M6

Terrigal is a scenic and peaceful coastal town well-known for its outstanding beaches, which are popular for surfing, swimming and surf-fishing. The Norfolk pines along the beachfront add to the relaxed feel and the boutique shops and restaurants add a sophisticated touch.

IN TOWN *Rotary Park:* pleasant for picnics and barbecues, backing onto Terrigal Lagoon, a good family swimming spot; Terrigal Dr.

WHAT'S ON *Artisans Market:* Rotary Park; 2nd Sat each month. *Terrigal Beach Food and Wine Festival:* July.

NEARBY **Bouddi National Park** This park ranges from secluded beaches beneath steep cliffs to lush pockets of rainforest, with several signposted bushwalks. Maitland Bay is at the heart of a 300 ha marine extension to protect marine life, one of the first in NSW, and contains the wreck of the PS *Maitland*. Fishing is allowed in all other areas. Putty Beach is safe for swimming and Maitland Bay is good for snorkelling. Tallow Beach not patrolled and is recommended for strong swimmers only. 17 km s. *The Skillion:* headland offering excellent coastal views; 3 km SE. *Erina:* pretty town with Fragrant Garden featuring a display garden, gift shop and cafe. The Central Coast Chilli Festival is held here in Mar. 4 km w. *Central Park Family Fun Centre:* water slide, fun cars and barbecues; 6 km N. *Ken Duncan Gallery:* largest privately owned photographic collection in Australia; 8 km NW. *Several excellent beaches:* Wamberal Beach, a safe family beach with rock pools (3 km N) and Avoca Beach (7.5 km s) and Shelly Beach (13 km N), both popular for surfing. *Sea-kayaking tours:* various routes available; bookings (02) 4342 2222.
ⓘ Rotary Park, Terrigal Dr; (02) 4385 4430 or 1300 130 708; www.cctourism.com.au

The Entrance
Pop. 2773

Map ref. 493 Q3, 496 H2, 509 M6

This immaculate seaside and lakeside town is named for the narrow channel that connects Tuggerah Lake to the Pacific Ocean. Given its proximity to Sydney and Newcastle, it has become a popular aquatic playground for residents of both cities.

IN TOWN *Memorial Park:* pelican-feeding with informative commentary at 3.30pm daily; Marine Pde. *The Waterfront:* town mall with 180 shops, pavement restaurants and children's playground.

WHAT'S ON *Craft market:* The Waterfront; Sat. *Art and craft market:* Bayview Ave; Sun. *Tuggerah Lakes Mardi Gras Festival:* Dec.

NEARBY **Wyrrabalong National Park** With sections lying north and south of town, this park conserves the last significant

Sturt National Park, near Tibooburra

coastal rainforest on the Central Coast. Signposted walking tracks lead along rocky cliffs and sandy beaches with lookouts and picnic spots along the way providing stunning coastal views. 5 km N and S.
Shell Museum: extensive shell collection; Dunleith Caravan Park; 1 km N. *Crabneck Point Lookout:* magnificent coastal views; 6 km S. *Nora Head Lighthouse:* attractive automated lighthouse built in 1903 after several ships were wrecked on the coast; 8 km N. *Toukley:* unspoiled coastal hamlet with breathtaking scenery. Holds markets each Sun in the shopping centre carpark and the Gathering of the Clans (Scottish festival) in Sept. 11 km N. *Munmorah State Recreation Area:* signposted bushwalking trails with magnificent coastal scenery; 21 km N. *Lakes:* 80 sq km lake system, on average less than 2 m deep and shark-free. The linked Tuggerah Lake, Budgewoi Lake and Lake Munmorah all empty into the ocean at The Entrance and are fabulous for fishing and prawning (in summer), as well as watersports.
ⓘ Memorial Park, Marine Pde; (02) 4334 4213 or 1300 130 708; www.cctourism.com.au

Thredbo   Pop. 2782

Map ref. 503 C13, 507 C10

Thredbo, a mountain village in Kosciuszko National Park (*see feature on p. 92*), was recently named the best major tourist attraction of the decade at the New South Wales Tourism Awards. It is unique in the region because it is truly a year-round resort with some of Australia's best skiing and winter sports in the colder months and angling, bushwalking and mountain-biking in summer. In winter the chalets and winding streets give Thredbo a genuine alpine-town ambience.

IN TOWN **Ski fields** Thredbo has 480 ha of skiable terrain and the longest ski runs in Australia (up to 5.9 km). Night skiing is a feature in July and Aug. There are slopes for beginners to advanced skiers and snowboarders with lessons and equipment hire available. The Outdoor Adventures School offers off-piste skiing, freeheeling, cross-country and snowshoeing lessons and excursions; bookings (02) 6459 4044.
Thredbo bobsled rides: 700 m luge-style track; adjacent to ski lifts. *Australian Institute of Sport Alpine Training Centre:* quality sporting facilities used by athletes for high-altitude training; northern end of the village. *Thredbo River:* excellent trout fishing. *Village walks:* include the Meadows Nature Walk through tea trees and the Thredbo Village Walk for diversity of alpine architecture; brochure from visitor centre. *Mountain-biking:* several tracks including the Village Bike Track; all bike and equipment hire available from Thredbo Service Station; bookings (02) 6457 6234. *Resort ponds:* several in the area with canoe hire available from the resort. *In-line skating:* several paths in and around town; skate hire and maps at resort.
WHAT'S ON *Blues Festival:* Jan. *Legends of Jazz:* May.
NEARBY *Pilot Lookout:* magnificent view dominated by The Pilot (1828 m) and The Cobberas (1883 m) in Vic. 10 km SE. *Skitube:* access to Perisher and Mt Blue Cow ski fields via this European-style train from Bullocks Flat. This winter-only service passes through Australia's largest train tunnel. 15 km NE. *Tom Groggin:* horseriding and accommodation at the historic station where Banjo Paterson met Irish brumby-hunter and horse-breaker Jack Riley, who was the inspiration for *The Man From Snowy River*; 24 km SW. *Mt Kosciuszko:* Australia's highest mountain,

with easy access in warmer months via chairlift from Thredbo and 13 km walk; guided walks also available, bookings 1800 020 589.
ⓘ Friday Dr; (02) 6459 4198; or Snowy Region Visitor Centre, Kosciuszko Rd, Jindabyne; (02) 6450 5600; www.thredbo.com.au

Tibooburra   Pop. 130

Map ref. 512 D3

Tibooburra is one of the hottest and most isolated town in New South Wales. Its name means 'heaps of rocks' in the local Aboriginal language and refers to the 450 million-year-old granite tors that surround the town. In a similar tale to the creation of the Blue Mountains' Three Sisters, three brothers were turned to stone after marrying women from another tribe, creating three large rocks (only one remains today). Gold was discovered in town in 1881 but a poor yield, outbreaks of typhoid and dysentery and a lack of water meant the sudden population explosion did not last.
IN TOWN *Courthouse Museum:* history of the region told with photographs, relics and documents in the restored 1887 courthouse; Briscoe St. *Tibooburra Aboriginal Land Council Keeping Place:* photographs and indigenous artefacts on display include a cockatoo-feather headdress; check opening times (08) 8091 3435; Briscoe St. *School of the Air:* most remote school in NSW servicing students of Tibooburra and the Cameron Corner region. Tours during school terms. Briscoe St. *Family Hotel:* the walls of the pub have been painted on by many artists including Russell Drysdale, Clifton Pugh and Rick Amor; Briscoe St.
WHAT'S ON *Tibooburra Festival:* July. *Gymkhana and Rodeo:* Oct.
NEARBY **Sturt National Park** This semi-desert park is noted for its wildlife, with wedge-tailed eagles, kangaroos and myriad reptiles. The landscape is diverse, ranging from wetlands and woodlands to white sand and the rolling red hills of the Strzelecki Desert. Temperatures range from well over 40°C in summer to below 0°C at night in winter. The Explorers Tree at the western end of the park marks the spot where Charles Sturt once buried food. There is an outdoor pastoralist museum and homestead accommodation at Mt Wood, the Golden Galley Mining Display, and the self-guide Granite Scenic Walk leading through sections of the park (details from visitor centre). Always check road conditions before travelling. The park lies north and east of town.
Milparinka This former gold town is now a virtual ghost town with the Albert Hotel (closed), a restored courthouse, and the remains of an old police station, bank, general store and post office. Recent efforts to rejuvenate the town include the Once a Jolly Swagman Festival each

Easter. 40 km s. Depot Glen Billabong, 14 km NW of Milparinka, is where Charles Sturt was marooned for 6 months in 1845 while on his search for an inland sea. One of the worst droughts in Australia's history kept the party there while waiting for rain to renew their diminishing water supply. The grave of James Poole, Sturt's second-in-command who died of scurvy, is 1 km further east under a grevillea tree. Poole's initials and the year of his death were carved into the tree and can still be seen. Poole's Cairn, commemorating the disastrous expedition, is located at Mt Poole, 7 km N of Depot Glen. *Cameron Corner:* where Qld, NSW and SA meet. The Wild Dog Fence, the longest fence in the world, runs through here from Jimbour in Qld to the Great Australian Bight. 133 km NW.
ℹ National Parks and Wildlife Service, Briscoe St; (08) 8091 3308; www.outbacknsw.org.au

Tocumwal   Pop. 1525

Map ref. 511 M12, 538 I2

This picturesque town ('Toc' to the locals) is on the northern bank of the Murray River. The region is a popular holiday destination thanks to its pleasant river beaches and laid-back lifestyle.
IN TOWN *Foreshore Park:* peaceful green park shaded by large gum trees, with a large fibreglass Murray cod. Foreshore markets are held 11 times during the year (dates from visitor centre). Deniliquin Rd. *Miniature World of Trains:* model train display; cnr Deniliquin Rd and Bridge St. *River cruises, walks, drives and bike tracks:* self-guide and guided tours of town and the river; brochures from visitor centre. *Art and craft shops:* several in town featuring local work; brochure from visitor centre.
WHAT'S ON *Tocumwal Classic:* fishing competition; Jan. *Pioneer Skills Day:* Mar. *Easter Eggs-travaganza:* Easter. *Country Craft Fiesta:* June. *Open Garden Weekend:* Oct.
NEARBY The Rocks and Blowhole This area is sacred to the Ulupna and Bangaragn people. The Rocks change colour according to weather conditions, and the Blowhole is a 25 m deep hole that legend says was home to a giant Murray cod that liked to eat young children who fell in to it. One young boy escaped the cod and was chased into the crevice, only to emerge in the Murray, suggesting that the blowhole and the river are linked. This has never been proved, but water has been known to flow from the Blowhole in times of drought. Adjacent to it is a working granite quarry. Rocks Rd; 8.5 km NE. *Tocumwal Aerodrome:* largest RAAF base in Australia during WW II, now home to international Sportavia Soaring Centre (glider joy-flights and learn-to-glide packages); 5 km NE. *Beaches:* around 25 attractive river beaches in the vicinity,

some with picnic areas; map from visitor centre. *Wineries:* 4 wineries in the area; brochure from visitor centre.
ℹ 41 Deniliquin St; (03) 5874 2131 or 1800 677 271; www.toconthemurray.com.au

Tumbarumba   Pop. 1499

Map ref. 507 B7

This former goldmining town in the foothills of the Snowy Mountains remains seemingly untouched by the modern world with old-style charm and well-preserved buildings. This has been helped by the fact that it has been bypassed by major road and rail routes. It experiences four distinct seasons and enjoys European-style vistas of snow-capped mountains, forested hills, rolling green pastures and a crystal-clear creek. Tumbarumba's name comes from the Wiradjuri language and is thought to mean 'sounding ground'. This relates to the suggestion that there are places in the region where the ground sounds hollow.
IN TOWN *Bicentennial Botanic Gardens:* mix of native and exotic trees, especially striking in autumn; Prince St. *Wool and Craft Centre:* local craft, fleece, homespun wool and spinning wheels. It is also home to the visitor centre and the Historical Society Museum, with a working model of a water-powered timber mill. Bridge St; open 10.30am–3.30pm Tues–Sun.
WHAT'S ON *New Year's Day Rodeo:* Jan. *Campdraft:* Jan. *Tumbafest:* food and wine festival; Feb. *Polocrosse Carnival:* May. *Christmas Street Carnival and Toy Run:* Dec.
NEARBY *Site of Old Union Jack Mining Area:* memorial to the students of the Union Jack school who died in WW I; 3 km N. *Henry Angel Trackhead:* starting point for a 12 km section of the Hume and Hovell Walking Track along Burra Creek. It includes waterfalls and the place where Hume and Hovell first saw the Snowy Mountains. The full walking trail is a 23-day, 440 km trek from Albury to Yass. For a kit (including maps), contact Department of Infrastructure, Planning and Natural Resources, Sydney (02) 9762 8044. Tooma Rd; 7 km SE. *Pioneer Women's Hut:* fascinating domestic and rural history museum focusing on the stories of women. The National Quilt Register, a record of quilts made by Australian women from the early 19th century to the mid-20th century, was an initiative of the women who run this museum. Wagga Rd, 8 km NW; open Wed, Sat and Sun. *Paddy's River Falls:* the waterfall cascades over a 60 m drop in a beautiful bush setting with a scenic walking track and picnic area. A concreted walkway is at the bottom and lookouts are at the top. 16 km S. *Tooma:* historic town with old hotel (c. 1880), tearooms and store; 34 km SE.

ℹ 10 Bridge St; (02) 6948 3444; www.tumbashire.nsw.gov.au

Tumut   Pop. 6195

Map ref. 507 C5, 508 D12

Tumut (pronounced 'Tyoomut') is an idyllic town located in a fertile green valley, surrounded by spectacular mountain scenery. The poplar and willow trees planted by early settlers help to make summer and autumn particularly striking. Prior to European settlement, Tumut was the seasonal meeting place for three Aboriginal tribes. Each summer the tribes would journey to the mountains to feast on Bogong moths.
IN TOWN *Old Butter Factory Tourist Complex:* local art and craft, and visitor centre; Snowy Mountains Hwy. *Millet Broom Factory:* 90 percent of the state's broom millet comes from the region and visitors can see the factory in action; Snowy Mountains Hwy; open Mon–Fri. *Tumut Art Society Gallery:* specialises in work by local artists; cnr Tumut Plains Rd and Snowy Mountains Hwy; open Tues and Sat. *Tumut Museum:* large collection of farm and domestic items and an excellent display of Miles Franklin memorabilia (the author was born in nearby Talbingo); cnr Capper and Merrivale sts; open 2pm–4pm Wed and Sat and school holidays. *River walk:* along Tumut River; from Elm Drive. *Historical and tree-identifying walks:* include Alex Stockwell Memorial Gardens with European trees and a WW I memorial; brochure from visitor centre.
WHAT'S ON *Festival of the Falling Leaf:* Autumn celebration; Apr/May.
NEARBY Blowering Reservoir This enormous dam is an excellent centre for watersports and fishing for rainbow trout, brown trout and perch. With the dam containing the largest trout hatchery in Australia almost everyone catches a fish. There is a spectacular lookout over the dam wall, and the Blowering Cliffs walk (19 km S) is a pleasant 5 km stroll in Kosciuszko National Park along stunning granite cliffs. 10 km S. *Air Escape:* powered hang-gliding; airport, off Snowy Mountains Hwy; 6 km E. *Tumut Valley Violets:* largest African violet farm in Australia with over 1000 varieties; Tumut Plains Rd; 7 km S. *Snowy Mountains Trout Farm:* NSW's largest trout farm with fresh trout sales; 10 km SE. *Talbingo Dam and Reservoir:* tall dam in steep, wooded country; 40 km S. *Power station tours:* Tumut 3 (45 km S) and Tumut 2 (115 km S); brochure from visitor centre. *Kosciuszko National Park:* massive alpine park to the south-east includes nearby Yarrangobilly Caves; *see feature on p. 92.*
ℹ Old Butter Factory Tourist Complex, Snowy Mountains Hwy; (02) 6947 7025; www.tumut.nsw.gov.au

NEW SOUTH WALES

Tweed Heads
Pop. 44 655

Map ref. 515 Q1, 600 I11, 607 Q11

Tweed Heads is the state's most northern town and – along with its twin town Coolangatta over the Queensland border – is a popular holiday destination at the southern end of the Gold Coast. The two towns developed independently, but as the Gold Coast expanded in the 1960s the border between them began to blur. The region is celebrated for its weather, surf beaches, night-life and laid-back atmosphere.

IN TOWN Point Danger This lookout is on the Qld/NSW border and overlooks Duranbah Beach, which is popular for surfing. It was named by Captain James Cook to warn of the dangerous coral reefs that lay under the waves off the coast. The world's first laser-beam lighthouse is located here. Dolphins may be seen off-coast along the pleasant cliff-edge walk. There are several picnic spots with stunning ocean views.
Tweed Maritime and Heritage Museum: 4 original Tweed Heads buildings house maritime, heritage and photographic collections; Pioneer Park, Kennedy Dr, Tweed Heads West. *Tweed Cruise Boats:* cruises visit locations along the Tweed River; River Tce. *Fishing and diving charters and houseboat hire:* guided and self-guide river excursions; bookings at visitor centre. *Spirit of the Bay Cruises:* whale- and dolphin-watching cruises in the waterways or open sea; bookings (07) 5527 6400.

WHAT'S ON *Craft market:* Florence St; Sun. *Jet Sprint Racing:* boat races; Jan. *Wintersun Carnival:* festival and parade; June. *Greenback Fishing Competition:* June. *Rainforest Week:* promoting ecosystem awareness; Sept.

NEARBY Minjungbal Aboriginal Cultural Centre The Aboriginal Heritage Unit of the Australian Museum is dedicated to self-determination and the importance of promoting, protecting and preserving Australian indigenous cultures. The unit runs this museum, which features displays on all aspects of Aboriginal life on the north coast. Tours include a dance demonstration and a bush tucker talk. There is also a walk encompassing a ceremonial bora ring and a mangrove and rainforest area. Located just over Boyds Bay Bridge.
Beaches: idyllic white sandy beaches for surfing and swimming, including Fingal (3 km s) and Kingscliff (14 km s). *Melaleuca Station:* re-created 1930s railway station in a tea tree plantation with train rides, a tea tree oil distillation plant and an animal nursery; 9 km s. *Tropical Fruit World:* home to the world's largest variety of tropical fruit with plantation safari, jungle riverboat cruise, fauna park and fruit tastings; 15 km s. *John Hogan Rainforest:* spectacular palm rainforest walks and picnic areas; 17 km sw.

ⓘ Tweed Shopping Centre; (07) 5536 4244 or 1800 674 414; www.tweed-coolangatta.com

Ulladulla
Pop. 9583

Map ref. 507 I6, 509 J13

This fishing town, built around a safe harbour, is surrounded by beautiful lakes, lagoons and white sandy beaches. It is a popular holiday resort and enjoys mild weather all year round. Visitors flock here each Easter Sunday for the Blessing of the Fleet ceremony.

IN TOWN Coomie Nulunga Cultural Trail This 30 min signposted walk along the headland was created by the local Aboriginal Land Council. Along the path are hand-painted and hand-carved information posts incorporating names of local plants and animals. Dawn and dusk are the best times to experience the wildlife along the walk, but visitors are advised to stay on the path for the good of the local fauna and for their own protection (from snakes). Starts Deering St opposite Lighthouse Oval carpark.
Funland: large indoor family fun park; Princes Hwy. *Warden Head:* lighthouse views and walking tracks. *South Pacific Heathland Reserve:* walks among native plants and birdlife; Dowling St. *Ulladulla Wildflower Reserve:* 12 ha with walking trails and over 100 plant types including waratah and Christmas bush; Warden St.

WHAT'S ON *Coastal Patrol Markets:* harbour wharf; 2nd Sun each month. *Blessing of the Fleet:* Easter. *Festival of Food and Wine by the Sea:* Aug.

NEARBY Pigeon House Mountain, Morton National Park The Ulladulla section of Morton National Park features this eye-catching mountain, which Captain James Cook thought looked like a square dovehouse with a dome on top, hence its name. The local Aboriginal people obviously had a different viewpoint and named it Didhol, meaning 'woman's breast'. The area is an Aboriginal women's Dreaming area. A 5 km return walk to the summit (for the reasonably fit) provides breathtaking 360-degree views taking in the Pacific Ocean, Budawang Mountains and Clyde River Valley. 25 km nw. *For other sections of the park see Bundanoon, Nowra and Robertson. Mollymook:* excellent surfing and beach fishing; 2 km n. *Narrawallee Beach:* popular surf beach with nearby Narrawallee Inlet featuring calm shallow water ideal for children; 4 km n. *Lakes:* good swimming, fishing and waterskiing at Burrill Lake (5 km sw) and Lake Conjola (23 km nw). *Milton:* historic town with art galleries and outdoor cafes. Village markets are held on the hwy 1st Sat each month, the Scarecrow Festival in April and the Settlers Fair in Oct. 7 km nw. *Pointer Gap Lookout:* beautiful coastal views; 20 km nw. *Sussex Inlet:* coastal hamlet with fishing carnival in May; 47 km n.

ⓘ Civic Centre, Princes Hwy; (02) 4455 1269 or 1300 662 808; www.shoalhaven.nsw.gov.au

Uralla
Pop. 2304

Map ref. 515 L9

This charming New England town is famous for its connection with bushranger Captain Thunderbolt, who lived and died in the area. It is no coincidence that this was a rich goldmining district at the time. Uralla's name comes from the Anaiwan word for 'ceremonial place'. As with other New England towns, Uralla is at its most striking when the European deciduous trees change colour in autumn.

IN TOWN McCrossin's Mill This restored 3-storey granite and brick flour mill (1870) is now a museum of local history. The ground floor and gardens are used for functions, but the upper levels have fascinating exhibitions including The Wool Industry, Gold Mining (featuring a replica Chinese joss house) and an Aboriginal diorama. The Thunderbolt exhibition includes a set of 9 paintings depicting the events leading up to his death. Salisbury St.
Hassett's Military Museum: large and impressive collection features displays on military history and memorabilia, including war vehicles, uniforms and a field kitchen. Many of the displays were donated by local families. Bridge St. *Thunderbolt statue:* of 'gentleman' bushranger Fred Ward. A complete dramatised version of his life can be heard by placing a dollar in the slot at the base of the statue. Bridge St. *Thunderbolt's grave:* he was hunted by police for over 6 years before being shot dead at nearby Kentucky Creek in 1870; Old Uralla Cemetery, John St. *New England Brass and Iron Lace Foundry:* beginning in 1872, it is the oldest of its kind still operating in Australia. Visitors are welcome and tours available. East St. *Self-guide heritage walk:* easy 2 km walk that includes 30 historic buildings, most built in the late 1800s; brochure from visitor centre.

WHAT'S ON *Youthfest:* Easter. *Thunderbolt Country Fair:* Nov.

NEARBY Mount Yarrowyck Nature Reserve This dry eucalypt environment is home to plentiful wildlife including kangaroos, wallaroos and wallabies, and is ideal for bushwalking and picnics. The highlight is the 3 km Aboriginal cultural walk – about halfway along the walk is a large overhang of granite boulders under which is a set of red-ochre paintings of circles and bird tracks. 23 km nw. *Dangars Lagoon:* bird sanctuary and hide; 5 km se. *Gold fossicking:* gold and small precious stones can still be found; map from visitor centre; 5 km sw. *Thunderbolt's Rock:* used by the bushranger as a lookout. Climb with care. 6 km s. *Tourist Drive 19:* signposted drive includes

Murrumbidgee River scenery near Wagga Wagga

historic Gostwyck Church (11 km se) and Dangars Falls and Gorge (40 km s); brochure from visitor centre.
ⓘ 104 Bridge St; (02) 6778 4496

Urunga   Pop. 2699
Map ref. 515 P9

Urunga is a sleepy but attractive town at the junction of the Bellinger and Kalang rivers and is regarded by locals as one of the best fishing spots on the north coast. Because it is bypassed by the Pacific Highway, the town has remained relatively untouched by tourism. A large percentage of the population are retirees drawn by a combination of natural beauty and serenity. There are some beautiful walks around the foreshore.
IN TOWN *Oceanview Hotel:* refurbished hotel with original furniture. Meals and accommodation are available. Morgo St. *Urunga Museum:* in historic building with photographs, documents and paintings from the local area; Morgo St. *Anchor's Wharf:* riverside restaurant and boat hire. *The Honey Place:* huge concrete replica of an old-style straw beehive with glass beehive display, honey-tasting, gallery and gardens; Pacific Hwy. *Watersports and fishing:* both on the rivers and beach; brochures at visitor centre.
NEARBY Bongil Bongil National Park
This stunning park is 10 km of unspoilt coastal beaches, pristine estuaries, wetlands, rainforest and magnificent views. The estuaries are perfect for canoeing and birdwatching, with abundant protected birdlife. The beaches provide outstanding fishing, surfing and swimming, as well as important nesting areas for a variety of wading birds and terns. There are signposted bushwalks and scenic picnic spots. 15 km n.

Hungry Head: beautiful beach for surfing and swimming; 3 km s. *Raleigh:* charming town with Prince of Peace Anglican Church (1900), winery, horseriding and a go-kart complex. 4 km n.
ⓘ Pacific Hwy; (02) 6655 5711 or 1800 808 611; www.bellingen.com

Wagga Wagga   Pop. 44 272
Map ref. 508 B12, 511 R10

Wagga Wagga ('place of many crows' in the Wiradjuri language) is the largest inland city in New South Wales and is regarded as the capital of the Riverina. In 1864 Wagga Wagga received international attention when a man arrived claiming to be Roger Tichborne, a baronet who was believed drowned when his ship disappeared off South America. While Tichborne's mother believed him, the trustees of the estate were not so sure. What followed is believed to be the longest court case in England's history. The man was found to be Arthur Orton, a butcher, and sentenced to 14 years for perjury. Mark Twain found this story so fascinating that he insisted on visiting Wagga Wagga when he visited Australia in the 1890s.
IN TOWN Museum of the Riverina The museum is divided into two locations, one at the historic Council Chambers (Baylis St) and the other at the Botanic Gardens (Lord Baden Powell Dr). The chambers museum features a regular program of travelling exhibitions. Inquiries (02) 6926 9655. The museum at the Botanic Gardens focuses on the people, places and events that have given Wagga Wagga its distinctive character. It also incorporates the Sporting Hall of Fame, which features local stars such as former Australian cricket captain Mark Taylor.
Botanic Gardens: themed gardens,

mini-zoo, free-flight aviary, miniature railway; picnic and barbecue facilities; Willans Hill. *Wagga Wagga Regional Art Gallery:* offers an extensive and changing exhibition program and includes the National Art Glass Collection; inquiries (02) 6926 9660; cnr Baylis and Morrow sts; closed Mon. *Tavenders Gourmet Produce:* regional gourmet products; Fitzmaurice St. *Bikeways:* along Lake Albert, Wollundry Lagoon, Flowerdale Lagoon and the Murrumbidgee River.
WHAT'S ON *Farmers market:* Wollundry Lagoon; 2nd Sat each month. *Australian Veterans Games:* even-numbered years, Mar. *Golden Cup Racing Carnival:* May. *Jazz Festival:* Sept.
NEARBY Junee This important railhead and commercial centre is located on Olympic Way. It has several historic buildings and museums. Monte Cristo Homestead is a restored colonial mansion with pleasant views of town and an impressive carriage collection. The Roundhouse Museum in Harold St contains an original workshop, locomotives, a model train and memorabilia. The visitor centre is located in Railway Sq in 19th-century railway refreshment rooms. 41 km ne.
Lake Albert: watersports, fishing, bushwalking and birdwatching; 7 km s. *Kapooka:* self-drive tours of the military base; brochure from visitor centre; 9 km sw. *RAAF Museum:* indoor and outdoor exhibits and barbecue facilities; 10 km e; open 10am–3pm. *The Rock:* small town noted for its unusual scenery. Walking trails through the reserve lead to the summit of The Rock. 32 km sw. *Aurora Clydesdale Stud and Pioneer Farm:* encounters with Clydesdales and other farm animals on a working farm; 33 km w; closed Thurs and Sun.

Timbertown's steam train, near Wauchope

Lockhart: historic town with National Trust-listed Green St for an impressive turn-of-the-century streetscape. Also several pleasant walking tracks in the area, and picnic races in Oct. 65 km w. *Wineries:* several in the area offering cellar-door tastings. Wagga Wagga Winery's tasting area and restaurant have an early-Australian theme. Brochure from visitor centre. *River cruises and walking tracks:* guided and self-guide tours of the city sights; brochures at visitor centre. ❶ Tarcutta St; (02) 6926 9621; www.tourismwaggawagga.com.au

Walcha   Pop. 1484
Map ref. 515 L10

Walcha (pronounced 'Wolka') is an attractive service town to the local farming regions on the eastern slopes of the Great Dividing Range. Modern sculptures are featured throughout the town and the beautiful Apsley Falls are a must-see for visitors.

IN TOWN Amaroo Museum and Cultural Centre This unique centre features Aboriginal art and craft with the artists working on-site. Visitors are invited to watch the artists at work. They use traditional designs combined with contemporary flair to make original clothing, homewares, gifts, jewellery and art. Also on display is a collection of local Aboriginal artefacts. Derby St. Open Mon–Fri.
Pioneer Cottage and Museum: includes a blacksmith's shop and the first Tiger Moth used for crop-dusting in Australia; Derby St. *Old School Gallery:* works by local artists and changing exhibitions; Fitzroy St. *Walking tour:* features sculptures, McKays Bakery (the lamington capital of the world) and historic buildings including the courthouse (1878) and the Anglican church (1862); brochure from visitor centre.

WHAT'S ON *Walcha Bushmans Carnival and Campdraft:* Jan. *Timber Expo:* even-numbered years, Sept . *Ride the Rim:* mountain-bike ride; Oct.

NEARBY Oxley Wild Rivers National Park This spectacular national park encompasses a high plateau, deep gorges and numerous waterfalls. The Walcha section of the park features Apsley Falls (20 km E) where 7 platforms and a bridge provide access to both sides of the gorge and waterfall. Tia Falls (35 km E) has beautiful rainforest scenery. Unique campsites at Riverside and Youdales Hut are accessible by 4WD.
Trout fishing: several good locations; brochure from visitor centre. ❶ 23e Fitzroy St; (02) 6777 1075; www.tourismnewengland.com

Walgett   Pop. 1817
Map ref. 514 C7

Walgett is the service centre to a large pastoral region. The name Walgett, which means 'the meeting of two waters', is apt, as the town is at the junction of the Barwon and Namoi rivers. The rivers provide excellent Murray cod and yellow-belly fishing. The area is rich in Aboriginal history, and archaeological digs in the shire have demonstrated that human life existed here up to 40 000 years ago.

IN TOWN *Norman 'Tracker' Walford Track:* signposted 1.5 km scenic walk includes the first European settler's grave on the banks of the Namoi River; from levee bank at end of Warrena St. *Hot artesian springs:* relaxing and therapeutic baths at swimming pool; Montekeila St; open in summer, key from visitor centre in winter.

WHAT'S ON *Campdraft and rodeo:* Aug.

NEARBY Come-by-Chance This town 'came by chance' to William Colless when all of the land in the area was thought to be allocated, but it was discovered that

some had been missed. Colless came to own most of the buildings, including the police station, post office, hotel, blacksmith shop and cemetery. It is now an attractive and quiet town with scenic riverside picnic spots, bushwalks and abundant wildlife. There are picnic races in Sept. 65 km SE.
Grawin, Glengarry and Sheepyard opal fields: go fossicking, but be warned that water is scarce so an adequate supply should be carried. Brochure from visitor centre; 70 km NW. *Narran Lake:* one of the largest inland lakes in Australia, it is a wildlife sanctuary without facilities for private visits. Flights over the lake can be arranged through the visitor centre. 96 km w.
❶ 88 Fox St; (02) 6828 6139; www.walgettshire.com

Warialda   Pop. 1201
Map ref. 514 I5

Warialda is a historic town in a rich farming district. Its situation on Warialda Creek gives the town a picturesque charm and contributes to its lush greenery. The origin of Warialda's name is uncertain but is thought to mean 'place of wild honey' and is presumed to be in the language of the original inhabitants, the Weraerai people.

IN TOWN *Carinda House:* historic home, now a craft shop featuring local work; Stephen St. *Pioneer Cemetery:* historic graves from as early as the 1850s in a bushland setting; Queen and Stephen sts. *Heritage Centre:* visitor centre and Well's Family Gem and Mineral collection; Hope St. *Koorilgur Nature Walk:* 3.6 km stroll through areas of wildflowers and birdlife; self-guide brochure from visitor centre. *Self-guide historical walk:* historic town buildings in Stephen and Hope sts; brochure from visitor centre.

WHAT'S ON *Flower Show:* Oct.

NEARBY Cranky Rock Nature Reserve It is rumoured that during the gold rush a 'cranky' Chinese man, after being challenged about a wrongdoing, jumped to his death from the highest of the balancing granite boulders. Today you'll find picnic spots, camping, fossicking, wildflowers and wildlife. A suspension bridge leads to an observation deck above Reedy Creek for breathtaking views. 8 km E.
❶ Heritage Centre, Hope St; (02) 6729 0046

Wauchope   Pop. 4759
Map ref. 515 O12, 516 E8

Wauchope (pronounced 'Waw-hope'), affectionately known as the 'heart of Hastings', is a centre for the local dairy and timber farms. Its popularity with visitors has vastly increased since the introduction of the fascinating Timbertown.

IN TOWN *Historical town walk:* self-guide walk past historic buildings such as the old courthouse and the bank; brochure from visitor centre.
WHAT'S ON *Lasiandra Festival:* community festival; Mar. *Demolition Derby:* April. *Rusty Iron Rally:* restored farm engines, tractors and machinery; April. *Timbertown Empire Day Celebrations:* May.
NEARBY Timbertown This re-created 1880s sawmillers' village features a craft gallery and leather-goods outlet, a working bullock team, horse-drawn wagons, a smithy and wood-turner, a restored steam train offering rides, and sleeper-cutting demonstrations. The authentic 1880s hotel offers damper and roast meats with accompanying Australian bush songs. The adjacent church houses the Historical Society Museum. 3 km w.
The Big Bull: dairy-farming display, hay rides and animal nursery. The 14 m bull offers panoramic views from the bullseye lookout. 2 km e. *Old Bottlebutt:* the largest known bloodwood tree in NSW; 6 km s. *Broken Bago Winery:* cellar-door tastings and sales; 8 km sw. *Billabong Koala and Nature Park:* 2.5 ha of lush parkland and waterways with animals and birds; 10 km e. *Bago Bluff National Park:* signposted bushwalks (various fitness levels) through rugged wilderness; 12 km w. *Werrikimbie National Park:* magnificent World Heritage-listed wilderness with rainforests, rivers and wildflowers (best viewed in spring). Also several excellent sites for camping and picnics. 80 km w.
ℹ High St; (02) 6586 4055

Wee Waa   Pop. 1815

Map ref. 514 F8

Wee Waa is a dynamic rural community near the Namoi River and also the base for the Namoi Cotton Cooperative, the largest grower-owned organisation in the country. Cotton has only been grown here since the 1960s, but the town has identified itself as the 'cotton capital of Australia'. Wee Waa's name comes from the local Aboriginal language and means 'fire for roasting'.
WHAT'S ON *Rodeo:* Aug.
NEARBY Guided cotton gin and farm tour First the tour visits a local cotton farm to view the picking and pressing of cotton into modules ready for transporting to the cotton gin. At the gin the cotton is transformed from modules into bales and then goes to the classing department for sorting. Bookings (02) 6795 4292. Runs April–Oct.
Cuttabri Wine Shanty The slab-construction shanty was built in 1882 and was once a Cobb & Co coach stop between Wee Waa and Pilliga. It was issued the second liquor licence in Australia and is the only wine shanty still operating in the country. 25 km sw.

Yarrie Lake: boating, swimming and birdwatching; 24 km s. *Cubbaroo Winery:* cellar-door tastings and sales; 48 km w. *Barren Junction:* hot artesian bore baths (over 100 years old) in a pleasant location surrounded by tamarind trees; 51 km w.
ℹ Newell Hwy, Narrabri; (02) 6799 6760 or 1800 659 931; www.weewaa.com

Wellington   Pop. 4672

Map ref. 508 F3

Set in the Wellington Valley at the foot of Mt Arthur, Wellington is a typical Australian country town with a wide main street, numerous monuments to significant local people and attractive parklands. It is best known for the nearby limestone Wellington Caves.
IN TOWN *Oxley Museum:* the history of Wellington is told with photographs and artefacts; in the old bank (1883); cnr Percy and Warne sts; open 1.30pm–4.30pm Mon–Fri. *Orana Aboriginal Corporation:* authentic Aboriginal ceramics, paintings, clothing and artefacts; Swift St. *Cameron Park:* known for its rose gardens and suspension bridge over the Bell River, it also has picnic and barbecue facilities; Nanima Cres. *Cumalonganavalook Train World:* model electric trains, train memorabilia and a restored Sydney tram; Macquarie St. *Self-guide town walk:* taking in historic buildings including hotels and churches; brochure from visitor centre.
WHAT'S ON *The Wellington Boot:* horseraces; Mar. *Vintage Fair:* Mar. *Festivale:* week of celebrations; Oct.
NEARBY Wellington Caves These fascinating limestone caves include Cathedral Cave, with a giant stalagmite, and Gaden Cave, with rare cave coral. There are guided tours through the old phosphate mine (wheelchair-accessible). Nearby is an aviary, an opal shop, Japanese gardens, picnic facilities and a kiosk. 9 km s.
Mount Arthur Reserve: walks to the lookout at the summit of Mt Binjang; maps from visitor centre; 3 km w. *Angora Rabbit Farm:* demonstrations of shearing angora rabbits and alpacas; 20 km sw. *Bakers Swamp Art Gallery:* paintings, pottery and crafts by local artists, including Bill O'Shea; 22 km s. A further 6 km s is the Eris Fleming Gallery with original oil paintings and watercolours by the artist. *Nangara Gallery:* Aboriginal art and craft with artefacts dating back over 20 000 years; 26 km sw. *Lake Burrendong State Park:* watersports, fishing, campsites and cabins, and spectacular lake views from the main wall. Burrendong Arboretum is a beautiful spot for birdwatching and features several pleasant walking tracks. Also excellent camping, picnic and barbecue sites at Mookerawa Waters Park. 32 km se. *Stuart Town:* small gold-rush town formerly known as Ironbark, made famous by Banjo Paterson's poem

The Man from Ironbark; 38 km se. *Wineries:* several in the area offering cellar-door tastings and sales. Glenfinlass Wines sell exclusively through cellar door; brochure from visitor centre.
ℹ Cameron Park, Nanima Cr; (02) 6845 1733 or 1800 621 614; www.wellington.nsw.gov.au

Wentworth   Pop. 1433

Map ref. 510 D6, 544 P2

At the junction of the Murray and Darling rivers, Wentworth was once a busy and important town. With the introduction of the railways it became quieter and is now an attractive and quiet holiday town with a rich history.
IN TOWN **Old Wentworth Gaol** The first Australian-designed gaol, Wentworth was designed by colonial architect James Barnett. The bricks were made on-site from local clay, and bluestone was transported from Victoria. Construcion took from 1879 to 1891. Closed as a gaol in 1927, the building is in remarkably good condition. Beverley St.
Pioneer World Museum: over 3000 historic artefacts including space junk, prehistoric animals and the country's largest collection of paddleboat photos; Beverley St. *Sturt's Tree:* tree on the riverbank marked by explorer Charles Sturt when he weighed anchor and identified the junction of the Murray and Darling rivers in 1830; Willow Bend Caravan Park, Darling St. *Fotherby Park:* PS *Ruby,* a historic paddlesteamer (1907), and statue of 'The Possum', a man who became a hermit during the depression and lived in trees for 50 years; Wentworth St. *Lock 10:* weir and park for picnics; south-west edge of town. *Historical town walk:* self-guide walk includes the town courthouse (1870s) and Customs House (one of two original customs houses still standing in Australia); brochure from visitor centre.
WHAT'S ON *Tri-state Polo Tournament:* Mar. *Henley on the Darling:* rowing regatta; Easter. *National Trust Festival Week:* April. *Country Music Festival:* Sept/Oct. *Wentworth Cup:* horserace; Nov.
NEARBY Perry Sandhills These magnificent dunes are estimated to have originated after an ice age 40 000 years ago. Skeletal remains of mega-fauna (kangaroos, wombats, emus and lions) have been found here. In WW II the area was used as a bombing range, but recently its bizarre and barren landscape has been used in film and television. The fantastic Music Under the Stars concerts are held here each Mar. Off Silver City Hwy; 5 km nw.
Yelta: former Aboriginal mission, now a Victorian town with model aircraft display; 12 km se. *Pooncarie:* 'outback oasis' with natural two-tier wharf, weir, museum and craft gallery; 117 km n. *Mungo National Park:* maps available;

157 km NE; *see feature on p. 55. Harry Nanya Aboriginal Cultural Tours:* brochure and bookings at visitor centre. *Heritage and nature driving tours:* various sites include Mildura and Lake Victoria; brochure from visitor centre. *Houseboat hire:* short- or long-term river holidays; brochure from visitor centre.
ⓘ 66 Darling St; (03) 5027 3624; www.wentworth.nsw.gov.au

West Wyalong   Pop. 3326

Map ref. 508 B8, 511 Q6

John Oxley was the first European explorer to visit West Wyalong. He disliked the region, claiming 'these desolate areas would never again be visited by civilised man'. He was proved wrong when squatters moved in, and the discovery of gold in 1893 meant the town became inundated with settlers eager to find their fortunes. West Wyalong is now in one of the state's most productive agricultural regions.
IN TOWN West Wyalong Local Aboriginal Land Council Arts and Crafts The craft shop features local Aboriginal work. Handcrafted items are on display and for sale and include boomerangs, didgeridoos, hand-woven baskets, clothing, and traditional beauty and skin-care products. The library features a collection of historic and contemporary titles relating to Aboriginal heritage, culture and modern issues. Main St. Open Mon–Fri and Sat morning.
Bland District Historical Museum: records of goldmining including a scale model of a goldmine and records from mines such as the Black Snake, the Blue Jacket and the Shamrock and Thistle; Main St.
NEARBY Lake Cowal When it is full, this is the largest natural lake in NSW and a bird and wildlife sanctuary. There are over 180 species of waterbird living in the area, with many rare or endangered. The lake is also excellent for fishing. No visitor facilities are provided, but this adds to the lake's untouched beauty. Via Clear Ridge; 48 km NE.
Barmedman: mineral-salt pool believed to help arthritis and rheumatism; 32 km SE.
Weethalle Whistlestop: Devonshire teas, art and craft; Hay Rd; 65 km W.
ⓘ 89–91 Main St; (02) 6972 3645

White Cliffs   Pop. 223

Map ref. 512 F8

White Cliffs is first and foremost an opal town. The first opal-field lease was granted in 1890. A boom followed with 4500 people flocking to the town. It is still known for its opals, particularly the unique opal 'pineapples' and the opalised remains of a plesiosaur, a two-metre-long 100 million-year-old fossil found in 1976. The intense heat has forced many people to build underground. The buildings left on the surface are surrounded by a pale and eerie

Mutawintji National Park, near White Cliffs

moonscape with an estimated 50 000 abandoned opal digs.
IN TOWN Solar Power Station The country's first solar power station was established by researchers from the Australian National University in 1981. White Cliffs was chosen because it receives the most solar radiation in NSW. The row of 14 giant mirrored dishes is a striking sight between the blue sky and the red ground. Next to council depot.
Outback Treasures: opal jewellery and Aboriginal art; Smith's Hill. *Jock's Place:* dugout home and museum with an opal seam along one wall; Turley's Hill. *Wellington's Underground Art Gallery:* paintings and polished opals by local artist; The Blocks. *Otto Photography:* gallery of photographs focusing on White Cliffs' stunning landscapes; Smith's Hill. *Self-guide and guided historical walks and fossicking:* include the old police station (1897) and school (1900) and several fossicking sites; brochures and maps from visitor centre. *Underground accommodation:* various standards available in dugout premises. Underground temperatures come as a relief at 22°C. Details at visitor centre. *Opal shops:* several in town sell local gems; details at visitor centre.
WHAT'S ON *Gymkhana and rodeo:* May.
NEARBY Mutawintji National Park Beautiful bushwalks lead through rugged terrain with colourful gorges, rock pools and creek beds. The park features magnificent scenery, and Aboriginal rock engravings and paintings tell stories of creation. The land was returned to its

traditional owners in 1998 and access to the site is on a 2 hr tour. Contact National Parks and Wildlife Service to check road conditions and book tour, (08) 8088 5933. 90 km SW.
Wilcannia: small and friendly town with many fine sandstone buildings, an opening bridge across the Darling River and a paddlesteamer wharf. Also a fascinating self-guide historical walk available; brochures from council offices in Reid St. 93 km S.
ⓘ Keraro Rd; (08) 8091 6611

Windsor   Pop. 1864

Map ref. 493 L6, 509 K7

Windsor, located on a high bank of the Hawkesbury River, is the third oldest European settlement on mainland Australia, after Sydney Cove and Parramatta. There are still many old buildings standing and this charming town is fascinating for history and architecture buffs. The surrounding national parks make breathtaking scenery.
IN TOWN Hawkesbury Museum Built as a home in the 1820s, the building became the Daniel O'Connell Inn in 1843. In the late 1800s it was used to print *The Australian*, a weekly newspaper. Today the historic building houses the history of the local area in photographs, documents and artefacts, with special displays on riverboat history and the Richmond Royal Australian Air Force base. Thompson Sq.

St Matthew's Church: the oldest Anglican church in the country, convict-built in 1817. The adjacent graveyard is even older. Moses St. *Self-guide tourist walk/drive:* historic sites include the original courthouse and doctor's house; brochure from visitor centre.
WHAT'S ON *Market:* Windsor Mall; Sun. *Bridge to Bridge Powerboat Classic:* May. *Fruits of the Hawkesbury Festival:* throughout region; Sept–Nov. *Bridge to Bridge Canoe Classic:* Oct. *Bridge to Bridge Waterski Classic:* Nov.
NEARBY Cattai National Park First Fleet assistant surgeon Thomas Arndell was granted this land and today the park features his 1821 cottage. There are also grain silos and the ruins of a windmill believed to be the oldest industrial building in the country. The old farm features attractive picnic and barbecue areas and campsites. In a separate section nearby, Mitchell Park offers walking tracks and canoeing on the scenic Cattai Creek. 14 km NE.
Ebenezer: picturesque town with Australia's oldest church (1809), Tizzana Winery, old cemetery and schoolhouse; 11 km N. *Rouse Hill Estate:* historic rural property (1813) with guided tours on Thurs and Sat; bookings at visitor centre; 15 km E. *Wollemi National Park:* Windsor section features the spectacular Colo River and activities including abseiling, canoeing and 4WD touring; via Colo; 26 km N.
ⓘ Tourism Hawkesbury, Bicentenary Park, Ham Common, Windsor–Richmond Rd, Clarendon; (02) 4588 5895; www.hawkesburyvalley.com

Wingham   Pop. 4659
Map ref. 509 O1, 515 N13, 516 B13

Heritage-listed Wingham is the oldest town in the Manning Valley. It has many Federation buildings surrounding the enchanting town common, which was based on a traditional English square. The wonderful Manning River and Wingham Brush bring nature to the centre of town.
IN TOWN Wingham Brush The unique brush, which begins near the centre of town, is part of the last 10 ha of subtropical flood-plain rainforest in NSW. It is home to orchids, ferns, giant Moreton Bay fig trees, endangered grey-headed flying foxes and 100 bird species. The brush has scenic picnic and barbecue facilities and a boat-launching area on the Manning River. Farquar St.
Manning Valley Historical Museum: housed in old general store (1880s) with displays on local farming, commercial and timber history; part of an attractive square bounded by Isabella, Bent, Farquar and Wynter sts. *Manning River:* picturesque waterway with several locations for swimming, boating, fishing and waterskiing. *Historical town walk:* tour of the town's Federation buildings; brochure from museum.

WHAT'S ON *Market:* Wynter St; 2nd Sat each month. *Summer rodeo:* Jan. *Manning Valley Beef Week:* May. *Show and rodeo:* Nov. *Killabakh Day in the Country:* country fair; Nov.
NEARBY Tourist Drive 8 This enjoyable drive begins in Wingham and passes through Comboyne and Bybarra before finishing in Wauchope. The highlight is the stunning Ellenborough Falls, 40 km N, one of the highest single-drop falls in NSW, with easy walking trails, lookouts and barbecue facilities. Brochure from visitor centre.
ⓘ Manning Valley Visitor Information Centre, 21 Manning St, Taree North; (02) 6592 5444 or 1800 801 522; www.manningvalley.info

Wisemans Ferry   Pop. 79
Map ref. 493 M3, 509 L6

Wisemans Ferry is a sleepy town built around what was once an important crossing on the Hawkesbury River. The mainland route from Sydney to Newcastle had always gone via this region, but when people started using the Castle Hill route, Solomon Wiseman, who had been granted a parcel of land and opened an inn, built a ferry to take people and cargo across the river. Today car ferries still cross at this point.
IN TOWN Wisemans Ferry Inn Before it was an inn, this was the home of Solomon Wiseman; he called it Cobham Hall. Wiseman later opened a section of the building as an inn and it is said to be haunted by his wife, whom he allegedly pushed down the front steps to her death. The inn provides food and accommodation. Old Northern Rd.
Cemetery: early settlers' graves include that of Peter Hibbs, who travelled with Captain Cook in 1770 and Captain Phillip in 1788; Settlers Rd.
NEARBY Dharug National Park The multi-coloured sandstone landscape provides striking scenery on this historic land. The convict-built Old Great North Road is a fantastic example of early 19th-century roadbuilding. Convicts quarried, dressed and shifted large sandstone blocks to build walls and bridges, but the road was abandoned before it was finished because of poor planning. Signposted walking tracks lead through beautiful bushland and to Aboriginal rock engravings. The clear-water tributaries are popular for swimming, fishing and canoeing. North side of the river.
Parr State Conservation Area: rugged land of gorges, cliffs and rocky outcrops. Discovery walks, talks and 4WD tours are conducted by the National Parks and Wildlife Service; bookings (02) 4739 2950; north-east side of the river (accessible by ferry). *Marramarra National Park:* wetlands and mangroves for canoeing, camping, picnicking, bushwalking (experienced bushwalkers), birdwatching; 28 km S.

ⓘ Tourism Hawkesbury, Bicentenary Park, Ham Common, Windsor–Richmond Rd, Clarendon; (02) 4588 5895; www.hawkesburyvalley.com

Wollongong   Pop. 227 522
Map ref. 500, 501 H6, 509 K10

As a major iron and steel producer, Wollongong has an undeserved reputation for being an unattractive industrial city. In fact, Wollongong enjoys some of the best coastal scenery and beaches in the state, superbly positioned with mountains to the west and ocean to the east. It has the facilities and sophistication missing in many smaller towns and has been awarded the title of 'Australia's most liveable regional city'.
IN TOWN Wollongong Botanic Gardens The gardens encompass 27 ha of undulating land and feature a sunken rose garden, a woodland garden, and flora representing a range of plant communities. Free guided walks are held at 2.30pm on the 1st Sun each month and the Discovery Centre runs programs, including craft workshops, during school holidays. The adjacent Glennifer Brae Manor House is a Gothic-style 1930s house now home to the Wollongong Conservatorium of Music and used for music recitals. Northfields Ave, Keiraville.
Illawarra Historical Society Museum: highlights include handicraft room and Victorian parlour; Market St; open weekends and 12pm–3pm Thurs. *Wollongong City Gallery:* collection of 19th- and 20th-century art including Aboriginal art; cnr Burelli and Kembla sts. *Mall:* soaring steel arches and water displays; Crown St. *Rhododendron Park:* rhododendrons and azaleas, with rare companion plants. A section of rainforest has walking trails. Parrish Ave, Mount Pleasant. *Flagstaff Point:* fish market and historic lighthouse (1872); Endeavour Dr. *Wollongong Harbour:* home to a huge fishing fleet, and Breakwater Lighthouse. *Surfing beaches and rock pools:* to the north and south, with excellent surfing and swimming conditions. *Foreshore parks:* several with superb coastal views and picnic facilities.
WHAT'S ON *Market:* Harbour St; Thurs and Sat. *Viva la Gong:* celebration of the city; Mar.
NEARBY Royal National Park Established in 1879, this is the second oldest national park in the world after Yellowstone in the USA. There is much natural diversity packed into a compact parkland. Highlights include walking and cycling along Lady Carrington Drive through rich forest, swimming at the beach or in the lagoon at Wattamolla, enjoying the Victorian-park atmosphere at Audley (with causeway, picnic lawns and rowboats) and walking the magnificent 26 km Coast Track. 35 km N.

NEW SOUTH WALES

Illawarra Escarpment: forms the western backdrop to the city and has spectacular lookouts at Stanwell Tops, Sublime Point, Mt Keira and Mt Kembla. *University of Wollongong Science Centre:* hands-on displays and activities for all ages; 2 km N. *Nan Tien Temple:* largest Buddhist temple in the Southern Hemisphere with a range of programs available; 5 km SW; closed Mon. *Lake Illawarra:* stretching from the South Pacific Ocean to the foothills of the Illawarra Range, the lake offers good prawning, fishing and sailing. Boat hire is available. 5 km S. *Port Kembla:* up-close view of local industry at Australia's Industry World with tours; bookings (02) 4275 7023. Also home to Harbourfest, with a street parade and fireworks, held each Nov. 10 km S. *Mount Kembla:* site of horrific 1902 mining disaster. Also here are several historic buildings and a historical museum featuring a pioneer kitchen, a blacksmith's shop and a reconstruction of the Mount Kembla disaster. The Mount Kembla Mining Heritage Festival is held each Aug in memory of those lost. 10 km W. *Bulli Pass Scenic Reserve:* steep scenic drive with stunning coastal views. Bulli Lookout at the top of the escarpment has great views and a walking path leads to Sublime Pt Lookout, which enjoys stunning views over Wollongong and has a restaurant. 16 km N. *Symbio Wildlife Gardens:* koalas, eagles, wombats and reptiles, as well as cow and goat milking; 32 km N. *Dharawal State Recreation Area:* swimming and canoeing in peaceful creeks and rock pools; 35 km N. *Lawrence Hargrave Memorial and Lookout:* on Bald Hill, this was the site of aviator Hargrave's first attempt at flight in the early 1900s. Now popular for hang-gliding. 36 km N. *Garawarra State Conservation Area:* undisturbed rainforest and spring wildflowers, with basic picnic facilities; 38 km N. *Heathcote National Park:* excellent for bushwalks through rugged bushland, past hidden pools and along gorges; 40 km N. *Guided walks and 4WD, canoe and kayak tours:* bookings at visitor centre.
ⓘ 93 Crown St;(02) 4227 5545 or 1800 240 737; www.tourism wollongong.com

Woolgoolga   Pop. 3788

Map ref. 515 P7

'Woopi' (as it is affectionately known to locals) is a charming and relaxed seaside town with a significant Sikh population. Punjabi migrants who were working on the Queensland canefields headed south for work on banana plantations, many settling in Woolgoolga. Today Indians make up between a quarter and a half of the town's population, providing a unique cultural mix. The beaches are popular for fishing, surfing and swimming.
IN TOWN *Guru Nanak Sikh Temple:* spectacular white temple with gold domes; River St. *Woolgoolga Art Gallery:* exhibits local works; Turon Pde.

WHAT'S ON *Market:* Beach St; 2nd Sat each month.
NEARBY **Yarrawarra Aboriginal Cultural Centre** The focus of the centre is to help Aboriginal and Islander people maintain their heritage while teaching others about it. Visitors are encouraged to browse through the rooms of locally produced art, craft, books and CDs. The Bush Tucker Cafe offers meals with an indigenous twist. Tours offered through the local area explore middens, ochre quarries and campsites while teaching about bush tucker and natural medicines. Stone and tool workshops are also offered. Red Rock Rd; 10 km N. *Yuraygir National Park:* Woolgoolga section is excellent for bushwalking, canoeing, fishing, surfing, swimming, picnicking and camping on unspoiled coastline; 10 km N. *Wedding Bells State Forest:* subtropical and eucalypt forest with walking trails to Sealy Lookout and Mt Caramba Lookout; 14 km NW.
ⓘ Cnr Pacific Hwy and McLean St, Coffs Harbour; (02) 6652 1522 or 1300 369 070; www.coffscoast.com.au

Woy Woy   Pop. 11 038

Map ref. 493 P4, 496 F8, 509 L6

Woy Woy is the largest of the numerous holiday villages clustered around Brisbane Water, a shallow but enormous inlet. Along with nearby Broken Bay, the Hawkesbury River and Pittwater, it draws visitors looking for aquatic holidays. The nearby national parks encompass breathtaking wilderness and lookouts.
IN TOWN *Woy Woy Hotel:* historic 1897 hotel offering meals and accommodation; The Boulevard. *Waterfront reserve:* picnic facilities with Brisbane Water view.
NEARBY **Brisbane Water National Park** A beautiful park of rugged sandstone with spring wildflowers, bushwalks and birdlife. Staples Lookout has superb coastal views. Warrah Lookout enjoys a sea of colour in spring when the wildflowers bloom. A highlight is the fascinating Bulgandry Aboriginal engravings on Woy Woy Rd. 3 km SW. *Ettalong Beach:* great swimming beach with markets each Sat and Sun (Mon on long weekends); 3 km S. *Milson Island:* recreation reserve once used as an asylum and then as a gaol. *HMAS Parramatta:* a WW I ship, it ran aground off the northern shore and the wreck is still there today; 5 km S. *Mt Ettalong Lookout:* stunning coastal views; 6 km S. *Pearl Beach:* chic holiday spot favoured by the rich and famous, with magnificent sunsets; 12 km S. *Boating, fishing and swimming:* excellent conditions on Brisbane Water, Broken Bay and Hawkesbury River.
ⓘ Shop 1, 18–22 The Boulevard; (02) 4385 4430 or 1300 130 708; www.cctourism.com.au

Wyong   Pop. 3172

Map ref. 493 P2, 496 F1, 509 M6

Wyong is an attractive holiday town surrounded by Tuggerah Lakes and the forests of Watagan, Olney and Ourimbah. After World War II it became a popular area for retirees and it retains that relaxed atmosphere today.
IN TOWN **District Museum** This museum features displays of local history, including early ferry services across the lakes and records of the logging era. It is situated in historic Alison Homestead, with picnic and barbecue facilities on 2 ha of rolling lawns. Cape Rd.
WHAT'S ON *Country Fair:* Racecourse Rd; 3rd Sun each month. *Wyong Shire Festival of the Arts:* Mar. *Cycle Classic:* Oct.
NEARBY **Olney State Forest** This native rainforest has several scenic walks. The Pines picnic area has an informative education shelter and Mandalong and Muirs lookouts have sensational views. 17 km NW.
Burbank Nursery: 20 ha of azaleas (flowering in Sept); 3 km S. *Fowlers Lookout:* spectacular forest views; 10 km SW. *Yarramalong Macadamia Nut Farm:* offers tours, talks and sales in beautiful Yarramalong Valley; 18 km W. *Frazer Park:* recreational park in natural bush setting; 28 km NE. *Bumble Hill Studio:* ceramics, glasswork and paintings; 30 km NW; open Fri–Sun.
ⓘ Rotary Park, Terrigal Dr, Terrigal; (02) 4385 4430 or 1300 130 708; www.cctourism.com.au

Yamba   Pop. 5622

Map ref. 515 Q5

This quiet holiday town at the mouth of the Clarence River offers excellent sea, lake and river fishing. It is the largest coastal resort in the Clarence Valley, with excellent facilities for visitors, but it manages to maintain a peaceful atmosphere. Fishing fleets from Yamba, Iluka and Maclean catch approximately 20 percent of the state's seafood, so this is a great spot for lovers of fresh seafood.
IN TOWN **Story House Museum** This quaint museum tells the story of the development of Yamba from the time it was merely a point of entry to the Clarence River. The collection of photographs and records tell a compelling tale of early development of a typical Australian coastal town. River St. *Clarence River Lighthouse:* coastal views from the base; via Pilot St. *Yamba Boatharbour Marina:* departure point for daily ferry service to Iluka, river cruises (Thurs and Sun), deep-sea fishing charters and whale-watching trips. Also houseboat hire. Off Yamba Rd. *Whiting Beach:* sandy river beach ideal for children. *Coastal beaches:* several in town with excellent swimming and surfing conditions; map from visitor centre.

WHAT'S ON *Market:* River St; 4th Sun each month. *Family Fishing Festival:* Oct.
NEARBY Maclean This quirky village is known as the 'Scottish town' because of the many Scots that settled the town. Some street signs are in Gaelic as well as English. Highlights in the town include Scottish Corner, Bicentennial Museum and a self-guide historical walk with a brochure available from the visitor centre. There is a market on the 2nd Sat each month and a Highland Gathering each Easter. A 24 hr ferry service crosses the river to Lawrence. 17 km w. *Lake Woolooweyah:* fishing and prawning; 4 km s. *Yuraygir National Park:* Yamba section offers sand ridges and banksia heath, and is excellent for swimming, fishing and bushwalking; 5 km s. *The Blue Pool:* deep freshwater pool 50 m from the ocean, popular for swimming; 5 km s. ⓘ Lower Clarence Visitor Centre, Ferry Park, Pacific Hwy, Maclean; (02) 6645 4121; www.tropicalnsw.com.au

Yass   Pop. 4886

Map ref. 507 D4, 508 F11

Yass is a rural town set in rolling countryside on the Yass River. Explorers Hume and Hovell passed through the area on their expedition to Port Phillip Bay. Hume returned in 1839. Yass is also the end of the Hume and Hovell Walking Track, which begins in Albury.
IN TOWN Cooma Cottage The National Trust has restored and now maintains this former home of explorer Hamilton Hume. He lived with his wife in the riverside house from 1839 until his death in 1873. It now operates as a museum with relics and documents telling of Hume's life and explorations. Yass Valley Way; open Thurs–Mon Aug–May. *Yass Cemetery:* contains the grave of explorer Hamilton Hume; via Rossi St. *Yass and District Museum:* historical displays including a war display encompassing the Boer War, WW I and WW II; Comur St. *Railway Museum:* history of the Yass tramway; Lead St; open Fri–Mon. *Self-guide town walk and drive:* highlight is the National Trust-listed main street; brochure from visitor centre.
WHAT'S ON *Market:* Railway Museum; 2nd Sat each month. *Picnic races:* Mar. *Rodeo:* Mar and Nov. *Yass River Festival:* Nov. *Yass Cup:* actually in Canberra; Dec.
NEARBY Wee Jasper This picturesque village, where Banjo Paterson owned a holiday home, is set in a pretty valley at the foot of the Brindabella Ranges. The Goodradigbee River is excellent for trout fishing. Carey's Caves are full of amazing limestone formations and were the site of the 1957 discovery of the spine of a large extinct wombat. 50 km sw. *Bookham:* village with historic cemetery, markets 2nd Sun each month and Sheep Show and Country Fair in Apr; 30 km w. *Binalong:* historic town with Motor

Royal National Park, north of Wollongong

Museum, Southern Cross Glass and the grave of bushranger Johnny Gilbert; 37 km nw. *Burrinjuck Waters State Park:* bushwalking, cruises, watersports and fishing. Burrinjuck Ski Classic is held each Nov (water level permitting). Off Hume Hwy; 54 km sw. *Brindabella National Park:* birdwatching, camping and bushwalking in alpine surrounds. 4WD access only; via Wee Jasper; 61 km sw. *Wineries:* in Murrumbateman area with cellar-door tastings, and the Days of Wine and Roses in Oct. Follow the signs on Barton Hwy; brochure from visitor centre. *Hume and Hovell Walking Track:* 23-day, 440 km trek from Albury to Yass. For a kit (including maps), contact Department of Infrastructure, Planning and Natural Resources, Sydney; (02) 9762 8044. ⓘ Coronation Park, Comur St; (02) 6226 2557; www.yass.nsw.gov.au

Young   Pop. 6821

Map ref. 507 C2, 508 D9

Young is an attractive town in the western foothills of the Great Dividing Range with a fascinating history of goldmining. The Lambing Flat goldfields were rushed after a discovery was announced in 1860. Within a year there were an estimated 20 000 miners in town, 2000 of whom were Chinese. A combination of lawlessness and racism boiled over in the Lambing Flat riots in 1861, which gave rise to the Chinese Immigration Restriction Act,

the first legislation of the infamous White Australia Policy. In contrast to its turbulent history, the town is today the peaceful centre of a cherry farming district.
IN TOWN Lambing Flat Folk Museum This museum is recognised as one of the finest in the country. Meticulously maintained photographs and relics tell the story of the town during the 1800s and 1900s. The full horrific story of the Lambing Flat riots is covered. Pieces on display include a 'roll-up' flag carried by miners during the riots. Campbell St. *Burrangong Art Gallery:* hosts changing exhibitions from guest and local artists; Olympic Hwy. *Blackguard Gully:* historic goldmining site featuring a reconstructed pug-mill, water racers, and remains of original diggings. Fossick for gold alongside the gully (hire equipment from museum). Boorowa Rd. *The Price of Peace Gardens and Cafe:* scenic garden overlooking town; Willawong St. *J. D.'s Jam Factory:* tours, tastings and Devonshire teas; Grenfell Rd.
WHAT'S ON *Hilltops Flavours of the Harvest Festival:* Feb. *National Cherry Festival:* Nov/Dec.
NEARBY *Chinaman's Dam Recreation Area:* scenic walks, playground, and picnic and barbecue facilities; 4 km se. *Yandilla Mustard Seed Oil farm and processing plant:* tours by appt; bookings (02) 6943 2516; 20 km s. *Murringo:* historic buildings, a glassblower and engraver; 21 km e. ⓘ 2 Short St; (02) 6382 3394 or 1800 628 233

AUSTRALIAN CAPITAL TERRITORY

CANBERRA

CANBERRA IS . . .

A dawn hot-air balloon flight
over the waking city

A picnic in the Australian
National Botanic Gardens

A bike ride around picturesque
Lake Burley Griffin

A bushwalk in the beautiful
Brindabella Range

A visit to Parliament House

Fine dining in one of Manuka's
many restaurants

A wander through the
National Gallery of Australia's
Sculpture Garden

Fun science activities at
Questacon – the National
Science and Technology
Centre

City views from the top
of Mt Ainslie

A trip to the National Museum
of Australia

Counting the country's dollars
at the Royal Australian Mint

Floriade in spring

Visitor information

Canberra Visitor Centre
333 Northbourne Ave, Dickson
(02) 6205 0044 or 1300 554 114
www.visitcanberra.com.au

Aerial view of Parliament House atop Capital Hill

Canberra really is the bush capital – kangaroo-dotted nature reserves are scattered throughout the city and the Brindabella mountain range bounds the south-western edge. As the national capital, Canberra claims some of the nation's most significant institutions, including a magnificent art gallery and one of the best war museums in the world. Grand public buildings and monuments complement the order and beauty of the city's original design, and the landmark flagpole of Parliament House can be seen from many parts of the city.

Many visitors are attracted by Canberra's national collections or the experience of federal politics, but Canberra has much more to offer. As well as superb parklands and thousands of hectares of natural bushland to explore, the capital boasts cool-climate wineries, top-class restaurants, attractions for children and a full calendar of cultural and sporting events. Its creation solved the debate between Sydney and Melbourne over which city should be Australia's capital, and Canberra became one of the few completely planned cities in the world.

Life in Canberra moves at a comfortable pace. The city offers all the cultural facilities and public institutions of larger cities without the traffic congestion and pollution. It is an easy city to get around and residents make the most of its many recreational opportunities. With the snow and the sea both only two hours away, the locals have the best of both worlds.

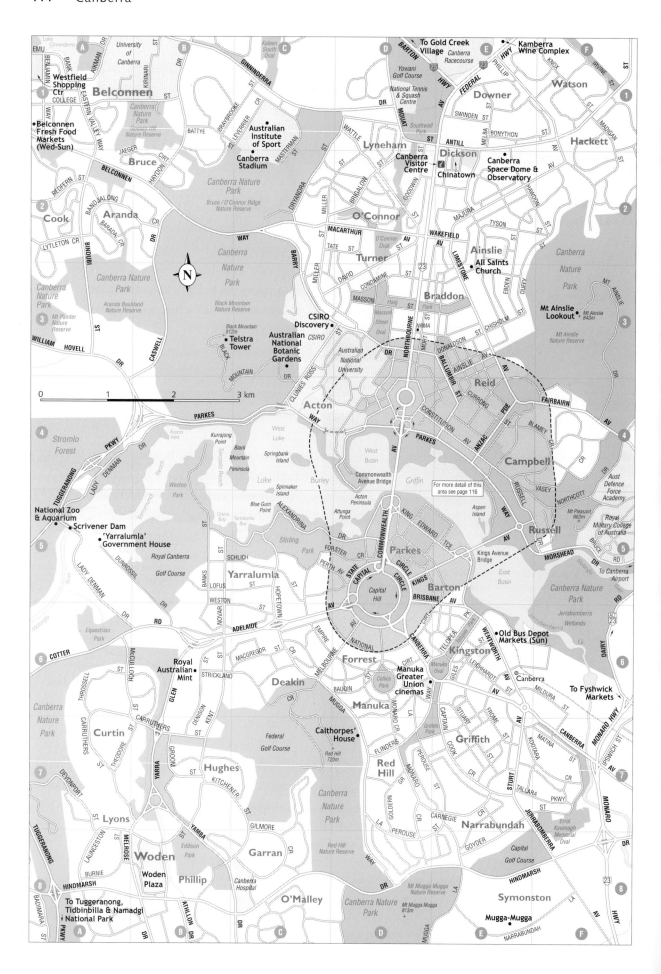

Central Canberra

The vision of Canberra's architect, Walter Burley Griffin, can be seen in the tree-lined avenues, spectacular lake views and spacious parks of central Canberra (*see A grand plan, p. 119*). The focal point is Parliament House, atop Capital Hill, situated at the apex of the Parliamentary Triangle. An integral part of Burley Griffin's plan was the vista from Capital Hill: one view leads straight to the Australian War Memorial, another to Canberra's CBD, known locally as 'Civic'.

PARLIAMENTARY TRIANGLE AND WAR MEMORIAL

The Parliamentary Triangle extends from Capital Hill to Lake Burley Griffin, bounded by Commonwealth and Kings avenues. This is where you'll find the country's national institutions and the home of the Australian democratic tradition. Across the lake and up the broad sweep of Anzac Parade is the Australian War Memorial.

National Capital Exhibition

The National Capital Exhibition tells the story of Canberra through interactive displays, rare photographs, a laser model of the city and varied audiovisual material. Learn about the area's indigenous inhabitants, European settlement and Walter Burley Griffin's design for the city. *Open daily; admission free.*

Parliament House

Designed by the American-based architects Mitchell/Giurgola & Thorp, Parliament House was officially opened by the Queen in 1988. It is home to both houses of Federal Parliament (the Senate and the House of Representatives). If your visit coincides with the sitting of parliament, you can see democracy in action from the public galleries (check parliament's website for sitting dates). Its permanent displays include an extensive collection of Australian art, the Great Hall Tapestry and one of only four surviving 1297 copies of the Magna Carta. Once inside, take the lift to the roof for magnificent views of the city. It is worth noting that the flag flying atop the 81-metre flagpole is roughly the size of the side of a double-decker bus. Guided tours of the complex are recommended; brochures also give visitors the option of self-guided tours. Those with a keen eye may spot the fossils in the main foyer's marble floor. Those who prefer outdoor attractions can walk through the 23 hectares of landscaped gardens. *Open daily; admission free; (02) 6277 5399 or www.aph.gov.au*

Old Parliament House

Old Parliament House was the 'temporary' home of Australia's Federal Parliament from 1927 to 1988. The heritage-listed building exhibits stories from Australia's political past, such as the decision to involve Australia in World War II. Make a grand entrance up the famous steps while enjoying the sweeping views across Lake Burley Griffin to the War Memorial. Free guided tours are available. Across the road is the **Aboriginal Tent Embassy**, established in 1972, and the **Old Parliament House Rose Gardens**. *King George Tce, Parkes; open daily; admission fee applies.*

National Portrait Gallery

Old Parliament House is also the main location for the National Portrait Gallery, which has a second gallery space just a few minutes away at **Commonwealth Place** (*see Waterside retreats, p. 121*). To get to the second gallery, head towards Lake Burley Griffin, pass **Reconciliation Place** (*see Monuments, p. 118*) and take the walkway to Commonwealth Place. The National Portrait Gallery has both a permanent display of Australian portraits in all media, and a variety of changing exhibitions. *Open daily; admission fee applies to Old Parliament House gallery.*

National Archives of Australia

The National Archives occupy what was Canberra's first GPO, opened in 1927. Enjoy a wander through the elegant building, designed by architect John Smith Murdoch. The National Archives collect valuable Commonwealth government records from the time of Federation to the present, including papers of prime ministers and governor-generals, cabinet documents and files from royal commissions. You will also find architectural plans, photographs, posters, and other records. On permanent display is Australia's 'birth certificate' – Queen Victoria's Royal Commission of Assent – and Australia's original Constitution. *Queen Victoria Tce; open daily; admission free.*

National Library of Australia

Collecting since 1901, this is the country's largest reference library. The present building contains over six million books as well as newspapers, periodicals, photographs, and other documents. *Parkes Pl, Parkes; open daily; admission free.*

Questacon – The National Science and Technology Centre

Making science fun and relevant for everyone, Questacon has many interactive exhibits – you can experience an earthquake and a cyclone, see lightning created and free-fall six metres on the vertical slide. *King Edward Tce, Parkes; open daily; admission fee applies.*

Getting around

Canberra is an easy city to get around if you have a car and a map. The road infrastructure is probably the best in Australia, with wide, well-planned roads, and visitors will find that they can cover long distances in a short time. Certainly in the central area of the city it is very easy to travel from one attraction to the next by car or public transport. Walking between the attractions in the Parliamentary Triangle is also very pleasant.

Buses are the only public transport available in Canberra, but these services can be variable at off-peak times. For a convenient way to get around the main attractions, catch one of the open-top double-decker City Sightseeing buses that depart from the Melbourne Building on Northbourne Avenue.

Canberra is a city full of cyclists and major roads have on-road cycling lanes, often marked with green where roads merge. Take care, as cyclists have right of way on the green lanes.

Public transport ACTION Buses 13 1710

Motoring organisation NRMA 13 1122, roadside assistance 13 1111

Car rental Avis 13 6333; Budget 13 2727; Capital Car Rentals (02) 6282 7272; Hertz 13 3039; Thrifty 1300 367 227; Rumbles (02) 6280 7444

Taxis Canberra Cabs 13 2227 or 13 1008

Bicycle hire Mr Spokes Bike Hire (02) 6257 1188

Climate

Canberra has a climate of extremes and seasons of beauty. Summer in the capital is hot and very dry, with temperatures sometimes reaching the mid 30s. Winter is cold and frosty, thanks to Canberra's altitude of roughly 600 metres, its inland location and its proximity to the Snowy Mountains. Don't let this stop you, though – Canberra winter days are breathtakingly crisp and usually fine, with cloudless, bright blue skies after the early morning fogs lift. Spring is Canberra at its most pleasant – the city is awash with colour and flowers abound – although some say that it is in autumn when Canberra is at its most beautiful.

	J	F	M	A	M	J	J	A	S	O	N	D
Max °C	28	27	24	20	15	12	11	12	16	19	23	26
Min °C	13	13	11	7	3	1	0	1	3	6	9	11
Rain (mm)	58	56	53	49	49	37	40	48	52	68	62	53
Raindays	8	7	7	8	9	9	10	11	10	11	10	8

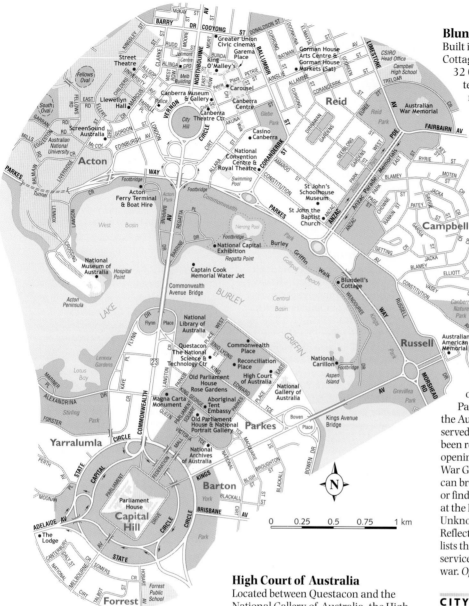

Top events

Summernats Car Festival *The ultimate car show, with street-machine exhibitions, burnout competitions and fireworks. January.*

National Multicultural Festival *A showcase of cultures in food, art and performance. February.*

Royal Canberra Show *Rural displays, fireworks and a grand parade. February.*

Canberra Balloon Fiesta *A ten-day festival with over 50 hot-air balloons launched daily from the lawns of Old Parliament House. March.*

Rally of Canberra *World-class car rally as part of the Asia Pacific Rally Championship. May.*

Floriade *A celebration of spring, flowers and fun. September–October.*

Days of Wine and Roses *Open weekend of the cool-climate vineyards, with music, food and much wine-tasting. November.*

High Court of Australia

Located between Questacon and the National Gallery of Australia, the High Court is notable for its glass-encased public gallery and timber courtrooms. Murals by artist Jan Senbergs reflect the history and functions of the court and the role of the states in Federation. Visitors can explore the building, talk to the knowledgeable attendants and view a short film on the court's work. *Parkes Pl, Parkes; open Mon–Fri; admission free.*

National Gallery of Australia

Established in 1911, the gallery has been housed across the road from the High Court since 1982. With over 100 000 works, the collection provides a brilliant overview of Australian art. The international collection is just as impressive and includes Jackson Pollock's *Blue Poles* and Australian-born Ron Mueck's *Pregnant Woman*. Enjoy a picnic lunch in the tranquil **Sculpture Garden**, which comprises a series of native gardens and contains over 50 sculptures set between the gallery and the lake. *Parkes Pl, Parkes; open daily; general admission free.*

Blundell's Cottage

Built in the 1860s, the historic Blundell's Cottage was part of the Campbell family's 32 000-acre estate and home to tenant farm workers. The cottage is now a museum that offers a close encounter with the region's early farming history. *Wendouree Dr, off Constitution Ave, Parkes; open daily; admission fee applies.*

St John the Baptist Church and St John's Schoolhouse Museum

Visit Canberra's oldest church and first schoolhouse, built in the 1840s. The buildings have been restored and now form an interesting museum. The adjoining cemetery has some of Canberra's oldest headstones. *Constitution Ave, Reid; open 10am–12pm Wed, 2pm–4pm Sat, Sun & public holidays; general admission free.*

Australian War Memorial

The War Memorial, set at the foot of Mt Ainslie and at the end of Anzac Parade, commemorates and honours the Australian men and women who have served in war. The memorial has recently been redeveloped, culminating in the opening of Aircraft Hall, the Second World War Gallery and ANZAC Hall. Visitors can browse over 20 exhibition galleries or find moments of silent contemplation at the Hall of Memory, the Tomb of the Unknown Australian Soldier, the Pool of Reflection and the Roll of Honour, which lists the names of over 102 000 Australian servicemen and servicewomen who died in war. *Open daily; admission free.*

CITY CENTRE

The modest size of Canberra's city centre, Civic, is a reminder that Canberra's population is only just over 300 000 people. There are many attractions in the centre, along with excellent shopping, great cafes and **Casino Canberra**.

Garema Place

The top end of Civic, this open public space is encircled by cafes and restaurants, and features a large movie screen (which shows movies at night during summer). Garema Place is a popular meeting place and is next to the Civic bus interchange. On Friday and Saturday evenings the Irish pub King O'Malley's is usually bursting at the seams, and the outdoor cafes are full of relaxed diners. If you head south from Garema Place down the tree-lined City Walk towards the large Canberra Centre mall, you will find Civic's landmark carousel. Built in 1914 in Melbourne, its hand-carved horses and two elephants were imported from Germany.

Canberra Museum and Gallery

CMAG's permanent collection reflects the history, environment, culture and community of the Canberra region. Dynamic exhibitions and diverse community events celebrate Canberra's social history and visual arts. *Cnr London Circuit & Civic Sq; open 10am–5pm Tues–Fri, 12noon–4pm weekends; admission free.*

ScreenSound Australia

Housed in the former Institute of Anatomy next to the landscaped grounds of the **Australian National University**, Australia's national screen and sound archive collects, preserves and shares Australia's film and sound heritage. The displays include film memorabilia, special exhibitions and interactive activities. *McCoy Circuit, Acton; open daily; admission free.*

National Museum of Australia

Opened in 2001, this thoroughly modern museum uses state-of-the-art technology and hands-on interactive displays to show stories about Australia's past, present, people, issues and future. Begin your experience in Circa, a rotating cinema, to get an overview of the three main themes of the museum: land, nation, people. The permanent displays include 'First Australians', an amazing display of indigenous culture, experience, dance and music; and 'Nation', where you can celebrate Australian icons such as the Hills hoist, Play School and Vegemite. 'Tangled Destinies' takes you through 20 000 years of environmental change, and in 'Eternity' you can share the joy and sorrow of ordinary and extraordinary Australians. Children will love 'kSpace', a virtual-reality experience, and 'Our Place', with four different cubbyhouses to explore. Fascinating temporary exhibitions change throughout the year. Guided tours available. *Lawson Cres, Acton Peninsula; open daily; general admission free.*

North-eastern suburbs

Incorporating some of the oldest suburbs in Canberra, this area is an enjoyable mix of relaxed cafes, interesting attractions and nature reserves with excellent walking and mountain-bike tracks.

Mt Ainslie Lookout 114 F3

Drive to the top of Mt Ainslie for a stunning view of the city and the surrounding mountain ranges. From here you will clearly see the geometry of Canberra's design. During autumn this is the best place to see Canberra's stunning array of natural colours.

Ainslie, Braddon and Dickson 114 E2

If you're in need of a good coffee, a tasty Chinese meal or a beer in the sun, head to the inner north-eastern suburbs. This is an area with an 'alternative' atmosphere, traditionally populated by Canberra's students. The shopping precincts of these suburbs offer small art galleries, interesting fashion and street cafes. **Ainslie** and **Braddon** have some of Canberra's earliest houses, and make for pleasant walking. Ainslie is also home to the historic **All Saints Church** (on Cowper Street). Further north, **Dickson** is a hive of activity and home to Canberra's Chinatown (on Woolley Street).

Canberra Space Dome and Observatory 114 E2

Discover the mysteries of the night sky in the observatory's planetarium. The dome features research-grade telescopes for fascinating night-time viewing, with tours run by experienced astronomers. The Flying Saucer is the audiovisual centre for the observatory and contains some space-art murals. For an insight into terrain of another type, there is also the Antarctic Igloo Exhibit, an Australian Antarctic Division survival igloo. *Hawdon Pl, Dickson; open Tues–Sat nights; admission fee applies; (02) 6248 5333.*

Kamberra wine complex 114 E1

With 7 hectares of landscaped gardens, vineyards, an outdoor amphitheatre, a glass-art gallery and a demonstration winery, this light and airy complex is well worth a visit. Wine-tastings and tours are available. *Cnr Northbourne Ave (Federal Hwy) & Flemington Rd, Lyneham; open daily; general admission free; (02) 6262 2333.*

North-western suburbs

The inner north-west of Canberra is a hub of activity, with the leafy suburbs of Turner, O'Connor and Lyneham particularly popular with students from the nearby Australian National University. **Canberra Nature Park**, which includes the Australian National Botanic Gardens, lies on the edge of the city centre. Further out is **Belconnen**, which is the main centre for northern Canberra. It offers a large shopping mall, a top-quality sports and aquatic centre and many other facilities. Also in Belconnen you will find **Lake Ginninderra**, a favourite recreational and picnic spot.

Australian National Botanic Gardens 114 C3

At the base of Black Mountain, these magnificent gardens (roughly 90 hectares, with 40 hectares developed and the remainder bushland) have the largest

Timeline

1820 *Charles Throsby Smith is the first European to explore the area, the land of the Ngunnawal and the Ngario people.*

1824–25 *Early settler Joshua Moore takes up 1000 acres on the banks of the Molonglo River, naming his farming property Canberry, an Aboriginal word meaning 'meeting place'. Robert Campbell also acquires land on the Molonglo, his family becoming the district's most prominent clan.*

1911 *The Federal Capital Territory comes into existence – the chosen site for Australia's capital city. Still mainly a farming area, the population of 1714 is outnumbered by the territory's 224 764 sheep.*

1912 *Walter Burley Griffin and Marion Mahony Griffin, American architects from Chicago, win an international competition for the design of the city.*

1913 *The capital is formally named Canberra at an official ceremony.*

1927 *The Duke of York opens the provisional Parliament House.*

1930s–40s *Canberra's population grows slowly, with government departments remaining in Melbourne and Sydney. The Australian National University is founded in 1946.*

1963 *The Molonglo River is dammed and Lake Burley Griffin created, inaugurated by Prime Minister Robert Menzies in 1964.*

1968–82 *The capital's icons spring into existence: the National Library (1968); the National Carillon (1970); the High Court (1980); and the National Gallery (1982).*

1988 *The new Parliament House is opened to coincide with the bicentenary of European settlement.*

2003 *Summer bushfires and a horrific firestorm burn 70 percent of the territory, destroying 95 percent of Namadgi National Park and around 500 homes. Four people lose their lives.*

Shopping

Canberra Centre, City *A stylish mall with department stores, a wide variety of smaller shops and specialty stores, in the heart of the CBD. See map on p. 116*

Kingston *Old-fashioned specialty shopping. 114 E6*

Manuka *Up-market fashion and homewares, streets lined with cafes, and a 24-hour supermarket. 114 D6*

Woden Plaza *One of Canberra's largest shopping malls with department stores, over 200 specialty shops, Hoyts 8 cinemas and plenty of parking. 114 B8*

Other suburban malls *These include Westfield Shopping Centre in Belconnen and the Tuggeranong Hyperdome. 114 A1 and 505 E8*

Monuments

Anzac Parade Memorials *Dramatic monuments set along the striking red gravel of Anzac Parade commemorate the war efforts of 11 different groups. See map on p. 116*

Australian–American Memorial *Celebrates America's World War II contribution to Australia's defence. See map on p. 116*

Captain Cook Memorial Water Jet *An impressive 150-metre water jet – hire a paddleboat to sail under the spray. See map on p. 116*

National Carillon *Recently upgraded and now the largest carillon in Australia, with 55 bells, it was a gift from the British government to celebrate Canberra's 50th anniversary. Recitals occur daily; tours Mon, Wed & Fri. See map on p. 116*

Reconciliation Place *An acknowledgement of the ongoing journey towards reconciliation. See map on p. 116*

See also Australian War Memorial, p. 116

Australian War Memorial

collection of Australian native flora in the world. The gardens are organised into sections representing Australia's various climatic zones and ecosystems. Follow the Aboriginal Plant Use Walk for an understanding of the species used for foods and medicines by the country's indigenous inhabitants. In summer, people flock here for evening picnics and weekend twilight jazz. *Clunies Ross St, Acton.*

Telstra Tower 114 B3
One of Canberra's landmarks, the communications tower rises 195 metres above the summit of Black Mountain and offers superb views of Canberra. It has two open viewing platforms, an exhibition gallery and a revolving restaurant. *Black Mountain Dr, Acton; open to 10pm daily; admission fee applies.*

CSIRO Discovery 114 C3
The centre showcases Australia's scientific research and innovation with exhibitions and interactive displays. Take part in the hands-on experiments, experience the virtual-reality theatre and find out about the latest research breakthroughs. *Off Clunies Ross St, Black Mountain; open Mon–Fri; admission fee applies.*

Australian Institute of Sport 114 C1
Providing world-class facilities across a broad range of disciplines, the AIS is the training ground for many elite athletes. The Sports Visitors Centre is the entrance point for visitors and has exhibitions and displays of sporting memorabilia. Tours of the AIS are led by athletes and give

visitors an insight into the life of an elite athlete. The tours include Sportex, an interactive exhibition where you can test your sporting skills against those recorded by our Olympians and see the latest in sport technology. *Leverrier Cres, Bruce; open daily; general admission free; (02) 6214 1444.*

Gold Creek Village

Gold Creek Village is a tourist attraction that takes its name from an old property established in the area in the mid-1800s. To make matters confusing, there is no Gold Creek, and no history of goldmining in this area – **Gold Creek Station** was apparently named after a racehorse. The station, north of the village, is still a large working merino property and is open to visitors wanting a taste of Australian rural life (groups only; bookings (02) 6230 9208). However, Gold Creek Village is the real drawcard here, with specialty shops, galleries, cafes, historic buildings and a host of modern attractions.

National Dinosaur Museum 505 E2
The museum has an extensive display of fossilised dinosaur remains, full skeletons and full-size replicas. During school holidays there are plenty of activities for children as well as guided tours. *Cnr Gold Creek Rd & Barton Hwy, Gold Creek Village; open daily; admission fee applies.*

Cockington Green 505 E2
Journey through a magical world of miniatures, from a Stonehenge replica to

a village cricket match amid beautifully manicured gardens, or take a ride on a miniature steam train. A heritage rose walk links the miniatures with the steam train. *11 Gold Creek Rd, Gold Creek Village; open daily; admission fee applies.*

Australian Reptile Centre 505 E2

The place for all things reptilian. Some of Australia's deadliest snakes are on display in exhibits that are divided into habitat types. The Prehistory Gallery takes you on a journey through reptile evolution and the Snake Shop offers a range of souvenirs and information. *O'Hanlon Pl, Gold Creek Village; open daily; admission fee applies.*

The Bird Walk 505 E2

Walk among over 500 birds representing 54 species from Australia and around the world in this aviary, which measures 1000 square metres. You can photograph and handfeed the colourful creatures, which fly free in the landscaped 9-metre-high enclosure. *Federation Sq, Gold Creek Village; open daily; admission fee applies.*

Ginninderra Village 505 E2

The old village of Ginninderra predates **Hall**, the nearby suburb that began life as a village well before the city of Canberra was created. Ginninderra serviced the surrounding farming districts, including the property of Gold Creek Station. The 'Ginninderra Village' that is today part of Gold Creek Village contains the old Ginninderra schoolhouse and the township's old Roman Catholic church. They can be found among giftware stores, craft studios and galleries. *Gold Creek Village; open daily.*

Inner south

Drive around Canberra's leafy inner-south suburbs to see official residences, Art Deco bungalows, carefully tended gardens and the diplomatic precinct. Most of the **embassies** are located in the suburbs of Yarralumla and Forrest, between State Circle and Empire Circuit. **The Lodge**, the Prime Minister's Canberra residence, situated next to Parliament House, is noticeable by the large cream brick wall that surrounds it. The house and grounds are not open to the public, but occasional open days are held. Likewise, **Government House**, the Governor-General's residence at Yarralumla, a grand 1820s building once part of a sheep station, is only open to the public once or twice a year. There are views of the grounds from a lookout on Lady Denman Drive.

Manuka and Kingston 114 D6

Over the years many of the original homes in these two suburbs have been replaced by townhouses and apartments – their proximity to both Lake Burley Griffin and the city centre has made them sought-after addresses. Both Manuka and Kingston have vibrant shopping precincts, with a fabulous variety of cafes, restaurants, nightclubs, bars and pubs (*see Eating out, on this page*). Up-market specialty shops and public squares add to the vibe, and the lovely **Telopea Park** is only a few minutes away from both suburbs. The nearby suburb of **Griffith** has some of Canberra's best organic and alternative shopping, along with a couple of excellent restaurants and cafes.

A grand plan

Canberra's design is perhaps the most interesting and functional urban design in the country. It was a planned city from day one, and the design was sought through a competition. From 137 entries, first prize (and a sum of 1750 pounds) was given to Chicago landscape architect Walter Burley Griffin. Griffin had never been to the actual site, but had seen a model (one of nine exhibited worldwide) and worked from maps of the area. He also wasn't alone in his success – his wife, architect Marion Mahony Griffin, was responsible for the stunning perspective drawings and plans that so impressed the judging panel.

The way Griffin's geometrical design related to the terrain was outstanding: he took full advantage of the area's natural features, from the hills and mountains to the waterways and broad plains. Today Black Mountain and Mt Ainslie stand as almost iconic features in the city, as Griffin ensured that development would be restricted to the valley floors.

Capital Hill, the site of Parliament House, became the physical centre of the city and the symbolic centre of the nation. Another feature was the spacious nature of the promenades and the sites of national institutions. Griffin made sure Canberra's national institutions didn't 'stand on end as in the congested American cities'.

It took many years for Griffin's grand plan to be fully realised. The lake, named in his honour, was not created until 1964.

However, as Griffin's design only allowed for a population of 25 000 and Canberra now stands at around the 300 000 mark, the design has since been expanded. The three suburban town centres of Woden, Belconnen and Tuggeranong were added between 1964 and 1973 to complement the existing city centre. Even now you will still find yourself five minutes out of the CBD and yet surrounded by forested hills, slowing down to let a kangaroo or two cross the road before you.

Eating out

Dickson *Home to Chinatown and a cosmopolitan range of cafes and restaurants. 114 E2*

Garema Place *In the city centre, choose from a wide range of restaurants and cafes, including Japanese, Indian, old-style Italian and Thai. See map on p. 116*

West Row *Enjoy a classy night out at Anise (modern Australian) or the excellent Mezzalira on London (Italian, modern Australian). See map on p. 116*

Manuka *A popular suburb with many cafes and restaurants. 114 D6*

Kingston *Here you will find restaurants, bars, pubs and cafes, most with some outdoor eating spaces. 114 E6*

Ainslie *Head to the Ainslie shops for fabulous vegetarian fare at Bernadette's Cafe and Restaurant. 114 E2*

Woden Plaza *For relaxed dining, try the Thai Spice or the Turkish Pide House. 114 B8*

Deakin *Just near the Mint, the Palette Cafe at Beaver Galleries is worth a visit for exquisite morsels and divine desserts. 114 B6*

Markets

Belconnen Fresh Food Markets *Fresh fruit, vegetables, produce and home to one of Australia's 'big things' – the Giant Mushroom. Wed–Sun. 114 A1*

Fyshwick Markets *Fresh produce markets with a great atmosphere and excellent value. Thurs–Sun. 505 G5*

Gorman House Markets, Braddon *Art and craft, home-baked treats, plants, clothes and a great up-beat atmosphere, near the city centre. Sat. See map on p. 116*

Hall Markets *Set in the historic showgrounds of Hall village on the outskirts of Canberra, with over 500 stalls of craft, home produce, plants and homemade designer clothing. 1st Sun each month (closed Jan). 505 E1*

Old Bus Depot Markets, Kingston *A local favourite, showcasing the creativity of the Canberra region, with handcrafted and home-produced art, craft and jewellery, gourmet food, New Age therapies, kids' activities and musical entertainment. Sun. 114 E6*

AUSTRALIAN CAPITAL TERRITORY

Walks and tours

Anzac Parade Walk *Follow the war memorials set along the regal Anzac Parade on this self-guided walk (2.5 kilometres). Brochure available from the visitor centre.*

Balloons Aloft! *Experience the beauty of Canberra as you float above in a hot-air balloon. Enjoy a champagne breakfast at the Hyatt afterwards. Bookings (02) 6285 1540.*

Black Mountain Wildflower Walk *Wander through the bushland of Black Mountain Nature Reserve. Brochure available from the visitor centre or the Australian National Botanic Gardens.*

Burley Griffin Walk or Ride *A self-guided walk takes in the north-eastern shores of Lake Burley Griffin, from the National Capital Exhibition at Regatta Point to the National Carillon (4.6 kilometres). Brochure available from the visitor centre. Or just ride around the lake on a bike.*

Lakeside Walk *Stroll past Canberra's major institutions on this self-guided walk that begins at Commonwealth Place and passes the National Gallery of Australia, the High Court of Australia and the National Library of Australia (1.8 kilometres). Brochure available from the visitor centre.*

Sport

*If a visit to the Australian Institute of Sport leaves you wanting more, then there is plenty of sport to see in Canberra. Watch a game of **basketball** as the two Canberra WNBL teams, the Capitals and the AIS, go head-to-head or play interstate teams. The Capitals play their home games at Southern Cross Stadium in Tuggeranong and the AIS team, of course, plays at the AIS.*

*See Canberra's **Rugby League** side, the Raiders, take on the rest of the nation at Canberra Stadium. The ACT Brumbies, the capital's **Rugby Union** team, also play at Canberra Stadium, to partisan capacity crowds. Canberra doesn't have an **AFL** (Australian Football League) team of its own, but one Melbourne team plays a couple of 'home' games a year at the picturesque Manuka Oval.*

*If **cricket** is more your thing, visit in summer to see the Prime Minister's XI take on one of the touring international sides at Manuka Oval.*

*In the lead-up to the Australian Open **tennis** in Melbourne, Canberra hosts the WTA Canberra Women's Classic.*

*If you like dust, mud and excitement, you can't go past the world-class Rally of Canberra **car rally** in May.*

Calthorpes' House 114 D7

Built in 1927 in Spanish Mission style, the house contains the original furnishings and photos, offering glimpses into what domestic life was like in the then-fledgling capital. Explore the 1920s garden or hide in the World War II air-raid shelter. There are guided tours during the week (phone for times) and open house on the weekend. *24 Mugga Way, Red Hill; open 1.30pm–4.30pm Sat–Sun; admission fee applies; (02) 6295 1945.*

National Zoo and Aquarium 114 A5

This modern zoo, with naturalistic enclosures rather than cages, has a strong commitment to breeding endangered species, and conservation. Animals range from the big cats to bears, otters and monkeys. Wander through the aquarium to see colourful marine life in the Great Barrier Reef exhibit and visit the shark-filled Predators of the Deep exhibit. Special tours include handfeeding the big cats and bears, meeting a cheetah, and seeing 'animals in action'. (These tours can cost significantly more than general admission, but include all-day zoo entry.) *Scrivener Dam, Lady Denman Dr, Yarralumla; open daily; admission fee applies; (02) 6287 8400.*

Royal Australian Mint 114 B6

Opened in 1965, the mint has the capacity to produce 2 million coins per day. You can learn how coins are made and see the production floor from an elevated gallery. There are displays of old coins, a video on coin production, and visitors can even make their own coins. *Denison St, Deakin; open daily; admission free.*

Southern Canberra

The suburbs south-west of the city are set against the forested slopes of the Brindabella Range. Explore the area via Tourist Drive 5, reached by following Adelaide Avenue onto Cotter Road. Scars from the 2003 bushfires are still visible throughout much of southern Canberra, but you can witness regeneration in progress as nature returns and facilities such as **Mount Stromlo Observatory** are rebuilt. The two southern town centres, **Woden** and **Tuggeranong**, have shopping malls and associated facilities. **Lake Tuggeranong** offers waterside recreation.

Mugga-Mugga 114 E8

Set on 17 hectares of grazing land, Mugga-Mugga is a collection of buildings and cultural objects dating from the 1830s to the 1970s. The highlight is the 1830s shepherd's cottage, which has been carefully conserved and furnished with household belongings from the early 1900s. The option of combined admission fees with Calthorpes' House offers good value. *Narrabundah La, Symonston; open 1.30pm–4.30pm Sat–Sun; admission fee applies.*

Tuggeranong Homestead 505 F8

This historic homestead, sitting on 31 hectares, is over 140 years old and includes a stone barn built by convicts in the 1830s. Owned by James and Mary Cunningham in the 1800s, it was bought by the Commonwealth government in 1917 for military purposes. War historian Charles Bean lived here from 1919 to 1925 while he wrote the official history of the Australian involvement in World War I. *Johnson Dr, opposite Calwell Shops, Richardson; open weekends or by appointment; (02) 6292 8888.*

Tidbinbilla Nature Reserve 505 A9

A special place for both locals and tourists, Tidbinbilla was burnt out in the 2003 bushfires. Areas are regenerating well and the visitor centre has a special exhibit of fire-affected items salvaged from the reserve. The wildlife is also returning. There are some great walking trails and ranger-guided activities. Contact the visitor centre to find out which walks are open at the time of your

AFL football at Manuka Oval

A year after the fires, the bush springs back to life in Namadgi National Park

visit. Expansion of current facilities is under way. *Paddys River Rd, Tidbinbilla; open daily; admission free; (02) 6205 1233.*

Canberra Deep Space Communication Complex 505 C8

This NASA facility is devoted to unravelling the mysteries of space. It is one of three facilities in the world that form NASA's Deep Space Network, a network of antennas that support deep-space tracking, radio and radar astronomy observations, and space missions. The Canberra Space Centre, the facility's visitor centre, has a genuine piece of moon rock that is 3.8 billion years old, astronaut suits, space food, spacecraft models and photographs. *Tourist Drive 5, off Paddys River Rd, Tidbinbilla; open daily; admission free.*

Corin Forest 505 B11

Destroyed in the 2003 bushfires, the recreation facilities at Corin Forest have been rebuilt and reopened to the public. The area has an 800-metre bobsled alpine slide, a flying fox, a new waterslide and some great picnic areas. *Corin Rd, Smokers Gap; open daily; general admission free; (02) 6235 7333.*

Lanyon 505 E11

Lanyon is one of Australia's most historic grazing properties and a beautiful 19th-century homestead. On the banks of the Murrumbidgee River, the homestead and its gardens provide a glimpse of the 1850s. The homestead's outbuildings (the kitchen, dairy, storerooms and workers' barracks) were built from wood and stone – the stone cut and quarried by convict labour. Parts of the homestead have been restored and furnished in the style of the period. The **Nolan Gallery**, featuring works by renowned Australian artist Sidney

Nolan and his contemporaries, is also located at Lanyon. *Tharwa Dr, Tharwa; open Tues–Sun; admission fee applies.*

Further on is **Cuppacumbalong Craft Centre**, a 1920s homestead with rambling gardens, an art gallery, a craft shop and a restaurant. *Naas Rd, Tharwa; open 11.00am–5.00pm Wed–Sun; admission free.*

Namadgi National Park 505 C12

Approximately 95 percent of this park was lost in the 2003 bushfires, but the Australian bush springs back to life with remarkable resilience. Namadgi is at the northern end of the Australian Alps and only a 45-minute drive from Canberra. It offers picnic and camping areas, walks, and an informative visitor centre. *Main access via Naas Rd from Tharwa.*

Day tours

Historic towns *A number of towns within easy driving distance of Canberra are noted for their heritage buildings and are filled with a sense of the area's farming and goldmining history. These towns include Captains Flat, Goulburn, Braidwood, Bungendore, Yass and Young; most are within an hour or so of the capital. The historic Bungendore, full of craft galleries and antique shops, is a great daytrip, although at only 30 minutes away it is easy enough to visit just for a fine meal or an enjoyable shopping expedition. For more details see p. 46*

Wine district *The Canberra district only has a few wineries, but they have a big reputation for the quality of the cool-climate varieties produced. Most are located to the immediate north and north-east of the territory (pick up a map from the Canberra Visitor Centre) and are open daily for tastings and sales. For more details see p. 46*

Entertainment

Cinema
The big suburban malls of Woden, Belconnen and Tuggeranong have Hoyts multiplexes, but for arthouse and independent cinema try Electric Shadows on Akuna Street in the city. Also in the city are Greater Union Civic cinemas. Manuka Greater Union has a wide range of interesting new releases. See the Canberra Times for details of current films.

Live music
Canberra has a surprisingly busy music scene and there is usually a good selection of live music around town, ranging from rock gigs at the ANU Union Bar to mellow jazz or soul at Tilley's Devine Cafe in Lyneham. Big acts play at the Canberra Theatre Centre or the Royal Theatre, both in the city centre. You will find nightclubs aplenty in Civic, Kingston, Manuka and Braddon, with a recent addition being the underground Academy in Civic. For gig details pick up a copy of the Canberra Times on Thursday for its lift-out entertainment guide, 'Times Out', or look for the free street magazine BMA.

Classical music and performing arts
The main venue for performing arts is the Canberra Theatre Centre. A couple of smaller venues around town, such as Gorman House Arts Centre in Braddon and the Street Theatre on Childers Street, cater to more eclectic tastes. Classical music concerts most often take place at Llewellyn Hall, part of the ANU's Canberra School of Music, in Acton. See the Canberra Times for details of what's on.

Waterside retreats

Black Mountain Peninsula *A picnic and barbecue spot on the edge of the lake in the shadow of Black Mountain. 114 C4*

Casuarina Sands *Where the Cotter and Murrumbidgee rivers meet. 505 B6*

Commonwealth Park *Formal gardens, parkland and public art on the edge of the lake. See map on p. 116*

Commonwealth Place *Promenade on the shores of the lake, with the International Flag Display and vistas of the Australian War Memorial and Parliament House. See map on p. 116*

Jerrabomberra Wetlands *A refuge for wildlife, including 77 species of birds. 114 F6*

Weston Park *A woodland and lakeside recreation area with play equipment for children. 114 B4*

VICTORIA

V ictoria is possibly Australia's most diverse state. In a half-hour drive from Melbourne you could be taking in mist-laden mountain ranges and ferny gullies. In an hour you could be lying on a sandy beach in a sheltered bay, or surfing in the rugged Southern Ocean. In around four hours you could be standing on the edge of the immense desert that stretches away into Australia's interior. In a country full of mind-numbing distances, nothing seems far away in Victoria.

Victoria has quiet places too . . . like the remote beaches of East Gippsland, where you can feel like Robinson Crusoe . . .

Victoria is Australia's second most populous state. Close to five million people live here, with 3.5 million in Melbourne. The city was only founded in 1835, as a kind of afterthought to Sydney and Hobart, but by the 1850s Victoria was off to a racing start. A deluge of people from all corners of the world fanned out across the state in response to the madness that was gold. It brought

prosperity to Victoria and it also brought the certain wildness treasured in the state's history – uprisings like the Eureka Rebellion and bushrangers like Ned Kelly.

Two centuries later Victoria has matured and recognised another form of wealth – the richness of its natural landscape. To the west of Melbourne, beyond Geelong, a tract of cool-temperate rainforest unravels on its way to the vivid, green Cape Otway, where a lighthouse stands on the cliff-top. The Great Ocean Road winds past here, en route to the state's iconic limestone stacks, the Twelve Apostles.

On the other side of Melbourne the land falls away into a series of peninsulas, islands and isthmuses. One leads to Wilsons Promontory, an untouched landscape of forested hills, tea-brown rivers and beaches strewn with enormous rust-red boulders.

Agriculture has rendered this part of the state a patchwork of green paddocks, from which come some of the finest cheeses in the country. And on Melbourne's doorstep, the amber-hued Yarra Valley produces some of the finest cool-climate wines.

From the Yarra Valley, the landscape begins its gradual climb up into the High Country. In winter it is a vista of snowfields, but before skiers – and before the rugged horsemen of the 19th century – these mountains were the domain of the Aboriginal

Mildura

Murray–Sunset National Park

Swan Hill

Little Desert National Park

Horsham

Grampians National Park

Ballarat

Geelong

Warrnambool

Portland

Echuca

Bendigo

Melbourne

Phillip Island

Wodonga

Bright

Lakes Entrance

Sale

Cann River

Wilsons Promontory

PREVIOUS PAGES *Croajingolong National Park*

Redmans Bluff, Grampians National Park

tribes of the north-east. They congregated here in summer to trade, arrange marriages, settle disputes and feast on bogong moths.

Perhaps Victoria's most cherished place is the Grampians, an offshoot of the Great Dividing Range that rises up from the wheat fields and paddocks of the Western District. With a quarter of the state's flora and 80 percent of its Aboriginal rock art, the Grampians is a living gallery and a superb place for bushwalking and camping.

Victoria has quiet places too, away from the crowds. Like the remote beaches of East Gippsland, where you can feel like Robinson Crusoe, or Little Desert National Park, in the state's west. This park may look plain on the surface, but if you're quiet and keep your eyes open, you might see a mallee fowl incubating its egg on an enormous, sprawling mound, and if you come in spring, you'll see ground orchids blooming across the plains. Little Desert National Park has more than 670 plant species within its borders, and across Victoria there are at least as many things to see and do for travellers.

F A C T   F I L E

Population 4 917 300
Total land area 227 010 sq km
People per square kilometre 21.7
Sheep per square kilometre 94
Length of coastline 1868 km
Number of islands 184
Longest river Goulburn River (566 km)
Largest lake Lake Corangamite (209 sq km)
Highest mountain Mt Bogong (1986 m), Alpine National Park
Hottest place Mildura (77 days per year above 30°C)
Wettest place Weeaproinah (1900 mm per year), Otway Ranges
Oldest permanent settlement Portland, 1834
Most famous beach Bells Beach, Torquay
Tons of gold mined 2500 (2 percent of world total)
Estimated tons of gold left 5000
Litres of milk produced on Victorian dairy farms per year 7 billion
Quirkiest festival Great Vanilla Slice Triumph, Ouyen
Famous people Germaine Greer, Barry Humphries, Kylie Minogue
Original name for the Twelve Apostles The Sow and Piglets
Best invention Bionic ear
First Ned Kelly film released *The Story of the Kelly Gang*, 1906 (also believed to be the world's first feature film)
Local beer Victoria Bitter

TIMELINE

1802
Lieutenant John Murray sails into Port Phillip Bay on the Lady Nelson.

1803
A party of settlers and convicts establish the first settlement near what is now Sorrento, but it is soon abandoned.

1835
John Batman sails up the Yarra River. The Port Phillip Bay area is 'purchased' from the Kulin people.

1851
The Port Phillip district is officially established as a separate colony and named after Queen Victoria. Gold is discovered shortly afterwards.

1854
In Ballarat, miners mount the Eureka Rebellion, protesting against the inequities of the goldfields licensing system.

1880–91
Victoria and Melbourne go through their boom years, with impressive new buildings signifying the immense wealth brought with the gold rush. Melbourne's first tram service begins in 1885.

1901
Australia's first federal parliament is held at Melbourne's Royal Exhibition Building.

1939
The worst fires in Australia's history sweep through Victoria, charring 1.4 million hectares and killing 71 people.

1956
Melbourne hosts the Olympic Games.

MELBOURNE

MELBOURNE IS . . .

A footy match at the MCG

A stroll along the St Kilda foreshore

Coffee in Degraves Street in the city

Shopping for produce at the Queen Victoria Market

A visit to Federation Square

Live music at a pub in Brunswick Street, Fitzroy

Views across the city from Melbourne Observation Deck

Sweating it out in the crowd at the Australian Open

Moonlight Cinema in the Royal Botanic Gardens

Waterside dining at Southgate or NewQuay, Docklands

A ferry trip to Williamstown

A picnic in the gardens of Heide Museum of Modern Art

A lap of the Australian Grand Prix circuit at Albert Park

Visitor information

Melbourne Visitor Information Centre
Federation Square
Cnr Flinders St and St Kilda Rd
(03) 9658 9658
www.visitmelbourne.com.au

A tram speeds past Flinders Street Station

Melbourne's city centre is a thick mesh of straight lines; within lies a world brimming with energy, ideas and diversity. Gothic banks and cathedrals give way to pockets of the most modern architecture you've seen. Department stores and shopping centres coexist with a vibrant string of laneways given over to cafe culture and boutique shopping. This city is renowned as Australia's seat of art and music, yet Melbourne wouldn't be Melbourne without sport – whether it is a footy match at the MCG or a game of backyard cricket.

Melbourne was born in 1835. John Batman thought it was 'the place for a village', but in just a few years Melbourne was well on its way to becoming a city. It was a humble British outpost with high hopes – hopes that were suddenly made possible with the boom of Victoria's goldfields. Unbelievable wealth was poured into treasury buildings and tramways, grand boulevards and Georgian masterpieces. European fashions and seaside holidays became the vogue.

Today Melburnians still enjoy the good life, and at the very centre of this is good food and fine dining. Comfort food in a cosy corner pub or meals with a view and a waterfront – a trend in so many of the country's coastal cities. Over a decade ago, Southbank, the shopping and eating precinct on the Yarra River, became an extension of the city centre, and now the city is on the move again – this time to Docklands.

You might come for the dining or the shopping. Or the gardens and the architecture. Or the arts and music. Or the football or cricket or tennis. Melbourne has as much diversity as it has suburbs and, at last check, these were marching right down the Mornington Peninsula.

City centre

Melbourne's central business district lies on the north bank of the Yarra River. The Met train system runs a ring around it and trams amble up and down most of the main streets. The block between Collins, Bourke, Swanston and Elizabeth streets comprises the main shopping district. Most of the attractions for visitors are in the eastern section of the CBD, between Elizabeth and Spring streets.

SOUTH-CENTRAL

Bounded by Flinders, Elizabeth, Little Bourke and Russell streets, this area is the heart of Melbourne. It takes in the eclectic corner of Swanston and Flinders streets, where a Gothic cathedral, a historically significant pub, the city's busiest station and the city's newest and most controversial piece of architecture stand facing one another. Further up is Melbourne Town Hall and a charming network of arcades and backstreets; further still is Bourke Street Mall, the centre of the shopping district.

A station, a pub and a cathedral

As the major train station in the CBD, **Flinders Street Station** is the first port of call for many people travelling in from the suburbs. Workers pour in and out of this elegant Edwardian Baroque building day and night, and the steps underneath the clocks at the Swanston Street entrance are a popular meeting spot. What lies above the platforms is one of the most under-utilised pieces of real estate in Melbourne, including an office space and an old ballroom.

On the three corners facing the station are three other landmarks, Federation Square (*see next entry*), St Paul's Cathedral and Young and Jacksons Hotel. In years gone by, **Young and Jacksons'** main attraction was the controversial *Chloe*, a painting of a French nude that has graced the hotel's walls for nearly 100 years. The pub has been restored recently, and with the birth of 'Fed Square', the corner's once seedy atmosphere has been transformed. Across Swanston Street is the grandiose **St Paul's Cathedral**, built in 1891. Its mosaic interior is well worth a look.

Federation Square

Federation Square is the biggest building project to occur in Melbourne in decades – if not in actual size, then at least in terms of its public significance and architectural ambition. It has created an open public space in a location that was once deemed one of Melbourne's ugliest sites, and a link at long last between the city and the Yarra River. If you have never made it to the Kimberley, then at least you can stroll across the piazza, paved with 7500 square metres of coloured Kimberley sandstone. After that, stop in at one of the bars, cafes or restaurants, many of them positioned with unique views over Flinders Street Station and the Yarra. The local wine industry is well represented

Getting around

Melbourne's trams are an icon, but also a very good way of getting around the city. The City Circle tram is free and now extends to Docklands. Trams depart every ten minutes between 10am and 6pm and run in both directions. Other (paid) services head out into the suburbs, with especially good coverage of the eastern, south-eastern and northern suburbs. A map of the different services can be found inside all trams, or in the Melway street directory.

Trains are generally a faster option if there is a service that goes to your destination. Many services go right to the outer suburbs. There are five stations in the city, three of them underground. Details of services can be found at all stations (see map on p. 130), or in the Melway street directory.

Buses tend to cover the areas that trains and trams don't service. Details of bus routes can be found in the Melway street directory.

All modes of public transport are covered by the one ticket, a Metcard. The price of the ticket depends on which 'zone' you need to travel to, and different kinds of Metcards are available such as two-hour and one-day tickets. Metcards are available at train stations, on trams (limited), on buses and at shops – usually newsagents – displaying a Metcard flag.

For drivers, the much-talked-about feature of Melbourne's roads is the hook-turn, a process of moving to the left of the road in order to turn right, and therefore getting out of the way of trams. Details of this rule can be found in the Melway street directory. Other than this, driving in Melbourne is a fairly standard procedure. If you wish to use the CityLink tollway, then either an e-TAG or a Day Pass is required (there are no tollbooths, but day passes can be purchased over the phone up to 24 hours after making a journey).

Public transport Tram, train and bus information line 13 1638

Airport shuttle bus Skybus (03) 9335 2811

Tollway CityLink 13 2629

Motoring organisation RACV 13 1955, roadside assistance 13 1111

Car rental Avis 13 6333; Budget 13 2727; Europcar 13 1390; Hertz 13 3039; Thrifty 1300 367 227

Taxis Black Cabs Combined 13 2227; Embassy 13 1755; Northern Suburban 13 1119; Silver Top 13 1008; West Suburban (03) 9689 1144

Water taxi Melbourne Water Taxis (Yarra River) (03) 9686 0914

Tourist bus City Explorer (03) 9650 7000

Bicycle hire Bicycles for hire 0412 616 633; Bike Now (03) 9696 8588; St Kilda Cycles (03) 9534 3074

Climate

'Four seasons in one day' is a familiar phrase to all Melburnians. It might reach 38°C in the morning then drop to 20°C in the afternoon – and the weather the next day is anyone's guess. Generally though, winter is cold – daytime temperatures of 11–12°C are not unusual – and spring is wet. January and February are hot, with temperatures anywhere between the mid 20s and high 30s. The favourite season of many locals is autumn, when the weather is usually dry and stable.

	J	F	M	A	M	J	J	A	S	O	N	D
Max °C	26	26	24	20	17	14	13	15	17	20	22	24
Min °C	14	14	13	11	8	7	6	7	8	9	11	13
Rain mm	48	47	52	57	58	49	49	50	59	67	60	59
Raindays	8	7	9	12	14	14	15	16	15	14	12	11

here – the Victorian Wine Precinct, as it is called, includes restaurants and a shop specialising in Victorian wines grouped towards the back of the square. For a gallery experience, make your way to the Ian Potter Centre: NGV Australia or to the Australian Centre for the Moving Image (*see entries on this page*).

Ian Potter Centre: NGV Australia

Australian art is a world of its own and here it has finally found a home that it doesn't have to share. Enjoy the stark and luminous landscapes of Fred Williams, the stylish lines of Brett Whiteley and the classic fifties photographs of Max Dupain. Also in the gallery are the best of the colonial artists such as Tom Roberts and Arthur Streeton. On the ground floor is a large space dedicated to indigenous art – from traditional sculptures and bark paintings to the bright and expressive works of modern Aboriginal artists. The third level features a series of changing exhibitions. *Federation Sq; open daily; general admission free.*

Australian Centre for the Moving Image (ACMI)

In the last 50 years pop culture has moved right along. For entertainment, people have turned to television and films, and more recently to computer games and the internet, but our arts institutions have remained largely in the realm of painting, sculpture and photography. Enter ACMI. This is a museum of the 21st century and an Australian-first, exploring all current guises of the moving image and ready to embrace any new formats that the future will bring. There are cinemas as well as darkened galleries displaying screen-based art, and the interactive component of the centre is growing. Check out the Booth, where you can have a private viewing of a short work then have your portrait taken and see it transformed into a character. *Federation Sq; open daily; general admission free.*

Swanston Street

Depending on which side of the road you walk on, your experience of Swanston Street can be totally different. On one side of the street it is a grand boulevard lined with trees, gently rattling with trams, and dotted with significant buildings and quirky public sculpture. The other side, the west side, seems overcrowded with discount stores, souvenir shops and fast-food outlets. Swanston Street is closed to cars other than taxis.

On the corner of Swanston and Collins streets is the prominent **Melbourne Town Hall**, a venue for various public events including the Melbourne Comedy Festival. Opposite is a statue of **Burke and Wills**, the two explorers who set out to make the first journey across Australia from south to north. They left Melbourne in a grand procession of horses, carts, camels, and even a boat for crossing the fabled inland sea. Stopping just short of the north coast because of an impenetrable tract of mangroves, the two men and most of their diminished party died on the return trip.

Swanston Street also boasts some fine historic buildings (*see Grand old buildings, p. 133*), and further north is the State Library of Victoria (*see p. 132*).

Collins Street

This is Melbourne's most dignified street, and the section between Swanston and Elizabeth streets has some fairly classy shopping on offer. Have a look at

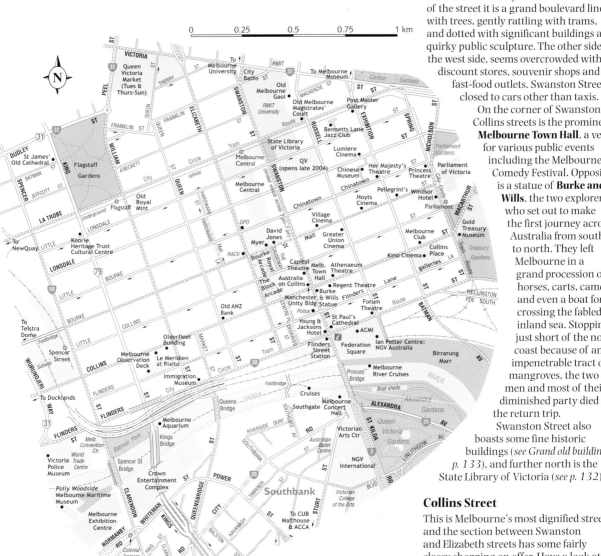

Australia on Collins, where you'll find all the big names in Australian fashion as well as a ground-floor food court. As Collins Street begins the climb up the hill to Spencer Street, some impressive buildings from Melbourne's old mercantile district appear.

Laneways and arcades

A part of Melbourne lives in its laneways. From Flinders Street Station to Bourke Street Mall, and very soon all the way to Latrobe Street, you can slip through a world of cafes, shoe shops, fashion boutiques and jewellers – many of them selling one-off items that you just don't find in malls and department stores. But it is worth it for the walk alone – time seems to stand still in these laneways, because in the shadows of the tall buildings that flank them they seem shut off from the rest of the city. You feel as though you could walk on forever.

You can access **Degraves Street** via a subway from Flinders Street Station. After years of neglect, the empty shops lining this subway are slowly filling up, mainly with clothing stores. The section of Degraves Street closest to Flinders Lane is closed to cars and is full of cafes spilling onto the paved street. Degraves Espresso is the old favourite here, with its worn theatre seating, dim lighting and great coffee.

Across from Degraves Street is **Centre Place**, with more cafes as well as bars and designer-fashion outlets. As you walk in, look up and see the Majorca Building, a Spanish-style building containing the most sought-after apartments in the inner city. Towards Collins Street, Centre Place becomes a covered arcade.

Block Arcade runs between Collins and Little Collins streets. It boasts Italian-imported mosaic floors, ornate glass ceilings, tearooms and exclusive clothing boutiques. Follow the arcade to Elizabeth Street, or to the laneway that joins it to Little Collins Street, where there are yet more cafes.

Over Little Collins Street is **Royal Arcade**, Australia's oldest surviving arcade. Black-and-white chequered tiles beckon you inside, and above the Little Collins Street entrance stand two giants, Gog and Magog, of ancient British legend. This arcade has not quite as much grandeur as the Block, but just as much charm. Walk through it to get to Bourke Street Mall and Elizabeth Street. (Alternatively, you can take the adjacent **Causeway**, a narrow laneway in the style of Centre Place, to get to the mall.)

West of the mall, between Bourke and Lonsdale streets, is **Hardware Lane**, which comes alive with office workers at lunchtime and with people seeking out cosy bars at night. The difference between this laneway and all the others is that, with a wider street, the sun actually shines here, making alfresco dining all the more pleasant. The

cobblestone paving, the window boxes and the brightly painted facades of the old buildings add to the charm.

Recent building works in the city such as the GPO development in Bourke Street Mall, the renovation of Melbourne Central and the new QV site are opening up more of the old laneways, restoring the original vision of Melbourne's designer, Robert Hoddle. In decades gone by many were bought out by private owners or closed up by department stores and plazas, but today's developers seem to have realised that Melbourne's laneways actually are unique.

Bourke Street Mall

Bourke Street Mall is the heart of Melbourne's shopping district, with big department stores and brand-name fashion outlets. Between Elizabeth and Swanston streets the mall is closed to cars, making it solely the territory of trams and pedestrians. **Myer**, Melbourne's favourite department store, and **David Jones**, a touch more up-market, both have entrances on the mall. Myer in particular is renowned for fine window displays at Christmas. At the west end of the mall is the **old GPO**, which was gutted by fire in 2001. Its restoration is under way (due for completion late 2004), though not as a post office (this has moved a block north) but as a smart shopping complex. Cafes will spill out onto the Elizabeth Street colonnade, and Postal Lane, between the GPO and Myer, will be reopened, linking Bourke and Little Bourke streets. The building will be home to around 60 food, clothing and homeware retailers.

If you fancy a break from shoppping, grab a seat along the mall and watch life wander by. More often than not there will be a busker performing for your entertainment.

SOUTH-EAST

This is Melbourne's most distinguished quarter, with some fine old buildings and the government district. The Victorian parliament occupies a suitably prominent position on Spring Street at the top of a hill. At the top end of Collins Street is the **Melbourne Club**, where Melbourne's male elite have been socialising and doing business since the city's earliest days. If dining interests you more than politicians and businessmen, then there is a food institution here too, at the top end of Bourke Street. **Pellegrini's** began serving real Italian espresso and pasta in 1954, at a time when Australian fare was all 'meat and three veg'. Today hardly a thing has changed behind its unassuming shopfront, including the furnishings, and the pasta is as good as ever.

Top events

Australian Open *One of the world's four major tennis Grand Slams. January.*

St Kilda Festival *A huge beachside party. February.*

Australian Grand Prix *The first round of the FIA World Championships. March.*

Melbourne Food and Wine Festival *Eat your way through Melbourne and regional Victoria. March–April.*

Melbourne International Comedy Festival *Just as many laughs as in Edinburgh and Montreal. April.*

Melbourne International Film Festival *Features, shorts and experimental pieces from around the world. July–August.*

AFL Grand Final *The whole city goes footy-mad. September.*

Melbourne International Arts Festival *Visual arts, theatre, dance and music in indoor and outdoor venues. The alternative Melbourne Fringe Festival is held around the same time. October.*

Melbourne Cup *The pinnacle of the Spring Racing Carnival. November.*

Boxing Day Test *Boxing Day in Melbourne wouldn't be the same without this cricket match. December.*

Shopping

Bourke Street Mall, City *With department stores Myer and David Jones. See map on p. 130*

Collins Street, City *Glamorous shopping strip with the big names in Australian fashion. See map on p. 130*

Southgate, Southbank *A classy range of clothing, art and gifts. See map on p. 130*

Smith Street, Collingwood *Sports stores and factory outlets to rival Bridge Road, along the top end of the street. 128 F2*

Bridge Road, Richmond *Back-to-back factory outlets and designer warehouses. 129 G4*

Chapel Street, South Yarra *Where shopping is an event to dress up for. 129 G6*

High Street, Armadale *Around 100 traders in antiques. 129 H7*

Eating out

Little Bourke Street, City *Chinatown, great for yum cha on Sundays. See map on p. 130*

Southgate and Crown Entertainment Complex, Southbank *Cafes, bars and restaurants along the Yarra. See map on p. 130*

Docklands *Melbourne's newest precinct, offering fantastic Indian, Moroccan and modern cuisine along the waterfront. 128 D4*

Lygon Street, Carlton *Pizza and pasta or coffee and cake. 128 E3*

Victoria Street, Abbotsford *Tasty, aromatic and cheap Vietnamese. 129 G3*

Brunswick Street, Fitzroy *Cafes, pubs and restaurants serving tasty modern meals. 128 F2*

Bridge Road, Richmond *A range of cuisines, from Argentinian to East Timorese. 129 G4*

Fitzroy Street, St Kilda *Restaurants galore and a hint of sea air. 128 F7*

Markets

Sunday Market, Southbank *Crafts galore, underneath the Victorian Arts Centre. See map on p. 130*

CERES Market *Old-style breads and organic produce on a community-run property in Brunswick East. While you're there, visit the bushfoods nursery and the multicultural village. Sat. 519 E6*

Collingwood Children's Farm Market *Victorian produce, from free-range eggs to olive oil, on a property dedicated to sustainability. 2nd Sat each month. 129 H3*

Flemington Upmarket *An inner-city Redhill Market at the Flemington Racecourse, with art, craft and regional produce. 4th Sun each month. 128 B1*

South Melbourne Market *Fruit, vegetables, deli items, clothing and homewares. Wed & Fri–Sat. 128 E5*

St Kilda Esplanade Market *Melbourne's oldest art and craft market, with over 200 artisans. Sun. 128 F7*

Camberwell Market *Melbourne's best trash and treasure event. Sun. 519 E6*

St Andrews Market *Laid-back market with alternative crafts, foods, music and clothing, an hour's drive from the city. Sat. 521 L4*

See also Queen Victoria Market, p. 134, and Prahran Market, p. 137

Parliament of Victoria

The Parliament of Victoria is entered via a grand run of steps. Built in stages between 1856 and 1929, the building remains incomplete in terms of the original vision of its architects – an ornate dome in the centre was supposed to double its height. From 1901 to 1927 this was the seat of federal government before it moved to Canberra. Free tours of the building run on days when parliament is not sitting. Sitting dates are published on the parliament's website. *Visit www.parliament.vic.gov.au for details. Spring St, facing Bourke St; (03) 9651 8568.*

Gold Treasury Museum

Not long after Victoria's first gold nugget was found there was a need for a place to store all the gold being exchanged for cash by the miners. In 1857 the Treasury building was built, with vaults for the gold and administrative offices for many of the colony's important figures. Today the vaults are home to a permanent exhibition on the gold era. Displays cover everything from bushrangers to the ships that took gold out of the country and brought thousands of migrants back. The building hosts other temporary exhibitions as well. *Spring St, facing Collins St; open daily; admission fee applies.*

Flinders Lane galleries

This laneway boasts the highest concentration of commercial galleries in Australia, mainly in the section between Spring and Swanston streets. There is a strong focus on indigenous and contemporary art, with standout galleries including the Anna Schwartz Gallery with international works, and the Gallery Gabrielle Pizzi with Aboriginal art from many of Australia's lesser known regions. Many local artists get a start in these galleries. Over in Swanston Street are the smaller artist-run spaces of the Nicholas Building, some with superb views over the city.

NORTH-EAST

This part of town is occupied mainly by office buildings, but there are some interesting places among them, such as the Old Melbourne Gaol, the State Library of Victoria and Chinatown. **QV** is here too, still in the throes of development at the time of publication. Occupying the block between Swanston, Lonsdale, Russell and Little Lonsdale streets, QV is planned as an entertainment, shopping and eating complex on the site of the old Queen Victoria Hospital. Laneways with hospital-related names will crisscross the site, with offices and apartments also part of the mix. On a small triangular block to the north, past RMIT, are the **City Baths**, which date back to the days when bathrooms were a luxury that few could afford. Today this building, a feast of domes on the skyline, houses a swimming pool, spas, saunas and a gymnasium.

State Library of Victoria

The front steps and lawn of the State Library of Victoria make a great spot for soaking up the sun. In fact, pre-Fed Square, this was the city centre's biggest public space and the meeting spot for many a demonstration. On the third floor of the Roman-style building is an impressive five-storey octagonal reading room, recently restored to its original sky-lit splendour. The library also incorporates two galleries – the Keith Murdoch Gallery, with changing exhibitions, and the Cowen Gallery, with a permanent exhibition of oil paintings and portrait sculpture. *Cnr Lonsdale & Swanston sts; open daily; admission free.*

Old Melbourne Gaol

Melbourne Gaol was the setting for the execution of some of early Victoria's most notorious criminals, including the infamous Ned Kelly. Closed now for over 80 years, today visitors can wander through the cells and corridors of this dark and tortured place. Discover the horrifying reality of death masks and the *Particulars of Execution*, a how-to book on this gruesome subject. If you are brave enough, you can join the candle-lit tours at night. *Russell St, between Victoria & Latrobe sts; (03) 9663 7228; open daily; admission fee applies.*

Chinatown

Melbourne's Chinatown has prospered and flourished in different eras and under different governments since the first Chinese migrated to Victoria at the beginning of the gold rush. Today it is a permanent feature of the city, and two big, red archways herald the entrance to the Little Bourke Street strip at the Swanston Street and Exhibition Street ends. Chinatown in Melbourne, like Chinatowns around Australia and the world, is like no other place in the city. Lanterns decorate the street at night, and exotic food aromas drift out through the doorways of small restaurants. During the day, clothing, grocery and discount stores open their doors to shoppers as well.

The **Chinese Museum**, in Cohen Place off Little Bourke Street, tells the tale of the Chinese who migrated to Australia in search of the 'New Gold Mountain', and is also the resting-place of Dai Loong (Big Dragon), which roams the streets during Chinese New Year. Old artefacts, travelling exhibitions and artwork by local Chinese artists are other features. *Open daily; admission fee applies.*

Federation Square

Grand old buildings

Old ANZ Bank *Known as the Gothic Bank, with an incredible, gold-leafed interior. 380 Collins St, City.*

Manchester Unity Building *Chicago-style building with stark vertical lines, once the city's tallest skyscraper. Cnr Collins & Swanston sts, City.*

Capitol Theatre *Designed by the architects of Canberra and with a ceiling that will amaze you. 109–117 Swanston St, City.*

St Patrick's Cathedral *Victoria's largest church building, built with tons of Footscray bluestone. 5 Gisborne St, East Melbourne.*

Princess Theatre *The dramatic exterior culminates in three cast-iron tiaras. 163–181 Spring St, City.*

Forum Theatre *Moorish domes, and a starry night sky on the inner ceiling. 150 Flinders St, City.*

St Paul's Cathedral *Gothic cathedral made of sandstone. 2 Swanston St, City.*

Old Melbourne Magistrates' Court *The rough sandstone exterior and deeply set archways make for a grim atmosphere. Cnr Russell & Latrobe sts, City.*

Olderfleet Building *An intricate Gotham City facade. Nearby is Le Meridien at Rialto Hotel, designed by the same architect. 477 Collins St, City.*

Regent Theatre *Melbourne's most glamorous theatre, with an interior of Spanish-style lattice and red carpet. 191 Collins St, City.*

St James' Old Cathedral *A humble relic of Melbourne's founding years. 419–435 King St, City.*

University of Melbourne *More historic buildings than you can count. Parkville.*

Windsor Hotel *Layered like a wedding cake and fit for a queen. 137 Spring St, City.*

See also Royal Exhibition Building, p. 138

VICTORIA

Lonsdale Street

The section of Lonsdale Street between Russell and Swanston streets is the centre of Melbourne's Greek community. On the southern side are Greek travel agents, bookshops, music stores and, of course, cafes and restaurants. Stop in for a coffee and some baklava.

Melbourne Central

Since the closure of Japanese department store Daimaru, Melbourne Central has undergone change and is still, at the time of publication, being reincarnated, with some serious thought being given to the way Melburnians like to shop. The central shot tower and pointed glass ceiling will stay, but the complex will offer less of a one-stop, all-under-the-one-roof shopping experience and more of an adventure through a network of arcades and laneways each with its own unique character. But this is not so much an innovation as a restoration of Melbourne as it was intended to be (*see Laneways and arcades, p. 131*). All manner of shops will be found within. An underground concourse lined with shops leads from the Lonsdale Street entrance to Melbourne Central Station. *Between Lonsdale & Latrobe sts (between Elizabeth & Swanston sts).*

WEST

This part of Melbourne stretches from the Queen Victoria Market down to the Yarra, taking in the legal district and many office blocks. The **Supreme Court**

of **Victoria** is located in William Street. **Flagstaff Gardens**, to the north, were Melbourne's first public gardens and are where many legal professionals and office workers go for time-out. Between the Supreme Court and the gardens is the **Old Royal Mint**, a plain building set off with a dazzling coat of arms, now home to the Royal Historical Society of Victoria.

Melbourne Aquarium

Beside the Yarra River, partly underground, is the Melbourne Aquarium. While the aquariums of northern Australia are devoted to the brightly coloured fish and corals of the tropics, here the creatures of the Southern Ocean and Victoria's inland waterways get a chance to grab the limelight. Take a journey into the depths of the ocean, past rock-pool and mangrove habitats and a surreal display of jellyfish, into a tunnel and the 'fishbowl' for a close-up encounter with sharks, stingrays and multitudes of fish. For kids there is the interactive 'Fishworks', and for those yearning for the colours of the tropics an impressive floor-to-ceiling coral atoll. For the brave there is also the option of a dive with the sharks. *Cnr Queens Wharf Rd & King St; open daily; admission fee applies.*

Immigration Museum

At first glance this might seem like a specialist museum, but nothing could be more generally relevant in Australia, where migration has been constant since the first day of European settlement. Soon after the British landed a new stream of people began flowing in, mostly by boat. This museum is about journeys and

Entertainment

Cinema
The major cinemas can be found in the city centre, with Village and Hoyts both in Bourke Street east of the mall, and Greater Union nearby in Russell Street. For arthouse films, try the Lumiere at 108 Lonsdale Street or the Kino in Collins Place. Standout cinemas in the inner-city area include the Nova in Carlton for a great range of popular and arthouse films, the Rivoli in Camberwell for the old-world cinema experience, and the Astor in St Kilda East, where they play re-runs of the classics and recent releases. See daily newspapers for details.

Live music
Melbourne is renowned for its live-music scene. Fitzroy is one of the major centres of original music, with venues like the Rob Roy, Bar Open, the Laundry and the Evelyn hosting bands most nights. On the south side of town is The Esplanade Hotel in St Kilda, one of Melbourne's best original rock venues. For jazz, try Bennetts Lane Jazz Club, off Little Lonsdale Street east of Russell Street in the city, and for a boogie to anything from reggae to funk, try the relaxed and lamplit Night Cat in Johnston Street, Fitzroy. Bigger local and international acts play at other venues around town. Pick up one of the free street publications, Beat *or* Inpress, *or get the 'EG' lift-out from the* Age *on Fridays.*

Classical music and performing arts
The Victorian Arts Centre is Melbourne's premier venue for theatre, opera and ballet, and the Melbourne Concert Hall, next door, is the venue for classical music concerts. Popular musicals and theatrical productions are held at the Regent, Her Majesty's, the Princess and the Athenaeum theatres. The Playbox hosts Australian plays, and La Mama in Carlton is the venue for more experimental works. Check out the arts section of the Age *for details. Most performances are booked through Ticketmaster and Ticketek.*

tumultuous new beginnings, and about people coming from all corners of the world and bringing their traditions with them – traditions that became so much more important once they arrived. The museum is located in the Old Customs Building, opposite where ships once docked and waited as their captains sought trade clearance. *400 Flinders St; open daily; admission fee applies.*

Melbourne Observation Deck
Take a lift to the 55th level of Melbourne's tallest building, the Rialto Towers, and you'll find the Melbourne Observation Deck. Enjoy 360-degree views over the city, up the Yarra and over Port Phillip. From up here Melbourne seems flat, aside from the soft line of the Dandenong and Yarra ranges in the distance. *525 Collins St; open daily; admission fee applies.*

Koorie Heritage Trust Cultural Centre
Aboriginal culture has long been associated with Australia's lesser populated areas, such as the Red Centre, the Kimberley and Cape York. Most people are unaware that the Aboriginal tribes of Victoria dressed in possum skins in winter and built stone huts and fish traps near Lake Condah, north-east of Portland. As you walk through this centre you realise the drastic, violent and totally irreversible change to a culture that is over 40 000 years old. Displays take you through tribal traditions and lifestyle, including food and crafts, as well as the events that have occurred in the last two centuries. There are also changing exhibitions by local Aboriginal artists. *295 King St; open Mon–Fri; admission free.*

Queen Victoria Market
This famous market is spread across seven hectares under the shelter of a massive shed. At the Elizabeth Street end is a building containing the meat, fish and deli produce, while outside, all manner of fruit, vegetable and herb stalls extend towards the horizon. On weekends, Saturdays in particular, the aisles are crammed with shoppers from all over Melbourne, and the wide range of clothing and souvenirs make this a hot spot for tourists as well. *Main entrance on Elizabeth St near Victoria St; open Tues & Thurs–Sun.*

On Wednesday evenings during summer, the market takes on a whole new character with the **Gaslight Night Market**. At these times it feels more like a festival than a market, with live music, food ranging from Spanish to Guatemalan, and a healthy dose of alternative-clothing and craft stalls. The whole area is licensed, which means you can wander around at your leisure with a beer or wine in hand.

SOUTHBANK

This inner-city suburb takes in some of Melbourne's best leisure and dining precincts, as well as a concentration of public arts institutions. Behind Flinders Street Station is Southgate, a stylish shopping and dining precinct on the Yarra. A riverfront promenade extends all the way from here to Crown Entertainment Complex, another development that has helped give the Yarra River a leading role in the life of Melbourne. In summer these are lovely spots for a stroll and a drink or a meal in one of the many cafes, bars and restaurants that provide outdoor dining. On the riverbanks here are also some interesting pieces of public sculpture.

Southgate
Fifteen years ago Southgate was just like Docklands (*see p. 136*) – an industrial site being slowly reinvented. Apartments, office blocks, shops, restaurants and a tree-lined promenade have been added to form what is today an essential part of Melbourne. The sun shines for only a moment in many parts of the CBD, but at Southbank it is possible to stroll along the Yarra in the sunshine at almost any time of the day.

On the ground floor of the complex is a food court and a handful of shops, including one of Melbourne's Suga stores, where candy-making has been transformed into an art form. As you make your way to the top, the restaurants and bars become increasingly exclusive and the shops become boutiques, selling

The land of the Kulin

In 1835, a party of Europeans from Van Diemen's Land sailed into Port Phillip and bought the land that Melbourne now stands on for a novelty selection of goods – knives, mirrors, blankets and a few sacks of flour, among other items. The way of life of the Kulin people, in existence for tens of thousands of years, would never be the same again.

If you look closely, you'll notice sites throughout the city that stand in silent tribute to a way of life now largely extinct. Today Yarra Park is the home of the MCG, but it was once a Koorie camping ground. Several scarred trees can be found in the park, their bark having been stripped to make canoes. There are also ceremonial bora rings in the

north-western suburbs, man-made rock wells near Sandringham, and shell middens scattered over the shores of Port Phillip.

There has been a surge of interest in Aboriginal culture in recent years, and while some of it has come from the local population, much of it has come via international tourism. In Melbourne you can visit the fantastic Bunjilaka, part of the Melbourne Museum (*see p. 138*), and the Koorie Heritage Trust Cultural Centre (*see entry on this page*), or you can go on one of the Aboriginal Heritage Walks at the Royal Botanic Gardens. Aboriginal culture is slowly coming out of a 200-year period of oblivion, and its emergence is well overdue.

The Bolte Bridge in the moonlight

glassware, art and jewellery. Some of Melbourne's finest restaurants are located on the top level.

Crown Entertainment Complex

Crown Entertainment Complex begins just over Queensbridge Street. For many Victorians the sight of its oval-shaped tower and the eight water walls along the riverfront that spew fireballs at night is intertwined with the memory of controversial former state premier, Jeff Kennett. He was the driving force behind this development and many others, including the Bolte Bridge and Melbourne Exhibition Centre. As well as a casino, Crown contains shops, restaurants, nightclubs and cinemas. The food range here is like Southgate's, with a food court at one end of the scale and a handful of top-notch restaurants at the other. The big names in fashion such as Versace and Armani reside here too, and items regularly top the $1000 mark.

Melbourne Exhibition Centre and *Polly Woodside*

Over Clarendon Street from Crown is the Melbourne Exhibition Centre, with its striking entrance angled upwards over the water. This is the venue for most of Melbourne's major expos, from car shows to food and wine shows and wedding exhibitions.

Next to the centre is the *Polly Woodside* Melbourne Maritime Museum, whose centrepiece is the *Polly Woodside*, a restored iron barque afloat in Melbourne's original, wooden-walled dry dock. Venture into the bows of the ship and then learn about the city's maritime history in the

1930s cargo sheds. *Open daily; admission fee applies.*

Victorian Arts Centre

The Victorian Arts Centre, on St Kilda Road over the bridge from Flinders Street Station, consists of two buildings – the Melbourne Concert Hall and the Theatres Building, with its distinctive lattice spire. This building plunges to six levels below St Kilda Road and includes three theatres: the State Theatre, with seating for 2000 and a venue for opera, ballets and musicals; the Playhouse, for drama; and the George Fairfax Studio, a smaller drama venue.

If you are not heading to a concert or a theatre show you can still visit the **George Adams Gallery**, also under the spire. This is the main exhibition space for the **Performing Arts Museum**, which preserves a variety of Australian performing-arts memorabilia. Exhibitions in the gallery focus on anything from Barry Humphries to the costumes of the *Phantom of the Opera*. *Open daily; admission free.*

NGV International

The National Gallery of Victoria recently split its collection in two, with Australian art moving to Federation Square (*see p. 129*) and the international collection staying at the home of the NGV since 1968 – the tall, oriental-style building next to the Arts Centre. Renovations were completed in 2003, with the water curtain at the entrance and the magnificent stained-glass roof by Leonard French remaining intact. There are now much bigger and better spaces for displaying touring exhibitions, including

Museums and galleries

Jewish Museum of Australia *A record of the experiences of Australia's many Jewish migrants. 26 Alma Rd, St Kilda; 10am–4pm Tue–Thurs, 11am–5pm Sun; admission fee applies.*

Monsalvat *An artist's colony that began in 1934, with magnificent French provincial buildings and art works for view in the gallery. 7 Hillcrest Ave, Eltham; open daily; admission fee applies.*

Australian Racing Museum and Hall of Fame *Celebrating Australia's horses, jockeys, trainers and owners. Federation Sq; open daily; general admission free.*

ANZ Banking Museum *Old money boxes, staff uniforms and historic displays in the glorious Gothic setting of the Old ANZ Bank. 380 Collins St, City; Mon–Fri; admission free.*

Post Master Gallery *For the stamp enthusiast, but also for those interested in art and design. Cnr Latrobe & Exhibition sts; open daily; admission free.*

Ian Potter Museum of Art *Victoria's second largest art collection, including cultural artefacts and contemporary artworks. University of Melbourne, opposite 800 Swanston St. (Note that the museum was closed for renovations at the time of publication and is expected to reopen early in 2005.)*

Victoria Police Museum *Victoria's life of crime revealed, from the capture of Ned Kelly to the Hoddle Street shootings. World Trade Centre Complex, 637 Flinders St; 10am–4pm Mon–Fri; admission free.*

Fire Services Museum *Huge collection of fire brigade memorabilia, including vintage vehicles and historic photos. 39 Gisborne St, East Melbourne; 9am–3pm Fri, 10am–4pm Sun; admission fee applies.*

Railway Museum *Open-air museum with historic locomotives. Champion Rd, North Williamstown; 12 noon–5pm weekends; admission fee applies.*

See also Melbourne Museum, p. 138, Gold Treasury Museum, p. 132, Immigration Museum, p. 133, Koorie Heritage Trust Cultural Centre, facing page, ACCA, p. 136, Heide, p. 139, Ian Potter Centre: NGV Australia, p. 130, NGV International, on this page, Australian Centre for the Moving Image, p. 130, Chinese Museum, p. 132, Flinders Lane galleries, p. 132, Polly Woodside, on this page, Performing Arts Museum, on this page

Parks and gardens

Birrarung Marr *Melbourne's newest park, with a Korean bell installation playing commissioned works. City. See map on p. 130*

Albert Park *A great spot for exercising around the lake, and the site for the Australian Formula One Grand Prix. Albert Park. 128 F6*

Gasworks Arts Park *Sculptures, native gardens, barbecues and artist studios in the former South Melbourne Gasworks. South Melbourne. 128 D6*

Yarra Bend Park *Closest bushland to the city, with boats for hire, great views and a strong Aboriginal heritage. Kew/Fairfield. 129 H2*

Eltham Lower Park *Featuring the Diamond Valley Miniature Railway, which offers rides for kids on Sundays. Eltham. 519 F5*

Brimbank Park *With wetlands, a children's farm and walking trails along the Maribyrnong River. Keilor. 519 C5*

Jells Park *A haven for waterbirds and a great place for a stroll through the bush. Wheelers Hill. 519 F7*

Wattle Park *Native bush and birds, and accessible by tram. Surrey Hills. 519 F6*

Westerfolds Park *On the Yarra and popular for canoeing and cycling, with the Mia Mia Aboriginal Gallery on top of the hill. Templestowe. 519 F5*

See also Royal Botanic Gardens, facing page, and Fitzroy Gardens, p. 139

cutting-edge film and installation art. With more than 30 galleries, more of the gallery's own extensive collection is also on display, covering everything from antiquities to painting and sculpture. *Open daily; general admission free.*

Contemporary arts on Sturt Street
Behind St Kilda Road is Sturt Street, an industrial and fairly quiet street since the CityLink tunnel bypassed it. But it is home to two more arts institutions – the CUB Malthouse and the Australian Centre for Contemporary Art (ACCA). Once a malt factory, the **CUB Malthouse** is home to the Playbox Theatre Company, dedicated to contemporary and all-Australian theatre. It is also the venue for the Melbourne Writers' Festival held each August. *113 Sturt St.*

Next to the Malthouse, the **ACCA** is housed in a rusted-steel building – the colour of Uluru against a blue sky. Inside the stark structural forms are changing contemporary Australian and international exhibitions, more confronting and interactive than conservative and traditional. Also based in the building is Chunky Move, a leading Australian dance company. 'Vault', otherwise known as the Yellow Peril, Melbourne's most controversial public sculpture, has finally found a resting place in the grounds of the ACCA. *111 Sturt St; open Tues–Sun; admission free.*

Docklands

Melbourne's CBD is once again on the move, this time west across Spencer Street and the railyards to Victoria Harbour and Docklands. Until the 1960s this was a busy shipping port, but the volume of shipping containers eventually grew too large for the space and Victoria Harbour fell into disuse. Now it is slowly being transformed into a residential, business, entertainment and retail precinct. So far the features include **Telstra Dome**, a major venue for AFL matches and other events, and **NewQuay**, a waterfront development with stylish bars, restaurants and cafes. It is estimated that by 2015 Docklands will be home to around 15 000 people and a workplace for around 20 000. It will also grow as a major destination for visitors, for both the dining possibilities and the harbour tours on offer.

The maritime feel and the distinctive waft of sea air is a brand-new feature of inner-city Melbourne, and something that the locals are very excited about. And while you can dine in some high-end restaurants overlooking the harbour, fish and chips and ice-cream are also on offers – essential features of any good wharf.

Inner south-east

Across the river from Federation Square, Melbourne's finest public gardens stretch away to the south-east. Beyond these gardens are some of the city's most exclusive suburbs: South Yarra, Toorak, Malvern and Armadale. South Yarra and Toorak centre around **Toorak Road**, where exclusive clothing, footwear and jewellery stores as well as cafes and gourmet food shops line the street. Over Williams Road in Toorak, a quaint Tudoresque shopping village houses all the top names in fashion. Chapel Street runs in the other direction, from South Yarra into

Sunrise in Alexandra Gardens, north of Kings Domain

St Kilda, and is virtually non-stop shops for three major blocks, from Toorak Road to Dandenong Road.

Gardens 128 F5

Bordered by the curve of the Yarra and the bitumen of St Kilda Road is a series of public gardens, including Kings Domain and the Royal Botanic Gardens. In **Kings Domain** is the **Sidney Myer Music Bowl**, a venue for outdoor concerts in summertime, and the imposing **Shrine of Remembrance**. Deep within the shrine stands a statue of two soldiers, representing the generations of Australians who have fought in various wars around the world. You access the shrine from the chambers below, through a new visitor centre. From the balcony at the top there are views straight down St Kilda Road. The shrine is the centre for ANZAC Day commemorations, and on 11 November (Armistice Day) each year, a ray of sunlight appears through a mathematically positioned gap in the roof to light up the Stone of Remembrance. *Open daily; admission free.*

To the east of the shrine is **La Trobe's Cottage**, a prefabricated house built in England and brought to Australia in 1839 to become the residence of Victoria's first lieutenant governor.

Directly opposite the shrine, across Birdwood Avenue, is Observatory Gate, behind which are the renowned **Royal Botanic Gardens**. Inside the gate is a cafe and the Old Melbourne Observatory. The visitor centre here has information on walks and activities in the gardens, including a National Trust tour taking in **Government House**, located just behind Observatory Gate but hidden from view by a tangle of vegetation. This impressive Italianate mansion is the official residence of the governor of Victoria.

Other walks and activities include the Night Sky Experience at the Observatory and the Aboriginal Heritage Walk (*see Walks and tours, on this page*). In summer the gardens host the **Moonlight Cinema**, a great way to enjoy this lush, green setting. Programs are available around town, and the films on offer range from new releases to the classics.

If you are after a riverfront picnic spot, look just outside the gardens across Alexandra Avenue. Free gas barbecues dot the Yarra bank from Swan Street Bridge to Anderson Street.

Chapel Street 129 G6

Chapel Street, between Toorak and Commercial roads, is the place to come for the latest in fashion – and you'd probably want to be wearing it while you're there. About halfway down this stretch is the **Jam Factory**, a shopping complex inside the old premises of the Australian Jam Company. Facing the street is Borders, one of Melbourne's favourite bookshops, and inside is a cinema complex that screens most of the new releases as well as some arthouse titles.

Just around the corner from Chapel Street on Commercial Road is the **Prahran Market**, which is Australia's oldest continually running market and a great place for everything from gourmet potatoes to dolmades, coffee beans and cookware (closed Mondays and Wednesdays).

A little further up, off Chapel Street is **Greville Street**, a narrow strip lined with cafes, bars, record stores and retro clothing shops. On Sunday afternoons Greville Street hosts a market, with clothing, food and handmade goods.

Como House and Herring Island 129 H5

While mansions today boast home-entertainment centres and swimming pools, those of yesteryear had croquet lawns and ballrooms. Como House is a National Trust-listed mansion at the end of Williams Road. Stroll around the gardens and take a tour of the house, complete with the original furnishings of the Armytage family, who resided here for 95 years. Nearby is Como Landing, where you can take a punt across to Herring Island in the middle of the Yarra. This artificial island boasts a sculpture park and picnic/barbecue facilities. *Como House is open 10am–5pm daily; admission fee applies; punt operates 12 noon–5pm, Thurs–Sun, during daylight saving.*

Inner north

Carlton and Fitzroy are two lively inner suburbs to the north and north-east of the city. Carlton is the heart of Victorian terrace territory: row upon row of them line the streets, fringed with Melbourne's distinctive cast-iron lace. Fitzroy is where many young Melburnians would choose to live if they could afford it – real estate has skyrocketed around here in recent years, but the alternative feel of Brunswick Street has so far remained intact. **Smith Street**, the next major street to the east, is like Brunswick Street a decade ago – still a little seedy, but slowly blossoming with cafes, health-food shops and independent fashion designers (and also with factory outlets towards Alexandra Parade; *see Shopping, p. 131*).

Lygon Street, Carlton 128 E3

This is Carlton's main artery and the centre of Melbourne's Italian population, with many restaurants and cafes as well as bookstores, clothing shops and a good cinema, the Nova. But in true Italian style, food is definitely the main focus here. Stop for authentic pasta, pizza or gelati and, of course, some first-rate coffee. You can also head to **Rathdowne Street**, parallel to Lygon Street. Beyond Elgin Street, cafes, restaurants and food stores line this leafy neighbourhood street too.

Walks and tours

Golden Mile Heritage Trail *Walk with a guide or navigate this trail on your own. There are two tours, one from the Immigration Museum to the Town Hall, and one from Federation Square to Melbourne Museum. Walkers gain discounted entry to heritage attractions along the way. Bookings 1300 130 152, or get a self-guide brochure from the visitor centre.*

Aboriginal Heritage Walk *With an Aboriginal guide and a gum leaf for a ticket, stroll through the Royal Botanic Gardens and learn about the bushfoods, medicines and traditional lore of the Boonwurrung and Woiworung people, whose traditional lands meet here. Bookings (03) 9252 2429.*

Swanston Street Art Walk *Stroll down Melbourne's street-cum-gallery, dotted with many a quirky sculpture. The walk begins at Federation Square and finishes at the art-as-architecture buildings of the Royal Melbourne Institute of Technology. Brochure available from the visitor centre.*

Haunted Melbourne Ghost Tour *Get the adrenalin pumping as you traipse down dark alleys and enter city buildings that the ghosts of early Melbourne are known to haunt. Bookings (03) 9670 2585.*

Chocoholic Tours *A range of tours to get you drooling, taking in Melbourne's best chocolatiers, candy-makers, ice-creameries and cafes. Bookings (03) 9815 1228.*

Harley Davidson Tour *Take the Introduction to Melbourne Tour around the bay and over the West Gate Bridge with the wind whistling through your hair. Bookings (03) 9877 3004.*

Foodies Dream Tour *Get tips on picking the best fresh produce, meet the specialist traders and taste samples from the deli at Queen Victoria Market. Bookings (03) 9670 2585.*

Murder and Mystery Tour *Find out about the illegal operations of Champagne Jimmy and the gruesome Gun Alley atrocity. Melbourne is not so innocent after all. Bookings (03) 9662 9010.*

River Cruise *A trip down the Yarra or the Maribyrnong will give you new views of Melbourne. Melbourne River Cruises (Yarra) (03) 9614 1215; City River Cruises (03) 9650 2214; Williamstown Bay and River Cruises (03) 9397 2255; Maribyrnong River Cruises (03) 9689 6431.*

VICTORIA

Sport

*Melbourne is possibly Australia's most sporting city, with hardly a gap in the calendar for the true sports enthusiast. **AFL** (Australian Football League) is indisputably at the top of the list. The season begins at the end of March and as it nears the finals in September, footy madness eclipses the city. Melbourne has nine teams in the league, and the blockbuster matches are played at the MCG and Telstra Dome.*

*After the football comes the **Spring Racing Carnival**, as much a social event as a horseracing one. October and November are packed with events at racetracks across the state, with the city events held at Caulfield, Moonee Valley, Sandown and Flemington racetracks. The Melbourne Cup, 'the race that stops the nation', is held at Flemington on the first Tuesday in November, and is a local public holiday.*

***Cricket** takes Melbourne through the heat of summer. One Day International and Test matches are usually played at the MCG, and the popular Boxing Day Test gives Christmas in Melbourne a sporting twist.*

*In January Melbourne hosts the **Australian Open**, one of the world's four major tennis Grand Slams. The venue is Melbourne Park, home to the Rod Laver Arena and the Vodafone Arena, both of which host other sporting events and concerts throughout the year.*

*Come March, and the **Australian Formula One Grand Prix** comes to town, attracting a large international crowd. The cars race around Albert Park Lake, which for the rest of the year is the setting for rather more low-key sporting pursuits such as jogging and rollerblading.*

Brunswick Street, Fitzroy 128 F2

Brunswick Street offers an eclectic mix of cafes, pubs and shops at both ends of the scale. Anything goes in Brunswick Street – young professionals come here for leisurely weekend breakfasts, *Big Issue* vendors ply the streets, and people in colourful clothing and with grungy haircuts always seem to be on their way to somewhere else. For a cheap meal and a great atmosphere, the Vegie Bar is always a favourite, and if you wander off the main drag you will find a few quaint corner pubs, such as the Napier, offering decent meals. This is also the centre of Melbourne's live-music scene (*see Entertainment, p. 134*).

Melbourne Museum and the Royal Exhibition Building 128 F3

These two buildings are set in Carlton Gardens, facing Nicholson Street. There is a contrast in styles here – the regal splendour of the long-standing exhibition building meets the spaceship-like structure of the new museum.

Melbourne Museum is the home of Phar Lap, Australia's champion horse, standing proud and tall in a dimly lit room. This is the most popular exhibit, but since the move from its previous premises in Russell Street, the place has become decidedly more upbeat. Inside the huge complex is Bunjilaka, an Aboriginal cultural centre telling the Koorie story from the Koorie perspective – not just an academic selection of Aboriginal artefacts. Other features of the museum include dinosaur skeletons, a living rainforest and impressive displays on science, the mind and the body. Located in the same building is the **IMAX Theatre**, screening films in 2D and 3D. *Open daily; admission fee applies.*

The Royal Exhibition Building is arguably Melbourne's most important historic building, with an application currently pending for World Heritage status. It was built during the exhibition movement that began in London in the 19th century, and it hosted the International Exhibition of 1880, a major event that showcased the technological and industrial achievements of over 20 countries. Today the building still hosts public exhibitions, though not on such a grand scale. Tours to marvel at the interior, including the detailed frescoes on the walls and ceiling, run from the museum daily whenever the building is not in use.

Melbourne Zoo 128 E1

This is Australia's oldest zoo, and the single iron-barred enclosure that remains is testimony to the days when animals were kept in minuscule cages. Today things are rather different – the zoo recently spent $10 million on a new feature, the Trail of the Elephants. Now the elephants live in a re-creation of an Asian rainforest, complete with an elephant-sized plunge pool. For visitors, there is an Asian Village with hawker stalls, vegetable gardens and interactive displays. Another perennial favourite here is the Butterfly House, where butterflies are quite happy to land on you as you pass through. During January and February the zoo runs a popular program of open-air jazz sessions called Zoo Twilights. *Open daily; admission fee applies.*

Inner east

Richmond and Abbotsford lie to the east of the city, and for both food and clothing here the combination of quality and price is hard to beat. Between the city and these suburbs are Melbourne's biggest sporting venues, scattered on either side of the railyards like giant, resting UFOs. The two major ones are the MCG and **Melbourne Park**, home of the Australian Open and various big concerts. Further out is a stretch of parkland that follows the winding path of the Yarra.

Bridge Road, Richmond 129 G4

Bridge Road is Richmond's main artery, and between Hoddle and Church streets it is a shopper's heaven. Many a tour bus pulls up here, with starry-eyed shoppers pouring into the designer-clothing stores and factory outlets. In the next block,

Cricket, football and the MCG

In 1838 Melbourne was little more than a ragged collection of tents, yet it already had a cricket club. It is proof that Melbourne hasn't always been footy-mad, and that once upon a time this city was absolutely cricket-crazy.

The Melbourne Cricket Club finally found a permanent home – the MCG – in 1853 and international teams started visiting in 1862. If the growing skills of the Melbourne team lured them, you could say that the MCG, slowly gaining a reputation as one of the world's great grounds, clinched the deal. Cricket in Melbourne was becoming serious business.

Meanwhile, another sport was developing. A hotchpotch of local men began thinking about what cricketers could do to keep fit in the off-season. Rugby was seen as too likely to cause injury, so they set about making rules for a brand-new game. The first official match of what has become AFL was played between two private boys' schools. Slowly the marks became more spectacular and the long, soaring kicks more accurate. Football began weaving its way into Melbourne's psyche.

AFL – fast, athletic, and probably just as likely to cause injury as rugby ever was – has surpassed the popularity of cricket in Melbourne, and indeed in much of Australia. Local matches can pull crowds of between 30 000 and 80 000, and the city's favourite venue is by far the MCG – revamped and remodelled many a time, but still going strong.

Kangaroos football supporters

between Church and Burnley Streets, is a strip of reasonably priced restaurants offering various cuisines, from Burmese to Mediterranean to Thai.

Swan Street, Richmond 129 G4
Swan Street, south of Bridge Road, is another good spot for wining and dining, especially if the flavours of Greece are high on your list. The original Dimmeys store is on Swan Street too, with its distinctive domed clock tower. This has been a great place for a bargain since 1853.

Victoria Street, Abbotsford 129 G3
Victoria Street, north of Bridge Road, is a living, breathing piece of Vietnam. From Hoddle Street to Church Street it overflows with Asian grocery stores and Vietnamese restaurants, where the focus is not on sophisticated dining but on authentic food, fast.

Melbourne Cricket Ground (MCG) 128 G4
A footy or cricket match at the MCG would have to be one of Melbourne's top experiences, but if you visit in the off-season or simply can't get enough sport in your system, then you could take a tour of the MCG, a stadium thoroughly intertwined with Australian sport – past and present. Tours run on every non-event day, 10am–3pm on the hour, from the Great Southern Stand. Subject to availability, the tour includes a walk on the legendary ground. (Owing to the MCG's redevelopment, the Australian Gallery of Sport and Olympic Museum and the Australian Cricket Hall of Fame are closed until late 2005/early 2006.)

Fitzroy Gardens 128 F3
Fitzroy Gardens are one of a handful of public gardens surrounding the CBD, but the only one that can boast Cook's Cottage, a fairy tree and a model Tudor village. The quaint, thatch-roofed cottage was the Yorkshire home of Captain Cook's parents, and was shipped out from London in 1934 as a centenary gift to Victoria. *Cottage open daily; admission fee applies.*

Yarra Bend Park 129 H2
Yarra Bend Park is a bushland sanctuary that feels far, far away from the city even though it is, in fact, just a few minutes drive from it. It features walking tracks and golf courses, and boat-hire facilities at the historic **Studley Park Boathouse**. Go boating on the river, then dock for a spot of Devonshire tea.

Heide 519 E5
Further upstream along the Yarra is Heide, which incorporates the Museum of Modern Art, the restored old weatherboard house that was the home of founders John and Sunday Reed, and beautiful parklands. The Reeds emerged as patrons of the arts in the 1930s and 1940s, and artists such as Albert Tucker, Sidney Nolan and Joy Hester found constant support at Heide. Today the support for modern art continues in the museum, which has changing exhibitions in its three galleries. This is the kind of place where you could spend a whole day looking at the art, wandering through the Reeds' home and kitchen garden, and finishing off with a picnic in the park. *7 Templestowe Rd, Bulleen; open daily; admission fee applies to galleries and house.*

Outer suburbs

Brunswick *Sydney Road is the place to come to for cheap fabrics, authentic Turkish bread and a healthy dose of Middle Eastern culture. 519 E6*

Footscray *A mini-Saigon that is the lesser known version of Victoria Street, Abbotsford. Jam-packed with cheap eateries and one of Melbourne's best produce markets. 128 A2*

Camberwell and Canterbury *In Melbourne's eastern money belt, with fashion outlets lining Camberwell's Burke Road and the elegant Maling Road shopping precinct in Canterbury. 519 E6*

Yarraville *A gem tucked away in a largely industrial sweep of suburbs, with cafes and a superb Art Deco cinema. 128 A4*

Hawthorn *With a strong student culture from the nearby university, and a strip of shops on Glenferrie Road offering everything from Asian groceries to smart fashion. 519 E6*

Balaclava *Kosher butchers mixed with an emerging cafe culture. Here and neighbouring Elwood are the affordable alternatives to St Kilda. 129 G8*

Black Rock *One of many bayside suburbs shifting from sleepy village into sought-after real estate, fronting two of Melbourne's best beaches. 519 E8*

Dandenong *The base for Melbourne's Indian community – with food stores galore and also one of Melbourne's oldest markets. 519 F9*

Eltham *All native trees and mud-brick architecture, this suburb feels like a piece of the country only 30 minutes from the city. 519 F5*

VICTORIA

Day tours

The Dandenongs *These scenic hills at the edge of Melbourne's eastern suburbs are apopular daytrip. Native rainforests of mountain ash and giant ferns, extensive cool-climate gardens, the popular steam train Puffing Billy and cafes, galleries and craft shops are among the many attractions. For more details see p. 142*

Yarra Valley and Healesville *High-quality pinot noir and sparkling wines are produced across one of Australia's best-known wine areas. Pick up a brochure from the information centre in Healesville and map out your wine-tasting tour. Worthy of its own daytrip is Healesville Sanctuary, featuring around 200 native animal species in a bushland setting. For more details see p. 142*

Mornington Peninsula *This holiday centre features fine-food producers, around 40 cool-climate vineyards, historic holiday villages, quiet coastal national parks, 20 golf courses and many attractions for children. For more details see p. 143*

Phillip Island *The nightly Penguin Parade on Phillip Island is one of Victoria's signature attractions. For the avid wildlife-watcher, seals and koalas are the other stars of the show, though the island also boasts magnificent coastal scenery and great surf breaks. For more details see p. 144*

Sovereign Hill *Ballarat's award-winning re-creation of a 19th-century goldmining village conjures up the detail and drama of life during one of the nation's most exciting periods of history. Stay into the evening for the on-site show that re-enacts the events of the Eureka Rebellion. For more details see Ballarat, p. 162*

Bellarine Peninsula *The Bellarine Peninsula separates the waters of Port Phillip from the famously rugged coastline of Victoria's south-west. Beyond the historic buildings, streets and waterfront of Geelong are quaint coastal villages, excellent beaches, golf courses and wineries. For more details see p. 147*

Mount Macedon and Hanging Rock *Country mansions and superb 19th- and 20th-century European-style gardens sit comfortably in the native bush and volcanic landscape. Here you'll find wineries, cafes, nurseries, galleries and the mysteriously beautiful Hanging Rock. For more details see p. 146*

Spa country *For a few hours of health-giving indulgence, visit the historic spa complex at Hepburn Springs. Afterwards explore the colourful shops of Daylesford, enjoy a meal at one of the region's excellent eateries, or take a peaceful forest drive. For more details see p. 146*

Eastern bayside

Melbourne's eastern bayside suburbs sprawl down towards the long arm of the Mornington Peninsula. These days the real estate here has quite a hefty price tag attached. At the top of the bay is **Port Melbourne**, once the entry point for many thousands of migrants and now the docking point for *Spirit of Tasmania* ferries. Bay Street has a range of pubs, shops and restaurants, as does Clarendon Street, South Melbourne. On Cecil Street is the **South Melbourne Market**, where meats, deli items, fruit, vegetables, flowers, homewares and clothing are all displayed under the one roof. South of South Melbourne is **Albert Park**, the venue for the Australian Formula One Grand Prix each March as well as a spot for bike riding, rollerblading, jogging and boating on and around the lake. Various other sports are also on offer in Albert Park's **Melbourne Sports and Aquatic Centre**. Further south again is St Kilda – and the charm of this suburb is pretty much irresistible.

St Kilda 128 F7

St Kilda began life as a seaside holiday destination, so separate from the city that on the sandy track that was then St Kilda Road, travellers ran the risk of a run-in with a bushranger. Today it has the feeling of a city within a city. **Fitzroy Street** is a long line of shoulder-to-shoulder cafes, restaurants, bars and pubs. Straight ahead is the palm-lined foreshore and the beach, and around the corner is **St Kilda Pier** – the iconic kiosk that once stood midway along the pier was sadly devastated by a fire in 2003. South of the pier are the **St Kilda Sea Baths**. Now a swanky relaxation complex, the baths date back to the days when swimming in the open ocean was not the done thing, and warm saltwater baths opening onto the sea were a much more acceptable option.

The path along the foreshore goes from Port Melbourne in the north to beyond Brighton in the south and is almost always busy with cyclists, rollerbladers and walkers. **The Esplanade Hotel** on The Esplanade is an integral part of Melbourne's live-music scene, and **The Palais**, a grand, French-style theatre further on, is the venue for some big-billed concerts. Luna Park (*see next entry*) is right next door to The Palais, and there is an art and craft market on The Esplanade every Sunday (*see Markets, p. 132*).

The Esplanade eventually runs into **Acland Street**, the quieter alternative to Fitzroy Street. Just around the corner from The Esplanade are the continental cake shops that have made this street famous.

South from St Kilda is a string of swimming beaches, including **Brighton Beach** with its trademark bathing boxes and views of the city. **Rippon Lea**, on Hotham Street in Elsternwick, is a grand, Romanesque mansion set in beautiful gardens and open daily. Visitors can go on a tour of the mansion or just visit the gardens.

Luna Park 128 F8

Even with its recent revamp, Luna Park still feels like a chunk of the early 20th century, when a ride on the Scenic Railway and a walk through the Palais de Foiles (the Palace of Giggles) was a big night out, and when live entertainment involving animals and midgets was perfectly acceptable. Since it opened in 1912, many things about the park live on, including the huge and famous (and much-renovated) face that forms its entrance. It is either laughing or screaming, according to how you look at it. Among the traditional rides such as the carousel, Ferris wheel and rollercoaster are the more modern Shock Drop, Enterprise and G-Force. *Open weekends as well as Fri nights in warm weather and daily during school holidays. Admission is free (though the rides are not).*

Western suburbs

Travel over the West Gate Bridge and you'll find a landscape of factories leading to more far-flung suburbs. But south of the West Gate Bridge, on the western arm of Hobsons Bay, is Williamstown – one of Melbourne's true gems.

Williamstown 128 B7

If St Kilda feels like a city within a city, then Williamstown feels like a village, perhaps even an island. It is bounded by a vast industrial area on two sides and by the sea on the other two, across which are superb views of the Melbourne skyline. Bobbing up and down in its harbour are a fleet of yachts, and along Nelson Place are restaurants, bars and cafes in old maritime buildings. People spill out onto the pavement in summer to sip lattes and sniff the sea air (despite all the industry, the sea does seem cleaner on this side of the bay). Alternatively, they buy fish and chips and ice-creams and spread out on the grass in front of the harbour. Williamstown's main swimming beach is around the other side of the bay. For those who care to use it, there is a ferry service to Willamstown from St Kilda and Southgate, with an optional stop at Scienceworks (*for information on the ferry, see Walks and tours, p. 137*).

Scienceworks 128 A5

This is the place to come to 'push it, pull it, spin it, bang it', and inadvertently get a grasp on science. It is a great place to bring the kids, with interactive exhibitions on all things science-related. Also in the complex is the **Melbourne Planetarium**, with simulated night skies and 3D adventures through space. A historic pumping station is located on site, and tours are available. *2 Booker St, Spotswood; open daily; admission fee applies.*

VICTORIA'S REGIONS

YARRA & DANDENONGS

Yarra Valley winery

Top events

Jan	Upper Yarra Draughthorse Festival (Warburton)
Feb	Jazz Festival (Olinda)
	Grape Grazing Festival (throughout Yarra Valley wine district)
April	Great Train Race (Emerald)
July	Winterfest (Warburton)
Aug–Nov	Rhododendron Festival (Olinda)
Sept–Oct	Tesselaar's Tulip Festival (Silvan, near Olinda)
Nov	Gateway Festival (Healesville, odd-numbered years)

W ineries, fine-food outlets, historic gardens, ancient forests, snowfields and excellent activities for children combine to make this a fantastic place for a daytrip or an extended holiday. The scenic Yarra Valley, about an hour's drive from Melbourne, is responsible for some of Australia's best cool-climate wines. The Dandenong Ranges, east of the city, offer a mix of tall, native forests and expansive European-style gardens. Beyond the two areas, a series of charming villages form a gateway to Victoria's magnificent alpine country.

Focus on

Tours of the forest

This area has some of the state's best forest scenery. Bushwalkers, horseriders and cyclists can travel the 38-kilometre Warburton Rail Trail, starting in Lilydale. The Beeches, an area of rainforest near Marysville, has a 5-kilometre stroll through forests of ancient beech and mountain ash. The less energetic can take a forest drive through or around Yarra Ranges National Park, choosing from the Black Spur Drive (between Healesville and Marysville), Acheron Way (from Warburton to Marysville) and the Lady Talbot Forest Drive (a shorter drive in the Marysville region). For something special, visit Mt Donna Buang Rainforest Gallery (near Warburton), which includes a viewing platform and a raised walkway through the rainforest.

Yarra Valley wineries

The 30 or so wineries of this district produce high-quality chardonnay, cabernet sauvignon and pinot noir. Visit Domaine Chandon, built by French champagne makers Moët & Chandon; the magnificent tasting-room offers fine views across the vine-covered valley. TarraWarra Estate features an impressive art gallery with work by artists such as Brett Whiteley, Sidney Nolan and Arthur Boyd, and De Bortoli is home to a restaurant serving fine Italian-style fare.

CLIMATE HEALESVILLE

	J	F	M	A	M	J	J	A	S	O	N	D
Max °C	26	26	24	19	16	12	12	14	16	19	22	24
Min °C	11	12	11	9	7	4	4	5	6	8	9	11
Rain mm	58	68	64	91	96	82	87	98	94	106	93	86
Raindays	7	7	8	11	14	14	16	17	15	14	12	10

Gardens of the Dandenongs

Mountain ash forests and fern gullies frame the historic cool-climate gardens of one of Australia's best-known gardening regions. Many of the private gardens are open daily. Public gardens include the National Rhododendron Gardens and the R. J. Hamer Forest Arboretum (both near Olinda), the William Ricketts Sanctuary (Mt Dandenong) and the Alfred Nicholas Memorial Gardens (Sherbrooke).

Experience it!

1 **Ride** the famous Puffing Billy steam train on its 25 km journey through lush forest and tree ferns from Belgrave to Gembrook and back again

2 **Follow** the Yarra Valley Regional Food Trail for berries, trout, chocolates and cheese (get a brochure from the visitor centre in Healesville)

3 **Have** some fun in the winter snow on Mt Donna Buang, near Warburton

For more detail see maps 519, 521, 524 & 534.
For descriptions of ❶ towns see Towns from A–Z (p. 159).

Marysville and Lake Mountain

This beautiful subalpine village, with its excellent cafes and art and craft outlets, provides access to the magnificent 84 m Steavenson Falls. Lake Mountain to the east is a popular tobogganing and cross-country skiing resort in winter, but also a great bushwalking destination in summer.

Healesville Sanctuary

Spread across 32 ha of bushland, this world-renowned native animal sanctuary has over 200 species, most roaming in natural settings. Special features include talks by keepers, a nocturnal viewing area, the bird-of-prey displays and the platypus exhibit.

MORNINGTON PENINSULA

Jumping off the
Portsea Pier

Top events

Jan Portsea Swim Classic

Feb Rye Beach Sand Sculpting
Championship

Mar Maize Maze Festival (Arthurs Seat)

Pinot Week (throughout wine district)

Cool Climate Wine Show (Red Hill)

Street Festival (Sorrento)

Oct Mornington Food and Wine Festival
(throughout wine district)

Nov Film Festival (Rosebud)

This broad peninsula separating Port Phillip and Western Port has a long history as a summer retreat for Melburnians. It offers a clutch of well-serviced seaside towns with access to three seafronts: the sheltered 'front' beaches of Port Phillip, the wild 'back' beaches of Bass Strait, and the relatively unpopulated surf beaches of Western Port. During winter, holiday-makers turn their attention to the region's scenic hinterland, with its cool-climate vineyards and gourmet-food producers. In any season, popular activities are walking, fishing, golfing (a choice of 20 courses), and eating out at the many restaurants, pubs and cafes.

Focus on

Wineries

The grape came relatively late to the peninsula: the oldest vineyard, Elgee Park, north of Merricks, was established early in the 1970s. Viticulture exploded during the 1980s and 90s; now there are nearly 40 wineries in this cool-climate region, most clustered around Red Hill and many set in postcard-perfect landscapes. The vineyards tend to be small and concentrate on the classic varieties of pinot noir and chardonnay. Stonier, Tucks Ridge and Main Ridge Estate are a few of the names to look out for.

CLIMATE MORNINGTON

	J	F	M	A	M	J	J	A	S	O	N	D
Max °C	25	25	23	19	16	14	13	14	16	18	20	23
Min °C	13	14	13	11	9	7	7	7	8	10	11	12
Rain mm	45	42	50	63	70	71	69	71	72	71	59	54
Raindays	7	7	8	11	14	15	15	16	14	13	10	8

For more detail see maps 519, 520–1, 522–3 & 534.
For descriptions of ☉ towns see Towns from A–Z (p. 159).

Portsea

Near the north-west tip of the peninsula, this village has long been favoured by Melbourne's wealthy. It has large houses (some with private boathouses), elegant hotels, B&Bs, good restaurants and a legendary pub. Further west, don't miss Fort Nepean, once an important defence site, and London Bridge, a rock formation off Portsea Surf Beach.

Mornington Peninsula National Park

This park extends along the south-west coast of the peninsula, where the Bass Strait surf pounds windswept beaches and headlands. A 32 km walking track runs from Portsea Surf Beach right down to Cape Schanck, with its historic 1858 lighthouse (offering accommodation).

Sorrento sojourns

The Queenscliff–Sorrento car ferry crosses Port Phillip several times a day, offering visitors a tour of the two peninsulas – Bellarine and Mornington – without a long drive by land. Dolphin cruises, some including a swim with Port Phillip's bottlenose dolphins, operate in summer.

Experience it!

1 **Shop** till you drop at the popular community market at Red Hill (first Saturday of the month, September–May)

2 **Ride** along the ocean beach on horseback, on a trail-ride from Ace Hi Wildlife Park at Cape Schanck

3 **Take** a ferry from Stony Point to French Island – hire a bike from the general store, let loose on the unsealed tracks, and keep your eyes peeled for koalas

Arthurs Seat

Just inland from Dromana, Arthurs Seat offers superb views across Melbourne and the bay. The 300 m summit is reached by foot or vehicle – at the top are picnic facilities and a restaurant. Nearby is Arthurs Seat Maze with a series of themed gardens and mazes, including the large Maize Maze each autumn.

PHILLIP ISLAND & GIPPSLAND

Road in Tarra–Bulga National Park

This is an area as diverse as it is beautiful. Along the coast, wild beaches and calm inlets give way to historic fishing, mining and farming towns, and spectacular stretches of bushland. Wildlife thrives, most famously in the penguin colony of Phillip Island. Inland, the forested ridges of the Strzelecki Ranges meet the central Gippsland plain, where Australia's largest deposits of brown coal are mined. Well-watered fields and rolling hills support one of Australia's biggest dairy industries, as well as burgeoning wine and gourmet-food production. In the north, gentle foothills rise to the high country of the Great Dividing Range, offering skiing in winter and walking tracks through grasslands and wildflowers in summer.

Top events

Jan	King of the Mountain Woodchop (Erica)
	South Gippsland Food and Wine Festival (Leongatha)
Mar	Jazz Festival (Inverloch)
	Jazz Festival (Moe)
	Blue Rock Classic (cross-country horserace, Moe)
	Fishing Contest (Port Albert)
Mar/April	World Superbike Championships (Phillip Island)
Easter	Tarra Festival (Yarram)
Oct	Italian Fest (Wonthaggi)
	Australian Motorcycle Grand Prix (Phillip Island)
Nov	Seabank Fishing Contest (Yarram)

CLIMATE WARRAGUL

	J	F	M	A	M	J	J	A	S	O	N	D
Max °C	26	26	24	20	16	13	13	14	16	19	21	23
Min °C	13	13	12	9	7	5	4	5	6	8	9	11
Rain mm	62	52	69	84	94	93	91	103	104	109	89	80
Raindays	8	7	10	13	15	16	16	17	16	15	13	11

Experience it!

❶ **Tour** the State Coal Mine at Wonthaggi with an old-time miner as a guide

❷ **Take** a Sunday ride on the South Gippsland Railway, across farmland and rolling hills, on a historic route between Leongatha and Korumburra

❸ **Fish** at Anderson Inlet near Inverloch, one of the state's best fishing spots

❹ **Spend** a day at Korumburra's Coal Creek Heritage Village, a re-creation of a 19th-century coalmining town

❺ **Drive** the 132 km Grand Ridge Road from Seaview to Carrajung, and stop for a walk through the rainforest at Tarra–Bulga National Park

Focus on
Phillip Island wildlife

The Penguin Parade on Summerland Beach is a major international tourist attraction. Just after sunset, little penguins – the world's smallest at 33 centimetres tall – come home to their burrows in the sand dunes after a day in the sea. To protect the penguins, visitors are restricted to designated viewing areas and no cameras are allowed. Bookings are essential during peak holiday periods. The visitor centre also offers a simulated underwater tour showing the penguins foraging for food and avoiding predators. On the island's western tip you can walk along a cliff-top boardwalk for views across to Seal Rocks, two kilometres offshore, where thousands of Australian fur seals live. For an up-close view of the frolicking animals, take a cruise from Cowes. Another popular resident on the island is the koala. Visit the Koala Conservation Centre near Cowes, where you can stroll along a network of raised walkways and see the delightful marsupials snoozing in the treetops.

Baw Baw National Park

The Aboriginal word for 'echo' gives this alpine park its name. The highest part of the park, Mt Baw Baw (via Moe), has ski facilities and unlike many other slopes is seldom crowded. The eastern section (via Erica and Walhalla) is popular in summer with bushwalkers, wildflower enthusiasts and campers.

Gourmet Deli Trail

Central Gippsland is home to producers of trout, venison, cheese, berries, potatoes, herbs and wine – many of them are linked by the Gourmet Deli Trail. The trail covers the area north and south of Warragul, and annotated maps are available from visitor centres. Included on the trail are a dozen or so cool-climate wineries; try Bass Phillip's pinot noir at Leongatha.

Walhalla

Tourist Route 91, from Moe or Traralgon, leads to the perfectly preserved former goldmining town of Walhalla, set in a steep valley. Historic buildings from the boom days include an old post office, bakery and bank, and Windsor House, now a B&B. Take the signposted town walk or a 45-minute ride on the Walhalla Goldfields Railway (weekends and holidays), or inspect the Long Tunnel Mine.

Phillip Island

Although best known for its little penguins, Phillip Island has other impressive attractions. The main town, Cowes, has sheltered beaches that are safe for swimming and watersports. Visitors can walk around the island's highest point, Cape Woolamai, drive across the bridge to Churchill Island to see a historic homestead, or immerse themselves in motor-racing history and culture at the Phillip Island Grand Prix Circuit Visitor Centre.

The power track

At the centre of the Latrobe Valley lies one of the world's largest brown-coal deposits – it is mined and converted into electricity to supply 85 percent of Victoria's power. The PowerWorks museum at Morwell explains the process and offers tours to the open-cut mines and power stations.

Port Albert

Today Port Albert is a quaint fishing village, but as the state's first official port, this town was once the gateway to Gippsland and Victoria. About 40 old buildings survive. For anglers, plentiful snapper, whiting, flathead, bream and trevally are found in the protected waters offshore.

Wilsons Promontory

The Prom is a remote and beautiful landscape supporting diverse native flora and fauna in a near-wilderness. The 30 km access road ends at Tidal River, where there are cabins and camping facilities. Around 150 km of walking tracks along bays and through bush begin at Tidal River and other points along the road.

Little penguins,
Phillip Island

For more detail see maps 521, 523 & 534–5.
For descriptions of ❶ towns see Towns from A–Z (p. 159).

VICTORIA

SPA & GARDEN COUNTRY

Convent Gallery, Daylesford

Ancient volcanic eruptions, lava flows and erosion have formed a stunning mountain landscape rising out of the coastal plains to the north-west of Melbourne. Gold and timber attracted the first European settlers to the district. Soon afterwards, Melbourne's elite arrived – lured by the health-giving waters of the area's mineral springs – and established grand, European-style gardens on the basalt-rich soil. Today the district retains the air of a 19th-century hill retreat, with historic spa towns, mansions, gardens, galleries, craft shops, forest walks and drives, and gracious guesthouses and B&Bs.

Top events

Jan	New Year's Day and Australia Day races (Hanging Rock, near Woodend)
	Lavandula Harvest Festival (Shepherds Flat)
May	Hepburn Swiss–Italian Festival (Daylesford)
July	Fine Food and Wine Fayre (Glenlyon)
Sept	Daffodil and Arts Festival (Kyneton)
Oct	Macedon Ranges Budburst Festival (throughout wine district)
Dec	Highland Gathering (Daylesford)
	Woodend Village Festival

Focus on

Country gardens

Gardens flourish in the volcanic soil and cool, moist climate of the spa country. There are botanic gardens in Daylesford and Malmsbury. Around the beautiful village of Mount Macedon, classic mountainside gardens surround large houses; check with a visitor centre for their spring and autumn open days. Cope-Williams Vineyard at Romsey is well known for its English-style garden and cricket green, while at Blackwood the beautiful Garden of St Erth offers two hectares of exotic and native species (closed Wednesday and Thursday). For something special, visit the Lavandula Lavender Farm at Shepherds Flat, where the lavender crop sits beside other cottage-style plants.

Daylesford and Hepburn Springs

The spa complex at Hepburn Springs offers heated mineral spas, flotation tanks, saunas and massages. The adjacent town of Daylesford is an attractive weekend destination with galleries, antique shops, heritage buildings, B&Bs and fantastic restaurants and cafes. Worth a visit is the Convent Gallery, a 19th-century former convent that houses local artwork, sculpture and jewellery.

Lerderderg State Park

The Lerderderg River has cut a deep gorge through sandstone and slate in this 14 250 ha park. Rugged ridges enclose much of the river, and there are also some interesting relics of old goldmining days. Explore on foot, or take a scenic drive via O'Briens Road (turn off south of Blackwood).

CLIMATE KYNETON

	J	F	M	A	M	J	J	A	S	O	N	D
Max °C	27	27	24	18	14	11	10	12	15	18	22	25
Min °C	10	10	8	6	4	2	2	2	3	5	7	9
Rain mm	37	39	47	54	75	90	82	84	74	69	52	50
Raindays	5	5	6	9	12	15	16	16	13	11	9	7

Map showing: MALMSBURY, KYNETON, KILMORE, SHEPHERDS FLAT, HEPBURN SPRINGS, DAYLESFORD, GLENLYON, WOODEND, ROMSEY, Mt Macedon 1013m, MOUNT MACEDON, MACEDON, TRENTHAM, BLACKWOOD, LERDERDERG STATE PARK, SUNBURY, BACCHUS MARSH, ORGAN PIPES NP. 0–10 km scale. Labelled points ①②③

Hanging Rock

This impressive rock formation north-east of Woodend was created by the erosion of solidified lava. The spot was inspiration for Joan Lindsay's novel *Picnic at Hanging Rock*, and a setting for the subsequent film. Walking tracks lead up to a superb view, with glimpses of koalas along the way, and the Discovery Centre tells the story of the site.

Organ Pipes National Park

Lava flows have created a 20 m wall of basalt columns in this small park near Sunbury. The 'organ pipes', within a gorge, can be seen close-up via an easy walking trail. A regeneration program is gradually bringing this formerly denuded area back to its native state.

Experience it!

❶ **Visit** Trentham Falls, the state's highest single-drop waterfall – it is most impressive in winter or spring

❷ **Dine** at the Lake House on Lake Daylesford, one of regional Victoria's finest restaurants

❸ **Shop** for cool-climate plants at the nurseries of Macedon

For more detail see maps 520–1, 531, 533, 534 & 538. For descriptions of ❶ towns see Towns from A–Z (p. 159).

WERRIBEE & BELLARINE

Bollards along the Geelong waterfront

The Bellarine Peninsula lies at the western entrance to Port Phillip, connected by car ferry to the Mornington Peninsula. Geelong, at the base of the peninsula, is a large regional city with strong links to the great days of the wool industry. Beyond Geelong are resort towns that offer surfing, swimming, sailing, scuba diving, fishing and golf. Visitors can dine opulently in Queenscliff's Victorian-era hotels or take in the sea air from a camping spot at Point Lonsdale. For wine buffs, some superb cool-climate varieties are offered for tasting at wineries on the peninsula and around Geelong.

Top events

Jan	Waterfront Festival (Geelong)
Feb	Australian International Air Show (Avalon Airfield, near Geelong, odd-numbered years)
Feb–Mar	Spray Farm Winery Summer Concert Series (near Drysdale)
Mar	Highland Gathering (Geelong)
April	Alternative Farmvision (Geelong)
June	National Celtic Folk Festival (Geelong)
Sept	Geelong Cup (horseracing)
Nov	Queenscliff Music Festival

Focus on

Holiday havens

Just an hour or so from Melbourne, this district is enormously popular for weekend getaways. Queenscliff offers luxurious accommodation and fine dining, and the Maritime Centre and Museum in town displays the region's historic relationship with the sea. The tiny historic town of Point Lonsdale has great views of the turbulent entrance to Port Phillip. Ocean Grove, the peninsula's biggest town, is popular with retirees, surfers and scuba divers. A bridge across the estuary leads to Barwon Heads, which was the setting for the television series *SeaChange*. This is a small town with an excellent surfing beach and good accommodation and restaurants.

CLIMATE GEELONG

	J	F	M	A	M	J	J	A	S	O	N	D
Max °C	25	26	24	20	17	14	14	15	17	19	21	24
Min °C	14	14	13	10	8	6	5	6	7	8	10	12
Rain mm	44	38	35	39	47	43	42	47	53	63	52	48
Raindays	8	6	9	12	14	16	16	17	16	15	13	10

The You Yangs

These granite tors rise abruptly from the Werribee Plains. There is a fairly easy walk (3.2 km return) from the carpark to the top of Flinders Peak. On a clear day the view extends to Mt Macedon, Geelong and the skyscrapers of Melbourne.

Geelong

Geelong, Victoria's second largest city, is a bustling port that grew with the state's wool industry. The redeveloped Eastern Beach Waterfront district features cafes, restaurants and colourful sculptures, with the historic Cunningham Pier as a centrepiece. Take a stroll along the promenade or cool off in the restored 1930s sea baths.

Werribee Park

Built in Italianate style during the 1870s, Werribee Mansion is now preserved in all its splendour, grandly furnished to re-create the lifestyle of a wealthy family in Victoria's boom years. Take a tour through the house, then visit the Victoria State Rose Garden before heading off on a safari at the Werribee Open Range Zoo.

Geelong wine region

Vines were first planted around Geelong in the 1850s, but were uprooted during the 1870s phylloxera outbreak. Today's industry was established in the 1960s and there are now around 20 wineries, including eight on the Bellarine Peninsula. Scotchmans Hill, near Drysdale, has views to the coast and a growing reputation for pinot noir and chardonnay.

Experience it!

❶ **See** fat-tailed dunnarts and rufous bettongs on a night walk at Little River Earth Sanctuary

❷ **Buy** fresh local mussels from the Portarlington pier

❸ **Play** at Barwon Heads Golf Club, one of Victoria's top-three public courses

For more detail see maps 519, 520, 522, 525, 527 & 534. For descriptions of ⓣ towns see Towns from A–Z (p. 159).

SOUTH-WEST COAST

The south-west coast of Victoria is one of Australia's great scenic destinations. The Great Ocean Road, the region's main touring route, weaves a breathtaking course across a coastal landscape of rugged cliffs and limestone formations, quiet bays and wild surf beaches, rainforests and waterfalls. En route is a string of charming holiday towns with many attractions – Torquay, a town forever entwined with surfing, and Lorne and Apollo Bay, with their rich, green hinterlands. Further afield are Port Fairy and Portland, with their superb 19th-century architecture. Inland, ancient volcanoes have formed a landscape of craters and scoria cones, now lakes and mountains. The accommodation choices throughout the region include everything from gourmet retreats to B&Bs, hillside cabins and remote camping spots.

Scenery around Loch Ard Gorge, Port Campbell National Park

Experience it!

1 **Spot** *southern right whales at Logans Beach in Warrnambool (June–September)*

2 **Walk** *to Red Rock Lookout, north of Colac, for views across the crater-dotted volcanic plains*

3 **Learn** *to surf at one of Torquay's surf schools*

4 **Admire** *the dry-stone walls around Terang, Camperdown and Derrinallum, built by early Anglo-Celtic settlers*

5 **Watch** *for glow worms after sunset at Melba Gully State Park*

Focus on

Shipwrecks

There are about 160 wrecks along the vital yet treacherous south-west-coast shipping route. Victoria's Historic Shipwreck Trail, between Moonlight Head (in Port Campbell National Park) and Port Fairy, marks 25 sites with plaques telling the history of the wrecks. Not to be missed is the evocative *Loch Ard* site, near Port Campbell. On a direct route from London to Melbourne, the *Loch Ard* ran to trouble while negotiating the entrance to Bass Strait; fog and haze prevented the captain from seeing that the ship was only a short distance from the cliffs. In the struggle to change direction the ship hit the cliffs and soon sank – only two people managed to swim ashore to the now well-known Loch Ard Gorge. At Flagstaff Hill Maritime Museum in Warrnambool you can see a magnificent statue of a peacock, which was being transported on the *Loch Ard* for display in Melbourne's International Exhibition of 1880 and was washed ashore after the wreck. At the museum you can also watch the sound-and-laser spectacular 'Shipwrecked', shown nightly, which brings the tale of the *Loch Ard* to life.

Top events

Jan	*Pier to Pub Swim and Mountain to Surf Foot Race (Lorne)*
Feb	*Wunta Fiesta (Warrnambool)*
	Food and Wine Festival (Heywood)
	Go Country Music Festival and Truck Show (Colac)
Mar	*Port Fairy Folk Festival*
Easter	*Rip Curl Pro (Bells Beach, near Torquay)*
May	*Racing Carnival (horseracing, Warrnambool)*
July	*Fun 4 Kids (Warrnambool)*
Sept	*Angair Wildflower and Art Show (Anglesea)*
Dec–Jan	*Falls Festival (Angahook–Lorne State Park)*

CLIMATE WARRNAMBOOL

	J	F	M	A	M	J	J	A	S	O	N	D
Max °C	23	24	22	19	16	14	13	14	15	17	19	21
Min °C	11	12	11	9	7	6	5	6	7	7	9	10
Rain mm	49	35	53	69	75	101	96	107	109	82	66	63
Raindays	11	9	12	15	17	20	20	20	19	16	15	13

Mount Eccles National Park
This park is at the far edge of the 20 000-year-old volcanic landscape that extends west from Melbourne. Geological features of the park include a complex cave system, scoria cones and a large lake (suitable for swimming) enclosed within three volcanic craters. There are excellent walking trails, and camping is available.

Surf coast
Torquay is Victoria's premier surfing town. This is where young surfers start out and old surfers settle down, where surfing is business as well as fun. Factory outlets offer great bargains on surf gear and the local Surfworld Australia museum celebrates the wonders of the wave. Bells and Jan Juc beaches are just around the corner.

Cape Bridgewater
A two-hour walk leads to a viewing platform overlooking one of the country's largest Australian fur seal colonies; take a boat trip into the mouth of a cave for a closer look at these charming creatures. Nearby you can see a petrified forest, thunderous blowholes and tranquil freshwater springs.

Lorne
This popular resort village could be called the capital of the south-west coast, with excellent cafes and restaurants and a lively summertime crowd. It also offers good beaches and surfing opportunities. Nearby, in Angahook–Lorne State Park, beautiful forests and waterfalls provide time-out for bushwalkers and nature lovers.

Port Fairy
Port Fairy is a superbly preserved whaling port, with historic bluestone buildings lining the main street. In summer it offers lazy beachside holidays, and in winter a refuge from the cold in one of the many cosy restaurants and B&Bs. The Port Fairy Folk Festival, in March, grows bigger each year, attracting large local and international acts.

The Twelve Apostles
These spectacular limestone stacks were part of the cliffs until wind and water carved them into their present shape and left them stranded in wild surf off the shore. Preserved in Port Campbell National Park, they are one of Australia's most photographed sights and the region's signature attraction.

The Otways
Here the contrast between rugged coastline and tranquil, temperate rainforest is at its most impressive. In the north, the recently opened Otway Fly takes visitors on a suspended walkway to a lookout in the treetops, 45 m above ground; in the south, at Cape Otway, a lighthouse offers views over the shipwreck-strewn sea.

VICTORIA

For more detail see maps 520, 526–7 & 532–3.
For descriptions of ⊕ towns see Towns from A–Z (p. 159).

Port Fairy harbour

GOLDFIELDS

The Goldfields region of central Victoria is one of the historic jewels of rural Australia. The discovery of gold near Ballarat in 1851 transformed a sleepy farming district into a rowdy, anarchic, cosmopolitan and fantastically wealthy goldmining frontier as immigrants from all over the world poured in to try their luck. Development took place on a massive scale between the 1850s and 1890s. Today the area preserves an intense concentration of Victorian architecture in both the grand public buildings, parks and gardens of Ballarat and Bendigo and the charming streetscapes of smaller towns like Castlemaine, Creswick, Clunes, Maldon and St Arnaud. The region's many galleries, museums, preserved mines and interpretive centres recall the drama and detail of the goldfields, while stylish B&Bs, hotels, restaurants and cafes supply visitors with modern comforts.

Sovereign Hill, Ballarat

Experience it!

❶ Book *a weekend's indulgence at Warrenmang Vineyard Resort, north-west of Avoca in the Pyrenees wine district*

❷ Enjoy *the begonias in March at Ballarat's historic Botanic Gardens on the shores of Lake Wendouree*

❸ Visit *Castlemaine Art Gallery, with its impressive collection of local and international art*

❹ See *potters in action at the long-established Bendigo Pottery*

❺ Ride *a camel at Sedgwick's Camel Farm, south-east of Bendigo*

Top events

Jan	*Organs of the Ballarat Goldfields*
	Highland Gathering (Maryborough)
Feb	*Gold King Festival (Buninyong)*
Mar	*Begonia Festival (Ballarat)*
Easter	*Bendigo Easter Festival*
	Maldon Easter Fair
April	*Pyrenees Vignerons' Gourmet Food and Wine Race Meeting (Avoca)*
	Castlemaine State Festival (odd-numbered years)
	Food, Wine and Jazz Festival (Smeaton)
Sept–Nov	*Royal South Street Eisteddfod (Ballarat)*
Oct	*Vintage Car Hill Climb (Maldon)*
	Gourmet, Grapes and Gardens Weekend (Maryborough)
Oct–Nov	*Maldon Folk Festival*
Nov	*Festival of Gardens (Castlemaine, odd-numbered years)*
	Racing Carnival (Bendigo)

CLIMATE BENDIGO

	J	F	M	A	M	J	J	A	S	O	N	D
Max °C	29	29	26	21	16	13	12	14	16	20	24	26
Min °C	14	15	13	9	7	4	3	5	6	8	11	13
Rain mm	33	32	36	41	55	61	56	59	54	52	37	33
Raindays	5	4	5	7	10	12	13	13	11	10	7	6

Focus on

Gold-rush history

Sovereign Hill in Ballarat is one of the country's best historic theme parks. It offers a complete re-creation of life on the 1850s goldfields. The nearby Gold Museum, part of the Sovereign Hill complex, features displays of gold nuggets and coins, and changing exhibits on the history of gold. The Eureka Stockade Centre offers interpretive displays on Australia's only armed insurrection, which took place in 1854. See the original Eureka Flag at the Ballarat Fine Art Gallery, which also houses an excellent collection of work by artists such as Tom Roberts, Sidney Nolan, Russell Drysdale and Fred Williams. In Eureka Street is the tiny Montrose Cottage (1856), an ex-miner's house furnished in the style of the period; here a museum display movingly recalls the lives and contribution of women in the gold-rush era. In Bendigo, the Central Deborah Gold Mine offers tours 80 metres down a reef mine, and excellent displays on goldmining techniques.

Backblocks of the goldfields

Some of the quieter gold towns are tucked away in a rural pocket north-west of Bendigo. In Dunolly 126 nuggets were found in the town itself – see replicas of some of the most impressive finds at the Goldfields Historical and Arts Society. St Arnaud boasts the beautiful Queen Mary Gardens and a number of old pubs and verandah-fronted shops. There are eucalyptus distilleries at Inglewood and Wedderburn.

Bendigo's Chinese sites

The restored Joss House on the city's northern outskirts and the Golden Dragon Museum in Bridge Street are reminders of the substantial presence of Chinese immigrants on the goldfields. The museum has an excellent display of Chinese regalia. A ceremonial archway leads from the museum to the Garden of Joy, built in 1996 to represent the Chinese landscape in miniature.

Maryborough Old Railway Station

Mark Twain described Maryborough as 'a railway station with a town attached'. Grand for the size of the town, the former railway station now houses a tourist complex that includes an antique emporium, a woodworking shop and a restaurant and cafe.

Pall Mall

The tree-lined, French-style boulevard of Pall Mall in Bendigo is probably country-Australia's most impressive street, with many of its buildings dating back to the gold rush. To complete the picture, Bendigo's vintage trams rattle up and down the street.

Castlemaine

This historic goldmining town has a community of painters, potters, instrument makers and other craftspeople. The original market building, with its classical Roman facade, now houses visitor information and a gold-diggings interpretive centre. Worth a visit is the 1860s Buda Historic Home, with its heritage-listed garden.

Sovereign Hill

One of Victoria's top tourist attractions, Ballarat's Sovereign Hill is a living museum. Blacksmiths, bakers and storekeepers in period dress ply their trades amid the tents, while miners pan for gold. In the evenings 'Blood on the Southern Cross', a sound-and-light re-enactment of the Eureka Rebellion, is played out across the town streets.

Maldon

The 1860s streets of Maldon are shaded by European trees and lined with old buildings of local stone. Declared a Notable Town by the National Trust, Maldon has historic B&Bs and a tourist steam train. Take in the view from the Anzac Hill lookout.

Map labels:
WEDDERBURN
ST ARNAUD
INGLEWOOD
BENDIGO ④
DUNOLLY
MALDON ⑤
MARYBOROUGH
CASTLEMAINE ③
PYRENEES WINE REGION
AVOCA ①
CLUNES
SMEATON
CRESWICK
BALLARAT
BUNINYONG ②
N
0   20 km

VICTORIA

For more detail see maps 520, 528, 529, 530–1, 533, 538 & 543.
For descriptions of ❶ towns see Towns from A–Z (p. 159).

Historic buildings in Bendigo

GRAMPIANS & CENTRAL-WEST

Victoria's central west is a mix of ancient mountains, semiarid plains and classic farming landscapes. In the south, the rugged 400 million-year-old blue-grey shapes of the Grampians – a dense and awe-inspiring environment of forests, fern gullies, soaring cliffs, waterfalls, creeks, lakes and swampland – rise from the plains. In the many rock shelters of the area, details of ancient Aboriginal life are impressively recorded. Anglo-Celtic settlement has made its mark with the thousands of hectares of wheat crops and sheep paddocks that dominate what is one of Australia's richest farming areas. The region's agriculture has kept pace with modern trends as well, with a growing number of olive groves and vineyards tucked in among the traditional farm holdings. In the north, timeless, pink-tinged salt lakes and claypans mark the limits of agricultural expansion and a return to a native landscape.

The Balconies, Grampians National Park

Experience it!

❶ **Take** *a dawn hot-air balloon flight from Stawell over the Grampians*

❷ **Fish** *for brown trout and redfin at Rocklands Reservoir*

❸ **Swim** *in summer at Lake Bellfield, just south of Halls Gap*

❹ **See** *the colourful display of ground orchids in spring and the massive mounds of the mallee fowl in Little Desert National Park*

❺ **Drive** *to the top of One Tree Hill near Ararat for a 360-degree view of the region*

Focus on

Aboriginal culture in the Grampians

The Djab Wurrung and Jardwadjali people shared the territory they called Gariwerd for at least 5000 years before European settlement, although some evidence suggests up to 30 000 years of habitation. The Brambuk Aboriginal Cultural Centre near Halls Gap, run by five Koorie communities, is an excellent first stop for information about the region's indigenous heritage. There is a ceremonial ground for everything from dance performances to boomerang-throwing, while bush tucker-inspired meals are served in the cafe. The region contains 100 recorded rock-art sites, representing more than 80 percent of all sites in Victoria. A Brambuk-guided tour of some of the sites (most are in Grampians National Park) is probably the most rewarding way to experience the meaning and nature of the art. Notable sites include Gulgurn Manja, featuring over 190 kangaroo, emu and handprint motifs, and Ngamadidj, a site decorated with 16 figures painted in white clay. Bunjil's Shelter is just outside the park near Stawell, and is the only site in the area where more than one colour is used and a known figure is represented. Bunjil was a creator spirit from the Dreaming, responsible for the people, the land and the law.

CLIMATE STAWELL

	J	F	M	A	M	J	J	A	S	O	N	D
Max °C	27	28	25	20	16	13	12	14	16	19	22	26
Min °C	13	13	12	9	7	5	4	5	6	8	9	11
Rain mm	36	28	33	41	57	60	67	67	64	58	36	29
Raindays	6	5	7	9	12	16	18	18	14	12	9	7

Top events

Jan	Champagne Picnic Races (Great Western)
Feb	Grampians Jazz Festival (Halls Gap)
	Country Muster (Penshurst)
Mar	Jailhouse Rock Festival (Ararat)
	Vintage Car Rally (Casterton)
Easter	Stawell Easter Gift (professional footrace)
	Y-Fest (Warracknabeal)
April	Wimmera German Festival (Dimboola)
May	Grampians Gourmet Weekend (Halls Gap)
June/July	Australian Kelpie Muster and Kelpie Working Dog Auction (Casterton)
Sept	Australian Orchid Festival (Ararat)
Oct	Golden Gateway Festival (Ararat)
	Southern Grampians Open Gardens (Cavendish)
	Spring Garden Festival (Horsham)
Nov	Kannamaroo Rock 'n' Roll Festival (Horsham)

Mt Arapiles
Mt Arapiles, part of Mount Arapiles–Tooan State Park, is regarded as Australia's best rockclimbing venue. It attracts interstate and international enthusiasts with its 2000 rockclimbing routes marked out across 365 m of sandstone cliffs. Courses and tours are available.

The olive groves of Laharum
Mount Zero Olives at Laharum is the largest olive plantation in the Southern Hemisphere, with 55 000 trees on 730 ha. The first trees were planted in 1943, after World War II stopped olive oil imports. You can buy oil, vinegar and lentils, and stay overnight.

Grampians day drive
From Halls Gap, drive to Boroka Lookout, Reed Lookout and MacKenzie Falls. Take a break for lunch at Zumsteins, a historic site and picnic area home to a large kangaroo population. Return to Halls Gap via Silverband Falls and through the stringybark forests and tree ferns of Delleys Dell.

Wines of Great Western
Grapevines were first planted at Seppelt's Great Western vineyards in 1865. Today the winery is best known for its red and white sparkling wines, cellared in 1.6 km of National Trust-classified tunnels dug by miners in the late 19th century. Other wineries in the area include Best's and Garden Gully.

Hamilton
Hamilton is the commercial hub of the wool-rich Western District. Gracious houses and churches on its tree-lined streets testify to over a century of prosperity. Close to town are historic homesteads in magnificent gardens; these properties are generally open in spring.

Gum San Chinese Heritage Centre
Ararat's Gum San is a surprising sight on the Western Highway – a little piece of China interrupting the Australian landscape. The centre, built in traditional Southern Chinese style, tells the story of the Chinese on the goldfields and the immense lead of gold they happened upon here accidentally. The centre also features an original mining tunnel uncovered during construction.

Byaduk Caves
These caves, located in Mount Napier State Park, are part of a giant, 24 km lava flow stretching to Mt Eccles in the south-west, evidence of the volcanic activity that shaped the region's landscape. The caves, one of which is open, are a wonderland of ropey lava, columns, stalactites and stalagmites.

VICTORIA

Tinsel lily, Little Desert National Park

For more detail see maps 530, 532–3 & 542–3.
For descriptions of T towns see Towns from A–Z (p. 159).

MALLEE COUNTRY

Lake Hattah,
Hattah–Kulkyne
National Park

The Murray River is the lifeblood of the mallee country. After several attempts, Australia's first large-scale irrigation scheme was established in Mildura by two Canadian brothers, the Chaffeys, around 1900. Since then, water from the Murray has allowed the cultivation of citrus fruit, olives, avocados and grapes, and the development of the major riverside settlements of Mildura and Swan Hill. Despite intensive farming, vast tracts of mallee scrub, intercut by lakes and rivers, are preserved in the expansive national parks.

Top events

Mar	Arts Festival (Mildura)
	Redgum Festival (Swan Hill)
July	International Balloon Fiesta (Mildura)
	Italian Festival (Swan Hill)
Aug/Sept	Great Australian Vanilla Slice Triumph (Ouyen)
Sept	Country Music Festival (Mildura)
	Big Lizzie Festival of Vintage Tractors (Mildura)
Nov	Sunraysia Jazz and Wine Festival (Mildura)

Focus on

Murray and mallee wildlife
This landscape of rivers and plains is home to abundant wildlife. Most notable is the birdlife: spoonbills, herons, eagles, mallee fowl, harriers and kites are to be found in the parks and on the roadsides and riverbanks. Hattah–Kulkyne National Park protects around 200 bird species as well as the red kangaroo. Murray–Sunset National Park – true desert country in parts – includes riverine plains. It supports an array of native fauna, including mallee fowl and the rare black-eared miner. To see the kangaroos and birdlife of Wyperfeld National Park, follow the Brambruk Nature Trail.

CLIMATE MILDURA

	J	F	M	A	M	J	J	A	S	O	N	D
Max °C	32	32	28	23	19	16	15	17	20	24	27	30
Min °C	17	16	14	10	8	5	4	5	7	10	12	15
Rain mm	21	22	19	19	27	23	26	28	29	31	24	23
Raindays	4	3	4	4	7	8	9	9	8	7	6	4

Mildura
With its museums and galleries, excellent dining and surrounding wineries and orchards, Mildura is like a colourful Mediterranean oasis. Go to the zoo, visit the Mildura Arts Complex and the Rio Vista museum (once the home of William Chaffey), or book a day tour with indigenous guides to Mungo National Park in New South Wales.

Wyperfeld National Park
A park of brilliant sunsets, huge open spaces and spring wildflowers, Wyperfeld is explored via walks from Wonga Campground and Information Centre, 50 km west of Hopetoun. The park is home to the endangered mallee fowl, a turkey-size bird that makes nesting mounds up to 5 m across.

River district wines
The wine-producing areas of Mildura and Swan Hill are an unrecognised heartland of the Australian wine industry, producing 37 percent of the total output – most for the bulk market, although prestige production is rising. The dozen or so wineries include the large Lindemans Karadoc estate, with cellar-door tastings and sales.

Experience it!

1 **Learn** about local bush tucker at the Robinvale Indigenous Gardens

2 **Take** your camera and your walking shoes to the Pink Lakes in Murray–Sunset National Park – their colour is best on overcast days

3 **Dine** at Stefano's in Mildura, home to television chef Stefano de Pieri

For more detail see maps 542–3 & 544–5.
For descriptions of ⊕ towns see Towns from A–Z (p. 159).

Swan Hill Pioneer Settlement
This 7 ha park offers a lively experience of river-port life in early Australia. Wander through the 19th-century-style streets, complete with staff in period dress. Ride on a paddlesteamer or book for the popular Sound and Light Tour. Also in the park is an Aboriginal canoe tree.

GOULBURN & MURRAY

Port of Echuca

This region centres around the Goulburn River on its path towards the Murray. Victoria's richest farming country lies north of Nagambie in the Goulburn Valley, and the canneries of Shepparton, the region's hub, process much of the harvest from the irrigated land. On the Murray are attractions of great historical interest, particularly the paddlesteamers of Echuca (the Goulburn enters the Murray near here, and Echuca is an Aboriginal word meaning 'meeting of the waters'). There are also ecologically significant wetlands and ancient river red gum forests, and excellent opportunities for fishing.

Barmah State Park and State Forest
These neighbouring areas form the state's biggest river red gum forest. This is a popular area for bushwalking, canoeing and camping. Walking trails take in various Aboriginal sites, and the Dharnya Centre interprets the culture of the local Yorta Yorta people.

Echuca
The historic port of Echuca, with its impressive red-gum wharf, recalls the late 19th century, when the Murray carried wool and other goods from farms and stations. A number of beautifully restored paddlesteamers are moored here, including some offering cruises up the river.

Cobram
This lovely fruit-growing town is surrounded by peach, nectarine, pear and orange orchards. It also offers access to a number of wide, sandy beaches on the Murray, perfect for swimming, fishing, picnicking and watersports. Camping facilities are available, and across the river in New South Wales is the renowned 36-hole Cobram Barooga golf course.

Top events

Jan   Peaches and Cream Festival (Cobram, odd-numbered years)

Feb   Riverboats, Jazz, Food and Wine Festival (Echuca)

      Southern 80 Ski Race (Torrumbarry Weir to Echuca)

Mar   Bridge to Bridge Swim (Cohuna)

      Goulburn Valley Vintage Festival (Nagambie)

April Barmah Muster (Barmah State Forest)

June Steam, Horse and Vintage Car Rally (Echuca)

Oct   Port of Echuca Steam Heritage Festival

Focus on

Food and wine
Irrigation has transformed the once dusty Goulburn Valley into the fruit bowl of Victoria. Orchards, market gardens and farms supply the canneries in Shepparton, which are among the largest in the Southern Hemisphere. The valley is dotted with outlets for venison, poultry, smoked trout, berries, organic vegetables, honey, jams, preserves, fruit juices, mustards, pickles, vinegar and liquored truffles. The region's nine wineries make reliable reds and distinctive whites. Near Nagambie, Mitchelton Wines is known for marsannes and rieslings grown on sandy, riverine soils. At nearby Avenel, Plunkett Wines makes long-finishing chardonnay from grapes grown high in the Strathbogie Ranges.

CLIMATE ECHUCA

	J	F	M	A	M	J	J	A	S	O	N	D
Max °C	31	31	27	22	18	14	13	15	18	22	26	29
Min °C	15	15	13	9	7	5	4	5	6	9	11	14
Rain mm	27	27	31	33	42	43	41	43	40	43	32	28
Raindays	4	4	5	6	9	10	11	11	10	9	6	5

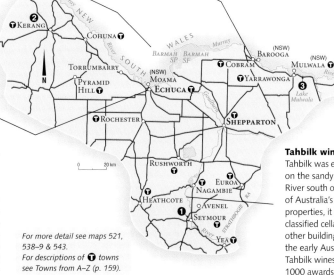

Experience it!

1 **Have** a drink in Seymour's Royal Hotel, made famous in Russell Drysdale's painting The Cricketers

2 **Go** birdwatching at Reedy Lakes near Kerang – Middle Reedy Lake is reputedly the world's largest breeding ground for ibis

3 **Run** amuck in the aquatic playground of Lake Mulwala, offering waterskiing, wakeboarding and tube rides

For more detail see maps 521, 538–9 & 543.
For descriptions of ⊕ towns see Towns from A–Z (p. 159).

Tahbilk winery
Tahbilk was established in 1860 on the sandy loam of the Goulburn River south of Nagambie. One of Australia's most beautiful wine properties, it has a National Trust-classified cellar, which – along with other buildings – is a timepiece of the early Australian wine industry. Tahbilk wines have won over 1000 awards.

VICTORIA

HIGH COUNTRY

Craig's Hut near Mansfield

The Victorian Alps form the lower reaches of the Great Dividing Range. Mt Hotham and Falls Creek, both on the Bogong High Plains, offer some of the state's most challenging skiing. Fast-flowing trout streams originate in these mountains and feed into the upper reaches of the Murray River. The foothills to the north of the alps are used for growing hops and walnuts, and – more traditionally – for grazing cattle. In this area are several old gold towns of great charm and historical interest. Lake Eildon, Victoria's largest constructed lake, stores water flowing west from the near-wilderness of Alpine National Park. Just west of Wodonga, grapes from the hot, alluvial flats on the south side of the Murray are made into the widely known fortified wines of Rutherglen.

Focus on

Ski country

Victoria's ski resorts are within easy reach of Melbourne. They include, in order of their distance from the city: Mt Buller (via Mansfield), Mt Buffalo (via Myrtleford), Mt Hotham (via Bright) and Falls Creek (via Mount Beauty). The ski season starts officially on the Queen's Birthday weekend, early in June, and ends on the first weekend in October. Snowsport conditions, however, depend on the weather. All resorts offer a range of skiing, from protected runs for beginners to cross-country ski trails. Mt Hotham, known as the 'powder snow capital' of Australia, has the most challenging runs for experienced downhill skiers and snowboarders. After the snow melts a range of summer activities come in to play. The adventurous can try mountain-bike riding, tandem paragliding, abseiling or caving. Mountain lakes and streams offer trout fishing, swimming, sailing and canoeing. Trails across the mountains, ablaze with wildflowers in summer, can be explored on horseback or on foot. The less energetic can just breathe the crystalline air and gaze across the hazy blue ridges.

Experience it!

1. **Wander** around Wandiligong's enormous hedge maze

2. **Indulge** in a weekend of fine dining at Howqua Dale Gourmet Retreat, near Howqua

3. **Ride** the High Country on horseback via the mountain town of Corryong

4. **Visit** the childhood home of novelist Henry Handel Richardson and see a remarkable grapevine, both at historic Chiltern

5. **Shop** for gourmet cheese at Milawa

Top events

Mar	Harvest Festival (Mansfield)
	Tobacco, Hops and Timber Food and Wine Festival (Myrtleford)
	Tastes of Rutherglen (district wineries)
Mar/April	Mansfield Balloon Festival
Easter	Golden Horseshoes Festival (Beechworth)
April	Music Muster (Mount Beauty)
April/May	The Man from Snowy River Bush Festival (Corryong)
	Autumn Festival (Bright)
June	Winery Walkabout (Rutherglen wineries)
Aug	Kangaroo Hoppet (cross-country ski race, Falls Creek)
Oct	Alpine Spring Festival (Bright)
	Great Alpine Bike Ride (Myrtleford to Bright)
Nov	Brown Brothers Wine and Food Weekend (Milawa)
	Celtic Festival (Beechworth)
	Festival of Jazz and Blues (Wangaratta)
Dec	Golden Spurs Rodeo (Myrtleford)

CLIMATE MOUNT BULLER

	J	F	M	A	M	J	J	A	S	O	N	D
Max °C	16	17	14	10	7	3	2	2	5	8	12	14
Min °C	8	8	6	4	1	–1	–3	–2	–1	1	4	6
Rain mm	83	66	79	136	161	160	190	185	156	185	155	124
Raindays	7	5	8	12	14	14	15	16	14	16	13	11

Wines of Rutherglen
The vines on the alluvial flats in a shallow loop of the Murray produce some of the world's great fortified wines. The region is known for tokays and muscats, big reds and – more recently – lighter reds such as gamay. There are over a dozen wineries near Rutherglen; look out for All Saints, with its historic building, and Pfeiffer, Chambers, Gehrig Estate and Campbells.

The Upper Murray
The Murray River rises in rugged alpine country in the north-east of the state, on the border of New South Wales. The swift mountain streams that feed the Murray are a trout-fishing paradise. The river and its rapids can be negotiated by canoe, and the adjacent Burrowa–Pine Mountain National Park features waterfalls, lyrebirds, wallabies and wombats, and offers challenging bushwalks.

Historic Beechworth
The National Trust has classified over 30 buildings in what is now one of Australia's best-preserved gold-rush towns. Many of these are built in a distinctive, honey-coloured granite. Dine in a stately former bank, visit the powder magazine, wander through an evocative cemetery for Chinese goldminers, and sample the delectable cakes, pastries and bread of the famous Beechworth Bakery.

Kelly country
A giant effigy of Ned Kelly greets visitors to Glenrowan. After killing three local policemen in 1878, the Kelly gang hid for two years in the Warby Range, raiding nearby towns. Ned was captured in 1880 after a shoot-out in Siege Street and was later hanged. Visit the Ned Kelly Memorial Museum and Homestead in Gladstone Street.

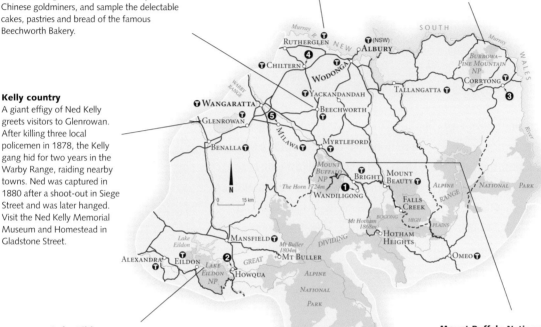

Lake Eildon
Created by damming the Goulburn River in the 1950s, this lake, with six times the capacity of Sydney Harbour, is popular with watersports enthusiasts, anglers and houseboat holiday-makers. The surrounding Lake Eildon National Park offers bushwalking, camping, and 4WD tracks through the foothills of the Victorian Alps.

Mount Buffalo National Park
This 31 000 ha national park is the state's oldest, declared in 1898. A plateau of boulders and tors includes The Horn, the park's highest point and a great place for views at sunrise. Walking tracks are set among streams, waterfalls, stunning wildflowers, and snow gum and mountain ash forest. There is summer camping, swimming and canoeing at Lake Catani. In winter, the Mt Buffalo ski area is popular with families and the pretty Mt Buffalo Chalet provides cosy accommodation.

For more detail see maps 521, 536, 539 & 540–1. For descriptions of ❶ towns see Towns from A–Z (p. 159).

Chinese burning towers, Beechworth Cemetery

EAST GIPPSLAND

Cape Howe, at the Victoria/New South Wales border

The natural features of East Gippsland include Australia's largest system of inland waterways, the remote splendour of Ninety Mile Beach and the scenic foothills of the High Country. Some of Victoria's most magnificent national parks are found here – including Croajingolong National Park, with its wild, rocky beaches, and Snowy River National Park, with areas still completely untouched. Activities include boating, fishing, sailing, swimming, surfing and, in the foothills, bushwalking, whitewater rafting, abseiling and caving. Accommodation ranges from caravan parks, motels, B&Bs and houseboats to the secluded campgrounds of the national parks.

Top events

Jan	Lakes Summer Festival (Lakes Entrance)
	Foothills Festival (Buchan)
Feb	Blues Bash (Bruthen)
	Jazz Festival (Paynesville)
Mar	Marlay Point–Paynesville Overnight Yacht Race (from Marlay Point, near Sale)
Easter	Rodeo (Buchan)
April	Australian Line Dancing Championships (Bairnsdale)
Oct	International Festival of the Lakes (Lakes Entrance)

Focus on

Fishing

Fishing is a huge drawcard in East Gippsland. Fish for trout in the mountain streams and rivers – such as the Delegate River – or head for the coast. The lakes, rivers and inlets around Paynesville, Marlo, Bemm River and Mallacoota are great for bream, trevally and flathead. Boat-angling is the best choice here, although land-based angling also yields results. Ninety Mile Beach and the remote beaches of The Lakes National Park provide some of the best surf-fishing in Victoria, with salmon, tailor and flathead among the prospects.

CLIMATE LAKES ENTRANCE

	J	F	M	A	M	J	J	A	S	O	N	D
Max °C	24	24	22	20	17	15	15	16	17	19	20	22
Min °C	15	15	13	11	9	7	6	6	8	9	11	13
Rain mm	56	41	56	63	67	65	54	51	59	64	71	70
Raindays	9	7	10	10	11	13	12	14	13	13	12	11

Mallacoota

Surrounded by the remote ocean beaches, estuarine waterways and unspoiled bush of Croajingolong National Park, this old-fashioned resort offers one of the best nature-based holidays in the state, with excellent fishing, walking, boating and swimming. Hire a boat in town and explore Mallacoota Inlet.

Snowy River National Park

The much-celebrated Snowy River begins as a trickle near Mt Kosciuszko and passes through wild limestone-gorge and forest country before reaching a coastal lagoon. McKillops Bridge (via Buchan) is a beautiful area with camping and barbecue facilities, swimming spots, and some good short walks.

Large lakes and a long beach

The Gippsland Lakes are fed by five major rivers and contained on the coastal side by Ninety Mile Beach. At the system's centre, the water-bound Lakes National Park offers birdwatching, walking, swimming and camping. Access is via boat from Paynesville or road and foot from Loch Sport.

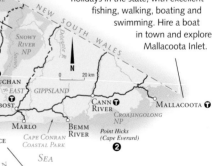

Experience it!

❶ Drive the Bataluk Cultural Trail, taking in sites significant to the Kurnai people (pick up a brochure from the Sale Visitor Centre)

❷ Stay at the remote Point Hicks Lightstation in Croajingolong National Park

❸ Tour the Royal and Fairy caves at Buchan Caves Reserve

For more detail see maps 535 & 536–7.
For descriptions of ❶ towns see Towns from A–Z (p. 159).

Lakes Entrance

Lakes Entrance, at the head of the lakes, is a great base for fishing and boating, and offers accommodation at all levels. For a holiday afloat, book a self-drive cruiser from nearby Metung. There are several wineries in the area – Wyanga Park Winery offers a lakes cruise from town to its cellar door and restaurant.

The cliffs on the coast near Anglesea

Alexandra
Pop. 2084

Map ref. 521 O1, 539 J11

Alexandra was apparently named after Alexandra, Princess of Wales, although, coincidentally, three men named Alexander discovered gold here in 1866. Situated in the foothills of the Great Dividing Range, Alexandra is supported primarily by agriculture. Nearby, the Goulburn River is an important trout fishery.

IN TOWN *Timber and Tramways Museum:* housed in the original railway station and offering an insight into the timber industry around Alexandra; Station St; open 2nd Sun each month. *Art and craft galleries:* many outlets around town displaying and selling local art, pottery and glassware.

WHAT'S ON *Bush market:* 3rd Sat each month (excluding winter); Perkins St. *Picnic Races:* Jan, Mar, Oct and Nov. *Truck, Bus and Ute Show:* June. *Open Gardens Weekend:* Oct. *Rose Festival:* Nov.

NEARBY *McKenzie Nature Reserve:* established in virgin bushland, with orchids and wildflowers during winter and spring; on the southern edge of town. *Self-guide tourist drives:* the Skyline Rd in particular, from Alexandra to Eildon, features a number of lookouts along the way; information at visitor centre. *Coach Stop Gallery:* 8 km s. *Taggerty:* home to the Willowbank Gallery and a bush market; open 4th Sat every month; 18 km s. *Trout*

fishing: in the Goulburn, Acheron and Rubicon rivers. *Lake Eildon National Park:* excellent walking trails in the north-west section of the park, to the east of town; *for more details see Eildon. Bonnie Doon:* a good base for exploring the lake region. Activities include trail-riding, bushwalking, watersports and scenic drives. 37 km NE near Lake Eildon.
ⓘ 45a Grant St; 1800 652 298 or (03) 5772 1100; www.murrindindi tourism.com.au

Anglesea
Pop. 2192

Map ref. 520 E12, 527 N8, 533 Q9

A pretty and sheltered part of the surf coast, Anglesea is one of the smaller holiday hamlets along the Great Ocean Road. The main beaches are patrolled from Christmas through to Easter, making it a favourite destination for both swimmers and beginner surfers.

IN TOWN Coogoorah Reserve Set on the Anglesea River, the name of this park means 'swampy reed creek'. Coogoorah was established after the 1983 Ash Wednesday fires and now features a network of boardwalks weaving through the distinctive wetland vegetation. Keep an eye out for fascinating local birdlife, including the peregrine falcon.
Anglesea Golf Course: golf enthusiasts share the green with kangaroos; Golf Links Rd. *Melaleuca Gallery:* Great Ocean Rd. *Viewing platform:* overlooks open-cut brown-coal mine and power station;

behind town in Coalmine Rd. *Paddleboats:* for hire on the banks of the Anglesea River.
WHAT'S ON *Markets:* local crafts and produce, held over summer, Easter and Melbourne Cup weekend; by the Anglesea River. *Rock to Ramp Swim:* Feb. *Anglesea Art Show:* June. *Angair Wildflower and Art Show:* Sept.
NEARBY Aireys Inlet This pretty little town is overlooked by a lighthouse built to guide passing ships along this treacherous coastline. Painkalac Creek flows out to the ocean here, creating the inlet of the town's name and a safe swimming spot. Horseriding and fishing are favourite activities along the sheltered beaches. South of town is the Great Ocean Road Memorial Arch, built in 1939. 11 km sw.
J. E. Loveridge Lookout: 1 km w. *Point Roadknight Beach:* a shallow, protected beach, popular with families; 2 km sw. *Ironbark Basin Reserve:* features ocean views, local birdlife and good bushwalking. The Point Addis Koorie Cultural Walk leads through the park, highlighting sites of indigenous significance. 7 km nw, off Point Addis Rd. *Angahook–Lorne State Park:* begins south-west of town and stretches down the coast. The northern section features unique heathland flora and good walking trails. Access via Aireys Inlet, 11 km sw. *For more details see Lorne. Surf Coast Walk:* 30 km from Torquay to Moggs Creek (south of Aireys Inlet). The track passes through Anglesea. *Surf schools:* learn to surf on one of the beginner courses available at nearby beaches; contact visitor centre for details.
ⓘ Off Great Ocean Rd; or ring Torquay Information Centre, (03) 5261 4219; www.visitsurfcoast.com

Apollo Bay   Pop. 1339

Map ref. 527 J12, 533 N12

Named after a local schooner, Apollo Bay has become the resting place of many shipwrecks, yet it maintains an appeal for all lovers of the ocean. The town is situated near Otway National Park with a wonderful contrast between rugged coastline and tranquil green hills. The seaside town is popular with fishing enthusiasts and, like many other towns along this stretch of coast, its population swells significantly over summer as visitors flock here for the holidays.
IN TOWN *Old Cable Station Museum:* features artefacts from Australia's telecommunications history and displays exploring the history of the region; Great Ocean Rd; open 2pm–5pm weekends and school and public holidays. *Bass Strait Shell Museum:* holds an impressive array of shells and provides many facts about the marine life along the Victorian south-west coast; Noel St.
WHAT'S ON *Foreshore Market:* each Sat. *Aquathon:* swimming and running race; Dec. *Apollo Bay Music Festival:* Mar.

NEARBY Otway National Park The park covers 13 000 ha and includes some of the most rugged coastline in Victoria, particularly around Cape Otway and the stretch of coast towards Princetown. It is an ideal location for a bushwalking adventure taking in sights through the park to the sea, from the scenic Elliot River down to adjacent Shelly Beach. Many species of wildlife inhabit the park, including koalas and the rare tiger quoll. Also look out for the historic Cape Otway Lighthouse, built in 1848. The Great Ocean Rd, west of Apollo Bay, passes through the park. 13 km sw.
Otway Fly The recently opened Otway Fly is a steel-trussed walkway perched high among the temperate rainforest treetops of the Otway Ranges. The 'Fly' is 25 m high and stretches for 600 m. It is accessible to all ages and levels of mobility. Get a bird's-eye view of ancient myrtle beech, blackwood and mountain ash while looking out for a variety of wildlife, including pygmy possums and the raucous yellow-tailed black cockatoo. A springboard bridge takes you over Youngs Creek, where you might spot a shy platypus. 62 km nw via Lavers Hill. *Marriners Lookout:* with views across Skenes Creek and Apollo Bay; 1.5 km nw. *Barham Paradise Scenic Reserve:* in the Barham River Valley, it is home to a variety of distinctive moisture-loving trees and ferns; 7 km nw. *Tanybryn Gallery:* displays and sells art and craft work in the magnificent surrounds of the Otway Ranges; Skenes Creek Rd; 19 km ne. *Fauna Australia:* wildlife sanctuary with kangaroos, wallabies and koalas; Lavers Hill; 47 km nw. *Melba Gully State Park:* temperate rainforest complete with mossy gullies, ferns and myrtle beech trees. In the evenings, watch as glow worms light up their surroundings. Near Lavers Hill; 47 km nw. *Forests and Waterfall Drive:* 109 km loop drive featuring spectacular Otway Ranges scenery. Waterfalls include Marriners, Triplet and Carisbrook falls. Drive starts at Apollo Bay, travels west to Lavers Hill and around to Skenes Creek. Map from visitor centre. *Charter flights:* views of the Twelve Apostles, the Bay of Islands and the 'Shipwreck Coast'; contact visitor centre for details.
ⓘ Great Ocean Road Visitor Information Centre, 100 Great Ocean Rd; (03) 5237 6529; www.greatoceanrd.org.au

Ararat   Pop. 7043

Map ref. 530 B8, 533 K2, 543 K13

Ararat is a city with a vibrant history. Once inhabited by the Tjapwurong Aboriginal people, the promising lands soon saw squatters move in, and the area really started to boom when gold was discovered in 1854. Thousands of prospectors arrived, and Ararat finally came into existence when Chinese immigrants rested on the town's site

in 1857 after walking from South Australian ports in order to avoid Victorian poll taxes. One member of the party discovered alluvial gold, and Ararat was born. Today Ararat is a service centre to its agricultural surrounds.
IN TOWN J Ward The town's original gaol, 'J Ward' served as an asylum for the criminally insane for many years and offers an eerie glimpse into the history of criminal confinement. Now guided tours reveal in chilling detail what life was like for the inmates. Girdlestone St; tours daily, (03) 5352 3357.
Gum San Chinese Heritage Centre Gum San means 'hill of gold', a fitting name for this impressive centre built in traditional Southern Chinese style and incorporating the principles of Feng Shui. The centre celebrates the contribution of the Chinese community both to Ararat, which is said to be the only goldfields town founded by Chinese prospectors, and to the surrounding Goldfields region. The experience is brought to life with interactive displays and an original Canton lead-mining tunnel, uncovered during the building of the centre. Western Hwy.
Alexandra Park and Botanical Gardens: an attractive formal garden featuring ornamental lakes, fountains and an orchid glasshouse; Vincent St. *Historical self-guide tours (walking or driving):* of particular note are the Bluestone buildings in Barkly St, including the post office, town hall, civic square and war memorial; details from visitor centre. *Ararat Art Gallery:* a regional gallery specialising in wool and fibre pieces by local artists; Barkly St. *Oth Art Gallery:* features work by resident artists; Birdwood Ave. *Langi Morgala Museum:* displays Aboriginal artefacts; Queen St.
WHAT'S ON *Jailhouse Rock Festival:* Mar. *Australian Orchid Festival:* Sept. *Golden Gateway Festival:* held over 10 days; Oct.
NEARBY Mount Buangor State Park The park features the Fern Tree Waterfalls and the three impressive peaks of Mt Buangor, Mt Sugarloaf and Cave Hill. Its diverse terrain with many varieties of eucalypts offers great sightseeing, bushwalking and picnicking. There are more than 130 species of birds, as well as eastern grey kangaroos, wallabies and echidnas. Access to the southern section is via Ferntree Rd off the Western Hwy; 30 km e. Mt Buangor and Cave Hill can be accessed from the main Mount Cole Rd in the Mount Cole State Forest.
Montara Winery: hosts a scarecrow competition each April, with ingenious entries from across the state scattered through the vineyard; 3 km s. Many more of the region's wineries can be accessed on the Great Grape Rd, a circuit through Ballarat and St Arnaud. This region is famous for sparkling whites and traditional old shiraz varieties. Brochure and map available from visitor centre.

Green Hill Lake: great for fishing and water activities; 4 km E. *McDonald Park Wildflower Reserve:* an extensive display of flora indigenous to the area, including wattles and banksias, particularly impressive during the spring months; 5 km N on Western Hwy. *One Tree Hill Lookout:* 360-degree views across the region; 5 km NW. *Langi Ghiran State Park:* Mt Langi Ghiran and Mt Gorrin form the key features of this park. A popular walk starts at the picnic area along Easter Creek, then goes to the Old Langi Ghiran Reservoir and along the stone water race to a scenic lookout. Access via Western Hwy, Kartuk Rd; 14 km E. *Mount Cole State Forest:* adjoins Mount Buangor State Park, with bushwalking, horseriding, four-wheel driving and trail-bike riding. The Ben Nevis Fire Tower offers spectacular views. 35 km E.
ℹ Old Railway Station, 91 High St; 1800 657 158 or (03) 5352 2096; www.visitararat.com.au

Avoca   Pop. 957

Map ref. 530 H6, 543 M12

Avoca was built during the gold boom of the 19th century and is renowned for its wide main street, divided by a stretch of park complete with trees and a war memorial. Avoca is set in the picturesque Pyrenees Ranges, with the Avoca River flowing by the town.

IN TOWN *Historic walk:* takes in the original courthouse, one of the oldest surviving courts in Victoria, as well as the powder magazine and Lalor's, one of the state's earliest pharmacies. Map available from visitor centre. *Cemetery:* Chinese burial ground from the goldmining period; on outskirts of town. *Avoca Rock Museum:* opals and local gemstones; High St; open 2pm–5pm weekends.
WHAT'S ON *Art and craft market:* RSL Hall, 2nd Sat each month. *Pyrenees Pink Lamb and Purple Shiraz Race Meeting:* country race meeting, Mar. *Petanque Tournaments (French Bowls):* Mar and Nov. *Pyrenees Vignerons' Gourmet Food and Wine Race Meeting:* April. *Avoca Taltarni Cup:* Oct.
NEARBY **Pyrenees Ranges State Forest** Covering an extensive stretch of bushland, these ranges are great for bushwalking and are popular for picnics and camping. Visitors can see a variety of wildlife, including koalas, wallabies, kangaroos and goannas. Orchids and lilies can be found growing around the base of the ranges in season. An 18 km walking track starts at The Waterfall camping area and finishes at Warrenmang–Glenlofty Rd. Access via Sunraysia or Pyrenees hwys.
Blue Pyrenees Estate: with underground cellar, petanque piste and gourmet lunches on weekends; 7 km W. *Mount Lonarch Arts:* displays and sells fine bone china made on the premises; Mount Lonarch; 10 km S. *Warrenmang Vineyard Resort:* with cottage-style accommodation

One of Montara Winery's competition scarecrows, near Ararat

and a restaurant specialising in regional produce. The vineyard is also the venue for A Sparkling Affair each Nov, an event celebrating the release of sparkling wines. 22 km NW. *Oasis Crystal Gallery:* local art and craft; Elmhurst; 26 km SW. *Fishing:* in the Avoca River near town, or in the Wimmera River, 42 km W. *Wine-tasting tours:* including self-guide Great Grape Rd; contact visitor centre for details.
ℹ 122 High St; (03) 5465 3767; www.pyreneestourism.com.au

Bacchus Marsh   Pop. 12 107

Map ref. 520 G5, 531 Q13, 533 R4, 534 A3

Bacchus Marsh shares part of its name with the Roman god of wine, but is actually better known for the apples that grow so well in the fertile valley region between the Werribee and Lerderderg rivers. Although it is now considered a satellite town within commuting distance of Melbourne, Bacchus Marsh retains a certain charm with stunning heritage buildings and a rural atmosphere.

IN TOWN **Avenue of Honour** Visitors to the town are greeted by the sight of the renowned Avenue of Honour, an elm-lined stretch of road built in honour of the Australian soldiers who fought in WW I. Eastern approach to town.
Big Apple Tourist Orchard: fresh produce market; Avenue of Honour. *Historic buildings:* include The Manor, the original home of the town's founder, Captain Bacchus (now privately owned), and Border Inn, built in 1850, thought to be the state's first service stop for Cobb & Co coaches travelling to the goldfields; contact visitor centre for details.
Local History Museum: connected to the blacksmith cottage and forge; Main St.

Express Building Art Gallery: Gisbourne Rd. *Ra Ceramics and Crafts:* Station St.
WHAT'S ON *Australian Speed Car Championships:* Mar. *Rotary Art Show:* June. *Cup Day in the Park:* Nov.
NEARBY **Lerderderg State Park** Featuring the imposing Lerderderg Gorge, the park is a great venue for picnics, bushwalking and swimming, while the Lerderderg River is ideal for trout fishing. The area was mined during the gold rush, and remnants from the water races used for washing gold can still be found upstream from O'Brien's Crossing. Late winter and spring are good times to see wildflowers and blossoming shrubs. Look out for koalas nestled in giant manna gums and for the magnificent sulphur-crested cockatoo and the wedge-tailed eagle. Access via Western Fwy to Bacchus Marsh–Gisborne and Lerderderg Gorge rds; 10 km N.
Werribee Gorge State Park Over time the Werribee River has carved through ancient seabed sediment and lava flows to form a spectacular gorge. The name 'Werribee' comes from the Aboriginal word 'Wearibi', meaning 'swimming place' or 'backbone', perhaps in reference to the snake-like path of the river. Rockclimbing is permitted at Falcons Lookout and a popular walk follows the Werribee River from the Meikles Point picnic area, providing views of the river and the gorge cliff-faces. Access via Western Fwy and Pentland Hills Rd to Myers Rd, or via Ironbark Rd (the Ballan–Ingliston Rd) from the Bacchus Marsh–Anakie Rd; 10 km W.
Long Forest Flora Reserve: a great example of the distinctive mallee scrub that once covered the region; 2 km NE. *St Anne's Vineyard:* with a bluestone cellar built from the remains of the old Ballarat Gaol; Western Fwy; 6 km W. *Merrimu Reservoir:* attractive park area with picnic facilities; about 10 km NE. *Melton:* now virtually a satellite suburb of Melbourne, this town has a long and rich history of horse breeding and training. Visit the Willow Homestead to see exhibits detailing the life of early settlers (open Wed, Fri and Sun), picnic on the Werribee River at Melton Reservoir, or taste the fine wines in the nearby Sunbury Wine Region. 14 km E. *Brisbane Ranges National Park:* with good walking tracks, wildflowers during spring and the imposing, steep-sided Anakie Gorge; 16 km SW. *Ballan:* try the refreshing mineral-spring water at Bostock Reservoir, or join in the festivities at the Vintage Machinery and Vehicle Rally in Feb, and an Autumn Festival held each Mar. 20 km NW. *Blackwood:* places to visit include the Mineral Springs Reserve and Garden of St Erth (closed Wed, Thurs). Blackwood is also the start of the 53 km return scenic drive through the Wombat State Forest. 31 km NW.
ℹ Council offices, 197 Main St; (03) 5366 7100

Bairnsdale
Pop. 10 557

Map ref. 535 P4, 536 F13

Bairnsdale is an attractive rural centre situated on the Mitchell River Flats and considered to be the western gateway to the lakes and wilderness region of East Gippsland. The area has a rich Koorie history brought to life through local landmarks, especially in Mitchell River National Park, where a fascinating piece of Aboriginal folklore is based around the Den of Nargun.

IN TOWN Aboriginal culture The Krowathunkoolong Keeping Place, on Dalmahoy St, details the cultural history of the region's Kurnai Aboriginal people and provides an insight into the impact of white settlement. To explore local Aboriginal history further, visit Howitt Park, Princes Hwy – a tree here has a 4 m scar where bark has been removed to make a canoe. The Bataluk Cultural Trail from Sale to Cann River takes in these and other indigenous sites of East Gippsland. Details of the trail available from Krowathunkoolong. *Historical Museum:* built in 1891, contains relics from Bairnsdale's past; Macarthur St. *Self-guide heritage walks:* take in St Mary's Church, with wall and ceiling murals by Italian artist Francesco Floreani, and the Court House, a magnificent, castle-like construction; contact visitor centre for details.

WHAT'S ON *Howitt Park Market:* 4th Sun each month. *Antiques and Collectibles Fair:* Mar. *East Gippsland Agricultural Field Days:* popular event with family entertainment; April. *Country Music Festival:* April. *Bairnsdale Easter Races:* Easter. *Line Dancing Championships:* Easter. *Bairnsdale Cup:* Sept.

NEARBY Mitchell River National Park Set in the remnants of temperate rainforest, this park has its own piece of mythology. According to Koorie history, Nargun was a beast made all of stone except for his hands, arms and breast. The fierce creature would drag unwary travellers

to his den, a shallow cave beneath a waterfall on the Woolshed Creek. This Den of Nargun can be found within the park, as can giant kanooka trees, wildflowers, and over 150 species of birds. There is a circuit walk to Bluff Lookout and Mitchell River, and Billy Goat Bend is a good spot for picnics. Princes Hwy; 15 km w near Lindenow. *McLeods Morass Wildlife Reserve:* a boardwalk extends over the freshwater marshland, allowing a close-up view of the many species of waterbirds found here; southern outskirts of town, access via Macarthur St; 2 km s. *Jolly Jumbuck Country Craft Centre:* woollen products for sale; 5 km E on Princes Hwy. *Wineries:* include Nicholson River Winery, for tastings and sales, 10 km E. *Bruthen:* hosts a Blues Bash each Feb; 24 km NW. *Dargo:* historic township in Dargo River valley and major producer of walnuts. Dargo Valley Winery has accommodation and cellar-door sales. The road beyond Dargo offers a scenic drive through high plains to Hotham Heights, stunning in spring when wattles bloom (unsealed road, check conditions). 93 km NW.
ⓘ 240 Main St; (03) 5152 3444; www.lakesandwilderness.com.au

Ballarat
Pop. 72 766

Map ref. 520 C4, 529, 531 K11, 533 O3, 538 A13

Ballarat is Victoria's largest inland city and features grand old buildings and wide streets that create an air of splendour. Built on the wealth of the region's goldfields, Ballarat offers activities ranging from fine dining in the many restaurants to real-life experiences of the area's goldmining past. Lake Wendouree provides a beautiful backdrop for picnics and the many festivals that take place during the year. Ballarat was the site of the infamous Eureka Rebellion of 3 December 1854. When goldfields police attempted to quell the miners' anger over strict mining-licence laws, a bloody massacre eventuated. The

Eureka Rebellion is viewed by many as a symbol of the Australian workers' struggle for equity and a 'fair go'. The best place to get a feel for this historic event is at Sovereign Hill.

IN TOWN Sovereign Hill This is the main destination for visitors to Ballarat and a good place to get a taste for what life was like on the Victorian goldfields. Spread over 60 ha, Sovereign Hill is a replica goldmining town, complete with authentically dressed townspeople. Panning for gold is a popular activity, while in the evening the Blood on the Southern Cross show re-enacts the Eureka Rebellion. Main St. *Eureka Stockade Centre:* a uniquely designed building, with information about the infamous battle; Eureka St. *Ballarat Botanic Gardens:* an impressive collection of native and exotic plants; along the shores of Lake Wendouree. *Ballarat Wildlife Park:* houses native Australian animals such as koalas, kangaroos, quokkas and crocodiles; cnr Fussel and York sts. *Ballarat Fine Art Gallery:* holds a significant collection of Australian art. The original Eureka Stockade flag is also on display. Lydiard St. *Gold Museum:* details the rich goldmining history of the area; opposite Sovereign Hill. *Historic buildings:* include Her Majesty's Theatre, built in 1875 and Australia's oldest intact, purpose-built theatre, and Craig's Royal and the George hotels, with classic old-world surroundings; Lydiard St. *Vintage Tramway:* via Wendouree Pde; rides weekends, and public and school holidays. *Montrose Cottage:* first masonry cottage built in the goldfields, now houses a museum displaying the history of women in the gold rush; Eureka St. *Avenue of Honour and Arch of Victory:* honours those who fought in WW I; western edge of city.

WHAT'S ON *Pleasant St Market:* 4th Sun each month. *Organs of the Ballarat Goldfields:* music festival held in historic venues; Jan. *Annual Rowing Regatta:* Feb. *Begonia Festival:* popular event for garden

Ballarat city centre

lovers; Mar. *Antique Fair:* Mar. *Eureka Jazz Festival:* April. *Winter Festival:* July. *Royal South Street Eisteddfod:* Sept–Nov. *Springfest Extravaganza:* market stalls and entertainment held around the perimeter of Lake Wendouree; Nov. *Ballarat Cup:* Nov. *Eureka Week:* major event commemorating the Eureka Rebellion; Nov–Dec.

NEARBY Enfield State Park Great for bushwalking or horseriding, the park is home to many species of orchids and numerous animals including echidnas, koalas, bats and frogs. There is a pretty picnic ground at Remote Long Gully, and numerous walking tracks. Also featured are the remnants of early goldmining settlements, including the Berringa Mines Historic Reserve. Access via Incolls and Misery Creek rds; 16 km s.
Buninyong Buninyong features many fine art and craft galleries. The Buninyong Flora and Bird Park, home to many species of parrots, has raised walkways through the aviaries. Visit in February for the Gold King Festival, which celebrates the early history of the town, and in March for the Buninyong Film Festival. The Mt Buninyong Lookout east of town offers great views. 13 km SE.
Kirks and Gong Gong reserves: ideal for picnics and bushwalking, these parks include many unique, indigenous plants; on opposite sides of Daylesford Rd; 5 km NE. *Kryal Castle:* replica of a medieval castle, with daily tours and family entertainment; 9 km E. *Yuulong Lavender Estate:* set in scenic landscaped gardens, the estate produces and sells lavender products; 15 km SW at Yendon. *Lal Lal Falls:* plunge 30 m into the Moorabool River; 18 km SE. *Lal Lal Blast Furnace:* fascinating 19th-century archaeological remains; 18 km SE. *Lake Burrumbeet:* this 2100 ha lake is a popular fishing spot, especially for redfin in spring and summer. Watersports and family activities are available on the lake; various boat ramps provide access. Caravan parks are set on the lakeside and are popular with holiday-makers. 22 km NW. *Skipton:* in town is an eel factory selling smoked eel and other products; 51 km SW. South of town are the Mt Widderin Caves – one has been named the Ballroom, as it was once a venue for dances and concerts. The caves are on private property; tours by appt (03) 5340 2081. *Beaufort:* a small town on the shores of Lake Beaufort, an artificial lake surrounded by gardens, providing a picturesque location for picnics and leisurely walks; 54 km W. South of town is Lake Goldsmith, home of a major rally of steam-driven machinery and vehicles each May and Nov. *Mooramong Homestead:* built in the 1870s and then altered during the 1930s by its ex-Hollywood owners. It is surrounded by beautiful gardens and a flora and fauna reserve, and is open for tours 3rd Sun each month. 56 km NW via Skipton. *Great Grape Rd:* circuit through Avoca, St Arnaud and Stawell, visiting local wineries.

ⓘ Cnr Sturt and Albert sts; 1800 446 633 or (03) 5320 5741; www.ballarat.com

Beechworth   Pop. 2781

Map ref. 539 O6, 536 A3

Set in the picturesque surrounds of the Australian Alps, Beechworth is one of the state's best preserved 19th-century gold towns, with over 30 buildings listed by the National Trust. The grandeur of Beechworth's buildings can be explained by the fact that during the 1850s over four million ounces of gold were mined here. There is a delightful tale about Beechworth's heyday: the story goes that Daniel Cameron, a political candidate vying for support from the Ovens Valley community, rode at the head of a procession through the town on a horse shod with golden shoes. Sceptics claim they were merely gilded, but the tale offers a glimpse into the wealth of Beechworth during the gold rush.

IN TOWN The Beechworth Gaol Built in 1859, the original wooden gates of this gaol were replaced with iron ones when it was feared prisoners would break out in sympathy with Ned Kelly during his trial. The gaol is still in operation and is located in William St.
Historic and cultural precinct This fantastic precinct provides a snapshot of 19th-century Beechworth. Featuring fine, honey-coloured granite buildings, the area incorporates the telegraph station, gold office, Chinese prospectors' office, town hall and powder magazine. Of particular interest is the courthouse, site of many infamous trials including Ned Kelly's, and where Sir Isaac Isaacs began his legal career. Also in the precinct is the Robert O'Hara Burke Memorial Museum, with the interesting 'Strand of Time' exhibition where 19th-century Beechworth shops are brought to life. Various guided tours are available, highlights being the 'Ned Kelly Trial Re-enactment' and the Lantern Tours. Tickets from the visitor centre. *Harness and Carriage Museum:* run by the National Trust; Railway Ave. *Ned Kelly's Cell:* under the shire offices, where he was once briefly held; Albert Rd. *Buckland Gallery:* country arts and crafts; Ford St. *Berringa Antiques:* Ford St. *Beechworth Gallery:* touring regional and international exhibitions; Albert St. *The Beechworth Pantry:* gourmet cafe and centre for produce of the north-east; Ford St. *Beechworth Bakery:* famous for its pastries and cakes; Camp St.
WHAT'S ON *Market at Police Reserve, Ford St:* 4 times a year, check visitor centre for details. *Golden Horseshoes Festival:* a celebration of the town's past, with street parades and a variety of market stalls; Easter. *Drive Back in Time:* vintage car rally; May. *Celtic Festival:* music festival; Nov.
NEARBY Beechworth Cemetery This cemetery is a fascinating piece of

goldfields history. More than 2000 Chinese goldminers are buried here. Twin ceremonial Chinese burning towers stand as a monument to those who died seeking their fortune far from home. Northern outskirts of town.
Beechworth Historic Park: surrounds the town and includes Woolshed Falls Historical Walk through former alluvial goldmining sites. *Gorge Scenic Drive (5 km):* starts north of town and covers areas designated for gold fossicking. *Beechworth Forest Drive:* takes in Fletcher Dam; 3 km SE towards Stanley. *Kellys Lookout:* at Woolshed Creek, about 4 km N. *Mt Pilot Lookout:* views of Murray Valley, plus signposted Aboriginal cave paintings nearby; 5 km N. *Stanley:* a historic goldmining settlement with fantastic views of the alps from the summit of Mt Stanley; 10 km SE. *Wineries:* 5 cellar doors in and around Beechworth for tastings and sales; map from visitor centre.
ⓘ Ford St; 1 300 366 321 or (03) 5728 3233; www.beechworth.com

Benalla   Pop. 8593

Map ref. 539 K7, 540 A2

Motorists from Melbourne entering Benalla will notice the Rose Gardens positioned beside the highway a short distance before Lake Benalla – gardens for which the city has become known as the 'Rose City'. The town is Sir Edward 'Weary' Dunlop's birthplace and proudly advertises the fact with a museum display and a statue in his honour at the Benalla Botanical Gardens.

IN TOWN The Benalla Regional Art Gallery Set by picturesque Lake Benalla, the gallery features an impressive collection including contemporary Australian art, works by Sidney Nolan, Arthur Streeton, Tom Roberts and Arthur Boyd, and a substantial collection of indigenous art. Built in 1975, the gallery is a striking work of modern architecture. There is a permanent exhibition featuring the works of Laurie Ledger, a local resident, and examples of the Heidelberg School and early colonial art. Bridge St.
Benalla Ceramic Art Mural: a Gaudi-inspired community construction, this fascinating 3D mural is opposite the Regional Art Gallery on Lake Benalla. *The Creators Gallery:* paintings, pottery and craft; at the information centre. *The Costume and Pioneer Museum:* displays period costumes, a Ned Kelly exhibit (including Kelly's cummerbund) and a feature display of Benalla's 'famous sons', in particular, Sir Edward 'Weary' Dunlop; Mair St. *Lake Benalla:* created in Broken River, it has good recreation and picnic facilities and is a haven for waterbirds. Take the self-guide walk around the lake. *Botanical Gardens:* features a splendid collection of roses and memorial statue of Sir Edward 'Weary' Dunlop; Bridge St. *Aerodrome:* centre for the Gliding Club of Victoria,

offering hot-air ballooning and glider flights; northern outskirts of town; bookings (03) 5762 1058.

WHAT'S ON *Craft and produce market:* Fawckner Dr; 4th Sat each month. *Rotary Art Show:* Easter. *Rose Festival:* Nov.

NEARBY Reef Hills State Park The forest here features grey box, river red gum, wildflowers in spring and wattle blossom in winter. The park is popular for scenic drives, bushwalks, picnics, and horseriding. There are more than 100 species of birds, including gang-gang cockatoos and crimson rosellas, plus animals such as eastern grey kangaroos, sugar gliders, brush-tailed possums, echidnas and bats. 4 km sw, western side of the Midland Hwy.

Lake Mokoan: great for fishing, boating and waterskiing; 10 km NE. *1950s-style cinema:* showing classic films, at Swanpool; 23 km s.
ⓘ 14 Mair St; (03) 5762 1749

Bendigo
Pop. 68 480

Map ref. 528, 531 P2, 538 C8, 543 Q10

Bendigo is one of Victoria's best-known goldmining centres, and perhaps the most impressive in terms of architecture, with lavish sandstone buildings funded by the gold discovered in the region in 1851. Bendigo has a rich and diverse multicultural history and is one of only two cities in the world outside China to have been granted a Chinese name (San Francisco is the other one). The name, Dai Gun Sun, meaning Big Gold Mountain, tells of the promise that the Bendigo region held for the large number of Chinese immigrants who arrived during the gold rush.

IN TOWN The Golden Dragon Museum The museum commemorates the contribution of the Chinese community to life on the goldfields. On display are exhibitions depicting the daily life and hardships of Chinese immigrants and an impressive collection of Chinese memorabilia and processional regalia, including what is said to be the world's oldest imperial dragon, 'Loong' (which first appeared at the Bendigo Easter fair in 1892), and the world's longest imperial dragon, 'Sun Loong'. Adjacent to the museum is the classical Chinese Garden of Joy. Bridge St.

Central Deborah Gold Mine Perhaps the best way to get a feel for life in a goldmining town is to take a trip down this mine, where you can still see traces of gold in the quartz reef 20 storeys below the ground. The Central Deborah Gold Mine was the last commercial goldmine to operate in Bendigo. From 1939 to 1954 around a ton of gold was excavated. Violet St; (03) 5443 8322 for tour details. *Bendigo Art Gallery:* features temporary exhibitions plus an extensive permanent collection with a focus on Australian artists, including Arthur Boyd, Tom Roberts and Arthur Streeton; guided tours

daily; View St. *Bus tours of major attractions:* in red double-decker buses. *Self-guide heritage walk:* takes in landmarks including the Shamrock Hotel, built in 1897, cnr Pall Mall and Williamson St; Sacred Heart Cathedral, the largest outside Melbourne, Wattle St; Alexandra Fountain, built in 1881, one of the largest and most ornate fountains in regional Victoria, at Charing Cross; and the Renaissance-style post office and law courts at Pall Mall. Details on heritage walks available from visitor centre. *Dudley House:* National Trust-classified building; View St. *Vintage Trams:* run from mine on 8 km city trip, including a stop at the Tram Depot Museum; taped commentary provided. *Chinese Joss House:* temple built by Chinese miners; included on the vintage tram trip; Finn St, Emu Point (North Bendigo). *Rosalind Park:* includes a lookout tower, Cascade and Conservatory gardens; Barnard St. *Discovery Science and Technology Centre:* features more than 100 hands-on displays; Railway Pl. *Bendigo Woollen Mills:* tours available, Lansell St West. *Making of a Nation Exhibition:* details Bendigo's role in Federation; at the visitor centre, Pall Mall.

WHAT'S ON *Large undercover market:* each Sun at the Prince of Wales Showgrounds, Holmes St. *Craft market:* 4th Sun each month (except winter); Pall Mall Rd. *Madison 10 000 Cycling Race:* Mar. *Bendigo Easter Festival:* first held in 1871, the festival spans 4 days and is a major event on the town's calendar, with free music and entertainment, craft markets, art exhibits, food and wine. *Eaglehawk Dahlia and Arts Festival:* Easter. *Bendigo by Bike:* April. *Chrysanthemum Championships:* April. *Bendigo Heritage Uncorked:* Oct. *Orchid Club Spring Show:* Oct. *National Swap Meet:* Australia's largest meet for vintage cars and bikes; Nov. *Racing Festival:* Bendigo Cup as a highlight; Nov.

NEARBY Greater Bendigo National Park The park, which extends to the north and south of town, protects some high-quality box-ironbark forest and is popular for scenic driving, cycling, walking and camping. Relics of the region's goldmining and eucalyptus-oil industries can be found, with the nearby Hartland's Eucalyptus Factory built in 1890 (open daily for sales). Fauna includes over 170 species of birds including the grey shrike-thrush, a pretty songbird. In the early morning and later in the evening, look out for eastern grey kangaroos, black wallabies and echidnas. Access via Loddon Valley Hwy through Eaglehawk; 8 km N.

Bendigo Pottery: Australia's oldest working pottery, with potters at work, a cafe and sales. Living Wings and Things wildlife display is adjacent to the pottery. Epsom, northern outskirts of town. *Fortuna Villa:* mansion built in 1871; Chum St; 2 km s; open Sun. *Bendigo Cactus Gardens:* established in 1937, the gardens are National Trust-classified; White Hills;

3 km NE. *One Tree Hill observation tower:* panoramic views; 4 km s. *Iron Bark Riding Centre:* 4 km N. *Eaglehawk:* site of the gold rush in 1852, it features remnants of goldmining days and fine examples of 19th-century architecture; details of self-guide heritage tour from visitor centre; 6.5 km NW. *Mandurang:* features historic wineries, an orchid nursery, Tannery Lane Pottery and Rupertswood Country Home Open Garden; 8 km SE. *Goldfields Mohair Farm:* guided tours; at Lockwood; 11 km SW. *Arakoon Resort:* aquatic fun park, open during summer; 18 km SE. *Sedgwick's Camel Farm:* offers rides and treks on weekends, or weekdays by appt; 20 km SE; (03) 5439 6367. *Bendigo wine region:* many wineries to the south and east of town, offering tastings and sales; brochure from visitor centre. *Goldfields Tourist Route:* information on this and guided prospecting tours from visitor centre.
ⓘ Old Post Office, 51–67 Pall Mall; 1800 813 153 or (03) 5444 4445; www.bendigotourism.com

Bright
Pop. 2086

Map ref. 536 C6, 539 P8, 541 L5

Bright is situated in the Ovens Valley in the foothills of the Victorian Alps. A particularly striking element of the town is the avenues of deciduous trees, at their peak during the autumn months. The Bright Autumn Festival is held annually in celebration of the spectacular seasonal changes. The Ovens River flows through the town, providing a delightful location for picnics or camping. The town also offers off-the-mountain accommodation for nearby Mt Hotham and Mt Buffalo.

IN TOWN Old Tobacco Sheds You could easily spend half a day here – wandering through the sheds filled with antiques and bric-a-brac and through the makeshift museums, which give an insight into the local tobacco industry and the gold rush. Also on the site there is a historic hut, and the Sharefarmers Cafe serves Devonshire tea. Great Alpine Rd. *Gallery 90:* local art and craft; at the visitor centre. *Centenary Park:* with a deep weir, children's playground and picnic facilities; Gavan St. *Bright Art Gallery and Cultural Centre:* community-owned gallery, displays and sells fine art and handicrafts; Mountbatten Ave. *Lotsafun Amusement Park:* Mill Rd. *Bright and District Historical Museum:* in the old railway station building, with artefacts and photographs from the town's past; cnr Gavan and Anderson sts; open by appt (contact visitor centre). *Walking tracks:* well-marked tracks around the area include Canyon Walk along the Ovens River, where remains of gold-workings can be seen; contact visitor centre for details.

WHAT'S ON *Bright Street Market:* 2nd Sat each month. *Craft market:* 3rd Sat each month; Burke St.

Bright Blues Festival: 7–9 Mar. *Autumn Festival:* activities include craft markets and entertainment; April/May. *Alpine Spring Festival:* free entertainment, displays and open gardens, celebrating the beauty of Bright in spring; Oct.

NEARBY Wandiligong A National Trust-classified hamlet, the area contains well-preserved historic buildings from the town's goldmining days. The tiny village is set in a rich green valley, with an enormous hedge maze as the dominant feature and over 2 km of walkways surrounded by lush gardens. The maze is well signposted and is open 10am–5pm Wed–Sun. 6 km s.

Mount Buffalo National Park This is not a large park, but it is one of Victoria's favourites. In winter it is a haven for skiers, many staying at Mount Buffalo Chalet. In summer bushwalkers and campers descend on the park, taking in the superb views from the granite peaks, the gushing waterfalls, and the display of alpine wildflowers. Lake Catani is a popular spot for canoeists, and rockclimbing and hang-gliding are also popular. 10 km NW.

Tower Hill Lookout: 4 km NW. *Boyntons of Bright Winery:* for sales and tastings; at junction of Ovens and Buckland rivers, Porepunkah; 6 km NW. *Snowline Deer and Emu Farm:* Hughes La, Eurobin; 16 km NW. *Harrietville:* a former goldmining village located just outside the Alpine National Park. Attractions include Pioneer Park, an open-air museum and picnic area; Tavare Park, with a swing bridge and picnic/barbecue facilities; and a lavender farm, with sales of lavender products. 20 km SE. *Alpine National Park:* to the south-east of town; *see feature on p. 186.*
ℹ 119 Gacan St; 1800 500 117 or (03) 5755 2275

Buchan   Pop. 134

Map ref. 507 B13, 536 I11

Situated in East Gippsland, Buchan is primarily an agricultural town renowned for offering some of the best caving in Victoria. Although the origin of the town's name is disputed, it is said to be derived from the Aboriginal term for either 'smoke-signal expert' or 'place of the grass bag'.

IN TOWN *Conorville Heritage Model Village:* model buildings from 1780 to 1914, including miniature sculptures of people. Also here is a full-sized, furnished 1840s bark-house replica. Main St.

WHAT'S ON *Foothills Festival:* Jan. *Canni Creek Races:* Feb. *Rodeo:* Easter. *Flowers and Craft Show:* Easter.

NEARBY The Buchan Caves Reserve The reserve features more than 350 limestone caves, of which the Royal and Fairy caves are the most accessible – the Fairy Cave alone is over 400 m long, with impressive stalactites. Europeans did not discover the caves until 1907, but from then on they

became a popular tourist destination. Now visitors can cool off in the spring-fed swimming pool after exploring the caves. Tours of the Royal and Fairy caves run daily. Off Buchan Rd, north of town.

Snowy River Scenic Drive The drive takes in the Buchan and Snowy rivers junction and runs along the edge of Snowy River National Park to Gelantipy. Beyond Gelantipy is Little River Gorge, Victoria's deepest gorge. A short walking track leads to a cliff-top lookout. Near the gorge is McKillops Bridge, a safe swimming spot, a good site to launch canoes, and the starting point for 2 walking tracks. Care is required on the road beyond Gelantipy. 4WD is recommended. Contact visitor centre for details.

Suggan Buggan: this historic townsite, surrounded by Alpine National Park, features an 1865 schoolhouse and the Eagle Loft Gallery, for local art and craft; 64 km N.
ℹ General Store, Main St; (03) 5155 9202; www.lakesandwilderness.com.au

Camperdown   Pop. 3126

Map ref. 526 F6, 533 L8

Situated at the foot of Mt Leura, a volcanic cone, Camperdown is more famous for its natural attractions

than for the town itself, being situated on the world's third largest volcanic plain. But that should not detract from Camperdown – National Trust-listed Finlay Avenue features two kilometres of regal elm trees, while in the town centre the Gothic-style Manifold Clock Tower proudly stands as a tribute to the region's first European pioneers.

IN TOWN *Manifold Clock Tower:* an imposing structure built in 1896; cnr Manifold and Pike sts; open 1st Sun each month. *Historical Society Museum:* displays Aboriginal artefacts, local historical photographs, and household and farming implements; Manifold St. *Courthouse:* built in 1886–87, described as one of the most distinctive courthouses in Australia; Manifold St. *Buggy Museum:* collection of 30 restored horse-drawn buggies; Ower St.

WHAT'S ON *Craft market:* Finlay Ave or Theatre Royal; 1st Sun each month. *One Act Play Festival:* July. *Vintage Motorsport Weekend:* Nov.

NEARBY Crater lakes Surrounding Camperdown are spectacular crater lakes that provide an interesting history of volcanic activity over the past 20 000 years, as well as opportunities for watersports and excellent fishing. Travelling west of town, take the scenic

The Cathedral, Mount Buffalo National Park, near Bright

Childers Cove, on the Great Ocean Road towards Warrnambool

The Great Ocean Road

Until the Great Ocean Road opened in 1932, Lorne and the surrounding coastal towns were just small, isolated communities. In the 1870s the only route to Lorne was a rough coach track through dense bushland, and before this the ocean provided the main link to the outside world. But World War I and the decision of Geelong mayor Howard Hitchcock soon changed things. Hitchcock saw a road as an opportunity to employ the many returning soldiers who were coming home to a bleak future with no jobs. He created the Great Ocean Road Trust and began raising money.

Thousands of soldiers flocked to the area when work began in August 1918. Most of the work was done with picks and shovels and horses and drays. Stage one, Lorne to Eastern View, was completed in 1922, and in November 1932 the full spectacular route was officially opened as one of the country's first tollways, costing drivers two shillings and sixpence (25 cents) and passengers one shilling and sixpence (15 cents).

Today the Great Ocean Road is one of Australia's most popular attractions. Particularly popular are the Twelve Apostles, sitting in the Southern Ocean beyond 70-metre-high limestone cliffs. The stormy water adds to the rugged beauty of the landmarks, and a comprehensive visitor centre tells of the history of the area and how the Apostles were formed.

The Great Ocean Road has a great deal more to offer visitors than just the Twelve Apostles. It also has excellent surf beaches, including the world-class Bells Beach, Bancoora and Jan Juc. Calmer beaches for safe swimming can be found at the holiday towns of Apollo Bay, Lorne and Torquay. And immediately inland are the rainforests, ferny gullies and waterfalls of various national and state parks, offering everything from treetop walks to close encounters with glow worms.

But perhaps even more than this, visitors flock to these parts for the simple and unbeatable experience of the drive itself, particularly exhilarating between Anglesea and Apollo Bay. Here it hugs the coast, winding around headlands and squeezed up against sheer cliffs – nothing lies between you and the ocean but fresh sea air.

drive around the rims of lakes Bullen Merri and Gnotuk and join in the watersports and swimming at South Beach. The lakes are regularly stocked with Chinook salmon and redfin. For a scenic picnic spot, and some of the best fishing, visit Lake Purrumbete, 15 km se. By far one of the most impressive lakes is Lake Corangamite, the Southern Hemisphere's largest permanent salt lake. This lake lies 25 km e, but the best viewing spot is Red Rock Lookout; *see Colac.*
Derrinallum and Mt Elephant Mt Elephant rises to almost 200 m behind the small township of Derrinallum – it doesn't sound like a lot, but across the plains of the Western District you can see it

from up to 60 km away. A gash in the elephant's western side is the result of decades of quarrying – the mountain is actually the scoria cone of an extinct volcano, and inside is a 90 m deep crater. Now owned by the community, there is a walking trail to the top, and the Music on the Mount festival is held here in Nov. Lake Tooliorook on the other side of town offers good fishing for trout and redfin, and watersports. 40 km n.
Camperdown–Timboon Rail Trail: walking or riding track through bush, following historic railway line. *Mt Leura:* extinct volcano close to the perfect cone of Mt Sugarloaf. A lookout offers excellent views over crater lakes and volcanoes,

and north across the plains to the Grampians. 1 km s. *Camperdown Botanic Gardens:* feature rare examples of Himalayan oak and a lookout over lakes Bullen Merri and Gnotuk; 3 km w. *Cobden Miniature Trains:* operates 3rd Sun each month; Cobden; 13 km s.
ℹ️ Old Courthouse, Manifold St; (03) 5593 3390

Cann River   Pop. 227

Map ref. 507 E13, 537 N11

Cann River is situated at the junction of the Princes and Cann Valley highways, and is notable for its proximity to several spectacular national parks. The area boasts excellent fishing, bushwalking and camping in the rugged hinterland, with nearby Point Hicks notable for being the first land on the east coast of Australia to be sighted by Europeans.
NEARBY Lind National Park The park includes Euchre Valley Nature Drive through temperate rainforest gullies. It also supports open eucalypt forests with grey gum, messmate and silvertop ash. Watch for wildlife such as the pretty masked owl and the elusive, long-footed potoroo. Has picnic facilities. 15 km w.
Coopracambra National Park In one of the most remote sections of Victoria, the park remains largely undisturbed. Ancient fossil footprints have been found in the red sandstone gorge of the Genoa River, and the surrounding granite peaks create a spectacular scene. The 35 000 ha area protects unique ecosystems and rare flora and fauna. Only experienced and well-equipped hikers should undertake walks in the rugged and remote parts of this park. A 'trip intentions' form needs to be lodged at the Cann River or Mallacoota office of Parks Victoria prior to departure, and parks staff must be notified upon return. 30 km n near NSW border.
Croajingolong National Park: the road travelling south of Cann River leads to Point Hicks and its historic 1890 lighthouse (daily tours offered). *For further details on the park see Mallacoota.*
ℹ️ Snowy River–Orbost Visitor Centre, 13 Lochiel St, Orbost; (03) 5154 2424; or Parks Victoria Cann River office; (03) 5158 6351; www.lakesandwilderness.com.au

Casterton   Pop. 1667

Map ref. 532 C4

Casterton is a Roman name meaning 'walled city', given to the town because of the natural wall of lush hills surrounding the valley where it lies. These hills, combined with the Glenelg River that flows through town, create an idyllic rural atmosphere. The region is colloquially known as 'Kelpie Country' as it is the birthplace of this world-famous breed of working dog. In the mid-1800s a prized Scottish collie female pup from nearby Warrock Homestead was sold to a stockman named Jack Gleeson, who named her 'Kelpie' – she was bred out with various 'black and tan' dogs, and so began the long line of the working man's best friend.

IN TOWN *Historical Museum:* housed in the old railway station, the museum displays local artefacts; cnr Jackson and Clarke sts; open by appt. *Alma and Judith Zaadstra Fine Art Gallery:* Henty St. *Mickle Lookout:* a great view across the town at Moodie St; off Robertson St on the eastern edge of town.

WHAT'S ON *Vintage Car Rally:* Mar. *Polocrosse Championships:* Mar. *Casterton Cup:* May. *Australian Kelpie Muster and Kelpie Working Dog Auction:* June/July. *Woodturning Demonstration Exhibition:* Aug. *Christmas Lights Festival:* bus tours available, contact visitor centre; Dec.

NEARBY Dergholm State Park The park features a great diversity of vegetation, including woodlands, open forests, heaths and swamps. In this tranquil setting an abundance of wildlife thrives, including echidnas, koalas, kangaroos, reptiles and the endangered red-tailed black cockatoo. A key attraction is Baileys Rocks, unique giant green-coloured granite boulders. 50 km N. *Long Lead Swamp:* waterbirds, kangaroos, emus, and a trail-bike track; Penola Rd; 11 km W. *Geological formations:* in particular, The Hummocks, 12 km NE, and The Bluff, off Dartmoor Rd, 20 km SW. Both rock formations are around 150 million years old. *Warrock Homestead:* a unique collection of 33 buildings erected by its founder, George Robertson. The homestead was built in 1843 and is National Trust-classified. 26 km N; open day on Easter Sun. *Bilston's Tree:* 50 m high and arguably the world's largest red gum; on Glenmia Rd; 30 km N. ℹ Shiels Tce; (03) 5581 2070

Castlemaine   Pop. 6822

Map ref. 531 O6, 538 C10, 543 Q11

Castlemaine is a classic goldmining town known for its grand old buildings and sprawling botanical gardens. The gold discovered in the 1850s ran out quite quickly. Now the town relies largely on agriculture, as well as being home to a thriving artistic community that takes inspiration from the area's red hills.

IN TOWN Castlemaine Art Gallery Housed in an elegant Art Deco building, the gallery was designed in 1931 by Peter Meldrum and is renowned for its collection of Australian art. Along with the permanent collection, many exhibitions appear here. Works by Rembrandt, Francisco Goya and Andy Warhol have all been displayed at this delightful gallery. Lyttleton St. **Buda Historic Home and Garden** Buda is considered to have one of the most significant examples of 19th-century

gardens in Victoria. The house itself is furnished with period pieces and art and craft created by the Leviny family, who lived here for 118 years. Ernest Leviny was a silversmith and jeweller. Five of his 6 daughters never married, but remained at Buda and pursued woodwork, photography and embroidery. Hunter St. *Diggings Interpretive Centre:* housed in the restored 19th-century Castlemaine Market building, the centre features interactive displays about the area's many goldmines as well as various exhibitions; Moyston St. *Theatre Royal:* recently restored, the theatre hosts live shows and films and also offers accommodation; Hargraves St. *Castlemaine Botanic Gardens:* one of Victoria's oldest and most impressive 19th-century gardens; cnr Walker and Downes rds. *Old Castlemaine Gaol:* the recently restored gaol offers tours and accommodation. Bowden St.

WHAT'S ON *Market:* each Sat at Wesley Hill, 2.5 km E. *Castlemaine State Festival:* odd-numbered years, April. *Festival of Gardens:* odd-numbered years, Nov.

NEARBY Castlemaine Diggings National Heritage Park The wealth on Castlemaine's streets springs from the huge hauls of gold found on the Mount Alexander Diggings, east and south of town. Thousands of miners worked the fields. Towns such as Fryerstown, Vaughan and Glenluce, now almost ghost towns, supported breweries, schools, churches and hotels. Today visitors can explore Chinese cemeteries, mineral springs, waterwheels and old townsites. Fossicking is popular. Details of self-guide walks and drives from visitor centre. *Chewton:* historic buildings line the streets of this former gold town; 4 km E. *Dingo Farm:* a chance to meet and pat purebred dingoes; 4 km SE, near Chewton. *Harcourt:* this town is known for its many wineries, including Harcourt Valley Vineyard and Blackjack Vineyards, with tastings and cellar-door sales. Also at Harcourt is the Skydancers Orchid and Butterfly Gardens. The town hosts the Apple Festival in Mar and spring, and the Orchid Festival in Oct. 9 km NE. *Big Tree:* a giant red gum over 500 years old; Guildford; 14 km SW. *Koala Reserve:* Mt Alexander; 19 km NE. ℹ Old Market, Moyston St; 1800 171 888 or (03) 5470 6200

Chiltern   Pop. 1035

Map ref. 511 P13, 536 A2, 539 O4

Now surrounded by rich pastoral farmland, Chiltern was once at the centre of a goldmining boom and had as many as 14 suburbs. After the Indigo gold discovery in the 1850s, there was a major influx of miners and settlers. Although the gold boom was brief, farming was soon prominent in the town's economy. Today the rich heritage of the 19th century can be seen in the well-preserved streetscapes, a vision not

lost on Australian filmmakers keen for that 'authentic' 1800s scene.

IN TOWN *Athenaeum Museum:* historic building with heritage display; Conness St. *Dow's Pharmacy:* old chemist shop with original features; Conness St. *Star Theatre and Grapevine Museum:* the quaint theatre still operates and the museum, formerly the Grapevine Hotel, boasts the largest grapevine in Australia, planted in 1867 and recorded in the *Guinness Book of Records;* Main St. *Federal Standard newspaper office:* open by appt for groups; Main St. *Lakeview House:* former home of author Henry Handel Richardson; Victoria St; open afternoons on weekends and public and school holidays. *Stephen's Motor Museum:* motoring memorabilia; Conness St. *Lake Anderson:* picnic and barbecue facilities; access via Main St.

WHAT'S ON *Antique Fair:* Aug. *Ironbark Fair:* Oct.

NEARBY Chiltern–Mount Pilot National Park This park stretches from around Chiltern south to Beechworth and protects remnant box-ironbark forest, which once covered much of this part of Victoria. Also featured are significant goldmining relics, including the impressive Magenta Goldmine (around 2 km E). Of the park's 21 000 ha, 7000 were exposed to bushfire in January 2003 – the regeneration already occurring is evidence of the hardiness of the forest. An introduction to the forest scenery and goldmining history is on the 25 km scenic drive signposted from Chiltern. Other activities include canoeing and rafting, fishing, and cycling and walking trips along the many marked trails. Access via Hume Hwy and the road south to Beechworth. *Koendidda Historic Homestead:* wonderfully landscaped gardens and B&B; near Barnawartha, 10 km NE. ℹ 30 Main St; (03) 5726 1611

Clunes   Pop. 1088

Map ref. 520 C2, 531 J8, 533 O2, 538 A11, 543 O13

The first registered gold strike in the state was made at Clunes on 7 July 1851. The town, north of Ballarat, is said to be one of the most intact gold towns in Victoria, featuring historic buildings throughout, including the imposing town hall and courthouse. Surrounding the town are a number of extinct volcanoes. A view of these can be obtained three kilometres to the south, on the road to Ballarat.

IN TOWN *Clunes Museum:* local history museum featuring displays on the gold-rush era; Fraser St; open weekends and school and public holidays. *Bottle Museum:* in former South Clunes State School; Bailey St. *Queens Park:* on the banks of Creswick Creek, the park was created over 100 years ago. *Butter Factory Art Gallery:* Cameron St. *The Weavery:* features hand-woven fabrics; Fraser St. *Clunes Homestead Furniture:* Talbot Rd.

VICTORIA

The fertile lands around Colac

WHAT'S ON *Caloma Day Garden Party:* Jan.
NEARBY Talbot This delightful, historic
town has many 1860–70 buildings,
particularly in Camp St and Scandinavian
Cres. Attractions include the Arts
and Historical Museum in the former
Methodist Church; the Bull and Mouth
Restaurant in an old bluestone building,
formerly a hotel; and a market selling local
produce, 3rd Sun each month. 18 km NW.
Mount Beckworth Scenic Reserve: popular
picnic and horseriding reserve with
panoramic views from the mountain's
summit; 8 km W.
ⓘ Old School Complex, 70 Bailey St;
(03) 5345 3896

Cobram   Pop. 4542

Map ref. 511 M13, 539 J3

At Cobram and nearby Barooga (across
the New South Wales border) the Murray
River is bordered by sandy beaches,
making it a great spot for fishing,
watersports and picnics. The stretch
of land between the township and the
river features river red gum forests and
lush wetlands, with tracks leading to
various beaches, the most accessible of
which is Thompsons Beach, located near
the bridge off Boorin Street. The town
is supported by orchards and dairies,
earning it the nickname 'peaches and
cream country'. A biennial festival is held
in honour of these industries.

IN TOWN *Historic log cabin:* built in
Yarrawonga in 1875, then moved piece
by piece to its current location; opposite
the information centre on Station St.
Station Gallery: at the railway station,
displays a collection of art by local
artists.
WHAT'S ON *Craft market:* Punt Rd;
1st Sat each month. *Peaches and Cream
Festival:* free peaches and cream, a rodeo,
fishing competitions and other activities;
odd-numbered years, Australia Day. *River*

Beaches Festival: Thompsons Beach; Easter
Sun. *Rotary Art Show:* May. *Antique Fair:*
June. *Open Gardens Display:* Oct.
NEARBY *Quinn Island Flora and Fauna
Reserve:* home to abundant birdlife and
Aboriginal artefacts, including scar
trees, flint tools and middens, the island
can be explored on a self-guide walk;
on the Murray River, accessed via a
pedestrian bridge off River Rd. *Binghi
Boomerang Factory:* large manufacturer
and exporter of boomerangs. Free
throwing demonstrations with purchases.
Tocumwal Rd, Barooga, across the
river. *Wineries:* east and west of Cobram,
including Heritage Farm Wines, with a
116 m woodcarving depicting scenes of
early Murray Valley life (Murray Valley
Hwy, 5 km W). *Scenic Drive Strawberry
Farm:* strawberry-picking during warmer
months; Torgannah Rd, Koonoomoo;
11 km NW. *Cactus Country:* Australia's
largest cacti gardens; Strathmerton;
16 km W. *Ulupna Island:* part of Barmah
State Park; turn-off after Strathmerton; *see
Echuca for details. Murray River Horse Trails:* a
fantastic way to explore the Murray River
beaches; (03) 5868 2221.
ⓘ Cnr Station St and Punt Rd; 1800 607
607 or (03) 5872 2132

Cohuna   Pop. 1953

Map ref. 511 J12, 538 C2, 543 Q3

A peaceful, small service centre located
on the Murray River. Cohuna's claim to
fame is that its casein factory developed
produce that became part of the diet of
the astronauts flying the *Apollo* space
missions. East of town is Gunbower Island,
at the junction of the Murray River and
Gunbower Creek. The island is home to
abundant wildlife, including kangaroos
and emus, plus breeding rookeries for
birdlife during flood years.
IN TOWN *Cohuna Historical Museum:*
housed in the former Scots Church, the

museum features memorabilia relating
to explorer Major Mitchell; Sampson St.
WHAT'S ON *Bridge to Bridge Swim:* Mar.
NEARBY Gunbower Island This island,
surrounded by Gunbower Creek and
the Murray River, is an internationally
recognised wetland, with a great variety
of waterbirds and stands of river red gum
forest. A 5 km canoe trail flows through
Safes Lagoon and bushwalking is another
highlight.
Cohuna Grove Cottage: for local art and
craft; on the Murray Valley Hwy; 4 km SE.
Mathers Waterwheel Museum: features
waterwheel memorabilia and an outdoors
aviary; Brays Rd; 9 km W. *Kraft Factory and
Shop:* cheese factory with demonstrations
and sales; open mornings; Leitchville;
16 km SE. *Kow Swamp:* bird sanctuary with
picnic spots and fishing at Box Bridge;
23 km S. *Section of Major Mitchell Trail:*
1700 km trail that retraces this explorer's
footsteps from Mildura to Wodonga
via Portland. From Cohuna, follow the
signposted trail along Gunbower Creek
down to Mt Hope, 28 km S. *Torrumbarry
Weir:* during winter the entire weir
structure is removed, while in summer
waterskiing is popular; 40 km SE.
ⓘ Golden Rivers Tourism, 15 Murray St,
Barham; 1800 621 882 or (03) 5453
3100; www.goldenrivers.com.au

Colac   Pop. 10 164

Map ref. 520 B11, 526 I7, 533 N9

Colac was built by the shores of Lake
Colac on the volcanic plain that covers
much of Victoria's Western District. It is a
popular destination for all kinds of water
activities, including fishing, boating and
waterskiing. The area was once described
by novelist Rolf Boldrewood as 'a scene
of surpassing beauty and rural loveliness
. . . this Colac country was the finest, the
richest as to soil and pasture that I had up
to that time ever looked on'.

IN TOWN *Performing Arts and Cultural Centre:* incorporates the Anderson Cinema, open daily; and the Historical Centre, open 2pm–4pm Thurs, Fri, Sun; cnr Gellibrand and Ray sts. *Botanic Gardens:* unusual in that visitors are allowed to drive through the gardens. Picnic, barbecue and playground facilities are provided. By Lake Colac. *Barongarook Creek:* prolific birdlife, and a walking track leading from Princes Hwy to Lake Colac; on the northern outskirts of town.

WHAT'S ON *Lions Club Market:* Memorial Sq, Murray St; 3rd Sun each month. *Go Country Music Festival and Truck Show:* Feb. *Kana Festival:* community festival with family entertainment, music and displays; Mar. *Colac Cup:* Mar. *Garden Expo:* at the Colac Showgrounds; Oct.

NEARBY **Red Rock Lookout** The lookout features a reserve with picnic and barbecue facilities, plus spectacular views across 30 volcanic lakes, including Lake Corangamite, Victoria's largest saltwater lake. At the base of the lookout is the Red Rock Winery, which includes a gallery and cafe. Near Alvie; 22 km N. The Volcano Discovery Trail goes from Colac to Millicent in SA, and follows the history of volcanic activity in the region; details from visitor centre.
Art and craft galleries: at Barongarook (12 km SE) and Gellibrand (26 km S); details from visitor centre. *Burtons Lookout:* features Wanawong Gardens and views of the Otways; 13 km S. *Tarndwarncoort Homestead:* wool displays and sales; off Warncoort Cemetery Rd; 15 km E. *Floating Island Reserve:* a lagoon with islands that shift with the tides; off Princes Hwy; 18 km W. *Carlisle State Park:* remote wilderness park with walking and vehicle trails; access via Gellibrand; 26 km S. *Forrest:* old timber and logging town in the Otway Ranges; 32 km SE. Popular attractions nearby include fishing, walking and picnics at the West Barwon Reservoir (2 km S), or spotting a platypus at Lake Elizabeth, formed by a landslide in 1952 (5 km SE).
ⓘ Cnr Murray and Queen sts (Princes Hwy); (03) 5231 3730; www.visitotways.com

Coleraine   Pop. 1011

Map ref. 532 E4

Situated in Victoria's Western District, Coleraine is a small, picturesque town supported by wool and beef industries. The area is home to a diverse range of native flora, many of which can be found in the Points Arboretum.

IN TOWN *Historic Railway Station:* also site of the visitor centre, it displays and sells local arts and crafts; Pilleau St. *Matthew Cooke's Blacksmith Shop:* Whyte St; open by appt. *Chocolate Factory:* open daily for tastings; Whyte St.

WHAT'S ON *Autumn Festival:* April. *Art Show:* Aug. *Coleraine Cup:* Sept.

NEARBY **Peter Francis Points Arboretum** Two thousand species of native flora are found here, including 500 species of eucalyptus. 'The Points' sprawls up the hillside behind the town, with great views from the top. Portland–Coleraine Rd; 2.2 km S. In town is the Eucalyptus Discovery Centre (Whyte St), designed to complement the arboretum and give an insight into the natural history and commercial applications of eucalypts. *Balmoral:* historic township west of the Grampians; 49 km N. Nearby features include the Glendinning Homestead, just east of town, with gardens and a wildlife sanctuary. The town is also the gateway to Rocklands Reservoir, for watersports and fishing, and Black Range State Park, popular for bushwalking.
ⓘ Old Railway Station, Pilleau St; (03) 5575 2733

Corryong   Pop. 1132

Map ref. 507 B8, 536 G2

The district offers superb mountain scenery and excellent trout fishing in the Murray River and its tributaries. The town is proud of its association with Jack Riley, who is believed to be the original 'Man from Snowy River' and is buried in the Corryong cemetery. An annual festival honours Riley's memory, and horseriding competitions are held to find his modern-day equivalent. The town is also the Victorian gateway to Kosciuszko National Park across the New South Wales border (*see feature on p. 92*).

IN TOWN **The Man from Snowy River Folk Museum** Banjo Paterson's poem brought to life the struggles and triumphs of the settlers of the High Country. This charming folk museum proudly does the same, with local exhibits, memorabilia and photos depicting the hardships of local life, as well as a unique collection of historic skis. Hanson St.
Jack Riley's grave: Corryong cemetery. *Large wooden galleon:* Murray Valley Hwy. *Playle's Hill Lookout:* for a great view of the township; Donaldson St.

WHAT'S ON *The Man from Snowy River Bush Festival:* music, art, and horsemanship challenges; April.

NEARBY **Burrowa–Pine Mountain National Park** Pine Mountain is one of Australia's largest monoliths. Mt Burrowa is home to wet-forest plants and unique wildlife, including wombats and gliders. Both mountains provide excellent and diverse opportunities for bushwalkers, campers, climbers and birdwatchers. The Cudgewa Bluff Falls offer fabulous scenery and bushwalking. Main access is from the Cudgewa–Tintaldra Rd, which runs off Murray Valley Hwy; 27 km W.
Khancoban This NSW town was built by the Snowy Mountains Authority for workers on the hydro-electric scheme. Its willow- and poplar-lined streets, historic rose garden and mountain surrounds

give the town a European feel. Huge trout are caught in Khancoban Pondage. Nearby, Murray 1 Power Station Visitor Centre reveals the workings of this 10-turbine station. South, along Alpine Way through Kosciuszko National Park, is the spectacular Scammell's Spur Lookout and historic Geehi Hut. 32 km E. *Emu Farm:* Murray Valley Hwy; 4 km W. *Lookouts:* Embereys Lookout over Mt Mittamatite, 10 km N; lookout with views over Kosciuszko National Park at Towong, 12 km NE. *Upper Murray Fish Farm:* 38 km S. *Nariel:* Nariel Creek is a good spot for trout fishing. Town hosts the Black and White Folk Music Festival each Dec. 45 km SW. *Walwa:* hire canoes and mountain bikes from Upper Murray Holiday Resort and Winery; 47 km NW. *4WD tours:* details from visitor centre. *Touring routes:* Murray River Rd, Lakeside Loop, Mitta Valley Loop; details at visitor centre. *Horse trail-rides:* details at visitor centre.
ⓘ Hanson St; (02) 6076 2277

Creswick   Pop. 2445

Map ref. 520 C3, 531 K9, 533 O2, 538 A12, 543 O13

Creswick is an attractive and historic town, a symbol of the rich and heady life of the gold-rush days of the 1850s. Unfortunately, the goldmining also meant that the surrounding forests were decimated. Today the town is surrounded by pine plantations over 100 years old; they exist thanks to the initiative and foresight of local pioneer John La Gerche and – while they are no replacement for the Australian bush – they have given Creswick the title of 'the home of forestry'. Creswick was the birthplace of renowned Australian artist Norman Lindsay, many of whose paintings can be seen in the local historical museum.

IN TOWN *Giant Mullock Heaps:* Ullina Rd. *Historical Museum:* photos and memorabilia from the town's goldmining past as well as an exhibition of Lindsay paintings; Albert St. *Gold Battery:* Battery Cres.

WHAT'S ON *Forestry Fiesta:* Oct. *Brackenbury Classic Fun Run:* Oct.

NEARBY **Creswick Regional Park** After La Gerche set about replanting the denuded hills around Creswick in the 1890s, the state established a nursery and it continues to operate today. The Landcare Centre and Nursery, within this park, has an excellent interpretive display that details this important history of conservation. Further natural history can be explored on the various walking trails, including the 30 min Landcare Trail or the longer La Gerche Forest Walk. Visit St Georges Lake, once a mining dam now popular for picnics and watersports, and Koala Park, an old breeding ground for koalas that was highly unsuccessful (they escaped over the fences). Slaty Creek is great for gold panning or picnics, with abundant birdlife. The park stretches east and south-east of town.

VICTORIA

World of Dinosaurs: features life-size models; off Midland Hwy; 1.5 km E. *Tangled Maze:* a maze formed by climbing plants; 5 km E. *Smeaton:* pretty little town with attractions including the historic Smeaton House, the Tuki Trout Farm and a Food, Wine and Jazz Festival held each April. 16 km NE.

ⓘ 1 Raglan St; (03) 5345 1114

Daylesford   Pop. 3395

Map ref. 520 E2, 531 N9, 533 Q2, 538 B12, 543 Q13

Daylesford is at the centre of Victoria's spa country. The area developed with the discovery of gold, which lured many Swiss-Italian settlers, but it was the discovery of natural mineral springs that proved a more lasting attraction. Of the 72 documented springs in the area, the most famous are nearby Hepburn Springs. The water is rich with minerals that dissolve into it as it flows from the crest of the Great Dividing Range through underground rocks, and it is known for its rejuvenating and healing qualities. Daylesford has grown as a destination in itself, complete with beautiful gardens, interesting shopping, great eating and a huge range of accommodation. The streets are lined with trees that blaze with colour in autumn, and inside the attractive old buildings are restaurants, cafes, galleries, bookshops, bakeries and chocolate shops. Overlooking the lake is one of regional Victoria's most highly regarded restaurants, the Lake House.

IN TOWN Convent Gallery A magnificent building surrounded by delightful cottage gardens, this former convent and girls school has been restored and features an impressive collection of artwork, sculptures and jewellery. A cafe serves local produce and Devonshire tea. Daly St. *Historical Museum:* features a collection of photographs from the region's past and artefacts from the local Djadja Wurrung people; Vincent St; open weekends and public and school holidays. *Timeless Timber Gallery:* variety of art and furniture for sale in former silent-movie house; Vincent St. *Lake Daylesford:* a lovely spot for picnics, with paddleboats and rowboats for hire in the warmer months. The Tipperary walking track starts here and ends at the Mineral Springs Reserve. Access to lake is from Bleakly Rd. *Wombat Hill Botanical Gardens:* established in 1861, these lovely gardens are situated on the hill overlooking town. *Daylesford Spa Country Train:* leaves railway station for Bullarto (11 km SE) each Sun.

WHAT'S ON *Market:* for arts, crafts and local produce, on Sun mornings; near railway station. *Silver Streak Champagne Train:* train journey with gourmet food; 1st Sat each month. *Steam Rally:* steam engines on display; Easter. *Hepburn Swiss–Italian Festival:* May. *Highland Gathering:* Dec.

NEARBY Hepburn Spa Resort Complex Located in the Mineral Springs Reserve, the complex features baths, pools and flotation tanks making use of the renowned mineral waters, as well as saunas and a range of health and beauty therapies. Forest Ave, Hepburn Springs; 4 km N.

Lavandula Lavender Farm A sprawling estate featuring fields of lavender, cottage gardens and sales of lavender-based products. The Lavandula Harvest Festival is a popular event with a variety of family entertainment, held in January. Shepherds Flat; 10 km N.
Hepburn Regional Park: located around Daylesford and Hepburn Springs, this park features old goldmining relics, mineral springs and the impressive Mt Franklin, an extinct volcano, with panoramic views from the summit and picnic, barbecue and camping facilities around the base. There are good walking tracks throughout the park. *Waterfalls:* several in area, including Sailors Falls, 5 km S; Loddon Falls, 10 km NE; Trentham Falls, 21 km SE. *Breakneck Gorge:* early goldmining site; 5 km N. *Glenlyon:* small town that hosts the popular Glenlyon Sports Day on New Year's Day, and the Fine Food and Wine Fayre in July; 8 km NE. *Lyonville Mineral Springs:* picnic and barbecue facilities; 15 km SE. *Yandoit:* historic Swiss–Italian settlement; 18 km NW.

ⓘ Vincent St; (03) 5348 1339; www.visitdaylesford.com

Dimboola   Pop. 1493

Map ref. 542 F7

Dimboola, on the Wimmera River, is a key access point to the Little Desert National Park. The area was home to the Wotjobaluk Aboriginal people until the first European settlers arrived. The district was known as 'Nine Creeks' because of the many little streams that appear when the river recedes after floods. Many of the early white settlers were German – an annual festival celebrates their heritage.

IN TOWN *Historic buildings:* include the mechanics institute in Lloyd St and the Victoria Hotel, a grand 2-storey structure with grapevines hanging from the verandahs (cnr Wimmera and Victoria sts). *Walking track:* follows a scenic stretch of the Wimmera River. The track can be followed all the way to the Horseshoe Bend camping ground in the Little Desert National Park 7 km away. For details of walks, contact visitor centre.

WHAT'S ON *Wimmera German Festival:* with German food and music; April. *Garden Party:* fundraising event for Dimboola Hospital; Oct. *Rowing Regatta:* on the Wimmera River; Nov.

NEARBY Little Desert National Park The park covers 132 647 ha. The eastern block (nearest to Dimboola) has picnic and camping facilities and good walking tracks. The park does not resemble the typical desert – it contains extensive heathlands and, during spring, more than 600 varieties of wildflowers and over 40 types of ground orchids. The park is home to the distinctive mallee fowl, and the large ground-nests built by the male birds can be seen during breeding season. Kangaroos, possums and bearded dragons are just some of the wildlife that inhabit the park. 6 km SW. *See also Nhill.*
Pink Lake: a salt lake that reflects a deep pinkish colour, particularly impressive at sunset; 9 km NW. *Ebenezer Mission Station:* founded in 1859 in an attempt to bring Christianity to the local Aboriginal people. The site contains fascinating ruins of the original buildings, a cemetery and a recently restored limestone church; off the Dimboola–Jeparit Rd; 15 km N. *Kiata Lowan Sanctuary:* the first part of Little Desert National Park to be reserved, in 1955. Home to the mallee fowl. Kiata; 26 km W.

ⓘ Dim E-Shop, 109–111 Lloyd St; (03) 5389 1588

Donald   Pop. 1326

Map ref. 543 K7

Donald is on the scenic Richardson River and referred to by locals as 'Home of the Duck', owing to the many waterbirds that live in the region. The town also features Bullocks Head, a tree on the riverbank with a growth that looks like its namesake. The 'bull' is the emblem for the local primary school and is also used as a flood gauge – according to how high the waters are, the 'bull' is either dipping his feet, having a drink or, when the water is really high, going for a swim.

IN TOWN *Bullocks Head Lookout:* beside Richardson River in Byrne St. *Steam Train Park:* a restored steam locomotive, an adventure playground and barbecue facilities; cnr Hammill and Walker sts. *Historic Police Station:* dates back to 1865; Wood St. *Shepherds hut:* built by early settlers; Wood St. *Agricultural Museum:* an impressive collection of agricultural machinery; Hammill St. *Scilleys Island:* reserve on the Richardson River featuring wildlife, walking tracks and picnic facilities; access by footbridge from Sunraysia Hwy. *Kooka's Country Cookies:* tours and sales; Sunraysia Hwy.

WHAT'S ON *Scottish Dancing Country Weekend:* June. *Antique and Collectibles Fair:* Oct.

NEARBY Lake Buloke The lake is filled by the flood waters of the Richardson River, so its size varies greatly with the seasons. This extensive wetland area is home to a variety of birdlife and is a popular venue for fishing, picnicking and bushwalking. The end of the park closest to town is a protected bird sanctuary. 10 km N.
Fishing There is good fishing for redfin and trout in the many waterways close to town. Good spots include Lake Cope Cope, 10 km S; Lake Batyo Catyo and Richardson River Weir, both 20 km S; Watchem Lake,

35 km N; and the Avoca River, which runs through Charlton, 43 km NE.
Mt Jeffcott: flora, kangaroos and views over Lake Buloke; 20 km NE.
ⓘ Council Offices, cnr Houston and McCulloch sts; (03) 5497 1300

Drysdale   Pop. 1727

Map ref. 519 A11, 520 H9, 527 Q5, 534 B6

Drysdale, situated on the Bellarine Peninsula, is primarily a service centre for the local farming community. The town is close to the beaches of Port Phillip Bay and there are a number of wineries in the area, including the delightful Spray Farm Winery. Drysdale is now considered a satellite town of Geelong, yet retains a charming, holiday-resort atmosphere.
IN TOWN *Old Courthouse:* home of the Bellarine Historical Society; High St. *Drysdale Community Crafts:* High St.
WHAT'S ON *Community Market:* at the reserve on Duke St; 3rd Sun each month; Sept–April.
NEARBY **Wineries** For over 150 years vines have been grown on the Bellarine Peninsula, and most vineyards here today remain family owned and operated. Owing to the peninsula's varying soil conditions, a range of white and red wines are produced. Many wineries offering cellar-door tastings and sales, include the historic Spray Farm Winery, which also runs the Summer Concert Series each Febuary and March in a natural amphitheatre. Great views to the sea can be had from Scotchmans Hill Winery. Winery map available from visitor centre.
Bellarine Peninsula Railway: steam-train rides from Queenscliff to Drysdale and return; *see Queenscliff. Lake Lorne picnic area:* 1 km SW. *Soho Nursery and Fine Arts Gallery:* 6 km E. *Portarlington:* a popular seaside resort. Attractions include a restored flour mill with displays of agricultural history, a safe bay for children to swim in and fresh mussels for sale near the pier. There is a market at Parks Hall, last Sun each month. 10 km NE. *St Leonards:* a small beach resort, which includes Edwards Point Wildlife Reserve, a memorial commemorating the landing of Matthew Flinders in 1802 and of John Batman in 1835; 14 km E.
ⓘ Queenscliff Visitor Information Centre, 55 Hesse St, Queenscliff; (03) 5258 4843; www.greatoceanrd.org.au

Dunkeld   Pop. 402

Map ref. 532 H4

Dunkeld is considered the southern gateway to the Grampians, and its natural beauty has long been recognised since the explorer Major Thomas Mitchell camped here in 1836. It was originally named Mount Sturgeon after the mountain that towers over the town. Both Mt Sturgeon and Mt Abrupt (to the north of town) have been renamed to recognise the ancient Aboriginal heritage of the landscape;

MacKenzie Falls

Grampians National Park

Aboriginal occupation of the area known as the Grampians dates back over 5000 years. To local Koorie communities, this magnificent landscape of rock-encrusted mountain ranges perched high above the agricultural plains of the Western District is known as Gariwerd.

Within the 167 000-hectare park is a startling array of vegetation and wildlife, including 200 bird species and a quarter of Victoria's native flora species. The Grampians are renowned for striking displays of wildflowers each spring – the heathlands abound in colourful shows of Grampians boronia, blue pincushion lily and Grampians parrot-pea. Twenty of the park's 8000 plant species are not found anywhere else in the world.

The National Parks Visitor Centre, a short walk or drive south of Halls Gap, is an excellent first stop in the park. It features interactive displays and written information about the park's attractions, and rangers are available to advise on camping and activities.

Adjacent to the centre is the Brambuk Aboriginal Cultural Centre, bringing to life the culture of the local Jardwadjali and Djab Wurrung people. Within the award-winning building you can learn the creation stories of Gariwerd in the Dreamtime Theatre and explore displays on indigenous art, clothing, tools and bush tucker. You can also arrange tours to nearby rock-art sites.

Natural highlights of the Grampians include MacKenzie Falls, the largest of the park's many picturesque waterfalls; Zumsteins picnic ground, a beautiful spot with tame and friendly kangaroos; and the Balconies, a rock ledge once known as the Jaws of Death, offering views over Victoria Valley. The most popular section of the park is the Wonderland Range, true to its name with features including Elephants Hide, Grand Canyon, Venus Baths and Silent Street.

The Grampians are one of Victoria's premier destinations for bushwalking, with over 90 walks available, all varying in length and degree of difficulty. Visitors are advised to consult a ranger before embarking on one of the longer treks.

VICTORIA

they are now known as Mt Wuragarri and Mt Murdadjoog respectively.

IN TOWN Historical Museum Housed in an old church, the museum features displays on the history of the local Aboriginal people, the wool industry and the journeys of explorer Major Mitchell. It also offers dining and accommodation. Templeton St; open weekends or by appt. *Botanic Gardens:* with picnic and barbecue facilities; opposite the visitor centre.

WHAT'S ON *Dunkeld Cup:* Nov.

NEARBY Lake Bolac This small town is set on the shores of a large freshwater lake. The lake features a sandy shoreline, making it popular for swimming and boating. There is also great fishing for eels, trout, perch and yellow-belly. Several boat-launching ramps are provided. At Easter, the town hosts a yachting regatta. 35 km E.

Arboretum: exotic species from around the world; Old Ararat Rd; 4 km E. *Grampians National Park:* the southern section of the park includes Victoria Valley Rd, a scenic drive that stops at Freshwater Lake Reserve (8 km N), popular for picnics. Also near Dunkeld are various hiking destinations and the Chimney Pots, a formation popular for rockclimbing (access via Henty Hwy). *For further details on the park see feature on p. 171.*

ⓘ Glenelg Hwy; (03) 5577 2558

Dunolly   Pop. 662

Map ref. 531 J3, 543 O10

Dunolly, Wedderburn and Inglewood formed the rich goldfield region colloquially known in the 1850s as the 'Golden Triangle'. The district has produced more gold nuggets than any other goldfield in Australia, with 126 unearthed in Dunolly itself. The 'Welcome Stranger', considered to be the largest nugget ever discovered, was found 15 kilometres north-west of Dunolly, at Moliagul.

IN TOWN *Restored courthouse:* offers a display relating to gold discoveries in the area; Market St; open Sat afternoons. *Original lock-up and stables:* Market St. *Goldfields Historical and Arts Society Collection:* includes replicas of spectacular gold nuggets found in the region; Broadway; open weekends. *Gold-themed tours of the region:* include gold panning in local creeks; contact visitor centre for details.

WHAT'S ON *Market:* with local produce, crafts and second-hand goods; Market St; 3rd Sat each month.

NEARBY *Moliagul:* the Welcome Stranger Discovery Walk leads to a monument marking the spot where the Welcome Stranger nugget was found in 1869. Moliagul is also the birthplace of Rev. John Flynn, founder of the Royal Flying Doctor Service. 15 km NW. *Laanecoorie Reservoir:* a great spot for swimming, boating and waterskiing, with camping and picnic facilities available; 16 km E. *Tarnagulla:* a small mining town with

splendid Victorian architecture and a flora reserve nearby; 16 km NE. *Bealiba:* hosts a market 2nd Sun each month; 21 km NW.

ⓘ 109 Broadway; (03) 5468 1205

Echuca   Pop. 1096

Map ref. 511 K13, 538 E4

Visitors to this delightful town are transported back in time by the sight of beautiful old paddleboats cruising down the Murray River. The town is at the junction of the Murray, Campaspe and Goulburn rivers. Once Australia's largest inland port, its name comes from an Aboriginal word meaning 'meeting of the waters'. A historic iron bridge joins Echuca to Moama, in New South Wales.

IN TOWN Port of Echuca The massive red gum wharf has been restored to the grandeur of its heyday, with huge paddlesteamers anchored here. Cruises are available on many boats, including the paddlesteamer *Pevensey,* renamed *Philadelphia* for the TV miniseries *All the Rivers Run;* the D26 logging barge; PS *Alexander Arbuthnot;* and PS *Adelaide.* Cruises and accommodation are also available on PS *Canberra, Pride of the Murray* and PS *Emmylou.* The MV *Mary Ann* also features a fine restaurant. *Historic buildings:* many along Murray Esplanade include the Star Hotel, with an underground bar and escape tunnel, and the Bridge Hotel, built by Henry Hopwood, the founder of Echuca, who ran the original punt service. *Red Gum Works:* wood-turning demonstrations; Murray Esplanade. *Sharp's Magic Movie House and Penny Arcade:* award-winning attractions; Murray Esplanade. *Echuca Historical Society Museum:* housed in former police station; High St; open 11am–3pm daily. *World in Wax Museum:* High St. *National Holden Museum:* Warren St.

WHAT'S ON *Southern 80 Ski Race:* from Torrumbarry Weir to Echuca; Feb. *Riverboats, Jazz, Food and Wine Festival:* Feb. *Steam, Horse and Vintage Car Rally:* June. *Winter Blues Festival:* July. *Port of Echuca Steam Heritage Festival:* Oct.

NEARBY Barmah State Park This park combines with Barmah State Forest to contain the largest river red gum forest in Victoria. Within the park, the Dharnya Centre features a display on the forest from the local Yorta Yorta people's perspective. Nearby are Barmah Lakes, a good location for fishing and swimming. Canoes and barbecue pontoons are available for hire. Ulupna Island, in the eastern section of the park (near Strathmerton), has river beaches, camping, and a large population of koalas. Barmah Muster, a cattle muster, is held in the state forest in April. 39 km NE. *Moama:* attractions include the Silverstone Go-Kart Track and the Horseshoe Lagoon nature reserve; 2 km N. *Mathoura:* set among the mighty red gums, Mathoura is a charming Murray town over the

NSW border. Fishing is popular, with sites including Gulpa Creek and the Edward and Murray rivers. To see the forest in its splendour, take the Moira Forest Walkway or, for that authentic Murray River experience, visit nearby Picnic Point, popular for camping, picnics, waterskiing and fishing. 40 km N. *Nathalia:* a town on Broken Creek with many historic buildings. Walking tracks along the creek take in fishing spots, old homesteads and a lookout. 57 km E.

ⓘ 2 Heygarth St; 1800 804 446 or (03) 5480 7555; www.echucamoama.com

Edenhope   Pop. 774

Map ref. 542 C11

Just 30 kilometres from the South Australian border, Edenhope is set on the shores of Lake Wallace, a haven for waterbirds. The town is renowned as the site where, in 1868, Australia's first all-Aboriginal cricket team trained – their coach was T. W. Wills, who went on to establish Australian Rules football. A cairn in Lake Street honours the achievements of this early cricket team.

IN TOWN *Edenhope Antiques:* offers an extensive variety of antique wares; Elizabeth St. *Edenhope bakery:* Elizabeth St. *Lake Wallace:* walking tracks and birdwatching hides; Wimmera Hwy.

WHAT'S ON *Henley-on-Lake Wallace Festival:* with market and family entertainment; Feb. *Gourmet Food Day:* Mar. *Races:* Mar.

NEARBY Harrow One of Victoria's oldest inland towns, Harrow has many historic buildings in Main St, including the Hermitage Hotel, the police station and an early log gaol. Harrow is now infamous for the 'Beaut Blokes' event, a search by country men for women, involving activities such as a Bachelors and Spinsters Ball. Kelly's Garage and Transport Museum in Main St is popular with car enthusiasts, and the National Bush Billycart Championship is held here in March. 32 km SE.

Dergholm State Park: 26 km S; *see Casterton. Naracoorte Caves National Park:* World Heritage site of fabulous caves with extensive fossil history to explore; around 50 km W over SA border; *for further details see feature on p. 251. Fishing:* redfin, trout and yabbies in many lakes and swamps nearby. Availability depends on water levels; contact visitor centre for locations.

ⓘ 96 Elizabeth St; (03) 5585 1509

Eildon   Pop. 669

Map ref. 521 P2, 539 K11, 540 A12

Eildon established itself as a town to service dam workers, and later holiday-makers, when the Goulburn River was dammed to create Lake Eildon. This is the state's largest constructed lake, irrigating a vast stretch of northern Victoria and providing hydro-electric power. In recent years low water levels have revealed homesteads that were submerged when the dam was constructed; they stand on the lake bed in a more or less preserved state. The lake and the surrounding national park are popular summer holiday destinations, especially for watersports, fishing and boating.

IN TOWN *Eildon Lake Charters:* boat hire; contact visitor centre for details.

WHAT'S ON *Power on the Pondage:* drag boat races; Feb. *Lions Club Monster Market:* Easter. *Opening of Fishing Season Festival:* Sep.

NEARBY Lake Eildon National Park Comprising the lake and surrounding woodlands, hills and wilderness areas, this national park provides a venue for many water- and land-based activities. When full, Lake Eildon has 6 times the capacity of Sydney Harbour. Hire a kayak, boat or houseboat from the outlets in Eildon to explore the waters, or enjoy the thrills of waterskiing with the picturesque foothills of the Alps providing a backdrop. In the surrounding hills and woodlands there are various nature walks, scenic drives and panoramic lookout points. Many of the walks start at the campgrounds; contact visitor centre for details. *Lake Eildon Wall Lookout:* 1 km N. *Eildon Pondage and Goulburn River:* for excellent fishing – there is no closed season for trout in Lake Eildon. *Minigolf:* an 18-hole course in a bush-garden setting; Back Eildon Rd; 3 km w. *Mt Pinniger:* for views of Mt Buller, the Alps and the lake; 3 km E. *Freshwater Discovery Centre:* native-fish aquariums and displays; Snobs Creek; 6 km sw. *Waterfalls:* include Snobs Creek Falls and Rubicon Falls; 18 km sw via Thornton. *Eildon Trout Farm:* towards Thornton on Back Eildon Rd.
ℹ Main St; 1800 003 713 or (03) 5774 2909

Emerald   Pop. 6111

Map ref. 519 H9, 521 M7, 524 C13, 534 F5

Emerald is a delightful little town set in the Dandenong Ranges, which lie behind Melbourne's eastern suburbs. Over the weekend many people flock from the city into 'the hills' to take in the scenic forests and visit the many cafes, galleries, and antique and craft stores.

IN TOWN **Emerald Lake** The lake is a lovely, tranquil spot ideal for picnics and walks. Attractions include the Environmental Centre, paddleboats (hire available adjacent to the Environmental Centre) and tearooms. Puffing Billy stops at Emerald Lake and many passengers spend a day here before returning on the train in the late afternoon. Emerald Lake Rd.
Galleries and craft shops: a wide variety, specialising in locally made products; along Main St.

WHAT'S ON *Great Train Race:* runners attempt to race Puffing Billy from Belgrave to Emerald Lake Park; April.

NEARBY **Puffing Billy** Victoria's favourite train runs between Belgrave and Gembrook, stopping at Emerald Lake. The view outside the red carriage windows is of tall trees and ferny gullies, and if you time your trip for the last Saturday of the month you could catch the local craft and produce market at Gembrook station. Also at Gembrook is the Motorist Cafe and Museum. Puffing Billy operates daily. Belgrave is 9 km w; Gembrook is 14 km E.
Menzies Creek This town is home to the Puffing Billy Steam Museum, which is open Wed, weekends and public holidays. Also in the town is Cotswold House, where visitors enjoy gourmet food amid fantastic views. Nearby is Cardinia

Reservoir Park, where picnic spots are shared with free-roaming kangaroos, and Lake Aura Vale, a popular spot for sailing. 4 km NW on the Belgrave–Gembrook Rd. *Sherbrooke Equestrian Park:* trail-rides; Wellington Rd; 3 km w. *Australian Rainbow Trout Farm:* at Macclesfield; 8 km N. *Sherbrooke Art Gallery:* impressive collection of local artwork; Monbulk Rd, Belgrave; 11 km NW. *Bimbimbie Wildlife Park:* Mt Burnett; 12 km SE.
ℹ Dandenong Ranges Information Centre, 1211 Burwood Hwy, Upper Ferntree Gully; (03) 9758 7522; www.dandenongrangestourism.asn.au

Euroa   Pop. 2699

Map ref. 538 I8

Euroa was the scene of one of Ned Kelly's most infamous acts. In 1878 the notorious bushranger staged a daring robbery, rounding up some 50 hostages and making off with money and gold worth nearly 2000 pounds. The Strathbogie Ranges, once one of the Kelly Gang's hideouts, now provide a pretty backdrop to the town, and the region really comes to life in spring, when stunning wildflowers bloom. During this time and in autumn a number of private gardens are open to the public.

IN TOWN **Farmers Arms Historical Museum** The museum features displays explaining the history of Ned Kelly and Eliza Forlonge; Eliza and her sister are said to have imported the first merino sheep into Victoria. Kirkland Ave; open Fri–Mon afternoons.
Walking trail: self-guide trail to see the rich history and architecture of the town, including the National Bank building and the post office, both in Binney St; brochure

Puffing Billy, which passes through Emerald

Looking south to Refuge Cove and beyond, east of Tidal River

Wilsons Promontory National Park

Wilsons Promontory is well-loved across the state for its wild and untouched scenery – massive lichen-covered boulders strewn at the edges of long sandy beaches, and tree-covered mountains that sweep down into calm, tea-brown rivers. It is a landscape made all the more special by the fact that it is bordered on all sides by sea – like a mini-Tasmania hanging from Victoria by a thin, sandy isthmus. It has limited road access, but this just makes the opportunities for walking all the more magnificent.

The Prom, as it is locally known, has been home to several Aboriginal groups for at least 6500 years. It is featured in various Dreamtime stories and has long been a spiritually significant site. Today local Aboriginal communities are active in establishing cultural and spiritual links with the park and in undertaking park-management activities.

The first European known to sight the Prom was George Bass in 1798. He returned from his trip with 9000 seal pelts and several tons of oil, sparking a sealing frenzy that carried on until numbers dwindled in the 1830s. The area also became popular for whaling and timber-cutting, but both were just as quickly abandoned once resources were exhausted. A battle between cattle farmers and naturalists was waged for control of the land, which was resolved at the turn of the century when the government gazetted the land as a national park. Apart from a brief closure for use as a commando training camp during World War II, the park has been open to the public ever since, with the remnants of the training camp now used as the visitor centre.

The park features dozens of walking tracks, all of which are described and mapped in the book *Discovering the Prom on Foot*, which is available from the visitor centre. Some are easy strolls, such as the 5-kilometre Lilly Pilly Gully nature walk, taking in the region's native flora and fauna, and the 6-kilometre Pillar Point walk, which boasts views over Tidal River. The Mt Oberon walk is only 3.2 kilometres long, with the 1-hour mountain climb rewarding hikers with fantastic views of Tidal River, Normal Bay and the headlands to the north. One of the excellent longer walks goes to Sealers Cove on the eastern shore of the Prom (20 kilometre return).

For those with more energy and who wish to experience the Prom as most never see it, overnight hikes (from one to five nights in duration) take visitors to one of 11 campsites that are only accessible by foot. Hikes range from beginner to intermediate, and permits are required (available from the visitor centre). The 40-kilometre-return walk from Tidal River to the lighthouse at South East Point is a highlight. Walkers can either camp overnight near the lighthouse or book a night in one of the cottages at its base.

available from visitor centre. *Seven Creeks Park:* good freshwater fishing, particularly for trout; Kirkland Ave. *Parachuting School:* Drysdale Rd; open weekends.
WHAT'S ON *Miniature steam-train rides:* Turnbull St; last Sun each month. *Wool Week:* Oct.

NEARBY *Faithfull Creek Waterfall:* 9 km NE. *Longwood:* includes the delightful White Hart Hotel, the Lavender Art Gallery and horse-drawn carriage rides; 14 km SW. *Gooram Falls:* a scenic drive takes in the falls and parts of the Strathbogie Ranges; 20 km SE. *Locksley:* popular for

gliding and parachuting; 20 km SW. *Polly McQuinns Weir:* historic river crossing and reservoir; Strathbogie Rd; 20 km SE. *Stone Crop Art Gallery:* for local arts and crafts; Violet Town; 24 km NE. *Mt Wombat Lookout:* spectacular views of surrounding country and the Alps; 25 km SE. *Balloon Flights:* hot-air balloon flights over region; (03) 5444 1127 for details.
ⓘ Strathbogie Ranges Tourism Information Service, BP Service Centre, Tarcombe St; (03) 5795 3677

Flinders   Pop. 511

Map ref. 521 J12, 523 J11, 534 D9

Flinders is set on the south coast of the Mornington Peninsula, a region famous for its wineries. During the 1880s, Flinders became known as a health and recreation resort and a number of guesthouses and hotels began to emerge. Today Flinders remains a popular holiday spot, and when standing on the cliff-tops looking at the view across the bay to The Nobbies and Seal Rocks, it is easy to understand the town's perennial appeal.
IN TOWN *Foreshore Reserve:* popular for picnics and fishing from the jetty. *The Old Vicarage Lavender Garden:* arts, crafts, pottery and lavender products; King St. *Historic buildings:* 'Bimbi', built in the 1870s, is the earliest remaining dwelling in Flinders; King St. 'Wilga', another fine Victorian-era home, is also on King St. *Flinders Golf Links:* great views across Bass Strait; on West Head, Wood St.
WHAT'S ON *Pinot Week:* gourmet food and wine events held across the wine district; Mar.
NEARBY **Red Hill** This small town in the hills of Mornington Peninsula is famous for its market held on the first Saturday of each month from September to May. It specialises in local crafts, clothing and fresh produce. The town also features a number of galleries and The Cherry Farm, where you can 'pick your own' cherries and berries in a pleasant setting (in season); Arkwells La. The Red Hill Truck Show and Festival is held in January and the Cool Climate Wine Show is in March.
Mornington Peninsula National Park The park covers 2686 ha and features a diverse range of vegetation, from the basalt cliff-faces of Cape Schanck to banksia woodlands, coastal dune scrubs and swampland. One of the park's many attractions is the Cape Schanck Lighthouse, built in 1859, which provides accommodation in the lighthouse keeper's house. Historic Point Nepean retains its original fortifications and has information displays and soundscapes. There are ocean beaches for swimming and surfing, while the Bushranger Bay Nature Walk, starting at Cape Schanck, and the Farnsworth Track at Portsea are just two of the many walks on offer.

Access to Cape Schanck is from the Rosebud–Flinders Rd; 15 km w.

French Island National Park French Island once served as a prison where inmates kept themselves entertained with their own 9-hole golf course. This unique reserve features a range of environments from mangrove saltmarsh to open woodlands. During spring more than 100 varieties of orchids come into bloom. The park is home to the most significant population of koalas in Victoria. Long-nosed potoroos and majestic sea-eagles can also be spotted. There is a variety of walking tracks on the island and bicycles can be hired from the general store. There are also guesthouses, and camping and picnic facilities. Access is via a 30 min ferry trip from Stony Point, 30 km NE of Flinders. *Ashcombe Maze and Water Gardens:* a large hedge maze surrounded by beautifully landscaped gardens; Red Hill Rd, Shoreham; 6 km N; closed Aug. *Ace Hi Horseriding and Wildlife Park:* beach and bush trail-rides and a native-animal sanctuary; Cape Schanck; 11 km w. *Main Ridge:* Sunny Ridge Strawberry Farm – pick your own berries in season, Mornington–Flinders Rd. Also The Pig and Whistle, English-style pub, Purves Rd. 11 km NW. *Point Leo:* great surf beach; 12 km NE via Shoreham. *The Barn Art and Craft Centre:* displays and sells local art and crafts; on the Bittern–Dromana Rd, Merricks; 13 km NE; open Wed–Mon. *Balnarring:* hosts the Emu Plains Market, specialising in handmade crafts, 3rd Sat each month Nov–May; 17 km NE. Nearby is Coolart Homestead, an impressive Victorian mansion with historical displays, gardens, wetlands and a bird-observation area.
ⓘ Nepean Hwy, Dromana; 1800 804 009 or (03) 5987 3078

Foster
Pop. 987

Map ref. 535 J10

Originally called Stockyard Creek, Foster was renamed in 1871 when magistrate William Henry Foster was called into the town to settle disputes arising between gold prospectors. He asked the residents to suggest a new name for the town and, seeking to win his favour, someone suggested 'Foster', a name the magistrate readily accepted. From these beginnings, Foster has grown into a prosperous little farming community. The town is set in Victoria's fertile Gippsland region and is within easy reach of a spectacular stretch of coastline, which includes Waratah Bay, Corner Inlet and Wilsons Promontory.

IN TOWN *Historical Museum:* in old post office; Main St. *Stockyard Gallery:* Main St. *Kaffir Hill Walk:* scenic walk past old goldmining sites; starts at town carpark.

NEARBY Corner Inlet Protected by one of 13 marine national parks in Victoria, Corner Inlet conserves an important ecosystem that includes large numbers of migratory waterbirds and sea-floor animals, and one of the state's few seagrass beds. Onshore, this inlet consists of mangroves and mudflats, and the calm waters protected by Wilsons Promontory are popular for boating and kayaking (tours available). The long Aboriginal history of this region is proven by the shell middens still dotting the shore. Access south of Foster and 6 km E of Yanakie. *Foster North Lookout:* 6 km NW. *Wineries:* several in the area, including Windy Peak Winery; 10 km S. *Beaches:* many nearby, including Port Franklin, 12 km SE; Waratah Bay, 34 km SW; and Walkerville, 36 km SW. *Fish Creek:* a quaint little township with art and craft outlets, including Fish Creek Potters; 13 km SW. *Turtons Creek:* old gold-rich area. Lyrebirds can be spotted in the tree-fern gullies nearby. 18 km N. *Shallow Inlet Marine and Coastal Park:* a quiet inlet for boating, birdwatching, and fishing for King George whiting, flathead and trevally. During summer the bright colours of windsurfers' sails can be seen slicing the waters. Access around 20 km S, near Sandy Point. *Sandy Point:* a popular coastal holiday town with a good surf beach; 22 km S. *Wilsons Promontory National Park:* 32 km S; *see feature on facing page. Cape Liptrap:* views over rugged coastline and Bass Strait; 46 km SW. *Gourmet Deli Trail:* ask at visitor centre for details.
ⓘ Stockyard Gallery, Main St; 1800 630 704 or (03) 5682 1125; www.promcountrytourism.com.au

Geelong
Pop. 129 668

Map ref. 520 F9, 525, 527 O5, 533 R7, 534 A6

Situated on Corio Bay, Geelong is the largest provincial city in Victoria. Geelong was traditionally a wool-processing centre, and the National Wool Museum in Brougham Street details its early dependence upon the industry. The town was first settled by Europeans in the 1830s, but Geelong and its surrounds were originally home to the Wathaurong people, with whom the famous convict escapee William Buckley lived for many years. Buckley later described the unique culture of the Aboriginal tribes who welcomed him into their lives, and his writing is now one of the most priceless historical records of indigenous culture in southern Australia. Geelong is a well-laid-out city, and a drive along the scenic Esplanade reveals magnificent old mansions built during its heyday.

IN TOWN Waterfront Geelong This superbly restored promenade stretches along Eastern Beach and offers a variety of attractions. Visitors can relax in the historic, 1930s-built sea-baths, enjoy fine dining in seaside restaurants and cafes or stroll past an array of colourful sculptures and public artworks. The Waterfront district is on Eastern Beach Rd, with the beautiful old Cunningham Pier as a centrepiece.

National Wool Museum Housed in a historic bluestone wool store, the centre features audiovisual displays plus re-created shearers' quarters and a mill-worker's cottage. There is a licensed restaurant and bar in the cellar, and a souvenir shop selling locally made wool products. Cnr Moorabool and Brougham sts. *Geelong Art Gallery:* this regional gallery is considered one of the finest in the state. The focus is on late 19th- and early 20th-century paintings by British artists and members of the Royal Academy, such as Tom Roberts and Arthur Streeton; Little Mallop St. *Historic buildings:* there are over 100 National Trust-classifications in Geelong, including Merchiston Hall, Osborne House and Corio Villa. 'The Heights' is a 14-room prefabricated timber mansion set in landscaped gardens; Aphrasia St, Newtown; contact visitor centre for details of open days. Christ Church, still in continuous use, is the oldest Anglican Church in Victoria; Moorabool St. *Ford Discovery Centre:* Geelong has long been a major manufacturing centre for Ford and this centre details the history of Ford cars with interactive displays; cnr Brougham and Gheringhap sts; closed Tues. *Wintergarden:* a historic building housing a gallery, a nursery, antiques and a gift shop; McKillop St. *Pottage Crafts:* Moorabool St. *Botanic Gardens:* overlooking Corio Bay and featuring a good collection of native and exotic plants; part of Eastern Park; Garden St. *Johnstone Park:* picnic and barbecue facilities; cnr Mercer and Gheringhap sts. *Queens Park:* walks to Buckley Falls; Queens Park Rd, Newtown. *Balyang Bird Sanctuary:* Shannon Ave, Newtown. *Barwon River:* extensive walking tracks and bike paths in parkland by the river. *Norlane Water World:* waterslides and fun park (summer only); Princes Hwy, Norlane. *Corio Bay beaches:* popular for swimming, fishing and sailing; boat ramps provided.

WHAT'S ON *Steampacket Gardens Market:* on foreshore at Eastern Beach; 1st Sun each month. *Geelong Farmers Market:* Little Malop St; 2nd weekend each month. *Waterfront Festival:* Jan. *Highland Gathering:* Mar. *Alternative Farmvision:* April. *National Celtic Folk Festival:* June. *Momenta Arts:* celebrates local arts industries; Sept. *Geelong Cup:* Sept. *Christmas Carols by the Bay:* Eastern Beach; Dec.

NEARBY You Yangs Regional Park These granite outcrops that rise 352 m above Werribee's lava plains have an ancient link to the Wathaurong people as they provided a much-needed water source – rock wells were created to catch water, and many of them can still be seen at Big Rock. The park is a popular recreational area: activities include the 12 km Great Circle Drive and the climb to Flinders Peak for fantastic views of Geelong, Corio Bay, Mt Macedon and Melbourne's skyline. 24 km N.

Werribee Park and the Open Range Zoo
The key feature of Werribee Park is a beautifully preserved 1870s mansion with the interior painstakingly restored to its original opulence. The mansion is surrounded by 12 ha of gardens, including a grotto and a farmyard area, complete with a blacksmith. Within the grounds is the Victoria State Rose Garden with over 500 varieties of flowers. Next to the park is the Werribee Open Range Zoo, developed around the Werribee River. The zoo covers 200 ha and has a variety of animals native to the grasslands of Africa, Asia, North America and Australia, including giraffes, rhinos, meerkats, cheetahs and vervet monkeys. Guided safaris through the replicated African savannah are a must. Access from the Princes Hwy; 40 km NE. *Fyansford:* one of the oldest settlements in the region, with historic buildings including the Swan Inn, Balmoral Hotel and Fyansford Hotel. The Monash Bridge across the Moorabool River is thought to be one of earliest reinforced-concrete bridges in Victoria; outskirts of Geelong; 4 km W. *Brownhill Observation Tower:* excellent views of the surrounding area; Ceres; 10 km SW. *Avalon Airfield:* hosts the Australian International Air Show in odd-numbered years; off Princes Hwy; 20 km NE. *Serendip Sanctuary:* a wildlife research station that includes nature trails, bird hides and a visitor centre; just south of the You Yangs. *Fairy Park:* miniature houses and scenes from fairytales; north of Anakie (29 km N). *Steiglitz:* once a gold town, now almost deserted. The restored courthouse is open on Sun. 37 km NW. *Little River Earth Sanctuary:* 200 animals live here in the open grassy woodland, including species that had been extinct in Victoria for over 100 years and were reintroduced right here. Take the Wildlife Adventure Walk at sunset to see such creatures as potoroos and pademelons. Also on-site is the set used in the recent film *Ned Kelly*. 45 km NE; guided tours only, bookings (03) 5283 1602. *Geelong Wine Region:* stretching north past Anakie, around Geelong and south along the Bellarine Peninsula, this region produces a diverse range of red and white wines. Cellar doors offer tastings and sales. Contact visitor centre for map.
ⓘ Stead Park, Princes Hwy, Corio; 1800 620 888 or (03) 5275 5797; www.greatoceanrd.org.au

Glenrowan   Pop. 347

Map ref. 539 M6, 540 D1

Glenrowan is a town well known to most Victorians as the site of Ned Kelly's final showdown with the police in 1880. Most of the attractions in Glenrowan revolve around the legends surrounding Kelly's life – a giant statue of Kelly himself towers over shops in Gladstone Street.
IN TOWN *Kate's Cottage Museum:* with an extensive collection of Kelly

memorabilia as well as a replica of the Kelly homestead and blacksmith shop; Gladstone St. *Cobb & Co Museum:* an underground museum featuring notorious stories of Kelly and other bushrangers; Gladstone St. *Kellyland:* a computer-animated show of Kelly's capture; Gladstone St. *Kelly Gang Siege Site Walk:* discover the sites and history that led to the famous siege on this self-guide walk (brochure available), or take a guided walk with a local historian; details from visitor centre. *Wine and produce outlets:* over 22 local wines are offered for tastings and sales at the Buffalo Mountain Wine Centre in Gladstone St. Gourmet jams and fruit products are also available at Smiths Orchard and The Big Cherry in Warby Range Rd. *White Cottage Herb Garden:* herb sales; Hill St.
NEARBY Warby Range State Park The 'Warbys', as they are known locally, extend for 25 km north of Glenrowan. The steep ranges provide excellent viewing points, especially from Ryans Lookout. Other lookouts include the Pangarang Lookout near the Pine Gully Picnic Area and the Mt Glenrowan Lookout, the highest point of the Warbys at 513 m. There are well-marked tracks for bushwalkers and a variety of pleasant picnic spots amid open forests and woodlands, with wildflowers blossoming during the warmer months. Access from Taminick Gap Rd.
ⓘ Kate's Cottage, Gladstone St (Old Hume Hwy); (03) 5766 2448; www.wangaratta.vic.gov.au

Halls Gap   Pop. 256

Map ref. 532 I1, 542 I12

The little village of Halls Gap is set in the heart of the Grampians. It was named after Charles Browing Hall, who discovered the gap and valley in 1841. The valley was later developed by cattle-station owners, but the town really took off in the early 1900s when tourists, nature-lovers and botanists caught on to the beauty and diversity of the mountain ranges that would later become Grampians National Park. The town itself has its own charm – shops, galleries and cafes lend a laid-back atmosphere that befits the location, while in the evening long-billed corellas arrive to roost opposite the shops in the main street.
WHAT'S ON *Grampians Jazz Festival:* Feb. *Grampians Gourmet Weekend:* May. *Wildflower Exhibition:* Oct.
NEARBY *Grampians National Park:* attractions close to Halls Gap include Lake Bellfield, to the south of town, for swimming, canoeing, fishing and picnics, and Lake Wartook, to the north, for canoeing and fishing. Also nearby are Boroka Lookout, Reeds Lookout and the Brambuk Aboriginal Cultural Centre. *For further details on the park see feature on p. 171. The Gap Vineyard:* cellar-door

tastings and sales of award-winning white and red wine varieties, as well as port; Pomonal Rd; 2 km E; closed Mon and Tues. *Roses Gap Recreation Centre:* scenic walks, fitness track, fauna park, accommodation and camping; Roses Gap Rd; 21 km N.
ⓘ Grampians Rd; 1800 065 599 or (03) 5356 4616; www.visithallsgap.com.au

Hamilton   Pop. 9118

Map ref. 532 F5

Hamilton is a prominent rural centre in the heart of a sheep-grazing district. This industry is such an important part of the town's economy that it has been dubbed the 'Wool Capital of the World'. It is located on a volcanic basalt plain with a deep valley formed by Grange Burn, a tributary of the Wannon River.
IN TOWN Hamilton Art Gallery This gallery is said to be one of regional Australia's finest, featuring a diverse collection of fine arts and museum pieces dating back to the earliest of European settlements in Australia. Many trinkets and treasures of the region's first stately homes are on display, as well as English and European glass, ceramic and silver work. There is also a good collection of colonial art from the Western District. Guided heritage tours of the gallery and district are available. Brown St.
Botanic Gardens First planted in 1870 and classified by the National Trust in 1990, these gardens have long been regarded as one of the most impressive in rural Victoria. Designed by the curator of the Melbourne Botanic Gardens, William Guilfoyle, the gardens feature his 'signature' design elements of sweeping lawns interrupted by lakes, islands, and contrasting plant and flower beds. Keep an eye out for the free-flight aviary, enormous English oaks and historic band rotunda. French St.
Big Woolbales Complex: woolshed memorabilia and crafts; Coleraine Rd. *Hamilton Country Spun Woollen Mill and Factory:* sales and tours; Peck St. *Hamilton Institute of Rural Learning:* offers a nature trail, and a breeding program for the endangered eastern barred bandicoot; North Boundary Rd; open Mon–Wed. *Land-care tours:* contact visitor centre for details. *Lake Hamilton:* the lake is good for watersports, fishing and cycling, and features lovely sandy beaches and picnic facilities; Ballarat Rd. *Sir Reginald Ansett Transport Museum:* details the history of Ansett, with aviation artefacts; on the banks of Lake Hamilton, Glenelg Hwy. *Hamilton Pastoral Museum:* features pastoral relics and history displays housed in the former St Luke's Lutheran Church; Glenelg Hwy; check opening times. *Hamilton History Centre:* features history of early Western District families; Gray St. *Mary MacKillop Pilgrims Drive:* takes in sites related to MacKillop's life; see visitor centre for details.

WHAT'S ON *Beef Expo:* Feb. *Hamilton Cup:* April. *Sheepvention:* sheep and wool inventions and farmdog championships; Aug.

NEARBY **Mount Eccles National Park** The key feature of this park is a large volcanic crater lake. A range of walks let visitors explore the scoria cones and caves formed thousands of years ago by volcanoes. The 3 main craters hold a 700 m long lake, Lake Surprise, fed by underground springs. Near Macarthur; 40 km s. *Waterfalls:* Nigretta Falls has a viewing platform; 15 km NW. Also Wannon Falls; 19 km W. *Mount Napier State Park:* features Byaduk Caves (lava caves) near the park's western entrance. Only one cave is accessible to the public. 18 km s. *Cavendish:* a small town en route to the Grampians, notable for the 3 beautiful private gardens open during the Southern Grampians Open Gardens Festival each Oct; 25 km N. *Penshurst:* a lovely historic town at the foot of Mt Rouse. Excellent views from the top of the mountain, where there is a crater lake. Country Muster each Feb. 31 km SE. ⓘ Lonsdale St; 1800 807 056 or (03) 5572 3746; www.sthgrampians.vic.gov.au

Healesville   Pop. 7133

Map ref. 519 I4, 521 N5, 524 E6, 534 F3

To the west of Yarra Ranges National Park and within easy reach of Melbourne, Healesville has a charming rural atmosphere. There are good restaurants and cafes in town, all focusing on quality local produce, especially the world-class Yarra Valley wines. On top of this is a host of art and craft boutiques and two major attractions – the recently opened TarraWarra Museum of Art and the famous Healesville Sanctuary, one of the best places in Victoria to experience Australia's unique wildlife up close.

IN TOWN *Art, craft and antiques:* Healesville Art Gallery, in a bushland setting with local artworks; Nigel Crt. Silvermist Studio Gallery; handmade gold and silver jewellery; Maroondah Hwy. Jacques Antiques and Collectibles; furniture, china and glass; Maroondah Hwy. The Church Street Gallery and Cafe; handpainted crafts; Church St. Tuscany Galleries; local art and pottery; Maroondah Hwy. *Open-air trolley rides:* from Healesville railway station to Yarra Glen; open Sun and public holidays.

WHAT'S ON *Market:* River St; 1st Sun each month. *Grape Grazing Festival:* variety of events held throughout wine district to celebrate the harvest; Feb. *Australian Car Rally Championship:* Sept. *Gateway Festival:* odd-numbered years, Dec.

NEARBY **Healesville Sanctuary** The 32 ha reserve accommodates an extensive range of native birds and animals from common kangaroos to rare creatures such as the Tasmanian devil. The sanctuary runs an important platypus-breeding program and is one of the few places in the world

Ned Kelly

Many books, films, websites and artworks later, Ned Kelly persists as an Australian legend – the son of an Irish convict father and an immigrant mother.

Ned Kelly

Born in December 1854, Ned Kelly was forced to leave school at the age of 12 to become the family breadwinner when his father died. The family moved to Greta (10 kilometres south of Glenrowan), known as a lawless outpost, and Ned became an accomplished troublemaker. His first brush with the law was an assault charge when he was 13, and it wasn't long before he was serving three years for receiving a stolen horse. After his release, Ned fell into stealing horses with his stepfather, but his real problem with police began in 1878. There is no record of what happened the day a police officer named Fitzpatrick visited the Kelly house. Some accounts suggest that Fitzpatrick assaulted one of Ned's sisters, but Fitzpatrick claimed he was assaulted by Ned's mother, Ellen, and shot in the wrist by Ned. Ellen was sentenced to three years in prison and Ned escaped. A £100 reward was offered for his capture.

Not surprisingly, no one came forward to inform on Ned. As his reputation as a fearsome bushranger and bank robber grew, so did his stance against authority and the wealthy, and the injustice they heaped on the poor with their power to tip people from their property or send them to gaol without reason. He was an eloquent man and regularly wrote letters to the authorities such as this:

'I have no intention of asking mercy for myself or any mortal man, or apologising, but wish to give timely warning that if my people do not get justice, and those innocents released from prison, and the police wear their uniform, I shall be forced to seek revenge of everything of the human race for the future.'

The gang that Ned had formed with his brother Dan and their friends Joe Byrne and Steve Hart largely kept to the bush. But on 26 October 1878, they came across police camped at Stringybark Creek. The Kelly gang assumed the police were there to kill them, and called on them to surrender. Three officers resisted and were shot dead by Ned. The reward for the gang's capture rose to £2000 and would later rise to £8000 (equivalent today to about $2 million). But the gang's supporters helped them to evade capture for the next two years.

The last stand of the Kelly gang came in June 1880 at the Glenrowan Hotel, where the men had taken the whole town hostage. Police surrounded the hotel and opened fire. Ned had donned his famous homemade iron armour and, despite being hit by dozens of bullets, managed to escape through police lines into the bush. His loyalty was his undoing; Ned returned to rescue his brother and friends (who were already dead) and this time the police aimed their guns low. Ned collapsed with 28 bullet wounds to his arms, legs, hands, feet and groin. Sentenced to hang, Ned Kelly stood at the gallows in the Melbourne Gaol and uttered his famous last words, 'Such is life'.

to have successfully bred these unique marsupials in captivity. Allow at least half a day to fully explore the sanctuary. Badger Creek Rd; 4 km s.

TarraWarra Museum of Art TarraWarra Estate has been operating as a vineyard since 1983, producing a selection of fine chardonnay and pinot noir. Now, among the vines and rolling hills, is a striking building housing an extensive private collection of modern art. The collection focuses on the 3 key themes of Australian Modernism – landscape, figuration and abstraction – and works by artists such as Howard Arkley, Arthur Boyd and Brett Whiteley can be found within. Healesville–Yarra Glen Rd.

HCP Antique Emporium: large undercover antique market; Badger Creek Rd; 2 km s. *Hedgend Maze:* giant maze and fun park; Albert Rd; 2.5 km s. *Corranderrk Aboriginal*

Cemetery: once the burial ground for an Aboriginal mission, and the final resting place of well-known Wurundjeri leader William Barak; 3 km s. *Maroondah Reservoir Park:* a magnificent park set in lush forests with walking tracks and a lookout nearby; 3 km NE. *Donnelly's Weir Park:* starting point of the 5000 km Bicentennial National Trail to Cooktown (Qld). The park also has short walking tracks and picnic facilities. 4 km N. *Galeena Beek Living Cultural Centre:* offers an experience in Aboriginal culture including live dance performances and guided bushwalks; 4 km s, opposite entry to Healesville Sanctuary. *Badger Weir Park:* picnic area in a natural setting. The weir is a popular swimming spot. 7 km SE. *Mallesons Lookout:* views of Yarra Valley to Melbourne; 8 km s. *Mt St Leonard:* good views from the summit; 14 km N. *Toolangi:* attractions include the Singing Garden of

Wheat field near Horsham

C. J. Dennis, a beautiful, formal garden; the Toolangi Forest Discovery Centre, for a fascinating insight into the local forests and how they were formed; and Toolangi Pottery. 20 km NW. *Wineries:* around 30 in the area open for tastings and sales. Tours available; contact visitor centre for details. *See also Yarra Glen.*

ⓘ Yarra Valley Visitor Information Centre, Old Courthouse, Harker St; (03) 5962 2600; www.yarravalleytourism.com

Heathcote   Pop. 1554

Map ref. 538 E9

Heathcote is located near the outskirts of the scenic Heathcote–Graytown National Park, with the McIvor Creek flowing by the town. Heathcote was established during the gold rush, but is now known as a prominent wine region with good red wines produced from a number of new vineyards.

IN TOWN *Courthouse Crafts:* displays relating to the gold rush, plus arts and crafts; High St. *Pink Cliffs:* eroded soil from gold sluices gave the cliffs their remarkable pink colour; Pink Cliffs Rd, off Hospital Rd. *McIvor Range Reserve:* off Barrack St. *Heathcote Winery:* this winery, in the old Thomas Craven Stores building, has an art gallery and cellar-door sales; High St.

WHAT'S ON *Rodeo:* Easter. *Heathcote Heartland Festival:* May. *Wine and Food Festival:* Oct.

NEARBY Heathcote–Graytown National Park Compared with many of Victoria's national parks, Heathcote–Graytown was declared only recently (2002) as part of a state-wide plan to preserve box-ironbark forest. Now protecting the largest forest of this type in the state, the park is not only an important nature reserve but also has a long history of settlement.

Take one of the many walks or scenic drives to explore evidence of Aboriginal, goldmining and pioneering history, or take in scenic views from the lookouts at Mt Black, Mt Ida and Viewing Rock (just near Heathcote). Access from Northern Hwy and Heathcote–Nagambie Rd. *Central Victorian Yabby Farm:* catch your own, take a farm tour and enjoy picnic/barbecue facilities; 6 km S. *Lake Eppalock:* one of the state's largest lakes, great for fishing, watersports and picnics. A powerboat race, the Eppalock Gold Cup, is held here each Feb. 10 km W. *Wineries:* this is a renowned shiraz region with many wineries offering cellar-door tastings and sales; details from visitor centre.

ⓘ Cnr High and Barrack sts; (03) 5433 3121; www.heathcote.org.au

Hopetoun   Pop. 624

Map ref. 510 E12, 542 H3, 544 H13

This small Mallee town, south-east of Wyperfeld National Park, was named after the first governor-general of Australia, the Earl of Hopetoun. The Earl was a friend of Edward Lascelles, who played a major role in developing the Mallee Country by eradicating vermin, developing water strategies to cope with the dry conditions, and enticing settlers to the region.

IN TOWN *Hopetoun House:* the residence of Lascelles, this majestic building is now National Trust-classified; Evelyn St. *Mallee Mural:* depicts history of the region, in shire offices along with leadlight windows; Lascelles St. *Lake Lascelles:* good for boating, swimming and fishing; access from end of Austin St.

NEARBY Wyperfeld National Park Outlet Creek connects the network of lake beds that are the main highlight for visitors to this park. They fill only when Lake Albacutya overflows, which in turn fills

only when Lake Hindmarsh overflows. Once a corroboree ground, the main lake bed, Wirrengren Plain, has flooded only once in the last 100 years. Eastern grey kangaroos can be seen grazing on Wirrengren and the other lake beds, and the Eastern Lookout Nature Drive is a great way to see the range of vegetation in the park – river red gums, black box, mallee and cypress pine, and wildflowers in spring. A variety of walking trails leave from the two campgrounds – Wonga Campground in the south and Casuarina Campground in the north, near the lakes. 50 km NW. *Patchewollock:* hosts the Easter Sports and Camel Cup, part of Warracknabeal Y-Fest; 35 km NW.

ⓘ Gateway Beet, 75 Lascelles St; (03) 5083 3001

Horsham   Pop. 13 201

Map ref. 542 G9

Horsham is an important centre for the Wimmera district. Prior to European settlement, Horsham and its surrounds were occupied by the Jardwa and Wotjobaluk Aboriginal people who referred to the region as 'Wopetbungundilar'. This term is thought to have meant 'place of flowers', a reference to the flowers that grow along the banks of the Wimmera River. Flowers continue to play an important role in Horsham, considered to be one of the prettiest regional towns in Victoria – the town prides itself on its clean streets and picturesque gardens. Although the Wimmera is a renowned wheat-growing region, Horsham is also a centre for fine wool production.

IN TOWN Horsham Regional Art Gallery This is one of Victoria's key regional galleries, with an extensive collection housed in a 1930s Art Deco building. Most of the artwork is centred around

the Mack Jost collection of Australian art, with contemporary Australian photography another specialty. Wilson St. *Botanic Gardens:* picturesquely set on the banks of the Wimmera River; cnr Baker and Firebrace sts. *Horsham Rocks and Gems:* sales and displays of local pieces; Golf Course Rd. *Country Crafts:* Golf Course Rd. *The Wool Factory:* produces extra-fine wool from Saxon-Merino sheep; Golf Course Rd; tours daily. *Wimmera River:* key attraction for the town, with scenic picnic spots along the river's edges. Visit the river at dusk for spectacular sunsets.
WHAT'S ON *Market:* showgrounds on McPherson St; 2nd Sun each month. *Fishing Competition:* Mar. *Art Is:* community festival; Mar. *Spring Garden Festival:* Oct. *Kannamaroo Rock 'n' Roll Festival:* Nov.
NEARBY Murtoa This town lies on the edge of Lake Marma, a small but scenic lake stocked with trout and redfin. The Water Tower Museum (open Sun) displays the history of the area as well as James Hill's 1885–1930 taxidermy collection of some 500 birds and animals. On the eastern side of town, among the grain silos, is an unusual relic called the Stick Shed. The roof of this now empty storage shed is held up with 640 unmilled tree trunks, and the interior is an evocative sight. An open day once a year in Oct allows access. 31 km NE. *Jung:* market on last Sat each month; 10 km NE. *Fishing:* good fishing for redfin and trout in local lakes, including Green Lake, 13 km SE; Pine Lake, 16 km SE; Taylors Lake, 18 km SE; Toolondo Reservoir, 44 km SW; and Rocklands Reservoir, 90 km S. *Do See View Farm:* an operating farm with Clydesdale horses and a blacksmith; 15 km NW. *Mount Zero Olives:* the largest olive grove in the Southern Hemisphere, with tastings and sales of olive oil; Laharum; 30 km S.
ⓘ 20 O'Callaghan Pde; 1800 633 218 or (03) 5382 1832; www.horsham vic.com.au

Inglewood   Pop. 685

Map ref. 538 A7, 543 O8

North along the Calder Highway from Bendigo is the 'Golden Triangle' town of Inglewood. Sizeable gold nuggets were found in this area during the gold rush and are still being unearthed. Inglewood is also known as the birthplace of Australian aviator Sir Reginald Ansett.
IN TOWN *Old eucalyptus oil distillery:* Calder Hwy, northern end of town. *Old courthouse:* local historical memorabilia; Southey St; open by appt. *Blue Mallee Crafts:* Brooke St.
WHAT'S ON *Blue Eucalyptus Festival:* Oct.
NEARBY Kooyoora State Park The park sits at the northern end of the Bealiba Range and features extensive box-ironbark forests. The Eastern Walking Circuit offers a great opportunity for bushwalkers, passing through strange

rock formations and giant granite slabs. The Summit Track leads to Melville Caves Lookout. The caves were once the haunt of the notorious bushranger Captain Melville. Camping is allowed around the caves. 16 km W.
Bridgewater on Loddon: fishing and watersports, Old Loddon Vines Vineyard, Water Wheel Vineyards, and horse-drawn caravans for hire; 8 km SE. *Loddon Valley wineries:* the warm climate and clay soils of this region are known for producing outstanding red varieties and award-winning chardonnays. Taste the wines at the cellar doors at Bridgewater on Loddon (8 km SE) and Kingower (11 km SW). Winery map from council offices.
ⓘ Council offices, High St, Wedderburn; (03) 5494 1200

Inverloch   Pop. 2448

Map ref. 534 G10

Inverloch is a small seaside resort set on the protected waters of Anderson Inlet, east of Wonthaggi. It is characterised by long stretches of pristine beach that offer good surf and excellent fishing.
IN TOWN *Bunurong Environment Centre:* natural history displays with special focus on dinosaur diggings. Also sales of natural products. The Esplanade. *Shell Museum:* The Esplanade.
WHAT'S ON *Jazz Festival:* Mar.
NEARBY Bunurong Coastal Drive Stretching the 14 km of coastline between Inverloch and Cape Paterson is this spectacular coastal drive with magnificent views to Venus Bay and beyond. Carparks offer access to beaches and coastal walks along the drive. The waters offshore are protected within Bunurong Marine and Coastal Park, and offer opportunities to surf, snorkel, scuba dive or simply explore the numerous rock pools that are dotted along the coast. *Anderson Inlet:* The most southerly habitat for mangroves in Australia, this calm inlet is popular for windsurfing and watersports, and nearby Townsend Bluff and Maher's Landing offer good birdwatching. Adjacent to town. *Fishing:* in nearby waterways such as the Tarwin River (20 km SE).
ⓘ A'Beckett St; (03) 5671 2233; www.phillipislandgippsland.com.au

Jeparit   Pop. 371

Map ref. 542 F6

This little town in the Wimmera is five kilometres south-east of Lake Hindmarsh, the largest natural freshwater lake in Victoria. Sir Robert Menzies, the long-serving prime minister, was born here in 1894.
IN TOWN Wimmera–Mallee Pioneer Museum This unique museum details what life was like for early settlers in the Wimmera through a collection of colonial buildings furnished in the style

of the period. The buildings on display are spread over a 4 ha complex and include log cabins, a church and a blacksmith's shop. The museum also features displays of restored farm machinery. Southern entrance to town, Charles St. *Menzies Square:* site of the dwelling where Menzies was born; cnr Charles and Roy sts. *Wimmera River Walk:* 6 km return; starts at museum.
WHAT'S ON *Museum Open Day:* Mar. *Fishing Competition:* Easter.
NEARBY Lake Hindmarsh Victoria's largest freshwater lake is fed by the Wimmera River. Boating, waterskiing and fishing are all popular pastimes (Schulzes Beach has a boat ramp) and the lake's shores provide a perfect spot for picnics and camping. The lake is home to breeding colonies of pelicans and many other waterbirds. A historic fisherman's hut can also be seen. Visitors should note that recent dry years have led to very low water levels at Lake Hindmarsh. Contact the visitor centre for an update. 5 km NW. *Rainbow:* a charming little Wimmera township, with Pasco's Cash Store, an original country general store, and Yurunga Homestead, a beautiful Edwardian home with a large collection of antiques and original fittings (northern edge of town, key available). 32 km N. *Pella:* former German settlement with Lutheran church and old schoolhouse; 40 km NW via Rainbow. *Lake Albacutya:* fills only when Lake Hindmarsh overflows; 44 km N. *Wyperfeld National Park:* great for bushwalking. Known for its birdlife, including the endangered mallee fowl, and wildflowers in spring. 60 km NW via Rainbow; *for details see Hopetoun.*
ⓘ Wimmera–Mallee Pioneer Museum, Dimboola Rd; (03) 5397 2102

Kerang   Pop. 3715

Map ref. 510 I12, 538 A2, 543 P3, 545 P13

Kerang, situated on the Loddon River just south of the New South Wales border, lies at the southern end of the Kerang wetlands and lakes. They extend from Kerang 42 kilometres north-west to Lake Boga and offer a wonderland for watersports enthusiasts and birdwatchers; the lakes contain what is reputedly the world's largest ibis breeding grounds. The town itself is a service centre for its agricultural surrounds.
IN TOWN *Lester Lookout Tower:* town views and gemstone museum; cnr Murray Valley Hwy and Shadforth St. *Historical Museum:* focuses on cars and antique farm machinery; Riverwood Dr.
WHAT'S ON *Jazz by the Lake:* Jan. *Woodworking Expo:* Oct/Nov.
NEARBY *Reedy Lakes:* a series of 3 lakes. Apex Park, a recreation reserve for swimming, picnicking and boating, is set by the first lake, and the second features a large ibis rookery. Picnic facilities are available at the third lake. 8 km NW.

Ninety Mile Beach and the Gippsland Lakes, near Lakes Entrance

Leaghur State Park: on the Loddon River flood plain, this peaceful park is a perfect spot for a leisurely walk through the black box woodlands and wetlands, or a picnic on the shores of Lake Meran; 25 km sw. *Murrabit:* a historic timber town on the Murray surrounded by picturesque forests, with a country market 1st Sat each month; 27 km n. *Quambatook:* hosts the Australian Tractor Pull Championship each Easter; 40 km sw. *Lake Boga:* popular for watersports, with good sandy beaches; 42 km nw. *Fishing:* Meran, Kangaroo and Charm lakes all offer freshwater fishing; details from visitor centre.
ⓘ Golden Rivers Tourism, 15 Murray St, Barham; 1800 621 882 or (03) 5453 3100; www.goldenrivers.com.au

Kilmore   Pop. 3520

Map ref. 521 J2, 538 F11

Kilmore is Victoria's oldest inland town, known for its historic buildings and for the many horseracing events held throughout the year. Like many towns in the central goldfields, Kilmore was the scene of a Kelly family saga. In this case, it was Ned Kelly's father who had a run-in with the law. In 1865 John 'Red' Kelly was arrested for killing a squatter's calf to feed his family, and was locked

away in the Kilmore Gaol for six months. It was a crime that Ned had actually committed. Soon after Red's release, he died of dropsy and was buried somewhere on the outskirts of town in an unmarked grave.
IN TOWN Old Kilmore Gaol This impressive bluestone building, established in 1859, has been carefully restored and is now a major tourist attraction. Guided tours go through the male and female cells and the exercise and labour yards, showing visitors what life was like for inmates. Other features include the 'Lock Up' restaurant and an antique centre. Sutherland St; closed Mon.
Hudson Park: cable-tram rides and picnic/barbecue facilities; cnr Sydney and Foote sts. *Historic buildings:* Whitburgh Cottage, Piper St, and a number of 1850s shops and hotels along Sydney St.
WHAT'S ON *Celtic Festival:* June. *Antique Fair:* Oct. *Kilmore Cup:* Oct.
NEARBY *Tramways Museum at Bylands:* extensive display of cable cars and early electric trams, with tram rides available; just south of town. *Broadford:* a small town featuring a historic precinct on High St. Hosts a Scottish Festival each Oct and a Hells Angels Concert each Dec. 17 km ne. Near Broadford is the Mt Piper Walking Track where wildlife and wildflowers can be spotted along the way (1 hr return).

Strath Creek: walks to Strath Creek Falls and a drive through the Valley of a Thousand Hills; starts at outskirts of Broadford.
ⓘ Library, 12 Sydney St; (03) 5781 1319

Koo-wee-rup   Pop. 1304

Map ref. 519 I11, 521 M10, 534 F7

Koo-wee-rup and the surrounding agricultural area exist on reclaimed and drained swampland. It has given rise to Australia's largest asparagus-growing district. The town's name derives from the Aboriginal name meaning 'blackfish swimming', a reference to the fish that were once plentiful in the swamp.
IN TOWN *Historical Society Museum:* local history; Rossiter Rd; open Sun.
NEARBY Bunyip Byways Tourist Trail A great way to see the area, this self-drive tour takes in a range of attractions including historic homesteads, antique stores, golf courses and tearooms. The trail is marked by road signs and follows a circular route from Gembrook, through Berwick, to Tooradin, 12 km w of Koo-wee-rup.
Swamp Observation Tower: offers views of remaining swampland and across to Western Port. A market with local produce operates regularly at the base. South Gippsland Hwy; 2 km se. *Bayles Fauna Reserve:* native animals; 8 km ne. *Harewood House:* restored 1850s house with original furnishings; South Gippsland Hwy towards Tooradin. *Tooradin:* offers good boating and fishing on Sawtells Inlet; 10 km w. *Australian Pioneer Farm:* provides opportunities to shear sheep and milk cows; Cardinia; 11 km nw. *Pakenham:* now considered a suburb of Melbourne, Pakenham is home to the Military Vehicle Museum, Army Rd, and the Berwick Pakenham Historical Society Museum, John St; 13 km n. *Tynong:* attractions include Victoria's Farm Shed, featuring farm animals and shearing, and Gumbaya Park, a family fun park; 20 km ne. *Royal Botanic Gardens Cranbourne:* renowned, wonderfully maintained native gardens; 22 km nw. *Grantville:* hosts a market 4th Sun each month; 30 km s.
ⓘ Newsagency, 277 Rossiter Rd; (03) 5997 1456

Korumburra   Pop. 3032

Map ref. 521 O12, 534 H8

Korumburra is set in the scenic South Gippsland countryside, a lush, fertile part of the state devoted to farming, particularly dairying. In recent years this part of Gippsland has become synonymous with arts and crafts as well as good food and wine. The Gourmet Deli Trail leads visitors on a hunt for everything from cheese and smoked meats to berries and chardonnay.
IN TOWN Coal Creek Heritage Village This is a delightful re-creation of a 19th-century coalmining village, complete

with old-fashioned shops, blacksmith, miners' cottages and carriage rides. Visitors can go for a ride on a small locomotive that meanders through tranquil bushland or take a guided tour through a coalmine. Located on the original site of the Coal Creek mine. Cnr South Gippsland Hwy and Silkstone Rd. **NEARBY South Gippsland Railway** Jump on one of the historic diesel trains that operate between Leongatha, Loch, Korumburra and Nyora. Travelling through some of the most picturesque scenery that Gippsland has to offer, see native animals roaming among the hills of the Strzelecki Ranges and cast your eye over the farmlands to the crystal blue waters of the coast. Trains operate Sun and public holidays; 1800 442 211. *Quilters' Barn:* arts and crafts, coffee shop and accommodation; Arawata; 12 km NE. *Loch:* a small town known for its antiques and arts and crafts shops; 14 km NW. *Poowong:* Poowong Pioneer Chapel is a fine example of German architecture. Also here is Mudlark Pottery with sales of ceramics. 18 km NW. *Gourmet Deli Trail:* self-guide tour; contact visitor centre for details.
ℹ Prom Country Information Centre, cnr South Gippsland Hwy and Silkstone Rd; 1800 630 704 or (03) 5655 2233; www.promcountrytourism.com.au

Kyneton   Pop. 4110
Map ref. 520 G1, 531 Q8, 533 R1, 538 D11, 543 R12

Part of Victoria's picturesque spa and garden country, Kyneton is a well-preserved town with many attractive bluestone buildings. Caroline Chisholm, who helped many migrants find their feet in this country, lived in Kyneton, where her family owned a store and her husband worked as a magistrate. While living in the town, she established a series of affordable, overnight shelters for travellers on the Mount Alexander Road (now the Calder Highway), a road frequented by gold prospectors. Remnants of the shelters can be seen at the historic township of Carlsruhe, south-east of Kyneton. **IN TOWN** *Historical Museum:* in a former bank building, with a drop-log cottage in the grounds; Piper St; open Fri–Sun. *Meskills Woolstore:* features a spinning mill, with yarns and handmade garments for sale; Piper St. *Botanic Gardens:* 8 ha area scenically located above Pipers Creek. The gardens feature rare varieties of trees. Clowes St. *Historic buildings:* many in town, including mechanics institute, Mollison St; and old police depot, Jenning St. *Campaspe River Walk:* scenic walk with picnic spots; access from Piper St. **WHAT'S ON** *Autumn Flower Show:* Mar. *Daffodil and Arts Festival:* Sept. *Kyneton Cup:* Nov. *Christmas Lights:* tours available; Dec. **NEARBY Trentham and Wombat State Forest** This picturesque spa country town

has a mixed history of gold, timber and farming. It has a charming streetscape and attractions include a historic foundry and Minifie's Berry Farm, where you can pick your own berries in season. Just north-east of town is Wombat State Forest – deep within is Victoria's largest single-drop waterfall, Trentham Falls. Cascading 32 m onto a quartz gravel base, the falls are an impressive backdrop for a picnic. 22 km SW. *Reservoirs:* several offering scenic locations for walks and picnics. Upper Coliban, Lauriston and Malmsbury reservoirs all nearby. *Carlsruhe Gallery and Campaspe Art Gallery:* both at Carlsruhe; 5 km SE. *Malmsbury:* a town noted for its old bluestone buildings. It features historic Botanic Gardens; Bleak House, with rose gardens; and The Mill, National Trust-classified, with gallery, restaurant and accommodation. Also wineries in the area. 10 km NW. *Art and Craft Gallery:* Tylden; 13 km W. *Turpins and Cascade Falls:* with picnic area and walks; near Metcalfe; 22 km N.
ℹ Jean Haynes Playground, High St; (03) 5422 6110

Lakes Entrance   Pop. 5476
Map ref. 535 R5, 536 H13

Lakes Entrance is a lovely holiday town situated at the eastern end of the Gippsland Lakes, an inland network of waterways covering more than 400 square kilometres. The artificially created 'entrance' of the town's name allows the Tasman Sea and the lakes to meet, making a safe harbour that is home to one of the largest fishing fleets in Australia. While many of the attractions in Lakes Entrance are based around the water, there is also opportunity for gourmets to indulge themselves with a variety of cafes and restaurants lining The Esplanade, plus sales of fresh fish and local wines. **IN TOWN** *Fishermen's Co-operative:* viewing platform and sales of freshly caught fish; Bullock Island. *Seashell Museum:* The Esplanade. **WHAT'S ON** *Lakes Summer Festival:* Jan. *International Festival of the Lakes:* Oct. *New Year's Eve Fireworks:* Dec. **NEARBY Gippsland Lakes** Five rivers end their journey to the sea here, forming a vast expanse of water tucked in behind Ninety Mile Beach. The lakes are a true playground for anyone with an interest in water activities, especially fishing and boating. Explore the lakes on a sightseeing cruise, including one to Wyanga Park Winery, or on the ever-popular houseboats that can be hired over summer. Contact visitor centre for details. *Jemmys Point:* great views of the region; 1 km W. *Lake Bunga:* nature trail along foreshore; 3 km E. *Kinkuna Country Family Fun Park:* on Princes Hwy; 3.5 km E. *Braeburne Park Orchards:* 6 km N. *Woodsedge Craft Centre:* gallery,

furniture workshop and glass-blowing demonstrations; Baades Rd; 8 km N. *Lake Tyers:* sheltered waters ideal for fishing, swimming and boating. Cruises depart from Fishermans Landing in town. Lake is 6–23 km NE, depending on access point. Lake Tyers Forest Park is great for bushwalking, wildlife-spotting, picnicking and camping. 20 km NE. *Nyerimilang Heritage Park:* 1920s homestead, with original farm buildings and the wonderfully maintained East Gippsland Botanic Gardens. Rose Pruning Day, with demonstrations, is held in July. 10 km NW. *Swan Reach:* Rosewood Pottery; Malcolm Cameron Studio Gallery, open weekends; 14 km NW. *Metung:* a scenic town on Lake King with boat hire, cruises and a marina regatta each Jan. Chainsaw Sculpture Gallery has chainsaw sculpture and a display of Annemieke Mein's embroidery art. 15 km W. *Nicholson River Winery:* 22 km NW. *East Gippsland Carriage Co:* restored horse-drawn carriages, and tours; 30 km E. *Bataluk Cultural Trail:* driving tour taking in Aboriginal cultural sites in the East Gippsland region; self-guide brochure available from visitor centre.
ℹ Lakes and Wilderness Tourism, cnr Esplanade and Marine Pde; 1800 637 060 or (03) 5155 1966; www.lakesentrance.com

Leongatha   Pop. 4222
Map ref. 521 P13, 534 H9

Leongatha is a thriving town, considered the commercial centre of South Gippsland. Despite this, it has maintained its small-town charm and visitors can pause for a coffee in the tree-lined main street before heading out into the rolling green hills in the distance. **IN TOWN** *Historic Society Museum:* McCartin St; check opening times. *Art and Craft Gallery:* McCartin St. *Mushroom Crafts and Pottery:* craft sales and gallery; Bair St. **WHAT'S ON** *South Gippsland Food and Wine Festival:* Jan. *Cycling Carnival:* Feb. *South Gippsland Golf Classic:* Feb. *Riverfest:* Mar. *Daffodil and Floral Festival:* Sept. **NEARBY Koonwarra** Your tastebuds will be delighted in this small village on the highway, with its growing reputation for gourmet produce and wine. Drop in at the Koonwarra Food and Wine Store to taste some of the flavours the region has to offer, or visit on the 1st Sat of each month for the farmers market. The village also has a thriving arts and crafts industry, and offers seasonal cooking and pottery classes. Surrounding the town are a number of cool-climate wineries that offer tastings and sales. 8 km SE. *Great Southern Rail Trail:* following the old railway line, this 7.5 km walking trail winds through farmland on its route from Leongatha to Koonwarra. *Brackenhurst Rotary Dairy:* 300 cows, milked daily from 3.30pm. Also a museum with dairy

VICTORIA

displays. Christoffersens Rd; 5 km E. *Gooseneck Pottery:* for locally produced ceramics; Ruby; 9 km NW. *Firelight Museum:* features antique lights and firearms; 9 km N. *Meeniyan:* a delightful small town with many craft shops; 16 km SE. *Mossvale Park:* impressive plantation of exotic trees with good barbecue/picnic facilities. A soundshell in the park is the venue for a Victorian Orchestra performance each Feb. 16 km NE. *Mirboo North:* Grand Ridge Brewing Company, for sales and viewing of beer-brewing process, Colonial Bank Antiques, and Erinae Lavender Garden and Tea Rooms; 26 km NE. *Gourmet Deli Trail:* takes in gourmet food and wine outlets in the South Gippsland region; contact visitor centre for details. *South Gippsland Railway: see Korumburra.*
ⓘ Michael Place Complex; (03) 5662 2111; www.promcountrytourism.com.au

Lorne   Pop. 1180

Map ref. 520 D13, 527 L9, 533 P10

Lorne is one of Victoria's most attractive and lively coastal resorts. The approach into town along the Great Ocean Road is truly spectacular with the superb mountain scenery of the Otways nearby. The village of Lorne was established in 1871 and quickly became popular with pastoralists from inland areas, leading to its development in the style of an English seaside resort. When the Great Ocean Road opened in 1932 Lorne became much more accessible, however the area has remained relatively unspoiled with good beaches, surfing and bushwalking in the hills – activities made all the more enjoyable by the pleasant, mild climate of the area.

IN TOWN *Teddys Lookout:* excellent bay views; behind the town, at the edge of George St. *Shipwreck Walk:* walk along the beach taking in sites of the numerous shipwrecks along this stretch of coast; details from visitor centre. *Foreshore Reserve:* great spot for a picnic, with paddleboats available for hire. *Qdos Contemporary Art Gallery:* Allenvale Rd. *Lorne Fisheries:* on the pier with daily supplies.

WHAT'S ON *Pier to Pub Swim:* Jan. *Mountain to Surf Foot Race:* Jan.

NEARBY **Angahook–Lorne State Park** The park covers 22 000 ha and includes a range of environments, from the timbered ridges of the eastern Otways to fern gullies, waterfalls and a coastline with tall cliffs, coves and sandy beaches. There are more than 100 walking tracks and the rock platforms along the coast provide ideal spots for ocean fishing. The Falls Festival, a major rock-music festival, is held over New Year's Eve at Erskine Falls, 9 km NW. For the rest of the year the falls are a peaceful location and drop 30 m over moss-covered rocks. As well as driving, you can walk to the falls from Lorne along the river. The park surrounds

Lorne and can be accessed from various points along the Great Ocean Rd. *Cumberland River Valley:* walking tracks and camping; 4 km SW. *Mt Defiance Lookout:* 10 km SW. *Wye River:* a small coastal village, good for rock and surf fishing, surfing and camping; 17 km SW. *Gentle Annie Berry Gardens:* pick your own; 26 km NW via Deans Marsh; open Nov–April. *Scenic drives:* west through the Otway Ranges, and south-west or north-east on the Great Ocean Rd.
ⓘ 144 Mountjoy Pde; (03) 5289 1152; www.greatoceanrd.org.au

Maffra   Pop. 3904

Map ref. 535 M5

Maffra, settled in the 1840s, retains the charm and old-style hospitality of another era. The town experienced a major boost when a sugar beet industry was established in the 1890s; its early days were fraught with drought, but the start of the Glenmaggie Irrigation Scheme in 1919 not only signalled a new heyday, but also ensured the viable and lengthy success of today's dairy industry. The sugar beet factory closed in 1948 owing to World War II's labour shortages and the competing dairy industry, but Maffra continues to support its rich agricultural surrounds.

IN TOWN *Maffra Sugar Beet Historic Museum:* local history museum with special interest in the sugar beet industry; River St; open Sun afternoon. *Mineral and gemstone display:* large collection of rare gemstones and fossils at the information centre; Johnson St. *All Seasons Herb Garden:* Foster St.

WHAT'S ON *Scotfest:* Feb. *Gippsland Harvest Festival:* Mar. *Mardi Gras:* Mar.

NEARBY *Stratford:* the scenic Avon River flows through town. Knobs Reserve is a site where the local Aboriginal people once sharpened axe heads on sandstone grinding stones – it is part of the Bataluk Cultural Trail, which takes in significant indigenous sites throughout East Gippsland. Stratford hosts the Shakespeare Celebration in May. 9 km E. *Australian Wildlife Art Gallery and Sculpture:* Princes Hwy near Munro; 25 km E. *Lake Glenmaggie:* popular watersports venue; 42 km NW via Heyfield. *Alpine National Park:* sprawls from Licola, 75 km NW, to the NSW border. Near Licola is Lake Tali Karng, which lies 850 m above sea level and is a popular bushwalking destination during the warmer months. *See feature on p. 186. Scenic drives:* the Traralgon to Stratford Tourist Route highlights attractions of the area. For stunning scenery, drive north along Forest Rd, through the Macalister River Valley to Licola and Mt Tamboritha in Alpine National Park; or to Jamieson (166 km NW via Heyfield), with access to snowfields or Lake Eildon.
ⓘ 96 Johnson St; (03) 5141 1811

Maldon   Pop. 1231

Map ref. 531 M5, 538 B10, 543 P11

Maldon is one of Victoria's best-known gold towns and a popular spot for a weekend getaway for Melburnians. The town has been wonderfully preserved, with the wide, tree-lined main street featuring delightful old buildings and shopfronts. It seems the town has hardly changed since the gold rush, aside from the cafes and galleries that now prosper. Maldon was declared Australia's first 'notable town' by the National Trust in 1966.

IN TOWN *Historic town walk:* grab a brochure from the visitor centre and take to the wide, old footpaths to discover the historic delights of Maldon. See preserved 19th-century shopfronts and old stone cottages. Highlights include the restored Dabb's General Store in Main St, and the Maldon Hospital in Adair St. *Museum:* displays on mining as well as domestic memorabilia from Maldon's past, in heritage building; High St; open 1.30pm–4pm daily. *The Beehive Chimney:* southern end of Church St. *Anzac Hill:* the walk to the top is rewarded with magnificent views of the area; southern end of High St.

WHAT'S ON *Campdraft:* Feb. *Fair:* Easter. *Vintage Car Hill Climb:* Oct. *Folk Festival:* Oct–Nov.

NEARBY **Porcupine Township** This award-winning tourist attraction is a reconstruction of an early 1850s goldmining town, with an array of slab, shingle and mudbrick buildings moved here from other goldfields. The village, complete with a blacksmith's, a doctor's surgery and even a bowling alley, is located in rugged bushland on the site of the original Porcupine diggings, where the first gold discovery between Castlemaine and Bendigo was made. Visitors can pan for gold, handfeed emus, or take a ride on the Little Toot train, which does a circuit through the diggings. Cnr Maldon–Bendigo and Allans rds; 3 km NE. *Mt Tarrangower Lookout Tower:* town views; 2 km W. *Carman's Tunnel Reserve:* guided mine tours feature relics from goldmining days; 2 km SW. *Nuggetty Ranges and Mt Moorol:* 2 km N. *Cairn Curran Reservoir:* great for watersports and fishing, features picnic facilities and a sailing club near the spillway; 10 km SW. *Victorian Goldfields Railway:* historic steam trains run from Maldon Railway Station (Hornsby St) through scenic forest to Castlemaine; operates Wed, Sun and public holidays; bookings (03) 5470 6658.
ⓘ High St; (03) 5475 2569; www.maldon.org.au

Mallacoota   Pop. 1031

Map ref. 507 G13, 537 Q11

Mallacoota is a popular holiday centre in far East Gippsland, surrounded by the scenic Croajingolong National Park, which features Point Hicks, notable for

Mt Buller ski resort, east of Mansfield

being the first land on the east coast of Australia to be sighted by Europeans. There are spectacular surf beaches near the town, with Mallacoota Inlet offering great fishing.

WHAT'S ON *Festival of the Great Southern Ocean:* Easter.

NEARBY Croajingolong National Park This park takes up a vast portion of what has been dubbed the Wilderness Coast. It protects remote beaches, tall forests, heathland, rainforest, estuaries and granite peaks, as well as creatures such as wallabies, possums, goannas and lyrebirds. Offshore, you might be lucky enough to spot dolphins, seals or southern right and humpback whales. Point Hicks Lighthouse is a popular spot to visit, and Tamboon and Mallacoota inlets are good spots for canoeing. Access the park via a track west of town or various roads south of the Princes Hwy. *Surf beaches:* Bastion Point, 2 km s; Bekta, 5 km s. *Gabo Island Lightstation Reserve:* take a scenic daytrip or stay in the Lightkeeper's Residence; 11 km E (offshore). *Gipsy Point:* a quiet holiday retreat overlooking the Genoa River; 16 km NW. ❶ Mallacoota Real Estate, 62 Maurice Ave; (03) 5158 0600; www.mallacoota.com

Mansfield   Pop. 2658

Map ref. 539 L10, 540 C10

Mansfield is located in Victoria's High Country at the junction of the Midland and Maroondah highways. It is within

easy reach of both Lake Eildon and Alpine National Park, so is an ideal destination for anyone with a love of hiking or, in winter, skiing.

IN TOWN *Troopers' Monument:* monument to police officers shot by Ned Kelly at Stringybark Creek; cnr High St and Midland Hwy. *Hot-air balloon trips:* depart from Highton Manor; bookings essential, 1800 627 661.

WHAT'S ON *Harvest Festival:* Mar. *Mansfield Balloon Festival:* Mar/April. *Mountain Country Festival:* Nov.

NEARBY Mt Buller Victoria's largest and best alpine skiing resort is Mt Buller, whose summit stands 1804 m above sea level. The 25 lifts give access to 180 ha of ski trails, from gentle 'family runs' to heart-stopping double black diamond chutes. If you're a beginner, take on the friendly Bourke Street (Green Run) to find your 'ski legs', or join one of the ski schools there. There is also a Half Pipe at Boggy Creek and Terrain Park, or cross-country skiing at nearby Mt Stirling. Mt Buller Village offers resort accommodation, and the ski season runs between early June and late Sept. 47 km E. **Craig's Hut** The High Country is synonymous with courageous and hardy cattlemen, transformed into Australian legends by Banjo Paterson's iconic ballad *The Man from Snowy River.* The men would build huts on the high plains for shelter during summer cattle drives. Craig's Hut on Mt Stirling is a replica of one such shelter, used as a set on the

1983 film *The Man from Snowy River.* The last 1.2 km of the track to the hut is 4WD or walking only. 50 km E. *Delatite Winery:* Stoneys Rd; 7 km SE. *Mount Samaria State Park:* scenic drives, camping and bushwalking; 14 km N. *Lake Eildon:* houseboat hire, fishing and sailing; 15 km s; *see Eildon for further details. Lake Nillahcootie:* popular for boating, fishing and watersports; 20 km NW. *Howqua Dale Gourmet Retreat:* 26 km s. *Jamieson:* an old goldmining town on the Jamieson River with historic buildings; 37 km s. *Alpine National Park:* begins around 40 km SE; *see feature on p. 186. Scenic drive:* take the road over the mountains to Whitfield (62 km NE), in the King River Valley, passing through spectacular scenery, including Powers Lookout (48 km NE) for views over the valley. *Lake William Hovell:* for boating and fishing; 85 km NE. *Mt Skene:* great for bushwalking, with wildflowers in summer; 85 km SE via Jamieson. *Fishing:* good spots include the Delatite, Howqua, Jamieson and Goulburn rivers. *Camel treks and horse trail-riding:* a different way to explore the region; see visitor centre for details. ❶ Old Railway Station, Maroondah Hwy; 1800 039 049 or (03) 5775 1464; www.mansfield-mtbuller.com.au

Maryborough   Pop. 7741

Map ref. 531 J5, 543 011

Maryborough is a small city set on the northern slopes of the Great Dividing Range. Its historic 19th-century buildings, particularly around the civic square, are a testament to the riches brought by the Maryborough gold rush of the 1850s. Take a stroll through the streets to enjoy the cafes, craft shops and magnificent buildings, such as the National Trust-listed courthouse, post office and town hall.

IN TOWN Maryborough Railway Station So immense and impressive is this building that Mark Twain, on his visit to the town, remarked that Maryborough was 'a station with a town attached'. Rumour has it that the building was actually intended for Maryborough in Queensland. The beautifully preserved station houses the visitor centre, the extensive Antique Emporium, the Woodworkers Gallery (open weekends only), and Twains Wood and Craft Gallery. Station St. *Pioneer Memorial Tower:* Bristol Hill. *Worsley Cottage:* a historical museum featuring local relics; Palmerston St; open Sun. *Central Goldfields Art Gallery:* features an impressive collection of local artworks, housed in the old fire station; Neill St. *Phillips Gardens:* Alma St.

WHAT'S ON *Highland Gathering:* New Year's Day. *Gourmet, Grapes and Gardens Weekend:* Oct. *Energy Breakthrough:* energy expo; Nov.

NEARBY Paddys Ranges State Park This park offers the chance to enjoy red ironbark and grey box vegetation on one

Citrus and apricot orchards near Mildura

of the scenic walks or drives. The majority of walks start from the picnic area – see old goldmines and relics, enjoy the spring wildflowers, or keep an eye out for the rare painted honeyeater and other birdlife. There is also fossicking within the park, but in designated areas only. Access to the park is just south of Maryborough. The scenic Golden Way Tourist Drive travels through parts of the ranges.
Aboriginal wells: impressive rock wells; 4 km s. *Carisbrook:* holds a popular tourist market 1st Sun each month; 7 km E.
ⓘ Cnr Alma and Nolan sts; 1800 356 511 or (03) 5460 4511; www.centralgoldfields.com.au

Marysville
Pop. 593

Map ref. 521 O4, 524 I3, 534 G2, 539 J13

Marysville is a pretty town, set in the lush forest of the Yarra Ranges. In town there are a number of charming arts and crafts shops and B&Bs, making it a popular destination for daytrips from Melbourne and romantic weekends away.
IN TOWN *Old Fashioned Lolly Shop:* Murchison St. *Country Touch Pottery:* Murchison St. *Hidden Talents:* for local arts and crafts; Murchison St. *Bruno's Art and Sculpture Garden:* Falls Rd. *Sawyer's Marysville Museum:* features vintage cars and accessories; Darwin St. *Nicholls Lookout:* excellent views; Cumberland Rd.

WHAT'S ON *Market:* Murchison St; 2nd Sun each month.
NEARBY Cathedral Range State Park
The word 'imposing' does not do justice to the 7 km rocky ridge that forms the backbone of this park. Gentle walks reveal a landscape of mountain streams and historic sites, while the challenging hikes up the ridge to lookout points offer unparalleled views to the valley below. Walks can include overnight stays at the Farmyard, so named because lyrebirds imitate the noises of the domestic animals in the farmyards below. 15 km N.
Lake Mountain Renowned for first-rate cross-country skiing, Lake Mountain has 40 km of scenic ski routes through the snow gum forests, and is also a great venue for tobogganing. When the snow melts and the wildflowers bloom, take the Summit Walk (4 km return) over the mountain, stopping at lookouts with spectacular views. Ski and walk brochure available from visitor centre.
Lady Talbot Forest Drive: this 46 km route begins east of town and takes in ferny gullies, tall gum trees and gushing waterfalls. Stop en route to enjoy picnic spots, walking tracks and lookouts.
Scenic walks: many tracks in the area, including a short walk to Steavenson Falls, from Falls Rd; 4 km loop walk in Cumberland Memorial Scenic Reserve, 16 km E; 4 km Beeches Walk through ancient beech and mountain ash forests

(accessed via Lady Talbot Forest Drive). *Buxton:* attractions include a zoo, a trout farm and the Australian Bush Pioneer's Farm at the foot of Mt Cathedral; 11 km N. *Big River State Forest:* camping, fishing and gold fossicking; 30 km E.
ⓘ 11 Murchison St; (03) 5963 4567

Milawa
Pop. 120

Map ref. 539 N6, 540 G1

Milawa is the perfect destination for lovers of fine food and wine. It is positioned on the Snow Road that links Oxley, Markwood and Wangaratta to the north-west and the Great Alpine Road to the east. The town boasts an excellent array of fresh, local-produce outlets, plus the Brown Brothers vineyard, a renowned winery set in gorgeous grounds.
IN TOWN *Milawa Mustards:* a wide range of locally produced mustards. Set in attractive cottage gardens. Snow Rd. *Milawa Cheese Company:* sales and tastings of specialist, gourmet cheeses; Factory Rd. *Brown Brothers:* cellar-door tastings and sales; Bobinawarrah Rd.
WHAT'S ON *Brown Brothers Wine and Food Weekend:* Nov.
NEARBY King Valley Wine Region
Stretching from Milawa and Oxley south to Whitfield and Cheshunt, this region produces wines with a distinctly Italian influence. The first vines were planted in the 1890s, and varieties including cabernet sauvignon, merlot, pinot noir, riesling and chardonnay are offered for tastings at various cellar doors, as well as the Italian varieties of sangiovese, pinot grigio and nebbiolo. The King Valley Virgin Wine, Food and Arts Festival is held each Nov in Whitfield and Cheshunt. Winery map available from visitor centre.
Oxley: home to many wineries as well as the Blue Ox Blueberry Farm, Churchworks, Earthly Gems, and King River Cafe; 4 km w.
ⓘ Wangaratta and Region Visitors Information Centre, cnr Handley St and Tone Rd, Wangaratta; 1800 801 065 or (03) 5721 5711

Mildura
Pop. 27 931

Map ref. 510 D7, 544 G3

Mildura offers a Riviera lifestyle, with the Murray River flowing by the town and sunny, mild weather throughout the year. It is one of Victoria's major rural cities. Its development has been aided by the expansion of irrigation, which has allowed the city to become a premier fruit-growing region.
IN TOWN Mildura Arts Centre Complex
The complex is set on the banks of the Murray River and includes an art gallery, an amphitheatre and the Rio Vista museum. Rio Vista was the home of the town's founders, the Chaffey brothers, and is now preserved as a museum displaying colonial household items.

The art gallery houses an impressive permanent collection and includes Australia's largest display of Brangwyn and Orpen paintings, as well as frequent temporary exhibitions. Outside, a delightful Sculpture Trail winds through the landscaped gardens surrounding the centre. Cureton Ave.
The Alfred Deakin Centre: interactive exhibitions and displays of the region; Deakin Ave. *Langtree Hall:* Mildura's first public hall now contains antiques and memorabilia; Walnut Ave; open Tues–Sun. *Mildura Wharf:* paddlesteamers departing here for river cruises include PS *Melbourne*, PS *Avoca* for lunch and dinner cruises, PS *Coonawarra* for 3-, 5- or 6-day cruises, and PV *Rothbury* for daytrips to Trentham Winery each Thurs. The wharf can be accessed from Madden Ave. *Snakes and Ladders:* fun park featuring 'dunny' collection; Seventeenth St. *Aquacoaster waterslide:* cnr Seventh St and Orange Ave. *Stefano's:* Italian restaurant in the majestic Grand Hotel, featuring the culinary skills of television chef Stefano di Pieri; Seventh St. *Dolls on the Avenue:* Benetook Ave. *Pioneer Cottage:* Hunter St. *The Citrus Shop:* locally produced citrus products; Deakin Ave.
WHAT'S ON *Arts Festival:* Mar. *International Balloon Fiesta:* July. *Golf Week:* July. *Racing Cup Carnival:* July. *Country Music Festival:* Sept. *Big Lizzie Festival of Vintage Tractors:* Sept. *Sunraysia Oasis Rose Festival:* Oct. *Sunraysia Jazz and Wine Festival:* Nov. *World Jet Sprint Boat Championships:* Nov.
NEARBY **Murray Darling Wine Region** The Mediterranean-style climate mixed with irrigated lands has contributed to making this wine region Victoria's largest. Noted mainly for its bulk table-wine, the region is well regarded for its varieties of chardonnay, cabernet sauvignon and shiraz. Among the large-scale wineries such as Lindemans Karadoc, smaller boutique wineries offer specialty wines for tastings and sales. Brochure available from visitor centre.
Golden River Fauna Park: native and exotic species are housed here in natural surroundings; 5 km NW. *Woodsies Gem Shop and Murray Gum Pottery:* 6 km W. *Sunbeam Dried Fruits:* tours available; Irymple; 6 km S. *Australian Inland Botanic Gardens:* 6 km N; open Sun–Fri. *Orange World:* tours of citrus-growing region; 6 km N. *Angus Park:* dried fruits and confectionery; 10 km SE. *Red Cliffs:* an important area for the citrus and dried fruit industries. The town features the 'Big Lizzie' steam traction engine. 15 km S. *Hattah–Kulkyne National Park:* 70 km S; *see Ouyen. Murray–Sunset National Park:* attractions near Mildura include Lindsay Island, for boating, swimming and fishing. Access from Sturt Hwy, about 100 km W of Mildura. *See Murrayville for further details on park. Mungo National Park:* 104 km NE over NSW border; *see feature on p. 55.*
🛈 Alfred Deakin Centre, 180–190 Deakin Ave; 1300 550 858 or (03) 5018 8380; www.visitmildura.com.au

Moe   Pop. 15 352

Map ref. 521 R10, 535 J7

Moe is a rapidly growing city in the La Trobe Valley. Although Moe, like many of the towns in this region, is supported by the power station industries, it has managed to avoid becoming a grim industrial centre. Instead Moe has a small-town feel and is home to a number of pretty gardens and public parks.

IN TOWN **Gippsland Heritage Park** This is a re-creation of a 19th-century community with over 30 restored buildings and a fine collection of fully restored horse-drawn carriages; Lloyd St. *Cinderella Dolls:* Andrew St. *Race track:* picturesque country horse track with regular meetings; Waterloo Rd.
WHAT'S ON *Market:* at Heritage Park, with local crafts and produce; 2nd Sun each month. *Modelling and Hobby Exhibition:* Jan. *Fairies in the Park:* Feb. *Jazz Festival:* Mar. *Blue Rock Classic:* cross-country horserace; Mar. *Moe Cup:* horserace; Oct.
NEARBY **Baw Baw National Park** The landscape of Baw Baw ranges from densely forested river valleys to alpine plateaus and the activities on offer are equally varied – from canoeing river rapids and fishing for trout to skiing, horseriding and bushwalking. Wildflowers carpet the alpine areas in spring. Baw Baw Alpine Resort is located 90 km north of Moe, while the popular Aberfeldy picnic and camping area is accessed via a track north of Walhalla. *Edward Hunter Heritage Bush Reserve:* 3 km S via Coalville St. *Trafalgar Lookout and Narracan Falls:* near Trafalgar; 10 km W. *Blue Rock Dam:* fishing, swimming and sailing; 20 km NW. *Thorpdale:* a town renowned for its potatoes. A bakery sells potato bread and a potato festival is held each Mar. 22 km SW. *Walhalla Mountain River Trail:* leads to picturesque old mining township of Walhalla; Tourist Route 91; see visitor centre for details. *See Walhalla.*
🛈 Gippsland Heritage Park, Lloyd St; (03) 5127 3082; www.phillipisland gippsland.com.au

Mornington   Pop. 13 692

Map ref. 519 E11, 521 K10, 523 J3, 534 D7

Mornington was once the hub of the Mornington Peninsula, which is the reason this long arm of land was eventually given the same name. Today Melbourne's urban sprawl has just about reached the town, and it has virtually become a suburb. Mornington overlooks Port Phillip and features calm swimming beaches. At Schnapper Point a jetty provides a fishing spot or boat launch. In the 19th century, paddlesteamers used to depart from here to transport Melbourne tourists to the various seaside resorts in the region.

IN TOWN **TV World** This unique family tourist destination has displays relating to the early 'golden days' of Australian television, cinema and radio. There are over 5000 exhibits in the centre. At the Cool Stores on Moorooduc Hwy.
Historic Mornington Pier: built in the 1850s, the pier remains popular today for walks and fishing. *Mornington Peninsula Regional Gallery:* print and drawing collection, including works by Dobell, Drysdale and Nolan; Dunns Rd; open Tues–Sat. *Motorised-trolley rides:* operate from Bungower Rd level crossing every Sun afternoon. *National Antique Centre:* Tyabb Rd. *World of Motorcycles Museum:* Tyabb Rd. *Old post office:* now home to a local history display; cnr Main St and The Esplanade. *Mornington Tourist Railway:* 10 km journey on steam train; departs from cnr Yuilles and Watt rds; 1st, 2nd and 3rd Sun each month, with additional trips running on Thurs in Jan.
WHAT'S ON *Street Market:* Main St; each Wed. *Mornington Racecourse Craft Market:* 2nd Sun each month. *Mornington Food and Wine Festival:* Oct. *Tea Tree Festival:* Nov.
NEARBY **Arthurs Seat State Park** At 309 m, Arthurs Seat is the highest point on the Mornington Peninsula. The summit can be reached by foot or vehicle and offers panoramic views of the bay and surrounding bushland. Picnic facilities and a restaurant are on the summit. There are many short walks, plus the historic Seawinds Park with gardens and sculptures. The Arthurs Seat Maze is set in superb gardens, with a variety of mazes and the Maize Maze Festival in March. Arthurs Seat Rd, near Dromana; 16 km SW.
Mornington Peninsula Wine Region Although the first vines were planted in 1886, the wine industry on the peninsula did not truly take off until the 1970s. Comprising over 170 vineyards, the region consists predominantly of boutique wineries, including around 40 cellar doors. While enjoying the sunshine, beaches and coastal resorts, it seems appropriate to try the crisp chardonnay that is famed in this region – or even a pinot noir or cabernet sauvignon as the chilly sea breeze kicks in of an evening. Wine festivals include Pinot Week each Mar, Queen's Birthday Wine Weekend each June and the Cool Whites Festival each Nov. Winery map available from visitor centre.
Mount Martha: here is The Briars with a significant collection of Napoleonic artefacts and furniture. The town also features many gardens, plus wetlands great for birdwatching and bushland walks. 7 km S. *Ballam Park:* historic, French-farmhouse-style homestead built in 1845; Cranbourne Rd, Frankston; 14 km NE; open Sun. *Mulberry Hill:* former home of artist Sir Daryl Lindsay and author Joan Lindsay, who wrote *Picnic at Hanging Rock*; Golf Links Rd, Baxter; 14 km NE; open Sun afternoons. *Tyabb Packing House:* antiques and collectibles; Mornington–Tyabb Rd, Tyabb; 16 km E. *Hastings:* coastal town

VICTORIA

Davies Plain, in the remote eastern section of the park

Alpine National Park

Covering 646 000 hectares in four sections, Alpine National Park is Victoria's largest and contains the highest mountains in the state. Most of Australia's south-east rivers, including the mighty Murray, have their source in these mountains. The area is known for its outstanding snowfields during winter, and bushwalking and wildflowers in the summer months. Other activities include horseriding, canoeing, rafting and mountain-bike riding.

Cobberas–Tingaringy

Adjoining New South Wales' Kosciuszko National Park to the north and Snowy River National Park to the south is the northernmost section of the park, Cobberas–Tingaringy. This section is largely wilderness, but there are some excellent drives as well, particularly along the Black Mountain–Benambra Road, which offers outstanding mountain views, and where groups of brumbies are a common sight.

Dartmouth

To the west of Cobberas–Tingaringy lies the Dartmouth section of the park. Dartmouth offers well-signed bushwalking tracks, where it is common to come across native wildlife such as swamp wallabies, eastern grey kangaroos and wombats. Dominating the area, though, is Lake Dartmouth, a massive freshwater lake popular for trout fishing (both rainbow and brown) and boating.

Bogong

Bogong is south-west of Dartmouth and is known for its outstanding winter sports at two of Victoria's most popular ski resorts, Mount Hotham and Falls Creek. Both areas offer excellent skiing for all abilities as well as snow camping (overnight cross-country ski tours). The Bogong High Plains have some of the finest mountain scenery in the state, and in summer the mountains and plains are carpeted with spectacular wildflower. The area is also scattered with historic huts that are still used by farmers grazing their cattle in the lush green mountains during summer.

Wonnangatta–Moroka

South-west of Bogong is Wonnangatta–Moroka, the southernmost and largest of the four sections. The region offers scenic bushwalks through rugged mountains and gorges. One highlight is Lake Tali Karng, the only natural lake in the alps, which was created by a landslide thousands of years ago. The lake can be reached by a popular overnight bushwalk that follows the Wellington River up through the Valley of Destruction to Lake Tali Karng at the river's head. The rugged terrain, rapids, waterfalls, cataracts and swimming holes at Moroka Gorge make this another popular destination, and Bryces Gorge is a spectacular abyss well-hidden in the upper reaches of Conglomerate Creek.

on Western Port with 2 km walking trail through wetlands and mangrove habitat; 21 km SE. *Beaches:* the stretch of coast between Mornington and Mount Martha features sheltered, sandy bays popular with holiday-makers.
ⓘ Mornington Peninsula Visitor Information Centre, Point Nepean Rd, Dromana; 1800 804 009 or (03) 5987 3078; www.melbournesbays.org/morningtonpeninsula

Morwell   Pop. 13 505

Map ref. 535 J7

Morwell is primarily an industrial town and Victoria's major producer of electricity. It is situated in the La Trobe Valley, which contains one of the world's largest deposits of brown coal. But among all the heavy machinery is the impressive Centennial Rose Garden, featuring over 3000 rose bushes and regarded as one of the finest rose gardens in the Southern Hemisphere.

IN TOWN *PowerWorks:* dynamic displays on the electrical industries; Ridge Rd; tours of mines and power stations daily. *Rose Garden:* off Commercial Rd.

WHAT'S ON *Market:* La Trobe Rd; each Sun.

NEARBY **Morwell National Park** This park protects some of the last remnant vegetation of the Strzelecki Ranges, including pockets of rainforest and fern gullies. The area was once occupied by the Woollum Woollum people, who hunted in the ranges. In the 1840s European settlers cleared much of the surrounding land. On the Fosters Gully Nature Walk, keep your eyes peeled for orchids (over 40 species are found here) and native animals such as koalas, kangaroos and greater gliders. 16 km S. *Hazelwood Pondage:* warm water ideal for year-round watersports; 5 km S. *Arts Resource Collective:* housed in an old butter factory; Yinnar; 12 km SW. *Lake Narracan:* fishing and waterskiing; 15 km NW. *Narracan Falls:* 27 km W. *Scenic drives:* routes along the Strzelecki Ranges and Baw Baw mountains offer impressive views over the La Trobe Valley.
ⓘ PowerWorks Visitor Centre, Ridge Rd; (03) 5135 3415; www.latrobe.vic.gov.au

Mount Beauty   Pop. 1621

Map ref. 536 D6, 539 Q8, 541 N5

Mount Beauty was originally an accommodation town for workers on the Kiewa Hydro-electric Scheme. Today the town is an ideal holiday destination at the foot of Mt Bogong, Victoria's highest mountain at 1986 metres.

IN TOWN *Heritage Museum:* at the visitor centre. *Mount Beauty Pondage:* for watersports and fishing; just north of Main St.

WHAT'S ON *Markets:* Main St; 1st Sat each month. *Music Muster:* April.

NEARBY Falls Creek Surrounded by Alpine National Park (*see feature on facing page*), Falls Creek is a winter playground for downhill and cross-country skiers. When the snow is falling, the ski resort caters for skiers and snowboarders with a variety of runs and terrain, including some to suit beginners. Novelty tours are also available, such as the Snowmobile Tours or the fantastic Sled Dog Tours, the only tour of its type offered in Australia. Each August, Falls Creek hosts the Kangaroo Hoppet cross-country ski race. In spring and summer, take a walk on the Bogong High Plains or fly-fish in one of the lakes and rivers nearby. 30 km SE. *Tawonga Gap:* features a lookout over valleys; 13 km NW. *Bogong:* scenic walks around nearby Lake Guy; 15 km SE. *Scenic drives:* to Falls Creek and the Bogong High Plains (not accessible in winter beyond Falls Creek); contact visitor centre for details.
ⓘ Kiewa Valley Hwy; (03) 5754 1962; www.mtbeauty.com

Murrayville   Pop. 355

Map ref. 510 B11, 544 B10, 555 R10

Murrayville is a small town on the Mallee Highway near the South Australia border. It is near three major, remote national parks: Murray–Sunset National Park; Wyperfeld National Park; and Big Desert Wilderness Park, one of Victoria's largest wilderness zones.
IN TOWN *Historic buildings:* include the restored railway station and the old courthouse. *Walking tracks:* several.
NEARBY Murray–Sunset National Park Millions of years ago this area was submerged beneath the sea. When the sea retreated, large sand ridges and dunes were left. Now there is a variety of vegetation including grasslands, saltbush and mallee eucalypts. In spring, wildflowers abound; look out for Victoria's largest flower, the Murray lily. Access roads to the park are off Mallee Hwy. The Pink Lakes saltwater lakes, with a distinctive, pinkish hue, are a key attraction and are especially remarkable at sunset. There are many good walking tracks near the lakes, as well as excellent camping facilities. Lakes access via Pink Lakes Rd (turn-off at Linga, 50 km E). *For north section of park see Mildura. Cowangie:* a small, historic town with several 19th-century buildings, including Kow Plains Homestead; 19 km E. *Big Desert Wilderness Park:* a remote park with no access other than by foot. True to its name, this park has remained relatively untouched by Europeans and includes many reptile species and plants adapted to arid conditions. The track south of town takes you close to the park boundary. *Wyperfeld National Park:* access via Underbool or by 4WD track south of Murrayville; *for further details see Hopetoun.*

ⓘ Murrayville Newsagency; 10 Reed St; (03) 5095 2181

Myrtleford   Pop. 2512

Map ref. 536 B5, 539 O7, 541 J2

Myrtleford is a pretty town in Victoria's High Country known for the large walnut groves that grow in the area. Hops and tobacco are other industries.
IN TOWN *The Phoenix Tree:* a sculpture created by Hans Knorr from the trunk of a red gum; Lions Park. *The Big Tree:* a huge old red gum; Smith St. *Old School:* the town's original school, now fully restored; Albert St; open Thurs, Sun or by appt. *Myrtleford Mart:* antiques and bric-a-brac; Myrtle St. *Swing Bridge over Myrtle Creek:* Standish St. *Reform Hill Lookout:* a scenic walking track from Elgin St leads to the lookout, which has great views across town; end of Halls Rd. *Parks:* Rotary Park in Myrtle St and Apex Park in Standish St are both delightful picnic spots. *Jan Mitchell Art Gallery:* collection of works by local artists; Power St. *Michelini Wines:* Great Alpine Rd.
WHAT'S ON *Market:* local produce; Great Alpine Rd; each Sat, Jan–April. *Tobacco, Hops and Timber Food and Wine Festival:* Mar. *Great Alpine Bike Ride:* here to Bright; Oct. *Golden Spurs Rodeo:* Dec.
NEARBY *Mount Buffalo National Park:* 7 km S; *see Bright. Wineries:* several in the region, including Rosewhite Vineyards and Winery; Happy Valley Rd; 8 km SE; open weekends, public holidays and throughout Jan. *Gapsted:* home to the Victorian Alps Winery and Valley Nut Groves, which produce walnuts and offers tours and sales; 8 km NW. *Eurobin:* a number of farms near the town with sales of local produce include Snowline Deer and Emu Farm; Leita Berry Farm, offering homemade jams and berries in season, Dec–Mar; and Bisinella Rose Farm; 16 km SE. *Nug Nug Quarter Horse Stud and Dingo Breeding:* 16 km S; open by appt. *Fishing:* in the Ovens and Buffalo rivers and Lake Buffalo (25 km S).
ⓘ Ponderosa Cabin, 29–31 Clyde St; (03) 5752 1727

Nagambie   Pop. 1404

Map ref. 538 G8

Nagambie is found between Seymour and Shepparton on the Goulburn Valley Highway. The town is on the shores of Lake Nagambie, which was created by the construction of the Goulburn Weir in 1891. Rowing, speedboat and waterskiing tournaments are held here.
IN TOWN *Colonial Doll Shop:* High St. *The Nut House:* sales of Australian products; High St.
WHAT'S ON *Goulburn Valley Vintage Festival:* Mar. *Shiraz Challenge:* a search for the best shiraz in the region; Nov. *Rowing Regatta:* Dec.

NEARBY Goulburn Valley Wine Region In the 1850s a group of farmers got together and planted some vines; they were to form the Tahbilk Vineyard Proprietary that would become the Tahbilk Winery, one of the most successful in the region. The vineyard features National Trust-classified buildings, plus a museum detailing the history of the estate. The Goulburn Valley's warm climate and proximity to the Goulburn River has allowed for a prosperous industry, with the vineyards producing high-quality grenache and mourvedre varieties as well as the old-time favourites. Brochure and map detailing Tahbilk and other wineries available from visitor centre.
ⓘ 145 High St; 1800 444 647 or (03) 5794 2647

Natimuk   Pop. 418

Map ref. 542 F9

Natimuk is part of the state's Wimmera region, and is popular for its proximity to Mt Arapiles, a 369-metre sandstone monolith that has been described as 'Victoria's Ayers Rock'. The mountain was first climbed by Major Mitchell in 1836, and today is a popular rockclimbing destination with over 2000 marked climbing routes. Brigitte Muir, the first Australian woman to climb Mt Everest, trained here.
IN TOWN *Arapiles Historical Society Museum:* housed in the old courthouse; Main St; open by appt. *Arapiles Craft Shop:* features local arts and crafts; Main St. *Self-guide heritage trail:* contact visitor centre for details.
NEARBY Mount Arapiles–Tooan State Park This park is divided into 2 blocks, the larger Tooan block and the smaller Mt Arapiles block, but Mt Arapiles offers the rockclimbing and is by far the most popular. Mitre Rock presents a smaller climbing challenge if required. Should you choose not to scale one of the various rock faces, great views are still available from the walking tracks, or you can drive to the summit. Nature study is another possibility – a huge 14 percent of the state's flora is represented in the Mt Arapiles section alone. Access is from the Wimmera Hwy; 12 km SW.
Lake Natimuk: good for watersports and picnics; 2 km N. *Banksia Hill Flower Farm:* 10 km E. *Duffholme Museum:* 21 km W. *Toolondo Reservoir:* trout fishing; 30 km S.
ⓘ National Hotel, Main St; (03) 5387 1300

Nhill   Pop. 1977

Map ref. 542 D7

The name of this town may be derived from the Aboriginal word 'nyell', meaning 'white mist on water'. Nhill is exactly halfway between Melbourne and Adelaide and claims to have the largest single-bin silo in the Southern Hemisphere. The town

Alfred Nicholas Gardens, near Olinda

is a good starting point for tours of Little Desert National Park.

IN TOWN *Historical Society Museum:* McPherson St; open by appt. *Cottage of John Shaw Neilson (lyric poet):* in Jaypex Park; Victoria St; open by appt. *Boardwalk:* scenic walk from Jaypex Park to Nhill Lake, with a bird hide along the way. *Lowana Craft Shop:* local crafts; Victoria St. *Self-guide historical walk and drive:* contact visitor centre for details.

WHAT'S ON *Country Music Festival:* Mar.

NEARBY *Little Desert National Park:* the Little Desert Lodge is in the central section of the park, south of Nhill, and is a departure point for day tours and a popular place to stay. There are walking trails in the central and western sections. *See also Dimboola. Mallee Dam:* offers fantastic birdwatching with bird hides provided; 20 km sw.

ⓘ Victoria St; (03) 5391 3086

Ocean Grove   Pop. 12 581

Map ref. 520 G10, 527 P6, 533 R8, 534 A7

Ocean Grove is a popular summer-holiday destination near the mouth of the Barwon River. The town's main street is at the top of a hill with excellent views of the pristine coastline along Bass Strait. The beaches here offer great surfing and safe swimming, with surf patrols operating during the summer months.

IN TOWN Ocean Grove Nature Reserve This reserve contains the only significant example of woodland on the Bellarine Peninsula, preserved virtually as it was prior to European settlement. There are a number of good walks in the park, which is known as a haven for birdlife. A bird

hide lets visitors look out for any number of the 130 different species that live here, including the eastern rosella and red-browed finch. Grubb Rd.

NEARBY Barwon Heads This is a pretty seaside town on the Barwon River made famous as the location for the television series *SeaChange*. There are several good restaurants in the area, including one right on the Barwon River that provides a scenic environment for fine dining. The Barwon Heads Golf Club is one of the top 3 public courses in the state. The Jirrahlinga Koala and Wildlife Reserve on Taits Rd lets visitors encounter the delightful, yet often elusive, koala in a natural environment. Barwon Heads is a short drive from Ocean Grove. 3 km s. *Lake Connewarre State Game Reserve:* with mangrove swamps and great walks, the reserve is home to a variety of wildlife, including wallabies; 7 km n. *Wallington:* on the Bellarine Hwy between Geelong and Ocean Grove, the town is home to A Maze'N Games, a timber maze with minigolf, picnic/barbecue facilities and a cafe, Koombahla Park Equestrian Centre, the Country Connection Adventure Park and Bellarine Adventure Golf. A strawberry fair is held in town in Nov. 8 km n.

ⓘ Geelong Visitor Information Centre, Stead Park, Princes Hwy, Corio; 1800 620 888 or (03) 5275 5797; www.greatoceanrd.org.au

Olinda   Pop. 949

Map ref. 519 G7, 521 M7, 524 B11, 534 E4

Olinda is in the centre of the Dandenong Ranges, a landscape of towering

mountain ash forests, lush fern gullies, waterfalls, English gardens and picnic spots. The ranges have been a retreat for Melburnians since the 1800s. Olinda and nearby Sassafras are known for their many galleries and cafes, particularly the numerous tearooms serving traditional Devonshire teas.

WHAT'S ON *Jazz Festival:* Feb. *Rhododendron Festival:* Aug–Nov.

NEARBY Dandenong Ranges National Park This park offers great walking tracks and picnic facilities. Visitors may be lucky enough to spot an elusive lyrebird, a species renowned for its ability to mimic sounds – from other bird calls to human voices and even chainsaws. Most walking tracks leave from picnic grounds, such as the Thousand Steps Track from Fern Tree Gully Picnic Ground (south-west via the Mount Dandenong Tourist Rd) and the walk to Sherbrooke Falls from the Sherbrooke Picnic Ground (via Sherbrooke Rd from the Mount Dandenong Tourist Rd). The park extends to the east and west of town.

William Ricketts Sanctuary William Ricketts was a well-known artist and conservationist whose intricate sculptures carved from wood focus on Aboriginal people and the complexities of Australia's native vegetation. Many sculptures are displayed in a lovely bushland setting on the scenic Mount Dandenong Tourist Rd. 3 km n. *National Rhododendron Gardens:* gardens begin just east of town and are something of a mecca for garden enthusiasts, with superb displays of rhododendrons and azaleas in season. *R. J. Hamer Arboretum:* good walking tracks through 100 ha of rare and exotic trees; Olinda–Monbulk Rd, shortly after turn-off to Rhododendron Gardens. *Cloudehill Gardens:* twilight concerts are held here in summer; south of R. J. Hamer Arboretum. *Mt Dandenong Lookout:* spectacular views over Melbourne; picnic/barbecue facilities; 3 km n. *Alfred Nicholas Gardens:* a quaint ornamental lake with the original boathouse and the George Tindale Memorial Garden, with flowering plants beneath mountain ash trees. The original Nicholas family home (built 1920s) is here. Sherbrooke; 4 km se. *Kawarra Australian Plant Garden:* an impressive collection of native plants; Kalorama; 4.5 km n. *Markets:* markets every weekend offer art, craft, plants and homemade goods. Nearby markets include Kallista Market, 6 km s, 1st Sat each month; Montrose Market, 8 km n, 3rd Sat of the month; Upper Ferntree Gully Market, 12 km se, every Sat and Sun. *Burrinja Gallery:* a memorial to artist Lin Onus, with Aboriginal and Oceanic sculptures and paintings; Upwey; 10 km sw. *Silvan:* prominent flower-growing region with many tulip farms. The famous Tesselaar's Tulip Farm hosts a popular festival each Sept–Oct with sales of flowers and bulbs,

and traditional Dutch music and food. Monbulk Rd; 15 km NE. *Silvan Reservoir:* an area to the north of this major Melbourne water supply has walking tracks and picnic/barbecue facilities; turn-off after Silvan. *Mont De Lancey:* wonderfully preserved house, built in 1882 and set in landscaped gardens, includes a museum and a chapel; Wandin North; 22 km NE via Mt Evelyn; open Wed–Sun and public holidays.
ⓘ Dandenong Ranges Information Centre, 1211 Burwood Hwy, Upper Ferntree Gully; (03) 9758 7522; www.dandenongrangestourism.asn.au

Omeo   Pop. 262

Map ref. 507 A12, 536 F8

Omeo is an Aboriginal word meaning mountains – appropriate for this picturesque town in the Victorian Alps. Today Omeo is a peaceful farming community, but it wasn't always so. During the gold rush, Omeo was an unruly frontier town, which early Australian novelist Rolf Boldrewood described as the roughest goldfield in Australia. The town was badly damaged by earthquakes in 1885 and 1892, and half-destroyed by the 1939 Black Friday bushfires. Despite such natural disasters, several distinctive old timber buildings remain.
IN TOWN A. M. Pearson Historical Park The park preserves a piece of Omeo's rich history in a peaceful, bushland setting. Buildings on display include the old courthouse, which now houses a museum, a log gaol, stables and a blacksmith's. Located on Day Ave (Great Alpine Rd). *Historic buildings:* many distinctive timber structures from the 19th century can be seen around town, including the CWA Hall and Petersens Gallery; Day Ave. *German Cuckoo Clock Shop:* traditional German clocks and artefacts; Day Ave.
WHAT'S ON *Picnic Races:* Mar. *Rodeo and Market:* Easter.
NEARBY Oriental Claims The Claims was a major goldmining area, with miners from all over the world. French-Canadians, Americans and Europeans all worked alongside Australians and Chinese. The word 'Oriental' in the mine's name refers to the fact that the mining company was Chinese-owned. There are a variety of walks around the site and visitors should look out for the wild orchids that grow here. High cliffs, left by the gold-sluicing process, offer impressive views across town, and signs throughout the site explain the history of the Claims. 1.5 km W on Great Alpine Rd.
Mt Hotham This popular downhill ski resort is suited to both budding and experienced skiers. Skiing areas range from the beginners' Big D Playground through to the more advanced slopes around Mary's Slide and the black diamond chutes of Heavenly Valley. For an introduction to the mountain, take

the free guided ski tour that leaves at 2pm each Mon and Sat from Hotham Central. In summer, the mountain is a popular hiking and mountain-bike-riding destination. 56 km W. *Livingstone Creek:* pleasant swimming hole adjacent to the Oriental Claims. *Mount Markey Winery:* Cassilis Rd, Cassilis; 15 km S. *Lake Omeo:* huge, scenic salt lake in an extinct volcano with abundant waterbirds; just beyond Benambra; 21 km NE. *Anglers Rest:* historic Blue Duck Inn, a good base for fishing; 29 km NW. *Taylors Crossing suspension bridge:* part of the scenic Australian Alps Walking Track; off Tablelands Rd; 44 km NE. *Scenic drives:* many self-guide driving tours include the Tambo River valley between Swifts Creek and Bruthen, 97 km S; to Benambra, then Corryong, 144 km NE; and from Omeo through Dinner Plain and on to Mt Hotham. Note that some drives cross state forests or alpine areas, so be alert for timber trucks and check conditions in winter. *Mitta Mitta and Cobungra rivers:* great trout fishing, waterskiing and whitewater rafting (only available in spring); contact visitor centre for details. *High Country tours:* explore the high plains around Omeo – on horseback, by 4WD or, for keen hikers, in challenging bushwalks; details from visitor centre.
ⓘ German Cuckoo Clock Shop, Day Ave (Great Alpine Rd); (03) 5159 1552; www.omeoregion.com.au

Orbost   Pop. 2086

Map ref. 537 J12

Situated on the banks of the legendary Snowy River, Orbost is on the Princes Highway and surrounded by spectacular coastal and mountain territory. For those who love arts and crafts, there are many shops in the area supplying and displaying local products.
IN TOWN *Information Centre:* display explains complex rainforest ecology; Lochiel St. *Old Pump House:* behind relocated 1872 slab hut; Forest Rd. *Historical Museum:* details local history with displays of artefacts; Forest Rd. *Croajingolong Mohair Farm:* sells garments, yarns, fabrics and leather goods; Forest Rd. *Snowy River Country Craft:* Forest Rd. *Lorna's Doll Display:* Forest Rd. *Netherbyre Gemstone and Art Galley:* cnr Browning and Carlyle sts.
WHAT'S ON *Australian Wood Design Exhibition:* Jan. *Craft Expo:* Nov.
NEARBY Errinundra National Park The park is one of the largest remaining stands of cool temperate rainforest in Victoria, and features giant eucalypt forests – take a stroll along the rainforest boardwalk for a closer look at these majestic, ancient trees. For keen hikers there are walking tracks, as well as camping and picnic facilities. Enjoy superb views from Ellery View, Ocean View Lookout and the peak of Mt Morris. In winter, snow and rain can make access difficult. Errinundra Rd, off Princes Hwy; 54 km NE.

Marlo: a popular fishing spot also known for its galleries and its Bush Races in Jan; 14 km S. *Cape Conran Coastal Park:* rugged coastal scenery and excellent walks. Turn south after Cabbage Tree Creek (26 km E) or take the coastal route from Marlo. *Cabbage Tree Palms Flora Reserve:* 27 km E. *Bemm River Scenic Reserve:* a 1 km signposted rainforest walk and picnic facilities; off Princes Hwy; 40 km E. *Snowy River National Park:* in the south of the park is Raymond Creek Falls. A 40 min return walk leads to the falls, with a further 1 hr walk leading to the Snowy River. 42 km N; 2WD access, check road conditions. McKillops Bridge, 148 km N via Deddick, is one of the most accessible parts of this park; *for more details see Buchan. Sydenham Inlet:* a good spot for bream fishing; 58 km E. *Tranquil Valley Tavern:* on the banks of the Delegate River near the NSW border; about 115 km NE. *Baldwin Spencer Trail:* a 262 km scenic drive following the route of this explorer, taking in old mining sites and Errinundra National Park; details from visitor centre.
ⓘ 13 Lochiel St; (03) 5154 2424; www.lakesandwilderness.com.au

Ouyen   Pop. 1156

Map ref. 510 E10, 544 H9

Ouyen was once little more than a station on the Melbourne–Mildura train route, but it has since grown to become an important service town. Ouyen is at the centre of the Mallee region, which was developed in the early 1900s – relatively late when compared with other regions of rural Victoria. This was mainly due to the difficulties in clearing the land as well as the harsh climate. The current success of agriculture in the region, in particular wheat-growing, is a testament to the hardiness of early farmers and settlers.
WHAT'S ON *Autumn Art Show:* April. *Great Australian Vanilla Slice Triumph:* Aug/Sept.
NEARBY Hattah–Kulkyne National Park This park protects an area of 48 000 ha that includes typical mallee country with both low scrub and open native pine woodlands. The freshwater Hattah Lakes are seasonally filled by creeks connected to the Murray River, which brings the area to life with plants and waterbirds. Activities within the park include bushwalking, canoeing, fishing and scenic drives. There are picnic and camping facilities at Mournpall and Lake Hattah. Off the Calder Hwy; 35 km N. *Speed:* Mallee Machinery Field Days: Aug; 39 km S.
ⓘ Mallee Tourism, Oke St; (03) 5092 1000; www.murrayoutback.org.au

Paynesville   Pop. 2850

Map ref. 535 Q5

Paynesville is a popular tourist resort close to the rural city of Bairnsdale, on the McMillan Straits. The town is

VICTORIA

Cape Woolamai, Phillip Island

set on the Gippsland Lakes and the beaches of the Tasman Sea, making it a favourite destination for fishing and waterskiing.

IN TOWN *St Peter-by-the-Lake Church:* built in 1961, this unique structure incorporates seafaring images in its design; The Esplanade. *Community Craft Centre:* displays and sells local arts and crafts; The Esplanade.

WHAT'S ON *Market:* at Gilsenan Reserve; 2nd Sun each month. *Jazz Festival:* Feb. *Marlay Point–Paynesville Overnight Yacht Race:* Mar.

NEARBY **Gippsland Lakes** This area incorporates The Lakes National Park, Gippsland Lakes Coastal Park, and the famous Ninety Mile Beach – an incredible stretch of scenic coastline offering great swimming beaches. Lake cruises, boat charters and organised scenic tours of the region are all available; contact the visitor centre for details.
Eagle Point: a small fishing community set by Lake King. The Mitchell River empties here, where it forms curious silt jetties that stretch out into the distance. The town hosts the annual Australian Powerboat Racing Championships at Easter. 2 km NW. *Raymond Island:* Koala Reserve, and Riviera Meadows, an animal farm that specialises in miniature breeds. The island is just east of Paynesville and can be accessed by a ferry that departs from the foreshore.
ⓘ Community Craft Centre, Esplanade; (03) 5156 7479; www.lakesand wilderness.com.au

Phillip Island   Pop. 7072

Map ref. 521 L13, 523 N12, 534 E9

Phillip Island is one of Australia's most popular holiday destinations, attracting over 3.5 million visitors each year. The fantastic wildlife attractions delight visitors, as do the coastal scenery and fabulous surf beaches. The first settlement was on Churchill Island, connected to the main island by a bridge. It was just a small shack, built by Lieutenant James Grant after his 1800 passage through Bass Strait. Farming was attempted in the mid-1800s and tracts of land were sold off in the 1860s, but it wasn't until the late 1800s that tourists discovered Phillip Island. Ferries brought passengers to the grand mansions of Cowes, and they would explore the island on horseback. The island has a long history of motor racing as well – the first race was held in 1928, and the International Motorcycle Grand Prix is still held each October.

EAST **Cowes** Situated on the north side, Cowes is the island's major town. The foreshore offers fantastic coastal walks and safe swimming beaches, and the jetty is a popular fishing spot. Seal-watching cruises to Seal Rocks also operate from the jetty and are the best way to see the fascinating fur seals close-up.
Koala Conservation Centre: view these lovely creatures in their natural habitat. An elevated boardwalk runs through the park. The centre also has an informative display giving interesting facts and

figures. Phillip Island Rd; 3 km s of Cowes. *Phillip Island Wildlife Park:* features native fauna, with visitors able to handfeed kangaroos and wallabies; 3 km s of Cowes. *Grand Prix Circuit:* the circuit is steeped in both old and recent history, which is detailed thoroughly in the visitor centre; Back Beach Rd; 6 km s of Cowes. *A Maze 'N Things:* family fun park featuring a large timber maze, optical-illusion rooms and 'maxi-golf'; Phillip Island Rd; 1 km SE of Five Ways. *Rhyll:* a small town on the eastern side of the island. The nearby Rhyll Inlet has wetlands of international significance, with the marshes and mangroves providing an important breeding ground for wading birds that migrate annually to breed here. There are various loop walks, as well as an excellent view from the Conservation Hill Observation Tower. *Cape Woolamai:* the beach here is renowned Australia-wide for its fierce and exciting surf (patrolled in season). From the beach there are a number of 2–4 hr loop walks, many to the southern end of the cape and passing the Pinnacles rock formations on the way. South of Cape Woolamai township. *Churchill Island:* a road bridge provides access to this protected parkland, which features a historic homestead, a walking track and abundant birdlife. 2 km NW of Newhaven. *Pelicans:* see these unusual birds up-close, with feeding time at 11.30am daily at the San Remo Pier (opposite the Fishing Co-op). *Wildlife Wonderland:* this place is easy to spot on the road in to Phillip Island; just look out for the giant earthworm. The centre includes an Earthworm Museum and Wombat World. 9 km E of San Remo.

WEST **Penguin Parade** The nightly penguin parade is the island's most popular attraction. During this world-famous event, little penguins emerge from the sea after a tiring fishing expedition and cross Summerland Beach to their little homes in the dunes. Tours run at sunset each night, and the penguins can be spotted from the boardwalks and viewing platforms. The site also has an interactive visitor centre with fascinating details about these adorable creatures. Note that no cameras are allowed beyond the visitor centre. Enquiries and bookings: (03) 5951 2800. 6 km SW of Ventnor.
The Nobbies and Seal Rocks A nature reserve on the rugged south-west tip of the island features a cliff-side boardwalk that provides views across the southern coast of the island to Western Port and beyond. See the fantastic natural landmark, The Nobbies, and further out see Seal Rocks, home to the country's largest colony of Australian fur seals. Walk around to the Blowhole to hear the thunderous noise of huge waves, or look out for the nesting sites of vast colonies of seagulls and short-tailed shearwaters that migrate to the island annually. The extensive boardwalks have informative displays explaining each

natural attraction. Ventnor Rd; 8 km sw of Ventnor.
Phillip Island Vineyard and Winery: offers tastings, sales and casual dining; Berrys Beach Rd; 4 km se of Ventnor.
WHAT'S ON *Market:* crafts and second-hand goods; each Sun; Settlement Rd, Cowes. *Farmers market:* 4th Sat each month; Churchill Island. *World Superbike Championships:* Grand Prix Circuit; Mar/April. *V8 Supercars:* Grand Prix Circuit; April. *Australian Motorcycle Grand Prix:* Grand Prix Circuit; Oct.
ⓘ 805 Phillip Island Rd, Newhaven; (03) 5956 7447 or 1300 366 422; www.visitphillipisland.com

Port Albert
Pop. 220

Map ref. 535 L10

Port Albert is a tiny town on the south-east coast. Looking at this peaceful village now, it's hard to believe that it was the first established port in Victoria, with ships from Europe and America once docking at its jetty. Ships from China arrived here during the gold rush bringing thousands of prospectors to the Gippsland goldfields. Today the sheltered waters of Port Albert are popular with anglers and boat-owners. Ninety Mile Beach begins north-east of town and is fantastic for fishing, surfing and swimming.
IN TOWN **Port Albert Hotel** This pretty old building has wide verandahs, and offers genuine country hospitality and a glimpse into the area's past. The hotel was first licensed in 1842, which makes it one of the oldest hotels in Victoria still operating. Wharf St.
Historic buildings: include original government offices and stores, and the Bank of Victoria, which now houses a maritime museum with photographs and relics from the town's past; Tarraville Rd. *Warren Curry Art:* a gallery featuring country-town streetscapes; Tarraville Rd.
WHAT'S ON *Fishing Contest:* Mar.
NEARBY **Nooramunga Marine and Coastal Park** Surrounding Port Albert and comprising the waters and sand islands offshore, this marine park is a fishing enthusiast's delight. Snapper, flathead and Australian salmon can be caught from the surf beaches or from a boat. The Aboriginal middens that dot the shorelines prove that fishing has been carried on here for many thousands of years. This park is an important reserve for migratory wading birds.
Christ Church: built in 1856, this was the first church to be established in Gippsland; at Tarraville; 5 km ne. *Beaches:* Manns, for swimming, 10 km ne; and Woodside, on Ninety Mile Beach, for good surfing, 34 km ne. Note that both beaches are patrolled during summer. *St Margaret Island:* a protected area featuring a wildlife sanctuary; 12 km e.
ⓘ Old Courthouse, 9 Rodgers St, Yarram; (03) 5182 6553

Port Campbell
Pop. 231

Map ref. 526 E10, 533 K11

This small seaside resort is supported by crayfishing and is in the centre of Port Campbell National Park on a spectacular stretch of coast on the Great Ocean Road. The Twelve Apostles, one of Victoria's most famous tourist attractions, are here and offer a truly breathtaking experience, especially at sunset.
IN TOWN *Historical Museum:* Lord St; open school holidays. *Loch Ard Shipwreck Museum:* relics from the *Loch Ard*, wrecked in 1878 at nearby Loch Ard Gorge; Lord St. *Fishing:* good from rocks and pier. Boat charters available.
WHAT'S ON *Market:* Lord St; each Sun in summer.
NEARBY **Port Campbell National Park** The park is a major attraction on the Great Ocean Rd, with magnificent rock formations jutting out into the ocean. Particularly impressive when viewed at dusk and dawn, the key coastal features are The Arch, 5 km w; London Bridge – the section connecting it to land has recently collapsed – 6 km w; Loch Ard Gorge, 7 km se; and the world-famous Twelve Apostles, which begin 12 km se of Port Campbell and stretch along the coast (Gibsons Steps give access to the beach here). There are walking tracks throughout the park, and shipwrecks in the area are popular with scuba divers. The Historic Shipwreck Trail, a self-guide drive between Moonlight Head and Port Fairy, marks 25 sites.
Mutton Bird Island: attracts short-tailed shearwaters, best viewed at dawn and dusk Sept–Apr; just off coast. *Glenample:* the first homestead in the area, with survivors from the *Loch Ard* recuperating there; Great Ocean Rd; 12 km e; check opening times. *Timboon:* a pretty town in the centre of a dairy district. Timboon Farmhouse Cheese offers tastings and sales of gourmet cheeses. A scenic drive goes from Port Campbell to the town. 19 km n. Pick your own berries in season at nearby Berry World. *Otway Deer and Wildlife Park:* 20 km e.
ⓘ 26 Morris St; 1300 137 255 or (03) 5598 6053; www.greatoceanrd.org.au

Port Fairy
Pop. 2520

Map ref. 532 G9

Port Fairy was once a centre for the whaling industry and one of the largest ports in Australia. Today many visitors are attracted to it for its charming old-world feel, its legacy of historic bluestone buildings and the small fleet of fishing boats that line the old wharf. But this town truly comes alive in summer and during March, when the Port Fairy Folk Festival is held. International folk and blues acts play, and tickets are best booked well in advance.

IN TOWN *History Centre:* displays relating to local history housed in the old courthouse; Gipps St. *Battery Hill:* old fort and signal station at the river mouth; end of Griffith St. *Port Fairy Wharf:* sales of fish and crayfish when in season. *Historic buildings:* many are National Trust-classified, including the splendid timber home of Captain Mills, Gipps St; Mott's Cottage, Sackville St; Caledonian Inn, Bank St; Seacombe House, Cox St; St John's Church of England, Regent St; and the Gazette Office, Sackville St.
WHAT'S ON *Port Fairy Folk Festival:* Mar. *Spring Music Festival:* Oct. *Moyneyana Festival:* family entertainment; Dec.
NEARBY **Griffiths Island** Connected to town by a causeway, this island is home to a large colony of short-tailed shearwaters. Each year they travel across the Pacific Ocean from North America to nest in the same burrows (Sept–April). Also on the island is a much-photographed lighthouse.
The Crags: rugged coastal rock formations; 12 km w. *Yambuk:* a small township centred around old inn with Yambuk Lake nearby, featuring a slide in the sand dunes; 17 km w. *Lady Julia Percy Island:* home to a fur seal colony; 22 km off coast; charters can be arranged from Port Fairy Wharf. *Codrington Wind Farm:* Victoria's first wind-power station; 27 km w. *Mahogany Walk to Warrnambool:* a 6–7 hr walk (one-way, return by bus) taking in a magnificent stretch of coastline; contact visitor centre for details. *Historic Shipwreck Trail:* between Port Fairy and Moonlight Head with 25 wreck sites signposted along the way.
ⓘ 22 Bank St; (03) 5568 2682; www.greatoceanrd.org.au

Portland
Pop. 9566

Map ref. 532 D9

Portland is the most westerly of Victoria's major coastal towns and the only deep-water port between Melbourne and Adelaide. It was also the first permanent settlement in Victoria, founded in 1834 by the Hentys. The township, which features many National Trust-classified buildings, overlooks Portland Bay. The Kerrup–Tjmara people, who once numbered in the thousands, were the original inhabitants of the district and referred to it as 'Pulumbete' meaning 'Little Lake' – a reference to the scenic lake now known as Fawthorp Lagoon.
IN TOWN **Portland Maritime Discovery Centre** The centre features a 13 m sperm whale skeleton, and the lifeboat used to rescue 19 survivors from the *Admella* shipwreck in 1859. Another wreck, the *Regia*, is displayed in 2 m of water. The centre shares the building with the information centre. Lee Breakwater Rd.
Botanical Gardens: established in 1857, with both native and exotic plant life. A restored 1850s bluestone worker's

cottage is within the grounds and open to the public. Cliff St. *Historical buildings:* more than 200 around town, many National Trust-classified. The best way to explore buildings such as the courthouse, Steam Packet Inn and Mac's Hotel is to take either a guided or a self-guide walk; contact visitor centre for details. *History House:* a historical museum and family research centre in the old town hall; Charles St. *Burswood:* a bluestone, regency-style mansion that was once the home of pioneer settler Edward Henty. The house is set amid 5 ha of gardens. B&B accommodation available. Cape Nelson Rd. *Fawthorp Lagoon:* prolific birdlife; Glenelg St. *Powerhouse Car Museum:* Percy St. *Watertower Lookout:* displays of WW II memorabilia on the way up the 133 steps to magnificent 360-degree views across Portland and the ocean, where whales and dolphins can sometimes be spotted; Percy St. Another good spot for whale-watching is Battery Hill. *Kingsley Winery:* tastings and sales; Bancroft St.

WHAT'S ON *Go Kart Street Grand Prix:* Feb. *Yachting Regatta:* Feb. *Three Bays Marathon:* Nov.

NEARBY Cape Bridgewater This cape is home to a 650-strong colony of Australian fur seals. A 2 hr return walk leads to a viewing platform, or you can take a 45 min boat ride that leads into the mouth of a cave to see them up close (bookings essential, (03) 5526 7247). Across the cape towards Discovery Bay are the Petrified Forest and the Blowholes – spectacular during high seas. 21 km sw. **Lower Glenelg National Park** The Glenelg River is a central feature of the park. It

has cut an impressive 50 m deep gorge through a vast slab of limestone. Keep an eye out for platypuses, water rats, moorhens and herons around the water's edge. Bushwalking, camping, fishing and canoeing are all popular, and Jones Lookout and the Bulley Ranges offer great views. Also in the park are the Princess Margaret Rose Caves on the north side of the river – you can drive there via Nelson or Dartmoor. Alternatively, boat tours operate from Nelson. The park begins 44 km nw.

Cape Nelson: here a lighthouse perches on top of tall cliffs; 11 km sw. *Narrawong State Forest:* a short walk leads to Whalers Point, where Aboriginal people once watched for whales; 18 km ne. *Discovery Bay Coastal Park:* Cape Bridgewater is included in this park, though the majority of it is remote and relatively untouched. The Great South West Walk (*see below*) offers the best chance to take in the park's scenery. Behind Cape Bridgewater are the Bridgewater Lakes (19 km w) – popular for waterskiing and fishing. A walking track leads from here to the beach. *Mount Richmond National Park:* a 'mountain' formed by an extinct volcano. The area has abundant spring wildflowers and native fauna, including the elusive potoroo; 25 km nw. *Heywood:* home to the Bower Birds Nest Museum and a food and wine festival in Feb; 28 km n. *Nelson:* a charming hamlet near the mouth of the Glenelg River. Good waterskiing in the area. 70 km nw. *Great South West Walk:* this epic 250 km walking trail takes in the full range of local scenery – the Glenelg River, Discovery and Bridgewater bays and Cape Nelson are some of the highlights. It is

possible to do just small sections of the walk. Contact visitor centre for maps and details.
🛈 Lee Breakwater Rd; 1800 035 567 or (03) 5523 2671; www.greatoceanrd.org.au

Pyramid Hill   Pop. 498

Map ref. 510 I13, 538 B4, 543 Q5

Pyramid Hill's namesake is an unusually shaped, 187-metre-high hill. The town, which is located in a wheat-growing district about 30 kilometres from the New South Wales border, was a source of inspiration to notable Australian author Katherine Susannah Pritchard, who based a character in her book *Child of the Hurricane* on a woman she met while staying in Pyramid Hill during World War I.

IN TOWN Pyramid Hill A climb to the top of this eerily symmetrical hill reveals views of the surrounding irrigation and wheat district. A 'Braille trail', which goes halfway up the hill, offers a commentary for the visually impaired. There are abundant wildflowers in spring. *Historical Museum:* features local story displays; McKay St; open Sun afternoons or by appt.

WHAT'S ON *Pioneer Machinery Display:* Oct. *Sidewalk Sale:* for local produce and fun; Nov. *Quarterhorse Show:* Nov.

NEARBY Terrick Terrick National Park The park is a large Murray pine forest reserve, with numerous granite outcrops, including Mitiamo Rock. There are a variety of good walking tracks, and the park is a key nesting area for the

Cape Nelson Lighthouse, near Portland

distinctive brolga. Access is via the Pyramid Hill–Kow Swamp Rd; 20 km SE. *Mt Hope:* named by explorer Major Mitchell, who 'hoped' he would be able to spot the sea from the mountain's peak. Now known for its wildflowers. 16 km NE. *Boort:* nearby lakes provide a habitat for swans, ibis, pelicans and other waterbirds, and a place for watersports, fishing and picnics; 40 km W.
ⓘ Newsagency, 12–14 Kelly St; (03) 5455 7036

Queenscliff   Pop. 3733

Map ref. 519 B12, 520 H10, 522 B5, 527 R6, 534 B7

Queenscliff is a charming seaside town on the Bellarine Peninsula. It began life as a resort for wealthy Victorians in the 1800s, as testified by lavish buildings such as the Queenscliff Hotel, with its ornate lattice work and plush interiors. The town's wide main street is lined with cafes and restaurants, plus an array of art galleries, and the nearby beaches become a playground for holiday-makers during summer. A ferry runs between Queenscliff and Sorrento, a resort town across Port Phillip.

IN TOWN Queenscliff Maritime Centre and Museum The centre explores the town's long association with ships and the sea through a collection of maritime memorabilia. It features a re-created fisherman's cottage, a diving-technology display and an array of navigational equipment. Weeroona Pde.
Marine Studies Centre This is a great family destination where visitors can learn all about the local marine life. It has a number of aquariums and touch-tanks. The centre also runs various tours, including boat cruises of Port Phillip and 'rock-pool rambles'. Adjacent to the Maritime Centre, Weeroona Pde.
Fort Queenscliff: built during the Crimean War, it includes the unique 'Black Lighthouse'. Tours of the fort run most days; contact visitor centre for further details. *Bellarine Peninsula Railway:* beautifully restored steam trains run between Queenscliff and Drysdale. There are many engines on display around the station. Symonds St; trains run Sun, public holidays, and other times during school holidays.
WHAT'S ON *Market:* with crafts and second-hand goods; Princes Park, Gellibrand St; last Sun each month Sept–May. *Queenscliff Music Festival:* major event attracting local and international music acts; Nov.
NEARBY Point Lonsdale This peaceful holiday town offers gorgeous beaches suitable for either surfing or swimming. A lookout from the cliff-top provides a great view of the treacherous entrance to Port Phillip known as 'The Rip'. A market is held here on the 2nd Sunday of each month. 6 km SW.

Lake Victoria: an important waterbird habitat; 7 km SW via Point Lonsdale. *Harold Holt Marine Reserve:* incorporates Mud Island and coastal reserves. Guided boat tours can be arranged from the Marine Studies Centre.
ⓘ 55 Hesse St; (03) 5258 4843; www.greatoceanrd.org.au

Robinvale   Pop. 2080

Map ref. 510 F8, 545 J6

Robinvale is set on the New South Wales border by a pretty stretch of the Murray River. The Robinswood Homestead, built in 1926, was home to the town's founder, Herbert Cuttle (you can find the homestead in River Road). Herbert's son, Robin, was killed during World War I, so he named both the homestead and the town in Robin's honour. As another form of remembrance, the town has a sister city in France, near where young Robin died.
IN TOWN *McWilliams Wines:* established in 1961 and specialising in a range of cream sherries made with local grapes; Moore St. *Rural Life Museum:* housed in the information centre, with locally grown almonds for sale; Bromley Rd; open by appt. *Murray River:* the beaches around Robinvale are popular for picnics and fishing, while in the river waterskiing and swimming are favourite summer pastimes.
WHAT'S ON *80 Ski Classic:* Mar. *Tennis Tournament:* Mar.
NEARBY *Euston Weir and Lock on Murray:* created as an irrigation water store, it features a 'fish ladder' that enables fish to jump over the weir. Picnic and barbecue facilities are provided. Pethard Rd, south-west edge of town. *Robinvale Organic and Bio-dynamic Wines:* tastings and sales of these distinctive, preservative-free wines. Also a children's playground. Sea Lake Rd; 5 km S. *Robinvale Indigenous Gardens:* learn about the local bush tucker; River Rd. *Hattah–Kulkyne National Park:* 66 km SW; *see Ouyen.*
ⓘ Kyndalyn Park Information Centre, Bromley Rd; (03) 5026 1388

Rochester   Pop. 2622

Map ref. 538 E6

On the Campaspe River, near Echuca, Rochester is the centre of a rich dairying and tomato-growing area. There are several lakes and waterways near town, making Rochester a popular destination for freshwater fishing.
IN TOWN The 'Oppy' Museum The museum details the history of Sir Hubert Opperman, affectionately known as Oppy, a champion cyclist who competed in the Tour de France. There is a collection of memorabilia related to Oppy's career as a cyclist, as well as artefacts from the town's past. The museum is in Moore St; opposite it is a statue of Oppy.
Heritage walk: take in the town's attractive old buildings; contact visitor centre for

details. *Campaspe River Walk:* a pleasant, signposted walk by the river.
NEARBY Kyabram Fauna Park This park, owned by the Kyabram community, is home to over 140 animal species – everything from wombats to waterfowl. It has been built from the ground up on a piece of degraded farmland, and is now heavily involved in breeding programs for endangered species such as the eastern barred bandicoot. Check out the walk-through aviary and Australia's first energy-efficient reptile house. 35 km NE. Opposite the park is The Stables, for pottery and crafts.
Random House Homestead: set in 4 ha of wonderfully landscaped gardens; Bridge Rd, eastern edge of town. *Campaspe Siphon:* an impressive engineering feat, where the Waranga–Western Main irrigation channel was redirected under the Campaspe River; 5 km N. *Fishing:* nearby channels, rivers and lakes are popular with anglers for redfin and carp. Lakes include Greens Lake and Lake Cooper (14 km SE), also popular for picnicking and watersports. *Elmore:* Here is the Campaspe Run Rural Discovery Centre, which explains Koorie and colonial history and heritage. Elmore Field Days are held each Oct. 17 km S.
ⓘ Council offices, 43 Mackay St; (03) 5484 4500; www.rochester.org.au

Rushworth   Pop. 1000

Map ref. 538 G7

Situated in central Victoria off the Goulburn Valley Highway, this delightful little town was once a goldmining settlement. The original site of the township was known as Nuggetty owing to the numerous gold nuggets found during the 19th century. Rushworth has retained much of its original character, with well-preserved early buildings lining the main street.
IN TOWN *Historic buildings:* many along High St are National Trust-classified, including the Church of England, the Band Rotunda, the former Imperial Hotel, the Glasgow Buildings and the Whistle Stop. Take the High St Heritage Walk to see these and others; map from visitor centre. *History Museum:* housed in the old mechanics institute with displays relating to the town's goldmining heritage; cnr High and Parker sts. *Growlers Hill Lookout Tower:* views of the town, Rushworth State Forest and the surrounding Goulburn Valley; Reed St.
NEARBY Rushworth State Forest The largest natural ironbark forest in the world, Rushworth State Forest is also renowned for the orchids and wildflowers that blossom here in spring. Picnics and bushwalks are popular activities in this attractive reserve where over 100 species of birds, along with echidnas and kangaroos, can be seen. Access via Whroo Rd; 3 km S.

Gehrig Estate, a winery near Rutherglen

Jones's Eucalyptus Distillery: eucalyptus oil is extracted from blue mallee gum; Parramatta Gully Rd, just south of town. *Waranga Basin:* an artificial diversion of the Goulburn weir constructed in 1916, now a haven for boating, fishing, swimming and watersports; 6 km NE. *Whroo Historic Reserve:* Balaclava Hill, an open-cut goldmine, along with camping and picnic facilities, the Whroo cemetery and an Aboriginal waterhole; 7 km S. *Murchison:* a small town picturesquely set on the Goulburn River. Town attractions include the Italian war memorial and chapel; Meteorite Park, the site of a meteorite fall in 1969; Longleat Winery; and Campbell's Bend Picnic Reserve. 21 km E. *Days Mill:* a flour mill with buildings dating from 1865; 39 km NE via Murchison. *Town ruins:* goldmining played a huge role in the development of this region, but not all towns survived the end of the gold rush. Ruins of Angustown, Bailieston and Graytown are all to the south of Rushworth.
ⓘ Council offices, 33 High St; (03) 5481 2200

Rutherglen   Pop. 1838

Map ref. 511 O13, 539 N4

Rutherglen is the centre of one of the most important winegrowing districts in Victoria, with a cluster of vineyards surrounding the town. Many of the local wineries are best known for their fortified wines. Rutherglen's main street features preserved late-19th-century architecture.

IN TOWN Rose of Sharon Museum
This is a goldmining museum based around the remnants of an old mine. Guided tours take visitors through a walk-in underground mine and explain the area's goldmining past. There are gold-panning exhibitions, and a collection of memorabilia and photographs housed in a replica miner's hut. The museum features an iris garden, a restaurant and barbecue facilities. Hopetoun Rd, on the outskirts of town. *Common School Museum:* local history displays and a re-creation of a Victorian-era schoolroom; behind Main St. *Walkabout Cellars:* sells a variety of local wines; Main St. *Historic tours:* the best way to explore the town's numerous old buildings is to take a self-guide walk, bike ride or drive, following maps provided at the visitor centre.
WHAT'S ON *Bush Market:* Main St; 4th Sun each month. *Tastes of Rutherglen:* celebration of the region's gourmet food and wine; Mar. *Easter in Rutherglen:* Easter. *Winery Walkabout:* June. *Country Fair:* June. *Wine Show:* Sept. *Tour de Muscat:* cycling race; Oct. *Campbell's Spring Picnic:* Oct/Nov.
NEARBY Wineries In Rutherglen, the most difficult task you'll face will be finding the time to visit all the fantastic wineries in the region. At many of them the appeal extends beyond cellar-door tastings and sales, such as at the All Saints Estate, 10 km NW, which features a National Trust-classified, castle-like

building and a fine restaurant. The All Saints Live concert is held here in January. In the grounds of the Bullers Calliope Vineyard, 6 km W, is a bird park, with over 100 native and exotic species. Gehrig Estate, 21 km E, is Victoria's oldest continuously operating vineyard. It displays historic farming implements and has a charming restaurant. *Great Northern Mine:* marked by mullock heaps associated with the first alluvial goldmine in the district. Historical details are provided on-site. Great Northern Rd, 5 km E. *Lake Moodemere:* found near the winery of the same name, the lake is popular for watersports and features ancient Aboriginal canoe trees by the shores; 8 km W. *Old customs house:* a relic from the time when a tax was payable on goods from NSW; 10 km NW.
ⓘ 57 Main St; 1800 622 871 or (02) 6032 9166; www.visitrutherglen.com.au

St Arnaud   Pop. 2398

Map ref. 543 L9

This is a former goldmining town surrounded by forests and scenic hill country. St Arnaud is a service centre for the district's farming community, yet retains a peaceful rural atmosphere. The main street is lined with well-preserved historic buildings, many of which feature impressive ornate lacework. Together, these buildings form a nationally recognised historic streetscape.
IN TOWN *Art Gallery:* impressive collection of works by local artists; Napier St. *Queen Mary Gardens:* great spot for a picnic; Napier St. *Old Post Office:* now a B&B and restaurant; Napier St. *Police lock-up:* built in 1862; Jennings St.
WHAT'S ON *Heritage Festival:* Nov.
NEARBY St Arnaud Range National Park
The park protects an oasis of dense box-ironbark forest and woodland surrounded by agricultural land. Over 270 different species of native flora have been recorded here and provide a glimpse of what the area would have looked like before the land-clearing that occurred during and after the gold rush. Within the park are the Teddington Reservoirs, popular for brown trout and redfin fishing. The rugged terrain throughout provides a great opportunity for keen bushwalkers or 4WD enthusiasts. Wedge-tailed eagles can be seen soaring above the steep, forested ranges. Sunraysia Hwy; 15 km S. *Great Grape Rd:* wine-themed circuit through Stawell and Ballarat; details from visitor centre.
ⓘ Old Post Office, 2 Napier St; (03) 5495 2313

Sale   Pop. 12 793

Map ref. 535 N6

Sale sits by the Thomson River near the La Trobe River junction, and is the main city in Gippsland. Although Sale is largely considered an industrial town, with the nearby Bass Strait oilfields providing a large part of the town's economy, it has a lot more to offer. There are many good cafes and restaurants, and a number of fine-art galleries and craft outlets. The lakes near Sale are home to the unique Australian black swan – the bird that has become a symbol for the town.

IN TOWN **Gippsland Regional Arts Gallery** The gallery was developed to promote the work of artists and craftspeople in central Gippsland. Works range from traditional landscapes to visual statements on environmental and cultural issues, and may be in any medium from painting and photography to film and video. Foster St. *Lake Guthridge:* a great recreation reserve where on a walk around the shoreline pelicans and black swans can be seen. There is an adventure playground provided for children, a series of parks, tennis courts, and a swimming pool. Foster St. *Historical Museum:* local history memorabilia; Foster St. *Ramahyuck Aboriginal Corporation:* offers local arts and crafts and is part of the Bataluk Cultural Trail, which takes in sites of Aboriginal significance in the region; Foster St. *Historical buildings:* include Our Lady of Sion Convent and the Criterion Hotel, which has beautiful lacework verandas; both in York St. *RAAF base:* home of the famous Roulettes aerobatic team; Raglan St. *Sale Common and State Game Refuge:* protected wetland area with a boardwalk; south-east edge of town.
WHAT'S ON *Bush Races:* bush horserace carnival; Jan. *Sale Cup:* Feb.
NEARBY **Holey Plains State Park** The open eucalypt forests in this park are home to abundant wildlife, while swamps provide a habitat for many frog species. There is a good swimming lake, and a series of fascinating fossils can be seen nearby in a limestone quarry wall. Bushwalking, picnicking and camping are all popular activities, particularly around Harriers Swamp. Access from Princes Hwy; 14 km sw.
Fishing: good fishing for trout in the Avon River near Marlay Point and also in the Macalister, Thomson and La Trobe rivers, especially at Swing Bridge, 5 km s. *Marlay Point:* on the shores of Lake Wellington with boat-launching facilities provided. The yacht club here sponsors an overnight yacht race to Paynesville each Mar. 25 km e. *Seaspray:* a popular holiday spot on Ninety Mile Beach, offers excellent surfing and fishing; 32 km s. *Golden and Paradise beaches:* two more townships on Ninety Mile Beach with great surfing and fishing; 35 km se. *Loch Sport:* set on Gippsland Lakes and popular for camping and fishing. *For details on Gippsland Lakes see Lakes Entrance and Paynesville.* 65 km se. *Howitt Bike Trail:* 13-day round trip beginning and ending in Sale; details from visitor centre. *Bataluk*

Cultural Trail: takes in sites of indigenous significance from Sale to Cann River; brochure from the visitor centre.
ⓘ Central Gippsland Information Centre, Princes Hwy; (03) 5144 1108; www.gippslandinfo.com.au

Seymour   Pop. 6422

Map ref. 538 G10

Seymour is a commercial, industrial and agricultural town on the Goulburn River. The area was recommended for a military base by Lord Kitchener during his visit in 1909. Nearby Puckapunyal became an important training place for troops during World War II, and remains a major army base today.

IN TOWN *Royal Hotel:* featured in Russell Drysdale's famous 1941 painting *Moody's Pub;* Emily St. *Old Courthouse:* built in 1864, it now houses local art; Emily St. *Fine Art Gallery:* in the old post office; Emily St. *Goulburn River:* a walking track goes by the river and the Old Goulburn Bridge has been preserved as a historic relic. *Goulburn Park:* for picnics and swimming; cnr Progress and Guild sts. *Seymour Railway Heritage Centre:* restored steam engines and carriages; Railway Pl; open by appt.
WHAT'S ON *Mobby's Market:* Wimble St; every 2nd Sun. *Alternative Farming Expo:* Feb. *Rafting Festival:* Mar. *Seymour Cup:* Oct.
NEARBY *Wineries:* several in the area, including Somerset Crossing Vineyards, 2 km s; Hankin's Wines, Northwood Rd, 5 km nw; and Hayward's Winery, 12 km se. *Historic Railway Station:* in the scenic Trawool Valley; 5 km se. *Mangalore:* hosts the National Air Show each Easter Sunday; 5 km n. *Army Tank Museum:* Puckapunyal army base; 10 km w.
ⓘ Old Courthouse, Emily St; (03) 5799 0233

Shepparton   Pop. 35 754

Map ref. 538 I6

Shepparton has recently become a popular destination for conferences and sporting events, and so has plenty of modern accommodation and good restaurants in town. Indeed, Shepparton is a thriving city and is considered the 'capital' of the Goulburn Valley. It is home to many orchards and market gardens irrigated by the Goulburn Irrigation Scheme.
IN TOWN *Art Gallery:* features Australian paintings and ceramics; Welsford St. *Aboriginal Keeping Place:* displays and dioramas on local Aboriginal culture; Parkside Dr; check opening times. *Historical Museum:* in the Historical Precinct; High St; open even-dated Sun afternoons. *Emerald Bank Heritage Farm:* displays of 1930s farming methods; Goulburn Valley Hwy. *Victoria Park Lake:* scenic picnic spot; Tom Collins Dr. *Reedy Swamp Walk:* prolific birdlife; at the end of Wanganui Rd.
WHAT'S ON *Trash and treasure market:*

Melbourne Rd; each Sun. *Craft market:* in Queens Gardens, Wyndham St; 3rd Sun each month. *International Dairy Week:* Jan. *Bush Market Day:* Feb. *Shepparton Fest:* major local festival with family entertainment; Mar. *Spring Car Nationals:* car competitions; Nov.
NEARBY **Tallarook State Forest** Tallarook is a popular destination for bushwalking, camping, rockclimbing and horseriding. The key features are Mt Hickey, the highest point in the park and the location of a fire-lookout tower, and Falls Creek Reservoir, a scenic picnic spot. Warragul Rocks offers great views over the Goulburn River. 5 km sw.
Ardmona KidsTown: a fun tourist attraction with a maze, flying fox, enormous playground and miniature railway, and camel rides on the weekends; Midland Hwy; 3 km w. *Mooroopna:* a small town in the fruit-growing district. It hosts the popular Fruit Salad Day in Feb. 5 km w. *Kialla:* Ross Patterson Gallery, with displays and sales of local artwork. Also here is Belstack Strawberry Farm, where you can pick your own berries. Goulburn Valley Hwy; 9 km s. *Tatura:* a museum with displays on local WW II internment camps. Taste of Tatura is held each Mar. 17 km sw. *Wunghnu:* (pronounced 'one ewe') the town is centred around the well-known Institute Tavern in the restored mechanics institute building. A tractor-pull festival is held each Easter. 32 km n.
ⓘ 534 Wyndham St; 1800 808 839 or (03) 5831 4400

Sorrento   Pop. 1328

Map ref. 519 B13, 520 I11, 522 D7, 527 R7, 534 B8

Just inside Port Phillip Heads on the Mornington Peninsula, in 1803 Sorrento was the site of Victoria's first European settlement. The town is close to historic Point Nepean and major surf and bayside beaches. Its population swells significantly over summer as visitors flock to soak up the holiday-resort atmosphere. A ferry links Sorrento to Queenscliff on the Bellarine Peninsula.
IN TOWN *Collins Settlement Historic Site:* marks the state's first European settlement and includes early graves; on Sullivan Bay. *Historic buildings:* include Sorrento Hotel, Hotham Rd; Continental Hotel, Ocean Beach Rd; and Koonya Hotel, The Esplanade. All are fine examples of early Victorian architecture. The visitor centre can give details of self-guide historical walks. *Nepean Historical Society Museum and Heritage Gallery:* a collection of local artefacts and memorabilia in the National Trust-classified mechanics institute. Adjacent is Watt's Cottage and the Pioneer Memorial Garden. Melbourne Rd. *Dolphin and seal cruises:* depart from the pier; not in winter months.
WHAT'S ON *Craft market:* at primary school, cnr Kerferd and Coppin rds; last

VICTORIA

Sat each month. *RACV Vintage Car Rally:* Jan. *Street Festival:* Mar.

NEARBY Mornington Peninsula National Park The park incorporates Sorrento, Rye and Portsea back beaches and stretches south-east to Cape Schanck and beyond (*see* Flinders). Walks, picnics and swimming are the main attractions, but there is also excellent sightseeing to visit landmarks such as the unique rock formation of London Bridge, at Portsea. The rugged coastline offers good surfing. Other attractions include Point Nepean and historic Fort Nepean, which can be accessed by a daily transport service departing from Portsea. There is a former Quarantine Station on Point Nepean with tours that include a visit to the Army Health Services Museum. Tours run on Sundays and public holidays.
Portsea: an opulent holiday town with good, safe swimming beaches. It hosts the Portsea Swim Classic each Jan. 4 km NW. *Popes Eye Marine Reserve:* an artificially created horseshoe-shaped island and reef, now popular for diving. Gannets nest here. Cruises available; ask at visitor centre. 5 km offshore at Portsea. *Rye:* a beachside holiday spot with horseriding trips on offer and the annual Beach Sand Sculpting Championship each Feb; 8 km E. *Rosebud:* a bayside resort town with gorgeous, safe swimming beaches. Summer fishing trips depart from Rosebud pier. A film festival is held each Nov. 15 km E. *McCrae Homestead:* National Trust drop-slab property built in 1844, one of the peninsula's earliest buildings; McCrae, 17 km E; open afternoons.
ℹ️ Mornington Peninsula Visitor Information Centre, Point Nepean Rd, Dromana; 1800 804 009 or (03) 5987 30 78

Stawell   Pop. 6133

Map ref. 530 A5, 543 J11

Pastoral runs were established in the Stawell region in the 1840s, but it was the discovery of gold in 1853 by a shepherd at nearby Pleasant Creek that was the catalyst for creating a town. With the interval of a century or so, Stawell is again a goldmining centre with Victoria's largest mine. But all gold aside, Stawell is actually better known as the home of the Stawell Gift, Australia's richest footrace.

IN TOWN Stawell Gift Hall of Fame Museum In 1878 the Stawell Athletic Club was formed by local farmers and businessmen who were keen to have a sports day each Easter. The club put up the prize-pool of £110, and the race was on. The annual Stawell Gift has run almost continuously since and is now one of the most prestigious races in the world. Visit the museum to discover the glory and heartbreak of the race since its inception. Main St; open 9am–11am Mon–Fri. Or visit nearby Central Park where the race has been held since 1898.

Big Hill: local landmark and former goldmining site. The Pioneers Lookout at the summit indicates positions of famous mines. *Casper's Mini World:* miniature tourist park with working models of famous world attractions such as the Eiffel Tower and including dioramas and commentaries; London Rd. *Fraser Park:* displays of mining equipment; Main St. *Pleasant Creek Court House Museum:* local history memorabilia; Western Hwy. *Stawell Ironbark Forest:* spring wildflowers, including rare orchids; northern outskirts of town, off Newington Rd.
WHAT'S ON *Market:* Sloane St; 1st Sun each month. *Stawell Easter Gift:* Easter.
NEARBY Bunjil's Shelter This is Victoria's most important Aboriginal rock-art site. It depicts the creator figure, Bunjil, sitting inside a small alcove with his two dingoes. Bunjil created the geographical features of the land, and then created people, before disappearing into the sky to look down on the earth as a star. The site is thought to have been used for ceremonies by the local Djab Wurrung and Jardwadjali people. Off Pomonal Rd; 11 km s.
The Sisters Rocks: huge granite tors; beside Western Hwy; 3 km SE. *Overdale Station:* guided tours by appt; Landsborough Rd; 10 km E. *Lakes:* include Lake Lonsdale for all watersports, 12 km NW; and Lake Fyans for sailing, 17 km SW. *Great Western:* a picturesque wine village with attractions including The Diggings pottery; Seppelt Great Western Winery, est. 1865, featuring National Trust–classified underground tunnels of cellars; and the Champagne Picnic Races in Jan. 16 km SE. *Tottington Woolshed:* rare example of a 19th-century woolshed; road to St Arnaud; 55 km NE. *Great Grape Rd:* circuit through Ballarat and St Arnaud, stopping at wineries; details from visitor centre.
ℹ️ Stawell and Grampians Visitor Information Centre, 50–52 Western Hwy; 1800 330 080 or (03) 5358 2314

Swan Hill   Pop. 9738

Map ref. 510 H11, 545 N11

In 1836 explorer Thomas Mitchell named this spot Swan Hill because of the black swans that kept him awake all night. The town's swans remain, but there are many other attractions in this pleasant city on the Murray Valley Highway.

IN TOWN Swan Hill Pioneer Settlement This museum, in the vein of Ballarat's Sovereign Hill, re-creates the Murray and Mallee regions from the 1830s to the 1930s. Wander through the street lined with barber shops and chemists, and take a ride on the PS *Pyap* or a horse-drawn cart. There is also the Sound and Light Tour; bookings required. End of Gray St on Little Murray River.
Regional Gallery of Contemporary Art: an impressive permanent collection plus touring exhibitions; opposite the Pioneer Settlement.

WHAT'S ON *Market:* Curlewis St; 3rd Sun each month. *Redgum Festival:* Mar. *Racing Cup Carnival:* June. *Italian Festival:* July.
NEARBY Swan Hill Wine Region The region, which starts around Tresco to the south-east and ends around Piangil to the north-west, takes advantage of the Murray River and the Mediterranean-style climate. The first vines were planted here in 1930, but the proliferation of vineyards really began when Sicilian immigrants arrived on the Murray after WW II. Today cellar doors offer tastings and sales of predominantly shiraz, colombard and chardonnay varieties. Winery map available from the visitor centre.
Lake Boga The town has an interesting history as an RAAF flying-boat repair depot during WW II. The depot serviced over 400 flying boats, one of which can be seen at the Flying Boat Museum. The underground museum is in the original communications bunker in Willakool Dr. Lake Boga the water mass is popular for watersports, fishing and camping, and is home to a variety of bird species that can be seen on the various walks. A yachting regatta is held here each Easter. 17 km SE. *Murray Downs Homestead:* historic sheep, cattle and irrigation property with daily cruises (from private wharf) on MV *Kookaburra*; Moulamein Rd, just over bridge into NSW; 2 km NE; check opening times. *Lakeside Nursery and Gardens:* over 300 varieties of roses; 10 km NW. *Tyntyndyer Homestead:* built in 1846; Murray Valley Hwy; 20 km NW; open public holidays or by appt, (03) 5037 6506. *Nyah:* good market with local produce; 2nd Sat each month; 27 km NW. *Tooleybuc:* situated in NSW, it has a tranquil riverside atmosphere and good fishing, picnicking and riverside walks. The Bridgekeepers Cottage has sales and displays of dolls and crafts. 46 km N.
ℹ️ 306 Campbell St; 1800 625 373 or (03) 5032 3033

Tallangatta   Pop. 920

Map ref. 536 D2, 539 Q5

When the old town of Tallangatta was going to be submerged in 1956 after construction of the Hume Weir, the residents simply moved the entire township eight kilometres west. Tallangatta now has an attractive lakeside location and sits directly north of Victoria's beautiful Alpine region.

IN TOWN *The Hub:* local art and craft, and Lord's Hut, the only remaining slab hut in the district; Towong St.

WHAT'S ON *Dairy Festival:* April. *Hairy Lemon Festival:* celebrates local lemon harvest; May. *Fifties Festival:* Oct. *Garage Sale Day:* Oct.

NEARBY Lake Hume Tallangatta is on the shores of this enormous and attractive lake, formed when the then largest weir in the Southern Hemisphere

A lazy day's fishing off the Portsea Pier, near Sorrento

was constructed. It is now a picturesque spot for swimming, waterskiing, windsurfing and fishing. The foreshore reserves are perfect for barbecues. *Traron Alpacas:* alpacas and other animals, plus sales of yarns and garments. Also ornamental Chinese Paulownia trees. Bullioh; 15 km E. *Gold-panning tour:* leads to Granya; 28 km NE; ask at visitor centre for details. *Eskdale:* craft shops, and trout-fishing in the Mitta Mitta River; 33 km S. *Lake Dartmouth:* great for trout fishing and boating; 58 km SE. *Mitta Mitta:* remnants of a large open-cut goldmine. Also a gallery, Butcher's Hook Antiques and Baratralia Emu Farm. 60 km S. *Australian Alps Walking Track:* passes over Mt Wills; 108 km S via Mitta Mitta. *Scenic drives:* to Cravensville, to Mitta Mitta along Omeo Hwy and to Tawonga and Mount Beauty.
ⓘ The Hub, 35–37 Towong St; (02 6071 2611

Terang
Pop. 1856

Map ref. 526 D6, 533 K8

Terang is in a fertile dairy-farming district. It is a well-laid-out town with grand avenues of deciduous trees, and is known throughout the state for its horseracing carnivals.

IN TOWN *Cottage Crafts Shop:* in the old courthouse on High St. *District Historical Museum:* old railway station and memorabilia; Princes Hwy. *Lions Walking Track:* 4.8 km, beside dry lake beds and majestic old trees; begins behind Civic Centre on High St. *Historic buildings:* many examples of early 20th-century commercial architecture. A Gothic-style Presbyterian church is in High St.
WHAT'S ON *New Year's Day Family Picnic:* Jan. *Australian Stockhorse Weekend:* Jan.
NEARBY *Demo Dairy:* demonstrates dairy-farming practices; Princes Hwy, 3 km W; open first Mon each month. *Lake Keilambete:* 2.5 times saltier than

the sea and reputed to have therapeutic properties; 4 km NW. *Model Barn Australia:* collection of model cars, boats and planes; Robertson Rd, 5 km E; open by appt. *Noorat:* birthplace of Alan Marshall, author of *I Can Jump Puddles*. The Alan Marshall Walking Track here involves a gentle climb to the summit of Mt Noorat, an extinct volcano, with excellent views of the crater, the surrounding district and the Grampians. 6 km N. *Mortlake:* holds a Buskers Festival in Feb; 22 km N.
ⓘ Clarke Saddlery, 105 High St; (03) 5592 1164

Torquay
Pop. 7943

Map ref. 520 F11, 527 O7, 533 Q9

Torquay was one of the first seaside resort towns on Victoria's coast, and remains one of the most popular today. It was named in honour of the famous English resort town, but its heritage is very different. Not only does Torquay and its coast have some of the best surf beaches in the world, it was also the birthplace of world-leaders in surfboards, wetsuits and other apparel, including Rip Curl and Billabong, founded here in the 1960s and 1970s.

IN TOWN Surf City Plaza Once a run of old surfie stores, this modern plaza now houses some of the biggest names in surfing retail alongside smaller outlets. The complex also boasts the world's biggest surfing museum, Surfworld. See how board technology has developed over the last century, find out exactly what makes a good wave, and learn about the history of surfing at Bells Beach. A theatre also screens classic 1960s and 1970s surf flicks and the latest surf videos. Beach Rd.
Craft Cottage: locally produced arts and crafts; Anderson St. *Fishermans Beach:* good spot for fishing, with a sheltered swimming beach and a large sundial on the foreshore. *Tiger Moth World:* theme

park based around the 1930s Tiger Moth biplane. Joy-flights available. Blackgate Rd. *Surf schools:* programs available to suit all abilities, with many courses run during summer school holidays; for further details, ask at visitor centre.
WHAT'S ON *Cowrie Community Market:* 3rd Sun each month on foreshore. *Danger 1000 Ocean Swim:* Jan. *Surf for Life Surfing Contest:* Jan. *Strapper Junior Pro:* Feb. *Hightide Festival:* fireworks display; Dec.
NEARBY The Surf Coast It's no wonder the coast that runs from Torquay through to Eastern View (past Anglesea) has dubbed itself the Surf Coast. Submerged reefs cause huge waves that are a surfer's paradise. Most famous is Bells Beach, around 5 km SW of Torquay. The clay cliffs provide a natural amphitheatre for one of the best surf beaches in the world. It is also home to the longest running surf competition, the Rip Curl Pro, which started in 1973 and still attracts the top competitors each Easter. Other good surf beaches include Jan Juc, Anglesea and Fairhaven. To see the coast on foot, take the 30 km Surf Coast Walk, starting at Torquay and travelling south to Moggs Creek.
Bellbrae: this pretty little town off the Great Ocean Rd has pottery studios and a museum featuring early-Australian horse-drawn carriages; 5 km W. *Bicycle track:* goes along Surfcoast Hwy from Grovedale to Anglesea.
ⓘ Surfworld Australia, Surf City Plaza, cnr Surfcoast Hwy and Beach Rd; (03) 5261 4219; www.greatoceanrd.org.au

Traralgon
Pop. 19 569

Map ref. 535 K7

Traralgon is one of the La Trobe Valley's main cities. It is primarily a service centre for neighbouring agricultural communities, yet also retains a certain village atmosphere with historic buildings in its wide streets and attractive public gardens.

IN TOWN *Historic buildings:* include the old post office and courthouse; cnr Franklin and Kay sts. *Victory Park:* a great spot for picnics. Also here is a band rotunda and miniature railway. Princes Hwy.
WHAT'S ON *International Junior Tennis Championships:* Jan. *Traralgon Cup:* Nov.
NEARBY *Walhalla Mountain Rivers Trail:* this scenic drive (Tourist Route 91) winds through pretty hills to the north of town. *Loy Yang power station:* tours available; 5 km S. *Toongabbie:* a small town that hosts Festival of Roses each Nov; 19 km NE. *Hazelwood Cooling Pond:* year-round warm water make this a popular swimming spot; outskirts of Churchill; 20 km SW.
ⓘ Latrobe Visitor Information Centre, The Old Church, Princes Hwy; 1800 621 409 or (03) 5174 3199; www.latrobe.vic.gov.au

Walhalla
Pop. 15

Map ref. 535 K5

This tiny goldmining town is tucked away in dense mountain country in Gippsland – in a steep, narrow valley with sides so sheer that some cemetery graves were dug lengthways into the hillside. The town has a tiny population and is a relic from a long-gone era – it was not even connected to electricity until 1998.

IN TOWN Long Tunnel Gold Mine
This was one of the most prosperous goldmines in the state during the 19th century with over 13 tons of gold extracted here. Guided tours take visitors through sites such as Cohen's reef and the original machinery chamber 150 m below the ground. Main St; tours operate daily at 1.30pm.
Historic buildings and goldmining remains: include the old post office, bakery, and Windsor House, now a B&B. *Walks:* excellent walks in the town area, including one to a cricket ground on top of a 200 m hill. Another walk leads to a historic cemetery with graves of early miners. Details from visitor centre. *Old Fire Station:* with hand-operated fire engines and fire-fighting memorabilia; open weekends and public holidays. *Museum and Corner Store:* local history displays plus goldmining artefacts; Main St. *Walhalla Goldfields Railway:* wonderfully restored old steam engine; departs from Thomson Station on Wed, Sat, Sun and public holidays. *Gold panning:* try your luck along pretty Stringers Creek, which runs through town.

NEARBY *Deloraine Gardens:* terraced gardens; just north of town. *Thomson River:* excellent fishing and canoeing; 4 km s. *Rawson:* a town built to accommodate those who helped construct the nearby Thomson Dam. Mountain Trail Rides are available. 8 km sw. *Erica:* visit this small timber town to see a timber-industry display at the Erica Hotel. The King of the Mountain Woodchop is held in town each Jan. 12 km sw. *Baw Baw National Park:* park areas accessible from Walhalla include the Aberfeldy River picnic and camping area; 12 km n. *See Moe. Moondarra State Park:* great for walks and picnics. Moondarra Reservoir is nearby. 30 km s. *4WD tours:* to gold-era 'suburbs' such as Coopers Creek and Erica. Tours can be organised through Mountain Top Experience, (03) 5134 6876. *Australian Alps Walking Track:* starts at Walhalla and goes for an incredible 655 km. It can be done in sections; details from visitor centre.
ⓘ Latrobe Visitor Information Centre, The Old Church, Princes Hwy, Traralgon; 1800 621 409 or (03) 5174 3199; www.phillipislandgippsland.com.au

Wangaratta
Pop. 16 310

Map ref. 539 M6

Wangaratta lies in a rich agricultural district in north-eastern Victoria that produces a diverse range of crops from kiwifruit, wine grapes and walnuts to wheat, hops and tobacco. The town's cemetery, in Tone Road, has the grave of infamous bushranger Daniel 'Mad Dog' Morgan. His headless body was buried here – his head was sent to Melbourne for examination.

IN TOWN *Wangaratta Exhibitions Gallery:* changing exhibitions by national and regional artists; Ovens St. *Brucks Textile Factory:* a factory outlet for Sheridan sheets; Sicily Ave. *Australian Country Spinners:* an outlet for local wool products; Textile Ave.
WHAT'S ON *Paddys Market:* council carpark, Ovens St; each Sun. *Wangaratta Stitched Up Festival:* textile displays; June/July. *Festival of Jazz:* well-known jazz festival; Nov.
NEARBY Warby Range State Park The steep ranges of the 'Warbys', as they are known locally, provide excellent viewing points, especially from Ryan's Lookout. Other lookouts include the Pangarang Lookout, near Pine Gully Picnic Area, and Mt Glenrowan Lookout, the highest point of the Warbys at 513 m. There are well-marked tracks for bushwalkers and a variety of pleasant picnic spots amid open forests and woodlands, with wildflowers blossoming during the warmer months. 12 km w.
Eldorado Eldorado is a fascinating old goldmining township named after the mythical city of gold. The main relic of the gold era is a huge dredge, the largest in the Southern Hemisphere, which was built in 1936. There is a walking track with information boards around the lake where the dredge now sits. The Eldorado Museum provides details of the town's mining past, alongside WW II relics and a gemstone collection. There are several potteries in the region with displays and sales. 20 km NE.
Reids Creek: popular with anglers, gem fossickers and gold panners; near Beechworth; 28 km E. *Wombi Toys:* old-fashioned, handmade toys for sale; Whorouly; 25 km SE. *Newton's Prickle Berry Farm:* pick your own blackberries and buy organic berry jams; Whitfield; 45 km S. *Scenic drives:* one goes for 307 km along the Great Alpine Rd through the Alps to Bairnsdale. The road south leads through the beautiful King Valley and to Paradise Falls. A network of minor roads allows you to fully explore the area, including a number of tiny, unspoiled townships such as Whitfield, Cheshunt and Carboor.
ⓘ Old Library, Murphy St; 1800 801 065 or (03) 5721 5711; www.wangaratta.vic.gov.au

Warburton
Pop. 2677

Map ref. 521 O6, 524 H9, 534 G3

Warburton was established when gold was discovered in the 1880s, but its picturesque location and proximity to Melbourne meant it quickly became a popular tourist town, with many guesthouses built over the years. It lies in the foothills of the Great Dividing Range, and the Yarra River flows through town. Its tree-lined banks provide great spots for picnics and walks. Look closely at the river and you may spot an elusive

Scenery in the Yarra Ranges, north of Warburton

platypus. There are many fine cafes and antique and craft shops in town.
IN TOWN *Information Centre:* local history display and an old-style, operating waterwheel, 6 m in diameter. A wood-fired bakery is adjacent to the centre. Warburton Hwy. *River Walk:* 9 km return walk, following a pretty stretch of the Yarra River; starts at Signs Bridge on Warburton Hwy. *Upper Yarra Arts Centre:* cinema with regular screenings and a variety of live performances held during the year; Warburton Hwy. *Warburton Golf Course:* with great views across the river valley; Dammans Rd.
WHAT'S ON *Upper Yarra Draughthorse Festival:* Jan. *Film Festival:* Upper Yarra Arts Centre: June. *Winterfest:* wood festival; July. *Strawberry Festival:* Nov.
NEARBY Yarra Ranges National Park
Here, tall mountain ash trees give way to pockets of cool temperate rainforest. Mt Donna Buang, a popular daytrip destination – especially during winter, when it is often snow-covered – is 17 km NW of Warburton. The recently built Rainforest Gallery on the southern slopes of the mountain features a treetop viewing platform and walkway. Night walk tours here reveal some of Victoria's unique nocturnal creatures. Acheron Way is a scenic 37 km drive north through the park to Marysville. Along the way are views of Mt Victoria and Ben Cairn. Drive starts 1 km E of town. *Tommy Finn's Trout Farm:* catch your own or purchase some of the farm's smoked fish products; 2 km W. *Yarra Junction Historical Museum:* local history displays; Warburton Hwy; 10 km W. *Upper Yarra Reservoir:* picnic and camping facilities; 23 km NE. *Walk into History:* takes in the goldmining and timber region from Warburton East to Powelltown (25 km S); details from visitor centre. *Ada Tree:* a giant mountain ash over 300 years old; access from Powelltown. *Yellingbo State Fauna Reserve:* good for nature spotting. Home to the helmeted honeyeater, a state emblem. 25 km SW. *Vineyards:* several in the region, many with tastings and sales. They include the Yarra Burn Winery, the Five Oaks Vineyard and the Brahams Creek Winery. *Rail trails:* former railway tracks now used for walking, bike riding or horseriding; details from visitor centre. ⓘ Warburton Hwy; (03) 5966 5996; www.tourism.warburton-ranges.net.au

Warracknabeal   Pop. 2479
Map ref. 542 H6

The town's Aboriginal name means 'the place of the big red gums shading the watercourse', a name that is both beautifully descriptive and accurate, especially for the part of town around Yarriambiack Creek. Warracknabeal is a major service town at the centre of a wheat-growing district.
IN TOWN *Historical Centre:* includes a pharmaceutical collection, clocks, and

antique furnishings of child's nursery; Scott St; open afternoons. *Black Arrow Tour:* a self-guide drive tour of historic buildings. *Walks:* including the Yarriambiack Creek Walk; details from visitor centre. *National Trust-classified buildings:* include the post office, the Warracknabeal Hotel and the original log-built town lock-up. *Lions Park:* by the pleasant Yarriambiack Creek with picnic spots and a flora and fauna park; Craig Ave.
WHAT'S ON *Y-Fest:* golf, horseracing, machinery and country music; Easter.
NEARBY *North Western Agricultural Machinery Museum:* displays of farm machinery from the last 100 years; Henty Hwy; 3 km S.
ⓘ 119 Scott St; (03) 5398 1632

Warragul   Pop. 10 405
Map ref. 521 P10, 534 H6

Warragul was once little more than a few shacks built to accommodate rail workers in the 19th century – standout architecture of that era can be seen in Queen Street. Today it is a sprawling rural centre with a delightful country charm that has attracted a growing Melbourne commuter population keen to escape the rush of city living. Warragul is also known as a major dairying region, supplying the major part of Melbourne's milk.
IN TOWN West Gippsland Arts Centre
Part of the town's fantastic, architect-designed civic centre complex, the centre is a mecca for art lovers from across the state. It houses a good permanent collection of contemporary visual arts and is known for the variety of theatre productions and events held here throughout the year. Ask inside for a full program of events. Civic Pl.
WHAT'S ON *Gippsland Field Days:* Mar.
NEARBY Mount Worth State Park
This park protects a rich variety of native flora including the silver wattle and the Victorian Christmas bush. The Giant's Circuit is a walk that takes in a massive old mountain ash that is 7 m in circumference. Other walks include the Moonlight Creek and MacDonalds tracks, both of which are easily accessible. No camping is permitted. Access via Grand Ridge Rd, 19 km SE.
Yarragon Yarragon is a delightful country village that forms part of the Gourmet Deli Trail, a self-guide tour through Gippsland visiting some of the best food and wine producers (details from visitor centre). The town has an excellent array of gourmet outlets that stock cheeses, wines and meats from local producers, as well as specialty antique and craft shops. Even the accommodation is quaint, with an abundance of B&B and cottage-style accommodation offered. Yarragon hosts a Harvest Festival each April. 13 km SE. *Darnum Musical Village:* a complex of buildings housing a collection of musical instruments dating back to the 1400s; Princes Hwy; 8 km E. *Oakbank Angoras*

and Alpacas: sales of yarn and knitted goods; near Drouin, 8 km W. *Waterfalls:* Glen Cromie, Drouin West (10 km NW); Glen Nayook, south of Nayook; and Toorongo Falls, just north of Noojee. *Labertouche:* wildflower sanctuary; 16 km NW. *Neerim South:* visit Tarago Cheese Company for tastings and sales of top-quality cheeses, or enjoy a picnic or barbecue at the pleasant reserve near the Tarago Reservoir. Scenic drives through mountain country start from town. 17 km N. *Grand Ridge Road:* 132 km drive that starts at Seaview, 17 km S, and traverses the Strzelecki Ranges to Tarra Bulga National Park (*see Yarram for park details*). *Nayook:* good fresh produce, a fruit-and-berry farm, and the Country Farm Perennials Nursery and Gardens; 29 km N. *Childers:* Sunny Creek Fruit and Berry Farm, and Windrush Cottage; 31 km SE. *Noojee:* a mountain town featuring a historic trestle bridge and the Alpine Trout Farm; 39 km N.
ⓘ Gippsland Food and Wine, 123 Princes Hwy, Yarragon; 1300 133 309 or (03) 5634 2451; www.phillipislandgippsland.com.au

Warrnambool   Pop. 26 669
Map ref. 526 A8, 532 I9

Warrnambool lies at the end of the Great Ocean Road on a notorious section of coastline that has seen over 80 shipwrecks. The best known was the *Loch Ard* in 1878, which claimed the lives of all but two of those on board. While the wreck site itself is closer to Port Campbell, impressive relics from the ship are held at the Flagstaff Hill Maritime Museum in town. Warrnambool, as Victoria's fifth largest city, offers first-rate accommodation and dining as well as a fantastic swimming beach. The southern right whales that migrate here in winter are another major drawcard.
IN TOWN Flagstaff Hill Maritime Museum This reconstructed 19th-century maritime village is complete with a bank, hotel, schoolhouse and surgery. There are also two operational lighthouses with an authentic keeper's cottage, now housing the Shipwreck Museum, where relics retrieved from the *Loch Ard* – including the famous earthenware Loch Ard Peacock – are kept. On display is the Flagstaff Hill tapestry, an intricate work depicting themes of Aboriginal history, sealing, whaling, exploration, immigration and settlement. At night, visitors can watch the sound-and-light show 'Shipwrecked', which details the story of the *Loch Ard*. Merri St. *Main beach:* a safe swimming beach, with a walkway along the foreshore from the Breakwater to near the mouth of the Hopkins River. *Lake Pertobe Adventure Playground:* a great spot for family picnics; opposite main beach, Pertobe Rd. *Art Gallery:* local artwork, plus European

VICTORIA

and avant-garde collections; Timor St. *Customs House Gallery:* Gilles St. *Botanic Gardens:* pretty regional gardens designed by Guilfoyle (a curator of Melbourne's Royal Botanic Gardens) in 1879. A swimming pool complex is opposite. Botanic Rd. *Fletcher Jones Gardens:* award-winning landscaped gardens in front of former Fletcher Jones factory; Raglan Pde, eastern approach to town. *History House:* local history museum; Gilles St; open 1st Sun each month or by appt. *Portuguese Padrao:* monument to early Portuguese explorers; Cannon Hill, southern end of Liebig St. *Heritage walk:* 3 km self-guide walk taking in the many historic buildings around town; details from visitor centre. *Middle Island:* home to a colony of little (fairy) penguins and the site of Aboriginal middens. Only accessible at low tide; access off road to Breakwater. *Hopkins River:* great for fishing and boating, with Blue Hole, at the river's mouth, a popular spot for surfing and rock-pool exploration. Cruises are available. East of town. *Proudfoots Boathouse:* National Trust-classified boathouse on the Hopkins. *Wollaston Bridge:* an unusual bridge, built over 100 years ago; northern outskirts of town.

WHAT'S ON *Trash and treasure market:* showgrounds on Koroit St; each Sun. *Craft market:* showgrounds; 2nd Sun each month. *Wunta Fiesta:* family entertainment, food stalls; Feb. *Tarerer Festival:* indigenous culture and music; Feb. *Racing Carnival:* May. *Fun 4 Kids:* July. *Melbourne–Warrnambool Cycling Classic:* Oct. *Flower Shows:* held in spring.

NEARBY Tower Hill State Game Reserve This is a beautiful piece of preserved bushland featuring an extinct volcano and a crater lake, with tiny islands. A nature walk starts at the Natural History Centre in the reserve. 12 km NW, just after the turn-off to Koroit. *Logans Beach:* see southern right whales, in season, from a viewing platform; eastern edge of town; *see feature on facing page. Warrnambool Trout Farm:* catch your own trout and have them cleaned on-site, or buy trout products prepared at the farm; Wollaston Rd; 4 km N. *Allansford Cheeseworld:* for cheese tastings and sales; 10 km E. *Hopkins Falls:* scenic picnic spot, particularly spectacular in winter after heavy rain. In spring hundreds of baby eels migrate up the falls, creating a most unusual sight. 13 km NE. *Cudgee Creek Wildlife Park:* deer, crocodiles and other native fauna, plus an aviary. Picnic and barbecue facilities are provided. Cudgee; 17 km E. *Koroit:* see National Trust-classified buildings, good local arts and crafts shops, botanic gardens, and an Irish Festival in April; 18 km NW. *Mahogany Walk:* from Warrnambool to Port Fairy, a 22 km (one-way) walk along a stunning stretch of coastline.

ⓘ Adjacent Flagstaff Hill Maritime Museum, Merri St; 1800 637 725 or (03 5564 7837; www.warrnamboolinfo.com.au

Wedderburn   Pop. 656

Map ref. 543 N7

Wedderburn, part of the 'Golden Triangle', was once one of Victoria's richest goldmining towns. Many large nuggets have been unearthed here in the past and – for some lucky people – continue to be discovered now. The town's annual Gold Festival, with music, historical re-enactments and family entertainment, is growing every year and recognises the importance of gold in the development of so many towns in Victoria.

IN TOWN Hard Hill Hard Hill is a fascinating former mining district with original gold diggings and Government Battery. There is a good walking track through the site, where old mining machinery can be seen. Hard Hill is in a pleasant bushland setting, and picnic facilities are provided. Nearby is a fully operational eucalyptus distillery offering tours and selling eucalyptus products. Northern outskirts of town. *Kuku-Yalinji:* an Aboriginal art and craft gallery with artwork on display and for sale; Wallaby Dr. *Coach House Cafe and Museum:* a 1910 building restored to its original appearance, with authentic, old-fashioned stock; High St. *Coach-building factory:* High St. *Old bakery:* now used as a pottery, with local ceramics for sale; High St. *Heritage walk:* takes in the key historic buildings around town; ask at visitor centre for map.

WHAT'S ON *Gold Festival:* Mar. *Wool Expo:* Aug. *Historic Engine Exhibition:* Sept.

NEARBY *The Chandelier Man:* workshop for manufacturer of crystal chandeliers; Korong Vale; 13 km NW. *Mt Korong:* rockclimbing and bushwalking; 16 km SE. *Wychitella Forest Reserve:* wildlife sanctuary set in mallee forest, home to mallee fowl; 16 km N. *Fossickers Drive:* takes in goldmining sites, places of Aboriginal significance, local wineries and the Melville Caves; details from visitor centre.

ⓘ Council offices, High St; (03) 5494 1200

Welshpool   Pop. 138

Map ref. 535 K10

Welshpool is a small dairying community in South Gippsland. On the coast nearby, Port Welshpool is a deep-sea port servicing the local fishing and oil industries. Barry Beach Marine Terminal, a short distance west of Port Welshpool, services the offshore oil rigs in Bass Strait.

NEARBY Port Welshpool This popular coastal town has all the natural attractions that a seaside village could want. It is frequented by families who enjoy the safe beaches and fabulous coastal walks, and has fantastic views

across to Wilsons Promontory. Fishing enthusiasts should drop a line from the historic jetty, or try from a boat. The port's long link with the sea is detailed in the Port Welshpool and District Maritime Museum, which exhibits shipping relics and local history displays as well. 2 km S. *Franklin River Reserve:* great bushwalking with well-marked tracks; near Toora; 11 km W. *Agnes Falls:* the highest single-span falls in the state, spectacular after heavy rain; 19 km NW. *Scenic drive:* head west to see magnificent views from Mt Fatigue; off South Gippsland Hwy. *Fishing and boating:* excellent along the coast.

ⓘ Old Courthouse, 9 Rodgers St, Yarram; (03) 5182 6553

Winchelsea   Pop. 1098

Map ref. 520 D10, 527 L6, 533 P8

This charming little town on the Barwon River west of Geelong was first developed with cattle runs in the 1830s. Many of the historic buildings that grew from this development can still be seen around town, the most impressive being the nearby Barwon Park Homestead – a mansion by anyone's standards. Winchelsea soon became a key stopover for travellers taking the road from Colac to Geelong, and it still serves that purpose for travellers on the Princes Highway.

IN TOWN *Barwon Bridge:* an impressive arched bridge, built from stone in 1867; Princes Hwy. *Alexandra's Antiques and Art Gallery:* Princes Hwy. *Barwon Hotel:* a museum with Australiana memorabilia; Princes Hwy. *Old Shire Hall:* beautifully restored bluestone building, now housing popular tearooms and a craft and woodwork gallery; Princes Hwy. *Old Library:* art gallery featuring works by local artists; Princes Hwy. *Horserides:* available from Sea Mist Holiday Farm; Wensleydale Station Rd.

WHAT'S ON *Wool Sports:* shearing competition; Nov.

NEARBY Barwon Park Homestead Only the greatest estate would satisfy Elizabeth Austin, and her husband, Thomas, acquiesced. Barwon Park, built in 1869, was the biggest mansion in the Western District. Featuring 42 rooms furnished largely with original pieces, the bluestone building is an impressive example of 19th-century design. The name Austin might be familiar: Thomas Austin reputedly imported the first of Australia's devastating rabbit population and Elizabeth Austin contributed to major charities, and established the Austin Hospital in Melbourne. Inverleigh Rd; 3 km N; open 11am–4pm Wed and Sun. *Country Dahlias Gardens:* beautiful gardens, best viewed during spring, with sales of dahlia plants; Mathieson Rd; 5 km S; open Feb–April. *Killarney Park Lavender Farm:* lavender plants and products; 6 km S; open Sept–May.

ⓘ Old Shire Hall, Princes Hwy; (03) 5267 2769

A quick appearance above the surface

Warrnambool's whales

Each year in June, southern right whales (also known as smiling whales) return to the waters along the south coast of Australia to give birth, raise their young and start the breeding cycle again. Each female seems to have a favourite spot to give birth, to which she will return year after year. The area off Warrnambool's Logans Beach is a favourite spot for many to calve, earning it the nickname of 'Australia's whale nursery'. The beach features a purpose-built viewing platform above the sand dunes (binoculars or a telescope are recommended), and the local visitor centre releases information on whale sightings daily.

The whales regularly come within 100 metres of the coast and breach (launch their bodies partially out of the water), blow water into the air and splash their tails. The adults, up to 18 metres in length, can often be seen with calves, which start life at around 6 metres but grow rapidly. The whales spend the cooler months along the Australian coast before heading back to Antarctica to feed in September.

The southern right whale is one of the largest mammals on earth, only slightly smaller than the blue and humpback whales. It was given this name by early whalers who noted that these whales swim slowly in herds and close to the shore, and when harpooned they float to the surface. They also produced a large amount of oil and whalebone, making them a bountiful catch. This resulted in southern right whales being hunted almost to extinction, but since whaling was outlawed in 1935 their numbers have steadily increased.

Wodonga   Pop. 27 659

Map ref. 511 P13, 536 B2, 539 P4

Wodonga and its twin town, Albury (*see New South Wales*), sit astride the Murray River. There are many attractions around the Murray and nearby Lake Hume, making the region a popular holiday destination.
IN TOWN *National Museum of Australian Pottery:* displays work of 19th-century potters; South St. *Gateway Village:* includes working craft shops and cafes. Also houses the visitor centre. Lincoln Causeway. *Wiradjuri Walkabout:* a self-guide walk along the Murray's shores taking in sites of Aboriginal significance such as canoe trees, and fish and tortoise carvings in tree trunks. Starts behind Gateway Village; ask at visitor centre for details. *Harvey's Fish Farm:* catch your own freshwater fish; Lincoln Causeway. *Sumsion Gardens:* a pretty lakeside park with picnic and barbecue facilities; Church St. *Indoor Tennis Centre:* the largest centre of its kind in Australia; Melrose Dr.

WHAT'S ON *Border Country Fair:* Gateway Village; 2nd Sun each month. *Sports Festival:* Feb. *Wodonga Show:* Mar. *In My Backyard Festival:* raises environmental awareness; Mar. *Wine and Food Festival:* Oct. *World Cup Show Jumping:* Nov.
NEARBY **Mount Granya State Park** The park displays a great contrast between steep, rocky slopes and open eucalypt forests. Bushwalking is a popular pastime and the display of wildflowers in spring is magnificent. There is a pleasant picnic spot at Cottontree Creek, and a short walk leads to the Mt Granya summit, which offers spectacular views of the alps. Murray River Rd; 56 km E.
Military Museum: Bandiana; 4 km SE. *Hume Weir:* good spot for walks and picnics; 15 km E. *Tours:* winery and fishing tours, as well as scenic drives through the Upper Murray region, the mountain valleys of north-east Victoria and the Riverina; details from visitor centre.
ⓘ Gateway Visitor Information Centre, Lincoln Causeway; 1300 796 222 or (02) 6051 3650; www.albury.wodonga.com

Wonthaggi   Pop. 6137

Map ref. 534 G10

Once the main supplier of coal to the Victorian Railways, Wonthaggi, near the beachside town of Cape Paterson, is South Gippsland's largest town. There are good tourist facilities in town and a number of pretty beaches nearby.
WHAT'S ON *Italian Fest:* Oct.
NEARBY **State Coal Mine** The demand for black coal created a thriving industry in Wonthaggi from 1909 until 1968, and the mine site has been retained to show visitors the lifestyle and working conditions of the miners. Daily underground tours offer close-up views of the coalface, a short walk into the East Area Mine and a cable-hauled skip ride to the surface. Above ground, visit the museum for an introduction to the history of the mine and of Wonthaggi itself, or take a walk around the historic buildings. Cape Paterson Rd; 1.5 km S. *Cape Paterson:* waters offshore are protected by Bunurong Marine and Coastal Park and are good for surfing, swimming, snorkelling and scuba diving; 8 km S. *George Bass Coastal Walk:* starts at Kilcunda; 11 km NW. Ask at visitor centre for details of other walks. *Gourmet Deli Trail:* takes in central Gippsland's gourmet food and wine producers; details from visitor centre.
ⓘ Watt St; (03) 5671 2444; www.phillip islandgippsland.com

Woodend   Pop. 3010

Map ref. 520 G2, 531 R9, 533 R2, 534 A1

During the gold rushes of the 1850s, travellers sought refuge from mud, bogs and bushrangers at the 'wood's end' around Five Mile Creek, where a town eventually grew. In the late 1800s Woodend became a resort town, and its lovely gardens and proximity to spectacular natural sights, such as Hanging Rock and Mt Macedon, still make it a popular daytrip and weekend getaway for visitors from Melbourne.
IN TOWN *Bluestone Bridge:* built in 1862, the bridge crosses Five Mile Creek on the northern outskirts of town. *Clock Tower:* built as a WW I memorial; Calder Hwy. *Insectarium of Victoria:* insect and invertebrate research and interpretation centre; Calder Hwy. *Courthouse:* historic structure built in 1870; Forest St.
WHAT'S ON *Craft market:* 3rd Sun each month Oct–May. *Macedon Ranges Budburst Festival:* held throughout the wine district; Oct. *Woodend Village Festival:* Dec.
NEARBY **Hanging Rock** A massive rock formation made famous by *Picnic at Hanging Rock*, the novel by Joan Lindsay that was later made into a film. The story, about schoolgirls who mysteriously vanished while on a picnic in the reserve, became something of a legend. There is

certainly something eerie about Hanging Rock with its strange rock formations and narrow tracks through dense bushland. Hanging Rock is renowned for the annual races held at its base, especially the New Year's Day and Australia Day races. Other events include a Vintage Car Rally and Harvest Picnic, both held in February. The reserve also has a discovery centre and cafe. Access from South Rock Rd, off Calder Hwy; 8 km NE.

Macedon: a town at the foot of Mt Macedon. Home to the Church of the Resurrection, with stained-glass windows designed by Leonard French, and excellent plant nurseries. 8 km SE. *Mount Macedon:* a township located higher up the mountain, 2 km from Macedon, renowned for its beautiful gardens, many open to the public in autumn and spring. *Macedon Regional Park:* bushwalking and scenic drives. The Camels Hump marks the start of a signposted walk to the summit of the mountain where there stands a huge WW I memorial cross. Access via turn-off after Mount Macedon township. *Wineries:* several in region include Hanging Rock Winery at Newham; 10 km NE; further details from visitor centre. *Paramoor Working Farm:* offers a first-hand experience of an old-fashioned farm, complete with trained Clydesdale horses; Carlsruhe; 10 km NW. *Gisborne:* a variety of craft outlets. Gisborne Steam Park holds a steam-train rally each May. 16 km SE. *Barringo Wildlife Reserve:* native and exotic animals, cafe and picnic facilities; New Gisborne; 17 km SE. *Cape Williams Country Club and Winery:* tastings and sales, surrounded by charming English-style gardens, tennis courts and a cricket green; Romsey; 19 km E. *Llapaca Picnics:* offers scenic walks with picnics carried by llamas or alpacas; McGiffords Rd,

Fern Hill; 20 km W; by appt. *Lancefield:* historic buildings and wineries. Home to a woodchopping competition in Mar and a Farmers Market, for local produce, 4th Sat each month. 25 km NE. *Monegeetta:* in town is the Mintaro Homestead, a smaller replica of Melbourne's Government House, but not open to the public; 27 km E via Romsey.

ⓘ High St, beside Five Mile Creek; 1800 244 711 or (03) 5427 2033

Wycheproof   Pop. 692

Map ref. 510 G13, 543 L5

Wycheproof is renowned for the long wheat trains that travel right down the middle of the main street, towing up to 60 carriages behind them. There are many historic buildings in town, as well as rare, old peppercorn trees. Mt Wycheproof, at a mere 43 metres, has been named the smallest mountain in the world.

IN TOWN **Mt Wycheproof** A walking track leads up and around the mountain. Emus and kangaroos can be seen up close in a fauna park at the mountain's base. *Willandra Museum:* farm machinery, old buildings and historical memorabilia; Calder Hwy; open by appt. *Centenary Park:* aviaries, two log cabins and barbecue facilities; Calder Hwy.

WHAT'S ON *Racing Carnival:* Nov.

NEARBY *Tchum Lakes:* artificially created lakes, great for fishing and watersports; 23 km W. *Birchip:* visitors to town are greeted by the town's beloved 'Big Red' mallee bull in the main street. Also in town is the Soldiers Memorial Park with large, shady Moreton Bay fig trees, a great spot for a picnic. 31 km W.

ⓘ Buloke Shire Office, Broadway; (03) 5493 7400; www.buloke.gov.au

Yackandandah   Pop. 627

Map ref. 536 B3, 539 P5

Yackandandah, with its avenues of English trees and traditional buildings, is so rich with history that the entire town is National Trust-classified. It is situated south of Wodonga in the heart of the north-east goldfields region. Many of the town's creeks still yield alluvial gold.

IN TOWN *Historic buildings:* in High St, the post office. Also several banks and general stores, with the Bank of Victoria now preserved as a museum, open Sun and school holidays. Explore these and other buildings on a self-guide walk; details available from visitor centre. *Ray Riddington's Premier Store and Gallery:* displays and sales of local art; High St. *The Old Stone Bridge:* a beautiful old structure, built in 1857; High St. *Arts and crafts:* many outlets in town, including Yackandandah Workshop, cnr Kars and Hammond sts, and Wildon Thyme, High St. *Antiques:* Finders Bric-a-Brac and Old Wares, High St; Frankly Speaking, High St; and Vintage Sounds Restoration, specialising in antique gramophones, radios and telephones, Windham St. *Rosedale Garden and Tea Rooms:* Devonshire teas; Kars St.

WHAT'S ON *Lavender Harvest Festival:* Jan. *Folk Festival:* Mar. *Vintage Engine Swap Meet:* June.

NEARBY *Kars Reef Goldmine:* take a tour of this fascinating old goldmine, or try your hand at gold panning (licence required). Kars St; details of tours at visitor centre. *Lavender Patch Plant Farm:* sales of plants and lavender products; Beechworth Rd; 4 km W. *Kirbys Flat Pottery and Gallery:* Kirbys Flat Rd; 4 km S; open weekends or by appt. *Indigo Valley:* a picturesque area with a scenic

Hanging Rock, near Woodend

drive leading along the valley floor to Barnawatha; 6 km NW. *Allans Flat:* a great destination for food-lovers, with The Vienna Patisserie for coffee, ice-cream and delicious Austrian cakes (closed Tues). Also here are Parks Wines and Schmidt's Strawberry Winery, both with tastings and sales. 10 km NE. *Wombat Valley Tramways:* a small-gauge railway; at Leneva, 16 km NE; open Easter or by appt for groups.
ⓘ The Athenaeum, High St; (02) 6027 1988

Yarra Glen   Pop. 1369

Map ref. 519 H4, 521 M5, 524 B6, 534 E3

Yarra Glen is in the heart of the Yarra Valley wine region, a gorgeous area featuring lush, vine-covered hills and fertile valleys, all within easy reach of Melbourne. Indulgence – in fine wines and top-quality local produce – is definitely the focus here.
IN TOWN *Yarra Glen Grand Hotel:* National Trust-classified hotel built in 1888; Bell St. *Old bank:* now houses Watsons, a restaurant specialising in local produce; Bell St.
WHAT'S ON *Craft market:* racecourse; 1st Sun each month Oct–June.
NEARBY Yarra Valley Wine Region Victoria's first vines were reputedly planted in the valley by the Ryrie brothers in the early 1800s – these plantings would develop into Yering Station, today home to one of the region's finest wineries and restaurants. Over 55 wineries operate in the Yarra Valley, with the majority offering cellar-door tastings and sales; look out for the famed pinot noir and sparkling varieties. Tour companies offer bus tours through the region, and a popular Grape Grazing Festival is celebrated each Feb. Winery map from visitor centre.
Kinglake National Park Divided into three sections, Kinglake features messmate forests, fern gullies and waterfalls. A number of lookouts offer impressive views of the Yarra Valley and, on clear days, the Melbourne skyline, Port Phillip and the You Yangs. For keen bushwalkers, there are a number of good walks. In spring, wildflowers feature along the Mount Everard Track in the Everard section, just north of Yarra Glen. Access is via points along Melba Hwy.
Gulf Station: this National Trust-owned pastoral property, preserved as it was during pioneering days, features old-fashioned farming implements and early animal breeds. It is also home to the Pioneer and Working Horse Fest in Jan. 2 km NE; open Wed–Sun and public holidays. *Yarra Valley Dairy:* a working dairy with sales of specialty cheeses and clotted cream. A cafe serves local produce. 4 km S. *Ponyland Equestrian Centre:* trail-rides and riding lessons; 7 km W. *Sugarloaf Reservoir Park:* sailing, fishing and walking, with barbecue and picnic

facilities available; 10 km W. *Yarra Valley Regional Food Trail:* a self-guide tour, taking in the many gourmet food outlets in the region; details from visitor centre.
ⓘ Yarra Valley Visitor Information Centre, Old Courthouse, Haker St, Healesville; (03) 5962 2600; www.yarra valleytourism.asn.au

Yarram   Pop. 1786

Map ref. 535 L9

Yarram is deep in the dairy country of South Gippsland. It was originally settled on a swamp, and its name is derived from an Aboriginal word meaning 'plenty of water'. In town are some notable examples of early architecture, including the Regent Theatre and the old courthouse.
IN TOWN *Regent Theatre:* built in 1930, this theatre has been wonderfully restored. Cinemas operate on weekends and school holidays. Commercial Rd.
WHAT'S ON *Tarra Festival:* Easter. *Seabank Fishing Contest:* Nov.
NEARBY Tarra–Bulga National Park Tarra Bulga is a lovely, tranquil park where visitors will be amazed by the spectacular river and mountain views. Fern Gully Walk, starting from the Bulga picnic ground, takes in the dense temperate rainforests of mountain ash, myrtle and sassafras. The walk leads across a suspension bridge high among the treetops. A walk to Cyathea or Tarra falls, surrounded by lush fern gullies, completes the rainforest experience. Keep an eye out for rosellas, lyrebirds and the occasional koala. The Tarra Bulga Visitor Centre is on Grand Ridge Rd near Balook. From Yarram, access the park from Tarra Valley Rd. 20 km NW.
Won Wron Forest: great for walks, with wildflowers in spring; Hyland Hwy; 16 km N. *Beaches:* many attractive beaches in the region, including Manns, for fishing, 16 km SE; McLoughlins, 23 km E; and Woodside Beach, which is patrolled in summer, 29 km E. *Tarra Valley:* there are many attractive gardens in the region, including Eilean Donan Gardens and Riverbank Nursery; just north-west of Yarram. *Scenic drive:* a 46 km circuit goes from Yarram through Hiawatha and takes in Minnie Ha Ha Falls on Albert River, where picnic and camping facilities are provided and gypsy wagons can be hired.
ⓘ Old Courthouse, 9 Rodgers St; (03) 5182 6553

Yarrawonga   Pop. 4020

Map ref. 511 N13, 539 K3

Yarrawonga and its sister town Mulwala, across the New South Wales border, are separated by a pleasant stretch of the Murray River and the attractive Lake Mulwala. The 6000-hectare lake was created in 1939 during the building of the Yarrawonga Weir, which is central to irrigation in the Murray Valley.

Yarrawonga's proximity to such great water features has made it a popular holiday resort. The sandy beaches and calm waters are ideal for watersports, and are also home to abundant wildlife.
IN TOWN *Yarrawonga and Mulwala foreshores:* great locations for walks and picnics, with shady willows, waterslides, barbecue facilities and boat ramps. *Old Yarra Mine Shaft:* large collection of gems, minerals and fossils; visitor centre, Irvine Pde. *Canning A.R.T.S Gallery:* work by local artists; Belmore St. *Tudor House Clock Museum:* Lynch St. *Cruises:* daily cruises along the Murray on paddleboats *Paradise Queen* or *Lady Murray*; depart from Bank St.
WHAT'S ON *Bush Market:* railway station on Sharp St; 2nd and 4th Sun each month. *Rotary Market:* local crafts and second-hand goods; showgrounds; 3rd Sun each month. *Rowing Regatta:* Jan. *Powerboat Racing:* Jan. *Linga Longa Festival:* Oct. *Murray Marathon:* Dec.
NEARBY *Fyffe Field Wines:* tastings and sales; Murray Valley Hwy; 19 km W. *Guided tours:* of Ovens River or local wineries; book at visitor centre. *Fishing:* Murray River for Murray cod and yellow-belly.
ⓘ Irvine Pde; 1800 062 260 or (03) 5744 1989

Yea   Pop. 971

Map ref. 521 M1, 538 I11

This town sits by the Yea River, a tributary of the Goulburn River. Hume and Hovell, the first explorers through the region, discovered this wonderfully fertile area – a discovery that led in part to the settlement of the rest of Victoria. Near the Yea–Tallarook Road there are beautiful gorges and fern gullies, a reminder of what Yea looked like thousands of years ago.
IN TOWN *Historic buildings:* Beaufort Manor, High St; General Store, now a restaurant, High St. *Wetlands Walk:* sightings of abundant birdlife and glider possums; eastern outskirts of town.
WHAT'S ON *Market:* local craft and produce; Main St; 1st Sat each month Sept–May. *Autumn Fest:* Mar.
NEARBY *Murrindindi Reserve:* see the impressive Murrindindi Cascades and a variety of wildlife including wombats, platypuses and lyrebirds; 11 km SE. *Ibis Rookery:* Kerrisdale; 17 km W. *Flowerdale Winery:* Whittlesea–Yea Rd; 23 km SW. *Grotto:* a beautiful old church set in the hillside; Caveat; 27 km N. *Berry King Farm:* pick your own fruit; Two Hills Rd, Glenburn; 28 km S. *Wilhelmina Falls:* spectacular falls and a great spot for walks and picnics; access via Melba Hwy; 32 km S. *Kinglake National Park:* 32 km S; *see Yarra Glen. Mineral springs:* Dropmore, off back road to Euroa; 47 km N. *Scenic drives:* many in the region. Best time is Aug–Sept when wattles are in bloom. Ask at visitor centre for maps.
ⓘ Old Railway Station, Station St; (03) 5797 2663

VICTORIA

SOUTH
AUSTRALIA

South Australia is one million square
kilometres of ancient Dreamtime
landscapes and wild coastal beauty. It
is also a land of incredible contrast: the endless
desert of the north and the fertile vales of the
south-east are a world apart.

**South Australians are
proud of their history
of social innovation,
and their state has a
well-earned reputation
for tolerance and
cultural diversity.**

Imagined as an
ideal society in a
verdant paradise,
the colony of South
Australia was
formed on Edward
Gibbon Wakefield's
philosophy
of freedom,
enlightenment
and integrity.

In 1836 Colonel William Light chose the site
for the capital on Kaurna land beside the River
Torrens, and a month later South Australia
was proclaimed a colony in a brief ceremony
conducted under a gum tree.

The settlement's early days were far from ideal
as Governor Hindmarsh and the first colonists
huddled in squalid mud huts, perhaps regretting
they had no convict labour to call on, but today
the world's first planned city is a gracious capital
of wide streets and generous public parks – a
tribute to Light's visionary ideas.

In the 1840s German Lutherans fleeing
persecution in Europe settled in the Adelaide
Hills and the Barossa Valley, bringing traditions
of wine-growing and social liberty that have
flourished here ever since. The 1950s saw large
numbers of Italians
arrive, introducing
espresso, Mediterranean
food and European style.
In the early 1970s the
election of flamboyant
rebel Don Dunstan as
premier launched a
decade of social reform
unmatched in any other
state. South Australians
are proud of their history
of social innovation, and
their state has a well-
earned reputation for
tolerance and cultural
diversity.

For travellers seeking
their own level of
adventure, South Australia
is the perfect place to get
off the beaten track. This is
the nation's most urbanised

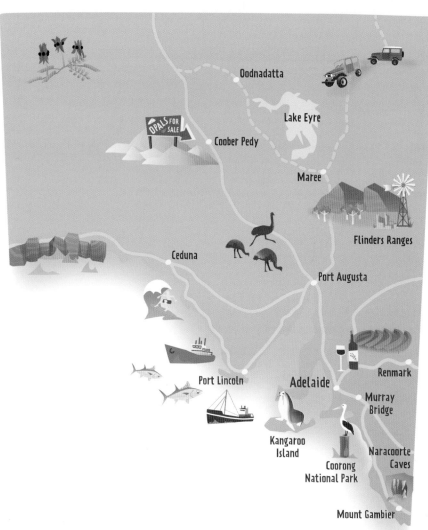

Grasstrees, Flinders Ranges

state, so the outback begins just an hour or two up the road from Adelaide. First there are the crumbling farmhouses of settlers who tried to farm the desert north of Goyder's Line, tricked by a few seasons of fickle rainfall. Further north are the open plains where it is possible to stop and get out of the car and hear . . . nothing.

The Flinders Ranges are one of the oldest mountain ranges on earth and hold rich cultural significance for the Adnyamathanha people. At its centre, Wilpena Pound (Ikara) is a lost world of cypress pines and hidden creeks, its gorges created by Akurra the serpent as he travelled north with a grumbling belly full of salt water from lakes Frome and Callabonna.

The state's Southern Ocean coastline includes the sheer cliffs of the Great Australian Bight and the sheltered wetlands of the Coorong, at the mouth of the Murray. This refuge for native and migratory birds would have to be one of the world's best places to sit quietly with a pair of binoculars.

South Australia is a state with many layers. Visitors here are treated to a little of the good life spiced with as much adventure as they care to seek. No wonder they call it Australia's best kept secret.

FACT FILE

Population 1 502 000
Total land area 984 377 sq km
People per square kilometre 1.5
Sheep per square kilometre 13.25
Length of coastline 3816 km
Number of islands 346
Longest river Murray River (650 km)
Largest lake Lake Eyre (9500 sq km)
Highest mountain Mt Woodroffe (1440 m), Musgrave Ranges, Pitjantjatjara Land
Lowest place Lake Eyre, 15 m below sea level (Australia's lowest point)
Hottest place 50.7°C – Australia's hottest recorded temperature – was reached in Oodnadatta in 1960
Driest place Lake Eyre is Australia's driest place with a mere 125 mm of rainfall per year
Longest place name Nooldoonooldoona, a waterhole in the Gammon Ranges
Best surf Cactus Beach, near Ceduna
Best discoveries and inventions penicillin by Howard Florey (he describes the discovery as 'a terrible amount of luck'); the wine cask by Tom Angove
Most dangerous coast There are 80 shipwrecks around Kangaroo Island
Best political stunt Premier Don Dunstan wore pink hot pants into parliament to campaign for gay law reform in the 1970s
Favourite take-away food Adelaide's pie floater (a meat pie floating in a bowl of pea soup – with or without tomato sauce)
Local beer West End Draught
Interesting fact Adelaide boasts a higher ratio of restaurants to residents than any other state

TIMELINE

1627
Dutch explorer Pieter Nuyts sails along the south coast as far as the Nuyts Archipelago, off present day Ceduna.

1802
Matthew Flinders and Nicholas Baudin meet unexpectedly at the mouth of the Murray.

1836
The first migrants land at Kangaroo Island on 20 July. By year's end South Australia is proclaimed a province and the site for Adelaide is chosen.

1947
Australian and British governments establish the Woomera Prohibited Area to test weapons.

1951
The first vintage of Grange Hermitage is produced; winemaker Max Schubert gives most of it away. Fifty years later a single bottle is valued at over $40 000.

1960
The first Adelaide Festival, created by a newspaper reporter and a professor of music, is declared a success.

1970
Don Dunstan is elected premier and begins the 'Dunstan Decade' of social and political reforms.

1971
The Aboriginal flag is flown for the first time ever, in Adelaide's Victoria Square.

1988
Production of uranium begins at Olympic Dam near Roxby Downs, tapping into the largest known body of uranium ore in the world.

ADELAIDE

ADELAIDE IS . . .

Coffee at Lucia's in Adelaide Central Market

A Popeye cruise along the River Torrens

A tram trip to Glenelg

Watching a game of cricket at the Adelaide Oval

Surveying the city from Light's Vision

A visit to the Aboriginal Cultures Gallery at the South Australian Museum

A walk along North Terrace

Henley Square on a Sunday afternoon, for lunch and a stroll by the sea

Being at Showdown – the annual AFL derby between the two local teams

A night out in East End

Visitor information

South Australian Visitor and Travel Centre
18 King William St
(08) 8303 2220 or 1300 655 276
www.southaustralia.com

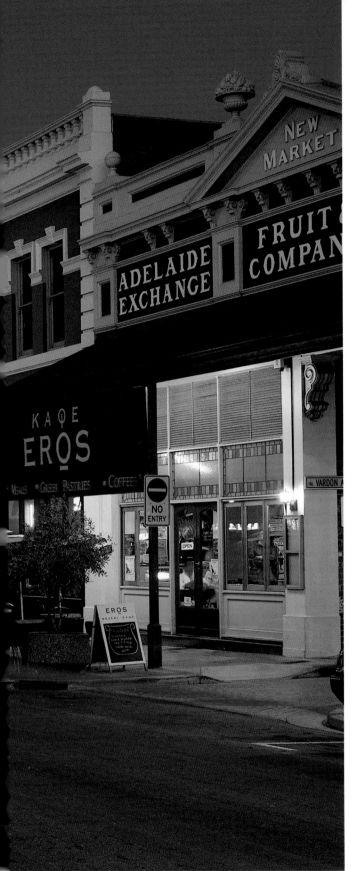

East End, the place to go for a great night out

One of the best-planned cities in the world, Adelaide remains testament to the work of its first surveyor, Colonel William Light, whose statue stands on Montefiore Hill, overlooking Adelaide Oval.

Settled in 1836, Adelaide was Australia's first free settlement. It was created by a British Act of Parliament and managed by the London-based South Australia Company. Like other well-planned cities around the world, Adelaide has few skyscrapers and retains a 'human scale' about its architecture, which blends both heritage and contemporary styles. Locals joke that they endure peak-minute rather than peak-hour traffic; you can take a trip from the picturesque Adelaide Hills to the white sands of Gulf St Vincent in around half an hour.

Since the 1970s Adelaide – and more generally South Australia – have been famous for the production of food and wine. The state is the powerhouse of the booming Australian wine industry, producing almost 60 percent of the total output, and is also a major exporter of fish and fresh vegetables, while Adelaide Central Market is possibly the finest fresh-produce market in Australia. The city is renowned for its restaurants – from the fish cafes of Gouger Street to master chef Cheong Liew's adventurous creations at the Grange, in the Hilton on Victoria Square.

Adelaide also knows how to throw a party and the city is compact enough to generate a feeling of all-over revelry. First on the calendar is the Adelaide Festival of Arts, one of the world's great arts festivals. In February, the festival and the coinciding Adelaide Fringe festival take over the city, and both residents and visitors are caught up in the festivities.

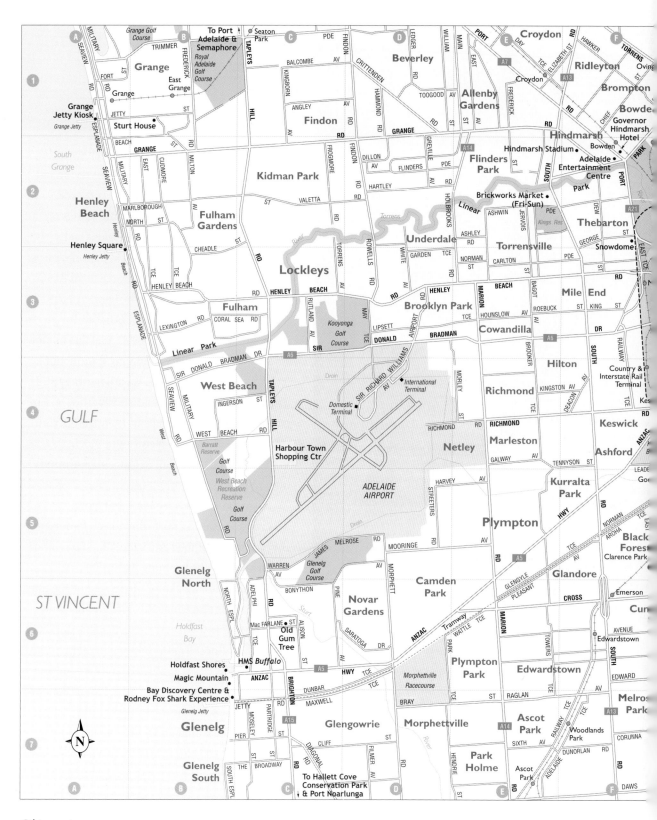

Climate

Adelaide's weather is described as temperate Mediterranean, with temperatures in summer rising to around 40ºC on a number of days, and falling to a minimum near zero a couple of times in winter. The in-between seasons are near-perfect, with maximum temperatures in the mid 20s for much of March, April, September and October.

	J	F	M	A	M	J	J	A	S	O	N	D
Max ºC	29	29	26	22	19	16	15	16	18	21	24	27
Min ºC	17	17	15	13	10	9	8	8	9	11	13	15
Rain mm	20	21	24	44	68	72	67	62	51	44	31	26
Raindays	4	4	5	9	13	15	16	16	13	11	8	6

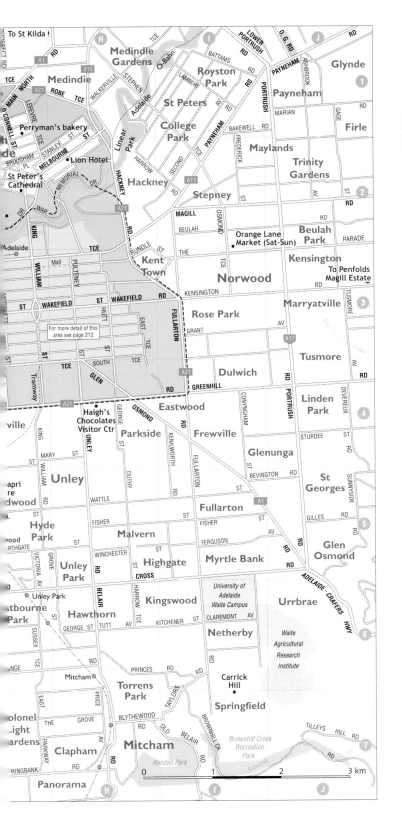

Getting around

Adelaide has quite a quirky range of public transport on offer. First there is the city's sole tram, which heads from Victoria Square in the city to the seaside suburb of Glenelg. Then there is the Adelaide O-Bahn – a kind of cross between a bus and a tram that forms the longest and fastest guided bus service in the world. It travels along Currie and Grenfell streets in the city, then heads out to Westfield Tea Tree Plaza in Modbury, in the north-eastern suburbs.

The Loop and the Beeline are two free buses that operate around the city centre. The Loop runs every 15 minutes and takes in North Terrace and Light, Hindmarsh and Victoria squares; while the Beeline runs every five minutes and includes Victoria Square, King William Street and the railway station. Both services operate during shopping hours.

Four train routes operate from the CBD to Adelaide's suburbs (to Gawler in the north, Outer Harbour in the north-west, Noarlunga in the south and Belair in the Adelaide Hills). There are also plenty of bus services operating around the suburbs. All public transport in Adelaide is covered by one ticketing system, and tickets can be purchased at train stations and on buses and trams.

Public transport Passenger Transport InfoLine (08) 8210 1000 or 1800 182 160

Airport shuttle bus Skylink Airport Shuttle (08) 8332 0528

Motoring organisation RAA (08) 8202 4600, roadside assistance 13 1111

Car rental Avis 13 6333; Budget 13 2727; Hertz 133039; Thrifty 1300 367 227

Taxis Suburban Taxis 13 1008; Yellow Cabs 13 2227

Tourist bus Adelaide Explorer (replica tram) (08) 8231 7172

Bicycle hire Contact Bicycle SA for operators (08) 8232 2644

SOUTH AUSTRALIA

Markets

Fisherman's Wharf Market, Port Adelaide
Fresh seafood and other produce are the main drawcards, but other food stalls and bric-a-brac make up the mix. Sun. 548 B6

Torrens Island Open Market, Port Adelaide *Buy fish direct from the boat. Other food stalls also showcase quality local produce. Sun. 548 C5*

Brickworks Market, Torrensville *Located in an old kiln, the market's 100 stalls offer a wide range of wares, including clothing and crafts, as well as produce. Fri–Sun. 210 E2*

Junction Market, Kilburn *Popular market offering fresh produce and specialty stores. Sat–Sun. 548 D6*

Orange Lane Market, Norwood *Art and craft, second-hand goods, tasty food and other treasures. Sat–Sun. 211 I2*

See also Adelaide Central Market, p. 215

City centre

Central Adelaide sits on a square street-grid bounded by four terraces that are named after the major compass points. Victoria Square is in the middle of the grid, with four smaller squares (Hindmarsh, Light, Whitmore and Hurtle) surrounding it. Just beyond North Terrace, down a gentle hill, is the River Torrens, which meanders through the CBD's northern fringe.

NORTH

The northern section of central Adelaide is based around North Terrace and Rundle Mall. **North Terrace,** a wide, tree-lined boulevard with a university located at either end, is the most spectacular of the four terraces in the CBD. Around the King William Street intersection is South Australia's centre of government, and in one blockbuster stretch from Kintore Avenue to the University of Adelaide, North

Terrace hosts three of South Australia's most important cultural institutions – the state library, the museum, and the art gallery. Rundle Mall lies one block south.

Rundle Mall

Australia's first shopping mall, developed during the Dunstan years (*see Adelaide Festival Centre, p. 215*). The mall and the arcades that shoot off it form the city's shopping heart, with major department stores, specialty clothing outlets, souvenir and craft stores, food outlets and music shops. Public sculptures dot the mall including two silver balls colloquially known as the 'Malls Balls'. While you're here, visit **Haigh's Chocolates** on historic Beehive Corner (*you can also visit the Haigh's factory in Parkside, see p. 218*) and **Balfour's Bake Cafe**, for one of their famous frog cakes. These frog-shaped cup cakes, traditionally iced with green fondant, have been a local hit since the 1920s and are listed with the National Trust, along with foods such as the pie floater (*see Eating out, p. 215*).

Rundle Mall runs parallel to Grenfell Street, and they are joined by Gawler Place, James Place and Twin Street. This network contains two treasures – Adelaide Arcade and Regent Arcade. Opened in 1885, **Adelaide Arcade** is a special delight and was the first retail establishment in the country to have electric lights. It is a thoroughly Victorian affair, lined with small shops of every kind on the ground floor and charming balcony level.

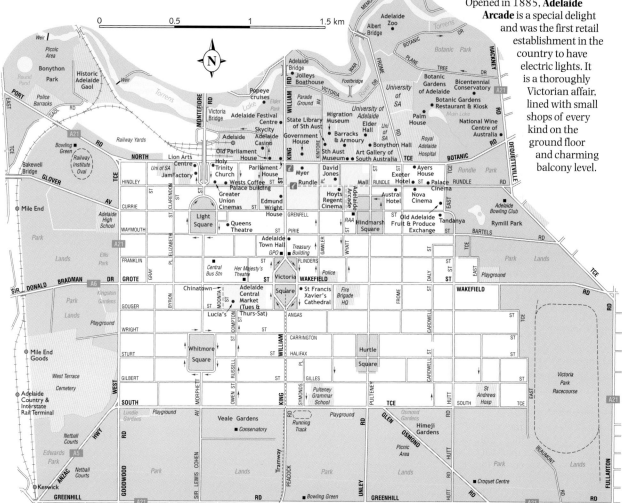

East End
The east end of Rundle Mall, beyond the main shopping zone, is the hub of Adelaide's nightlife. Friday and Saturday nights in East End are like being on Dublin's Temple Bar on a summer weekend. It throbs with longstanding pubs – such as the Austral and the Exeter – among newer bars and clubs, all of them bursting with revellers. With over 50 cafes and restaurants, this is also a superb place to come for food – there are wine bars, cafes with plenty of outdoor seating – and the shopping is great too.

Hindley Street
At the other end of Rundle Mall, Hindley Street, sometimes known as West End, is another lively part of Adelaide. On the seedier side of things, it is home to strip joints and pubs that stay open till dawn, but among these are popular student hang-outs, Lebanese restaurants and important government arts bodies. The ornate Wests Coffee Palace building, constructed in 1903 as the Austral Stores and serving as a coffee palace (unlicensed hotel) from 1908 onwards, is now the home of Arts SA.

Parliament House and Government House
These impressive buildings adorn the northern corners of the intersection of North Terrace and King William Road. Government House, the oldest in Australia, is set on a sweep of manicured lawns and was once the meeting place of the first council of government. As the council expanded, new buildings were constructed, including what is now **Old Parliament House**. In 1889 the first chamber of the current Parliament House was opened, and with its colonnaded facade adorned with local marble, was an impressive front for the government. These buildings, along with several statues and monuments – including the War Memorial at the corner of Kintore Avenue – make for an interesting and informative walk. *Guided tours of Parliament House run on non-sitting days (weekdays only) at 10am and 2pm; sitting days are published on the parliament's website www.parliament.sa. gov.au. Government House normally has two open days a year; (08) 8203 9800.*

State Library of South Australia
The State Library complex is a wonderful blend of charming 19th-century buildings and modern technology. It prides itself on bringing the history of South Australian culture to the people, as well as showcasing some of the library's collection items on the Treasures Wall. The most notable exhibition, which attracts both local and international visitors, is the **Bradman Collection**. Housed in the Institute Building, this is an outstanding collection of cricket memorabilia belonging to Sir Donald Bradman, who lived in Adelaide for much of his life. Over the years, Bradman donated many bats, 'baggy green' caps and personal documents to the library. Today there are over 100 items on display. *North Tce; open daily; admission free.*

Migration Museum
This museum details immigrant life from pioneering days up to today. The museum building itself has a long history connected with refuge – it was once Adelaide's Destitute Asylum, where many of the city's aged, homeless and underprivileged lived (and died). The women and children who lived there from the mid-1800s to 1918 tell their stories in the 'Behind the Wall' exhibition. *82 Kintore Ave; open 10am–5pm Mon–Fri & 1pm–5pm weekends & public holidays; entry by donation.*

South Australian Museum
For over a century, the South Australian Museum has played a crucial role in researching, documenting and exhibiting every facet of Aboriginal culture, and this continues to be a major focus of the museum today. The excellent **Aboriginal Cultures Gallery** contains over 3000 objects and is the world's most comprehensive Aboriginal cultural exhibition. It exhibits traditional items such as shields, canoes and boomerangs, as well as displays relating to the lives of Aboriginal people today.
In the **Origin Energy Fossil Gallery** is a fascinating collection of opalised fossils, representing a distinctive part of South Australia's natural history – look up to see the impressive model skeleton of the *Addyman plesiosaur*, a marine animal over 100 million years old. *North Tce; open daily; admission free.*

Art Gallery of South Australia
This gallery has grouped its permanent collection in three major categories. The Australian collection is one of the country's most comprehensive chronological collections and includes some fine works from distinguished South Australian artists Margaret Preston and Stella Bowen. An impressive collection of contemporary British artwork is housed in the European collection, as is an array of major works by French sculptor Auguste Rodin, bequeathed by a generous benefactor. The Asian collection includes delicate Japanese artworks and South-East Asian ceramics. There is also a program of changing exhibitions. *North Tce; open daily; general admission free.*

Ayers House
In the early days, North Terrace was where the wealthy and prestigious lived – figures such as Premier Henry Ayers, whose name identified the country's most recognisable landmark (Ayers

Top events

Schützenfest *Traditional German folk festival with music, food, and frivolity. January.*

Jacobs Creek Tour Down Under *Bike riders descend on Adelaide for this race into the hills. January.*

Adelaide Festival of Arts *The city's defining event, and one of the world's highest regarded arts festivals. February–March (even-numbered years).*

Adelaide Fringe *Alongside the Festival of Arts, the edgy performances of this world-renowned festival are great entertainment. February–March (even numbered years).*

WOMADelaide *A huge festival of world music and dance in Botanic Park. March.*

Clipsal 500 Adelaide *V8 supercars race on city streets in what is said to be Australia's best motor event. March.*

Glendi Festival *Greek culture, food, song and dance. March.*

Tasting Australia *International event celebrating food, wine and beer as well as chefs and writers. October (odd-numbered years).*

Bay to Birdwood Run *Costumed drivers sit at the wheel of pre-1950s vehicles in a race from West Beach to Birdwood. September.*

Shopping

Rundle Mall, City *The CBD's main shopping area, with major department stores as well as individual offerings of clothing, chocolates and much more. See map on p. 212*

Melbourne Street, North Adelaide *Adelaide's most exclusive strip, with designer fashion boutiques. 211 H2*

The Parade, Norwood *Very cosmopolitan, with an array of stores and plenty of places to stop for a coffee, a meal or a drink. 211 I3*

King William Road, Hyde Park *Hip fashion outlets sprinkled among cafes, and furniture and homeware stores. 211 G5*

Jetty Road, Glenelg *A great mix of stores, and food and drink outlets. 210 C7*

Harbour Town *This complex offers seconds and discount stores. 210 C4*

Magill Road, Stepney *For antiques and second-hand treasures. 211 I2*

See also Adelaide Central Market p. 215, Gouger Street p. 215, and O'Connell Street p. 216

SOUTH AUSTRALIA

Grand old buildings

Barracks and Armoury *Built in 1855, these magnificent examples of colonial architecture were the local Australian Army headquarters from 1857 to 1870. Behind South Australian Museum, City.*

Central Railway Station *Built in 1856, the main feature is the Great Hall, with marble floors, Corinthian columns and a domed ceiling. Skycity Adelaide casino now occupies much of the station's upper floors. North Tce, City.*

Edmund Wright House *Wright was the architect of some of Adelaide's grandest buildings, including Parliament House, the GPO and the Adelaide and Glenelg town halls. This elaborate Italianate creation was completed in 1878 and used as a banking chamber. 59 King William St, City.*

Adelaide Town Hall *Opened in 1866, this building is much admired for its magnificent tower and classic portico, and its equally grand interior. Free tours run on Monday at 10am; bookings essential (08) 8203 7203. 128 King William St, City.*

Bonython Hall *Part of Adelaide University, the hall has an unusual sloping floor. This was insisted upon by benefactor Langdon Bonython, a strict Methodist, to prevent dancing. North Tce, City.*

Elder Hall *This church-like building in the grounds of the University of Adelaide is in fact a concert venue with a spectacular pipe organ. Next to Bonython Hall, City.*

Churches *As well as St Francis Xavier's Cathedral near Victoria Square, there's St Peter's Cathedral in North Adelaide and the Holy Trinity Church on North Terrace.*

Old Adelaide Fruit and Produce Exchange *The charming facade of this old wholesale market still stands on East Terrace. The rear has been converted into apartments. City.*

Queens Theatre *For a theatre, this is a surprisingly humble affair – perhaps because it is the oldest theatre on the mainland, built in 1840. Cnr Gilles Arcade & Playhouse La, City.*

Sturt House *The home of Charles Sturt, the man who sailed into South Australia on a whaleboat down the Murray, which led to the settlement of the state. Many original furnishings remain. Sun. Jetty St, Grange.*

See also Ayers House, p. 213, Migration Museum, p. 213, Parliament House and Government House, p. 213, and Carrick Hill, p. 218

Jolleys Boathouse, on the banks of the River Torrens

Rock) until it was changed back to its indigenous name, Uluṟu. Ayers made his money through the Burra coppermine, and wasn't afraid to spend it on lavish decorations and furniture. After years in the hands of the Royal Adelaide Hospital, the original decorations of the building have now been painstakingly restored, and one wing has been transformed into a luxurious restaurant. *288 North Tce; house is open for viewing 10am–4pm Tues–Fri & 1pm–4pm Sat–Sun; admission fee applies.*

Tandanya – National Aboriginal Cultural Institute

This is a vibrant meeting place of cultures with a strong emphasis on the culture of the Kaurna people, the traditional owners of the land on which Adelaide stands. Tandanya aims to exhibit the contemporary culture, art and lifestyle of Australia's indigenous people while still acknowledging the traditions the culture was built on. In the gallery, see the exciting work of emerging artists, or taste modern versions of traditional bush tucker in the cafe. Indigenous tours are also offered, encompassing both the centre and the grounds. *253 Grenfell St; open daily; admission fee applies.*

Botanic Gardens of Adelaide

The gardens were laid out in the mid-1800s and retain a northern-European style. The **Palm House**, in particular, is a fine example of German engineering – it was imported in 1875 and has been recently restored to its original splendour. A more recent construction is the impressive **Bicentennial Conservatory**, considered to be the largest single-span conservatory in the Southern Hemisphere. Inside, walkways guide visitors through a lush rainforest environment, past endangered native and exotic plant species. *North Tce; open daily; admission fee applies to Bicentennial Conservatory.*

National Wine Centre of Australia

Here visitors can take a Wine Discovery Journey though the different stages of wine-production, meet winemakers and try winemaking – all through virtual technology. The centre has its own vineyard and a retail centre for wine-tasting. Sample and buy wines from around the country. Affiliated with the University of Adelaide, the centre is also where the modern vigneron comes to learn the trade. *Cnr Botanic & Hackney rds; open daily; admission fee applies.*

Adelaide Zoo

The preservation of the zoo's 19th-century buildings and landscaped gardens has led many to call it the most attractive zoo in Australia. The Elephant House is a highlight of 1900s architecture – the enclosure's design was based on an Indian Temple, and is now classified by the National Trust. The zoo is also renowned for its fabulous bird collection; see a colourful exhibition of native Australian birds at the Australian Rainforest Aviary, or more exotic displays, such as the macaws, in the Amazon Aviary. *Frome Rd; open daily; admission fee applies.*

The River Torrens

The river provides a scenic setting for a host of leisure activities including walking, cycling, paddling and enjoying a ride on Adelaide's **Popeye** cruises and motor launches. From the Elder Park

44444444444444

Wharf, Popeye cruises operate every hour, on the hour, on weekdays, and every 20 minutes on weekends. Paddleboats can be hired on weekends from **Jolleys Boathouse** under the Adelaide Bridge on King William Road. For those less inclined to venture into the river, a restaurant with good food and lovely views can also be found at the boathouse.

Adelaide Festival Centre
In the 1970s, South Australia had a premier who not only loved the arts, but had worked as a competent stage and radio personality. Don Dunstan was determined to turn the arts into a viable industry rather than just a pastime. His accomplishments include developing the South Australian Film Corporation and increasing support for the state's other major arts groups. The construction of the Festival Centre was completed during his tenure in government. Overlooking Elder Park and the River Torrens, the centre consists of four theatres, from the large Festival Theatre to the outdoor Amphitheatre, and is an architectural landmark. Visitors can take in a show or wander through the foyer to view the centre's collection of artworks as well as the changing displays of the Performing Arts Collection of South Australia, which includes costumes, props and photographs.

JamFactory – Contemporary Craft and Design
Each year a rigorous application process sifts through hopefuls keen on becoming a Design Associate of the JamFactory. Only the best make it into one of the four training programs of this institution, which are split into ceramics, furniture, metal (including jewellery) and glass work. The pieces produced by each studio are said to be some of the most innovative and impressive craft designs on the Australian market. Changing exhibits of international and JamFactory works are showcased in the gallery, and many one-off designs are available for purchase in the store. *19 Morphett St; open daily; admission free.*

Nearby is another Adelaide arts institution, the **Experimental Art Foundation** at the Lion Arts centre. This centre has some of the best in new artistic media, such as video and installation art.

Historic Adelaide Gaol
Today you can tour the cells and yards of this antiquated complex – which operated as a gaol from 1841 to 1988 – and imagine the days when Sister Mary MacKillop visited the prisoners. The truly obsessed can take a night tour or even stay overnight. *Gaol Rd (turn right after the railway line as you head north-west from North Tce); open 11am–4pm Wed & Sun, with guided tours on Sun and at night by appointment; admission fee applies.*

SOUTH

The southern part of central Adelaide is home to some stellar attractions – the Adelaide Central Market is an absolute must-see, and there is superb dining on Gouger Street.

Adelaide Central Market
Located just off Victoria Square, the market fills the block between Grote and Gouger streets. A showcase for South Australia's fresh produce, the market has evolved into a significant shopping and social centre. It's a wonderland of fruit, vegetables, fish, breads, cheeses, meats and nuts, with rows of stalls surrounded by alleys and arcades that are crammed with shops and cafes. 'Meet you at the market' must be one of Adelaide's most common exhortations. Grab lunch at Zuma's, Malacca Corner or Lucia's (Adelaide's original pizza joint, now serving breakfast and lunch as well), or just wander the aisles of the market, and experience its sensory delights. *Open Tues, Thurs, Fri & Sat.*

Gouger Street
Originally a spin-off from Central Market, Gouger Street has grown into an attraction in its own right with restaurants, cafes, bars and clubs. Gouger Street winds down earlier than East End, but has its own character and appeal. And it has the very Adelaide feature of cheap, simple, but high-quality fish cafes where patrons can feast on King George whiting – one of the most popular catches from the waters of Gulf St Vincent.

There are five Chinese restaurants on Gouger Street, but Adelaide's **Chinatown** is centred on Moonta Street – between Gouger and Grote streets – with its noodle bars, Chinese shops and T-Chow, another popular dining spot. The restaurant Ying Chow is famous for its sought-after tables and late-night service.

North Adelaide
With a vision of elegance and symmetry, Colonel Light designed a residential area on the northern bank of the River Torrens to mirror the business complex on the southern bank. The belt of parklands that surrounds the CBD extends across the river. Visitors going to North Adelaide from the city should take in **Light's Vision** on Montefiore Hill, where a bronze statue of the colonel gazes over the city.

North Adelaide is one of the city's most exclusive residential addresses. It is also rich in history, with a mix of stately Georgian mansions and humble workers' cottages. From Light's Vision you can take a walk through Lower North

Eating out

Hutt Street, City *A belt of cafes that is a touch more up-market. See map on p. 212*

Hindley Street, City *Lebanese and Italian are among the offerings. See map on p. 212*

The Parade, Norwood *For a range of cafes and a couple of good pubs. 211 I3*

Henley Square *Everything from fish and chips to Greek, Thai and Italian. 210 A3*

City pie carts *Every visitor should try a pie floater (a unique Adelaide creation featuring a meat pie floating in a bowl of pea soup) at least once. There are two regular carts: one outside the Railway Station on North Terrace; the other on Victoria Square by the GPO.*

See also East End p. 213, Adelaide Central Market p. 215, Gouger Street p. 215, and O'Connell Street p. 216

Parks and gardens

Rymill Park *The centrepiece is Rymill Lake, with rowboats for hire, but there is also a large rose garden. City. See map on p. 212*

Himeji Gardens *Created in conjunction with Himeji, Adelaide's sister city, this garden blends two classic Japanese styles: 'senzui' (lake and mountain garden) and 'kare senzui' (dry garden). City. See map on p. 212*

Veale Gardens *For some years the green belt around Adelaide was more paddock than parkland, but a town clerk named William Veale started beautifying the gardens around the middle of the last century. Veale Gardens were his pièce de résistance and feature a rose garden, rockeries, fountains and a conservatory. City. See map on p. 212*

Bonython Park *A park with a more native style. The river attracts birdlife, and the paths are well trodden by joggers and cyclists. The park also contains a children's playground and a popular picnic area. Thebarton. See map on p. 212*

Linear Park *This park follows the curves of the Torrens all the way from West Beach to Paradise, and is great for bike riding. The sections near the city offer fantastic views, while further out the track runs through a thick corridor of bushland. 210 E2*

SOUTH AUSTRALIA

Entertainment

Cinema

Adelaide has the usual range of multiplex cinemas in the city – Hoyts Regent Cinema is located in Rundle Mall and Greater Union Cinemas is on Hindley Street. Those who want a bit more atmosphere should head for the Piccadilly in North Adelaide, which has three cinemas and screens both mainstream and art-house films. A similar line-up is available at the Palace and Nova cinemas in Rundle Street's East End. Adelaide's main alternative cinema is the Mercury at the Lion Arts Centre – it shows cult classics, foreign language and arthouse movies, and holds short film festivals. The Capri Theatre, in Goodwood, is notable for the live organ recitals that introduce film screenings on Tuesday, Saturday and Sunday nights. Check the Adelaide Advertiser for daily listings.

Live music

The best live-music venue in Adelaide, without question, is the Governor Hindmarsh Hotel on Port Road, opposite the Adelaide Entertainment Centre. Offering everything from Irish fiddlers in the front bar to major international acts in the large, barn-like concert room at the back, The Gov (as it's known to the locals) has been the top venue in town for at least a decade. Plenty of other pubs also offer live music, and the best way to find out what's on is to pick up a copy of Rip It Up, the local contemporary-music paper.

Classical music and performing arts

The Adelaide Festival Centre is the hub of mainstream performing arts activity in Adelaide, hosting the three major and highly regarded state companies: State Theatre SA, State Opera of South Australia and Adelaide Symphony Orchestra (ASO). The ASO also holds small recitals at its Grainger Studio in Hindley Street. Adelaide nurtures a diverse range of theatre companies – look out for performances by the Australian Dance Theatre (contemporary dance), Vitalstatistix (women's theatre) and Windmill Performing Arts (children's theatre). The Lion Arts Centre is the venue for two innovative companies: Nexus (cabaret) and Doppio Teatro (multicultural). Indigenous dance is also on display in daily performances at Tandanya. The Adelaide Advertiser publishes a listing of entertainment events each Thursday.

Adelaide (comprising the two smaller blocks that sit at angles off the main block) to get the full picture. Take Palmer Place (the section that runs parallel to Jeffcott Street) into Brougham Place to see old mansions that command views across the city.

Brougham Place continues into Stanley Street. Down the hill you'll find small stone cottages that formed part of South Australia's first subdivision. **Melbourne Street** is the heart of this area and is Adelaide's classiest street, with art galleries, boutiques, restaurants and the restored Lion Hotel.

To find the true cafe heart of North Adelaide, head to **O'Connell Street** – it has old pubs bedecked with Victorian iron lace, as well as restaurants and cafes. There's pizza, pasta, and coffee – and the vibe is as good as ever. **Tynte Street**, which runs off O'Connell Street and was once North Adelaide's main street, has many fine 19th-century buildings. One of these buildings houses **Perryman's**, a bakery that has been producing bite-sized pies and pastries since 1925. During the Depression these miniature treats were all that many customers could afford; today they're a novelty, and the locals keep coming back for more.

Seaside suburbs

One of Adelaide's great features is its long frontage to Gulf St Vincent. This coastline is hugely varied – there are glitzy suburbs, such as Glenelg, as well as more low-key areas such as Semaphore in the north and Port Noarlunga in the south. At either end of the suburban sprawl the environment is also varied – in the north are the impenetrable mangrove swamps that the first settlers wrestled with and eventually overcame to create Port Adelaide; in the south are classic Fleurieu beaches, with yellow cliffs and sweeping stretches of sand.

Glenelg 210 B7

High-rise apartments are slowly creeping across the Glenelg foreshore, but they haven't spoiled the fun or ambience offered by this popular beachside suburb. Cafes line busy Jetty Road, and Adelaide's only tramline runs to Victoria Square in the city.

Holdfast Shores sits on the waterfront – a development with restaurants, boutique shopping and a marina. For eating with a difference, try the nearby **HMS Buffalo**. A replica of the ship that carried the first South Australian settlers, it offers some fine seafood dining. On the upper deck is a museum with illustrations, logbooks and other relics telling the history of the ship.

And, just as all prominent seaside suburbs seem to be incomplete without an amusement park, Glenelg doesn't disappoint. **Magic Mountain** is located behind the marina, with waterslides, dodgem cars and other rides. In the warmer

months, other activities on offer include mini go-karts and bungee trampolining. Add to these things the revolving restaurant atop the Atlantic tower on Anzac Highway, and Glenelg can feel a little overdone. But then there are also some fascinating historic sites to visit, such as the **Old Gum Tree**, with a spectacularly bent trunk, in a park in Glenelg North. This was where the colony of South Australia was officially proclaimed in 1836, shortly after the first European settlers arrived.

Visit the **Bay Discovery Centre** in the old Glenelg Town Hall (Moseley Square) for more history. Also in the town hall is the **Rodney Fox Shark Experience**, with full-size models of sharks and displays of shark jaws and fossilised teeth, as well as a huge collection of photographs. The display was collected by Rodney Fox, a shark-attack victim, filmmaker and researcher. The town hall also has information on various walking trails around Glenelg and along the coast.

Henley Beach to Semaphore 210 A2

At Henley Beach a long wooden jetty extends into Gulf St Vincent, flanked on either side by a long strip of sand that in summer is filled with sunbathers. Nearby **Henley Square** is a drawcard, especially on weekends, with restaurants, bars and cafes often humming with live music.

Straight up Seaview Road is the suburb of **Grange**, which has its own combination of beach and jetty. The transformed Grange Jetty Kiosk offers fine food in a casual setting.

Further along is **Semaphore**, a suburb with fine heritage buildings, many cafes and uninterrupted sea views. This suburb grew as a village, separated from Adelaide and Port Adelaide by the Port River. It served as the government's official signal

A Glenelg tram

station from 1856. With the construction of a sturdy bridge, Semaphore later developed into a seaside resort, and a 1920s carousel on the foreshore survives from those early days. The carousel still offers rides at weekends and on public and school holidays. A waterslide operates during the warmer months, and visitors can take historic train rides from the jetty to nearby **Fort Glanville**, built as defence against a Russian invasion. The Art Deco Semaphore Palais offers dining right on the waterfront, and a popular walking and bike-riding track heads north to Largs Bay and North Haven Marina.

Port Adelaide 548 C6

Melbourne has St Kilda, Perth has Fremantle, Hobart has Salamanca Place – and Adelaide has Port Adelaide. Without being overly commercialised, 'the Port', established in 1840, retains the charm of its maritime history and serves as an interesting destination in its own right, with weekend wharf markets, pubs and cafes, and galleries and antique shops. This was South Australia's first State Heritage Area, with historic buildings and a sense of the days when the old ports were busy trading and social centres. There's even a tunnel from a brig in the basement of one old pub to a platform under a wharf on the Port River. Drunken sailors would be taken back to their ships via this passage, after sleeping off a night's indulgence.

This is, however, still very much a working port, with a grain terminal, a tug-base, and fishing and pleasure boats in the inner port – on the upper reaches of the Port River – and a container terminal and wharves for large ships in the outer harbour, at the mouth of the river. On a trip down the river, visitors pass three power stations as well as the construction base for Australia's Collins Class submarines.

South Australian Maritime Museum 548 B6

A red-and-white lighthouse stands right in the middle of Port Adelaide, on Queens Wharf. Although not in its original location and now owned by the maritime museum, it signifies just how important the great days of seafaring were to this suburb. Behind the lighthouse is the Maritime Museum proper, where visitors can immerse themselves in South Australia's beach-going lifestyle, climb aboard a replica ketch, or learn about the tentative beginnings of the state's rock-lobster industry. You might even pick up a few trade secrets, such as the reason prawn fishermen never go out to sea on a full-moon night. This is a first-class centre with a program of permanent and changing exhibitions. *126 Lipson St, Port Adelaide; open daily; admission fee applies.*

Port Adelaide's dolphins

The environment of thick mangroves, mud and mosquitoes didn't endear the Port Adelaide area to the early settlers and they named it Port Misery. Today this environment is more popular, and is known as a haven for birdlife and the home of animals including a pod of playful bottlenose dolphins. Visitors can drive along the Dolphin Trail to the six hotspots where dolphins are commonly sighted (maps are available from the visitor centre) or take a cruise from Queens Wharf near the lighthouse – the dolphins often swim alongside the boat. On Sundays there are several cruises throughout the day; those wishing to take cruises on other days are advised to book ahead. For a special outing, visitors can also book a cruise on one of the tall ships docked at the wharf – the *One and All* and the *Falie*. *Port Adelaide Visitor Centre, 66 Commercial Rd.*

Ships' Graveyard 548 C5

Many shipwrecks and other sunken vessels around Australia provide magnificent sites for divers – but the one in Port Adelaide can be accessed from land. Around 25 wrecks were abandoned on the south side of Garden Island, including barges, sailing ships and steamers – their disintegrating skeletons create an eerie skyline above the water. Visitors can view this watery graveyard from the Garden Island Bridge, or – for a closer look – on a kayak tour with Blue Water Sea Kayaking (phone (08) 08 8295 8812).

St Kilda 548 C4

St Kilda is more of an outer village than an outer suburb, even though it is only a short distance (as the crow flies) from Port Adelaide and the Lefevre Peninsula. The access road crosses vast salt crystallisation pans, but beyond them is an idyllic little marina and other attractions that make this an excellent daytrip destination. First is the Mangrove Trail and Interpretive Centre, which gives a fascinating insight into this little-understood ecosystem and its inhabitants. Then there is the Tramway Museum, open on Sundays, which has 20 historic trams and provides tram rides to the nearby adventure playground. The playground is St Kilda's pièce de résistance, with a range of unique play equipment that includes a wooden ship, giant slides and a monorail.

Towards the Fleurieu

The southern suburbs of Adelaide begin to blur into the Fleurieu Peninsula just south of Brighton. Here you'll find **Hallett Cove Conservation Park** (548 B10), which protects an incredible record of glaciation. Over a period of 600 million years this part of the coast has changed from tidal flats to mountain ranges, ice-scape, shallow seas and alluvial plains – it has created some spectacular ochre- and sand-coloured

Walks and tours

Adelaide Oval Tours *Get an up-close view of this Adelaide icon as well as access to the Adelaide Oval Museum. Weekdays at 10am, departing from the southern end.*

Market Adventures *Follow the experts through Adelaide's famous Central Market. The same company also runs a 'Grazing on Gouger' tour, giving people the chance to eat five courses at five of Gouger Street's best restaurants. Bookings (08) 8336 8333.*

Taoundi Aboriginal Cultural Tour *Learn about the bush tucker and medicines of the Kaurna people on this guided walk through the Botanic Gardens of Adelaide. Mon–Fri; tickets from garden kiosk.*

City of Adelaide Historical Walking Trails *Pick up a brochure from the visitor centre and head out on one of a series of themed walks, covering everything from the grand buildings of North Adelaide to the places of interest around Rundle Mall and Adelaide's historic cinemas and theatres.*

Port Walks *Take a walk through historic Port Adelaide. Contact the Port Adelaide Visitor Centre for details. 66 Commercial Rd; (08) 8405 6560.*

Yurrebilla Trail *Take in the magnificent bushland on Adelaide's doorstep on this 52 km trail that links Black Hill and Morialta conservation parks in the north with Belair National Park in the south. The scenery includes gorges, waterfalls, thick forest and, around some corners, unsurpassed views of the city. Walkers can also opt to do smaller sections of the hike. Contact the visitor centre for details or go to www.environment.sa.gov.au/parks/yurrebilla*

SOUTH AUSTRALIA

Sport

*Adelaide has been passionate about **cricket** from its earliest beginnings. Until his death in 2001, Adelaide was the proud home of Australia's greatest cricketer, Sir Donald Bradman. The city is also home to the Adelaide Oval, regarded as one of the most beautiful sporting arenas in the world. The oval has a charming blend of historic and contemporary grandstand architecture, a hill at the northern end shaded by enormous Moreton Bay fig trees, and a scoreboard more than a century old next to a modern replay screen. Adelaide's cricket test, usually in December, is a great event, marked by the attendance of what seems to be South Australia's entire farming community and thousands of school children.*

*With two local **AFL** teams, Adelaide and Port Adelaide, football is the city's other sporting passion. Showdown is the twice-yearly match between the two teams, and the whole city stops to watch what seems like Adelaide's own grand final. Football Park at West Lakes is the city's home of AFL.*

*In March there is a **motor race** that literally takes over the city. Sections of the Clipsal 500 Adelaide track, centring on Victoria Park Racecourse, are run on Wakefield Road and East Terrace in the south-east of the city. This V8 event was created after Adelaide lost the Australian Formula One Grand Prix to Melbourne and, interestingly, is more popular than Formula One ever was. Some say it is now the best event on Australia's racing calendar.*

*Also on the calendar is the AAPT Championships, the international **tennis** tournament held at Memorial Drive near the Adelaide Oval in late December/early January. Adelaide's United **soccer** team matches are held at Hindmarsh Stadium, and the NBL 36ers play **basketball** on their home court at Beverley.*

rock formations. A walking trail takes visitors on a guided geological tour. A little further south the state's second longest river flows through **Onkaparinga River Recreation Reserve** and **National Park** (549 F3). In the park the river has created a gorge 50 metres deep, and there are some excellent – but steep – walking trails.

City surrounds

While the majority of Adelaide's attractions centre on the city and the coast, some interesting attractions can also be found in a broad band of inland suburbs.

Snowdome 210 F2

To compensate for the fact that South Australia is a state without snow, Snowdome boasts the world's first indoor ski slope. It has 200 tons of real snow, and is suited to both children and adult skiers and snowboarders. All equipment is available for hire, and skiing lessons are available. There is also an ice-skating rink in the complex. *23 East Tce, Thebarton; open daily (until late on Fri & Sat); admission fee applies.*

Haigh's Chocolates 211 H4

Australia's oldest chocolate-maker is located just south of Adelaide's CBD. A visitor centre is attached to the factory and includes a viewing area, displays of original factory machinery and a delightful, old-world shop with a tempting array of chocolates. While you'll be sure to find all your favourites, Haigh's also has some unique creations, such as quandong-filled chocolates. *154 Greenhill Rd, Parkside; closed Sun.*

R. M. Williams Outback Heritage Museum 548 D7

Reginald Murray Williams was a classic example of the 1930s battler – he spent his life moving from digging wells to mining, droving and whatever else he could do to earn a living. He made his first pair of boots in outback South Australia and later started up a 'factory' in his father's back shed. Out of this grew an Australian legend. This museum, on the site of that shed, charts the story of his life in fascinating photographs, objects and displays. *5 Percy St, Prospect; open Mon–Sat; admission free.*

Investigator Science and Technology Centre 548 C7

This is an excellent place to bring children, with its emphasis on making science both fun and interactive. Learn about a range of subjects, from sound waves and the arrangement of the night sky to the way the human mind works. During school holidays, a range of different shows are held throughout the day. *Days Rd, Regency Park; open daily; admission fee applies.*

Carrick Hill 211 I7

This 1930s house was once the home of Edward and Ursula Hayward – Edward was the son of wealthy retailers, and Ursula was the daughter of wealthy pastoralists. On their year-long honeymoon they collected many of the fittings for their house, including 16th- to 18th-century windows, doors, staircases and panelling. When they returned, their house was built in the style of a 17th-century English manor. The gardens surrounding the house contain a citrus orchard, a pleached pear arbour and avenues of poplars. The house also has an impressive collection of art. *46 Carrick Hill Dr, Springfield; open Wed–Sun; admission fee applies.*

Penfolds Magill Estate 548 E8

This winery, located between the city and the hills, was the first venture of Penfolds, one of Australia's best known winemakers. Established in 1844, the vintage cellar is still used for making shiraz, and the Still House, once used for making brandy, is now used for cellar-door tastings and sales. *78 Penfold Rd, Magill; open daily.*

Day tours

Adelaide Hills *The hills directly east of Adelaide have long been a retreat for citysiders including, most famously, 19th-century governors. Today the attractions of this beautiful semirural area include cool-climate wineries, gourmet produce, forests, and lookouts over the city. For more detail see p. 222*

Barossa Valley *Australia's best-known winegrowing region is a landscape of rolling yellow hills carpeted with vines. It boasts around 50 wineries, including some of the top names in the business. The district owes much to its strong German heritage, which is also expressed in the local food, architecture, and many cultural events. For more detail see p. 223*

Clare Valley *Boutique wineries, attractive 19th-century buildings and magnificent food and accommodation make the scenic Clare Valley a favourite weekend retreat. Just east of Clare is another world altogether – the old mining region of Burra, with landmarks that recall the immense copper boom. For more detail see p. 224*

Fleurieu Peninsula *The small seaside villages along Gulf St Vincent and the historic maritime town of Victor Harbor are irresistible seaside destinations close to the capital. En route to the peninsula, visitors can stop in at one of the cellar doors around McLaren Vale, one of the country's top wine regions. For more detail see p. 220*

SOUTH AUSTRALIA'S
REGIONS

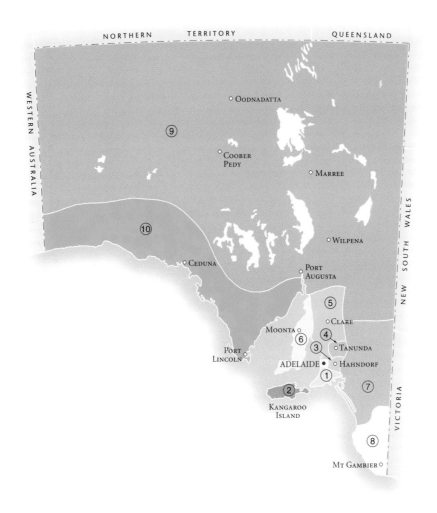

FLEURIEU PENINSULA

Port Noarlunga

This peninsula is one of South Australia's most popular and accessible holiday destinations. It is known for its wineries, magnificent coastline, scenic hinterland and gourmet produce. Some of the Fleurieu's rural villages date back 160 years, while on the south-east coast Goolwa and Port Elliot – and later Goolwa and Victor Harbor – were once linked in the great days of Murray River transport. Along the remote southern coastline are protected coves, rugged headlands, and creeks cutting a path through deep valleys; from the cliff-tops are views across to Kangaroo Island. The 1200-kilometre Heysen Trail, one of the country's premier long-distance bushwalks, begins at Cape Jervis.

Focus on
Wine districts
The Fleurieu Peninsula has two main wine-producing districts: McLaren Vale and Langhorne Creek. The McLaren Vale district is set against a landscape of weathered hills and rolling acres. With a viticulture history dating back to 1838, the region is highly regarded particularly for its full-bodied reds, most notably its shiraz. Over 50 wineries, ranging from boutique outfits to big players, are located in the district – Tourist Route 60 is an excellent way to explore both the wineries and the region. The second district is based around the highly productive Langhorne Creek area on the flood plains of the Bremer and Angas rivers. Vines have been grown here since the 1850s, however only five cellar doors offer tastings and sales. Many of the grapes grown here are sold to wine-producers in other regions around the country.

McLaren Vale
This is the heart of the wine region, but vines are not the only side to agriculture here – olives, almonds, avocados and stone fruits are also grown in the fertile surrounds. In town, visit the Almond and Olive Train and the McLaren Vale Olive Grove for local produce, and head to Medlow Confectionary for high-quality gels and chocolates.

Gulf St Vincent coast
The Fleurieu Peninsula's western coastline includes spectacular scenery and popular holiday towns. While visiting, go snorkelling at Port Noarlunga, dive off Aldinga Beach, bathe at one of a number of family beaches or visit the heritage-listed sand dunes at Normanville.

CLIMATE **VICTOR HARBOR**

	J	F	M	A	M	J	J	A	S	O	N	D
Max °C	25	25	23	21	19	16	15	16	18	20	22	24
Min °C	15	15	14	12	10	8	8	8	9	10	12	14
Rain mm	21	20	23	43	62	71	75	67	56	46	28	24
Raindays	5	4	6	10	14	15	17	16	14	11	8	7

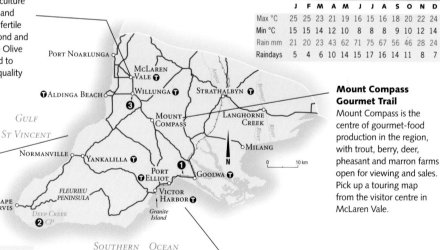

Mount Compass Gourmet Trail
Mount Compass is the centre of gourmet-food production in the region, with trout, berry, deer, pheasant and marron farms open for viewing and sales. Pick up a touring map from the visitor centre in McLaren Vale.

Victor Harbor
Historic Victor Harbor on Encounter Bay began as a whaling port in the 1830s, later becoming the ocean port for trade up and down the Murray (linked by rail to Goolwa at the Murray mouth). Today visitors can soak up the relaxed atmosphere of this popular holiday resort. Take a walk around the many heritage sites in town, or jump on a horse-drawn tram to Granite Island to see penguins, dolphins and maybe even whales.

Experience it!

1 **Ride** around Encounter Bay on the Cockle Train, between Goolwa and Victor Harbor

2 **Pack** a picnic and hike to secluded Deep Creek Cove, in Deep Creek Conservation Park

3 **Shop** for local produce at the Willunga Farmers Market, held each Saturday

For more detail see maps 548, 549, 550, 552 & 555.
For descriptions of T towns see Towns from A–Z (p. 230).

KANGAROO ISLAND

Australia's third largest island is located in the remote Southern Ocean, 16 kilometres off the tip of the Fleurieu Peninsula. Its most popular attraction is a large population of native creatures who live undisturbed in pristine natural habitats. Other attractions include its coastal scenery – rugged surf beaches in the south and idyllic coves in the north – its maritime history and its local produce. The island is reached by vehicular ferry from Cape Jervis or by plane from Adelaide. Accommodation options include camping spots in the forest, beachfront apartments and eco cabins.

Remarkable Rocks, Flinders Chase National Park

Top events

Feb   Racing Carnival (Kingscote)
Street Fair (Kingscote)

Easter Kangaroo Island Easter Fair (Parndana)
Art Exhibition (Penneshaw)

Focus on

Wildlife-watching

As a result of its isolation from the mainland, Kangaroo Island has one of Australia's most impressive concentrations of wildlife. Seal Bay is home to a colony of Australian sea lions, while at Cape du Couedic in Flinders Chase National Park there is a 600-strong colony of New Zealand fur seals. This national park is also the best place to see land animals like kangaroos, tammar wallabies, brush-tailed possums and the occasional koala or platypus. Little penguins can be seen on tours operating from Kingscote or Penneshaw. There is a large and varied bird population (240 species) across the island, with Murray Lagoon (en route to Seal Bay) home to many waterbirds.

CLIMATE KINGSCOTE

	J	F	M	A	M	J	J	A	S	O	N	D
Max °C	24	24	22	20	18	15	15	15	17	19	21	22
Min °C	15	15	14	13	11	9	8	8	9	10	12	14
Rain mm	15	17	18	35	58	73	77	65	47	37	23	19
Raindays	4	4	5	9	13	16	18	17	13	10	7	5

SOUTH AUSTRALIA

Cape Borda Lighthouse

This unusually shaped lighthouse – squat and square rather than tall and round – was built in 1858 and converted to automatic operation in 1989. Guided tours are conducted regularly and accommodation is available in the old lighthouse-keeper's residence.

Kingscote

The island's largest town, Kingscote is situated on the Bay of Shoals. It was the site of the state's first European settlement (1836), and its long pioneering history is presented in the excellent National Trust Museum. Other attractions include tours to see the nearby colony of little penguins.

Flinders Chase National Park

This park is the location of the Remarkable Rocks, enormous weathered boulders that perch precariously on a cliff. It is also known for its wonderfully varied springtime wildflowers and for its wildlife – including the New Zealand fur seal colony at Cape du Couedic and the Cape Barren geese often seen wandering around the visitor centre. Walking trails lead into the wilderness.

Experience it!

1 **Taste** the island's gourmet produce, including superb cheese and honey, at the various farms and outlets inland from Kingscote

2 **Fish** for King George whiting off the jetty in Kingscote

3 **Climb** the stairs to Mt Thisby Lookout for the view Matthew Flinders saw when he surveyed Kangaroo Island

For more detail see maps 549, 552 & 554–5.
For descriptions of 🛈 towns see Towns from A–Z (p. 230).

Seal Bay Conservation Park

Some 500 Australian sea lions feed their young and rest between fishing expeditions at Seal Bay. See the creatures from a boardwalk or up-close on a ranger-guided tour, which takes you down onto the beach.

ADELAIDE HILLS

*Piccadilly Valley,
north of Stirling*

Top events

Easter	Oakbank Easter Racing Carnival
April	Mount Lofty Spring Bulb Festival (Stirling)
May	Autumn Leaves Festival (Aldgate)
	Highland Gathering and Heritage Festival (Mount Barker)
Sept	Bay to Birdwood Run (vintage vehicles)
	Hills Affare (wine and food, Stirling)
Oct	Heysen Festival (Hahndorf)
Nov	Rock and Roll Rendezvous (Birdwood)
Dec	Lights of Lobethal Festival

T his magnificent landscape of hills and valleys rises in the east above the coastal plains of Adelaide. It is well known for its interesting mix of Australian bushland and European-style farmland, and for its historic villages, gardens, museums and galleries. The Adelaide Hills are a feast for the senses – taste the wines of a boutique vineyard, breathe in the clean air in the parks and gardens, and take in fantastic views from lookouts high in the hills. Visit on a daytrip from Adelaide, just 20 minutes away, or stay longer at one of the many B&Bs and guesthouses.

Focus on

Food and wine

The Adelaide Hills are becoming increasingly well known as a touring destination for those with gourmet inclinations. Highlights include a visit to Petaluma's Bridgewater Mill, an old flour mill, for tastings and sales of Petaluma wines or lunch at the restaurant attached. In Hahndorf try German-style produce, including breads and smallgoods, at the many outlets. Here you can also buy full-flavoured berry produce at the Beerenberg Strawberry Farm or go wine-tasting at Hahndorf Hill Winery or Hillstowe Wines. There is an excellent introduction to South Australia's regional wine and cheese at the Birdwood Wine and Cheese Centre, which offers tastings. Fine boutique wineries are also found around Birdwood.

Mt Lofty Lookout

Enjoy spectacular views of Adelaide and the hills from the lookout at the 727 m summit of Mt Lofty. Drop in to the information centre to plan your day, and enjoy 'food with a view' in the adjacent restaurant and cafe.

Cleland Wildlife Park

Within Cleland Conservation Park, this excellent wildlife park has a large collection of everybody's favourite animals, including kangaroos, emus and wallabies. Nocturnal walks reveal some of the rarer species, including bettongs and bandicoots. Daytime visits could be combined with a picnic in the adjacent Mount Lofty Botanic Gardens.

CLIMATE **MOUNT BARKER**												
	J	F	M	A	M	J	J	A	S	O	N	D
Max °C	27	27	25	20	17	14	13	14	16	19	22	25
Min °C	12	12	10	8	7	5	5	5	6	7	9	10
Rain mm	26	26	31	59	89	100	105	103	86	68	40	34
Raindays	6	5	7	11	15	16	17	18	15	13	9	7

Experience it!

❶ **Visit** Birdwood National Motor Museum, with over 300 vintage vehicles tracing the history of motoring

❷ **Journey** back in time along the historic interpretive trail at the Jupiter Creek Goldfields near Echunga

❸ **Hear** ancient Dreamtime stories on a guided walk along the Yurridla Trail in Cleland Conservation Park

Hahndorf

This distinctive town was settled in the 1830s by Prussian refugees. Its heritage is preserved in the village architecture and German-style shops, museums and cafes. Visit The Cedars, former home of artist Hans Heysen, and see contemporary artworks at the Hahndorf Academy.

Belair National Park

South Australia's oldest national park, established in 1891, offers a natural landscape of eucalypt forests and brilliant flowering plants. Green-thumbs will enjoy a stroll through the gardens of the governor's old summer residence, which dates back to 1859.

*For more detail see maps 548, 549, 550, 552 & 555.
For descriptions of ❶ towns see Towns from A–Z (p. 230).*

BAROSSA VALLEY

The Barossa is Australia's best-known wine region. Along with nearby Eden Valley, it offers a landscape of vine-covered hills dotted with historic villages, stone cottages and the grand buildings of old wine estates. The wine traditions are based on a 150-year history of German settlement, which can be seen in every aspect of life – from the spires of the Lutheran churches to the local German breads and pastries. Only an hour from Adelaide, the Barossa also boasts some of the best restaurants and accommodation of any regional area.

Eden Valley winery

Top events

Feb   Barossa under the Stars (Rowland Flat)

Easter Gawler Gourmet and Heritage Festival

April Barossa Vintage Festival (throughout region, odd-numbered years)

Oct   Barossa International Music Festival (throughout region)

Brass Band Contest (Tanunda)

Focus on

Gourmet tradition

While many parts of Australia have developed gourmet credentials over the last decade or so, the Barossa has a culinary heritage that dates back to the mid-1800s. German-style baking is a highlight: try the Lyndoch Bakery, or the Apex Bakery in Tanunda, established 70 years ago. Old-fashioned ice-cream is made and served at Tanunda's Nice Ice and in Angaston you'll find the shopfront for Australia's biggest processor of dried fruit – the Angas Park Fruit Company. Maggie Beer's Farm Shop at Nuriootpa sells the cook's renowned products – everything from quince paste to verjuice – while Angaston Gourmet Foods is a showcase for all the best local foods.

CLIMATE NURIOOTPA

	J	F	M	A	M	J	J	A	S	O	N	D
Max °C	29	29	26	21	17	14	13	14	17	20	24	26
Min °C	14	14	12	9	7	5	4	5	6	8	10	12
Rain mm	19	19	22	38	55	56	66	64	60	49	29	24
Raindays	5	4	5	8	12	13	16	16	13	11	8	6

SOUTH AUSTRALIA

Barossa wineries

In this famed region is a landscape of old, gnarled shiraz vines planted as early as the 1840s adding character to the newer vines and varieties. The Barossa is best known for its shiraz, semillon and chardonnay. The biennial Barossa Vintage Festival is a time of great activity and colour.

Seppeltsfield

The Seppelts estate, established in the 1850s, is one of the grandest in the country. Elegant bluestone buildings are surrounded by superb gardens, and the property is accessed by an avenue of 2000 date palms. Don't miss the hilltop mausoleum built in the style of a Doric temple.

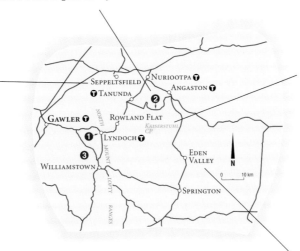

Kaiserstuhl Conservation Park

This rugged mountainside park offers a view of what the Barossa would have looked like before European settlement. A couple of excellent walking trails allow visitors to explore the varied terrain and glimpse the local wildlife.

Eden Valley wineries

This elevated wine-producing area is regarded as a distinct region. A small number of wineries are open for tastings. In Springton stands the Herbig Tree, a giant, hollow red gum that was the temporary home of a German family in the 1850s.

Experience it!

1 **Look** down over the Barossa Valley on a hot-air-balloon flight from Lyndoch

2 **Travel** Menglers Hill Road Scenic Drive between Angaston and Tanunda

3 **Whisper** messages at one end of the Whispering Wall near Williamstown and have them heard at the other

For more detail see maps 548, 550, 551 & 555.
For descriptions of ⊤ towns see Towns from A–Z (p. 230).

MID-NORTH

Sevenhill winery

Top events

Feb   Jailhouse Rock Festival (Burra)

Mar   Twilight Jazz Affair (Burra)

Easter Clare Races (horseracing)

April   Celtic Music Festival (Kapunda)

Spanish Festival (Clare)

May   Antique and Decorating Fair (Burra)

Farm Fair (odd-numbered years, Kapunda)

Clare Gourmet Weekend

Aug   Balaklava Cup (horseracing)

Nov   Spring Garden Festival (Clare)

The mid-north was settled in the 1840s as a major mining and farming district. The area today is renowned for its scenic countryside, with old stone cottages and a spread of rolling hills and vineyards. The wineries of the Clare Valley are the prime attraction, followed by the old coppermining sites of Burra – said to be among the most important historic industrial sites in Australia. These attractions combine with galleries, antique and craft stores, B&Bs and restaurants to make this a great place for a weekend away.

Focus on

History

Historically, this is one of the most interesting and well-preserved areas of rural South Australia. In 1839 Edward Eyre explored the Clare Valley and his favourable reports led quickly to pastoral settlement. Jesuit priests planted the first Clare Valley vines at Sevenhill in 1851, and a booming wine industry followed. Copper deposits found at Burra and Kapunda in the 1840s drove a huge mining industry, but this fell into decline in the 1870s. The community's perseverance in preserving Burra's history led to the town's State Heritage Area listing in 1993. Kapunda had a change of direction after mining, with cattle baron Sir Sidney Kidman initiating an agricultural industry that has since grown exponentially. This mixture of viticulture, agriculture and mining history is a Clare Valley attraction in itself – endless stories of survival and success can be found in the museums and displays throughout the region.

Clare Valley wineries

This wine-producing district extends for 35 km across the fertile valley, including big names as well as charming boutique establishments. Although the climate is generally Mediterranean in style, many Clare Valley wines have cool-climate characteristics. Clare Valley rieslings are regarded as among the best in Australia.

Sevenhill

Austrian Jesuit priests established the Clare Valley's first winery here in the early 1850s to ensure a steady supply of altar wine. There have been seven Jesuit winemakers since then, and the wine range now includes table wine. Next to the cellars, St Aloysius Church (1875) is worth a visit.

CLIMATE CLARE

	J	F	M	A	M	J	J	A	S	O	N	D
Max °C	30	29	27	22	17	14	13	15	18	21	25	27
Min °C	13	13	12	8	6	4	3	4	5	7	10	12
Rain mm	25	24	25	47	73	80	82	80	73	57	37	29
Raindays	4	4	5	8	12	14	15	15	13	11	7	6

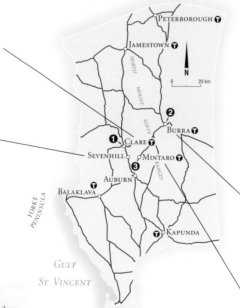

Burra

Located in the sparse landscape of the Bald Hills Range, this former coppermining centre is a timepiece of the mid-19th century. Pick up a Burra Heritage Passport and visit mine shafts, museums and heritage buildings. Marvel at the creek-bed dugouts that were home to over 1800 miners, and see the working conditions on a guided mine tour.

Experience it!

❶ **Buy** local gourmet produce – chutneys, jams, olive oil and more – from Clare retailers

❷ **Explore** the Bald Hills Range on horseback, on a trail-ride near Burra

❸ **Cycle** or walk the Riesling Trail, a scenic 27 km path following the old railway line between Clare and Auburn

For more detail see maps 550, 555 & 557.
For descriptions of ❶ towns see Towns from A–Z (p. 230).

Mintaro

Mintaro is an almost-intact 19th-century village, with many attractive stone buildings incorporating the region's unique slate. It was the first town in South Australia to be declared a State Heritage Area. Just south-east is Martindale Hall, an 1879 mansion used in the film *Picnic at Hanging Rock* (1975) and now open to the public.

YORKE PENINSULA

Wallaroo
jetty

This long, boot-shaped peninsula is flanked by the calm waters of Gulf St Vincent on one side and by Spencer Gulf on the other. The area was put on the map in the late 1850s by the discovery of rich copper-ore deposits – many of the now peaceful resort towns along the coast were once busy ports. Today the area is one of the world's richest barley- and wheat-growing regions, and is also a popular beachside holiday destination (around two hours from Adelaide). The surrounding waters offer excellent fishing, diving and surfing.

Top events

May	Kernewek Lowender (Cornish festival, odd-numbered years, Kadina, Moonta and Wallaroo)
Sept	Blessing of the Fleet (Port Pirie)
Oct	Moonta Garden Fair
	Yorke Surfing Classic (Innes National Park)
	Festival of Country Music (Port Pirie)
Nov	Copper Coast Fishing Competition (Wallaroo)
	Copper Coast Spring Garden Fair (Kadina)

Focus on

Fishing

The Yorke Peninsula is one of South Australia's top fishing destinations, with jetties at Wallaroo, Moonta Bay, Edithburgh, Stansbury and Port Victoria, and rocky points and sandy coves all through the region, providing excellent opportunities for land-based anglers. Snapper, squid, tommy ruff, garfish and whiting are among the more commonly caught species. Reef-fishing is also popular. Browns Beach, on the western side of Innes National Park, is renowned for its big hauls of salmon. Near Goose Island, just north of Wardang Island on the west coast, are two reefs that offer excellent boat-fishing for a variety of species.

Port Victoria

This town was once the main port of call for the clippers and windjammers that transported grain to the Northern Hemisphere, a period of history recorded in the local Maritime Museum. Port Victoria is now a resort town, offering access to swimming beaches and to Wardang Island, a popular diving spot with an underwater heritage trail featuring eight wrecks.

Innes National Park

At the southern tip of the peninsula, Innes National Park protects salt lakes, low mallee scrub, wildflowers, sandy beaches and rugged cliffs. Browns Beach, West Cape and Pondalowie Bay are popular for surfing, diving and fishing. A 1904 shipwreck can be glimpsed from Ethel Beach, and the interesting remains of Inneston mining town are found in the south of the park.

Little Cornwall

The Cornish miners that flocked to Wallaroo, Moonta and Kadina in the early 1860s prompted the colloquial name for this triangle of towns – Little Cornwall. The discovery of substantial copper deposits led to a prosperous mining industry, revealed in the heritage architecture of the towns. Visit the Moonta Mines State Heritage Area, with walking trails to mining ruins.

Edithburgh

The town's jetty was once the site of a large shipping operation, when thousands of tons of salt harvested from the nearby lakes were exported from here. Edithburgh is now a popular resort town. Attractions include a tidal pool for safe swimming, good diving locations, and access to Troubridge Island, home to populations of little penguins, black-faced shags and crested terns.

Experience it!

❶ Travel on the historic diesel train between Wallaroo and Bute

❷ Follow the Investigator Strait Maritime Heritage Trail – taking in 26 dive sites to sunken vessels

❸ Taste fresh oysters at the oyster farms in Stansbury

For more detail see map 554–5.
For descriptions of ❶ towns see Towns from A–Z (p. 230).

CLIMATE KADINA

	J	F	M	A	M	J	J	A	S	O	N	D
Max °C	31	30	28	24	19	16	15	17	20	23	26	28
Min °C	16	16	14	11	9	7	6	6	8	10	12	14
Rain mm	15	19	19	33	46	52	49	45	39	34	23	18
Raindays	3	3	4	6	10	12	13	13	10	8	6	4

SOUTH AUSTRALIA

MURRAY

The Murray River runs through South Australia for 650 kilometres. It crosses a variety of landscapes – rugged cliff-lined river valleys, mallee scrub, river red gum forests, lagoons, orchards and vineyards. The river empties into the massive Lake Alexandrina on the coast and feeds the wondrous Coorong wetlands. Its rich history of trade and agriculture has been preserved in the many river towns along the way. As South Australia's only river of significance, it provides a welcome focus in a state known for its aridity and is a popular destination for relaxing summer holidays.

Murray River scenery near Berri

Top events

Feb	Mardi Gras (Loxton)
	Riverland Run, Rally and Rock (Renmark)
Mar	Rotary Food Fair (Waikerie)
	Riverland Greek Festival (Renmark)
May	Riverland Rock 'n' Roll Festival (Waikerie)
	Riverbank Balloon Fiesta (Renmark)
June	South Australian Country Music Festival (Barmera)
Oct	Rose Festival (Renmark)
Nov	Steam Rally Festival (Murray Bridge)

Focus on

Paddlesteamers

Paddlesteamers were first used in South Australia when PS *Mary Ann* was launched at Mannum in 1853. Carrying goods and passengers, they were vital in the development of the all-important trade route that ran from the mouth of the river into New South Wales and Victoria (and vice versa). Two of the original boats, PS *Mayflower* and PS *Marion*, operate as day-cruisers, departing from Morgan and Mannum respectively. Longer tours are available from Mannum on PS *River Murray Princess* – the largest paddleboat ever built in the Southern Hemisphere – and from Murray Bridge on PS *Proud Mary*, which specialises in nature tours.

Riverland produce

The Riverland is the fruit bowl of South Australia, producing over 90 percent of the state's citrus fruit, stone fruit and nuts. Wine is also produced here; tastings and sales are available at half-a-dozen estates, including Angoves near Renmark, Berri Estates Winery near Berri, and Banrock Station Wine and Wetland Centre at Kingston-on-Murray.

CLIMATE RENMARK

	J	F	M	A	M	J	J	A	S	O	N	D
Max °C	33	32	29	24	20	17	16	18	21	24	28	30
Min °C	17	17	14	11	8	6	5	6	8	11	13	15
Rain mm	16	19	14	18	25	25	23	25	28	28	21	18
Raindays	3	3	3	4	6	8	8	9	7	6	4	4

Morgan

Morgan's days as a busy river port may be over, but a rich legacy of sites and buildings preserves something of the excitement of the 19th-century river trade. Look out for the wharves (built in 1877), the customs house and the courthouse. For a thorough look at the history of Morgan, drop in to the Port of Morgan Historical Museum in the old railway buildings.

The Coorong

The Coorong, a shallow lagoon protected within Coorong National Park, is one of Australia's most significant wetlands. It stretches 135 km along the coast, separated from the Southern Ocean by the dunes of the Younghusband Peninsula. The Coorong is best known for its abundant birdlife (and for birdwatching). Over 240 species have been recorded, including many migratory species.

Camping and watersports

From Murray Bridge to Renmark there are caravan parks and camping grounds with river frontage and access to a wide range of watersports, including canoeing, fishing and swimming. Murray River National Park provides a couple of quiet spots at the north-east end of the river for those who like their recreation in a park setting.

Experience it!

1 **Hop** on a safari bus at the open-range Monarto Zoological Park near Murray Bridge

2 **Captain** your own houseboat for a few days of Murray River sightseeing

3 **Discover** the rich Aboriginal history of the Coorong in the museum at Camp Coorong

For more detail see maps 550, 552 & 555.
For descriptions of ⊤ towns see Towns from A–Z (p. 230).

SOUTH-EAST

The south-east follows the coastline from Kingston S.E. to the Victorian border, and includes the fertile country inland. It is a major holiday region, featuring historic fishing villages and stunning beach scenery as well as the prestigious wineries of the Coonawarra. Impressive natural attractions include the World Heritage-listed Naracoorte Caves and the numerous coastal parks and wetland regions to be explored. The region's major service centre, Mount Gambier, is picturesquely set in pine forests on the edge of an ancient volcano.

Coastal scenery with Robe jetty in the background

Top events

Jan	Cape Jaffa Seafood and Wine Festival
	Yachting Regatta (Kingston S.E.)
	Bayside Festival (Port MacDonnell)
	Vigneron Cup (Penola)
	Lazy Days of Summer (Coonawarra/ Penola)
Feb	Taste the Limestone Coast (Naracoorte)
	South-East Country Music Weekend (Mount Gambier)
May	Penola Coonawarra Festival
	Mount Gambier Racing
Nov	Cabernet Celebrations (Coonawarra/ Penola)

Focus on
Seaside towns
In summer the quiet fishing towns of the coast transform into busy holiday centres, offering great beaches and fantastic seafood. Visit Kingston S.E., a major lobster port at the southern end of Coorong National Park – nearby lakes and lagoons are havens for birdlife. Head further south to Robe, with its lovely combination of maritime history and windswept scenery, or to Beachport, settled as a whaling station in the 1830s. Today the town's long jetty is a popular spot for fishing. For more fishing, don't miss Port MacDonnell, where it is the main focus of life and where you'll find South Australia's largest lobster fleet.

SOUTH AUSTRALIA

Robe
Settled in the 1840s, Robe is one of the state's oldest and best-preserved towns. It boasts a fine collection of stone cottages, shops, public buildings and hotels, many of them National Trust-classified. Set around Guichen Bay along a beautiful stretch of coast, Robe combines a quaint fishing-village atmosphere with excellent facilities for holiday-makers.

The Coonawarra
The Coonawarra is Australia's most valuable piece of wine real estate. The first vines were planted by John Riddoch in the late 1800s. Since then this 12 km long and 2 km wide stretch of terra rossa soil has continually produced wine of the highest quality, chiefly bold red varieties. The region's cabernet sauvignon is outstanding. Over 20 wineries offer cellar-door tastings and sales.

Experience it!

1 **Go** birdwatching at Bool Lagoon Game Reserve, one of southern Australia's most important wetlands

2 **Walk** the massive dunes of Canunda National Park

3 **Visit** the Mary MacKillop Interpretive Centre at Penola to learn about this pioneering woman

For more detail see map 552.
For descriptions of ⊕ towns
see Towns from A–Z (p. 230).

CLIMATE MOUNT GAMBIER

	J	F	M	A	M	J	J	A	S	O	N	D
Max °C	25	25	23	19	16	14	13	14	16	18	20	23
Min °C	11	12	10	9	7	6	5	5	6	7	8	10
Rain mm	26	25	35	55	72	84	99	94	73	63	47	37
Raindays	9	8	11	14	18	19	21	21	19	17	14	12

Naracoorte Caves
Along with Queensland's Riversleigh Fossil Site, this is one of Australia's most significant cave systems, a fact reflected by its World Heritage listing. There are 60 known caves, several of which are open to the public. At the excellent Wonambi Fossil Centre, displays show how the fossils found in the caves have played a key role in charting the continent's evolutionary history.

Mount Gambier
This major regional centre is set on the slopes of an extinct volcano – its crater contains the intensely coloured Blue Lake. Beneath the town, stretching from the coast all the way to Bordertown in the north, is an enormous wedge of limestone that has given rise to many caves. Nearby examples include Engelbrecht Cave (popular with divers) and the Umpherston Sinkhole.

FLINDERS RANGES & OUTBACK

Oodnadatta

This vast and varied region covers around 70 percent of South Australia, including some of the country's most legendary landscapes. The Flinders Ranges ripple through the south-east, rich with magnificent gorges and waterholes, Aboriginal sites, and the evocative ruins of many failed attempts at European settlement. To get to the real outback, head north and west; here you'll find the quintessential outback town of Coober Pedy, modern oases like Roxby Downs, and remote outposts like Innamincka and Oodnadatta. While many attractions are easily reached along well-maintained roads, others require four-wheel-drive vehicles and safety precautions.

Top events

Jan	Night Rodeo (Wilmington)
Feb	Wilpena under the Stars
Feb/Mar	Outback Surfboat Carnival (Port Augusta)
Mar	Outback Fringe Festival (Roxby Downs)
Easter	Opal Festival (Coober Pedy)
May	Race Meeting (Oodnadatta)
July	Pichi Richi Marathon (Quorn)
	Australian Camel Cup (Marree)
Aug	Picnic Race Meeting (Innamincka)

Focus on
Trails and tracks

Beginning (or ending) in the Flinders Ranges are two long-distance trails for bushwalkers and bike-riders. The longest track is the 1200 km Heysen Trail, which begins at Cape Jervis and follows the mountain ranges to Parachilna Gorge north of Flinders Ranges National Park, taking in the best of the scenery of the Fleurieu Peninsula, Adelaide Hills and Barossa Valley en route. The 800-kilometre Mawson Trail is a bike track that runs between Adelaide and Blinman – it was named after explorer Sir Douglas Mawson. The trail explores the lesser known parts of the Mount Lofty and Flinders ranges, travelling along unmade and rarely used roads, farm-access tracks and national-park trails. Beyond the ranges are some of Australia's premier four-wheel-drive treks, including the Oodnadatta Track – taking in hot springs, old railway sidings and sections of the Dog Fence – and the Birdsville Track, crossing impressive sandhills and Cooper Creek.

Innamincka Regional Reserve

Four-wheel-drive enthusiasts flock to this remote reserve to tackle the terrain, but there is more here than just adventure driving. The area's wetlands are internationally significant, particularly Coongie Lakes, which provide a vital refuge for waterbirds. Closer to Innamincka is the Cullyamurra Waterhole, on Cooper Creek, where visitors can see Aboriginal rock carvings.

Coober Pedy

Coober Pedy is considered the opal capital of the world, producing an incredible 90 percent of the world's gem-quality supply. It is also Australia's most famous underground town, with homes, churches and art galleries all set into the hills to keep cool. Visit the museums and mines, and try your hand at prospecting.

For more detail see maps 553, 556–7, 558–9 & 560–1.
For descriptions of ⓣ *towns see Towns from A–Z (p. 230).*

Wilpena Pound

The Pound, part of Flinders Ranges National Park, is one of the most extraordinary geological formations in Australia. It is a vast natural amphitheatre, ringed with sheer cliffs and jagged rocks that change colour according to the light. An old homestead within the pound, built by the Hill family in 1902 and abandoned after floods in 1914, stands as a reminder of the difficulties of farming in this environment.

Experience it!

❶ Take a Ridgetop Tour via Arkaroola, scaling hairy ridges to be rewarded with jaw-dropping views

❷ Rest aching muscles in the therapeutic Dalhousie Springs in remote Witjira National Park

❸ Take a flight over the vast saltpan of Lake Eyre from Marree or William Creek

Port Augusta

This prosperous port city stands at the northern tip of Spencer Gulf. It has some excellent attractions for visitors – the award-winning Wadlata Outback Centre provides an indigenous, natural and social history of the outback and ranges, while the Australian Arid Lands Botanic Garden offers an in-depth look at the country's little-understood arid environments.

CLIMATE HAWKER

	J	F	M	A	M	J	J	A	S	O	N	D
Max °C	34	33	30	25	20	16	16	18	22	26	29	32
Min °C	18	18	15	11	7	5	4	4	7	10	13	16
Rain mm	19	21	17	20	31	39	35	33	28	25	22	21
Raindays	3	3	2	3	5	7	7	7	6	5	4	3

EYRE PENINSULA & NULLARBOR

This region of vast landscapes stretches 1000 kilometres from the large town of Whyalla to the remote border of Western Australia, taking in the calm waters of Spencer Gulf and the wild seas of the Great Australian Bight. Fishing and surfing spots here are among the best in the world. Wildlife, wildflowers, coastal scrub and low hills dominate the eastern reaches; in the west vast, treeless plains and the spectacular sea-cliffs of the Nullarbor take over. Travel in the cooler months to avoid extreme heat, and take precautions when crossing the Nullarbor.

Whale-watching at Head of Bight

Top events

Jan	Tunarama Festival (Port Lincoln)
	Family Fish Day Contest (Streaky Bay)
Feb/Mar	Adelaide to Lincoln Yacht Race and Lincoln Week Regatta (Port Lincoln)
Mar–May	Sculptures on the Cliff (odd-numbered years, Elliston)
Easter	Australian Amateur Snapper Fishing Championship (Whyalla)
April	Mediterraneo Festival (Port Lincoln)
	World Championship Kalamazoo Classic (Cummins)
June–Aug	Australian Salmon Fishing Competition (Elliston)
Oct	Oysterfest (Ceduna)
	'Beyond and Back' Gawler Ranges Outback Challenge (even-numbered years, Kimba)

Focus on
Wildlife
This sparsely settled district remains a wildlife haven. Rare and endangered bird species find refuge in many of the parks and reserves; at Nullarbor National Park look out for Major Mitchell cockatoos, or see migrating birds land at Lincoln National Park after their journey from the chilly Arctic Circle. Lolling about on the sands after days of fishing far out at sea are the rare and endangered Australian sea lions of Point Labatt Conservation Park – they are Australia's only resident mainland colony. One of the most important parks in the region is the Sir Joseph Banks Group Conservation Park, on islands offshore from Tumby Bay. This park is Australia's largest breeding ground for Cape Barren geese, a breeding ground for dolphins, and a home for New Zealand fur seals and Australian sea lions.

Nullarbor Plain
The Nullarbor, Latin for 'treeless', is a plain of 250 000 sq km, resting on a massive area of limestone riddled with caves. Along the coast a long line of sheer-faced cliffs drop suddenly into the foaming waters of the Great Australian Bight. Head of Bight offers some of the country's best whale-watching, between June and October.

Surf coast
This 73 km stretch of coast between Ceduna and the tiny settlement of Penong justifiably promotes itself as a surfing paradise. There are renowned surf beaches along the remote coastline, the most famous being Cactus Beach, just south of Penong, which boasts three world-famous breaks.

WARNING: Sharks have been known to frequent these waters – seek local advice before entering.

Experience it!
❶ **Drive** the Whalers Way south of Port Lincoln for cliff-top views and sightings of kangaroos and emus

❷ **Swim** with the sea lions at Baird Bay, with Baird Bay Charters and Ocean Ecotours

❸ **Visit** the Stonehenge-like Murphy's Haystacks, south-east of Streaky Bay

Coffin Bay National Park
This park protects a pristine coastal wilderness of exposed cliffs, small coves and beaches. Bush camping, surfing, walking and fishing are all popular activities. Many of the vehicle tracks are 4WD only, but for conventional vehicles there is a popular scenic tour called the Yangie Trail, beginning at Coffin Bay township.

CLIMATE PORT LINCOLN

	J	F	M	A	M	J	J	A	S	O	N	D
Max °C	25	26	24	22	19	17	16	17	18	20	22	24
Min °C	15	16	15	13	11	9	8	8	9	11	12	14
Rain mm	13	15	20	37	57	75	79	69	50	36	22	19
Raindays	4	4	5	10	14	16	18	17	13	11	7	6

Spencer Gulf coast
Here calm waters lap at peaceful holiday villages and the northern regional centre of Whyalla. At Port Lincoln in the south, the huge natural harbour is home to Australia's foremost tuna fleet. Beaches, museums, golf, walks and drives all feature, but the biggest drawcard is fishing – jetty-fishing or gamefishing – in some of the best grounds in Australia.

For more detail see maps 554, 556, & 562–3.
For descriptions of ☗ towns see Towns from A–Z (p. 230).

Hauling in the day's catch at Port Willunga, near Aldinga Beach

TOWNS

Aldinga Beach — Pop. 5518

Map ref. 549 E4, 552 B3, 555 K10

The rolling hills of the southern Mount Lofty Ranges form the backdrop to Aldinga Beach, a long curve of white sand facing Gulf St Vincent. One and a half kilometres off the coast is one of the state's best diving spots – the Aldinga Drop Off, an underwater cliff where divers say the marine life has to be seen to be believed. The township – to the west of the original Aldinga, which grew as a small farming centre in the mid-1800s – is a popular holiday spot.

IN TOWN *Gnome Caves:* 5 theme 'caves', great for kids; Aldinga Beach Rd.
NEARBY *Star of Greece* In 1888 the *Star of Greece* plunged to the ocean floor in a wild storm. The ship was only a short distance from land, but at 3am, and in gigantic swells, 17 of the 28 people on board drowned. Today a portion of the vessel can be seen from shore at low tide. A plaque lies on the seabed for the benefit of divers, but for those wanting to stay dry, pictures of the wreck line the walls of the Star of Greece Cafe. Port Willunga, 3 km N. *Aldinga Scrub Conservation Park:* walk through remnant coastal vegetation; end of Dover St, off Aldinga Beach Rd; 1 km S. *Aldinga:* Uniting Church cemetery has the graves of those that died in the *Star of Greece* shipwreck. Aldinga Country Market, held in Institute Hall, Old Coach Rd, 1st Sat each month. 4 km NE. *Beaches:* many north and south of Aldinga Beach including Port Willunga Beach, with the remains of an old jetty and caves built in the cliff by anglers (3 km N); Sellicks Beach, with boat access and good fishing (8 km S); and Maslin Beach, Australia's first official nudist beach (10 km N). *Lookouts:* one south of Sellicks Beach (11 km S) and another over the Myponga Reservoir (23 km S).
❶ McLaren Vale and Fleurieu Visitor Centre, Main Rd, McLaren Vale; 1800 628 410 or (08) 8323 9944

Andamooka — Pop. 496

Map ref. 556 G4

If Queen Elizabeth II had ever been to Andamooka, perhaps she would have thought differently about the Andamooka Opal given to her as a gift in 1954 on her first visit to Australia. The opal weighed 203 carats and glistened in blues, reds and greens. It was the result of an extensive search for the most beautiful opal in the state, yet Andamooka itself is a misshapen collection of tin sheds, dugouts and fibros in the middle of the desert. With constant water shortages, no local council and an all-consuming drive to find opals, residents have become experts in making do. The town offers old-fashioned outback hospitality to an increasing number of tourists.

IN TOWN *Opal showrooms:* showrooms in town include Andamooka Gems and Trains, attached to Dukes Bottlehouse Motel, with opals and a model railway.

Historic miners' huts: a handful of old semi-dugouts line the creek bed in the centre of town, complete with old tools and furnishings. Access is by tour, which includes a visit to an underground mine. Details from post office. *Cemetery:* with miners' nicknames on the headstones.

WHAT'S ON *Market and barbecue:* local art and craft; Sat of long weekends (Easter, June and Oct).

NEARBY *Fossicking:* noodling in unclaimed mullock dumps surrounding town; details from post office. *Lake Torrens:* one of the state's largest salt lakes stretches away to the south-east; 4WD recommended for access.
ⓘ Dukes Bottlehouse Motel (incorporating post office), 275 Opal Creek Blvd; (08) 8672 7007; www.andamookaopal.com.au

Angaston   Pop. 1930

Map ref. 550 G4, 551 I5, 555 M8

Angaston takes its name from George Fife Angas who purchased the original plot of land on which the town now stands. He was a prominent figure in the South Australian Company and one of the shareholders who used his substantial buying power to get the best plots of land and dictate the terms of purchase. Many of the town's public buildings were funded by him, even before he emigrated. In a sense, the town's strong German heritage was also funded by him as he sponsored many Lutherans to make the journey to South Australia. Angaston still has strong ties with its history. In town is a German butcher that has been making wursts for more than 60 years, a blacksmith shop over a century old and a cafe and specialty food shop named the South Australian Company Store. Jacarandas and Moreton Bay figs line the main street.

IN TOWN **A. H. Doddridge Blacksmith Shop** This is the town's original blacksmith, started by Cornish emigrant William Doddridge. The shop closed in 1966 and 15 years later it was purchased by local townspeople. On Saturdays and Sundays it operates as a working smithy, complete with the original bellows that Doddridge brought out from England. Murray St.
Angas Park Fruit Co: retail outlet for Angas Park dried fruits and nuts; Murray St. *The Abbey:* second-hand clothing and period pieces inside the old church; Murray St; open Thurs–Sun. *The Lego Man:* one of Australia's largest Lego collections; 37 Jubilee Ave. *Food outlets:* include Angaston Gourmet Foods, famous for their baguettes, and the Barossa Valley Cheese Company, which makes cheese on the premises; Murray St. *Angaston Heritage Walk:* brochure from visitor centre.

WHAT'S ON *Farmers market:* Sat morning; behind Vintners Bar and Grill, Nuriootpa Rd. *Barossa Vintage Festival:* celebration of locally produced food and wine in various locations; odd-numbered years, April. *Barossa Jazz Weekend:* Aug. *Barossa International Music Festival:* Oct.

NEARBY *Barossa wine region:* wineries near Angaston include Saltram Estate, with historic Mamre Brook House and Salters Restaurant (1 km w), and Yalumba, one of the oldest in the Barossa with beautiful gardens and a distinctive clock tower (2 km s); *for more information on the region see Tanunda, Lyndoch and Nuriootpa. Collingrove Homestead:* the old Angas family home, now owned by the National Trust and open for tours, boutique accommodation and dining; 7 km se. *Mengler Hill Lookout:* views over the Barossa Valley; 8 km sw. *Kaiserstuhl Conservation Park:* a small pocket of native flora and fauna, with walking trails; 10 km s. *Butcher, Baker, Winemaker Trail:* between Lyndoch and Angaston, taking in wineries and gourmet-food producers along the way; brochure from visitor centre.
ⓘ Barossa Wine and Visitor Information Centre, 66–68 Murray St, Tanunda; 1300 852 982 or (08) 8563 0600

Ardrossan   Pop. 1080

Map ref. 555 J7

A cluster of bright white grain silos sit atop the red clay cliffs at Ardrossan, an industrial town on Yorke Peninsula. The town has two jetties – one for the export of grain, salt and dolomite and the other for the benefit of local anglers. Ardrossan is well known for its blue swimmer crabs that are found under the jetty or in the shallows at low tide. The best season for crabbing is between September and April.

IN TOWN **Stump Jump Plough** A lonely stump-jump plough stands in the cliff-top park opposite East Tce. Mallee scrub once covered much of this area and caused endless grief to early farmers because it was so difficult to clear. The invention of the stump-jump plough made it possible to jump over stumps left in the ground and plough on ahead. The plough's design was perfected in Ardrossan. The original factory, on Fifth St, now houses a historical museum (open Sun 2.30pm–4.30pm).

NEARBY *Zanoni wreck* South Australia's most complete shipwreck is 15 km south-east of Ardrossan off Rogues Point. The wreck was lost for over 100 years, but was eventually rediscovered by some local fishermen. It lies virtually in one piece on the seabed. Some artefacts from the ship can be found at the Ardrossan historical museum, but divers wanting to see the wreck in situ need a permit from Heritage South Australia; (08) 8204 9245.
Walking trail: 3 km track along cliff-tops to Tiddy Widdy Beach; begins at the boat ramp in town. *BHP Lookout:* view of Gulf St Vincent and dolomite mines; 2 km s. *Clinton Conservation Park:* mangrove swamps and tidal flats with an array of birdlife; begins after Port Clinton. 25 km n, and stretches around the head of Gulf St Vincent.
ⓘ Ardrossan Bakery, 39 First St; (08) 8837 3015

Arkaroola   Pop. 25

Map ref. 553 H1, 557 M3

Arkaroola is set in an incredible landscape of ranges laced with precious minerals, waterholes nestled inside tall gorges and place names such as Nooldoonooldoona, Weetootla and Bararranna. What's more, the Flinders Ranges are still alive, rumbling with up to 200 small earthquakes a year. It was a place that geologist Reg Sprigg found fascinating, and certainly worth conserving. He purchased the Arkaroola property in 1968 and created a wildlife sanctuary for endangered species. Today a weather station, seismograph station and observatory (tours available) add to its significance and the spectacular four-wheel-drive tracks entice many visitors. The village has excellent facilities for such a remote outpost.

NEARBY **Ridgetop Tour** This, the signature attraction of the northern Flinders Ranges, is a 4WD tour along an insanely steep track. The original track, built for mining exploration, wound through the creek beds, but run-off from the ridges washed the road away in just a few years. The idea was formed to create a track along the ridges themselves. A few bulldozers later, the track was complete. This is a guided tour, but Arkaroola Wilderness Sanctuary also has 100 km of self-guide 4WD tracks, including the popular Echo Camp Backtrack.
Gammon Ranges National Park This park is directly south of Arkaroola, taking in much of the distinctive scenery of the northern Flinders Ranges and extending across to Lake Frome. The Adnyamathanha people believe that the Dreamtime serpent, Arakaroo, drank Lake Frome dry and carved out Arkaroola Gorge as he dragged his body back to his resting spot, inside Main Pound. His restlessness is the cause of all the earthquakes. Features include the surprisingly lush Weetootla Gorge, fed by a permanent spring, and Italowie Gorge, the unlikely spot where an impoverished R. M. Williams began making shoes. Park Headquarters at Balcanoona.
Waterholes: many picturesque waterholes along Arkaroola Creek and tributaries west and north-east of the village. *Bolla Bollana Smelter ruins:* where the ore from surrounding mines was once treated. It includes a Cornish beehive-shaped kiln. 7 km nw. *Paralana Hot Springs:* the only active geyser in Australia where water, heated by radioactive minerals, bubbles through the rocks. Swimming or extended exposure is not recommended. 27 km ne. *Big Moro Gorge:* rock pools surrounded by limestone outcrops. The gorge is on Adnyamathanha land and a permit is needed from Nepabunna Community Council, (08) 8648 3764. 59 km s.

Scenic flights: over the ranges or further afield; details from village reception.
ⓘ Arkaroola Village reception; 1800 676 042 or (08) 8648 4848; www.arkaroola.on.net

Balaklava   Pop. 1520

Map ref. 555 K6

Balaklava is set on the Wakefield River in an area dominated by traditional wheat and sheep farms. It sprang up as a stopping point between the Burra copperfields and Port Wakefield, but a grain merchant from Adelaide, Charles Fisher, soon turned the focus to agriculture. He built grain stores here before there was any sign of grain. This proved a canny move, as it lured farmers to the area. The town features old sandstone buildings and a 'silent cop', a curious keep-left sign in the middle of a main intersection.

IN TOWN Courthouse Gallery The arts are alive and well in Balaklava, as shown by this community-run art gallery, that has a changing program of local and visiting exhibitions, plus a popular art prize in July. Edith Tce. Open 2pm–4pm Thurs, Fri and Sun.
Balaklava Folk Museum: old household items and local memorabilia; Old Centenary Hall, May Tce; open 2pm–4pm, 2nd and 4th Sun each month. *Urlwin Park Agricultural Museum:* old agricultural machinery, 2 old relocated banks and a working telephone exchange; Short Tce; open Sat mornings. *Walking trail:* scenic 3 km track along the riverbank.
WHAT'S ON *Balaklava Cup:* major regional horserace; Aug.
NEARBY Port Wakefield Behind the highway's long line of takeaways and petrol stations is a quiet town that began life as a cargo port to carry the copper mined in Burra's Monster Mine back to Port Adelaide. It is set on the mangrove-lined Wakefield River at the top of Gulf St Vincent. The wharf, which has a floor of mud at low tide, is now used by the local fishing industry. A historical walk brochure is available from the caravan park. This is a popular spot for fishing, crabbing and swimming. 25 km w.
Devils Garden: a picnic spot among river box gums, once a 'devil of a place' for bullock wagons to get through as the black soil quickly turned to mud; 7 km NE. *Rocks Reserve:* walking trails and unique rock formations by the river; 10 km E. *Balaklava Gliding Club:* offers weekend 'air experience flights' with an instructor; bookings (08) 8864 5062; Whitwarta Airfield; 10 km NW.
ⓘ Council offices, 10 Edith Tce; (08) 8862 1811

Barmera   Pop. 1937

Map ref. 555 P7

Barmera lies in the middle of a swooping hairpin bend of the Murray River, close to the Victorian border, but it is hard to tell where the river stops and where the flood plains and tributaries begin in the area to the west of town. The wetlands eventually flow into Lake Bonney, a large body of water to the north of Barmera. Swimming, waterskiing, sailing and fishing are some of the activities popular on the lake. The town was established in 1921 as a settlement for returned World War I soldiers, who were all promised a patch of well-irrigated farmland.

IN TOWN Rocky's Country Music Hall of Fame Dean 'Rocky' Page established Barmera's famous country music festival and was a well-known musician in his own right. Within the centre is an array of country music memorabilia and a display of replica guitars with the handprints of the legends who used them. The pièce de résistance is Slim Dusty's hat. Barwell Ave. Open Wed–Fri.
Donald Campbell Obelisk: commemorates an attempt in 1964 to break the world water-speed record, but 347.5 km/h was not quite enough to make the books; Queen Elizabeth Dr.
WHAT'S ON *Lake Bonney Yachting Regatta:* Easter. *South Australian Country Music Festival:* June. *Riverland Field Days:* Sept. *Barmera Bonnie Sheepdog Trials:* Oct.
NEARBY Banrock Station Wine and Wetland Centre Fruity wines mix with a cacophony of birds and frogs at Banrock Station. In these new times of sensitive agriculture, Banrock is working with environmental organisations to breathe life back into a pocket of wetland that was ruined by irrigation (almost 70 percent of all Murray wetlands have been affected). The natural cycles of flooding and drying have seen the return of black swans, native fish and ibis, and a boardwalk gives visitors a close-up look. Kingston-on-Murray; 10 km W.
Overland Corner This was the first settlement in the area, a convenient stop en route for drovers and people travelling to the goldfields. By 1855 a police post had been established to deal with the odd bushranger and quell the problems flaring between drovers and the indigenous inhabitants. In 1859 the Overland Corner Hotel opened its doors. Its thick limestone walls and red gum floors have seen many floods. A walking track into the adjacent Herons Bend Reserve leaves from the hotel. 19 km NW.
Cobdogla Irrigation and Steam Museum: has the world's only working Humphrey Pump, used in the early days of irrigation. Also local memorabilia and steam-train rides. 5 km W; open Sun of long weekends. *Highway Fern Haven:* features an indoor rainforest; 5 km E. *Napper's Old Accommodation House:* ruins of a hotel built in 1850 on the shores of the lake; turn east over Napper Bridge; 10 km NW. *Loch Luna Game Reserve:* linking Lake Bonney and the Murray, these wetlands form an important refuge for waterbirds

and one of the few inland nesting sites for sea-eagles. Chambers Creek, which loops around the reserve, is popular for canoeing. Turn west over Napper Bridge; 16 km NW. *Moorook Game Reserve:* these wetlands surround Wachtels Lagoon; 16 km SW. *Loveday Internment Camps:* guided tour or self-guide drive to the camps where Japanese, Italian and German POWs were held during WW II; details from visitor centre.
ⓘ Barwell Ave; (08) 8588 2289

Beachport   Pop. 406

Map ref. 552 F11

Beachport started out as a whaling port, set up by the enterprising Henty brothers who founded Portland, Victoria. Today the crayfish industry has taken over and the town has South Australia's second longest jetty, its length made necessary by the shallow waters of Rivoli Bay. People flock here for summer holidays to loll about on the beautiful sandy beaches, to swim in the bay and the nearby lakes, and to fish. Regular catches from the jetty include whiting, flathead and garfish.

IN TOWN Old Wool and Grain Store Museum In the late 1800s Beachport became a shipping port for local wool and grain. Were it not for some bureaucrats who confused Robe with Beachport, Rivoli Bay might have been dredged and the jetty lengthened to create a port to rival Portland's. Now a museum, the old store contains displays and historic items, including harpoons and relics from shipwrecks. Railway Tce. Open 10am–4pm daily over holiday period, 10am–2pm Sun at other times.
Lanky's Walk: a short walk through bushland to Lanky's Well, where the last full-blood member of the Boandik tribe camped while working as a police tracker; begins on Railway Tce North; details on this and other walks from visitor centre. *Pool of Siloam:* this small lake, 7 times saltier than the sea, is said to be a cure for all manner of ailments. Also a popular swimming spot. End of McCourt St. *Lighthouse:* the original lighthouse was located on Penguin Island, a breeding ground for seals and penguins offshore from Cape Martin, where the current lighthouse now stands. It offers good views of the island from the cape. South of town.
WHAT'S ON *Festival by the Sea:* stalls and entertainment; Feb/Mar. *Market:* Sat of long weekends (Easter, June and Oct).
NEARBY Beachport Conservation Park This park is a succession of white beaches, sand dunes and rugged limestone cliffs, with the southern shore of Lake George lying inland. The coast is dotted with ancient shell middens and is accessed primarily by 4WD or on foot. Five Mile Drift, a beach on Lake George, is a good base for swimming, sailing and windsurfing. Access to the coast side is via Bowman Scenic Dr, which begins at

the lighthouse. Access to the Lake George side is via Railway Tce North.
Woakwine Cutting: an incredible gorge, cut through Woakwine Range by one man to drain swampland and allow farming, with viewing platform, information boards and machinery exhibit; 10 km N.
ⓘ Millicent Rd; (08) 8735 8029

Berri
Pop. 4213

Map ref. 555 Q7

Orange products and wine are big business in this Riverland town, which has the country's largest winery and is one of the major growing and manufacturing centres of the country's biggest orange-juice company. The Big Orange, on the north-west outskirts of town, makes this rather clear. The name 'Berri' has nothing to do with fruit, though. It comes from the Aboriginal 'Bery Bery', thought to mean 'bend in the river'. The town was established in 1911, the year after irrigation of the Murray began.

IN TOWN *Berri Ltd:* makers of Berri Fruit Juice and other products, with sales and a video presentation detailing production history of the Riverland; Old Sturt Hwy. *Riverlands Gallery:* local and touring art exhibitions; Wilson St; open Mon–Fri. *Berri Community Mural:* enormous community-painted mural commemorating the past and present fruit industry; Old Sturt Hwy next to Berri Ltd. *Berri Lookout Tower:* panoramic views of river, town and surrounds from a converted water tower; cnr Fiedler St and Vaughan Tce. *Lions Club Walking Trail:* 4 km riverfront walk from Berri Marina to Martin Bend Reserve, a popular spot for picnics and waterskiing. An Aboriginal mural and totems are under the bridge and further along are monuments to famous Aboriginal tracker Jimmy James. *Birdwatching safaris:* to Bookmark Biosphere Reserve; tours offered by Jolly Goodfellows Birding (08) 8583 5530.
WHAT'S ON *Riverland Rodeo:* Jan. *Riverland Gem and Mineral Show:* Australia Day weekend; even-numbered years, Jan. *Speedboat Spectacular:* Feb (subject to river conditions). *Art and Craft Fair:* Nov.
NEARBY Berri Estates Winery This impressive winery was founded in 1922 and has grown to be the largest winery and distillery in Australia. The Murray River and the temperate climate have much to do with the quality of the wines here, including reds, whites and fortified wines, as well as brandy. Between Berri and Glossop.
Murray River National Park, Katarapko Section In this park, see the merging of two distinct vegetations – of the famous Murray River flood plains and the equally renowned Mallee region. The 6 km Mallee Drive takes the visitor into the heart of the park and to the distinctive mallee terrain. There are also walking trails to see some of the park's inhabitants,

Berri and the surrounding Riverland is a major centre for orange-growing

including the ever-popular kangaroo. Just south of Berri.
The Big Orange: inside the enormous fruit it seems appropriate to taste the local wares at the cafe and juice bar. On the second level is a 360-degree mural depicting the surrounding region – to see it first-hand, head to the lookout at the top. Old Sturt Hwy, just north-east of Berri. *Monash:* a small irrigation town best known for the free family attractions at the Monash Adventure Park on Morgan Rd. Enjoy delicate handmade chocolates at the Chocolates and More store opposite the park, or taste the wines at nearby Pandau Wines. 12 km NW. *Glossop:* a service town featuring a pottery and glass factory, and Winmante Arts Centre with sales of Aboriginal arts and crafts; just west of Berri. *Angas Park Fruit Company:* dried fruits and other products; Old Sturt Hwy; 3 km W; open 8.30am–5pm Mon–Fri, 10am–midday Sat and public holidays. *Wilabalangaloo:* a flora and fauna reserve with incredible coloured cliffs, marked river walks and a historic homestead; Old Sturt Hwy; 5 km N; open 10am–4pm Thurs–Mon (open 7 days in school holidays).
ⓘ Riverview Dr; (08) 8582 5511; www.berribarmera.sa.gov.au

Birdwood
Pop. 724

Map ref. 550 F8, 552 C1, 555 L9

The small town of Birdwood is set picturesquely in the Torrens Valley in the northern part of the popular Adelaide Hills district. The region's beauty would have been a welcome site for German settlers escaping religious persecution in the 1840s. Like many of the German-settled towns in the area, Birdwood was originally named after a Prussian town, Blumberg. However, anti-German sentiment during World War I created a feeling of unrest and the town's name

was changed to Birdwood after the commander of the ANZAC forces in Gallipoli, Sir William Birdwood.
IN TOWN National Motor Museum The largest in the Southern Hemisphere, this impressive collection of over 300 vintage cars, motorcycles and commercial vehicles is housed in the 1852 flour mill. The vehicles are lovingly restored, often from simply a shell. Visit the workshop complex to see the process of restoration as coach builders and mechanics work tirelessly on these old machines. The building's original history as a flour mill can be seen in the Mill Building. Shannon St. *Birdwood Wine and Cheese Centre:* introduces visitors to boutique wines and cheeses of regional SA with tastings and sales; Shannon St; open Wed–Sun. *Blumberg Inn:* imposing 1865 inn harking back to German-settler days; Main St.
WHAT'S ON *Bay to Birdwood Run:* vintage motoring event attracting more than 1600 vehicles; Sept. *Rock and Roll Rendezvous:* Nov.
NEARBY Lobethal The quaint town of Lobethal features historic German-style cottages and an 1842 Lutheran Seminary. Fairyland Village takes the visitor into the world of fairytales; open weekends. The National Costume Museum houses a collection of dresses, suits and accessories dating from 1812; closed Mon. The town lights up each Christmas in the 'Lights of Lobethal' festival. 13 km SW. *The Toy Factory:* a family business manufacturing wooden toys from a shop adjacent to an 18 m giant rocking horse; Gumeracha; 7 km W. *Chain of Ponds Wine:* boutique winery with tastings, sales, viewing platform, restaurant and B&B (1880s cottage); 9 km W. *Malcolm Creek Vineyard:* boutique winery with cellar door and friendly deer; Bonython Rd, Kersbrook; 20 km NW; open weekends and public holidays. *Roachdale Reserve:* self-guide nature trail with brochure;

23 km nw via Kersbrook. *Torrens Gorge:* spectacular cliffs and streams make this a popular spot for picnics; 25 km w. *Samphire Wines and Pottery:* a small boutique winery and handmade pottery shop; cnr Watts Gully and Robertson rds; 27 km nw via Kersbrook. *Warren Conservation Park:* difficult trails, including part of the long-distance Heysen Trail, lead to spectacular views over countryside and Warren Gorge; adjacent to Samphire Wines and Pottery. *Mount Crawford Forest:* walkers, horseriders and cyclists will enjoy the forest tracks of this park, which is scattered in various locations north, west and south-west of Birdwood. Visit the information centre on Warren Rd (signposted turn-off between Kersbrook and Williamstown) for a map.
ℹ Shannon St; (08) 8568 5577

Blinman   Pop. 27

Map ref. 553 E5, 557 K6

During the 19th century numerous mining townships dotted the landscape in the northern part of the Flinders Ranges. Blinman is the sole surviving town surveyed at the time. The discovery of copper in 1859 was accidental. The story goes that a shepherd, Robert Blinman, used to watch the sheep from a boulder. One day he absentmindedly broke off a chunk and discovered it was copper. Historic buildings in the main street are reminders of those rich and heady days.
WHAT'S ON *Land Rover Jamboree:* May. *Picnic Gymkhana and Races:* Oct. *Art Show:* Oct. *Cook Outback:* food/wine festival with camp oven comp; Oct long weekend.
NEARBY *Blinman Mine Historic Site:* a 1 km self-guide walk explains the history and geology of the site. Contact the caretaker on (08) 8648 4874 for a guided tour. Just north-east of Blinman. *Great Wall of China:* impressive limestone ridge; Wilpena Rd; 10 km s. *Angorichina Tourist Village:* accommodation ranging from tents to cabins; 14 km w. Village is also the start point for 4 km walk along creek bed to Blinman Pools, permanent spring-fed pools in scenic surrounds. *Glass and Parachilna gorges:* along the loop road north-west of town are these two beautiful gorges. Parachilna Gorge is the end point of the 1200 km Heysen Trail (bushwalking trail), which begins at Cape Jervis (for information on the trail contact Parks SA (08) 8124 4792). *Flinders Ranges National Park:* 26 km s; *see feature on p. 260.* *Prairie Hotel:* a historic hotel at Parachilna offering cuisine with a bush-tucker twist as well as first-rate accommodation. Hotel staff can arrange activities including 4WD tours, scenic flights, and visits to nearby Nilpena Station on the edge of Lake Torrens to sample the outback life. 32 km w; (08) 8648 4844. *Scenic drive:* travel east through Eregunda Valley (around 20 km e), then north-east to

Mt Chambers Gorge (around 75 km ne), with its rock pools and Aboriginal carvings. Further north is Gammon Ranges National Park, *see Arkaroola*. *Mawson Trail:* this 900 km bike trail from Adelaide ends in Blinman. It is named after famous Australian explorer Sir Douglas Mawson and traverses the Mount Lofty and Flinders ranges. For details contact Bicycle SA (08) 8411 0233.
ℹ General Store, Mine Rd; (08) 8648 4370

Bordertown   Pop. 2440

Map ref. 552 H6

In spite of its name, Bordertown is actually 18 kilometres from the South Australia–Victoria border in the fertile country of the Tatiara District. Its name, thought to be the Aboriginal word for 'good country', is justified by the region's productive wool and grain industries. For a different native-animal experience, look out for Bordertown's famous white kangaroos, Australia's only known colony. Former Australian prime minister Robert (Bob) J. L. Hawke was born here.
IN TOWN *Robert J. L. Hawke's childhood home:* includes memorabilia. Visit by appt only; contact visitor centre for details. Farquhar St. *Bordertown Wildlife Park:* native birds and animals, including pure-white kangaroos; Dukes Hwy. *Hawke Gallery:* in foyer of council chambers; Woolshed St. *Bordertown Recreation Lake:* popular spot for fishing, canoeing and walking, with artwork on display; northern outskirts of town.
WHAT'S ON *SA State Championships Working Dog Trial:* showgrounds; July.
NEARBY **Padthaway** The Padthaway district has long been regarded as a leader in Australian wine production. An excellent place to start the tasting of such wines is the Padthaway Estate Winery, where meals and wine-tastings enrich the palate. Adjacent is the historic Padthaway Homestead, an 1882 building rising regally above the surrounding region. After indulging in gastronomic delights, walk among the magnificent red gums and stringybarks at nearby Padthaway Conservation Park. 42 km sw. *Clayton Farm:* incorporates the Bordertown and District Agricultural Museum and features vintage farm machinery and a National Trust-classified thatched-roof building and homestead. Clayton Farm Vintage Field Day is held here each Oct long weekend. 3 km s. *Mundulla:* a historic township featuring the heritage-listed Mundulla Hotel; 10 km sw. *Bangham Conservation Park:* a significant habitat for the red-tailed black cockatoo; 30 km se.
ℹ 81 North Tce; (08) 8752 0700

Burra   Pop. 1096

Map ref. 555 L5

The Burra region exploded into activity when copper was found by two shepherds

in 1845. Settlements were established based on the miners' country of origin: Aberdeen for the Scottish, Hampton for the English, Redruth for the Cornish and Llwchwr for the Welsh. The combined settlement grew to be the second largest in South Australia, but the miners were fickle – with riches promised on the Victorian goldfields, they did not stay for long. In 1877 the Monster Mine closed. Luckily, Burra did not turn into a ghost town. Instead, the rich heritage of its past has been carefully preserved by the community, resulting in the town being declared a State Heritage Area in 1993. Burra is in the Bald Hill Ranges, named for the 'naked' hills around the town.
IN TOWN **Burra Heritage Passport** This 'passport' allows visitors to discover the major heritage sites of Burra – armed with an unlimited-access 'key' and a brief history of each site outlined in the pamphlet *Discovering Historic Burra.* Included in the passport is the Burra Historic Mine Site (off Market St), with an ore dressing tower and powder magazine offering views of the open-cut mine and town. At the site is Morphetts Enginehouse Museum (additional entry fee), featuring an excavated 30 m entry tunnel and engine displays. Another site is the Burra Creek Miners' Dugouts (alongside Blyth St) – these dugouts cut into the creek beds housed 1800 people in the boom. Visit the Unicorn Brewery Cellars (Bridge Tce) that date back to 1873, the police lock-up and stables (Tregony St) – these were the first built outside Adelaide – and Redruth Gaol (off Tregony St), which served as a gaol, then a girls reformatory from 1856 to 1922. You can also visit the ruins of a private English township called Hampton, on the northern outskirts of town. Passports are available from the visitor centre and can be upgraded to provide access to the town's museums.
Bon Accord Mine Complex: National Trust interpretive centre with working forge and model of Burra Mine. Guided tours available. Railway Tce; closed Mon and Fri. *Market Square Museum:* an old-style general store, post office and family home returned to its heyday; opposite visitor centre. *Malowen Lowarth Cottage:* restored 1850s Cornish miner's cottage; Kingston St. *Ryan's Deer Farm:* includes an animal nursery and restaurant; Tregony St. *Burra Regional Art Gallery:* local and touring exhibitions; Market St. *Antique shops:* in Commercial and Market sts. *Burra Creek:* swimming, canoeing and picnicking.
WHAT'S ON *Jailhouse Rock Festival:* Feb. *Twilight Jazz Affair:* Mar. *Antique and Decorating Fair:* May.
NEARBY *Burra Trail Rides:* horseriding adventures in Bald Hills Range; bookings (08) 8892 2627. *Burra Gorge:* picnics, camping and walking tracks around gorge and permanent springs; 23 km se. *Dares Hill Drive:* scenic 90 km drive with

The cliffs of the Nullarbor, west of Ceduna

lookout; begins 30 km N near Hallett; map available from visitor centre.
ℹ 2 Market Sq; (08) 8892 2154

Ceduna   Pop. 2569

Map ref. 563 N9

The name Ceduna is derived from the Aboriginal word 'chedoona', meaning resting place, which is apt for those who have just traversed the Nullarbor. Ceduna is also the last major town for those about to embark on the journey west – the place to check your car and stock up on food and water. The difficulty of obtaining supplies and provisions has a long history around Ceduna. Denial Bay, where the original settlement of McKenzie was situated, was where large cargo ships brought provisions for the early pioneers. Ceduna was established later, in 1896, and is situated on the shores of Murat Bay with sandy coves, sheltered bays and offshore islands. In the 1850s there was also a whaling station on St Peter Island (visible from Thevenard).

IN TOWN *Old Schoolhouse National Trust Museum:* pioneering artefacts, including those from British atomic testing at Maralinga; Park Tce; closed Sun. *Ceduna Arts Cultural Centre:* original paintings, local pottery and ceramics; cnr Eyre Hwy and Kuhlmann St; open Mon–Fri. *Oyster tours:* offered to Denial Bay, Thevenard and Smoky Bay; book at visitor centre. *Ceduna Oyster Bar:* fresh oysters year-round; western outskirts, on Eyre Hwy. *Local beaches:* swimming, boating, waterskiing and fishing. The foreshore is an ideal spot for walks and picnics (sharks have been known to frequent these waters – seek local advice). *Encounter Coastal Trail:* 4 km interpretive trail from the foreshore to Thevenard.

WHAT'S ON *Ceduna Race Meeting:* major horseracing event; Jan. *Oysterfest:* community festival including street parade and fireworks; Oct long weekend.

NEARBY Great Australian Bight Marine Park The park protects the habitats of marine animals and preserves the fragile ecosystem of the Great Australian Bight. It has spectacular wildlife sights, including the breeding and calving of endangered southern right whales from June to Oct. Spend a day observing these giant creatures from the viewing platform at the Head of Bight. There are spectacular views of the Bunda Cliffs, where the Nullarbor reaches the ocean. Permits are required from Yalata Roadhouse or ranger station. 300 km w. **Nullarbor National Park** Aboriginal culture is closely linked with the semiarid cave landscape of this park, the largest karst landscape in the world. Vast and mainly flat, the park's most beautiful scenery is along the coast where the cliffs stretch for 200 km overlooking the Southern Ocean. Visitors should take care along the cliff edges, as they are unstable. Rare and endangered species such as the Major Mitchell cockatoo and the peregrine falcon live in the park. Watch out for the ambling hairy-nosed wombat. 300 km w. *Thevenard:* a deep-sea port that handles bulk grain, gypsum and salt, as well as a large fishing fleet noted for whiting hauls. Tour the fishing factories; contact visitor centre for details. A 3.8 km interpretive trail, 'Tracks Along the Coast', runs from the Sailing Club to Pinky Point. 4 km sw. *Denial Bay:* visit the McKenzie ruins to see an early pioneering home and the heritage-listed landing where cargo was brought to shore. Denial Bay jetty is good for fishing and crabbing. 14 km w. *Davenport Creek:* see pure-white sandhills and swim in the sheltered creek. Beyond the sandhills is excellent surfing and waterskiing. 40 km w. *South-east towns and beaches:* Decres Bay for swimming, snorkelling and rock-fishing (10 km se); Laura Bay with cove-swimming near the conservation park (18 km se); Smoky Bay for safe swimming, fishing and boating (40 km se); Point Brown for surf beaches, salmon fishing and coastal walks (56 km se). *Penong:* more than 40 windmills draw the town's water from underground. See historical memorabilia and local crafts at the Penong Woolshed Museum. Goanywea camel day-rides and safaris (May–Oct). 73 km w. *Cactus Beach:* renowned for its 'perfect' surfing breaks; 94 km w. *Fowlers Bay:* this town, surrounded by a conservation park, offers long, sandy beaches and excellent fishing; 139 km sw. *North-east conservation parks and reserves:* comprising Yellabinna, Yumbarra, Pureba, Nunnyah and Koolgera, an extensive wilderness area of dunes and mallee country. Rare species of wildlife, including dunnarts and mallee fowl, find refuge in the waterways and salt lakes. 4WD is essential, and visitors must be experienced in outback travel. North of Ceduna. *Googs Track:* 4WD trek from Ceduna to Malbooma (154 km N) and the Trans-Australia railway track through Yumbarra Conservation Park and Yellabinna Regional Reserve; contact visitor centre for details.
ℹ 58 Poynton St; 1800 639 413 or (08) 8625 2780; www.ceduna.net

Clare   Pop. 2920

Map ref. 555 L5

Clare is known as the 'Garden of the North' and has always been considered picturesque. Edward John Eyre reported favourably on the area on his travels in the mid-1800s. Pastoral settlement followed and the town came to be known as Clare after the county in Ireland. From this small beginning the land has proved as favourable as Eyre claimed and Clare continues to boast a rich agricultural industry, including the famous Clare Valley

SOUTH AUSTRALIA

wine region. The first vines were planted by Jesuit priests at Sevenhill in 1851. The Sevenhill Cellars are still operated by Jesuit brothers and the monastery buildings, including the historic St Aloysius Church, are of special interest.

IN TOWN *Old Police Station Museum:* the building has a chequered past as a prison, a casualty hospital and housing for government employees. It is now a National Trust museum with historic artefacts and photographs. Neagles Rock Rd; open weekends and public holidays. *Lookouts:* Billy Goat Hill from Wright St and Neagles Rock Lookout on Neagles Rock Rd. *Town walk:* self-guide trail; brochure from visitor centre.

WHAT'S ON *Clare Races:* horseraces among the vines; Easter. *Spanish Festival:* April. *Clare Gourmet Weekend:* May. *Spring Garden Festival:* Nov.

NEARBY Clare Valley Wineries The Clare Valley wine region consists of 12 valleys of undulating hills and lowlands, home to over 30 boutique and commercial wineries. The area is most famous for producing a fine riesling, grown to perfection because of the high terrain and continental climate. The wineries are around Clare, Polish Hill River, Mintaro, Sevenhill, Penwortham, Watervale and Auburn. For those wanting to see the villages and wineries on foot or bicycle, the 27 km Riesling Trail is a good option. It starts from either Clare or Auburn and follows an old railway line. Contact the visitor centre for a winery map. *Watervale:* a historic town with a self-guide walk leaflet available from Clare Town Hall; 12 km s. *Blyth:* a little country town overlooking the western plains. Take a short walk on the interpretive botanical trail or picnic at Brooks Lookout. Medika Gallery, originally a Lutheran church, offers an art gallery and Australian craft sales. 13 km w. *Geralka Rural Farm:* an operating farm that offers tours introducing visitors to past and present farming life, including an old farm machinery display, historic buildings, animal feeding and Shetland pony rides for children. Walking trail, camping facilities and guided tours 1.30pm Sun and public holidays and daily in school holidays, other times by appt (08) 8842 3318. 25 km N. *Auburn:* the birthplace in 1876 of poet C. J. Dennis. Take a self-guide walk through National Trust historic precinct in St Vincent St. 26 km s. *Scenic drive:* travel south to Spring Gully Conservation Park with its walking tracks and rare red stringybarks.
ⓘ Town Hall, 229 Main North Rd; 1800 242 131 or (08) 8842 2131; www.clarevalley.com.au

Coffin Bay   Pop. 451

Map ref. 554 C8

A picturesque holiday town and fishing village on the shores of a beautiful estuary, Coffin Bay is popular particularly in summer, when the population quadruples. The bay offers sailing, waterskiing, swimming and fishing. The town was originally known as Oyster Town because of the abundant natural oysters in the bay, but they were dredged to extinction last century. Today the cultivated oysters are among the best in the country. The bay – in spite of what some locals will try to tell you – was named by Matthew Flinders in 1802 in honour of his friend Sir Isaac Coffin.

IN TOWN *Fishing:* in the bay or to game fishing areas; boat hire and charters available. *Oyster Walk:* 12 km walkway along foreshore and bushland from a lookout (excellent view of Coffin Bay) to Long Beach; brochure from visitor centre.

NEARBY Coffin Bay National Park A mixture of rugged coastal landscapes and calm bays and waterways makes this diverse park a pleasure to wander and drive through. Conventional vehicles can access the eastern part of the park where walks through she-oak and samphire swamps reveal incredible birdlife. The beaches and lookouts provide a different perspective on this remote wilderness. 4WD vehicles and bushwalkers can access the western part, which includes Gunyah Beach, Point Sir Isaac and the Coffin Bay Peninsula. The park extends south and west of town.
Kellidie Bay Conservation Park: a limestone landscape popular for walking and canoeing; eastern outskirts of Coffin Bay. *Yangie Trail:* the 10 km trail starts at Coffin Bay and travels south-west via Yangie Bay Lookout, which offers magnificent views to Point Avoid and Yangie Bay. *Mount Dutton Bay:* features the restored heritage-listed jetty and woolshed, the latter now a shearing and farming museum that holds the annual Easter Art and Craft Festival; 40 km N. *Farm Beach:* popular swimming spot; 50 km N. *Gallipoli Beach:* location for the film *Gallipoli* (1981); 55 km N. *Scenic coast drive:* between Mount Hope and Sheringa; 105 km N.
ⓘ Beachcomber Agencies, Esplanade; (08) 8685 4057; www.tep.com.au

Coober Pedy   Pop. 2440

Map ref. 561 R11

On 1 February 1915 a group of gold prospectors discovered opal in the area surrounding Coober Pedy. It was to become the biggest opal field in the world and provide over 90 percent of the world's gem-quality opals. The name Coober Pedy is derived from the Aboriginal phrase 'Kupa Piti', loosely translating to 'white man's hole in the ground'. The town's unique underground system of living was first established by the soldiers returning from World War I who were used to trench life. Today around 80 percent of the population call the 'dugouts' home – as ideal places to escape the severe summer temperatures and cold winter nights. The countryside of Coober Pedy is desolate and harsh, dotted with thousands of mines.

IN TOWN Umoona Underground Mine and Museum This award-winning underground centre provides an all-round look at Coober Pedy. A detailed town history and an Aboriginal interpretive centre comprehensively document Coober Pedy's evolution. Experience 'dugout' life in an underground home or mine life on an on-site mine tour. An excellent documentary on Coober Pedy is seen in the underground cinema. Hutchison St.
Old Timers Mine: museum in an original 1916 mine featuring 3 large opal seams and interpretive centre with self-guide walk; Crowders Gully Rd. *Underground churches:* St Peter and St Pauls was the first underground church in the world; Hutchison St. Other interesting churches include the Catacomb Church, Catacomb Rd, and the Serbian Orthodox Church with its 'ballroom' style. *Desert Cave:* international underground hotel with shopping complex and display gallery detailing the early hardships of miners in Coober Pedy; Hutchison St; open 8am–8pm daily. *Underground Art Gallery:* works of central Australian artists, including Aboriginal pieces; Hutchison St. *Opal retailers:* outlets offer jewellery and stone sales. Many demonstrate the skill required to cut and polish opals. *Big Winch Lookout:* monument and lookout over town; Italian Club Rd. *Outback scenic and charter flights:* both local and outback tours; depart from airport; bookings (08) 8672 3067. *Mine tours:* to local mines; contact visitor centre.

WHAT'S ON *Opal Festival:* Easter. *Coober Pedy Greek Glendi:* celebration of Greek culture; July. *Amateur Race Meeting and Gymkhana:* Oct long weekend.

NEARBY Moon Plain and the Breakaways The rocky landscape of Moon Plain, 15 km NE, has been the backdrop for many movies, especially those with a science-fiction bent. Likewise, the 40 sq km reserve of the Breakaways, 30 km N. The unique arid landscape of flat-topped outcrops and stony gibber desert is breathtaking, as is the wildlife that has adapted to these harsh conditions. Passes to the reserve are available from the visitor centre and other outlets in town. Return via the road past part of the Dog Fence, a 5300 km fence built to protect sheep properties in the south from wild dogs.

The Mail Run This overland adventure is a unique way of discovering the remote outback of SA. Travelling with Coober Pedy's mailman, the tour travels past waterholes and through scenic landscapes on its delivery run to Oodnadatta, William Creek and the remote cattle stations in between. Travelling 600 km over outback roads and the renowned Oodnadatta Track, the mailman offers up fascinating stories and

history of the landscape and people. Tours depart from the Underground Bookshop at 9am on Mon and Thurs. Bookings 1800 069 911 or (08) 8672 5226. *Underground Pottery:* handmade pottery depicting colours and landscape of the desert; 2 km w. *William Creek:* the smallest town in SA, situated in Anna Creek station, the world's largest cattle station. A race meeting is held the weekend before Easter each year. Flights offered over Lake Eyre. 166 km E. *Painted Desert:* rich colours paint the Arckaringa Hills, also noted for flora and fauna; 234 km N. *Travellers note: Opal fields are pocked with diggings. Beware of unprotected mine shafts. Avoid entering any field area unless escorted. For safety reasons, visitors to the mines are advised to join a tour. Trespassers on claims can be fined a minimum of $1000. Coober Pedy is the last stop for petrol between Cadney Homestead (151 km N) and Glendambo (252 km S).*
ⓘ Council offices, Hutchison St (Mon–Fri); 1800 637 076 or (08) 8672 5298; www.opalcapitaloftheworld.com.au

Coonawarra   Pop. 35

Map ref. 532 A2, 542 A13, 552 H10

Unlike many other Australian wine regions, Coonawarra was a planned horticulture scheme – and a very successful one at that. John Riddoch, a Scottish immigrant, acquired extensive lands in South Australia's south-east in the late 1800s. He subdivided 800 hectares of his landholding specifically for orchards and vineyards. Named the Coonawarra Fruit Colony, the verdant lands would later become Wynns Coonawarra Estate.
WHAT'S ON *Coonawarra Cup:* Jan. *Lazy Days of Summer:* music, wine and food; Jan. *Coonawarra After Dark:* cellar doors open in the evenings; April. *Penola Coonawarra Festival:* arts, food and wine; May. *Cabernet Celebrations:* Nov.
NEARBY **Coonawarra wine region** An inland sea once covered much of south-east SA. The ancient shore of limestone decayed to produce the unique terra rossa soil of the region. Now this small area is completely covered in vines. The incredible soil produces some of the boldest and most famous red wines in Australia and, indeed, the world. The cool climate is ideal for long ripening, with harvest from early March to late April. Over 20 cellar doors operate in the 12 km strip of terra rossa soil south of Coonawarra, producing shiraz, cabernet sauvignon, chardonnay and riesling.
ⓘ 27 Arthur St, Penola; (08) 8737 2855; www.thelimestonecoast.com

Cowell   Pop. 792

Map ref. 554 G5

This pleasant Eyre Peninsula township is on the almost land-locked Franklin Harbour – its entrance is merely 100 metres wide. Matthew Flinders sailed

Opal fields at Coober Pedy

South Australian opals

Since ancient Roman times the opal has been revered – worn by royal families around the world and used in literary symbolism by Shakespeare. At one time, Eastern Europe and parts of South America were the only regions to produce these wondrous gems. But in 1849 common opal was found near Angaston by the geologist Johannes Menge. Although Australian opals did not appear on the world market until the 1890s, and then did not dominate until the 1930s, this was the start of a booming industry in Australia.

The first major discovery of opals was made by a 14-year-old boy who was actually prospecting for gold north-west of Adelaide in 1915. This area was to become Coober Pedy, which today produces 90 percent of the world's gem-quality opals, mostly of the white or milky varieties. The next South Australian discovery was in Andamooka, south-west of Coober Pedy, in 1930. This opal field was to become one of Australia's most famous, producing top-quality matrix and crystal opals. Mintabie opals were also discovered in the 1930s, but the harshness of the conditions and lack of water discouraged serious mining there until 1976, when big earth-moving machinery was introduced.

The source of Australia's prosperous opal industry is the Great Artesian Basin, the vast body of water found beneath a broad sweep of the continent's desert region, including large parts of Queensland and South Australia and smaller parts of New South Wales and the Northern Territory. Before it sank underground, the Great Artesian Basin was a vast inland sea, surrounded by a shoreline of silica-rich sands. Over time and with changes in the weather, the silica dissolved to form a gel, which flowed into gaps and crevices in the ground and slowly began to harden.

The 'play of colour' so sought-after in opals occurs when a uniform arrangement of spheres occurs, allowing them to reflect light. The most prized opals look like all gemstones rolled into one, shimmering with the purple of amethyst, the green of emerald and the red of ruby. Looking close into a boulder or a black opal can be like looking through a high-powered telescope at a far-off constellation, or at the brightest Expressionist painting. Black opals fetch the highest price; they are a specialty of Lightning Ridge in New South Wales, but are also found around Mintabie and Coober Pedy.

Along with the commercial enterprises, many individuals are on quests to find opals, that ultimate flash of colour among the dust and dirt. Those wanting to go out to the opal fields and do more than just fossick (simply turn over rocks) must obtain a permit. The alternative is fossicking or noodling (using sieves or other tools) in the public areas surrounding the towns of Andamooka and Coober Pedy.

Contact Primary Industries and Resources South Australia (Minerals department) for more information; Head Office (08) 8463 4154; www.pir.sa.gov.au

past here in 1802 and, understandably, mistook the harbour for a large lagoon. The sandy beach is safe for swimming and the fishing is excellent. Oyster farming is a relatively new local industry, and fresh oysters can be purchased year-round. The world's oldest jade deposit is in the district and is considered one of the largest in the world. Discovered in the Minbrie Range in 1965, the deposit is believed to have been formed around 1700 million years ago by the shifting of the earth's surface.
IN TOWN *Franklin Harbour Historical Museum:* in the old post office and its

attached residence (1888), now operated by the National Trust and featuring local history displays; Main St. *Ruston Proctor Steam Tractor Museum:* open-air agricultural museum; Lincoln Hwy. *Cowell Jade Motel:* showroom and sales of local jade jewellery; Lincoln Hwy. *Turner Aquaculture:* tours of an oyster factory; Oyster Dr. *Boat hire:* from the caravan park.
WHAT'S ON *Fireworks Night:* includes street party; Dec.
NEARBY *Scenic drive:* 20 km drive south to Port Gibbon along a coast renowned for its history of wrecked and sunken

ketches. Interpretive signs detail the history at each site. *Franklin Harbour Conservation Park:* coastal peninsula park of sand dunes and mangrove habitat, popular for bush camping and fishing; 5 km s. *May Gibbs Memorial:* marks the location of children's author May Gibbs's first home; Cleve Rd; 10 km s. *The Knob:* good fishing from sheltered beach and rocks; 13 km s. *Lucky Bay:* safe swimming for children and the start of a 4WD track to Victoria Point with excellent views of the harbour. 16 km E. *Port Gibbon:* old shipping port with remains of original jetty. Sea lions are visible from the short walk to the point. 25 km s. *Yeldulknie Weir and Reservoir:* picnics and walking; 37 km w. *Cleve:* a service town with murals depicting its early days and an observation point at Tickleberry Hill; 42 km w. *Arno Bay:* a holiday town with sandy beaches and a jetty for fishing. Regular Sunday yacht races are held in summer. 44 km sw.
ⓘ Main St; (08) 8629 2588; www.tep.com.au

Crystal Brook   Pop. 1258

Map ref. 555 J4

Crystal Brook serves the sheep and wheat country at the southern point of the Flinders Ranges. It once formed part of a vast sheep station, Crystal Brook Run, which extended from the current town to Port Pirie in the north-west. The country feel of the town begins on entering the tree-lined main street.

IN TOWN *National Trust Old Bakehouse Museum:* local history collection in the town's first 2-storey building; Brandis St; open 2pm–4pm Sun and public holidays, or by appt (08) 8636 2328. *Crystal Crafts:* local craft; Bowman St. *Creekside parks:* popular spots for picnics.

NEARBY *Bowman Fauna Park:* enjoyable walks, including part of the Heysen Trail, around ruins of the Bowman family property, Crystal Brook Run (1847); 8 km E. *Koolunga:* a small community, home to the mythical bunyip – in 1883 two attempts to capture the beast were unsuccessful. Also craft outlets and the Bunyip River Walk on the banks of Broughton River. 10 km E. *Gladstone:* set in rich rural country in the Rocky River Valley. Heritage-listed Gladstone Gaol offers daily tours. Try traditional soft drinks, including Old Style Ginger Beer, at the Trends Drink Factory in Sixth Ave (open Mon–Fri) or discover the town's history on foot by picking up a map from the caravan park. 21 km NE. *Redhill:* riverside walk, museum, craft shop and antique shop; 25 km s. *Laura:* boyhood home of C. J. Dennis, author of *The Songs of a Sentimental Bloke*, known for its cottage crafts, art galleries and historic buildings. Leaflet available for self-guide walking tour from Biles Art Gallery, Herbert St. The Folk Fair each

Tidal pool at Edithburgh

April brings thousands of visitors to the town. 32 km N. West of town is the Beetaloo Valley and Reservoir, a pleasant picnic spot in cooler months. *Snowtown:* surrounded by large salt lakes that change colour according to weather conditions. Lake View Drive is a scenic 6 km drive around the lakes. Lochiel–Ninnes Rd Lookout provides panoramic country and lake views. 50 km s.
ⓘ Port Pirie Regional Tourism and Arts Centre, 3 Mary Elie St, Port Pirie; 1800 000 424 or (08) 8633 8700

Edithburgh   Pop. 428

Map ref. 554 I10

Edithburgh is located on the foreshore at the south-eastern tip of Yorke Peninsula. This is an area synonymous with shipwrecks and, although reflecting tragic maritime days of old, it is a source of excitement for the diving enthusiast. Despite the construction of a lighthouse in 1856, over 26 vessels were wrecked on the coast between West Cape in Innes National Park and Troubridge Point just south of Edithburgh. Today Edithburgh is a popular coastal holiday destination overlooking Gulf St Vincent and Troubridge Island.

IN TOWN *Edithburgh Museum:* a community museum with local history of the town and region featuring a historical maritime collection; Edith St; open 2pm–4pm Sun and public holidays, or

by appt (08) 8852 6187. *Native Flora Park:* walk through eucalypts and casuarinas and see a variety of birdlife; Ansty Tce. *Bakehouse Arts and Crafts:* local handcrafts and produce in a historic 1890 building; Blanche St. *Town jetty:* built in 1873 to service large shipments of salt found inland, it offers views to Troubridge Island and is popular with anglers. End of Edith St. *Natural tidal pool:* excellent for swimming; foreshore. *Fishing and offshore diving tours:* tours to local 'hotspots'; contact visitor centre for details. *Nature walks:* south to Sultana Point or north to Coobowie.

WHAT'S ON *Gala Day:* family day of entertainment and stalls; Oct.

NEARBY *Dive sites* Discover the south coast of Yorke Peninsula with *The Investigator Strait Maritime Heritage Trail* brochure that includes the history and maps of 26 dive sites. By far the worst recorded shipwreck was of the *Clan Ranald*, a huge steel steamer that, through incompetence and greed, was wrecked in 1909 just west of Troubridge Hill. The disaster claimed 40 lives – 36 bodies were later buried in the Edithburgh Cemetery. *Sultana Point:* fishing and swimming; 2 km s. *Coobowie:* a coast town popular for swimming; 5 km N. *Troubridge Island Conservation Park:* home to penguins, black-faced shags and crested terns; tours available (30 min by boat) from town. *Scenic drive:* west along the coast to Innes National Park; *see Yorketown.*
ⓘ Cnr Weaver and Towler sts, Stansbury; (08) 8852 4577

Elliston   Pop. 234

Map ref. 554 A5

Nestled in a range of hills on the shores of picturesque Waterloo Bay is the small community of Elliston. The waters of the bay used to have rich abalone beds, but fierce exploitation in the 1960s led to their ruin. The rugged and scenic coastline is spectacular and – with its excellent fishing and safe swimming beaches – Elliston is becoming a popular holiday destination. The 12-kilometre stretch of coast north of Elliston, known as Elliston's Great Ocean View, is said to rival the landscape of Victoria's Great Ocean Road, but on a smaller scale.

IN TOWN *Town Hall Mural:* the Southern Hemisphere's largest mural, which represents the history of town and district; Main St. *Jetty:* the heritage-listed 1889 jetty has been restored and is lit by night.

WHAT'S ON *Sculptures on the Cliff:* odd-numbered years, Mar–May. *Australian Salmon Fishing Competition:* June–Aug.

NEARBY *Elliston's Great Ocean View:* scenic cliff-top drive north of town to adjacent Anxious Bay, with fabulous coastal views. Along the way is Blackfellows, reputedly one of the best surfing beaches in Australia. *Anxious Bay:* good fishing from beach and ledges for

King George whiting. The boat ramp here provides access to Waldegrave Island (4 km offshore) and Flinders Island (35 km offshore), both good for fishing and seal-spotting (seek local advice about conditions before departing). *Locks Well:* a long stairwell down to a famous salmon-fishing and surf beach with coastal lookout; 12 km SE. *Walkers Rock:* good beaches for swimming and rock-fishing; 15 km N. *Lake Newland Conservation Park:* significant dunes separate the park's salt lakes and wetlands from the sea. Walk along bush tracks or try a spot of fishing. 26 km N. *Scenic drive:* to Sheringa (40 km S). From Sheringa Beach, a popular fishing spot, see whales, dolphins and seals offshore. *Talia Caves:* spectacular scene of caves with waves crashing on edge. Another good spot for beach-fishing. 45 km N.
ⓘ Town Hall, 6 Memorial Dr; (08) 8687 9200; www.tep.com.au

Gawler   Pop. 16 779

Map ref. 550 D5, 555 L8

Set in the fork of the North and South Parra rivers and surrounded by rolling hills, it is no wonder that Gawler was picked, in 1839, as the site of South Australia's first country town. The grand architecture of that era can be seen in its stately homes and buildings, especially in the Church Hill State Heritage Area, which comprises three main squares. Gawler is today a major service centre to a thriving agricultural district and has a growing Adelaide commuter population.

IN TOWN Historical Walking Trail The excellent trail brochure (available from the visitor centre) guides the visitor past stately buildings and homes, many with original cast-iron lacework. The Church Hill State Heritage Area provides a fascinating snapshot of town planning in the 1830s, and the 2.4 km walk around it includes a look at several churches, the old school, the courthouse, and cottages of the Victorian era. Also on the way are Gawler Mill, Eagle Foundry (now a popular B&B), the Anglican Church with its pipe organ (open Sun) and the Para Para Mansion (1862), a grand mansion that features a domed ballroom and has had British royalty as its guests (closed to public). *Gawler Museum:* located in the Old Telegraph Station, this National Trust museum displays the history of Gawler's pioneer past; Murray St; closed Mon and Sat. *Dead Man's Pass Reserve:* so named because an early pioneer was found dead in the hollow of a tree. It has picnic facilities and a walking trail. Southern end of Murray St. *Adelaide Soaring Club:* glider flights over Gawler and region; contact visitor centre for details.
WHAT'S ON *Gawler South Markets:* Gawler Railway Station; Sun mornings. *Gawler Gourmet and Heritage Festival:* Easter.

NEARBY *Roseworthy Agricultural Museum:* a dryland farming museum featuring vintage farm implements, engines and working tractors, located at the Roseworthy campus of the University of Adelaide. Open Wed and 3rd Sun each month; 15 km N. *Freeling:* a rural town with a self-guide historical walk; 17 km NE. *Two Wells:* named for 2 Aboriginal wells found by original settlers, forgotten, then recovered in 1967. It has craft shop with local crafts, Main Rd. 24 km W. *Stockport Astronomical Facility:* run by the Astronomical Society of SA, this complex has an impressive observatory with public viewing nights; contact (08) 8338 1231. 30 km N.
ⓘ 2 Lyndoch Rd; (08) 8522 6814; www.gawler.sa.gov.au

Goolwa   Pop. 4330

Map ref. 549 I7, 552 C3, 555 L11

Goolwa is a rapidly growing holiday town on the last big bend of the Murray River before it reaches open waters. Goolwa was originally surveyed as the capital of South Australia, but Adelaide was later thought to be a better option. Goolwa did, however, boom as a river port from the 1850s to the 1880s – in the golden days of the riverboats. The area is excellent for fishing, with freshwater fishing in the Murray and saltwater fishing in the Southern Ocean and the Coorong, as well as boating, surfing, watersports, birdwatching and photography.

IN TOWN Signal Point River Murray Interpretive Centre Learn about the river and district before European settlement and see the impact of later development. There is also a detailed history on Goolwa's river port, the paddlesteamers, and local Aboriginal people. A highlight is the 3D model showing how the Murray River interacts with the SA landscape. The Wharf.
National Trust Museum: documents the history of Goolwa and early navigation of the Murray River; Porter St. *South Coast Regional Arts Centre:* explore the restored old court and police station and see exhibitions by local artists; Goolwa Tce. *Goolwa Barrage:* desalination point to prevent salt water from reaching the Murray River; Barrage Rd; open Mon–Fri. *Armfield Slipway:* a working exhibition of wooden boatbuilding and restoration; Barrage Rd; open Tues mornings and Fri afternoons. *Horse-drawn railway carriage:* first carriages used in SA between Goolwa and Port Elliot from 1854; Cadell St. *Goolwa Beach:* popular surfing and swimming beach with large cockles to be dug up (in season); end of Beach Rd. *Cockle Train:* journey around Encounter Bay from Goolwa Wharf to Victor Harbor, stopping at Port Elliot. The train has been operating since 1887, and its name comes from the abundance of large cockles found on Goolwa's surf beach.

It forms part of the longer *SteamRanger* tourist railway from Mount Barker; *see Hahndorf.* Operates most weekends and public and school holidays; bookings (08) 8231 4366. *Cruises:* day tours to the mouth of the Murray, the Coorong, the Barrages and the Lower Murray; details and bookings at visitor centre. *Scenic flights:* over the region; contact visitor centre for details. *Goolwa Heritage Walk:* a self-guide tour to see the 19th-century architecture of the river port's boom days; brochure available from visitor centre.
WHAT'S ON *Goolwa Wharf Markets:* 1st and 3rd Sun each month. *Milang to Goolwa Freshwater Sailing Classic:* Jan. *Wooden Boat Festival:* odd-numbered years, Mar.
NEARBY *Hindmarsh Island:* Captain Sturt located the mouth of the Murray River from here in 1830 – visit the Captain Sturt Lookout and monument. The island is now popular for both freshwater and saltwater fishing. East of town. *Currency Creek Game Reserve:* feeding grounds, breeding rookeries and hides for many waterbirds; access by boat only; 3 km E. *Currency Creek:* Lions Park is a popular picnic spot with a walking track along the creek. Near town is an Aboriginal canoe tree (a eucalypt that has been carved to make a canoe) and also the Currency Creek Winery with a restaurant and fauna park. 7 km N.
ⓘ Signal Point River Murray Interpretive Centre, Goolwa Wharf; (08) 8555 3488; www.visitalexandrina.com

Hahndorf   Pop. 1902

Map ref. 549 I2, 550 D11, 552 C2, 555 L9

In the heart of the Adelaide Hills is Hahndorf, Australia's oldest surviving German settlement. Prussian Lutheran refugees fleeing religious persecution in their homelands settled the area in the late 1830s. The town has retained a distinctly Germanic look and many local businesses and attractions are still operated by descendants of the original German pioneers. The surrounding countryside with its rolling hills, historic villages, vineyards, gourmet-produce farms and native bushland is renowned as a tourist destination.

IN TOWN *Main Street:* a mix of historic buildings, German-style bakeries, delis, cafes, restaurants and art and craft shops. *The Cedars:* historic paintings, gardens and home of famous landscape artist Hans Heysen; Heysen Rd; closed Sat. *Hahndorf Academy:* displays work of local artists in SA's largest regional gallery; Main St. *Model Train Land:* housed in a historic butcher shop with a model railway in miniature Bavarian countryside; Mount Barker Rd. *Hahndorf Farm Barn:* interactive farm animal shows, with petting and feeding; Mount Barker Rd. *Hillstowe Wines:* wine and cheese tastings; Main St. *Hahndorf Hill Winery:* boutique cool-climate winery

SOUTH AUSTRALIA

with tastings and sales; Pains Rd; open weekends. *Beerenberg Strawberry Farm:* balcony viewing of the farm and packing area, jam and condiment sales, and berry-picking Oct–May; Mount Barker Rd. *Historic Hahndorf:* obtain *A Guide to Historic Hahndorf,* which lists 42 historic properties; available from visitor centre.

WHAT'S ON *Heysen Festival:* major 10-day event celebrating the life of Hans Heysen, with the Heysen Art Prize, food, wine and entertainment; Oct.

NEARBY **Cleland Conservation Park** This park protects a variety of vegetation, from the stringybark forests in the highlands to the woods and grasses of the lowlands. It also includes panoramic views from the Mount Lofty Summit viewing platform. A highlight is the award-winning Cleland Wildlife Park where many native animals wander freely about. Kids will enjoy the daily animal-feeding shows at 10am and 3pm or the fabulous guided night tours. Bookings (08) 8339 2444. For a rich cultural experience, take the guided Aboriginal tour on the Yurridla Trail where Dreamtime stories come alive. Mount Lofty Summit Rd. 14 km NW.
Belair National Park The oldest national park in SA was declared in 1891. There are plenty of activities, including 5 defined bushwalks ranging from the easy Wood Duck Walk to the more challenging 6.5 km Waterfall Walk, and cycling and horseriding tracks. Visitors can also visit Old Government House, built in 1859 to serve as the governor's summer residence (open Sun and public holidays). 19 km W. *Mount Barker:* a historic town renowned for its gourmet outlets. The *SteamRanger* tourist train operates from here, including regular trips to Strathalbyn and on to the coastal section from Goolwa to Victor Harbor (this section is known as the Cockle Train; *see Goolwa*). For *SteamRanger* information and bookings contact 1300 655 991. Local events include the Highland Gathering and Heritage Festival in May. 6 km SE. *Bridgewater:* a historic town with excellent gardens and Petaluma's Bridgewater Mill, which has wine-tastings, sales and an up-market restaurant for lunch in a historic flour mill; 6 km W. *Oakbank:* craft shops and historic buildings with self-guide heritage-walk brochure available from local businesses. The Oakbank Easter Racing Carnival, held each April, is the Southern Hemisphere's biggest picnic race meeting and brings thousands of visitors to the town each year. 7 km N. *Aldgate:* a historic village features art and craft shops and historic sites that include the Aldgate Pump and the National Trust-listed Stangate House with its extensive camellia garden. Aldgate holds the annual Autumn Leaves Festival each May. 8 km W. *Stirling:* renowned for its European gardens and architecture, including the National Estate-listed Beechworth Heritage Garden (Snows Rd).

See colourful parrots in the aviaries at Stirling Parrot Farm (Milan Tce). Stirling is home to the Mount Lofty Spring Bulb Festival (April) and the Hills Affare (Sept). 10 km W. *Warrawong Sanctuary:* large native animal reserve for reintroduced and endangered species, with walking trails and a boardwalk around Platypus Lakes. Guided dawn and evening tours are available; bookings (08) 8370 9197. 10 km SW via Mylor. *Jupiter Creek Goldfields:* walking trails with interpretive signs across historic fields discovered in 1852; 12 km SW. *Woodside Heritage Village:* includes Melba's Chocolate Factory (with guided tours and sales) as well as craft studios with artisans at work; Woodside; 13 km NE. *Mount Lofty Botanic Gardens:* Australia's largest botanic gardens, with walking trails past cool-climate garden species, on the eastern face of Mt Lofty; access via Summit or Piccadilly rds; 14 km NW. *Wittunga Botanic Gardens:* native plants; Shepherds Hill Rd; 21 km W at Blackwood.
ⓘ Adelaide Hills Visitor Information Centre, 41 Main St; (08) 8388 1185; www.visitadelaidehills.com.au

Hawker   Pop. 292

Map ref. 553 D10, 557 J9

This small outback town was once a thriving railway centre. The historic buildings from this boom era are still well preserved in its streets. Hawker was also once an agricultural region producing bumper crops of wheat. Serious drought sent the crops into decline and the industry died. Today Hawker is the place to begin exploring the fantastic natural attractions of the region, including the South Flinders Ranges.

IN TOWN *Museum:* local history displays; Hawker Motors, cnr Wilpena and Cradock rds. *Scenic flights and 4WD tours:* around the region; contact visitor centre for details. *Heritage walk:* self-guide walk on numbered path; brochure from visitor centre.
WHAT'S ON *Horseraces:* May. *Art Exhibition:* Sept/Oct.
NEARBY *Jarvis Hill Lookout:* walking trail with views over the countryside; 7 km SW. *Yourambulla Caves:* Aboriginal rock paintings in caves and surrounds; 12 km SW. *Willow Waters:* popular picnic spot with a short walk to Ochre Wall; 20 km E off Cradock Rd. *Moralana Scenic Drive:* 22 km drive with superb views of Wilpena Pound and the Elder Range; leaves Hawker–Wilpena Rd; 23 km N. *Cradock:* a tiny town with National Heritage-listed St Gabriel's Church (1882); 26 km SE. *Kanyaka Homestead Historic Site:* ruins of the homestead, stables and woolshed once part of a large sheep run, with informative displays explaining the history of each ruin; 28 km SW. *Kanyaka Death Rock:* once an Aboriginal ceremonial ground, it

overlooks a permanent waterhole; near Kanyaka Homestead ruins. *Long-distance trails:* close to Hawker you can pick up sections of the Heysen (walking) and Mawson (cycling) trails; information from visitor centre.
ⓘ Hawker Motors, cnr Wilpena and Cradock rds; (08) 8648 4014; www.hawkersa.info

Innamincka   Pop. 14

Map ref. 559 Q7, 616 H10

This tiny settlement is built around a hotel and trading post on the Strzelecki Track. The first European explorer to visit the area was Charles Sturt, who discovered nearby Cooper Creek in 1846 while vainly searching for an inland sea. It was also the final destination of the ill-fated Burke and Wills expedition. In 1860 all but one of Burke and Wills' party perished near the creek. John King survived owing to the outback skills of the Aboriginal people who found him. Innamincka was once a customs depot and service centre for surrounding pastoral properties, but now mainly services a burgeoning tourist industry.

IN TOWN **Australian Inland Mission** Built in 1928 to service the medical needs of remote pastoral properties, this mission was attended by a rotating staff of 2 nurses who reached the town on horseback. Injured workers, flood victims and even fallen jockeys from the races called on their expertise. The mission was abandoned in the early 1950s when the Royal Flying Doctor Service began providing their services. The restored classic outback building now houses the national parks headquarters as well as a tribute museum to the nurses who faced the trials of this isolated region. *Boat hire and tours:* fishing and cruising trips; contact hotel for details.
WHAT'S ON *Picnic Race Meeting:* Aug.
NEARBY **Innamincka Regional Reserve** This isolated but spectacular reserve is popular with 4WD enthusiasts and nature lovers. It covers 13 800 sq km and comprises important wetland areas, the most impressive being Coongie Lakes, 112 km NW. This internationally significant wetland area is a haven for wildlife, particularly waterbirds. Closer to Innamincka is Cullyamurra Waterhole, on Cooper Creek, 16 km NE, for bush camping and fishing. Aboriginal rock carvings and the Cullyamurra Choke are accessible by foot at the eastern end of the waterhole. 4WD is essential in parts of the park; after heavy rains roads become impassable. Entry permits are required; visit the Inland Mission in Innamincka or contact 1800 816 078 for details. *Memorial plaques:* to Charles Sturt and Burke and Wills; 2 km N. *Burke and Wills Dig Tree:* famous Dig Tree where supplies were buried for their expedition; 71 km across border in Qld. *Strzelecki*

Regional Reserve: sand-dune desert country with birdwatching facilities at Montecollina Bore; 167 km sw. ***Travellers note:*** *motorists intending to travel along the Strzelecki Track should ensure road conditions are suitable by phoning the Northern Roads Condition Hotline on 1300 361 033 before departure. There are no supplies or petrol between Lyndhurst and Innamincka.*
ⓘ Innamincka Hotel, South Tce; (08) 8675 9901

Jamestown   Pop. 1348

Map ref. 555 L3, 557 K13

Jamestown survived the demise of wheat crops in the late 1800s to become an important service town to the thriving agricultural farmlands of the Clare Valley. John Bristow Hughes took up the first pastoral lease in 1841 and the strength of stud sheep and cattle farms, cereals, dairy produce and timber grew rapidly. A look at the names of towns in South Australia will reveal that the governors, politicians and surveyors of the day were bent on commemorating themselves or people they liked. Jamestown followed this trend, named after Sir James Fergusson, then state governor.

IN TOWN *Railway Station Museum:* a National Trust museum detailing local rail and Bundaleer Forest history and featuring the Both-designed iron lung (invented at Caltowie); Mannanarie Rd; closed Wed. *Heritage murals:* on town buildings. *Belalie Creek:* parks for picnics along the banks; floodlit at night. *Town and cemetery walks:* self-guide tours; brochure available from caravan park.
WHAT'S ON *Jamestown Show:* largest 1-day show in SA; Oct. *Christmas Pageant:* Dec.

NEARBY Bundaleer Forest Reserve This original plantation forest, established in 1876, was the first in the world. Walking tracks start from the Arboretum, Georgetown Rd and the picnic area, and range from botanic walks to historic trails past building ruins and extensive dry-stone walls. The longer Mawson (cycling) and Heysen (walking) trails also travel through the reserve, as does a scenic drive from Jamestown, which then continues on towards New Campbell Hill, Mt Remarkable and The Bluff. Each Easter Sunday the Bilby Easter Egg Hunt is held in the reserve. Spalding Rd; 9 km s. *Appila Springs:* scenic picnic and camping spot; 31 km nw via Appila. *Spalding:* a town the Broughton River valley. Picnic areas and excellent trout fishing. 34 km s.
ⓘ Country Retreat Caravan Park, 103 Ayr St; (08) 8664 0077; www. clarevalley.com.au

Kadina   Pop. 3742

Map ref. 554 I6

Kadina exists solely as a result of the digging habits of wombats. In 1860

Hindmarsh Island lies across the water from Goolwa, near the mouth of the Murray and the start of the Coorong

upturned ground from wombat diggings revealed copper. This was the starting point of coppermining on Yorke Peninsula. The wombats were commemorated by the naming of Kadina's 1862 hotel: Wombat Hotel. Kadina, along with Wallaroo and Moonta, formed part of a copper triangle colloquially named Little Cornwall because of the number of Cornish immigrants recruited to work on the mines. Kadina is now the commercial centre and largest town on Yorke Peninsula.

IN TOWN *Kadina Museum Complex:* comprises the National Dryland Farming Interpretive Centre; National Trust-listed Matta House (1863), former home of the mine manager; and a 1950s-style schoolroom. Also here are the old Matta Mine and the Kadina Story, a display of town history. Moonta Rd. *Banking and Currency Museum:* unique private museum with banking memorabilia including money boxes and coins, and a 130-year-old strongroom; Graves St; closed Fri, Sat and all of June. *Ascot Theatre Gallery:* cultural centre exhibiting local artists' work, with sales; Graves St; closed Sun. *Victoria Square Park:* historic band rotunda and Wallaroo Mine Monument; Main St. *Heritage walk:* self-guide walk includes historic hotels such as the Wombat and the Royal Exchange with iron-lace

balconies and shady verandahs; brochure from visitor centre.
WHAT'S ON *Kernewek Lowender:* Cornish festival held with Wallaroo and Moonta; odd-numbered years; May. *Copper Coast Spring Garden Fair:* Nov.
NEARBY *Yorke Peninsula Field Days:* Australia's oldest field days, started in 1884, held each Sept (odd-numbered years); Paskeville; 19 km SE.
ⓘ Yorke Peninsula Regional Visitor Information Centre, 50 Moonta Rd; 1800 654 991 or (08) 8821 2333; www.yorke peninsula.com.au

Kangaroo Island   Pop. 4384

Map ref. 549 A11, 554 F11

In the early days of Australia's European settlement, Kangaroo Island was a haven for some of the country's most rugged characters – escaped convicts and deserters from English and American whaleboats. These men formed gangs, hunted more than their fair share of whales, seals, kangaroos, wallabies and possums, and went on raids to the mainland to kidnap Aboriginal women. It was an island truly without law. Two centuries on, the only ruggedness to speak of is found along the island's southern coast, where the surf is Southern Ocean-style and the seals

Australian sea lions at Seal Bay, Kangaroo Island

are now left in peace. The north shore is a rippling line of bays and coves, with grass-covered hills sweeping down into Investigator Strait. The island is a mecca for wildlife-watchers and fishing enthusiasts, and also has a growing reputation for gourmet produce. Travel to the island is by air from Adelaide (30 minutes) or vehicle and passenger ferry from Cape Jervis (45 minutes).

EAST Kingscote Kangaroo Island's largest town, Kingscote was SA's first official settlement (est. 1836). Its long pioneering and maritime history is illustrated in the National Trust Museum in Centenary Ave and also at the town's cemetery, SA's oldest, in Seaview Rd. Visit St Alban's Church in Osmond St to see impressive stained-glass windows and pioneer memorials. In true 'KI' style there is a wildlife attraction too, in the little (fairy) penguins that come ashore nightly. To view them, take the Discovering Penguins Tour, which starts at the Penguin Centre at 15 Kingscote Tce. There are 2 tours every night, and times vary during the year; contact visitor centre for details. *Emu Bay:* excellent swimming at the beach with fishing from the jetty. *Parndana:* a small town known as The Place of Little Gums, featuring the Soldier Settlement Museum. *Stokes Bay:* natural rock tunnel leads to a rock pool, ideal for swimming. *Island Pure Sheep Dairy:* tasting and sales of produce, and milking demonstrations; Cygnet River; open 1pm–5pm daily. *Emu Ridge Eucalyptus Oil Distillery:* sales of eucalyptus-oil products; Wilsons Rd, off South Coast Rd; 20 km s of Kingscote; open 9am–2pm daily. *Clifford's Honey Farm:* sales and free tasting of honey produced by pure Ligurian bees; Hundred Line Rd; 25 km s of Kingscote. *American River:* a fishing village overlooking Eastern Cove and Pelican Lagoon, havens for birdlife.

Mt Thisby Lookout: spectacular views from the spot where Matthew Flinders surveyed island; on narrow neck to Dudley Peninsula. *Penneshaw:* a small town on Dudley Peninsula where the vehicular ferry arrives from Cape Jervis. The town features a National Trust folk museum and nightly penguin tours from the Penguin Interpretive Centre at Hog Bay Beach. *Antechamber Bay:* picturesque beach and area excellent for bushwalking, fishing and swimming; 20 km SE of Penneshaw.

SOUTH Seal Bay Conservation Park
This park protects the habitat of the rare Australian sea lion, which almost faced extinction on the SA coast during the 1800s. Guided beach tours provide close-up encounters with the snoozing creatures. There are also views down to the beach from the 400 m boardwalk that runs through dunes to an observation deck. 58 km SW of Kingscote. *Murray Lagoon:* well-known waterbird area with tea-tree walk; 40 km SW of Kingscote. *Little Sahara:* large sand dunes surrounded by bush; 6 km W of Seal Bay turn-off. *Vivonne Bay:* popular beach for surfing and fishing (beware of strong undertow – safe swimming near the jetty, boat ramp and Harriet River). *Kelly Hill Conservation Park:* sugar gum forest walks and guided tours of limestone caves; 2 km W of Karatta.

WEST Flinders Chase National Park On the south coast of this vast park are the precariously positioned granite boulders called the Remarkable Rocks, gradually being eroded by wind and sea to form spectacular shapes. Nearby is the Cape du Couedic lighthouse, and a colony of New Zealand fur seals that can be seen from the boardwalk down to Admirals Arch, a sea cave. There are many walking

trails throughout the park and a detailed map is available from the visitor centre at Rocky River. Watch for the Cape Barren geese around the visitor centre. *Cape Borda Lightstation:* historical tours offered of 1858 lighthouse. Also here is the Cape Borda Heritage Museum. Cannons are fired at 12.30pm. *Scotts Cove:* from here you can view the highest coastal cliffs in the state, at 263 m; near Cape Borda. *Western River Wilderness Protection Area:* 2.5 km track to winter waterfall; turn-off 30 km or 37 km east of Cape Borda.

WHAT'S ON *Racing Carnival:* Kingscote; Feb. *Street Fair:* Kingscote; Feb. *Kangaroo Island Easter Fair:* Parndana; Easter. *Art Exhibition:* Penneshaw; Easter.
ℹ Kangaroo Island Gateway Visitor Information Centre, Howard Dr, Penneshaw; (08) 8553 1185; www.tour kangarooisland.com.au

Kapunda   Pop. 2295

Map ref. 550 E3, 555 L7

Kapunda is between two wine districts – the Barossa Valley and the Clare Valley – but its history is very different. Copper was discovered here by Francis Dutton, a sheep farmer, in 1842. It was to be the highest grade copper ore found in the world. Settlement followed, and Kapunda came into existence as Australia's first coppermining town. When the mines closed in 1878, Australia's 'cattle king' Sir Sidney Kidman moved in, eventually controlling 26 million hectares of land across Australia.

IN TOWN *Kapunda Museum:* excellent folk museum with a short Kapunda history film and displays of old agricultural machinery, an original fire engine and other vehicles in the pavilion. Detailed mining history is in Bagot's Fortune interpretive centre. Hill St; open 1pm–4pm daily. *Community Gallery:* significant regional gallery with local and touring art exhibitions; cnr Main and Hill sts; open Tues–Sat. *'Map Kernow':* 8 m bronze statue commemorating early miners, many of whom migrated from Cornwall in England; end of Main St at southern entrance of town. *High school's main building:* former residence of Sir Sidney Kidman; West Tce. *Gundry's Hill Lookout:* views over township and surrounding countryside; West Tce. *Heritage trail:* 10 km self-guide tour through town and historic Kapunda Copper Mine; *Discovering Historic Kapunda* brochure available at visitor centre.

WHAT'S ON *Celtic Music Festival:* April. *Farm Fair:* including fashion, craft and antiques; odd-numbered years, May.

NEARBY *Pines Reserve:* nature and wildlife reserve; 6 km NW on road to Tarlee. *Anlaby Station:* historic Dutton Homestead and gardens, once a setting for large prestigious parties. Also a coach collection and historic station buildings. Anlaby Rd; 16 km NE; open 10am–4pm Wed–Sun. *Tarlee:* historic local-stone buildings; 16 km NW. *Riverton:* a historic town in the Gilbert Valley, once a stopover point for copper-hauling bullock teams. Many historic buildings remain, including the heritage-listed railway station and Scholz Park Museum, which incorporates a cottage, blacksmith and wheelwright shop; 30 km NW; open 1pm–4pm weekends. *Scenic drive:* 28 km drive north-east through sheep, wheat and dairy country to Eudunda. ⓘ Cnr Hill and Main sts; (08) 8566 2902; www.clarevalley.com.au

Keith   Pop. 1126

Map ref. 552 G6, 555 P13

Keith is a farming town in the area formerly known as the Ninety Mile Desert. Settlers found the original land unpromising, but the area has since been transformed from infertile pasture to productive farmland with the addition to the soil of missing trace elements and water piped from the Murray.

IN TOWN *Congregational Church:* National Trust church with 11 locally made leadlight windows depicting the town's life and pioneering history; Heritage St. *Early Settler's Cottage:* limestone pioneer cottage; open by appt (08) 8755 1118; Heritage St. *Keith Water Feature:* water sculpture; Heritage St.

NEARBY Ngarkat group of conservation parks Protecting 262 700 ha of sand dunes, mallee and heath are the 4 adjacent conservation parks – Ngarkat, Scorpion Springs, Mount Rescue and Mount Shaugh. The walking trails are an excellent introduction to the region's vegetation. Birdwatching is particularly good at Rabbit Island (Mount Rescue) and Comet Bore (Ngarkat). For panoramic views, try walking to the summit of Mt Rescue, Goose Hill or Mt Shaugh. Visitors can drive through the parks on the Pinaroo–Bordertown Rd. The main entrance is via Snozwells Rd near Tintinara. *Monster Conservation Park:* scenic views and picnic spots; 10 km S. *Tintinara Homestead:* one of the first homesteads in the area, with woolshed, shearers quarters and pioneer cottage, it caters for visitors. 38 km NW. *Mount Boothby Conservation Park:* mallee scrub, granite outcrops and wildflowers in spring; 58 km NW via Tintinara. ⓘ Mobil Roadhouse, cnr Riddock and Dukes hwys; (08) 8755 1700

Kimba   Pop. 684

Map ref. 554 F3, 556 E13

A small town on the Eyre Peninsula, Kimba is 'halfway across Australia' according to the huge sign on the Eyre Highway. It is the gateway to the outback, a fact that explorer Edward John Eyre

confirmed when he traversed the harsh landscape in 1839. Early settlers thought the country too arid for settlement and it wasn't until demand for wheat production grew, and rail services were extended to the area in 1913, that the Kimba region developed. It is now major sheep- and wheat-farming country.

IN TOWN *Kimba and Gawler Ranges Historical Museum:* a 'living' museum featuring local history and a Pioneer House (1908), a blacksmith's shop and 'Clancy' the fire truck; Eyre Hwy; open 1.30pm–4pm Sat or by appt (08) 8627 2349. *Halfway Across Australia Gem Shop and the Big Galah:* standing 8 m high, the Big Galah is in front of the gem shop, which offers sales of local gemstones, carved emu eggs, opal and locally mined jade, including rare black jade; Eyre Hwy. *Pine 'n' Pug Gallery:* local craft; High St. *Roora Walking Trail:* meanders through 3 km of bushland to White Knob Lookout; starts at north-eastern outskirts of town.

WHAT'S ON *'Beyond and Back' Gawler Ranges Outback Challenge:* teams cycle, run and horseride; even-numbered years, Oct.

NEARBY *Lake Gilles Conservation Park:* habitat for mallee fowl; 20 km NE. *Caralue Bluff:* popular for rockclimbing; 20 km SW. *Carappee Hill Conservation Park:* bush camping and walking; 25 km SW. *Darke Peak:* excellent views from the summit and a memorial at the base to John Charles Darke, an explorer who was speared to death in 1844. 40 km SW. *Pinkawillinie Conservation Park:* the largest mallee vegetation area on the peninsula and a habitat for small desert birds, emus and western grey kangaroos; turn-off 50 km W. ⓘ Kimba Mobil Roadhouse, Eyre Hwy; (08) 8627 2040; www.tep.com.au

Kingston S.E.   Pop. 1477

Map ref. 552 F8

Known as the 'Gateway to the South East', Kingston S.E. is at the southern end of Coorong National Park on Lacepede Bay. The area was once home to the Ngarranjerri, river people who mastered the waterways of the Coorong and the Murray River. This famous lobster town was established in 1858 and its shallow lakes and lagoons are a haven for birdlife and a delight for photographers.

IN TOWN *National Trust Museum:* pioneer museum; Cooke St; open 2pm–4.30pm daily during school holidays, or by appt (08) 8767 2114. *Cape Jaffa Lighthouse:* built in the 1860s on the Margaret Brock Reef, it was dismantled and re-erected on its current site in the 1970s; Marine Pde; open 2pm–4.30pm daily during school holidays, or by appt (08) 8767 2591. *Analematic Sundial:* an unusual sundial, 1 of only 8 in the world; on an island in the creek adjacent to Apex Park in East Tce. *Aboriginal burial ground:* Dowdy St. *Power House engine:* historic engine that produced the town's energy until 1974;

Lions Park, Holland St. *The Big Lobster:* 17 m high 'Larry Lobster' has sales of cooked lobster; Princes Hwy.

WHAT'S ON *Fishing Contest:* Jan. *Yachting Regatta:* Jan.

NEARBY *Butchers Gap Conservation Park:* this important coastal park provides a winter refuge for bird species. Follow walking trail from the carpark. 6 km SW. *The Granites:* rocky outcrops, a striking site from the beach; 18 km N. *Cape Jaffa:* scenic drive south-west from Kingston S.E. leads to this small fishing village popular with anglers and divers. The Cape Jaffa Seafood and Wine Festival is held here each Jan. 18 km SW. *Mount Scott Conservation Park:* part of a former coastal dune system, with walks through stringybark forest; 20 km E. *Jip Jip Conservation Park:* features a prominent outcrop of unusually shaped granite boulders; 50 km NE. ⓘ BP Roadhouse, 1 Princes Hwy; (08) 8767 2404

Leigh Creek   Pop. 627

Map ref. 553 D3, 557 J4

Located in the Flinders Ranges, Leigh Creek is a modern coalmining town that services a huge open-cut mine to the north. The original township (13 kilometres north) was unfortunately placed, as it was situated over a large coal seam. The lure of the dollar led to the town's relocation in 1982 to its current site. A tree-planting scheme has transformed the town from a barren landscape to an attractive oasis.

NEARBY *Coalmine tours:* tours to the open-cut mine each Sat from Mar to late Oct and during school holidays; contact visitor centre for details. *Aroona Dam:* in a steep-sided valley with coloured walls; picnic area near gorge; 4 km W. *Coalmine viewing area:* turn-off 14 km N (area is 3 km down road to coalmine). *Beltana:* almost a ghost town, it has a historic reserve and holds a Picnic Race Meeting and Gymkhana each Sept; 27 km S. *Lyndhurst:* starting point of the famous Strzelecki Track. It also features a unique gallery of sculptures by well-known talc-stone artist 'Talc Alf'; tours by appt (08) 8675 7781. 39 km N. *Ochre Cliffs:* here Aboriginal people used to dig for ochre. The colours range from white to reds, yellows and browns. 44 km N via Lyndhurst. *Sliding Rock Mine ruins:* access track is rough in places; 60 km SE. *Gammon Ranges National Park:* 64 km E; see Arkaroola. **Travellers note:** *care must be taken on outback roads. Check road conditions with Northern Roads Condition Hotline on 1300 361 033 before departure.* ⓘ Shop 13, town centre; (08) 8675 2723

Loxton   Pop. 3350

Map ref. 555 Q7

Although the area around Loxton was originally settled largely by German immigrants, the town's boom began when servicemen returned from World War II. The enticement of irrigated allotments brought a great number of them to town and the success of current-day industries, such as the production of citrus fruits, wine, dried fruit, wool and wheat, was due to their skill on the land. Loxton's delightful setting on the Murray River has made the town the 'Garden City of the Riverland'.

IN TOWN Loxton Historical Village The Riverland's pioneering history comes to life in the 30 historic buildings, all fully furnished in the styles of late 1880s to mid-1900s. A highlight is the pine-and-pug building, Loxtons Hut, built by boundary rider William Loxton. The town is his namesake. Visit on one of the Village Alive days held regularly in the village. Locals dress up in period costume and the whole village steps back 100 years. Riverfront. *Terrace Gallery:* local art and pottery displays and sales; part of visitor centre; Bookpurnong Tce. *Art and craft shops:* main street. *Pepper tree:* grown from a seed bought by Loxton over 110 years ago; near the historical village. *Nature trail:* along riverfront; canoes for hire. *Heritage Walk:* brochure from visitor centre.

WHAT'S ON *Mardi Gras:* Feb. *Loxton Gift:* SA's largest and richest footrace; Feb. *Riverland Field Days:* Sept. *Loxton Lights Up:* Christmas lights throughout town; self-guide tour map available; Dec.

NEARBY *Medea Cottage:* fresh and preserved local produce; Bookpurnong Rd, Loxton North. *Australian Vintage:* wine-tasting and sales; Bookpurnong Rd, Loxton North. *Lock 4:* picnic/barbecue area; 14 km N on Murray River.
ⓘ Bookpurnong Tce; (08) 8584 7919; www.riverland.info

Lyndoch   Pop. 1244

Map ref. 550 E6, 551 C9, 555 L8

Lyndoch is one of the oldest towns in South Australia. The first European explorers, led by Colonel Light in 1837, described the area around Lyndoch as 'a beautiful valley'. The undulating landscape and picturesque setting attracted Lutheran immigrants and English gentry, who began growing grapes. By 1850 Johann Gramp had produced his first wine from the grapes at Jacob's Creek.

IN TOWN *Stone mill wheel:* in the mid-1800s water from the Para River was used to operate a flour mill with this wheel; on display in Flebig Square. *Helicopter and balloon flights:* scenic flights over the Barossa region; contact visitor centre for details. *Historic Lyndoch Walk:* self-guide walk featuring buildings from the mid-1800s, including many built from locally quarried hard ironstone; brochure from visitor centre.

WHAT'S ON *Barossa under the Stars:* food, wine and music; Rowland Flat; Feb. *Barossa Vintage Festival:* celebration

of food and wine in various locations; odd-numbered years, April. *Barossa Jazz Weekend:* Aug. *Barossa International Music Festival:* various venues; Oct.

NEARBY Para Wirra Recreation Park Para Wirra comes from the Aboriginal words for 'river with scrub'. The park has been developed into a large recreational area with extensive facilities including tennis courts, picnic and barbecue areas, and walking trails ranging from short 800 m walks to more extensive 7.5 km trails. The major part of the park consists of eucalypts and is home to a large variety of native birds – including inquisitive emus that meander around the picnic areas. The historic Barossa Goldfield Trails (1.2 km or 5 km loop walks) cover the history of the old goldmines. 12 km SW. *Barossa wine region:* wineries and cellar doors lie around Lyndoch and Rowland Flat, just north-east, with rich red varieties as well as crisp whites. At Rowland Flat is the Jacob's Creek Visitor Centre Gallery where viticulture history is on display. For a total Barossa experience, take the self-drive Butcher, Baker, Winemaker food and wine trail from Lyndoch to Angaston; brochure available from visitor centre. *For more information on the region see Tanunda, Angaston and Nuriootpa. Sandy Creek Conservation Park:* on undulating sand dunes, with walking trails and birdlife. See western grey kangaroos and echidnas at dusk. 5.5 km W. *Lyndoch Lavender Farm:* wander through rows of over 60 lavender varieties. The nursery and farm shop offer lavender-product sales. Cnr Hoffnungsthal and Tweedies Gully rds; 6 km SE; open daily Sept–Feb, Mon–Fri Mar–April. *Barossa Reservoir and Whispering Wall:* acoustic phenomenon allowing whispered messages at one end to be audible at the other end, 140 m away; 8 km SW.
ⓘ Kies Family Wines, Lot 2, Barossa Valley Hwy; (08) 8524 4110; www.barossa-region.com

McLaren Vale   Pop. 2583

Map ref. 549 F4, 550 A13, 552 B2, 555 K10

McLaren Vale is recognised not so much as a single township, but as a region of vineyards, orchards and gourmet-produce farms. Serious wine-making began here in 1853 when Thomas Hardy bought Tintara Vineyards. Today Hardy's remains a stronghold among the region's 50 wineries. The fabulous coastal vistas to the west provide ample subject matter for the many artists who exhibit in McLaren Vale's galleries.

IN TOWN *McLaren Vale and Fleurieu Visitor Information Centre:* picturesque landscaped grounds with a vineyard and a centre that features changing art exhibitions, sales of local craft and produce, a wine bar and a cafe; Main Rd. *The Old Bank Artel:* community cooperative of local crafts including pottery, jewellery and metalwork; Main Rd. *Almond and Olive*

Train: sales of local produce, including fine local almonds, in a restored railway carriage; Main Rd. *McLaren Valley Bakery:* produces unique 'wine pies'; Central Shopping Centre, Main Rd. *McLaren Vale Olive Grove:* grows over 26 varieties of olives and sells olive products, arts and crafts and local gourmet produce; Warners Rd. *Medlow Confectionery and FruChocs Showcase:* tastings and sales of gourmet chocolate and other confectionery. Interactive confectionary machine for kids. Main Rd. *McLaren Vale Heritage Trail:* self-guide trail of historic sites, including wineries; audio CD available; starts at visitor centre.

WHAT'S ON *Sea and Vines Festival:* music, food and wine; June. *Wine Bushing Festival:* according to European tradition, tree branches are hung over cellar doors to signify the new season's wines, and the makers of the year's best wines are crowned king and queen; Oct.

NEARBY Onkaparinga River National Park The Onkaparinga River, SA's second longest river, travels through valleys and gorges to Gulf St Vincent. The walks in Onkaparinga Gorge are impressive, but very steep. More regulated walking trails are on the northern side of the gorge. The estuary section of the park is an altogether different environment and is best explored on the 5 km interpretive trail. Look out for the 27 species of native orchids. Access is via Main South Rd, Old Noralunga; 7 km NW.
McLaren Vale Wineries First planted in the 1830s by British settlers, the grapes of McLaren Vale have produced a wide range of wine varieties as a result of the diverse soil conditions of the area. The region is renowned for its bold red varieties, such as shiraz and grenache, as well as white-wine varieties and minor releases of sangiovese and marsanne. Around 50 wineries operate in the region, most with cellar-door tastings and sales. Follow the scenic Tourist Route 60 to get a taste of the landscape. A winery map is available from the visitor centre. *Old Noarlunga:* self-guide tour of historic colonial buildings (brochure available). Walks into Onkaparinga National Park start from here. 7 km NW. *Port Noarlunga:* popular holiday destination with historic streetscapes. A marked underwater trail along the reef is provided for divers and snorkellers. 11 km NW. *Coastal beaches:* safe family beaches to the north-west include O'Sullivan, Christies and Moana.
ⓘ McLaren Vale and Fleurieu Visitor Centre, Main Rd; 1800 628 410 or (08) 8323 9944

Maitland   Pop. 992

Map ref. 554 I7

Maitland represents a much smaller version of the city of Adelaide, with the town layout in the same pattern of radiating squares. It is in the heart of

Yorke Peninsula and is central to a rich agricultural region. In recent years tourism has grown dramatically on the peninsula, but barley and wheat industries remain strong.

IN TOWN *Maitland Museum:* located in the former school, this National Trust museum documents local indigenous and settlement history; cnr Gardiner and Kilkerran tces; open 2pm–4pm Sun and public holidays, other times by appt (08) 8832 2220. *St John's Anglican Church:* stained-glass windows depict biblical stories in an Australian setting; cnr Alice and Caroline sts. *Lions Bicycle Adventure Park:* off Elizabeth St. *Aboriginal Cultural Tours:* 5-day tagalong tours in Adjahdura Land (Yorke Peninsula), with an Aboriginal guide, include Dreamtime stories, cultural ceremonies and water-based activities such as spearfishing; bookings and inquiries (08) 8410 8833. *Heritage town walk:* interpretive walk; brochure from council in Elizabeth St.

WHAT'S ON *Maitland Art/Craft Fair:* Nov.

NEARBY *Gregory's Wines:* Yorke Peninsula's only commercial vineyard. Cellar-door tastings and sales 10.30am–4pm weekends. 13 km s. *Balgowan:* this coastal town has safe, sandy beaches and is popular with anglers; 15 km w.
ⓘ Council offices, 8 Elizabeth St; (08) 8832 0000; www.yorkepeninsula.com.au

Mannum   Pop. 2187

Map ref. 550 I9, 552 D1, 555 M9

Mannum is one of the oldest towns on the Murray River, at the romantic heart of the old paddlesteamer days. In 1853 the 'Father of Mannum', William Randell, built the first Murray River paddlesteamer, *Mary Ann* (named after his mother), in order to transport his flour to the Victorian goldfields. The paddlesteamer set out from Mannum in 1853 and started a boom in the river transport industry. Another first for Mannum was Australia's first steam car, built in 1894 by David Shearer.

IN TOWN **Mannum Dock Museum**
This excellent museum documents the changing history of the Mannum region from ancient days through indigenous habitation, European settlement and river history to the present day. Outside is the renowned Randell's Dry Dock, where the grand lady of the Murray, PS *Marion*, is moored. Passenger cruises on the restored paddlesteamer still operate. Randell St. *Mary Ann Reserve:* popular recreation reserve on the riverbank with PS *Mary Ann's* original pumping engine. PS *River Murray Princess* is moored here between cruises. *Ferry service:* twin ferries operate to the eastern side of the river. *River cruises and houseboat hire:* afternoon, day and overnight cruises are available. Hire a houseboat to discover the Murray River your own way. Contact visitor centre for details. *Town lookout:* off Purnong Rd

to the east. *Scenic and historical walks:* brochures from visitor centre.

WHAT'S ON *Mannum Big River Fishing Competition:* Feb. *Houseboat Hirers' Open Days:* May. *Christmas Pageant:* Dec.

NEARBY *Mannum Falls:* picnics and scenic walks, best visited in winter (after rains) when the waterfall is flowing; 6 km SE. *Kia Marina:* the largest river marina in SA holds an open day in Oct. Boats and houseboats for hire. 8 km NE. *Lowan Conservation Park:* mallee vegetation park with varied wildlife, including fat-tailed dunnarts, mallee fowl and western grey kangaroos; turn-off 28 km E at Bowhill. *Purnong:* scenic drive north-east, runs parallel to excellent Halidon Bird Sanctuary; 33 km E.
ⓘ 6 Randell St; (08) 8569 1303; www.murraylands.info

Marree   Pop. 115

Map ref. 556 I1, 558 I13

Marree is a perfect illustration of a tiny, outback desert town. It is frequented by four-wheel-drive enthusiasts taking on the legendary Birdsville and Oodnadatta tracks. The settlement was established as a camp for the Overland Telegraph Line as it was being constructed. It soon serviced all travellers and workers heading north, including the famous Afghan traders who drove their camel trains into the desert in the 1800s and played a significant role in opening up the outback.

IN TOWN *Aboriginal Heritage Museum:* features artefacts and cultural history; in Arabunna Aboriginal Community Centre. *Marree Heritage Park:* includes Tom Kruse's truck that once carried out the famous outback mail run on the Birdsville Track in the 1950s. *Camel sculpture:* made out of railway sleepers. *Scenic flights:* including

over Lake Eyre and the Marree Man, a 4 km long carving in a plateau of an Aboriginal hunter. The carving, visible only from the air, appeared in 1998, and its creator remains anonymous. Contact visitor centre for details.

WHAT'S ON *Picnic Races and Gymkhana:* June. *Aust. Camel Cup:* July. *Gymkhana:* Oct.

NEARBY **Lake Eyre National Park** This breathtaking park epitomises the vast and isolated Australian outback. Lake Eyre is a salt lake of international significance, dry for most of the time – filled to capacity on only 3 occasions in the last 150 years. When water does fill parts of the lake, birds flock to it. Avoid visiting in the hotter months (Nov–Mar). Lake Eyre North is accessed via the Oodnadatta Track, 195 km w of Marree. Lake Eyre South is accessed via the 94 km track from Marree. Both access routes are 4WD only. Lake Eyre South also meets the Oodnadatta Track about 90 km w of Marree, where there are good views. A Desert Parks Pass is required for the park and is available from Marree Post Office or by contacting the Desert Parks Hotline on 1800 816 078. Scenic flights are perhaps the most rewarding option, from both Marree and William Creek. *Oodnadatta Track:* a 600 km 4WD track from Marree to Marla. Highlights along the track include the Dog Fence (around 40 km w) and the railway-siding ruins at Curdimurka Siding and Bore (90 km w) from the original *Ghan* railway line to Alice Springs. Curdimurka is also the setting for the Outback Ball in Oct (even-numbered years), which attracts thousands of Australian and international visitors. A short distance beyond Curdimurka is Wabma Kadarbu Mound Springs Conservation Park, with a series of mound

Vineyards in McLaren Vale

springs – fed by water from the Great Artesian Basin – supporting a variety of plants and animals. Between Marree and Marla, fuel is available only at William Creek (202 km NW) and Oodnadatta (405 km NW). *Birdsville Track:* the famous 4WD track from Marree to Birdsville (in Qld) of just over 500 km, once a major cattle run. Highlights on the track include the failed date palm plantation at Lake Harry Homestead (30 km N) and the meeting of the Tirari and Strzelecki deserts at Natterannie Sandhills (140 km N, after Cooper Creek crossing). Cooper Creek may have to be bypassed if flooded (with a 48 km detour to a ferry). Between Marree and Birdsville, fuel is available only at Mungerannie Roadhouse (204 km N). ***Travellers note:*** *care must be taken when attempting the Birdsville and Oodnadatta tracks. These tracks are unsealed, with sandy patches. Heavy rain in the area can cut access for several days. Motorists are advised to ring the Northern Road Condition Hotline on 1 300 361 033 before departure.* ❶ Marree Outback Roadhouse and General Store; (08) 8675 8360

Melrose   Pop. 452
Map ref. 555 J2, 557 J12

Melrose, a quiet settlement at the foot of Mt Remarkable, is the oldest town in the Flinders Ranges. Indigenous groups who occupied the southern Flinders Ranges around Mt Remarkable and Melrose resisted European settlement in the 1840s, but after just a few decades the population was reduced to a handful. Pastoral properties were established on the mountainous slopes of the ranges, but Melrose truly took off when copper deposits were found nearby in 1846. Bushwalking through Mt Remarkable National Park is a highlight of any visit to this area. The arid north country meets the wet conditions of southern regions to provide a diverse landscape to explore. **IN TOWN** *National Trust Museum:* documents local history, with particular focus on early law enforcement. Original stone buildings include the courthouse and lock-up. Stuart St; open 2pm–5pm Thurs–Tues. *Bluey Blundstone Blacksmith Shop:* a restored shop with a cafe and B&B; Stuart St; closed Tues. *Serendipity Gallery:* Australiana arts and crafts; Stuart St. *War Memorial and Lookout Hill:* views over surrounding region. *4WD tours:* to local landmarks; contact visitor centre for operators. *Heritage walk:* self-guide walk includes ruins of Jacka's Brewery and Melrose Mine; brochure from visitor centre. **NEARBY Mount Remarkable National Park** Part of the southern Flinders Ranges and popular with bushwalkers. Marked trails through the park's gorges and ranges vary in scope from short scenic walks to long 3-day hikes. Highlights include the wildflowers in Alligator Gorge and

the tough but worthwhile 5 hr return walk from Melrose to the summit of Mt Remarkable (960 m), with breathtaking views from the top. Access to the park by vehicle is via Mambray Creek or Wilmington. Foot access is from carparks and Melrose. 2 km W. *Cathedral Rock:* an impressive rock formation on Mount Remarkable Creek; just west of Melrose. *Murray Town:* a farming town with nearby scenic lookouts at Box Hill, Magnus Hill and Baroota Nob. Remarkable View Wines offers tasting and sales on weekends. Starting point for a scenic drive west through Port Germein Gorge. 14 km S. *Booleroo Centre:* this service town to a rich farming community features the Booleroo Steam Traction Preservation Society's Museum; open by appt (08) 8667 2193. Annual Rally Day is held in Mar/April. 15 km SE. *Wirrabara:* you could easily lose half a day in this town's bakery-cum-antiques shop, wandering through the rooms of relics and antiques just to work up an appetite for another homemade pastry; 25 km S. ❶ Melrose Tourist Park; (08) 8666 2060; www.mountremarkable.com.au

Meningie   Pop. 896
Map ref. 552 D4, 555 M12

Today Meningie is an attractive lakeside town, but it was once a wilderness area home to the Ngarrindjeri people, who had a self-sufficient lifestyle on the water. They made canoes to fish on the waterways and shelters to protect themselves from the weather. However, European settlement – after Captain Charles Sturt's journey down the Murray from 1829 to 1830 – soon wiped out much of the population, largely through violence and the introduction of smallpox. Stretching south from the mouth of the Murray and located just south of Meningie, the Coorong, with its lakes, birdlife, fishing and deserted ocean beaches, attracts visitors year-round. **IN TOWN** *The Cheese Factory Museum Restaurant:* a restaurant and separate community museum with special interest in the changing population of Meningie and the Coorong; Fiebig Rd; closed Mon. *Coorong Cottage Industries:* local craft and produce; The Chambers, Princes Hwy. **NEARBY** *Scenic drive:* follows Lake Albert to the west, adjacent to Lake Alexandrina, which is the largest permanent freshwater lake in the country (50 000 ha). Ferry crossing at Narrung. *Coorong National Park:* 10 km S; *see feature on facing page. Camp Coorong:* cultural centre offering bush-tucker tours and other traditional Aboriginal experiences; 10 km S; (08) 8575 1557. *Coorong Wilderness Lodge:* operated by the Ngarrindjeri people, this accommodation lodge offers Aboriginal heritage tours of the Coorong as well as traditional bush

tucker and other cultural experiences; Hacks Point; 25 km S; (08) 8575 6001. *Poltalloch Station:* a historic pastoral property established in the 1830s as a sheep station. Guided tours take in a heritage-listed farm village and museum, historic farm machinery, and past and present farm life. Cottage accommodation available; bookings (08) 8574 0043. Poltalloch Rd near Narrung; 30 km NW. ❶ Melaleuca Centre, 76 Princes Hwy; (08) 8575 1259

Millicent   Pop. 4430
Map ref. 552 G11

The locals in Millicent were not always as welcoming and friendly as they are today. In 1876 the unfortunate barque *Geltwood* was wrecked off the Canunda Beach, with debris, bodies and cargo littering the sands. Many locals were charged with stealing the washed-up goods. They were acquitted, claiming that they did not realise to do so was illegal. Relics from the *Geltwood* can now be found in the award-winning National Trust Living History Museum. The town's distinctive aroma can be attributed to the surrounding pine forests, which support a pulp mill, a paper mill and sawmill. **IN TOWN** *Visitor Centre, Admella Gallery and National Trust Living History Museum:* mixed in together in one building are the Visitor Centre, a wealth of Millicent information; local art and craft at the Admella Gallery; and indigenous and settlement history (including a buggy and carriage display) in The Living History Museum. Mount Gambier Rd. *Lake McIntyre:* boardwalks and bird hides to view the lake's prolific birdlife, native fish and yabbies; northern edge of town. **WHAT'S ON** *Two Tall Timbers Exhibition and Competition:* pine and red-gum craft; April. *Geltwood Craft Festival:* April. **NEARBY Canunda National Park** The massive sand-dune system of the southern part of the park rises to cliffs and scrublands in the north. These 2 sections provide quite different experiences. In the north (accessed via Southend and Millicent) the walking trails pass along cliff-tops and through the scrubland. In the south (accessed via Carpenter Rocks and Millicent) the beaches and wetlands provide picturesque coastal walks. You can surf, birdwatch, bushwalk and fish (excellent from the beaches and rocks). 10 km W. *Mount Muirhead Lookout:* a large viewing platform provides views of Millicent, pine plantations and Mount Burr Range. It is also the start of the Volcanoes Discovery Trail (brochure from Millicent Visitor Centre); 6 km NE. *Mount Burr:* a historic timber town, the first to plant pines for commercial use on the Limestone Coast; 10 km NE. *Tantanoola:* home of the famous 'Tantanoola Tiger', a Syrian wolf shot in the 1890s, now stuffed and displayed in the Tantanoola Tiger Hotel; 20 km SE. *Tantanoola Caves Conservation Park:* daily tours of an imposing dolomite cavern in an ancient limestone cliff. Also walks and picnic areas. 21 km SE. *Glencoe Woolshed:* National Trust limestone woolshed once occupied by 38 shearers; 29 km SE. ❶ 1 Mount Gambier Rd; (08) 8733 3205; www.thelimestonecoast.com

Minlaton　　Pop. 753

Map ref. 554 I9

A small rural centre on Yorke Peninsula. It was originally called Gum Flat, because of the giant eucalypts in the area, but was later changed to Minlaton – from the Aboriginal word 'minlacowrie', thought to mean 'sweet water'. Aviator Captain Harry Butler, pilot of the *Red Devil,* a 1916 Bristol monoplane, was born here.

IN TOWN *Butler Memorial:* in a hangar-like building stands the *Red Devil,* a fighter plane – thought to be the only one of its type left in the world – that fought in France and, less romantically, flew mail between Adelaide and Minlaton; Main St. *Minlaton Museum:* National Trust museum in the historic general store features a local history display and Harry Butler memorabilia; Main St; open 9.30am– 1pm Tues–Fri, 9.30am–12pm Sat. *Harvest Corner Visitor Information Centre:* tourist information, craft and local produce sales, a gallery and tearooms; Main St. *The Creamery:* crafts, ceramics and an art exhibition in a historic building; Maitland Rd. *Gum Flat Gallery:* art workshop and gallery; Main St; open 10am–4pm Wed and 2pm–4.30pm Fri. *Shell Museum:* displays of old and rare shells; Maitland Rd. *Minlaton Fauna Park:* popular spot for picnics, with kangaroos, emus and wallabies; Maitland Rd. *River Red Gum Walk:* a trail to the river red gums that are rare on Yorke Peninsula. View salt lakes and birdlife from the bird hide. Contact visitor centre for details.

NEARBY *Ramsay Park:* native flora and fauna park; between Minlaton and Port Vincent to the east. *Port Rickaby:* quiet swimming and fishing spot; 16 km NW. ❶ Harvest Corner Visitor Information Centre, 29 Main St; (08) 8853 2600; www.yorkepeninsula.com.au

Mintaro　　Pop. 100

Map ref. 555 L5

Although it is in the Clare Valley region, Mintaro's prosperity is not linked with the valley's booming wine industry. Instead, its buildings date back to the 1840s and 50s, when bullock drays carried copper from the Monster Mine at Burra to Port Wakefield in the south. Many of the buildings use local slate. In 1984 Mintaro became the state's first town to be classified a State Heritage Area.

IN TOWN *Mintaro Cottage Garden:* one of the town's fine garden displays; enter

Tea trees surround a salt lake in the Coorong

Coorong National Park

Coorong National Park is listed as a 'wetland of international importance'. Featuring a long finger of water beside a long, sandy peninsula facing the Southern Ocean, its waterways, islands and vast saltpans demonstrate a diverse ecological environment invaluable for the refuge and habitat of migratory and drought-stricken birds.

Throughout the park are reminders of the long history of habitation by the Ngarrindjeri people. There are ancient midden heaps and burial grounds, and the park's name comes from their word 'kurangh', meaning long neck of water – at 163 kilometres, this is exactly what it is. Ngarrindjeri people continue to have strong links with the Coorong, running bush-tucker and cultural tours via Camp Coorong and Coorong Wilderness Lodge (*see Meningie*). In 1999 the Ngarrindjeri held their first corroboree in 100 years, a symbol that – after almost two centuries of European colonisation – Aboriginal culture on the Coorong is now able to return to its roots.

There are a number of ways to see the park: take a boat, canoe or cruise on the waterways; walk one of the varied tracks offered; drive your four-wheel drive onto the Southern Ocean beach; or simply sit and soak up the park's atmosphere.

Walking is the best way to access great coastal views, birdwatching spots and historic ruins. The most comprehensive walk in the park is the Nukan Kungun Hike. This 27-kilometre hike starts at Salt Creek and includes smaller, side trails, including the informative walk to Chinaman's Well, the ruins of a temporary settlement that sprang up en route to the goldfields. The hike ends at the 42-Mile Crossing Sand Dune Walk, which leads to the breathtakingly wild Southern Ocean.

Coorong National Park is a vital habitat for over 200 bird species, and perhaps the most famous of these are the pelicans. Colin Thiele's book *Storm Boy* and the subsequent film, both set in the Coorong, made them into Australian icons along with Mr Percival, the pelican companion of Storm Boy. To see Australia's largest colony of pelicans, take the short walk to the viewing area at Jacks Point. High-powered binoculars assist in observing the nearby islands and their pelican and tern populations. Dawn and dusk are the best times for viewing.

Access to the waterways is from boat launches at Goolwa and between Meningie and Policemans Point. The Princes Highway hugs much of the Coorong where it meets the mainland, providing scenic views and access to most of the attractions.

via Timandra Nursery, Kingston St.
Mintaro Garden Maze: kids will love getting
lost in the maze, comprising over 800
conifers; Jacka St; open 10am–4pm
Thurs–Mon. *Reillys Wines:* wine-tastings,
cellar-door sales and a restaurant; Burra
Rd. *Mintaro Cellars:* wine-tastings and sales;
Leasingham Rd. *Mintaro Slate Quarries:* fine-
quality slate, produced since the quarry
opened in 1854, is used world-wide
for billiard tables; viewing platform in
Kadlunga Rd; open 7.30am–3pm Mon–
Fri. *Heritage walk:* self-guide trail includes
18 heritage-listed colonial buildings and
2 historic cemeteries; brochure available.
NEARBY Martindale Hall This 1879
mansion was built for Edmund Bowman
who, the story goes, commissioned it for
his bride-to-be from English high society.
The lady declined his offer of marriage,
and Bowman lived there on his own until
1891. Today visitors can explore the
National Trust, Georgian-style home with
its Italian Renaissance interior. A room
in the mansion was used in the 1975 film
Picnic at Hanging Rock as a girls' dormitory.
Accommodation and dining are available.
Manoora Rd; 3 km SE. Open 11am–4pm
Mon–Fri, noon–4pm weekends.
Polish Hill River Valley: a subregion of the
Clare Valley wine region, with cellar
doors offering tastings and sales; between
Mintaro and Sevenhill. *Waterloo:* features
the historic Wellington Hotel, once a
Cobb & Co staging post; 23 km SE.
ⓘ Town Hall, 229 Main North Rd, Clare;
1800 242 131 or (08) 8842 2131;
www.clarevalley.com.au

Moonta   Pop. 3080

Map ref. 554 I6

The towns of Moonta, Kadina and
Wallaroo form the 'Copper Coast' or
'Little Cornwall', so called because of
abundant copper finds and the significant
Cornish population. Like so many other
copper discoveries in South Australia,
Moonta's was made by a local shepherd –
in this case, Paddy Ryan in 1861. It
was to prove a fortunate find: Moonta
Mining Company paid over £1 million
in dividends. Thousands of miners,
including experienced labourers from
Cornwall, flocked to the area. The mines
were abandoned in the 1920s because
of the slump in copper prices and rising
labour costs. Moonta has survived as
an agricultural service town with an
increasing tourist trade.
IN TOWN *All Saints Church of England:*
features a locally constructed copper bell;
cnr Blanche and Milne tces. *Queen Square:*
park for picnics, with the imposing town
hall opposite; George St. *Heritage walks
and drives:* self-guide trails to see heritage
stone buildings and historic mine-sites;
brochure from visitor centre.
WHAT'S ON *Kernewek Lowender:*
prize-winning Cornish festival held with
Kadina and Wallaroo; odd-numbered

years, May. *Moonta Garden Fair:* Oct.
Moonta Antiques and Collectible Fair: Nov.
**NEARBY Moonta Mines State Heritage
Area** Take a historical walk or drive
from Moonta to this significant heritage
area. Interpretive walking trails guide
the visitor to the major sites, including
the Hughes Pump House, shafts, tailing
heaps and ruins of mine offices. A 50
min historical railway tour runs from the
museum (tours depart each hour, 1pm–
4pm, weekends and public holidays).
Also on the site is a historic 1880 pipe
organ in the Moonta Mines Heritage
Uniting Church; Cornish lifestyle history
and memorabilia at the Moonta Mines
Museum; and the National Trust-
furnished Miners Cottage and Heritage
Garden (all open 1.30pm–4pm Wed, Fri,
Sun and daily in school holidays). Enjoy
old-style sweets at the Moonta Mines
Sweet Shop. Via Verran Tce; 2 km SE.
Wheal Hughes Copper Mine: underground
tour of one of the original mines, which
closed in 1993; Wallaroo Rd; 3 km N;
tours at 1pm daily except Fri. *Moonta Bay:*
a popular seaside town for fishing and
swimming. See native animals at the
Moonta Wildlife Park. 5 km W.
ⓘ Railway Station, Blanche Tce; (08)
8825 1891; www.yorkepeninsula.com.au

Morgan   Pop. 424

Map ref. 555 N6

This Murray River town was once a
thriving port and a stop on the rail
trade route to Adelaide. Settlers saw
the potential of the region, and Morgan
boomed as soon as it was declared a
town in 1878. Now it is a quiet holiday
destination, but evidence of its boom days
can still be seen in the streetscapes and
the historic wharf and rail precinct.
IN TOWN Port of Morgan Museum This
comprehensive museum is dedicated to
the rail- and river-trade history of Morgan.
In the old railway buildings are museum
exhibits focusing on the paddlesteamers
and trains that were the lifeblood of the
town. The Landseer Building, an old
warehouse, has vintage vehicles and a
12 m mural depicting the old Murray River
lifestyle. Other highlights are the restored
wharf and the permanently moored PS
Mayflower. Riverfront. Open 2pm–4pm
Wed, Sat and Sun.
Houseboats: for hire; contact visitor centre
for details. *Heritage walk:* self-guide trail
covers 41 historic sites, including the
impressive wharves (1877) standing
12 m high, the customs house and
courthouse, the sunken barge and
steamer, and the rail precinct; brochure
from visitor centre.
NEARBY *Morgan Conservation Park:* a
diverse landscape of river flats, sand
dunes and mallee scrub with abundant
birdlife; across the Murray River from
Morgan. *White Dam Conservation Park:* well-
known for red and western grey kangaroo

populations; 9 km NW. *Cadell:* scenic
12 km drive east from Morgan via a ferry
crossing (operates 24 hrs) to Cadell, a
major citrus-growing region.
ⓘ Shell Morgan Roadhouse,
14–18 Fourth St; (08) 8540 2354;
www.riverland.info

Mount Gambier   Pop. 22 656

Map ref. 552 H12

Mount Gambier is set on an extinct
volcano – the area boasts a fascinating
network of volcanic craters above sea
level and one of limestone caves beneath.
Lieutenant James Grant named the
volcano in 1800 – he sighted it from HMS
Lady Nelson, off the coast. The original
settlement was known as Gambier Town.
Today Mount Gambier is at the centre of
the largest softwood pine plantation in
the Commonwealth and is surrounded by
farming, viticulture and dairy country.
IN TOWN Blue Lake The lakes formed
in the craters of the extinct volcano
have become an important recreational
area for locals and visitors alike. The
most spectacular is Blue Lake, so-called
because the water's dull, blue-grey winter
colour changes to a vibrant blue each
November and stays that way until March
the following year. The sudden colour
change is yet to be explained scientifically.
Discover the area on the 3.6 km walking
track around the shores. Aquifer Tours
offers a trip in a glass lift down an old well
shaft to experience the underwater world
(without getting wet!); (08) 8723 1199.
The area also includes a wildlife park
and an adventure playground. Southern
outskirts of town.
Old Courthouse: a National Trust dolomite
building with a local history museum
and an art and craft gallery; Bay Rd;
open 11am–3pm daily. *Lady Nelson Visitor
Information and Discovery Centre:* full-scale
replica of HMS *Lady Nelson,* interactive
displays on the region's history and
geography, and free local information
packs; Jubilee Hwy East. *Riddoch Art
Gallery:* changing exhibitions of local and
touring art and sculpture; Commercial St
East; open Tues–Sat. *Cave Garden:* a cave
used as a water supply for early settlers,
now a rose garden with a suspended
viewing platform; Bay Rd. *Umpherston
Sinkhole:* a sunken garden on the floor of
a collapsed cave; floodlit at night; Jubilee
Hwy East. *Engelbrecht Cave:* guided tour
of the limestone cave system under the
city; book at visitor centre. *Centenary
Tower:* views of the city, the lakes area
and surrounding countryside; top of Mt
Gambier, 190 m above sea level. *Heritage
walk:* self-guide tour of historic buildings,
many constructed of white Mt Gambier
stone; brochure from visitor centre.
WHAT'S ON *Mount Gambier Market:*
Fletcher Jones Complex; Sat. *World Series
Sprintcars:* Jan. *South-East Country Music
Weekend:* Feb. *Mount Gambier Racing:* May.

Limestone Coast Art and Craft Fair: Aug.
Christmas Parade: Nov.
NEARBY *Blue Lake Papermill:* offers
tours to see traditional paper-making
techniques; Pollard Cl; 2 km E. *Haig's
Vineyards:* wine tastings and sales;
4 km SE. *Mt Schank:* excellent views of the
surrounding district from the summit of an
extinct volcano. Note that the 2 summit
walks are very steep. 17 km S. *Nelson
and Lower Glenelg National Park:* over the
Victorian border; *see Portland (Vic).*
ⓘ Lady Nelson Visitor Information and
Discovery Centre, Jubilee Hwy East; 1800
087 187 or (08) 8724 9750; www.mount
gambiertourism.com.au

Murray Bridge   Pop. 12 998

Map ref. 550 I12, 552 D2, 555 M10

Murray Bridge, just as its name suggests, is
all about bridges. The town was established
in 1879 when a road bridge was built over
the Murray River. The plan to make the
river a major trade route from east to west
and back had become a reality. In 1886
the construction of a railway line between
Adelaide and Melbourne cemented the
town's importance. Now watersports, river
cruises and a relaxed river atmosphere
make Murray Bridge, South Australia's
largest river town, a perfect holiday spot.
IN TOWN *Captain's Cottage Museum:*
local history museum; Thomas St; open
10am–4pm weekends. *Dundee's Wildlife
Park:* crocodiles, a bird sanctuary and
renowned Butterfly House; Jervois Rd.
Puzzle Park: fun park for kids and adults
alike with slides, flying fox, 3.5 km maze
and minigolf; Jervois Rd. *Heritage and
Cultural Community Mural:* depicts significant
aspects of Murray Bridge; Third St. *Sturt
Reserve:* offers fishing, swimming, picnic
and playground facilities, as well as the
mythical Aboriginal creature, The Bunyip
(coin-operated attraction); Murray Cod
Dr. *Long Island Marina:* houseboat hire and
recreational facilities; Roper Rd. *Charter
and regular cruises:* on the Murray River;
various operators; contact visitor centre.
Town and riverside walks: brochure from
visitor centre.
WHAT'S ON *International Pedal Prix:*
novelty bikes and endurance event; Sept.
Waterski Race: over 110 km; Oct. *Steam
Rally Festival:* Nov.
NEARBY Monarto Zoological Park
This open-range 1000 ha zoo features
Australian, African and Asian animals.
It also runs a breeding program for rare
and endangered species. Jump on a safari
bus tour to see the animals up close. On
the way you might encounter the huge
giraffe herd or some cheetahs, zebras or
rhinoceroses. The first safari tour departs
at 10.30am, then hourly until 3.30pm.
There are also walking tracks through
native bushland and mallee country.
Princes Hwy; 10 km W.
Thiele Reserve: popular for waterskiing;
east of the river. *Avoca Dell:* a popular

Mount Gambier and Blue Lake from the air

picnic spot with boating, waterskiing,
minigolf, and caravan facilities;
5 km upstream. *Swanport Wetlands:*
recreational reserve with raised walkways
and bird hides; adjacent to Swanport
Bridge; 5 km E. *Sunnyside Reserve Lookout:*
views across the wetlands and Murray
River; 10 km E. *Willow Point Winery:* cellar-
door tastings and sales of famous ports,
sherries and muscats; Jervois Rd; 10 km S;
closed Sun. *Ferries–McDonald and Monarto
conservation parks:* walking trails through
important mallee conservation areas,
prolific birdlife, and blossom in spring;
16 km W. *Tailem Bend:* a historic railway
town with views across the Murray River.
A children's playground features an old
steam locomotive, and over 90 historic
buildings are displayed at the Old Tailem
Town Pioneer Village. 25 km SE. *Wellington:*
situated where Lake Alexandrina meets
the Murray River. A museum is in the
restored courthouse. Wellington and
nearby Jervois have free 24 hr vehicle
ferries. 32 km S. *Karoonda:* the heart of the
Mallee, Karoonda is well known for the
1930 meteorite fall nearby (monument
at RSL Park). Natural attractions include
the limestone caves of Bakara Plains and
walking trails in Pioneer Historical Park.
66 km E.
ⓘ 3 South Tce; (08) 8539 1142;
www.rcmb.sa.gov.au

Naracoorte   Pop. 4745

Map ref. 552 H9

Naracoorte dates from the 1840s, but
its growth has been slow. In the 1850s
it was a stopover point for Victorian gold
escorts and miners. Since then it has
gradually developed a rich agricultural
industry. Today it is renowned for its
natural attractions, including the parks
and gardens but more significantly the
Naracoorte Caves, protected within South
Australia's only World Heritage area.

IN TOWN *The Sheep's Back:* a
comprehensive museum in the former
flour mill (1870) details the history and
community of the wool industry, with
a craft gallery and information centre;
MacDonnell St. *Naracoorte Art Gallery:*
local and touring exhibitions; Ormerod
St; open Tues–Sat. *Mini Jumbuck Centre:*
display gallery and sales of woollen
products; Smith St. *Pioneer Park:* restored
locomotive on display; MacDonnell St.
Walking trail: starts at the town centre and
winds 5 km along the Naracoorte Creek.
WHAT'S ON *Taste the Limestone Coast:*
wine and gourmet festival; Feb. *Naracoorte
3-Day Equestrian Event:* May. *Limestone Coast
Children's Expo:* Nov. *Christmas Pageant:* Dec.
NEARBY *Naracoorte Caves National Park:*
12 km SE; *see feature on p. 251. Wrattonbully
Wine Region:* a recently established wine
region focusing mainly on red wine
varieties; 15 km SE. *Bool Lagoon Game
Reserve:* wetland area of international
significance, a haven for ibis and
numerous waterbird species. It includes
boardwalks and a bird hide. 17 km S.
Lucindale: a small country town featuring
a Historical Society Museum and Jubilee
Park with a lake, island and bird haven.
It holds mammoth South East Field Days
each Mar. 26 km W. *Frances:* a historic
railway town that attracts visitors each
Mar to the Frances Folk Gathering;
40 km NE. *Padthaway:* prominent wine
region; 47 km NW; *see Bordertown.*
ⓘ The Sheep's Back, MacDonnell St;
1800 244 421 or (08) 8762 1518;
www.naracoortetourism.com.au

Nuriootpa   Pop. 3845

Map ref. 550 F4, 551 G4, 555 M8

The long history of winemaking in this
Barossa Valley town is apparent when
travelling down the main street. Old
vines that glow red in autumn drape
the verandahs of equally old buildings.

Surprisingly, the town actually began life as a pub. As a trade route was being established northwards to the Kapunda coppermines, William Coulthard foresaw the demand for rest and refreshment. He built the Old Red Gum Slab Hotel in 1854 and the town developed around it. The Para River runs through Nuriootpa, its course marked by parks and picnic spots.

IN TOWN *Coulthard Reserve:* popular recreation area; off Penrice Rd.

WHAT'S ON *Barossa Vintage Festival:* celebration of food and wine in various locations; odd-numbered years, April. *Barossa Jazz Weekend:* Aug. *Barossa International Music Festival:* various venues; Oct.

NEARBY *Barossa wine region:* many wineries surround Nuriootpa, including Penfolds, one of the largest and most reputable establishments, located just south of town, offering tours, tastings, sales and fine dining; *for more information on the region see Tanunda, Lyndoch and Angaston. Maggie Beer's Farm Shop:* tastings and sales of gourmet farm produce from renowned chef and writer Maggie Beer, as well as Pheasant Farm and Beer Brothers wines. Enjoy a gourmet lunch (bookings essential). Pheasant Farm Rd; 5 km sw. *Light Pass:* a small, historic township with notable Lutheran churches and Luhrs Pioneer German Cottage, displaying German artefacts; 3 km e.
ⓘ Barossa Wine and Visitor Centre, 66–68 Murray St, Tanunda; 1300 812 662 or (08) 8563 0600; www.barossa-region.org

Oodnadatta   Pop. 164

Map ref. 558 B6

Oodnadatta is a tiny outback town on the legendary Oodnadatta Track. It was once a major railway town, but the line's closure in 1981 left it largely deserted. Local Aboriginal people have successfully kept the town operating since then. Today it is a refuelling and supply point on the Oodnadatta Track and provides access to major desert parks to the north. It is believed that the name Oodnadatta originated from an Aboriginal term meaning 'yellow blossom of the mulga'.

IN TOWN *Railway Station Museum:* well-preserved sandstone station (1890) now a local museum; key from retail outlets.

WHAT'S ON *Race Meeting:* May. *Bronco Branding:* Aug/Sept. *Cattle Drive:* Sept/Oct.

NEARBY *Witjira National Park* This arid-landscape park is most famous for the Dalhousie Springs. The thermal springs emerge from the Great Artesian Basin deep below the surface and are said to be therapeutic. They are also a unique environment for many fish species that adapt to the changing water conditions. A Desert Parks Pass must be obtained before entering the park; available from Mount Dare Homestead, Dalhousie Springs, Pink Roadhouse or from Parks

SA (1800 816 078). 180 km n. *Oodnadatta Track:* an old Aboriginal and European trade route that runs from Marree (404 km se) through Oodnadatta and joins the Stuart Hwy at Marla (212 km nw). *Neales River:* swim in permanent waterholes. *The Painted Desert:* rich colours paint the Arckaringa Hills, noted for their flora and fauna; 100 km sw. *Simpson Desert Conservation Park and Regional Reserve:* incredible sand dunes with ridges up to 500 km long. Visitors must be totally self-sufficient. 4WD only; access via Witjira National Park.
ⓘ Pink Roadhouse, Ikaturka Tce; 1800 802 074 or (08) 8670 7822

Penola   Pop. 1220

Map ref. 532 A3, 552 I10

One of the oldest towns in south-east South Australia, and with some of Australia's best wineries nearby, Penola is a popular overnight destination on the Limestone Coast. Penola is noted for its association with Mary MacKillop, a Josephite nun who in 1866 established Australia's first school to cater for children regardless of their family's income or social class. In 1995 she was beatified by the Vatican, the second-last step in the process of being declared a saint. Penola is also noted for its literary roots – several Australian poets were inspired by the landscape and lifestyle.

IN TOWN *Mary MacKillop Interpretive Centre and Woods MacKillop Schoolhouse:* details the lives of Mary MacKillop and Father Julian Tenison (who shared Mary's dream) through photos, memorabilia and displays. Delve into the world of 19th-century schooldays in the schoolhouse furnished in 1860s style. Portland St. *Petticoat Lane:* heritage area of original cottages, including Sharam Cottage, the first built in town; many are now retail outlets. *Penola Coonawarra Visitor Information Centre:* incorporates the Local History Exhibition and Hydrocarbon Centre, featuring hands-on and static displays on natural gas; Arthur St. *Toffee and Treats:* old-fashioned sweet sales; Church St. *Heritage walk:* details from visitor centre.

WHAT'S ON *Harvest Festival:* Jan. *Vigneron Cup:* Jan. *Lazy Days of Summer:* music, wine and food; Jan. *Petanque Festival:* Feb. *Penola Coonawarra Festival:* arts, food and wine; May. *Cabernet Celebrations:* Nov. *Roses and Wine:* Nov.

NEARBY *Yallam Park:* a magnificent 2-storey Victorian home with original decorations; 8 km w; by appt (08) 8737 2435. *Penola Conservation Park:* signposted woodland and wetland walk; 10 km w. *Coonawarra wine region:* more than 20 wineries, most open for tastings and cellar-door sales; north to Coonawarra.
ⓘ Penola Coonawarra Visitor Information Centre, 27 Arthur St; (08) 8737 2855; www.wattlerange.sa.gov.au

Peterborough   Pop. 1680

Map ref. 555 L2, 557 L13

Peterborough is a town obsessed with the railway. Its very existence and growth can be claimed by that industry. In 1881 the line to Jamestown was opened and over the next few years the town became a key intersection between all the major South Australian towns. Locals boast about how, in a mammoth one-day effort, 105 trains travelled the Broken Hill to Port Pirie line. The rail passion continued even after many of the lines closed, and today each town entrance has a welcoming model steam train.

IN TOWN **Steamtown** Preservation of a 100-year-old rail history is the key to this dynamic museum. Located in and around the old locomotive workshops is a collection of historic rolling stock, including a converted Morris (a car) that rides the tracks. Also on display is Australia's only 3-gauge roundhouse and turntable. Main St. Open daily. *Town Hall:* a beautiful, ornate 1927 building with its original theatre and a Federation wall hanging in the foyer. Main St; open Mon–Fri. *Rann's Museum:* 19th-century exhibits include engines and farm implements; Moscow St. *Ley's Museum:* antiques; Queen St. *The Gold Battery:* ore-crushing machine; contact visitor centre; end Tripney Ave. *Saint Cecilia:* a gracious home with splendid stained glass, once a bishop's residence. It offers accommodation and dining. Callary St. *Victoria Park:* features a lake and islands with deer and kangaroo enclosure and a playground; Queen St. *Bus tour:* guided tour of sights and history of town; contact visitor centre. *Town walk and drive:* self-guide tour; brochure from visitor centre.

NEARBY *Terowie:* an old railway town with well-preserved 19th-century main street. Self-guide drive or walk tour; brochure *A Tour of Terowie* available from tearooms. 24 km se. *Magnetic Hill:* park the car, turn off the engine and watch it roll uphill! 32 km nw via Black Rock.
ⓘ Main St; (08) 8651 2708; www.peterborough.au.com

Pinnaroo   Pop. 594

Map ref. 510 A11, 544 A10, 552 I3, 555 R10

This little township is on the Mallee Highway close to the Victorian border. In the 19th century the harshness of the land prevented settlers from properly establishing a farming community here. Instead, they chose the more fertile conditions south-west. The arrival of rail in 1906 and the influx of farming families allowed the community to grow. Although conditions remained tough, the now-renowned Mallee spirit of the farmers allowed the region's agricultural industry to strengthen to what it is today.

IN TOWN **Mallee Tourist and Heritage Centre** This major historical complex, housed in the old railway station building, comprises the D. A. Wurfel Grain Collection, featuring the largest cereal collection in Australia (1300 varieties); working printing and letter presses in the Printing Museum; dioramas, interpretive displays and photos depicting local history in the Heritage Museum; and a collection of restored farm machinery in the Gum Family Collection. Railway Tce South; open 10am–1pm Mon–Sat. *Animal Park and Aviary:* South Tce.

NEARBY *Karte Conservation Park:* includes a walking trail through low scrub and 40 m high sand dunes; 30 km NW. *Billiatt Conservation Park:* the 1 km walk through mallee scrub and dune country ends with panoramic views from Trig Point; 37 km NW. *Lameroo:* Mallee town with historic 1898 Byrne pug-and-pine homestead (Yappara Rd) and railway station (Railway Tce); 40 km W. *Ngarkat group of conservation parks:* south-west of town; *see Keith.* *Peebinga Conservation Park:* important reserve for the rare western whipbird; on Loxton Rd; 42 km N.
ⓘ Mallee Tourist and Heritage Centre, Railway Tce South; (08) 8577 8644

Port Augusta   Pop. 13 153

Map ref. 553 A13, 556 I11

A thriving industrial city at the head of Spencer Gulf, Port Augusta is the most northerly port in South Australia. The difficulty of land transportation in the 1800s prompted the town's establishment in 1854. It was a major wool and wheat shipping depot until its closure in 1973 – luckily the power stations built by the State Electricity Trust were already generating the city's chief income. Fuelled by coal from the huge open-cut mines at Leigh Creek, the stations generate more than a third of the state's electricity. Port Augusta is today a supply centre for outback areas, an important link on the Indian–Pacific railway and a stopover for the Adelaide to Darwin *Ghan* train.

IN TOWN **Wadlata Outback Centre** This award-winning complex covers the natural history of the outback and Flinders Ranges, as well as the people that have called it home throughout the ages. There are interpretive displays, audiovisual presentations and artefacts. Discover the landscape of 15 million years ago in the Tunnel of Time, and hear ancient Dreamtime stories. The centre is a place in which to learn – Wadlata is an Aboriginal word for communicating. Flinders Tce.
Homestead Park Pioneer Museum: picnic areas, re-creation of a blacksmith's shop, an old steam train and crane, and the restored 130-year-old pine-log Yudnappinna homestead; Elsie St. *Fountain Gallery:* local and touring art and cultural exhibitions; Flinders Tce; open Mon–Fri.

The underground world of the Naracoorte Caves

Naracoorte Caves

For thousands of years the 26 Naracoorte Caves – today protected by national park and World Heritage listing – have acted as a natural trap for animals. It was a simple process at work: the hidden openings surprised passing animals and they fell to their deaths at the bottom of the caves. Countless numbers must have died in similar ways across the world, but in these caves the environment happened to be just right for fossilisation. Twenty fossil deposits have been found – an incredible record of Australia's evolution over the last 500 000 years.

Cave tours

The ancient cave systems are an adventure playground for the senses, be it on one of the guided walks or the exhilarating adventure tours. Not all the caves are open to the public, but the tours offered provide a fabulous opportunity to explore the cave world.

Guided walking tours take in the chambers, extensive stalagmite and stalactite deposits and fossil collections. The Victoria Fossil Cave Tour is an introduction to the ancient animal history of Australia, while the natural delights of the caves, including helictites and fabulous domed ceilings, are accessed on the 30-minute Alexandra Cave Tour. The world of bats is celebrated on The Bat Tour, the highlight being unhindered views of the bats' activity from infra-red cameras – you might even see them drinking from the tiny straw stalactites.

Adventure caving allows visitors to see the caves in their raw state, while also providing an opportunity for exciting squeezes and crawls through some very tight spaces. For caving beginners, try the Blackberry and Stick-Tomato tours. For the more experienced cavers, enjoy the crawls and sights on the Starburst Chamber Tour. The Fox Cave Tour is the ultimate caving experience, with access to the cave system by a small entrance, leading to great fossil collections, vast speleothem development and incredible scenery.

You can get details on these tours from Wonambi Fossil Centre, located within the park (visit or phone (08) 8762 2340). At the centre you'll also find some of the fossils retrieved from the caves, displays detailing the caves' ability to 'trap' animals, and life-size replicas of the ancient creatures and their habitats. Also in the centre is the Flinders University Gallery with exhibits on the work done and discoveries made by Flinders University scientists and students in piecing together the incredible evolutionary history of the Naracoorte Caves.

Gladstone Square: landscaped square surrounded by historic sites, including the courthouse, barracks and Presbyterian church; cnr Jervois and Marryatt sts. *Australian Arid Lands Botanic Garden:* walks through 20 ha of arid-zone vegetation; northern outskirts, on the Stuart Hwy. *McLellan Lookout:* site of Matthew Flinders' landing in 1802; Whiting Pde. *Water Tower Lookout:* spectacular views from the balcony of the 1882 tower; Mitchell Tce.

Matthew Flinders Lookout: excellent view of Spencer Gulf and the Flinders Ranges; end of McSporran Cres. *Boat cruises, fishing charters and adventure tours:* contact visitor centre. *Heritage walk:* self-guide town walk includes the Kapunda marble cells in the courthouse and the magnificent stained glass in St Augustine's Church; brochure from visitor centre.
WHAT'S ON *Outback Surfboat Carnival:* Feb/Mar. *Cup Carnival:* horseracing; June.

SOUTH AUSTRALIA

Sleaford Bay, Lincoln National Park

NEARBY *Spencer Gulf:* watersports, yachting and fishing for King George whiting in northern waters. *Scenic drive:* north-east to the splendid Pichi Richi Pass, historic Quorn and Warren Gorge. See the same sights by train on Pichi Richi Railway, a 33 km round trip operating from Quorn; *see Quorn.*
ℹ️ Wadlata Outback Centre, 41 Flinders Tce; (08) 8641 0793; www.portaugusta.sa.gov.au

Port Broughton   Pop. 730

Map ref. 555 J4

This Yorke Peninsula holiday town has a quiet coastal feel in winter and bustles with sun-seeking holiday-makers in summer. Set on a quiet inlet on Spencer Gulf, it has a long fishing history. In the 1900s the fishing fleets and ketches operated from the jetty. Today the town is still a major port for fishing boats and each week truckloads of blue swimmer crabs depart for city restaurants.
IN TOWN *Heritage Centre:* local history museum in the old school; Edmund St. *Fishlab Aquaculture:* 1 hr tour of land transformed into a habitat for marine plants and animals; (08) 8635 2220; Fishermans Bay Rd. *Sailboat hire and fishing charters:* from foreshore. *Town jetty:* popular fishing spot. *Historical walking trail:* grab a *Walk Around Port Brought* booklet from the visitor centre and navigate the historical sights of the town, including the Heritage Plaques on the foreshore.
NEARBY *Fisherman Bay:* fishing, boating and holiday spot with over 400 holiday shacks; 5 km N along the coast.
ℹ️ Bay St; (08) 8635 2261; www.yorke peninsula.com.au

Port Elliot   Pop. 1516

Map ref. 549 H8, 552 C3, 555 L11

Port Elliot is a charming historic town set on scenic Horseshoe Bay. Its popularity as a holiday destination lies in the fabulous beaches and the relaxed coastal atmosphere. The town was established in 1854, the year Australia's first public

(horse-drawn) railway began operating between Goolwa and the town. Port Elliot's intended purpose as an ocean port for the Murray River was, however, unsuccessful. The bay proved less protected than was first thought and the port was moved to Victor Harbor.
IN TOWN *National Trust Historical Display:* interpretive centre detailing local history in the old railway station; The Strand. *The Strand:* historic street of art and craft shops, cafes and restaurants. *Cockle Train:* stops at the railway station on Henry St on its journey from Goolwa wharf to Victor Harbor, so you can do a section of the journey from here; *for more details see Goolwa. Freeman Nob:* spectacular views and coastal walks; end of The Strand. *Encounter Bikeway:* scenic coastal route between Goolwa and Victor Harbor. *Horseshoe Bay:* safe family beach with fishing from jetty. *Boomer Beach:* popular surfing beach; western edge of town. *Maritime Heritage Trail:* the town's story illustrated in foreshore displays. *Heritage walk:* brochure from railway station.
WHAT'S ON *Market:* Lakala Reserve; 1st and 3rd Sun each month.
NEARBY *Basham Beach Regional Park:* scenic coastal trails with interpretive signage and southern right whale sightings during their migration season, June–Sept; just north-east of Port Elliot. *Middleton:* coastal town with Heritage Bakery, the old flour mill and fabulous beaches; 3 km NE. *Crows Nest Lookout:* excellent views of the coast; 6 km N. *Middleton Winery:* with restaurant, wine-tastings and sales; 8 km NE via Middleton.
ℹ️ Information Bay, Port Elliot Rd; or at the foreshore adjacent to The Causeway, Victor Harbor; (08) 8552 5738; www.visitalexandrina.com

Port Lincoln   Pop. 12 630

Map ref. 554 D8

Each January this township on the Eyre Peninsula celebrates the life of the tuna – one of the few festivals in Australia devoted to a fish and a fair indication of the reign tuna has over this town.

Lincoln Cove, the marina, is the base for Australia's largest tuna fleet and tuna-farming industry. Port Lincoln is set on attractive Boston Bay, which is three times the size of Sydney Harbour. The townsite was reached by Matthew Flinders in his expedition of 1802. The place was so picturesque he named it in honour of his home, Lincolnshire, in England. Thirty years later settlers were still taken by it and considered it as a site for the state's capital. Sheltered waters, a Mediterranean climate and scenic coastal roads make this a popular holiday spot.
IN TOWN *Mill Cottage:* National Trust museum with early pioneering artefacts and paintings; Flinders Hwy; open 2.30pm–4.30pm Mon, Wed and Sat. *Railway Museum:* relics of the railway past displayed in a historic 1926 stone building; Railway Pl. *Axel Stenross Maritime Museum:* features original boatbuilding tools and working slipway; Lincoln Hwy. *Rose-Wal Memorial Shell Museum:* extensive shell display; grounds of Old Folks Home; Flinders Hwy. *Settler's Cottage:* stone cottage with early pioneer photos and documents; in Flinders Park, Flinders Hwy. *Kotz Stationary Engines:* museum collection of oil and petrol engines; Baltimore St. *Nautilus Theatre:* features 2 galleries of local and touring art, a gallery shop and a wine bar; Tasman Tce. *Kuju Arts and Crafts:* Aboriginal craft sales; Ravendale Rd. *Mayne Gallery:* local arts and crafts; King St; open 12.30pm–4.30pm daily. *Apex Wheelhouse:* original wheelhouse from the tuna boat *Boston Bay;* adjacent to Kirton Point Caravan Park; Hindmarsh St. *South Australian Seahorse Marine Centre:* informative tours of breeding farm to see several species of seahorse; contact visitor centre for bookings. *Lincoln Cove:* includes marina, leisure centre with water slide, holiday charter boats, and the base for the commercial fishing fleet (tastings of local catches available). Guided walking tours of the marina are available from the visitor centre. Off Ravendale Rd. *Boston Bay:* swimming, waterskiing, yachting and excellent fishing.

Yacht and boat charters: for gamefishing, diving, day fishing and for viewing sea lions, dolphins and birdlife around Sir Joseph Banks Group Conservation Park and Dangerous Reef; contact visitor centre for details. *Aquaculture Cruise:* features a visit to the tuna, kingfish and mussel farms; contact visitor centre for details. *Boston Island boat tours:* cruises around bay and island; contact visitor centre for details. *Adventure tours and safaris:* Eyre Peninsula; offshore and land adventures offered; contact visitor centre for details. *Old Mill Lookout:* panoramic views of town and bay; Dorset Pl. *Parnkalla Walking Trail:* 14 km trail with coastal views and abundant wildlife. It forms part of the longer Investigator Walking Trail from North Shields to Lincoln National Park. Brochure from visitor centre.

WHAT'S ON *Tunarama Festival:* Jan. *Adelaide to Lincoln Yacht Race and Lincoln Week Regatta:* Feb/Mar. *Mediterraneo Festival:* April.

NEARBY Lincoln National Park This spectacular coastal park has a network of walking trails through rugged wilderness areas to fantastic coastal scenery. The park is an important sanctuary for migrating birds that arrive in summer from the chilly Arctic Circle. To see the park from a height, take the 1.1 km return hike up Stamford Hill. At the top is the Flinders Monument and panoramic views of the coast. For a true, uninterrupted wilderness experience, grab a key and permit from the visitor centre and head on to Memory Cove, a calm bay with a fantastic beach. There is also a replica of the plaque placed by Matthew Flinders in 1802 in memory of 8 crew members lost in seas nearby. 4WD enthusiasts would enjoy the challenges of the Sleaford Bay coast with its rolling sand dunes and surf beaches. 20 km s. *Delacolline Estate Wines:* well known for blended variety of sauvignon blanc/ semillon; tastings and sales; Whillas Rd; 1 km w; open 1.30pm–4pm weekends. *Winters Hill Lookout:* views to Boston Bay, Boston Island and Port Lincoln; Flinders Hwy; 5 km nw. *Boston Bay Winery:* tastings and sales; Lincoln Hwy; 6 km n; open 11.30am–4.30pm weekends. *Roseview Emu Park and Rose Gardens:* picturesque gardens in bush setting, with sales of emu produce; Little Swamp La; 10 km nw. *Skirmish Down Under:* paintball games; Big Swamp; 15 km n. *Glen-Forest Tourist Park:* native animals, bird-feeding and miniature golf course; Greenpatch; 15 km nw. *Poonindie Church:* quaint old church built in 1850 with the unique feature of two chimneys; 20 km n. *Mikkira Station and Koala Park:* historic 1842 homestead, with bushwalks to see native wildlife. Off Fishery Bay Rd; 26 km sw. *Constantia Designer Craftsmen:* guided tours of world-class furniture factory and showroom; on road to Whalers Way; open Mon–Fri. *Whalers Way:* cliff-top drive

through privately owned sanctuary inhabited by seals, ospreys, kangaroos and emus. It finishes at Flinders Lookout. Permit from visitor centre. 32 km s.
ⓘ 3 Adelaide Pl; 1800 629 911 or (08) 8683 3544; www.visitportlincoln.net

Port MacDonnell   Pop. 605

Map ref. 552 H13

Port MacDonnell is a quiet fishing town that was once a thriving port. The establishment of the breakwater in 1975 has ensured the southern rock-lobster trade many more years of fruitful operation. The fleet is now the largest in Australia. While fishing is the main focus of the area, the rich maritime history, fascinating crystal pools and coastal scenery attract visitors year-round.

IN TOWN Port MacDonnell and District Maritime Museum The long maritime history of this stretch of coast is littered with stories of shipwrecks and bravery. Here photos and salvaged artefacts bring the old days to life. A particularly tragic story is the crash of the *Admella* on an off-coast reef in 1859. Only 24 of the 113 people aboard survived. The ship's bell and cannon are on display in the museum. There is also a focus on community history and on the rock-lobster industry. Meylin St. Open 12.30pm–4.30pm Mon, Wed and Sun. *Clarke's Park:* popular picnic spot with natural spring; northern outskirts. *Fishing:* anglers will enjoy fishing from the jetty and landing. Boat charters available for deep-sea catches of tuna; details from visitor centre. *Heritage walk:* includes historic cemetery with hidden headstones; contact visitor centre.

WHAT'S ON *Bayside Festival:* Jan.

NEARBY Ewens Ponds and Piccaninnie Ponds conservation parks For a unique snorkelling or diving experience, visit the crystal-clear waters of these parks. At Ewens Ponds (7 km e) there are 3 ponds, connected via channels. Snorkel on the surface to see the amazing plant life underwater, or go diving for the ultimate experience. The deep caverns in Piccaninnie Ponds (20 km e) offer visitors an insight into the underwater world. Snorkellers can gaze into the depths of the Chasm, while divers can explore the limestone-filtered waters of the Cathedral, so named because of its regal white walls. While no experience is necessary for snorkelling, divers require qualifications. Inquiries and bookings to SA Parks and Wildlife; (08) 8735 1177. *Cape Northumberland Heritage and Nature Park:* a coastal park famous for sunrises and sunsets. Other highlights include a historic lighthouse, a penguin colony and unusual rock formations; just west of town. *Dingley Dell Conservation Park:* the historic 1862 restored cottage that is located here was once the home of Australian poet Adam Lindsay Gordon

and features displays on his life and work; 2 km w; tours 10am–4pm daily. *Germein Reserve:* 8 km boardwalk (loop track) through wetlands; opposite Dingley Dell. *Southern Ocean Shipwreck Trail:* over 89 vessels came to grief on the section of coast from the Victorian border to the Murray River mouth. The drive trail includes 10 interpretive sites. Brochure from visitor centre.
ⓘ Rural Transaction Centre, 7 Charles St; (08) 8738 2576; www.thelimestonecoast. com.au

Port Pirie   Pop. 13 253

Map ref. 555 J3, 556 I13

Industry in its splendour greets the visitor at this major industrial and commercial centre. The oil tanks, grain silos and 250-metre-high smokestack all tower over the city, while on the waterfront huge local and overseas vessels are loaded and discharged. Broken Hill Proprietary Company (BHP) began mining lead in 1889 and various South Australian ports at that time vied for BHP's smelting business. Port Pirie eventually won, and created what is today the largest lead-zinc smelter in the world. Wheat and barley from the mid-north are also exported from here. Port Pirie shows great character in its old buildings and attractive main street, and Spencer Gulf and the Port Pirie River offer swimming, waterskiing, fishing and yachting.

IN TOWN Regional Tourism and Arts Centre This award-winning centre comprises an eclectic mix of exhibitions, art and information. A lifelike fibreglass model of the largest white pointer shark taken from SA's waters is on display. Local and regional history is presented through a series of art pieces and on the miniature railway, Pirie Rail Express, which replicates the journey from Port Pirie to Broken Hill (runs 1st and 3rd Sun each month). There are local and touring art exhibitions in the art gallery and the centre runs tours to the Pasminco smelter every Wed at 12.45pm. Mary Elie St. *National Trust Museum:* located in historic town buildings, including the old customs house (1882) and the Victorian pavilion-style railway station, the museum houses a local history display and rooms furnished in early-1900s style; Ellen St. *Memorial Park:* features the John Pirie anchor, memorials, and the Northern Festival Centre; Memorial Dr. *Fishing:* good local spots, include the main wharf. *Self-guide walks:* including National Trust Walking Tours and The Journey Landscape, a 1.6 km nature trail representing changes in vegetation from Broken Hill to Port Pirie; brochures from visitor centre.

WHAT'S ON *Regional Masters Games:* even-numbered years, April. *Blessing of the Fleet:* celebrates the role of Italians in establishing the local fishing industry; Sept. *Festival of Country Music:* Oct.

SOUTH AUSTRALIA

NEARBY *Weeroona Island:* good fishing and holiday area accessible by car; 13 km N. *Port Germein:* a quiet beachside town with a tidal beach safe for swimming. At 1.7 km, the town's jetty is one of the longest in Australia. 23 km N. *Telowie Gorge Conservation Park:* follow the marked Nukunu Trail from the park's entrance to the breathtaking Telowie Gorge on the south-west edge of the Flinders Ranges. Care should be taken on less-formal tracks in the park. 24 km NE. ℹ️ Regional Tourism and Arts Centre, 3 Mary Elie St; 1800 000 424 or (08) 8633 8700

Port Victoria   Pop. 333

Map ref. 554 H7

A tiny township on the west coast of Yorke Peninsula, Port Victoria was tipped to be a thriving port town after James Hughes travelled up the coast in 1840. Hughes, a land surveyor, studied the coastline from his schooner, *Victoria*, and reported favourably on the region. It became an important port for grain exports, with windjammers transporting wheat from here to Europe. The town still proudly proclaims that it is the 'last of the windjammer ports'.

IN TOWN *Maritime Museum:* displays, relics and artefacts of the great era of the windjammer; Main St; open 2pm–4pm weekends and public holidays. *Jetty:* original 1888 jetty that hosted the great sailing ships; good swimming and fishing; end of Main St. *Geology trail:* 5 km interpretive track along the foreshore explains the coast's ancient volcanic history; brochure from visitor centre.

NEARBY *Goose Island Conservation Park:* important breeding area for several bird species and the Australian sea lion; 13 km offshore; access by private boat. *Wardang Island:* this large island is an Aboriginal reserve, and permission for access is required from Goreta (Point Pearce) Aboriginal Community Council, (08) 8836 7205; near Goose Island. *Wardang Island Maritime Heritage Trail:* this scuba diving and overland trail includes 8 shipwreck sites with underwater plaques around Wardang Island and 6 interpretive signs at Port Victoria; waterproof self-guide leaflet available from visitor centre. ℹ️ Port Victoria Kiosk, Esplanade; or Yorke Peninsula Regional Visitor Information Centre, 50 Moonta Rd, Kadina; 1800 654 991 or (08) 8821 2333; www.yorkepeninsula.com.au

Quorn   Pop. 985

Map ref. 553 B12, 556 I10

Nestled in a valley in the Flinders Ranges, Quorn was established as a town on the Great Northern Railway line in 1878. The line was built by Chinese and British workers and operated for over 45 years (it closed in 1957). Part of the line through Pichi Richi Pass has been restored as a tourist railway, taking passengers on a scenic 33-kilometre round trip via Port Augusta. The town's old charm has not been lost on movie producers – the historic streetscapes and surrounding landscapes have been used in many movies.

IN TOWN *Railway Workshop Tours:* guided tours of the workshop where locomotives travelling on the Pichi Richi line are maintained and restored; tours at 2pm Tues and Thurs; book at visitor centre. *Junction Art Gallery:* local art exhibition; Railway Tce. *Pichi Richi Railway:* historical tourist train travels through dramatic countryside to Port Augusta and back; tour options available; bookings 1800 440 101. *Town walks:* the Walking Tour of Quorn and the Quorn Historic Buildings walk; brochures from visitor centre.
WHAT'S ON *Race Meeting:* May. *Pichi Richi Marathon:* July. *Spring Craft Fair:* Oct. *Campdraft and Field Days:* Oct.
NEARBY *Buckaringa Gorge Scenic Drive:* drive past Buckaringa Sanctuary and Proby's Grave (he was the first settler at Kanyaka Station) to a lookout accessed via a short walk; drive signposted north of town. *Quorn Native Flora Reserve:* stone reserve, once the town's quarry, with informative brochure available that details the reserve's flora; Quarry Rd; 2 km NW. *The Dutchmans Stern Conservation Park:* colourful rocky outcrops observed on 2 trails through the park. The Ridge Top Trail (8.2 km return) offers spectacular views of the Flinders Ranges and Spencer Gulf; 8 km W. *Devil's Peak Walking Trail:* panoramic views up steep climb to the summit; 10 km S; closed Nov–April (fire season). *Mount Brown Conservation Park:* mixed landscape of ridges and woodland. The loop trail, starting at Waukarie Falls, offers a side climb to the Mt Brown summit. Richman Valley Rd; 15 km S. *Warren Gorge:* imposing red cliffs popular with climbers. Also the habitat of the rare yellow-footed rock wallaby. 23 km N. ℹ️ 3 Seventh St; (08) 8648 6419; www.flindersrangescouncil.sa.gov.au

Renmark   Pop. 4448

Map ref. 555 Q6

It is hard to imagine that the lush lands around Renmark, thriving with orchards and vineyards, were once a veritable wasteland. In 1887 the Canadian-born Chaffey brothers were granted 30 000 acres (12 000 hectares) by the South Australian government to test their irrigation scheme. Theirs was the first of its type to succeed in Australia and today the farmlands are still irrigated with water piped from the Murray River.

IN TOWN *Olivewood:* National Trust historic building, formerly the Chaffey homestead, dressed in period furnishings, set in the grounds of a still-operating orangery and with famous olive trees in the orchard; cnr Renmark Ave and Twenty-first St; closed Wed. *PS Industry:* 1911 grand lady of the river still operates on steam when taking visitors out on her monthly cruises; 90 min tours run at 11am, 1.30pm and 3pm the first Sun each month; bookings at visitor centre. *Renmark Hotel:* historic community-owned and -run hotel; Murray Ave. *Renmano Wines:* premium table-wine producers offer cellar-door tastings and sales; Industrial Rd; closed Sun. *Nuts About Fruit:* sales of local dried fruit, nuts and other produce; Renmark Ave; closed Sun. *Renmark North Lookout:* views of town and Murray River; northern outskirts of town. *Murray River cruises:* houseboat hire or paddlesteamer tours to cruise the mighty Murray; contact visitor centre for details.
WHAT'S ON *Riverland Run, Rally and Rock:* Feb. *Riverland Greek Festival:* Mar. *Riverland Balloon Fiesta:* May. *Rose Festival:* Oct. *Renmark Rose Run:* race along the riverfront; Oct.

NEARBY Bookmark Biosphere Reserve
This reserve incorporates the mallee country and arid outback landscapes of Chowilla Regional Reserve and Danggali Conservation Park. In Chowilla (50 km N) are stretches of flood plains interspersed with native woodland and scrubland. Fishing, canoeing and birdwatching are popular and the history of the flood plains is explained on the Old Coach Road Vehicle Trail. Danggali (90 km N) is a vast wilderness area with interesting trails to explore. The two drive tours, Nanya's Pad Interpretive Drive (100 km circuit, 2WD accessible) and Tipperary Drive (100 km circuit, 4WD only), are both excellent introductions to the mallee scrub region, while the 10 km Target Mark Walking Trail passes through native vegetation to the dam. *Lock and Weir No. 5:* picnic in surrounding parklands; 2 km SE. *Paringa:* small farming community featuring a historic suspension bridge (1927), Bert Dix Memorial Park, and nearby Headings Cliffs Lookout; 4 km E. *Angove's:* producers of St Agnes Brandy as well as wine, with cellar-door tastings and sales; Bookmark Ave; 5 km SW. *Bredl's Wonder World of Wildlife:* unique fauna, particularly reptiles. Handling and feeding times between 11am and 3pm. 7 km SW. *Ruston's Rose Garden:* the Southern Hemisphere's largest rose garden with over 50 000 bushes and 4000 varieties; off Sturt Hwy; 7 km SW; open Oct–May. *Dunlop Big Tyre:* spans the Sturt Hwy at Yamba Roadhouse and marks the fruit-fly inspection point (no fruit allowed between Vic and SA); 16 km SE. *Murray River National Park, Bulyong Island section:* popular park for water-based activities, fishing and birdwatching; just upstream from Renmark on the Murray River. ℹ️ 84 Murray Ave; (08) 8586 6704; www.renmarkparinga.info

Robe   Pop. 950

Map ref. 552 F9

Guichen Bay and Robe's coastline would have been a welcome sight to the Chinese immigrants arriving in the mid-1800s. During the Victorian gold rush, around 16 500 Chinese disembarked here and travelled overland to the goldfields to avoid the Poll Tax enforced at Victorian ports. Robe had a thriving export trade before rail was introduced, which has left a legacy of historic buildings, from quaint stone cottages to the Caledonian Inn, with internal doors salvaged from shipwrecks. Today Robe is one of the state's most significant historic towns, but also a fishing port and holiday centre, famous for its crayfish and its secluded beaches.

IN TOWN *Robe Institute Building:* incorporates the visitor centre, library and Historic Interpretation Centre with photographic and audiovisual displays on Robe's history; Mundy Tce. *Robe Customs House:* historic 1863 building, once the hub of Robe's export trade, now a museum featuring Chinese artefacts and displays on the explorers and governors significant in Robe's past; Royal Circus; open 2pm–4pm Tues, Sat and daily in Jan. *Art and craft galleries:* throughout town, especially in Smillie and Victoria sts. *Fishing and dive charters:* to the deep sea; bookings (08) 8768 1968. *Crayfish fleet:* anchors in Lake Butler (Robe's harbour); sells fresh crayfish and fish Oct–April. *Walk and scenic drive tours:* self-guide tours available. Take the town walk past 81 historic buildings and sites. Brochures from visitor centre.

WHAT'S ON *Robe Rodeo:* New Year's Day. *Robe Easter Surfing Classic:* Easter. *Blessing of the Fleet:* Sept. *Robe Village Fair:* last full weekend in Nov.

NEARBY *Lake Fellmongery:* popular spot for waterskiing; 1 km SE. *Long Beach:* 17 km pristine beach for surfing and swimming. Cars are allowed on the sand. 2 km N. *Little Dip Conservation Park:* features a complex, moving sand-dune system, salt lakes, freshwater lakes and abundant wildlife. Drive or walk through native bush to beaches for surfing and beach-fishing. Some areas 4WD only; 2 km S. *Beacon Hill:* panoramic views of Robe, lakes and coast from lookout tower; Beacon Hill Rd; 2 km SE. *The Obelisk:* navigational marker at Cape Dombey. Scenic access via cliff walk from the Old Gaol at Robe; 2 km W. *Mount Benson wine region:* young wine region specialising in varieties of shiraz and cabernet sauvignon. Five cellar doors offer tastings and sales. 18 km N.
ⓘ Robe Institute Building, Mundy Tce; (08) 8768 2465; www.robe.sa.gov.au

Roxby Downs   Pop. 3607

Map ref. 556 F4

In 1975 Roxby Downs station was a hard-working property on the red sand dunes of central South Australia. That was until a body of copper and uranium, the largest in the world, was discovered near a dam. Roxby Downs, the township, was built to accommodate the employees of the Olympic Dam mining project and has many modern facilities.

IN TOWN *Cultural Precinct:* incorporates the visitor centre, cinema, cafe, art gallery with local and touring exhibitions, and interpretive display that introduces visitors to town and dam history; Richardson Pl. *Arid Discovery:* area of native landscape with sunset tours to see reintroduced native animals, including bilbies and burrowing bettongs. A highlight is the close viewing of animals in the observation hide. Contact visitor centre for tour details. *Emu Walk:* self-guide flora walk through town; contact visitor centre.

WHAT'S ON *Market:* Richardson Pl; closest Sat to the 15th each month. *Outback Fringe Festival:* Mar.

NEARBY *Olympic Dam Mining Complex:* an extensive underground system of roadways and trains services the mine that produces refined copper, uranium oxide, gold and silver. The mine is 9 km N, but limited views are available at the site. Olympic Dam Tours run surface tours at 9am each Mon, Thurs and Sat from Roxby Downs; book at the visitor centre.
ⓘ Roxby Downs Cultural Precinct; (08) 8671 2001; www.roxbydowns.com

Stansbury   Pop. 530

Map ref. 554 I9

Situated on the lower east coast of Yorke Peninsula and with views of Gulf St Vincent, Stansbury was originally known as Oyster Bay because of its claim to the best oyster beds in the state. The town has always serviced the farms inland, but its mainstay today is tourism. The bay

The Murray River, near Renmark

is excellent for fishing and watersports, including diving and waterskiing.

IN TOWN *Schoolhouse Museum:* this local history museum in Stansbury's first school features cultural and environmental displays as well as the headmaster's rooms furnished in early-1900s style; North Tce; open 2pm–4pm Wed and Sun, daily in Jan. *Oyster farms:* see daily operations of local oyster farms and try fresh oysters. Southern Yorke Oysters offers short tours of its farm; (08) 8852 4363. *Fishing:* popular spots include the jetty, rocks and beach. *Mills' Gully Lookout:* popular picnic spot with panoramic views of bay, town and Gulf St Vincent; northern outskirts of town. *Coastal trails:* walking and cycling trails past reserves, lookouts and a historic cemetery; start at foreshore caravan park; brochure from visitor centre.

WHAT'S ON *Stansbury Seaside Markets:* monthly Oct–May; check dates with visitor centre. *Stansbury and Port Vincent Wooden and Classic Boat Regatta:* April. *Sheepdog Trials:* May.

NEARBY *Kleines Point Quarry:* SA's largest limestone quarry offers morning tours of the quarry and ship-loading; bookings essential (08) 8852 4104; 5 km S. *Lake Sundown:* one of the many salt lakes in the area and a photographer's delight at sunset; 15 km NW. *Port Vincent:* popular holiday destination with good swimming, yachting and waterskiing; 17 km N.
ⓘ Cnr Weaver and Towler sts; (08) 8852 4577; www.stansburysa.com

Strathalbyn   Pop. 3203

Map ref. 549 I4, 552 C3, 555 L10

This heritage town has some of the most picturesque and historic streetscapes in country South Australia. It has a predominantly Scottish heritage,

Murphy's Haystacks, near Streaky Bay

first settled by Dr John Rankine, who emigrated with 105 other Scotsmen in the late 1830s. The town is set on the Angas River, with the Soldiers Memorial Gardens following the watercourse through the town. Strathalbyn is renowned for its antique and craft shops.

IN TOWN *National Trust Museum:* features an early history display in the courtroom, Victorian-era relics in the courthouse, and a historical room and photographic displays in the Old Police Station; Rankine St; open 2pm–5pm Wed, Thurs, Sat and Sun. *Old Railway Station:* complex includes the visitor centre, the Station Master's Gallery with local and touring art exhibitions (open Wed–Sun), and the station for the tourist railway from Mount Barker, the *SteamRanger (see Hahndorf)*; South Tce. *St Andrew's Church:* impressive church with castle-like tower; Alfred Pl. *Original Lolly Shop:* old-fashioned lollies and fudge; High St. *Antiques, art and craft shops:* outlets in High St. *Heritage walk:* self-guide trail featuring over 30 heritage buildings and the architectural delights of Albyn Tce; brochure available from visitor centre.

WHAT'S ON *Collectors, Hobbies and Antique Fair:* Aug. *Glenbarr Highland Gathering:* Oct. *Rotary Duck Race:* plastic ducks; Nov.

NEARBY **Milang** This old riverboat town is now a popular holiday destination on the shores of Lake Alexandrina, Australia's largest freshwater lake. The lake offers fishing, sailing and windsurfing. In town, visit the Port Milang Railway for its local history display and pick up a Heritage Trail brochure for a self-guide walk. Each Australia Day weekend the Milang–Goolwa Freshwater Classic fills the town with visitors who come to watch hundreds of yachts begin the race. 20 km SE. *Lookout:* views over town and district; 7 km SW. *Ashbourne:* buy local produce at roadside stalls and at the country market held the 3rd Sun each month; 14 km W. *Langhorne Creek wine region:* on

the Bremer and Angas rivers flood plains, the first vines were planted in the 1850s. This winemaking region has always specialised in red varieties, particularly cabernet sauvignon and shiraz. Five cellar doors offer tastings and sales, and The Vintage Affair is held here each May. 15 km E. *Meadows:* features Pottery at Paris Creek and Iris Gardens (open Oct–Mar) nearby. The Country Fair is held each Oct. 15 km NW.

ℹ Old Railway Station, South Tce; (08) 8536 3212; www.visitalexandrina.com

Streaky Bay   Pop. 1080

Map ref. 563 P12

A holiday town, fishing port and agricultural centre for the cereal-growing hinterland. The bay was first sighted in 1627 by Dutch explorer Peter Nuyts, but it wasn't fully explored until 1802 by Matthew Flinders. Flinders named the bay after the 'streaky' colour of the water, caused by seaweed oils. While this town is pretty, it is the surrounding bays and coves, sandy beaches and towering cliffs that bring the visitors.

IN TOWN *National Trust Museum:* early pioneer history displays in the old school, as well as a restored pioneer cottage and a doctor's surgery; Montgomerie Tce; open 2pm–4pm Tues and Fri, or by appt (08) 8626 1443. *Powerhouse Restored Engine Centre:* display of old working engines; Alfred Tce. *Visitor Centre:* fishing information and Great White Shark replica (original caught with rod and reel); Alfred Tce. *Fishing:* for King George whiting, southern rock-lobster, abalone and shark (check with visitor centre).

WHAT'S ON *Family Fish Day Contest:* Jan. *Perlubie Sports Day:* Jan. *Cup Race:* April.

NEARBY *Scenic drives:* include Westall Way Scenic Drive, which starts 9 km S, taking in rock formations, high cliffs, quiet pools and the Yanerbie Sand Dunes. Also the drive west of town to Cape Bauer and

the Blowhole (20 km NW), for views across the Bight. *Calpatanna Waterhole Conservation Park:* bushwalking in coastal park to an important Aboriginal waterhole; excellent birdwatching; 28 km SE. *Murphy's Haystacks:* a much-photographed cluster of pink granite boulders, with interpretive signage and paths; 40 km SE. *Baird Bay:* a small coastal town with an attractive beach for swimming, boating and fishing. Baird Bay Charters and Ocean Ecotours offer swims with sea lions and dolphins; (08) 8626 5017. 45 km SE. *Point Labatt Conservation Park:* from the cliff-top viewing platform, see the rare and endangered Australian sea lions sleeping on the beach (this colony is the only permanent one on the Australian mainland). Parts of access road unsealed; 50 km SE. *Venus Bay Conservation Park:* important reserve for breeding and reintroduction of native species. The park includes the peninsula and 7 islands with beach-fishing and swimming. Peninsula access is 4WD only; turn-off 50 km SE. *Acraman Creek Conservation Park:* this mangrove and mallee park is an important refuge for coastal birds. Popular activities include canoeing and fishing. 2WD access to beach, 4WD to Point Lindsay; turn-off 53 km N. *Port Kenny:* this small township on Venus Bay offers excellent fishing, boating and swimming, with sea lion and dolphin tours available; 62 km SE. *Venus Bay:* fishing village renowned for catches of King George whiting, trevally, garfish and many more. Its waters are safe for swimming and watersports, and nearby beaches are good for surfing. Needle Eye Lookout nearby provides fantastic views, with southern right whale sightings June–Oct. 76 km S.

ℹ Stewarts Roadhouse, 15 Alfred Tce; (08) 8626 1126; www.tep.com.au

Swan Reach   Pop. 266

Map ref. 555 N8

This quiet little township on the Murray River was once one of five large sheep stations; the original homestead is now the Swan Reach Hotel. Established as one of the first river ports for Murray River trade, the introduction of rail, and Morgan's rise as one of the state's busiest ports, saw the era of paddlesteamers in Swan Reach decline. Today the picturesque river scenery and excellent fishing make the town a popular holiday destination.

IN TOWN *Swan Reach Museum:* local history displays with special interest in Swan Reach's flood history, the waters having devastated the town in the early 1900s; Nildottie Rd. *Murray River Educational Nature Tours:* tours offering environmental education; inquiries (08) 8570 2212.

NEARBY Yookamurra Sanctuary This sanctuary represents an initiative to restore 1100 ha of land to its original state. Fittingly, the sanctuary is named Yookamurra after the Aboriginal word for 'yesterday'. The mallee vegetation that was found here before European habitation has been replanted, feral animals have been eradicated and native animals are being reintroduced. Keep an eye out for the rare and endangered numbat or the bilby and woylie. Walking tours and overnight stays are available. Bookings are essential, (08) 8562 5011. Pipeline Rd, Sedan; 21 km w. *Murray Aquaculture Yabby Farm:* catch your own yabbies; 1.5 km E. *Ridley and Swan Reach conservation parks:* both parks represent typical western Murray vegetation and protect the habitat of the hairy-nosed wombat; 7.5 km s and 10 km w respectively. *Ngaut Ngaut Boardwalk:* guided tours of archaeological site, established when an ancient skeleton was discovered in rock; 14 km s at Nildottie. *Big Bend:* imposing Murray cliffs, the tallest found on the river, home to diverse flora and fauna. Spectacular nightly 'Big Bend By Night' tours are available, inquiries (08) 8570 1097; 20 km downstream. *Bakara Conservation Park:* mallee-covered plains and sand dunes, important habitat for the mallee fowl; 32 km E. *Brookfield Conservation Park:* bushwalking in limestone country to see hairy-nosed wombats, red kangaroos and a variety of bird species; 40 km NW.
ⓘ General Store, 47 Anzac Ave; (08) 8570 2036; www.murraylands.info

Tanunda   Pop. 3841

Map ref. 550 F5, 551 E6, 555 L8

Tanunda is at the heart of the Barossa and surrounded by vineyards. The modern-day township grew out of the village of Langmeil, which was the focal point for early German settlement. The German Lutherans found it only natural to plant vines, as it was a basic part of their lifestyle. Many of the Barossa's shiraz vines date back to those early days. Tanunda has a boisterous German spirit and fine examples of Luthern churches.

IN TOWN *Barossa Historical Museum:* situated in the former post and telegraph office (1865), its collections specialise in German heritage; Murray St. *Barossa Wine and Visitor Centre:* sales of souvenirs and produce. Also incorporates the Wine Interpretation Centre that details the region's history. Murray St. *Gourmet produce:* specialty stores include Tanunda Bakery for German breads (Murray St), Tanunda's Nice Ice for homemade ice-cream (Kavel Arcade) and Apex Bakery for traditional pastries (Elizabeth St). *Heritage walk:* includes many historic Lutheran churches; brochure available from visitor centre.

WHAT'S ON *Barossa Market:* stalls and live entertainment; Sun; Chateau Dorrien Winery, Barossa Valley Way, north of town. *Barossa Vintage Festival:* celebration of locally produced food and wine in various locations; odd-numbered years, April. *Barossa Jazz Weekend:* Aug. *Barossa International Music Festival:* various venues; Oct. *Brass Band Contest:* Oct.

NEARBY Barossa wine region The Mediterranean-style climate, varying soils, specialised winemakers and long history (dating back to the 1840s) have created a world-renowned wine region in the Barossa Valley. Among the big names, such as Penfolds, Yalumba and Seppelt, are smaller boutique wineries, and nearly all outfits offer cellar-door tastings and sales. Close to Tanunda is the Barossa Small Winemakers Centre, housed in the cellar door at Chateau Tanunda, Basedow Rd, and showcasing the rare and handmade varieties of the Barossa's small producers. At the Chateau Dorrien Winery Tourism Centre in Barossa Valley Way there is an interesting mural depicting Barossa heritage. Winery map available from visitor centre. *For more information see Angaston, Lyndoch and Nuriootpa. Norm's Coolies:* see performances by a unique breed of sheepdog, Norm's coolie, at 2pm Mon, Wed and Sat; just south on Barossa Valley Way. *Bethany:* this pretty village was the first German settlement in the Barossa. The creekside picnic area, pioneer cemetery, attractive streetscapes and walking trail along Rifle Range Rd make it well worth a visit. 3 km SE. *The Keg Factory:* makers of American and French oak kegs, as well as barrel furniture and wine racks; St Halletts Rd; 4 km SW.
ⓘ Barossa Wine and Visitor Centre, Murray St; 1300 812 662 or (08) 8563 0600; www.barossa-region.org

Tumby Bay   Pop. 1226

Map ref. 554 E7

Tumby Bay is a pretty coastal town on the east coast of Eyre Peninsula. Its development was slow – Matthew Flinders discovered the bay in 1802, settlers arrived in the 1840s and the jetty was built in 1874 to ship the grain produce, but still there was no town. It

took until the early 1900s for any official settlement to be established. Now the famous long, crescent beach, white sand and blue water attract holiday-makers.

IN TOWN *C. L. Alexander National Trust Museum:* depicts early pioneer history in an old timber schoolroom; West Tce; open 10am–11am Wed, 2.30pm–4.30pm Sun. *Rotunda Art Gallery:* local art display and a fantastic mural on the outside of the rotunda; Tumby Tce; open 10am–noon Mon and Wed, 1.30pm–4.30pm Sun. *Mangrove boardwalk:* 70 m walkway with interpretive signs explaining ecology of mangroves; Berryman St. *Fishing:* from the recreational jetty, beach, rocks or boats (hire and charters available).

NEARBY Koppio Smithy Museum Time disappears and the early 1900s come to life in this extensive National Trust museum in the Koppio Hills. Consisting of the restored Blacksmith's Shop (1903), historic log cottage 'Glenleigh' (1893) and schoolrooms, the museum houses an eclectic collection of Aboriginal artefacts, early pioneer furniture, firearms and vestiges of 1900s schooldays. Early machinery, engines and farming tools are also displayed. 30 km SW. Closed Mon. *Trinity Haven Scenic Drive:* travels south from town along the coast and offers scenic coastal views and secluded beaches and bays. *Island Lookout Tower and Reserve:* views of town, coast and islands. Enjoy a picnic in the reserve. Harvey Dr; 3 km s. *Lipson Cove:* popular spot for anglers. Walk to the coastal sanctuary on Lipson Island at low tide. 10 km NE. *Ponta and Cowleys beaches:* fishing catches include snapper and bream; 15 km NE. *Moody Tanks:* State Heritage-listed water-storage tanks once used to service passing steam trains; 30 km w. *Cummins:* rich rail heritage celebrated each April at the World Championship Kalamazoo Classic; 37 km NW. *Port Neill:* an old port town with a safe beach for fishing and watersports. Also Ramsay Bicentennial Gardens, and vintage vehicles at Vic and Jill Fauser's Living Museum. Port Neill Lookout, nearby, provides fantastic views of the coast. 42 km NE. *Sir Joseph Banks Group Conservation Park:* comprising around 20 islands and reefs, this park is a breeding area for migrating coastal birds and the Australian sea lion colony at Dangerous Reef. Boat access is from Tumby Bay, Port Lincoln and 250 m north of Lipson Cove.
ⓘ Hales MiniMart, 1 Bratten Way; (08) 8688 2584; www.tumbybay.sa.gov.au

Victor Harbor   Pop. 8923

Map ref. 549 G8, 552 B4, 555 L11

In the 1830s the crystal waters of Encounter Bay – and the Southern Ocean beyond – throbbed with the whalers and sealers of the south. Granite Island housed a whaling station, Victor Harbor was its port, and life revolved around the ocean slaughters. Today the whalers

SOUTH AUSTRALIA

and sealers are gone, Granite Island is a recreation park and Victor Harbor is a holiday town. The naming of Encounter Bay comes from the unexpected meeting in the bay in 1802 between explorers Matthew Flinders and Nicolas Baudin.

IN TOWN South Australian Whale Centre This unique centre focuses on the 25 species of whale and dolphin found in southern Australian waters, with an aim to conserve their species. Past atrocities of the whaling industry are displayed alongside interactive displays and presentations that reveal the wonders of these amazing creatures. Between June and September each year, southern right whales mate and breed in Encounter Bay. The centre offers whale-cruise information, as well as a Whale Info Hotline for the latest sightings (in season); 1900 931 223. Railway Tce. Open 11am–4.30pm daily. *Encounter Coast Discovery Centre:* National Trust museum that covers Aboriginal, whaling, settler and recent local history. A museum walk finishes at the Old Customs House, which has period furnishings. Flinders Pde; open 1pm–4pm daily. *Cockle Train:* departs from Railway Tce for return journey to Goolwa, bookings (08) 8391 1223; *for more details see Goolwa. Camel rides:* on foreshore; start near Causeway entrance from 11am weekends and school holidays (weather permitting). *Parasailing:* in Encounter Bay on weekends and school holidays (Nov–April); details (08) 8277 3233.

WHAT'S ON *Regional Art Show:* Jan. *Triathlon:* Mar. *Whale Season Launch:* June.

NEARBY Granite Island Recreation Park Granite Island has a long and varied history. It has significance in the Ramindjeri people's Dreamtime; in 1837 a whaling station was established; and today the island is a recreation park. This history is detailed on the Kaiki Trail, a 1.5 km walk around the island. A highlight is the Below Decks Oceanarium, just off the Screwpile Jetty, with close-up views of marine life and tours daily. At dusk, take a guided Penguin Discovery Tour to see the penguins scuttle in and out of their burrows. (Book for both tours on (08) 8552 7555). The island is linked to the mainland by a 630 m causeway. Walk or take the horse-drawn tram, operating since 1894 (tickets from visitor centre). *Hindmarsh River Estuary:* peaceful picnic and fishing spot with boardwalk through coastal scrub; 1 km NE. *Sawtooth Ridge:* winery with cellar-door tastings and sales; 3 km N; open weekends. *Scotts Greenhills Adventure Park:* family-fun activities including go-karts, jumping castle and waterslide; Waggon Rd; 3.5 km N. *Victor Harbor Winery:* cellar-door tastings and sales; 4 km N in the Hindmarsh Valley; open Wed–Sun. *Urimbirra Wildlife Park:* popular fauna park with a wetland bird sanctuary, crocodile-feeding and children's farmyard; Adelaide Rd; 5 km N. *Wild Rose Garden and*

Miniature Village: minute replicas of SA's historical attractions in landscaped gardens, with tearooms and fruit sales (in season) at the Apple Shed; next to Urimbirra Wildlife Park. *Nangawooka Flora Reserve:* tranquil walks through native bushlands with over 1250 native plant varieties on show; opposite Urimbirra Wildlife Park. *The Bluff (Rosetta Head):* 500 million-year-old mass of granite, well worth the 100 m climb for the views; 5 km SW. *Newland Head Conservation Park:* known for its wild surf and coastal vegetation, this park protects the headland and Waitpinga and Parsons beaches, which offer surf-fishing opportunities and beach walks; turn-off 15 km SW. *Hindmarsh Falls:* pleasant walks and spectacular waterfall (during winter); 15 km NW. *Mount Billy Conservation Park:* mallee and forest park renowned for its rare orchid species; 18 km NW. *Inman Valley:* features Glacier Rock said to be the first recorded discovery of glaciation in Australia; 19 km NW.
ⓘ Causeway Building, Esplanade; (08) 8552 5738; www.tourismvictorharbor.com.au

Waikerie   Pop. 1764

Map ref. 555 O6

Waikerie, the citrus centre of Australia, is surrounded by an oasis of irrigated orchards and vineyards in the midst of the mallee-scrub country of the Riverland. Owing to its position on cliff-tops, the area around Waikerie was not a promising settlement. However, in an experiment by the South Australian government in 1894 that attempted to alleviate unemployment and decentralise capital, 281 people were relocated from Adelaide. It was an instant town. Waikerie has beautiful views of the river gums and sandstone cliffs along the Murray River, which is a popular spot for fishing, boating and waterskiing – and the skies above are a glider's paradise due to the fantastic thermals and flat landscape.

IN TOWN *Rain Moth Gallery:* local art exhibitions; Peake Tce; open 10.30am–2.30pm Mon–Fri, 10am–1pm Sat. *Waikerie Murray River Queen:* unique floating motel, restaurant and cafe; moored near the ferry. *Harts Lagoon:* wetland area with bird hide; Ramco Rd. *Thomsons Woolpunda Wines:* wine and local produce sales. Wine-tastings include rare cabernet tempranello. O'Loughlin St; open weekdays. *Houseboat hire:* scenic trips along the Murray; contact visitor centre for details. *Bush Safari:* camel or 4WD tours to the river and outback country north-east of Waikerie; bookings (08) 8543 2280. *Scenic walk:* along cliff-top to lookout; northern outskirts of town.

WHAT'S ON *Rotary Food Fair:* Mar. *Horse and Pony Club Easter Horse Show:* Easter. *Riverland Rock 'n' Roll Festival:* May. *Riverland Field Days:* Sept.

NEARBY *Orange Tree Giftmania:* local produce sales – including citrus and

dried fruits – and souvenirs. Enjoy Murray River views from the viewing platform. Sturt Hwy. *Waikerie International Soaring Centre:* offers recreational flights, beginner courses and cross-country training; Waikerie Aerodrome, off Sturt Hwy, east side of town; inquiries (08) 8541 2644. *Maize Island Conservation Park:* this waterbird reserve has fantastic cliffs and lagoons. Beware of strong currents when swimming. 2 km N. *Pooginook Conservation Park:* both dense and open mallee country, home to kangaroos, hairy-nosed wombats and the ever-busy mallee fowl; 12 km NE. *Stockyard Plain Disposal Basin Reserve:* varied plant and birdlife – over 130 bird species identified; key available from visitor centre; 12 km SW. *Broken Cliffs:* abundant crystallised gypsum fossils and a popular fishing spot; Taylorville Rd; 15 km NE. *Birds Australia Gluepot Reserve:* important mallee area that forms part of the Bookmark Biosphere Reserve (*see Renmark*). Also significant bird refuge, with over 17 threatened Australian species to be seen on the 14 walking trails. Access key from Shell Service Station in Waikerie. 64 km N.
ⓘ Orange Tree Giftmania, Sturt Hwy; (08) 8541 2332

Wallaroo   Pop. 2717

Map ref. 554 I6

Vast grain silos greet visitors to Wallaroo, a coastal town and shipping port on the west coast of Yorke Peninsula. The town is an interesting mix of tourism and industry. The safe beaches and excellent fishing prove popular with holiday-makers, while the commercial port controls exports of barley and wheat. Wallaroo exists thanks to a lucky shepherd's discovery of copper in 1859. Vast deposits were uncovered and soon thousands of Cornish miners arrived. The area boomed until the 1920s, when copper prices dropped and the industry slowly died out. Wallaroo's buildings and old Cornish-style cottages are a reminder of its colourful past. Wallaroo and nearby towns Moonta and Kadina are part of the 'Copper Coast' or 'Little Cornwall'.

IN TOWN Wallaroo Heritage and Nautical Museum This National Trust museum in Wallaroo's original 1865 post office features shipwreck displays, maps, charts, model ships and records, as well as local cultural and religious history. Meet George, the unlucky giant squid eaten then recovered from a whale's belly 30 years ago. Jetty Rd. Open 2pm–4pm Tues, Thurs, Sat and Sun, 10.30am–4pm Wed and public holidays. *Yorke Peninsula Railway:* historical diesel-train journey from Wallaroo to Bute; runs 2nd Sun each month and school holidays; contact visitor centre for details. *Ausbulk:* informative drive through grain-handling facility; Lydia Tce. *Boat hire and charters:* for the ultimate gulf-fishing experience. *Self-guide historical walk*: highlight is the 1865 Hughes chimney stack, which contains over 300 000 bricks and measures more than 7 sq m at its base; brochure available from museum or town hall.

WHAT'S ON *Kernewek Lowender*: Cornish festival held in conjunction with Moonta and Kadina; odd-numbered years, May. *Copper Coast Fishing Comp*: Nov.

NEARBY *Bird Island*: crabbing; 10 km s. 🛈 Yorke Peninsula Regional Visitor Information Centre, 50 Moonta Rd, Kadina; 1800 654 991 or (08) 8821 2333; www.yorkepeninsula.com.au

Whyalla
Pop. 21 211

Map ref. 554 I2, 556 H13

Whyalla, northern gateway to Eyre Peninsula, has grown from the small settlement of Hummock Hill to the largest provincial city in South Australia. It has become known for its heavy industry since iron ore was found in the 1890s around Iron Knob and the steelworks opened in 1964. Whyalla also has an interesting natural attraction. Each year, from May to August, an incredible number of cuttlefish spawn on the rocky coast just north – a must-see for diving enthusiasts. The city is modern and offers safe beaches, good fishing and boating.

IN TOWN **Whyalla Maritime Museum** The central attraction is HMAS *Whyalla*, a 650-ton corvette, the largest permanently land-locked ship in Australia. It was the first ship built in the BHP shipyards. Guided tours of the ship are included in the entry price and run on the hour from 11am to 3pm. The lives of the 4 wartime corvettes built by BHP are documented, as are histories of the shipbuilding industry and maritime heritage of Spencer Gulf. Lincoln Hwy. *Mount Laura Homestead Museum*: National Trust museum featuring the original homestead with progressive city-history displays, period furnishings in the 1914 Gay St Cottage, and the Telecommunications Museum; Ekblom St; open 10am–noon Mon–Fri, 2pm–4pm Sun. *Tandera Craft Village*: art and craft shops, market and tearooms; next to Maritime Museum; open 10am–4pm last weekend each month. *Whyalla Wildlife Sanctuary*: walking trails through exhibits, including an aviary and a children's zoo; Lincoln Hwy. *Whyalla Wetlands*: park and wetlands area with walking trails and a picnic/barbecue area; Lincoln Hwy. *Foreshore and marina*: safe beach, jetty for recreational fishing, picnic/barbecue area, access to Ada Ryan Gardens, and a marina with boat-launching facilities. *Ada Ryan Gardens*: mini-zoo with picnic facilities under shady trees; Cudmore Tce. *Steelworks Tour*: 2 hr guided tour explains steelmaking process (for safety, visitors must wear long-sleeved top, trousers and closed footwear); departs 1pm Mon, Wed

Aerial view of Victor Harbor and Granite Island

and Fri; book at visitor centre. *Hummock Hill Lookout*: views of city, gulf, steelworks and coast from WW II observation post; Queen Elizabeth Dr. *Flinders and Freycinet Lookout*: Farrel St. *Whyalla Tourist Drive*: self-guide drive (Route 61 Tourist Drive) shows development of city; *Whyalla Visitor's Guide* from visitor centre.

WHAT'S ON *Australian Amateur Snapper Fishing Championship*: Easter. *Whyalla Show*: family activities, rides and stalls; Aug.

NEARBY *Whyalla Conservation Park*: 30 min walking trail through typical semiarid flora and over Wild Dog Hill; 10 km N off Lincoln Hwy. *Port Bonython and Point Lowly*: this area of coast offers beautiful views of Spencer Gulf, fishing from rocks, and dolphin sightings. Lowly Beach is a popular swimming beach and the Freycinet Trail is a scenic drive from just before Port Bonython along Fitzgerald Bay to Point Douglas (parts are gravel). 34 km E. *Iron Knob*: a mining town with museum and mine lookout tours (depart from the museum at 10am and 2pm Mon–Fri); 53 km NW. 🛈 Lincoln Hwy; 1800 088 589 or (08) 8645 7900; www.whyalla.com

Willunga
Pop. 1902

Map ref. 549 F4, 550 B13, 552 B3, 555 K10

The historic town of Willunga grew rapidly around the slate quarries, which drove the town's economy until the late 1800s. Fortunately, by that time Willunga already had a thriving new industry – almonds. The town sits at the southern edge of the McLaren Vale wine region and is surrounded by farmlands and olive groves. Its name is derived from the Aboriginal word 'willa-unga', meaning 'the place of green trees'.

IN TOWN *Willunga Courthouse Museum*: National Trust-run museum featuring

local history displays in the original 1855 courtroom, cells and stables; guided 'Willunga Walks and Talks' tours (check times); High St; open 11am–4pm Tues, 1pm–5pm weekends. *Quarry*: having operated for 60 years (1842–1902), this is now a National Trust site; Delabole Rd. *Historical walk*: self-guide town walk featuring historic pug cottages, fine colonial architecture and an Anglican church with an Elizabethan bronze bell; brochure available from museum.

WHAT'S ON *Willunga Farmers Market*: Hill St; Sat mornings. *Willunga Quarry Market*: country market with local produce and crafts; Aldinga Rd; 2nd Sat each month. *Almond Blossom Festival*: running since 1970, celebrates the blooming of almond trees; July.

NEARBY *Mount Magnificent Conservation Park*: explore virtually untouched rocky landscapes and vegetation popular for picnics and scenic walks. The highlight is the walk to the Mt Magnificent summit for coastal views. 12 km SE. *Mount Compass*: a small farming town featuring the Wetlands Boardwalk and many farms open for viewing and sales, offering both primary products and gourmet food. Australia's only Cow Race is held here each Feb. 14 km S. *Fleurieu Big Shed*: local produce, art and craft sales; 15 km S. *Kyeema Conservation Park*: completely burnt out in the 1983 Ash Wednesday fires and then again in the fires of 1994 and 2001, this park is evidence of nature's ability to constantly regenerate. It is home to over 70 species of birdlife and offers good hiking and camping. Part of the Heysen Trail passes through it. 14 km NE. 🛈 McLaren Vale and Fleurieu Visitor Centre, Main Rd, McLaren Vale; 1800 628 410 or (08) 8323 9944; www.visitorcentre.com.au

A road into the Flinders Ranges

Flinders Ranges National Park

For thousands of years the ancient landscapes of the Flinders Ranges were home to the Adnyamathanha people – the hill and rock people. Their ancient Yura Muda (Dreamtime) stories tell of the creation of the mountainous slopes and gorges that ripple across the landscape for over 400 kilometres from south-east of Port Augusta to north of Arkaroola.

The 1850s brought change to the ranges. Stock runs were established at Arkaba, Wilpena and Aroona. Foreign plant and animal species were introduced and the natural balance of the ranges was altered. Within 50 years of European settlement many endemic animals of the ranges had been pushed to extinction. Today conservationists are trying to recover the natural balance of the area. Permanent waterholes have been established and many introduced feral animals have been eradicated.

Flinders Ranges National Park in the central Flinders Ranges is a fabulous place for hikers. There are 17 walks and hikes to choose from and the choice is difficult. All provide a different historical, geological or scenic look at the ranges. For a look into early European settlement history, take the 5.4-kilometre-return Hills Homestead Walk into the extraordinary natural rock formation of Wilpena Pound. Impressive rock paintings of the Adnyamathanha people that depict the creation of the ranges can be seen on the Arkaroo Rock Hike (3-kilometre loop track). For nature lovers, don't miss the Bunyeroo Gorge Hike, a 7.5-kilometre-return trail that follows the gorge and reveals fantastic wildlife and rock formations.

There are also scenic drive tours that reveal some of the park's most spectacular scenery. The popular Brachina Gorge Geological Trail is a 20-kilometre drive that details the long history of the ranges. The gorge is also one of the most impressive natural attractions of the park. Look out for the yellow-footed rock wallaby in the rocky upper slopes. The Bunyeroo–Brachina–Aroona Scenic Drive is a great introduction to the Aboriginal, European and natural history of the ranges, as well as an opportunity to see some spectacular mountain scenery. All the roads north of Wilpena are unsealed, but are two-wheel-drive accessible.

Among all of this, at Wilpena, is some of the best accommodation and facilities north of Adelaide. Drop in at the Wilpena Pound Visitor Information Centre for a park guide.

Wilmington
Pop. 242

Map ref. 555 J1, 556 I11

Robert Blinman had the foresight to build an inn, called the Roundwood Hotel, at the base of Horrocks Pass in 1861, and soon the Cobb & Co coaches were stopping there on their passenger routes. The town was built around the first hotel, and before long the farming community was thriving. Originally named Beautiful Valley by European explorers, the name was changed to Wilmington in 1876, although the original name still persists in many local establishments. Today the town retains much of its old-time feel and is renowned for its stone buildings.

IN TOWN *Wilmington Hotel:* built around 1876, the hotel is one of the town's oldest buildings and was first called The Globe Hotel. Original Cobb & Co coach stables are at the rear of the building. Main North Rd. *Mount Maria Walking Trail:* 2 km walking trail starting from town leads to vantage point over Wilmington; brochure available from general store.

WHAT'S ON *Night Rodeo:* Jan.
NEARBY *Spring Creek Mine Drive:* 24 km scenic loop beginning south of town, passing mountain and farm scenery and an old copper mine, now the town's water supply; brochure from general store. *Horrocks Pass and Hancocks Lookout:* this historic pass was named after explorer John Horrocks who traversed the pass in 1846. Hancocks Lookout, at the highest point of the pass, offers magnificent views to Spencer Gulf. 8 km W off road to Port Augusta. *Mount Remarkable National Park:* 13 km S; see Melrose. *Winninowie Conservation Park:* coastal park of creeks and samphire flats, home to abundant birdlife; 26 km SW. *Hammond:* historic ghost town; 26 km NE. *Bruce:* historic railway town featuring 1880s architecture; 35 km N. *Carrieton:* historic buildings and Yanyarrie Whim Well in town. A rodeo is held here each Dec. 56 km NE. See Aboriginal carvings a further 9 km along Belton Rd.
ⓘ Wilmington General Store, Main North Rd; (08) 8667 5155

Wilpena
Pop. 35

Map ref. 553 E8, 557 K7

Wilpena consists of a resort and caravan/camping park near the entrance to Wilpena Pound. It services visitors to the surrounding Flinders Ranges National Park. In 1902 the Hill family, wheat farmers, built a homestead inside the pound, but abandoned it after a flood washed away the access road in 1914. The pound is a vast natural amphitheatre surrounded by peaks that change colour with the light, and is a fantastic destination for bushwalking.

IN TOWN *Wilpena Pound Resort:* the resort is partly powered by the largest solar-power system in the Southern Hemisphere (viewing area accessed by a walking trail). The visitor centre at the resort has extensive information on nearby walks, 4WD and organised tours, self-guide drives, scenic flights, bushwalking and mountain climbing.

WHAT'S ON *Wilpena Under the Stars:* black-tie dinner and dance to raise funds for the RFDS; Feb. *Tastes of the Outback:* April. *Flinders Ranges Event Program:* events run in autumn and spring, including guided walks, tours and cultural activities; details from visitor centre.

NEARBY *Flinders Ranges National Park: see feature on this page. Sacred Canyon:* Aboriginal rock carvings and paintings; 19 km E. *Rawnsley Park Station:* holiday-unit accommodation, scenic flights, horseriding and 4WD tours; inquiries (08) 8648 0030; 20 km S on Hawker Rd. *Moralana Scenic Drive:* includes Blacks Gap Lookout (also accessible by 12 km walking trail); drive starts 25 km S.
ⓘ Wilpena Pound Visitor Information Centre; (08) 8648 0048; www.wilpena pound.com.au

Woomera   Pop. 596

Map ref. 556 F6

Woomera and its testing range were established in 1947 as a site for launching British experimental rockets during the Cold War era. The town was a restricted area until 1982. The Woomera Prohibited Area remains today and is still one of the largest land-based rocket ranges in the world. Until 2003, Woomera was the site of a controversial detention centre for refugees. The detainees are now held at the Baxter Detention Centre near Port Augusta.

IN TOWN *Woomera Heritage and Visitor Information Centre:* provides a detailed history of the area through videos, exhibitions, rocket relics and photographic displays. It includes a bowling alley. Tours of the Rocket Range can be booked and depart here. Dewrang Ave. *Missile Park:* open-air defence display of rockets, aircraft and weapons; cnr Banool and Dewrang aves. *Baker Observatory:* viewing the night sky through a computer-controlled telescope; contact visitor centre for details.
ℹ Dewrang Ave; (08) 8673 7042; www.woomerasa.com.au

Wudinna   Pop. 535

Map ref. 554 C3, 556 B13

The enormous silos in Wudinna are indicative of the town's major grain industry, predominantly wheat and barley, grown here since the first pastoral lease was granted in 1861. Wudinna was proclaimed a town in 1916 and has since grown as a service centre to Eyre Peninsula. A little travelling in the surrounding countryside will reveal unusually shaped granite outcrops – the area is known as granite country.

IN TOWN *Gawler Ranges Cultural Centre:* dedicated to the exhibition of artwork with a ranges theme; Ballantyne St.

NEARBY Gawler Ranges National Park This rugged national park offers fantastic gorge and rocky-outcrop scenery, spectacular when the spring wildflowers are in bloom. There are no marked trails, but highlights of drive tours include the Organ Pipes, a large and unique formation of volcanic rhyolite, the Kyolay Mirica Falls and Yandina Gorge. Some areas are accessible by 2WD, but 4WD is generally recommended. Roads may be impassable after rain. Guided tours into the ranges are offered by two operators: Gawler Ranges Wilderness Safaris (ph 1800 243 343) and Xplore Eyre (ph (08) 8680 5220). 40 km N. *Wudinna Granite Trail:* signposted 25 km tourist drive to all major rock formations in the area. *Mount Polda Rock Recreation Reserve:* walking trail for excellent birdwatching with views from the top of Polda Rock; 7 km NE.

Mount Wudinna Recreation Reserve: the mountain is thought to be the second largest granite outcrop in the Southern Hemisphere. At its base is a picnic area, a 30 min return interpretive walking trail, and original stone walls used as water catchments. Enjoy scenic views at the mountain's summit. 10 km NE. On the road to the reserve look out for Turtle Rock. *Ucontitchie Hill:* isolated and unique granite formations, similar to Kangaroo Island's Remarkable Rocks; 32 km S. *Minnipa:* home to the Agricultural Centre, which provides invaluable research into sustainable dryland farming. Tours run at 10am Tues and Thurs. Nearby are granite formations of geological significance, including Yarwondutta Rock (2 km N), Tcharkulda Rock (4 km E) and the wave-like formation of Pildappa Rock (15 km N). 37 km NW. *Koongawa:* memorial to explorer John Charles Darke; 50 km E.
ℹ 44 Eyre Hwy; (08) 8680 2969; www.tep.com.au

Yankalilla   Pop. 440

Map ref. 549 D7, 552 B3, 555 K11

Since the first land grant in 1842, Yankalilla has been the centre of a thriving farming industry. It is a growing settlement just inland from the west coast of the Fleurieu Peninsula, but it still retains its old country flavour. It has even adopted the slogan 'Yankalilla Bay – you'll love what we haven't done to the place'. In recent times it has seen an influx of visitors keen to see the apparition at Our Lady of Yankalilla Shrine. The Blessed Virgin Mary was first sighted here in 1996.

IN TOWN *Yankalilla District Historical Museum:* local history display with interpretive trail; Main South Rd; open 1pm–4pm Sun. *Anglican Church:* historic and known for apparition of Mary; Main St.

WHAT'S ON *Twilight Rodeo:* Jan.

NEARBY Deep Creek Conservation Park Take one of the many walks offered in this park and each turn will reveal a new and exciting sight: rugged coastal cliffs, tranquil creeks, majestic forests and scenic waterfalls. The extensive walking network offers easy short walks to more challenging long-distance hikes. Add them together for a longer, overnight trek. Keep an eye out for the western grey kangaroos at dusk on the Aaron Creek Hiking Trail or – for the fishing enthusiast – drop a line at Blowhole Creek and Boat Harbour beaches. Permits are required in the park (self-registration). 26 km SW. *Normanville:* a seaside town with beach and heritage-listed sand dunes. Shipwrecks off the coast are popular with divers. 3 km W. *Myponga Conservation Park:* popular bushwalking and birdwatching park; 9 km NE.

Myponga: a historic town with fantastic views from the Myponga Reservoir; 14 km NE. *Second Valley:* a peaceful picnic spot with a jetty for fishing; 17 km SW. *Rapid Bay:* this seaside town offers excellent fishing and diving opportunities. Sightings of the endangered leafy sea dragon in the bay make diving a must for any enthusiast. 27 km SW. *Talisker Conservation Park:* an interpretive trail explains the old silver-mine workings in the park; 30 km SW. *Cape Jervis:* breathtaking sea and coastal views on entering town. Vehicular ferries to Kangaroo Island depart from here, and it is also the starting point of the 1200 km Heysen Trail (bushwalking trail) to the Flinders Ranges. Morgan's and Fishery beaches nearby have good fishing. 35 km S.
ℹ 104 Main South Rd; (08) 8558 2999; www.yankalillabay.com

Yorketown   Pop. 645

Map ref. 554 I9

Yorketown is a small rural community at the southern end of Yorke Peninsula. The surrounding landscape is dotted with many inland salt lakes, some of which are still mined. In the late 1840s farmers were eager to take up land here as it was prime crop-producing land. The town was settled in 1872 and has remained an important service centre on the peninsula since.

NEARBY Innes National Park In summer, soak up the sun at one of the park's beaches or bays with excellent (but challenging) surf breaks at Chinamans Reef, Pondalowie Bay and West Cape. In winter, keep an eye out at Stenhouse Bay and Cape Spencer for the migrating southern right whales off the coast. Diving is a popular activity in the park, especially near The Gap, an eroded gap in a 60 m high cliff. Other activities include beach and jetty fishing, and walking. Both coastal and inland tracks are available. Accommodation is something special in this park – enjoy fabulous coastal camping in the mallee scrub or stay at the heritage lodge in the old mining township of Inneston. The annual Yorke Surfing Classic is held here each Oct. 81 km SW. *Bublacowie Military Museum:* educates the young about their ancestors' sacrifices through personal stories, memorabilia and documents, and is also a craft centre; 25 km N; closed Mon. *Corny Point:* coastal town featuring a lighthouse and lookout, and fishing and camping opportunities; 69 km NW. *Daly Head:* great surfing spot with nearby blowhole; 75 km W. *Marion Bay:* popular with surfers and visitors to nearby Innes National Park; 79 km SW.
ℹ Council offices, 15 Edithburgh Rd; (08) 8852 0200; www.yorkepeninsula.com.au

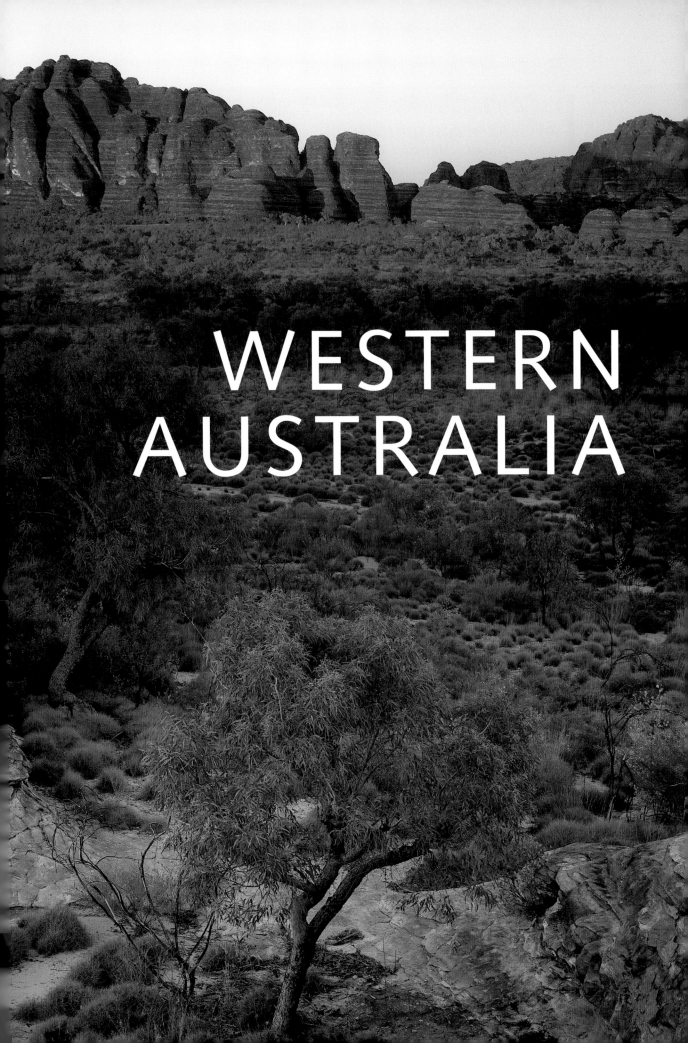

WESTERN AUSTRALIA

f there is one thing that defines Western Australia, it is its size. Spanning an area of 2.5 million square kilometres, it covers one-third of the Australian continent. In dramatic contrast to its size is its population of just 1.9 million, one-tenth of Australia's total population. Over 72 percent of Western Australians live in or around the capital city of Perth.

After driving for hours along empty highways, you'll get a true feeling for the state's vastness.

Within this great state are incredibly diverse landscapes – an ancient terrain of rugged ranges and dramatic gorges to the north, towering forests to the south, arid deserts to the east and 12 889 kilometres of the world's most pristine coastline to the west. To match the huge variety in landscape is a huge variety in climate – from the tropical humidity of the north and the dryness of the desert to the temperate Mediterranean-style climate of the South-West.

Travelling in Western Australia requires time and, in remote regions, care. After driving for hours along empty highways, you'll get a true feeling for the state's vastness. But you will be amply rewarded when you reach your destination. Western Australia boasts some of the world's most precious natural features, including the 350 million-year-old Bungle Bungle Range, the limestone sentinels of the Pinnacles Desert, and the majestic karri forests of the South-West. There is the extraordinary

marine life of Ningaloo Reef, the friendly dolphins of Monkey Mia, and Rottnest Island's famous quokkas. Stunning wildflowers carpet the countryside after spring rains. Up to 12 500 species can be found within the state's borders; some 75 percent are found nowhere else in the world.

But it is not only Western Australia's natural beauty that is worth seeing. The Aboriginal people who first inhabited the land – between 40 000 and 60 000 years ago – left a legacy of some of the most distinctive rock art in Australia. Albany, the site of the state's first European settlement in 1826, boasts well-preserved heritage buildings that give you an insight into Western Australia's historic past.

Kununurra

Derby   Purnululu
          National Park
Broome

Fitzroy   Halls
Crossing   Creek

Port Hedland

Ningaloo Reef

Newman

Karijini
National Park

Gibson Desert

Carnarvon

Meekatharra

Laverton

Geraldton

90 MILE
STRAIGHT

Kalgoorlie-Boulder

Eucla

Perth

Norseman

Bunbury

Esperance

Albany

PREVIOUS PAGES Sunrise at the Bungle Bungles, Purnululu National Park

Geographe Bay, Dunsborough

Gracious 19th-century buildings in the capital city of Perth and its nearby port of Fremantle hark back to the days of the Swan River Colony, established in 1829 at the mouth of the Swan River by Captain James Stirling.

The great gold discoveries around Coolgardie and Kalgoorlie in the 1890s attracted the immigrants and capital that transformed Western Australia from a remote pastoral backwater into one of the world's great producers of gold, iron ore, nickel, diamonds, mineral sands and natural gas. In addition, Western Australia has a thriving primary industry, involved principally with wheat, sheep, beef and, controversially, hardwood from the southern forests. Tourism is the latest industry to develop as a result of the state's natural resources, and each year increasing numbers of visitors experience the unspoiled beauty and compelling vastness of this ancient landscape.

FACT FILE

Population 1 952 300
Total land area 2 529 875 sq km
People per square kilometre 0.7
Sheep and cattle per square kilometre 9.8
Nearest interstate city Adelaide, 2700 km east
Length of coastline 12 889 km
Number of islands 3747
Longest river Gascoyne River (760 km)
Largest constructed reservoir Lake Argyle (storage volume 10 760 million cubic metres)
Highest mountain Mt Meharry (1253 m), Karijini National Park
Highest waterfall King George Falls (80 m), northern Kimberley
Highest town Tom Price (747 m)
Hottest place Marble Bar (160 days a year over 37.5°C)
Coldest place Bridgetown (33 days a year begin at below 2°C)
Most remote town Warburton
Strangest place name Walkaway
Most famous person Rolf Harris
Quirkiest festival Milk Carton Regatta, Hillarys Boat Harbour
Number of wildflowers 12 500 species
Most challenging road Gibb River Road, the Kimberley
Best beach Cable Beach, Broome
Most identifiable food Pavlova (created at Perth's Esplanade Hotel)
Local beer Swan Lager

TIMELINE

1616
Dirk Hartog makes a brief landing at Shark Bay.

1826
Major Lockyer and party establish a military outpost at King George Sound (present-day Albany).

1829
Captain Fremantle raises the British flag at the head of the Swan River. Captain Stirling arrives with settlers and establishes the Swan River Colony.

1850–68
Convicts are sent from Britain to alleviate labour shortages.

1885–93
Gold is discovered at Halls Creek. Major gold strikes are made at Coolgardie and nearby Kalgoorlie.

1933
Western Australians vote 2:1 to secede from the Commonwealth. A House of Commons ruling disallows it.

1941
HMAS Sydney sinks off the WA coast, with entire crew of 645 lost, after battle with German raider Kormoran.

1942
Broome, Wyndham, Derby and Onslow are bombed by the Japanese.

1948
First shipment of iron ore leaves Yampi Sound.

1961
The Ord Irrigation Scheme is established in the Kimberley.

1987
Fremantle hosts the America's Cup yacht race.

PERTH

PERTH IS . . .

Views across the city from Kings Park

Swimming at any of Perth's beaches

Sipping a coffee on the 'cappucino strip' of South Terrace, Fremantle

A ferry trip down the Swan River

Seeing black swans at Lake Monger

A cricket match at the WACA

A picnic on the Matilda Bay foreshore

A visit to the Western Australian Museum

Eating out in Northbridge

Browsing the eclectic offerings at the Fremantle Markets

A footy match at Subiaco Oval

Touring the forbidding Fremantle Prison

Visitor information

Western Australian Visitor Centre
Albert Facey House
Cnr Forrest Pl & Wellington St, Perth
(08) 9483 1111 or 1300 361 351
www.westernaustralia.net

Indiana Tea House, Cottesloe Beach

Perth is set on the banks of the magnificent Swan River, which widens to lake-size near the city centre. Overlooking the city's modern skyline of concrete-and-glass skyscrapers is the natural bushland and botanic garden of Kings Park. To the west is the Indian Ocean, with its endless white-sand beaches; to the east is the Darling Range, with its tranquil forest.

Claimed to be the sunniest state capital in Australia, Perth has a Mediterranean climate: hot and dry in summer, cool and wet in winter. This climate, and the city's proximity to both river and ocean, fosters a relaxed lifestyle. One of Perth's great attributes is that these water frontages are public land, accessible to everyone. Picnicking is a popular pastime, while cafes and bars spill their tables and chairs out onto pavements to make the most of the glorious weather.

Yet for all Perth's natural beauty, it is the river that defines the city. North of the river is Kings Park and the old-money riverside suburbs with their grand homes; further on are the beaches and the newer northern beach suburbs stretching up the coast. The zoo, the casino, the riverside suburbs of modern mansions and a suburban heartland of 1960s and 70s homes lie south of the river. At the mouth of the Swan is the historic port city of Fremantle, with its rich maritime history, creative community and street-cafe culture. Upstream from Perth – where the river rapidly dwindles to a meandering waterway – is the Swan Valley, the state's oldest wine district.

Perth is the most isolated capital city in the world, and is closer to Singapore than it is to Sydney. Its nearest neighbour, Adelaide, is 2700 kilometres away by road. Yet it is exactly this isolation that has allowed Perth to retain a feeling of space and a relaxed charm.

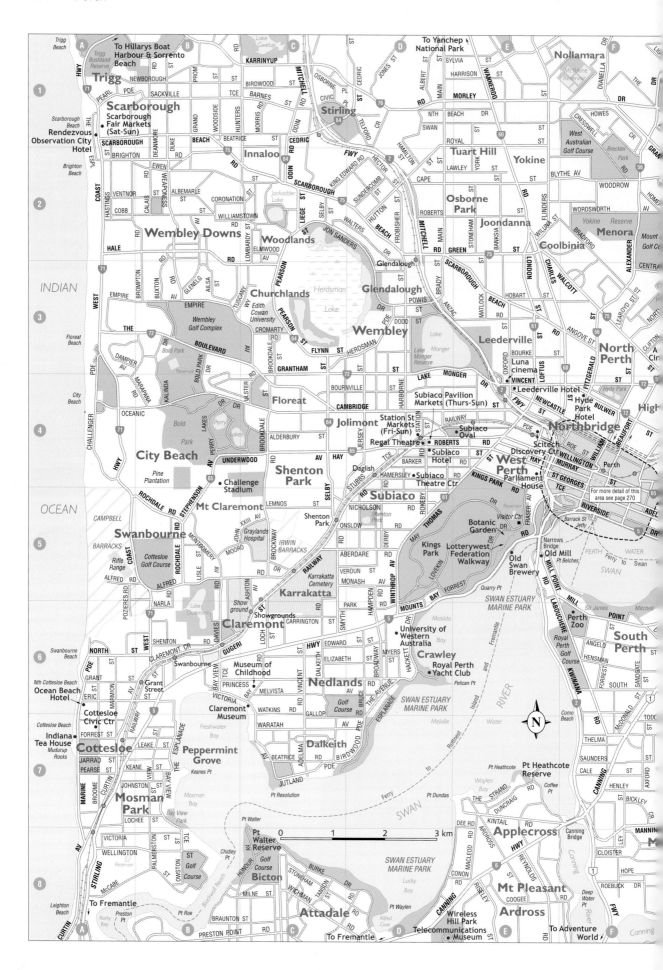

Central Perth

Perth's city centre is a compact mix of towering skyscrapers and elegant colonial buildings. It is bordered to the south and east by the Swan River, with stretches of grassy parkland fringing the riverbank. East Perth is where you'll find the Western Australian Cricket Association oval, known colloquially as the WACA, where cricket matches entertain the crowds over the summer months. Northbridge, which lies north of the city centre across the train line, is Perth's centre for the arts and the heart of the city's cafe culture.

CITY CENTRE

Perth's central business district harbours the city's large pedestrian-only shopping precinct, made up of a series of malls and arcades. This is connected northwards to the Perth train station by an overhead walkway across Wellington Street. To the west, the ultra-hip King Street is renowned for its gourmet cafes, galleries and fashion houses. St Georges Terrace, the main commercial street, has high-rise buildings interspersed with remnants of Perth's early British heritage and lies to the south. Just beyond it is the main bus depot, and at the river end of Barrack Street is the city's jetty.

Malls, arcades and a touch of old England

Perth's central shopping precinct is in the blocks bounded by St Georges Terrace and William, Wellington and Barrack streets. These three main shopping blocks encompass the vehicle-free zones of **Hay Street Mall**, **Murray Street Mall** and **Forrest Place**. Between them, the two malls contain a swag of brand-name fashion outlets, bookstores and homeware shops. The big department stores of Myer and David Jones both have entrances on Murray Street Mall, and the western side of Forrest Place is home to the GPO. A series of arcades and underground walkways run from Murray Street Mall through to Hay Street Mall and on to St Georges Terrace, making it possible to shop in the city without ever crossing a street. **London Court**, an arcade with the appearance of a quaint Elizabethan street, runs from Hay Street Mall to St Georges Terrace, and is Perth's only open-air arcade. At the mall end, knights joust above a replica of Big Ben every 15 minutes, while St George and the Dragon do battle above the clock at the St Georges Terrace end.

King Street

This historic precinct of commercial buildings between Hay and Wellington streets dates from the 1890s gold rush. While the street has been restored to its turn-of-the-century character, its commercial interests are entirely modern: designer fashion houses, specialist bookstores, art galleries and gourmet cafes, such as the ever-popular **No 44 King Street**, with its homemade bread and extensive wine list.

St Georges Terrace

The city's main commercial street is lined with modern office towers that overshadow a number of historic buildings. At the western end of the

Getting around

The city is compact and easy to explore. A free bus service known as the CAT (Central Area Transit) System operates regular services, every 5–10 minutes, around central Perth. The blue CAT runs in a north-south loop, the red CAT operates in an east-west loop, and the yellow CAT travels to the city centre from East Perth. (Note that a CAT bus also services Fremantle.) You can also travel free on Transperth buses or trains within the Free Transit Zone in the city centre, but only on trips that start and finish within the zone.

Trains run from the city out to the northern suburbs and down to Fremantle. Ferries and cruise boats depart regularly from Barrack Street Jetty to various destinations, including Fremantle, South Perth, Rottnest Island and the Swan Valley wine region. (Transperth runs the ferry to South Perth, while private operators travel further afield.) Perth, with its largely flat landscape, is also excellent for cycling; maps of the city's 700-kilometre bike network are available from the Department for Planning and Infrastructure (441 Murray Street) and at bike shops.

Public transport Transperth (bus, ferry and train) 13 6213

Airport shuttle bus Airport–city shuttle (08) 9475 2900

Motoring organisation RAC of WA (08) 9421 4444 or 13 1703

Car rental Avis 13 6333; Budget 13 2727; Hertz 13 3039; Thrifty 13 6139

Taxis Black and White Taxis 13 1008; Swan Taxis 13 1330

Swan River ferries and cruises Captain Cook Cruises (08) 9325 3341; Boat Torque Cruises (08) 9421 5888; Oceanic Cruises (08) 9325 1191

Bicycle hire About Bike Hire, (08) 9221 2665

See also Getting to Fremantle, p. 277

Climate

Perth is Australia's sunniest capital, with an annual average of eight hours of sunshine per day. All this sunshine gives Perth a Mediterranean climate of hot, dry summers and mild, wet winters. The average maximum temperature in summer is 31˚C; however, heat waves of temperatures in the high 30s and low 40s are not unusual. Fortunately, an afternoon sea breeze affectionately known as 'the Fremantle Doctor' eases the heat of summer.

	J	F	M	A	M	J	J	A	S	O	N	D
Max ˚C	30	31	29	25	21	19	18	18	20	22	25	27
Min ˚C	18	19	17	14	12	10	9	9	10	12	14	17
Rain mm	8	12	19	45	123	184	173	136	80	54	21	14
Raindays	3	3	4	8	14	17	18	17	14	11	6	4

WESTERN AUSTRALIA

Top events

Hopman Cup *Prestigious international tennis event. January.*

Perth Cup *Western Australia's premier horseracing event. January.*

Australia Day Skyworks *A day-long party of events, culminating in a spectacular fireworks display. January.*

Perth International Arts Festival *Music, theatre, opera, dance, visual arts and film. February.*

Kings Park Wildflower Festival *Australia's premier native plant and wildflower exhibition. September–October.*

Perth Royal Show *Showcases the state's primary and secondary resources. October.*

Telstra Rally Australia *Four days of action-packed, world-class motor sport. November.*

See also Top events in Fremantle, p. 276

terrace is the **Barracks Archway**, the only remains of the Pensioners' Barracks, a structure that originally had two wings and 120 rooms. This building housed the retired British soldiers who guarded convicts in the mid-1800s. The **Central Government Building** on the corner of Barrack Street marks the spot where Perth was founded with a tree-felling ceremony in 1829. Around 50 years later, convicts and hired labour commenced work on the building that stands there today. At one stage it housed the GPO, and a plaque on the building's east corner marks the point from which all distances in the state are measured. Other historic buildings along the terrace include the Cloisters, the Old Perth Boys' School, the Deanery, St George's Cathedral, Government House and the Old Court House (*see Grand old buildings, on facing page*).

City gardens

Two delightful city gardens are located in the block bounded by St Georges Terrace, Riverside Drive, Barrack Street and Victoria Avenue. **Stirling Gardens** offer ornamental trees, well-kept lawns and lots of shady spots. Along the footpath near St Georges Terrace there are large statues of kangaroos – a great photo opportunity. Within the gardens is the oldest public building in Perth, now the Francis Burt Law Museum (*see Museums, p. 272*), and an ore obelisk, a memorial acknowledging the state's role as one of the world's foremost producers of minerals. The **Supreme Court Gardens**, further towards Riverside Drive, are a popular location for concerts on warm summer evenings, including the annual Carols by Candlelight.

Bells and a jetty

Barrack Square, at the water's edge south of the city, is where you'll find the **Swan Bells** and the **Barrack Street Jetty**. This jetty is the departure point for ferry services to Fremantle, South Perth, Rottnest Island and Carnac Island, along with various leisure cruises on the Swan River and to the vineyards of the Swan Valley.

The Swan Bells consist of 18 'change-ringing' bells, which form the largest set in the world. Twelve of the bells, given to the state in 1988 by the British government, come from London's St Martin-in-the-Fields church. The bell tower – which cost $6 million to build amid great controversy – offers galleries from which you can view the bellringers and the bells in action. A viewing platform at the top of the bell tower provides excellent views of the river and city. *Barrack Sq, intersection of Barrack St & Riverside Dr; open daily; admission fee applies.*

NORTHBRIDGE

Northbridge, across the train line and just north of the city, is the centre for culture, good food and nightlife. This inner-city suburb is connected to the city centre via a walkway that crosses Perth Railway Station and leads directly to the Perth Cultural Centre. This complex, bounded by Roe, Francis, Beaufort and William streets, includes the state museum, art gallery, state library, and Perth's institute of contemporary arts. **William Street** and the streets further west are packed with restaurants and bars that offer great eating, drinking and nightclubbing (*see Entertainment, p. 274*). Many of the restaurants open out onto the streets to take advantage of the mild Perth evenings.

Art Gallery of Western Australia

The state's principal public art gallery, founded in 1895, houses collections of Australian and international paintings, sculpture, prints, craft and decorative arts. The gallery's collection of Aboriginal art is one of the finest in Australia. *Perth Cultural Centre, James St Mall; open daily; general admission free; free guided tours available.*

Western Australian Museum

At this comprehensive museum you can see a 25-metre whale skeleton, the 11-ton Mundrabilla meteorite, and 'Megamouth', one of the largest species of shark. There are exhibitions concerning the state's Aboriginal people; the origins of the universe; and dinosaur, bird, butterfly, mammal and marine galleries. The interactive Discovery Centre is great for children. Within the museum complex is the **Old Gaol**, built in 1856

[Map of Perth and Northbridge showing streets and landmarks including: Aberdeen St, John St, Fitzgerald St, Shenton St, Parker St, Francis St, Northbridge, Russell Square, Elephant & Wheelbarrow, Cinema Paradiso, Mustang Bar, Rosie O'Grady's Pub, The Paramount Nightclub, Brass Monkey Pub & Brasserie, Wellington St, Murray St, Perth Entertainment Centre, Perth Institute of Contemporary Arts, Australian Woodcraft Galleries, Greenhill Galleries, Creative Native, His Majesty's Theatre, Barracks Archway, QV1 Building, The Cloisters, Old Perth Boys' School, Central Park Building, London Court, Transperth Busport, Alexander Library, Perth Cultural Centre, WA Museum, Galleria Art & Craft Markets (Sat-Sun), Art Gallery of WA, Perth Police Station, Forrest Place, GPO, Myer, David Jones, Perth Town Hall, Transperth Plaza Arcade, Gov Stirling Statue, St George's Cathedral, Central Government Building, Playhouse Theatre, Fire Safety Education Ctr & Museum, Former Gov't Printer's Office, Royal Perth Hospital, Kirkman House, McIver, Wittenoom St, Wellington Square, St Mary's Cathedral, Perth Mint, Queens Gardens & the WACA, Perth Concert Hall, Government House, Old Court House, Stirling Gardens, Supreme Court Gardens, The Esplanade Reserve, Barrack St, Swan Bells, Barrack Street Jetty, Ferry Terminal, Riverside Dr, Langley Park, To Kings Park, Mitchell Fwy, Mounts Bay Rd, WATER, PERTH. Scale: 0, 0.25, 0.5, 0.75, 1 km. Compass pointing N]

Inside the Swan Bells tower

and used as the Swan River Colony's gaol for Colonial prisoners until 1888. *Perth Cultural Centre, James St Mall; open daily; general admission free.*

Perth Institute of Contemporary Arts

Commonly referred to by its acronym, PICA, the Perth Institute of Contemporary Arts is where you can sample the latest in visual and performance art. There is an ever-changing program of exhibitions. *Perth Cultural Centre, James St Mall; 11am–6pm Tues–Sun; general admission free.*

EAST PERTH

This is the WACA end of town, with Gloucester Park Raceway nearby. Once the dead end of town – except when night matches or race meets lit up the night sky – East Perth is now an enclave of offices and hip inner-city apartments. There are two historically important sites in this precinct, the Perth Mint and Queens Gardens.

Perth Mint

The mint's imposing façade was built in 1899 from Rottnest Island limestone, and is one of the best examples of Perth's gold-boom architecture. Here at Australia's oldest operating mint you can see the world's largest collection of natural gold specimens, including the 'Golden Beauty', a 11.5 kg nugget. Visitors can hold a 400-ounce gold bar, mint their own coins and watch gold being poured. *310 Hay St (cnr Hill St); 9am–4pm weekdays, 9am–1pm weekends; admission fee applies.*

Queens Gardens

The serene, English-style Queens Gardens feature a tranquil water garden complete with a replica of the famous Peter Pan statue that graces London's Kensington Gardens. These gardens were originally clay pits, where bricks were kilned for use in early colonial buildings such as the Perth Town Hall. *Cnr Hay & Plain sts.*

Across Hale Street from Queens Gardens is the **WACA**. True lovers of the sport should visit the WACA's cricket museum (*see Museums, p. 272*).

Tranby House

Just beyond East Perth in the suburb of Maylands is historic Tranby House. Built on the Swan River in 1839, it is one of the oldest and finest colonial houses in Western Australia. It has been beautifully restored by the National Trust. *Johnson Rd, Maylands; Aug–June (closed July); 10am–4pm Tues–Sun; admission fee applies.*

Kings Park and foreshore

Just minutes from the city centre, Kings Park is one of Perth's major attractions. Below Kings Park, Mounts Bay Road winds its way along the river's edge to the suburb of Crawley, passing the **Old Swan Brewery** site, now a riverside complex of up-market offices, apartments and restaurants. The distinctive clock tower of the University of Western Australia's Winthrop Hall is an easily spotted landmark. Across Matilda Bay Road from the university is the grassy **Matilda Bay** shoreline, with shady spots and views back up the river towards the city.

Kings Park and Botanic Garden 268 E5

The first stop for any visitor to Perth has to be Kings Park. Standing on top of Mount Eliza, you enjoy sweeping views of the city and the Swan River, with the

Shopping

London Court, City *Mock-Tudor arcade with souvenir, jewellery and antique stores. See map on p. 270*

Hay Street Mall, Murray Street Mall and Forrest Place, City *The CBD's main shopping precinct with brand-name fashion outlets and major department stores Myer and David Jones. See map on p. 270*

King Street, City *High fashion, galleries and cafes with style. See map on p. 270*

Rokeby Road, Subiaco *Funky local designers sit alongside more established labels. 268 D4*

Bay View Terrace, Claremont *Perth's up-market fashion hotspot. 268 B6*

Napoleon Street, Cottesloe *Cafes, boutiques and designer homewares. 268 A7*

Grand old buildings

Government House *Gothic arches and turrets reminiscent of the Tower of London. St Georges Tce (opposite Pier St), City.*

His Majesty's Theatre *'The Maj', built in 1904, features an opulent Edwardian exterior. Free foyer tours 10am–4pm Mon–Fri. 825 Hay St, City.*

Kirkman House *In front of this gracious edifice is an immense Moreton Bay fig tree, planted in the 1890s and now classified by the National Trust. 10 Murray St, City.*

Old Court House *Perth's oldest surviving building (1836), now home to the Francis Burt Law Museum. Cnr St Georges Tce & Barrack St, City.*

Old Perth Boys' School *Perth's first purpose-built school was made from sandstone ferried up the Swan River by convict labour. 139 St Georges Tce, City.*

Perth Town Hall *Built by convict labour (1867–70) in the style of an English Jacobean market hall. Cnr Hay & Barrack sts, City.*

St George's Cathedral *This 1879 Anglican church features an impressive jarrah ceiling. 38 St Georges Tce, City.*

St Mary's Cathedral *Grand Gothic-style cathedral, one end of which was built in 1865. Victoria Sq, City.*

The Cloisters *Check out the decorative brickwork of this 1858 building, originally a boys' school. The old banyan tree adjoining it is something special too. 200 St Georges Tce, City.*

See also Fremantle's grand old buildings, p. 278

WESTERN AUSTRALIA

Eating out

King Street, City *Up-market cafe-style fare.*
See map on p.270

Northbridge *International cuisine to suit all*
tastes and budgets. See map on p. 270

Oxford Street, Leederville *An eclectic collection*
of eateries. 268 E4

Rokeby Road, Subiaco *Street cafes, stylish pubs*
and fine restaurants. 268 D4

Marine Parade, Cottesloe *Beachside cafes with*
glorious views. 268 A7

South Perth Esplanade, South Perth *For fine*
dining with views across the river to the city.
268 F5

See also Eating out in Fremantle, p. 278

Museums

Fire Safety Education Centre and Museum *This*
1900 limestone building houses exhibitions on
the history of the Perth fire brigade, including
fire rescue and old Big Red engines. Cnr Murray
& Irwin sts; 10am–12pm, 1pm–3pm Mon–Fri;
admission free.

Francis Burt Law Museum *The history of the*
state's legal system is housed in the Old Court
House. Stirling Gardens, cnr St Georges Tce &
Barrack St; 10am–2.30pm Mon–Wed & Fri;
admission free.

Museum of Performing Arts *Entertainment*
history brought to life through exhibitions
of costumes and memorabilia taken from
backstage archives. His Majesty's Theatre,
825 Hay St; 10am–4pm Mon–Fri; admission
by gold coin donation.

WACA Museum *Offers cricket memorabilia*
for fans of the sport. Gate 2, Nelson Cres,
East Perth; 10am–3pm Mon–Fri; tours of
ground and museum 10am & 1pm Tues–Thurs;
admission fee applies.

Army Museum of Western Australia *Houses*
army memorabilia dating from colonial times
to WWII. Artillery Barracks, Burt St, Fremantle;
11am–3pm Wed, 12.30pm–4.30pm Sat & Sun;
admission fee applies.

World of Energy *Offers fascinating interactive*
displays tracing the development of gas and
electricity. 12 Parry St, Fremantle; 9am–5pm
Mon–Fri; admission fee applies.

See also Perth Mint, p. 271, and Western
Australian Museum, p. 270.

Lotterywest Federation Walkway, Kings Park

Darling Range in the distance. Within this huge 400-hectare natural bushland reserve there are landscaped gardens and walkways, lakes, playgrounds, a restaurant and cafes.

Fraser Avenue, the main entrance road into the park, is lined with towering lemon-scented gums, honouring those who perished in war. The clock tower and bronze portrait bust at this entrance is a memorial to Edith Cowan, the first woman elected to an Australian parliament. A tireless advocate for women's rights and children's welfare, she now lends her name to one of Perth's universities.

Opened in 2003, the Lotterywest Federation Walkway is a combination of on-ground pathways, elevated walkway and spectacular steel-and-glass bridge extending in all 620 metres through the gardens. Spread over 17 hectares and planted with more than 1700 native species, the gardens are well worth a visit. In spring, the annual Kings Park Wildflower Festival showcases the best of the state's wildflowers, attracting over 50 000 visitors from around the world. During summer, the park is a favourite venue for live outdoor entertainment and moonlight movies. The park also has a number of bike tracks – bikes can be rented from the western side of the main carpark. *Fraser Ave; open daily; free guided walks from the visitor centre at 10am and 2pm daily.*

University of Western Australia
268 D6

With its distinctive Mediterranean-style architecture and landscaped gardens, the University of Western Australia is renowned as one of Australia's most beautiful campuses. Here you'll find

Winthrop Hall, with its majestic clock tower and reflection pond, and the **Sunken Garden**, backdrop for many a wedding photo. Also within the university grounds is the **Berndt Museum of Anthropology**, which houses one of Australia's finest collections of traditional and contemporary Australian Aboriginal art and artefacts. *Social Sciences Building, off Hackett Dr, Crawley; 2pm–4.30pm Mon & Wed, 10am–2pm Fri; admission free.*

The **Lawrence Wilson Art Gallery**, home to the university's extensive collection of Australian art, includes works by Sidney Nolan, Arthur Boyd, Fred Williams and Rupert Bunny. *35 Stirling Hwy, Crawley; 11am–5pm Tues–Fri, 12pm–5pm Sun; admission free.*

Foreshore suburbs 268 C6
Extending along the river foreshore from Matilda Bay towards the ocean is a series of exclusive waterfront suburbs with charming village-style shopping areas, fashionable galleries and foreshore restaurants. **Nedlands** is the suburb closest to the University of Western Australia; Steve's Nedlands Park Hotel, on the river, is the local student hang-out. **Dalkeith**'s Jutland Parade takes you to Point Resolution, with magnificent views of the river to the south and west. Follow the walking paths down the hillside to White Beach on the foreshore, a popular recreational spot.

Claremont is home to Perth's most up-market shopping area, centred around Bay View Terrace. Towards the river, in the Edith Cowan University's Claremont campus, is the **Museum of Childhood**. With displays of toys, dolls and games, this collection of childhood memorabilia is open 10am–4pm Mon–Fri; admission fee applies. The **Claremont Museum**, on

Victoria Avenue, was built in 1862 by convicts and the Pensioner Guards as the Freshwater Bay School. It now offers an interesting social history display 12pm–4pm Mon–Fri; admission fee applies. Nearby is a children's playground and picnic area.

Peppermint Grove boasts some of Perth's grandest homes. A drive along The Esplanade takes you past grass-backed riverside beaches, natural bushland and shady picnic areas. Follow the road around to Bay View Park – another great place for picnicking – in Mosman Park, and up the hill for sweeping views of Mosman Bay, the Swan River and Perth city skyline.

Inner west

Overlooking the city to its west is Parliament House. It marks the city end of West Perth, a business district that centres around the shops and eating establishments of **Hay Street**. Beyond West Perth is the popular shopping, cafe and market precinct of **Subiaco**, with its village-style main street, Rokeby Road (pronounced 'Rock-a-bee'). 'Subi', as it is known to the locals, is one of Perth's oldest suburbs, and there are some fine old homes in the back streets behind Rokeby Road. The word Subiaco rings a bell for AFL supporters too, as it is the home of **Subiaco Oval**. Nearby **Lake Monger** in Leederville is the best place in Perth to see Western Australia's famous black swans.

Parliament House 268 E4
Go inside the corridors of power on a free, hour-long guided tour. *Harvest Tce, West Perth; tours at 10.30am Mon & Thurs; no booking required.*

Scitech Discovery Centre 268 E4
This interactive science and technology centre has more than 160 hands-on exhibits. Children can touch, switch, climb, crank and explore – all in the name of science. *City West, cnr Sutherland St & Railway Pde, West Perth; open daily; admission fee applies.*

Along the coast

With pristine white-sand beaches stretching northwards up the coast, swimming and surfing are a way of life in Perth. Several stunning beaches – including **Cottesloe**, **Swanbourne** (a nude bathing beach), **City**, **Floreat**, **Scarborough** and **Sorrento beaches** – are close to the city. Scattered along these beach-fronts are lovely cafes, restaurants and bars. Enjoy the sublime Perth experience of sipping a glass of Western Australian wine as you watch the sun sink into the Indian Ocean. Further north is **Hillarys Boat Harbour**, where you can swim, shop, dine out, visit one of Australia's most spectacular aquariums and whale-watch in season. Nearby is **Marmion Marine Park**, a great area for fishing, snorkelling and diving.

Cottesloe 268 A7
Cottesloe is distinguished by its towering Norfolk Island pines and the **Indiana Tea House**, a neo-colonial building of grand proportions that sits right on the beach. *99 Marine Pde.*

The Spanish-style **Cottesloe Civic Centre**, once the private mansion

Galleries

Artplace *Exclusively represents emerging local artists. 24 Church St, Perth.*

Australian Woodcraft Galleries *Sculpture, furniture and homewares made from Western Australian hardwoods. 381 Murray St, Perth.*

Creative Native *Offers a large range of original Aboriginal art and artefacts. 32 King St, Perth and also at 65 High St, Fremantle.*

Greenhill Galleries *New York-style gallery features works of leading Australian artists. 37 King Street, Perth.*

Holmes à Court Gallery *Changing display of works from Australia's finest private art collection. 11 Brown St, East Perth; 11am–6pm Tues–Sun; general admission free.*

Bannister Street Craftworks *A cooperative of artisans create, display and sell their work. 8–12 Bannister St, Fremantle.*

Indigenart *Aboriginal art on canvas, paper and bark, plus sculpture, artefacts and craft. 82 High St, Fremantle.*

Kailis Australian Pearls *Perfectly matched strands and handcrafted pieces made from exquisite cultured and seedless pearls. Cnr Marine Tce & Collie St, Fremantle.*

See also Art Gallery of Western Australia, p. 270, and Perth Institute of Contemporary Arts, p. 271

Markets

Galleria Art and Craft Markets *Handcrafted items in the grounds of the Perth Cultural Centre, Northbridge. Sat–Sun. 268 F4*

Subiaco Pavilion Markets *Art and craft stalls in restored warehouse adjacent to station. Thurs–Sun. 268 D4*

Station Street Markets, Subiaco *Eclectic array of goods and live entertainment. Fri–Sun. 268 D4*

Scarborough Fair Markets *Specialty stalls and a food hall on Scarborough Beach. Sat–Sun. 268 A1*

Canning Vale Markets *Huge undercover flea markets. 7am–2pm Sun. 566 E7*

Stock Road Markets *Lively weekend markets on the shores of Bibra Lake. Sat–Sun. 566 D8*

Wanneroo Markets, Wangara *Variety of stalls and a food hall. Sat–Sun. 566 D4*

See also Fremantle Markets, p. 276

WESTERN AUSTRALIA

The view to Perth from Matilda Bay

Entertainment

Cinema
The major cinemas can be found in the city centre, at the Hoyts complexes of Cinema City in Hay Street, and Cinecentre in Murray Street. For arthouse films, try Cinema Paradiso in Northbridge, the Luna in Leederville, and the Astor in Mount Lawley. In Fremantle, the major cinema complex is Queensgate Cinemas on William Street; for arthouse films, check out the Luna on SX (Essex Street) and the FTI (Film and Television Institute) Cinema on Adelaide Street. Programs and session times, including those for the open-air cinemas over summer, are listed daily in the West Australian.

Live music
Northbridge, Leederville and Subiaco are the places to go for live music, as a healthy pub scene supports local musicians. In Northbridge popular venues include the Brass Monkey Pub & Brasserie, the Mustang Bar, the Paramount, the Elephant and Wheelbarrow, and Rosie O'Grady's. The Leederville Hotel on Oxford Street has a legendary Sunday afternoon session; the Ocean Beach Hotel in Cottesloe (known locally as the 'OBH') adds sunset views from the bar. In Fremantle, the premier live music venues are the Fly by Night club on Parry Street, Kulcha on South Terrace and Mojos in North Freo. Pick up one of the free street publications, Xpress or Hype, for gig guides. Jazz venues include the Hyde Park Hotel in Bulwer Street, North Perth, and the Fremantle Hotel in High Street; aficionados should phone the recorded information Jazzline on 9357 2807 or Jazzwa, the Jazz Coordination Association of WA, on 9243 0401.

Classical music and performing arts
His Majesty's Theatre, Australia's only remaining Edwardian theatre, is Perth's premier venue for high-end theatre, opera and ballet. The Regal Theatre in Subiaco often has touring productions from interstate or overseas. Local productions can be seen at The Playhouse in Pier Street and the Subiaco Theatre Centre, while Fremantle is home to the Deckchair Theatre in High Street and Spare Parts Puppet Theatre in Short Street. The Perth Concert Hall in St Georges Terrace and the Perth Entertainment Centre off Wellington Street are venues for concerts by local and international performers. The Burswood Casino in Burswood hosts international acts and popular musicals. There are free concerts under the stars in the Supreme Court and Queens Gardens, and in Kings Park during the Perth International Festival. Check out the entertainment section of the West Australian for details.

of flamboyant millionaire Claude de Bernales, boasts magnificent gardens with sweeping views of the Indian Ocean. *109 Broome St; open daily; admission free.*

Scarborough 268 A1
Renowned for its beachside cafe society, the beach here is a top spot for surfers and sailboarders. The five-star Rendezvous Observation City Hotel dominates the landscape, reminiscent of the Gold Coast resorts. On weekends the Scarborough Fair Markets set up stalls just opposite the hotel – shop here for antiques, collectables and curios. *Cnr Scarborough Beach Rd & West Coast Hwy.*

Hillarys Boat Harbour 566 C4
This ocean-side complex houses a marina, a world-class aquarium (*see next entry*), and Sorrento Quay, a 'village' of shops, cafes, restaurants and resort apartments. If the beautiful sandy beaches are too tame for you, try The Great Escape, a leisure park with waterslides, miniature golf and trampolines. Ferries to Rottnest Island run from Hillarys, and there are whale-watching cruises from September to November. If you visit in March, be sure to attend the Milk Carton Regatta. Competitors in this wacky boatrace build their craft entirely from milk cartons and then paddle for prize money and glory. The sand sculpture competition prior to the race produces fantastic creations.

Aquarium of Western Australia (AQWA) 566 C4
The highlight of the aquarium is an incredible 98-metre underwater tunnel aquarium, surrounded by approximately 3 million litres of the Indian Ocean. Here you'll see thousands of marine creatures including sharks, stingrays, seals, crocodiles, sea dragons and turtles. For the ultimate underwater sensation, visitors can snorkel or dive with sharks, or swim with seals. *91 Southside Dr, Hillarys Boat Harbour, Hillarys; open daily; admission fee applies.*

South of the Swan
There are a host of interesting attractions south of the Swan River, including the Burswood International Resort Casino, the Perth Zoo, and the Old Mill, one of Perth's oldest buildings. Cross the Canning River – a large tributary of the Swan River – via Canning Bridge and wind your way through the affluent suburb of Applecross to **Point Heathcote Reserve** on Duncraig Road. This hilltop playground and parkland area, which includes a local museum, art gallery, restaurant, kiosk and free barbecue facilities, is the best spot south of the Swan for sweeping views of the river and city.

Burswood International Resort Casino 269 H5
Built on an artificial island on the southern banks of the Swan River, this complex includes a casino, hotel, convention centre, tennis courts, golf course and Burswood Dome indoor stadium (the venue for the Hopman Cup). The casino's Atrium Lobby has an impressive 47-metre-high pyramid of shimmering glass containing a tropical garden and waterfall. Burswood Park, the beautifully landscaped gardens that surround the casino complex, offers paths for walkers, cyclists and joggers, a heritage trail and a children's playground. *Great Eastern Hwy, Burswood.*

Perth Zoo 268 F6
Perth Zoo, with its shady gardens, walkways and picnic areas, is just a short ferry ride across the river from the city. Visit the Australian Walkabout for a close-up look at native animals in a bush setting. Other exhibits include the Penguin Plunge, African Savannah, Reptile Encounter and Rainforest Retreat. *20 Labouchere Rd, South Perth; open daily; admission fee applies.*

Old Mill 268 E5
This picturesque whitewashed windmill at the southern end of the Narrows Bridge is one of the earliest buildings in the Swan River Colony – the foundation stone was laid by Captain James Stirling, the first governor, in 1835. The mill, the

The City of Lights

Midnight, 20 February 1962 – in Perth and neighbouring Rockingham, lights shone out from homes and buildings. Fairy lights festooned gardens and Hills hoists were draped with sheets and lit from beneath. One hundred and sixty-three miles above the city, astronaut John Glenn was making his historic orbit of the earth in the spacecraft *Friendship 7* – the first American to do so. He circled the earth three times in less than five hours, while 18 radar stations around the world kept track of the spacecraft. On the first orbit, after crossing the Indian Ocean, Glenn saw the lights of Perth and more lights to the south and east – presumably Bunbury and Kalgoorlie. 'Thank everyone for turning on the lights,' he told the radar station ground crew at Muchea, just north of Perth. The next morning, the *West Australian's* headline proudly proclaimed, 'Glenn Orbits Earth, Says Thanks to Perth'. Around the world, Perth claimed a brief moment of fame. From then on, Perth became known as the 'City of Lights'.

The beach at Hillarys Boat Harbour

adjacent miller's cottage and the recently established Education Centre review the development of flour milling in the early days of the colony. Coloured lights turn the huge Norfolk Island pine next to the Old Mill into a giant Christmas tree every December, making a festive display in the summer night sky. *Mill Point Rd, South Perth; open 10am–4pm Sun–Fri, 1pm–4pm Sat; admission fee applies.*

Wireless Hill Park 268 D8

This natural bushland area boasts a magnificent springtime wildflower display. Three lookout towers provide views of the Swan River and the city skyline. A **Telecommunications Museum** is housed in the original Wireless Station and is open on weekdays by appointment only (08) 9364 0155. *Almondbury Rd, Ardross.*

Point Walter Reserve 268 C8

This recreation area on the river is a pleasant spot for a picnic. Pick a shady peppermint tree by the water's edge to sit under and watch children paddling in the river. A kiosk, cafe and children's playground area are nearby. Stroll out on the jetty to see what's biting, and walk out on the huge sandbar for great views both up and down river. *Honour Ave, Bicton.*

Adventure World 566 D8

The state's biggest fun park offers over 30 rides and attractions, including the Tunnel of Terror, Turbo Mountain Rollercoaster, the Grand Prix Raceway, Powersurge and the Lagoon Pool, an enormous free-form swimming pool. Nearby Bibra Lake is a great place to see black swans and other waterbirds. *179 Progress Dr, Bibra Lake; 10am–5pm Sept–May.*

Fremantle

Although now linked to Perth by a sprawl of suburbs, Fremantle ('Freo' to the locals) has a feel that is quite different in both architecture and atmosphere. Today it is a major boat and fishing centre at the mouth of the Swan River, but it also has the streetscape of a 19th-century port. It is a place to stay, unwind and watch the world go by. You can shop at the famous Fremantle Markets, or rest at a cafe on South Terrace and wait for the arrival of the 'Fremantle Doctor', the refreshing afternoon wind that blows in off the Indian Ocean.

European settlers arrived at Fremantle in 1829. The settlement developed gradually, its existence dependent on whaling and fishing. The population was boosted with the arrival in 1850 of British convicts, who constructed the forbidding Fremantle Prison (now open to the public) and the imposing lunatic asylum, now the Fremantle Arts Centre and History Museum. Many heritage houses and terraces with cast-iron balconies from this period have survived.

Fremantle was at the centre of the world stage in 1987 when it hosted the America's Cup series of yacht races, following the win by *Australia II* – a Fremantle yacht – in 1983. Preparations for this huge event included the restoration of many old buildings in Fremantle, and the boost to its tourist economy has lasted to the present day.

HISTORIC CENTRE

This precinct is roughly bordered by Queen, Phillimore, Norfolk and Parry streets and Marine Terrace. The **Town Hall**, which now

Walks and tours

Boom or Bust *This self-guided two-hour walking trail follows Perth's historic buildings from 1890 to 1930. Brochure available from the visitor centre.*

Kings Park Guided Walks *Volunteer guides lead you from wildflowers to memorials, 10am and 2pm daily from the park's visitor centre.*

Perth Coffee Cruise *This leisurely two-hour voyage takes you up the Swan River as far as Claisebrook Cove, then down to the Royal Perth Yacht Club. Bookings (08) 9325 1191.*

Spirit of the West – City to Port Indulgence *Fine dining aboard this Federation restaurant train from Perth to Fremantle. Bookings (08) 9250 7011.*

Swan Brewery Tour *This state-of-the-art brewery is renowned for its Swan and Emu beers. Bookings (08) 9350 0222.*

'Tram' Tours *Take in all the inner-city attractions aboard a replica of the city's first trams. For an all-day adventure take the Tourist Trifecta, a full-day tour including a tram tour of Perth, a cruise on the Swan River and a tram tour of Fremantle. Bookings (08) 9322 2006.*

Fremantle Historic Walking Tours *Learn about Fremantle's history, culture and art. Bookings (08) 9431 8455.*

Sport

AFL *(Australian Football League) is the most popular spectator sport in Perth, with crowds flocking to Subiaco Oval and Fremantle during the winter months to support their local teams, the West Coast Eagles and the Fremantle Dockers.*

Winter is also the time of the year for **basketball** *fans, who can catch the popular Perth Wildcats basketball team – or their female counterparts, the Perth Breakers – in games at the Perth Entertainment Centre.*

The summer's **cricket** *season takes up where footy and basketball leave off, with the famous WACA hosting both interstate and international test matches.*

In January Perth's Burswood Dome hosts the Hopman Cup, a prestigious international **tennis** *event.*

Horseracing *is a year-round event, split between two venues: Ascot racecourse in summer and Belmont Park in winter. Events such as the Perth Cup (held on New Year's Day), the Easter Racing Carnival and the Opening Day at Ascot draw huge crowds. Night harness racing can be seen at Gloucester Park.*

WESTERN AUSTRALIA

houses the Fremantle Tourist Bureau, is in the heart of the port city. Built in 1887, it can be easily distinguished by its clock tower. It is also the departure point for Tram Tours. From here it is an easy stroll to many fine historic buildings, galleries, museums and the 'cappucino strip' of **South Terrace**. The Fremantle Markets, also along South Terrace, are one of the city's most popular attractions.

Shipwreck Galleries

Part of the Western Australian Maritime Museum, the galleries are one of three sites showcasing Western Australia's maritime history. The state's treacherous coastline has doomed many ships to a watery grave. The Shipwreck Galleries, housed in the restored convict-built Commissariat building, document this chapter of maritime history. The most popular exhibit is the stern of the *Batavia*, wrecked in 1629, which has been reconstructed from recovered timbers. *Cliff St; open daily; admission by donation.*

Fremantle Markets

These National Trust-classified markets, with their ornate gold-rush era architecture, were opened in 1897. They offer a diversity of stalls: fresh produce, food, books, clothes, bric-a-brac, pottery and crafts. There is also a great tavern bar where buskers often perform. *Cnr South Tce & Henderson St; 9am–9pm Fri, 9am–5pm Sat, 10am–5pm Sun.*

Top events in Fremantle

Fremantle International Jazz Festival *Popular summer music event. January.*

Fremantle Seafood Celebration *Family fun day that celebrates Freo's fishing culture. February.*

St Patrick's Day Parade and Concert *Celebrates the Irish national holiday with much gusto. March.*

Fremantle Street Arts Festival *Local, national and international buskers perform on the streets. April.*

Blessing of the Fleet *Traditional Italian blessing of the fishing fleet. October.*

Fremantle Festival *Performing arts and community activities culminating in a street parade and dance party. November.*

Visitor information

*Fremantle Tourist Bureau
Fremantle Town Hall
Cnr William and Adelaide sts
(08) 9431 7878
www.fremantle.wa.gov.au*

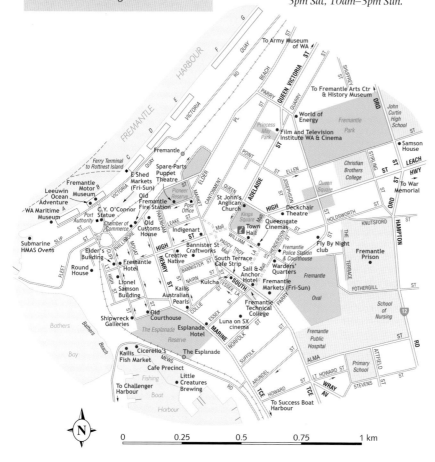

HARBOURSIDE

Although north Fremantle is the centre of industrial activity, the south side of the harbour still has an industrial feel and contains plenty of attractions for visitors. At Arthur Head, west of the city centre, is the Round House, the state's oldest public building, and beyond that is the tourist-friendly Victoria Quay where you can catch a ferry to Rottnest Island. Also at the quay are the **E Shed Markets**, with produce, arts and crafts and a food court (open Fri–Sun). Fanning out towards South Fremantle is a series of harbours. The first is **Challenger Harbour**, built for the America's Cup. Next is **Fishing Boat Harbour**, where Fremantle's 500-strong fishing fleet moors, and where a strip of restaurants line the wharf south of The Esplanade Reserve, giving you the chance to sample the fresh catch – the lobster in particular is delicious. Furthest south is **Success Boat Harbour**, home to the yachts of the Fremantle Sailing Club.

The Round House

Its name a misnomer, the Round House is actually a dodecahedron, with its twelve sides erected around a central yard. Built in 1831 by the first settlers as a prison, it is the oldest public building in the state. At 1pm each day, the Round House's signal station fires a cannon – the time gun – and this activates a time ball (an instrument once used to give accurate time readings to vessels out at sea). The Whalers' Tunnel underneath the Round House was cut by a whaling company in 1837 for access to Bathers Bay. *10 Arthur Head; 10.30am–3.30pm daily; admission free.*

Western Australian Maritime Museum

This stunning, nautically inspired building perched on the waterfront has six galleries, each of which explores a different theme in the state's maritime history. A highlight of the collection of historic and significant boats on display is the yacht that won the America's Cup, *Australia II*. The *Parry Endeavour*, in which Western Australian Jon Sanders circumnavigated the world three times, is mounted at an angle to replicate the way the yacht was driven down mountainous waves off Cape Horn. Next door to the museum is another of its prize exhibits, the submarine HMAS *Ovens*, which was in service during World War II. Take the tour to see what conditions are really like inside a real submarine. *Victoria Quay; open daily; admission fee applies.*

Fremantle Motor Museum

Australia's foremost collection of veteran, vintage, classic and racing cars ranges

C. Y. O'Connor

Outside the Fremantle Port Authority in Cliff Street stands the statue of a man inextricably linked to Western Australia's economic prosperity. Charles Yelverton O'Connor arrived in 1891 to take up the position of the state's first engineer-in-chief. In just over a decade O'Connor's many accomplishments included designing the inner harbour at Fremantle and the Goldfields Water Supply Scheme, which ranks as one of Australia's greatest engineering achievements.

Finding a reliable water supply to support the eastern goldfields' booming population became imperative after the 1890s gold rush. O'Connor's solution was radically brilliant: the construction of a reservoir at Mundaring in the hills outside Perth and a 556-kilometre water pipeline to Kalgoorlie. Although criticised by many as unfeasible, O'Connor's three-year water scheme was approved by Premier John Forrest, and by 1899 the project was under way.

The criticism from politicians, the press and the public was relentless, and affected O'Connor deeply. On Monday, 19 March 1902, he went for his usual morning ride along the beach south of his home in Fremantle. As he neared Robb Jetty, he rode his horse into the sea and shot himself.

By the end of that year – as O'Connor had predicted – the water scheme was successfully completed for the estimated cost. In the new year of 1903, the water was turned on. Kalgoorlie received the promised five million gallons (22 million litres) a day.

A century later, O'Connor's water scheme is still operating and is the longest freshwater pipeline in the world. It provides water to an area of 44 000 square kilometres (two-thirds the size of Tasmania), 100 000 people and 6 000 000 sheep. Its replacement value today is estimated to be $760 million.

On the coast just south of Fremantle is a statue of a man on a horse, half submerged in the waters of the Indian Ocean – a poignant tribute to this man of genius.

Getting to Fremantle

By car *A drive of 20–30 minutes, either via Stirling Highway on the north bank of the Swan River or via Canning Highway on the south.*

By train *A 30-minute journey from Perth Railway Station, Wellington Street. Trains depart every 15 minutes on weekdays and less frequently on weekends.*

By bus *Many buses and routes link both cities. Timetables and route details from Transperth 13 6213.*

By ferry *Various ferry operators travel twice daily between Perth and Fremantle, departing Barrack Street Jetty, Perth. See Getting around, p. 269.*

Combined travel packages *For combined ferry, train and 'tram' tours of Perth and Fremantle, contact either Fremantle Tram Tours (08) 9339 8719 or Perth Tram Company (08) 9322 2006.*

Once you've arrived, *look out for the free orange CAT bus, which runs regular services from Victoria Quay, through the city centre and down to South Fremantle. 'Tram' tours are another option, and depart hourly between 10am and 5pm from the town hall. Bike hire is available at the Boat Torque Cruises terminal in North Fremantle (08) 9430 5844.*

from an 1894 Peugeot to the Williams driven by Formula One Grand Prix World Champion Alan Jones. *B Shed, Victoria Quay; open daily; admission fee applies.*

Leeuwin Ocean Adventure

The *Leeuwin II* – a 55-metre, three-masted barquentine – is rated as the largest tall ship in Australia. It is available for full-day, morning or twilight sails in spring and summer. In the winter months there are longer trips up the north-west coast. When in Fremantle, it is open to

the public. *B Shed, Victoria Quay; (08) 9430 4105.*

Duyfken

The first recorded chart of the Australian coastline was made during the 1606 voyage of the Dutch ship *Duyfken*, the 'Little Dove'. This replica of the ship was built in Fremantle and launched in 1999. At the time of writing, tours on board were no longer available; however, you can still enjoy the sight of this beautiful boat, moored in Fishing Boat Harbour.

A tempting array of fresh produce, Fremantle Markets

WESTERN AUSTRALIA

Eating out in Fremantle

South Terrace *Numerous cafes and restaurants line Fremantle's 'cappucino strip'. The historic 1854 Sail & Anchor Hotel specialises in locally brewed Matilda Bay beers. See map on p. 276*

Fishing Boat Harbour *The place to go for fish 'n' chips and seafood. Cicerello's is a long-time favourite; Little Creatures Brewing is an up-market must-do for food and beer lovers. See map on p. 276*

West End *Vietnamese, Indian and vegetarian fare are easy to find here. Check out the old fire station building in Phillimore Street for good Indian food. Or cross the railway line and visit the renovated E Shed at Victoria Quay, with its large food court. See map on p. 276*

East Fremantle *Two great places to eat lie under the Queen Victoria Street and Stirling Highway bridges on Riverside Road: the Left Bank cafe, bar and restaurant, and the swanky Red Herring restaurant. 566 C7*

Fremantle's grand old buildings

Elder's Building *Georgian-style building, made of brick and Donnybrook stone, once the hub of Fremantle's overseas trade. 11 Cliff St.*

Esplanade Hotel *This 1890s hotel has been extended to blend in with the original facade. Cnr Marine Tce & Essex St.*

Fremantle Technical College *Now the Challenger TAFE e-Tech, this building boasts Donnybrook stone facings and plinth with Art Nouveau decorative influences. Cnr South Tce & Essex St.*

Lionel Samson Building *A rich facade epitomises the optimistic style of gold-rush architecture. 31–35 Cliff St.*

Samson House *Grand old 1900 house, originally built for Michael Samson, who later became mayor of Fremantle. Cnr Ellen & Ord sts; 1pm–5pm Sun.*

St John's Anglican Church *Features a stone belltower and large stained-glass window. Cnr Adelaide & Queen sts.*

Warders' Quarters *A row of convict-built cottages built in 1851, used until recently to house warders from the Fremantle Prison. Henderson St.*

See also Fremantle Town Hall, p. 275, The Round House, p. 276, and Fremantle Prison, on this page

CITY OUTSKIRTS

The Fremantle Prison dominates the outer ring of the city. However there are a number of other interesting buildings and museums in the area, including the beautifully restored Samson House (*see Fremantle's grand old buildings, on this page*), the Army Museum of Western Australia, and the World of Energy (*see Museums, p. 272*). Visit the **War Memorial**, on the corner of High and Swanbourne streets, for fantastic views of Fremantle Harbour.

Fremantle Prison
The first convicts arrived in Fremantle in 1850 and were immediately set to work to build a prison. The limestone used in construction was quarried on-site. Huge, forbidding and full of history, the Fremantle Prison was in use from 1855 until 1991. Now visitors can experience the atmosphere on a guided tour, taking in the isolation chamber and the gallows. The entrance can be reached via steps and a walkway around Fremantle Oval from Parry Street. *1 The Terrace; 10am–6pm daily; tours conducted half-hourly 10am–5pm; bookings essential for candlelight tours from 7.30pm on Wed & Fri; (08) 9336 9200; admission fee applies.*

Fremantle Arts Centre and History Museum
Like the Fremantle Prison, this magnificent limestone building was built by convicts. A striking building of steeply pitched roofs and Gothic arches, it was the colony's first lunatic asylum. It now offers an interesting display on the history of Fremantle, contemporary art exhibitions, a craft shop, a ghost walk and a garden area with a cafe. *1 Finnerty St; open daily; admission free.*

Day tours

Rottnest Island *Just off the coast of Perth, the low-key island resort of Rottnest makes for a perfect day tour. Access is via ferry from Fremantle, Perth or Hillarys Boat Harbour. No private cars are permitted: island transport is by foot, bicycle or bus. Visitors to Rottnest can divide their time between the beach and the scenic and historic attractions of the island. For more details see p. 280*

Darling Range *Follow the Great Eastern Highway for a tour of the Darling Range and its 80 000 hectares of escarpment and jarrah forest in the Hills Forest area. Highlights include a scenic drive through John Forrest National Park and a visit to the huge, forest-fringed Mundaring Weir. For more details see p. 281*

Swan Valley *A premier winegrowing district, with vineyards along the scenic Swan River. Other attractions include the historic town of Guildford; Woodbridge House, a Victorian mansion in West Midland; Walyunga National Park; and Whiteman Park, a 2500-hectare area that includes Caversham Wildlife Park. For more details see p. 281*

Yanchep National Park *On the coast north of Perth, Yanchep has long been one of the city's favourite recreation areas. Have your photo taken with a koala; see didgeridoo and dance performances; or take a guided tour of Crystal Cave, where stalactites hang above the inky waters of an underground pool. For more details see Yanchep, p. 329*

Aerial view of Fishing Boat Harbour, Fremantle

WESTERN AUSTRALIA'S
REGIONS

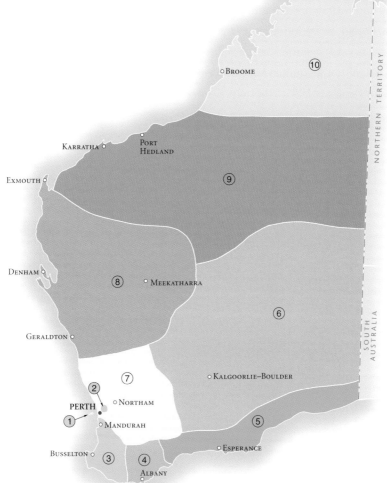

ROTTNEST ISLAND

An idyllic, relaxed lifestyle draws about half a million holiday-makers to Rottnest Island each year. The island, 11 kilometres long and 4.5 kilometres wide, lies in azure waters only 18 kilometres west of Perth, just a short ferry or plane ride from the mainland. Its crystal-clear bays and white, sandy beaches are perfect for a range of aquatic pleasures, while on land there are heritage sites and interesting flora and fauna – including the famous quokka – to

The famous Rottnest Island quokka

discover. The island's fishing and surfing are at their best during the cooler months. Daytrips are popular, as are longer stays in the low-key accommodation. With no private cars permitted on the island, bicycles are the main mode of transport, although limited bus services operate and a light railway takes visitors to Oliver Hill, in the centre of the island, for spectacular views.

Top events

Jan–Feb	Peters Trumpet Twilights (free evening concerts)
Feb	Rottnest Channel Swim
Mar	Rottnest Kite Surf Classic
May	WA Open Surfing Series
Aug	WA Surf Industry Cup
Oct	Marathon and Fun Run
Dec	Rottnest Swim Through

Focus on

Island heritage

Known as Wadjemup to the Nyungar people, Rottnest was unoccupied when Europeans arrived although there is evidence of Aboriginal occupation around 7000 years ago, when the island was linked to the mainland. The island was given the unflattering name Rotte-nest, meaning 'rats' nest', in 1696 by the explorer Willem de Vlamingh, who mistook the island's quokkas for large rats. Europeans settled on the island in 1831. From 1838 to 1903 it was used as a prison for Aboriginal people. During World War I it became an internment camp and in 1917 it was declared an A-class reserve. World War II saw it used as a military post. Many heritage sites can be found, including an original 1840s streetscape – Thomson Bay's Vincent Way. Other interesting sites are the Chapel (1858), the octagonal prison building known as the Quad (1864), the Oliver Hill Gun Battery (1930s) and Rottnest Lighthouse (1859) on Wadjemup Hill.

Underwater wonderland

The diversity of fish and coral species and the numerous shipwrecks found around the island make Rottnest a favourite site for scuba divers and snorkellers. Dive charters and snorkelling tours are popular; if you prefer not to get wet, enjoy the underwater scenery aboard the glass-bottomed *Underwater Explorer*.

CLIMATE ROTTNEST ISLAND

	J	F	M	A	M	J	J	A	S	O	N	D
Max °C	26	27	25	23	20	18	17	17	18	20	22	24
Min °C	18	19	18	16	14	13	12	12	12	13	15	17
Rain mm	7	13	14	37	106	156	149	104	61	39	17	10
Raindays	2	2	4	8	15	18	20	18	14	11	6	3

The Basin

An outer reef surrounds Rottnest, protecting the clear waters and creating calm conditions for family swimming. The Basin provides one of a number of beautiful sandy beaches on the eastern end of the island. It is within easy walking distance of Thomson Bay and has basic facilities.

Experience it!

❶ Fish the recreational waters of Rottnest for species such as flathead, tailor, moon wrasse, marlin and tuna

❷ Visit the Rottnest Museum, charting the fascinating cultural, environmental and maritime history of the island

❸ Enjoy a late-afternoon drink in the beer garden at the Rottnest Hotel

West End

The 'West End' of Rottnest can be reached on an 11 km bike ride along a sealed road, or on a bus tour. There are stunning ocean views from Cape Vlamingh (where you may also spot a humpback whale in winter) and a 1 km heritage trail that affords sightings of wedge-tailed shearwaters, fairy terns, quokkas and bottlenose dolphins.

Quokka country

The quokka is a native marsupial found primarily on Rottnest. It is seminocturnal and furry, and grows to the size of a hare. There are about 10 000 quokkas on the island. Find the interpretive signs about a kilometre south of Thomson Bay, just before Kingstown Barracks; if you don't see a quokka here, then there are good viewing spots along the boardwalk at Garden Lake.

DARLING & SWAN

Houghton's
Vineyard,
Swan Valley

Barely half an hour from the centre of Perth are two distinct country landscapes perfect for picnicking, walking, sampling local produce and looking for wildflowers. To the north-east is the Swan Valley, Western Australia's oldest wine region. Here among lush bushland, orchards and vineyards you'll enjoy cellar-door tastings, restaurants and cafes, galleries, fresh produce and charming B&B accommodation. Directly east is the Darling Range, incorporating the Hills Forest area. This 80 000-hectare stretch of unique Western Australian jarrah forest includes five national parks and is interspersed with historic towns, lakes and weirs, scenic drives with spectacular views, and a superb botanic garden.

Top events

Mar–April	Taste of the Valley (food, wine and art festival, throughout Swan Valley)
April	Mundaring Hills Festival (Mundaring)
Aug	Avon Descent (whitewater race down Avon and Swan rivers, from Northam to Perth)
Oct	Spring in the Valley (wine festival, throughout Swan Valley)
Nov	Darlington Arts Festival

Focus on

Heritage sites

In historic Guildford, roam among yesteryear's farm tools, fashions and household items at the Old Courthouse, Gaol and Museum. Then enjoy a drink at the nearby Rose and Crown Hotel (1841), the oldest trading hotel in the state. The faithfully restored Woodbridge House (1885), picturesquely located on the banks of the Swan River, is a fine example of late Victorian architecture. And just south of Upper Swan, at Henley Brook on the western bank of the river, All Saints Church (1839–41) is the state's oldest church.

CLIMATE GUILDFORD

	J	F	M	A	M	J	J	A	S	O	N	D
Max °C	32	32	30	27	22	19	18	19	21	23	27	30
Min °C	17	17	15	13	10	8	7	8	9	10	13	15
Rain mm	8	10	17	43	122	177	172	139	86	56	20	13
Raindays	2	2	4	7	14	17	19	17	14	11	6	4

Swan Valley wineries

The Swan Valley region is renowned for its chardonnay, shiraz, chenin blanc and verdelho. It boasts over 40 wineries; of these, Houghton, Evans & Tate, and Sandalford are the best known. For a treat that offers scenery as well as wine-tasting, take a Swan River wineries cruise from Perth.

John Forrest National Park

Declared a national park in 1947, John Forrest is one of the oldest and best-loved picnic spots in the Perth Hills. A drive through the park has vantage points with superb views across Perth and the coastal plain. A popular walk is the Heritage Trail on the western edge, past waterfalls and an old rail tunnel.

Experience it!

1 **Travel** the one-way Zig Zag Scenic Drive, an old train route with spectacular views, via Kalamunda

2 **Picnic** in Walyunga National Park and enjoy wildflowers in spring

3 **See** Lesmurdie Brook drop 50 m over the Darling Escarpment in Lesmurdie Falls National Park

For more detail see maps 566, 567, 572 & 574.
For descriptions of 🚉 towns see Towns from A–Z (p. 292).

Mundaring Weir

The rolling lawns and bush-clad surrounds of the weir reserve make it ideal for picnics. At the foot of the weir, the Number 1 Pump Station commemorates C. Y. O'Connor's extraordinary engineering feat in piping water to the goldfields some 600 km east. Nearby, at the Hills Forest Discovery Centre, you can sign up for nature-based activities such as bushcraft.

Araluen Botanic Park

Tall forest trees (jarrah, eucalypt and marri) frame the rock pools, cascades and European-style terraces of these beautiful 59 ha gardens. Established in the 1930s by the Young Australia League, the gardens have picturesque walking trails, picnic and barbecue areas and, in spring, magnificent tulip displays.

THE SOUTH-WEST

Western Australia's South-West is renowned for its world-class wines, excellent surf breaks and towering old-growth forests. At the coast, the calm waters of Koombana and Geographe bays are ideal for swimming and fishing. The rocky Limestone Coast runs from Cape Naturaliste to Cape Leeuwin, where the Indian and Southern oceans meet. Whales migrate along this coastline from July to September, and onshore is one of the world's most beautiful limestone cave systems. Margaret River, the town at the centre of the state's famed wine region, is a few kilometres inland. Over 65 wineries in the area produce a huge 20 percent of Australia's premium wines. Further east is tall-timber country, lush and green, with rolling hills, orchards and forests of jarrah and karri. Scenic drives link historic towns, while national parks offer superb bushwalking. The Bibbulmun Track, a 963-kilometre long-distance trail, passes through some of the state's most picturesque southern towns, including Dwellingup, Collie, Balingup, Pemberton, Northcliffe and Walpole.

Busselton Jetty

Experience it!

❶ Surf the Hawaiian-style surf breaks around Margaret River

❷ Dive the Wreck Trail at Hamelin Bay, where 11 wrecks form the state's most unusual heritage trail

❸ Visit the Old Cheese Factory Craft Centre in Balingup, the largest art and craft centre in the state

❹ Visit the magnificent Lake Cave, one of 360 limestone caves found beneath the Leeuwin–Naturaliste Ridge

❺ Enjoy a drink at Yallingup's legendary Caves House Hotel, surrounded by acres of gardens

Top events

Jan	Festival of Busselton
Feb/ Mar	Leeuwin Estate Concert (near Margaret River)
Mar/ April	Margaret River Masters (surfing competition)
July	Winterfest and Forest Heritage Festival (Dwellingup)
Aug	Collie–Donnybrook Cycle Race
Sept	Gloucester Tree Birthday Celebration (Pemberton)
Oct	Blackwood Marathon (Boyup Brook to Bridgetown)
Nov	Ironman Western Australia Triathlon (Busselton)
	Margaret River Wine Region Festival
	Blues at Bridgetown Festival
Dec	Cherry Harmony Festival (Manjimup)
	Yallingup Malibu Surfing Classic

Focus on

Jarrah, karri, tuart and tingle

Western Australia's only forests are in the cool, well-watered South-West. The grey-barked tuart tree grows only on coastal limestone; just outside Busselton is the largest remaining pure tuart forest in the world. Jarrah, a beautifully grained, deep-red hardwood, flourishes between Dwellingup and Collie. The Forest Heritage Centre at Dwellingup has interpretive displays on the issues of forest management, and a treetop walk. Forests of karri – one of the world's tallest trees, reaching 90 metres in 100 years – are found in the wetter areas, from Manjimup to Walpole. Near Pemberton, 4000 hectares of old-growth karri forest are protected by Warren and Beedelup national parks. In Gloucester National Park, right outside the town, is the 61-metre Gloucester Tree, with a spiral ladder to the top. The Valley of the Giants, east of Walpole, is home to towering red tingle trees. Here you'll find the Tree Top Walk (the region's most famous walk through the trees). Nearby is the 25-metre-wide Giant Red Tingle, a huge fire-hollowed tree that is regarded as one of the ten largest living things on the planet.

CLIMATE BUSSELTON

	J	F	M	A	M	J	J	A	S	O	N	D
Max °C	29	28	26	23	19	17	16	17	18	20	24	27
Min °C	14	14	13	11	9	8	8	8	9	11	13	
Rain mm	10	11	22	42	118	175	167	117	75	52	24	13
Raindays	3	2	4	8	15	19	22	19	16	13	7	4

Peel Coast
The coastal towns south of Rockingham offer swimming, boating, fishing and crabbing. Yalgorup National Park protects ten coastal lakes, with views over the ocean and dunes at high points. From Preston Beach a walking track crosses tuart and peppermint woodlands to Lake Pollard, where black swans gather from October to March.

Swim with dolphins
In Bunbury's Koombana Bay you can swim under ranger guidance with wild bottlenose dolphins. If you prefer not to get wet, take a dolphin-spotting cruise. Learn about the dolphins and other marine life at the Dolphin Discovery Centre's interpretive museum and theatre.

Pemberton
At tiny Pemberton you can take a tramway through the heart of the great karri and marri forests, and visit the virgin forests of Warren and Beedelup national parks. You can also sample the marron (a freshwater crayfish bred in local hatcheries) and go wine-tasting at the local wineries – the Pemberton region is gradually becoming known for excellent cool-climate wines.

Busselton Jetty
Stretching a graceful 2 km into Geographe Bay, this wooden jetty is the longest in the Southern Hemisphere. Built in 1865, the jetty originally serviced American whaling ships; later it was extended to take a railway line for the loading of timber. Today a small tourist train will take you from the Interpretive Centre at one end to the Underwater Observatory at the other.

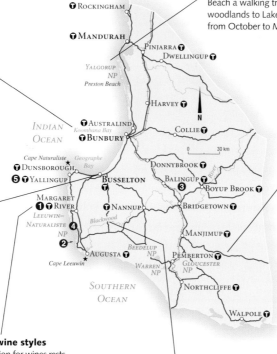

Tree Top Walk
Gain a unique perspective on the majestic southern forests as you walk through the upper branches of giant tingle and karri trees. East of Walpole, this walkway 38 m above the forest floor is one of the highest and longest of its kind in the world. Down at ground level, the Ancient Empire interpretive boardwalk weaves its way through the veteran tingle trees.

Margaret River wine styles
The region's reputation for wines rests principally on cabernet sauvignon and chardonnay grown on grey-brown, gravelly-sandy soils. Try the cabernet from Vasse Felix, Moss Wood and Cullen, and the chardonnays from Leeuwin, Voyager and Ashbrook.

Blackwood Valley
The Blackwood River meanders for 500 km through wheat-belt plains and forested valleys to its broad estuary at Augusta. Secluded spots along the river between Nannup and Alexandra Bridge offer tranquil camping, fishing, swimming and canoeing. The Sheoak Walk is a one-hour loop through the forest close to Nannup.

Climbing the Dave Evans Bicentennial Tree, Warren National Park

For more detail see maps 566, 567, 568, 569, 570, 572 & 574. For descriptions of ⓣ towns see Towns from A–Z (p. 292).

HEARTLANDS

The Pinnacles

Top events

Jan	Lancelin Ocean Classic (windsurfing competition)
	State Gliding Championships (Narrogin)
Mar	Wimbledon of the Wheatbelt (Carnamah)
	Wagin Woolorama
	Keela Dreaming Cultural Festival (odd-numbered years, Kellerberrin)
May	Moondyne Festival (Toodyay)
Aug	Avon Descent (whitewater race down Avon and Swan rivers, from Northam to Perth)
Sept	Jazz Festival (York)
Oct	Kulin Bush Races
	Spring Garden Festival (York)
Nov	Blessing of the Fleet (Jurien Bay)

Western Australia's wheat belt dominates this region: a vast, golden landscape of grain, sheep and cattle farms and quaint historic towns. Only an hour's drive from Perth lies the Avon Valley, a forested countryside with an almost English character, while northwards the imposing Spanish-inspired buildings of New Norcia provide an unexpected sight among the gum trees. Along the coast a string of surf beaches and lobster ports beckon holiday-makers, and the extraordinary Pinnacles Desert draws visitors from around the world. Each spring, from the coast to the wheatfields, wildflowers provide a common theme for this otherwise diverse region.

Focus on

Wildflowers
Western Australia, home to some 12 500 species of wildflowers, has one of the richest floras in the world. The Heartlands is one of the most accessible places to see magnificent wildflower displays. Top spots include the Chittering Valley near Gingin, Lesueur and Badgingarra national parks near Jurien Bay, and the sand plains around Southern Cross. Up to 20 species of native orchids flourish around Hyden in spring; yellow wattles light up the countryside around Dalwallinu; and massed displays of white, pink and yellow everlastings line the road from Moora to Wubin.

The Pinnacles
Thousands of limestone pillars, the eroded remnants of what was once a thick bed of limestone, create a weirdly beautiful landscape in Nambung National Park. Other park attractions include a beautiful coastline with superb beaches where visitors can fish, swim, snorkel, walk or picnic.

New Norcia
This town, with its Spanish Colonial architecture, was built in 1846 by Benedictine monks who established a mission for the local indigenous population. It remains Australia's only monastic town. Visitors can tour the buildings and visit the fascinating museum and art gallery.

CLIMATE NORTHAM

	J	F	M	A	M	J	J	A	S	O	N	D
Max °C	34	34	31	26	21	18	17	18	20	24	28	32
Min °C	17	17	15	12	9	7	5	6	7	9	12	15
Rain mm	10	13	19	23	57	83	84	62	37	25	12	9
Raindays	2	2	3	6	11	15	16	14	11	7	4	2

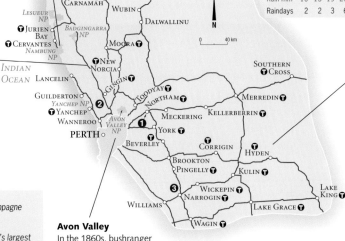

Wave Rock and Mulka's Cave
Wave Rock, east of Hyden, is a 2.7 billion-year-old piece of granite, 15 m high and 100 m long. It looks like a giant wave frozen at the moment of breaking and has vertical bands of colour created by algal growth. To the north is Mulka's Cave, decorated with Aboriginal rock art.

Experience it!

❶ **Float** over the Avon Valley on a champagne hot-air-balloon flight from Northam

❷ **Gaze** at the stars through the state's largest telescope at the Gravity Discovery Centre, south-west of Gingin

❸ **See** rare wildlife in natural surroundings at Dryandra Woodland's Barna Mia Animal Sanctuary, north-west of Narrogin

Avon Valley
In the 1860s, bushranger Moondyne Joe hid in the forests, caves and wildflower fields of this lush valley. Now Avon Valley National Park preserves much of the landscape. In the valley's heart, and marking the start of the wheat belt, are the historic towns of Northam and York.

For more detail see maps 566, 567, 572 & 574. For descriptions of ⊕ towns see Towns from A–Z (p. 292).

GREAT SOUTHERN

The Stirling Range

T he Great Southern region begins at Katanning and Kojonup, small towns at the southern extremity of the wheat belt. The road south crosses sheep country, with views of the jagged peaks of the blue and purple Stirling Range. A stop at Mount Barker offers a chance to taste the intensely floral rieslings grown in the district's burgeoning wine region. Albany, on panoramic King George Sound, is the centre of the district. This comfortable historic town, with its range of accommodation and restaurants, is the ideal base for exploring the rugged coast east to Bremer Bay and west to the surfing beaches near the secluded riverside town of Denmark.

Top events

Jan	Mount Barker Wine Festival
Mar	Wine Summer Festival (Porongurup)
Easter	Brave New Works (new performance art, Denmark)
Sept	Wildflower Display (Cranbrook)
Sept/Oct	Great Southern Wine Festival (Albany)
Oct	Mount Barker Wildflower Festival
Oct	Wildflower Festival (Porongurup)
Nov	Art Show (Cranbrook)
Dec/Jan	Vintage Blues Festival (Albany)

Focus on

Albany heritage

Albany, the oldest white settlement in Western Australia, was officially founded on 21 January 1827. The founders were a party of soldiers and convicts, under the command of Major Edmund Lockyer, who had arrived on the *Amity* a month earlier. Albany's magnificent harbour, once commanding the sea lanes running between Europe, Asia and eastern Australia, became a whaling station and later a coaling port for steamships. Museums now occupy several of the town's historic buildings, and a full-size replica of the *Amity* stands next to one of them, the Residency Museum. Stirling Terrace has some evocative Victorian shopfronts, while Princess Royal Fortress on Mt Adelaide has restored buildings and gun emplacements, and offers fine views.

CLIMATE ALBANY

	J	F	M	A	M	J	J	A	S	O	N	D
Max °C	25	25	24	22	19	17	16	16	17	19	21	24
Min °C	14	14	13	12	10	8	7	8	7	8	9	11	12
Rain mm	27	24	28	63	102	103	124	106	82	78	48	25
Raindays	8	9	11	14	18	19	21	21	18	15	13	10

WESTERN AUSTRALIA

Torndirrup National Park

This park, 15 minutes from Albany, features The Blowholes, The Gap and Natural Bridge, all sculpted into their current form by the treacherous Southern Ocean. Granite outcrops and cliffs alternate with dunes, and sandy heath supports peppermint, banksia and karri. Easy walking trails take in some of the most spectacular sights.

For more detail see maps 571, 572 & 574.
For descriptions of ❂ towns see Towns from A–Z (p. 292).

Stirling Range National Park

The Stirling Range rises abruptly above the surrounding plains; its rock faces are composed of the sands and silts laid down in the delta of an ancient river. The highest peaks can be veiled in swirling mists, which creates a cool and humid environment that supports a proliferation of flowering plants. Bluff Knoll, at 1073 m, is one of the state's premier hiking challenges.

Great Southern wineries

This region has over 40 wineries, extending from Frankland east through Mount Barker to Porongurup. Since the first plantings in 1967, the region has gained an international reputation for its aromatic rieslings. More recently, premium-quality chardonnay, shiraz, cabernet sauvignon and pinot noir are also proving popular. Many of the wineries are open for tastings and sales.

Experience it!

❶ Surf the mighty Southern Ocean at Denmark's Ocean Beach

❷ See southern right whales with their newborn calves around Bremer Bay, from August to November

❸ Enjoy Devonshire tea at The Old Farm (the state's oldest farm) at Strawberry Hill, 2 km west of Albany

Albany Whaleworld

The bloody realities of whaling are displayed at the old Cheynes Beach Whaling Station on Frenchman Bay, 25 km south-east of Albany. Visitors can explore *Cheynes IV*, a restored whalechaser, and relive the sights and sounds of the hunt. A 3D theatrette occupies one of the old whale-oil storage tanks.

ESPERANCE & NULLARBOR

*Sand dunes on
the Nullarbor*

This is a coastline of rare and remote beauty. The beaches of Esperance are among the most spectacular in Australia, famed for their white sand, brilliant turquoise waters and views across a network of offshore islands. To the north-east, beyond the desert beaches, underwater caves, sheer fossil-encrusted cliffs and drifting dunes, lies the vast Nullarbor Plain. While Esperance is a large and well-serviced holiday centre, the Nullarbor is as remote as you can get. Advance bookings should be made for the limited accommodation en route, and travellers should observe basic outback travel precautions, such as ensuring adequate fuel and water supplies.

Top events

Jan	Summer Festival (Hopetoun)
Feb	Offshore Angling Classic (Esperance)
Sept	Wildflower Show (Ravensthorpe)
	Wildflower Show (Esperance)
Oct	Agricultural Show (Esperance)
Oct/ Nov	Border Dash (Border Village to Eucla)

Focus on

The Nullarbor

The Nullarbor is one of the country's essential touring experiences. This 250 000-square-kilometre treeless limestone slab was initially part of the seabed, and has been formed in part by deposits of marine fossils. The terrain is riddled with sinkholes, caverns and caves, the largest of which is the six-kilometre Cocklebiddy Cave (just north-west of Cocklebiddy), one of the longest underwater caves in the world. Although it can seem featureless, the country is far from monotonous, particularly where the highway veers to the coast for a view of dramatic cliffs and the wild Southern Ocean, and perhaps a lucky sighting of migrating southern right whales.

CLIMATE ESPERANCE

	J	F	M	A	M	J	J	A	S	O	N	D
Max °C	26	26	25	23	20	18	17	18	19	21	23	25
Min °C	16	16	15	13	11	9	8	9	10	11	13	14
Rain mm	22	27	31	43	76	82	98	84	58	50	36	17
Raindays	6	6	8	11	14	16	17	17	14	12	10	7

Cape Le Grand National Park

Swimming beaches, sheltered coves, heathlands, sand plains and the Whistling Rock are all features of this park, 56 km east of Esperance. There are easy walking trails and two camping areas. Scenic spots include Thistle Cove, Hellfire Bay and Lucky Bay (where luck might have you spot a kangaroo on the beach).

Great Ocean Drive

A 38 km circuit drive explores the coast west of Esperance. Attractions include Australia's first wind farm, sheltered swimming at Twilight Cove, and Pink Lake, rendered lipstick-colour by algae. There are coastal lookouts, and sightings of southern right whales from June to November.

Eucla

This isolated outpost was established in 1877 as a telegraph station. Coastal dunes partially obscure the station's ruins. On the beach, a lonely jetty stretches out into startlingly blue waters, and in Eucla National Park, under mallee scrub and heathland, lies the 45 m high chamber of Koonalda Cave.

Archipelago of the Recherche

This group of 105 granite islands and 1500 islets stretches for 250 km along the Esperance coast. Boat tours, available from Esperance, may provide sightings of fur seals, sea lions, dolphins and, in season, southern right whales. Visitors can stay overnight in safari huts or camp on Woody Island.

Experience it!

1 **Windsurf** *on Esperance harbour, or fish for salmon, snapper and whiting on the nearby beaches and rock ledges*

2 **See** *the many species of orchids in spring in remote Cape Arid National Park*

3 **Have** *your photo taken beside the signpost marking the western end of the longest straight stretch of road in Australia – the '90-mile straight'*

*For more detail see maps 574–5.
For descriptions of 🌐 towns see Towns from A–Z (p. 292).*

GOLDFIELDS

The Exchange Hotel,
Kalgoorlie–Boulder

Top events

Feb	Undies 500 Car Rally (Kalgoorlie–Boulder)
Mar	Norseman Cup
	Laverton Day
June	Leonora Mile Festival
Sept	Fishing in the Desert (Kambalda)
	Race Round (Kalgoorlie–Boulder)
	Balzano Barrow Race (Kanowna to Kalgoorlie–Boulder)
Sept/ Oct	Metal Detecting Championships (Coolgardie)
Nov	Boulder Blues Festival
Dec	St Barbara's Mining and Community Festival (Kalgoorlie–Boulder)

W estern Australia's historic Goldfields region occupies a landscape of alluvial flats and salt plains broken by rocky outcrops and a surprising diversity of native vegetation – around 100 species of eucalypt, as well as brilliant displays of wildflowers in spring. Gold continues to be mined here, while sheep stations the size of small nations produce fine wool. The area offers an excellent opportunity to delve into its fascinating heritage and explore the long and lingering stretches of Western Australia's outback. April to October is the best time to visit. Those planning to explore beyond the main centres should observe basic outback safety precautions.

Focus on
Goldfields history
The discovery of gold in the region in 1892 secured the economic success of Western Australia. Since then, goldmines from Norseman to Laverton have yielded well over 1000 tons. A railway from Perth in 1896 and a water pipeline in 1903 helped Kalgoorlie and Boulder sustain a population of 30 000, the liquor requirements of which were met by 93 hotels. By 1900 surface gold was exhausted and big companies went underground. Exhausted mines have left a belt of ghost towns north of Kalgoorlie, while nickel mining since the 1960s has allowed towns such as Kambalda, Leonora and Laverton to survive.

CLIMATE KALGOORLIE–BOULDER

	J	F	M	A	M	J	J	A	S	O	N	D
Max °C	34	32	30	25	20	18	17	18	22	26	29	32
Min °C	18	18	16	12	8	6	5	5	8	11	14	17
Rain mm	22	28	19	19	28	31	26	20	15	16	18	15
Raindays	3	4	4	5	7	8	9	7	5	4	4	3

Experience it!

1 Drive the 965 km Golden Quest Discovery Trail, starting in Coolgardie, which traces the 1890s gold rushes

2 View the few remaining 'starting stalls' of Kalgoorlie's red-light district

3 Visit Warburton's Tjulyuru Cultural and Civic Centre, home to artworks of the Ngaanyatjarra people, including world-famous Warburton Glass

Kalgoorlie–Boulder
Kalgoorlie–Boulder produces half of Australia's gold, and the adjacent Golden Mile is the richest square mile of gold-bearing ore in the world. Take a circuit of the Golden Mile on the Loopline Tourist Railway, see the gold vault at the Museum of the Goldfields, and sample the rigours of 1890s mining at Hannan's North Tourist Mine.

Coolgardie
The 100 street markers scattered through Coolgardie are a good introduction to this town, the first settlement in the eastern goldfields. Coolgardie's splendid historic buildings include the Marble Bar Hotel, now the RSL, and the 1898 Warden's Court. The latter, an architectural treasure, houses the comprehensive Goldfields Exhibition Museum and the visitor centre.

North of Kalgoorlie
Menzies has 130 people and several intact old buildings, while Kookynie has retained its spacious 1894 Grand Hotel. Gwalia, almost a ghost town, has a museum, the restored State Hotel, and tin houses preserved in their lived-in state. Laverton, 100 km east, has historic buildings saved by the nickel industry.

For more detail see maps 574–5 & 577. For descriptions of ❖ towns see Towns from A–Z (p. 292).

Peak Charles National Park
In this park south-west of Norseman, granite mountains rise in wave-cut platforms to a height of 651 m. Walking trails to the summit of Peak Charles and its twin, Peak Eleanora, should only be attempted in favourable weather, but at the top are fantastic views across saltpans, sand plains and dry woodlands.

WESTERN AUSTRALIA

OUTBACK COAST & MID-WEST

Meeting the
dolphins at
Monkey Mia

The ancient landforms of Western Australia's interior meet the startlingly blue waters of the Indian Ocean in this vast area known for the richness and rarity of its natural features. Reefs, eroded cliffs and gorges, and life-forms billions of years old are all to be found. A series of towns (mostly coastal) offer good holiday facilities as well as glimpses of Western Australia's pioneer and maritime history. Much of this country is remote; for those planning to explore beyond the main tourist routes, outback safety precautions are essential.

Top events

Jan	Windsurfing Classic (Geraldton)
Mar	Sport Fishing Classic (Kalbarri)
	Whale Shark Festival (Exmouth)
June	Batavia Celebrations (Geraldton)
	Carnarfin (fishing competition, Carnarvon)
Aug	Carnarvon Festival and Rodeo
Aug/Sept	Mullewa Wildflower Show
Oct	Airing of the Quilts (Northampton)
	Sunshine Festival (Geraldton)
Oct/Nov	Gamex (gamefishing competition, Exmouth)
Nov	Blessing of the Fleet (Kalbarri)

Focus on

Shark Bay

World Heritage-listed Shark Bay is a sunny paradise of bays, inlets and shallow azure waters, blessed with a great number of unusual features. It boasts the world's most diverse and abundant examples of stromatolites – the world's oldest living fossils – which dot the shores of Hamelin Pool in rocky lumps. The bay region supports the largest number and greatest area of seagrass species in the world. Covering 4000 square kilometres, these vast underwater meadows are home to around 10 000 dugongs, ten percent of the world's total number. The bay's extraordinary marine population also includes humpback whales resting on their long migrations, manta rays, green and loggerhead turtles and, most famously, the dolphins that regularly visit Monkey Mia.

Ningaloo Reef

Ningaloo Marine Park protects the state's largest reef, a stunning underwater landscape of fish and corals located directly off the beach. For a quintessential Ningaloo experience, take a swim with the whale sharks, the gentle giants that migrate to the reef between March and June. Tours can be arranged in Exmouth.

Kalbarri National Park

This park is best known for its 80 km of gorges carved out by the Murchison River. Watersports are popular on the river's lower reaches. The park is also one of the world's richest wildflower areas. Dolphins, whale sharks and whales frequent the coastal waters, and the fishing is excellent.

Monkey Mia

The wild bottlenose dolphins of Monkey Mia are world famous for their daily morning ritual of swimming into the shallows to be handfed with fish. Under the guidance of rangers, visitors can wander into the water and witness this rare event. For a total marine encounter, dugong-watching cruises can also be arranged from here.

CLIMATE CARNARVON

	J	F	M	A	M	J	J	A	S	O	N	D
Max °C	31	33	31	29	26	23	22	23	24	26	27	29
Min °C	22	23	22	19	15	12	11	12	14	16	19	21
Rain mm	12	21	16	14	38	48	47	19	6	6	4	2
Raindays	2	3	2	3	5	7	7	5	3	2	1	1

Geraldton

Geralton is surrounded by superb swimming and surfing beaches, but if you prefer architecture to aquatics follow the Hawes Heritage Trail, which highlights the remarkable church buildings (1915–39) of architect-priest Monsignor John Cyril Hawes. In Geraldton, the Byzantine-styled St Francis Xavier Cathedral is considered to be one of Hawes' masterpieces.

Experience it!

❶ Tour a working banana plantation at Carnarvon's Westoby Plantation

❷ Dive around the Houtman Abrolhos Islands, a group of over 100 coral islands

❸ Stay at Wooleen Station near Murchison – in the shearers' quarters, rammed-earth guest houses or National Trust-listed homestead

For more detail see maps 573, 574 & 576.
For descriptions of ❂ towns see Towns from A–Z (p. 292).

Map labels

NINGALOO MARINE PARK
EXMOUTH
CAPE RANGE NATIONAL PARK
CORAL BAY
TROPIC OF CAPRICORN
INDIAN OCEAN
CARNARVON ❶
Shark Bay
FRANCOIS PERON NATIONAL PARK
DENHAM
MONKEY MIA
Hamelin Pool
MT AUGUSTUS NATIONAL PARK
GASCOYNE JUNCTION
Murchison River
MURCHISON
KALBARRI NATIONAL PARK
KALBARRI
❸
MEEKATHARRA
CUE
MOUNT MAGNET
NORTHAMPTON
GERALDTON
Houtman Abrolhos Is ❷
GREENOUGH
DONGARA
MULLEWA
YALGOO
MORAWA
PERENJORI
N
0   80 km

PILBARA

This region's centrepiece is the vivid, ochre-hued Hamersley Range, which stretches for 300 kilometres on its south-easterly path towards Newman. In the 1860s, pastoralists settled in the western Pilbara and established Roebourne and Cossack. Iron-ore discovery in the 1960s saw the establishment of modern towns such as Tom Price and Newman, which today provide comfortable bases for touring the area's magnificent rust-red landscapes. The Pilbara coast from Exmouth Gulf to Eighty Mile Beach is a place of vast tidal flats broken by mangroves. Coral reefs and offshore islands offer swimming, boating and beachcombing.

Karijini National Park

Top events

May   Welcome to Hedland Night (Port Hedland)

June Black Rock Stakes (wheelbarrow race, Karratha)

July Game Fishing Classic (Port Hedland)

Aug   FeNaClNG Festival (Karratha)
          Campdraft and Rodeo (Newman)
          Roebourne Cup and Ball

Sept Cultural Festival (Roebourne)
          Pilbara Music Festival (Port Hedland)

Oct   Octoberfest (Newman)

Focus on

Hamersley Range resources

One of the world's richest deposits of iron ore was discovered in the Hamersley in 1962, spearheading the Hamersley Iron Project. Towns with swimming pools, gardens and golf courses sprang up in this landscape of mulga scrub, spinifex and red mountains. Visitors can inspect open-cut mines at Tom Price and Newman. At Dampier and Port Hedland there are iron-ore shipping ports; the latter boasts the largest iron-ore export centre in Australia. Offshore from Karratha is the massive North West Shelf Gas Project; a visitor centre at the processing plant on Burrup Peninsula explains its operations.

WESTERN AUSTRALIA

CLIMATE ROEBOURNE

	J	F	M	A	M	J	J	A	S	O	N	D
Max °C	39	38	38	35	30	27	27	29	32	35	38	39
Min °C	26	26	25	22	18	15	14	15	17	20	23	25
Rain mm	59	67	63	30	29	30	14	5	1	1	1	10
Raindays	3	5	3	1	3	3	2	1	0	0	0	1

Pilbara islands

The Damper Archipelago and the Montebello and Mackerel islands seem a far-flung beach paradise from the industrial ports of the Pilbara. In reality, the nearest islands – those of the Dampier Archipelago – are just 20 minutes by boat from Dampier. The islands are a haven for marine life, including turtles, dolphins and migrating humpback whales, and are a renowned location for fishing.

Millstream–Chichester National Park

Amongst the arid beauty of Millstream–Chichester National Park, spring-fed Chinderwarriner Pool has an almost mirage-like quality. Encircled by remnant rainforest, the oasis is a haven for a range of plants and animals, many of them rare. Visit historic Millstream homestead, and take a refreshing dip in the pool.

Cossack

This first port in the north-west was built between 1870 and 1898 and is now a ghost town. Many buildings have been restored. The old post office houses a gallery and the courthouse has a museum, while the police barracks offer budget accommodation.

Experience it!

1 **Tour** the world's largest open-cut iron-ore mine at Mt Whaleback, Newman

2 **Walk** Karratha's 3 hr Jaburara Heritage Trail to see Aboriginal rock carvings and artefacts

3 **Visit** Australia's hottest town, Marble Bar, named for a unique bar of red jasper found nearby

Karijini National Park

Karijini was the name given to this area by the original inhabitants, the Banjima. It is renowned for extraordinary gorges, multicoloured walls, and hidden pools and waterfalls. Brilliant wildflowers carpet the rust-red hills in spring. Camping is available inside the park.

For more detail see maps 573, 576–7 & 578–9.
For descriptions of ☮ towns see Towns from A–Z (p. 292).

KIMBERLEY

Gantheaume Point, Broome

Remote and rugged, the Kimberley is one of the world's great wilderness areas. Covering more than 420 000 square kilometres – an area three times the size of England – it has a population of just 25 000 people. It is an ancient landscape of mighty ranges, spectacular gorges and arid desert. Along its coastline, pristine beaches fringe the turquoise waters of the Indian Ocean. The Kimberley has two distinct seasons: the Wet and the Dry. The wet season extends from November to March and is a time of hot, humid days, when thunderstorms deliver most of the annual rainfall to the region. The dry season, from April to October, is characterised by blue skies, clear days and cool nights. At all times of the year, travelling conditions are highly variable. While the coastal town of Broome is well known as a resort, there are large tracts of the Kimberley that are completely inaccessible by road – or accessible by four-wheel drive only – and offer only the most basic facilities. Travellers should familiarise themselves with prevailing conditions and carry adequate supplies.

Focus on

Aboriginal art

The Kimberley is one of Australia's most important regions for Aboriginal rock art. It is renowned for two styles – the Bradshaw and the Wandjina. The Bradshaw figures, as they are known, are painted in red ochre. According to one Aboriginal legend, birds drew the figures using their beaks. One rock-face frieze shows figures dancing and swaying; another depicts figures elaborately decorated with headdresses, tassels, skirts and epaulets. Significant Bradshaw sites have been found on the Drysdale River. The more recent Wandjina figures, depictions of ancestor spirits from the sky and sea who brought rain and fertility, are in solid red or black, outlined in red ochre, and sometimes on a white background. Wandjina figures are typically human-like, with pallid faces and wide, staring eyes, halos around their heads and, for reasons of religious belief, no mouths. Good examples of Wandjina art have been found near Kalumburu on the King Edward River and at the burial site known as Panda-Goornnya on the Drysdale River.

Experience it!

1 **Drive** the Gibb River Road, a 649 km outback adventure from Derby with detours to magnificent falls and gorges

2 **Marvel** at 130 million-year-old dinosaur footprints at Gantheaume Point near Broome

3 **Stay** at El Questro Station, Australia's most luxurious outback resort, and enjoy the hot springs

4 **See** the 1000-year-old boab tree near Derby, once used as a prison

5 **Fly** from Kununurra to a camp on the remote Mitchell Plateau to take in gushing waterfalls and Aboriginal art

Top events

Easter Dragon Boat Regatta (Broome)

May Ord Valley Muster (Kununurra)

King Tide Day (celebrating Australia's highest tide, Derby)

June Moonrise Rock Festival (Derby)

July Mowanjum Festival (indigenous art and culture, Derby)

Rodeo (Fitzroy Crossing)

Boab Festival (mardi gras, mud football and Stockmen and Bushies weekend, Derby)

Aug Opera Under the Stars (Broome)

Shinju Matsuri (Festival of the Pearl, Broome)

Nov Mango Festival (Broome)

CLIMATE HALLS CREEK

	J	F	M	A	M	J	J	A	S	O	N	D
Max °C	37	36	36	34	30	27	27	30	34	37	38	38
Min °C	24	24	23	20	17	14	13	15	19	23	25	25
Rain mm	153	137	74	22	13	5	6	2	4	17	37	77
Raindays	13	13	8	3	2	1	1	1	1	3	6	11

Cruising the Wandjina Coast

This coastline is a succession of capes, gulfs, bays and mangrove swamps, and rivers emptying onto mudflats. There are 3000 islands, including the 800 that make up the Buccaneer Archipelago, and countless reefs, including the spectacular Montgomery Reef uncovered twice a day at low tide. Explore these regions on a charter boat or sea plane from Broome or Derby.

Lake Argyle

The massive Lake Argyle was formed in the 1960s as part of the Ord River Scheme, the success of which is evident in the lush crops within its irrigation area. It has transformed a dusty, million-acre cattle station into a habitat for waterbirds, fish and crocodiles; the hills and ridges of the former station have become islands. Take a boat cruise and experience the magnificent scenery and abundant wildlife of the area.

Dampier Peninsula

The 200 km unsealed route from Broome to Cape Leveque traverses open eucalypt country and Aboriginal reserve land. Within the reserve is the Sacred Heart Church at Beagle Bay, with a beautiful pearl-shell altar. The Aboriginal community at Lombadina offers sightseeing, fishing and mudcrabbing tours.

Purnululu National Park

A rough 50 km track off the Great Northern Highway leads to the spectacular Bungle Bungle Range in Purnululu National Park, on the Ord River. A fantastic landscape of huge black-and-orange sandstone domes is intersected by narrow, palm-lined gorges where pools reflect sunlight off sheer walls. For an aerial view, take a scenic flight from Halls Creek or Kununurra.

Wolfe Creek Crater

Two hours south of Halls Creek by unsealed road, across some inhospitable country, is the world's second largest meteorite crater. It is 850 m across and was probably formed by a meteorite weighing at least several thousand tons crashing to earth a million years ago. Like so many of the Kimberley's attractions, it is perhaps most impressive from the air; scenic flights run from Halls Creek.

Port of pearls

Broome's attractions include its tropical climate, cosmopolitan character and world-famous pearling industry. Visit restored luggers and the Japanese Cemetery for tales of the town's pearling history, then see today's pearls on display in Chinatown. Enjoy a camel ride at sunset along 22 km Cable Beach, renowned as one of the most beautiful beaches in the world.

Geikie Gorge

The Fitzroy River cuts through the Geikie Range to create a 7 km gorge just north-east of Fitzroy Crossing. Its sheer walls are bleached by annual flooding. The riverbanks are inhabited by freshwater crocodiles, fruit bats and many bird species, and the only way to see the gorge is by boat – during the Dry.

For more detail see maps 578–9 & 580–1.
For descriptions of ⊕ towns see Towns from A–Z (p. 292).

Wandjina rock art

Cape Freycinet in Leeuwin–Naturaliste National Park, north-west of Augusta

Albany
Pop. 22 256

Map ref. 571 N12, 572 H13, 574 F12

Albany, a picturesque city on Western Australia's south coast, is the site of the state's first European settlement. On Boxing Day 1826 – three years before the Swan River Colony was founded – Major Edmund Lockyer, with a party of soldiers and convicts from New South Wales, came ashore to establish a military and penal outpost. Ninety years later, Albany was the embarkation point for Australian troops during World War I and, for many, their last view of the continent. A whaling industry, which began in the 1940s, defined the town until 1978 when the Cheynes Beach Whaling Company closed. Nowadays, whale-watching has taken its place. Lying within the protected shelter of the Princess Royal Harbour on the edge of King George Sound, Albany is one of the state's most popular tourist destinations.

IN TOWN Historic buildings Albany boasts more than 50 buildings of historical significance dating back to the early years of the settlement. Two of the oldest were built in the 1830s: Patrick Taylor Cottage on Duke St, which houses an extensive collection of period costumes and household goods, and the Old Farm at Strawberry Hill on Middleton Rd, site of the first government farm in WA. Other heritage buildings include the Old Gaol (1851), with its collection of social history artefacts, and the Residency Museum (1850s), a showcase of historical and environmental exhibits, both in Residency Rd. There are self-guide walks available, including the Colonial Buildings Historical Walk; contact visitor centre for brochures.
The Amity: full-scale replica of the brig that brought Albany's first settlers from Sydney in 1826; Princess Royal Dr. *St. John's Church:* 1848 Anglican church is the oldest in the state; York St. *Vancouver Arts Centre:* gallery, craft shop, studio and workshop complex, originally the Albany Cottage Hospital (1887); Vancouver St. *House of Gems:* extensive range of gemstones and jewellery; Frenchman Bay Rd. *Dog Rock:* granite outcrop resembling the head of an enormous labrador is a photo opportunity not to be missed; Middleton Rd. *Princess Royal Fortress:* commissioned in 1893, Albany's first federal fortress was fully operational until the 1950s; off Forts Rd. *Spectacular views:* lookouts at the peaks of Mt Clarence and Mt Melville have 360-degree views. Near the top of Mt Clarence is the Desert Mounted Corps Memorial statue, a recast of the original statue erected at Suez in 1932; Apex Dr. John Barnesby Memorial Lookout at the top of Mt Melville is 23 m high, with observation decks; Melville Dr. *Bibbulmun Track:* 963 km walking track to Perth begins at Albany's Old Railway Station in Proudlove Pde; *see feature on p. 323. Whale-watching:* cruises daily from town jetty; July–Oct.

WHAT'S ON *Farmers markets:* Aberdeen St; Sat mornings. *Great Southern Wine Festival:* Sept/Oct. *Vintage Blues Festival:* Dec/Jan.

NEARBY Torndirrup National Park Torndirrup is one of the most visited parks in the state, featuring abundant wildflowers, wildlife and bushwalking trails. The park is renowned for its rugged coastal scenery, including such features as the Gap, a chasm with a 24 m drop to the sea, and the Natural Bridge, a span of granite eroded by huge seas to form a giant arch. Exercise extreme caution on this dangerous coastline; king waves can rush in unexpectedly. 17 km s.

Whale World Even before the Cheynes Beach Whaling Company closed in 1978, Albany's oldest industry was a major tourist attraction. In its heyday, the company's chasers took up to 850 whales a season. View the restored whale-chaser *Cheynes IV*, whale skeletons, the old processing factory, an aircraft display and the world's largest collection of marine mammal paintings. This is the only whaling museum in the world created from a working whaling station. Free guided tours are available. 25 km SE. *Albany Bird Park:* undercover walk-in aviary with over 250 native and exotic birds; Frenchman Bay Rd; 3.5 km SW. *Deer-O-Dome:* showcases the Australian deer industry; 6 km N. *Mount Romance Sandalwood Factory:* skincare products, perfumes, therapeutics and free guided tours; 12 km N. *Albany Wind Farm:* 12 giant turbines, each 100 m high; 12 km SW. *Point Possession Heritage Trail:* views and interpretive plaques; Vancouver Peninsula; 20 km SE. *Fishing:* Emu Point (8 km NE), Oyster Harbour (15 km NE), Jimmy Newhill's Harbour (20 km S), Frenchman Bay (25 km SE). *Diving:* former HMAS *Perth* was scuttled in 2001 as an artificial dive reef; Frenchman Bay; 25 km SE. *West Cape Howe National Park:* walking, fishing, swimming and hang-gliding; 30 km W. *Two Peoples Bay Nature Reserve:* sanctuary for the noisy scrub bird, thought to be extinct but rediscovered in 1961; 40 km E.
ℹ Old Railway Station, Proudlove Pde; (08) 9841 1088 or 1800 644 088; www.albanytourist.com.au

Augusta   Pop. 1096

Map ref. 568 C13, 569 D12, 572 B11, 574 B11

The town of Augusta lies in the south-west corner of Western Australia. The state's third oldest settlement sits high on the slopes of the Hardy Inlet, overlooking the mouth of the Blackwood River and the waters of Flinders Bay. Just beyond it lies Cape Leeuwin with its unforgettable signpost dividing the oceans: the Southern Ocean to the south and the Indian Ocean to the west.

IN TOWN Augusta Historical Museum Augusta's difficult beginning in 1830 is documented in this collection of artefacts and photographs. An exhibit details the 1986 rescue of whales that beached themselves near the town. Blackwood Ave. *Crafters Croft:* locally made handcrafts, jams, emu-oil products; Ellis St.

WHAT'S ON *Spring Flower Show:* Sept/Oct.

NEARBY Leeuwin–Naturaliste National Park The park extends 120 km along the rugged south-west coast from Cape Naturaliste in the north to Cape Leeuwin in the south. Close to Augusta are three major attractions: Cape Leeuwin, Jewel Cave and Hamelin Bay. Cape Leeuwin, 8 km SW, marks the most south-westerly point of Australia. Climb 176 steps to the top of the limestone lighthouse for a sensational view. Nearby is the Old Water Wheel, built in 1895 from timber that has since calcified, giving it the appearance of stone. Jewel Cave, 8 km NW on Caves Rd, is renowned for its abundant limestone formations, including the longest straw stalactite found in any tourist cave. Nearby is Moondyne Cave, which has guided adventure tours. Bookings essential; contact visitor centre. At Hamelin Bay, 18 km NW, a windswept beach and skeleton of an old jetty give little indication of the massive amounts of jarrah and karri that were once transported from here. In the heyday of the local timber industry, the port's exposure to the treacherous north-west winds resulted in 11 wrecks. These now form the state's most unusual Heritage Trail: the Hamelin Bay Wreck Trail, for experienced divers. *See also Margaret River and Dunsborough. The Landing Place:* where the first European settlers landed in 1830; 3 km s. *Whale Rescue Memorial:* commemorates the 1986 rescue of beached pilot whales; 4 km s. *Matthew Flinders Memorial:* Flinders began mapping the Australian coastline from Cape Leeuwin in December 1801; 5 km s. *Alexandra Bridge:* picnic and camping spot with towering jarrah trees and beautiful wildflowers in season; 10 km N. *Boranup Maze and Lookout:* the maze offers a short walking track under trellis, while the lookout provides a picnic area with panoramic views of the coast and the Leeuwin–Naturaliste ridge; 18 km N. *Augusta–Busselton Heritage Trail:* 100 km trail traces the early history of the area through the movements of the pioneering Bussell and Molloy families, who settled in Augusta only to move further up the coast looking for suitable agricultural land; contact visitor centre for map. *Cruises:* Blackwood River and Hardy Inlet. *Marron in season:* fishing licence required and available at the post office; Blackwood Ave. *Whale-watching:* charter boats and coastal vantage points offer sightings of migrating humpback and southern right whales, plus pods of dolphins and fur seals; July–Sept; contact visitor centre for details.
ℹ Blackwood Ave; (08) 9758 0166; www.downsouth.com.au

Australind   Pop. 9596

Map ref. 568 G4, 572 C8, 574 C10

Lying on the Leschenault Estuary and bordered by the Collie River, Australind offers a multitude of aquatic pleasures including fishing, crabbing, prawning, swimming, boating, sailing and windsurfing. The town's unusual name is a contraction of Australia and India coined by its founders in the hope of a prosperous trade in horses between the two countries.

IN TOWN *St Nicholas Church:* reputedly the smallest church in Australia at only 3.6 m wide and 8.2 m long; Paris Rd. *Henton Cottage:* early 1840s heritage building now houses the visitor centre, Cottage Fairies and an art and craft gallery; cnr Old Coast and Paris rds. *Featured Wood Gallery:* fine furniture and craft made from the local timbers of jarrah, she-oak, marri, banksia and blackbutt; Piggot Dr. *Pioneer Memorial:* site of the first settlers' landing in 1840; Old Coast Rd. *Cathedral Ave:* scenic 2 km drive through arching paperbark trees with sightings of kangaroos and black swans, especially at sunset; off Old Coast Rd.

WHAT'S ON *Spring Fair:* Nov.

NEARBY Leschenault Inlet The inlet offers recreational attractions from the simple pleasure of fishing from the Leschenault Inlet Fishing Groyne to picnicking, camping and bushwalking in the Peninsula Conservation Park. The park is a haven for native wildlife with over 60 species of birds recorded. Only walking or cycling is permitted in the park except for 4WD beach access from Buffalo Rd; 1 km s. The Leschenault Waterway Discovery Centre has an interpretive gazebo with information on the estuary environment. Old Coast Rd; 2 km s. *Pioneer Cemetery:* graves dating back to 1842 and beautiful wildflowers in season; Old Coast Rd; 2 km N. *Binningup and Myalup:* pleasant beach towns north of Leschenault. *Australind–Bunbury Tourist Drive:* coastal scenery, excellent crabbing and picnic spots; contact visitor centre for brochure.
ℹ Henton Cottage, cnr Old Coast and Paris rds; (08) 9796 0102

Balingup   Pop. 795

Map ref. 568 I8, 570 C2, 572 D9, 574 C11

This small town, nestled in the Blackwood River Valley, is surrounded by rolling hills, forests and orchards. Balingup is renowned for its glowing summer sunsets, amazing autumn colours and misty winter mornings.

IN TOWN *Birdwood Park Fruit Winery:* unique award-winning fruit wines, chutneys, jams and fruits; Brockman St. *Tinderbox:* herbal and natural products; South Western Hwy. *Old Cheese Factory Craft Centre:* the largest art and craft centre in WA, offering pottery and timber products; Balingup–Nannup Rd.

The view from Mt Ragged, Cape Arid National Park, south of Balladonia

WHAT'S ON *Small Farm Field Day:*
roadside scarecrows; April. *Medieval Fayre:*
Aug. *Festival of Country Gardens:* Oct/Nov.
Balingup Jalbrook Classic Concert: Nov.

NEARBY **Golden Valley Tree Park** This
60 ha arboretum boasts a superb
collection of exotic and native trees. Other
attractions include a tree information
gazebo, walk trails, lookout and the
historic Golden Valley Homestead. Old
Padbury Rd; 2 km s.
Jalbrook Alpacas and Knitwear Gallery:
alpacas to feed and alpaca knitwear;
2 km e. *Lavender Farm:* oil-producing
lavender farm with open gardens, picnic
area, art gallery and gift shop. Take
a distillation tour. Balingup–Nannup
Rd; 2.5 km w; open Sept–April. *Balingup
Heights Scenic Lookout:* stunning views
of town and orchards; off Balingup–
Nannup Rd; 2.5 km w. *Greenbushes:*
small town nearby boasts WA's first
metal-producing mine (1888), still in
production and now the world's largest
tantalum producer. There is an excellent
lookout at the mine. 10 km w. *Heritage
Country Cheese:* cheese-producing factory
with viewing window and tastings;
13 km w. *Wineries:* several in area; contact
visitor centre for details. Balingup–Nannup
Rd: enjoy wonderful scenery, interesting
and historic landmarks and great
marroning, fishing and picnic sites.
Bibbulmun Track: sections of this trail pass
through Balingup; *see feature on p. 323.*
ⓘ Cnr Jayes Rd and South Western Hwy;
(08) 9764 1818; www.balinguptourism.
com.au

Balladonia   Pop. 13

Map ref. 575 L8

Balladonia lies on the Eyre Highway on
the western edge of the Nullarbor Plain.
Its closest towns are Norseman, 191
kilometres to the west, and Caiguna,

182 kilometres to the east. This arid
desert woodland is one of the world's
oldest landscapes, containing seashells
millions of years old from when the area
was ocean floor. Balladonia made world
headlines in 1979 when space debris
from NASA's *Skylab* landed 40 kilometres
east on Woorlba Sheep Station.

IN TOWN **Cultural Heritage Museum**
Learn about the crash-landing of *Skylab,*
early explorers, Afghan cameleers and
the area's history. Balladonia Roadhouse.

NEARBY **90-Mile Straight** Have your
photo taken beside the signpost marking
the western end of the longest straight
stretch of road in Australia, which
runs for 90 miles (146.6 km) between
Balladonia and Caiguna. 35 km e.
Newman Rocks: superb views from rocky
outcrop, with picnic and camping areas
on-site; 50 km w. *Cape Arid National Park
and Israelite Bay:* great birdwatching and
fishing; access via 4WD track, south
of town; check track conditions at
roadhouse.
ⓘ Balladonia Roadhouse, Eyre Hwy;
(08) 9039 3453; www.users.bigpond.
com/balladonia

Beverley   Pop. 815

Map ref. 572 F4, 574 D8

Beverley is a small town set on the banks
of the Avon River 130 kilometres east
of Perth. Its main street boasts some
beautifully preserved buildings from
Federation to Art Deco style. This farming
community has long been associated
with wheat and wool. Today these staples
are joined by more exotic products such
as grapes, olives, emus, deer and yabbies.

IN TOWN **Aeronautical Museum** This
museum offers a comprehensive display
of early aviation in WA. The star attraction
is the 'Silver Centenary', a biplane built
between 1928 and 1930 by local man

Selby Ford and his cousin Tom Shackles.
Ford designed the plane in chalk on the
floor of the powerhouse where he worked.
The plane first flew in July 1930, but
was never licensed because of the lack of
design blueprints. Vincent St.
Dead Finish Museum: the oldest building
in town (1872) now houses memorabilia
and historic items from wooden cotton
wheels to washing boards; Hunt Rd; open
11am–3pm Sun, April–Dec.

WHAT'S ON *Yabbie Races:* Feb. *Annual
Quick Shear:* Aug.

NEARBY **Avondale Discovery Farm**
Avondale is an agricultural research
station with displays of historic farming
machinery. The 1850s homestead is
furnished in period style and set in
traditional gardens. There is also an
animal nursery, Clydesdale horses
and a picnic area with barbecues and
a children's playground. A land-care
education centre houses interactive
displays on agriculture in the wheat belt.
The farm hosts the Avondale Harvest
Festival every November. Waterhatch Rd;
6 km w.
Brookton: attractions of this nearby town
include the Old Police Station Museum
and the Brookton Pioneer Heritage Trail,
which highlights places significant to the
local Aboriginal people; 32 km s. *County
Peak Lookout:* spectacular views from the
summit; 35 km se. *The Avon Ascent:* take a
self-drive tour of the Avon Valley; contact
visitor centre for map.
ⓘ 139 Vincent St; (08) 9646 1555;
www.beverleywa.com

Boyup Brook   Pop. 544

Map ref. 570 E2, 572 E9, 574 D11

Boyup Brook is on the tranquil Blackwood
River in the heart of grass tree country.
The town's name is thought to derive from
the Aboriginal word 'booyup', meaning
'place of big stones' or 'place of much
smoke', which was given to the nearby
Boyup Pool. Wildflowers are abundant
during September and October.

IN TOWN **Carnaby Beetle and Butterfly
Collection** Keith Carnaby was such a
leading light in the field of entomology
that beetles have been named after him.
His collection of Jewel beetles, part of
which is on display at the Boyup Brook
Tourist Information Centre, is regarded
as the best outside the British Museum of
Natural History. Cnr Bridge and Abel sts.
Pioneers' Museum: displays of agricultural,
commercial and domestic equipment;
Jayes Rd; open 2–5pm Mon, Wed, Fri or
by appt. *Sandakan War Memorial:* honours
1500 Australian POWs sent to Sandakan
to build an airfield for the Japanese;
Sandakan Park. *The Flax Mill:* built during
WW II for processing flax needed for war
materials. At its peak it operated 24 hours
a day and employed over 400 people.
Now the site of the local caravan park. Off
Barron St. *Heritage walk:* follows 23 plaques

around town centre; self-guide pamphlet available from visitor centre. *Bicentennial Walking Trail:* pleasant walk around town and beside the Blackwood River.
WHAT'S ON *Country Music Festival:* Feb. *Autumn Art Affair:* May. *Blackwood Marathon:* running, canoeing, horseriding, cycling and swimming the 58 km course to Bridgetown; Oct.
NEARBY Harvey Dickson's Country Music Centre This entertainment shed with a difference is decorated wall-to-wall and floor-to-rafter with music memorabilia spanning 100 years. The 'record room' contains hundreds of records and a variety of Elvis memorabilia. Music shows occur throughout the year and there is also a rodeo. Arthur River Rd; 5 km N; open by appt, contact visitor centre. *Gregory Tree:* remaining stump of a tree blazed by explorer Augustus Gregory in 1845; Gibbs Rd; 15 km NE. *Glacial rock formations:* Glacier Hill; 18 km S; view by appt. *Norlup Homestead:* built in 1874, this is one of the district's first farms; to view ph (08) 9767 3034; off Norlup Rd; 27 km SE. *Wineries:* Scotts Brook Winery (20 km SE) and Blackwood Crest Winery (at Kilikup, 40 km E); both open by appt. *Haddleton Flora Reserve:* displays of brown and pink boronia in season; 50 km NE. *Farm tours:* visit a wheat, sheep, pig, goat or deer farm; arrange through visitor centre. *Boyup Brook flora drives:* self-guide maps available from visitor centre.
ⓘ Cnr Bridge and Abel sts; (08) 9765 1444; www.wn.com.au/bbvisitor

Bremer Bay
Pop. 239

Map ref. 574 G11

Bremer Bay on Western Australia's south coast is a wide expanse of crystal-clear blue water and an endless stretch of striking white sand. The main beach, only a ten-minute walk from the town, has a sheltered cove that is perfect for swimming and fishing. Just north of Bremer Bay is the magnificent Fitzgerald River National Park with its four rivers, dramatic gorges, wide sand plains, rugged cliffs, pebbly beaches and spectacular displays of wildflowers between August and October.
IN TOWN *Watersports:* fishing, boating, swimming, surfing, waterskiing, scuba diving, bay cruises and seasonal whale-watching are the town's main attractions. *Rammed earth buildings:* the Bremer Bay Hotel/Motel on Frantom Way and Catholic Church on Mary St are excellent examples of rammed earth construction.
NEARBY Fitzgerald River National Park This huge 242 739 ha park, lying between Bremer Bay and Hopetoun to the east, is renowned for its diverse scenery and flora, which in turn supports threatened native animals. A staggering 1800 species of flowering plants have been recorded. Royal hakea, endemic to this region, is one of the most striking. Quaalup Homestead (1858), restored as a museum, offers

meals and accommodation in the park. Point Ann has a viewing platform for whale-watching; best times Aug–Nov. Campgrounds, barbecues and picnic areas available. 17 km N.
Fishery Beach: good boat-launching facilities; 6 km W. *Wellstead Homestead Museum:* the first residence in the area, now incorporating a gallery and museum with family heirlooms, historic farm equipment and vintage cars; Peppermint Grove, Wellstead Rd; 9 km SW. *Surfing:* nearby beaches include Native Dog Beach, Dillon Bay, Fosters Beach and Trigelow Beach; ask at visitor centre for directions.
ⓘ BP Roadhouse, 5 Gnombup Tce; (08) 9387 4093

Bridgetown
Pop. 2091

Map ref. 570 C3, 572 D10, 574 D11

Bridgetown is a picturesque timber town nestled among rolling hills on the banks of the Blackwood River. Crossing the river, Bridgetown boasts the longest wooden bridge in the state, made of the area's famous jarrah. Along with timber and tin mining, fruit growing has been one of the town's enduring industries.
IN TOWN Brierley Jigsaw Gallery The only public jigsaw gallery in the Southern Hemisphere, Brierley has over 170 jigsaws from around the world on display. They range from the world's smallest wooden puzzle up to a huge 9000-piece jigsaw. A highlight is an 8000-piece jigsaw of the Sistine Chapel. Wander around the gallery or sit and do a jigsaw at the tables provided. Back of visitor centre, Hampton St. *Bridgedale:* historic house owned by John Blechynden, one of the first European settlers to the area, constructed in 1862 of local timber and bricks made from the clay of the riverbank; South Western Hwy. *Memorial Park:* picnic area with a replica of the ship the town was named after and a chessboard with 3 ft high chess pieces; South Western Hwy.
WHAT'S ON *Blackwood River Park Markets:* fortnightly; Sun mornings. *Blackwood River Chamber Festival:* April. *State Downriver Kayaking Championships:* Aug. *Blackwood Classic Powerboat Race:* Sept. *Blackwood Marathon:* between Boyup Brook and Bridgetown; Oct. *Blues at Bridgetown Festival:* Nov. *Festival of Country Gardens:* Nov.
NEARBY The Cidery Discover the history of Bridgetown's apple industry and sample fresh juice and cider. The orchard contains over 80 varieties of apple. Cnr Forrest St and Gifford Rd; 2 km N; open 11am–4pm Wed–Sun. *Excellent views:* Sutton's Lookout, off Phillips St and Hester Hill, 5 km N. *Greenbushes Historical Park:* displays of tin-mining industry, and Gwalia Mine Site Lookout; 18 km N. *Bridgetown Jarrah Park:* ideal place for a picnic or bushwalk. The Tree Fallers and Shield Tree trails commemorate the early timber

history of the town. Brockman Hwy; 20 km W. *Karri Gully:* bushwalking and picnicking; 20 km W. *Geegelup Heritage Trail:* 52 km walk retraces history of agriculture, mining and timber in the region. It starts at Blackwood River Park. *Scenic drives:* choose from 8 scenic drives in the district through green hills, orchards and valleys into karri and jarrah timber country; self-guide maps available at visitor centre.
ⓘ 154 Hampton St; (08) 9761 1740 or 1800 777 140; www.bridgetowntourist.com

Broome
Pop. 15 242

Map ref. 578 G9

Broome is distinguished by its pearling history, cosmopolitan character and startling natural assets: white sandy beaches, turquoise water and red soils. The discovery of pearling grounds off the coast in the 1880s led to the foundation of the Broome township in 1883. A melting pot of nationalities flocked to its shores in the hope of making a fortune. Japanese, Malays and Koepangers joined the Aboriginal pearl divers, while the Chinese became the shopkeepers in town. By 1910 Broome was the world's leading pearling centre. In those early, heady days, over 400 pearling luggers operated out of Broome. The industry suffered when world markets collapsed in 1914, but stabilised in the 1970s as cultured-pearl farming developed. Today remnants of Broome's exotic past are everywhere, with the town's multicultural society ensuring a dynamic array of cultural influences. Broome's beaches are ideal for swimming and there is good fishing all year round.
IN TOWN Pearl Luggers Experience Broome's pearling heritage. Visit two restored pearling luggers in Chinatown and take a historical journey through the life and times of the divers. Former divers conduct daily tours; Dampier Tce.
Japanese Cemetery The largest Japanese cemetery in Australia contains the graves of over 900 Japanese pearl divers, dating back to 1896. This is a sobering reminder of the perils of the early pearling days when the bends, cyclones and sharks claimed many lives. Port Dr.
Staircase to the Moon This beautiful optical illusion is caused by a full moon reflecting off the exposed mudflats of Roebuck Bay at extremely low tides. Town Beach; Mar–Oct; check dates and times at visitor centre.
Chinatown: an extraordinary mix of colonial and Asian influences, Chinatown was once the bustling hub of Broome where pearl sheds, billiard saloons and Chinese eateries flourished. Now it is home to some of the world's finest pearl showrooms. *Buildings on Hamersley Street:* distinctive Broome-style architecture including the courthouse, made of teak inside and corrugated iron outside; Captain

Gregory's House, a classic old pearling master's house, built in 1915, now an art gallery; and Matso's Cafe, once the Union Bank Building. *Historical Society Museum:* pearling display and collection of photographs and literature on Broome's past; Saville St. *Bedford Park:* war memorial, replica of explorer William Dampier's sea chest and an old train coach; Hamersley St. *Shell House:* one of the largest shell collections in Australia; Guy St. *Sun Pictures:* the world's oldest operating outdoor cinema, opened in 1916; Carnarvon St. *Heritage trail:* 2 km walk introduces places of interest; contact visitor centre for self-guide pamphlet.

WHAT'S ON *Courthouse Markets:* Hamersley St; Sat mornings. *Town Beach Markets:* Robinson St; first two nights of full moon; check with visitor centre for dates and times. *Dragon Boat Regatta:* Easter. *Pentathlon:* April. *Race Round:* horseracing; June–Aug. *Opera Under the Stars:* Aug. *Shinju Matsuri:* Festival of the Pearl, recalls Broome's heyday; Aug. *National Indigenous Art Awards:* Sept. *Worn Arts:* theatrical performance of wearable art; Sept/Oct. *Mango Festival:* Nov.

NEARBY Cable Beach With its 22 km of pristine white sands fringing the turquoise waters of the Indian Ocean, Cable Beach is one of the most stunning beaches in the world. Every day the beach is washed clean by 10 m high tides. It takes its name from the telegraph cable laid between Broome and Java in 1889. The $55 million Cable Beach Resort, which fronts onto the beach, is a popular tourist destination. While you're here, why not do that quintessential Broome activity and ride a camel along this famous beach; contact visitor centre for details. 7 km NW.

Gantheaume Point Dinosaur footprints believed to be 130 million years old can be seen at very low tide. A plaster cast of the tracks has been embedded at the top of the cliff. 5 km NE.
Crocodile Park: home to some of Australia's biggest crocodiles; Cable Beach Rd; 7 km NW. *Reddell Beach:* enjoy the dramatic sight of Broome's distinctive red soils, known as 'pindan', meeting

white sands and brilliant blue water; 7 km SW. *Manbana Indigenous Aquaculture Centre:* WA's first indigenous-owned aquaculture hatchery and interpretive centre, with tours daily; Murakami Rd; 10 km S. *Buccaneer Rock:* at entrance to Dampier Creek, this landmark commemorates Captain William Dampier and HMAS *Roebuck*; 15 km E. *Broome Bird Observatory:* see some of the 310 species of migratory wader birds that arrive each year from Siberia; 17 km E. *Willie Creek Pearl Farm:* the Kimberley's only pearl farm open to the public, with daily tours; 35 km N. *Dampier Peninsula:* this remote area north of Broome boasts unspoiled coastline; 4WD access only. The Sacred Heart Church at Beagle Bay, 118 km NE, was built by Pallotine monks in 1917 and boasts a magnificent pearl-shell altar. Lombadina, 200 km NE, is a former mission now home to an Aboriginal community that offers sightseeing, fishing and mudcrabbing tours. Cape Leveque, at the north of the peninsula, is well known for its pristine beaches and rugged pindan cliffs; 220 km NE. *Buccaneer Archipelago:* in Broome you can arrange scenic flights over this magnificent landscape that stretches north-east of the Dampier Peninsula; *see feature on p. 325. Hovercraft Spirit of Broome:* tours of Roebuck Bay; details from visitor centre.
ⓘ Cnr Bagot St and Broome Rd; (08) 9192 2222; www.broomevisitorcentre. com.au

Bunbury   Pop. 45 153

Map ref. 568 F4, 572 C8, 574 C10

Bunbury, known as the 'harbour city', is the major commercial and regional centre of the South-West. It lies on a scenic peninsula surrounded by the waters of the Indian Ocean, Koombana Bay and the Leschenault Inlet. This is an angler's paradise with good deep-sea fishing, bay fishing for bream, flounder, tailor and whiting, and succulent blue manna crabs in season in the estuary. Bunbury is also known for its wild dolphins that come close to the beach at Koombana Bay. Bunbury was

settled by Europeans in 1838 and the Koombana Bay whalers were a source of initial prosperity. Today the port is the main outlet for the timber industry, mineral sands and produce of the fertile hinterland.

IN TOWN Dolphin Discovery Centre Wild bottlenose dolphins regularly visit Koombana Bay. The centre has interpretative displays on dolphins and other marine life and offers visitors the chance to swim with dolphins under ranger guidance. Dolphin visits usually occur in the mornings, however times and days of visits are unpredictable. If you prefer not to get wet, take a dolphin-spotting cruise on the bay. Koombana Dr; open 8am–5pm daily Nov–May; open 9am–3pm daily June–Aug.
Historic buildings: many date back to the early decades of the settlement, including the 1865 Rose Hotel, cnr Victoria and Stephen sts; contact visitor centre for details. *King Cottage:* built in 1880 and one of the oldest buildings in Bunbury, this cottage was built by Henry King using homemade bricks. It now displays items of domestic life from the early 20th century. Forrest Ave; open 2pm–4pm daily. *Sir John Forrest Monument:* born in Picton on the outskirts of Bunbury in 1847, Sir John Forrest was elected the first Premier of WA in 1890 and entered Federal Parliament in 1901; cnr Victoria and Stephen sts. *Victoria Street:* a 'cappuccino strip' of sidewalk cafes and restaurants. *Bunbury Regional Art Galleries:* built in 1887, formally a convent for the Sisters of Mercy and now the largest art gallery in the South-West; Wittenoom St. *Miniature Railway Track:* take a ride on this 800 m track through the trees at Forest Park; Blair St; 3rd Sun of each month. *Lookouts:* Boulter's Heights, Haig Cres and Marlston Hill, Apex Dr. *Lighthouse:* painted in black-and-white check, this striking landmark has a lookout at the base; end of Ocean Dr. *Basaltic rock:* formed by volcanic lava flow 150 million years ago; foreshore at end of Clifton St, off Ocean Dr. *Mangrove boardwalk:* 200 m elevated boardwalk lets you view the southern-most mangrove colony in WA, estimated

A camel trek along Cable Beach, Broome

to be 20 000 years old; Koombana Dr. *Big Swamp Wildlife Park*: handfeed kangaroos, see bettongs, wombats, swamp wallabies and more, and enjoy the South-West's largest walk-through aviary with 60 species of native birds; Prince Phillip Dr. *Heritage trail*: 12 km walk from the Old Railway Station; contact visitor centre for brochure.

WHAT'S ON *Three Waters Festival*: Feb/Mar.

NEARBY *St Marks Anglican Church*: built in 1842, this is the second oldest church in WA. The churchyard contains the graves of many early Bunbury settlers. 5 km SE at Picton. *South West Gem Museum*: over 2000 gemstones; 12 km S. *Wineries*: many in the area offer cellar-door tastings, including Killerby Wines (10 km S) and Capel Vale Wines (27 km S); contact visitor centre for details. *Australind–Bunbury Tourist Drive*: coastal scenery, excellent crabbing and picnic spots; contact visitor centre for map. *Abseiling tours*: on the quarry face of the Wellington Dam; contact visitor centre for details. *Scenic flights*: over Bunbury and surrounds. ℹ️ Old Railway Station, Carmody Pl; (08) 9721 7922 or 1800 286 287; www.bunburybreaks.com.au

Busselton   Pop. 13 863

Map ref. 568 D7, 569 F3, 572 B9, 574 C10

First settled by Europeans in 1834, Busselton is one of the oldest towns in Western Australia. It is situated on the shores of Geographe Bay and the picturesque Vasse River. Sheltered from most prevailing winds, the tranquil waters of the bay are an aquatic playground edged with 30 kilometres of white sand beaches. Over the past three decades, the traditional industries of timber, dairying, beef cattle and sheep have been joined by grape-growing and winemaking. Fishing is also important, particularly crayfish and salmon in season. In spring, the wildflowers are magnificent.

IN TOWN Busselton Jetty The longest timber jetty in the Southern Hemisphere was built over a 95-year period, beginning in 1865, principally for the export of timber. Over 5000 ships from all over the world docked here through the ages of sail, steam and diesel, before the port closed in 1972. The jetty stretches a graceful 2 km into Geographe Bay and has always been a popular spot for fishing, snorkelling and scuba diving because of the variety of marine life beneath it. An Interpretive Centre at the base of the jetty displays historical and environmental exhibits. At the seaward end is an Underwater Observatory that opened at the end of 2003. An observation chamber with viewing windows 8 m beneath the surface allows visitors to marvel at vividly coloured corals, sponges and fish. Tours

are available; bookings essential. A small tourist train runs the length of the jetty on most days, weather permitting. End of Queen St. *Ballarat Engine*: first steam locomotive in WA; Pries Ave. *St Mary's Anglican Church*: built in 1844 of limestone and jarrah, with a she-oak shingle roof. The churchyard has many pioneer graves, including John Garrett Bussell's, after whom Busselton was named. Peel Tce. *Nautical Lady Entertainment World*: family fun park with giant water slide, flying fox, mini golf, skate park, racing cars, lookout tower and nautical museum; on beachfront at end of Queen St. *Old Courthouse*: restored gaol cells and arts complex; Queen St. *Busselton Historical Museum*: originally a creamery, now houses historic domestic equipment; Peel Tce. *Vasse River Parkland*: barbecue facilities; Peel Tce.

WHAT'S ON *Festival of Busselton*: Jan. *Beach Festival*: Jan. *Busselton Jetty Swim*: Feb. *Geographe Bay Race Week*: yachting; Feb. *Naturaliste Bluewater Classic*: fishing; Mar. *Respect Yourself Forest Rally*: Mar. *Heritage Festival Day*: April. *Busselton Fine Wine and Food Fair*: Oct. *Busselton Agricultural Show*: one of the oldest and largest country shows in WA; Oct/Nov. *Busselton Winedowner*: Nov. *Ironman Western Australia Triathlon*: Nov.

NEARBY Tuart Forest National Park The majestic tuart tree grows only on coastal limestone 200 km either side of Perth. Known locally as the Ludlow Tuart Forest, this 2049 ha park protects the largest natural tuart forest in the world. It also has the tallest and largest specimens of tuart trees on the Swan Coastal Plain, up to 33 m high and 10 m wide. Enjoy scenic drives, forest walks and picnics in a magnificent setting. 12 km SE. *Wonnerup House*: built in 1859, now a National Trust museum and fine example of colonial architecture, furnished in period style; 10 km E. *Whistle Stop*: miniature railway with picnic area; Vasse Hwy; 11 km SE; check opening times. *Bunyip Craft Centre*: Ludlow; 15 km E. *Wineries*: numerous vineyards and wineries in the area. Many are open for cellar-door tastings; contact visitor centre for map. *Augusta–Busselton Heritage Trail*: contact visitor centre for map. ℹ️ 38 Peel Tce; (08) 9752 1288; www.downsouth.com.au

Caiguna   Pop. 10

Map ref. 575 N8

Caiguna, on the Nullarbor Plain, consists of a roadhouse, caravan park, restaurant and service station. The nearest town west is Balladonia, 183 kilometres away, so whichever way you're travelling, Caiguna is for most an essential stop for food and petrol. From immediately east of Caiguna until Border Village, locals operate on Central Western Time, 45 minutes ahead of the rest of Western Australia.

NEARBY John Baxter Memorial In 1841 John Baxter, with an Aboriginal guide known as Wylie and two unnamed Aboriginal men, accompanied Edward John Eyre on his epic journey across the Nullarbor. The party left Fowlers Bay in SA on 25 February and reached the site of modern-day Eucla on 12 March. Later the two unnamed Aboriginal men killed Baxter and, taking most of the supplies, fled into the desert. Eyre and Wylie walked for another month and eventually reached Thistle Cove (near Esperance), where they were rescued by a French whaler. The Baxter memorial is on the Baxter Cliffs overlooking the Great Australian Bight. 4WD access only; 38 km S. *90-Mile Straight*: have your photo taken beside the signpost marking the eastern end of the longest straight stretch of road in Australia, which runs for 90 miles (146.6 km) between Caiguna and Balladonia; 4 km W. *Caiguna Blowhole*: only a few metres from the highway; 5 km W. *Nuytsland Nature Reserve*: covers 400 000 ha of the coastland of the Great Australian Bight; 22 km S. ℹ️ Caiguna Roadhouse; (08) 9039 3459

Carnamah   Pop. 358

Map ref. 574 C5

Carnamah is a typical wheat-belt town servicing the surrounding wheat and sheep properties. From late July through to December the shire of Carnamah and the rest of the wheat belt blossoms into a wildflower wonderland. This is one of Western Australia's richest areas of flowering plants, with more than 600 species.

IN TOWN *Historical Society Museum*: displays historic domestic equipment and old farm machinery; McPherson St.

WHAT'S ON *Wimbledon of the Wheatbelt*: Mar. *North Midlands Agricultural Show, Rodeo and Ute Parade*: Sept.

NEARBY Tathra National Park This park, with its diverse range of spring wildflowers, is named after the Nyungar word for 'beautiful place'. 25 km SW. *McPherson's Homestead*: an excellent example of pioneering architecture (1869), once the home of Duncan McPherson, the first settler in the area; Bunjil Rd; 1 km E; open by appointment. *Yarra Yarra Lake*: this salt lake changes from pink in summer to deep blue in winter. View it from the Lakes Lookout. 16 km S. *Three Springs*: tours to open-cut talc mine; 23 km NW. *Lake Indoon*: a freshwater lake popular for waterskiing, swimming, sailing, camping, picnics and barbecues; 61 km SW. ℹ️ Council offices, McPherson St; (08) 9951 1055

Carnarvon   Pop. 7189

Map ref. 573 B8

Carnarvon is a large coastal town at the mouth of the Gascoyne River. The river and the fertile red earth surrounding it are crucial to the town's thriving agricultural industry. Plantations stretching for 15 kilometres along the riverbanks draw water from the aquifer of the river basin to grow a host of tropical fruits such as bananas, mangoes, avocados, pineapples, pawpaws and melons. Carnarvon gained national prominence when a NASA tracking station operated nearby at Browns Range from 1964 to 1974.

IN TOWN Robinson Street In 1876 the region's founding fathers, Aubrey Brown, John Monger and C. S. Brockman, overlanded 4000 sheep from York and established themselves in the district. Carnarvon was gazetted in 1883 and developed into the centre of an efficient wool-producing area. Camel teams, driven by Afghan camel drivers, brought the wool to Carnarvon from the outlying sheep stations. This is the reason for the extraordinary width of the town's main street, which, at 40 m, gave the camel teams enough room to turn around. *Jubilee Hall:* built in 1887 as the Roads Board building, now used as a craft market. In 1960 a cyclone blew the roof off and all the shire papers blew away. Francis St. *Pioneer Park:* good picnic spot; Olivia Tce. *Murals:* up to 15 buildings in the town, including the Civic Centre, are adorned with murals painted by local artists. *Heritage walking trail:* 20 historic landmarks around the town; contact visitor centre for map.

WHAT'S ON *Fremantle–Carnarvon Yacht Race:* even-numbered years, May. *Growers' market:* Sat mornings; May–Nov. *Courtyard Markets:* Robinson St; first Sat each month; May–Dec. *Carnarfin:* fishing competition; June. *Carnarvon Festival and Rodeo:* Aug. *Gascoyne Showcase Gala Concert:* Aug.

NEARBY Carnarvon Heritage Precinct On Babbage Island, and connected to the township by a causeway, the heritage precinct incorporates one of Carnarvon's most popular tourist attractions, the One Mile Jetty. Built in 1897, this is the longest jetty in WA's north, stretching for 1493 m into the Indian Ocean. It offers excellent fishing and a jetty train runs its length. Other attractions in the precinct include the Lighthouse Keeper's Cottage museum, a steam train that runs between One Mile Jetty and the town bridge, a prawning factory at the old whaling station (tours in season, check times at visitor centre) and Pelican Point, for picnics, swimming and fishing. **Blowholes** Jets of water shoot up to 20 m in the air after being forced through holes in the coastal rock. When you arrive at the Blowholes, you are greeted by a huge sign declaring 'KING WAVES KILL' – a cautionary reminder that this picturesque coastline has claimed the lives of over 30 people in freak waves. 73 km N. A further 7 km down

The stromatolites at Lake Thetis, near Cervantes

the road from the blowholes is a cairn commemorating the loss of HMAS *Sydney* in 1941. *Westoby Plantation:* a working banana plantation. Tours are available; contact visitor centre for details. 5 km E. *'The Big Dish':* a huge 29 m wide reflector, part of the old NASA station, with views of town and plantations from the base; 8 km E. *Bibbawarra Artesian Bore:* hot water surfaces at 65 degrees Celsius; picnic area nearby; 16 km N. *Bibbawarra Trough:* 180 m long, believed to be the longest in the Southern Hemisphere; adjacent to bore; 16 km N. *Miaboolya Beach:* good fishing, crabbing and swimming; 22 km N. *Rocky Pool:* picnic area and deep billabong ideal for swimming; Gascoyne Rd; 55 km E. *Red Bluff:* world-renowned surfing spot with waves 1–6 m, depending on the time of the year; 143 km N. *Fishing:* excellent fishing for snapper or groper and game fishing for marlin or sailfish; charter boats available.
ⓘ Civic Centre, Robinson St; (08) 9941 1146; www.shireofcarnarvon.com

Cervantes   Pop. 242

Map ref. 574 B6

This small but thriving fishing town was established in 1962 and named after the American whaling ship *Cervantes*, which sank off the coast in 1844. The town's fishing fleet nearly doubles in rock lobster season, and in spring the town is surrounded by spectacular displays of wildflowers with vistas of wattles stretching from horizon to horizon. Not

far from Cervantes is one of Australia's best-known landscapes, the Pinnacles Desert, lying at the heart of Nambung National Park.

IN TOWN *Pinnacle Wildflowers:* displays of native WA flora, dried flower arrangements, souvenirs; Bradley Loop.

NEARBY Nambung National Park In the Pinnacles Desert thousands of limestone pillars rise out of a stark landscape of yellow sand. In places they reach over 3 m. The Pinnacles are the eroded remnants of a bed of limestone, which was created from sea-shells breaking down into lime-rich sands. See such formations as the Indian Chief, Garden Wall and Milk Bottles. The loop drive is one-way and not suitable for caravans. 17 km S. *Lake Thetis Stromatolites:* one of WA's six known locations of stromatolites, the oldest living organism on earth; 5 km S. *Kangaroo Point:* good picnic spot; 9 km S. *Hangover Bay:* a stunning white sandy beach ideal for swimming, snorkelling, windsurfing and surfing; 13 km S.
ⓘ Cervantes Service Station, cnr Aragon and Seville sts; (08) 9652 7041

Cocklebiddy   Pop. 9

Map ref. 575 O8

This tiny settlement, comprising a roadhouse with motel units, caravan sites and camping facilities, lies between Madura and Caiguna on the Nullarbor Plain. The Nuytsland Nature Reserve extends southwards, a 400 000 hectare strip running along the Great Australian Bight. Locals operate on Central Western Time, 45 minutes ahead of the rest of Western Australia.

NEARBY Eyre Bird Observatory Housed in the fully restored 1897 Eyre telegraph station, Australia's first bird observatory offers nature lovers the opportunity to birdwatch, bushwalk and beachcomb in the wilderness of the Nuytsland Nature Reserve. Over 240 species of birds have been recorded at Eyre, including Major Mitchell cockatoos, brush bronze-wings, honeyeaters and mallee fowl. It is near the site where Edward John Eyre found water and rested during his Nullarbor journey in February 1841. Tours and whale-watching (Aug–Oct) can be arranged with 24 hrs notice on (08) 9039 3450 or through the visitor centre. 4WD access only; 50 km SE. *Chapel Rock:* picnic area; 4 km E. *Cocklebiddy Caves:* the Nullarbor Plain is honeycombed with caves, some containing water-filled passages that are among the largest known in the world. In 1983 a French team of speleologists set an underground record in the Cocklebiddy Caves when they made the deepest cave dive in the world. For adventure caving, contact CALM on (08) 9071 3733 or visitor centre. 21 km NW. *Twilight Cove:* fishing and whale-watching spot famous for its 70 m high limestone

cliffs overlooking the Great Australian Bight; 4WD access only; 32 km s.
ⓘ Wedgetail Inn; (08) 9039 3462

Collie   Pop. 6946

Map ref. 572 D8, 574 C10

Collie is Western Australia's only coalmining town. The surrounding area was first explored in 1829 when Captain James Stirling led a reconnaissance party to the land south of Perth. The region was originally considered ideal for timber production and as pasturelands. However, the discovery of coal along the Collie River in 1883 changed the region's fortunes. In 1896 Collie was declared a township. In dense jarrah forest, near the winding Collie River, the town has many parks and gardens. The drive into Collie on the Coalfields Highway along the top of the Darling Scarp offers spectacular views of the surrounding forests, rolling hills and farms.

IN TOWN Tourist Coal Mine Step back in time and gain an insight into the mining industry and the working conditions in underground mines. This replica mine was constructed in 1983 to commemorate the centenary of coal discovery. Tours by appt only; contact visitor centre. Throssell St.
Coalfields Museum: displays of historic photographs, coalmining equipment, rocks and minerals, woodwork by local miner Fred Kohler, a doll house and art housed in the historic Roads Board building; Throssell St. *Steam Locomotive Museum:* superbly restored collection includes an old front-end loader, a puffing billy and F, V and W class locomotives; Throssell St. *All Saints Anglican Church:* impressive Norman-style church distinctive for its unusual stained-glass windows, extensive use of jarrah timbers and elaborate mural, which in 1922 took renowned stage artist Philip Goatcher 8 months to complete; tours by appt; contact visitor centre; Venn St. *Old Collie Goods Shed:* restoration of rolling stock; Forrest St. *Central Precinct Historic Walk:* self-guide walk of historic buildings; contact visitor centre for map. *Collie River Walk:* pleasant walk along riverbank; contact visitor centre for map.

WHAT'S ON *Market at Westrail Reserve:* Forrest St; first and third Sun each month (except winter). *Busy Fingers Art and Craft Show:* Feb. *Collie–Donnybrook Cycle Race:* Aug. *Collie River Valley Marathon:* Sept.

NEARBY Wellington National Park Covering 4000 ha, this park features heavy tracts of magnificent jarrah forest. Picnic, swim, canoe or camp at Honeymoon Pool or Potters Gorge, or go rafting in winter on the rapids below the Wellington Dam wall. 18 km w.
Minninup Pool: where the Collie River is at its widest, ideal for swimming, canoeing or picnicking; off Mungalup Rd; 3 km s.

Stockton Lake: camping and waterskiing; 8 km E. *Harris Dam:* beautiful picnic area; 14 km N. *Collie River Scenic Drive:* views of jarrah forest and wildflowers in season; contact visitor centre for map. *Bibbulmun Track:* sections of this trail pass through Collie; *see feature on p. 323.*
ⓘ 156 Throssell St; (08) 9734 2051; www.collierivervalley.org.au

Coolgardie   Pop. 1081

Map ref. 574 I6

After alluvial gold was found in 1892, Coolgardie grew in ten years to a town of 15 000 people, 23 hotels, six banks and two stock exchanges. The main street, lined with some magnificent buildings, was made wide enough for camel trains to turn around in. As in many outback towns, the heat and the isolation lead to innovation, in this case that of the Coolgardie safe, which used water and a breeze to keep food cool before the days of electricity.

IN TOWN Historic buildings There are 23 buildings in the town centre that have been listed on the National Estate register, many of them on the main street, Bayley St. Over 100 markers record the history of the town through these buildings and historic sites, using stories and photographs to recapture the gold-rush days. The index to markers is in Bayley St next to the visitor centre.
Railway Station Built in 1896, the railway station is now a museum housing a transport exhibition and a display on the famous Varischetti mine rescue. In 1907 Modesto Varischetti was trapped underground in a flooded mine for 9 days. Varischetti survived in an air pocket until divers eventually found him. The dramatic rescue captured world attention. Woodward St.
Pharmacy Museum: recreated turn-of-the-century pharmacy; Bayley St. *Ben Prior's Open-Air Museum:* unusual collection of historic memorabilia; cnr Bayley and Hunt sts. *Warden Finnerty's House:* striking 1895 example of early Australian architecture and furnishings; McKenzie St; open 11am–4pm daily except Wed. *C. Y. O'Connor Dedication:* fountain and water course in memory of O'Connor, who masterminded the Coolgardie Water Scheme; McKenzie St. *Gaol tree:* used for prisoners in early gold-rush days, before a gaol was built; Hunt St. *Lindsay's Pit Lookout:* over open-cut goldmine; Ford St.
WHAT'S ON *Coolgardie Day:* Sept. *Metal Detecting Championships:* Sept/Oct.

NEARBY Coolgardie Cemetery The town cemetery gives you an inkling of how harsh the early gold-rush years were. The register of burials records that of the first 32 burials, the names of 15 were unknown. There are frequent entries for 'male child' and 'female child' with the cause of death cited as 'fever'. Between 1894 and 1899 there were 1108 burials.

From 1961 to 1966 there were only 43. One of the most significant graves is that of Ernest Giles, an Englishman whose name is associated with the exploration of inland Australia. 1 km w.
Stamp Battery: tours available of this fully operational battery; contact visitor centre for details; Coolgardie–Esperance Hwy. *Coolgardie Camel Farm:* ride the 'ships of the desert'; 4 km w. *Gnarlbine Rock/Hunts Well:* one of the few known watering holes for the early prospectors; 30 km sw. *Kunanalling Hotel:* once a town of over 800 people, the ruins of the hotel are all that remain; 32 km N. *Victoria Rock:* spectacular views from the summit; 55 km sw. *Burra Rocks:* popular picnic area; 55 km s. *Rowles Lagoon Nature Reserve:* freshwater wetlands ideal for swimming, boating, canoeing, bushwalking, birdwatching, picnicking and camping; 65 km N. *Wallaroo Rocks:* three dams with scenic views and good bushwalking; 90 km w. *Cave Hill Nature Reserve:* spectacular granite outcrop with large cave formation and waterholes; 4WD access only; 90 km s. *Golden Quest Discovery Trail:* Coolgardie forms part of this 965 km self-guide drive trail of the goldfields; book, map and CD available at visitor centre.
ⓘ Goldfields Exhibition Building, Bayley St; (08) 9026 6090; www.kalgoorlie.com

Coral Bay   Pop. 1008

Map ref. 573 B5

Coral Bay is famous for one thing – its proximity to the Ningaloo Marine Park. The Ningaloo Reef is Western Australia's equivalent of the Great Barrier Reef, boasting an incredible diversity of marine life and stunningly beautiful coral formations. At Coral Bay the coral gardens lie close to the shore, which makes access to the reef as easy as a gentle swim. Lying at the southern end of the Ningaloo Marine Park, Coral Bay is blessed with pristine beaches and a near-perfect climate: it is consistently warm and dry, regardless of the season, and the water temperature only varies from 18 to 28 degrees. Swimming, snorkelling, scuba diving, and beach, reef and deep-sea fishing (outside sanctuary areas) are available year-round.

NEARBY *Ningaloo Marine Park: see feature on p. 305. Point Cloates:* the wrecks of the *Zvir, Fin, Perth* and *Rapid* lie on the reef just off the point; 4WD access only; 8 km N. *Tours:* including glass-bottomed boat cruises, snorkel and dive tours, kayak tours, fishing charters, scenic flights, and marine wildlife-watching tours to see whale sharks (April–June), humpback whales (June–Nov) and manta rays (all year); contact visitor centre for details.
ⓘ Coastal Adventure Tours, Coral Bay Arcade, Robinson St; (08) 9948 5190

WESTERN AUSTRALIA

Corrigin   Pop. 724

Map ref. 572 H5, 574 E8

Corrigin was established in the early
1900s and was one of the last wheat-belt
towns to be settled. Today the town has a
healthy obsession with dogs, as testified
by its Dog Cemetery and the national
record the town holds for lining up 1527
utes with dogs in the back.

IN TOWN Corrigin Pioneer Museum
Superb collection of old agricultural
equipment including an original
Sunshine harvester and some early
steam-driven farm machinery. A small
working steam train carries passengers
on a short circuit around the museum
and local rest area. Kunjin St.
RSL Monument: a Turkish mountain gun
from Gallipoli; Gayfer St.

WHAT'S ON *Dog in a Ute event:* held
in varying years in April; contact visitor
centre for dates.

NEARBY Dog Cemetery Loving dog
owners have gone to the considerable
expense of having elaborate headstones
placed over the remains of their faithful
four-footed friends. There are over
80 dogs buried in the cemetery, with
gravestones dedicated to Dusty, Rover,
Spot, et al. There is even one statue of a
dog 6 ft high. Brookton Hwy; 7 km w.
Wildflower scenic drive: signposted with
lookout; 3 km w. *Kunjin Animal Farm:*
kangaroos, emus, alpacas, donkeys and
goats; 18 km w. *Gorge Rock:* large granite
outcrop with picnic area; 20 km se.
ℹ️ Corrigin Telecentre, Campbell St;
(08) 9063 2778

Cranbrook   Pop. 267

Map ref. 571 L6, 572 H11, 574 E11

The small town of Cranbrook greets
travellers with a large sign announcing
that it is 'The Gateway to the Stirlings'.
A mere ten kilometres away is Stirling
Range National Park, a mecca for
bushwalkers and climbers. The nearby
Frankland area has gained a national
reputation for its premium-quality wines.

IN TOWN *Station House Museum:*
restored and furnished 1930s-style;
Gathorne St. *Wildflower walk:* 300 m walk
to Stirling Gateway with displays of
orchids in spring; Salt River Rd.

WHAT'S ON *Cranbrook Shire on Show:*
April. *Wildflower Display:* Sept. *Art Show:* Nov.

NEARBY Stirling Range National Park
Surrounded by a flat, sandy plain, the
Stirling Range rises abruptly to over
1000 m, its jagged peaks veiled in swirling
mists. The cool, humid environment
created by these low clouds supports
1500 flowering plant species, many
unique to the area. This is one of WA's
premier destinations for bushwalking.
Best time to visit is Oct–Dec. 10 km se.
Sukey Hill Lookout: expansive views of
farmland, salt lakes and Stirling Range;

off Salt River Rd; 5 km e. *Lake Poorrarecup:*
swimming and waterskiing; 40 km sw.
Wineries: the nearby Frankland River
region boasts several wineries, including
Alkoomi, Frankland Estate and Ferngrove;
50 km w. *Wildflower Drive and Heritage Trail:*
contact visitor centre for brochure.
ℹ️ Council offices, Gathorne St;
(08) 9826 1008

Cue   Pop. 290

Map ref. 573 H13, 574 E1, 576 B13

This town was once known as the
'Queen of the Murchison'. In 1891
Mick Fitzgerald and Ed Heffernan found
large nuggets of gold not far from what
was to become the main street. It was
their prospecting mate, Tom Cue, who
registered the claim on their behalf and
when the town was officially proclaimed
in 1894, it bore his name. Within ten
years the population of this boom town
of the Murchison goldfields had exploded
to about 10 000 people. While Cue's
population has significantly dwindled
over time, the legacy of those heady
gold-rush days is evident in the town's
remarkably grandiose buildings.

IN TOWN Heritage buildings Many
magnificent early buildings still stand
and are classified by the National Trust.
A stroll up the main street takes in
the elegant band rotunda, the former
Gentleman's Club (now the shire offices,
housing a photographic display of the
region's history), the Old Gaol, the
courthouse, the post office and the police
station. One block west in Dowley St is the
former Masonic lodge. This two-storey
residence built in 1899 is reputed to be
the largest corrugated iron structure in
the Southern Hemisphere.

NEARBY Walga Rock This monolith is
1.5 km long and 5 km around the base.
It has several Aboriginal rock paintings.
One of the most extraordinary paintings,
considering that Cue is over 300 km
from the sea, is of a white, square-rigged
sailing ship. It is believed to depict one
of the Dutch ships that visited WA's mid-
west shores in the 17th century. 50 km w.
Day Dawn: once Cue's twin town, thanks
to the fabulous wealth of the Great Fingall
Mine. The mine office, a magnificent
century-old stone building now perched
precariously on the edge of a new open-
cut mine, is all that remains of the town;
5 km w. *Heritage trail:* includes old hospital
ruins; contact visitor centre for brochure.
ℹ️ Lot 35, Robinson St (April–Nov): (08)
9963 1216; or shire offices, Austin St;
(08) 9963 1041

Denham   Pop. 1388

Map ref. 573 B10

On the middle peninsula of Shark Bay,
Denham is the most westerly town in
Australia. Dirk Hartog, the Dutch
navigator, landed on an island at the bay's

entrance in 1616, the first known
European to land on the continent.
Centuries later, in 1858, Captain H. M.
Denham surveyed the area and a town
bearing his name was established. The
Shark Bay region was once known for its
pearling and fishing, and the streets of
Denham were literally paved with pearl
shells. In the 1960s, however, the local
roads board poured bitumen over the
pearl shells, and so destroyed what could
have been a unique tourist attraction.
Fortunately, several buildings made from
coquina shell block still stand in the town.
Today Shark Bay is renowned for the wild
dolphins that come inshore at Monkey
Mia (pronounced 'my-a'). As a World
Heritage area, it also protects dugongs,
humpback whales, green and loggerhead
turtles, important seagrass feeding
grounds and a colony of stromatolites,
the world's oldest living fossils.

IN TOWN *Shell block buildings:*
St Andrews Anglican Church, cnr
Hughes and Brockman sts, and the Old
Pearlers Restaurant, cnr Knight Tce
and Durlacher St, were both built from
coquina shell block. *Town Bluff:* popular
walk for beachcombers; from town along
beach to bluff. *Pioneer Park:* contains the
stone on which Captain Denham carved
his name in 1858; Hughes St.

NEARBY Monkey Mia The daily shore
visits by the wild bottlenose dolphins
at Monkey Mia are a world-famous
phenomenon. The dolphins swim right
into the shallows, providing a unique
opportunity for humans to make contact
with them. It began in the 1960s when a
local woman started feeding the dolphins
that followed her husband's fishing boat
to a campsite on the shoreline. Feeding
still occurs, although now it is carefully
monitored by rangers to ensure that the
dolphins maintain their hunting and
survival skills. Visiting times, and the
number of dolphins, vary. 26 km ne.

Hamelin Pool and the stromatolites The
shores of Hamelin Pool are dotted with
stromatolites, the world's largest and
oldest living fossils. These colonies of
micro-organisms resemble the oldest
and simplest forms of life on earth,
dated at around 3.5 million years old.
The Hamelin Pool stromatolites are
relatively new colonies however, about
3000 years old. They thrive here because
of the extreme salinity of the water, the
occurrence of calcium bicarbonate and
the limited water circulation. Visitors
can view these extraordinary life forms
from a boardwalk. Close by is the Flint
Cliff Telegraph Station and Post Office
Museum (1884) with a history of the
region. 88 km se.

Dugongs The Shark Bay World Heritage
Area has the largest seagrass meadows
in the world, covering about 4000 sq km.
These meadows are home to around
10 000 dugongs, 10 percent of the
world's remaining population. An

endangered species, the dugong is nature's only vegetarian sea mammal. Also known as a sea cow, the dugong can live for up to 70 years and grow up to 3 m long. Tours are available offering visitors a unique opportunity to see dugongs in the wild. Contact visitor centre for details. *Little Lagoon:* ideal fishing and picnic spot; 3 km N. *Francois Peron National Park:* Peron Homestead with its 'hot tub' of artesian water; 4WD access only; 7 km N. *Ocean Park:* marine park with aquarium and touch pool; 9 km S. *Eagle Bluff:* habitat of sea eagle and a good viewing spot for sharks and stingrays; 20 km S. *Blue Lagoon Pearl Farm:* working platform where black pearls are harvested; Monkey Mia; 26 km NE. *Shell Beach:* 120 km of unique coastline comprising countless tiny coquina shells; 45 km SE. *Steep Point:* western-most point on mainland with spectacular scenery; 4WD access only; 260 km W. *Zuytdorp Cliffs:* extend from beneath Shark Bay region south to Kalbarri; 4WD access only. *Tours:* boat trips and charter flights to historic Dirk Hartog Island (*see feature on p. 325*), catamaran cruises, safaris and coach tours; contact visitor centre for details.
ⓘ 71 Knight Tce; (08) 9948 1253; www.outbackcoast.com

Denmark
Pop. 2433

Map ref. 571 K12, 572 G13, 574 E12

Denmark lies at the foot of Mt Shadforth, overlooking the tranquil Denmark River and Wilson Inlet. It is surrounded by forests of towering karri trees that sweep down to meet the Southern Ocean. The Aboriginal name for the Denmark River is 'koorabup', meaning 'place of the black swan'. Originally a timber town, Denmark's economy is today sustained by a combination of dairying, beef cattle, fishing, timber and tourism. The town's appeal lies in its proximity to some of the most beautiful coastline in the state.

IN TOWN *Bandstand:* located on the riverbank with seating for the audience on the other side of the river; Holling Rd. *Arts and crafts:* galleries abound, including the Old Butter Factory in North St; contact visitor centre for details. *Pentland Alpaca Stud and Tourist Farm:* diverse collection of animals, including alpacas, koalas, kangaroos, bison, water buffalo, llamas and many more; cnr McLeod and Scotsdale rds. *Mt Shadforth Lookout:* magnificent views; Mohr Dr. *Berridge and Thornton parks:* shaded picnic areas; along riverbank in Holling Rd.
WHAT'S ON *Pantomime:* Berridge Park; Jan. *Craft Market:* riverbank; Jan, Easter and Dec. *Music Festival:* Howard Park Winery; Feb. *Brave New Works:* new performance art; Easter.
NEARBY William Bay National Park
This relatively small 1867 ha park protects stunning coastline and forest between Walpole and Denmark on

WA's south coast. It is renowned for its windswept granite tors, which have a striking primeval appearance. Green's Pool, a natural rock pool in the park, remains calm and safe for swimming and snorkelling all year round. Nearby are the Elephant Rocks, massive rounded boulders resembling elephants; Madfish Bay, a good fishing spot; and Waterfall Beach for swimming. 17 km SW.
Ocean Beach: one of the finest surfing beaches in WA; 8 km S. *Bridget's Orchard:* fresh fruit and preserves; 9 km W; check opening times. *Monkey Rock:* lookout with panoramic views; 10 km SW. *Bartholomew's Meadery:* honey, honey wines, gourmet honey ice-cream and other bee products, as well as a live beehive display; 20 km W. *Eden Gate Blueberry Farm:* spray-free fruit and blueberry wines; 25 km E; open Thurs–Mon Dec–April. *Whale-watching:* viewing platform above Lowlands Beach (July–Oct); 28 km E. *Fishing:* at Wilson Inlet, Ocean Beach (8 km S) and Parry Beach (25 km W). *West Cape Howe National Park:* Torbay Head, WA's most southerly point, and Cosy Corner, a protected beach perfect for swimming; 30 km SW. *Aqua Blue Marron Farm:* tours available; contact visitor centre for details; 40 km W. *Wineries:* many wineries open for cellar-door tastings, including Howard Park Winery, West Cape Howe and Tinglewood Wines; contact visitor centre for map. *Scenic drives:* the 25 km Mt Shadforth Scenic Drive and the 34 km Scotsdale Tourist Drive both feature lush forests, ocean views, wineries and galleries; contact visitor centre for maps. *Heritage trails:* 3 km Mokare trail, 5 km Karri Walk or 9 km Wilson Inlet trail; contact visitor centre for maps. *Bibbulmun Track:* a section of this world-class 963 km long-distance trail passes through Denmark; *see feature on p. 323. Valley of the Giants Tree Top Walk: see Walpole.*
ⓘ 60 Strickland St; (08) 9848 2055; www.denmarkvisitorcentre.com.au

Derby
Pop. 3661

Map ref. 579 J7, 580 B9

It is said that Derby, known as the 'Gateway to the Gorges', is where the real Kimberley region begins. It was the first town to be settled in the Kimberley and features some of its most spectacular natural attractions nearby: the Devonian Reef Gorges of Windjana and Tunnel Creek are only a few hours' drive along the Gibb River Road, and the magnificent islands of the Buccaneer Archipelago are just a short cruise away. Although King Sound was first explored in 1688, it wasn't until the early 1880s that the Port of Derby was established as a landing point for wool shipments and Derby was proclaimed a townsite. The first jetty was built in 1885, the same year that gold was discovered at Halls Creek. Miners and prospectors poured into the port on their way to the goldfields but by the 1890s, as gold fever died, the port was used almost exclusively for the export of live cattle and sheep. In 1951 iron-ore mining began at Cockatoo Island, which revitalised the town. Derby is now a service centre for the region's rich pastoral and mining industries. Rain closes some roads in the area from November to March, so check conditions before setting out on any excursion.

IN TOWN *Old Derby Gaol:* built in 1906, this is the oldest building in town; Loch St. *Library and Botanical Gardens:* the library houses a collection of historic memorabilia and Aboriginal artefacts. The adjacent gardens feature a rockery of Jowalenga sandstone, also known as 'Kimberley colourstone'. Clarendon St. *Wharfinger House Museum:* built in the 1920s for the local harbourmaster, the design is typical of the tropics; Loch St. *Derby Jetty:* the highest tides in Australia, up to 12 m, can be seen from the jetty. The last commercial

Dugongs in Shark Bay, near Denham

WESTERN AUSTRALIA

ship visited the port in 1983 and the ramps used for loading live cattle are still in place.

WHAT'S ON *King Tide Day:* festival celebrating highest tide in Australia; May. *Market:* Clarendon St; every Sat; May–Sept. *Moonrise Rock Festival:* June. *Garden Competition:* June. *Derby Races:* June/July. *Mowanjum Festival:* indigenous art and culture; July. *Boab Festival:* mardi gras, mud football and Stockmen and Bushies Weekend; July. *Derby Rodeo:* Aug. *Croc Festival:* 2-day festival for schoolchildren; Aug. *Flower and Produce Show:* Aug. *Craft Show:* Sept. *Ike Stohl Fishing Competition:* Sept. *Boxing Day Sports:* Dec.

NEARBY Windjana Gorge National Park A 350 million-year-old Devonian reef rises majestically above the surrounding plains. An easy walking trail winds through the gorge, taking in primeval life forms fossilised within the gorge walls. 145 km E. **Tunnel Creek National Park** Wear sandshoes, carry a torch and be prepared to get wet as you explore the 750 m long cave that runs through the Napier Range. Nearby Pigeon's Cave was the hideout of an 1890s Aboriginal outlaw, Jandamarra, also known as 'Pigeon'. For tours, contact visitor centre. 184 km E.
Prison tree: 1000-year-old boab tree formerly used as a prison; 7 km S. *Myall's Bore:* beside the bore stands a 120 m long cattle trough reputed to be the longest in the Southern Hemisphere; 7 km S. *Gorges:* Lennard Gorge (190 km N), Bell Gorge (214 km E), Manning Gorge (306 km E), Barnett River Gorge (340 km NE), Sir John Gorge (350 km E); 4WD access only. *Mitchell Plateau:* highlights include the Wandjina rock art and spectacular Mitchell Falls, King Edward River and Surveyor's Pool. In this remote region, visitors must be entirely self-sufficient. Via Gibb River Rd and Kalumburu Rd; 580 km NE. Scenic flights can also be arranged from Derby and Kununurra. *Pigeon Heritage Trail:* follow the story of the Aboriginal outlaw Jandamarra, nicknamed Pigeon, and his people, the Bunuba; contact visitor centre for map. *Gibb River Rd:* 4WD road between Derby and Wyndham traverses some of the most spectacular gorge country of the Kimberley; contact visitor centre for guidebook and current road conditions. *Buccaneer Archipelago:* in Derby you can arrange a scenic flight or cruise around this archipelago which begins north of King Sound; *see feature on p. 325.*
ℹ 2 Clarendon St; (08) 9191 1426 or 1800 621 426; www.derbytourism.com.au

Dongara–Denison Pop. 2199

Map ref. 574 B4

Dongara and its nearby twin town of Port Denison lie on the coast 359 kilometres north of Perth. Dongara–Denison is the self-proclaimed 'Lobster Capital' of the state with its off-shore reefs supporting

a profitable industry. Dongara's main street is lined with magnificent Moreton Bay fig trees while Port Denison provides local anglers with a large marina and harbour.

IN TOWN Irwin District Museum Housed in Dongara's Old Police Station, Courthouse and Gaol (1870), the museum features exhibits on the history of the buildings, the invasion of rabbits into WA and the Irwin Coast shipwrecks. Waldeck St; open 10am–4pm Mon–Fri, 10am–12pm Sat. *Russ Cottage:* a beautifully restored farmworker's cottage (1870). The hard-packed material of the kitchen floor was made from scores of anthills, and the flood-level marker near the front door indicates how high the nearby Irwin River rose during the record flood of 1971. St Dominic's Rd, Dongara; open 10am–12pm Sun, or by appt. *The Priory Lodge:* this 1881 building has been an inn, a priory and a boarding college for girls and is now once again a hotel; St Dominic's Rd, Dongara. *Church of St John the Baptist:* (1884) its pews were made from the driftwood of shipwrecks and its church bell is said to have come from Fremantle Gaol; cnr Waldeck and Church sts, Dongara. *The Royal Steam Flour Mill:* (1894) it served the local wheat-growing community until its closure in 1935; northern end of Waldeck St, Dongara. *Cemetery:* headstones dating from 1874 and a wall of remembrance to Dominican sisters; Dodd St, Dongara. *Town Heritage Trail:* 1.6 km walk that features 28 historic Dongara sites; contact visitor centre for map. *Live Rock Lobster Facility:* with a holding capacity of 35 000 kg of live lobster. Daily tours at 2pm, Nov–June. Denison Marina. *Fisherman's Lookout:* one remaining of two obelisks built in 1869, with panoramic views of Port Denison; Point Leander Dr, Port Denison.

WHAT'S ON *Dongara Races:* Easter. *Craft Market:* at old police station; Easter and Christmas. *Country Music Festival and Craft Market Day:* Oct. *Larry Lobster Festival and Blessing of the Fleet:* at the start of each rock lobster season; Nov.

NEARBY *Silverdale Olive Orchards:* olive oil products; 10 km N; open April–Nov by appt. *Mingenew:* small town in agricultural surrounds. Nearby is Fossil Cliff, filled with marine fossils over 250 million years old. 47 km E.
ℹ 9 Waldeck St; (08) 9927 1404; www.lobstercapital.com.au

Donnybrook Pop. 1611

Map ref. 568 H6, 572 C8, 574 C10

Donnybrook is the centre of the oldest and largest apple-growing area in Western Australia. This is the home of the Granny Smith apple and where Lady William apples were developed. Gold was found here in 1897 but mined for only four years. Donnybrook is famous for its sandstone, which has been used in construction statewide since the early 1900s. In Perth, the

GPO, St Mary's Cathedral and the University of Western Australia buildings have all been faced with Donnybrook stone. The quarry can be seen from the Upper Capel Road out of town.

IN TOWN *Memorial Hall:* built of Donnybrook stone; Bentley St. *Anchor and Hope Inn:* (1862) the oldest homestead in the district, now a private property; view outside from South Western Hwy. *Trigwell Place:* picnic and barbecue facilities, and canoeing on nearby Preston River; South Western Hwy. *Apple Harvest:* tours of sheds Mar–May; arrange through visitor centre.

WHAT'S ON *Apple Festival Ball:* even-numbered years, Easter. *Marathon Relay:* Nov.

NEARBY Old Goldfields Orchard and Cider Factory Combines goldfield history with a working orchard. Climb the reconstructed poppet head over the mine, study the history of gold on the property and try your hand at gold prospecting. The orchard provides seasonal fruit for sale and you can enjoy tastings of cider, fruit juice and wines. Goldfields Rd; 6 km S; open 9.30am–4.30pm Wed–Sun and public and school holidays. *Boyanup:* features a Transport Museum; 12 km NW. *Ironstone Gully Falls:* barbecue area en route to Capel; 19 km W. *Gnomesville:* surprising roadside collection of garden gnomes; by the side of the Wellington Mills roundabout on the road between Dardanup and Lowden; 25 km SE. ℹ Old Railway Station, South Western Hwy; (08) 9731 1720; www.donnybrook tourism.com.au

Dunsborough Pop. 1611

Map ref. 568 C7, 569 C2, 572 B9, 574 B10

Dunsborough is a picturesque coastal town on the south-western tip of Geographe Bay. Just west of the town is the Leeuwin–Naturaliste National Park with its dramatic coastline and seasonal wildflower displays. Many of the wineries of the South-West region are only a short drive from the town.

WHAT'S ON *Market:* Dunsborough Hall; cnr Gibney St and Gifford Rd; 2nd Sat each month. *Margaret River Wine Festival:* throughout region; Nov.

NEARBY Leeuwin–Naturaliste National Park Close to Dunsborough at the northern end of the park is Cape Naturaliste with its lighthouse, museum and whale-watching platform (best time Sept–Dec). Walking tracks offer spectacular views of the coastline. Sugarloaf Rock is a dramatic formation just south of the lighthouse – it is also the home of the endangered red-tailed tropic bird. 13 km NW. *See also Margaret River and Augusta.*
Country Life Farm: animals galore, plus merry-go-round, giant slide, bouncing castles and wild-west saloon; Caves Rd; 1 km W. *Simmo's Icecreamery:* 39 flavours of homemade ice-cream made fresh daily; Commonage Rd; 5 km SE. *Quindalup*

Thistle Cove, Cape Le Grand National Park, near Esperance

Fauna Park: specialises in birds, fish, tropical butterflies and baby animals; 5 km E. *Wreck of HMAS Swan:* the largest accessible dive-wreck site in the Southern Hemisphere; tour bookings and permits at visitor centre; off Point Picquet, just south of Eagle Bay; 8 km NW. *Beaches:* to the north-west, popular for fishing, swimming and snorkelling, include Meelup (5 km), Eagle Bay (8 km) and Bunker Bay (12 km). *Wineries:* as part of the Margaret River wine region, there are many wineries nearby; contact visitor centre for details. *In the area:* whale-watching boat charters (Sept–Dec); deep-sea fishing charters; scuba diving, snorkelling and canoeing; wildflower displays in season.
ⓘ Seymour Blvd; (08) 9755 3299; www.downsouth.com.au

Dwellingup   Pop. 345

Map ref. 567 D11, 572 D6, 574 C9

Set among pristine jarrah forest, this is a thriving timber town that was virtually destroyed in 1961 when lightning started a bushfire that lasted for five days, burnt 140 000 hectares of forest and destroyed several nearby towns. Dwellingup was the only town to be rebuilt, and is now a forest-management centre. The Hotham Valley Tourist Railway operates here.

IN TOWN Forest Heritage Centre This centre records WA's jarrah forest heritage and promotes fine wood design, training and education. The building is built of rammed earth, and designed to represent three jarrah leaves on a bough. Each 'leaf' of the building houses a different facility: an Interpretive Centre, a School of Wood and a Forest Heritage Gallery. Learn about conservation and walk among the treetops on an 11 m high canopy walkway. Acacia Rd. *Historical Centre:* includes a photographic display depicting life in the mill towns along the Darling Scarp in the early 1900s. Also a 1939 Mack Fire Truck, the only one in WA. Visitor centre, Marrinup St. *Community Hotel:* last community hotel in WA; Marrinup St.

WHAT'S ON *Log Chop and Community Fair:* Feb. *Giant Pumpkin Competition:* April.

Winterfest and Forest Heritage Festival: July.

NEARBY Lane–Poole Reserve This popular recreational area provides opportunities for picnicking, swimming, canoeing, rafting, fishing and camping. There are several walk trails in the reserve, including sections of the Bibbulmun Track, the 18 km King Jarrah Track from Nanga Mill, the 17 km Nanga Circuit and a 1.5 km loop from Island Pool. 10 km S.
Marrinup Forest Tour: unique 16 km vehicle and walk tour that features many aspects of the Darling Scarp including the Marrinup POW camp and remnants of old mills and towns of days gone by; contact visitor centre for map. *Hotham Valley Tourist Railway:* travel from Perth via Pinjarra to Dwellingup by train, taking in lush green dairy country before climbing the Darling Range, WA's steepest and most spectacular section of railway, and finishing in the heart of the jarrah forest; steam-hauled May–Oct, diesel-hauled Nov–April; check times; Dwellingup Railway Station. *Etmylin Forest Tramway:* takes visitors 8 km through farms and old-growth jarrah forest to the pioneer settlement of Etmylin; check times. *Bibbulmun Track:* long-distance walk trail runs through the middle of the town; *see feature on p. 323. Munda Biddi Trail:* WA's first long-distance off-road bike track begins in Mundaring on the outskirts of Perth and winds 182 km through national parks and state forest to Dwellingup. It will eventually be extended all the way to Albany. Contact visitor centre for details.
ⓘ Marrinup St; (08) 9538 1108

Esperance   Pop. 9365

Map ref. 575 J10

Known to the local Aboriginal people as 'kepa kurl' – the place where the water lies down like a boomerang – Esperance was a sleepy backwater until, in the 1950s, it was found that adding trace elements to the sandy soil made farming feasible. The town became a port and service centre for the agricultural and pastoral hinterland. However, it is the magnificent scenery, the pristine beaches

and the proximity of many national parks that draw visitors to this town. Stand on the jetty and gaze at the sugar-white sandy beaches edged by brilliant blue water, with the islands of the Recherche Archipelago dotting the horizon. Then take the Great Ocean Drive, 38 kilometres of postcard-perfect scenery, and you'll understand why Esperance is a popular holiday spot.

IN TOWN Municipal Museum Visit one of WA's outstanding regional museums. See exhibits about shipwrecks, including the famous *Sanko Harvest*, and learn of Australia's only recorded pirate, the bloodthirsty Black Jack Anderson, who roamed the Recherche Archipelago. There is also a comprehensive display about *Skylab*, which crashed and spread debris through the area in 1979. James St; open 1.30pm–4.30pm daily. *Museum Village:* collection of historic buildings housing craft shops, blacksmith, art gallery, cafe and visitor centre; Dempster St. *Mermaid Leather:* unique range of leather products made from fish and shark skins; Wood St. *Aquarium:* 14 aquariums and touch pool; The Esplanade.

WHAT'S ON *Offshore Angling Classic:* Feb. *Wildflower Show:* Sept. *Agricultural Show:* Oct.

NEARBY Great Ocean Drive One of Australia's most spectacular scenic drives, this 38 km loop road passes wind farms, which supply 30 percent of the town's electricity, and some of the region's best-known natural attractions. Contact visitor centre for map.

Cape Le Grand National Park This stretch of spectacular coastline is littered with pristine beaches, including Hellfire Bay and Thistle Cove. At Lucky Bay, kangaroos can often be spotted lying on the beach. Visit Whistling Rock, which 'whistles' under certain wind conditions, and climb Frenchman's Peak for breathtaking views. There are magnificent displays of wildflowers in spring, and many bushwalks. Camping at Cape Le Grand and Lucky Bay. 56 km E.

Recherche Archipelago The Esperance region is known as the Bay of Isles because of this collection of 110 islands dotted along the coast that provide a haven for seals and sea lions. Daily cruises (3 hrs 30 min) take you around Cull, Button, Charlie, Woody and other islands; landing is permitted only on Woody Island. For an extraordinary camping experience, try a safari hut on Woody Island. These canvas huts set high on timber decking overlook an idyllic turquoise bay framed by eucalyptus trees. Woody Island also has an interpretive centre to provide information to visitors. *Rotary Lookout:* views of bay, town and archipelago; Wireless Hill; 2 km w. *Pink Lake:* a pink saltwater lake; 5 km w. *Twilight Cove:* sheltered swimming; 12 km w. *Observatory Point and Lookout:* dramatic views of bay and islands; 17 km w. *Mojingup Lake Nature Reserve:* walk trails, birdwatching and wildflowers in spring; 20 km w. *Telegraph Farm:* proteas, deer, buffalo and native animals; farm tours available; 21 km N; closed Tues and Wed. *Hellfire Gallery:* local and Australian fine-art gallery, set in garden of 1000 lavender plants; 30 km E; closed Tues and Wed. *Dalyup River Wines:* the most isolated winery in WA; 42 km w; open weekends and public holidays. *Stokes National Park:* beautiful coastal and inlet scenery; 80 km w. *Cape Arid National Park:* birdwatching, fishing, camping and 4WD routes; 120 km E. *Whale-watching:* southern right whales visit bays and protected waters to calve; June–Nov; along the Great Ocean Drive and at Cape Arid. ● Museum Village, Dempster St; (08) 9071 2330 or 1300 664 455; www.visitesperance.com

Eucla   Pop. 30

Map ref. 562 A8, 575 R7

Eucla is the largest settlement on the Nullarbor Plain, located just near the South Australian border. The much-photographed ruin of a telegraph station exists at the original townsite, among slowly advancing sand dunes. Beyond the ruins are the remains of a jetty, a reminder of pioneering days when supplies were transported by boat. Eucla operates on Central Western Time, 45 minutes ahead of the rest of Western Australia.

IN TOWN Telegraph station ruins Opened in 1877 (just 33 years after Samuel Morse invented the telegraph), the Eucla Telegraph Station helped link WA with the rest of Australia and the world, sending 11 000 messages a year. The first message, sent to Perth in December 1877, stated simply, 'Eucla line opened. Hurrah.' 4 km s. *Eucla Museum:* local history told through newspaper clippings and old photographs; Eucla Motel. *Travellers' Cross:* dedicated to travellers and illuminated at night; on the escarpment, west of town. *Bureau of Meteorology:* visitors welcome; east of town; open

10am–2pm daily. *9-hole golf course:* site of the Golf Classic; north of town.
WHAT'S ON *Border Dash:* Border Village to Eucla; Oct/Nov.
NEARBY Eucla National Park This park extends between Border Village and Eucla. Within it lies Koonalda Cave, with a 40 m wide entrance that plunges to a lake more than 100 m below the surface of the Nullarbor. There are ladders and walkways, but the entrance to the cave is dangerous and entry should be attempted only by experienced cavers. *Border Village:* quarantine checkpoint for people entering WA (travellers should ensure they are not carrying fruit, vegetables, honey, used fruit and produce containers, plants or seeds); 13 km E. ● Eucla Motel; (08) 9039 3468

Exmouth   Pop. 3027

Map ref. 573 C3

One of the newest towns in Australia, Exmouth was founded in 1967 as a support town for the Harold E. Holt US Naval Communications Station, the main source of local employment. Excellent year-round fishing and its proximity to the Cape Range National Park and Ningaloo Marine Park have since made Exmouth a major tourist destination. The town is on the north-eastern side of North West Cape, the nearest point in Australia to the continental shelf. In March 1999 Exmouth was hit by Cyclone Vance, which caused extensive damage. At the height of the cyclone a wind gust speed of 267 kilometres per hour was recorded.

WHAT'S ON *Whale Shark Festival:* Mar. *Mall Market:* Sun, April–Sept. *Arts Quest:* July. *Octoberfest:* Oct. *Gamex:* world-class game-fishing competition; Oct/Nov.
NEARBY *Cape Range National Park: see feature on facing page. Ningaloo Marine Park: see feature on facing page. Naval Communication Station:* the centre tower in its antenna field, at 388 m, is one of the tallest structures in the Southern Hemisphere; 5 km N; not open to public. *Vlamingh Head Lighthouse and Lookout:* built in 1912, Australia's only kerosene-burning lighthouse served as a beacon to mariners until 1967. The lookout offers panoramic 360-degree views. 19 km N. *Learmonth Jetty:* destroyed by Cyclone Vance, a few solitary pylons mark this popular fishing spot; 33 km s. *Wildlife-watching:* turtle-nesting (Nov–Jan); coral-spawning (Mar–April); boat cruises and air flights to see whale sharks (Mar–June); humpback whales (Aug–Nov) from lighthouse (17 km N) and from whale-watching boat tours. Snorkellers can swim with whale sharks and manta rays located by cruise boats. Also coral-viewing boat cruises. Contact visitor centre for details. ● Murat Rd; (08) 9949 1176 or 1800 287 328; www.exmouth-australia.com

Fitzroy Crossing   Pop. 1448

Map ref. 579 L9, 580 G11

Fitzroy Crossing is in the heart of the Kimberley region. As its name suggests, the original townsite was chosen as the best place to ford the mighty Fitzroy River. In the wet season, the river has been known to rise over ten metres and to spread out from its banks for a distance of up to 15 kilometres. Fitzroy Crossing's main attraction is its proximity to the magnificent 30-metre-deep Geikie Gorge with its sheer yellow, orange and grey walls. Check road conditions before any excursions from December to March, as this area is prone to flooding.

IN TOWN Crossing Inn First established in the 1890s as a shanty inn and trade store for passing stockmen, prospectors and drovers, it has operated on the same site ever since, and is one of the very few hotels in the state to retain a true outback atmosphere. A stop-off and drink are a must for all travellers passing by. Skuthorp Rd.
WHAT'S ON *Rodeo:* July. *Garnduwa Festival:* sporting events; Oct. *Fishing Competition:* Nov.
NEARBY Geikie Gorge National Park Nearby is the spectacular Geikie Gorge with colourful cliffs and sculptured rock formations carved by water through an ancient limestone reef. The Fitzroy River is home to sharks, sawfish and stingrays that have, over centuries, adapted to the fresh water. Freshwater crocodiles up to 3 m long and barramundi are plentiful, best seen on a guided boat tour. Aboriginal heritage and cultural tours are run by guides from the local Bunaba tribe; bookings essential. CALM rangers run tours on the geology, wildlife and history of the area. Contact visitor centre for details. Entry to park is restricted during wet season (Dec–Mar). 18 km NE. *Tunnel Creek National Park:* unique formation created by waters from the creek cutting a 750 m tunnel through the ancient reef; 4WD access only; 110 km NW. *Windjana Gorge National Park:* 350 million-year-old Devonian reef rising majestically above the surrounding plains. An easy walking trail takes you past primeval life forms fossilised within the gorge walls. 4WD access only; 145 km NW. *4WD tours:* to Tunnel Creek and Windjana Gorge; bookings essential, contact visitor centre for details. ● Cnr Great Northern Hwy and Flynn Dr; (08) 9191 5355

Gascoyne Junction   Pop. 51

Map ref. 573 D8

Lying at the junction of the Lyons and Gascoyne rivers, Gascoyne Junction is a small administration centre for the pastoral industry. Sheep stations in the area, ranging in size from around 36 000 to 400 000 hectares, produce a wool clip exceeding 1.5 million kg annually.

IN TOWN *Junction Hotel:* see the high-water mark from the 1982 floods on the wall of this Aussie pub; Carnarvon–Mullewa Rd. *Old Roads Board Museum:* memorabilia of the area; Scott St.
WHAT'S ON *Dry Bed River Dash:* Oct.
NEARBY Kennedy Range National Park Along with spectacular scenery, the park is home to fossils of the earliest known species of banksia in Australia, and marine fossils that reflect the history of the region as an ocean bed. Ideal for sightseeing, hiking and bush camping. 60 km N.
Mount Augustus National Park Mt Augustus is the world's largest monolith, twice the size of Uluṟu. It is also known as Burringurrah, named after a boy who, in Aboriginal legend, broke tribal law by running away from his initiation. On capture, his punishment was to be speared in the upper right leg. The spear broke as the boy fell to the ground, leaving a shortened section protruding from his leg. It is said that, as you look at Mt Augustus, you can see the shape of the boy's body with the stump of the spear being the small peak at the eastern end called Edney's Lookout. 294 km NE.
ⓘ Shire offices, Scott St; (08) 9943 0988

Geraldton   Pop. 25 324

Map ref. 574 A3

Situated on the spectacular Batavia Coast, Geraldton is the largest town in the mid-west region. As a port city, it is the major centre for the surrounding wheat belt and is renowned for its lucrative rock lobster industry. Geraldton is also regarded as one of the best windsurfing locations in the world. The nearby Houtman Abrolhos Islands are the site of 16 known shipwrecks. The most infamous is that of the Dutch ship *Batavia*, which foundered on a reef in 1629. A mutiny among the survivors resulted in the massacre of 125 people. The wreck site was discovered in 1963 and skeletons of victims of the mutiny have been found on Beacon Island.
IN TOWN HMAS *Sydney* Memorial A memorial has been built on Mt Scott overlooking the town to commemorate the loss of 645 men from HMAS *Sydney* on 19 November 1941, the wreck of which has never been found. The ship was lost somewhere off Steep Point, between Carnarvon and Geraldton, after a sunset encounter with the German raider HSK *Kormoran*. Seven pillars representing the seven seas hold aloft a 9 m high domed roof formed of 645 interlocking figures of seagulls. At night an eternal flame lights the cupola. Near the memorial is the bronze sculpture of a woman looking out to sea, representing the women left behind waiting for those who would not return. Cnr George Rd and Brede St.
WA Museum Geraldton Exhibits focus on the cultural and natural heritage of

Yardie Creek, Cape Range National Park

Reef to range

Ningaloo Marine Park stretches from Bundegi Beach north of Exmouth to Amherst Point south of Coral Bay. The park protects the 260-kilometre-long Ningaloo Reef, the longest fringing coral reef in Australia. It is the only large reef in the world found so close to a continental land mass: about 100 metres offshore at its nearest point and less than seven kilometres at its furthest. This means that even novice snorkellers and children can access the coral gardens bursting with brightly coloured tropical fish.

The reef is home to over 500 species of fish, 250 species of coral, manta rays, turtles and a variety of other marine creatures, with seasonal visits from humpback whales, dolphins and whale sharks. The latter is the world's biggest species of fish and can reach up to 12 metres long and weigh more than 11 tons. Ningaloo Reef is the only easily accessible place in the world where whale sharks appear in large numbers at predictable times of the year. From April to June visitors from around the world converge on Ningaloo to swim with these gentle giants.

The arrival of the whale sharks corresponds with the extraordinary phenomenon of mass coral-spawning. This three-day event begins a week or so after the full moon in March/April and results in abundant food for the sharks.

Cape Range National Park, near Exmouth on the western side of North West Cape, is a rugged landscape of arid rocky gorges edged by the stunning coastline of Ningaloo Marine Park. Wildlife is abundant, with emus, euros, rock wallabies and red kangaroos often sighted. In late winter there is a beautiful array of wildflowers including the Sturt's desert pea and the superb bird flower. Recreational activities include swimming, bushwalking, birdwatching and camping.

On the eastern side of the park are Shothole Canyon, an impressive gorge, and Charles Knife Canyon, with spectacular views. To the west is Mangrove Bay, a sanctuary zone with a bird hide overlooking a lagoon, and Mandu Mandu Gorge where you can walk along an ancient river bed. Yardie Creek is the only gorge in the area with permanent water, fed from the ocean. Of the many beaches along the coastline, Turquoise Bay is one of the most popular for swimming and snorkelling. The Milyering Visitor Centre, made of rammed earth and run by solar power, is 52 kilometres from Exmouth on the western side of the park and offers information on both Cape Range and Ningaloo.

the Geraldton region. Maritime displays include finds from Australia's oldest shipwrecks, notably the original stone portico destined to adorn the castle gateway in the city of Batavia and lost to the sea when the *Batavia* sank in 1629. Museum Place, Batavia Coast Marina. Adjacent in the Geraldton Marina is a replica of the *Batavia* Longboat.
Historic buildings: explore the town's historic architecture dating back to the mid-1800s with works of noted architect Monsignor John Cyril Hawes a highlight. Many of the buildings have been restored and are open to the public, including the Old Geraldton Gaol (1858), which is now a craft centre, and the Bill Sewell Complex (1884), which was built as a hospital and subsequently became a prison. In Cathedral Ave, St Francis Xavier Cathedral offers free tours (10am Mon and 2pm Fri), and the Cathedral of the Holy Cross has one of the largest areas of stained glass in Australia. Self-guide walks are available, including the Heritage Trail; contact visitor centre for details. *Geraldton Regional Art Gallery:* the original Geraldton Town Hall (1907) converted to house art exhibitions and workshops; Chapman Rd; closed Mon. *Leon Baker Jewellers:* international jeweller works with Abrolhos pearls and Argyle diamonds. Workshop tours are available. Marine Tce Mall. *Rock Lobster Factory:* take a tour and follow the journey of Geraldton's most famous export, the western rock lobster, from processor to plate; covered shoes required; Willcock Dr, Fisherman's Wharf; tours 9.30am Mon–Fri Nov–June. *Point Moore Lighthouse:* assembled in 1878 from steel sections prefabricated in England, and standing 34 m tall, this is the only lighthouse of its kind in Australia; Willcock Dr.
WHAT'S ON *Windsurfing Classic:* Jan. *Batavia Celebrations:* June. *Sunshine Festival:* Oct.
NEARBY Houtman Abrolhos Islands These 122 reef islands with a fascinating history span 100 km of ocean and are the main source of rock lobster for the local lobster fishing industry. They also offer diving, snorkelling, surfing, windsurfing, fishing and birdwatching. Access is via boat or plane; tours and charters are available. Contact visitor centre for details and bookings. 65 km w. *For more information see feature on p. 325.*
Fishing: good fishing spots at Sunset Beach (6 km N) and Drummond Cove (10 km N). *Mill's Park Lookout:* excellent views over Moresby Range and coastal plain; 10 km NE. *Oakabella Homestead:* one of the region's oldest pioneering homesteads with a rare buttressed barn; tours available; 30 km N. *Chapman Valley:* an area of scenic drives and spectacular scenery, once home to the first coffee bean plantation in Australia. Also a huge diversity of wildflowers on display July–Oct. Wineries include Chapman Valley Wines, the northernmost winery

in WA. Enjoy free tastings. 35 km NE. *Scenic flights:* tours over nearby Abrolhos Islands, Murchison Gorges or the coastal cliffs of Kalbarri; contact visitor centre.
ⓘ Bill Sewell Complex, Chapman Rd; (08) 9921 3999 or 1800 818 881; www.geraldtontourist.com.au

Gingin   Pop. 548

Map ref. 572 C2, 574 C7

Gingin is one of the oldest towns in Western Australia, having been settled in 1832, only two years after the establishment of the Swan River Colony. For tourists, it has the charm of old original stone buildings within a picturesque natural setting. Situated 84 kilometres north of Perth, it is an ideal destination for a daytrip from the city.
IN TOWN Historic buildings Enjoy a pleasant self-guide stroll around the town on the Gingin Walkabout Trail, which features many fine examples of early architecture including Philbey's Cottage and St Luke's Anglican Church, both made from local stone. Contact visitor centre for map.
Granville Park: in the heart of the town with free barbecue facilities, playground and picnic area. *Self-guide walks:* stroll along the Gingin Brook on the Jim Gordon VC Trail or try the Three Bridges Recreation Trail, rebuilt after being destroyed by fire in Dec 2002; contact visitor centre for maps.
WHAT'S ON *Horticultural Expo:* April. *British Car Club Day:* May. *Lily Festival:* Sept.
NEARBY Gravity Discovery Centre Opened in 2003, this $4 million centre offers hands-on and static scientific displays on gravity, magnetism and electricity. It includes the biggest public astronomy centre in the Southern Hemisphere and the largest telescope in WA. Visitors can take a high-tech look at heavenly bodies in an evening presentation (bookings essential) and see a number of WA inventions relating to physics. Military Rd; 15 km SW.
Cemetery: with a spectacular display of kangaroo paws in early spring; northern outskirts of town. *Colamber Bird Park:* a walk-through aviary and exotic parrots; 1 km w; April–Oct or by appointment. *Jylland Winery:* open to public, wine tastings and cellar-door sales; 2 km s. *West Coast Honey:* live bee display, honey extraction, tastings, sales of honey and bee products; 3 km w; open 9am–4pm weekdays, weekends by appointment. *Moore River National Park:* special area for conservation featuring banksia woodlands and wildflower displays in spring.
ⓘ Council offices, Brockman St; (08) 9575 2211; www.gingin.wa.gov.au

Greenough   Pop. 100

Map ref. 574 B4

Lying 24 kilometres south of Geraldton, the Greenough Flats form a flood plain close to the mouth of the Greenough

River. At its peak in the 1860s and 1870s, Greenough (pronounced 'Grennuff') was a highly successful wheat-growing area. However, the combined effects of drought, crop disease and floods led to the area's decline and from 1900 the population dropped dramatically. The historic hamlet that was once the centre of this farming community has been extensively restored and is classified by the National Trust.
IN TOWN *Pioneer Museum:* folk display located in an original limestone cottage; tours available; Brand Hwy. *Greenough Hamlet:* precinct of restored stone buildings dating from the 1860s; self-guide maps available; cnr Brand Hwy and McCartney Rd. *The Walkaway Railway Station:* built in the style of a traditional British railway station, now housing a railway and heritage museum; Evans Rd; closed Mon. *Leaning trees:* these trees are a unique sight, having grown sideways in response to the harsh salt-laden winds that blow from the Indian Ocean; seen from Brand Hwy on the Greenough Flats. *Hampton Arms Inn:* fully restored historic inn (1863) now houses the Out of Print and Rare Book Shop, one of the most isolated bookshops in the world. Browse with a beer and become acquainted with the resident ghost. Company Rd.
NEARBY *Greenough River mouth:* ideal for swimming, canoeing, beach and rock fishing, birdwatching and photography. River cruises are available. 14 km N. *Flat Rocks:* surfing, swimming and rock fishing. A round of the State Surfing Championships is held here in June every year. 10 km s. *Ellendale Pool:* this deep, freshwater swimming hole beneath spectacular sandstone cliffs is an ideal picnic area; 23 km E. *Greenough River Nature Trail:* self-guide walk; contact visitor centre for brochure. *The Greenough Heritage Trail:* 57 km self-drive tour of the area; contact visitor centre for map.
ⓘ Greenough Hamlet, cnr Brand Hwy and McCartney Rd; (08) 9926 1660; www.greenough.wa.gov.au

Halls Creek   Pop. 1266

Map ref. 579 P9, 581 N11

In the heart of the Kimberley region and on the edge of the Great Sandy Desert, Halls Creek is the site of the first payable gold discovery in Western Australia. In 1885 Jack Slattery and Charlie Hall (after whom the town is named) discovered gold, thereby sparking a gold rush that brought over 15 000 people to the area. In 1917 a stockman named James 'Jimmy' Darcy was taken into Halls Creek from a nearby station where he had been seriously injured. With neither doctor nor hospital in the town, and doctors from both Wyndham and Derby unable to be contacted, the local postmaster carried out an emergency operation using a penknife as instructions were telegraphed by Morse code from Perth. The Perth doctor then set out on the ten-day journey to Halls Creek via cattle boat, model-T Ford, horse-drawn sulky and, finally, on foot, only to discover that the patient had died the day before his arrival. The event inspired Reverend John Flynn to establish the Royal Flying Doctor Service in 1928, a development that helped to encourage settlement throughout the outback.

IN TOWN *Russian Jack Memorial:* tribute to a prospector who pushed his sick friend in a wheelbarrow to Wyndham for medical help; Thomas St. *Trackers Hut:* restored original hut of Aboriginal trackers; behind police station.

NEARBY Wolfe Creek Crater National Park Wolfe Creek Crater is the second largest meteorite crater in the world. Named after Robert Wolfe, a Halls Creek prospector, it is 870–950 m across and, in Aboriginal legend, said to be the site of the emergence of a powerful rainbow serpent from the earth. 148 km s. Scenic flights afford magnificent views; contact visitor centre for details. *China Wall:* white quartz formation said to resemble Great Wall of China; 6 km e. *Caroline's Pool:* deep pool ideal for swimming and picnicking; 15 km e. *Old Halls Creek:* remnants of original town including graveyard where James Darcy is buried; prospecting available; 16 km e. *Palm Springs:* fishing, swimming and picnicking; 45 km e. *Sawpit Gorge:* fishing, swimming, picnicking; 52 km e. *Purnululu National Park:* 160 km e; scenic flights can be arranged in town; *see feature on p. 308. Billiluna Aboriginal Community:* fishing, swimming, camping, birdwatching and bushwalking, and bush tucker and cultural tours; 180 km s.
ⓘ Hall Street; (08) 9168 6262

Harvey   Pop. 2544

Map ref. 568 H2, 572 C7, 574 C10

On the Harvey River, kilometres from the coast, the thriving town of Harvey is surrounded by fertile, irrigated plains. Beef production, citrus orchards and viticulture flourish in the region and intensive dairy farming provides the bulk of Western Australia's milk supply. Bordered by the Darling Range, Harvey offers a wealth of natural attractions from the magnificent scenic drives through the escarpment to the pristine white beaches and excellent fishing on the coast.

IN TOWN *Tourist and Interpretive Centre:* tourist information and display of local industries; James Stirling Pl. *Harvey Museum:* memorabilia housed in renovated railway station; Harper St; open 2pm–4pm Sun or by appointment. *Stirling Cottage:* replica of the home of Governor Stirling, which later became the home of May Gibbs, author of *Snugglepot and Cuddlepie*; James Stirling Pl tourist precinct. *Internment Camp Memorial*

Boabs are found around Halls Creek and throughout the Kimberley

Shrine: the only roadside shrine of its type in the world, built by prisoners of war in the 1940s; collect key from visitor centre; South Western Hwy. *Heritage trail:* 6.2 km self-guide walk includes historic buildings and sights of town; map available at visitor centre.

WHAT'S ON *Summer Series Concerts:* Jan–Mar. *Harvest Festival:* Mar. *Spring Fair:* Sept.

NEARBY *Harvey Dam:* landscaped park with viewing platform, amphitheatre, barbecues and playground. Fishing is allowed in season with permit. Scenic flights over dam are available. 3 km e. *Harvey Cheese:* tour and gourmet cheese tasting; 3 km s. *Stirling Dam:* walking trails and picnic sites; 12 km e. *White Rocks Museum and Dairy:* founded in 1887. Compare current technology with display of machinery from the past. 15 km s; open 2pm–4pm or by appt. *Logue Brook Dam:* horseriding and water activities including ski-boat rides, wave/knee boarding, ski tubes and waterskiing; 15 km ne. *Beaches:* Myalup Beach provides good swimming, surfing and beach fishing; 21 km w. Binningup Beach is protected by a reef that runs parallel to shore and is ideal for sheltered swimming, snorkelling, beach fishing and boating; 25 km sw. *Wineries:* wineries open to the public are only a short distance from town; contact visitor centre for details.
ⓘ James Stirling Pl; (08) 9729 1122; www.harveytourism.com

Hyden   Pop. 400

Map ref. 574 F8

The small wheat-belt town of Hyden is synonymous with its famous nearby attraction, Wave Rock, originally known as Hyde's Rock in honour of a sandalwood cutter who lived in the area. A typing error by the Lands Department

made it Hyden Rock, and the emerging town soon became known as Hyden. The area around the town boasts spectacular wildflowers in spring, including a wide variety of native orchids.

NEARBY Wave Rock Resembling a huge breaking wave, this 100 m long and 15 m high granite cliff owes its unique shape to wind action over the past 2.7 billion years. Vertical bands of colour are caused by streaks of algae and chemical staining from run-off waters. 4 km e. At Wave Rock Visitor Centre see the largest lace collection in the Southern Hemisphere with fine examples of antique lace, including lace worn by Queen Victoria. There are local wildflower species on display, an Australiana collection at the Pioneer Town, fauna in a natural bush environment, and daily Aboriginal culture tours (bookings essential). *Hippo's Yawn:* rock formation; 5 km e via Wave Rock. *Stargate Observatory:* view magnificent southern skies; 8 km e via Wave Rock. *The Humps and Mulka's Cave:* Aboriginal wall paintings; 22 km n via Wave Rock. *Rabbit Proof Fence:* see the fence where it meets the road; 56 km e.
ⓘ Wave Rock; (08) 9880 5182

Jurien Bay   Pop. 1145

Map ref. 574 B6

Jurien Bay, settled in the mid-1850s, is the centre of a lobster fishing industry. The early success of the pastoralists led to the construction of a jetty in 1885 to enable a more efficient route to markets for locally produced wool and hides. Located within a sheltered bay protected by reefs and islands, the town has wide beaches and sparkling waters ideal for swimming, waterskiing, windsurfing, snorkelling, diving and surfing. The Jurien Bay boat harbour services the fishing fleet and has facilities for holiday

Inside Echidna Chasm

Purnululu National Park

In 2003 Purnululu National Park was declared a World Heritage Area. It joins Western Australia's only other World Heritage site, Shark Bay, as an internationally recognised area of natural and cultural significance. This remote park in the outback of the east Kimberley is home to the Bungle Bungle Range, a remarkable landscape of tiger-striped, beehive-shaped rock domes.

Formed by uplift and erosion over the last 20 million years, the distinctive domes are made of sandstone so fine that it crumbles when touched. Thin layers of black lichens and orange silica cover and protect the sandstone, giving the domes their distinctive horizontal black and orange banding. A scenic flight from Halls Creek, Kununurra or Warmun is the best way to gain a perspective of the Bungle Bungle's massive size and spectacular scenery.

The most visited site in Purnululu is Cathedral Gorge, a fairly easy walk. A couple of days and a backpack allow you to explore nearby Piccaninny Creek and Gorge, camping overnight. If you do this, make sure you are well prepared. The deeper you go, the more spectacular the scenery, but for your safety you must tell a ranger before setting out. On the northern side of the park is Echidna Chasm, a narrow gorge totally different from those on the southern side. Purnululu is also rich in Aboriginal art, and there are many traditional burial sites within its boundaries.

Purnululu is open to visitors between April and December, and is accessible by 4WD. There are few facilities and no accommodation; visitors must carry in all food and water.

boating and fishing enthusiasts. Anglers can fish from boat, jetty and beach.
IN TOWN *Jurien Bay Charters:* boat and fishing charters, scuba diving, sea lion tours; bookings at dive shop; Carmella St. *Old jetty site:* plaque commemorates site of original jetty. Remains of jetty's timber piles have been discovered 65 m inland from high-water mark, which indicates gradual build-up of coastline over time. Hastings St.
WHAT'S ON *Kite-surfing Carnival:* Jan. *Easter Fair:* April. *Badgingarra Shears Competition:* Aug. *Blessing of the Fleet:* Nov.
NEARBY **Jurien Bay Marine Park** Established in August 2003, this marine park extends from Wedge Island to Green Head and encompasses major sea lion and seabird breeding areas. The reefs within the park are populated by a wide range of plants and animals, and the seagrass meadows are a breeding ground for western rock lobsters. *Lions Lookout:* spectacular views of town and surrounds; 5 km E. *Drovers Cave National Park:* rough limestone country with numerous caves, all of which have secured entrances limiting public access; 4WD access only; 7 km E. *Grigsons Lookout:* panoramic views of ocean and hinterland. Also wildflowers July–Nov. 15 km N. *Lesueur National Park:* with over 900 species of flora, representing 10 percent of the state's known flora, Lesueur is an important area for flora conservation. Enjoy coastal views from a lookout. 23 km E. *Stockyard Gully National Park:* walk through 300 m Stockyard Gully Tunnel along winding underground creek; 4WD access only; 50 km N.
ⓘ Council offices, 110 Bashford St; (08) 9652 1020

Kalbarri   Pop. 2123

Map ref. 573 C13, 574 A2

Kalbarri lies at the mouth of the Murchison River, flanked by Kalbarri National Park. Established in 1951, the town is a popular holiday resort, famous for the magnificent gorges up to 130 metres deep along the river. Just south of the township a cairn marks the spot where in 1629 Captain Pelsaert of the Dutch East India Company marooned two crew members implicated in the *Batavia* shipwreck and massacre. These were the first, albeit unwilling, white inhabitants of Australia.
IN TOWN *Oceanarium:* large aquariums and touch pools; Grey St. *Pelican feeding:* daily feeding by volunteers on the river foreshore; off Grey St; starts 8.45am. *Museum:* displays of dolls and gemstones; opposite pelican feeding on Grey St. *Family Entertainment Centre:* trampolines, minigolf, bicycle hire; Porter St.
WHAT'S ON *Sport Fishing Classic:* Mar. *Blessing of the Fleet:* Nov.
NEARBY **Kalbarri National Park** Gazetted in 1963, the park offers spectacular

scenery from the dramatic coastal cliffs along its western boundary to towering river gorges and seasonal wildflowers, many of which are unique to the park. The Murchison River, running through the heart of the park, has carved a gorge through sedimentary rock known as Tumblagooda sandstone, creating a striking contrast of brownish red and purple against white bands of stone. Embedded in these layers are some of the earliest signs of animal life on earth. There are many lookouts including 'Nature's Window' at the Loop, which overlooks the Murchison Gorge, and the breathtaking scenery at Z Bend Lookout. Along the 20 km coastal section of the park, lookouts such as Mushroom Rock, Pot Alley and Eagle Gorge offer panoramic views and whale-watching sites. Bushwalking, rockclimbing, abseiling, canoeing tours, rafting, cruises, camping safaris, coach and wilderness tours, and barbecue facilities are all available. Contact visitor centre for details. 57 km E.

Rainbow Jungle: breeding centre for rare and endangered species of parrots, cockatoos and exotic birds set in landscaped tropical gardens. Also here is the largest walk-in parrot free-flight area in Australia. Red Bluff Rd; 3 km S. *Seahorse Sanctuary:* aquaculture centre focused on the conservation of seahorses and other tropical marine fish; Red Bluff Rd; 3 km S. *Wildflower Centre:* view over 200 species on display along a 1.8 km walking trail. Visit the plant nursery and herbarium, where you can purchase seeds and souvenirs. Ajana–Kalbarri Rd; 3km E; July–Nov. *Murchison House Station:* tours available of one of the oldest and largest stations in WA, which includes historic buildings and cemetery, display of local arts and crafts, and wildflowers. Seasonal, check with visitor centre. Ajana–Kalbarri Rd; 4 km E. *Big River Ranch:* enjoy horseriding through the spectacular countryside; Ajana–Kalbarri Rd; 4 km E. *Wittecarra Creek:* cairn marking the site where two of the mutineers from the Dutch ship *Batavia* were left by Captain Pelsaert as punishment for their participation in the murders of 125 survivors of the wreck; 4 km S. *Hutt River Province:* founded in 1970 under the sovereignty of Prince Leonard and his wife, Princess Shirley. Have your passport stamped, visit the war memorial, cemetery or post office and purchase Hutt River Province stamps. 50 km SE. ⓘ Grey St; (08) 9937 1104 or 1800 639 468; www.kalbarriwa.info

Kalgoorlie–Boulder Pop. 28 196

Map ref. 574 I6

Kalgoorlie is the centre of Western Australia's goldmining industry. It was once known as Hannan's Find in honour of Paddy Hannan, the first prospector to discover gold in the area. In June 1893 Hannan was among a party of about 150 men who set out from Coolgardie to search for some lost prospectors near Yerilla. After a stop at Mt Charlotte the main party continued on, leaving Hannan and two others behind as one of their horses had lost a shoe. Some idle 'specking' (looking on the ground for nuggets) led them to stumble on the richest goldfield the world had known. Hannan returned to Coolgardie to report his find. Other prospectors soon located large gold deposits five kilometres south in an area that became known as the 'Golden Mile', reputedly the richest square mile of gold-bearing ore in the world. Rapid development of Kalgoorlie and nearby Boulder followed with thousands of men travelling from all over the world, reaching a maximum population of about 30 000 in 1903. Shortage of water was always a problem on the goldfields, but in 1903 the genius of engineer C. Y. O'Connor enabled a pipeline to be opened that pumped water 560 kilometres from Perth. In its heyday Kalgoorlie and Boulder boasted eight breweries and 93 hotels. The two towns amalgamated in 1989 to form Kalgoorlie–Boulder, the main commercial centre of the goldfields region.

IN TOWN Historic buildings Although only a few kilometres apart, Kalgoorlie and Boulder developed independently for many years. The amalgamated towns now form a city with two main streets lined with impressive buildings. Built at the turn of the century, when people were flocking to the area, many of these buildings display ornamentation and fittings that reflect the confidence and wealth of the mining interests and are fine examples of early Australian architecture. In Hannan St, the Kalgoorlie Town Hall (1908) displays a collection of memorabilia including some impressive furniture. Dame Nellie Melba performed in this building on several occasions. The offices of the *Kalgoorlie Miner* and the *Old Western Argus*, where the first newspaper was published, was the first three-storey building in town. Burt St in Boulder is regarded as one of the most significant streetscapes in WA. Buildings to see include the Grand Hotel (1897), the old chemist shop (1900), which now houses a pharmaceutical museum, and the post office (1899), which once was so busy that it employed 49 staff. Guided and self-guide heritage walks are available. Contact visitor centre for details.

Paddy Hannan's Statue: a monument to the first man to discover gold in Kalgoorlie; Hannan St. *St Mary's Church:* built in 1902 of Coolgardie pressed bricks, many of which are believed to contain gold; cnr Brookman and Porter sts. *WA School of Mines Mineral Museum:* displays include over 3000 mineral and ore specimens and many gold nuggets; Egan St; open 8.30am–12pm Mon–Fri. *WA Museum Kalgoorlie–Boulder:* panoramic views of the city from the massive mining headframe at the entrance. Known locally as the Museum of the Goldfields, displays include a million-dollar gold collection, nuggets and jewellery. See the narrowest pub in the Southern Hemisphere, a re-created 1930s miner's cottage and other heritage buildings. Guided tours available; 17 Hannan St; open 10am–4.30pm daily. *Goldfields Arts Centre:* art gallery and theatre; Cassidy St. *Goldfields Aboriginal Art Gallery:* examples of local Aboriginal art and artefacts for sale; Dugan St; open 9am–5pm Mon–Fri, 9am–3pm Sat, Sun by appointment. *Paddy Hannan's Tree:* a plaque marks the spot where Paddy Hannan first discovered gold; Outridge Tce. *Red-light district:* view the few remaining 'starting stalls', in which women once posed as prospective clients walked by, and visit the only working brothel in the world that visitors can tour. Tours at 1pm, 3pm and 7pm daily. Hay St. *Superpit Lookout:* view one of the world's biggest open-cut gold mines, which operates 24 hrs a day. Visitors can view the daily mine blast. Check times at tourist information. Scenic flights are also available. Outram Rd. *Boulder Town Hall:* beautifully preserved building, built in 1908, is home to one of the world's last remaining Goatcher stage curtains, which elaborately depicts the Bay of Naples. Phillip Goatcher lived in Victorian times and was one of the greatest scenic painters of his time. His remarkable stage curtains could be found from London and Paris to New York. Public viewing of the curtain is 9am–12pm and 1pm–4pm Mon–Fri, except Wed, when viewing is 10am–12pm and 1pm–3pm. Cnr Burt and Lane sts. *Mount Charlotte:* the reservoir holds water pumped from the Mundaring Weir in Perth via the pipeline of C. Y. O'Connor. A lookout provides good views of the city. *Hammond Park:* miniature Bavarian castle made from thousands of local gemstones. Also here is a sanctuary for kangaroos and emus, and aviaries for a variety of birdlife. Enjoy twilight outdoor cinema Fri and Sat nights in summer months; check at visitor centre; Lyall St. *Miners' Monument:* tribute to mine workers; Burt St. *Goldfields War Museum:* war memorabilia and armoured vehicles on display; 106 Burt St; open 10am–2pm Mon–Fri, 9am–1pm weekends and public holidays. *WMC Nickel Pots:* massive nickel pots and interpretive panels describe the story of the development of the nickel industry in the region; Goldfields Hwy. *Loopline Railway:* take a steam-train journey on the line that once carried hundreds of miners and tour the surrounds of the Golden Mile; Boulder Station; departs 10am daily. *Royal Flying Doctor Visitor Centre:* climb on board an authentic RFDS plane; tours available; Airport, Hart

Kerspien Dr; open 10am–3pm Mon–Fri. *Karlkurla Bushland:* pronounced 'gullgirla', this natural regrowth area of bushland offers a 4 km signposted walk trail, picnic areas and lookout over the city and nearby mining areas; Riverina Way. *Walks:* guided and self-guide heritage walks; details and maps at visitor centre.

WHAT'S ON *Boulder Market Day:* Burt St, Boulder; 3rd Sun each month. *Undies 500 Car Rally:* Feb. *Community Fair:* April. *Menzies to Kalgoorlie Cycle Race:* May. *Rhythms in the Outback Festival:* May. *Diggers and Dealers Mining Conference:* Aug. *Balzano Barrow Race:* Sept. *Goldfields Mining Expo:* Oct. *Art Prize Exhibition:* Oct. *Back to Boulder Festival:* Oct. *Spring Festival:* Oct. *Boulder Blues Festival:* Nov. *St Barbara's Mining and Community Festival:* Dec.

NEARBY **Australian Prospectors and Miners Hall of Fame** Tour a historic underground mine, watch a gold pour or visit the Exploration Zone, which is designed specifically for young people. You will find interactive exhibits on exploration, mineral discoveries and surface and underground mining, including panning for gold. The Environmental Garden details the stages and techniques involved in mine-site rehabilitation. At Hannan's North Tourist Mine, historic buildings re-create an early gold-rush town and visitors can take a first-hand look at the cramped and difficult working conditions of the miners. Eastern Bypass Rd; 7 km N. *Arboretum:* a living museum of representative species of the semi-arid zone and adjacent desert areas, this 26.5 ha of parklands with interpretive walk trails has recreation facilities; Hawkins St; 3 km NW. *Bush 2-Up:* visit the unique original corrugated iron shack and bush ring where Australia's only legal bush 2-up school used to operate; off Goldfields Hwy; 8 km E. *Kanowna Belle Gold Mine lookouts:* wander the ghost town and see day-to-day mining activities from two lookouts over a previously mined open pit and processing plant; 20 km E. *Broad Arrow:* see the pub where scenes from the Googie Withers movie *Nickel Queen* were shot in the 1970s. Every wall is autographed by visitors. 38 km N. *Ora Banda:* recently restored inn; 54 km NW. *Kambalda:* Red Hill Lookout, Lake Lefroy, and Fishing in the Desert competition where the local swimming pool is stocked with fish each Sept; 55 km S. *Rowles Lagoon:* ideal spot for watersports after good rain. Also birdwatching, bushwalking, picnics and camping. 80 km NW. *Abandoned townsites:* some abandoned townsites lie beyond the outskirts of town; maps available at visitor centre. *Prospecting:* visitors to the area may obtain a miner's right from the Department of Mineral and Petroleum Resources in Brookman St; strict conditions apply; details from the visitor centre. *Golden Quest Discovery Trail:* 965 km drive that traces the gold

rushes of the 1890s through Coolgardie, Kalgoorlie–Boulder, Menzies, Kookynie, Gwalia, Leonora and Laverton. Pick up the map, book and CD at the visitor centre. *Golden Pipeline Heritage Trail:* when it began operating in 1903 the pipeline opened up vast inland areas for settlement *(for information see feature on p. 277).* Follow the course of the pipeline from Mundaring Weir to Mt Charlotte. Guidebook available at visitor centre. *Tours:* self-drive or guided 4WD tours available to many attractions. Also fossicking, prospecting, camping and museum tours; Aboriginal heritage, culture and bush tours by Aboriginal guides; and self-guide wildflower tours. Details at visitor centre. *Scenic flights:* flights over Coolgardie, the Superpit, Lake Lefroy; details at visitor centre.
ⓘ 250 Hannan St; (08) 9093 1083 or (08) 9021 1966 or 1800 00 4653; www.kalgoorlie.com

Karratha   Pop. 10 730

Map ref. 573 G1

Karratha is the Aboriginal word for 'good country'. Founded in 1968 as a result of expansion of the iron-ore industry, Karratha was originally established for workers on the huge industrial projects nearby. For visitors, Karratha is an ideal centre from which to explore the fascinating Pilbara region.

IN TOWN *TV Hill Lookout:* excellent views over town centre and beyond; off Millstream Rd. *Jaburara Heritage Trail:* 3 hr walk features Aboriginal rock carvings; pamphlet available at visitor centre.

WHAT'S ON *Blackrock Stakes:* June. *FeNaCING Festival:* this celebration takes its name from the town's mining roots (Fe is the chemical symbol for iron ore, NaCl is the symbol for salt, and NG is an abbreviation for natural gas); Aug. *Gamefishing Classic:* Aug.

NEARBY **Millstream–Chichester National Park** Rolling hills, spectacular escarpments and tree-lined watercourses with hidden rock pools characterise this park. The remarkable oasis of Millstream is an area of tropical palm-fringed freshwater springs, well known to the Afghan cameleers of Pilbara's past. Other notably scenic spots are Python, Deepreach and Circular pools, and Cliff Lookout. The Millstream Homestead Visitor Centre, housed in the Gordon family homestead (1919), has displays dedicated to the local Aboriginal people, early settlers and the natural environment. Popular activities include bushwalking, picnicking, camping, fishing, swimming and boating. Tours are available; contact visitor centre for details. 124 km S. *Salt Harvest Ponds:* Australia's largest evaporative salt fields. Tours are available; details at visitor centre. 15 km N. *Dampier:* port facility servicing the iron-ore operations at Tom Price and Paraburdoo. Watersports and boat hire are available.

22 km N. *Hamersley Iron Port Facilities:* 2 hr tour and audiovisual presentation daily; booking essential; 22 km N. *Cleaverville Beach:* scenic spot ideal for camping, boating, fishing and swimming; 26 km NE. *North-West Shelf Gas Project Visitor Centre:* displays on the history and technology of Australia's largest natural resource development, with panoramic views over the massive onshore gas plant; Burrup Peninsula; 30 km N; open 10am–4pm Mon–Fri April–Oct, 10am–1pm Mon–Fri Nov–Mar. *Aboriginal rock carvings:* there are more than 10 000 engravings on the Burrup Peninsula alone, including some of the earliest examples of art in Australia. A debate is currently raging over the damage being done to this magnificent outdoor gallery by the adjacent gas project. Check with visitor centre for locations and tours. *Dampier Archipelago:* 42 islands and islets ideal for swimming, snorkelling, boating, whale-watching and fishing. Take a boat tour from Dampier. *Montebello Islands:* site of Australia's first shipwreck, the *Tryal*, which ran aground and sank in 1622. It is now a good spot for snorkelling, beachcombing, fishing and diving. Beyond Dampier Archipelago. *Tours:* scenic flights and day or safari tours of the Pilbara outback; details at visitor centre.
ⓘ 4548 Karratha Rd; (08) 9144 4600; www.pilbara.com/karratha.html

Katanning   Pop. 3676

Map ref. 571 L1, 572 H9, 574 E10

Katanning lies in the middle of a prosperous grain-growing and pastoral area. A significant development in the establishment of the town was the completion in 1889 of the Great Southern Railway, which linked Perth and Albany. It was begun at both ends, and a cairn to the north of town now marks the spot where the lines were joined.

IN TOWN *Old Mill Museum:* built in 1889, it features an outstanding display of vintage roller flour-milling process; cnr Clive St and Austral Tce. *All Ages Playground and Miniature Steam Railway:* scenic grounds with equipment for all ages. Covered shoes required to ride the train, which runs on the 2nd and 4th Sun of each month; cnr Great Southern Hwy and Clive St. *Kobeelya:* a majestic residence (1902) with 7 bedrooms, ballroom, billiard room, tennis courts and croquet lawn; Brownie St; open by appt. *Old Winery Ruins:* inspect the ruins of the original turreted distillery and brick vats, with old ploughs and machinery on display; Andrews Rd. *Historical Museum:* the original school building has been converted into a museum of local memorabilia; Taylor St; open 2pm–4pm Sun, or by appt. *Piesse Memorial Statue:* unveiled in 1916, this statue of Frederick H. Piesse, the founder of Katanning, was sculpted by P. C. Porcelli, a well-known

artist in the early days of WA; Austral Tce.
Art Gallery: a changing display and local
collection; Austral Tce; closed Sun.
WHAT'S ON *Farmers markets:* Pemble
St; 3rd Sat of each month. *Prophet
Mohammad's Birthday:* part of Muslim
religious festival; varies. *Triathlon:* Feb.
Multicultural Day: Mar. *Saltbush Youth Festival:*
Nov. *Caboodle Street Party:* Dec.

NEARBY *Police Pools:* site of the original
camp for the district's first police officers.
Enjoy swimming, picnicking and
bushwalking. 3 km s. *Lake Ewlyamartup:*
picturesque freshwater lake ideal for
picnicking, swimming, boating and
waterskiing, particularly in early summer
when the water level is high; 22 km E.
Katanning–Piesse Heritage Trail: 20 km self-
drive/walk trail; map at visitor centre.
Watersports: the lakes surrounding the
town are excellent for recreational
boating, waterskiing and swimming;
details at visitor centre.
🛈 Old Mill; cnr Austral Tce and Clive St;
(08) 9821 2634; www.katanning.wa.
gov.au

Kellerberrin   Pop. 817

Map ref. 572 H3, 574 E7

Centrally located in the wheat belt,
Kellerberrin is 200 kilometres east of
Perth. In springtime, magnificent displays
of wildflowers adorn the roadsides, hills
and plains around the town.

IN TOWN **International Art Space
Kellerberrin Australia** This contemporary
art gallery, built in 1998, is home to
an ambitious art project. International
artists are given the opportunity to live
and work within the local community
for a three-month period. Workshops
and mentoring programs provide
collaboration between these established
artists and emerging Australian talent.
Many of the exhibitions created are then
displayed in larger venues throughout
Australia and the world. Massingham St.
Pioneer Park and Folk Museum: located in
the old Agricultural Hall, displays include
local artefacts, farming machinery and
photographic records. Pick up the key
from tourist information or Dryandra
building next door. Cnr Leake and
Bedford sts. *Centenary Park:* children's
playground, in-line skate and BMX track,
maze, heritage walkway and barbecue
facilities all in the centre of town; Leake
St. *Golden Pipeline Lookout:* interpretive
information at viewing platform with
views of the countryside and pipeline;
via Moore St. *Railway Station:* the original
station is about 1 km out of town, so in
1995 the locals built a new station set
in landscaped gardens; Massingham St.
Heritage trail: self-guide town walk that
includes historic buildings and churches;
brochure available.
WHAT'S ON *Keela Dreaming Cultural
Festival:* odd-numbered years, Mar. *Central
Wheatbelt Harness Racing Cup:* May.

The entrance to the Exchange Hotel, Kalgoorlie–Boulder

NEARBY *Sharks Mouth:* this granite
formation on private property is an
Aboriginal protected site. It can be
viewed from the road. 5 km NE. *Durokoppin
Reserve:* take a self-guide scenic drive
through this woodland area, which is
particularly beautiful in the wildflower
season. Contact visitor centre for map.
27 km N. *Kokerbin Wave Rock:* the third
largest monolith in WA. The Devil's
Marbles and a historic well are also at
the site. Vehicle access is available to the
top, which provides panoramic views.
30 km s. *Golden Pipeline Heritage Trail:*
one of the main stops along the trail,
which follows the water pipeline of C. Y.
O'Connor from Mundaring Weir to the
goldfields; guidebook available at visitor
centre.
🛈 Shire offices, 10 Massingham St; (08)
9045 4006; www.kellerberrin.wa.gov.au

Kojonup   Pop. 1127

Map ref. 571 J2, 572 G9, 574 E11

A freshwater spring first attracted white
settlement of the town now known as
Kojonup. In 1837 Alfred Hillman arrived
in the area after being sent by Governor
Stirling to survey a road between Albany
and the Swan River Colony. He was
guided to the freshwater spring by local
Aboriginal people and his promising
report back to Governor Stirling resulted
in a military outpost being established.
The Shire of Kojonup was the first shire in
Western Australia to have a million sheep
within its boundaries.

IN TOWN *Kodja Place Visitor and
Interpretive Centre:* fascinating and fun
displays about the land and its people,
with stories of Aboriginal heritage
and white settlement. It also includes
the Australian Rose Maze, the only
rose garden in the world growing
exclusively Australian roses. 143
Albany Hwy. *Kojonup Museum:* in historic
schoolhouse building with displays of

local memorabilia; Spring St; open by
appointment. *Kojonup Spring:* grassy picnic
area; Spring St. *Military Barracks:* built in
1845, this is one of the oldest surviving
military buildings in WA and features
historical information about the building;
Spring St; by appointment. *Elverd's
Cottage:* display of pioneer tools and farm
machinery; Soldier Rd; by appointment.
Town Walk Trail: self-guide signposted walk
of historic sights; map at visitor centre.
WHAT'S ON *Country and Wildflower
Festival:* Oct. *Kojonup Show:* Oct.

NEARBY *Myrtle Benn Memorial Flora and
Fauna Sanctuary:* walk one of the many
trails among local flora and fauna
including many protected species;
Tunney Rd; 1 km W. *Farrar Reserve:* scenic
bushland and spectacular wildflower
display in season; Blackwood Rd; 8 km W.
Australian Bush Heritage Block: natural
woodland featuring wandoo and species
unique to the South-West; 16 km N.
Lake Towerinning: boating, waterskiing,
horseriding, camping; 40 km NW.
Aboriginal guided tours: tours of Aboriginal
heritage sites; details and bookings at
visitor centre.
🛈 143 Albany Hwy; (08) 9831 0500;
www.kojonup.gov.wa.au

Kulin   Pop. 287

Map ref. 572 I6, 574 F9

The sheep- and grain-farming districts
surrounding Kulin provide spectacular
wildflower displays in season. The
flowering gum, *Eucalyptus macrocarpa,*
is a particularly beautiful example of
Australia's natural flora and is the floral
emblem of the town. A stand of jarrah
trees, not native to the area and not
known to occur elsewhere in the wheat
belt, grows near the town. According to
Aboriginal legend, two tribal groups met
at the site and, as a sign of friendship,
drove their spears into the ground. From
these spears, the jarrah trees grew. The

Kulin Bush Races event has expanded from horseracing to a major attraction including a weekend of live music, an art and craft show, camel racing, foot races and Clydesdale horserides. In the months prior to the Kulin Races, tin horses appear in the paddocks lining the road on the way to the racetrack. These, along with the tin horses from past years, create an unusual spectacle.

IN TOWN *Tin Horse Highway:* starting in town and heading to the Jilakin racetrack, the highway is lined with horses made from a wide variety of materials. *Kulin Herbarium:* specialising in local flora; Johnston St; open by appointment. *Butlers Garage:* built in the 1930s, this restored garage houses a museum of cars and machinery; cnr Johnston and Stewart sts; open by appointment. *Memorial Slide and Swimming Pool:* the longest waterslide in regional WA; Holt Rock Rd; open 12pm–6pm Tues–Fri, 10am–6pm weekends/public holidays, summer months; check for opening hours of waterslide. *Macrocarpa Walk Trail:* 1 km self-guide signposted walk trail through natural bush; brochure available at visitor centre; 1 km w.

WHAT'S ON *Charity Car Rally:* Sept. *Kulin Bush Races:* Oct. *Longneck Roughneck Des Cook Memorial Quick Shears Shearing Competition:* Oct.

NEARBY *Jilakin Rock and Lake:* granite monolith overlooking a 1214 ha lake; 16 km e. *Hopkins Nature Reserve:* important flora conservation area; 20 km e. *Buckley's Breakaways:* unusual pink and white rock formations; 58 km e. *Dragon Rocks Nature Reserve:* wildflower reserve with orchids and wildlife; 75 km e.
ⓘ Resource Centre, Johnston St; (08) 9880 1021; www.kulin.wa.gov.au

Kununurra   Pop. 5220
Map ref. 579 Q5, 581 P2

Kununurra lies in the East Kimberley region not far from the Northern Territory border. It was established in the 1960s alongside Lake Kununurra on the Ord River at the centre of the massive Ord River Irrigation Scheme. Adjacent is the magnificent Mirima National Park. Lake Argyle to the south, in the Carr Boyd Range, was created by the damming of the Ord River and is the largest body of fresh water in Australia. Islands in the lake were once mountain peaks. The word 'Kununurra' means 'meeting of big waters' in the language of the local Aboriginal people. The climate in Kununurra and the East Kimberley is divided into two seasons, the Dry and the Wet. The Dry extends from April to October and is characterised by blue skies, clear days and cool nights. The Wet, from November to March, is a time of hot, humid days, when frequent thunderstorms deliver most of the annual rainfall to the region.

IN TOWN *Historical Society Museum:* artefacts and photos of the development of the town; Coolibah Dr. *Diversion Gallery:* art gallery exhibiting Kimberley artworks for sale; Konkerberry Dr; check opening times. *Warringarri Aboriginal Arts:* large and varied display of Aboriginal art and artefacts for sale; Speargrass Rd; open daily, weekends by appt. *Red Rock Gallery:* a gallery and studio for indigenous painters from across the Kimberley; 223 Victoria Hwy; open Mon–Fri. *Kelly's Knob Lookout:* panoramic view of town and Ord Valley; off Speargrass Rd. *Celebrity Tree Park:* arboretum on the shore of Lake Kununurra where celebrities, including John Farnham, HRH Princess Anne, Harry Butler and Rolf Harris, have planted trees. Lily Creek Lagoon at the edge of the park is a good spot for birdwatching. The boat ramp was once part of the road to Darwin. Off Victoria Hwy. *Historical Society walk trails:* choose between two trails of different lengths; maps available from visitor centre.

WHAT'S ON *Ord Valley Muster:* May. *Mardi gras:* June. *Kununurra Races:* Aug. *Rodeo:* Aug. *Night Rodeo:* Sept. *Apex Barra Bash:* Sept.

NEARBY **Mirima National Park** Known by locals as the 'mini-Bungles', a striking feature of this park are the boab trees that grow on the rock faces, the seeds having been carried there by rock wallabies and left in their dung. There are walking trails within the park, and between May and August guided walks are available. Details at visitor centre. 2 km e. *Lake Kununurra:* formed after the completion of the Diversion Dam as part of the Ord River Scheme, the lake is home to a large variety of flora and fauna and is ideal for sailing, rowing, waterskiing, and boat tours. Details at visitor centre. 2 km s. *City of Ruins:* unusual sandstone formation of pinnacles and outcrops that resemble the ruins of an ancient city; off Weaber Plains Rd; 6 km n. *Ord River and Diversion Dam:* abundance of wildlife and spectacular scenery and a variety of watersports and cruises available; details at visitor centre; 7 km w. *Barra Barra:* tastings and sales of a wide variety of tropical fruits; 9 km n; daily April–Oct. *Top Rockz Gallery:* exhibits gemstones and precious metals; 10 km n; open May–Sept. *Melon Farm:* tastings and sales of melons and other local produce with tours of the farm daily; 12 km n; open May–Sept. *Ivanhoe Crossing:* permanently flooded causeway is an ideal fishing spot; Ivanhoe Rd; 12 km n. *Hoochery Distillery:* visit a traditional old Country and Western Saloon Bar or take a tour of the only licensed distillery in WA; Weaber Plains Rd; 15 km n; closed Sun. *Zebra Rock Gallery:* view the amazing display of zebra rock, nearly 600 million years old and believed to be unique to the Kimberley, or feed fish from the lakeside jetty. Packsaddle Rd; 16 km s. *Middle Springs:*

picturesque spot with diverse birdlife; 30 km n; 4WD access only. *Black Rock Falls:* spectacular waterfall during the wet season that spills over rocks stained by the minerals in the water; 4WD access only; 32 km n; April–Oct (subject to road conditions). *Parry Lagoons Nature Reserve:* enjoy birdwatching from a shaded bird hide at Marlgu Billabong or scan the wide vistas of the flood plain and distant hills afforded from the lookout at Telegraph Hill; 65 km nw. *The Grotto:* ideal swimming hole at the base of 140 stone steps with a waterfall in the wet season; 70 km nw. *Argyle Downs Homestead Museum:* built in 1884 and relocated when the lake was formed, the building is a fine example of an early station homestead; Parker Rd; 70 km s; closed Nov–Mar. *Lake Argyle:* the view of the hills that pop out of the main body of water is said to resemble a crocodile basking in the sun and is known locally as Crocodile Ridge. Fishing, birdwatching, camping, bushwalking, sailing, canoeing and lake cruises are all available. 72 km s. *El Questro Station:* featuring Aboriginal rock art, hot springs, spectacular scenery, camping, boating and fishing. Also the Barrafest Competition held in Oct. 110 km e. *Argyle Diamond Mine:* the largest producing diamond mine in the world. Access is via tour only, or take a scenic flight over Lake Argyle, the Ord Dam and the Bungle Bungles. Details at visitor centre. 120 km s. *Purnululu National Park:* 375 km s; scenic flights available in town; *see feature on p. 308.* *Mitchell River National Park:* one of the Kimberley's newest national parks protects this scenic and biologically important area. Mitchell Falls and Surveyor's Pool are the two main attractions to visitors. The area is remote. Access to the park is 4WD only and is about 16 hours' drive from Kununurra. 680 km nw. *Scenic flights:* flights from town take visitors over the remarkable Bungle Bungles, Argyle Diamond Mine, Mitchell Plateau or Kalumburu; details and bookings at visitor centre. *Tours:* bushwalks, safaris, camping, canoeing, 4WD or coach; details at visitor centre.
ⓘ Coolibah Dr; (08) 9168 1177; www.eastkimberley.com

Lake Grace   Pop. 529
Map ref. 574 F9

The area around Lake Grace is a major grain-growing region for the state, producing wheat, canola, oats, barley, lupins and legumes. Sandy plains nearby are transformed into a sea of colour at the height of the wildflower season in September and October.

IN TOWN *Inland Mission Hospital Museum:* the only remaining inland mission hospital in WA, this fully restored building (est. 1926) is now a fascinating medical museum. Approach the building via Apex Park along the interpretive walkway; Stubbs St; by appt. *Mural:* artwork depicting pioneering women was begun in 1912; Stubbs St. *Memorial Swimming Pool:* includes water playground for children; Bishop St; open 11am–6pm daily Oct–April.

WHAT'S ON *Speed Shearing Competition:* Sept. *Art Exhibition:* Oct.

NEARBY *Wildflower walk:* easy walk through natural bushland with informative signage; details at visitor centre; 3 km E. *Lake Grace:* combination of two shallow salt lakes that gives the town its name; 9 km w. *Lake Grace Lookout:* ideal spot to view the north and south lakes system; 12 km w. *White Cliffs:* unusual rock formation and picnic spot on private property; details at visitor centre; 17 km s. *Holland Track:* in 1893 John Holland and his partners cut a track from Broomehill through bushland to Coolgardie in the goldfields. Hundreds of prospectors and their families trudged along this track in search of fortune, and cartwheel ruts are still evident today. A plaque marks the place where the track crosses the road. Newdegate Rd; 23 km E. *Dingo Rock:* now on private property, this reservoir for water run-off was built by labourers from Fremantle Gaol. Wildflowers are spectacular in season. Details at visitor centre. 25 km NE. *Newdegate:* small town with a pioneer museum in the heritage-listed Hainsworth building. One of WA's major agricultural events, the Machinery Field Days, are held here in September each year. 52 km E. ⓘ Stationmaster's house; (08) 9865 1105; www.lakegrace.wa.gov.au

Lake King   Pop. 40

Map ref. 574 G9

This small rural town lies on the fringe of sheep- and wheat-farming country. With a tavern and several stores, Lake King is a stopping place for visitors travelling across the arid country around Frank Hann National Park to Norseman (adequate preparations must be made as there are no stops en route). Outstanding wildflowers in late spring include rare and endangered species.

IN TOWN *Self-guide walks:* signposted walk trails; maps at visitor centre.

NEARBY *Lake King and Causeway:* 10 km road across the salt lake studded with native scrub and wildflowers; 5 km w. *Pallarup Reserve:* pioneer well and lake with abundant wildflowers in season; 15 km s. *Mt Madden:* cairn and lookout with picnic area that forms part of the Roe Heritage Trail; 25 km SE. *Frank Hann National Park:* good example of inland sand plain heath flora with seasonal wildflowers. The rabbit-proof fence forms a boundary to the park. Access is subject to weather conditions. 32 km E. *Roe Heritage Drive Trail:* begins south of Lake King and covers natural reserves and

historic sites. It offers panoramic views from the Roe Hill lookout and retraces part of J. S. Roe's explorations in 1848. Map available at visitor centre. ⓘ Lake's Breaks, Church Ave; (08) 9874 4007

Laverton   Pop. 440

Map ref. 575 J3

Surrounded by old mine workings and modern mines, Laverton is on the edge of the Great Victoria Desert. In 1900 Laverton was a booming district of gold strikes and mines, yet gold price fluctuations in the late 1950s made it almost a ghost town. In 1969 nickel was discovered at Mt Windarra, which sparked a nickel boom. Early in 1995 a cyclone blew through Laverton, leaving it flooded and isolated for three months. Mines closed down and supplies were brought in by air. During this time, locals held a 'wheelie bin' race from the pub to the sports club. The race has become an annual event as part of Laverton Day. Today the town has two major gold mines and one of the world's largest nickel mining operations. Wildflowers are brilliant in season.

IN TOWN **Historic buildings** Restored buildings include the courthouse, the Old Police Station and Gaol, the railway station and the Mount Crawford Homestead. The original Police Sergeant's House is now the local museum with displays of local memorabilia. Contact visitor centre for details.

WHAT'S ON *Laverton Day:* Mar. *Outback Weekend:* Sept.

A sunflower farm near Kununurra, made possible by the colossal Ord River Irrigation Scheme

NEARBY *Giles Breakaway:* scenic area with interesting rock formation; 25 km E. *Lake Carey:* swimming and picnic spot exhibiting starkly contrasting scenery; 26 km w. *Windarra Heritage Trail:* walk includes rehabilitated mine site and interpretive plaques; Windarra Minesite Rd; 28 km NW. *Empress Springs:* discovered in 1896 by explorer David Carnegie and named after Queen Victoria. The spring is in limestone at the end of a tunnel that runs from the base of a 7 m deep cave. A chain ladder allows access to the cave. Enclosed shoes and torch required. 305 km NE. *Warburton:* the Tjulyuru Arts and Culture Regional Gallery showcases the art and culture of the Ngaanyatjarraku people; 565 km NE. *Golden Quest Discovery Trail:* Laverton forms part of the 965 km self-guide drive trail of the goldfields; book, map and CD available. *Outback Highway:* travel the 1200 km to Uluru from Laverton via the Great Central Rd. All roads are unsealed but regularly maintained. *Travellers note: Permits are required to travel through Aboriginal reserves and communities – they can be obtained from the Aboriginal Lands Trust in Perth, the Department of Aboriginal Affairs in Kalgoorlie–Boulder, or the Ngaanyatjarra Council, Alice Springs. Water is scarce. Fuel, supplies and accommodation are available at Tjukayirla Roadhouse, Warburton and Warakurna Roadhouse. Check road conditions before departure at the Laverton Police Station or Laverton Shire Offices; road can be closed due to heavy rain.* ⓘ Laver Pl; (08) 9031 1750

WESTERN AUSTRALIA

Leonora   Pop. 1072

Map ref. 574 I3

Leonora is the busy railhead for the north-eastern goldfields. Mt Leonora was discovered in 1869 by John Forrest. Gold was later found in the area and, in 1896, the first claims were pegged in Leonora. By 1908 the town boasted seven hotels and was the largest centre on the north-eastern goldfields. Many of the original buildings were constructed of corrugated iron and hessian, as these were versatile materials and light to transport. Today Leonora is the service centre for the mining and pastoral industries of the area.

IN TOWN *Historic buildings:* buildings from the turn of the century include the Police Station, Courthouse, Fire Station and Masonic Lodge; details at visitor centre. *Tank Hill:* excellent view over town; Queen Victoria St.

WHAT'S ON *Leonora Mile Festival:* June. *Art Prize:* Oct.

NEARBY **Gwalia** With a unique historical precinct, including WA's first state-built and -operated hotel (1903), Gwalia is a ghost town that has been restored to show visitors life in the pioneering gold-rush days. The original mine manager's office now houses the Gwalia Historical Museum with displays of memorabilia that include the largest steam winding engine in the world and a headframe designed by Herbert Hoover, the first mine manager of the Sons of Gwalia mine and eventually the 31st President of the United States. Self-guide heritage trail walk available. 4 km s. *Mt Leonora:* sweeping views of the surrounding plains and mining operations; 4 km s. *Malcolm Dam:* picnic spot at the dam, which was built in 1902 to provide water for the railway; 20 km E. *Kookynie:* the old mine in this small town is still operational. View restored shopfronts and historic memorabilia on display at the Grand Hotel. The nearby Niagara Dam was built in 1897 with cement carried by camel from Coolgardie. 92 km SE. *Menzies:* small goldmining town with an interesting and historic cemetery. View controversial 'stick figure' artworks, for which locals posed, about 55 km west of town. The Menzies Muster is held every year in Oct. 110 km s. *Golden Quest Discovery Trail:* self-guide drive trail of 965 km takes in many of the towns of the northern goldfields; maps, book and CD available at visitor centre.
ⓘ 34c Tower St; (08) 9037 6888; www.leonora.wa.gov.au

Madura   Pop. 9

Map ref. 575 P8

Madura, a roadhouse, motel and caravan park on the Eyre Highway, lies midway between Adelaide and Perth on the Nullarbor Plain. It is remarkable, given the isolation of the area, that Madura Station was settled in 1876 to breed horses, which were then shipped across to India for use by the British Army. Now Madura is surrounded by private sheep stations. Locals operate on Central Western Time, 45 minutes ahead of the rest of Western Australia.

NEARBY *Blowhole:* look for the red marker beside the track; 1 km N. *Madura Pass Lookout:* spectacular views of the Roe Plains and Southern Ocean; 1 km w on hwy. *Madura Caves:* take a good torch and sturdy shoes; 12 km s.
ⓘ Madura Pass Oasis Motel and Roadhouse; (08) 9039 3464

Mandurah   Pop. 46 549

Map ref. 566 C13, 567 B9, 572 C5, 574 C9

Mandurah has long been a popular holiday destination for Perth residents. Today, with better roads, it has also become the southernmost point of Perth's ever-expanding commuter belt. The Murray, Serpentine and Harvey rivers meet at Mandurah to form the vast inland waterway of Peel Inlet and the Harvey Estuary. This river junction was once a meeting site for Aboriginal groups who travelled here to barter. The town's name is derived from the Aboriginal word 'mandjar', meaning trading place. The river and the Indian Ocean offer a variety of watersports and excellent fishing and prawning. But the aquatic activity for which Mandurah is perhaps best known is crabbing. It brings thousands during summer weekends, wading the shallows with scoop nets and stout shoes.

IN TOWN **Christ's Church** Built in 1870, this Anglican church has hand-worked pews believed to be the work of early settler Joseph Cooper. Many of the district's pioneers are buried in the churchyard, including Thomas Peel, the founder of Mandurah. In 1994 the church was extended and a belltower added to house eight bells from England. Cnr Pinjarra Rd and Sholl St. *Abingdon Miniature Village:* display of miniature heritage buildings and gardens from UK and Australia with maze, picnic area and children's playground; Husband Rd; 3 km E. *Barragup Botanical Gardens:* award-winning gardens; Caponi Rd; 3 km E. *Hall's Cottage:* built in 1832, restored home of one of the original settlers, Henry Hall; Leighton Rd. *Community Museum:* (1898) displays on Mandurah's social, fishing and canning histories; Pinjarra Rd; open Tues–Sun. *King Carnival Amusement Park:* funfair attractions including merry-go-rounds, ferris wheel and more; Layton Pl, Hall Park. *Estuary Drive:* scenic drive along Peel Inlet and Harvey Estuary.

Surfing near Margaret River

WHAT'S ON *Mandurah Murray Markets:* Pinjarra Rd; Sat and Sun. *Jazz at Ravenswood:* Jan–Mar. *Crab Festival:* Mar. *WA Boat Show:* Oct.

NEARBY *Coopers Mill:* the first flour mill in the Murray region, located on Cooleenup Island near the mouth of the Serpentine River. Joseph Cooper built it by collecting limestone rocks and, every morning, sailing them across to the island. Accessible only by water. Contact visitor centre for information. *Castle Water Gardens:* miniature cottage garden and Japanese garden; Halls Head; 2 km s. *Marapana Wildlife World:* handfeed and touch native and imported animals; 14 km N at Karnup. *Yalgorup National Park:* swamps, woodlands and coastal lakes abounding with birdlife. Lake Clifton is one of only three places in Australia where the living fossils called thrombolites survive. A boardwalk allows close-up viewing. 45 km s. *Wineries:* several in the area, contact visitor centre for details. *Tours:* estuary cruises, dolphin interaction tours, horseback treks; contact visitor centre for details.
ⓘ 75 Mandurah Tce; (08) 9550 3999; www.peeltour.net.au

Manjimup   Pop. 4387

Map ref. 570 D6, 572 D10, 574 D11

Manjimup is the gateway to the South-West region's tall-timber country. Magnificent karri forests and rich farmlands surround the town. While timber is the town's main industry, Manjimup is also the centre of a thriving fruit and vegetable industry that supplies both local and Asian markets. The area is well known for its apples, and is the birthplace of the delicious Pink Lady apple.

IN TOWN **Timber and Heritage Park** A must-see for any visitor to Manjimup, this 10 ha park is packed full of attractions. Displays include the state's only timber museum, an exhibition of old steam engines, an 18 m climbable fire lookout tower and a historic village with an early settler's cottage, blacksmith's shop, old police station and lockup, one-teacher school and early mill house. Set in natural bush and parkland, there are many delightful spots for picnics or barbecues. Cnr Rose and Edwards sts.

WHAT'S ON *Manjimup Show:* Mar. *Festival of Country Gardens:* Oct/Nov. *Horticultural Expo:* Nov. *Cherry Harmony Festival:* Dec.

NEARBY **One Tree Bridge** Marvel at the ingenuity of Manjimup's early settlers. In 1904 a single enormous karri tree was felled so that it dropped across the 25 m wide Donnelly River, forming the basis of a bridge. Winter floods in 1966 swept most of the bridge away; the 17 m piece salvaged is displayed near the original site with information boards recounting the history of the region. Nearby is Glenoran Pool, a scenic spot for catching rainbow

trout and marron in season, with walking trails and picnic areas. Graphite Rd; 21 km w.
King Jarrah: estimated to be 600 years old, this massive tree is the centrepiece for several forest walks; Perup Rd; 3 km w. *Dingup Church:* built in 1896 by the pioneer Giblett family and doubling as the school, this church is one of the few remaining local soapstone buildings; Balbarrup Rd; 8 km E. *Pioneer Cemetery:* poignant descriptions on headstones testify to the hardships faced by first settlers; Perup Rd; 8 km E. *Diamond Tree Lookout:* one of 4 tree towers constructed from the late 1930s as fire lookouts. Climb to the wooden cabin atop this 51 m karri, used as a fire lookout from 1941 to 1947. 9 km s. *Fonty's Pool:* dammed in 1925 by Archie Fontanini for the irrigation of vegetables, it is now a popular swimming pool and picnic area in landscaped grounds; Seven Day Rd; 10 km s. *Fontanini's Nut Farm:* gather chestnuts, walnuts, hazelnuts and fruit in season; Seven Day Rd; 10 km s; open April–June, check times. *Black George's Winery and Alpaca Centre:* historic cottage, alpaca stud and wine-tasting; Black Georges Rd; 12 km s. *Nyamup:* old mill town redeveloped as a tourist village; 20 km SE. *Four Aces:* four giant karri trees 220–250 years old and 67–79 m high stand in Indian file; Graphite Rd; 23 km w. *Great Forest Trees Drive:* self-guide drive through Shannon National Park; 45 km s; contact visitor centre for map. *Perup Forest Ecology Centre:* night spotlight walks to see rare, endangered and common native animals; 50 km E; contact CALM on (08) 9771 7988 for details. *Lake Muir Lookout/Bird Observatory:* boardwalk over salt lake to bird hide; 55 km E. *Wineries:* several in area; contact visitor centre for map.
ⓘ 80 Giblett St; (08) 9771 1831

Marble Bar   Pop. 241

Map ref. 576 D2

Marble Bar has gained a dubious reputation as the hottest town in Australia. For 161 consecutive days in 1923–24 the temperature in Marble Bar did not drop below 100 degrees Fahrenheit (37.8 degrees Celsius). This mining town was named after a bar of mineral deposit that crosses the nearby Coongan River and was originally mistaken for marble. It proved to be jasper, a coloured variety of quartz.

IN TOWN *Government buildings:* built of local stone in 1895, now National Trust listed; General St.

WHAT'S ON *Marble Bar Races:* July.

NEARBY **Comet Gold Mine** Experience Marble Bar's goldmining past at this old mine site. A working mine from 1936 to 1955, the Comet is now a museum and tourist centre with displays of gemstones, rocks, minerals and local history. Also here is a 75 m high smoke stack, reputed to be the tallest in the Southern

Hemisphere. Underground mine tours occur daily; check times. 10 km s. *Marble Bar Pool:* site of the famous jasper bar (splash water on it to reveal its colours) and a popular swimming spot; 4 km w. *Corunna Downs RAAF Base:* built in 1943 as a base for long-range attacks on the Japanese-occupied islands of the Indonesian archipelago; 40 km SE. *Doolena Gorge:* watch the cliff-face glow bright red as the sun sets; 45 km NW.
ⓘ Marble Bar Travellers' Stop, Lot 232, Halse Rd; (08) 9176 1166; www.pilbara.com/marble.html

Margaret River   Pop. 3629

Map ref. 568 C10, 569 C7, 572 A10, 574 B11

One of the best known towns in Western Australia, Margaret River is synonymous with world-class wines, magnificent coastal scenery, excellent surfing beaches and spectacular cave formations. A pretty township, it lies on the Margaret River near the coast 280 kilometres south-west of Perth.

IN TOWN **Wine Tourism Showroom** Although the first grapevines were only planted in the area in 1967, Margaret River is now considered to be one of the top wine-producing regions in Australia. A huge 20 percent of Australia's premium wines are made here. The 'terroir' is perfect for grape-growing: cool frost-free winters, good moisture-retaining soils and low summer rainfall provide a long, slow, ripening period. These conditions produce greater intensity of fruit flavour, the starting point for all great wines. There are now more than 100 wine producers in the region, many of which are open to the public for tastings and cellar-door sales. Others have restaurants and tours of their premises. A good place to start a wine tour is the Margaret River Wine Tourism Showroom at the visitor centre. It provides information about the regional wineries and vineyards as well as bottle and glass displays, an interactive wineries screen, videos, a sensory display and wine-making paraphernalia. Bussell Hwy.
Rotary Park: picnic area on riverbank with a display steam engine; Bussell Hwy. *Museum Heritage Tea Room:* displays of historic farm buildings and machinery; on riverbank, Bussell Hwy. *St Thomas More Catholic Church:* one of the first modern buildings built of rammed-earth; Wallcliffe Rd. *Fudge Factory:* fudge and chocolate made before your eyes; Bussell Hwy. *Arts and crafts:* many in town, including Margaret River Gallery on Bussell Hwy; contact visitor centre for details.

WHAT'S ON *Town Square Markets:* 11am–1pm every Sun in summer, every 2nd Sun rest of year. *Margaret River Masters:* surfing competition; Mar/Apr. *Margaret River Wine Region Festival:* Nov.

NEARBY **Mammoth and Lake caves, Leeuwin–Naturaliste National Park** Lying beneath the Leeuwin–Naturaliste Ridge

WESTERN AUSTRALIA

that separates the hinterland from the coast is one of the world's most extensive and beautiful limestone cave systems. Mammoth Cave is home to the fossil remains of prehistoric animals. An audio self-guide tour lets you travel through the cave at your own pace. Mammoth is one of the few caves in Australia with partial disabled access. 21 km sw. Only a few kilometres away is the beautiful Lake Cave with its delicate formations and famous reflective lake. The adjacent interpretive centre, CaveWorks, features a walk-through cave model, interactive displays and a boardwalk with spectacular views of a collapsed cavern. 25 km sw. Further south, also in the national park, are Jewel and Moondyne caves; *see Augusta. See also Dunsborough.*

Eagles Heritage: the largest collection of birds of prey in Australia, with free flight displays at 11am and 1.30pm daily; Boodjidup Rd; 5 km sw. *Leeuwin Estate Winery:* the picturesque venue for the world-renowned open-air Leeuwin Estate Concert, held each Feb/Mar; 8 km s. *Candy Cow:* free tastings of fudge, nougat and honeycomb, with demonstrations at 11am Wed–Sun; 10 km NW, at Cowaramup. *Prevelly Park:* huge waves attract surfers from around the world; 12 km w. *Gnarabup Beach:* safe swimming beach for all the family; 13 km w. *Cheese outlets:* Fonti Farm and Margaret River Cheese Factory; Bussell Hwy; 13–15 km N. *The Berry Farm:* jams, pickles, naturally fermented vinegars, fruit and berry wines; Bessell Rd; 15 km SE. *Ellensbrook Homestead:* this wattle-and-daub homestead (1857) was once the home of Alfred and Ellen Bussell, the district's first pioneers. Nearby is the beautiful Meekadarabee Waterfall, a place steeped in Aboriginal legend. 15 km NW. *Olio Bello:* boutique, handmade olive oil, with tastings available; 17 km NW, at Cowaramup. *Grove Vineyard:* learn about and make your own sparkling wine. It includes Yahava KoffeeWorks with coffee appreciation sessions. 20 km N, at Willyabup. *Arts and crafts:* many in area, including Boranup Galleries, 20 km s on Caves Rd; contact visitor centre for details. *Margaret River Chocolate Company:* free chocolate tastings, interactive displays, and viewing windows to watch the chocolate products being made; Harmans Mill Rd, at Metricup; 30 km NW. *Bootleg Brewery:* enjoy naturally brewed boutique beers in a picturesque setting; cnr Pusey and Johnson rds, Wilyabrup; 45 km NW. *Bushtucker River and Winery Tours:* experience the Margaret River region through its wine, wilderness and food; open 12pm–5pm daily, bookings essential. *Land-based activities:* abseiling, caving, canoeing, coastal treks, horseriding and hiking; contact visitor centre for details. *Heritage trails:* including the Rails-to-Trails and Margaret River heritage trails; contact visitor centre for maps.

🛈 Cnr Tunbridge St and Bussell Hwy; (08) 9757 2911; www.margaretriver.com

Meekatharra   Pop. 948
Map ref. 573 I11, 576 C12

The name Meekatharra is believed to be an Aboriginal word meaning 'place of little water' – an apt description for a town sitting on the edge of a desert. Located 764 kilometres north-east of Perth, Meekatharra is now the centre of a vast mining and pastoral area. Like the rest of the East Murchison, Meekatharra came into existence in the 1880s when gold was discovered in the area. However, the gold rush was short-lived and it was only the arrival of the railway in 1910 that ensured Meekatharra's survival. The town became the railhead at the end of the Canning Stock Route, a series of 54 wells stretching from the East Kimberleys to the Murchison. The railway was closed in 1978, but the town continues to provide necessary links to remote outback areas through its Royal Flying Doctor Service and School of the Air.

IN TOWN *Royal Flying Doctor Service:* operates an important base in Meekatharra; Main St; open to public 9am–2pm daily. *School of the Air:* experience schooling outback-style; High St; open to public during school terms, 8am–10.30am Mon–Fri. *Old Courthouse:* National Trust building; Darlot St. *Meekatharra Museum:* photographic display and items of memorabilia from Meekatharra's past; shire offices, Main St; open 8am–4.30pm Mon–Fri.

NEARBY *Peace Gorge:* this area of granite formations is an ideal picnic spot; 5 km N. *Bilyuin Pool:* swimming (but check water level in summer); 88 km NW. *Old Police Station:* remains of the first police station in the Murchison; Mt Gould; 156 km NW.
🛈 Shire offices, 54 Main St; (08) 9981 1002; www.meekashire.wa.gov.au

Merredin   Pop. 2803
Map ref. 572 I2, 574 F7

Merredin, at the heart of the wheat belt, is a main junction 260 kilometres east of Perth on the Perth–Kalgoorlie railway line. It started as a shanty town where miners stopped on their way to the goldfields. In 1893 the railway reached the town and a water catchment was established on Merredin Peak, guaranteeing the town's importance to the surrounding region. An incredible 40 percent of the state's wheat is grown within a 100-kilometre radius of the town.

IN TOWN *Cummins Theatre:* the oldest theatre (1926) outside Perth; Bates St; open 10am–4pm daily; operates in evenings as a cinema. *Military Museum:* the state's largest collection of restored military vehicles and equipment. Tours arranged through visitor centre. Great

Eastern Hwy. *Old Railway Station Museum:* prize exhibits are the 1897 locomotive that once hauled the Kalgoorlie Express and the old signal box with 95 switching and signal levers; Great Eastern Hwy; open 9am–3pm daily. *Railway Water Tower:* fresh water was once channelled off Merredin Peak into a railway dam and then pumped into this tower, built in 1893. An advertisement for the long-gone goldfields beer, Kalgoorlie Bitter, can still be seen. Great Eastern Hwy. *Merredin Peak Heritage Walk:* self-guide walk that retraces the early history of Merredin and its links with the goldfields and the railway; contact visitor centre for map.

WHAT'S ON *Undies 2000:* drive in your underwear in this car rally with a difference; Feb. *Community Show:* Oct.

NEARBY *Pumping Station No. 4:* built in 1902 but closed in 1960 to make way for electrically driven stations, this fine example of early industrial architecture was designed by C. Y. O'Connor; 3 km w. *Hunt's Dam:* one of several wells sunk by convicts under the direction of Charles Hunt in 1866. It is now a good spot for picnics and bushwalking. 5 km N. *Totadgin Rock:* wave formation similar to Wave Rock; 16 km sw in Totadgin Dam Reserve. *Lookout over Edna May Goldmine:* 32 km E at Westonia. *Mangowine Homestead:* now a restored National Trust property, in the 1880s this was a wayside stop en route to the Yilgarn goldfields; 40 km NW at Nungarin; open 1pm–4pm Mon–Fri (closed Wed), 10am–4pm Sat and Sun. *Lake Chandler:* salt lake for swimming, waterskiing and picnics; 45 km N. *Bruce Rock:* museum, craft centre and Australia's smallest bank; 50 km sw. *Kokerbin Rock:* superb views from summit; 90 km sw. *Koorda:* museum and several wildlife reserves in area; 140 km NW.
🛈 Barrack St; (08) 9041 1666

Moora   Pop. 1711
Map ref. 574 C6

On the banks of the Moore River, Moora is the largest town between Perth and Geraldton. The area in its virgin state was a large salmon gum forest. Many of these attractive trees can still be seen.

IN TOWN *Historical Society Genealogical Records and Photo Display:* Clinch St; open by appointment. *Yuat Aboriginal Crafts:* artefacts and craft; Padbury St; open 10am–12pm daily. *Painted Roads Initiative:* murals by community artists on and in town buildings.

WHAT'S ON *Country Campout:* country music festival; Easter. *Moora Races:* Oct.

NEARBY The Berkshire Valley Folk Museum James Clinch, who came from England in 1839, created a village in the dry countryside of WA based on his home town of Berkshire. Over a 25-year period from 1847 Clinch built a homestead, barn, manager's cottage, stables, shearing shed and bridge. The elaborate buildings were made from adobe, pise, handmade bricks and unworked stone. 19 km E; open by appointment.

Western Wildflower Farm: one of the largest exporters of dried wildflowers in WA with dried flowers, seeds and souvenirs for sale; Midlands Rd, Coomberdale; 19 km N; open 9am–5pm daily Easter–Christmas. *Watheroo National Park:* site of Jingamia Cave; 50 km N. *Moora Wildflower Drive:* from Moora to Watheroo National Park, identifying flowers on the way; contact visitor centre for map.
ⓘ 34 Padbury St; (08) 9651 1401; www.moora.wa.gov.au

Morawa   Pop. 622

Map ref. 574 C4

Morawa, a small wheat-belt town, has the distinction of being home to the first commercial iron-ore to be exported from Australia. In springtime the area around Morawa is ablaze with wildflowers.

IN TOWN Church of the Holy Cross and Old Presbytery From 1915 to 1939, the famous WA architect-priest Monsignor John C. Hawes designed a large number of churches and church buildings in WA's mid-west region. Morawa boasts two of them: the Church of the Holy Cross and an unusually small stone hermitage known as the Old Presbytery. The latter, which Hawes used when visiting the town, is reputed to be the smallest presbytery in the world with only enough room for a bed, table and chair. Both buildings are part of the Monsignor Hawes Heritage Trail. Davis St; church usually open; if not, contact council offices.
Historical Museum: housed in the old police station and gaol with displays of farm machinery, household items and a collection of windmills; cnr Prater and Gill sts; open by appt.

NEARBY *Koolanooka Mine Site and Lookout:* scenic views and a delightful wildflower walk in season; 9 km E. *Perenjori:* nearby town has historic St Joseph's Church, designed by Mgr Hawes, and the Perenjori–Rothsay Heritage Trail, a 180 km self-drive tour taking in Rothsay, a goldmining ghost town; 18 km SE. *Bilya Rock Reserve:* with a large cairn, reportedly placed there by John Forrest in the 1870s as a trigonometrical survey point; 20 km N. *Koolanooka Springs Reserve:* ideal for picnics; 26 km E.
ⓘ Windfield St (Aug–Oct); (08) 9971 1421; or council offices, cnr Dreghorn and Prater sts; (08) 9971 1204; www.morawa.wa.gov.au

Mount Barker   Pop. 1723

Map ref. 571 M9, 572 H12, 574 E12

Mount Barker lies in the Great Southern region of Western Australia, with the Stirling Range to the north and the Porongurups to the east. The area was settled by Europeans in the 1830s.

The Pilbara region is well known for its pink mulla mullas

Wildflowers of the west

Western Australia is renowned for its spectacular wildflowers. With up to 12 500 species within its borders and many unique to the state, Western Australia's wildflower season draws visitors from around the world.

The season spans several months and regions, its timing influenced by rain and sunshine. In the north of the state, wildflowers will appear in July with early rains hastening their arrival. Down south, it may be as late as November before the bush bursts forth in a completely different array of blooms.

The mid-west region, three hours north of Perth by car, is the heart of wildflower country. Here fields of fine, papery everlastings carpet the inland countryside in soft white, gold and pink colours. They are joined by bright orange wild pomegranate, pink native foxgloves, orchids, grevillea, smoke bush, woody pear, blue cornflower, yellow bells and the region's star attraction, the wreath flower (*Lechenaultia macrantha*). The annual Mullewa Wildflower Show celebrates the beauty of these wheat-belt wildflowers.

Northwards on the coast is Kalbarri National Park, which has around 1000 species of wildflowers. Unique to the area are the Kalbarri catspaw and several orchids, including the Kalbarri spider orchid and the Murchison hammer orchid.

Further north, the Gascoyne region features wattles, hakeas, dampieras, purple peas and Shark Bay daisies. Up in the Pilbara region the dry, red earth yields yellow native hibiscus, bluebells, sticky cassia, mulla mulla, native fuchsias and many more. East of Perth the goldfields combine mass displays of everlastings with acacia, hakea and Sturt's desert pea.

The southern regions offer their own magnificent floral displays. More than 150 species of orchids are known to exist here, along with the exquisitely scented brown boronia and green kangaroo paws. The region also boasts carnivorous plants such as the Albany pitcher plant, and mistletoes including the amazing Western Australian Christmas tree. Fitzgerald River National Park on the south coast – a recognised Biosphere Reserve in the UNESCO program – is botanically one of the most significant parks in Australia, protecting more than 1800 species of flowering plants. This represents nearly 20 percent of the total number of plant species in Western Australia, in an area that covers only a tiny fraction of the state.

Don't have time to tour these regional areas? Then go no further than Kings Park, which overlooks the city of Perth. Here in the Botanic Gardens you'll find more than 1700 native species on display. The annual Kings Park Wildflower Festival, which attracts over 50 000 visitors each year, showcases the best of Western Australia's wildflowers.

Travellers note: Picking wildflowers is prohibited by law.

WESTERN AUSTRALIA

Vineyards were first established here in the late 1960s. Today, Mount Barker is a major wine-producing area.

IN TOWN *Old Police Station and Gaol:* built by convicts in 1867–68, it is now a museum of memorabilia; Albany Hwy, north of town; open10am–4pm Sat and Sun, daily during school holidays. *Banksia Farm:* complete collection of banksia and dryandra species, with guided tours daily; Pearce Rd; closed July.

WHAT'S ON *Mount Barker Wine Festival:* Jan. *Machinery Field Day:* Mar. *Mount Barker Wildflower Festival:* Sept/Oct. *Goundrey's Celtic Festival:* Nov.

NEARBY Porongurup National Park This is a park of dramatic contrasts, from stark granite outcrops and peaks to lush forests of magnificent karri trees. Many unusual rock formations, such as Castle Rock and Balancing Rock, make the range a fascinating place for bush rambles. The Tree in the Rock, a mature karri, extends its roots down through a crevice in a granite boulder. 24 km E.
Lookout and TV tower: easily pinpointed on the summit of Mt Barker by 168 m high television tower, it offers panoramic views of the area from the Stirling Ranges to Albany; 5 km SW. *St Werburgh's Chapel:* small mud-walled chapel (1872) overlooking Hay River Valley; 12 km SW. *Kendenup:* historic town, location of WA's first gold find; 16 km E. *Porongurup:* hosts Wine Summer Festival each Mar, and Wildflower Festival each Oct; 24 km E. *Wineries:* wineries include Goundrey, Marribrook and Plantagenet; contact visitor centre for map. *Mount Barker Heritage Trail:* 30 km drive tracing the development of the Mount Barker farming district; contact visitor centre for map. *Stirling Range National Park:* 80 km NE; *see Cranbrook.*
ⓘ Old Railway Station, Albany Hwy; (08) 9851 1163; www.mountbarkerwa.com

Mount Magnet   Pop. 890

Map ref. 574 E2

In 1854 the hill that rises above this Murchison goldmining town was named West Mt Magnet by surveyor Robert Austin after he noticed that its magnetic ironstone was playing havoc with his compass. Now known by its Aboriginal name, Warramboo Hill affords a remarkable view over the town and mines. Located 562 kilometres north-east of Perth on the Great Northern Highway, Mount Magnet offers visitors a rich mining history, rugged granite breakaway countryside and breathtaking wildflowers in season.

IN TOWN *Historical Society Museum:* collection of mining and pioneering artefacts includes a Crossley engine from the original State Battery; Hepburn St. *Heritage trail:* see the surviving historic buildings and sites of the gold-rush era on this 1.4 km walk; contact visitor centre for map.

NEARBY *The Granites:* rocky outcrop with picnic area and Aboriginal rock paintings; 7 km N. *Heritage drive:* 37 km drive of local historic and natural sights, including views of old open-cut goldmine. Also takes in The Granites and various ghost towns; contact visitor centre for map. *Fossicking for gemstones:* take care as there are dangerous old mine shafts in the area.
ⓘ Hepburn St; (08) 9963 4172

Mullewa   Pop. 532

Map ref. 574 B3

Mullewa, 100 kilometres north-east of Geraldton, is in the heart of wildflower country. In spring, the countryside surrounding the town bursts forth with one of the finest displays of wildflowers in Western Australia. The wreath flower is the star attraction of the annual Mullewa Wildflower Show.

IN TOWN Our Lady of Mount Carmel Church This small church is widely considered to be the crowning achievement of noted priest-architect Monsignor John C. Hawes. Built of local stone, this gem of Romanesque design took 7 years to build with Hawes as architect, stonemason, carpenter, modeller and moulder. The adjoining Priest House is now a museum in honour of Hawes, housing his personal belongings, books, furniture and drawings. Cnr Doney and Bowes sts. Both of these buildings are part of the Monsignor Hawes Heritage Trail, which also features the Pioneer Cemetery (Mullewa–Carnarvon Rd; 1 km N) and a site at the old showground just outside town, where a rock carved by Monsignor Hawes was once a simple altar where he held mass for the local Aboriginal people (Mount Magnet Rd; 1.5 km E). Details of trail from visitor centre.
Kembla Wildlife Sanctuary: collection of Australian fauna, and a haven for injured wildlife; Stock St; open 10am–3pm daily, June–Oct.

WHAT'S ON *Autumn Roundup:* series of craft workshops; April. *Mullewa Wildflower Show:* Aug/Sept. *Lions Street Festival:* Dec.

NEARBY Butterabby Gravesite This gravesite is a grim reminder of the harsh pioneering days. A stone monument recalls the spearing to death in 1864 of a convict labourer and the hanging in 1865 of five Aboriginal people accused of the crime. Mullewa–Mingenew Rd; 18 km S.
Tenindewa Pioneer Well: example of the art of stone pitching that was common at the time of construction, reputedly built by Chinese labourers en route to Murchison goldfields; 18 km W. *Bindoo Hill:* glacial moraine where ice-smoothed rocks dropped as the face of the glacier melted around 225 million years ago; 40 km NW. *Coalseam Conservation*

Park: remnants of the state's first coal shafts, now a picnic ground; 45 km SW. *Tallering Peak and Gorges:* ideal picnic spot; Mullewa–Carnarvon Rd; 59 km N; check accessibility at visitor centre. *Wooleen homestead:* stay on a working sheep and cattle station in the central Murchison district. Visit Boodra Rock and Aboriginal sites, and experience station life. 194 km N.
ⓘ Jose St (July–Oct); (08) 9961 1505; or council offices, cnr Padbury and Thomas sts; (08) 9961 1007; www.mullewa.wa.gov.au

Mundaring   Pop. 2652

Map ref. 566 H5, 567 E4, 572 D3, 574 C8

Mundaring is virtually an outer suburb of Perth, only 34 kilometres east. Nearby, the picturesque Mundaring Weir is the water source for the goldfields 500 kilometres further east. The original dam opened in 1903. The hilly bush setting makes the weir a popular picnic spot.

IN TOWN *Mundaring Arts Centre:* contemporary WA fine art and design; Great Eastern Hwy. *Mundaring and Hills District Museum:* displays on the diverse history of the shire; Great Eastern Hwy. *Mundaring Sculpture Park:* collection of sculptures by WA artists, set in natural bush park with grassed areas for picnics and children's playground; Jacoby St.

WHAT'S ON *Mundaring Hills Festival:* April. *Perth Hills Wine Show:* Sept.

NEARBY Mundaring Weir The Number 1 Pump Station, formerly known as the C. Y. O'Connor Museum, houses an exhibition on the mammoth project of connecting the weir to the goldfields (8 km S; Mundaring Weir Rd; open 12pm–5pm Sun). This is also the starting point of the 560 km Golden Pipeline Heritage Trail to Kalgoorlie, which follows the route of O'Connor's water pipeline, taking in towns and heritage sites. Nearby, the Hills Forest Discovery Centre offers activities such as abseiling and bushcraft, and performances by Aboriginal dance groups and bush bands (contact visitor centre for details). The Mundaring Weir Gallery, built in 1908 as a Mechanics Institute Hall, showcases the work of local craftspeople (cnr Hall and Weir Village rds; open 11.30am–5pm Sat, Sun and public holidays). Fred Jacoby Park, opposite the Weir, offers picnic and barbecue facilities.
John Forrest National Park: on a high point of the Darling Range with sensational views and lovely picnic spot beside a natural pool at Rocky Pool; 6 km W. *Karakamia Sanctuary:* native wildlife sanctuary with guided dusk walks; bookings essential; Lilydale Rd at Chidlow; 8 km. *Quatre Saisons Heritage Rose Garden:* one of the state's largest private collections; 9 km W; open Sun in spring and autumn; check times. *Kalamunda Camel Farm:* camel rides; Paulls

Valley Rd; 10 km s. *Lake Leschenaultia:* swimming, canoeing, bushwalks and camping with picnic/barbecue facilities and miniature railway on shore; 12 km NW. *Kalamunda National Park:* walking trails through jarrah forest, including the first section of the 963 km Bibbulmun Track (*see feature on p. 323*); 23 km s. *Kalamunda History Village:* collection of historic buildings; 23 km s; open Sat–Thurs. *Lesmurdie Falls National Park:* good views of Perth and Rottnest Island near spectacular falls over the Darling Escarpment; 29 km s. *Walyunga National Park:* beautiful bushland and wildflowers, and venue for the Avon Descent, a major whitewater canoeing event held each Aug; 30 km NW. *Wineries:* several in area; contact visitor centre for map. *Mundaring Loop Trail:* 16 km mountain-bike trail starting from Hills Forest Discovery Centre carpark; details from centre.
ℹ The Old School, 7225 Great Eastern Hwy; (08) 9295 0202; www.mundaring tourism.com.au

Nannup   Pop. 529

Map ref. 568 G10, 570 A4, 572 C10, 574 C11

Nannup is a historic mill town in the Blackwood Valley south of Perth. Known as 'The Garden Village', it has beautiful private and public gardens, tulip farms, daffodils and wildflowers. The countryside is a series of lush, rolling pastures alongside jarrah and pine forests.

IN TOWN *Old Police Station:* now a visitor centre surrounded by Blythe Family Gardens; Brockman St. *Town Arboretum:* fine collection of old trees planted in 1926; Brockman St. *Kealley's Gemstone Museum:* displays of rocks, shells, gemstones, bottles and stamps; Warren Rd; closed Wed. *Marinko Tomas Memorial:* memorial to the local boy who was the first serviceman from WA killed in the Vietnam War; Warren Rd. *Blackwood Wines:* beautiful winery overlooking an artificial lake; Kearney St; closed Wed. *Arts, crafts and antiques:* many in town, including Crafty Creations for quality timber goods on Warren Rd (closed June). *Heritage trail:* in two sections, with a 2.5 km town walk highlighting historic buildings, and a 9 km scenic drive featuring sites of historic and natural significance; contact visitor centre for map.
WHAT'S ON *Market:* Warren Rd; second Sat of each month. *Music Festival:* Feb/Mar. *Respect Yourself Forest Car Rally:* Mar. *Flower and Garden Month:* Aug. *Daffodil Week:* Aug/Sept. *Rose Festival:* Nov.
NEARBY *Condill Park:* bushwalks and wildflowers in season; 3 km w. *Barrabup Pool:* largest of several pools, ideal for swimming, fishing and camping. Also has barbecue facilities. 10 km w. *Carlotta Crustaceans:* marron farm; 14 km s off

Vasse Hwy. *Tathra:* fruit winery and restaurant; 14 km NE; open 11am–4.30pm daily. *Donnelly River Wines:* open for cellar-door tastings; contact visitor centre for details; 45 km s. *Blackwood River:* camping, swimming, canoeing and trout fishing. *Self-guide walks:* wildflower (in spring), waterfall (in winter) and forest walks; contact visitor centre for maps. *Scenic drives:* through jarrah forest and pine plantations, including 40 km Blackwood Scenic Drive; contact visitor centre for maps.
ℹ 4 Brockman St; (08) 9756 1211; www.nannup.net

Narrogin   Pop. 4424

Map ref. 572 G6, 574 E9

Narrogin, 192 kilometres south-east of Perth on the Great Southern Highway, is the commercial hub of a prosperous agricultural area. Sheep, pigs and cereal farms are the major industries. First settled in the 1870s, the town's name is derived from an Aboriginal word 'gnarojin', meaning waterhole.

IN TOWN *Gnarojin Park* This park is a national award winner for its original designs and artworks portraying local history and culture, which include the Centenary Pathway, marked with 100 locally designed commemorative tiles, Newton House Barbecue and Noongar Cultural Sites. Gordon St.
History Hall: local history collection; Egerton St. *Old Courthouse Museum:* built in 1894 as a school, it later became the district courthouse; Egerton St; open Mon–Sat or by appointment. *Narrogin Art Gallery:* exhibitions; Federal St; open 10am–4pm Tues–Fri, 10am–12pm Sat. *Lions Lookout:* excellent views; Kipling St. *Heritage trail:* self-guide walk around the town's historic buildings; contact visitor centre for map.
WHAT'S ON *State Gliding Championships:* Jan. *Spring Festival:* Sept. *Rev Heads:* car rally; Nov/Dec.

NEARBY **Dryandra Woodland** One of the few remaining areas of virgin forest in the wheat belt, Dryandra is a paradise for birdwatchers and bushwalkers. The open, graceful eucalypt woodlands of white-barked wandoo, powderbark and thickets of rock she-oak support many species of flora and fauna including numbats, the state's animal emblem, woylies, tammar wallabies, brush-tailed possums and many others. Over 100 species of birds have been identified, including the mound-building mallee fowl. Tune your radio to 100FM for 'Sounds of Dryandra', a 25 km radio drive trail with 6 stops featuring tales of the local Nyungar people, early forestry days, bush railways and Dryandra's unique wildlife. There are day-visitor facilities and accommodation, walk trails, a weekend Ecology Course (runs in autumn and spring; try your hand at radio-tracking, trapping and spotlighting) and school holiday programs.
Barna Mia Animal Sanctuary The sanctuary, within the Dryandra Woodland, has guided spotlight walks at night that show some of Australia's most threatened marsupials, including the bilby and boodie. Bookings essential; contact CALM on (08) 9881 9200 or visitor centre. Narrogin–Wandering Rd; 26 km NW; contact visitor centre for map. *Yilliminning and Birdwhistle Rocks:* unusual rock formations; 11 km E. *District Heritage Trail:* contact visitor centre for map.
ℹ Old Courthouse, Egerton St; (08) 9881 2064; www.dryandratourism.org.au

New Norcia   Pop. 75

Map ref. 572 D1, 574 C6

In 1846 Spanish Benedictine monks established a mission 132 kilometres north of Perth in the secluded Moore Valley in an attempt to help the local Aboriginal population. They named their mission after the Italian town of Norcia, the birthplace of the order's founder, St Benedict. Today, the handsome and

Our Lady of Mount Carmel Church, Mullewa

imposing Spanish-inspired buildings of New Norcia, surrounded by the gum trees and dry grasses of the wheat belt, provide a most unexpected vista. The town still operates as a monastery and is Australia's only monastic town. Visitors may join the monks at daily prayers.

IN TOWN Abbey Church This fine example of bush architecture was built using a combination of stones, mud plaster, rough-hewn trees and wooden shingles. It is the oldest Catholic church still in use in WA and contains the tomb of Dom Rosendo Salvado, the founder of New Norcia and its first Abbot. Hanging on a wall is the painting of Our Lady of Good Counsel (also called The Mother of Good Counsel) given to Salvado before he left for Australia in 1845 by Bishop (later Saint) Vincent Palotti. One of New Norcia's most famous stories relates how, in 1847, Salvado placed this revered painting in the path of a bushfire threatening the mission's crops. The wind suddenly changed direction and drove the flames back to the part already burnt, and the danger was averted. *Museum and art gallery:* the museum tells the story of New Norcia's history as an Aboriginal mission, while the art gallery houses priceless religious art from Australia and Europe as well as Spanish artefacts, many of which were gifts from Queen Isabella of Spain. The Museum Gift Shop features New Norcia's own produce including bread, nutcake, pan chocolatti, biscotti, wine, honey and olive oil. *Monastery:* daily tours of the interior. A guesthouse allows visitors to experience the monastic life for a few days. *Hotel:* this magnificent building, featuring a massive divided central staircase and high, moulded pressed-metal ceilings, was opened in 1927 as a hostel to accommodate parents of the children who were boarding at the town's colleges. *Flour Mill:* built in 1879, and reputed to be the oldest working flour mill in WA. The flour is baked into bread at the Monastery Bakehouse. There is an interpretive display inside; ask at visitor centre for access. *Old Flour Mill:* the oldest surviving building in New Norcia dates from the 1850s. *Heritage trail:* 2 km self-guide walk highlights New Norcia's historic and cultural significance and the role of the Benedictine monks in colonial history; contact visitor centre for map. *Guided tour:* 2 hr tour of the town with an experienced guide takes you inside buildings not otherwise open to the public; 11am and 1.30pm daily.

NEARBY Mogumber: town with one of the state's highest timber-and-concrete bridges; 24 km sw. *Piawaning:* magnificent stand of eucalypts north of town; 31 km ne. *Bolgart:* site of historic hotel; 49 km se. *Wyening Mission:* former mission, now a historic site; 50 km se; open by appt. ℹ Museum and art gallery, Great Northern Hwy; (08) 9654 8056; www.newnorcia.wa.edu.au

Newman
Pop. 3515

Map ref. 576 D6

Located in the heart of the Pilbara, Newman was built in the late 1960s by the Mount Newman Mining Company to house the workforce required at nearby Mt Whaleback, the largest open-cut iron-ore mine in the world. At the same time a 426-kilometre railway – the longest privately owned railway in the world – was constructed between Newman and Port Hedland to transport the ore for export to Japan.

IN TOWN Mt Whaleback Mine Tours: the mine produces 30 million tons of iron ore every year. Tours run Mon–Sat May–Sept, Tues and Thurs Oct–April; minimum 4 people; book through visitor centre. *BHP Iron Ore Silver Jubilee Museum and Gallery:* mining museum features a magnificent 9 x 2.5 m leadlight window, depicting the Pilbara landscape; located at visitor centre. *Mining and Pastoral Museum:* interesting display of relics from the town's short history, including the first Haulpak (giant iron-ore truck) used at Mt Whaleback; located at visitor centre. *Radio Hill Lookout:* panoramic view of town and surrounding area; off Newman Dr.

WHAT'S ON Campdraft and Rodeo: Aug. *Fortescue Festival:* Aug. *Octoberfest:* beer festival; Oct.

NEARBY Ophthalmia Dam: swimming, sailing, barbecues and picnics (no camping); 15 km e. *Mt Newman:* excellent views; 20 km nw. *Eagle Rock Falls:* permanent pools and picnic spots nearby; 4WD access only; 69 km nw. *Wanna Munna:* site of Aboriginal rock carvings; 70 km w. *Rock pools and waterholes:* at Kalgans Pool (65 km ne), Three Pools (75 km n) and Weeli Wolli (90 km w). *Newman Waterholes and Art Sites Tour:* tours arranged and maps available at the visitor centre. *Karijini National Park:* 196 km n; *see feature on p. 327.* ℹ Cnr Fortescue Ave and Newman Dr; (08) 9175 2888; www.newman-wa.org

Norseman
Pop. 1058

Map ref. 575 J8

Norseman is the last large town on the Eyre Highway for travellers heading east towards South Australia. Gold put Norseman on the map in the early 1890s with one of the richest quartz reefs in Australia. The town is steeped in goldmining history, reflected in its colossal tailings dump. If visitors could stand atop this dump – the tallest in the state – they could have up to $50 million in gold underfoot (although the rock has been processed, much residual gold remains). The story behind the town's name has become folklore. The settlement that sprang up in 1892 as a result of gold being discovered in the area was originally called Dundas. Two years later, a horse owned by prospector Laurie Sinclair pawed the ground and unearthed

a nugget of gold on a site that proved to be a substantial reef. The horse's name was Norseman, and the township was renamed in its honour.

IN TOWN Historical Collection: mining tools and household items; Battery Rd; open 10am–1pm Mon–Sat. *Phoenix Park:* open-plan park with displays, stream and picnic facilities; Prinsep St. *Statue of Norseman:* bronze statue by Robert Hitchcock commemorates Norseman, the horse; cnr Roberts and Ramsay sts. *Camel Train:* corrugated iron sculptures represent the camel trains of the pioneer days; cnr Ramsay St and Coolgardie Hwy. *Dollykissangel Toy Museum:* display of antique dolls, collectable dolls, teddy bears, cars, trains, bottles and toys; Roberts St. *Gem fossicking:* gemstone permits are available from the visitor centre.

WHAT'S ON Norseman Cup: Mar.

NEARBY Beacon Hill Lookout: spectacular at sunrise and sunset, this lookout offers an outstanding 360-degree panorama of the salt lakes, Mt Jimberlana, the township and surrounding hills and valleys; Mines Rd; 2 km n. *Mt Jimberlana:* reputed to be one of the oldest geological areas in the world. Take the walking trail to the summit for great views. 5 km e. *Dundas Rocks:* barbecue and picnic area near old Dundas townsite, where the lonely grave of a 7-month-old child is the only sign that the area was once inhabited; 22 km s. *Buldania Rocks:* picnic area with beautiful spring wildflowers; 28 km e. *Bromus Dam:* freshwater dam with picnic area; 32 km s. *Peak Charles National Park:* good-weather track for experienced walkers and climbers to Peak Eleanora, with a magnificent view from top; 50 km s, then 40 km w off hwy. *Cave Hill Nature Reserve:* spectacular granite outcrops, caves, waterholes and wildlife; 4WD access only; 55 km n, then 50 km w. *Heritage Trail:* 33 km trail follows the original Cobb & Co route taken at the turn of the century; contact visitor centre for map. ℹ 68 Roberts St; (08) 9039 1071; www.norseman.info

Northam
Pop. 6137

Map ref. 567 H2, 572 E3, 574 D7

Northam lies in the heart of the fertile Avon Valley. The Avon River winds its way through the town and on its waters you'll find white swans, a most unusual sight in a state where the emblem is a black swan. White swans were brought to Northam from England in the 1900s and have flourished here. Northam is also synonymous with hot-air ballooning as it is one of the few areas in Western Australia ideally suited to this pastime. Northam is home to the famous Avon Descent, a 133 km whitewater race down the Avon and Swan rivers to Perth.

IN TOWN Historic buildings Of the many historic buildings in Northam, two are particularly noteworthy: Morby

Cottage (1836) on Avon Dr, the home of Northam's first settler, John Morrell, now a museum and open 10.30am–4pm Sun or by appt; and the Trust-classified Sir James Mitchell House (1905), cnr Duke and Hawes sts, with its elaborate Italianate architecture. Take the 90 min self-guide walk for the full tour of the town; contact visitor centre for map. *Old Railway Station Museum:* displays include a steam engine and renovated carriages, plus numerous artefacts from the early 1900s; Fitzgerald St West; open 10am–4pm Sun or by appt. *Visitor centre:* exhibition showcasing the area's significant postwar migrant history; Grey St. *Suspension bridge:* the longest pedestrian suspension bridge in Australia crosses the Avon River adjacent to visitor centre.

WHAT'S ON *Vintage on Avon:* car rally; Mar. *Avon Descent:* Aug.

NEARBY *Mt Ommanney Lookout:* excellent views of the township and agricultural areas beyond; 1.5 km w. *Hot-air ballooning:* Northam Airfield; 2 km NE; Mar–Nov; bookings essential. *Meckering:* small town made famous in 1968 when an earthquake left a huge fault line in its wake; 35 km E.
ⓘ Avon Valley Visitor Centre, 2 Grey St; (08) 9622 2100

Northampton   Pop. 801

Map ref. 574 A3

Northampton, nestled in the valley of Nokarena Brook, 51 kilometres north of Geraldton, was awarded Historic Town status by the National Trust in 1993. It was declared a townsite in 1864 and is one of the oldest settlements in Western Australia. A former lead-mining centre, its prosperity is now based on sheep- and wheat-farming.

IN TOWN *Chiverton House Historical Museum:* unusual memorabilia housed in what was originally the home of Captain Samuel Mitchell, mine manager and geologist; Hampton Rd; open 10am–12pm and 2pm–4pm Fri–Mon. *Church of Our Lady in Ara Coeli:* designed in 1936 by Monsignor John Hawes, WA's famous architect-priest; Hampton Rd. *Gwalla Church and Cemetery:* ruins of town's first church, built in 1864; Gwalla St. *Hampton Road Heritage Walk:* 2 km walk includes 37 buildings of historical interest including the Miners Arms Hotel (1868) and the Old Railway Station (1879); contact visitor centre for map.
WHAT'S ON *Market:* Kings Park, cnr Essex St and Hampton Rd; 1st Sat each month. *Airing of the Quilts:* quilts hung in main street; Oct.
NEARBY *Alma School House:* built in 1916 as a one-teacher school; 12 km N. *Aboriginal cave paintings:* at the mouth of the Bowes River; 17 km W. *Oakabella Homestead:* one of the first farms in WA to plant canola, or rapeseed as it was then

The view from Mt Meharry, north-west of Newman in the Hamersley Range

known. Take a guided tour of the historic homestead and outbuildings; 18 km s; open daily Mar–Nov. *Horrocks Beach:* beautiful bays, sandy beaches, good fishing and surfing; 20 km w. *Lynton Station:* ruins of labour-hiring depot for convicts, used in 1853–56; 35 km NW. *Lynton House:* squat building with slits for windows, probably designed as protection from hostile Aboriginal people; 35 km NW. *Hutt Lagoon:* appears pink in midday sun; 40 km w. *Port Gregory:* beach settlement, ideal for swimming, fishing and windsurfing; 47 km NW. *Warribano Chimney:* Australia's first lead smelter; 60 km N.
ⓘ Hampton Rd; (08) 9934 1488; www.wn.com.au/northampton

Northcliffe   Pop. 239

Map ref. 570 C9, 572 D12, 574 D12

Magnificent virgin karri forests surround the township of Northcliffe, 31 kilometres south of Pemberton in the state's South-West. Just a kilometre from the town centre is Northcliffe Forest Park, where you can see purple-crowned lorikeets, scarlet robins and, in spring, a profusion of wildflowers. Not far away is the coastal settlement of Windy Harbour, a popular swimming beach.

IN TOWN Pioneer Museum Northcliffe came into existence as a result of the Group Settlement Scheme, a WA government plan to resettle returned WW I soldiers and immigrants by offering them rural land to farm. The scheme was enthusiastically backed by the English newspaper magnate Lord Northcliffe (hence the town's name). Unfortunately by the 1920s, when the scheme began, all the good land in the state had already been settled. The group settlers were left to contend with pockets of inhospitable country such as the South-West timber country. With only crosscut saws and axes, they were faced with the daunting task of clearing some of the world's biggest trees from their land. It is not surprising that by the mid-1930s all of the Group Settlement projects in the South-West timber country had failed. A visit to the Pioneer Museum with its excellent displays is the best way to understand the hardships the group settlers experienced. Wheatley Coast Rd. Open 10am–2pm daily Sept–May, 10am–2pm Sat, Sun and school holidays June–Aug.
Visitor centre: houses one of WA's largest rock collections. Also Aboriginal displays and photographic folio of native flora and birds; Wheatley Coast Rd. *Canoe and mountain-bike hire:* contact visitor centre for details.

WHAT'S ON *Karri Cup:* Feb/Mar. *Mountain Bike Championship:* May/June. *Night-time Mountain Bike Race:* Nov.
NEARBY *Northcliffe Forest Park:* follow the Hollow Butt Karri and Twin Karri walking trails or enjoy a picnic; Wheatley Coast Rd. *Warren River:* trout fishing and sandy beaches; 8 km N. *Mt Chudalup:* spectacular views of the surrounding D'Entrecasteaux National Park and coastline from the summit of this giant granite outcrop; 10 km s. *Moon's Crossing:* delightful picnic spot; 13 km NW. *Lane–Poole Falls and Boorara Tree:* 3 km walking trail leads to the falls, passing the Boorara Tree with 50 m high fire-lookout cabin; 18 km SE. *Point D'Entrecasteaux:* limestone cliffs, popular with rock climbers, rise 150 m above the sea where 4 viewing platforms provide superb views of this dramatic coastline; 27 km s. *Windy Harbour:* swimming, snorkelling, fishing, camping and whale-watching (from platform, best times Sept–Nov); 27 km s. *Cathedral Rocks:* watch seals and dolphins; 27 km s. *Salmon Beach:* surf beach offers salmon fishing April–June; 27 km s. *The Great Forest Trees Drive:* 48 km self-guide scenic drive takes in the karri giants at Snake Gully Lookout,

the Boardwalk and Big Tree Grove; contact visitor centre for map. *Pemberton–Northcliffe Tramway:* tramcars based on 1907 Fremantle trams operate daily through tall-forest country between Northcliffe and Pemberton. Steam-train rides are available Easter–Nov; contact visitor centre for times. *Bibbulmun Track:* section of this long-distance walking trail links the three national parks around Northcliffe: D'Entrecasteaux (5 km s), Warren (20 km n) and Shannon (30 km e). *See feature on facing page. Mountain-bike trails:* 4 permanent trails have been established around Northcliffe; contact visitor centre for details.
ⓘ Wheatley Coast Rd; (08) 9776 7203; www.southernforests.com.au

Onslow   Pop. 795

Map ref. 573 D3

Onslow, on the north-west coast between Exmouth and Karratha, is the supply base for offshore gas and oil fields. This part of the coast is among the north's most cyclone-prone and Onslow has often suffered severe damage. The town was originally at the Ashburton River mouth and a bustling pearling centre. In the 1890s gold was discovered nearby. In 1925 the townsite was moved to Beadon Bay after cyclones caused the river to silt up. During World War II, submarines refuelled here and the town was bombed twice. In the 1950s it was the mainland base for Britain's nuclear experiments at Montebello Islands. In 1963 Onslow was almost completely destroyed by a cyclone. It is now an attractive tree-shaded town.
IN TOWN *Goods Shed Museum:* memorabilia from the town's long history and collections of old bottles, shells and rocks; in visitor centre; Second Ave. *Beadon Creek and Groyne:* popular fishing spot. *Ian Blair Memorial Walkway:* 1 km scenic walk; starts at Beadon Point; finishes at Sunset Beach. *Heritage trail:* covers sites of interest in town; contact visitor centre for map.
NEARBY *Termite mounds:* with interpretive display; 10 km s. *Mackerel Islands:* excellent fishing destination. Charter boats are available for daytrips or extended fishing safaris. 22 km off the coast; contact visitor centre for details. *Ashburton River:* swimming, camping and picnicking; 45 km sw. *Old Townsite Heritage Trail:* self-guide walk around original townsite; 45 km sw; contact visitor centre for map.
ⓘ Second Ave (April–Oct); (08) 9184 6644; or council offices, Second Ave; (08) 9184 6001

Pemberton   Pop. 898

Map ref. 570 C7, 572 D11, 574 C11

Pemberton sits in a quiet valley surrounded by some of the tallest trees in the world and, in spring, brilliant wildflowers. This is the heart of karri country, with 4000 hectares of protected virgin karri forest in the nearby Warren and Beedelup national parks. Pemberton is a centre for high-quality woodcraft and is renowned for its excellent rainbow trout and marron fishing.
IN TOWN *Karri Forest Discovery Centre:* interpretive centre includes museum with collection of historic photographs and forestry equipment; at visitor centre. *Pioneer Museum:* utensils, tools and other memorabilia from pioneer days plus a full-scale settler's hut; at visitor centre. *Craft galleries:* many in town, including the Fine Woodcraft Gallery in Dickinson St and the Peter Kovacsy Studio in Jamieson St.
WHAT'S ON *Mill Hall Markets:* 2nd Sat of every month; Brockman St. *CWA Markets:* 4th Sat of every month; Brockman St. *Gloucester Tree Birthday Celebration:* Sept. *Food and Wine Show:* Nov.
NEARBY **Gloucester National Park** In this park is the town's most popular tourist attraction, the Gloucester Tree. With its fire lookout teetering 61 m above the ground and a spine-tingling 153 rungs spiralling upwards, this is not a climb for the faint-hearted. Named after the Duke of Gloucester, who visited the site during construction of the lookout cabin, the Gloucester Tree is one of 8 tree towers constructed from the late 1930s as fire lookouts. As the extremely tall trees in the southern forests offered few vantage points for fire-lookout towers, it was decided to simply build a cabin high enough in one of the taller trees to serve the purpose. Also within the park are the Cascades, a scenic spot for picnicking, bushwalking and fishing. 1 km s.
Warren National Park This park boasts some of the most easily accessible virgin karri forest. The Dave Evans Bicentennial Tree has picnic facilities and walking tracks nearby. 9 km sw.
Beedelup National Park Here you'll find the Walk Through Tree, a 75 m, 400-year-old karri with a hole cut in it big enough for people to walk through. The Beedelup Falls, a total drop of 106 m, are rocky cascades best seen after heavy rain. Nearby are walk trails and a suspension bridge. 18 km w.
Lavender and Berry Farm: enjoy berry scones, lavender biscuits and other unusual produce; Browns Rd; 4 km n. *Big Brook Dam:* the dam has its own beach, picnic and barbecue facilities, trout and marron fishing in season, and walking trails; 7 km n. *Big Brook Arboretum:* established in 1928 to study the growth of imported trees from around the world, it offers daily tours; 7 km n. *King Trout and Marron Farm:* catch and cook your own trout; 8 km sw; closed Thurs. *Founder's Forest:* part of the 100-Year-Old Forest, with karri regrowth trees over 120 years old; 10 km n. *Wineries:* about 28 wineries in the area, many offering tours, tastings and sales; contact visitor centre for details.

Pemberton–Northcliffe Tramway: tramcars based on 1907 Fremantle trams operate daily through tall-forest country between Northcliffe and Pemberton. Steam-train rides are available Easter–Nov; contact visitor centre for times. *Fishing:* in rivers, inland fishing licence is required for trout and marron; contact visitor centre for details. *Tours:* Forest Industry tours into logging and regrowth areas, marron farm tours, scenic bus tours, 4WD adventure tours, self-guide forest drives, horseriding trails and walking trails; contact visitor centre for details. *Drive trails:* include the Heartbreak Trail, a one-way drive through the karri forest of Warren National Park; contact visitor centre for maps. *Walk trails:* include the 1 hr return Rainbow Trail; contact visitor centre for maps. *Bibbulmun Track:* walking trail passes through Pemberton; *see feature on facing page.*
ⓘ Brockman St; (08) 9776 1133 or 1800 671 133; www.pembertontourist.com.au

Pingelly   Pop. 729

Map ref. 572 F5, 574 D9

Located 158 kilometres south-east of Perth on the Great Southern Highway, Pingelly is part of the central-southern farming district. Sandalwood was once a local industry, but today sheep and wheat are the major produce.
IN TOWN *Courthouse Museum:* built in 1907, now houses historic memorabilia and photographs; Parade St. *Apex Lookout:* fine views of town and surrounding countryside; Stone St.
WHAT'S ON *Autumn Country Show and Ute Muster:* Mar.
NEARBY *Pingelly Heights Observatory:* audio tour and telescope viewing of the stars and constellations; bookings essential; 5 km ne. *Moorumbine Heritage Trail:* 1 hr self-guide walk through this old townsite features early settlers' cottages and St Patrick's Church, built in 1873; contact council office for map; 10 km e. *Tutanning Flora and Fauna Reserve:* botanist Guy Shorteridge collected over 400 species of plants from here for the British Museum between 1903 and 1906; 21 km e. *Boyagin Nature Reserve:* widely recognised as one of the few areas of original fauna and flora left in the wheat belt, this picnic reserve has important stands of powderbark, jarrah and marri trees and is home to numbats and tammar wallabies. 26 km nw.
ⓘ Council offices, 17 Queen St; (08) 9887 1066; www.pingelly.wa.gov.au

Pinjarra   Pop. 1866

Map ref. 567 C10, 572 C6, 574 C9

A pleasant 84-kilometre drive south of Perth along the shaded South Western Highway brings you to Pinjarra, picturesquely set on the Murray River. Predominantly a dairying, cattle-farming

The suspension bridge under Beedelup Falls

Bibbulmun Track

At 963 kilometres, the Bibbulmun Track is Western Australia's only long-distance walking trail and one of the longest continuously marked trails in Australia. It stretches from Kalamunda, a suburb on the outskirts of Perth, to Albany on the south coast. On the way it passes through some of the state's most picturesque southern towns including Dwellingup, Collie, Balingup, Pemberton, Northcliffe, Walpole and Denmark. The track is designed to give walkers ample opportunities to experience the beauty and diversity of the South-West.

Named after a local Aboriginal language group, the track is marked by a stylised image of the 'Waugal' (rainbow serpent), a spirit being from the Aboriginal Dreaming. Whether taking a short walk or a five-day hike, easy access points enable walkers of all ages and fitness levels to experience the Bibbulmun Track.

Walk the track in springtime and see the bush at its best with Western Australia's amazing array of wildflowers providing a spectacular backdrop of colour. Flats of pale-barked wandoo give way to stands of jarrah and marri, and forest dominated by the majestic karri, the second tallest flowering tree in the world. Near Walpole you'll encounter the massive red tingle trees of the Valley of the Giants. Other well-known natural attractions on the track include Mt Cook, the highest point in the Darling Range, Beedelup Falls and the Gloucester Tree lookout.

All campsites on the Bibbulmun Track provide a robust, wooden shelter designed to accommodate 8–15 people comfortably. These shelters are completely open on one side, providing an unbroken view of the bush or forest after a hard day on the trail. The shelter at the Brookton campsite has been modified to allow access and use by people with restricted mobility. The site is linked to the Brookton Highway by 2.5 kilometres of wheelchair-accessible trail, enabling hardy, outdoor-oriented people with disabilities to share in the magic of the Bibbulmun experience.

For maps and more information contact the Bibbulmun Track Office of CALM on (08) 9334 0265 or visit www.bibbulmuntrack.org.au

and timber-producing area, Pinjarra was also once known as the horse capital of Western Australia when horses were bred for the British Army in India. Today horseracing, pacing and equestrian events are a major part of Pinjarra culture. The Alcoa Refinery north-east of town is the largest alumina refinery in Australia.
IN TOWN Edenvale Complex Built in 1888 with locally fired clay bricks, Edenvale was the home of Edward McLarty, member of the state's Legislative Council for 22 years. It is now home to the visitor centre. Nearby is Liveringa

(1874), the original residence of the McLarty family (tours available). There is a Heritage Rose Garden featuring 364 varieties of old-fashioned roses, and a quilters' display in the Old School House. Cnr George and Henry sts. *Suspension bridge:* across the Murray River, with picnic areas at both ends; George St. *Heritage trail:* 30 min river walk follows series of tiles explaining the heritage of the area; contact visitor centre for map.
WHAT'S ON *Railway Markets:* 2nd Sun morning of each month; Lions Park. *Edenvale Markets:* 4th Sat morning of each

month. *Pinjarra Cup:* Mar. *Pinjarra Festival:* June. *Teddy Bears' Picnic:* Nov.
NEARBY Fairbridge This was established by Kingsley Fairbridge in 1912 as a farm school for British children, many of them orphans. Over the years more than 8000 English children were educated here. The boarding houses, which are today used as holiday cottages, have famous British names such as Clive, Shakespeare, Nightingale, Exeter, Evelyn and Raleigh. South Western Hwy; 6 km N.
Old Blythewood: beautiful National Trust property built in 1859 by John McLarty, who arrived in Australia in 1839; 4 km S; open 10am–4.30pm Sun and Mon or by appointment. *Alcoa Scarp Lookout:* good views of coastal plain, surrounding farming area and Alcoa Refinery; 14 km E. *North Dandalup Dam:* recreation lake, picnic area and coastal views from lookout; 22 km NE. *South Dandalup Dam:* barbecues and picnic areas; 30 km E. *Lake Navarino:* formerly known as Waroona Dam, it is good for watersports, fishing, walking and horseriding; 33 km S. *Tumbulgum Farm:* native and farm animals, Aboriginal culture, farm shows and WA product sales; 38 km N at Mundijong. *Coopers Mill:* first flour mill in the Murray region, located on Cooleenup Island near the mouth of the Serpentine River. It is accessible only by water; contact visitor centre for details. *Hotham Valley Tourist Railway:* travel from Pinjarra to Dwellingup by train, taking in lush green dairy country before climbing the steep and spectacular Darling Range and finishing in the heart of the jarrah forest. The train is steam-hauled May–Oct and diesel-hauled Nov–April. Check times with visitor centre.
ℹ️ Edenvale Complex, cnr George and Henry sts; (08) 9531 1438; www.peeltour.net.au

Port Hedland   Pop. 12 697

Map ref. 576 C1, 578 B13

Port Hedland was named after Captain Peter Hedland, who reached this deep-water harbour in 1863. An iron-ore boom that began in the early 1960s saw the town grow at a remarkable rate. Today, Port Hedland handles the largest iron-ore export tonnage of any Australian port. Iron ore from some of the world's biggest mines is loaded onto huge ore carriers. The 2.6-kilometre trains operated by BHP Iron Ore arrive nine times daily. Salt production is another major industry with about two million tonnes exported per annum.
IN TOWN *Don Rhodes Mining Museum:* open-air museum with displays of historic railway and mining machinery; Wilson St. *Pioneer and Pearlers Cemetery:* used between 1912 and 1968, it has graves of early gold prospectors and Japanese pearl divers; off Stevens St. *Town observation tower:* 26 m tower offers

WESTERN AUSTRALIA

wonderful views of the harbour, town, surrounding coast and hinterland; behind visitor centre, Wedge St. *Town Tour:* visit the town's many attractions; 11am Mon, Wed and Fri June–Oct; book through visitor centre. *BHP Iron Ore Tour:* see the enormous machinery required to run this industrial giant; departs 9.30am Mon–Fri from visitor centre.

WHAT'S ON *Australia Day Port Festival:* Jan. *Welcome to Hedland Night:* May. *Game Fishing Classic:* July. *Port Hedland Cup:* Aug. *Pilbara Music Festival:* Sept. *Hedland Octoberfest:* Oct.

NEARBY **Stairway to the Moon** Like the Broome version, this beautiful illusion is created when a full moon rises over the ocean at low tide. The moon's rays hit pools of water left by the receding tide, creating the image of a stairway leading up to the moon. It lasts for about 15 minutes. Check with visitor centre for dates and times. Coastal side of Goode St. *Heritage trail:* 1.8 km self-guide walk around the town; contact visitor centre for map. *Pretty Pool:* picnic, fish and swim at this scenic tidal pool; 8 km NE. *Dampier Salt:* see giant cone-shaped mounds of salt awaiting export; 8 km S. *Royal Flying Doctor Service:* operates an important base in Port Hedland at the airport; 15 km S. Open to public 8am–11am Mon–Fri; closed public holidays, school holidays and weekends. *School of the Air:* experience schooling outback-style at the airport; 15 km S. Open to public 8am–11am Mon–Fri; closed public and school holidays. *Turtle-watching:* flatback turtles nest in the area Oct–Mar at Pretty Pool, Cooke Point and Cemetery Beach. *Cruises:* scenic harbour and sunset cruises; contact visitor centre for details. *Travellers note: Poisonous stonefish frequent this stretch of coast, especially Nov–Mar, so wear strong shoes when walking on rocky reef areas and make local inquiries before swimming in sea.* ℹ️ 13 Wedge St; (08) 9173 1711; www.porthedlandtouristbureau.com

Ravensthorpe   Pop. 342

Map ref. 574 H10

Ravensthorpe is encircled by the Ravensthorpe Range. This unspoiled bushland is home to many plants unique to the area such as the Qualup bell, warted yate and Ravensthorpe bottlebrush. Gold was discovered here in 1898 and by 1909 the population had increased to around 3000. Coppermining reached a peak in the late 1960s; the last coppermine closed in 1972. Many old mine shafts can be seen around the district and fossicking is a favourite pastime.

IN TOWN *Historical Society Museum:* local history memorabilia; in Dance Cottage near visitor centre; Morgans St. *Historic buildings:* many in town including

the impressive Palace Hotel (1907) and the restored Commercial Hotel (now a community centre); both in Morgans St. *Rangeview Park:* local plant species, picnic and barbecue facilities; Morgans St.

WHAT'S ON *Art and Craft Exhibition:* July/Aug. *Wildflower Show:* Sept. *Wool and Show Day:* Sept.

NEARBY *WA Time Meridian:* plaque on a boulder marks the WA time meridian; at first rest bay west of town. *Eremia Camel Treks:* offers rides and bush tucker; Hopetoun Rd; 2 km SE; open by appt. *Old Copper Smelter:* in operation 1906–18, now site of tailings dumps and old equipment; 2 km SE. *Archer Drive Lookout:* extensive views over farms and hills; 3 km N in Ravensthorpe Range. *Mt Desmond Lookout:* magnificent views in all directions; Ethel Daw Dr; 17 km SE in Ravensthorpe Range. *Hopetown:* small seaside village surrounded by pristine beaches ideal for swimming, surfing, windsurfing, fishing and boating. Walk on the Hopetoun Trail Head Loop (part of the Hopetoun–Ravensthorpe Heritage Walk) or visit Fitzgerald River National Park to the west; *see Bremer Bay.* 49 km S. *Scenic drives:* include the 170 km circular Hamersley Drive Heritage Trail; contact visitor centre for maps. *Rock-collecting:* check locally to avoid trespass. ℹ️ Morgans St; (08) 9838 1277

Rockingham   Pop. 60 529

Map ref. 566 C10, 567 B7, 572 C4, 574 C8

Lying on the edge of Cockburn Sound just 47 kilometres south of Perth, the coastal city of Rockingham offers sheltered waters ideal for swimming, snorkelling, sailing, windsurfing, fishing and crabbing. Established in 1872 to ship timber from Jarrahdale to England, Rockingham was the busiest port in Western Australia until the end of the 19th century, after which all port activities were shifted north to Fremantle. It was only with the establishment of the industrial area nearby at Kwinana in the 1950s and the development of the HMAS *Stirling* Naval Base on Garden Island in the 1970s that the town was revitalised. Today, its magnificent golden beaches, protected waters and proximity to Perth are Rockingham's main attractions.

IN TOWN **Rockingham Museum** This folk museum features local history exhibits including displays on the Group Settlement farms, domestic items and antique photographic equipment. One of the highlights is the Z Force display. This clandestine force, formed during WW II from combined British and Australian forces, trained on Garden Island. During the war Z Force entered Singapore Harbour in tiny submarines and blew up a number of Japanese ships. They were eventually captured in Singapore near the end of the war. Cnr Flinders La and Kent

St. Open 1pm–4pm Tues, Wed, Thurs, Sat; 10am–4pm Sun. *The Granary:* museum of artefacts celebrating the history of WA's grain industry; northern end of Rockingham Rd; open by appt, bookings essential, minimum group size 4. *Mersey Point Jetty:* departure point for cruises and island tours; at Shoalwater. *Kwinana Beach:* hull of wrecked SS *Kwinana. Cape Peron:* the lookout was once the main observation post for a WW II coastal battery; Point Peron Rd. *Bell and Churchill Park:* family picnics and barbecues in shaded grounds; Rockingham Rd.

WHAT'S ON *Mussel Festival:* Mar. *Lions Sunset Jazz Festival:* Mar. *Spring Festival:* Nov. *Safety Bay Windsurfing Classic:* Dec. *Cockburn Yachting Regatta:* Dec. *Christmas Regatta:* Dec.

NEARBY **Penguin Island** Take a trip to this offshore island, which is home to a colony of little (fairy) penguins. The Discovery Centre allows you to see these little penguins up close in an environment similar to their natural habitat and to learn about them through daily feedings, commentaries and displays. The island also provides picnic areas, lookouts and a network of boardwalks, and you can swim, snorkel or scuba dive at any of the pristine beaches. The island is open to the public in daylight hours Sept–June. Ferries to the island leave regularly from Mersey Point, south of Rockingham. The ferry also provides bay cruises and snorkelling tours. *Sloan's Cottage:* restored pioneer cottage; 2 km W at Leda; open Mon–Fri. *Lake Richmond:* walks, flora and fauna, and thrombolites (domed rock-like structures like the famous stromatolites of Hamelin Pool near Denham, built by ancient micro-organisms); 4 km SW. *Marapana Wildlife World:* handfeed and touch native and imported animals; 15 km SE at Karnup. *Wineries:* in the area include Baldivis Estate (15 km SE) and Peel Estate (17 km SE); contact visitor centre for details. *Secret Harbour:* surfing, snorkelling and windsurfing; 20 km S. *Serpentine Dam:* major water storage with brilliant wildflowers in spring, bushland, and the nearby Serpentine Falls; 48 km SE. *Garden Island:* home to HMAS *Stirling* Naval Base, two-thirds of the island is open to the public but is accessible only by private boat during daylight hours. *Shoalwater Bay Islands Marine Park:* extends from just south of Garden Island to Becher Point. Cruises of the park are available; contact visitor centre for details. *Dolphin Watch Cruises:* swim with dolphins between Point Peron and Garden Island; daily Sept–May; contact visitor centre for details. *Scenic drives:* including Old Rockingham Heritage Trail, a 30 km drive that takes in 23 points of interest in the Rockingham–Kwinana area, and Rockingham–Jarrahdale Timber Heritage Trail, a 36 km drive retracing the route of the 1872 timber railway; contact visitor centre for maps.

ℹ 43 Kent St; (08) 9592 3464

Roebourne   Pop. 945

Map ref. 573 G1, 576 A2

Named after John Septimus Roe, Western Australia's first surveyor-general, Roebourne was established in 1866 and is the oldest town on the north-west coast. As the centre for early mining and pastoral industries in the Pilbara, it was connected by tramway to the pearling port of Cossack and later to Point Samson. Now Cossack is a ghost town and Point Samson is known for its beachside pleasures.

IN TOWN *Historic buildings:* some original stone buildings remain, many of which have been classified by the National Trust. The Old Gaol, designed by the well-known colonial architect George Temple Poole, now operates as the visitor centre and museum; Queen St. *Mt Welcome:* offers views of the coastal plains and rugged hills surrounding town. Spot the railroad from Cape Lambert to Pannawonica, and the pipeline carrying water from Millstream to Wickham and Cape Lambert. Fisher Dr.

WHAT'S ON *Roebourne Cup and Ball:* Aug. *Cultural Festival:* Sept.

NEARBY Cossack Originally named Tien Tsin after the boat that brought the first settlers there in 1863, Cossack was the first port in the north-west region. During its days as a pearling centre in the late 1800s the population increased dramatically. Although now a ghost town, the beautiful stone buildings have been restored. Visitors can hire boats at the wharf, and cruises are available. 14 km N. *Wickham:* the company town for Robe River Iron Ore offers a spectacular view from Tank Hill lookout; tours available; 12 km N. *Point Samson:* good fishing, swimming, snorkelling and diving. Boat hire and fishing charters are available. 19 km N. *Cleaverville:* camping and fishing; 25 km N. *Harding Dam:* ideal picnic spot; 27 km s. *Millstream–Chichester National Park:* 150 km s; see *Karratha. Emma Withnell Heritage Trail:* 52 km historic self-drive trail, named after the first European woman in the north-west, takes in Roebourne, Cossack, Wickham and Point Samson; map available at visitor centre. *Tours:* including Pearls and the Pastcoach tour from visitor centre and tours to Millstream–Chichester and Karijini national parks; contact visitor centre for details.

ℹ Old Gaol, Queen St; (08) 9182 1060; www.pilbara.com/roebourne.html

Southern Cross   Pop. 890

Map ref. 574 G7

A small, flourishing town on the Great Eastern Highway, Southern Cross is the centre of a prosperous agricultural and pastoral region. Its claim to fame is as the

Cruising down Crocodile Creek near Yampi Sound, Buccaneer Archipelago

Off the coast

Western Australia's vast 12 500-hectare coastline is dotted with over 3500 islands. Grouped in vast archipelagos or lying solitary in the ocean, these islands accommodate seals, turtles and seabirds, preserve relics of Australia's earliest European history, and provide great recreation.

To the north of Derby and King Sound off the Kimberley coast is the Buccaneer Archipelago. Also known as the Thousand Islands, this is a dramatic coastal area of rugged red cliffs, spectacular waterfalls and secluded white sandy beaches. Here you'll find whirlpools created by massive 11-metre tides and the amazing horizontal two-way waterfall of Talbot Bay. Tours leave from Derby and Broome.

Just off the industrial Pilbara coast is the Dampier Archipelago, a cluster of 42 islands that are a haven in particular for anglers. Record-breaking game fish have been caught in the surrounding waters, which may account for the fact that the coastal towns of the Pilbara boast the highest rate of private vessel ownership in the country. Charters and tours leave from Dampier.

Further south along the coast at Shark Bay is the state's largest and most historically significant island, Dirk Hartog Island. It was named after Dutchman Dirk Hartog, who landed here in 1616 – 154 years before Captain Cook stepped ashore at Botany Bay. Hartog left behind an inscribed pewter plate, which was removed in 1697 by his countryman Willem de Vlamingh and replaced with another plate. The original was returned to Holland; Vlamingh's plate is now housed in the Maritime Museum in Fremantle. Flights and cruises leave from Denham.

The Houtman Abrolhos Islands, off the coast of Geraldton, are the site of the first, albeit unwilling, white settlement in Australia, and were named in 1619 by the Dutch explorer Frederick Houtman. The word 'Abrolhos' is a contraction of the Portuguese term *abri vossos olhos* meaning 'open your eyes … keep a look out'. There are 16 known shipwrecks in the Abrolhos Islands of which the most infamous is that of the Dutch ship *Batavia*. In 1629 *Batavia*, with 316 people on board, was wrecked on a reef that forms part of the islands. Captain Pelsaert and 47 of the survivors sailed north to Batavia (modern day Jakarta) for help. When they returned three and a half months later, they discovered that a mutiny had taken place and 125 of the remaining survivors had been massacred. All of the mutineers were hanged, except for two who were marooned on the mainland, becoming Australia's first white inhabitants. There is no record of their subsequent fate. The wreck was discovered in 1963 and some skeletons of victims of the mutiny have been found on Beacon Island. *For more information on the islands see Geraldton.*

The Esperance region on the state's south coast is known as the Bay of Isles. Here the numerous islands of the Archipelago of the Recherche are scattered along the coastline. These islands provide a haven for myriad marine and bird life, including seals and sea lions. Cruise around the islands, go diving or snorkelling, or visit Woody Island, which provides an interpretive centre, walking trails and safari hut accommodation. Cruises leave from Esperance.

site of the first major gold discovery in the huge eastern goldfields and, although it never matched the fever-pitch of Kalgoorlie and Coolgardie, Southern Cross remains the centre for a significant gold-producing area. The town's wide streets once allowed camel trains to turn and, like the town itself, were named after stars and constellations.

IN TOWN *Yilgarn History Museum:* originally the town courthouse and mining registrar's office, it now houses displays on mining, agriculture, water supply and military involvement; Antares St. *Historic buildings:* including the post office in Antares St, the Railway Tavern in Spica St and the restored Palace Hotel in Orion St.

WHAT'S ON *King of the Cross:* motorcycle race; Aug. *2-day Enduro:* motorcycle race; Sept/Oct.

NEARBY *Hunt's Soak:* picnic area; 7 km N. *Frog Rock:* large rock with wave-like formations is a popular picnic spot; 34 km S. *Goldmining:* at Marvel Loch (35 km S) and Bullfinch (36 km N). *Baladjie Rock:* granite outcrop with spectacular views; 50 km NW. *Karalee Rock and Dam:* swimming and picnics; 52 km E.
ⓘ Council offices, Antares St; (08) 9049 1001; www.yilgarn.wa.gov.au

Tom Price   Pop. 3094

Map ref. 573 H4, 576 B5

The huge iron-ore deposit now known as Mt Tom Price was discovered in 1962 in the heart of the Pilbara, after which the Hamersley Iron Project was established. A mine, two towns (Dampier and Tom Price) and a railway line between them all followed. Today, the town is an oasis in a dry countryside. On the edge of the Hamersley Range at an altitude of 747 metres, this is the state's highest town, hence its nickname of 'Top Town in WA'.

NEARBY *Kings Lake:* constructed lake with nearby park offering picnic and barbecue facilities (no swimming); 2 km W. *Mt Nameless Lookout:* stunning views of district around Tom Price; 6 km W via walking trail or 4WD track. *Aboriginal carvings:* thought to be 35 000 years old; 10 km S. *Karijini National Park:* 50 km E; *see feature on facing page. Mine tours:* marvel at the sheer enormity of Hamersley Iron's open-cut iron-ore mine; bookings essential, arrange through visitor centre. *Hamersley Iron Access Road:* this private road is the most direct route between Tom Price and Karratha via Karijini and Millstream national parks. It requires a permit to travel along it; permits available from visitor centre. ***Travellers note:*** To the north-east is Wittenoom, an old asbestos-mining town. Although the mine was closed in 1966, there is still a health risk from microscopic asbestos fibres present in the abandoned mine tailings in and around Wittenoom. If disturbed and inhaled, blue asbestos

dust may cause cancer. The Ashburton Shire Council advocates avoidance of the Wittenoom area.
ⓘ Central Rd; (08) 9188 1112; www.tompricewa.com.au

Toodyay   Pop. 674

Map ref. 567 G1, 572 E2, 574 D7

This National Trust-classified town is nestled in the Avon Valley surrounded by picturesque farming country and bushland. The name originates from 'Duidgee', which means the 'place of plenty'. Founded in 1836, Toodyay was one of the first inland towns to be established in the colony. It was a favourite haunt of Western Australia's most famous bushranger, Joseph Bolitho Johns, who was more commonly known as 'Moondyne Joe'.

IN TOWN **Historic buildings** Some original buildings from the early settlement of Toodyay still stand, including Stirling House (1908), Connor's Mill (1870s) with displays of working flour-milling equipment, the Old Newcastle Gaol (1865) built by convict labour and where Moondyne Joe was imprisoned, and the Police Stables (1870) built by convict labour from random rubblestone. Self-guide walk available; pamphlet at visitor centre. *Cola Cafe:* with a huge selection of Coca Cola memorabilia on display and music from the 1950s playing, this is a cafe with a difference; Stirling Tce. *Duidgee Park:* popular picnic spot on the banks of the river has a miniature railway and a walking track; check at visitor centre for running times; Harper Rd. *Newcastle Park:* contains a unique stone monument of Charlotte Davies, the first white female to set foot on the soil of the Swan River Colony. Also here is a children's playground facility. Stirling Tce. *Pelham Reserve and Lookout:* nature walks, a lookout with views over the town and a memorial to James Drummond, the town's first resident botanist; Duke St.

WHAT'S ON *Moondyne Festival:* May. *Avon Descent:* Aug. *Healing Festival:* Sept. *Jazz Festival:* Oct.

NEARBY **Avon Valley National Park** The park offers spectacular scenery with abundant wildflowers in season. Being at the northern limit of the jarrah forests, the jarrah and marri trees mingle with wandoo woodland. This mix of trees creates diverse habitats for fauna, including a wide variety of birdlife. The Avon River, which in summer and autumn is a series of pools, swells to become impressive rapids during winter and spring. These rapids provide the backdrop for the Avon Descent, a well-known annual whitewater race held every August, which begins in Northam and passes through the park. The park is ideal for camping, bushwalking, canoeing and picnicking, although all roads are

unsealed. Whitewater rafting tours are available. 25 km SW. *Pecan Hill Tearoom Museum:* tearoom and museum set in a pecan nut orchard with a lookout offering spectacular views over the Avon Valley; Julimar Rd; 4 km NW. *Coorinja Winery:* dating from the 1870s; open for tastings and sales; 4 km SW; closed Sun. *Ringa Railway Bridge:* constructed in 1888, this timber bridge has 18 spans, but is not readily accessible; details from visitor centre; 6 km SW. *Windmill Hill Cutting:* the deepest railway cutting in Australia; 6 km SE. *Lavender Farm:* lavender products for sale; Dumbarton Rd; 7 km SE; guided tours; open 10am–4pm Thurs–Sun. *Avonlea Park Alpaca Farm:* alpacas and other farm animals, and sales of alpaca wool products; 12 km SE. *Emu Farm:* one of the oldest in Australia. Birds range free in natural bushland. Also crafts and emu products for sale. 15 km SW. *Cartref Park Country Garden:* 2 ha park of English-style landscaped gardens and native plants, with prolific birdlife; 16 km NW. *Oliomio Farm:* olive farm offers tastings and sales; Parkland Dr; 20 km NW. *Wannadoo Aquaculture:* go fishing in these well-stocked artificially made ponds (fishing gear provided); Julimar Rd; 21 km NW. *Toodyay Pioneer Heritage Trail:* honouring the pioneering spirit in the Avon Valley, this 20 km self-drive trail retraces the route of the first settlers; contact visitor centre for map. *Avon Valley Tourist Drive:* 95 km scenic drive includes Toodyay, Northam, York and Beverley; contact visitor centre for map. *Hotham Valley Steam Railway:* the famous steam-train service runs special trips including a monthly 'murder-mystery' night; contact visitor centre for details.
ⓘ 7 Piesse St; (08) 9574 2435; www.gidgenet.com.au/toodyay

Wagin   Pop. 1281

Map ref. 572 G8, 574 E10

Wagin, 177 kilometres east of Bunbury, is the sheep capital of Western Australia. The importance of the wool industry to the district is celebrated in its annual Wagin Woolorama, the largest rural show in the state, and its Giant Ram, an enormous structure that visitors from around the country come to photograph.

IN TOWN *Wagin Historical Village:* visit 24 relocated or re-created historic buildings providing a glimpse of pioneering rural life; Kitchener St; open 10am–4pm. *Giant Ram and Ram Park:* 9 m high statue provides a photo opportunity not to miss; Arthur River Rd. *Wagin Heritage Trail:* self-guide walk around the town; contact visitor centre for map.

WHAT'S ON *Wagin Woolorama:* Mar.

NEARBY *Marroblie Bird Place:* view a wide variety of native bird species; Bolt Rd; 2 km N; open by appt. *Corralyn Emu Farm:* tours available with hands-on experience;

3 km N; closed Sun. *Puntapin Rock:* spectacular views over the town and surrounding farmlands from the top of the rock. Enjoy the picnic and barbecue facilities nearby. Bullock Hill Rd; 4 km SE. *Mt Latham:* interesting rock formation with walk trails, a lookout and abundant wildflowers in season; Arthur River Rd; 8 km w. *Lake Norring:* swimming, sailing and waterskiing; picnic and barbeque facilities; water levels vary considerably; check conditions at visitor centre; 17 km SW. *Lake Dumbleyung:* where Donald Campbell established a world water-speed record in 1964. Swimming, boating and birdwatching are subject to water levels that vary considerably. Check conditions at visitor centre. 18 km E. *Wait-jen Trail:* self-guide 10.5 km signposted walk that follows ancient Aboriginal Dreaming. The word 'Wait-jen' means 'emu footprint' in the language of the local Aboriginal people. Contact visitor centre for map. *Wheat Belt Wildflower Drive:* self-guide drive that includes the Tarin Rock Nature Reserve; contact visitor centre for map.
ⓘ Council offices, Arthur Rd; (08) 9861 1177; www.wagin.wa.gov.au

Walpole   Pop. 294

Map ref. 570 G12, 572 F13, 574 D12

Walpole is entirely surrounded by national park and is the only place in the South-West where the forest meets the sea. The area is renowned for its striking ocean and forest scenery, which provides an idyllic setting for outdoor activities. The town of Walpole was established in 1930 through the Nornalup Land Settlement Scheme for city families hit by the Great Depression.

IN TOWN *Pioneer Cottage:* re-creation of a historic cottage to commemorate the district's pioneer settlers; South Coast Hwy.

WHAT'S ON *Easter Markets:* April. *Orchid Display:* Sept.

NEARBY Walpole–Nornalup National Park The many forest attractions near Walpole form part of this park and include the Valley of the Giants, the Hilltop Drive and Lookout, Circular Pool and the Knoll. The park is probably best known for its huge, buttressed red tingle trees that are unique to the Walpole area. The world-class Bibbulmun Track, between Perth and Albany, passes through the park; *see feature on p. 323.*

Valley of the Giants Tree Top Walk Here visitors can wander over a walkway suspended 38 m above the forest floor, the highest and longest walkway of its kind in the world. The Ancient Empire interpretive boardwalk weaves its way through the veteran tingle trees. 16 km E. *Giant Red Tingle:* a 25 m circumference defines this tree as one of the 10 largest living things on the planet; 2 km E. *Hilltop Lookout:* views over the Frankland River out to the Southern Ocean; 2 km w. *John Rate Lookout:* panoramic views over the mouth of the Deep River and of the nearby coastline and forests; 4 km w. *Thurlby Herb Farm:* herb garden display with sales of herbal products; Gardiner Rd; 13 km N. *Mandalay Beach:* the site of the 1911 shipwreck of the *Mandalay.* A boardwalk has descriptive notes about the wreck. 20 km w. *Bird and Reptile Centre:* a collection of native birds and reptiles, and exotic birds; 25 km E. *Mount Frankland National Park:* noted for its exceptional variety of birdlife, it also offers breathtaking views from the top of Mt Frankland, known as 'Caldyanup' to the local Aboriginal people; 29 km N. *Peaceful Bay:* small fishing village with an excellent beach for swimming; 35 km E. *Fernhook Falls:* ideal picnic spot at its best in winter, when it is popular for canoeing and kayaking; 36 km NW. *Walk trails:* many trails in the area, including self-guide Horseyard Hill Walk Trail through the karri forest and the signposted Coalmine Beach Heritage Trail from the coastal heathland to the inlets. Contact visitor centre for maps. *Tours:* take a guided cruise through the inlets and rivers, hire a boat or canoe, or go on a forest tour. Contact visitor centre for details.
ⓘ Pioneer Cottage, South Coast Hwy; (08) 9840 1111; www.southernforests.com.au

Karijini National Park

Set in the Hamersley Range, Karijini National Park offers scenery that is uniquely Western Australian: craggy ochre-coloured rock faces interrupted with bright-white snappy gums, all set against a rich blue sky. Across the parched, undulating plains, neat bundles of olive-green spinifex dot the red earth, but suddenly these plains sweep down into chasms up to 100 metres deep, where the gorge walls cast long shadows across the turquoise waterways. The waterfalls and rock pools of Karijini offer some of the best swimming in the state.

Karijini is the second largest national park in Western Australia, covering an area of 100 000 square kilometres. The park protects the many different wildlife habitats, plants and animals of the Pilbara. The landscape is dotted with huge termite mounds and the rock piles of the rare pebble mouse; other species include red kangaroos and rock wallabies, and every reptile from legless lizards to pythons.

At Ferns Pool, nestled between the walls of Dales Gorge and shaded by lush vegetation, two 10-metre waterfalls cascade into a crystal-clear rock pool. Nearby are the beautiful Fortescue Falls. Kalamina Gorge and Pool is the most accessible gorge, while at Hamersley Gorge a wave of tectonic rock acts as a backdrop to a swimming hole and natural spa. Oxer Lookout reveals where the Joffre, Hancock, Weano and Red gorges meet.

Mt Bruce, the second tallest peak in the state, offers spectacular views and interpretive signs along the trail to the top.

The Karijini Visitor Centre provides static and interactive displays on the flora, fauna and geology of the area and on the local Aboriginal people and their culture. The word Karijini is the Banyjima Aboriginal name for the Hamersley Range, and the design of the building, representing a goanna moving through the country, is symbolic to the local Banyjima people. The tail represents their history, the head the future direction of the traditional owners, and Aboriginal Law is in the centre or stomach. The high, weathered steel walls of the centre mimic the sheer-sided gorges that are a feature of the park.

The ideal time to visit Karijini National Park, east of Tom Price, is May–August. The visitor centre is located off the road to Dales Gorge and has information on camping.

Fortescue Falls, Dales Gorge

Wickepin
Pop. 216

Map ref: 572 G6, 574 E9

The first settlers arrived in the Wickepin area in the 1890s. Albert Facey's internationally acclaimed autobiography, *A Fortunate Life*, details these pioneering times. However, Facey is not the only major literary figure to feature in Wickepin's history. The poet and playwright Dorothy Hewett was born in Wickepin in 1923, and much of her work deals with life in the area.

IN TOWN *Historic buildings in Wogolin Rd:* excellent examples of Edwardian architecture. *Facey Homestead:* the home of author Albert Facey has been relocated and restored with its original furniture; open 10am–4pm daily Mar–Nov, 10am–4pm Sat, Sun and public holidays Dec–Feb.

WHAT'S ON *Oasis Christmas Bash:* Dec.

NEARBY *Tarling Well:* the circular stone well marks the original intended site for the town; 8 km w. *Malyalling Rock:* unusual rock formation; 15 km se. *Toolibin Lake Reserve:* see a wide variety of waterfowl while you enjoy a barbecue; 20 km s. *Yealering and Yealering Lake:* historic photographs on display in town, and swimming, boating, windsurfing and birdwatching at lake; 30 km ne. *Harrismith Walk Path:* self-guide trail through wildflowers in season, including orchids and some species unique to the area; contact visitor centre for brochure. *Albert Facey Heritage Trail:* 86 km self-drive trail brings to life the story of Albert Facey and the harshness of life in the early pioneering days of the wheat belt; contact visitor centre for map.
ⓘ District Resource and Telecentre; (08) 9888 1500

Wyndham
Pop. 787

Map ref: 579 P4, 581 N1

Wyndham, in the Kimberley region, is the most northerly town and safe port in Western Australia. The entrance to the town is guarded by the 'Big Croc', a 20-metre-long concrete crocodile.

IN TOWN *Historical Society Museum:* in the old courthouse building, its displays include a photographic record of the town's history, artefacts and machinery; O'Donnell St. *Warriu Dreamtime Park:* statues relating to the Aboriginal heritage of the area; Koolama St. *Zoological Gardens and Crocodile Park:* daily feeding of crocodiles, alligators and komodo dragons; Barytes Rd. *Durack's Old Store:* still operating as a shop, there is an informative plaque on this building with details of its history; O'Donnell St. *Pioneer Cemetery:* gravestones of some of the area's original settlers; Great Northern Hwy. *Boat charters:* scenic, fishing and camping cruises; contact visitor centre for details.

WHAT'S ON *Hall's Creek Fishing Competition:* April. *Races:* Aug. *Art and Craft Show:* Aug.

NEARBY Three Mile Valley On offer is spectacular scenery typical of the Kimberley region, with rough red gorges and pools of clear, cold water during the wet season. Walk trails lead the visitor through the brilliant displays of wildflowers in season. Three Mile Valley is the home of the 'Trial Tree', a sacred Aboriginal site into which, when a person died of unnatural causes, the body was placed. Rocks were placed around the base of the tree, each rock representing a relative of the deceased. When the body started to decompose, the first rock to be marked by the decomposition indicated the name of the person responsible for the death. This person was then banished from the tribe. 3 km n.
Afghan Cemetery: containing the graves of Afghan camel drivers who carried supplies throughout the Kimberley region. All the gravestones face towards Mecca. 1 km e. *Koolama Wreck Site:* the *Koolama* was hit by Japanese bombs near Darwin in 1942. After limping along the coast to Wyndham, it sank just 40 m from the jetty. The spot is marked by unusual swirling in the water. 5 km nw. *Five Rivers Lookout:* spectacular views of the Kimberley landscape from the highest point of the Bastion Range, particularly good for viewing the striking sunsets. Also a good picnic area with barbecue facilities. 5 km n. *Moochalabra Dam:* completed in 1971, the dam was constructed to provide an assured water supply to the Wyndham area. The construction is unique in Australia, designed to allow overflow to pass through the rock on the crest of the hill. 4WD access only; King River Rd; 18 km sw. *Aboriginal rock paintings:* 4WD access only; well signposted off the King River Rd; 18 km sw. *Parry Lagoons Nature Reserve:* visitors can enjoy birdwatching from a shaded bird hide at Marlgu Billabong or scan the wide vistas of the flood plain and distant hills afforded from the lookout at Telegraph Hill; 20 km se. *Prison tree:* 2000–4000-year-old boab tree once used by local police as a lock-up; King River Rd; 22 km sw. *The Grotto:* this rock-edged waterhole, estimated to be 100 m deep, is a cool, shaded oasis offering year-round swimming; 36 km e. *El Questro:* this extraordinary holiday destination, set in a million acres of wilderness park, offers a variety of accommodation. Attractions include the scenic Emma Gorge, Aboriginal rock art, hot springs, spectacular scenery, camping, boating and fishing. 100 km s; closed Nov–April.
ⓘ Kimberley Motors, Great Northern Hwy; (08) 9161 1281

Yalgoo
Pop. 116

Map ref: 574 D3

Alluvial gold was discovered in the 1890s in Yalgoo, which lies 216 kilometres east of Geraldton. Today, gold is still found in the district and visitors are encouraged to try their luck fossicking in the area. The name Yalgoo is from the Aboriginal word meaning 'blood', a rather odd fact given that in 1993 a Yalgoo resident was the first person in Australia to be the victim of a parcel bomb.

IN TOWN *Courthouse Museum:* exhibits of local artefacts; Gibbons St. *Gaol:* built in 1896 and recently relocated to the museum precinct, it has photographs illustrating the town's history; Gibbons St. *Chapel of St Hyacinth:* designed by Monsignor Hawes and built in 1919 for the Dominican Sisters who lived in a wooden convent school near the chapel; Henty St. *Heritage walk:* self-guide town walk; pamphlet available at visitor centre.

NEARBY *Cemetery:* the history of Yalgoo as told through headstones; 5 km w. *Joker's Tunnel:* a tunnel carved through solid rock by early prospectors and named after the Joker's mining syndicate, it has panoramic views near the entrance; 10 km se. *Meteorite crater:* discovered in 1961, a portion of the meteorite is held at the WA Museum in Perth; 100 km n.
ⓘ Old Railway Station, Geraldton–Mount Magnet Rd; (08) 9962 8157

Yallingup
Pop. 175

Map ref: 568 B7, 569 C2, 572 A9, 574 B10

Yallingup has long been known for its magnificent limestone caves and world-class surf breaks. It is also an ideal location for swimming, fishing and beachcombing, with the nearby Leeuwin–Naturaliste National Park offering spectacular scenery, interesting bushwalks and beautiful wildflowers in season. Art and craft galleries abound and many of the wineries of the South-West region are only a short drive from the town. Yallingup continues to live up to its Aboriginal meaning of 'place of love' with nearby Caves House Hotel being a favourite destination for generations of honeymooners and holiday-makers.

IN TOWN *Caves House Hotel:* originally built in 1903 as a holiday hotel, the building was damaged by fire in 1938 and rebuilt; off Caves Rd. *Yallingup Beach:* surfing, scuba diving, whale-watching and salmon fishing in season.

WHAT'S ON *Amberley Estate Seafood and Semillon Weekend:* Feb. *Yallingup Malibu Surfing Classic:* Dec.

NEARBY *Leeuwin–Naturaliste National Park:* stretches north and south of town; *see Dunsborough, Margaret River and Augusta.* *Ngilgi Cave:* (pronounced 'Nillgee') semi-guided tours are available

for this stunning display of stalactite, stalagmite and shawl rock formations. An interpretive area details the history of the cave. 2 km E. *Canal Rocks and Smith's Beach:* fishing, surfing, swimming, snorkelling and diving; 5 km SW. *Gunyulgup Gallery:* over 120 artists and craftspeople are represented, with paintings, prints, ceramics and sculpture on display and for sale; 9 km SW. *Yallingup Gallery:* specialises in custom-built furniture; 9 km SW. *Quinninup Falls:* scenic falls that are particularly attractive in winter months and can be reached only by 4WD or on foot; 10 km S. *Shearing Shed:* shearing demonstrations and sales; 11am demonstration, closed Fri; Wildwood Rd; 10 km E. *Surfing:* the popular surf breaks of Three Bears, Yallingup, Smith's Beach and Injidup are known all over the world. *Wineries and breweries:* many award-winning wineries and boutique breweries in the area and adjacent Margaret River offer tastings and sales; contact visitor centre for details.
ⓘ Seymour Blvd, Dunsborough; (08) 9755 3299; www.downsouth.com.au

Yanchep   Pop. 1955

Map ref. 566 B1, 567 A1, 572 C2, 574 C7

Only 58 kilometres north of Perth, Yanchep is a rapidly developing recreational area and popular tourist destination. It provides safe, sandy beaches and good fishing areas, and natural attractions such as the series of caves found within Yanchep National Park. The town derives its name from the Aboriginal word 'Yanjet', which means bullrushes, a feature of the area.

IN TOWN *The Stables and Cameleer Park Camel Farm:* horse and camel rides; bookings essential; Yanchep Beach Rd.

NEARBY Yanchep National Park Lying on a belt of coastal limestone, this 2842 ha park has forests of massive tuart trees, underground caves and spring wildflowers. Within the park, attractions include the Gloucester Lodge Museum with displays of local history (open 11.30am–4.30pm Sat, Sun, Tues, Wed); the historic Tudor-style Yanchep Inn; the Yonderup and Crystal caves, featuring magnificent limestone formations (tours available); a koala enclosure; row-boat hire on freshwater Loch McNess; self-guide walk trails; and Aboriginal cultural tours through the park (bookings essential). Other activities include didgeridoo and dance performances, Share the Dreaming and Meet the Koala (check times). Boomerang Gorge follows a collapsed cave system and has a nature trail for people with disabilities. Wide grassy areas with barbecues and picnic tables provide a perfect setting for a family outing. 5 km E.
Wild Kingdom: wildlife park with native fauna and farmyard animals; 3 km NE.
Marina: charter fishing boat hire; 6 km NW

at Two Rocks. *Guilderton:* peaceful town at the mouth of the Moore River. Estuary provides safe swimming, and upper reaches of the river can be explored by boat or canoe (hire on river foreshore). Also good fishing. 37 km N. *Ledge Point:* great destination for diving, with dive trail to 14 shipwrecks. Also the starting point for Lancelin Ocean Classic, a major windsurfing race to Lancelin each Jan. 62 km N. *Lancelin:* great base for fishing and boating because of a natural breakwater offshore. White sandy beaches provide safe swimming, and sand dunes at the edge of town have designated areas for off-road vehicles and sand-boarding. 71 km N.
ⓘ Information office, Yanchep National Park; (08) 9561 1004

York   Pop. 2015

Map ref. 567 I4, 572 F3, 574 D8

On the banks of the Avon River in the fertile Avon Valley, York is one of the best preserved and restored 19th-century towns in Australia. It is now classified by the National Trust as 'York Historic Town'. Settled in 1831, only two years after the establishment of the Swan River Colony, York was the first inland European settlement in Western Australia.

IN TOWN Historic buildings There are a significant number of carefully preserved historic buildings in York, many made from local stone and some built of mudbrick. The three remaining hotels are fine examples of early coaching inns, while the Romanesque-style Town Hall, built in 1911, with its ornate facade reflects the wealth brought into the town by the gold rushes. Contact visitor centre for details.
Avon Park: picturesque park on the banks of the river with playground and barbecue facilities; Low St. *Sandalwood Press Museum:* guided tours available of

York Motor Museum

WA's only working printing museum; cnr Macartney and Grey sts; open 10am–4pm Mon–Fri. *York Motor Museum:* vehicles on display represent the development of motor transport; Avon Tce. *Jah Roc Mill Gallery:* display and sales of unique and award-winning recycled jarrah furniture and craft; Broome St. *Residency Museum:* personal possessions, ceramics and silverware reflect aspects of civic and religious life in early York; Broome St; open 1pm–3pm Tues–Thurs, 11am–3.30pm Sat, Sun and public holidays. *Needle and I Costume Gallery:* display of old-world costumes, laces and sewing machines; cnr Macartney and Georgiana sts. *Avon Valley Historical Rose Garden:* informative display of roses and their development; children's playground; Osnaberg Rd. *Suspension bridge and walk trail:* built in 1906, the bridge crosses the Avon River at Avon Park. A 1.5 km nature and heritage walk starts at the bridge. Low St.

WHAT'S ON *Country Music Festival:* Feb. *York Society Photographic Awards:* April. *Antique Fair:* April. *Healing Fayre:* May. *Olive Harvest Festival:* June. *Festival of Cars:* July. *Jazz Festival:* Sept. *Spring Garden Festival:* Oct. *Flying 50s Car Rally:* Oct.

NEARBY *Mt Brown Lookout:* provides 360-degree views over town; 3 km SE. *Miniature Village:* scale reproductions; 3 km S. *Gwambygine Park:* picturesque picnic area overlooking the river with boardwalk and viewing platform; 10 km S. *Toapin Weir and Mt Stirling:* panoramic views; 64 km E. *York to Goldfields Heritage Trail:* follow the route of miners, prospectors and fossickers as they headed to the goldfields; contact visitor centre for map. *Avon Ascent:* self-drive tour through Perth's scenic hinterland to a series of special places in the Avon Valley; contact visitor centre for map.
ⓘ 81 Avon Tce; (08) 9641 1301; www.yorkwa.com.au

WESTERN AUSTRALIA

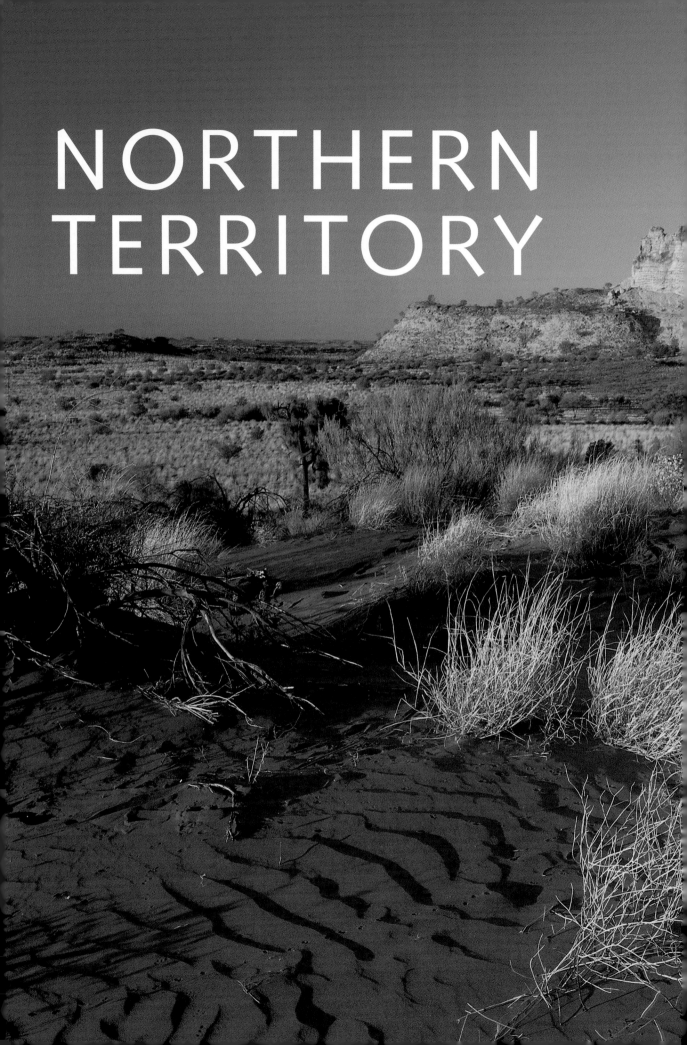

NORTHERN TERRITORY

The Northern Territory is Australia's least settled state or territory, with vast tracts of desert and tropical woodlands. To regard this country as empty though is to do it a disservice; Aboriginal people have lived and travelled across the Territory for thousands of years, and still do. Many non-Aboriginal Australians regard it as the last great frontier because of its remoteness, spectacular landscapes and hardy outback characters.

The Territory has its southern border in the desert regions of central Australia, and the tropical Top End is lapped by the Timor and Arafura seas. Although the diversity of landscape and wildlife makes it one of Australia's most inspiring destinations, visitors should expect a lot of distance between highlights.

The tropical coastline and offshore islands are places of special beauty – pearly white beaches interspersed with red, rocky cliffs and rich mangrove habitats. The coastal rivers are home to thousands of bird and marine species and have huge tidal flows and crystal clear waters at certain times of the year. Their flood plains carry the annual wet season deluge out into the Timor and Arafura seas and the Gulf of Carpentaria, and the rivers are spawning grounds for barramundi, which attract anglers from around the world.

The western border of the Top End abuts the Kimberley in Western Australia, sharing many of its rugged rock formations. The north-east includes Arnhem Land – the largest Aboriginal reserve in Australia and the home of many groups who still live a semitraditional lifestyle. Here visitors can explore parts of the Gove and Cobourg peninsulas, where thick, green vegetation, turquoise waters and great fishing sit with the ruins of European settlement and a rich Aboriginal heritage. This heritage includes everything from custodianship of Australia's most famous indigenous instrument, the didgeridoo, to the incredible trade and mingling of cultures that occurred between Yolngu people and Indonesian seafarers from the 1600s.

. . . thick, green vegetation, turquoise waters and great fishing sit with the ruins of European settlement and a rich Aboriginal heritage . . .

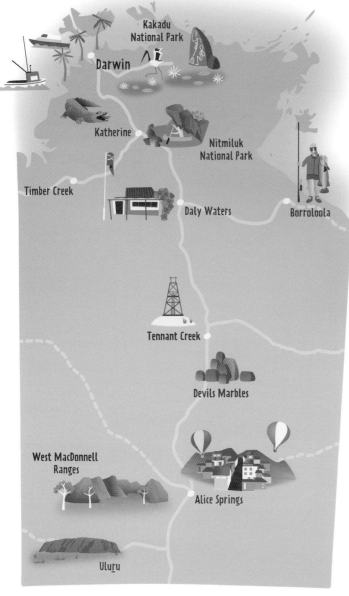

Kakadu National Park

Darwin

Katherine

Nitmiluk National Park

Timber Creek

Daly Waters

Borroloola

Tennant Creek

Devils Marbles

West MacDonnell Ranges

Alice Springs

Uluru

PREVIOUS PAGES Chambers Pillar, south of Alice Springs

Baringura (Little Bondi) Beach, Gove Peninsula, Arnhem Land

In the west, the Victoria River District is centred around the mighty Victoria ('Vic') River. This region south-west of Katherine is prime grazing land for Territory pastoralists. Although much of the area between Katherine and Alice Springs is regarded as desert or semidesert country, it is the base for a huge livestock industry that services nearby markets in Asia.

The Red Centre is ancient and breathtaking, with the MacDonnell Ranges home to some beautiful gorges, rock holes and vistas. While many travellers are drawn to Uluṟu and Kata-Tjuṯa, the surrounding countryside is equally impressive – from the rolling, red sandhills of the Simpson Desert to the undulating grasslands west of Glen Helen. North of Alice Springs, the Tanami Desert is incredibly remote and vastly interesting.

F A C T   F I L E

Population 198 700
Total land area 1 335 742 sq km
People per square kilometre 0.15
Beef cattle per square kilometre 1.3
Length of coastline 5437 km
Number of islands 887
Longest river Victoria River (560 km)
Highest mountain Mt Zeil (1531 m), West MacDonnell National Park
Highest waterfall Jim Jim Falls (160 m), Kakadu National Park
Highest town Areyonga (700 m), west of Hermannsburg
Hottest place Aputula (Finke), 48.3°C in 1960
Strangest place name Humpty Doo
Quirkiest festival Todd River Boat Races in the dry river bed, Alice Springs
Longest road Stuart Highway (approximately 2000 km)
Most scenic road Larapinta Drive, from Alice Springs to Hermannsburg
Most famous pub Daly Waters Pub
Most impressive gorge Nitmiluk (Katherine) Gorge, Nitmiluk National Park
Most identifiable tree Pandanus palm or desert she-oak
Most impressive sight Electrical storms in the build-up to the wet season, Darwin
Favourite food Barramundi
Local beer NT Draught
Interesting fact Some 50 percent of the Northern Territory is either Aboriginal land or land under claim

TIMELINE

80 000–50 000 years ago
The first Aboriginal people arrive.

1623
A Dutch ship, the Arnhem, sights the Territory coast.

1824–1849
British concerns about Dutch and French interest in northern Australia lead to three unsuccessful settlements on the coast.

1863
The Northern Territory becomes part of South Australia, with Palmerston selected as the main town in 1869.

1872
The Overland Telegraph Line links Adelaide to Palmerston and then overseas.

1870s and 80s
A gold rush at Pine Creek attracts prospectors, and pastoralists begin to settle the Barkly Tableland.

1911
South Australia surrenders the Territory to Commonwealth control. Palmerston is renamed Darwin.

1942
Darwin – and later Katherine – is bombed by the Japanese.

1974
Cyclone Tracy devastates Darwin.

1978
The Territory is granted full self-government.

1998
Territorians reject a referendum for statehood.

DARWIN

DARWIN IS . . .

A stroll along The Esplanade

**Sunset drinks at the Darwin
Sailing Club**

**Fish and chips at
the Wharf Precinct**

**Watching a thunderstorm in
the evening sky**

**Window-shopping for pearls in
Smith Street Mall**

**Exploring Aboriginal
art galleries**

A picnic at Fannie Bay

Fishing off Stokes Hill Wharf

**Watching a movie at the
Deckchair Cinema**

**Learning about cyclones at
the Museum and Art Gallery of
the Northern Territory**

**Handfeeding fish
at Aquascene**

**Enjoying the Mindil Beach
Sunset Markets**

**A safe encounter with reptiles
at Crocodylus Park**

Visitor information

*Tourism Top End
Cnr Mitchell and Knuckey sts, Darwin
(08) 8936 2499 or 1300 138 886
www.tourismtopend.com.au*

Outdoor dining at Stokes Hill Wharf

Regarded as Australia's northern outpost, Darwin's proximity to Asia and its immersion in Aboriginal culture makes it one of the world's most interesting cities. It retains a tropical, colonial feel despite having been largely rebuilt after devastation by Cyclone Tracy over 30 years ago.

The founding fathers of Darwin were bureaucrats and surveyors who laid out the city centre on a small peninsula that juts into one of the finest harbours in northern Australia. Their names live on in the wide streets of the CBD, which is easy to get around and lacks the winding alleyways and lanes of older Australian cities.

Built on the land of the Larrakia Aboriginal people, Darwin is a beautiful, green city. Manicured lawns, swaying palm trees, hedges of bougainvillea and frangipani, and huge, arching rain trees adorn parks and roadways, while the waters of the Timor Sea lap three sides of the city.

Over 50 ethnic groups live together harmoniously here – this diversity stretches back to the early days of Darwin's development when Aboriginal, European and Chinese people worked side by side. More recent arrivals include migrants from Greece, Timor and Indonesia.

Evidence of the early days remain, but Darwin is one of Australia's most modern cities. A new port, the AustralAsian Railway and international air services mean that Darwin will play a major role as Australia's front door to Asia. It is already the centre for a huge livestock export industry and Australia's northern defence headquarters.

With so much natural beauty around its harbour, along the beaches and in its tropical parks and reserves, Darwin remains one of the most attractive cities in the world.

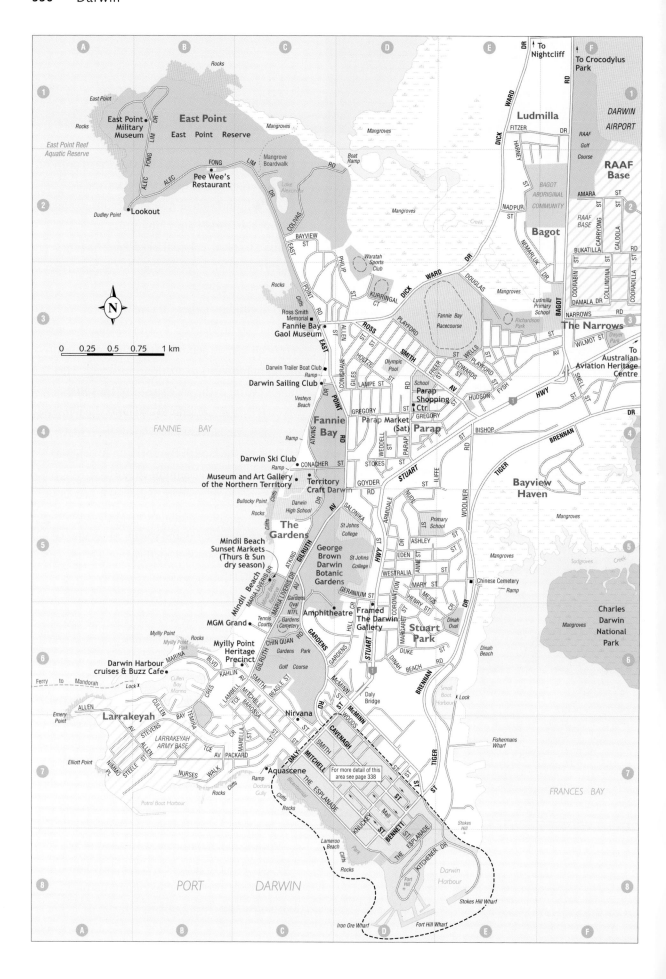

N

0   0.25   0.5   0.75   1 km

East Point

Rocks

East Point

Rocks

East Point Reef
Aquatic Reserve

East Point
Military
Museum

East Point   Reserve

Mangroves

Mangrove
Boardwalk

Boat
Ramp

Mangroves

To
Nightcliff

To Crocodylus
Park

DARWIN
AIRPORT

Ludmilla

RAAF
Base

Pee Wee's
Restaurant

Lake
Alexander

FONG

LIM

ALEC

ALEC

FONG

COLVAS   DR

Dudley Point   Lookout

BAYVIEW
ST

EAST

POINT

PHILIP   ST

Rocks

Cliffs

Mangroves

FITZER

HARNEY   ST

NADPUR   ST

NEMARLUK   DR

Creek

Mangroves

RAAF
Golf
Course

BAGOT
ABORIGINAL
COMMUNITY

Bagot

AMARA   ST

BUKATILLA   ST

COORABIN   ST

DAMALA   DR

COLLINDINA   ST

CARRYONG   ST

CALOOLA   ST

COORADILLA   RD

Waratah
Sports
Club

KURRINGAL
CT

DICK   WARD   DR

DOUGLAS   ST

Fannie Bay
Racecourse

Richardson
Park

Ludmilla
Primary
School

NARROWS   RD

The Narrows

Dwyer
Park

Ross Smith
Memorial

Fannie Bay
Gaol Museum

ALLEN   ST

HOUTZE   ST

GILES   ST

ROSS   ST

SMITH   ST

PLAYFORD   ST

WELLS   ST

FREER   ST

EDWARDS   ST

PLAYFORD   ST

FYSH   ST

WILMOT   ST

AV

To
Australian
Aviation Heritage
Centre

Darwin Trailer Boat Club
Ramp

Darwin Sailing Club

Vesteys
Beach

Ramp

FANNIE   BAY

Ramp

Darwin Ski Club

Ramp   CONACHER   ST

Museum and Art Gallery
of the Northern Territory

Territory
Craft Darwin

Bullocky Point
Rocks

Cliffs

CONSIGRAVE   DR

POINT   RD

ATKINS   DR

EAST   POINT   RD

LAMPE   ST

GREGORY   ST

WEDDELL   ST

STOKES   ST

GOYDER   RD

Olympic
Pool

School

Parap
Shopping
Ctr

Parap Market
(Sat)

PARAP   ST

SALONIKA   ST

Darwin
High School

Parap

HUDSON   ST

GREGORY   ST

BISHOP   ST

HWY

HWY

DR

Bayview
Haven

Mangroves

The
Gardens

Mindil Beach
Sunset Markets
(Thurs & Sun
dry season)

Mindil Beach

MGM Grand

MARIA LIVERIS DR

Mindil Beach
Reserve

MARIA LIVERIS DR

ATKINS   DR

GILRUTH   AV

George
Brown
Darwin
Botanic
Gardens

GERANIUM ST

St Johns
College

St Johns
College

WESTRALIA   ST

EDEN   ST

ANNE   ST

MARY   ST

MEIGS   ST

HENRY   ST

ASHLEY   ST

Primary
School

Mangroves

Chinese Cemetery
Ramp

HILL   CR

ARMIDALE   ST

NUDN   ST

WOOLNER   RD

TIGER

Charles
Darwin
National
Park

Mangroves

Myilly Point
Myilly Point
Park

Rocks

Darwin Harbour
cruises & Buzz Cafe

Ferry   to   Mandorah

Emery
Point

Larrakeyah

ALLEN

Elliott Point

Myilly Point
Heritage
Precinct

CHIN QUAN   DR

Gardens
Oval
NTFL

Tennis
Courts

Gardens
(Cemetery)

Amphitheatre

GILRUTH   ST

GARDENS   RD

Gardens
Park

Golf   Course

Framed
The Darwin
Gallery

Stuart
Park

Dinah
Oval

MARGARET   ST

CORONATION   DR

DUKE   ST

Dinah
Beach

DINAH   BEACH   RD

BRENNAN   ST

Small
Boat
Harbour   Lock

MARINA   BLVD

Cullen
Bay
Marina

Lock

KAHLIN   AV

CULLEN   BAY   CRES

LIAMBELL   TCE

MITCHELL   ST

BEAGLE   ST

BARADSSA   CR

TEMIRA   CR

STEVENS   AV

ALLEN   AV

NIMMO   PL

STEELE   ST

MARELLA   ST

PACKARD   AV

NURSES   WALK

Larrakeyah
Army Base

Nirvana

SMITH   ST

DALY   ST

CAVENAGH   ST

MITCHELL   ST

McMINN   RD

WOODS   ST

SMITH   ST

STUART   HWY

McMINN   ST

Daly
Bridge

Fishermans
Wharf

For more detail of this
area see page 338

Aquascene

Ramp
Doctors
Gully

Cliffs

Rocks

THE   ESPLANADE

Bicentennial
Park

KNUCKEY   ST

BENNETT   ST

Mall

THE   ESPLANADE

Lameroo
Beach

Cliffs

Rocks

Fort
Hill

Stokes
Hill

Lock

KITCHENER   DR

Darwin
Harbour

Stokes Hill Wharf

FRANCES   BAY

PORT   DARWIN

Iron Ore Wharf

Fort Hill Wharf

Central Darwin

Perhaps the most picturesque area of Central Darwin is The Esplanade, which looks over a long, cliff-top park to Darwin Harbour. This beautiful boulevard forms the western boundary of the precinct – the next street is Mitchell Street, renowned for its outdoor eateries, pubs and late-night entertainment. After that is Smith Street, home to a vibrant shopping mall that is Darwin's main retail centre. Parts of Cavenagh Street retain the flavour of Darwin's original Chinatown, while down on the harbour Stokes Hill Wharf is a magnet for anglers and people who enjoy dining by the water with a gentle sea breeze ruffling their hair.

CITY CENTRE

Like most of Darwin, the city centre is open and vibrant with wide streets, leafy parks, a cool mall and outdoor dining. Arching shade trees and towering palms are features of the lush parks and reserves, while stunning Aboriginal art and artefacts are characteristic of the retail areas. Tall, modern structures have begun to replace the old colonial-style buildings, but they still retain a fresh, tropical flavour with overhanging eaves, corrugated iron and lush vegetation.

Smith Street

Smith Street Mall is the retail heart of the CBD. Shady **Raintree Park** at the northern end is popular with tourists and locals at lunchtime, and many outdoor concerts are held here during the dry season. A walk down the mall between May and the end of August will reveal buskers from all over Australia who have travelled north to beat the southern winter. Plazas and small arcades reveal shops where visitors can buy Aboriginal art, locally made jewellery, and tropical clothing. Halfway down the mall is the **Victoria Hotel**, a Darwin landmark and one of its oldest pubs. Almost directly opposite is the Star Arcade, which used to house the old open-air Star Theatre. At the southern end of the mall are some of the city's grandest buildings where it is possible to look at or buy South Sea pearls – one of northern Australia's most valued exports.

Across Bennett Street, Smith Street continues south towards the harbour past **Brown's Mart**, which was built in 1883 and is now home to the Darwin Theatre Company. Across the street are the ruins of **Palmerston Town Hall** (Darwin was initially named Palmerston), which was built in 1883 and partially destroyed by Cyclone Tracy in 1974. It remains as a memorial to the city's early colonial days and to the ferocity of the cyclone.

Behind Brown's Mart are the Darwin City Council Chambers, where an ancient banyan tree known as the **Tree of Knowledge** castes a huge umbrella of shade. Planted at the end of the 19th century, the tree has been a meeting place, dormitory and soapbox for generations who lived in or passed through Darwin. At the southern end of Smith Street is **Christ Church Cathedral**, built in 1902 and damaged by both Japanese bombers and Cyclone Tracy.

Mitchell Street

One street to the west of Smith Street is Mitchell Street, a popular dining and entertainment area specialising in outdoor eateries. With backpacker accommodation, pubs and outdoor dining areas, Mitchell Street is the party precinct of Darwin. You'll find cinemas and the **Darwin Performing Arts Centre**, which hosts many exciting theatrical performances, particularly late in the dry season during the Festival of Darwin.

Cavenagh Street

Cavenagh Street is one street east of Smith Street. Among the commercial buildings and government departments, it boasts a few art galleries and cafes. At the **Roma Bar**, which is popular with politicians, journalists, writers, and members of the local arts community, people from all walks of life can rub shoulders over a coffee.

This street was the original Chinatown in Darwin. In the late 1800s the southern end was full of ramshackle huts and shops with the occasional opium den. While some of the original stone buildings remain up near Darwin Post Office, a reminder of the Asian history is at nearby Litchfield Street where a modern **Chinese Temple** is built on the site of an older temple that was constructed in 1887. People can visit this temple and the **Northern Territory Chinese Museum** next door, which has displays that take visitors through the history of Chinese people in Darwin from the establishment of Chinatown and market gardens to the bombing in World War II. *The Northern Territory Chinese Museum is open most days during the dry season; admission by gold coin donation.*

The Esplanade

Much of Darwin's up-market accommodation is built along The Esplanade, with balconies and windows looking out over Darwin Harbour. Oil rigs can often be seen being towed out to the offshore fields of the Timor Sea, as can cattle boats lying at anchor, awaiting shipments. There are many Australian and American wrecks at the bottom of the harbour, sunk by the Japanese bombers that struck without warning in February 1942. There are memorial sites all around the harbour recording the hundreds of bombing raids that were made on the city during World War II.

Getting around

Darwin is easy to get around – city streets are laid out in a grid, most attractions are within walking distance, and traffic is rarely heavy.

A regular public bus service covers many of the suburbs as well as the satellite town of Palmerston (the city terminus is on Harry Chan Avenue). Private mini-buses can be found near the northern end of Smith Street Mall and taxis are available at either end of the mall.

The Tour Tub is an open-air bus service to the city's top sights, departing every hour from the northern end of Smith Street Mall.

Darwin's network of bicycle paths extends from the city out to the northern suburbs, and bikes can be hired from many backpacker lodges, most of which can be found on Mitchell Street.

Public transport Bus Service (08) 8924 7666

Airport shuttle bus Darwin Airport Shuttle Bus 1800 358 945; Arafura Shuttle Minibus (08) 8981 3300

Motoring organisation AANT (08) 8981 3837, roadside assistance 13 1111

Police road report 1800 246 199 (a good source of information for travel outside Darwin, particularly in the wet season)

Car rental Avis 136 333; Britz Camperdown Rentals 1800 331 454; Budget 132 727; Four-wheel-drive hire service (08) 8981 6760; Hertz 133 039

Bus tours Tour Tub (08) 8985 6322

Taxis City Radio Taxis 131 008 or (08) 8981 3777

Bicycle hire Elkes Backpackers Inner City Lodge (08) 8981 8399

Swimming

Swimming in waters around Darwin is not recommended, particularly during the build-up to the wet season (October to December) and during the wet season (up until the end of April) because of the hidden dangers of box jellyfish and crocodiles. Although Darwin Harbour and the foreshores are patrolled regularly by Parks and Wildlife Commission officers, and saltwater crocodiles are relocated to farms, the seas are not completely free of dangerous creatures. Box jellyfish pose the biggest problem because they are small, almost transparent, and deadly. Some people do swim in the sea during the dry season, when box jellyfish are least threatening, but most locals do not. Preferred swimming spots include community pools at Parap, Nightcliff and Casuarina, East Point Reserve (see p. 341), and natural springs outside the city.

NORTHERN TERRITORY

Climate

Darwin has a constant temperature of around 30°C and the weather is always warm and humid – just how humid depends on the time of year. Most people visit during the dry season, which extends from May to the end of September. The 'build-up' period (between October and December) is famous for hot, stifling weather and massive electrical storms. During the wet season (which can last until late April), the Asian monsoon drops over Darwin, often bringing days of cleansing rain. When the inevitable cyclone comes, the streets of the city and surrounding landscape become waterlogged and flood-bound. The wet season may be uncomfortable, but it is the time when the landscape is green and lush. At the end of the season, native trees burst into flower and attract thousands of birds.

	J	F	M	A	M	J	J	A	S	O	N	D
Max °C	32	31	32	33	32	31	30	31	32	33	33	33
Min °C	25	25	24	24	22	20	19	21	23	25	25	25
Rain mm	406	349	311	97	21	1	1	7	19	74	143	232
Raindays	21	20	19	9	2	0	1	2	7	12	16	

Beautiful **Bicentennial Park** runs the length of The Esplanade and a walking/cycling track goes from Doctors Gully in the north to the Wharf Precinct in the south. The park is a great place for people to relax under shady trees, enjoy their lunch or simply watch the day go by; in the mornings and evenings this is also a popular area for joggers and walkers. There is a children's playground halfway along the park, an eagle's nest lookout at the northern end and a **Cenotaph** honouring service men and women at the southern end. A branch of the walking/cycling track goes past Lameroo Beach and the **Deckchair Cinema**. The cinema is open every night during the dry season.

On the corner of Knuckey Street, at the southern end of The Esplanade, is **Old Admiralty House**, built in 1937, which shows off tropical design and living standards in Darwin before the city was devastated in 1974. Further north is **Lyons Cottage**, the former British Australian Telegraph (BAT) headquarters for the Overland Telegraph. Built in 1925 for BAT staff, it now houses an excellent chronology of early Darwin life. *Lyons Cottage, cnr The Esplanade & Knuckey St; open daily; admission free.*

STATE SQUARE

This is one of Darwin's most outstanding precincts. The thoroughly modern Parliament House and Supreme Court buildings are either loved or hated by locals, but most people agree that Government House, one of the few intact reminders of the city's colonial days, is utterly charming. The wide, green lawns of Liberty Square and surrounding shade trees make this an ideal area in which to eat a sandwich or simply relax.

Parliament House, the Supreme Court and Liberty Square

Parliament House is a large, white rectangular building with one of the finest views of Darwin Harbour. Opened in 1994, this modern, imposing edifice also houses the **Northern Territory Library** and a cafe that opens out to an area of lawn, a large fountain and a great view. People are encouraged to look through the grand hall that displays art and photographic exhibitions. *Phone (08) 8946 1448 for details of guided tours.*

Across the wide courtyard at the front of Parliament House is the Supreme Court building, which was built in 1990. High ceilings and an atmosphere of modern grandeur are also a feature of this building – it has a spectacular foyer with a giant floor-mosaic designed by Aboriginal artist Norah Napaljarri Nelson, and a permanent exhibit of Arnhem Land burial poles. At the southern side of Parliament House, next to the Supreme Court, is an open, grassed area called Liberty Square. Edged by spreading rain trees, this is the place where unionists met early last century to protest against the administration of Dr John Gilruth, who was eventually forced to flee the city as a result of a popular uprising against him.

Government House, Old Police Station and Courthouse

Across the road from Liberty Square is Government House, an elegant, gabled, colonial-style building – built in 1879 – that survived both cyclones and bombs. The building is open to the public once a year and is the venue for formal government occasions and ceremonies. Further along The Esplanade, on the corner of Smith Street, is the Old Police Station and Courthouse which is today offices for the

A concert on the lawns of Liberty Square, outside Parliament House

Northern Territory administrator and his staff. Directly opposite these buildings is **Survivors Lookout**. It surveys the Wharf Precinct and Darwin Harbour to East Arm Port and the terminus of the AustralAsian Railway, which runs across the continent from Adelaide. The lookout also marks a spot where World War II battles were witnessed by journalists and photographers.

THE WHARF PRECINCT

Steeped in history and perched upon one of the largest natural harbours in Australia, this precinct is the original base of the city of Darwin. Stokes Hill and Fort Hill wharves date back more than a century to a time when clippers and steam ships used to call at Darwin to load exotic cargoes such as crocodile skins, buffalo hides and pearls. Today the port is used for luxury liners and warships, and as a venue for outdoor dining.

World War II Oil Storage Tunnels
A set of stairs leads from Survivors Lookout to the Wharf Precinct. At the bottom of the stairs are storage tunnels that were built underground after the above-ground tanks were bombed in early raids on Darwin. One of the five tunnels is open to the public and there are historical displays of the war years. *Kitchener Dr; open daily during the dry season; admission fee applies.*

Indo Pacific Marine
At this wonderful attraction local coral ecosystems can be viewed without dipping a toe in the water. Find out what lies in Darwin Harbour – from deadly stone fish that can inflict terrible pain – and even death – to the beautiful coral that lies hidden in the Top End's sometimes murky waters. Indo Pacific Marine is one of the few places in the world that has been able to transfer a living ecosystem from the water into a land-based exhibition. Also on show are creatures endemic to the Top End, such as the deadly box jellyfish. *Kitchener Dr, near the entrance to Stokes Hill Wharf; open daily; admission fee applies.*

Australian Pearling Exhibition
Housed in the same building as Indo Pacific Marine, this exhibition gives a detailed history of pearling in northern Australia. It highlights the important contribution Aboriginal, Islander and Japanese people made to this multimillion-dollar industry. Also on display are some wonderful examples of South Sea pearls, which are found in northern waters and are the largest pearls in the world. Pearling makes a huge contribution to the northern Australian economy and is still an important source of employment. *Open daily; admission fee applies.*

Stokes Hill Wharf
Once northern Australia's most important port catering to sailing vessels and steamers, Stokes Hill Wharf is now a berth for international cruise ships and a place for restaurants, bars and shops. Stokes Hill is popular with visitors and locals not only for dining, but also as a place to throw a line over. When the fish are biting, the wharf is one of the best places in Darwin to fish. During the build-up to the wet season, the wharf is an ideal place to watch storms as they gather across the harbour and travel towards Darwin. Often international naval vessels can be found berthed at Stokes Hill, with neighbouring Fort Hill Wharf used for commercial and cargo vessels.

Inner north

The beaches of the inner north are idyllic in the dry season, but can be deadly during the build-up to the wet season when box jellyfish float in shallow waters along the shoreline (*see Swimming, p. 337*). Most visitors content themselves with sunbathing and only swim at the peak of the dry season.

Top events

Touring Car Championships *Three days of V8 Supercars at Hidden Valley Raceway. Early dry season.*

Royal Darwin Show *Three days of rides, and equestrian and agricultural displays at the Darwin Showgrounds. July.*

Darwin Rodeo, Pearl of the North Cutting competition and Country Music Concert *A lot of skilled riding and yee-ha music. Mid-dry season.*

Darwin Cup Carnival *The city's premier horse-racing carnival. August.*

Darwin Beer Can Regatta *Darwin-style boat races in vessels built from beer cans. August.*

National Aboriginal Art Award *Exquisite Aboriginal art at the Museum and Art Gallery of the Northern Territory. August or September.*

Festival of Darwin *A feast of visual and performing arts that attracts people from around the world. September.*

Eating out

City centre *Good restaurants with a strong emphasis on Asian dining. The Hanuman in Mitchell Street offers great Thai food while the Nirvana, in Dashwood Crescent, specialises in exquisite Indian and Malaysian cuisine. For something more low-key try Rorke's Drift Bar and Cafe and Shenannigans Irish Pub, both in Mitchell Street. See map on p. 338*

The Wharf Precinct *A range of eat-in or takeaway cafes and restaurants make this one of Darwin's most eclectic and scenic dining areas. See map on p. 338*

Cullen Bay *Contemporary fine dining with a choice of spectacular views over the Cullen Bay Marina or the Timor Sea. One of the best is Buzz Cafe. 336 B6*

Parap Shopping Centre *Some good Asian restaurants, as well as the legendary Cyclone Cafe constructed from debris of Cyclone Tracy. It serves an excellent coffee. 336 D4*

East Point *Darwin's restaurant views are generally impressive, but none more so than at Pee Wee's – tables and chairs are placed among the swaying palms, with the Timor Sea lapping at the shore below. 336 B2*

NORTHERN TERRITORY

Shopping

Smith Street Mall, City *Darwin's major shopping precinct in the CBD, with interesting shops that carry Aboriginal art and artefacts interspersed with outdoor eateries, five arcades and a galleria. Paspaley Pearls is a good place to buy pearls and there are several shops near the top of the mall and in Knuckey Street where you can buy Aboriginal art. Territory Colours has great examples of local art and craft, while Animale in the Galleria is a terrific frock shop. See map on p. 338*

Casuarina Shopping Square *Every popular department and chain store is under one roof here, and there is also a huge eatery with more than 30 restaurants and cafes. 584 C5*

Framed – The Darwin Gallery, City *One of the oldest art galleries in Darwin, with some of the best Aboriginal and Islander art in northern Australia and also some of the best local craft. 336 D6*

Cullen Bay *Around the marina are some interesting shops and excellent outdoor dining venues. Shop, then eat; eat, then shop. Check out the bookshop Absolutely for a variety of local books, cards and alternative publications. 336 B6*

Walks and tours

The 'Discovering Trails' Walks *Eight self-guided walks, including the Wharf Precinct, The Esplanade, the city centre, the northern suburbs, East Point and Fannie Bay. Brochure available from the visitor centre.*

Heritage Carriage Tour *A relaxed tour of the CBD in a horse-drawn carriage. Bookings 0414 736 605.*

George Brown Darwin Botanic Gardens Walks *Self-guided walks through different habitats; pamphlets available from the visitor centre at the Geranium Street entrance. A guide can be organised if you book ahead (08) 8981 1958.*

Sunset Cruises *Take a cruise on one of the charter boats at Cullen Bay Marina to see the sun slip below the horizon over the Timor Sea. Operators include Azure Cruises (08) 8988 9835, City of Darwin Cruises 0417 855 829, Darwin Cruises and Charters (08) 8942 3131, and Spirit of Darwin (08) 8981 3711.*

Ferry to Mandorah *Cast a line off the Mandorah Jetty and enjoy the views of Darwin. It's 130 kilometres by road, but only a 20-minute ferry ride from Cullen Bay Marina. Mandorah Ferry Service (08) 8978 5015.*

See also the Tour Tub, Getting around p. 337

Handfeeding fish at Aquascene

Aquascene 336 C7

This is one of Darwin's most popular attractions, where visitors can handfeed fish that live in Darwin Harbour. Opening times depend on the high tide, but Aquascene publishes feeding times every day in the *Northern Territory News* and weekly timetables can be found at Tourism Top End. Aquascene is not only a chance to interact with the marine life of the harbour, but also an opportunity to learn about northern Australian creatures through informative talks. *Doctors Gully Rd; admission fee applies.*

Cullen Bay Marina 336 B6

Cullen Bay is a popular dining and recreational area where waterside mansions and berths for yachts are built alongside holiday apartments. A wide walking path fringes a gently sloping, sandy beach, while a variety of restaurants and cafes overlook the blue waters of the marina. A regular ferry service crosses Darwin Harbour to Mandorah, departing from the front of the lock at Cullen Bay, while sunset and evening charters are based within the marina itself.

At about a kilometre north of central Darwin, the road down to the marina (Kahlin Avenue) passes **Myilly Point Heritage Precinct**. This small group of pre-World War II houses was constructed for senior public servants and survived Cyclone Tracy; they are considered excellent examples of tropical residential architecture, with louvred windows and vibrant gardens. Burnett House is located here and is the headquarters of the National Trust. The buildings are open to the public at different times; check with the National Trust (08) 8984 2848.

Mindil Beach Sunset Markets 336 C5

The Mindil Beach Sunset Markets are Darwin's most popular tourist attraction. Located off Gilruth Avenue, the markets are set up on one to two kilometres of wide footpaths, starting at the CBD. They operate on Thursday evenings (with a smaller version on Sunday evenings) from the end of April to the end of October, taking advantage of the superb dry-season weather. Up to 10 000 people enjoy the food of more than 30 nations and wander between stalls that offer everything from Aboriginal arts and Asian crafts to tarot-card readings and massages. Live performances by theatrical and singing troupes are spiced with whip-cracking and poetry readings. Bands play at night and there is an occasional offshore fireworks display. At sunset, people often walk over the sand dunes to the beach to experience a quintessential Darwin moment.

MGM Grand 336 C6

Also on Mindil Beach, MGM Grand casino lies next to the market strips. As well as the attraction of gambling, the casino also frequently holds concerts on its lawns. With the beach only metres away, this is a very pleasant way to spend an afternoon or evening. There are several restaurants in the casino, and this is the hub of the horseracing scene in August when a gala ball is held on the lawns. *Gilruth Ave, Mindil Beach.*

George Brown Darwin Botanic Gardens 336 C5

The botanic gardens have paths that wind through one of the best collections of tropical plants in Australia. Established in the 1870s, the gardens cover an area of 42 hectares and contain attractions such as an extensive collection of tropical orchids and palms, and a self-guided Aboriginal plant-use trail. The gardens are popular with family groups and wedding parties. A wonderful tree house incorporated into a huge African mahogany is a hit with kids. *Geranium St, The Gardens.*

Museum and Art Gallery of the Northern Territory 336 C4
The Museum and Art Gallery of the Northern Territory is one of Darwin's main cultural icons. This institution houses one of the finest Aboriginal art collections in Australia, which is enhanced every year with the work of entrants in the Aboriginal and Torres Strait Islander Art Award. A spine-tingling Cyclone Tracy gallery details what happened during and after that fateful Christmas in 1974. The museum also possesses an excellent natural history display of fauna and flora of the Top End and South-East Asia. The Maritime Boatshed, a vast room filled with all sorts of vessels that have travelled to northern Australia over the years, is impressive in its size and in the diversity of its exhibits from tiny jukung with their slender outriggers and woven sails to the large fishing vessels that limped to Australian shores overloaded with refugees. The nearby **Territory Craft Darwin** exhibits the work of local artists and craft producers. *Conacher St, Bullocky Point; open daily; general admission free.*

Sunset dining 336 C4
One of the pleasures of visiting Darwin is being able to enjoy a meal by the beach as the sun sets over Fannie Bay. There are several popular dining venues, such as the **Darwin Ski Club**, on the beach at Fannie Bay next to the Museum and Art Gallery of the Northern Territory, and the **Darwin Sailing Club**, just 200 metres further along the coast on Atkins Drive, and one of the most popular dining venues in Darwin.

Fannie Bay Gaol Museum 336 C3
One of Darwin's most interesting destinations is Fannie Bay Gaol Museum, which served as Darwin's prison between 1883 and 1979. Located barely 300 metres from the Sailing Club, the gaol housed some of Darwin's most desperate criminals. The cells and gallows provide a sobering display for visitors, but are sometimes used as a backdrop for dinner parties and social events. *East Point Rd; open daily; admission free.*

East Point Reserve 336 B1
The cliff-top paths into and along East Point Reserve are spectacular and very popular with joggers, rollerbladers and cyclists. Early morning and sunset finds a range of people taking a constitutional along these paths that meander between palm trees and parks, and around barbecue areas. The waters of Fannie Bay are enticing but, like all beaches in Darwin, are unsafe for swimming, particularly late in the year because of the presence of box jellyfish. **Lake Alexander**, at East Point Reserve, is an alternative swimming area, along with public baths at Parap, Nightcliff and Casuarina and these are definitely the options preferred by the locals. A raised boardwalk on the northern side of the lake gives access to mangroves that are teeming with bird, fish and plant life.

East Point Military Museum, in the north of the reserve, sits in the shadow of two huge, cement gun emplacements that were manned during World War II to protect the city. The museum highlights the role of Darwin in World War II and the parts played by service personnel in the defence of northern Australia. *Alec Fong Lim Dr, East Point; open daily; admission fee applies.*

Outer suburbs

Darwin is blessed with a particularly attractive coastline, lush parks and excellent walking paths that meander through a beautiful urban environment. The suburbs of Fannie Bay, Nightcliff and Casuarina all front on to the Timor Sea which is flat, calm and often like liquid gold at sunset. Tall palm trees sway

Markets

Parap Market *This market is about waking up to the splendours of Asia. Colourful flowers, frozen-fruit ice-cream, silk-screened sarongs, Asian food, sensual massages and exotic blended drinks are all on offer. Parap Shopping Centre, Sat mornings. 336 D4*

Palmerston Night Market *A community event with lots of crafts for sale. Frances Mall, Fri evenings, May–Oct. 584 F8*

Rapid Creek Markets *Asian food, Top End craft, excellent fresh vegies and fruit. Rapid Creek Shopping Centre, Fri evenings & Sun mornings. 584 B5*

Nightcliff Markets *These markets are focused on relaxed Sunday mornings – visitors can drink coffee and read the newspapers, with an option to go Asian – all in an outdoor setting. Nightcliff Shopping Centre, Sun mornings. 584 B5*

See also Mindil Beach Sunset Markets, p. 340

Sport

Darwinites love their sport. **AFL** *is like a second religion in Darwin and the surrounding communities, particularly for Aboriginal and Torres Strait Islander players, many of whom go on to play for big clubs. In March the NTFL grand final is held at Marrara Stadium and the Tiwi Islands Football Grand Final is held on Bathurst Island – grand-final day is the only time Bathurst Island is open to visitors without a permit. Darwin and Territory teams often play a curtain-raiser to the Australian AFL season. Any match between the Aboriginal All Stars and an AFL team is a must-see game.*

*   **Rugby League** *and* **Rugby Union** *are also well supported in Darwin. Rugby League matches are played at Richardson Park in Fannie Bay, and Rugby Union is played at the headquarters at Marrara. The Marrara sporting complex is also home to* **hockey**, **basketball** *and* **gymnastics***.*

Fannie Bay and Darwin Harbour are great for **sailing***. The foreshore is also popular for recreational* **fishing***, with the possibility of catching a barramundi at any beach or wharf.*

The annual Darwin Cup **horseracing** *carnival in August draws people from around the country, and Darwin's Fannie Bay track turns on perfect conditions and weather.*

The Hidden Valley leg of the V8 Supercar series in May brings **motorsport** *to town. Three days of car racing is turned into a week of celebrations as Top Enders turn out in tens of thousands for this event.*

The female influence

Darwin and the Top End of the Northern Territory have long had a 'macho' reputation, encouraged by tales about the exploits of pearl divers, miners, crocodile hunters, buffalo shooters and hard-living cattlemen. In fact, women have had a powerful influence in the Top End, particularly in Darwin, where they made contributions to society as nurses, teachers, business people, governesses, missionaries, hotel owners, and strong matriarchs of large families.

Women were often better educated than men. Many ran vast cattle stations and large businesses either in their own right or in their husbands' absence. Ellen Ryan owned and operated the famous Victoria Hotel in Darwin, while May Brown, Fannie Hayes and Christina Gordon ran hotels in Top End goldfields, surrounded – and often outnumbered by more than a thousand to one – by men of different cultures (European, Aboriginal and Chinese).

Women continue to assert their influence on Northern Territory society into the 21st century. Former journalist Clare Martin was elected the first female chief minister of the Northern Territory and Marion Scrymgour was the first female Aboriginal minister in any Australian government.

Entertainment

Cinema

One of the first examples of entertainment infrastructure ever established in Darwin was the outdoor cinema that ran during the dry season – the nights were clear and balmy and the temperature perfect. That tradition continues to this day at the Deckchair Cinema (on the shores of Darwin Harbour just around from Lameroo Beach). There are also cinema complexes in Mitchell Street, Casuarina Shopping Square and The Hub in Palmerston. The Museum and Art Gallery of the Northern Territory also runs interesting documentaries, short films and movies at its theatrette. Check the Northern Territory News for daily showings.

Live Music

Darwin has a young population and is a regular stopover for naval and cruise vessels from many countries – an advantage of this is that Darwin is a city of many 'party' venues. There are plenty of clubs, pubs and restaurants in the centre of the city that provide live music. The MGM Grand has regular entertainment on its lawns during the dry season, while there is a jazz program at Cullen Bay and Stokes Hill Wharf on weekends. Nightclubs such as Discovery and Throb have disc jockey commentaries interspersed with live music, while the Amphitheatre in the Botanic Gardens is a popular venue for touring musicians. Friday's edition of the Northern Territory News publishes a round-up of what's on in the Gig Guide, or visitors can check what's on by visiting Top End Tourism.

Classical music and performing arts

Darwin has a vibrant arts community that has been deeply influenced by Aboriginal and Asian cultures. Local playwrights, dancers and artists are always producing some tropical gem that can be viewed at interesting venues such as Brown's Mart, the Palmerston Town Hall ruins in Smith Street or the Darwin Performing Arts Centre (DPAC) in Mitchell Street. During the dry season the Darwin Festival is particularly stimulating and includes a concert on The Esplanade. Check with Top End Tourism for the dates of the Darwin Festival as the timing changes each year. Otherwise, see the Northern Territory News for weekly programs.

in the breeze that blows onshore every afternoon, while parks full of fig trees and other sweet-smelling tropical foliage provide shade, shelter and food for the huge variety of birds that inhabit Darwin. The nature parks are full of wildlife and it is not unusual to see wallabies eating shoots of grass or goannas wandering the lawns and sandhills of the foreshore. Darwin is one of the few cities in Australia where sea turtles still come ashore to nest.

Australian Aviation Heritage Centre 584 D6

Darwin was the first port of call for many early aviators – Sir Charles Kingsford Smith touched down in present-day Parap on his historic flight between Britain and Australia. The Australian Aviation Heritage Centre houses an American B-52 bomber and the wreckage of a Japanese zero shot down over Darwin in 1942. The city's rich aviation history is detailed at the centre, along with superbly restored exhibits. *Stuart Hwy, Winnellie; open daily; admission fee applies.*

City and coastal nature parks

Mangroves merge with tropical woodland at **Charles Darwin National Park** (336 F6), off Tiger Brennan Drive, east of the city. There is an excellent view of the city from a lookout on the escarpment, and the park contains a number of Aboriginal shell middens and some World War II bunkers. It also incorporates some of the most pristine mangrove areas in northern Australia, and if accessed by boat there is excellent fishing.

At **Holmes Jungle Nature Park** (584 E6), off Vanderlin Drive in Karama, there is a monsoonal rainforest full of native fauna and flora. Excellent walking trails meander through Holmes Jungle and the reserve is home to many species of birds, mammals and reptiles.

Casuarina Coastal Reserve (584 C4) boasts a magnificent white, sandy beach that backs on to dunes and thickets of native she-oaks. Several hundred metres from Casuarina Beach is Free Beach, Darwin's only recognised nudist bathing area, popular with sunbathers and swimmers during the dry season.

Nightcliff foreshore 584 B5

The Nightcliff foreshore provides an excellent cliff-top walkway that runs from Nightcliff boat ramp to a bridge over Rapid Creek, on to Casuarina Beach. Parks, play areas for children and fishing spots can be found all along here.

Crocodylus Park 584 D6

Peoples' fascination with crocodiles can be satisfied at Crocodylus Park, where they can see the huge saltwater variety that inhabits waters around Darwin, as well as other species from around the world. Crocodylus Park is a research centre as well as a tourist attraction and there are other animals on show including monkeys and large cats, such as tigers. Crocodiles emerge from the murky waters at feeding times (10am, noon and 2pm) to take pieces of meat that are dangled over the side of their enclosures. Well-trained guides allow children –under supervision – to handle baby crocodiles with their jaws taped shut to avoid any sharp teeth. Work by scientists at Crocodylus Park helped establish the Northern Territory's ground-breaking policies on crocodile preservation. *End of McMillans Rd, past the airport, near the Police Centre; open daily; admission fee applies.*

Day tours

Palmerston *One of the nicest parts of Palmerston is Marlows Lagoon Nature Park. Gently sloping hills roll down to a beautiful lake surrounded by grassed open areas.*

Howard Springs Nature Park *A pleasant, shaded swimming area south of Darwin with many native birds and animals and a crocodile-free pool. For more details see p. 346*

Darwin Crocodile Farm *This working crocodile farm allows you to get up close to these remarkable reptiles. Feeding times are a highlight. For more details see p. 346*

Territory Wildlife Park and Berry Springs Nature Park *This award-winning park showcases the Top End's flora and fauna. Many exhibits are connected by a four-kilometre walk or shuttle train route. Berry Springs is next door with a swimming pool and picnic facilities. For more details see p. 346*

Window on the Wetlands *Looking out over the Adelaide River flood plains, this centre not only has excellent interpretive displays of Top End ecology, but also has excellent views. Nearby, popular jumping crocodile cruises run on the Adelaide River. For more details see p. 346*

Mary River *The river is a popular fishing area, with places such as Corroboree Billabong and Shady Camp popular for boating (houseboats can be hired at Corroboree) and fishing. But visitors should be careful: crocodiles are plentiful in these areas. For more details see p. 346*

Litchfield National Park *Two hours drive south of Darwin, this park is a wonderful place to visit or camp, with bubbling streams and gushing waterfalls that flow year-round. Visitors can take walks, admire the scenic views or take advantage of the picnic areas. While generally crocodile-free, you should still read the signs before venturing into any pools. For more details see p. 346*

NORTHERN TERRITORY'S
REGIONS

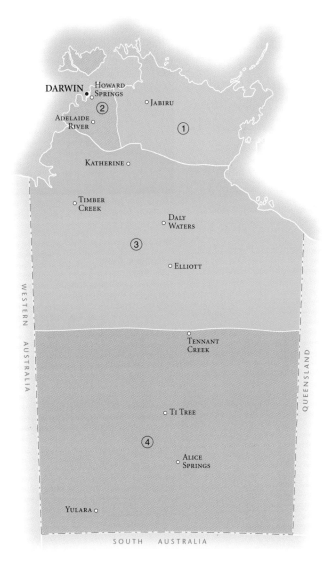

KAKADU & ARNHEM LAND

The ancient Arnhem Land escarpment meanders 500 kilometres north to south, separating Kakadu National Park in the west from Aboriginal-owned Arnhem Land in the east. World Heritage-listed Kakadu is of enormous cultural and environmental significance, protecting most habitats of northern Australia and one-third of the country's bird species, and preserving an incredible record of natural and Aboriginal history in the vast galleries of rock art. Before European settlement this was one of the most intensely populated areas on the continent. Today the park offers excellent facilities, tours across serene lily-strewn billabongs, and four-wheel-drive tracks for more intrepid explorers. Arnhem Land is the traditional home of a number of language groups and one of Australia's most remote and least-traversed regions. Permits are required for approaches by road.

Kakadu National Park

Top events

Aug	Garma Festival (Nhulunbuy)
	Gove Peninsula Festival (Nhulunbuy)
	Wind Festival (Jabiru)

Focus on

Yolngu culture
The Yolngu people have lived in north-east Arnhem Land for over 40 000 years and, despite Australia's European settlement, have managed to keep their culture relatively intact. It was only from the 1930s that Yolngu people had steady contact with Balanda (Europeans). They were not truly affected by this contact until 1963, when a proposal to develop part of Arnhem Land for mining was put forth. In a famous response, the Yolngu sent their opposing petition to the House of Representatives on a piece of bark. While mining went ahead, the petition now hangs in Parliament House in Canberra, seen as having been instrumental in the fight for Aboriginal land rights. The Yolngu people are well known for their art and craft – particularly for their bark paintings – and for their skill at playing the didgeridoo. In Yolngu Dreaming, an ancestor, Ganbulabula, brought the yidaki (didgeridoo) to the people – north-east Arnhem Land is said to be where the instrument originated. Most of the members of Australia's most prominent indigenous band, Yothu Yindi, are of Yolngu descent.

Experience it!

1. **Walk** to Sunset Lookout at Ubirr for spectacular escarpment views at sundown
2. **Join** a tour of the Ranger Uranium Mine near Jabiru in the dry season
3. **See** the landscape from above on a scenic flight from Jabiru
4. **Take** an Aboriginal-guided cultural tour of the East Alligator River, via Border Store
5. **Board** a fishing charter at Nhulunbuy, for species such as red emperor, mangrove jack and barramundi

CLIMATE JABIRU

	J	F	M	A	M	J	J	A	S	O	N	D
Max °C	34	33	33	35	33	32	32	34	36	38	37	35
Min °C	25	24	24	24	22	19	18	19	21	24	25	25
Rain mm	347	332	318	66	11	1	3	4	9	27	158	211
Raindays	22	21	20	7	2	0	0	0	1	3	12	16

Cobourg Peninsula

Four Iwaidja clan groups are custodians of this peninsula, which is protected by Garig Gunak Barlu National Park. Here visitors can fish and explore the remote and beautiful landscape. In Port Essington are the ruins of Victoria Settlement, set up by the British in 1838 to defend the north and now accessible by boat (boat hire and tours are available from Garig Store). Access is by four-wheel drive through Arnhem Land, or by charter flight.

Ubirr

Ubirr, on the Arnhem Land escarpment, houses one major rock-art gallery and some 36 smaller sites nearby. The paintings are predominantly in the X-ray style, although there are also Mimi paintings (depictions of delicate spirit figures), believed to be older. A circuit walk takes in the main sites.

Gove Peninsula

The Gove Peninsula is the traditional home of the Yolngu people, who have freehold title of the area. This remote paradise, with its islands and cays, reefs and beaches, is a frontier for anglers. Access is via charter flight, or by four-wheel drive through Arnhem Land.

Walks at South Alligator River

Towards the end of the Dry, thousands of magpie geese, jabirus and other waterbirds congregate to feed in the Mamukala Wetlands. A short nature trail through the wetlands starts just east of South Alligator River crossing on the Arnhem Highway. West of the river, the Gungarre Monsoon Rainforest Walk passes through a forest environment.

Yellow Water

Yellow Water (Ngurrungurrudjba) is a spectacular wetland area with prolific birdlife, especially in the dry season. Boat tours give visitors a close-up view of the birdlife and the Territory's crocodiles; the sunrise and sunset tours are particularly rewarding. Tours depart from Gagudju Lodge, Cooinda.

For more detail see maps 587 & 588–9.
For descriptions of ☕ towns see Towns from A–Z (p. 350).

Jim Jim Falls and Twin Falls

Jim Jim Falls (Barrkmalam) and Twin Falls (Gungkurdul) are reached via a four-wheel-drive track, 60 km and 70 km respectively off the Kakadu Highway. An incredible volume of water cascades over the 215 m Jim Jim Falls in the wet season, when the falls can only be seen from the air. Beside Twin Falls is a beautiful white sandy beach. Swimming is not recommended at either of the falls due to crocodiles.

Nourlangie Rock

Nourlangie, on the Arnhem Land escarpment, is one of Kakadu's main Aboriginal rock-art areas. On the Nourlangie Art Site Walk visitors see a variety of styles, including prime examples of Kakadu X-ray art, which shows the anatomy of humans and animals in rich detail. Enjoy great views as you walk.

NORTHERN TERRITORY

Port Essington, Garig Gunak Barlu National Park

AROUND DARWIN

Anglers catch a
huge barramundi
near the Mary River

T he attractions within easy reach of Darwin introduce visitors to the
natural wealth of the Territory and offer a glimpse of the local culture
as well. Litchfield National Park showcases some extraordinary geological
features, the Adelaide and Mary rivers teem with fish and birdlife, and the
Territory Wildlife Park offers up-close encounters with the creatures of
northern Australia. During the Wet (November to April), some parts of the
region may be inaccessible by road.

Top events

May	Gold Rush Festival (Pine Creek)
	Races (horseracing, Pine Creek)
June	Bush Race Meeting (horseracing, Adelaide River)
	Northern Territory Gold-panning Championships and Didgeridoo Festival (Pine Creek)
	Rodeo and Campdraft (Adelaide River)
	Rodeo (Pine Creek)
June/July	International Skydiving and Parachuting Championships (Batchelor)

Focus on

Crocodiles
Crocodiles are both compelling and deadly
creatures. Of the two types in northern Australia,
the most dangerous is the estuarine crocodile
('saltie'). This well-camouflaged reptile is found
out at sea, along the coastline, in tidal rivers and
creeks, and in rivers up to 100 kilometres from
the coast. Never go swimming where salties have
been seen. The freshwater crocodile ('freshie')
inhabits rivers and lagoons; it is smaller, but can
still inflict a serious wound. Both types nest and
sun themselves near the water's edge. Always
seek local advice before swimming, camping
or boating. View these reptiles safely at Darwin
Crocodile Farm, 40 kilometres south of the city,
and Crocodylus Park, an education and research
centre in Darwin's north-eastern suburbs.

Tiwi Islands
Bathurst and Melville islands form the Tiwi Islands,
80 km offshore from Darwin. They belong to
the Tiwi people, whose unique culture results
from their long isolation. The landscape includes
escarpments, lakes, waterfalls, beaches and forests,
but perhaps the biggest attraction to the islands is
the renowned Tiwi art and craft. One- and two-
day tours run from Darwin during the Dry.

Territory Wildlife Park
This award-winning park showcases northern
Australia's native fauna and flora. Features include
aviaries, raptor displays, an aquarium tunnel and
a large nocturnal house. Nearby, Berry Springs
Nature Park has a spring-fed pool – safe for
swimming – in natural bushland.

CLIMATE ADELAIDE RIVER

	J	F	M	A	M	J	J	A	S	O	N	D
Max °C	32	31	32	33	32	31	30	31	33	33	33	33
Min °C	25	25	25	24	22	20	19	21	23	25	25	25
Rain mm	429	353	322	103	21	1	1	6	16	73	141	250
Raindays	21	20	19	9	2	1	1	1	2	7	12	16

Mary River wetlands
Monsoon and paperbark forests
fringe the billabongs and riverbanks
of this magnificent wetland. Visitors
in conventional vehicles can picnic
and fish at Mary River Crossing on
the Arnhem Highway. Those with
four-wheel drives can head further
north to the famed fishing spots
of Corroboree Billabong, North
Rockhole and Shady Camp.

Litchfield National Park
Litchfield, two hours from Darwin,
has waterfalls, gorges, pockets of
rainforest, giant termite mounds,
and rock formations that resemble
lost civilisations. Enjoy the scenic
pools beneath the waterfalls – most
offer crocodile-free swimming, but
read the signs before you take the
plunge.

Experience it!

1 **Swim** in the spring-fed pool (crocodile free)
at Howard Springs Nature Park

2 **Visit** the Window on the Wetlands Visitor
Centre for an insight into this unique
environment and views across the Adelaide
River flood plains

3 **Visit** Fogg Dam at sunrise or sunset to
see the Top End's prolific wildlife in natural
surroundings

For more detail see maps 584,
586 & 588.
For descriptions of towns
see Towns from A–Z (p. 350).

GULF TO GULF

Katherine's
Jarraluk Dancers

L ying between the Red Centre and the Top End are areas where visitors can experience the natural riches of the Territory away from crowds. Some of these places are well known, particularly the world-famous gorges of Nitmiluk National Park. Other attractions are scarcely on the map: the rugged national parks of the far west, the string of remote barramundi-fishing destinations along the east and west coasts, and a number of four-wheel-drive destinations. Long distances separate towns here; travellers should familiarise themselves with prevailing conditions and carry adequate supplies.

Never Never country
Jeannie Gunn wrote *We of the Never Never* (1908) after living at Elsey Station. Now you can visit a faithful replica of Gunn's home on the property of Mataranka Homestead. Nearby in Elsey National Park visitors can enjoy the Mataranka thermal pool, which pumps out 20 million litres of water daily.

Nitmiluk National Park
The traditional home of the Jawoyn people, this park is world-renowned for its 13 stunning gorges, carved from red sandstone over a period of 20 million years. Visitors can navigate the gorges in canoes, take a boat tour with a Jawoyn guide, swim in the pools or explore the 100 km network of walking tracks.

Keep River National Park
This remote park includes the traditional land of the Miriwoong and Kadjerong people and contains many important rock-art sites, including the accessible Nganalam site. A major attraction is the rugged sandstone formations, similar to the Bungle Bungles over the Western Australian border. There are designated camping areas and good walking tracks.

Experience it!

❶ **Visit** the Gregory Tree, a boab in Gregory National Park inscribed by the explorer and his party in 1855–56

❷ **Take** a flight from Cape Crawford to the Lost City, an eerie landscape of pillars rising from the plains

❸ **See** the Jarraluk Dancers perform a corroboree (in Katherine on Wednesday evenings)

For more detail see maps 588–9 & 590–1.
For descriptions of ❶ towns see Towns from A–Z (p. 350).

Top events

Easter	*Barra Classic (Borroloola)*
April–May	*Fishing competitions (Timber Creek)*
May	*Back to the Never Never Festival (Mataranka)*
	Art Show (Mataranka)
June	*Katherine Cup (horseracing)*
	Canoe Marathon (Katherine)
Aug	*Bushman's Carnival and Rodeo (Mataranka)*
	Flying Fox Festival (Katherine)
Sept	*Races (horseracing, Timber Creek)*

Focus on

Barramundi fishing
Barramundi, Australia's premier native sport fish, is nowhere as prolific or accessible to anglers as it is in the Northern Territory. There is good barra fishing along both east and west coasts. The rugged west features tropical wetlands and a network of waterways. Popular spots include the Daly River (known for the size of its barramundi and its fishing lodges), Nitmiluk (Katherine Gorge), and Victoria River via Timber Creek. The numerous eastern rivers are smaller, with minimal tides but very clear water. Top spots east are Borroloola on the McArthur River and Roper Bar on the Roper River.

CLIMATE KATHERINE

	J	F	M	A	M	J	J	A	S	O	N	D
Max °C	35	34	35	34	32	30	30	33	35	38	38	37
Min °C	24	24	23	20	17	14	13	16	20	24	25	24
Rain mm	234	215	161	33	6	2	1	1	6	29	89	195
Raindays	15	14	10	2	1	0	0	0	1	3	8	12

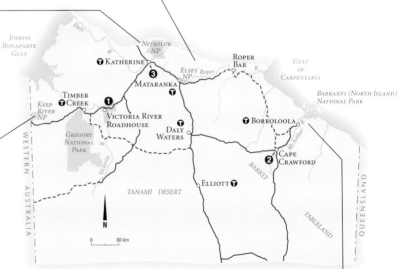

Eastern frontiers
The area adjoining the Gulf of Carpentaria is popular with four-wheel-drive travellers seeking new frontiers. The main settlement, Borroloola, is central for barramundi anglers and offers access to the waters around Barranyi (North Island) National Park.

NORTHERN TERRITORY

RED CENTRE

Uluṟu

This is Australia's geographic, scenic and mythic heart. With its spectacular landforms, deserts, blue skies and monumental sense of scale, it has become a powerful symbol of the ancient grandeur of the Australian continent. For many thousands of years the region has been home to Aboriginal people from numerous groups – including the Arrernte and the Anangu – who named, mapped and inscribed with spiritual meaning almost every one of the landforms, from massive Uluṟu to the ancient riverbeds and obelisks. Europeans colonised the area in the 1870s with the building of the Overland Telegraph Line. Tourism began in the 1940s and has flourished since the 1970s. The best time to visit is during the winter months; summer is extremely hot. Visitors intending to explore beyond the beaten track need to be fully self-sufficient, and those traversing Aboriginal land need to check if they require a permit.

Focus on

The story of Uluṟu

Uluṟu lies in the territory of the Anangu people. European explorer William Gosse named it Ayers Rock in 1873. Along with The Olgas (now Kata Tjuṯa) and surrounding land it became a national park in 1958. In 1985 it was returned to its traditional owners and gazetted as Uluṟu. The rock is Australia's most identifiable natural icon. It is a massive, red, rounded monolith rising 348 metres above the plain and 863 metres above sea level, and reaching 6 kilometres below the earth's surface. Uluṟu's circumference measures 9.4 kilometres. It has no joints – so despite its valleys, fissures and caves, it is a true monolith. Uluṟu attracts tourists because of its size and singularity. For the Anangu, however, the rock is not a single spiritual object but a thing of many parts; Uluṟu and Kata Tjuṯa were laid down during the Tjukurpa (creation period) and are joined by the iwara (tracks) of the ancestral beings that created all the land.

Experience it!

1 **Enjoy** a picnic at Ellery Creek Big Hole, surrounded by red cliffs, river red gums and ghost gums, in West MacDonnell National Park

2 **Inspect** the ruins at Arltunga Historical Reserve, site of central Australia's first gold rush in 1887

3 **Go** UFO-spotting at the renowned location of Wycliffe Well, near Wauchope

4 **Visit** Devils Marbles, a cluster of boulders that according to Aboriginal legend are the eggs of the Rainbow Serpent

5 **Walk** through different desert habitats and learn about desert animals at Alice Springs Desert Park

Top events

Jan	Lasseter's Indoor Challenge (Alice Springs)
Mar	Alice is Wonderland Festival (Alice Springs)
April–May	Country Music Festival (Alice Springs)
	Racing Carnival (horseracing, Alice Springs)
May	Bangtail Muster (Alice Springs)
	Cup Day (horseracing, Tennant Creek)
	Go-Kart Grand Prix (Tennant Creek)
June	Finke Desert Race (vehicles, Alice Springs)
July	Camel Cup (Alice Springs)
	Alice Springs Show
	Tennant Creek Show
Aug	Rodeo (Alice Springs)
Sept	Henley-on-Todd Regatta (Alice Springs)
	Desert Harmony Festival (Tennant Creek)
Oct	Masters Games (mature-age athletics, Alice Springs, even-numbered years)
Nov	Corkwood Festival (Alice Springs)

CLIMATE ALICE SPRINGS

	J	F	M	A	M	J	J	A	S	O	N	D
Max °C	36	35	33	28	23	20	20	23	27	31	34	35
Min°C	21	21	17	13	8	5	4	6	10	15	18	20
Rain mm	38	44	33	18	19	15	14	10	9	22	28	38
Raindays	5	5	3	2	3	3	3	2	2	5	6	6

Kings Canyon

Spectacular Kings Canyon has sandstone walls rising to 270 m. A 6 km return trail scales the side of the canyon and leads past beehive formations to the Garden of Eden. Within Watarrka National Park, this is the traditional land of the Luritja people, and also includes lush vegetation and classic red sand dunes.

Ruby Gap Nature Park

This far-flung park in the East MacDonnell Ranges is well worth the trip by four-wheel drive. Its 850 million-year-old landscape includes the garnet-strewn gorge at Glen Annie and, on the Hale River, another that is considered by many to be Australia's most beautiful. There are no facilities, although bush camping is permitted.

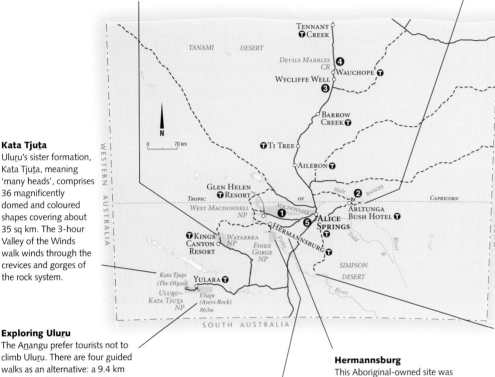

Kata Tjuta

Uluru's sister formation, Kata Tjuta, meaning 'many heads', comprises 36 magnificently domed and coloured shapes covering about 35 sq km. The 3-hour Valley of the Winds walk winds through the crevices and gorges of the rock system.

Exploring Uluru

The Anangu prefer tourists not to climb Uluru. There are four guided walks as an alternative: a 9.4 km walk around the base; the Mala walk to art sites; the Kuniya walk, which introduces creation stories; and the Liru walk, explaining the use of bush foods and materials, such as quandong fruit.

Finke Gorge National Park

This park has four-wheel-drive access only. Its unique feature is Palm Valley, a 10 000-year-old oasis with 3000 red fan palms. The Finke River, which has carved out Finke Gorge, has maintained its course for over 100 million years and is possibly the world's oldest river.

Hermannsburg

This Aboriginal-owned site was established as a German Lutheran mission in 1877. The missionaries started a school and learned the local Arrernte language, even translating the New Testament. Today the historic precinct displays preserved buildings from that time, as well as works of art from the acclaimed Hermannsburg School, of whom Albert Namatjira is the most famous.

Simpson Desert and Chambers Pillar

The world's largest sand-dune desert was formed around 18 000 years ago after the continent's central lakes dried up. Much of the desert is impossibly remote, however this northern section is accessible by four-wheel drive. The main attraction is Chambers Pillar, a sandstone obelisk towering 50 m above the plain.

NORTHERN TERRITORY

Old gaol at Arltunga

For more detail see maps 585, 590–1, 592–3 & 594–5. For descriptions of ⓣ towns see Towns from A–Z (p. 350).

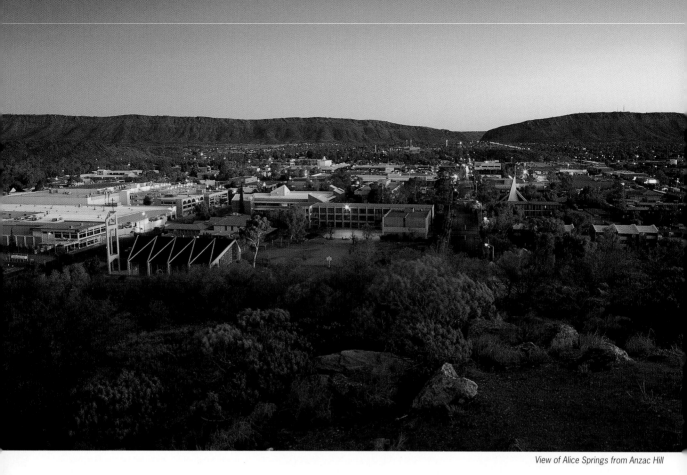
View of Alice Springs from Anzac Hill

Adelaide River   Pop. 228

Map ref. 586 E8, 588 E7

Adelaide River is a small town located near the headwaters of the river of the same name, known for its large population of saltwater crocodiles. A settlement was established here as a base for workers on the Overland Telegraph Line in the early 1870s. The population was boosted by gold discoveries at Pine Creek – Adelaide River was midway between Darwin and the goldfields – and the subsequent building of the Northern Australia Railway, which operated from 1888 to 1976. During World War II the relatively sheltered Adelaide River was a major military base for 30 000 Australian and US soldiers.

IN TOWN Adelaide River Inn The hotel was a favourite watering hole of soldiers during WW II and still has war photographs and memorabilia adorning the walls. Hard to ignore is the main attraction, Charlie the Buffalo, suitably stuffed, from the film *Crocodile Dundee*. Meals and accommodation are available. Stuart Hwy.
Adelaide River Railway Station: National Trust-classified station (1888), now a museum featuring relics of local history including the railway construction and WW II; Stuart Hwy. *Adelaide River Motor Cycle Haven:* collection of motorcycles and associated memorabilia; Stuart Hwy.
WHAT'S ON *Rodeo and Campdraft:* May. *Bush Race Meeting:* June.

NEARBY Daly River Copper was discovered here in 1883 and mining began in 1884, which led to a bloody conflict between miners and Aboriginal people. Mining ceased about 1909. Daly River is now a sleepy riverside town with a roadside inn and local Aboriginal art and craft. It is said that the country's best barramundi are caught in the Daly River and the area teems with crocodiles and other reptiles, buffalo, cockatoos and wild pigs. The Merrepen Arts Festival is held here each June. 102 km SW.
War Cemetery This is Australia's only war cemetery on Australian soil. There are graves of 434 military personnel and 54 civilians killed in the 1942 Japanese air raids, along with memorials for those lost in Timor and other northern regions. Just north of town.
Mount Bundy Station: rural experience with fishing, walking, swimming and a wide range of accommodation; 3 km NE.
Robin Falls: pleasant 15 min walk to falls that flow most of the year; 15 km S.
Snake Creek Armament Depot: wartime military base and weapon storage area with 40 buildings still intact; 17 km N.
Grove Hill Heritage Hotel and Museum: example of outback ingenuity made from recycled materials in a fashion designed to withstand the harsh weather of the Top End. Hotel offers meals and accommodation. Around 70 km SE. Goldfields Rd.
ⓘ Adelaide River Inn, Stuart Hwy; (08) 8976 7047

TOWNS

A–Z

Aileron
Pop. 5

Map ref. 592 I6

The highlight of the year at this popular rest stop on the Stuart Highway is the annual cricket match between local grape farmers and government officials from the Department of Primary Industries. There are even attendant seagulls, which are made by sticking parts of packing-cases onto sticks and painting them white.

IN TOWN Aileron Hotel Roadhouse
The roadhouse is a welcome oasis with a swimming pool, Aboriginal art, playground and picnic and barbecue facilities. The hotel offers meals, including a roast for Sunday lunch, and accommodation. There is also an adjoining campsite. Stuart Hwy.

WHAT'S ON *Cricket Match:* dates from visitor centre.

NEARBY Ryans Well Historical Reserve
The reserve is named after Ned Ryan, a 19th-century stonemason and bushman who was expert at sinking wells. He accompanied John McKinlay on his ill-fated exploration of Arnhem Land in 1866. When they became trapped on the East Alligator River during the wet season, Ryan and another bushman fashioned a raft out of the skins of 27 pack horses to negotiate their escape. Ryans Well was hand-dug in 1889 as part of an attempt to encourage settlement in the NT. Today there is a plaque beside the well explaining the process of raising water. 7 km SE. *Glen Maggie Homestead:* ruins of 1914 homestead, once used as a telegraph office but abandoned in 1934; 7 km SE. *Native Gap Conservation Reservation:* sacred Aboriginal site with picnic area surrounded by cypress pines and magnificent views of the Hahn Range; 12 km SE.
🛈 Aileron Roadhouse, Stuart Hwy; (08) 8956 9703

Alice Springs
Pop. 23 384

Map ref. 585, 593 J8, 595 N4

Located on the Todd River in the MacDonnell Ranges, Alice Springs is almost 1500 kilometres from the nearest capital city. In 1871 Overland Telegraph Line surveyor William Whitfield Mills discovered a permanent waterhole just north of today's city. Mills named the water source after Alice Todd, wife of South Australian Superintendent of Telegraphs Sir Charles Todd. A repeater station was built on the site. In 1888, the South Australian government gazetted a town 3 kilometres to the south. It was called Stuart until 1933, when the name Alice Springs was adopted. Supplies came to the slow-growing settlement by camel train from Port Augusta. The railway line from Adelaide, known as the Ghan after the original Afghan camel drivers, was completed in 1929. Today 'the Alice' is an oasis of modern civilisation in the middle of a vast and largely uninhabited desert,

made all the more likeable by not taking itself too seriously (as some of its annual events testify).

IN TOWN Alice Springs Desert Park
David Attenborough was so impressed by this desert park that he proclaimed, 'there is no museum or wildlife park in the world that could match it'. The park invites visitors to explore the arid lands and the relationship between its plants, animals and people. A walking trail leads through 3 habitats: Desert Rivers, Sand Country and Woodland. There are films, interactive displays, guided tours and talks about flora, fauna and the ability of Aboriginal people to survive in such harsh conditions. The park has a spectacular desert nocturnal house with native marsupials such as the bilby and mala, and there are free-flying birds of prey in daily shows. Larapinta Dr. *John Flynn Memorial Uniting Church:* in memory of founder of Royal Flying Doctor Service and Australian Inland Mission; Todd Mall. *Adelaide House:* originally a hospital designed by Rev Flynn, now a museum displaying pedal-radio equipment he used and other artefacts and photographs; Todd Mall; open 10am–4pm Mon–Fri and 10am–12noon Sat, Mar–Nov. *Sounds of Starlight Theatre:* musical journey through Central Australia; Todd Mall; open April–Nov. *Aboriginal Australia Art and Culture Centre:* exhibits of local Arrernte culture and an Aboriginal music museum including the only didgeridoo university in the world. Activities include boomerang and spear throwing, damper and billy tea and a bush tucker experience; Todd St. *Royal Flying Doctor Service Base:* operational base since 1939, with daily tours and presentations and an interactive museum; Stuart Tce; open 9am–5pm Mon–Sat and 1pm–4pm Sun and public holidays. *Panorama Guth:* remarkable 360-degree landscape painting by Henk Guth, 6 m high and 60 m around, featuring Ross River, Uluṟu and Palm Valley. A gallery features other work by the same artist. Hartley St; open Mon–Sat and Sun afternoon (last admission 4pm). *National Pioneer Women's Hall of Fame:* national project dedicated to preserving women's place in Australia's history. Located in the old courthouse in Hartley St; open Feb–mid-Dec. *Minerals House:* fossicking, geological and mineral displays; Hartley St; open Mon–Fri. *Old Stuart Town Gaol:* the harsh but functional design of stone and timber reflects the community attitude to prisoners at the time of construction (1907); Parsons St; open 10am–12.30pm Mon–Fri and 9.30am–12noon Sat, Feb–Dec. *Technology, Transport and Communications Museum:* relics are used to demonstrate the methods pioneers devised to overcome the hardships of isolation; Memorial Dr. *Araluen Galleries:* 4 galleries feature Aboriginal art with an emphasis on work from the central desert. The magnificent stained-glass window

by local artist Wenten Rubuntja is a highlight. Larapinta Dr. *Anzac Hill:* the most visited landmark in Alice Springs, this war memorial features panoramic views of town and the MacDonnell Ranges; Wills Tce. *Stuart Town Cemetery:* original town cemetery with graves of the earliest pioneers dating from 1889; George Cres. *School of the Air:* the first of its kind in Australia with a classroom size of 1.3 million sq km. See interpretive displays and hear lessons being broadcast. Head St. *Old Hartley Street School:* originally constructed in 1930 and closed in 1965, the school was added to several times as the population surged, reflecting the changing styles and requirements of school design through different periods; Hartley St; open 10am–2.30pm Mon–Fri. *Central Australian Aviation Museum:* Flying Doctor memorabilia and 2 original planes; cnr Larapinta Dr and Memorial Ave. *Museum of Central Australia:* interpretive centre focusing on natural history of region; cnr Larapinta Dr and Memorial Ave. *Limerick Inn:* part of Lasseters Casino complex, this Irish bar is seemingly at odds with its desert location. Barbecue in beer garden every Sun. Barrett Dr; open daily from 4pm. *Olive Pink Botanic Gardens:* named for an anthropologist who worked with Central Desert people, this is Australia's only arid-zone botanic garden. Covering 16 ha, it contains over 300 Central Australian plant species in simulated habitats such as sand dunes, woodlands and creeks. Barrett Dr. *The Residency:* grand home completed in 1927 and housing Central Australia's regional administrator until 1973, it has welcomed many VIPs, including Queen Elizabeth II, and now showcases local history; cnr Parsons and Hartley sts. *The Overlanders Steakhouse:* established in 1971 to honour the men and women involved in the largest movements of cattle in Australia's history. It dares diners to try the 'Drover's Blowout', a multi-course meal of soup, emu, crocodile, camel, barramundi, beef, kangaroo and dessert. Hartley St. *Red Centre Dreaming:* authentic, traditional and modern Aboriginal dance. Australian food is served including damper, kangaroo and barramundi. North Stuart Hwy. *Aboriginal art and artefacts:* many outlets with authentic products; brochure from visitor centre.

WHAT'S ON *Lasseter's Indoor Challenge:* several contests including scrabble, backgammon and bridge; Jan. *Alice is Wonderland Festival:* gay and lesbian event; Mar. *Market:* Todd Mall; 2nd Sun each month, Mar–Dec. *Racing Carnival:* April–May. *Country Music Festival:* April–May. *Bangtail Muster:* street parade and sports day; May. *Finke Desert Race:* car and motorbike racing; June. *Camel Cup:* July. *Show:* cooking, crafts and camels; July. *Rodeo:* Aug. *Henley-on-Todd Regatta:* boats wheeled or carried along a dry riverbed; Sept. *Masters Games:* mature-age athletics

NORTHERN TERRITORY

carnival; even-numbered years, Oct. *Corkwood Festival:* art, craft, music and dance; Nov.

NEARBY **Emily and Jessie Gaps Nature Park** Located in the East MacDonnells, Emily Gap (13 km E) and Jessie Gap (18 km E) both contain Aboriginal rock art and are important spiritual sites to the Eastern Arrernte people. The caterpillar beings of Mparntwe (Alice Springs) originated where Emily Gap lies today. They formed Emily Gap and other topographical features around Alice Springs and then spread across to the edge of the Simpson Desert. Both gaps are popular barbecue and picnic places. *Pitchi Richi Sanctuary:* open-air museum

with displays of William Ricketts' clay sculptures and lessons about the Dreamtime and bush tucker; 2 km E. *Alice Springs Telegraph Station Historical Reserve:* area protecting original stone buildings and equipment, with historical display, guided tours, bushwalking and wildlife (Alice Springs waterhole is located here); 3 km N. *Old Timers Traeger Museum:* unique museum set in a retirement home and run by volunteer residents. It displays photographs and memorabilia from the early days of white settlement in Central Australia; 5 km S. *John Flynn's Grave Historic Reserve:* at the foot of the MacDonnell Ranges with a plaque in memory of Rev Flynn; 5 km W. *Frontier Camel Farm:*

camel rides and tours, reptile house and museum with displays highlighting the importance of camels and Afghan workers to the area; 7 km E. *The Date Farm:* locally grown dates and a pleasant palm garden at Australia's first commercial date farm; 7 km E. *National Road Transport Hall of Fame:* impressive collection of old trucks, cars and motorbikes; 8 km S. *Ghan Railway Museum:* re-creation of a 1930s railway siding featuring the Old Ghan, which runs on 8 km of private line between MacDonnell Siding and Mt Ertiva; 10 km S. *West MacDonnell National Park:* includes Simpsons Gap, a picturesque area with rock wallabies and a Ghost Gum Walk that highlights native plant species. The gap is linked to Alice Springs by sealed bicycle path through 17 km of open woodland. 25 km W. *For more information on the park see feature on this page. Tropic of Capricorn Marker:* bicentennial project marking the Tropic of Capricorn; 30 km N. *Ewaninga Rock Carvings Conservation Reserve:* soft sandstone outcrops form natural galleries of sacred Aboriginal paintings. Custodians request that visitors do not climb on rocks or interfere with the paintings. 35 km SE. *Corroboree Rock Conservation Reserve:* significant Eastern Arrernte site for ceremonial activities with a short walk and information signs; 43 km E. *Standley Chasm:* spectacular narrow, sheer-sided gorge that is particularly striking at midday when sun lights up the rocks. An attractive 1 km creek walk leads to the chasm and picnic and barbecue facilities. 50 km W. *Camel Outback Safaris: 2–14-* day outback camel safaris; bookings (08) 8956 0925; 93 km SW. *Rainbow Valley Conservation Reserve:* stunning free-standing sandstone cliffs that change colour at sunrise and sunset. Access by 4WD only. 101 km S. *Mud Tank zircon field:* prospecting for zircons, guided fossicking tours and gem-cutting at the caravan park; 135 km NE. *Henbury Meteorites Conservation Reserve:* contains 12 craters created when meteorites (comprising 90 percent iron) crashed to earth 4700 years ago. The largest of the meteorites was over 100 kg and is now at the Museum of Central Australia in Alice Springs. 147 km SW. *Chambers Pillar Historical Reserve:* Chambers Pillar, named by John McDouall Stuart in 1860, is a 40 m high solitary rock pillar left standing on a Simpson Desert plain after 340 million years of erosion. It served as a landmark for early pioneers and explorers and is best viewed at dawn or dusk. 149 km S. *Mereenie Loop:* links Alice Springs, Kings Canyon, Uluru and Kata Tjuta via the West MacDonnell Ranges and Glen Helen. A permit is required because a section of the route passes through Aboriginal land; map and permit from visitor centre. *Tours:* experience scenic attractions and Aboriginal culture by foot, bus or coach, train, limousine, 4WD safari, Harley

The ancient hills of the West MacDonnell Ranges

West MacDonnell National Park

The majestic MacDonnell Ranges, once higher than the Himalayas, were formed over 800 million years ago. Over time the ancient peaks have been dramatically eroded so that what remains is a spectacular environment of rugged gorges, hidden waterholes, remnant rainforest, an unexpectedly large number of animal species and an incredible diversity of flora. The traditional owners of the land, the Western Arrernte people, have lived in the region for thousands of years.

Ormiston Gorge, considered the 'jewel of the MacDonnell Ranges' and one of the most beautiful gorges in the country, was the subject of several paintings by artist Albert Namatjira. The Ochre Pits are a natural quarry once mined by Aboriginal people for ochre, used in rock art, painting and ceremonial decoration. There are good campsites with breathtaking scenery at Redbank Gorge (4WD access only) and Serpentine Gorge, which runs snake-like through the Heavitree Range, with waterholes supporting rare and relict plant species. Ellery Creek Big Hole, a large waterhole with high red cliffs and a sandy creek fringed with river red gums, is also significant for folds in the rock that tell the geological history of the area over thousands of millennia. Walking trails provide access to all these natural attractions.

The **Larapinta Trail** is a 230-kilometre walk across the desert range, visiting the major sites in the West MacDonnells. Beginning at the old Telegraph Station just north of Alice Springs, the trail leads to Mount Sonder via 12 sections that can be walked either individually in several days, or in total over several weeks. For those who enjoy walking and sightseeing, but not carrying provisions and cooking, tours are available that provide a swag and a hot meal at the end of each day's trek. Walkers are advised to use the Walker Registration Scheme prior to departure, 1300 650 730, or contact the Parks and Wildlife Commission of the Northern Territory for maps and tour options, (08) 8951 8211.

Davidson motorcycle, camel, horse, aeroplane, helicopter or hot-air balloon; brochures at visitor centre.
❶ Central Australian Tourism Industry Association, 60 Gregory Tce; 1800 645 199 or (08) 8952 5800; www.centralaustraliantourism.com

Arltunga Bush Hotel   Pop. 7

Map ref. 593 K8, 595 Q3

Arltunga, a goldmining town that sprang up in the late 1800s, was named after a subgroup of the Arrernte people who had lived in the area for at least 22 000 years before Europeans arrived.When gold was discovered in 1887, prospectors travelled 600 kilometres from the Oodnadatta railhead, often on foot, to get there. When the gold ran out the people left and the only remaining signs of life today are the hotel and adjoining campground. Ruins of the town have been well-preserved by the dry climate.

IN TOWN Arltunga Bush Hotel: provides meals, accommodation at the adjoining campground and fossicking licences.

NEARBY N'Dhala Gorge Nature Park The shady gorge features extensive walking tracks that provide access to a large number of rock art sites with carvings and paintings, including more than 6000 petroglyphs. The carvings are of two distinct types – finely pecked and heavily pounded – and are thought to represent two different periods. There are also rare plants in the park such as the peach-leafed poison bush and the undoolya wattle. Access by 4WD only. 53 km SW. Arltunga Historical Reserve: ruins of Arltunga, some of which have been restored, including police station and gaol, mines and the Government Battery and Cyanide Works (1896). The visitor centre has displays on the history of the town; behind the hotel. Ruby Gap Nature Park: the site of Central Australia's first mining rush, in 1886, when rubies were thought to have been found. After the stones proved to be relatively valueless garnets the boom went bust and people left. The stunning gorges are now popular sites for bushwalking and camping. Track closures possible Nov–April due to wet conditions. 37 km E. Trephina Gorge Nature Park: known for its sheer quartzite cliffs, red river gums and sandy creek bed. Several waterholes attract native wildlife and provide a beautiful setting for bushwalking, swimming, camping and picnicking. 43 km W.
❶ Arltunga Historical Reserve Visitor Centre, (08) 8956 9770; or Arltunga Bush Hotel, (08) 8956 9797

Barrow Creek   Pop. 10

Map ref. 593 J4

Although its appearance today is one of a small wayside stop on the highway, Barrow Creek was originally an important telegraph station and resting place for cattle drovers on the North–South Stock Route. It was also the site of an 1874 punitive expedition against the Kaytej people by police after a telegraph station master and linesman were killed during an assault by 20 Kaytej men. This attack (thought to have been a reaction to the abuse of an Aboriginal woman), is the only known planned attck on staff of the Overland Telegraph.

IN TOWN Old Telegraph Station This restored stone building (1872) is set against the breathtaking backdrop of the Forster Ranges. It is one of 15 telegraph stations that formed the original network from Port Augusta to Port Darwin. A key is available from the hotel for those who wish to look inside. Stuart Hwy. Barrow Creek Hotel: outback pub (1932), with original bar, cellar and tin ceilings, and memorabilia of the area on display; Stuart Hwy. Cemetery: graves of early settlers and local characters. Information available at the hotel.
❶ Barrow Creek Hotel; (08) 8956 9753

Batchelor   Pop. 723

Map ref. 586 D7, 588 E7

Established as a large air force base during World War II, Batchelor became prominent with the discovery of uranium at nearby Rum Jungle in 1949. It was home for workers of Australia's first uranium mine, which prospered for over ten years until its closure in 1963, followed by closure of the uranium treatment plant in 1971. Today Batchelor thrives on tourism, in particular, because of its close proximity to the increasingly popular Litchfield National Park.

IN TOWN Karlstein Castle Czech immigrant Bernie Havlik worked at Rum Jungle then was a gardener there until his retirement in 1977. As a gardener he had been frustrated by a rocky outcrop that was too large to move and too difficult to keep tidy, so he decided to build over it. Havlik spent five years constructing a mini replica of the original Karlstein Castle that still stands in Bohemia. He added finishing touches, despite serious illness, and died just after completion. Rum Jungle Rd. Coomalie Cultural Centre: bush tucker garden plus display of Aboriginal works and culture; Batchelor Institute, cnr Awilla Rd and Nurudina St.

WHAT'S ON International Skydiving and Parachuting Championships: June/July.

NEARBY Lake Bennett Wilderness Resort This stunning resort is set in 125 ha of tropical bushland on the shore of an 81 ha freshwater lake. The area has a plethora of birdlife and native fauna that can be enjoyed in the many serene picnic areas. There are a diverse range of activities including abseiling, swimming, windsurfing, sailing, bushwalking, barramundi fishing or just lazing on a floating mattress. The restaurant offers veranda dining and there is accommodation available. Chinner Rd; 18 km NE.
Litchfield National Park Sandstone formations and monsoon rainforest feature in this easily accessible park. There are fantastic swimming spots: plunge into the rainforest-fringed pool at Wangi Falls, swim beneath the cascading Florence Falls or relax in the waters of Buley Rockhole. Do not miss the Lost City (access by 4WD only), a series of windswept formations that eerily resemble the ruins of an ancient civilisation, and the magnetic termite mounds, so-called because they all align north–south. 20 km W. Batchelor Air Charter: scenic flights, parachuting and gliding; Batchelor Aerodrome. Rum Jungle Lake: canoeing, kayaking, diving and swimming; 10 km W.
❶ Information booth, Tarkarri Rd; or general store, Tarkarri Rd; (08) 8976 0045

Borroloola   Pop. 769

Map ref. 589 O13, 591 O3

Located beside the McArthur River, Borroloola is a small settlement with a chequered past. As a frontier town and port in the 19th century it was a base for rum smuggling from Thursday Island. It became known as the home of criminals, murderers and alcoholics, a reputation it lost only when it was virtually deserted in the 1930s. Today Borroloola's fortunes have vastly improved and it is popular with fishing and four-wheel-drive enthusiasts. Although it lies on Aboriginal land, no permit is required to enter.

IN TOWN Police Station Museum: built in 1886, the museum is the oldest surviving outpost in the NT and displays memorabilia and photographs that illustrate the town's history. Robinson Rd. Cemetery: pioneer graves; Searcy St and other scattered sites; map from visitor centre.

WHAT'S ON Barra Classic: Easter. Rodeo: Aug.

NEARBY Cape Crawford Known as the gateway to the Gulf Country, Cape Crawford is a charming town and an excellent base for exploring Bukalara rocks (60 km E) and the Lost City (20 km SE). Bukalara rocks are a mass of chasms winding through ancient sandstone structures (the area is very remote and a guide is recommended). The Lost City is a collection of sandstone turrets, domes and arches formed by water seeping through cracks and eroding the sandstone. It is an important Aboriginal ceremonial site and accessible only by air. Flights can be arranged from Cape Crawford. 110 km SW. King Ash Bay: popular fishing spot all year round; 40 km NE. Caranbirini Conservation Reserve: protects weathered rock escarpments and semi-permanent waterhole rimmed by riverine vegetation and open woodland, along with many

NORTHERN TERRITORY

native birds. Surrounding the waterhole are 25 m sandstone spires providing a vivid contrast in colour and shape to the surrounding countryside. 46 km sw. *Barranyi (North Island) National Park:* sundrenched wilderness with long sandy beaches and excellent angling. No permit is required, but visitors are requested to register with the Borroloola Ranger Station. Offshore; 70 km ne. *Lorella Springs:* campground and caravan park at thermal springs. The road is unsealed and accessible only during the dry season. 170 km nw. *Limmen Bight River Fishing Camp:* ideal conditions for barramundi and mud crabs. Accommodation is available but check road access in wet season. 250 km nw. *Fishing charters:* river and offshore fishing trips; bookings at visitor centre. *Scenic flights:* over town and the islands of the Sir Edward Pellew Group; brochure at visitor centre. ⓘ Lot 384, Robinson Rd; (08) 8975 8799; www.grtpa.com.au

Daly Waters   Pop. 16

Map ref. 590 I3

The nearby springs, from which this tiny settlement takes its name, were named after the governor of South Australia by John McDouall Stuart during his south–north crossing of Australia in 1862. The town's size belies its historical importance as the first international refuelling stop for Qantas in 1935.
IN TOWN Daly Waters Pub This historic hotel (1893) once provided refreshment to stockmen and their cattle en route between Queensland and the Kimberley in WA. Today it is known as one of the great authentic Australian pubs with characters to match. The knickers donated by patrons and stapled to the beam above the bar have all been removed. Accommodation and meals are available with the menu including 'bumnuts on toast' and 'ambuggers'. Stuart St.
WHAT'S ON *Campdraft:* Sept.
NEARBY *Daly Waters Aviation Complex:* display on local aviation in the oldest hangar in the NT (1930). Key available from Daly Waters Pub. Off Stuart Hwy; 1 km ne. *Tree:* marked with an 'S', reputedly by explorer John McDouall Stuart; 1 km n. *Dunmarra:* roadhouse and accommodation; 44 km s. *Historic marker:* commemorates the joining of north and south sections of the Overland Telegraph Line; 79 km s. *Larrimah:* remains of historic WW II building at Gorrie Airfield and museum with relics of the local transport industry and WW II; 92 km n. ⓘ Daly Waters Pub, Stuart St; (08) 8975 9927

Elliott   Pop. 407

Map ref. 591 J6

Elliott is a shady one-street town that is used as a cattle service stop. Stock being

transported from the north are given a chemical tick bath here to prevent infection of herds in the south. The town was named after Lieutenant Snow Elliott, the officer in charge of an army camp on this site during World War II.
IN TOWN *Nature Walk:* meandering interpretive trail introduces visitors to native flora and its traditional Aboriginal uses; details from visitor centre.
NEARBY Renner Springs This roadside stop on the Stuart Hwy is thought of as the place where the tropical Top End gives way to the dry Red Centre. It was named after Frederick Renner, doctor to workers on the Overland Telegraph Line. Dr Renner discovered the springs when he noticed flocks of birds gathering in the area. Fuel, supplies and meals are available and there are pleasant picnic and barbecue facilities. 91 km s. *Newcastle Waters:* once-thriving old droving town featuring historic buildings and a bronze statue, *The Drover*; 19 km nw. ⓘ Elliott Hotel, Stuart Hwy; (08) 8969 2069

Glen Helen Resort   Pop. 16

Map ref. 592 H8, 594 I5

This small homestead-style resort is an excellent base for exploring the superb scenery of Glen Helen Gorge and other attractions in West MacDonnell National Park. Its facilities include accommodation, restaurant, bar, entertainment, tour information and an attractive natural swimming hole.
NEARBY Glen Helen Gorge This breathtaking sandstone formation was created by the erosive action of the Finke River over thousands of years. There is a beautiful walk along the Finke River, possibly the oldest river in the world. The towering cliffs provide a habitat for black-footed wallabies. Helicopter flights to the surrounding area provide awe-inspiring views over Mt Sonder. 300 m e. *West MacDonnell National Park:* majestic mountain range and wilderness surrounding Glen Helen Resort and featuring Ormiston Gorge (12 km ne), Ochre Pits (21 km e) and the Larapinta Trail; *for more details see feature on p. 352. Tnorala (Gosse Bluff) Conservation Reserve:* huge crater, 25 km in diameter, formed when a comet struck earth over 130 million years ago, with excellent views from Tylers Pass. Access permit, from visitor centre, is included with Mereenie Loop permit (Mereenie Loop links West MacDonnells with Kings Canyon Resort in the south-west); 50 km sw. ⓘ Namatjira Dr; (08) 8956 7489

Hermannsburg   Pop. 456

Map ref. 592 H9, 594 I6

This Aboriginal community lives on the site of a former mission station established by German Lutherans in 1877. In keeping

with the religious zeal of the period the missionaries established a church, school and other facilities. During the first 14 years, they recorded the Arrernte language and culture, compiled an Arrernte dictionary and translated the New Testament into the local language. From 1894 to 1922 the mission was run by Pastor Carl Strehlow, who restored and constructed most of the extant buildings. His son, T.G.H. Strehlow, assembled a vast collection of anthropological items relating to the Arrernte way of life. Renowned artist Albert Namatjira, the first Aboriginal to paint landscapes in a European style, was born at the mission in 1902. In 1982 the mission and its land was returned to the Arrernte people. Visitors are restricted to the shop, petrol station and historic precinct.
IN TOWN Historic precinct The National Heritage-listed mission site comprises about 13 main buildings, mostly stone, the earliest dating from 1877 but generally from the period 1897–1910. They include Strehlow's House (1879), home of the pastor in charge of the mission and now Kata-Anga Tea Rooms with a reputation for delicious apple strudel; old manse (1888), currently a watercolour gallery housing work by Aboriginal artists of the Hermannsburg school (guided tours available); old schoolhouse (1896); tannery (1941); and Old Colonists House (1885), now a museum displaying historic items from the missionary era.
NEARBY Finke Gorge National Park For millions of years the Finke River has carved its way through the weathered ranges, creating red-hued gorges and wide valleys. There are astonishing rock formations and dry creek beds that wind through sandstone ravines, where rare flora flourishes. The park's most famous feature, Palm Valley, is a refuge for about 3000 red cabbage palms (*Livistona mariae*), which are found nowhere else in the world. The 46 000 ha area is great for bushwalking: a 1.5 km climb leads to Kalarranga Lookout for views of the amazing Amphitheatre rock; the 5 km Mpaara Walk with informative signs explains the mythology of Western Arrernte culture; and the 2 km Arankaia Walk passes through the lush oasis of Palm Valley. Park access by 4WD only. 20 km s. *Monument to Albert Namatjira:* a 6 m red sandstone memorial to the legendary artist; Larapinta Dr; 2 km e. *Wallace Rockhole Aboriginal community:* cultural tours and camping; 46 km se. ⓘ Ntaria Supermarket; (08) 8956 7480

Jabiru   Pop. 1524

Map ref. 587 P4, 588 H6

Located deep within Kakadu National Park, Jabiru was first established because of the nearby uranium mine and, although this still operates, the town is

Magela Creek wetlands in the wet season

Kakadu National Park

Kakadu, a World Heritage site listed for both its natural value and cultural significance, is a place of rare beauty and grand landscapes, abundant flora and fauna, impressive rock art and ancient mythology. The largest national park in Australia, it encompasses the flood plain of the South Alligator River system and is bordered to the east by the massive escarpment of the Arnhem Land Plateau. In the wet season water surges across the plateau and cascades 300 metres to the lowlands below. The spectacularly rich wetlands once supported a large Aboriginal population. Today the traditional owners comprise many clans, who showcase their culture through guided tours and by exhibitions and displays at an on-site cultural centre. They recognise six distinct seasons in Kakadu: Gunumeleng (pre-monsoon storm season), Gudjewg (monsoon season), Banggerreng ('knock 'em down' storm season), Yegge (cooler, but still humid season), Wurrgeng (cold weather season) and Gurrung (hot and dry season).

The wide-ranging habitats, from arid sandstone hills, savannah woodlands and monsoon forests to freshwater flood plains and tidal mudflats, support an immense variety of wildlife, some rare, endangered or endemic. There are over 50 species of mammal, including kangaroos, wallabies, quolls, bandicoots, bats and dugong. More than 120 reptile species include saltwater and freshwater crocodiles, goannas and turtles. The park is home to over one-third of Australia's bird species, including more than two million migratory birds such as magpie geese and whistling ducks. Rare bird species include the hooded parrot and the Gouldian finch, and others such as the chestnut-quilled rock pigeon and white-throated grasswren are endemic to Kakadu and Arnhem Land. A quarter of the country's freshwater fish species inhabit the park's river systems.

Thermoluminescence dating suggests there has been human occupation of Kakadu for 50 000 to 60 000 years. With around 5000 rock-art sites, the park has the world's largest and possibly oldest rock-art collection. It is of inestimable significance, revealing the complex culture of Aboriginal people since the Creation Time, when their ancestors are believed to have created all landforms and living things. Some paintings depict animals that have since become extinct, such as the long-beaked echidna, thought to have disappeared from Australia 18 000 years ago but still found in New Guinea. There are drawings of the thylacine, thought to have vanished from the mainland to Tasmania up to 3000 years ago and now extinct there, and the Tasmanian devil – now found only in Tasmania. Other sites show spirit figures that are the embodiment of Aboriginal stories and mythology. Other paintings depict early contact between Aboriginal people and Macassan traders, and the first contact with Europeans.

Kakadu is a special place. It is important to respect the land and its people and refrain from entering restricted areas such as sacred sites, ceremonial sites and burial grounds.

Kakadu is managed jointly by its traditional owners and Parks Australia. *For information on things to see and do in the park, see Kakadu and Arnhem Land, p. 344–5.*

now a major centre for the thousands who come to explore Kakadu each year.

IN TOWN Gagudju Crocodile Holiday Inn This NT icon is a 250 m crocodile-shaped building that really only resembles a crocodile from the air. The entrance (the mouth of the crocodile) leads to a cool marble reception area, designed to represent a billabong, and accommodation is in the belly of the beast. The design was approved by the Gagudju people, to whom the crocodile is a totem, and was a finalist at the prestigious Quaternario Architectural Awards in Venice. Flinders St. *Aurora Kakadu Lodge and Caravan Park:* accommodation laid out in traditional Aboriginal circular motif; Jabiru Dr.

WHAT'S ON *Wind Festival:* music, dance and artistic expression celebrating Kakadu; Sept.

NEARBY *Tourist walk:* 1.5 km stroll from town centre through bush to Bowali Visitor Centre, which features an audiovisual presentation and interpretive displays on Kakadu. *Scenic flights:* over Kakadu parklands to see inaccessible sandstone formations standing 300 m above vast flood plains, seasonal waterfalls, wetland wilderness, remote beaches and ancient Aboriginal rock art sites; 6 km E. *Ranger Uranium Mine:* open cut mine with educational tours available; bookings through Tours Office, (08) 8979 2411; 9 km E. *Kakadu National Park:* highlights include art galleries of Nourlangie Rock (34 km S), flora and fauna of Yellow Water (cruises depart from Cooinda, 55 km SW), and educational displays and exhibitions at Warradjan Aboriginal Cultural Centre also in Cooinda. *For more detail see feature on this page.*

ⓘ 6 Tasman Plaza; (08) 8979 2548

Katherine   Pop. 6493

Map ref. 588 G10

Katherine, on the south side of the Katherine River, has always been a busy and important area for local Aboriginal groups, who used the river and gorge as meeting places. Explorer John McDouall Stuart named the river on his way through in 1862 after the second daughter of James Chambers, one of his expedition sponsors. The town grew up around an Overland Telegraph station and was named after the river. Today its economic mainstays are the Mount Todd goldmine, tourism and the Tindal RAAF airbase.

IN TOWN Jarraluk Dancers The Jarraluk Dancers share some of their culture and stories through the medium of dance in a traditional corroboree performance. The community sells its art and craft at the venue and refreshments are available. Lindsay St near visitor centre; Wed evenings; bookings at visitor centre. *Katherine Museum:* built as an air terminal in 1944–45, the museum houses artefacts, maps, photographs and farming displays.

There is also memorabilia relating to Dr Clyde Fenton, who as a pioneer medical aviator and Katherine's Medical Officer between 1934 and 1937, serviced an area of 8 000 000 sq km in a second-hand Gypsy Moth he bought for 500 pounds. The plane is on display. Check opening times, (08) 8972 3945; Gorge Rd. *Railway Station Museum:* displays of the area's railway history with an old steam engine adjacent to the museum; Railway Tce; open 10am–4pm Mon–Fri. *School of the Air:* see displays about the history of the school and listen in on lessons; Giles St; open Mon–Fri, April–Oct. *O'Keefe House:* built during WW II and used as the officers' mess, it became home to Sister Olive O'Keefe, whose work with the Flying Doctor and Katherine Hospital from the 1930s to 1950s made her a NT identity. The house is one of the oldest in town and is a classic example of bush ingenuity, using local cypress pine, corrugated iron and flywire. Riverbank Dr; open 1pm–3pm Mon–Fri, May–Sept. *NT Rare Rocks:* unusual rock and gem displays; Zimmin Dr. *Katherine Orchid Nursery:* 25 000 orchids on display; guided tours available; Stutterd St; open Wed–Sat. *Self-guide walks:* including Pioneer Walk and Arts and Crafts Trail; brochures from visitor centre.

WHAT'S ON *Tick Markets:* Lindsay St; 1st Sat each month, April–Sept. *Country Music Muster:* May. *Katherine Cup:* horse race; June. *Canoe Marathon:* June. *Flying Fox Festival:* community festival, theatre and music; Aug. *Carols on Horseback:* Dec.

NEARBY **Nitmiluk National Park** This 292 800 ha wilderness is owned by the Jawoyn people and managed jointly with NT Parks and Wildlife Commission. The Katherine River flows through a broad valley that narrows dramatically between the high sandstone cliffs of the magnificent Nitmiluk Gorge. High above the floodline, on the overhangs of the ancient rock walls, are Aboriginal paintings thousands of years old. The best way to explore the gorge is by flat-bottomed boat (daily cruises; bookings at visitor centre), but canoe hire is available. Another highlight of the park is Edith Falls (Leliyn), which drops into a paperbark and pandanus-fringed natural pool that is a popular swimming spot. There are signposted bushwalks, picnic areas and campsites. Fauna in Nitmiluk includes many reptile and amphibian species, kangaroos and wallabies in higher reaches and rare birds such as the hooded parrot and Gouldian finch. The countryside is at its best Nov–Mar although the weather is hot. 29 km NE. *Knotts Crossing:* site of region's first Overland Telegraph station (1870s) around which original township of Katherine developed. By 1888 there was a hotel, store and police station. The hotel lost its licence in 1916 and the store was given a Gallon Licence. The Gallon Licence Store (now a private residence)

A tour boat plies a gorge in Nitmiluk National Park, near Katherine

operated until 1942. Giles St; 2 km E. *Natural Hot Springs:* on the banks of the Katherine River with picnic facilities and pleasant walking trails; Victoria Hwy; 3 km S. *Low Level Nature Reserve:* weir built by US soldiers during WW II, now a popular waterhole for swimming and canoeing (bring own canoe). The river is teeming with barramundi, black bream and northern snapping turtles. 3 km S. *Springvale Homestead:* originally the home of Alfred Giles, this is oldest remaining homestead in NT (1879). Accommodation, restaurant, swimming pool and camping; Shadforth Rd; 8 km W. *Cutta Cutta Caves Nature Park:* 1499 ha of the only accessible tropical limestone caves in the NT with fascinating formations 15 m underground; regular tours each day; 37 km SE. *Manyallaluk Aboriginal Community:* camping and Aboriginal cultural tours; bookings essential, (08) 8975 4727; 100 km NE. *Flora River Nature Park:* great campsites, interesting mineral formations, pools and cascades along the river; 110 km SW. *Tours:* magnificent scenery can be enjoyed from helicopter tours, scenic flights, 4WD safaris, barramundi fishing expeditions and horseback trail rides; brochures at visitor centre.

ⓘ Cnr Lindsay St and Stuart Hwy; (08) 8972 2650; www.krta.com.au

Kings Canyon Resort   Pop. 55

Map ref. 592 F9

Kings Canyon Resort, in Watarrka National Park, is an excellent base from which to explore the region. It has various standards of accommodation, a petrol station, supermarket, laundry, tennis courts and swimming pools.

NEARBY **Watarrka National Park** This park encompasses the western reaches

of the rugged George Gill Range, as well as many rock holes and gorges that provide a refuge from the harsh conditions for many species of plants and animals. The great attraction is Kings Canyon, an enormous amphitheatre with sheer sandstone walls rising to 270 m. The 870 m Carmichael Crag is known for its majestic colours, which are particularly vibrant at sunset. There are well-signed trails. The Rim Walk is a boardwalk through prehistoric cycads in the lush Garden of Eden and takes in unusual rock formations such as the Lost City. There are wonderful views across the canyon. The Kings Creek Walk is a 1 hr return walk along the canyon floor. The 6 km (3–4 hr) Kings Canyon Walk is rough going and recommended only for experienced walkers. Tours of the park include Aboriginal tours and scenic flights; brochures available from visitor centre. *Kings Creek Station:* working cattle and camel station with campsites and accommodation. Quad (4-wheeled motorcycle), helicopter and camel tours of the area. 36 km SE. *Mereenie Loop:* links Alice Springs, Kings Canyon, Uluru and Kata Tjuta via the West MacDonnell Ranges and Glen Helen. Permit required because a section of the route passes through Aboriginal land; map and permit from visitor centre.

ⓘ Luritja Rd; (08) 8956 7442; www.voyages.com.au

Mataranka   Pop. 468

Map ref. 588 I11

Visitors are lured to Mataranka for its thermal springs and its sense of literary history. Jeannie Gunn, author of *We of the Never Never*, lived at nearby Elsey station in the early 20th century. The town has adopted the term 'Never Never', using it to name a museum and a festival. Generally the phrase now refers to the vast remote area of inland northern Australia.

IN TOWN *Stockyard Gallery:* showcases NT artists' work, including leather sculpture; Devonshire teas available; Stuart Hwy. *Territory Manor:* restaurant and accommodation with daily feeding of barramundi at 9.30am and 1pm (open to the public); Stuart Hwy. *We of the Never Never Museum:* outdoor displays of pioneer life, railway and military history and the Overland Telegraph; Stuart Hwy; open Mon–Fri. *Giant termite mound:* sculpture with recorded information; Stuart Hwy.

WHAT'S ON *Back to the Never Never Festival:* celebration of the outback including a cattle muster; May. *Art show:* May. *Bushmans Carnival and Rodeo:* Aug.

NEARBY **Elsey National Park** The park encircles the Roper River, with rainforest, paperbark woodlands, and tufa limestone formations at Mataranka Falls. The thermal pools at Mataranka Springs and nearby Bitter Springs are believed to have therapeutic powers. At Mataranka Thermal Pool water (34°C) rises from underground at the rate of 30.5 million litres per day to provide a beautiful swimming spot surrounded by palm trees. The Roper River offers excellent canoeing (hire available) and barramundi fishing. There are scenic walking tracks through pockets of rainforest with wildlife observation points and camping areas. The walk from Twelve Mile Yards leads to the small but beautiful Mataranka Falls. Mataranka Homestead Tourist Resort is a replica of Jeannie Gunn's home, Elsey Homestead, and offers accommodation and camping. The replica was used in the 1982 film *We of the Never Never.* 5 km E.

Elsey Cemetery: graves of outback pioneers immortalised by Jeannie Gunn, who lived on Elsey station from 1902 to 1903; 20 km SE. *We of the Never Never:* a cairn marks site of the original homestead near the cemetery; 20 km SE.

ⓘ Stockyard Gallery, Stuart Hwy; (08) 8975 4530

Nhulunbuy   Pop. 3768

Map ref. 589 P5

Located on the north-eastern tip of Arnhem Land on the Gove Peninsula, Nhulunbuy and its surrounds are held freehold by the Yolngu people. Originally a service town for the bauxite-mining industry, it is now the administrative centre for the Arnhem region and a pleasant and relaxed hideaway. Access is by a year-round daily air service from Darwin or Cairns or, with a permit, by four-wheel drive through Arnhem Land.

IN TOWN **Gayngaru Wetlands Interpretive Walk** The path surrounds an attractive lagoon that is home to around 200 bird species. There are two viewing platforms and a bird hide, enabling visitors to enjoy the wildlife without disturbing it. There

are also signs near local flora explaining their uses in Aboriginal food and bush medicine. Visitors can take the Winter walk or Tropical Summer walk, which is shorter as a result of higher water levels. Centre of Nhulunbuy.

WHAT'S ON *Beach Volleyball Day:* June. *Garma Festival:* celebration of the arts and culture; Aug. *Gove Peninsula Festival:* Aug.

NEARBY **Buku-Larrnggay Mulka** This renowned community-based Aboriginal art museum, which is run by senior ceremonial elders, was set up to educate visitors in the ways of local law and culture and to share the art of the Yolngu people. The artists at the centre have won many awards. 'Buku-Larrnggay' refers to the feeling on your face as it is struck by the first rays of the sun. 'Mulka' is a sacred but public ceremony and means to hold or protect. A permit is not required for a museum visit; open Mon–Fri and Sat morning. 20 km SE.

Dhamitjinya (East Woody Island) and Galaru (East Woody Beach): island with long sandy beaches, tropical clear blue water and amazing sunset views; 3 km N. *Nambara Arts and Crafts:* traditional and contemporary Aboriginal art and craft; 15 km NW. *Tours:* include boat charters for outstanding game, reef and barramundi fishing, eco and cultural tours with Yolngu guides, 4WD tours, birdwatching and croc-spotting tours and bauxite-mine tours. Details from visitor centre. ***Travellers note:*** *Visitors intending to drive to Nhulunbuy must obtain a permit from the Northern Land Council beforehand, (08) 8987 2602; conditions apply. Allow two weeks for processing. A recreation permit is also required for travel outside the Nhulunbuy Town Lease, available from Dhimurru Land Management, (08) 8987 3992.*

ⓘ Chamber of Commerce, Endeavour Sq; (08) 8987 1985

Noonamah   Pop. 12

Map ref. 584 I13, 586 E4, 588 E6

Noonamah is a tiny town outside Darwin at the centre of numerous parks and reserves. It is a great base to experience wildlife, native bushland and safe swimming spots (something of a rarity, considering the Northern Territory's crocodile population).

NEARBY **Territory Wildlife Park** This 400 ha bushland park provides an easy way to view native animals in their natural habitat. They can be seen from walking trails or a motorised open train. A tunnel leads through an extensive aquarium that represents a Top End river system, where visitors can come face to face with a 3.7 m crocodile. Other highlights include a bird walk, nocturnal house and daily show of birds of prey. 14 km SW. *Darwin Crocodile Farm:* around 10 000 crocodiles, from hatchlings to 5 m long, in a natural environment. The farm is

open daily, but be there around 2pm to see the crocs being fed. Just north of town. *Didgeridoo Hut:* see Aboriginal craftspeople make didgeridoos and weave baskets and dilly bags. Works are for sale in the gallery and there is an emu farm on-site. 8 km N. *Lakes Resort:* great facilities for watersports including waterski and jetski hire; accommodation available; 10 km SW. *Berry Springs Nature Park:* safe swimming in spring-fed pools in a monsoon forest with pleasant walking trails and picnic areas; 13 km SW next to Territory Wildlife Park. *Southport Siding Exotic Fruit Farm:* wander through the orchard and taste exotic fruits in season such as breadfruit and black sapote, then meet the wildlife; open Tues, Thurs and Sat mornings. 20 km SW. *Jenny's Orchid Garden:* huge and colourful collection of tropical orchids, many on sale in the nursery; 22 km NW. *Howard Springs Nature Park:* safe swimming, birdwatching and picnicking; 23 km NW. *Majestic Orchids:* more than 320 000 plants; farm tours daily Mar–Sept and weekdays Oct–Feb; bookings (08) 8988 6644; 24 km SW. *Manton Dam:* safe swimming, fishing, water sports and shady picnic spots; 25 km S. *Tumbling Waters Deer Park:* fauna enclosure and caravan park; 26 km SW. *Fogg Dam:* wetland with prolific wildlife that is best viewed at sunrise or sunset; 41 km NE. *Window on the Wetlands:* interpretive centre offering insight into the Top End's fascinating wetland environments plus superb views over the Adelaide River flood plains. 40 km NE (7 km beyond Fogg Dam turn-off). *Adelaide River Jumping Crocodile Cruises:* see crocodiles jump out of the water with the lure of food. Several tours each day; bookings (08) 8988 8144; 41 km NE (next to wetlands centre). *Fishing:* excellent barramundi fishing at Mary River Crossing (45 km E of Fogg Dam turn-off). Several 4WD tracks lead north from here to prime fishing spots in Mary River National Park such as Corroboree Billabong (houseboat hire available).

ⓘ Noonamah Tavern, Stuart Hwy; (08) 8988 1054

Pine Creek   Pop. 453

Map ref. 586 I13, 588 F8

The town, officially called Playford until 1973, was named Pine Creek by Overland Telegraph workers because of the prolific pine trees growing along the banks of the tiny creek. A brief gold rush was sparked in the early 1870s after an Overland Telegraph worker discovered alluvial gold. The surface gold soon appeared to have run out, but mining continued for uranium, iron ore, silver, lead and zinc. Today the town benefits from the reopened goldmine, one of the largest open-cut goldmines in the Northern Territory.

IN TOWN **Railway Station Museum** The station (1888) is at the terminus of the uncompleted 19th-century transcontinental railway system and now

NORTHERN TERRITORY

Artist, Tiwi Islands

The Tiwi Islands

Owned by the Tiwi Land Trust, Bathurst and Melville islands lie 80 kilometres north of Darwin and are the traditional homes of the Tiwi Aboriginal people. 'Tiwi' is said to mean 'the people' or 'we, the chosen people'. The first Europeans to visit the islands were probably the Dutch, and in 1824 a British garrison, Fort Dundas (near present-day Pirlangimpi), was established on Melville Island – to stave off any Dutch or French claims to the region. The settlement was abandoned in 1828, largely due to attacks from the Tiwi people. The legacy of Fort Dundas is some crumbling ruins and the wild water buffalo that roam the island today. In 1911 a Catholic mission was established on Bathurst Island (on the site of today's Nguiu), followed by several subsequent missions, but all were eventually abandoned and the Tiwi people were left in peace.

In 1978 the ownership of the islands was officially handed back to the Tiwi people. Before the arrival of Europeans, the islands had been isolated from the mainland for around 4000 years after a rise in sea levels. As a result the Tiwi developed a distinctive language, culture and religion.

Renowned artists, the Tiwi people produce beautiful silk-screened clothing, woven bangles, painted conch shells, carvings, pottery and elaborately decorated Pukumani burial poles.

Tiwi Tours run one- and two-day tours to Bathurst Island from Darwin and arrange permits, accommodation and transport via light aircraft. Tiwi Tours are part of Aussie Adventure Holidays, 1300 721 365.

houses photographs and memorabilia. The historic Beyer Peacock steam train was built at Manchester in England in 1877 and used in the film *We of the Never Never* (1982). The adjacent Miners Park points to an important visible link between the railway and the mines, which depended on the railway for survival. There are interpretive signs and displays of old mining machinery that reflect life on the goldfields. Main Tce. *Water Gardens:* ponds with walking trails, bird life and picnic spots; Main Tce. *Historical Society Museum:* once a doctor's residence, military hospital then post office, building now houses historical collection, including display on the Overland Telegraph; Railway Tce; open 11am–5pm Mon–Fri and 11am–1pm Sat, April–Oct; 1pm–5pm Mon–Fri, Nov–Mar. *Enterprise Pit Mine Lookout:* panoramic views of open-cut goldmine that was once Enterprise Hill, but is now a water-filled pit; Enterprise Pit. *Gun Alley Gold Mining:* features restored steam ore crusher and gold-panning tours; Gun Alley Rd. *Bird Park:* tropical birds in lush garden setting; Gun Alley Rd. *Old Timers Rock Hut:* rock and mineral display; Jenson St. *Town walk:* takes in historic buildings and mining sites; brochure from visitor centre.
WHAT'S ON *Races:* horseracing; May. *Northern Territory Gold-panning Championships and Didgeridoo Festival:* June. *Rodeo:* June.
NEARBY Butterfly Gorge Nature Park This park is the traditional home of the Wagiman people, who believe their ancestors still dwell here. It is a wilderness of sheer cliff faces, dense vegetation and scenic shady river walks. Butterfly Gorge was named for the butterflies that settle in its rock crevices and is a beautiful and safe swimming and picnic spot. Access is by 4WD only; open only during the dry season (May–Sept). 113 km NW. *Copperfield Recreation Reserve:* safe swimming in deep-water lake and picnicking on foreshore plus a Didgeridoo Jam held each May; 6 km SW. *Bonrook Lodge and Station:* wild horse sanctuary with trail rides and overnight camps; 6 km SW. *Umbrawarra Gorge Nature Park:* good swimming, rockclimbing and walking trails; 22 km SW. *Tjuwaliyn (Douglas) Hot Springs Park:* sacred place for Wagiman women with hot springs; camping available; off Stuart Hwy; 64 km NW. *The Rock Hole:* attractive secluded waterhole; 4WD access only (via Kakadu Hwy); 65 km NE. *Gold fossicking:* several locations; licence required (available along with maps from visitor centre). *Kakadu National Park:* best-known park in the Top End, this is a massive tropical savannah woodland and freshwater wetland. Highlights nearby include the spectacular views at Bukbukluk Lookout (87 km NE) and the beautiful falls and permanent waterhole at Waterfall Creek (113 km NE). *For more details see feature on p. 355.*

ⓘ Diggers Rest Motel, 32 Main Tce; (08) 8976 1442; www.pinecreek.nt.gov.au

Tennant Creek   Pop. 3184
Map ref. 591 K10

John McDouall Stuart named the creek in 1860 after an expedition sponsor, John Tennant. In the early 1870s an Overland Telegraph station sprang up north of the present-day town. According to legend, the settlement sprang up when a beer wagon broke down here. Gold was found in the area in the early 1930s and the town grew rapidly in the wake of Australia's last great gold rush. Gold and copper deposits still account for its role as a centre for the Barkly Tableland, an area larger than Victoria.

IN TOWN Nyinkka Nyunyu Cultural Centre This centre was built near a Warumungu sacred site and its name means 'home of the spiky-tailed goanna'. Dioramas illustrate the history of the area, an Aboriginal art gallery showcases the Tennant Creek art movement, and bush tucker, dance performances and displays explain the Aboriginal people's relationship with the land. The centre is set in landscaped gardens, which have plants used for bush tucker and medicine and feature two dance rings: one for men and one for women. Paterson St; open Mon–Sat and 10am–2pm Sun. *National Trust Museum:* housed in historic Tuxworth Fullwood House, an old WW II army hospital (1942), this museum has a photographic collection and displays of early mine buildings and equipment, a 1930s police cell and a steam tractor engine; Schmidt St; open 2pm–4pm May–Sept; other times by appt with the visitor centre. *Purkiss Reserve:* pleasant picnic area with swimming pool nearby; Ambrose St. *Anyinginyi Arts:* authentic Aboriginal art and craft; Irvine St. *Self-guide tours:* scenic drives and heritage walk; brochure from visitor centre.
WHAT'S ON *Cup Day:* horseracing; May. *Go-Kart Grand Prix:* May. *Show:* cooking, craft and camels; July. *Desert Harmony Festival:* arts and culture; Sept.
NEARBY Battery Hill This comprises an underground mine and operational gold-processing plant. Visitors can see a 10-head stamp battery, one of three in Australia still in working order. There are daily tours of a modern underground mine with working machinery that displays gold extraction and crushing techniques. Bill Allen Lookout, just past the battery, offers panoramic views, with plaques identifying significant sites. Off Peko Rd; 1.5 km E. *Historical building:* old Australian Inland Mission built in 1934 of prefabricated corrugated iron is oldest building in town; Paterson St. *Tennant Creek Cemetery:* pioneer graves with plaques telling stories

of battles with the elements and joys and hardships of pioneer life; just south of town. *Mary Ann Dam:* artificial dam ideal for swimming, canoeing, windsurfing and picnics; 5 km NE. *Juno Horse Centre:* horseriding and cattle drives; bush camping facilities; 10 km E. *Telegraph Station:* restored stone buildings (1872), once the isolated domain of telegraph workers, whose isolated lives are revealed by interpretive signs. 12 km N; open 10am–2pm Fri, May–Sept. *Nobles Nob:* once the richest open-cut goldmine in Australia, this was founded by William Weaber, who was totally blind, and Jack Noble, who had only one good eye; tours available; 16 km E. *The Pebbles:* spectacular in their quantity, these are miniature versions of the Devils Marbles (huge balancing boulders found north of Wauchope). The site is sacred to the Munga Munga women. 16 km NW. *Three Ways Roadhouse:* good roadhouse meals at the junction of Stuart and Barkly hwys, with memorial to John Flynn, founder of the Royal Australian Flying Doctor Service, nearby; 25 km N. *Memorial Attack Creek Historical Reserve:* memorial marks the encounter between John McDouall Stuart and local Aboriginal people; 73 km N. *Goldmining tours:* includes night tour of early goldmine and fossicking; brochure from visitor centre.
ⓘ Peko Rd; (08) 8962 3388; www.tennantcreektourism.com.au

Ti Tree   Pop. 80

Map ref. 592 I5

This rest stop on the Stuart Highway took its name from nearby Ti Tree Wells, the source of plentiful sweet water in the 1800s. Today the desert region supports remarkably successful fruit and vegetable industries.

IN TOWN *Gallereaterie:* Pmara Jutunta art with exhibitions and sales; food available; Stuart Hwy. *Ti Tree Park:* picnic area and playground; Stuart Hwy.
NEARBY *Central Mount Stuart Historical Reserve:* the sandstone peak was noted by John McDouall Stuart as the geographical centre of Australia; no facilities, but a monument at the base; 18 km N.
ⓘ Ti Tree Roadhouse, Stuart Hwy; (08) 8956 9741

Timber Creek   Pop. 292

Map ref. 588 D13, 590 D2

In 1855 explorer A. C. Gregory was the first European to visit this area as he followed the Victoria River south from the Timor Sea. His boat was wrecked at the site of Timber Creek, where he found the timber he needed to make repairs. The town today is growing in importance as a stop on the journey from the Kimberley in Western Australia to the major centres of the Northern Territory and as a gateway to Gregory National Park.

IN TOWN *National Trust Museum:* displays of historic artefacts in restored police station (1908); off Victoria Hwy; open 10am–12pm Mon–Fri. *Office for Parks and Wildlife Commission of the Northern Territory:* information for travellers to Gregory and Keep River national parks; Victoria Hwy. *Tours:* boat and fishing tours, river cruises (with abundant crocodiles) and scenic flights; brochures from visitor centre.
WHAT'S ON *Fishing competitions:* April–May. *Rodeo:* May. *Timber Creek Races:* horseracing; Sept.
NEARBY *Gregory National Park* Gregory is NT's second largest national park with two sections covering 13 000 sq km of ranges, gorges, sandstone escarpments, remnant rainforest, eucalypts and boab trees. There are opportunities for boating, canoeing and bushwalking, scenic flights and cruises, as well as Aboriginal and European heritage sites. Gregory's Tree (in the Victoria River section to the east) stands at Gregory's campsite with historic inscriptions and audio presentation. The tree also has special significance for the Ngarinman people and is a registered sacred site. The spectacular dolomite blocks and huge cliffs of Limestone Gorge can be found in the Bullita section to the west. Bullita station has traditional timber stockyards, old homestead, interpretive displays and shady camping spots in summer. Check with Parks and Wildlife Commission for current access details. 31 km W and 92 km E. *Jasper Gorge:* scenic gorge with permanent waterhole and Aboriginal rock art; 48 km SE. *Victoria River Roadhouse:* rest stop where the Victoria Hwy crosses the Victoria River; boat tours, fishing trips and accommodation; several scenic walks in the area including the Joe Creek Walk (10 km W); 92 km E. *Keep River National Park:* rugged scenery, Aboriginal rock art and wildlife. Most trails are 4WD only; check with Parks and Wildlife Commission for current access details; 180 km W.
ⓘ Max's Victoria River Boat Tours, Victoria Hwy; (08) 8975 0850

Wauchope   Pop. 10

Map ref. 591 K13, 593 K2

Wauchope (pronounced 'walk-up') was established to cater for the wolfram-mining and cattle-farming communities nearby. Today it is a service town and tourist destination thanks to its proximity to the popular Devil's Marbles.

IN TOWN *Wauchope Hotel* Once catering to workers at the old Wolfram Mines, this desert oasis now offers fuel, meals (licensed restaurant and take-away), various standards of accommodation and an adjacent campground. The walls of the pub are adorned with signed bank notes (a 'bush bank' where customers pin deposits to the wall to be retrieved on a later visit) and photographs of patrons.

The landscaped beer garden features native birdlife including Bill the talking cockatoo. Stuart Hwy.
NEARBY *Wycliffe Well* This roadhouse was the first in NT to be allowed to sell water (at a penny a gallon). Once a market garden supplying troops during WW II it now features pleasant picnic lawns surrounding Wycliffe Lake. The area is said to be at a cross-section of energy lines and has had many alleged UFO sightings (ranked 5th in the world for number of sightings). Wycliffe Well also claims to have Australia's largest range of beers, but any connection between that and the UFO sightings is yet to be proven. Accommodation available. 17 km S.
Devils Marbles: large, precariously balanced granite boulders; 8 km N. *Davenport Range National Park:* isolated area with important Aboriginal heritage and waterhole ecology sites; high clearance vehicles or 4WD access only; advise travel plans at the Wauchope Hotel; 118 km E.
ⓘ Wauchope Hotel, Stuart Hwy; (08) 8964 1963; www.tennantcreek tourism.com.au

Yulara   Pop. 1797

Map ref. 592 E11, 594 B12, 594 E9

Yulara is a resort town that was built specifically to cater for visitors coming to see Uluru and Kata Tjuta. It offers excellent visitor facilities and food and accommodation for all budgets. Advance bookings for accommodation are essential.
IN TOWN *Information Centre:* displays of geology, history, flora and fauna; spectacular photographic collection.
NEARBY *Uluru* Australia's most recognisable natural landmark and the largest monolith in the world, Uluru features stunning Aboriginal rock art sites that can be viewed on guided walks and tours around the base. These sites highlight the rock's significance for Aboriginal people. The traditional owners prefer visitors not to climb Uluru and there are countless tales of a curse befalling those who take a piece of the rock home as a souvenir. The spectacular changing colours of Uluru at sunrise and sunset are not to be missed. 20 km SE.
Uluru-Kata Tjuta Cultural Centre: designed in the shape of two snakes, with displays of Aboriginal culture and sales of artwork; on approach road to Uluru. *Kata Tjuta:* remarkable rock formations, with spectacular Valley of the Winds walk, fantastic views and a variety of flora and fauna; 50 km W. *Tours:* helicopter, coach and safari tours. The Uluru Experience Night Show offers viewing and narration of Aboriginal and European interpretations of the night sky. Bookings at visitor centre or at reception in accommodation centres.
ⓘ Ayers Rock Resort; (08) 8957 7377

NORTHERN TERRITORY

QUEENSLAND

Queensland is Australia's second largest state and has many unique attractions spread across its vast landscape. Fringed in the east with tropical beaches lapped by the warm waters of the Coral Sea and the South Pacific Ocean, the state offers idyllic holiday destinations.

Myriad islands, cays and atolls are scattered along Queensland's 6973-kilometre coastline. Stretching from Cape York to Bundaberg, the Great Barrier Reef offers the ultimate in diving. There are 1600 species of fish, as well as dugongs, turtles and extensive coral gardens living in the reef, all protected by World Heritage.

...fish, dugongs, turtles and extensive coral...all protected by World Heritage.

By contrast, the arid west gives visitors a chance to experience some of Australia's unique outback in towns such as Winton, established by those searching for the lost Burke and Wills expedition. Winton also has a special place in Australian folklore as the location of Dagworth woolshed where Banjo Paterson wrote the iconic 'Waltzing Matilda' in 1895.

Two-thirds of Queensland lies above the Tropic of Capricorn. In the monsoonal Far North, visitors can venture into magnificent ancient rainforests, like those of the Daintree, where cool respite lies in the boulder-strewn Mossman Gorge.

South of Brisbane is the famous Gold Coast. With more waterways than Venice and 300 days of sunshine each year, it's the perfect place for swimming and surfing. The theme parks here will terrify and astound with the world's tallest and fastest thrill rides, raging whirlpools and heart-stopping waterslides. Just 20 minutes away from all this is the hinterland, an emerald-green paradise where visitors can soak up magnificent views among waterfalls and 4000-year-old rainforest trees.

In between the luxurious resorts of Port Douglas in the Far North and the Gold Coast's high-rise glamour lie opportunities to sample more relaxing ocean experiences, such as watching humpback whales playing in the shelter of Hervey Bay or finding quiet solitude at Mission Beach.

Captain James Cook and his crew were the first Europeans to unexpectedly enjoy the Queensland coast after they ran aground on a reef near Cape Tribulation in 1770 and spent several weeks near the present-day Cooktown repairing their damaged ship.

THE TOP OF AUSTRALIA

Weipa

Cape York Peninsula

Cooktown

Cairns

Normanton

Boodjamulla (Lawn Hill) National Park

Townsville

Charters Towers

Mount Isa

Mackay

Winton

Boulia

Longreach

Lark Quarry Conservation Park

Emerald

Rockhampton

Birdsville

Bundaberg

Charleville

Maryborough

Roma

Toowoomba

Brisbane

Gold Coast

PREVIOUS PAGES Scuba diving in the Great Barrier Reef

Fitzroy Island, offshore from Cairns

Dutch explorer Willem Jansz had sailed along the western side of Cape York 164 years earlier, getting a hostile reception from local Aboriginal people, but becoming the first European to make a recorded sighting of Australia.

European settlement of Queensland occurred quite late compared with the rest of Australia. In 1824 a convict station was built near Moreton Bay to cater for the most intractable prisoners from southern gaols, but after a year of active resistance by Aboriginal tribes it was abandoned and relocated to where Brisbane stands today. The next hundred years were marred by similar conflicts as the frontier of pastoral settlement fanned outwards.

In recent years Queensland has shaken off its reputation as a quiet backwater. This modern state is fast becoming the envy of the rest of the country with its stunning natural features, relaxed pace and languid lifestyle, all enhanced by a climate close to perfect.

FACT FILE

Population 3 796 800
Total land area 1 722 000 sq km
People per square kilometre 2.2
Sheep and cattle per square kilometre 12
Length of coastline 6973 km
Number of islands 1955
Longest river Flinders River (840 km)
Largest lake Lake Dalrymple (dam), 220 km sq
Highest mountain Mt Bartle Frere (1622 m), Wooroonooran National Park
Highest waterfall Wallaman Falls (305 m), Girringun (Lumholtz) National Park
Highest town Ravenshoe (930 m)
Hottest place Cloncurry (average 37°C in summer)
Coldest place Stanthorpe (46 days per year begin at below 0°C)
Wettest place Tully gets 4300 mm per year, and has a giant gumboot to prove it
Sunniest town Townsville (average 300 days of sunshine per year)
Most remote town Birdsville
Major industries sugar and mining
Most famous person Steve Irwin, the 'Crocodile Hunter'
Quirkiest festival Cunnamulla–Eulo Lizard Races
Number of 'big things' 39
Best beach Whitehaven Beach, Whitsunday Island
Local beer XXXX

TIMELINE

1606

Dutchman Willem Jansz sails the Duyfken down the west coast of Cape York Peninsula – the first known European to sight Australia.

1824

The British establish a penal settlement at Moreton Bay. The settlement is moved to the site of Brisbane in 1825.

1842

The Moreton Bay district opens to free settlers and they quickly occupy the Brisbane River valley, the Darling Downs and the Burnett country.

1957–1989

The Country–Liberal coalition governs the state until being voted out following corruption allegations and inquiries. These are the infamous 'Joh years', named after Joh Bjelke-Petersen, premier from 1968 to 1987.

1974

The Brisbane River breaks its banks and Brisbane suffers its worst floods ever, with 16 people losing their lives and an estimated $300 million worth of damage caused.

1982

Eddie Koiki Mabo and other Torres Strait Islanders begin legal action to claim ownership of their traditional land. After a 10-year fight, this results in the Commonwealth Native Title Act 1993, which recognises the right of Australia's indigenous people to claim their traditional land.

1988

Brisbane holds World Expo '88. Tourism booms and Brisbane matures into the internationally renowned city it is today.

BRISBANE

BRISBANE IS . . .

*A CityCat trip on the iconic
Brisbane River*

*An ice-cold beer on the
deck of the historic riverside
Regatta Pub, Toowong*

*Retail therapy in fabulous
Queen Street Mall*

*Fine-dining overlooking the
river at Eagle Street Pier*

*A picnic in the shade at the
City Botanic Gardens*

*City views from atop
Mt Coot-tha*

*A swim in the lagoon at
South Bank Beach*

*A daytrip to the islands of
Moreton Bay*

*An afternoon of culture at the
Queensland Art Gallery*

*Hugging a koala at Lone Pine
Koala Sanctuary*

Visitor information

*Brisbane Visitor Information Centre
Cnr Albert and Queen sts
Queen Street Mall, Brisbane
(07) 3006 6200 or (07) 3006 6290
www.ourbrisbane.com.au*

Victoria Bridge to Conrad Treasury Casino and the city

The fabulous weather, abundant subtropical vegetation and all-round relaxed attitude make Brisbane a city distinctly different from any other. The Brisbane River winds through the city to Moreton Bay – its curves offer numerous spots for waterside recreation and spectacular views. Moreton and Stradbroke islands create a barrier to the Pacific Ocean, providing the city with a vast body of calm water at its foreshore. Inland, Brisbane's hilly terrain provides breathing space and a beautiful backdrop for the city, with its massed frangipanis, colourful jacarandas and renovated old Queenslanders on stilts. Gold-hued sandstone buildings sit among the gleaming skyscrapers of the city centre.

Brisbane has matured since beginning life as a convict settlement in 1825, playing host to the Commonwealth Games in 1982 and the World Expo in 1988. The population has increased at a rapid rate since the late 1980s – it currently stands at 1 653 000, large enough to give Brisbane a vibrant big-city feel, small enough to make it community-focused and easy to get around. New developments have created pleasant recreational spaces, such as the Roma Street Parkland, and easier ways to get around, such as the CityCat catamarans that speed up and down the river.

Brisbane is home to some of Australia's best restaurants, from fine-dining establishments to relaxed riverside fish-and-chip cafes. The wonderful warm climate means Brisbane is market-central – there are vibrant weekly markets along the river, in city parks, in the Valley, north of Brisbane, south of Brisbane – and that's not all of them!

With highlights such as South Bank – where else can you find a beach right in the centre of a city? – Brisbane is a superb destination for a holiday in a region known for its great holidays.

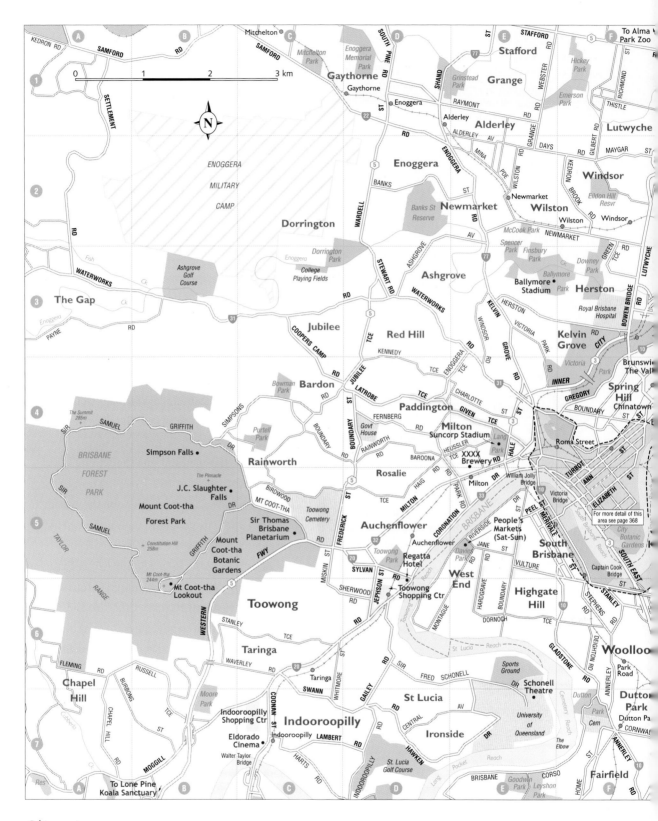

Climate

Queensland isn't called the sunshine state for nothing and, with an average of 300 days of sunshine each year, the south-east corner has (according to many) the most liveable climate in the state and possibly the country. Summers are hot and steamy; winters are mild and dry. Summer days in Brisbane average in the high 20s or low 30s.

The hot days often build up to spectacular evening thunderstorms, and Brisbane's annual rainfall of approximately 1400 mm occurs mostly in summer. In winter the average temperature is 21°C – a very pleasant 'winter' for anyone from down south! Winter evenings can be a bit cool though, so make sure you pack at least one jumper.

	J	F	M	A	M	J	J	A	S	O	N	D
Max °C	29	29	28	27	24	21	21	22	24	26	27	29
Min °C	21	21	20	17	14	11	10	10	13	16	18	20
Rain mm	169	177	152	86	84	82	66	45	34	102	95	123
Raindays	14	14	15	11	10	8	7	7	7	10	10	11

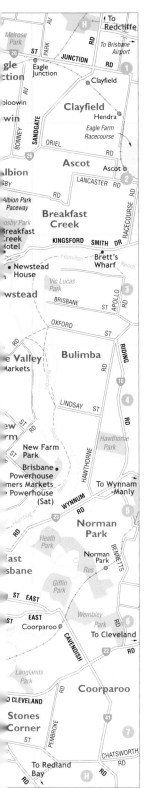

Central Brisbane

The centre of Brisbane is full of contrasts: young corporates in summer suits stride past relaxed locals and tourists in shorts, singlets, thongs and bikini tops; glass skyscrapers tower above old public squares landscaped with lush foliage and leafy trees; and modern restaurants and shopping malls contrast with historic public buildings from the 19th century. Set aside a day at least to wander through the streets – escape into the airconditioning of the shops and arcades of Queen Street Mall if the humid warmth gets too much for you.

CITY CENTRE

Brisbane is a beautiful city and the centre of town is no exception. Despite the fact that it is the commercial and retail heart of Brisbane, the city centre retains the buoyant holiday spirit that pervades the entire sunshine state. If ever you lose your way in the CBD grid, remember that the streets named after royal women all run north-east and parallel to each other, while the king-inspired streets run north-west.

Queen Street Mall

With the Myer Centre, Broadway on the Mall, the new Macarthur Central (between the mall and the GPO) and various other retail centres, Queen Street Mall is a shopper's paradise and the hub of the CBD. Catering only to pedestrians (but with a bus station conveniently located beneath), the mall is usually packed with shoppers, buskers and people simply enjoying the relaxed Brisbane pace. Along with a public stage, there are outdoor cafes and restaurants dotted down the centre of the mall. At the top of the mall is the Conrad Treasury Casino (*see next entry*) and the bridge over to South Bank. Look for the striking banquet-table water sculpture at this end of the mall. At the other end, the mall leads onto two of the city's most peaceful public squares, ANZAC Square (*see below*) and Post Office Square. Cutting through the middle of the mall is Albert Street, leading to more shopping on Elizabeth Street, including the interesting Elizabeth Arcade, and Adelaide Street. Get a literary insight into Brisbane by following the Albert Street Literary Walk – look for the 32 brass plaques in the pavement.

Conrad Treasury Casino

One of Brisbane's spectacular buildings, the Treasury Building, built between 1885 and 1928, is now the Conrad Treasury Casino. With restaurants, bars and live bands nightly, the casino is a top nightspot. Perhaps the popularity of the casino leads to a local name for the city – Brisvegas. *George St; open 24 hours daily; admission free.*

ANZAC Square

Often filled with pigeons, wandering herons and lunching office workers, ANZAC Square, between Ann and Adelaide streets, is a peaceful retreat. The square's Shrine of Remembrance, built in 1930, honours, with its eternal flame, the Australian soldiers who died in World War I. In the pedestrian

Getting around

Brisbane has well-signed, well-maintained roads and little traffic congestion (except at peak times), but it is not an easy city for the first-time visitor to negotiate. The city's phenomenal growth in recent times has resulted in a criss-crossing network of major motorways on the doorstep of the city centre. In the centre itself, there are many one-way streets. To make matters more confusing, the Brisbane River twists its way through the city and suburbs. An up-to-date road map and some careful route planning at the beginning of each day is a good idea.

Public transport is comprehensive and efficient. Trains, buses and ferries cater for all needs and a couple of bus routes are designed specifically for visitors (see below). A boat trip on the Brisbane River is a must. Plenty of tours are available to riverside tourist attractions (see Walks and tours, p. 373) and there is an excellent commuter ferry and catamaran (CityCat) service. Buy a Day Rover ticket for about $8 and travel on the CityCats all day, from the University of Queensland in St Lucia to Brett's Wharf downriver. The Cats travel at high speed; standing on the deck and feeling the cool wind in your hair is the best way to see Brisbane.

Public transport TransInfo (bus, ferry, CityCat and rail) 13 1230

Airport shuttle bus Coachtrans Airport Service (07) 3238 4700

Airtrain Citylink Train from airport to city and Gold Coast 13 1230 or (07) 3215 5000

Motoring organisation RACQ 13 1905, roadside assistance 13 1111

Car rental Avis 13 6333; Budget 13 2727; Hertz 13 3039; Thrifty 1300 367 227

Bus tours City sights bus tours and The Loop (free bus circling the CBD) 13 1230

Taxis Black and White Cabs 13 1008; Yellow Cabs 13 1924

Bicycle hire Brisbane Bike Sales and Hire (07) 3229 2433; Valet Cycle Hire 0408 003 198

QUEENSLAND

tunnel behind the square is the World War II Shrine of Memories (open Monday to Friday only) where you can see unit plaques, honour rolls and a mosaic made from hand-cut glass enamels and soils from official World War II cemeteries. From ANZAC Square take the steps to the walkways over Adelaide Street to reach **Post Office Square**, another of Brisbane's grassy public squares. Opposite the square is the **General Post Office**, built in the 1870s; even with the busy post-office crowds, you can still get an impression of its history.

Brisbane City Hall

In regal King George Square, home of the city's enormous Christmas tree in December, is the historic Brisbane City Hall. Opened in 1930, this impressive sandstone building is topped by a soaring 92-metre clock tower. Tours are available and include a trip up the clock tower. *Between Ann and Adelaide sts; (07) 3403 8888; open daily; general admission free (fees apply for tours and elevator trips up the clock tower).*

Museum of Brisbane

Within Brisbane City Hall, this museum is a recent addition to the cultural and creative life of the city. Also known as MoB, the museum has five exhibition spaces and celebrates the history, culture and people of Brisbane. Displays incorporate history, design, craft and the visual arts. The museum's Discovery Room offers online and text-based resources as well as objects from the collection. The MoB Store is a good spot to pick up something created by one of Brisbane's talented writers, artists or musicians. *Ground floor, Brisbane City Hall; open daily; admission free.*

St John's Cathedral

This striking example of Gothic-Revival architecture was built in three stages, the first beginning in 1906. It has the only fully stone-vaulted ceiling in Australia as well as extensive woodcarvings by Queensland artists, fossiliferous marble 350 million years old and beautiful stained-glass windows. Next to the cathedral is the **Deanery**, built in 1850 and formerly the residence of Queensland's first governor, Sir George Bowen. Free tours are conducted daily. *373 Ann St; (07) 3835 2248.*

St Stephen's Cathedral

This magnificent cathedral is a quiet place of worship amid the hustle and bustle of the city. The cathedral grounds include **St Stephen's Chapel**, the oldest surviving church in Queensland. Guided tours of the cathedral are available. *249 Elizabeth St; (07) 3224 3111.*

Commissariat Stores

Built by convicts in 1829 (with additions since), this solid-stone building is one of the oldest buildings in Brisbane. Today it is home to the offices, library and museum of the Royal Historical Society of Queensland. There is a convict display, and tours are available. *115 William St; (07) 3221 4198; open Tues–Sun; admission fee applies.*

FORESHORE

The serpentine Brisbane River curves around central Brisbane; developments along the riverside in the past few years have created new riverfront precincts offering award-winning restaurants, excellent shopping and spectacular vistas. Public water transport stops at Riverside Wharf and the marvellous RiverWalk (*see RiverWalk, p. 372*) takes you all the way to the City Botanic Gardens.

Customs House
Built in 1889 and beautifully restored, this magnificent building served as the city's Customs House for almost a century until port activities shifted closer to the mouth of the river. Now a cultural and educational facility of the University of Queensland, it is set right on the edge of the Brisbane River and includes an art gallery and brasserie with waterfront tables. On Sundays there are free guided tours. *399 Queen St; (07) 3365 8999; open daily; admission free.*

Riverside Centre
Home to the popular **Riverside Markets** on Sundays (*see Markets, p. 371*), the Riverside Centre also offers superb dining and beautiful water features. Riverside is the location for some of corporate Brisbane's newest skyscraper developments.

Eagle Street Pier
On the riverfront just south of the Riverside Centre, Eagle Street Pier has some of Brisbane's best and most-awarded restaurants (*see Eating out, p. 371*). If you would prefer something more casual, grab some fish and chips and sit on the boardwalk, enjoying the spectacular views of the river and the landmark **Story Bridge**, the largest steel cantilever bridge in Australia. On Sundays the **Eagle Street Pier Markets** (*see Markets, p. 371*), together with the Riverside Markets, dominate the northern city edge of the river and create a vibrant atmosphere.

City Botanic Gardens
These beautiful historic gardens, established in 1855 right in the heart of the city, are Queensland's oldest public gardens and recognised for both their natural and historic heritage. You could spend hours here, walking down the avenues lined with majestic bunya pines, resting beneath the weeping Moreton Bay figs, exploring the rainforest glade or taking the **Mangrove Boardwalk** along the bank of the river. Hidden gardens and shady nooks provide secluded lunch spots and, if you take the riverside path, you can enjoy stunning views of the river and Kangaroo Point cliffs. There are free guided tours, or hire a bike for a quicker journey. Look out for alfresco films with Sunset Cinema in the gardens between September and November. *Gardens Point, Alice St.*

QUT Cultural Precinct
Launched in 2000, Queensland University of Technology's Cultural Precinct, at Gardens Point next to the City Botanic Gardens, encompasses Old Government House, the QUT Arts Museum and the Gardens Theatre. Now run by QUT, **Old Government House** was home to the Queensland governor for most of the state's first 50 years. This graceful sandstone building, built in 1860, is open Monday to Friday and guided tours are available; phone (07) 3864 8005. **QUT Arts Museum** is housed in a 1930s Neoclassical building and is home to QUT's art collection as well as diverse contemporary exhibitions. Works by QUT students are also displayed. The Arts Museum is open Tuesday to Friday, 10am–4pm, and Saturday and Sunday, noon–4pm. Admission is free. The cultural venue of the **Gardens Theatre** offers shows by QUT students and visiting international and Australian theatre companies.

Parliament House
Overlooking the City Botanic Gardens, this grand public building was built in 1868 (new buildings have since been added to the parliamentary precinct). The two sandstone wings contain majestic staircases, stained-glass windows and ornate chandeliers. Fringed with palms, the parliamentary precinct is a showcase of Queensland's history and is still home to the Queensland parliament. Tours of Parliament House and the legislative chambers run from Tuesday to Thursday except when parliament is sitting. *Cnr George & Alice sts; (07) 3406 7562; open daily; admission free.*

AROUND ROMA STREET PARKLAND

Once a bit of a barren wasteland with railyards dominating the area, the landscape north-west of the CBD has changed dramatically with the creation of the lush Roma Street Parkland. If you're coming into town via train, hop off at Roma Street Station and head to the **Queensland Police Museum** and **Victoria Barracks**. The museum has displays on themes such as police heritage, the Dog Squad and police investigative techniques. The military museum at Victoria Barracks has a collection of weapons from wars between 1899 and 1972 (*open 1pm–4pm Sun*).

Top events

Queensland Winter Racing Carnival *Three months of excitement on and off the racecourse. May–June.*

Brisbane International Film Festival *Superb showcase of the latest in Australian and international film, with an international atmosphere. July–August.*

The Ekka (Royal Queensland Show) *A Brisbane institution; ten days of the city meeting the country, with fireworks and wild rides included. August.*

Riverfestival *Colourful festival on the Brisbane River with fireworks, fantastic food and live music. September.*

Spring Hill Fair *Brisbane's oldest fair, with markets, stalls, entertainment and delicious food. September.*

Brisbane Festival *Queensland's largest biennial celebration of the performing and visual arts. September (even-numbered years).*

Livid *A massively popular music festival with Australian and international bands (and lots of stage-diving). October.*

Festivus *A feast of festivals celebrating summer in Brisbane, including New Year's Eve and Australia Day events. November–January.*

Woodford Folk Festival *Huge award-winning folk festival, just out of Brisbane, with local, national and international musicians and artists, and lots of stalls. December.*

QUEENSLAND

Across Roma Street Parkland to the city

Shopping

Queen Street Mall, City *Brisbane's major shopping precinct, with major department stores and 10 malls and arcades including the Myer Centre, Brisbane Arcade, Macarthur Central and Wintergarden. Everything you'll ever need for retail therapy. See map on p. 368*

Fortitude Valley *For up-and-coming designer fashion and innovative chic, collectibles and books, art and trendy homewares, adventure gear and trinkets. 367 G4*

Little Stanley Street, Southbank *Edgy designer fashion, homewares and gifts. See map on p. 368*

Paddington *Antiques and boutique homewares on Latrobe and Given terraces. 366 D4*

Toowong Shopping Centre *Medium-sized mall with a department store, specialty shops and fresh-food market. 366 D6*

Indooroopilly Shopping Centre *Enormous mall with over 250 specialty shops, major department stores, a gym and a 16-cinema complex. Fabulous shopping. 366 C7*

Stones Corner *Factory outlets and fashion seconds only 15 minutes south from the CBD. 367 G7*

Chermside Shoppingtown *Huge northside mall with a department store, a 16-cinema complex and hundreds of specialty shops. 598 E6*

Old Windmill

Brisbane's oldest convict-built structure is the windmill, on Wickham Terrace overlooking the Roma Street Parkland. It was constructed in 1828 and used to grind flour for Brisbane's convict settlement. In 1861 it was converted to a signal station. Since then it has been used as both an observatory and a fire tower and, in 1934, the first successful experimental television transmittal was made from it. It no longer has its original sails and treadmill, but an information board lists its fascinating history and it is a pleasant walk from the CBD up the Jacobs Ladder steps through the leafy King Edward Park.

Roma Street Parkland

This huge subtropical garden is a wonderful haven in Brisbane's centre, just north of the Brisbane Transit Centre and Roma Street Station. The 16 hectares of parkland include landscaped gardens, Queensland's largest public art collection and hundreds of unique plants. Meander through the parkland on the network of pathways or simply escape from the summer heat under the shade of one of the many mature trees. Kids can spend time in the playground or play frisbee on the open Celebration Lawn. The lake precinct is beautiful and the subtropical rainforest is a cool retreat, while the **Spectacle Garden** is the parkland's horticultural heart. Enjoy a barbecue in one of the many picnic areas or get someone else to do the cooking at the parkland's cafe. You can also pick up one of the useful brochures for the self-guided themed walks, take a guided tour or hop on the trackless train that travels the paths.

SOUTH BANK

Set aside a day to spend at South Bank, Brisbane's fabulous leisure precinct incorporating parklands and some of Queensland's major cultural institutions. An easy walk across Victoria Bridge or the pedestrian- and cycle-only Goodwill Bridge from the city, South Bank was developed on the site of World Expo '88 and covers 125.5 hectares of prime riverfront.

There is much to see and do at South Bank. Explore the **Queensland Cultural Centre**, which comprises the buildings of the state's museum, gallery, library and performing arts centre, all within easy reach of one another. Follow the beautiful 1 km-long **Energex Arbour** – created by unusual, tendril-like metal columns covered in hot-pink bougainvillea – that winds through the full length of the precinct. South Bank always has plenty of live entertainment – from buskers and street performers to international acts in the 2600-seat **Suncorp Piazza**. The ornate **Nepalese Peace Pagoda**, featured in Expo '88, is set among tropical rainforest trees; enjoy a peaceful moment within this beautiful pagoda. Stroll along the shady **Rainforest Walk**, a raised boardwalk through the beautiful subtropical vegetation for which Queensland is famed.

South Bank is also a renowned dining spot; it has over 20 cafes and restaurants, so sit back, relax and enjoy a good meal or a coffee among sculptures, tropical foliage and water features. Ice-creams at **Cold Rock Ice-Creamery** are a must; choose your favourite ice-cream and a mix-in of other sweet treats, then watch as the staff mix it all up on the frozen 'cold rock' – definitely a Brisbane favourite.

If you're feeling energetic, the paths this side of the river are perfect for cycling or rollerblading (in South Bank bikes and rollerblades are only allowed along the Clem Jones Promenade). Get your wheels on and head down to Kangaroo Point for great views of the city. You can also watch the rockclimbers and abseilers do their stuff on Kangaroo Point Cliffs. If you're really keen, you can learn to abseil on the spot. From the **Kangaroo Point Cliffs City Lookout** there are great views of the city.

South Bank Beach
A sandy beach right in the centre of Brisbane. South Bank Beach has a crystal-clear lagoon that contains enough water to fill an Olympic swimming pool five times over. Surrounded by tropical palms, the area is patrolled by qualified lifesavers. Kids play among the sunbathers, and there are barbecues and covered picnic areas around the beach, which has views over the Brisbane River to the CBD.

Queensland Performing Arts Centre
The perfect spot in Brisbane for theatre, music and opera lovers, this centre, at the northern end of South Bank, has performance spaces to cater for all types of theatrical entertainment. The Cremorne Theatre provides a space for experimental theatre; the Playhouse offers cutting-edge technology in stage design; the Lyric Theatre is the flagship of the centre and host to everything from Opera Queensland performances to the latest blockbuster musical; and the Concert Hall is home to regular performances by the Queensland Orchestra as well as international classical, jazz and pop artists. At the ground-floor entrance of the Cremorne Theatre is the **Tony Gould Gallery**, the exhibition space for the QPAC Museum, which displays exhibitions related to the performing arts. There are cafes and a restaurant, perfect for post-theatre suppers. Outside the main entrance is the Cascade Court, where regular performances are held, including the popular World Music Cafe Series. Guided tours of the centre happen once a week. *Stanley St; see www.qpac.com.au for details of what's on; phone (07) 3840 7444 for details of guided tours; admission to gallery free.*

Queensland Museum
This excellent museum has an extensive natural-history collection, including a fascinating endangered species exhibit, and displays on Queensland's indigenous and European history. Interactive displays for kids sit alongside the skeleton of a humpback whale and dinosaur displays.

Plan to spend a few hours here and take in **Sciencentre**, an interactive science experience. *Cnr Grey & Melbourne sts; open daily; general admission free.*

Queensland Art Gallery
Overlooking the Brisbane River, this is Brisbane's premier cultural attraction. It houses the state's permanent art collection as well as a wide variety of special exhibitions. The highlight of the building is the peaceful Watermall, an internal water feature that forms one of the gallery's exhibition spaces. Free guided tours are available. The second venue of the gallery, the **Queensland Gallery of Modern Art**, is due to open late 2005. It will showcase the gallery's collections of cutting-edge contemporary art as well as becoming home to the highly successful Asia–Pacific Triennial of Contemporary Art. *Melbourne St; open daily; general admission free.*

State Library of Queensland
Since 1896 the State Library has been archiving and preserving books, images, prints, maps and other material charting the history and culture of Queensland. Located on the corner of Peel and Stanley streets right on the riverbank, the library is currently undergoing major redevelopment. Due to reopen in 2005/2006, the new building will be double its current size. New services will cater for the ever-increasing number of people using the library's facilities. In the meantime, the library's services and collections are located in the auditorium of the Cultural Centre between the Queensland Art Gallery and the library, in Griffith University's College of Art and Conservatorium of Music, and at a new location in the suburb of Cannon Hill. Free public transport operates between the Cultural Centre location and the Cannon Hill location. *Visit www.slq.qld.gov.au for up-to-date information and opening hours, or phone (07) 3840 7666.*

Grey Street Precinct
Recently redeveloped as a grand tree-lined boulevard, Grey Street sits between South Bank and the suburb of South Brisbane. It is home to a cinema complex as well as the **Brisbane Convention and Exhibition Centre**, a 7.5-hectare complex that houses the Great Hall, a ballroom, and exhibition halls used for regular trade and retail exhibitions. Running between Grey Street and South Bank, **Little Stanley Street** is home to designer fashion stores, smoky cigar bars, gourmet food shops and great cafes and restaurants. Closed to traffic, **Stanley Street Plaza** is usually buzzing with people enjoying its classy cafes and fantastic South Bank location.

Eating out

Brunswick Street, Fortitude Valley *Stylish restaurants, relaxed pubs, tapas bars, street cafes and food from the world over. 366 G4*

Central Brunswick, Fortitude Valley *One of the city's newest dining spots, offering Spanish, Brazilian, Indian and Thai cuisine, delicious gelati, and that's not all. 366 G4*

Chinatown, Fortitude Valley *Authentic pan-Asian food on offer, from yum-cha to sushi, with an authentic atmosphere. 366 F4*

Eagle Street Pier, City *Australia's most-awarded dining precinct, with elegant fine-dining and classic river views. See map on p. 368*

East End, City *Centred on Adelaide Street, some of the city's best and most innovative restaurants, with big-name chefs and modern dining. See map on p. 368*

South Bank *Contemporary fine-dining, outdoor cafes and easy takeaways in the superb surrounds of the South Bank Parklands. See map on p. 368*

West End *Perfect for brunch, cosmopolitan dishes and delicious cocktails. 366 E5*

Markets

Riverside and Eagle Street Pier markets *Two fabulous open-air markets become one along the city edge of the Brisbane River, with fashion, craft, food, plants and much more. Sun. See map on p. 368*

South Bank Art and Craft Markets *Street performances, art and craft, jewellery and live music make the lively South Bank markets popular. Fri night & Sat–Sun. See map on p. 368*

The Valley Markets *Brisbane's alternative markets, with vintage clothing, alternative fashion, tarot readings, interesting gifts, old books and an exciting atmosphere. Brunswick St Mall, Sat–Sun. 366 G4*

Farmers Markets at the Powerhouse *Farm-fresh produce, gourmet food, cut flowers and fresh seafood, all in the atmospheric surrounds of the Brisbane Powerhouse. New Farm, 2nd & 4th Sat each month. 367 H5*

People's Markets *Friendly, cosmopolitan markets on the river at Davies Park, West End, with bargains, art and craft, and free entertainment. Sat–Sun. 366 E5*

QUEENSLAND

Sport

*Brisbane's weather is perfect for sport, and Brisbane's stadiums are state of the art. If **AFL** (Australian Football League) is your passion, you can't miss the Brisbane Lions at their home ground, the Gabba, proving that Victoria is no longer the stronghold of AFL. The Gabba is also home to Queensland **cricket** – watch the Bulls defend the state's cricketing honour. You'll find the Gabba (known formally as the Brisbane Cricket Ground) in the suburb of Woolloongabba, south of Kangaroo Point.*

*   **Rugby League** is a way of life in Queensland, culminating in State of Origin. You can watch the Brisbane Broncos, the city's Rugby League team, at the redeveloped Lang Park (also known as Suncorp Stadium), a Brisbane sporting institution in Milton. Ticket-holders enjoy free public transport on match days.*

*   Show your true colours by supporting the Reds, Queensland's **Rugby Union** team, at their matches at Ballymore Stadium, Herston – the home of Queensland Rugby Union since 1967.*

*   If you're addicted to the speed and excitement of **basketball**, watch the Brisbane Bullets, the state's National Basketball League team, take on the nation at their home stadium in South Bank's Brisbane Convention and Exhibition Centre. The Townsville Fire, Queensland's team in the Women's National Basketball League, play some of their games at SEA FM Stadium in the Brisbane suburb of Annandale.*

*   If you prefer the sport of thoroughbreds, head to Brisbane's **horseracing** venues at Doomben and Eagle Farm. Or for car racing at its loudest and most thrilling, head south for the **Gold Coast Indy** in October.*

*   The Brisbane region is the place to be if you're a **golf** fanatic. Visit in November/ December to watch the Australian PGA Championship at the Royal Queensland Golf Club (in Eagle Farm, east of Hamilton).*

South Bank Beach

Queensland Maritime Museum

At the south-eastern end of South Bank, the museum is situated around the historic South Brisbane Dry Dock, built in 1881. Three galleries display relics, memorabilia and informative exhibits, such as the special wall map of vessels lost in Queensland seas – over 1500 since the first recorded wreck in 1791. There are displays on sailing, old diving equipment and the navigation instruments used by early explorers of Queensland's incredible coastline. There is also an impressive collection of historic seagoing craft, ocean-liner replicas and nautical machinery. In the Dry Dock you can explore Australia's only remaining World War II frigate, HMAS *Diamantina*. During spring and autumn months, take a leisurely cruise (lunch included) into Moreton Bay on the museum's coal-fired, steam-powered 1925 tug SS *Forceful*. *Sidon St; open daily; admission fee applies.*

West End 366 E5

Just behind South Bank, the riverside suburb of West End has become a popular choice for professionals, artists and students because of its proximity to the CBD, its multicultural mix of cafes and restaurants and its great alternative nightspots. Despite the recent rejuvenation of West End, you will still see unrestored 19th-century houses throughout the suburb, and the 1912 Gas Stripping Tower in Davies Park.

Fortitude Valley

Known simply as the Valley, this cosmopolitan area of inner-city Brisbane is a fascinating mix of seedy history, stylish restaurants and alternative chic. First settled in 1849 by 256 'free' settlers who arrived in Moreton Bay aboard the *Fortitude*, the Valley still retains much of its 19th-century heritage. Amid the old buildings and renovated Queenslanders are brand new high-rise apartment blocks, and old warehouses and woolstores are being converted into fashionable inner-city residences, particularly in the riverside precinct of

RiverWalk

New recreational facilities are being created all the time in Brisbane and one of the best developments in recent times is the RiverWalk.

    This ever-growing network of paths, currently spanning over 20 kilometres, follows the river and connects with Brisbane's bikeways and ferry routes. You can walk on the north bank of the river from the picturesque University of Queensland campus at St Lucia past the CBD to the trendy riverside precinct of Teneriffe, near New Farm.

    On the south bank you can walk downriver from West End through South Bank – stopping for an ice-cream or lunch – to Dockside at Kangaroo Point. Cross the river over the Goodwill Bridge or follow the RiverWalk paths to various ferry terminals. The latest

addition to RiverWalk is an 850-metre-long, 5.4-metre-wide pontoon, or floating walkway, across the river between New Farm and the wharves under the Story Bridge.

    When complete, RiverWalk will cover 34 kilometres of riverside paths and boardwalks from St Lucia to Breakfast Creek on the north side, and from Dutton Park to Bulimba on the south side. Brisbane City Council has a map of the paths that you can pick up at the visitor centre or download from the Brisbane City Council website, www.brisbane.qld.gov.au. Brisbane's weather makes it a perfect city to explore on foot, and following the winding curves of the city's stunning river on the RiverWalk is a great way to see the city.

Teneriffe. Nightclubs, bars and cafes abound, especially on Brunswick Street, and, even though old pubs are being given trendy facelifts, the Valley is still Brisbane's alternative and artistic centre, home to many private art galleries and artists' studios. The creative hub is the **Judith Wright Centre of Contemporary Arts**. Running across Brunswick Street, **Ann Street** has an older feel, but offers cutting-edge fashion and new pubs and bars, such as the GPO, in the old Fortitude Valley Post Office.

Brunswick Street Mall 366 G4
This is where crowds flock on weekends for the bohemian **Valley Markets** (*see Markets, p. 371*). This is also where you'll find the historic **McWhirters Apartments**. On the corner of Brunswick and Wickham streets, McWhirters was a department store built in 1912 and has recently been converted to stylish apartments – shops still fill the bottom levels. Free bands play in the mall on some Friday and Saturday nights and the vibe is busy but always relaxed. Enjoy the alfresco dining at any time of day. Further up Brunswick Street, you'll find the foodies' delight that is **Central Brunswick** (*see Eating out, p. 371*).

James Street Precinct 367 G4
James Street, the newest development in the Valley, runs parallel to Brunswick Street a few blocks north-east. It is a perfect example of urban renewal – James Street has undergone a transformation from an industrial zone dotted with old houses and the odd church to a vibrant (and some say Brisbane's hottest) lifestyle district. Homeware and furniture stores cater to cashed-up new inner-city residents, while outdoor cafes, restaurants and bars satisfy appetites for good coffee, fine dining and innovative cocktails. The **James Street Market** offers fresh food and produce along with flowers, nuts and juices. The **Centro** development includes a cinema complex – James Street offers the full entertainment package.

Chinatown 366 F4
With wonderful smells, bright colours and delicious food, Brisbane's Chinatown is a sensory delight. Restaurants offer excellent value and even better yum cha, supermarkets have traditional Chinese treasures and the busy Valley Markets extend into Chinatown on the weekends. Elements of Feng Shui were used in the design of the Chinatown Mall on Duncan Street and you can expect to see peaceful practitioners of tai chi in the mall on weekends. The **Chinese Museum of Queensland** (due to open early 2005) in the TC Beirne Building that links Chinatown with Brunswick Street Mall, will portray the history of Chinese in Queensland and the contributions

Chinese–Australians make to the broader community. If you're in Brisbane in late January/early February, head to Chinatown for spectacular Chinese New Year celebrations.

Inner north-east

Fortitude Valley is the heart of the inner north-east, but both south and north are other lively suburbs well worth a visit. The river winds its way around the district, and pockets of parkland on the riverbank create restful recreation spots. This is a great area for a picnic or to relax in a cafe.

New Farm 367 G4
Named in the 1800s to distinguish it from older farming areas in the Brisbane region, New Farm is another of Brisbane's inner-city suburbs with a growing population and changing dynamic. Still home to artists and a broad multicultural community, there are also streets lined with outdoor cafes, trendy fashion shops, art galleries and bookshops. Originally an 1846 racecourse until bought by the Brisbane City Council in 1913, the large tree-filled **New Farm Park** is a favourite spot for locals at any time, in any season. Enjoy a walk through the beautiful rose garden; kids can spend time in the playground or hide in the natural treehouse.

Brisbane Powerhouse 367 H5
This exciting new centre for live arts is based in the old New Farm Powerhouse, built in the 1920s. Now restored, the powerhouse offers a diverse program of contemporary music, theatre, dance and art. Rehearsal rooms, meeting areas and smaller performance spaces join with riverside outdoor spaces to create a new cultural precinct for Brisbane's north-east. A cafe, bar and fortnightly markets (*see Markets, p. 371*) add to the lively feel. *119 Lamington St, New Farm; phone (07) 3358 8622 or go to www.brisbanepower house.org for details of upcoming shows and opening hours.*

Miegunyah 367 G3
This historic 1886 house is set in shady grounds and reflects opulent 19th-century elegance. Built in traditional Queensland fashion with long verandahs and ornate ironwork, Miegunyah has been restored to its original style and portrays the life of the Queensland middle class in late Victorian times. It is now home to the Queensland Women's Historical Association and serves as a memorial to the state's pioneering women. *35 Jordan Tce, Bowen Hills; open 10.30am–3pm Wed and 10.30am–4pm Sat & Sun; admission fee applies.*

Walks and tours

Boutique Golf Tours *Explore Brisbane's many picturesque golf courses; perfect for the keen golfer. Bookings (07) 3378 0535.*

Brisbane Heritage Trails *Take a trip back in time with any one of the Brisbane City Council's Heritage Discovery Walks – excellent self-guided tours of historic districts in the city and its surrounds. Brochures available from the visitor centre and Brisbane City Council (07) 3403 8888.*

City Sights Bus Tours *See the cultural and historic attractions of Brisbane in comfort. Set your own pace – you can hop off and on the clearly signed buses at any time. The City Sights ticket extends to ferries, CityCats and commuter buses. Brochure and tickets available from the visitor centre or ring 13 1230 for more information.*

City Nights Tours *Get a real feel for Brisbane's night-life on the night version of the City Sights Bus Tours. See contact details above.*

Coastal Heritage Trails *Once you've explored historic Brisbane, do the same along the coast in Redcliffe, Cleveland and Wynnum–Manly. Brochures available from the visitor centres.*

Fly Me to the Moon *See the sun rise over Brisbane city at dawn – take a hot-air balloon flight, followed by a gourmet champagne breakfast. Bookings (07) 3423 0400.*

Gonewalking *Discover Brisbane on foot with the help of experienced Brisbane City Council volunteers, or buy a copy of Great Brisbane Walks from Brisbane City Council (07) 3403 8888 or a good bookshop, to plan your own.*

Ghost Tours *Scare yourself silly on one of a variety of serious ghost tours, exploring Brisbane's haunted history. Bookings (07) 3844 6606.*

Moreton Bay Cruises *Explore beautiful Moreton Bay on one of the many cruises on offer. Information at the visitor information centre.*

River Tours *Travel the river up to Lone Pine with Mirimar Cruises (07) 3221 0300 or enjoy a fine meal with stunning views on a Kookaburra River Queen cruise (07) 3221 1300.*

QUEENSLAND

Entertainment

Cinema

Movies are the best way to escape the mid-summer heat in Brisbane and there are many cinemas to choose from. Major cinemas can be found at the Myer Centre in the city (a Hoyts complex), and at most of the big suburban malls. For a more unusual experience, visit one of the restored Brisbane landmarks: the refurbished eight-cinema Eldorado in Indooroopilly, showing films since the mid-1900s; and the atmospheric Regent Theatre in Queen Street Mall, with its marble staircase and ornate ceilings. If you're after something independent or arthouse, try the Dendy Twin in George Street, the boutique Regal Twin in Graceville, or the Schonell at the University of Queensland in St Lucia. See the Courier Mail *for movie times.*

Live music

The Valley is the centre of Brisbane's live music scene and has been the birthplace of some of Australia's best and most innovative bands. Crowded with partying people most evenings, Brunswick Street and Ann Street are lined with fantastic bars, pubs, nightclubs – including the award-winning The Family – and alternative music venues such as the Zoo, a Brisbane institution. Kangaroo Point has some good live-music venues, including the renowned Story Bridge Hotel and the Brisbane Jazz Club. For jazz you could also head to West End. Popular alternative acts play gigs at the Tivoli in the Valley; international acts play the Brisbane Entertainment Centre out at Boondall. Buy a copy of the Courier Mail *on Fridays for the lift-out guide, or pick up one of the free street papers such as* TimeOff *for details of what's on.*

Classical music and performing arts

Brisbane has a pulsing creative life with theatres of all sizes spread throughout the city. For high-end performing arts and music the premier venue is the Queensland Performing Arts Centre, which includes the Concert Hall and the Lyric Theatre. West End is the address of the Queensland Ballet, in the Thomas Dixon Centre. The Valley has a number of smaller venues for experimental and alternative theatre, and there are often live street performances taking place in Brunswick Street Mall. The Roundhouse Theatre in the new Kelvin Grove Urban Village is the venue for the La Boite Theatre Company and some brilliant productions. See the Courier Mail *for details of what's on.*

Newstead House 367 G3

Brisbane's oldest residence, Newstead House was built in 1846 by Patrick Leslie, the first white settler on the Darling Downs. Beautifully restored, with its spacious verandahs, formal gardens and lawns down to the river, it offers an image of the quintessential Australian homestead. The house has a fascinating history – it was even occupied by the American military during World War II (there is an Australian–American War Memorial in the grounds). Today the house is furnished from the Victorian period. *Newstead Park, Breakfast Creek Rd, Newstead; open 10am–4pm Mon–Fri & 2pm–5pm Sun; admission fee applies.*

Breakfast Creek and Hamilton 367 G3

Downriver from the city, this area is becoming the latest part of Brisbane to undergo significant urban renewal. At the junction of Breakfast Creek and the Brisbane River, you'll find the historic **Breakfast Creek Hotel**. Built in 1889, this Queensland institution is still going strong. Head here if top-class steak and cold beer make your perfect evening out; the hotel is renowned across Brisbane for its incredible steaks. Nearby is **Breakfast Creek Wharf**, where you can take your pick from numerous seafood restaurants or take a boat tour on the river. Hamilton has some stunning examples of Queensland homes from the 1890s as well as **Brett's Wharf**, the last stop downriver for public water-transport and a short stroll away from the cafes and shops of **Racecourse Road**, which leads to the city's premier racecourse, **Eagle Farm**.

West of the city

The inner-west suburbs of the city follow the Brisbane River upstream and, with an eclectic mix of houses, subtropical greenery and steep hills, it is here you will experience the essence of Brisbane living. Many of the old houses have been restored and most have expansive decks and verandahs, perfect for Brisbane's year-round outdoor lifestyle. The suburbs of Paddington, Red Hill and Milton, closest to the CBD, are full of busy cafe strips, bars, clubs and upmarket shops. Toowong, St Lucia and Taringa are home to an interesting mix of professionals enjoying riverside life and students studying at the nearby **University of Queensland**. With one of Queensland's many unusual names, the suburb of Indooroopilly is home to one of the biggest shopping centres in Brisbane, **Indooroopilly Shopping Centre** (*see Shopping, p. 370*). On your way to the many attractions in the west, take a detour through some of these western suburbs to see the best of Brisbane.

Milton 366 E4

Not only home to the iconic XXXX Brewery (*see next entry*) and the legendary sportsground Lang Park, Milton also has the bustling Park Road, a lively street lined with stylish restaurants and cafes (and endowed with a mock mini Eiffel Tower), leading to the Brisbane River. Shop at the upmarket fashion, jewellery or furniture boutiques or browse in the quality bookshop Coaldrakes. The nearby small suburb of **Rosalie** is also home to some outstanding cafes and shopping – who could go past its dessert-only restaurant, Freestyle Tout?

XXXX Brewery 366 E4

The Castlemaine Perkins XXXX Brewery, at its Milton location since 1878, is a Queensland icon – as is the fourex beer itself. Brisbanites are used to the pungent smell of brewing beer occasionally wafting over nearby suburbs, and the brewery has always been a Brisbane landmark. For beer-loving tourists, the brewery's Ale House is a must. On offer is an interactive tour lasting just over an hour (bookings are recommended); gain an insight into the heritage and workings of the brewery. At the tour's completion,

Multicultural Brunswick Street is in the heart of the Valley

sample four of XXXX's most popular beers in the Ale House Bar. *Cnr Black & Paten sts (just off Milton Rd); (07) 3361 7597; open Mon–Fri; admission fee applies.*

Paddington 366 D4

The streets of this hilly inner-city suburb are lined with old Queenslanders, many lovingly restored. You could easily spend a relaxing day shopping, browsing and eating here. **Caxton Street**, at the Petrie Terrace end of Paddington, has a couple of pubs and a variety of bars and restaurants. **Given Terrace** has excellent restaurants, cafes and antique shops, lovely views of the city, and the popular Paddington Tavern (better known to locals as the Paddo). Some of Brisbane's oldest public buildings are to be found in Paddington (first settled in 1859), especially on Given Terrace and Latrobe Terrace, which also form the suburb's main commercial strips.

Toowong 366 C6

Toowong, between Mount Coot-tha and the Brisbane River, boasts an eclectic mix of modern apartments and classic old Queenslanders. The **Toowong Cemetery** contains about a hundred thousand graves, some dating back to 1875; headstones tell the story of the trials, tribulations and triumphs of Queensland's early settlers. On a lighter note, Toowong is also home to the very popular and beautifully renovated **Regatta Hotel**, built in 1886. Enjoy its fabulous river views in the classy restaurant, the cafe or one of the excellent bars (and make sure you take a trip to the much-talked-about loo with a view). The CityCat stops right outside the hotel.

Mount Coot-tha Forest Park 366 B5

A drive up Mt Coot-tha should be first on your list of things to do in Brisbane. From the **Mt Coot-tha Lookout**, you will see the Brisbane River snaking through leafy suburbs, impressive views of the CBD and, unless it's very hazy, the islands in Moreton Bay. To the west are rugged bush-covered ranges. Look down at your feet and you'll see that the lookout's paving reflects the layout of the city, the river and the ocean. Also in the park are some beautiful walks and picnic areas including the local favourite, **J. C. Slaughter Falls**. From here you can walk to the summit lookout (just over 2 kilometres), follow the Aboriginal Art Trail or simply relax over a barbecue while watching the scrub turkeys dig up the bush. The scenic **Sir Samuel Griffith Drive** links all the major sights in the park.

Mount Coot-tha Botanic Gardens
366 B5

Nestled in the foothills of Mt Coot-tha and only 7 kilometres from the city centre, these botanic gardens are well worth a visit. The highlight is the Tropical Dome, with its superb display of tropical plants. You can also wander through the Bonsai House, the Fern House and the elegant Japanese Garden. The Australian Plant Communities section occupies 27 of the gardens' 52 hectares and showcases an enormous number of native species. Free guided walks are available. The gardens are also home to the recently upgraded **Sir Thomas Brisbane Planetarium**, which features real-time digital star shows and re-creations of Brisbane's night sky. *Mt Coot-tha Rd, Toowong; (07) 3403 2535; open daily; admission free.*

Lone Pine Koala Sanctuary 598 D8

The world's largest koala sanctuary, Lone Pine was opened in 1927 and has over 130 koalas. Visitors can hold koalas, handfeed kangaroos and emus, and watch wombats, Tasmanian devils and many other species in a natural environment. The sanctuary is set on 20 hectares next to the Brisbane River. You can get to Lone Pine by road (it's only 11 kilometres from the city) or catch Mirimar's Wildlife Cruise (*see Walks and tours, p. 373*). There are informative talks daily. *Jesmond Rd, Fig Tree Pocket; open daily; admission fee applies.*

Along the coast

Brisbane may have a relaxed beach feel, but the city is actually set in off the coast. Head to suburbs like Redcliffe and Manly to soak up the beautiful and serene atmosphere of Moreton Bay.

Redcliffe 598 F4

The site of Queensland's first European settlement in 1824, Redcliffe has grown into a thriving seaside city just 30 minutes north-east of Brisbane. The relaxed lifestyle, golden beaches and beautiful foreshore parks are just part of the attraction. The Redcliffe peninsula juts into Moreton Bay and from the top of the volcanic red cliffs there are excellent views of the islands across the bay. Follow one of the heritage trails to see historic buildings (ask at the information centre for brochures). Redcliffe's beaches are perfect for swimming, and fishing from Redcliffe Jetty is a popular local pastime. For a colourful trip back to childhood, visit Pelican Park on the second and fourth Sunday of each month when the Queensland Kiteflyers Society have kite-flying days. (In May Redcliffe hosts the QKS Redcliffe KiteFest, a spectacular display of all things kite.) If watching wildlife is more your thing, tours depart from Redcliffe to watch the humpback whales migrate past the coast in the winter months. *Redcliffe Visitor Information Centre, Pelican Park, Hornibrook Espl, Redcliffe; (07) 3284 3500 or 1800 659 500.*

Day tours

Mount Glorious *The sleepy settlement of Mount Glorious lies to the north-west of Brisbane in Brisbane Forest Park, a 28 500-hectare reserve of subtropical forests and hills. Mount Glorious is the base for a number of enjoyable walking tracks. Nearby Wivenhoe Lookout offers extraordinary views of the surrounding country. For more details see p. 378*

Daisy Hill State Forest *Close to Brisbane's south-eastern suburbs is Daisy Hill State Forest, best known for its large colony of koalas. The Daisy Hill Koala Centre has a variety of displays and, from a tower, you can see koalas in their favourite place – the treetops. For more details see p. 378*

Bribie Island *Connected to the mainland by bridge at Caboolture, Bribie is the most accessible of the Moreton Bay islands. Fishing, boating and crabbing are popular activities. For a quiet picnic and walk, visit Buckleys Hole Conservation Park at the southern end. For more details see p. 379*

Moreton Island *This large scenic sand island is almost completely protected by national park. It is reached by vehicular or passenger ferry from Scarborough or the Brisbane River. Vehicle access is four-wheel drive only, but guided tours are available. Walking, swimming, fishing and dolphin-watching are some of the activities on offer. For more details see p. 379*

North Stradbroke Island *A favourite getaway for Brisbanites, Straddie (as it's known) is the most developed of the Moreton Bay islands. Visit Blue Lake National Park, at the centre of the island, for swimming and walking (access by four-wheel drive or a 45-minute walk), or enjoy ocean views along the North Gorge Headlands Walk. The island is reached by vehicular ferry from Cleveland. For more details see p. 379*

The Gold Coast *An hour's drive from Brisbane, the Gold Coast is Australia's busiest holiday region, with beautiful surf beaches and huge theme parks (perfect for kids of all ages). All activities on offer, from deep-sea fishing and golf to dining and shopping, are of international-resort standard. For more details see p. 380*

(See following page for continuation of Day tours)

QUEENSLAND

Day tours *cont'd*

Gold Coast Hinterland *The 'green behind the gold', as it's called, offers a peaceful retreat from the bustle of the coast. Follow the winding scenic road up to Lamington National Park, part of a World Heritage area and Queensland's most visited park. It preserves a beautiful rainforest environment and a large wildlife population with many bird species, including bowerbirds and lyrebirds. For more details see p. 380*

The Sunshine Coast *With the stylish resort town of Noosa Heads as its northern centre, the Sunshine Coast is a series of relaxed towns and golden beaches. Enjoy the beachside atmosphere, good shopping and scenic beaches (and the superb fish and chips) of Caloundra, Maroochydore and Mooloolaba – long-time favourite holiday spots for many Queenslanders. Inland are the iconic Glass House Mountains, with views all the way to the coast. For more details see p. 383*

Alma Park Zoo 598 E3

Set in award-winning rainforest gardens, the zoo is 28 kilometres north of the city, inland from Redcliffe. It features both Australian and exotic animals and offers many opportunities for interaction. You can touch koalas, feed kangaroos and deer in the walk-through enclosures, and see animals ranging from wombats to camels and monkeys. There are also lots of pretty spots for a picnic lunch. *Alma Rd, Dakabin; open daily; admission fee applies.*

Wynnum–Manly 598 G7

It's hard to believe that this beautiful coastal area is just 15 kilometres east of the city. **Pandanus Beach** is the largest sandy beach in the Wynnum area and offers great swimming. The **Wynnum North Mangrove Circuit** is worth a look, especially for wildlife – watch out for fish and migrating birds. If you're feeling active, a boardwalk skirts the foreshore; hire a bike to ride the 5-kilometre **Esplanade** from Manly to Lota. The **Manly Boat Harbour** is a vista of stunning yachts, and charters and hire boats for both fishing and sailing are available. Tours to the island of St Helena also depart from here. This island is two-thirds national park, and served as a penal settlement between 1867 and 1932. Prison life is recalled in the grim structures that remain. Wynnum–Manly's neighbouring suburbs have a history dating back to the 1860s and boast some interesting historic sights.

North of Wynnum, at the mouth of the Brisbane River, is the 19th-century **Fort Lytton**, surrounded by a moat. A museum at the fort (open only Sundays and public holidays) interprets Queensland's military and social history from 1879. Further north is the **Port of Brisbane**, which offers public tours and includes an informative visitor centre. *Wynnum–Manly Visitor Information Centre, 43A Cambridge Pde, Manly; (07) 3348 3524.*

Cleveland 598 H8

South of Manly, this leafy bayside suburb is the centre of the Redland Bay district. The area is rich in history, so follow the heritage trail from the Old Courthouse to explore it. Try one of the delicious counter meals at Brisbane's oldest pub, the 1851 **Grand View Hotel** – with Queensland's oldest banyan tree out the front. Another historic building **Ormiston House**, built in 1862 and now magnificently restored, was the home of the founder of the Queensland sugarcane industry. Catch a ferry from Cleveland to North Stradbroke Island (*see Day tours, p. 375*). Enjoy the colourful Cleveland Bayside Markets on Sundays.

Redland Bay 598 I10

This peaceful holiday village south of Cleveland has a quaint feel. Known for its markets, gardens and rich red farmlands, Redland Bay also offers good fishing. Boats can be hired along this section of coast – set off to fish and explore the tranquil waters of Moreton Bay.

Aerial view of Manly Boat Harbour

QUEENSLAND'S
REGIONS

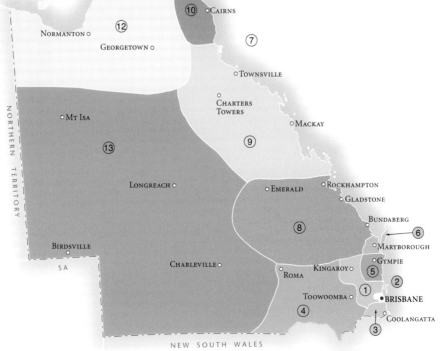

BRISBANE HINTERLAND

King parrots
are one species
to watch for in
the hinterland

Top events

Mar	Pine Rivers Heritage Festival (Strathpine)
	Wine and Food in the Park Festival (Kingaroy)
April	Great Horse Ride (Kilkivan)
May	Pumpkin Festival (Goomeri)
July	Multicultural Festival (Esk)
Aug	Camp Oven Bush Poets Festival (Strathpine)
Sept	Peanut Festival (Kingaroy)
	Spring Festival (Laidley)
Oct	Potato Carnival (Gatton)
	Annual Fishing Competition (Bjelke-Petersen Dam, south-east of Murgon)
	Pioneer Festival (Nanango)

A step away from the bustle of Brisbane are the many attractions of the Brisbane hinterland. The heavily forested hills of the D'Aguilar Range create a subtropical haven just 20 minutes west of the city; the main access point is the hamlet of Mount Glorious, in Brisbane Forest Park. Travel to the Valley of the Lakes near Esk and even further north-west to the South Burnett, with its diverse crops and heritage villages. Here the landscape, including stands of rare pine rainforest, is preserved in Bunya Mountains National Park. Children will love this area too, as there are many opportunities for encounters with native animals.

Focus on

Animal antics

The Walkabout Creek Wildlife Centre, in Brisbane Forest Park, features a freshwater creek environment populated with water dragons, frogs, platypuses, pythons and fish. The Australian Woolshed, just past Samford, re-creates life on a sheep station. Shearing demonstrations, ram shows and cattle-dog demonstrations are staged daily, while native animals roam freely around the property. Daisy Hill State Forest is a pocket of eucalypt forest and acacia scrub 25 kilometres south of Brisbane, where visitors can scan the canopy for koalas from a treetop tower. The Daisy Hill Koala Centre in the central picnic area has information about koalas and their habitats.

Bunya Mountains

This isolated spur of the Great Dividing Range is a cool, moist region of waterfalls, green and scarlet king parrots, and the remaining stands of bunya pine, a species much depleted by early timber-getters. Walk the easy 4 km Scenic Circuit from the Dandabah camping area, which winds through rainforest to Pine Gorge Lookout.

South Burnett

This comfortable slice of rural Queensland invites you to the historic timber towns of Blackbutt and Yarraman, and to wineries along the scenic Barambah Wine Trail. Go to Nanango or Kilkivan to fossick for gold and bed down for the night in a B&B or farmstay.

CLIMATE MOUNT GLORIOUS

	J	F	M	A	M	J	J	A	S	O	N	D
Max °C	25	24	24	21	18	16	15	17	20	22	24	25
Min °C	18	17	17	15	12	10	9	9	11	14	15	17
Rain mm	238	252	222	129	126	84	86	56	57	114	123	167
Raindays	15	16	16	12	11	8	8	7	7	10	11	13

Booubyjan Homestead

Two Irish brothers, the Clements, took up this run near Goomeri in 1847, beginning with sheep and then moving to cattle in the 1880s. Many generations later, the property is still in the family. The homestead, open daily, provides a glimpse of pioneering life in Queensland's early years.

Brisbane Forest Park

Few cities have an attraction such as Brisbane Forest Park on their doorstep, with its pristine rainforest, towering trees, cascading waterfalls, deep pools, mountain streams and incredible wildlife. The small settlement of Mount Glorious is a base for forest walking tracks. Wivenhoe Lookout, 10 km further on, has superb views west to Lake Wivenhoe.

Experience it!

1 **Tour** the Workshops Rail Museum in Ipswich, where Queensland's first train line was launched in 1864

2 **Take** a balloon flight from Laidley, over orchards and market gardens

3 **Drive** the Mount Glorious–Samford Road, one of the state's most scenic routes

For more detail see maps 598, 599, 601 & 607.
For descriptions of ⊕ towns see Towns from A–Z (p. 395).

BRISBANE ISLANDS

North
Stradbroke
Island

T he calm blue waters of Moreton Bay encircle the mouth of the
Brisbane River and extend along the Brisbane coastline. There are
over 350 islands in and around the fringe of this bay, including
the sizeable islands of Moreton, North Stradbroke, St Helena and Bribie.
Despite some development, these islands have managed to retain an
aura of wilderness, with endless white beaches, creeks, lakes, pockets
of eucalpyt forest, wildflowers and wildlife. All, with the exception
of St Helena, are major holiday destinations with a range of facilities
and accommodation. They offer surfing, snorkelling, diving, fishing,
bushwalking and scenic touring.

Top events

Aug Straddie Fishing Classic (North Stradbroke Island, biggest fishing competition in Australia)

Sept Festival in Ruins (celebrates history and ecology of St Helena Island)

Sept/ Oct Bribie Island Festival (including mullet-throwing competition)

Focus on
Marine life
The marine population of Moreton Bay includes dolphins, whales, dugongs and turtles. Visitors to Moreton Island can see dolphins at the Tangalooma Wild Dolphin Resort, where a care program has been developed, or at several spots along the western shore. Migrating humpback whales can be seen between July and November from Cape Moreton and from North Gorge Headland on North Stradbroke Island. Pumicestone Channel, between Bribie and the mainland, is a haven for turtles, dolphins and dugongs. Diving and snorkelling facilities are available on all three islands, allowing visitors to explore the crystal waters and rich underwater life of this magnificent bay.

CLIMATE **MORETON ISLAND**

	J	F	M	A	M	J	J	A	S	O	N	D
Max °C	33	32	32	32	31	30	30	31	32	34	35	34
Min °C	23	23	23	21	19	18	17	16	18	20	21	23
Rain mm	326	331	287	115	22	10	8	4	5	17	65	198
Raindays	20	20	19	11	6	4	4	2	2	2	5	12

Bribie Island
About a third of Bribie is protected by national park. See the magnificent birdlife and spectacular wildflower displays on one of the Bicentennial bushwalks, or go fishing, boating or crabbing. Woorim, in the south-east, is an old-fashioned resort with great surfing beaches. Nearby, Buckleys Hole Conservation Park has good picnic spots for daytrippers and walking tracks to the beach. The island is connected to the mainland by bridge east of Caboolture.

St Helena Island
This low sandy island, 8 km from the mouth of the Brisbane River, was used as a prison from 1867 to 1932. It was dubbed 'the hell-hole of the South Pacific'. Historic ruins remain and are protected in the island's national park. Tours of the island depart from the Brisbane suburbs of Manly and Breakfast Creek.

Experience it!
❶ **Swim** in the beautiful freshwater Blue Lake on North Stradbroke Island

❷ **Walk** to Queensland's oldest operating lighthouse (1857) at the tip of Cape Moreton

❸ **Go** crabbing in Pumicestone Channel off Bribie Island

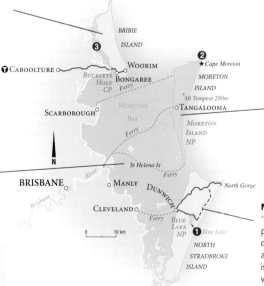

For more detail see maps 599, 601 & 607.
For descriptions of ❶ towns see Towns from A–Z (p. 395).

Moreton Island
Almost all of this large island is national park. It is also mainly sand, with 280 m Mt Tempest possibly the world's highest stable sandhill. On the east coast is an unbroken 36 km surf beach, with calmer beaches on the west coast. Get to the island by passenger or vehicular ferry from Scarborough or the Brisbane River. A four-wheel drive and a permit are required for self-drive touring.

North Stradbroke Island
'Straddie' is a coastal and bushland paradise, with contained pockets of development. Blue Lake National Park is an ecologically significant wetland; access is by four-wheel drive or a 45-minute walk. Other island walking trails include the popular North Gorge Headland Walk. Travel to North Stradbroke by vehicular ferry from Cleveland. The ferry arrives at Dunwich, the site of a 19th-century quarantine and penal centre.

QUEENSLAND

GOLD COAST & HINTERLAND

Some four million visitors arrive each year to holiday along the Gold Coast's 70 kilometres of coastline, which stretches from South Stradbroke Island to the New South Wales border and includes no less than 35 beautiful beaches. Shopping, restaurants, nightlife, family entertainment, high-rise hotels, golf, fishing, sailing, surfing and unbelievably good weather – around 300 days of sunshine per year – are the trademark features of what has become Australia's biggest and busiest holiday destination. To the west lies the Gold Coast hinterland, another world altogether. Here a superb natural landscape of tropical rainforests, unusual rock formations and cascading waterfalls – much of it protected by national park – offers visitors nature-based activities such as bushwalking, camping and wildlife-watching.

Surfers at Coolangatta

Experience it!

❶ **Try** your luck at Conrad Jupiters Casino at Broadbeach

❷ **Hop** on a trolley at Tamborine Mountain to see the sights of the mountain retreat

❸ **Stroll** across the treetops on the rainforest canopy walk at Green Mountains, in Lamington National Park

❹ **Board** a charter at Surfers Paradise to fish for mackerel, tuna, bonito and snapper

❺ **Take** a scenic flight from Broadbeach aboard a Tiger Moth plane

CLIMATE COOLANGATTA

	J	F	M	A	M	J	J	A	S	O	N	D
Max °C	28	28	27	25	23	21	20	21	22	24	26	26
Min °C	20	20	19	17	13	11	9	10	12	15	17	19
Rain mm	184	181	213	114	124	122	96	103	49	108	137	166
Raindays	14	15	16	14	10	9	7	9	9	11	11	13

Focus on
Golden beaches

The Gold Coast is a surfers' mecca and, mixed with the fabulous weather, also the perfect destination for a relaxing beach holiday. Best for surfers are the southern beaches, including Currumbin and Kirra Point (in Coolangatta), said to have one of the ten best breaks in the world. Greenmount Beach, also in Coolangatta, is great for families, as is Tallebudgera, north of Palm Beach, which offers both estuary and ocean swimming. Towards Surfers Paradise the crowds get larger, but the beaches are still spectacular. Surfers Paradise is renowned for its beachfront – try out your volleyball skills in the free competition near Cavill Avenue. There is an open-ocean beach on The Spit, near Main Beach, with the marine park Sea World close by. For a more remote option, try the 22 kilometres of beach on the east coast of South Stradbroke Island. Once you've soaked up enough magnificent Gold Coast sunshine, you could explore the island's wetlands and rainforest.

Top events

Jan	Magic Millions Racing Carnival (Gold Coast Turf Club)
Mar	Australian Beach Volleyball Championships (Surfers Paradise)
April	Carp Busters Fishing Competition (Beaudesert)
May	Blues Music Festival (Broadbeach)
May–June	Gold Coast Cup Outrigger Canoe Marathon (Coolangatta)
June	Wintersun Festival (Coolangatta)
	Country and Horse Festival (Beaudesert)
July	Gold Coast Marathon (Runaway Bay)
Aug	Australian Arena Polo Championships (Nerang)
Aug–Sept	Gold Coast Show (Southport)
Oct	Springtime on the Mountain (Tamborine Mountain)
	Indy 300 (Surfers Paradise)
	Gold Coast Tropicarnival (Surfers Paradise)
Nov	Australian Music Week (Surfers Paradise)

Warner Bros. Movie World
This popular theme park south of Oxenford offers visitors the chance to 'meet' their favourite Hollywood characters and see the business of movie-making up close. Studio tours, stunt shows and roving Looney Tune characters are a few of the many features. Rides include the Scooby Doo Spooky Coaster, Lethal Weapon, the Wild West Falls Adventure and the Road Runner Rollercoaster (for the toddlers).

Golf at Sanctuary Cove
With 40 courses, the Gold Coast is one of the Southern Hemisphere's great golfing destinations. Sanctuary Cove boasts two championship courses: the exclusive Pines, one of the toughest, and the immaculate Palms, designed around groves of cabbage palms. Pick up a golfing guide from the Gold Coast Tourism Bureau.

The Broadwater
This calm expanse, fringed by waterfront houses and protected by the long finger of South Stradbroke Island, is popular for boating and fishing. Land-based anglers can try the breakwalls inside the Broadwater's southern entrance. Here visitors can hire boats to explore this waterway and its tributaries.

South Stradbroke Island
South Stradbroke, separated from North Stradbroke by the popular fishing channel Jumpinpin, is a peaceful alternative to the Gold Coast. Access is by launch from Runaway Bay. Cars are not permitted; once on the island visitors must walk or cycle. There are two resorts, a camping ground, a range of leisure activities, and beautiful beaches.

Surfers Paradise
Surfers Paradise is the Gold Coast's signature settlement – high-rise apartments fronting one of the state's most beautiful beaches. The first big hotel was built here in the 1930s, among little more than a clutch of shacks. Since then the area has become an international holiday metropolis attracting every kind of visitor, from backpacker to jetsetter.

Tamborine Mountain
This 552 m plateau lies on the Darlington Range, a spur of the McPherson Range and a popular spot for hang-gliders. Tamborine National Park comprises 17 small areas, one being Witches Falls, the first national park area in the state. Nearby visitors will find villages full of galleries, cafes, antique stores and craft shops, and a couple of beautiful gardens.

Lamington National Park
Part of a World Heritage area, this popular park preserves a wonderland of rainforest and volcanic ridges, criss-crossed by 160 km of walking tracks and filled with rich plant and animal life. The main picnic, camping and walking areas are at Binna Burra and Green Mountains, sites of the award-winning Binna Burra Lodge and O'Reilly's Rainforest Guest House.

Currumbin Wildlife Sanctuary
Be captivated by the wild and roaming animals in this National Trust reserve. The crocodile wetlands let you get up close, and the daily feedings in the aviary make for a loud and exciting experience. For weary legs, take the miniature railway around this 20 ha sanctuary.

For more detail see maps 599, 600 & 607.
For descriptions of ⊕ towns see Towns from A–Z (p. 395).

Lush subtropical rainforest in Lamington National Park

DARLING DOWNS

Jondaryan Woolshed

Top events

Feb	Melon Festival (Chinchilla, odd-numbered years)
Mar	Cotton Week (Dalby)
Easter	National Rock Swap Festival (Warwick)
May	Opera in the Vineyards (Ballandean Estate Winery)
Aug	Australian Heritage Festival (Jondaryan Woolshed)
Sept	Miles Country Music Spectacular
	Carnival of Flowers (Toowoomba)
Oct	Granite Belt Spring Wine Festival (Stanthorpe)
	Rose and Rodeo Festival (Warwick)

The Darling Downs, beginning 100 kilometres west of Brisbane, is a huge agricultural district spread across 72 000 square kilometres of undulating plains, 900 metres above sea level. The region's rich volcanic soil yields grapes, oilseeds and wheat, as well as some of the country's most magnificent gardens. Throughout the countryside, English-style plantings of elms, plane trees and poplars fringe green pastures, neat grainfields and historic towns. National parks preserve a native landscape of eucalypt forests and granite outcrops. Part of the attraction to this region lies in its traditional winter season, something which much of the rest of Queensland lacks; winter, called the 'Brass Monkey Season', is a popular time for touring.

Focus on

Gardens of the Downs

The climate and soils of the Darling Downs have created one of Australia's great gardening districts. Toowoomba has 150 public parks and gardens, including Ju Raku En (a Japanese garden), the Scented Garden – for visually impaired people – and the 6 hectares mountainside Boyce Gardens, with 700 species of trees, shrubs and perennials. Warwick is known for its roses, particularly the red 'City of Warwick', best seen in the Jubilee Gardens. There are superb private gardens throughout the region – some open daily, some seasonally and some as part of the Open Garden Scheme; check with an information centre for details.

CLIMATE TOOWOOMBA

	J	F	M	A	M	J	J	A	S	O	N	D
Max °C	28	27	26	23	20	17	16	18	21	24	26	28
Min °C	17	17	15	12	9	6	5	6	9	12	14	16
Rain mm	135	122	95	63	60	58	54	40	48	73	89	120
Raindays	12	11	11	8	8	8	7	6	7	8	10	11

Jondaryan Woolshed

This 1859 woolshed on historic Jondaryan Station is the centrepiece of a complex of old farm buildings. Sheepdog and shearing demonstrations are held daily, and for a taste of yesteryear, sit down for a yarn over the billy tea and damper.

Allora

This evocative town lies just off the highway between Toowoomba and Warwick. Victorian verandahed shopfronts and three old timber hotels line the main street. St David's Anglican Church (1888) is one of Queensland's finest timber churches. Glengallan Homestead, south of town, was built in 1867, during the golden age of pastoralism.

For more detail see maps 606–7.
For descriptions of ❶ towns see Towns from A–Z (p. 395).

The Toowoomba Japanese garden

A thousand visitors a week stroll the 3 km of paths at Ju Raku En, a Japanese garden at the University of Southern Queensland. Opened in 1989, it showcases the harmony and beauty of ancient Japanese garden design with its lake, willowy beeches, islands, bridges, stream and pavilion.

Experience it!

❶ **Enjoy** magnificent views of the Lockyer Valley from Toowoomba's Picnic Point

❷ **Visit** Queen Mary Falls in the southern section of Main Range National Park

❸ **Take** in Warwick's magnificent sandstone architecture on the city's self-guide trail

Granite Belt wineries

Queensland's only significant wine region is on an 800 m plateau in the Great Dividing Range, around Ballandean and Stanthorpe. Over 40 boutique wineries, many with tastings and sales, grow major grape varieties on the well-drained granite soils, favouring soft reds made from shiraz and merlot grapes.

Map labels: ROMA, MILES, CHINCHILLA, SURAT, MOONIE, ST GEORGE, PITTSWORTH, DALBY, CROWS NEST, OAKEY, TOOWOOMBA, JONDARYAN, CLIFTON, MAIN RANGE NP, ALLORA, MILLMERRAN, WARWICK, KILLARNEY, GOONDIWINDI, STANTHORPE, BALLANDEAN, GIRRAWEEN NP, TEXAS, GREAT DIVIDING RANGE, NEW SOUTH WALES, RANGE, 0 50 km, N

SUNSHINE COAST

Glass House
Mountains

Beautiful beaches, bathed by the blue South Pacific and fringed by native bush, stretch from Rainbow Beach south to the tip of Bribie Island to form the Sunshine Coast. The weather is near-perfect, with winter temperatures around 25°C. Holiday towns cater for the varied interests of holidaymakers, from golf and fishing to fine dining and the cafe life. Inland are the forested folds and ridges of the hinterland, including the quaint villages and hamlets of the Blackall Range where visitors can enjoy waterfalls, walks, scenic drives and superb views. In the south of the region, the Glass House Mountains loom above the surrounding plains.

Top events

Jan	Ginger Flower Festival (Yandina)
April	Sunshine Coast Festival of the Sea (throughout region)
	Robert Pryde Memorial Surf Classic (Rainbow Beach)
Aug	Country Music Muster (Amamoor State Forest, near Gympie)
Sept	Bush to Bay Seafood Fun Day (Tin Can Bay)
	Jazz Festival (Noosa Heads)
Oct	Gold Rush Festival (Gympie)
	Scarecrow Festival (Maleny)
	Yarn Festival (Mapleton)

Focus on

Tropical produce

The Sunshine Coast hinterland, with its subtropical climate and volcanic soils, is renowned for its produce. Nambour's Big Pineapple symbolises the importance of food as an industry and a tourist attraction. Visitors can take a train, trolley and boat through a plantation growing pineapples and other fruit, macadamia nuts, spices and flowers. Yandina's Ginger Factory, the world's largest, sells ginger products including ginger ice-cream. For freshly picked local fruit and vegetables, visit the Saturday morning markets at Eumundi, north of Yandina. The Superbee Honey Factory, south of Buderim, has beekeeping demonstrations and 28 varieties of honey for tasting.

The coloured sands of Teewah

Located in the Cooloola section of Great Sandy National Park, these coloured sands rise in 40 000-year-old cliffs. It is thought that oxidisation or decaying vegetation has caused the colouring; Aboriginal legend attributes it to the slaying of a rainbow serpent.

Mountain villages

The 70 km scenic drive here is one of Queensland's best. Starting on the Bruce Highway near Landsborough, it passes the antique shops, B&Bs, galleries and cafes of the pretty mountain villages of Maleny, Montville, Flaxton and Mapleton, offering beautiful coastal and mountain views along the way. The drive ends near Nambour.

CLIMATE NAMBOUR

	J	F	M	A	M	J	J	A	S	O	N	D
Max °C	30	29	28	26	24	22	21	22	25	27	28	29
Min °C	19	20	18	15	12	9	8	8	10	14	16	18
Rain mm	242	262	236	149	143	91	92	53	48	105	141	176
Raindays	16	18	18	13	13	9	9	8	9	12	12	13

Coastal towns

The southern towns of Caloundra, Mooloolaba and Maroochydore make pleasant daytrips from Brisbane or good spots for an extended family holiday, with patrolled surfing beaches and protected lakes and rivers for boating and fishing. Central Noosa Heads offers luxury hotels, top restaurants, hip bars and stylish boutiques, as well as the pandanus-fringed beaches of Noosa National Park.

Glass House Mountains

These 20 million-year-old crags, the giant cores of extinct volcanoes, mark the southern entrance to the Sunshine Coast. Glass House Mountains Road leads to sealed and unsealed routes through the mountains, with some spectacular lookouts along the way. There are walking trails, picnic grounds, and challenges aplenty for rockclimbers.

Experience it!

1 **Glide** along Noosa River in a gondola at sunset, with champagne and music to set the scene

2 **Experience** the transparent tunnel at the UnderWater World complex, Mooloolaba

3 **Fish** for bream, flathead, whiting and dart in the surf along Rainbow Beach

For more detail see maps 601, 602 & 607.
For descriptions of towns see Towns from A–Z (p. 395).

FRASER ISLAND & COAST

*Fishing on
Fraser Island*

This region has two of Queenland's signature attractions: Hervey Bay, a large resort town with the best whale-watching in Australia, and Fraser Island, a nature-based holiday destination just offshore. Offering spectacular white beaches, coloured sand cliffs, dunes, creeks, lakes, wildflower heathland and rainforest, Fraser is best explored by four-wheel drive or on foot. Hervey Bay offers a range of accommodation and other facilities. The heritage town of Maryborough and the calm waters of Great Sandy Strait are among the region's other attractions.

For more detail see map 607.
For descriptions of ❶ towns
see Towns from A–Z (p. 395).

Top events

Feb	*Yagubi Festival (multicultural festival, Hervey Bay)*
Easter	*Amateur Fishing Classic (Burrum Heads)*
May	*Bay to Bay Yacht Race (Tin Can Bay to Hervey Bay)*
Aug	*Whale Festival (Hervey Bay)*

Focus on

Whale-watching

At the start of winter humpback whales begin migrating to the warmer waters of Hervey Bay. Visitors are never far behind them, many making their way up the coast for the chance to see these amazing creatures offshore. Each year around 2000 humpback whales migrate from the Antarctic to Australia's eastern subtropical coast. Between July and November, up to 400 rest and regroup in Hervey Bay. For an up-close view of the majestic whales, various tours operate from the boat harbour in town.

CLIMATE MARYBOROUGH

	J	F	M	A	M	J	J	A	S	O	N	D
Max °C	31	30	29	27	25	22	22	23	26	28	29	31
Min °C	21	21	19	17	13	10	9	9	12	15	18	20
Rain mm	166	173	159	90	80	67	54	40	43	75	85	128
Raindays	13	14	14	12	11	8	7	6	6	8	9	11

Great Sandy Strait

This narrow strait between the mainland and Fraser Island makes for good boating; there are houseboats and other vessels for hire. Drop into the Kingfisher Bay Resort and Village on Fraser Island, facing the strait. Look out for dugongs, the world's only plant-eating marine mammals, and fish at the mouth of the Mary River, around River Heads.

Maryborough Heritage Walk and Drive

Established in 1847, Maryborough is one of Queensland's oldest and best-preserved provincial cities. A self-guide brochure leads visitors through tree-lined streets, past heritage sites and well-restored Queenslander houses, and along the historic streetscape of Wharf Street.

Experience it!

❶ Visit the Thursday heritage markets in Maryborough

❷ Catch the July–October run of tailor on the northern half of Fraser Island's Seventy Five Mile Beach

❸ Swim in the dazzling blue Lake McKenzie on Fraser Island

Hervey Bay

This once sleepy settlement is now a booming resort town. The bay itself is a large, calm body of water warmed by tropical currents. The area's protected beaches are perfect for family swimming. Other popular activities include sailing, diving, windsurfing, fishing, kayaking and skydiving.

Fraser Island's dingoes

Roaming around on the world's largest sand island is what is thought to be the purest strain of dingoes in eastern Australia. By the time dingoes arrived on the mainland – they came with Asian seafarers around 5000 years ago – Fraser Island was already disconnected from the continent, and the dingoes swam the few kilometres across Great Sandy Strait. Unlike most mainland dingoes, they are largely free of hybridisation with domestic dogs.

WARNING: Dingoes have been known to attack. Stay with small children and never feed or coax animals.

Fraser Island's east coast

Fraser Island's east coast, also its surf coast, has an alluring list of attractions. It takes in the beautiful Seventy Five Mile Beach; The Cathedrals, 15 m sheer cliffs composed of different-coloured sands; the wreck of the *Maheno*, a trans-Tasman luxury liner; and Eli Creek, a freshwater creek filtered through the dunes, where visitors can float beneath the pandanus trees.

GREAT BARRIER REEF

Hardy Reef, near the Whitsundays

The reef is Australia's most prized and visited natural destination. Extending over 2000 kilometres along the coast of Queensland, this breathtakingly beautiful marine environment features tropical islands, aquamarine waters, rare and brilliantly coloured corals, seagrass beds, fish, and sea-going mammals and birds. It is considered to be one of the world's great destinations for diving, sailing and a large number of other activities, including fishing, swimming, windsurfing and kayaking. Only 22 of the reef's 900 islands cater for tourists. Some of these support large resorts with every level of accommodation, while others are completely protected by national park and offer camping only. Daytrips from the mainland are a popular way of seeing the reef for those with limited time.

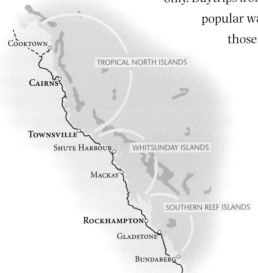

For more detail see maps 603, 604, 605, 607, 609 & 611. For descriptions of ⊤ towns see Towns from A–Z (p. 395).

ISLAND ACCESS

Tropical North Islands

Magnetic Island *8 km NE of Townsville*
From Townsville, by vehicular ferry, catamaran or water taxi.

Orpheus Island *80 km N of Townsville*
From Townsville or Cairns, by sea plane.

Hinchinbrook Island *5 km E of Cardwell*
From Cardwell, by launch.

Bedarra Island *35 km NE of Cardwell*
From Dunk Island, by launch.

Dunk Island *5 km SE of Mission Beach*
From Cairns, by plane. From Clump Point near Mission Beach, by launch. From Wongaling Beach and South Mission Beach, by water taxi.

Fitzroy Island *30 km SE of Cairns*
From Cairns, by catamaran.

Green Island *27 km NE of Cairns*
From Cairns, by catamaran, sea plane or helicopter.

Lizard Island *93 km NE of Cooktown*
From Cairns or Cooktown, by plane or sea plane.

Whitsunday Islands

Brampton Island *32 km NE of Mackay*
From Mackay, by light plane or launch. From Hamilton Island, by plane.

Lindeman Island *67 km N of Mackay*
From Airlie Beach or Shute Harbour, by light plane or boat. From Mackay, by plane. From Hamilton Island, by boat or plane.

Hamilton Island *16 km SE of Shute Harbour*
Direct flight from Sydney, Brisbane and Melbourne; connections from all major cities. From Shute Harbour, by launch.

Long Island *9 km SE of Shute Harbour*
From Shute Harbour or Hamilton Island, by launch or helicopter. From Whitsunday Airport (near Proserpine), by sea plane.

South Molle Island *8 km E of Shute Harbour*
From Shute Harbour or Hamilton Island, by launch.

Daydream Island *5 km NE Shute Harbour*
From Shute Harbour or Hamilton Island, by launch or helicopter.

Whitsunday Island *25 km E of Shute Harbour*
From Shute Harbour or Airlie Beach, by boat.

Hook Island *20 km NE of Shute Harbour*
From Shute Harbour or Airlie Beach, by launch.

Hayman Island *25 km NE of Shute Harbour*
Direct flight to Hamilton Island from Sydney and Brisbane (connections from all major cities), then by launch to Hayman Island. From Airlie Beach, by water taxi.

Southern Reef Islands

Lady Elliot Island *80 km NE of Bundaberg*
From Bundaberg or Hervey Bay, by plane.

Lady Musgrave Island *105 km N of Bundaberg*
From Bundaberg, by sea plane, catamaran or trimaran. From Seventeen Seventy, by catamaran.

Heron Island *72 km NE of Gladstone*
From Gladstone, by catamaran or charter helicopter.

North West Island *75 km NE of Gladstone*
From Gladstone, by charter boat.

Great Keppel Island *48 km NE of Rockhampton*
From Rockhampton, by light plane. From Yeppoon, by launch.

QUEENSLAND

Tropical North Islands

Fitzroy Island

Lizard Island
Northernmost island with tourist facilities. Gamefishing, snorkelling, diving and bushwalking. Small, luxurious resort with bungalow-style lodgings (max 80 people) or camping (max 20 people); camping permits from Cairns parks office.

Green Island
True coral cay covered with thick tropical vegetation. Glass-bottomed boats for reef viewing, also underwater observatory. Popular daytrip destination with small resort (max 90 people).

Dunk Island
National park with walking tracks through rainforest, and prolific birdlife, butterflies and wild orchids. Parasailing, waterskiing, sailing, clay-target shooting and horseriding. Resort accommodation (max 360 people) and camping (max 30 people).

Bedarra Island
Island of untouched tropical beauty, off-limits to day visitors and children under 15. Bushwalking, snorkelling, fishing, swimming, windsurfing, sailing and tennis. Exclusive resort (max 30 people).

CLIMATE FITZROY ISLAND

	J	F	M	A	M	J	J	A	S	O	N	D
Max °C	31	30	29	28	26	24	24	25	27	29	30	31
Min °C	12	12	10	8	7	5	4	5	6	7	9	10
Rain (mm)	27	25	31	60	89	100	106	103	86	68	40	35
Raindays	6	5	7	11		5	18	17	18	15	13	9	7

Fitzroy Island
Low-key destination with national park, white coral beaches and magnificent flora and fauna. Bushwalking, diving and snorkelling. Cabins and hostel-style accommodation (max 160 people) and camping (max 20 people).

Hinchinbrook Island
National park with wonderland of mountains, tropical vegetation, waterfalls and sandy beaches. Snorkelling, swimming, fishing and bushwalking. Small, low-key resort (max 45 people).

Orpheus Island
Small island surrounded by coral reefs and protected by national park. Birdwatching, watersports, glass-bottomed boat tours, island walks and fishing. Five-star resort (max 74 people) or bush camping (max 54 people); camping permits from Ingham parks office.

Magnetic Island
With national park and beautiful beaches. Horseriding, bushwalking, snorkelling, parasailing, swimming, fishing, sea-kayaking and reef excursions. Permanent population and range of accommodation from budget to deluxe.

Whitsunday Islands

Long Island
Part of Conway National Park. Walking tracks leading to scenic lookouts, plus watersports, fishing and resort activities. Three resorts: Club Crocodile (max 400 people), Palm Bay (max 60 people) and Whitsunday Wilderness Lodge (max 16 people).

Lindeman Island
Secluded beaches, national park, and prolific birds and butterflies. Golf course, and full range of watersports and other island activities. Club Med resort (max 460 people).

Brampton Island
National park and wildlife sanctuary with fine golden beaches. Snorkelling trail, bushwalking, sea-plane trips and watersports. Resort-style accommodation (max 280 people).

Daydream Island
Small island of volcanic rock, coral and dense tropical foliage. Kids Club, tennis, outdoor cinema, watersports centre, snorkelling, diving, and reef and island trips. Luxurious resort (max 900 people).

Hayman Island
Close to the outer reef. Fishing, sightseeing trips, scenic flights, diving, watersports, Kids Club, and whale-watching excursions. Luxury resort (max 450 people).

Hook Island
Small low-key wilderness resort with cabins and campsites (max 140 people). Snorkelling, scuba diving, fishing, reef trips, submarine trips and fish-feeding.

South Molle Island
Numerous inlets and splendid views of Whitsunday Passage, plus great wildflowers in spring and early summer. Golf, bushwalking, snorkelling, scuba diving, windsurfing and sailing. Medium-size resort (max 520 people).

Whitsunday Island
Entirely uninhabited national park. Beautiful 7 km white silica beach and complex mangrove system. Camping only (max 40 people); details from Airlie Beach parks office.

Hamilton Island
Large island with wide range of facilities and activities. Shops, marina and fauna park. Windsurfing, sailing, fishing, scuba diving, parasailing, helicopter rides, tennis, squash, and reef and inter-island trips. Resort (max 1500 people).

SHUTE HARBOUR
AIRLIE BEACH
MACKAY
N
0   100 km

CLIMATE HAMILTON ISLAND												
	J	F	M	A	M	J	J	A	S	O	N	D
Max °C	30	30	29	27	25	23	22	23	25	28	29	30
Min °C	25	25	24	23	21	19	18	18	20	22	23	24
Rain (mm)	13	322	262	242	159	100	80	59	23	52	89	215
Raindays	15	18	19	19	18	12	10	11	7	8	8	13

Southern Reef Islands

CLIMATE LADY ELLIOT ISLAND												
	J	F	M	A	M	J	J	A	S	O	N	D
Max °C	29	29	28	27	24	22	21	22	24	25	27	28
Min °C	24	24	23	22	20	18	17	17	19	20	22	23
Rain (mm)	27	174	133	106	120	93	99	58	38	59	71	86
Raindays	13	15	15	15	15	12	10	9	8	9	8	10

Heron Island
Small coral cay, entirely national park. Turtle-nesting site, birdwatching and prolific flora. Diving and snorkelling, and reef and ecology walks. Resort-style accommodation (max 250 people).

North West Island
Second largest coral cay on reef. Superb bird- and turtle-watching opportunities. Camping only (max 150 people); permit from Gladstone parks office.

Great Keppel Island
White, sandy beaches and unspoiled tropical island scenery. Tennis, waterskiing, diving, snorkelling, fishing, sea-kayaking, golf, parasailing, coral viewing and island cruises. Kids Club during holidays. Camping, cabins and lodge-style accommodation (max 650 people).

Lady Musgrave Island
Coral cay with navigable lagoon. Glass-bottomed boats, floating pontoon, submarine (semi-submersible), prolific birdlife and turtle-nesting site. Camping only (max 50 people); permit from Gladstone parks office.

ROCKHAMPTON
GLADSTONE
N
0   100 km
BUNDABERG

Snorkelling off Lady Elliot Island

Lady Elliot Island
Small coral cay with 19 major dive sites. Bird rookeries, turtle-nesting site and whale-watching opportunities. Low-key resort (max 140 people), ranging from budget to island suites.

QUEENSLAND

CAPRICORN

Spanning the Tropic of Capricorn, this highly productive region combines tourism with mining, industry, agriculture and cattle-raising. Offshore lie the southernmost islands of the Great Barrier Reef. The coastline is relatively untouched by commercial development. Remote beaches and river estuaries with unspoiled coastal bushland are found in the national parks of the Discovery Coast, south of Gladstone. Inland, the eroded sandstone plateaus of the Great Dividing Range rise abruptly from the plains, most notably in Carnarvon and Blackdown Tableland national parks. Most of Queensland's coal exports come from open-cut mines around Blackwater. Mining also occurs in gemfields west of Emerald. The area has three big towns: Bundaberg, a centre for sugarcane, subtropical fruits and vegetables; Gladstone, a major port and industrial centre; and Rockhampton, a cattle town servicing properties in the Fitzroy River valley and to the west.

The Chimneys, Mount Moffatt section, Carnarvon National Park

Experience it!

① **Visit** the Dreamtime Cultural Centre, north of Rockhampton, and learn about the Darumbal people, the original inhabitants of the Fitzroy River area

② **Savour** a mud-crab sandwich at Miriam Vale's Shell Roadhouse

③ **Watch** crocodiles feeding and baby crocs hatching at the Koorana Crocodile Farm, Keppel Sands

④ **Canoe**, fish, ski, sail or swim in the vast, calm Lake Awoonga

⑤ **See** the 25 million-year-old Mystery Craters, north-east of Gin Gin

Focus on

Discovery Coast
Seventeen Seventy, a small town on a narrow, hilly peninsula above an estuary, was named to mark Captain Cook's landing at Bustard Bay on 24 May 1770. The main access is from Miriam Vale on the Bruce Highway (a 60-kilometre journey on a partly sealed road). Today's visitors come for the views from the headland north across the bay, and for fishing, mudcrabbing and boating. Agnes Water, a few kilometres south, has Queensland's northernmost surfing beach; rolling surf and a balmy climate attract visitors all year round. Eurimbula National Park, just across Round Hill Inlet from Seventeen Seventy, has dunes, mangroves, salt marshes and eucalypt forests. From Agnes Water, an 8-kilometre track south to Deepwater National Park is suitable for four-wheel drives only. The long beaches of this park, broken by the estuaries of freshwater creeks, form a breeding ground for loggerhead turtles.

Top events

Mar	1770 Longboard Classic (surfing competion, Agnes Water)
Easter	Harbour Festival (Gladstone, includes finish of Brisbane–Gladstone Yacht Race)
	Sunflower Festival (Emerald)
June	Country Music Festival (Biloela)
	Rocky Roundup (Rockhampton)
	Orange Festival (Gayndah, odd-numbered years)
July	Multicultural Food and Wine Festival (Childers)
Aug	Gemfest (Emerald)
Sept	Yeppoon Tropical Pinefest
	Bundy in Bloom Festival (Bundaberg)
	Seafood Festival (Gladstone)
Oct	Rocky Barra Bounty (Rockhampton)

CLIMATE ROCKHAMPTON

	J	F	M	A	M	J	J	A	S	O	N	D
Max °C	32	31	30	29	26	23	23	25	27	30	31	32
Min °C	22	22	21	18	14	11	9	11	14	17	19	21
Rain mm	136	141	103	47	52	35	31	29	24	48	68	105
Raindays	11	12	10	7	7	5	5	4	4	7	8	10

The gemfields
Some of the world's richest sapphire fields are found around the tiny, ramshackle settlements of Anakie, Sapphire, Rubyvale and Willows Gemfields, some 50 km west of Emerald. The same area yields zircons, amethysts, rubies and topaz. Fossicking licences can be bought on the gemfields for a small fee. But if you don't find what you're after on the gemfields, you may have better luck in one of the area's many gemstone retail outlets.

Blackdown Tableland National Park
This undulating 800 m high sandstone plateau of open forest, heath, waterfalls and gorges lies 50 km south-east of Blackwater. There is a camping ground at Mimosa Creek, a gorge with swimming holes at Rainbow Falls, and a number of scenic trails. Visit Sunset Lookout for superb sunrise and sunset views.

Carnarvon National Park
Carnarvon Gorge, the signature attraction of Carnarvon National Park, bends and twists its way around 30 km of semi-arid terrain. Within its sandstone walls exists a cool, green world of delicate ferns and mosses fed by Carnarvon Creek. The 298 000 ha park, 250 km south of Emerald, also contains some magnificent Aboriginal rock-art sites. You can camp near the gorge during most school holidays, but accommodation is available year-round at two nearby lodges.

Australia's beef capital
Over two million cattle graze in the Fitzroy River valley and surrounding countryside, west of Rockhampton. The town has many heritage buildings – particularly grand are the buildings in Quay Street. There is also an excellent discovery centre at the Customs House, and the historic botanic gardens are worth a look. Try your luck in the Fitzroy River, especially in the section close to town, to snag a barramundi.

Rum town
On the southern coast of the Capricorn region is Bundaberg, home of 'Bundy' rum. This is an area of major sugar production – see the spectacular cane fires during harvest season (July–November). Bundaberg is also renowned for its parks and gardens, in particular the Botanical Gardens, with the excellent Hinkler House Memorial Museum and steam-train rides that operate every Sunday.

Capricorn Coast
Thirteen beaches stretch out along Keppel Bay, taking in Yeppoon, Emu Park and Keppel Sands. Picturesque bays are framed by rocky headlands, pockets of rainforest, peaceful estuarine waters and wetlands – some of the natural features that have helped make the sunny Capricorn Coast a popular resort area.

Industrial powerhouse
Gladstone has Queensland's biggest power station, the world's largest alumina plant and aluminium refinery, Australia's biggest cement plant and Queensland's largest multi-cargo port. Tours of the major industries are available. The town is built around a magnificent deep-water harbour, which, despite industry, retains much of its natural beauty.

Mon Repos turtle rookery
Mon Repos Conservation Park, 15 km north-east of Bundaberg, is one of Australia's most important turtle rookeries. Sea turtles lay eggs in the sand from November to January, and the young emerge and make for the sea from mid-January to March. In season there is an on-site interpretative centre and guided night tours.

Mount Morgan
This goldmining town south of Rockhampton has hardly changed in a century, except for the mountain of the town's name, which is now a large crater. Take a tour to the Southern Hemisphere's largest excavation, or see the ancient dinosaur footprints in nearby caves. Other highlights include the heritage railway station, the museum and the cemetery, containing graves of Chinese workers and other nationals.

Map labels:
RUBYVALE, SAPPHIRE, EMERALD, WILLOWS GEMFIELDS, ANAKIE, BLACKWATER, SPRINGSURE, BLACKDOWN TABLELAND NP, *Fitzroy R.*, YEPPOON, Gt Keppel Is, Emu Park, ROCKHAMPTON, Keppel Sands, *Tropic of Capricorn*, CAPRICORN COAST, GREAT BARRIER REEF, MOUNT MORGAN, *Lake Awoonga*, GLADSTONE, Bustard Bay, EURIMBULA NP, SEVENTEEN SEVENTY, AGNES WATER, DEEPWATER NP, BILOELA, MIRIAM VALE, *Dawson River*, CARNARVON NATIONAL PARK, GREAT DIVIDING RANGE, THEODORE, EXPEDITION NATIONAL PARK, MONTO, GIN GIN, MON REPOS CP, BUNDABERG, CHILDERS, TAROOM, MUNDUBBERA, BIGGENDEN, GAYNDAH, 0   50 km

For more detail see maps 606–7 & 608–9. For descriptions of ☉ towns see Towns from A–Z (p. 395).

Fossicking at Sapphire

THE MID-TROPICS

The World Theatre,
Charters Towers

Top events

Jan	Goldfield Ashes Cricket Carnival (Charters Towers)
Mar	Greek Festival (Townsville)
April–May	Towers Bonza Bash (Charters Towers)
May	Australian Italian Festival (Ingham)
	Country Music Festival (Charters Towers)
July	Australian Festival of Chamber Music (Townsville)
	Troy Dunn International Bull Riding (Mackay)
Aug	Gold Festival (Clermont)
Sept	Sugartime Festival (Mackay)
	Water Festival (Ayr)

Gold, cattle and sugar were the spearheads for settlement in this area. The regional centres of Mackay and Townsville were established in the 1860s, and today cattle and sugar remain key industries. Much of the coast – stretches of sandy shoreline, warm tropical waters, bush-covered headlands and large pockets of rainforest – remains intact despite development, and the district provides a great holiday alternative to some of Queensland's busier coastal areas. Accessible from several points is the Great Barrier Reef and its islands. Inland, on the edge of the outback, are a couple of the state's best preserved historic towns.

Focus on

Heritage

This region preserves some interesting pockets of heritage. Ravenswood, east of Charters Towers, is now almost a ghost town. It flourished in the second half of the 19th century as a centre for the surrounding goldfields, and many of its buildings from this period are in a near-original state. West of Mackay is Greenmount Historic Homestead – now a museum – built in 1915 on the Cook family's grazing property. Bowen, established in 1861, is north Queensland's oldest town. History here is recorded in 25 murals detailing the stories, personalities and events of the town.

Wallaman Falls

In Girringun (Lumholtz) National Park, part of the Wet Tropics World Heritage Area, Wallaman Falls has a 305 m sheer drop, the highest in Australia. Most of the park is trackless wilderness, and the one-hour drive from Ingham is mostly on unsealed road. Camping is available near the falls.

Marine attractions

At Reef HQ in Townsville, touch-tanks and underwater viewing-tunnels reveal some of the Great Barrier Reef's ecological mysteries. Next door, the Museum of Tropical Queensland features a full-scale reproduction of the bow of HMS *Pandora*, a British vessel wrecked on the reef in 1791.

CLIMATE **MACKAY**

	J	F	M	A	M	J	J	A	S	O	N	D
Max °C	30	29	28	27	24	22	21	22	25	27	29	30
Min °C	23	23	22	20	17	14	13	14	16	20	22	23
Rain mm	293	311	303	134	104	59	47	30	15	38	87	175
Raindays	16	17	17	15	13	7	7	6	5	7	9	12

Charters Towers

Charters Towers was Queensland's second largest city during the 1870s gold rush; at that time it was known as 'The World' because of its cosmopolitan population. Today it is a showpiece, with many beautifully preserved buildings including the Bank of Commerce, now restored as the New World Theatre Complex. The 'Ghosts of Gold' Heritage Trail allows visitors to indulge in the town's glamorous history.

Hibiscus Coast

Steep rainforest-clad hills plunge to rocky headlands and white sandy beaches in this lovely and surprisingly peaceful district north of Mackay. Cape Hillsborough National Park offers the most pristine scenery, with kangaroos often seen hopping along the deserted beaches.

[Map showing the Mid-Tropics region with locations including Cardwell, Girringun (Lumholtz) NP, Hinchinbrook Island, Orpheus Is, Ingham, Magnetic Island, Townsville, Cape Bowling Green, Ayr, Charters Towers, Ravenswood, White Mountains NP, Lake Dalrymple, Gloucester Island, Hayman Island, Bowen, Airlie Beach, Shute Harbour, Proserpine, The Whitsundays, Eungella NP, Brampton Island, Cape Hillsborough NP, Mackay, Sarina, Middle Island, South Island, Northumberland Isles, Moranbah, Clermont, Great Dividing Range. South Pacific Ocean, Great Barrier Reef, Hibiscus Coast labelled.]

Experience it!

1 Tour the Fairleigh Sugar Mill near Mackay during crushing season, July–October

2 Swim, saunter and savour the atmosphere at The Strand waterfront precinct, Townsville

3 Dive to the wreck of the SS *Yongala*, 16 km off Cape Bowling Green

For more detail see maps 603, 608–9 & 611.
For descriptions of ❶ towns see Towns from A–Z (p. 395).

CAIRNS & THE TROPICS

Whitewater rafting on the Tully River

Top events

May	Village Carnivale (Port Douglas)
	Folk Festival (Kuranda)
June	Endeavour Festival (Cooktown)
Sept	Wallaby Creek Folk Festival (Rossville, near Cooktown)
	Festival Cairns
	Palm Cove Fiesta
Oct	Country Music Festival (Mareeba, even-numbered years)
	Folk and Frog Festival (Yungaburra)
	Harvest Festival (Innisfail)
Nov	Music Festival (Mossman)

South and north of Cairns is a region of ancient rainforest, remote islands and a coastline that fronts part of the world's most spectacular reef. The national parks here form part of the World Heritage Wet Tropics and offer extensive opportunities for camping, fishing, walking and wildlife-watching. Four-wheel-drive enthusiasts flock to the rugged and spectacular Cape Tribulation, and visitors wanting to get in touch with the rainforest lifestyle head to Kuranda. The gateway to all of these attractions is Cairns – the first stop in the Far North for tourists from around the world.

Focus on

Tropical rainforests

The World Heritage Wet Tropics Area covers 894 000 hectares along the eastern escarpment of the Great Dividing Range between Townsville and Cooktown, and features rainforest, mountains, gorges, fast-flowing rivers and countless waterfalls. The rainforest here is one of the oldest continually existing rainforests on earth, with an estimated age of more than 100 million years. It represents major stages in the earth's evolutionary history and has the world's greatest concentration of primitive flowering plants, or 'green dinosaurs', as they are known. Its biological diversity is astounding; while the Wet Tropics covers just 0.1 percent of the continent, it contains 30 percent of Australia's marsupial species, 60 percent of its bats and 62 percent of its butterflies.

Daintree National Park

The Mossman Gorge section of this park takes visitors into the rainforest's green and shady heart via an easy 2.7 km walk to the Mossman River. The Cape Tribulation section is a rich mix of coastal rainforest, mangroves, swamp and heath.

Atherton Tableland

This 900 m high tableland south-west of Cairns is a productive farming district, thanks to the high rainfall and rich volcanic soil. Near Yungaburra is the remarkable Curtain Fig Tree, a strangler fig that has subsumed its host, sending down a curtain of roots. Volcanic lakes and spectacular waterfalls, including Millaa Millaa Falls and Zillie Falls, are among the other scenic attractions.

Experience it!

1 **Ride** a raft on the whitewater of the Tully River, which descends from the Atherton Tableland through rainforest gorges

2 **Marvel** at the Boulders, west of Babinda, rounded by fast-flowing river waters

3 **Travel** from Cairns to Kuranda on the Scenic Railway, through rainforest and over waterfalls

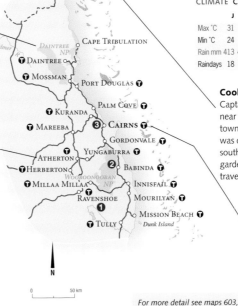

CLIMATE **CAIRNS**

	J	F	M	A	M	J	J	A	S	O	N	D
Max °C	31	31	30	29	28	26	26	27	28	29	31	31
Min °C	24	24	23	22	20	18	17	18	19	21	22	23
Rain mm	413	435	442	191	94	49	28	27	36	38	90	175
Raindays	18	19	20	17	14	10	9	8	8	8	10	13

Cooktown

Captain Cook beached the *Endeavour* near the site of Cooktown in 1770. The town was built a century later when gold was discovered on the Palmer River to the south-west. Cooktown has excellent botanic gardens dating from the 1880s, and cruises travel along the river and out to the reef.

Tjapukai Aboriginal Cultural Park

An Aboriginal group, originally a dance company, set up this park in Smithfield to make their unique Far North Queensland culture more accessible. In the theatres you can hear Aboriginal creation stories and watch Aboriginal dance, and in the Camp Villiage you can learn to throw a boomerang.

For more detail see maps 603, 604, 605 & 611.
For descriptions of ☻ towns see Towns from A–Z (p. 395).

QUEENSLAND

CAPE YORK

Fruit Bat Falls, Jardine River National Park

Cape York, a vast undeveloped region with a population of just 10 000, is one of Australia's last frontiers. Some of the country's finest Aboriginal rock art is found in the south near Laura – an area known as Quinkan country. On the west coast is the mining town of Weipa and several Aboriginal communities with strong ties to their traditional way of life. At the northern tip, via roads often impassable, is the town of Bamaga, and beyond is the rich cultural heritage of the Torres Strait. The national parks are rugged and wild, but the intrepid explorer will be rewarded with a rich experience of spectacular wildlife and amazing landscapes.

Top events

June	*Laura Dance and Cultural Festival (odd-numbered years)*
	Mabo Day (Torres Strait Islands)
July	*Coming of the Light Festival (Torres Strait Islands)*

Focus on

Aboriginal Cape York

Before white people arrived, the Aboriginal people of Cape York were divided into two main groups – East Cape and West Cape – with many language and cultural groups within this broad division. The distinctive art of the East Cape people survives in the rock-art galleries around Laura, some of the most extensive and unusual in Australia. The Aboriginal groups of West Cape, an area that proved largely resistant to European expansion, maintained sizeable pockets of land around Mapoon and Aurukun. Native title legislation since the 1950s has handed much of the West Cape back to its Aboriginal owners.

CLIMATE WEIPA

	J	F	M	A	M	J	J	A	S	O	N	D
Max °C	32	31	32	32	32	31	30	32	33	35	35	33
Min °C	24	24	24	23	21	20	19	19	20	21	23	24
Rain mm	421	401	338	82	6	2	1	1	1	14	98	256
Raindays	22	21	20	10	3	2	1	1	1	3	8	16

Torres Strait Islands

Australia's only non-Aboriginal indigenous people come from this group of around 100 islands off the northern tip of Cape York. The commercial centre is Thursday Island, reached by ferry from Seisia or Punsand Bay or by ship or plane from Cairns. The Torres Strait Islander people are of Melanesian descent and include among their number the late Eddie Mabo, famous for his successful 1992 land claim in Australia's High Court.

Weipa

The world's largest bauxite deposits are found around Weipa. In 1961 Comalco built a modern mining town, with all facilities, on the site of an Aboriginal mission station and reserve. Today the company offers tours of its mining operations. The fishing around Weipa (and indeed the whole of the cape) is excellent.

Lakefield National Park

Lakefield is Queensland's second largest national park, and the most accessible on the Cape York Peninsula. A near-wilderness of grassland, woodland, swamp and mangroves is cut by three major rivers and their tributaries. Access for conventional vehicles is via the township of Laura (during the Dry only). Visit the Old Laura Homestead, fish for barramundi and watch the wildlife.

Quinkan country

To the south-east of Laura are the spectacular Aboriginal rock-art sites of Split Rock and Gu Gu Yalangi. Encompassing the area between Laura and Cooktown, these form just a small part of one of the largest collections of prehistoric rock art in the world. The most distinctive works are the Quinkan figures, stick-like figures representing spirits that might emerge suddenly from the rock crevices.

Map labels

TORRES STRAIT
③ THURSDAY ISLAND
Cape York ①
SEISIA • BAMAGA
JARDINE RIVER NP
GREAT
MAPOON
CORAL SEA
WEIPA ②
AURUKUN
MUNGKAN KANDJU NP
GREAT DIVIDING
BARRIER
COEN
REEF
N
0   50 km
LAKEFIELD NATIONAL PARK
CAPE YORK PENINSULA
LAURA
Palmer
River

Experience it!

① **Indulge** yourself for a night or two at Pajinka Wilderness Lodge on the tip of Cape York, also the traditional meeting grounds of two incredible cultures

② **Absorb** West Cape history and culture at the Western Cape Cultural Centre in Weipa

③ **Take** a helicopter flight from Thursday Island to see this remote tip of Australia and its islands from up high

For more detail see maps 610–11 & 612. For descriptions of ❶ towns see Towns from A–Z (p. 395).

GULF SAVANNAH

Along the road to the Undara lava tubes

In this remote and far-flung area of Queensland, vast tracts of savannah grasslands give way to the lagoons and mangrove-lined estuaries of the Gulf of Carpentaria coastline. The waterways here match the Northern Territory's by any standard, especially if you measure it on the chance of catching a barra. Much of the region's history is related to the goldmining days, when the existence of towns was purely to service the growing number of incomers eager to find their riches. Earlier history was discovered at the Riversleigh Fossil Site, where ancient Australian animals – both bizarre and familiar – have been retrieved from their limestone tombs.

Top events

Easter Barra Classic (Normanton)
World Barramundi Championships (Burketown)

April Fishing Competition (Karumba)

May Gregory River Canoe Marathon (Gregory)

July Normanton Races
Tablelands Country Music Festival (Chillagoe)

Focus on
Fishing the Gulf
The Gulf is one of Australia's true fishing frontiers. Anglers can fish the rivers – the Nicholson, Albert, Flinders, Norman and Gilbert – as well as the coastal beaches and the offshore waters and reefs of the Gulf, accessible via the island resorts. Karumba, on the Norman River estuary, is a popular base for both river and offshore anglers. Sweers Island, in the Wellesley group, has a fishing resort offering access to thousands of hectares of reef, where coral trout, parrotfish, sweetlip and sea perch (and in winter, pelagics such as mackerel and tuna) are plentiful. Mornington Island is home to the Birri Fishing Resort, offering crabbing and sport- and bottom-fishing, all with professional masters. You can also stay at Escott Barramundi Lodge on the Nicholson River, reached via Burketown. Fishing charters take you along the nearby lagoons and rivers, where you can catch barramundi, catfish and mangrove jack.

QUEENSLAND

Tourist train
Every Wednesday the *Gulflander* leaves Normanton on a 153 km journey to the historic goldmining town of Croydon. With stops at points of interest along the line, the trip takes four hours. Travellers can explore Croydon with a local guide and return to Normanton on Thursday.

CLIMATE NORMANTON

	J	F	M	A	M	J	J	A	S	O	N	D
Max °C	35	34	34	34	32	29	29	31	34	36	37	36
Min °C	25	25	24	22	19	16	15	17	20	23	25	25
Rain mm	260	249	158	31	8	9	3	2	3	10	44	143
Raindays	14	14	9	2	1	1	1	0	0	1	4	9

Boodjamulla (Lawn Hill) National Park
Lawn Hill Gorge, about 205 km from Burketown, is this remote park's main attraction. The gorge has given life to an oasis of lush rainforest. Canoeing, swimming and walking are the main activities and Aboriginal art sites are accessible at two locations.

Map: GULF OF CARPENTARIA, Wellesley Islands, KARUMBA, BURKETOWN, Nicholson R, BOODJAMULLA (LAWN HILL) NP, GREGORY, Albert R, Norman, Flinders River, NORTHERN TERRITORY, CAPE YORK PENINSULA, Gilbert, NORMANTON, CROYDON, GEORGETOWN, GULF SAVANNAH, CHILLAGOE, CHILLAGOE–MUNGANA CAVES NP, MOUNT SURPRISE, UNDARA VOLCANIC NP, River, 0 100 km, N

Lava tubes
Undara, an Aboriginal word for long, accurately describes the tubes in Undara Volcanic National Park east of Mount Surprise. At 160 km, one of the lava tubes here is the longest on earth. The caves in nearby Chillagoe–Mungana Caves National Park are a feast for the senses, with bat colonies and richly decorative stalactites and stalagmites. Tours are necessary to visit both the tubes and the caves. The incredible geological history of the area is detailed at The Hub in Chillagoe.

Experience it!

1 **Spot** a croc at sunset on a river cruise from Karumba or Normanton

2 **Fossick** for topaz, quartz and aquamarine at the gemfields around Mount Surprise

3 **Discover** the landscape of the Gulf on a four-wheel-drive adventure trek; get clues and mud maps from The Hub in Chillagoe

Riversleigh Fossil Site
The fossils in this World Heritage-listed part of Boodjamulla (Lawn Hill) National Park record the evolution of mammals over 20 million years, as the vegetation changed from rainforest to semi-arid grassland. Guided tours provide an insight into the ancient world, and there is a self-guide interpretive trail.

*For more detail see maps 610–11 & 613.
For descriptions of ● towns see Towns from A–Z (p. 395).*

OUTBACK

Sandhills near Windorah

This is a remote, sparsely populated and – in parts – stunningly beautiful region extending west from the slopes of the Great Dividing Range. In the Channel Country of the south-west, dry waterholes and salt-pans dominate the landscape, except when floodwaters from the north bring brilliant life to the country in the form of native flowers, grasses and flocks of birds. Many of the stories and legends of Australia's pioneering days were born here, and the themes of mateship, egalitarianism and a 'fair go' are celebrated in the region's museums and monuments. Distances are vast and temperatures extreme – those intending to travel beyond sealed roads should plan their trips with care.

Focus on

Ancient animals

Queensland's outback is a veritable feast of fossils that document its changing ecological history. There is a fossil collection at Flinders Discovery Centre in Hughenden, its main exhibit being the replica skeleton of *Muttaburrasaurus langdoni*. In 1963 the skeleton of this unknown dinosaur was found in a creek near Muttaburra. Kronosaurus Korner in Richmond is well known for its vertebrate fossils, lovingly collected in hundreds of exhibits, and the Riversleigh Fossil Centre in Mount Isa showcases the tremendous findings, still being unearthed, of the nearby Riversleigh Fossil Site. For a bit of dinosaur drama, visit Lark Quarry Conservation Park south-west of Winton, where the preserved tracks of a dinosaur stampede lie protected under a shelter.

Mount Isa

This is Queensland's largest outback town. For a quintessential outback experience, visit Outback at Isa, complete with underground mining tunnels and mining machinery. Nearby is the Kalkadoon Tribal Centre and Cultural Keeping Place, with artefacts of the fierce and proud Kalkadoon Aboriginal people.

Channel Country

Monsoon rains in the tropical north flood the hundreds of inland river channels that meander through Queensland's south-west. Here cattle graze on huge semi-desert pastoral holdings. Spectacular red sandhills are found in the area, particularly in Simpson Desert National Park, beyond Birdsville.

CLIMATE LONGREACH

	J	F	M	A	M	J	J	A	S	O	N	D
Max °C	37	36	35	31	27	24	23	26	30	34	36	37
Min °C	23	23	20	16	12	8	7	8	12	17	20	22
Rain mm	58	68	43	10	13	5	4	3	3	16	16	44
Raindays	7	7	5	3	3	2	2	2	2	4	4	6

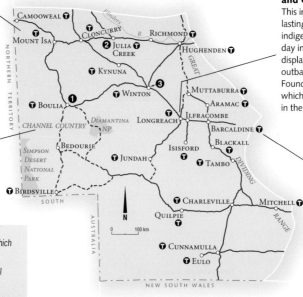

Australian Stockman's Hall of Fame and Outback Heritage Centre

This impressive institution is a lasting tribute to the outback people – indigenous, European settler, and current day inhabitants alike. The imaginative displays show the development of the outback. Don't miss the nearby Qantas Founders Outback Heritage Museum, which tells the story of the oldest airline in the English-speaking world.

Barcaldine

This 'Garden City of the West' was the first Australian town to tap the waters of the Great Artesian Basin, an event commemorated by the town's giant windmill. The Australian Workers Heritage Centre, in town, recollects the 1891 Shearers' Strike that led to the formation of the Australian Workers Party, forerunner of the Australian Labor Party. It also features recreated work precincts in tribute to all the workers who helped shape early Australia.

Experience it!

1 Watch for the mysterious Min Min light, which appears at night around Boulia

2 Spot the rare Julia Creek dunnart – a small marsupial only found within a 100 km radius of Julia Creek

3 Chart the history of Australia's favourite ballad at the Waltzing Matilda Centre in Winton

For more detail see maps 606, 608, 614–15 & 616–17. For descriptions of ❶ towns see Towns from A–Z (p. 395).

Hill Inlet, Whitsunday Island, offshore from Airlie Beach

Airlie Beach
Pop. 3017

Map ref. 609 K3

Airlie Beach is at the centre of the thriving Whitsunday coast. This tropical holiday town offers a cosmopolitan blend of bars, restaurants and shops just metres from the beach. From Abel Point Marina, daytrips to the outer Great Barrier Reef and Whitsunday Islands are on offer. Watersports available include sailing, snorkelling, diving and fishing. Nearby Shute Harbour is one of the largest marine passenger terminals in Australia and, along with Airlie Beach, services the majority of the Whitsunday islands.

IN TOWN *Airlie Beach Lagoon:* safe, year-round swimming in landscaped environment; foreshore. *Vic Hislop's Shark and Whale Expo:* informative show focusing on the 4 man-eating species of sharks plus a great white shark display; Waterson Rd. *Whale watching:* tours July–Sept depart Abel Point Marina; contact visitor centre for details.

WHAT'S ON *Community market:* Airlie Beach Esplanade; Sat mornings. *Whitsunday Fun Race:* competitions for cruising yachts; Aug. *Triathlon:* Sept.

NEARBY Conway National Park Covering 35 km of coastline, this park is renowned for its natural beauty and as the habitat of the Proserpine rock wallaby (endangered species). Walks start in Airlie Beach and Shute Harbour. The Mt Rooper Lookout is a highlight, featuring a panoramic view over Hamilton, Dent, Long and Henning islands. Access the park off the road to Shute Harbour. **Islands of Whitsunday Passage** These islands offer an abundance of sights and activities, whether they be the sports and social activities at the resorts on Hamilton, Daydream and Hayman islands, or the more secluded island experience on Whitsunday, Hook and South Molle islands. Whitsunday Island is famous for the pure white sand and clear water of Whitehaven Beach. The waterfalls on Hook Island are impressive, as are the butterflies on the shores of the island's aptly named Butterfly Bay. Big-game enthusiasts strive to get black marlin to bite on Hayman Island Sept–Nov.

Crocodile safaris and fishing trips: to nearby coastal wetlands; contact visitor centre for details. *Scenic flights:* various tours over the 74 Whitsunday Islands; contact visitor centre for details.

ⓘ 277 Shute Harbour Rd; 1800 819 366 or (07) 9496 6665; www.whitsunday tourism.com.au

Allora
Pop. 915

Map ref. 607 N10

Allora is a charming town in the Darling Downs, central to its rich agricultural surrounds. Explored and settled with stud farms in the 1840s, the main street is noted for its well-preserved historic buildings and old-time country feel.

IN TOWN *Allora Museum:* noted for its replica of the Talgai Skull, an Aboriginal cranium dating back 15 000 years; old courthouse, Drayton St; open Sun afternoons. *St David's Anglican Church:* built in 1888 and said to be one of the finest timber churches in country Queensland; Church St. *The Gnomery:* handcrafted items; New England Hwy.

NEARBY Goomburra Forest Reserve In the western foothills of the Great Dividing Range, the forest is an important refuge for wildlife. There are short walks around Dalrymple Creek and spectacular views from Mt Castle and Sylvesters lookouts. Take the Inverramsay Rd 40 km E to the forest. The last 6 km is unsealed and may be impassable following heavy rain. *Glengallan Homestead and Heritage Centre:* restored 1867 sandstone mansion. Documents and photos chronicle its history as a pastoral station. New England Hwy; 11 km S; open weekends. ❶ 49 Albion St (New England Hwy), Warwick; (07) 4661 3401; www.qldsoutherndowns.org.au

Aramac   Pop. 322

Map ref. 608 C10, 615 Q10

Aramac is a small service town west of the Great Dividing Range. The town was named by explorer William Landsborough; the name is an acronym of the name of 19th-century Queensland premier, Sir Robert Ramsay Mackenzie (RRMac). The town's sole water supply is from two bores that tap into the Great Artesian Basin.

IN TOWN *Harry Redford Interpretive Centre:* photographic exhibition of cattle drives, also local arts and crafts; Gordon St. *White Bull replica:* commemorating Captain Starlight's arrest for cattle stealing; Gordon St. *The Tramway Museum:* with old rail motor and historical exhibits; McWhannell St.

WHAT'S ON *Ballyneety Rodeo:* May. *Redford Muster:* May.

NEARBY Lake Dunn This freshwater lake and its surrounds have greatest appeal to birdwatchers. It is also a popular spot for swimming and fishing, with shady spots under the coolibahs to retreat from the heat. Follow signs to 'The Lake'; 68 km NE. **Forest Den National Park** This remote park is an important wildlife sanctuary due to its semipermanent waterholes. Have a picnic next to Torrens Creek and go birdwatching at dusk. 4WD recommended; Torrens Creek Rd; 110 km N. *Gray Rock:* large sandstone rock engraved with the names of hundreds of Cobb & Co travellers. This was once the site of a hotel – a nearby cave was used as the hotel's cellar. 35 km E. *Lake Galilee:* 15 000 ha saltwater lake with large waterfowl population; some of access road unsealed; 100 km NE. ❶ Post office, 22 Gordon St; (07) 4651 3147

The weathered window of an old Queenslander, Atherton

Atherton   Pop. 5846

Map ref. 611 M7

Originally called Prior's Pocket, the town was renamed Atherton in 1885. It is the commercial hub of the Atherton Tableland, an area renowned for its volcanic crater lakes, spectacular waterfalls and fertile farmlands. A patchwork of dense rainforest that abounds in birdlife surrounds the town, and the nearby parks and forests offer a variety of watersports, bushwalking and other outdoor activities.

IN TOWN Chinese Interpretive Centre and Old Post Office Gallery Atherton once had a large population of Chinese working for local timber cutters. This centre exhibits photos of these days and has artefacts and works by local artists and potters. Tours of the nearby Hou Wang Temple, built in 1903 and recently restored, depart from here. Herberton Rd. *Hallorans Hill Conservation Park:* walk to the rim of this extinct volcanic cone on the Atherton Tableland, where there is a spectacular lookout and informative displays; off Kennedy Hwy. *Crystal Caves:* explore underground tunnels and chambers lined with crystals, fossils and flourescent minerals. The above-ground Fascinating Facets shop sells a range of jewellery and gemstones. Main St.

NEARBY Lake Tinaroo With 200 km of shoreline, Lake Tinaroo is an ideal spot for fishing, waterskiing and sailing. Walking tracks circle the lake, and dinghies and houseboats are available for hire. The Danbulla Forest Drive is a scenic 28 km drive around lake. 15 km NE via Kairi. *Hasties Swamp National Park:* local and migratory birds visit this swamp, including whistling ducks and magpie geese. View them through the bird hide at the swamp's edge. 3 km S. *Tolga:* this town has a railway museum and craft outlets;

5 km N. *Wongabel State Forest:* important wildlife refuge in Wet Tropics World Heritage Area. An informative heritage trail gives an insight into Aboriginal culture and history. Kennedy Hwy; 8 km S. ❶ Cnr Silo and Main sts; (07) 4091 4222; www.athertontableland.com

Ayr   Pop. 8337

Map ref. 603 I10, 608 H1, 611 Q13

This busy town south-east of Townsville is surrounded by sugarcane fields – the most productive in Australia – and is the largest mango-growing area in the country. On the north side of Burdekin River, it is linked to Home Hill to the south by the 1097-metre Silver Link Bridge, which ensures the towns are not cut off when the river floods.

IN TOWN *Ayr Nature Display:* fine collection of emu-egg carvings, shells, butterflies and beetles; Wilmington St. *Burdekin Cultural Complex:* 530-seat theatre, library and activities centre. Distinctive 'Living Lagoon' in theatre forecourt. Queen St. *Juru Walk:* starting at Plantation Creek Park, this informative bush-tucker walk passes through remnant forest.

WHAT'S ON *Market:* Plantation Creek Park; Bruce Hwy; 3rd Sun each month. *Water Festival:* Sept.

NEARBY Home Hill This small town is just south of Ayr over the Silver Link Bridge. In town are the Lions Diorama, showing agricultural achievements of the Burdekin region, and the Eighth Avenue plaques illustrating the history of local pioneering families. A community market is held on the 2nd Sat of each month and there is a Harvest Festival in Nov. *Hutchings Lagoon:* watersports and picnics; 5 km NW. *Alva Beach:* beach walks, birdwatching, swimming and fishing; market 3rd Sun each month; 18 km N. *Cape Bowling Green:* wreck of SS *Youngala* 16 km off coast, great for diving; 20 km N. *Charlie's Hill:* WW II historic site; 24 km S. *Groper Creek:* great fishing spot with camping available; 24 km SE. *Mt Inkerman:* good views at top, plus picnic and barbecue facilities; 30 km S. ❶ Burdekin Visitor Information Centre, Bruce Hwy, Plantation Creek Park; (07) 4783 5988

Babinda   Pop. 1168

Map ref. 603 D1, 611 N7

A small sugar town south of Cairns, Babinda boasts abundant wildlife, secluded swimming holes and untouched rainforest in its surrounds. In adjacent Wooroonooran National Park are the state's two highest mountains, Mt Bartle Frere (1622 metres) and Mt Bellenden Ker (1592 metres).

NEARBY Wooroonooran National Park Part of the Wet Tropics World Heritage Area, the park has endemic species of

plants and animals and spectacular walks through tropical rainforest. Swim in the watering hole at Josephine Falls, located at the base of Mt Bartle Frere, or see The Boulders, a large group of boulders worn smooth by tropical rains. Access off Bruce Hwy, west of Babinda.
Deeral: departure point for cruises through rainforest and saltwater-crocodile haunts of the Mulgrave and Russell rivers. Deeral Cooperative makes footwear and Aboriginal artefacts. Nelson Rd; 14 km N. *Bramston Beach:* small community behind long palm-lined beach; Bruce Hwy s to Miriwinni, then 12 km E. *Russell River National Park:* small park on the coast with good birdwatching; no facilities; 4WD access; 6 km N of Brampton Beach.
🛈 Cnr Bruce Hwy and Munro St; (07) 4067 1008

Barcaldine   Pop. 1492

Map ref. 608 C11, 615 Q11

After the 1891 Shearers' Strike, the Australian Labor Party was born in this pastoral and rail town. Located east of Longreach, Barcaldine's good supply of artesian water ensures its status as 'Garden City of the West'; all the streets are named after trees.

IN TOWN Australian Workers Heritage Centre This centre was established as a tribute to the working men and women of Australia – the shearers, teachers, policemen and other workers who helped build the nation. The interpretive displays also cover the events leading to the formation of the Labor Party. Ash St. *Tree of Knowledge:* huge ghost gum where the striking shearers met in 1891; Oak St. *Mad Mick's Funny Farm:* 8 settlers' buildings including a Cobb & Co office (now studio and art gallery) and old shearing sheds; also hand-reared wildlife; cnr Pine and Bauhinia sts. *Folk Museum:* display of historical memorabilia from the area; cnr Gidyea and Beech sts. *National Trust-classified buildings:* Masonic lodge, Beech St; Anglican church, Elm St; shire hall, Ash St. *Artesian Country tours:* including some to Aboriginal carvings and caves; contact visitor centre for details.
WHAT'S ON *Mini steam-train rides:* depart Folk Museum; last Sun each month (Mar–Oct). *Easter in the Outback:* Easter.
NEARBY *Bicentennial Park:* has botanical walk through bushland; Blackall Rd; 9 km s.
🛈 Oak St; (07) 4651 1724; www.barcaldine.qld.gov.au

Beaudesert   Pop. 4452

Map ref. 599 D11, 607 P10

Beaudesert lies in the valley of the Logan River, in the Gold Coast hinterland. The town was built up around the homestead of Edward Hawkins – his property was immense, comprising land from the coast to Logan River. Those origins continue

today with the area being noted for its dairying, beef cattle, and fruit and vegetable produce, making the country markets a great attraction.
IN TOWN *Historical Museum:* displays of old machinery and tools; Brisbane St. *Community Arts Centre:* art gallery, tea house and craft shop; Enterprise Dr.
WHAT'S ON *Markets:* Westerman Park; 1st Sat each month. *Carp Busters Fishing Competition:* April. *Country and Horse Festival:* June. *Rodeo:* Oct.
NEARBY Mount Barney National Park
A remote park where the rugged peaks of Barney, Maroon, May and Lindesay mountains stand as remnants of the ancient Focal Peak Shield Volcano. The walks are not for the inexperienced, but picnicking at Yellow Pinch at the base of Mt Barney is an alternative. The challenging 10 hr ascent to Mt Barney's summit on the Logan's Ridge track rewards walkers with spectacular views. 55 km SW.
Woollahra Farmworld: dairy farm in action; 8 km N. *Darlington Park:* recreation area with picnic/barbecue facilities; 12 km s. *Tamrookum:* has fine example of a timber church; tours by appt; 24 km SW. *Bigriggen Park:* recreation area with picnic/barbecue facilities; 30 km SW. *Rathdowney:* great viewpoint from Captain Logan's Lookout in John St; 32 km s. *Lamington National Park:* 40 km SW; *see Nerang.*
🛈 Historical Museum, 54 Brisbane St; (07) 5541 3740

Biggenden   Pop. 635

Map ref. 607 N4

This agricultural town south-west of Bundaberg, known as the 'Rose of the Burnett', is proud of its impressive range of roses in the main street. Situated in a valley, the majestic ranges of nearby Mount Walsh National Park tower over the town.
IN TOWN *Historical Museum:* exhibits history of shire and life of the early pioneers; Brisbane St; open Thurs plus every 2nd Sat each month, or by appt (07) 4127 7185.
WHAT'S ON *Big Sky Country Fly-in:* April. *Auto Spectacular:* Aug.
NEARBY Mount Walsh National Park
Featuring the impressive Bluff Range, this wilderness park commands the skyline. Walks take in rugged granite outcrops and gullies and are for the experienced bushwalker only. From the picnic area the views are still commanding. Maryborough Rd; 8 km s.
Mt Woowoonga: bushwalking in a forestry reserve; picnic/barbecue facilities; 10 km NW. *Coalstoun Lakes National Park:* protects 2 volcanic crater lakes. Walk up the northern crater for a view over the rim. 20 km SW. *Coongara Rock:* a volcanic core surrounded by rainforest; 4WD access only; 20 km s. *Chowey Bridge:* 1905 concrete arch railway bridge, one of

two surviving in the country; 20 km NW. *Brooweena:* small town with Pioneer Museum; Biggenden Rd; 30 km SE.
🛈 Cafe Classic, 26 Edward St; (07) 4127 1440

Biloela   Pop. 5443

Map ref. 607 K1, 609 N13

This thriving town in the fertile Callide Valley is part of the Banana Shire, but do not expect to find any bananas grown here. The area was actually named after a bullock called 'Banana', whose job was to lure wild cattle into enclosures, a difficult feat that local stockmen applauded him for.
IN TOWN Silo Primary Industries Exhibition Originally an exhibition at the Expo '88 in Brisbane, this silo stands at 28 m. Inside are exhibits on hi-tech farming techniques, scenes of rural life and interactive displays – climb to the top of a coal haul truck. Also in the complex is Pioneer Place, Biloela's first church, where photographs and memorabilia document the area's past. Dawson Hwy. *Greycliffe Homestead:* original slab hut converted to a museum retells area's pioneering heritage; Gladstone Rd; open by appt (07) 4992 1572.
WHAT'S ON *Country Music Festival:* June.
NEARBY Mt Scoria Known locally as the 'Musical Mountain' because of the basalt columns at the top that ring when hit with another rock. Walks and trails around the mountain. 14 km s.
Thangool: renowned for its race days; 10 km SE. *Callide Dam:* excellent for boating, fishing and swimming; 12 km NE. *Callide Power Station:* tours available; near Callide Dam. *Callide Mine Lookout:* view over Biloela, the mine and the dam; 18 km NE, past dam. *Kroombit Tops National Park:* 25 km E; *see Gladstone.* *Baralaba:* historic village; watersports on the Dawson River; 100 km NW.
🛈 Callide St; (07) 4992 2405

Birdsville   Pop. 120

Map ref. 616 E5

Birdsville is a tiny town on the edge of the Simpson Desert and at the northern end of the Birdsville Track, a major cattle route developed in the 1880s. In the 1870s the first European settlers arrived in the area. By 1900 it was a flourishing town boasting three hotels, several stores, a customs office and a cordial factory. When, after Federation in 1901, the toll on cattle crossing the border was abolished, the town's prosperity slowly declined. The famous 'Flynn of the Inland' founded the first Australian Inland Mission at Birdsville. Cattle remains a major trade, as well as the tourism accompanying four-wheel-drive enthusiasts keen to take on the Birdsville Track and Simpson Desert National Park.
IN TOWN *Museum:* Australiana, domestic artefacts and working farm

QUEENSLAND

Two Mile Falls, Blackdown Tableland National Park

equipment; McDonald St. *Blue Poles Gallery:* local art; Graham St. *Artesian bore:* water comes out at near boiling point from this 1219 m deep bore; behind the bore is a geothermal power plant; Graham St. *Adelaide Street:* ruins of Royal Hotel (1883) – a reminder of Birdsville's boom days; Birdsville Hotel (1884) – still an important overnight stop for travellers.

WHAT'S ON *Birdsville Cup Racing Carnival:* the first meeting of this annual event was held in 1882 and the tradition continues on the claypan track south-east of town. Held the first Fri and Sat in Sept, the population swells to over 6000.

NEARBY **Simpson Desert National Park** West of Birdsville is this arid national park, the largest in Queensland. The parallel windblown sand dunes are enormous – up to 90 m high, about 1 km apart, and can extend up to 200 km. The traveller can follow a self-guide drive of 10 sites that starts at the eastern park boundary and follows the track to Poeppel's Corner. Walking any distance is not recommended and a 4WD is essential; visit only between April and Oct; 65 km w; *see note below*.
Waddi Trees and Dingo Cave Lookout: 14 km N. *Big Red:* huge sand dune; 35 km w. *Bedourie:* Eyre Creek runs through town providing waterholes that are home to endangered species of bilby and peregrine falcons; 191 km N.
Travellers note: Travel in this area can be hazardous, especially in the hotter months (approximately Oct–Mar). Motorists are advised to check the RACQ Road Conditions Report on 1300 130 595 (or www.racq.com.au) for information before departing

down the Birdsville Track and to advise police if heading west to Simpson Desert National Park. There is no hotel or fuel at Betoota, 164 km E, but fuel is available at Windorah, 375 km E.
🛈 Wirrari Centre, Billabong Blvd; (07) 4656 3300

Blackall   Pop. 1401

Map ref. 606 A1, 608 D13, 615 R13, 617 R1

Blackall is west of the Great Dividing Range in sheep and cattle country, and was home to the legendary sheep-shearer Jackie Howe. In 1892 he set the record of shearing 321 sheep with blade shears in less than eight hours at Alice Downs Station (north of town). The statue in Shamrock Street commemorates this feat, which was surpassed only after the introduction of electric shears.

IN TOWN *Petrified tree stump:* millions of years old; Shamrock St. *Major Mitchell Memorial Clock:* commemorates the founding of Blackall in 1846; Shamrock St. *Replica of the Black Stump:* the reference point used when area was surveyed in 1886; Thistle St. *Pioneer Bore:* first artesian bore sunk in Queensland, with display of replica drilling plant; Aqua St.
WHAT'S ON *Flower Show:* Sept. *Springtime Affair:* celebration of the season; Sept.
NEARBY **Idalia National Park** Renowned habitat of the yellow-footed rock wallaby, which can be spotted at Emmet Pocket Lookout (which also has amazing panoramic views) or along the Bullock Gorge walking track. The park can also be explored by car; a self-guide drive begins

at the information centre, which is 12 km beyond park entrance. 70 km SW on Yaraka Rd; at Benlidi siding turn south. *Blackall Wool Scour:* restored steam-driven wool-processing plant with demonstrations of machinery (steam operating May–Sept only); Evora Rd; 4 km N.
🛈 Shamrock St; (07) 4657 4637; www.blackall.qld.gov.au

Blackwater   Pop. 4914

Map ref. 609 K11

Blackwater is west of Rockhampton in the Capricorn region and is known as the coal capital of Queensland. The coal is transported directly from coalmines south of town to Gladstone by train. The name 'Blackwater' is not a reference to the effects of mining operations, however, but comes from the discolouration of local waterholes caused by tea trees.

IN TOWN **Japanese Garden complex** In conjunction with overseas experts, this ornate traditional Japanese garden was constructed over eight months in 1998. It symbolises the relationship Blackwater shares with its sister town Fujisawa in Japan. The complex also has a mining museum displaying the history of the industry and its equipment. The craft shop and information centre was once the town's station, and a restored steam locomotive still departs from its platform. Capricorn Hwy.
Lions Park: displays the flags of 37 nations to commemorate the nationality of every worker on the coalmines. In terms of size and variety, the display is second only to that of the United Nations' building in New York; Capricorn Hwy to the west of town. *Helicopter flights over Blackwater Coal Mine:* see the mine in action; contact visitor centre for details.
WHAT'S ON *May Day Festival:* May. *Charity Rodeo:* 1st Sat in Oct. *Craft Fair and Art Exhibition:* regional arts and crafts exhibit; 3rd Sat in Oct.
NEARBY **Blackdown Tableland National Park** At the north-eastern edge of the central-Queensland sandstone belt, this national park offers spectacular scenery over mountains and lowlands, including some beautiful waterfalls. It is the traditional home of the Ghungalu people, whose stencil art can be seen by walking the 2.8 km Mimosa Culture Track. Walk through to Rainbow Falls Gorge and swim in rock pools. 30 km E to turnoff. *Bedford Weir:* dam excellent for fishing; 20 km N. *Comet:* in town is the Leichhardt Dig Tree, where the explorer buried letters and marked the tree 'dig'; 30 km w.
🛈 Eliza's Craft Cottage, Capricorn Hwy; (07) 4982 5500

Boonah   Pop. 2185

Map ref. 599 A11, 607 P10

Boonah is set in the picturesque Fassifern Valley, surrounded by hills. Once noted as a 'beautiful vale' by 19th-century explorers, a little expedition in the surrounding region will reveal the beauty and ruggedness of the area. West of town is the Main Range National Park, part of the semicircle of mountains known as the Scenic Rim.

IN TOWN *Cultural Centre:* incorporates regional art gallery; High St. *Art and Soul:* local art and photography; Walter St. *Gliding and ultralight tours:* flights over the Scenic Rim; contact visitor centre for details.

WHAT'S ON *Country markets:* Springleigh Park, 2nd and 4th Sat each month. *Country Show:* May. *Orchid Show:* Oct.

NEARBY Main Range National Park A World Heritage-listed park of rugged mountains and landscapes with spectacular lookouts. There are walks starting at the Cunningham's Gap and Spicer's Gap campsites; from Spicer's Gap a traditional Aboriginal path leads from inland to the coast. See the varied birdlife, including the satin bowerbird, on the 8.4 km-return Box Forest track. 40 km w; access the park from Cunningham Hwy. In the south of the park are Queen Mary Falls; *see Killarney.*
Templin: has historical museum chronicling history of area; 5 km NW. *Moogerah Peaks National Park:* excellent for birdwatching, and with lookouts over the Fassifern Valley. The Frog Buttress at Mt French is one of the best rock-climbing sites in Queensland. 12 km w. *Lakes Maroon and Moogerah:* ideal for camping and watersports; 20 km s and sw.
ⓘ Boonah–Fassifern Rd; (07) 5463 2233; www.boonah.qld.gov.au

Boulia
Pop. 289

Map ref. 614 F9

Boulia is the capital of the Channel Country and is on the Burke River, named after the explorer Robert Burke. The town is famous for random appearances of the mysterious Min Min light, a ball of light that sometimes reveals itself to travellers at night (for the full story, see feature on this page). The isolated Diamantina National Park nearby is a haven for threatened species that are rarely seen in their natural habitat.

IN TOWN *Min Min Encounter:* high-tech re-creation of the Min Min light, with outback characters as your guide; Herbert St. *Stone Cottage:* National Trust-classified house and one of the oldest in western Queensland (1884), now a museum displaying Aboriginal artefacts, a local fossil collection and historic relics of the region; Pituri St. *Red Stump:* warns travellers of dangers of the Simpson Desert; Herbert St. *Corroboree Tree:* last known of the Pitta Pitta community; near Boulia State School.

WHAT'S ON *Rodeo Races and Campdraft:* Easter. *Desert Sands Camel Race and Festival:* July. *Back to Boulia:* traditional games weekend; Sept.

NEARBY Diamantina National Park This remote park south-east of Boulia is rich in colours and landscapes. Follow the 157 km Warracoota self-guide circuit drive to view the spectacular sand dunes, claypans and ranges and many rare and threatened species in their native habitat, including the greater bilby, kowari and peregrine falcon. Canoe or fish in the winding creeks and rivers. 4WD access only. Roads may become impassable after rain. Check road conditions before travelling.
Ruins of Police Barracks: 19 km NE. *Cawnpore Hills:* good views from summit; 108 km E. *Burke and Wills Tree:* on the west bank of the Burke River; 110 km NE. *Ruins of Min Min Hotel:* burned down in 1918, where Min Min light was first sighted; 130 km E. ⓘ Min Min Encounter, Herbert St; (07) 4746 3386; www.outbackholidays. tq.com.au

Bowen
Pop. 8368

Map ref. 609 J2

At the top of the Whitsundays is Bowen, positioned within five kilometres of eight pristine beaches and bays. Named after the state's first governor, Bowen was established in 1861 – the first settlement in north Queensland. The town and surrounding area is well known for its mangoes, the Big Mango being testimony to the fact.

IN TOWN **Historical murals** Around the buildings and streets of Bowen's town centre are 25 murals by local and national artists, each illustrating an aspect of the region's history. The mural by Australia's Ken Done was displayed at Expo '88. A new mural is commissioned every 2 years.
Historical Museum: covers history of area; Gordon St. *Golden Arrow's Tourist Drive:* self-guide drive past area's sights; starts at Salt Works, Don St.

WHAT'S ON *Multicultural Festival:* July. *Art, Craft and Orchid Expo:* Aug. *Bowen Family Fishing Classic:* Sept. *Coral Coast Festival:* Oct. *Food and Wine Festival:* Nov.

NEARBY Eight bays and beaches Choose from 8 excellent spots for swimming, snorkelling and fishing in spectacular surrounds. Rose and Horseshoe bays are connected by a walking track with panoramic views over the ocean; a sidetrack leads to Murray Bay. Impressive corals and fish can be found at Grays, Horseshoe, Murray and Rose bays. Diving enthusiasts should head to Horseshoe and Murray bays. For the more exclusive swim, visit secluded Coral Bay. Ask at visitor centre for locations.
Big Mango: tribute to local Kensington Mango, grown since the 1880s. A shop sells all things mango-related – the locally produced mango ice-cream is a highlight. Bruce Hwy, Mount Gordon; 7 km s. *Gloucester Island National Park:* group of secluded islands 23 km offshore, part of

The land of the Min Min

On certain nights and in certain conditions, Queensland's Channel Country is handed over to the realm of the Min Min. Not a bunyip or a creature of the Dreamtime, but something equally mysterious. The Min Min is a strange ball of white light that hovers above the ground, changing shape, disappearing, reappearing, and moving around at will. Some find it mesmerising, but others truly terrifying – the Min Min has been known to reduce hardened outback men to tears.

The territory of the Min Min encircles Boulia, and for at least 70 years it has been appearing at random intervals. It was first recorded at the site of the old Min Min Hotel, a pub for shearers and cattlemen who worked on nearby stations. The hotel was located between Boulia and Middleton, and after sundown things often got out of hand. 'So many were its crimes and murders of kerosene and brimstone, that in righteous anger they burnt it to the ground', wrote Ernestine Hill in *Walkabout*, referring to the hotel's demise in 1918.

Enter the Min Min. Soon after the hotel went up in smoke a stockman was passing the ruins and saw a strange light, seemingly emanating from the graveyard behind the hotel. The light followed him all the way to Boulia.

Some local Aboriginal people believe that the light did not make an appearance until the killings of many of their ancestors in the late 1800s, and that it is actually a kind of ghost that rose up out of an old Aboriginal burial ground.

Not nearly as fascinating are the scientific explanations of the phenomenon. Some have said that it is caused by a swarm of luminescent insects, or that it is the result of gas rising up out of a bore. But most convincing is the work of Professor Jack Pettigrew from the University of Queensland. He claims that the Min Min is an inverted mirage of light sources hundreds of kilometres away, over the horizon. The light gets trapped in a layer of air next to the ground and moves with the curve of the globe as if on a cable.

Whether supernatural or scientific, the possibility of seeing the phenomenon lures many travellers to the Channel Country. For most people, long cold nights peering into the darkness yield no results. The Min Min seems to have a kind of cunning – only after you have given up all hope of ever seeing it does it suddenly appear. The Min Min Encounter in Boulia is the next best thing, an impressive centre where visitors can come and soak up the stories surrounding this outback legend.

QUEENSLAND

the Great Barrier Reef, boasting beaches and rainforest. Campers must be self-sufficient and obtain a permit. Access via private boat from Dingo Beach, Hideaway Bay, Bowen or Airlie Beach. *Cape Upstart National Park:* remote granite headland flanked with sandy beaches; self-sufficient visitors only. Access by boat; ramps are at Molongle Bay and Elliot River. 50 km NW. *Collinsville:* coalmine tours can be arranged from Bowen visitor centre; 82 km SW.
ⓘ Bruce Hwy next to Big Mango, Mount Gordon; (07) 4786 4222; www.bowentourism.com.au

Buderim   Pop. 31 789

Map ref. 601 G4, 602 G9, 607 Q7

Buderim is just inland from the Sunshine Coast, high on the fertile red soil of Buderim Mountain, a plateau overlooking the surrounding bushland and ocean. It escapes the crush of nearby towns like Maroochydore and Mooloolaba with its wide streets and an abundance of small-scale art and craft galleries.

IN TOWN **Pioneer Cottage** This restored 1876 National Trust timber cottage is one of Buderim's earliest houses and retains many of its original furnishings. Now home to the local historical society, it has exhibits on the history of the town and its surrounds. Ballinger Cres; open Sun–Thurs.
Buderim Forest Park: subtropical rainforest reserve and a great place for a picnic or barbecue. In the south, via Quorn Cl, is the Edna Walling Memorial Garden and Serenity Falls; in the north, via Lindsay Rd, is Harry's Restaurant and a boardwalk along Martins Creek. *Foote Sanctuary:* rainforest walks and more than 80 bird species; car entry via Foote St. *Art and craft galleries:* various shops selling locally made things; Main St.

WHAT'S ON *Biennale:* festival of antiques, music and arts; April. *Street Festival:* Oct.

NEARBY **Tanawha to Forest Glen Tourist Drive** This self-guide tour takes in the area south-east of Buderim. Along the drive are the Superbee Honey Factory, the Bellingham Maze (a star-shaped hedge maze) and the Forest Glen Sanctuary where you can take the 'safari' excursion and see exotic deer and native fauna.
Mooloolah River National Park: 6 km SE; *see Mooloolaba.*
ⓘ Old Post Office, Burnett St; (07) 5477 0944; www.buderim.com

Bundaberg   Pop. 44 154

Map ref. 607 O2

Bundaberg, the southernmost access point to the Great Barrier Reef, is proud of its parks and gardens. Even more recognisable is its world-famous amber spirit, Bundaberg Rum, and the surrounding fields of sugarcane. In harvest season, from July to November,

the cane fires give the area a smoky haze. As the sugar industry was being developed in the 1880s, and Australian labour costs were rising, South Sea Islanders were placed under 'contract' to work on the canefields as a cheap alternative. In fact, the majority of these labourers had been lured from their island homes onto boats under the pretence of trading goods. In 1901, when Australia's commonwealth government was established, the Kanakas (as the labourers were known) were allowed to return home. A Kanaka-built basalt stone wall can still be seen near Bargara, a short distance north-east of town. Bundaberg more proudly claims the aviator Bert Hinkler as one of its own. In 1928 Hinkler was the first to successfully fly from England to Australia in a flight of just over 15 days.

IN TOWN **Botanical Gardens** In this picturesque setting stand many buildings from Bundaberg's past. Hinkler House Memorial Museum, inside Bert Hinkler's relocated Southampton home, is a tribute to him and to aviation history. Fairymead House Sugar Museum, a restored plantation house, recalls years of sugar production, and the nearby Historical Museum chronicles the general history of the area. To see more of the grounds, take the restored steam train around the lakes, which runs every Sun. Mount Perry Rd. *Bundaberg Rum Distillery:* discover the distillation process first-hand; tours daily; Avenue St. *Schmeider's Cooperage and Craft Centre:* demonstrations of barrel making and glass-blowing, and sales of local crafts and handmade crystal jewellery; closed Sun; Alexandra St. *Arts Centre:* 3 galleries devoted to local and visiting art exhibitions; cnr Barolin and Quay sts. *Baldwin Swamp Conservation Park:* boardwalks and pathways, waterlily lagoons, abundant birdlife and native fauna; Steindl St. *Tropical Wines:* taste unique wines made from local fruit; Mount Perry Rd. *Alexandra Park and Zoo:* historic band rotunda, cactus garden, zoo (free admission); riverbank, Quay St. *Whaling Wall:* a 7-storey-high whale mural; Bourbong St. *Heritage City Walk:* self-guide walking tour of 28 significant sites and buildings; starts at historic post office, Barolin St.

WHAT'S ON *Shalom College Markets:* local crafts; Fitzgerald St; every Sun. *West School Craft Markets:* George St; 2nd Sun each month. *Country Music Roundup:* Easter. *Multicultural Festival:* July. *Bundy in Bloom Festival:* celebration of spring; Sept. *Arts Festival:* Oct. *Food and Wine Festival:* Nov.

NEARBY **Mon Repos Conservation Park** This park contains the largest and most accessible mainland loggerhead turtle rookery in eastern Australia. Between November and March these giant sea turtles come ashore to lay their eggs. Hatchlings leave their nests for the sea from mid-January to late March. Access

to the park is restricted during these times – guided night tours depart from the park information centre for viewing turtles up close. When turtles are not hatching, snorkelling and exploring the rock pools are popular. 15 km NE.
Burrum Coast National Park Broken into two sections, this national park offers a variety of landscapes and activities. In the northern Kinkuna section it is relatively undeveloped. The vegetation along the beach is rugged and spectacular, and birdwatching in the wallum heath is a highlight. Access is via Palm Beach Road; 14 km SW; 4WD and sand-driving experience is necessary. The southern Woodgate section is more developed, with boardwalks and established tracks that allow the visitor to see abundant wildlife from every vantage. Access is via Woodgate, a small town with a magnificent ocean beach; 57 km S.
Hummock Lookout: panoramic view of Bundaberg, canefields and coast; 7 km NE. *Meadowvale Nature Park:* rainforest and walkway to Splitters Creek; 10 km W. *Sharon Nature Park:* rainforest, native fauna, and walkway to Burnett River; 12 km SW. *Bargara:* coastal town with a popular surf beach and year-round fishing on man-made reef. Turtles often nest at nearby Neilson Park, Kelly's and Rifle Range beaches; 13 km NE. *Fishing spots:* area renowned for its wide variety of fishing. Excellent spots at Burnett Heads, 15 km NE; Elliott Heads, 18 km SE; Moore Park, 21 km NW. *Mystery craters:* 35 small craters in sandstone slab, the origin of which causes much debate, but confirmed to be over 25 million years old; 25 km SW. *Littabella National Park:* lagoons and billabongs surrounded by tea tree forest. Many sand tracks for the 4WD enthusiast can be found at nearby Norval Park Beach. 38 km NW. *Lady Elliot and Lady Musgrave islands:* excellent spots for snorkelling and fishing. Wilderness camping on Lady Musgrave; seabird nesting on Lady Elliot during summer. Sea access from Bundaberg Port plus air access to Lady Elliot from Hinkler Airport.
ⓘ 271 Bourbong St; 1800 308 888 or (07) 4153 8888; www.bundaberg region.info

Burketown   Pop. 220

Map ref. 613 E8

Burketown is on the edge of the Gulf of Carpentaria, on the dividing line between the wetlands to the north and the Gulf Savannah plains to the south. It was named after the ill-fated explorer Robert Burke, who was the first European (with partner William John Wills) to arrive in the area. Regularly in spring, the natural phenomenon known as Morning Glory takes over the horizon at dawn between Burketown and Sweers Island, offshore. The clouds appear as rolling tube-like

A loggerhead turtle returns to sea after laying eggs on Mon Repos Beach, near Bundaberg

formations and can extend for more than 1000 kilometres.

IN TOWN *Museum and Information Centre:* in the original post office, with displays on the history of the area plus local arts and crafts; Musgrave St. *Artesian bore:* operating for over 100 years and quite a sight to see due to the build up of minerals; The Great Top Rd.

WHAT'S ON *World Barramundi Championships:* Easter. *Campdraft and Gymkhana:* May.

NEARBY *Original Gulf Meatworks:* machinery relics of this once thriving industry; just north of town. *Colonial Flat:* site of the Landsborough Tree. Blazed by the explorer in 1862 on his search for Burke and Wills, it became the depot camp for search parties and the resting place of Landsborough's ship *Firefly* – the first ship to enter the Albert River. 5 km E. *Nicholson River wetlands:* breeding ground for crocodiles, fish and birds; 17 km w. *Escott Barramundi Lodge:* operating cattle station offering camping and accommodation. Anglers can try and reel in a barramundi in the station's waterways. 18 km w over Nicholson River. *Bluebush Swamp:* large wetland area ideal for birdwatchers; 30 km sw. *Sweers Island:* excellent spot for lure and fly fishing, plus golden beaches and over 100 species of birds. Access by aircraft or boat, contact visitor centre for details; 30 km N. *Leichhardt Falls:* picturesque flowing falls in rainy months; 71 km SE. *Gregory:* small outback town that holds the Gregory River Canoe Marathon in May; 113 km s. *Boodjamulla (Lawn Hill) National Park:* around 90 km w of Gregory; *see feature on p. 424. Fishing and boat tours:* to nearby estuaries and Wellesley Islands;

contact visitor centre for details.
ⓘ Old Post Office (April–Sept) or council offices (Oct–Mar), both in Musgrave St; (07) 4745 5100; www.burkeshire council.com

Caboolture   Pop. 18 754

Map ref. 598 D1, 599 C1, 601 F8, 607 P8

At the northern edge of Greater Brisbane and the southern opening to the Sunshine Coast, Caboolture is surrounded by subtropical fruit farms. The town was settled in 1842 after the restricted land around Moreton Bay penal colony was opened up. The historical village north of town exhibits much of this history. Bribie Island to the east has spectacular aquatic and wildlife attractions, which bring many visitors to the region.

IN TOWN *Trail of Reflections:* self-guide trail of open-air artwork and sculptures around town that illustrate history of area; starts in King St; brochure available from visitor centre.

WHAT'S ON *Market:* showgrounds, Beerburrum Rd; Sun mornings. *Air Spectacular:* May. *Country Music Festival:* May. *Medieval Tournament:* July. *Rodeo:* Dec.

NEARBY *Bribie Island* This island park is separated from the mainland by Pumicestone Passage, where mangroves flourish and dugongs, dolphins, turtles and over 350 species of birds live. National park covers about a third of the island and offers secluded pristine white beaches. Follow the Bicentennial Bushwalks to discover the park on foot, boat along Pumicestone Passage or 4WD along the ocean beach (permit required). Fishing and surfing are popular at Woorim Beach,

just north of which are the old WW II bunkers. See the migratory birds in summer on Buckleys Hole Conservation Park on the south-west tip of the island. Bridge access to island; 21 km E. *Ferryman cruises:* cruise the waters of Pumicestone Passage; (07) 3408 7124. *Caboolture Historical Village:* over 50 restored buildings of historical importance house museums, with themes including maritime and transport; Beerburrum Rd; 2 km N; closed Sun. *Airfield:* Warplane and Flight Heritage Museum with displays of WW II memorabilia and restored fighter planes. Tiger Moth and Mustang flights, hot-air ballooning and gliding offered. McNaught Rd. 2 km E. *Sheep Station Creek Conservation Park:* walks through open forest. See the remains of old bridge on original road leading from Brisbane to Gympie. 6 km SW. *Abbey Museum:* traces growth of western civilisation with displays of art and antiques; just off road to Bribie Island; 9 km E. *Woodford:* the town has one of the largest narrow-gauge steam locomotive collections in Australia, in Margaret St; 22 km NW. *Mount Mee State Forest:* boardwalks through subtropical rainforest and lookouts over Neurum Valley, Moreton Bay and surrounds; 23 km w. *Donnybrook, Toorbul and Beachmere:* coastal fishing towns to the east.
ⓘ 55 King St; (07) 5495 3122; www.cabooltouretourism.com.au

Cairns   Pop. 90 085

Map ref. 604 G11, 611 N6

This modern, colourful city is the capital of the tropical north but was once a service town for the sugar plantations to the south. Tourism boomed with the airport's upgrade in 1984 and the influx of visitors and commercial enterprises resulted in the unusual mix of modern architecture and original Queenslander homes that can be seen today. The cosmopolitan Esplanade traces the bay foreshore and blends the city life of cafes and shopping with the natural attractions of the Coral Sea. With Cairns' superb location – the Great Barrier Reef to the east, mountain rainforests of the Wet Tropics and plains of the Atherton Tableland to the west, and palm-fringed beaches to the north and south – it is a good base for many activities. For fishing enthusiasts, Cairns is famous for its black marlin.

IN TOWN *Flecker Botanic Gardens* Established in 1886 as a recreational reserve, they are now the only wet tropical botanic gardens in Australia. The gardens display tropical plants from around the world, including a number of endangered species and over 200 species of palm. Follow the boardwalks through remnant lowland swamp to adjacent Centenary Lakes to see turtles and mangrove birds. Access gardens via Collins Ave.

QUEENSLAND

Mount Whitfield Conservation Park: 2 major walking tracks through forested mountain range to summit for views of Cairns and Coral Sea; behind botanic gardens. *Royal Flying Doctor Service Visitor Centre:* highlights the history and achievements of the service, with aircraft display; Junction St; closed Sun. *McLeod Street Pioneer Cemetery:* honours local pioneers. *Tank Centre:* multipurpose centre in revamped WW II oil storage tanks, including gallery with local art; Collins Ave. *Regional Gallery:* local artists exhibit in this National Trust-classified building; cnr Shields and Abbott sts. *Cairns Museum:* displays of Aboriginal, gold-rush, timber and sugarcane history; cnr Lake and Shields sts. *Undersea World Aquarium:* variety of tropical fish. See the sharks being fed by divers. Ground floor, Pier Marketplace. *Bulk Sugar Terminal:* guided tours during crushing season (June–Dec); Cook St. *Foreshore Lagoon:* landscaped area with safe swimming lagoon; foreshore; closed Wed mornings. *Kuranda Scenic Railway:* trip through Barron Gorge to rainforest village of Kuranda; leaves Cairns Railway Station in Bunda St; *see also Kuranda. Game fishing:* boats moor at Marlin Marina, Marlin Jetty and Trinity Wharf and you can arrange fishing trips from here; end of Spence St. *Dive schools:* contact visitor centre for details.

WHAT'S ON *Rusty's Bazaar:* Grafton and Sheridan sts; Fri nights and Sat and Sun mornings. *Pier Market:* every Sat and Sun. *Festival Cairns:* Sept.

NEARBY Great Barrier Reef and islands Take a tour, charter a boat or fly to see some of the spectacular sights just offshore. Rainforest-covered Fitzroy Island to the east has impressive snorkelling sites at Welcome and Sharkfin bays. Follow the Secret Garden track to see wildlife up close, including Ulysses butterflies and emerald doves. Green Island to the north-east is a true coral cay and the surrounding reef is home to magnificent tropical fish; they can be seen from a glass-bottom boat, in the underwater observatory or by snorkelling. Smaller Michaelmas and Upolo cays to the north-east are important sites for ground-nesting seabirds. The surrounding waters are excellent for reef swimming. For tours contact visitor centre.

Tjapukai Aboriginal Cultural Park The group began as an Aboriginal dance company in 1987, but the demand for more cultural information prompted the move to this large park. Four theatres, both live and film, illustrate the history and culture of the rainforest people of Far North Queensland. The interactive camp village and 'Tjapukai By Night' live-theatre experience are highlights. Smithfield; 11 km NW.

Beaches: incredible 26 km of beaches extending from Machans Beach on north bank of Barron River, 9 km N, north to Ellis Beach. *Skyrail:* spectacular gondola ride through rainforest to Kuranda; departs Caravonica Lakes, 11 km N. *Bungee tower:* bungee jump from platform through rainforest in Smithfield; 13 km N; contact visitor centre for details. *Crystal Cascades:* walks by cascades. Also an excellent spot for cooling off. End of Redlynch Valley; 18 km SW. *Lake Morris and Copperlode Dam:* walking tracks; 19 km SW. *Barron and Freshwater valleys:* bushwalking, hiking, whitewater rafting and camping to the west and north-west of Cairns; contact visitor centre for details. *Safaris:* 4WD to Cape York and the Gulf Country; contact visitor centre for details.
ℹ️ The Gateway Discovery Centre, 51 The Esplanade; (07) 4051 3588; www.tropicalaustralia.com

Caloundra
Pop. 33 817

Map ref. 601 H6, 602 I13, 607 Q7

This popular holiday spot at the southern tip of the Sunshine Coast was once a retirement haven. It now boasts a diverse population of retirees and young Brisbane commuters keen on the seaside lifestyle. The nearby beaches offer a variety of watersports – the calm waters of Golden Beach are especially popular with windsurfers. The fishing between Bribie Island and the mainland in Pumicestone Passage is excellent.

IN TOWN Queensland Air Museum This museum was founded by members of the Aviation Historical Society of Australia in 1973 in an attempt to collect and celebrate important relics of Queensland's aviation heritage. Memorabilia displayed include old fighter planes and bombers. Airport, Pathfinder Dr.
Caloundra Regional Art Gallery: local and touring art exhibitions; Omrah Ave; open Wed–Sun. *Ben Bennet Botanical Park:* easy walks through natural bushland; Queen St. *Suncruise Helicopter Flights:* over Glass House Mountains and Sunshine Coast; bookings: (07) 5499 6900. *Pumicestone Passage Cruises:* day and twilight tours, depart Maloja Avenue Jetty; daily cruises 11am and 1pm; sunset cruises Tues and Fri; bookings: (07) 5492 8280.

WHAT'S ON *Market:* West Terrace; Sun. *Art and Craft Show:* Aug.

NEARBY Currimundi Lake Conservation Park This unspoiled coastal park offers quiet walks beside the lake and through to the beach. Canoe and swim in the lake or see the finches and friar-birds in the remnant wallum heath. In spring the wildflowers are spectacular. Access from Coongara Esplanade; 4 km N. *Opals Down Under:* opal cutting demonstrations and 'scratch patch' where visitors may fossick for their own gemstones; 14 km NW. *House of Herbs:* nursery and herb house offering educational talk on qualities and uses of herbs; 15 km NW. *Aussie World:* has bush camp with demonstrations of sheepshearing and stock whipping.

Also features native reptile display and one of the country's growing number of Ettamogah Pubs, based on Ken Maynard's cartoon. 18 km NW. *Surrounding beaches:* including patrolled beaches of Bulcock, Kings and Dicky (here you'll find the wreck of SS *Dicky* – 1893); excellent fishing at Moffat and Shelly beaches. *Scenic drives:* taking in the beaches to the north; the Blackall Range with art galleries and views of the Sunshine Coast; the Glass House Mountains with magnificent walks and scenery. Details from visitor centre.
ℹ️ 7 Caloundra Rd; 1800 644 969 or (07) 5491 9233; www.caloundra tourism.com.au

Camooweal
Pop. 238

Map ref. 591 R11, 614 B2

North-west of Mount Isa, Camooweal is the last Queensland town before the Northern Territory border. It was once the centre for enormous cattle drives travelling south. Some say that the town is a suburb of Mount Isa, which would make the 188 kilometres of Barkly Highway between Mount Isa and Camooweal one of the longest main streets in the world. To the south of town are the incredible Camooweal Caves, a series of sinkhole caves that have evolved over millions of years.

IN TOWN *Barkly Tableland Heritage Centre:* museum in National Trust-classified building that exhibits the area's drover history; Barkly Hwy. *Historic buildings:* the Drovers and Freckleton's stores; Barkly Hwy.

WHAT'S ON *Drovers Camp and Reunion Festival:* April.

NEARBY Camooweal Caves National Park On the Barkly Tableland, this national park is still evolving as water continues to filter through the soluble dolomite to create and transform the extensive cave system. The underground caves are linked by vertical shafts and only the experienced caver should attempt them. The Great Nowranie Cave is excellent to explore with an 18 m drop at the opening (climbing gear is essential). Caves may flood during wet season. If exploring the caves, inform local police or ranger beforehand. 4WD access is recommended; 24 km S. *Cemetery:* headstones tell local history; 1 km E. *Boodjamulla (Lawn Hill) National Park:* around 300 km N via Gregory; *see feature on p. 424.*
ℹ️ Barkly Tableland Heritage Centre, Barkly Hwy; (07) 4748 2022

Cardwell
Pop. 1359

Map ref. 603 D5, 611 N10

Cardwell is a coastal town overlooking Rockingham Bay and the nearby islands of the Great Barrier Reef. Ferries transport visitors to nearby Hinchinbrook Island, the largest island national park

Zoe Creek, Hinchinbrook Island

in Australia. Between the island and the mainland is Hinchinbrook Channel (Cardwell is at the northern edge), a popular spot for fishing and snorkelling and a sheltered area for houseboats.

IN TOWN Bush Telegraph Heritage Centre This historical complex comprises the old post office and telegraph station, in operation 1870–1982, and the original magistrates court and gaol cells. An informative history of communications and the region is provided through interpretive displays. 53 Bruce Hwy; open 10am–1pm Tues–Thurs and Sat mornings.
Rainforest and Reef Information Centre: interpretive centre that acquaints visitors with landscape, flora and fauna of northern Queensland; 142 Bruce Hwy, near jetty. *Coral Sea Battle Memorial Park:* large war memorial that commemorates the WW II battle off the coast between Australian/US forces and the Japanese; beachfront. *Boat hire and cruises:* explore the tropical waters and islands to the east at the helm of a yacht, houseboat or cruiser, or travel with an organised cruise; contact visitor centre for details. *Snorkelling and scuba diving tours:* contact visitor centre for details.

WHAT'S ON *Market:* Cardwell Espl; 1st Sun each month. *Coral Sea Battle Memorial Commemoration:* May.

NEARBY Hinchinbrook Island National Park An amazing variety of vegetation covers this island park, including rainforest, wetlands, forests and

woodlands. The 32 km Thorsborne Trail on the east coast is renowned for its spectacular scenery as it winds past waterfalls and along pristine beaches. Many people allow 4 days or more for the walk, camping on a different beach each night. Hikers must be self-sufficient and bookings are essential (limited number of walkers allowed). Shorter walks are from the camping areas at Macushla and The Haven. Access the island via ferry from Cardwell or Lucinda.
Scenic drive in Cardwell State Forest: this 26 km circuit from Cardwell takes in a lookout, waterfalls, swimming holes and picnic spots; begins on Braesnose St. *Edmund Kennedy National Park:* boardwalk through extensive mangrove forests and variety of other vegetation to beach, with spectacular view of islands. This park is a habitat of the endangered mahogany glider. 4 km N. *Dalrymple's Gap:* original service path and stone bridge through range; 15 km S. *Brook Islands:* nesting area for Torresian imperial pigeons (Sep–Feb). Excellent snorkelling on reef of northern 3 islands. Sea access only; 30 km NE. *Murray Falls:* climb the steep 1 km path to viewing platform over falls and surrounds; 42 km NW. *Girringun (Lumholtz) National Park:* travel through World Heritage rainforest on road (dry weather only) to the 3-tier 91 m Blencoe Falls, 71 km W; *see Ingham for southern parts of park.*
ⓘ Rainforest and Reef Information Centre, 142 Bruce Hwy; (07) 4066 8601; www.gspeak.com.au/cardwell

Charleville Pop. 3507

Map ref. 606 B6

Charleville is in the heart of mulga country on the banks of the Warrego River and at the centre of a rich sheep and cattle district. By the late 1890s the town had its own brewery, ten hotels and 500 registered bullock teams. Cobb & Co recognised the value of Charleville as a major stock route and opened a coach-building factory in 1893. There are also strong links with the pioneers of aviation. The first London–Sydney flight landed here in 1919, Qantas' first fare-paying service took off in 1922 and record-setting aviator Amy Johnson landed nearby in 1930. Charleville marks the terminus of the Westlander rail service from Brisbane.

IN TOWN Cosmos Centre This centre explores the Australian night sky and its significance to Aboriginal culture. There are multimedia displays, nightly shows and interactive areas where the wonders of the sky are observed through telescopes. Of particular interest are the show in the Cosmos Theatre on the creation of the universe and the focus on Aboriginal cosmology in the Indigenous Theatre. Matilda Hwy.
Royal Flying Doctor Service Visitor Centre: museum displaying memorabilia from the past and present. View the documentary entitled 'A Day in the Life of the Flying Doctor'. Old Cunnamulla Rd. *National Parks and Wildlife Centre:* with captive breeding

program for endangered yellow-footed rock wallabies and bilbies; Park St; open weekdays; nightly Bilby tours April–Oct. *Historic House Museum:* machinery displays including steam engine and rail ambulance in restored Queensland National Bank building; Alfred St. *CDEP workshop:* displays and sales of Aboriginal art; Matilda Hwy. *Vortex Gun:* in 1902 this 5 m long gun was used in an unsuccessful rain-making experiment; Bicentennial Park, Matilda Hwy. *Heritage trail:* self-guide walk past heritage buildings; brochure available at visitor centre.

WHAT'S ON *Market:* Historic House Museum; 1st Sun each month. *Great Matilda Camel Races and Festival:* July.

NEARBY Tregole National Park This semi-arid national park has a vulnerable and fragile ecosystem. It is largely made up of ooline forest – rainforest trees dating back to the Ice Age. Follow the 2.1 km circuit track to see the diverse vegetation and spectacular birds of the park. 99 km E via Morven. *Monument:* marks the spot where Ross and Keith Smith landed with engine trouble on the first London–Sydney flight; 19 km NW.
ℹ️ Matilda Hwy; (07) 4654 3057

Charters Towers
Pop. 8454

Map ref. 603 E12, 608 E2

Charters Towers is in the Burdekin Basin south-west of Townsville. The town's gold rush began on 25 December 1871 when an Aboriginal horse-boy, Jupiter, made the first gold strike while looking for lost horses. He brought gold-laden quartz to his employer, Hugh Mosman, who rode to Ravenswood to register the claim, and the gold rush was on. Between 1872 and 1916 Charters Towers produced ore worth 25 million pounds. At the height of the gold rush it was Queensland's second largest city and was commonly referred to as 'The World' because of its cosmopolitan population. This rich history can be seen in the preserved streetscapes of 19th- and 20th-century architecture. To the north-west of Charters Towers is the 120-kilometre Great Basalt Wall, a lava wall created from the Toomba basalt flow.

IN TOWN Ghosts of Gold Heritage Trail This informative tour reveals the rich history of the town in the district known as 'One Square Mile'. Over 60 heritage-listed buildings are in the precinct. Of particular interest are the recreated workings of the Stock Exchange in Mosman St; the once heavily mined Towers Hill (1.5 km W) with interpretive walking trails and a film screening at night; and the Venus Gold Battery in Millchester Rd, an old gold processing plant where the 'ghosts' come alive. Starts in the orientation centre behind the visitor centre.
Zara Clark Museum: local historical memorabilia; Mosman St. *Civic Club:* once a men-only club, this remarkably restored

building (1900) still contains the original billiard tables; Ryan St. *Ay Ot Lookout:* actually a restored historic home; cnr High and Hodkinson sts; open Mon–Fri. *Rotary Lookout:* panoramic views over region; Fraser St.

WHAT'S ON *National Trust Markets:* Stock Exchange; 1st and 3rd Sun each month. *Showgrounds Markets:* cnr Mary and Show sts; 2nd Sun each month. *Goldfield Ashes Cricket Carnival:* Jan. *Rodeo:* Easter. *Towers Bonza Bash:* festival including music and bush poets; April–May. *Country Music Festival:* May Day weekend.

NEARBY Dalrymple National Park This small park on the Burdekin River comprises mainly woodland and is an important area for native animals including rock wallabies and sugar gliders. A highlight is the 4 million-year-old solidified lava wall, the Great Basalt Wall, parts of which are accessible from this park. The site of the old Dalrymple township is also of interest. Bushwalkers are advised to contact the ranger before setting out on any walks. 46 km N. *Ravenswood:* another gold-rush centre, but now 'not quite a ghost town'. Today visitors will find historic buildings, interesting old workings and perhaps a little gold. 85 km E. *Burdekin Falls Dam:* recreation area with barramundi fishing; 165 km SE via Ravenswood. *Blackwood National Park:* a woodland park of undulating hills and stony ridges. See the Belyando blackwood trees that give the park its name, and walk on fire trails to discover the park's interesting birdlife including squatter pigeons and speckled warblers. 180 km S.
ℹ️ 74 Mosman St; (07) 4752 0314; www.charterstowers.qld.gov.au

Childers
Pop. 1397

Map ref. 607 O3

Childers is a picturesque National Trust town south of Bundaberg, part of the state's sugarcane belt. With leafy streets and a lovely outlook over the surrounding valleys, the town's history has been blighted by fire. One ravaged the town in 1902 (though many of the heritage buildings survived) and another engulfed a backpacker's hostel in 2000, tragically killing 15 people and making international news. A memorial to those lost in this fire stands in Churchill Street. But life has returned to normal in Childers and the flow of backpackers on the fruit-picking trail is as strong as ever.

IN TOWN *Pharmaceutical Museum:* interesting collection of memorabilia including leather-bound prescription books. Also Aboriginal wares. Churchill St. *Historical complex:* area of historic buildings including school, cottage and locomotive; Taylor St. *Baker's Military and Memorabilia Museum:* 16 000 items on display covering all the major wars, including uniforms and communications

equipment; Ashby La; closed Sun. *Childers Art Gallery:* Churchill St. *Snakes Downunder:* informative exhibits on native snakes; Lucketts Rd; open Tues, Fri, Sat. *Historic Childers:* self-guide town walk past historic buildings; highlight is the Old Butcher's Shop (1896) in Churchill St.

WHAT'S ON *Multicultural Food and Wine Festival:* a week of celebrations also including workshops by visiting artists and performers; last Sun in July.

NEARBY Flying High Bird Habitat The native vegetation here is home to 600 bird species. Follow the boardwalk tracks to see the many Australian parrots and finches. Cnr Bruce Hwy and Old Creek Rd, Apple Creek; 5 km N. *Buxton and Walkers Point:* unspoiled fishing villages to the east. *Woodgate:* coastal town to the north-east with magnificent 16 km beach. Access to Burrum River National Park is from here; *see Bundaberg.* *Goodnight Scrub National Park:* 27 km W; *see Gin Gin.*
ℹ️ Palace Backpackers (Childers Memorial), 72 Churchill St; (07) 4126 1994

Chillagoe
Pop. 183

Map ref. 611 K7

Chillagoe is a small outback town west of Cairns and the Atherton Tableland. Once a thriving mining town after silver and copper deposits were found in 1887, the town was practically deserted after the smelter closed in 1940. Chillagoe's history and the well-preserved Aboriginal rock art and limestone caves in the area make it a popular spot with visitors.

IN TOWN The Hub This major interpretive centre is constructed from local materials including Dreamtime marble and copper. Informative displays cover the geographical history of the local landscape (dating back 2 billion years), the town's mining and pioneering past and the region's Aboriginal heritage. Queen St. *Heritage Museum:* displays on local history and relics of old mining days; Hill St. *Historic cemetery:* headstones from early settlement; Railway Line Rd. *Historical walks:* self-guide or guided walks taking in the old State Smelter and disused marble quarry just south of town; contact visitor centre for details.

WHAT'S ON *Rodeo:* May. *Tablelands Country Music Festival:* July.

NEARBY Chillagoe–Mungana Caves National Park The impressive rugged limestone outcrops and magnificent caves of this park, south of town, are studied by scientists world-wide. The cave system was originally an ancient coral reef and is home to a wide variety of bats. Fossilised bones, including those of a giant kangaroo, have been discovered in the caves. Guided tours only; tickets from The Hub. Above ground are magnificent Aboriginal rock paintings at Balancing Rock. 7 km S.

Almaden: small town where cattle own the main street; 30 km SE. *Mungana:* Aboriginal rock paintings at the Archways. Also a historic cemetery. 16 km W. *4WD self-guide adventure trek:* mud maps and clues provided; contact visitor centre for details. *Tag-along tours:* full- and half-day tours visiting Aboriginal sites, marble quarries and other interesting places; contact visitor centre for details.
ℹ The Hub, 23 Queen St; (07) 4094 7111; www.athertontableland.com

Chinchilla   Pop. 3366

Map ref. 607 K7

Chinchilla is a prosperous town in the western Darling Downs. Ludwig Leichhardt named the area in 1844 after the local Aboriginal name for the native cypress pines, 'jinchilla' – there are still many in town. Chinchilla is known as the 'melon capital' of Australia as it produces around 25 percent of the country's watermelons.

IN TOWN *Historical Museum:* a varied collection of memorabilia including steam engines, a replica 1910 sawmill and a slab cottage. Also an excellent display of local petrified wood known as 'Chinchilla Red'. Villiers St. *Pioneer Cemetery:* headstones tell early history. Also a monument to Ludwig Leichhardt. Warrego Hwy.

WHAT'S ON *Melon Festival:* odd-numbered years; Feb. *Market:* Warrego Hwy; Easter Sat. *Rotary May Day Carnival:* May. *Polocrosse Carnival:* July. *Lions Mardi Gras:* last Sat in Nov.

NEARBY *Cactoblastis Memorial Hall:* dedicated to the insect introduced from South America to eradicate the prickly pear cactus; Boonarga, 8 km E. *Fossicking:* for petrified wood at nearby properties; contact visitor centre for licences and details. *Fishing:* good spots include Charleys Creek and the Condamine River; contact visitor centre for details. *Chinchilla Weir:* popular spot for boating and waterskiing, plus excellent fishing for freshwater fish, including golden perch and jewfish; 10 km S.
ℹ Warrego Hwy; (07) 4668 9564; www.chinchilla.org.au

Clermont   Pop. 2038

Map ref. 608 H9

Clermont is in the central highlands south-west of Mackay. It was established over 130 years ago after the discovery of gold at Nelson's Gully. At first the settlement was at Hood's Lagoon, but was moved to higher ground after a major flood in 1916 in which 63 people died. To the east of Clermont are the prominent cone-shaped mountains of Peak Range National Park. The Wolfgang Peak between Clermont and Mackay is particularly spectacular.

IN TOWN **Hood's Lagoon and Centenary Park** Walk the boardwalks in this

A rustic scene in Clermont

picturesque setting to see the colourful birdlife. The park has interesting memorials and monuments that include the Sister Mary MacKillop grotto, an Aboriginal monument and a war memorial. The tree marker at the flood memorial plaque demonstrates how high the water rose. Access via Lime St. *Railway Wagon Murals:* paintings on four original wagons depict industries within the Belyando Shire; Hershel St. *The Stump:* memorial to the 1916 floods; cnr Drummond and Capricorn sts.

WHAT'S ON *Gold Festival:* Aug.

NEARBY *Cemetery:* headstones dating back to 1860s and mass grave of 1916 flood victims; just north of town. *Clermont Museum and Heritage Park:* museum exhibits historic artefacts and machinery, including the steam engine used to shift the town after floods. Complex also comprises historic buildings, such as the old Masonic lodge, with photo displays of local family histories. 4 km NW. *Remnants of Copperfield:* old coppermining town with museum in original Copperfield store, chimneystack, and cemetery containing 19th-century graves of copperminers; 5 km S. *Theresa Creek Dam:* popular spot for waterskiing, sailboarding and fishing (permit required). Bushwalks nearby. Off Peakvale Rd; 17 km SW. *Blair Athol open-cut mine:* free half-day tour to see the largest seam of steaming coal in the world; departs from Clermont Visitor Centre 8.45am Tues and Fri. Blair Athol is 23 km NW. *Blackwood National Park:* 187 km NW; *see Charters Towers. Fossicking for gold:* obtain licence and fossicking kit to start the search in nearby area; contact visitor centre for details.
ℹ 58 Capella St; (07) 4983 3001; www.belyando.qld.gov.au

Clifton   Pop. 885

Map ref. 607 N10

Clifton is south of Toowoomba in the fertile agricultural lands of the Darling Downs. The town's charming street facades have been a popular backdrop for many Australian movies, including the epic *Thornbirds*. The town is a vision of colour during the renowned annual Rose and Iris Show.

IN TOWN *Historical Museum:* in the old butter factory, with displays of early implements and farm life; King St. *Alister Clark Rose Garden:* largest Queensland collection of these roses; Edward St.

WHAT'S ON *Rose and Iris Show:* Oct.

NEARBY **Nobby** This small town provided inspiration to well-known writer Arthur Hoey Davis (Steele Rudd), author of *On Our Selection* and creator of the famous Dad and Dave characters. Rudd's Pub (1893) is dedicated to the author and has a museum of pioneering memorabilia. Nearby is the burial site of Sister Kenny along with a memorial and museum dedicated to her – she was renowned for her unorthodox method of treating poliomyelitis. 8 km N. *Leyburn:* holds the Historic Race Car Sprints in Aug; 30 km W.
ℹ Council offices, 70 King St; (07) 4697 4222; www.clifton.qld.gov.au

Cloncurry   Pop. 2731

Map ref. 614 G4

Cloncurry is an important mining town in the Gulf Savannah region. In 1861 John McKinlay, leading a search for Burke and Wills, reported traces of copper in the area. Six years later, pastoralist Ernest Henry discovered the first copper lodes. During World War I Cloncurry was the centre of a copper boom and the largest

QUEENSLAND

source of the mineral in Australia. Copper prices slumped postwar and a pastoral industry took its place. The town's interesting history extends to aviation as well. Qantas was conceived here – the original hangar can still be seen at the airport – and the town became the first base for the famous Royal Flying Doctor Service in 1928.

IN TOWN John Flynn Place This complex includes the RFDS Museum, with history on the service and memorabilia including the first RFDS aircraft and an original Traeger pedal wireless. There is also the Fred McKay Art Gallery, with changing exhibits of local art, the Alfred Traegar Cultural Centre and the Alan Vickers Outdoor Theatre. Cnr Daintree and King sts. *Mary Kathleen Park:* with buildings from abandoned uranium mining town of Mary Kathleen including Old Police Station and Town Office – now a museum with historic items such as Robert O'Hara Burke's water bottle, local Aboriginal artefacts and a comprehensive rock, mineral and gem collection; McIlwraith St. *Shire hall:* restored 1939 building; Scarr St. *Cemeteries:* varied cultural background of Cloncurry can be seen in the three cemeteries: Cloncurry Old Cemetery, including the grave of Dame Mary Gilmore (Sir Hudson Fyshe Dr); Afghan Cemetery (part of Cloncurry Old Cemetery); Chinese Cemetery (Flinders Hwy). *Original Qantas hangar:* airport, Sir Hudson Fyshe Dr.

WHAT'S ON *Market:* Florence Park, Scarr St; 2nd Sat each month. *Stockman's Challenge and Campdraft:* night rodeo; July. *Country Music and Bush Poets Festival:* July. *Merry Muster Rodeo:* Aug. *Clash of the Mines:* Oct.

NEARBY *Rotary Lookout:* over Cloncurry and the river; Mount Isa Hwy; 2 km w. *Chinamen Creek Dam:* peaceful area with abundant birdlife; 3 km w. *Ernest Henry Copper and Gold Mine:* tours available; 29 km NE. *Burke and Wills cairn:* near Corella River; 43 km w. *Kajabbi:* town holds Yabby Races in May; 77 km NW. *Kuridala:* this one-time mining town is now a ghost town. Explore the ruins including the old cemetery. 88 km s. *Fossicking:* for amethysts and other gemstones nearby; contact visitor centre for details. ⓘ Mary Kathleen Park, McIlwraith St; (07) 4742 1361; www.cloncurry.qld. gov.au

Cooktown   Pop. 1572

Map ref. 611 L3

Cooktown is the last main town before the vast wilderness that is Cape York. In 1770 Captain James Cook beached the *Endeavour* here for repairs after running aground on the Great Barrier Reef. Cooktown was founded more than 100 years later after gold was discovered at Palmer River. It became the gold-rush

port with 37 hotels and a transient population of some 18 000, including 6000 Chinese. Around Cooktown are some of the most rugged and remote national parks in Australia. They form part of the Wet Tropics World Heritage Area and are a special experience for the intrepid explorer.

IN TOWN James Cook Museum Housed in the old convent school (1888), this museum documents the varied history of the area, from Aboriginal times to Cook's voyages and the gold-rush past. Relics include the anchor from the *Endeavour.* Helen St.
Botanic Gardens: these are the second oldest botanic gardens in Queensland, with native, European and exotic plants. The 'Cooktown Interpretive Centre: Nature's Powerhouse' has botanical and wildlife illustrations, and there are also walking trails to Cherry Tree and Finch bays. Walker St. *Historic cemetery:* documents varied cultural heritage of Cooktown and includes grave of tutor, early immigrant and heroine Mary Watson; Boundary Rd. *Chinese Shrine:* to many who died on the goldfields; near cemetery. *Cooktown Wharf:* dates back to 1880s and is an excellent spot for fishing. *The Milibi Wall:* collage of traditional art by local Aboriginal people; near wharf.

WHAT'S ON *Markets:* Endeavour Lions Park; 2nd Sat each month. *Endeavour Festival:* re-enactment of Cook's landing; June.

NEARBY Lizard Island National Park Comprises six islands to the north-east of Cooktown surrounded by the blue waters and coral reefs of the northern Great Barrier Reef. Four of the islands are important seabird nesting sites. Lizard Island is a resort island and a popular destination for sailing and fishing. Also on offer is snorkelling in the giant clam gardens of Watsons Bay. Walk to Cooks Look for a spectacular view. There are eleven species of lizard here, and green and loggerhead turtles nest in late spring. Regular flights depart from Cairns; charter flights depart from Cairns and Cooktown; charter or private boat hire is available at Cooktown.
Endeavour River National Park: just north of town is this park of diverse landscapes, including coastal dunes, mangrove forests and catchment areas of the Endeavour River. Most of the park is accessible only by boat (ramps at Cooktown); southern vehicle access is via Starcke St, Marton. *Black Mountain National Park:* impressive mountain range of granite boulders and a refuge for varied and threatened wildlife; Cooktown Developmental Rd; 25 km s. *Helenvale:* small town with historic Lions Den Hotel (est. 1875) and rodeo in June; 30 km s. *Rossville:* town with markets every 2nd Sat and Wallaby Creek Folk Festival at Home Rule Rainforest Lodge in Sept; 38 km s. *Cedar Bay (Mangkal–Mangkalba)*

National Park: this remote coastal park is an attractive mix of rainforest, beaches and fringing reefs, with a variety of wildlife including the rare Bennett's tree kangaroo. Walk on the old donkey track once used by tin miners (remains of tin workings can be seen). Access by boat or by the walking track, which starts at Home Rule Rainforest Lodge, Rossville, 38 km s. *Elim Beach and the Coloured Sands:* spectacular beach with white silica sand hills and surrounding heathlands. The Coloured Sands are found 400 m along the beach (Aboriginal land, permit required from Hope Vale Community Centre). 65 km N. *Cape Melville National Park:* this rugged park on the Cape York Peninsula has spectacular coastal scenery. Much of the plant life is rare, including the foxtail palm. Visitors must be self-sufficient; 4WD access only in dry weather. Southern access via Starcke homestead; western access via Kalpower Crossing in Lakefield National Park. 140 km NW. *Flinders Group National Park:* comprising 7 continental islands in Princess Charlotte Bay. There are 2 self-guide trails taking in bushfoods and Aboriginal rock-art sites on Stanley Island. Access by charter or private boat or seaplane; 195 km NW. *Sportfishing safaris:* to nearby waterways; contact visitor centre for details. *Guurrbi Aboriginal Tours:* full- and half-day tours of Aboriginal rock-art sites and informative history of bush tucker and traditional medicine; contact visitor centre for details. *Bicentennial National Trail:* 5000 km trail that runs from Cooktown to Healesville in Victoria, for walkers, bike riders and horseriders. Possible to do just a section of trail. Contact visitor centre for details. ***Travellers note:*** *Before driving to remote areas check road conditions and restrictions with Queensland Parks and Wildlife Service, 5 Webber Espl, Cooktown, (07) 4069 5777.* ⓘ 101 Charlotte St; 1800 001 770 or (07) 4069 5446

Crows Nest   Pop. 1321

Map ref. 607 N8

On the western slopes of the Great Dividing Range north of Toowoomba is the small town of Crows Nest. It was named after Jimmy Crow, a Kabi-Kabi Aboriginal man who made his home in a hollow tree near the present police station. He was an invaluable source of directions for passing bullock teams staying overnight in the area. A memorial to Crow can be found in Centenary Park.

IN TOWN *Carbethon Folk Museum and Pioneer Village:* many interesting old buildings and over 20 000 items of memorabilia documenting the history of the shire; Thallon St; open Thurs–Sun. *Bullocky's Rest and Applegum Walk:* a 1.5 km track follows the creeks to Hartmann Park and a lookout over Pump Hole.

Visit in late winter to see the beautiful wildflowers. New England Hwy.

WHAT'S ON *Village Markets:* arts, crafts and local produce; 1st Sun each month. *Crows Nest Day:* children's worm races, fun run and painting competitions; Oct.

NEARBY Crows Nest National Park This popular park features a variety of landscapes, including granite outcrops and eucalypt forest. The wildlife is spectacular: see the platypus in the creek and the brush-tailed rock wallabies on the rocky cliffs. A steep track from the creek leads to an excellent lookout over Crows Nest Falls; follow this further to Koonin Lookout for spectacular views over the gorge, known locally as the Valley of Diamonds. 6 km E (look for sign to Valley of Diamonds).

Lake Cressbrook: set amongst picturesque hills is this excellent spot for windsurfing and boating. Fish the lake for silver perch. 17 km E. *Ravensbourne National Park:* a small park comprising remnant rainforest and wet eucalypt forest with over 80 species of birds, including the black-breasted button-quail that can be seen feeding on the rainforest floor on the Cedar Block track. Many bushwalks start at Blackbean picnic area. Esk–Hampton Rd; 25 km SE. *Beutel's Lookout:* picnic area with scenic views across the Brisbane Valley; adjacent to Ravensbourne National Park; 25 km SE. *Goombungee:* historic town with museum. Famous for running rural ironman and ironwoman competitions on Australia Day. 32 km W. *Walking and bike tracks to Toowoomba:* contact visitor centre for details.
ⓘ Hampton Visitor Information Centre, 8623 New England Hwy, Hampton (12 km s); 1800 009 066 or (07) 4697 9066; www.crowsnest.info

Croydon   Pop. 223

Map ref. 610 F10

Croydon is a small town on the grassland plains of the Gulf Savannah. It marks the eastern terminus for the *Gulflander* train service, which leaves each Thursday for Normanton. The train line was established in the late 1800s to service Croydon's booming gold industry. Many original buildings dating from 1887 to 1897, and classified by the National Trust and Australian Heritage Commission, have been restored to the splendour of the town's goldmining days.

IN TOWN *Historical Village:* historical precinct with many restored buildings brings the rich history of Croydon to life. Highlights include the courthouse, with original furniture and hospital documents, and the old hospital ward. Tours start at the visitor centre daily. *Outdoor Museum:* displays mining machinery from the age of steam; Samwell St. *Old Police Precinct and Gaol:* historic documents and access to gaol cells; Samwell St. *General Store*

The buttress roots of an enormous tree, Mossman Gorge section

Daintree National Park

'The Daintree' is arguably Australia's most beautiful and famous rainforest. The lush tangle of green protected within it is an incredible remnant from the days of Gondwana, forming part of the Wet Tropics World Heritage Area. This park will dazzle visitors with its diverse landscapes such as canopies of sprawling fan palms, deserted mangrove-lined beaches and boulder-strewn gorges.

Mossman Gorge section

The Mossman Gorge section is a picturesque landscape of swimming holes, granite boulders, coastal lowlands and rugged mountain terrain. Walk 400 metres from the carpark to the suspension bridge over Rex Creek – look out for freshwater turtles and platypus. Continue on to the informative 2.7-kilometre Rex Creek rainforest circuit. Another way to explore this part of the park is on a guided KuKu Yalanji Dreamtime Walk traversing an old Aboriginal trail through the rainforest. Walkers learn about bush tucker and the legends of the Dreamtime along the way. This section is around five kilometres west of Mossman.

Cape Tribulation section

The Cape Tribulation section is between the Daintree and Bloomfield rivers and was named by Captain Cook on his troubled voyage in 1770. It features crystal-clear creeks, forests festooned with creepers and vines, and palm-lined beaches. Visitors might catch a glimpse of rainforest birds such as the cassowary or the noisy pitta. There are informative rainforest and mangrove walks like the Maardja boardwalk at Oliver Creek or the Dubuji boardwalk at Cape Tribulation. Experienced hikers ready for a challenge would enjoy the full-day Mt Sorrow Ridge trail, with spectacular views over the Daintree coast. This section is accessed via the Daintree River cable ferry (runs 6am–12 midnight daily). Four-wheel drive is recommended and motorists are advised to check the RACQ Road Conditions Report on 1300 130 595 (or www.racq.com.au) for information before departing.

Snapper Island section

This island of rainforest and grassland lies near the mouth of the Daintree River, two kilometres east of Cape Kimberley. Queen Elizabeth and Prince Phillip lunched here on their 1970 tour of the area. Snorkelling in the surrounding reef is spectacular. There is a short walking track linking the beaches on the north-west and south-west coasts. Access is by private boat and visitors should anchor on the north-west side of the island.

Travellers note: Beware of estuarine crocodiles that live in the sea and estuaries; never cross tidal creeks at high tide, swim in creeks, prepare food at water's edge or camp close to deep waterholes. Beware of marine stingers between October and March.

Cotton crop near Dalby

and Museum: restored store in the old ironmongers shop; Sircom St.
WHAT'S ON *Rodeo:* June. *Campdraft:* Aug. *Poddy Dodger Music Festival Week:* Sept.
NEARBY *Mine Museum:* interesting display of early mining machinery including battery stamper; 1 km N. *Historic cemetery:* includes old Chinese gravestones; 2 km s. *Chinese Temple Site:* Heritage-listed archaeological site of 50 years of Chinese settlement. Follow the Heritage Trail to see how the Chinese lived. On road to Lake Belmore. *Lake Belmore:* one of many sites for birdwatching. Also swimming, waterskiing and fishing (limits apply). 5 km N.
ⓘ Samwell St; (07) 4745 6125; www.gulf-savannah.com.au

Cunnamulla   Pop. 1357

Map ref. 606 A10, 617 R10

Cunnamulla is on the Warrego River, north of the New South Wales border. It is the biggest wool-loading station on the Queensland railway network, with two million sheep in the area. Explorers Sir Thomas Mitchell and Edmund Kennedy were the first European visitors, arriving in 1846 and 1847 respectively, and by 1879 the town was thriving with regular Cobb & Co services to the west. In 1880 Joseph Wells held up the local bank but could not find his escape horse. Locals bailed him up in a tree that is now known as the Robber's Tree and can be found in Stockyard Street. The wetland birdlife in the area, particularly the black swans,

brolgas and pelicans, is spectacular.
IN TOWN *Bicentennial Museum:* photographs and memorabilia document town's history; John St. *Yupunyah Tree:* planted by Princess Anne; cnr Louise and Stockyard sts. *Lost Generation Arts and Crafts:* exhibits and sales of local Aboriginal art; Stockyard St. *Outback Botanic Gardens and Herbarium:* Matilda Hwy. *The Heritage Trail:* discover the days of the late 1880s on this self-guide trail; contact visitor centre for details.
WHAT'S ON *Races:* April. *Cunnamulla–Eulo Lizard Races:* Sept. *Bullride Championships:* Nov.
NEARBY *Wyandra:* small town featuring Powerhouse Museum and Heritage Trail; 100 km N. *Noorama:* remote sheep station that holds picnic races each April; 110 km SE. *Culgoa Floodplain National Park:* 195 km SE; *see St George.*
ⓘ Centenary Park, Jane St; (07) 4655 2481; www.paroo.info

Daintree   Pop. 70

Map ref. 605 C4, 611 M5

The unspoiled township of Daintree lies in the tropical rainforest of Far North Queensland, at the heart of the Daintree River catchment basin surrounded by the McDowall Ranges. Daintree began as a logging town in the 1870s. Now tourism is the major industry with the natural delights of the Daintree River and World Heritage rainforest nearby. Australia's prehistoric reptile, the saltwater crocodile, can be seen in the mangrove-lined creeks and tributaries of the Daintree River.

IN TOWN *Daintree Timber Museum:* hand-crafted pieces from local woods exhibited and sold. Also displays telling local history, including logging past. Stewart St.
NEARBY *Daintree National Park:* spectacular rainforest park to the north-east and south-east of Daintree; *see feature on p. 407. Daintree Discovery Centre:* informative displays introduce visitors to the area. A boardwalk and aerial walkway passes through rainforest and canopy tower. 11 km SE. *Wonga Belle Orchid Gardens:* 3.5 ha of lush gardens; 17 km SE. *Cape Tribulation:* spectacular beaches and reefs. Reef tours and horseriding on beach can be arranged at visitor centre or Mason's Shop in Cape Tribulation; for details phone (07) 4098 0070. Access via Daintree River cable ferry (car ferry, runs 6am–12midnight). *River cruises:* to see the saltwater crocodiles and plentiful birdlife; contact visitor centre for details.
ⓘ 5 Stewart St; (07) 4098 6120; www.pddt.com.au

Dalby   Pop. 9693

Map ref. 607 M8

Dalby is a large town on the volcanic black soil of the northern Darling Downs. It was a small rural town until the soldier resettlement program after World War II. The population influx allowed the surrounding agricultural industry to thrive. Dalby is now the centre of Australia's richest grain- and cotton-growing area.
IN TOWN *Pioneer Park Museum:* comprises historic buildings, household and agricultural items and a craft shop; Black St. *Cultural and Administration Centre:* regional art gallery, theatre, cinema and restaurant; Drayton St. *The Crossing:* an obelisk marks the spot where explorer Henry Dennis camped in 1841; Edward St. *Historic cairn:* pays homage to the cactoblastis, the Argentinean caterpillar that eradicated prickly pear in the 1920s; Myall Creek picnic area, Marble St. *Myall Creek Walk:* walkway along banks of Myall Creek to see varied birdlife. *Heritage walk:* self-guide walk provides insight into town's history. It starts at St Joseph's Catholic Church, Cunningham St; brochure available from visitor centre.
WHAT'S ON *Cotton Week:* 4-day festival; Mar. *Australian Stockhorse Show:* Dec.
NEARBY Lake Birdwater Conservation Park The 350 ha lake is an important breeding ground for waterfowl. There are over 240 species of bird that can be seen from the short walks around the lake. Waterskiing and boating are popular on the main body of the lake when it is full (permit required). 29 km SW. *Historic Jimbour House:* attractive French homestead, formal gardens and boutique winery; 29 km N. *Bell:* small town at the base of Bunya Mountains with traditional arts and crafts stores; 41 km NW. *Cecil Plains:* cotton town with historic

murals and Cecil Plains Homestead. Also a popular spot for canoeing down Condamine River. 42 km s. *Rimfire Vineyards and Winery:* boutique winery offering tastings; 47 km NE. *Bunya Mountains National Park:* 63 km NE; *see Kingaroy.*
ℹ️ Thomas Jack Park, cnr Drayton and Condamine sts; (07) 4662 1066; www.dalby.info

Emerald   Pop. 10 037
Map ref. 608 I11

Shady Moreton Bay fig trees line the main street in Emerald, an attractive town at the hub of the Central Highlands. The town was established in 1879 as a service town while the railway from Rockhampton to the west was being constructed. Several fires ravaged the town in the mid-1900s, destroying much of this early history. The largest sapphire fields in the Southern Hemisphere are nearby, where visitors can fossick for their own gems.
IN TOWN *Pioneer Cottage Complex:* historic cottage and lock-up gaol with padded cells. There is also a church and a communications museum. Harris St. *Botanic Gardens:* walk around native display, herb garden and Melaleuca maze. You can also visit a traditional bush chapel and ride the monorail. Banks of Nogoa River. *Railway station:* restored 1900 National Trust-classified station with attractive lacework and pillared portico; Clermont St. *Fossilised tree:* 250 million years old; in front of Town Hall. *Mosaic pathway:* 21 pictures depict 100 years of Emerald history; next to visitor centre. *Van Gogh Sunflower Painting:* largest one (on an easel) in the world; Morton Park, Clermont St.
WHAT'S ON *Sunflower Festival:* Easter. *Wheelbarrow Derby:* odd-numbered years, June. *Gems of Country:* music festival; June. *Gemfest:* Aug.
NEARBY **Sapphire Gemfields** To the west of Emerald is the largest sapphire-producing area in the Southern Hemisphere, incorporating the towns of Rubyvale, Sapphire, Anakie and Willows Gemfields. They feature walk-in mines, fossicking parks, gem-faceting demonstrations, jewellers and museums. Obtain a licence and map of the mining areas from local stores or the Department of Natural Resources in Emerald to start fossicking for precious gems. Rubyvale offers 4WD tours of local gemfields including Tomahawk Creek. *Kiely's Farm and Animal Sanctuary:* birds and wildlife including deer, alpacas and wallabies. Tour the cotton farm. 7 km E. *Lake Maraboon/Fairbairn Dam:* popular spot for watersports and fishing, especially for the red claw crayfish; 19 km s. *Capella:* first town settled in the area. See its history at the Capella Pioneer Village. The Pioneer Village Arts and Crafts Fair is held every April. 51 km NW. *Local cattle stations*

and farm stays: day tours in nearby area; contact visitor centre for details.
ℹ️ Clermont St; (07) 4982 4142; www.emerald.qld.gov.au

Esk   Pop. 894
Map ref. 601 B10, 607 O8

Esk is a heritage town in the Upper Brisbane Valley renowned for its beautiful lakes and dams where watersports enthusiasts are well catered for. Deer roam in the fine grazing country north of town, progeny of a small herd presented to the state by Queen Victoria in 1873.
IN TOWN *Antiques and local crafts:* numerous shops in town.
WHAT'S ON *Market:* Highland St; each Sat. *Multicultural Festival:* July. *Picnic Races:* July.
NEARBY **Lakes and dams** Known as the Valley of the Lakes, this region is popular for swimming, fishing and boating. Lake Wivenhoe (25 km E) is the source of Brisbane's main water supply and the state's centre for championship rowing. Walk to the Fig Tree Lookout for a panoramic view over the dam and lake area or ride a horse around the lake. Lake Somerset (25 km NE) is on the Stanley River and is a popular waterskiing spot. Atkinson Dam (30 km s) also attracts watersports enthusiasts. *Caboonbah Homestead:* museum that houses the Brisbane Valley Historical Society, with superb views over Lake Wivenhoe; 19 km NE; closed Thurs. *Coominya:* small historic town that holds the Watermelon Festival in Jan; 22 km SE. *Ravensbourne National Park:* 33 km W; *see Crows Nest. Skydiving:* take a tandem dive over valley; contact visitor centre for details.
ℹ️ 82 Ipswich St; (07) 5424 2923; www.esk.qld.gov.au

Eulo   Pop. 75
Map ref. 617 Q11

Eulo is on the banks of the Paroo River in south-west Queensland and was once a centre for opal mining. The town was originally much closer to the river but, after severe flooding, moved to where it currently stands. Eulo's population is variable as beekeepers travel from the south every winter so their bees can feed on the precious eucalypts in the area.
IN TOWN *Eulo Queen Hotel:* owes its name to Isobel Robinson who ran the hotel and reigned over the opal fields in the early 1900s; Leo St. *Eulo Date Farm:* taste the famous date wine; western outskirts; open Easter–Oct. *WW II air-raid shelter:* part of Paroo Pioneer Pathways; self-guide brochure available from visitor centre. *Destructo Cockroach Monument:* commemorates the death of a champion racing cockroach; near Paroo Track, where annual lizard races are held. *Fishing:* on the Paroo River; contact visitor centre for details.

WHAT'S ON *Cunnamulla–Eulo Lizard Races:* Sept.
NEARBY **Currawinya National Park** The lakes and waterholes of Paroo River form an important refuge for the abundant birdlife of this park. The 85 km circuit track for vehicles starts at the Ranger Station and is the best way to view the park. See the black swans and grebes at Lake Wyara or go canoeing at Lake Numulla. For an excellent outlook over the park, climb the Granites. 4WD necessary to reach the lakes. 60 km SW. *Mud springs:* natural pressure valve to artesian basin that is currently inactive; 9 km W. *Yowah:* small opal-mining town where visitors can fossick for opals or take a tour of the minefields. The 'Bluff' and 'Castles' provide excellent views over the minefields. Yowah holds a craft day in June and the Opal Festival in July, which includes an international opal jewellery competition. 87 km NW. *Lake Bindegolly National Park:* walk to the lakes to see pelicans and swans. The 9.2 km lake circuit track may flood after rain. No vehicles are allowed in the park. 100 km W. *Thargomindah:* pick up a mud map at visitor centre for Burke and Wills Dig Tree site; 130 km W. *Noccundra Waterhole:* good fishing spot on Wilson River; 260 km W.
ℹ️ Centenary Park, Jane St, Cunnamulla; (07) 4655 2481; www.paroo.info

Gatton   Pop. 5027
Map ref. 607 O9

In the Lockyer Valley west of Brisbane, Gatton was one of the first rural settlements in Queensland. The much recorded and debated 'Gatton Murders' that occurred in 1898 were the subject of Australian writer Rodney Hall's novel *Captivity Captive.* The graves of the three murdered siblings can still be seen in the cemetery. The Great Dividing Range provides a scenic backdrop to the surrounding fertile black soil, excellent for vegetable produce.
IN TOWN *Lake Apex:* park and complex include the historic village with preserved heritage buildings, memorabilia and Aboriginal carvings. Follow the walking tracks to see the diverse birdlife. Old Warrego Hwy.
WHAT'S ON *Clydesdale and Heavy Horse field days:* May. *Potato Carnival:* Oct.
NEARBY *Agricultural College:* opened in 1897. Drive through the grounds that are now part of the University of Queensland. 5 km E. *Helidon:* town noted for its sandstone – used in many Brisbane buildings – and spa water; 16 km W. *Glen Rock Regional Park:* at the head of East Haldon Valley, this park boasts rainforest gorges, creeks and excellent valley views; 40 km s. *Tourist drive:* 82 km circuit through surrounding countryside that includes farm visits; contact visitor centre for details.
ℹ️ Lake Apex Dr; (07) 5462 3430; www.gatton.qld.gov.au

Gayndah
Pop. 1788

Map ref. 607 N4

Gayndah, in the Capricorn region, is one of Queensland's oldest towns. Founded in 1849, it was once competing with Brisbane and Ipswich to be the state's capital. Main Street's heritage buildings and attractive landscaped gardens illustrate the long history of the town. Gayndah is now central to a rich citrus-growing industry.

IN TOWN **Historical Museum** An award-winning museum that documents the area's pioneer heritage. In several historic buildings, displays, photographs and memorabilia illustrate the town's changing history from small settlement to thriving agricultural centre – a highlight is a restored 1884 Georgian cottage. There is also an interesting display on the lungfish and its link between sea and land animals. Simon St.

WHAT'S ON *Orange Festival:* odd-numbered years, June.

NEARBY *Lookouts:* several in area offering views over Burnett Valley. Closest to town is Archers Lookout, atop the twin hills 'Duke and Duchess' overlooking town. *Claude Warton Weir:* excellent spot for fishing and picnics; 3 km w. *Ban Ban Springs:* natural springs and picnic area; 26 km s.
ⓘ Historical Museum, 3 Simon St; (07) 4161 2226

Gin Gin
Pop. 890

Map ref. 607 N2

Some of Queensland's oldest cattle properties surround this pastoral town south-west of Bundaberg. The district is known as 'Wild Scotchman Country' after James McPherson, Queensland's only authentic bushranger. His antics are re-enacted every March at the Wild Scotchman Festival.

IN TOWN *Historical Society Museum:* displays memorabilia of pioneering past in 'The Residence' – a former police sergeant's house. The old sugarcane locomotive *The Bunyip* forms part of the historic railway display. Mulgrave St. *Courthouse Gallery:* fine-arts gallery in old courthouse; Mulgrave St.

WHAT'S ON *Wild Scotchman Festival:* Mar.

NEARBY **Goodnight Scrub National Park** A dense remnant hoop pine rainforest in the Burnett Valley, this park is home to over 60 species of butterfly. Have a bush picnic at historic Kalliwa Hut, used during the logging days of the park. Drive up to One Tree Hill (4WD only) for a spectacular panoramic view over the area, on a clear day, all the way to Bundaberg. Turn-off is 10 km south of Gin Gin. *Lake Monduran:* an excellent spot for watersports and fishing (permit from

The coastline at Coolangatta, on the Gold Coast

kiosk). Catch a barramundi or Australian bass, or walk the 6 km of walking tracks in the bush surrounds. 24 km NW. *Boolboonda Tunnel:* longest non-supported tunnel in the Southern Hemisphere. It forms part of a scenic tourist drive; brochure available from visitor centre. 27 km w. *Mount Perry:* small mining town, home to the Mount Perry Mountain Cup, a mountain-bike race, in June; 55 km SW.
ⓘ Mulgrave St; (07) 4157 3060

Gladstone
Pop. 26 509

Map ref. 609 P12

Gladstone is a modern city on the central coast of Queensland. Matthew Flinders discovered Port Curtis, Gladstone's deep-water harbour, in 1802, but the town did not truly develop until the

1960s. Today it is an outlet for central Queensland's mineral and agricultural wealth – a prosperous seaboard city with one of Australia's busiest harbours. Set among hills with natural lookouts over the harbour and southern end of the Great Barrier Reef, Gladstone's waterways and beaches are popular for swimming and surfing. They are also good fishing spots – especially for mud crabs and prawns.

IN TOWN *Tondoon Botanic Gardens:* displays of all-native species of the Port Curtis region with free guided tours on weekends. Also offers a recreational lake and Mount Biondello bushwalk. Glenlyon Rd. *Gladstone Regional Art Gallery and Museum:* local and regional art with history exhibitions; cnr Goondoon and Bramston sts. *Maritime Museum:* artefacts and memorabilia document 200 years of port history; Auckland Point; Thurs–Sun. *Potter's Place:* fine-art gallery and craft shop; Dawson Hwy. *Gecko Valley Vineyard:* tastings and sales of award-winning wines; Bailiff Rd. *Barney Point Beach:* historic beach including Friend Park; Barney St. *Waterfall:* spectacular at night when floodlit; Flinders Pde.

WHAT'S ON *Harbour Festival:* includes the finish of the Brisbane to Gladstone Yacht Race; Easter. *Multicultural Festival:* Aug. *Seafood Festival:* Sept.

NEARBY **Capricornia Cays National Park** This park, 60–100 km offshore from Gladstone, protects the nine coral islands and cays that form the southern end of the Great Barrier Reef. The islands are important nesting sites for seabirds and loggerhead turtles. North West Island has walking tracks through forests dominated by palms and she-oaks. The most popular activities are reef walking, diving and snorkelling in the spectacular reefs or visiting the renowned dive sites on Heron Island. Access is by private boat or charter from Gladstone; air access to Heron Island. There is seasonal closure to protect nesting wildlife. *Boyne Island:* with beautiful foreshore parks and beaches. Home to the Boyne–Tannum Hookup Fishing Competition in June. The Boyne Aluminium Smelter is Australia's largest and has an information centre and tours every Fri. The island and its twin town of Tannum Sands are linked by bridge. 25 km SE. *Tannum Sands:* small community offers sandy beaches with year-round swimming, picturesque Millennium Way along the beach and 15 km of scenic walkways known as the Turtle Way. Wild Cattle Island, an uninhabited national park at the southern end of the beach, can be reached on foot at low tide. 25 km SE. *Calliope:* small rural community with excellent fishing in nearby Calliope River with abundant mud crabs, salmon and flathead. The Calliope River Historical Village documents Port Curtis history in restored buildings and holds regular art and craft markets. 26 km SW. *Lake*

Awoonga: a popular spot for swimming, skiing (permit required) and fishing. It has walking tracks and recreational facilities, and holds the Lions Lake Awoonga Family Fishing Festival each Sept. 30 km s. *Mt Larcom:* spectacular views from the summit; 33 km w. *Castle Tower National Park:* a rugged park of granite cliffs and the outcrops of Castle Tower and Stanley mountains. Only experienced walkers should attempt the climb to Mt Castle Tower summit, where there are superb views over the Boyne Valley and Gladstone. Access by foot or boat from Lake Awoonga; access by car from Bruce Hwy. 40 km s. *Kroombit Tops National Park:* this mountain park is on a plateau with sandstone cliffs and gorges, waterfalls and creeks. Drive the 90 min return loop road to explore the landscapes and walk to the site of a WW II bomber crash. 4WD recommended. 75 km sw via Calliope. *Curtis Island National Park:* at the north-east end of the island is this small park with a variety of vegetation and excellent spots for birdwatching. There are no walking tracks, but the 3–4 day hike along the east coast is worthwhile. Access by boat from Gladstone or The Narrows. *Great Barrier Reef tours:* cruises depart from the Marina; Bryan Jordan Dr. ⓘ Marina Ferry Terminal, Bryan Jordan Dr; (07) 4972 4000; www.gladstoneregion.org.au

Gold Coast · Pop. 361 964

Map ref. 599 H11, 600, 607 Q10

The famous Gold Coast lies between Brisbane and the New South Wales border. It comprises towns and suburbs famous for their coastal pleasures – beaches, surfing and watersports. The sunny subtropical climate, the international-standard accommodation and the exciting attractions mean the Gold Coast is an appealing destination for a wide range of holidaymakers.

WEST OF THE BROADWATER
South Stradbroke Island This resort island boasts peaceful coves to the west and lively ocean beaches to the east, separated by wetland and remnant rainforest. See the abundant bird and butterfly species and discover the pleasures of windsurfing and sailing on either a daytrip or longer stay. Access is by ferry or private boat from Runaway Bay Marina.
The Broadwater: sheltered waterways excellent for boating (hire available), watersports and shore walks; access from Labrador and Southport. *Surfers Riverwalk:* scenic 9 km walk from Sundale Bridge at Southport to Pacific Fair at Broadbeach. *Fishing platforms:* excellent spot for testing the line; Marine Pde, Labrador. *Southport Spit Jetty:* excellent spot to fish, with nearby dive site around the wreck of the *Scottish Prince. Sanctuary Cove:* famous area for championship golf courses. Hire a houseboat or take

Gold Coast theme parks

Warner Bros. Movie World
The movies come to life at 'Hollywood on the Gold Coast'. The rides, stunts and shows will delight the movie buff as well as entertain the kids. For the fast-paced visitor, try the upside-down thrills of Lethal Weapon – The Ride, or be spooked by ghouls and gargoyles on the Scooby-Doo Spooky Coaster. For a gentler adventure, visit Looney Tunes Village and chase the Road Runner with the ever-unsuccessful Wile E. Coyote. Pacific Motorway, Oxenford; (07) 5573 3999; www.movieworld.com.au

Wet 'n' Wild Water World
As the name suggests, getting wet is the aim of this theme park. There are rides for the thrill seekers – like the tube slide, Speedcoaster – or, for the more leisurely visitor, relaxing at Calypso Beach. The Giant Wave Pool is always popular with its constant one-metre swell. A highlight is watching a movie at the Dive In Movies from the comfort of a floating tube. They run every Saturday night throughout the year and every night during the January school holidays. Pacific Motorway, Oxenford; (07) 5556 1610; www.wetnwild.com.au

Sea World
Sea World displays all the delights that our oceans have to offer. At Polar Bear Shores the visitor can get up close to these amazing animals and watch as they play up to the crowds. There are excellent presentations at Dolphin Cove and the sea lions get the limelight at the Quest for the Golden Seal show. There are also adventure rides, waterslides, a skyway to see the park from on high and the Dolphin Nursery Pools. Sea World Drive on The Spit (Main Beach); (07) 5588 2205; www.seaworld.com.au

Dreamworld
Dedicated to 'the happiness of all people', Dreamworld has a diverse range of attractions for the visitor. The Giant Drop, the tallest freefall in the world, is a heart-stopping 120-metre drop from 38 stories high. For those seeking a quieter thrill, cuddle a koala in Koala Country or see the Bengal tigers play at Tiger Island. Kennyland features rides, shows and characters to delight the children. There is also the six-storey-high Imax Theatre featuring spectacular films. Dreamworld Parkway, Coomera; 1800 073 300 or (07) 5588 1111; www.dreamworld.com.au

a cruise. *Warner Bros. Movie World, Wet 'n' Wild Water World and Dreamworld:* major theme parks at Oxenford and Coomera; *see feature on this page. High-speed racing:* 3 professional circuit tracks to test the visitor's driving skills in V8 Supercars, Commodores and WRXs. Courses at Ormeau and Pimpama; Pacific Hwy towards Brisbane.

AROUND MAIN BEACH
The Spit: ocean beach featuring Marine Mirage and Mariner's Cove, both tourist complexes with specialty shops, restaurants, outdoor cafes and weekend entertainment. Sea World is also found here; *see feature on this page. Main Beach Bathing Pavilion:* historic 1934 building.

AROUND SURFERS PARADISE
Ripley's Believe It or Not The 12 galleries of amazing feats, facts and figures will surprise and amaze. There are interactive displays and movies that bring events to life. Raptis Plaza, Cavill Ave, Surfers Paradise.
Adventure activities and tours: try surfing lessons or scenic flights to see 'Surfers' in a new light or take a tour to the Gold Coast hinterland; contact visitor centre for details. *KP Go Karting:* Ferny Ave, Surfers Paradise. *Flycoaster and Bungee Rocket:* thrill rides; Cypress Ave, Surfers Paradise. *Gold Coast Arts Centre:* theatre, art gallery and cafe, with Evandale sculpture walk nearby; Bundall Rd, Bundall. *Royal Pines Resort:* famous golf

course that holds the Australian Ladies Masters each year.
AROUND BROADBEACH
Oasis: shopping centre with monorail to Conrad Jupiters, Broadbeach. *Pacific Fair:* Australia's largest shopping centre. *Conrad Jupiters:* casino and entertainment complex. *Mermaid Beach:* the surfing beach here is the main focus of the suburb. *Miami:* popular spot for fishing off platform at Dunlop's Canal, or swimming at nearby Nobby Beach.
AROUND BURLEIGH HEADS
Burleigh Head National Park Escape the bustle of the Gold Coast at this coastal park. Take the 2.8 km Ocean View circuit to experience the coastal vegetation, rainforest and mangroves or go to Tumgun Lookout to watch for dolphins and humpback whales (seasonal). Access from Goodwin Tce, Burleigh Heads. *David Fleay Wildlife Park:* displays Queensland's native animals in a natural setting with the only display of Lumholtz's tree kangaroo and mahogany gliders in the world. The park also has crocodile feeding in summer and Aboriginal heritage programs. West Burleigh Rd. *Tallebudgera:* swimming in estuary and ocean.
AROUND CURRUMBIN
Currumbin Wildlife Sanctuary This 20 ha reserve is owned by the National Trust. There are free-ranging animals in open areas, the new Crocodile Wetlands with

raised walkways over pools harbouring freshwater and saltwater crocodiles, a walk-through rainforest aviary and rides through the sanctuary on a miniature railway. A highlight is the twice-daily feeding of wild rainbow lorikeets. The 'Wildnight Tours' is an interactive tour to see the nocturnal wildlife. Tomewin St.

Springbrook National Park, Mount Cougal section This small section of the park contains a subtropical rainforest remnant and is part of the Central Eastern Rainforest Reserves World Heritage Area. Mt Cougal's twin peaks and the Currumbin Valley are an interesting and diverse landscape. There is a scenic drive through the valley and a walking track through rainforest, past cascades, to the remains of an old bush sawmill. End of Currumbin Creek Rd; 22 km sw. *Natural Bridge section: see Nerang.*
Superbee Honeyworld: live displays, Walks with Bees tour, honey making and sales; opposite sanctuary. *Palm Beach:* popular golden-sands beach that has won Queensland's Cleanest Beach Award in previous years. *Olson's Bird Gardens:* large landscaped aviaries in subtropical setting with a lilly pilly hedge maze; Currumbin Creek Rd.

AROUND COOLANGATTA

Greenmount and Coolangatta beaches: sheltered white-sand beaches with beautiful views of the coast. *Rainbow Bay:* sheltered beach excellent for swimming. Walk along the coast to Snapper Rocks. *Point Danger:* named by Captain Cook as he sailed by. It offers excellent panoramic views over the ocean and coast. Catch a glimpse of dolphins from the Captain Cook Memorial Lighthouse. North Head. *Kirra Beach:* top surf beach to the north with a dive site off coast. *Coolangatta Airport:* services Gold Coast for domestic flights, charters, scenic flights and tandem skydiving; Bilinga. *Tom Beaston Outlook (Razorback Lookout):* excellent views; behind Tweed Heads.
WHAT'S ON *Cavill Mall Markets:* Surfers Paradise; Fri nights. *Farmers markets:* Marina Mirage; 1st Sat each month. *Coolangatta Markets:* beachfront; 2nd Sun each month. *Magic Millions Racing Carnival:* Gold Coast Turf Club; Jan. *Queensland Short Course Championship:* in Gold Coast Triathlon; Southport; Feb. *Australian Beach Volleyball Championships:* Surfers Paradise; Mar. *Blues Music Festival:* Broadbeach; May. *Prime Minister's Cup:* racing event; Gold Coast Turf Club; May. *Gold Coast Cup Outrigger Canoe Marathon:* May–June. *Wintersun Festival:* Coolangatta; Queen's Birthday weekend, June. *Gold Coast Marathon:* July. *Gold Coast Show:* Aug–Sept. *Indy 300:* racing through many streets of Surfers; Oct. *Gold Coast Tropicarnival:* Oct. *Broadbeach Festival:* Nov. *Australian Music Week:* Nov.
ⓘ Gold Coast Tourism Bureau, Cavill Walk, Surfers Paradise; (07) 5538 4419; or Shop 14b, Coolangatta Pl, cnr Griffith and Warner sts, Coolangatta; (07) 5536 7765; www.goldcoasttourism.com.au

Goondiwindi   Pop. 5475

Map ref. 514 H2, 607 K11

Beside the picturesque MacIntyre River in the western Darling Downs is this border town. Explored by Allan Cunningham in 1827 and settled by pastoralists in the 1830s, the town derives its name from the Aboriginal word 'gonnawinna', meaning 'resting place of the birds'.
IN TOWN *Customs House Museum:* explore local history in the restored 1850 customs house; McLean St; closed Tues. *Victoria Hotel:* renowned historic pub with tower; Marshall St. *Cotton Gin:* one of the largest in Australia. It runs tours in season; contact visitor centre for details. *River Walk:* watch abundant birdlife and wildlife on 2 km walk along MacIntyre River; starts at Riddles Oval, Lagoon St. *'Goondiwindi Grey' Statue:* tribute to famous racing horse Gunsynd; Apex Park, MacIntyre St.
WHAT'S ON *Market:* Town Park, Marshall St, 2nd Sun each month. *Hell of the West Triathlon:* Feb. *Rodeo:* Sept. *Spring Festival:* coincides with flowering of jacarandas and silky oaks; Oct.
NEARBY **Southwood National Park** This brigalow–belah forest park was once known as 'Wild Horse Paradise'. Have a bush picnic and look for the black cockatoos in the belah trees, or visit at night and go spotlighting for feathertail gliders. 4WD is recommended. Access from Moonie Hwy; 125 km nw. *Botanic Gardens of Western Woodlands:* 25 ha of native plants of the Darling Basin. Also here is a lake popular for swimming and canoeing. Access from Brennans Rd; 1 km w. *Toobeah:* small town famous for its horse events; 48 km w.
ⓘ Cnr McLean and Bowen sts; (07) 4671 2653; www.goondiwindi.qld.gov.au

Gordonvale   Pop. 3553

Map ref. 611 N7

Gordonvale is a sugar-milling town just south of Cairns. Its charm lies in the well-preserved streetscapes, its historic buildings and the 922-metre-high Walsh's Pyramid that forms the backdrop to the town. People flock to the mountain in August for a race to the top. The town's less glorious claim to fame is that cane toads were released here in 1935 in an attempt to eradicate sugarcane pests.
NEARBY **Goldsborough Valley State Forest** The lowland rainforest along the Goldsborough Valley is protected here. Walk to the falls along the 1.6 km Kearneys Falls track and learn about the local Aboriginal culture and customs from the informative displays. The 18 km historic Goldfields Trail travels through nearby Wooroonooran National Park to The Boulders near Babinda. 25 km sw via Gillies Hwy.

Mulgrave River: runs next to Gordonvale and is popular for swimming, canoeing, kayaking and bushwalking. *Wooroonooran National Park:* waterfalls, walking tracks and Walsh's Pyramid; 10 km s. (For the southern sections: *see Babinda and Millaa Millaa.*) *Orchid Valley Nursery and Gardens:* tours of tropical gardens; 15 km sw. *Cairns Crocodile Farm:* crocodiles and other native wildlife. There are daily tours. Around 5 min north on road to Yarrabah.
ⓘ Cnr Bruce Hwy and Munro St, Babinda; (07) 4067 1008

Gympie   Pop. 10 582

Map ref. 607 P6

On the banks of the Mary River on the Sunshine Coast is the major heritage town of Gympie. Its history began when James Nash discovered gold in the area in 1867 and started Queensland's first gold rush to save the state from near bankruptcy. The field proved extremely rich – four million ounces had been found by the 1920s. The gold slowed to a trickle soon after, but the dairy and agricultural industries were already well established. See the attractive jacarandas, silky oaks, cassias, poincianas and flame trees that line the streets.
IN TOWN **Mary Valley Heritage Railway** Known locally as the 'Valley Rattler', this restored 1923 steam train takes the visitor on a 40 km journey through the picturesque Mary Valley. The train departs Gympie every Wed and Sun on its way to Imbil where it stops before returning. Special tours run each Sat. For tickets and information contact the visitor centre (07) 5482 2750.
Woodworks, Forestry and Timber Museum: exhibits memorabilia and equipment from old logging days including a steam-driven sawmill; Fraser Rd. *Deep Creek:* gold-fossicking area; permits available from visitor centre; Counter St. *Public Gallery:* local and visiting art exhibitions in heritage building; Nash St. *Heritage walk:* self-guide walk includes the Stock Exchange and Town Hall; contact visitor centre for details.
WHAT'S ON *Market:* Gympie South State School; 2nd and 4th Sun each month. *Race the Rattler:* a race against the historic steam train; June. *Gold Rush Festival:* Oct.
NEARBY **Amamoor State Forest** Over 120 species find shelter in this protected forest, a remnant of the woodlands and vegetation that used to cover the Cooloola region. See the platypus in Amamoor Creek at dusk or take the Wonga walk or Cascade circuit track starting from across the road from Amama. The renowned outdoor music festival, the Country Music Muster, is held in the forest on the last weekend in Aug. 30 km s.
Gold Mining Museum: delve into the area's goldmining history. It includes Andrew Fisher House (Fisher was the first Queenslander to become prime

Lake McKenzie from the air

Fraser Island

World Heritage-listed Fraser Island is the largest sand island in the world. It is an ecological wonder with lakes and forests existing purely on sand. This alone would make it a worthwhile holiday destination, but add to this the beauty of the beaches, the coloured sand cliffs, more than 40 freshwater lakes and the spectacular tall rainforests.

Protected within Great Sandy National Park, the island is home to a variety of wildlife, including migratory birds and rare animals such as the ground parrot and Illidge's ant-blue butterfly. Fraser Island's dingoes are one of the purest strains in the country. Offshore, see the turtles, dugong and dolphins soak up the warm waters and, between August and November, look out for migrating humpback whales.

There are a variety of walks – ranging from short scenic walks to longer hikes. During holiday periods, spotlight tours and guided walks are run by the rangers. Scenic drives (four-wheel drive and permit necessary) start at Central Station and Happy Valley and are an excellent introduction to the island.

Some of the more spectacular sights include Lake McKenzie, with shallow, aquamarine waters that are ideal for swimming, and Lake Wabby, slowly being engulfed by an enormous sand blow. There is also the shipwreck of *The Maheno*, beached near Happy Valley, the coloured sands of The Cathedrals, crystal-clear Eli Creek and the lovely Champagne Pools at Middle Rocks.

Getting there

Visitors can access Fraser Island by air, boat or barge. Commercial barges operate from Inskip Point (near Rainbow Beach), River Heads and Urangan Boat Harbour at Hervey Bay. Bookings are recommended. A passenger ferry service runs from Urangan Boat Harbour to Kingfisher Bay, which boasts a popular resort. Private boats can anchor at Kingfisher Bay Resort, Wathumba and Garry's Anchorage. Flights operate out of Hervey Bay.

Obtain vehicle and camping permits from Queensland Parks and Wildlife Service online at www.qld.gov.au or by phoning 13 13 04. For general information ring Hervey Bay Tourism on 1800 811 728 or (07) 4125 9855.

Travellers note: Care should be taken around the island's dingo population. Stay with children, walk in groups, never feed or coax the dingoes and keep all food and rubbish in vehicles or campground lockers.

minister). 5 km s. *Mothar Mountain:* rock pools and forested area for bushwalking and excellent views; 20 km se. *Imbil:* picturesque town with excellent valley views. There is a market every Sun, and the nearby Lake Borumba offers great watersports and fishing – especially for golden perch and saratoga. Take the 14 km Imbil Forest Drive through scenic pine plantations just south of town. 36 km s. *Mary Valley Scenic Way:* enjoy this scenic route through towns of the valley, pineapple plantations and grazing farms. It runs south between Gympie and

Maleny, via Kenilworth.
ⓘ Mary Street Information Booth; (07) 5483 6656; or Cooloola Regional Information Centre, Matilda's Roadhouse Complex, Bruce Hwy, Kybong (15 km s); 1800 444 222 or (07) 5483 5554; www.cooloola.org.au

Herberton   Pop. 944

Map ref. 603 B1, 611 M8

Known as the 'Village in the Hills', Herberton sits about 1000 metres above sea level on the south-west ranges of the

Atherton Tableland. It was established in 1880 – the first settlement on the tableland. It was a thriving tin-mining town in the Herbert River field until the mine's closure in 1978.
WHAT'S ON *Tin Festival:* Sept.
NEARBY Mount Hypipamee National Park Set on the Evelyn Tableland, this park boasts high-altitude rainforests and a climate that attracts birdlife and possums, including the green and lemuroid ringtail possums. The park is known locally as 'The Crater' because of its sheer-sided volcanic explosion crater 70 m wide. Walk to the viewing deck for the best prospect, or see the Dinner Falls cascade down the narrow gorge. 25 km s. *Herberton Range State Forest:* the temperate climate attracts a variety of wildlife in this rainforest park, including the attractive golden bowerbird. Walk to the summit of Mt Baldy for panoramic views over the tableland (the steep ascent should be attempted only by experienced walkers). Rifle Range Rd, between Atherton and Herberton. *Irvinebank:* many heritage-listed buildings including Mango House, Queensland National Bank Building and Loudoun House Museum; 26 km w on unsealed road. *Emuford:* small town featuring a historic stamper battery and museum; 51 km w.
ⓘ 45 Grace St; (07) 4096 3474; www.athertontableland.com

Hervey Bay   Pop. 35 106

Map ref. 607 P3

Hervey (pronounced 'Harvey') Bay is the large area of water between Maryborough and Bundaberg, protected by Fraser Island. It is also the name of a thriving city spread out along the bay's southern shore. The climate is ideal and during winter there is an influx of visitors, not only for the weather, but also for the migrating humpback whales that frolic in the bay's warm waters between July and November. Hervey Bay is promoted as 'Australia's family aquatic playground' – there is no surf and swimming is safe, even for children. Fishing is another popular recreational activity, especially off the town's kilometre-long pier.
IN TOWN *Botanic Gardens:* interesting orchid conservatory; Elizabeth St. *Historical Museum:* recalls pioneer days in 14 historic buildings, including an 1898 slab cottage; Zephyr St; open Fri–Sun afternoons. *Sea Shell Museum:* shell creations and displays, including 100 million-year-old shell; Esplanade. *Neptune's Reefworld:* animals of the ocean, including performing seals; Pulgul St. *M & K Model Railways:* award-winning miniature gardens and model trains. Ride the replica diesel train. Old Maryborough Rd; open Tues–Fri. *Thrillseeker's Amusement Park:* rides include the Bungee Rocket; Hervey Bay Rd. *Dayman Park:* memorial commemorates landing of Matthew

Flinders in 1799 and the Z-Force commandos who trained there on the Krait in WW II. *Scenic walkway:* cycle or walk 15 km along the waterfront. *Whale-watching tours:* half- and full-day tours to see the migratory whales off the coast, departing from Boat Harbour; contact visitor centre for details.

WHAT'S ON *Nikenbah Markets:* Nikenbah Animal Refuge; 1st and 3rd Sun each month. *Koala Markets:* Elizabeth St; 2nd, 4th and 5th Sun each month. *Yagubi Festival:* multicultural festival; Feb. *Gladstone–Hervey Bay Blue Water Classic:* April. *Whale Festival:* Aug.

NEARBY *Fraser Island: see feature on p. 413. Great Sandy Strait:* the Mary and Susan rivers to the south of Hervey Bay run into this strait where the visitor can see spectacular migratory birds, including the comb-crested jacana. Hire a houseboat to travel down the strait; contact visitor centre for details. *Toogoom:* quiet seaside resort town. Feed the pelicans on the boardwalk. 15 km w. *Burrum Heads:* pleasant holiday resort at the mouth of the Burrum River with excellent beaches and fishing. Visit at Easter for the Amateur Fishing Classic. 20 km NW. *Burrum Coast National Park:* 34 km NW; *see Bundaberg. Brooklyn House:* historic old Queenslander pioneer house; Howard; 36 km w. *Lady Elliot Island:* fly to island for a day to snorkel on the fabulous reef; contact visitor centre for details. *Scenic flights:* over Hervey Bay and Fraser Island in a Tiger Moth or other small plane; contact visitor centre for details.
ⓘ Cnr Urraween and Maryborough–Hervey Bay rds; 1800 811 728 or (07) 4125 9855; www.herveybay tourism.com.au

Hughenden   Pop. 1397

Map ref. 608 A4, 615 O4

Hughenden is on the banks of the Flinders River, Queensland's longest river, west of the Great Dividing Range. The first recorded Europeans to pass here were members of Frederick Walker's 1861 expedition to find the explorers Burke and Wills. Two years later Ernest Henry selected a cattle station and Hughenden came into existence. The black volcanic soil in the region is rich with fossilised bones, particularly those of dinosaurs.

IN TOWN **Flinders Discovery Centre** Learn about the Flinders Shire's history in this complex. The fossil exhibition's centrepiece is the 7 m replica skeleton of *Muttaburrasaurus langdoni*, a dinosaur found in Muttaburra (206 km s) – it was the first entire fossil skeleton found in Australia. The Historical Society also documents the shire history in their display. Gray St.
Historic Coolibah Tree: blazed by Walker in 1861 and again by William Landsborough in 1862 when he was also searching for the Burke and Wills

expedition; east bank of Station Creek, Stansfield St East.

WHAT'S ON *Country Music Festival:* April. *Dinosaur Festival:* even-numbered years, Sept. *Night Rodeo:* Oct.

NEARBY **Porcupine Gorge National Park** The coloured sandstone cliffs of this park are a visual delight and contrast with the greenery surrounding Porcupine Creek. The gorge, known locally as the 'mini Grand Canyon', has formed over millions of years and can be seen from the lookout just off Kennedy Development Rd. Walk down into the gorge on the 1.2 km track, but be warned, the steep walk back up is strenuous. 61 km N.
Basalt Byways: discover the Flinders Shire landscapes on these 4WD tracks. Cross the Flinders River and see the Flinders poppy in the valleys. The longest track is 156 km. Access on Hann Hwy; 7.3 km N. *Prairie:* small town with mini-museum and historic relics at Cobb & Co yards; 44 km E. *Mount Emu Goldfields:* fossicking and bushwalking; 85 km N. *Torrens Creek:* the town, a major explosives dump during WW II, was nearly wiped out by 12 explosions when firebreaks accidentally hit the dump. Visit the Exchange Hotel, home of the 'dinosaur steaks'. 88 km E. *Kooroorinya Falls:* the small falls cascade into a natural waterhole, excellent for swimming. Walk and go birdwatching in surrounding bushland. 109 km SE via Prairie. *White Mountains National Park:* rugged park with white sandstone outcrops and varied vegetation. Burra Range Lookout on Flinders Hwy has excellent views over the park. There are no walking tracks. 111 km E. *Chudleigh Park Gemfields:* gem-quality peridot found in fossicking area (licence required); 155 km N. *Moorrinya National Park:* important conservation park protecting 18 different land types of the Lake Eyre Basin. The park is home to iconic Australian animals, such as koalas, kangaroos and dingoes, and includes remains of the old sheep-grazing property 'Shirley Station'. Walking is for experienced bushwalkers only. 178 km SE via Torrens Creek.
ⓘ Flinders Discovery Centre, Gray St; (07) 4741 1021

Ingham   Pop. 4666

Map ref. 603 E6, 611 N11

Ingham is a major sugar town near the Hinchinbrook Channel. Originally, Kanaka labour was employed in the surrounding sugarcane fields, but after the change in laws at the beginning of the 20th century, Italian immigrants replaced them. This strong Italian heritage is celebrated in the Australian Italian Festival each May. Ingham is at the centre of a splendid range of national parks. The Wallaman Falls in Girringun (Lumholtz) National Park are a highlight as the largest single-drop falls in Australia.

IN TOWN *Hinchinbrook Heritage Walk*

and Drive: displays at each historic site in Ingham and the nearby township of Halifax illustrate the dynamic history of the shire. It starts at the Shire Hall in Ingham; brochure available from visitor centre. *Memorial Gardens:* picturesque waterlily lakes and native tropical vegetation. They include Bicentennial Bush House with displays of orchids and tropical plants (open weekdays). Palm Tce.

WHAT'S ON *Conroy Hall Markets:* McIlwraith St; 2nd Sat each month. *Raintree Market:* Herbert St; 3rd Sat each month. *Australian Italian Festival:* May. *Maraka Festival:* Oct.

NEARBY **Girringun (Lumholtz) National Park** The Wallaman Falls section (50 km w) of the park is in the Herbert River Valley and features waterfalls, gorges and tropical rainforest. See the crimson rosellas on the 4 km return walk from the Falls Lookout to the base of Wallaman Falls – look out for platypus and water dragons. Take a scenic drive around the Mt Fox section of the park (75 km SW) or walk the 4 km return ascent to the dormant volcano crater. There are no formal tracks and the ascent is for experienced walkers only. 4WD is recommended in both sections during the wet season. *See Cardwell for northern parts of park.*
Paluma Range National Park The Jourama Falls section of the park (24 km s) is at the foothills of the Seaview Range. Walk the 1.5 km track through rainforest and dry forest to the Jourama Falls Lookout (take care crossing the creek) to see the vibrant birdlife including azure kingfishers and kookaburras. The Mt Spec section of the park (40 km s) features casuarina-fringed creeks in the lowlands and rainforest in the cooler mountain areas. Drive to McClelland's Lookout for a spectacular view and take the two short walks from there to see the varied park landscapes. *Tyto Wetlands:* 90 ha of wetlands with birdlife and wallabies. See the rare grass owl from the viewing platform. Outskirts of town. *Cemetery:* interesting Italian tile mausoleums; 5 km E. *Forrest Beach:* sandy 16 km beach overlooking Palm Islands. Stinger-net swimming enclosures are installed in summer. 20 km SE. *Taylors Beach:* popular family seaside spot for sailing with excellent fishing and crabbing in nearby Victoria Creek; 24 km E. *Hinchinbrook National Park:* resort island to the north-east; sea access from Lucinda; 25 km NE; *see also Cardwell. Lucinda:* coastal village on banks of the Herbert River at the southern end of the Hinchinbrook Channel. Take a safari or fishing tour through the channel. Stinger-net swimming enclosures are installed in summer. 27 km NE. *Broadwater State Forest:* swimming holes, walking tracks and birdwatching; 45 km w. *Orpheus Island National Park:* this rainforest and woodland park is a continental resort island in the Palm Islands surrounded by a marine park and fringing reefs. Snorkel

and dive off the beaches or take in the wildlife on the short track from Little Pioneer Bay to Old Shepherds Hut. Access is by private or charter boat from Lucinda or Taylors Beach.

ℹ Hinchinbrook Visitor Centre, cnr Lannercost St and Townsville Rd; (07) 4776 5211; www.hinchinbrooknq. com.au

Innisfail   Pop. 8396

Map ref. 603 D2, 611 N8

Innisfail is a prosperous, colourful town on the banks of the North Johnstone and South Johnstone rivers south-east of Cairns. The parks and walks on the riverside, as well as the classic Art Deco buildings in the town centre, create the charm of this town. Sugar has been grown here since the early 1880s and is celebrated at the Harvest Festival each October. There is a strong Italian influence in the town, as immigrants were a prominent labour force on the sugarcane fields throughout the 20th century. There was even a local mafia group known as the 'Black Hand', which reigned during the 1930s. The area is renowned for the tropical fruits grown and the excellent fishing in nearby rivers, beaches and estuaries.

IN TOWN Innisfail and District Historical Society Museum: documents local history; Edith St. Chinese Joss House: reminder of Chinese presence during gold-rush days; Owen St. Warrina Lakes and Botanical Gardens: recreational facilities and walks; Charles St. Historical town walk: see classic architecture of the town and historic Shire Hall on self-guide or guided town walk; contact visitor centre for details.

WHAT'S ON Market: ANZAC Memorial Park; 3rd Sat each month. Harvest Festival: Oct.

NEARBY Eubenangee Swamp National Park This important park protects the last of the remnant coastal lowland rainforest around Alice River, part of the Wet Tropics Region. See the rainforest birds on the walk from Alice River to the swamp where jabirus and spoonbills feed. 13 km NW.

Flying Fish Point: popular spot for swimming, camping and fishing; 5 km NE. Johnstone River Crocodile Farm: daily feeding shows at 11am and 3pm; 8 km NE. Ella Bay National Park: small coastal park with beach and picnic spot; 8 km N. North Johnstone River Gorge: walking tracks to several picturesque waterfalls; 18 km W via Palmerston Hwy. Wooroonooran National Park: 33 km W; see Millaa Millaa. Crawford Lookout: spectacular views of North Johnstone River; 38 km W off Palmerston Hwy.

ℹ Cnr Eslick St and Bruce Hwy; (07) 4061 7442; www.greatgreenway.com

Ipswich   Pop. 65 694

Map ref. 598 B9, 599 B7, 607 P9

Ipswich is Queensland's oldest provincial city. Its charm lies in the abundance of diverse heritage buildings throughout its streets. In 1827 a convict settlement was established alongside the Bremer River to quarry the nearby limestone deposits used in Brisbane's stone buildings. In 1842 the settlement, simply called 'Limestone', opened to free settlers and was in 1843 renamed Ipswich. Ipswich has commemorated its honour as the birthplace of Queensland Railways in the impressive Workshops Rail Museum. Australia's largest RAAF base is in the suburb of Amberley.

IN TOWN Workshops Rail Museum In the North Ipswich railyards, this museum offers diverse historical displays, interactive exhibitions and an impressive variety of machinery. Watch workers restore old steam trains, or look into the future of rail by taking a simulated ride in the high-speed tilt train. North St.

Global Art Links Gallery This art gallery and social history museum merges heritage and present day at the Old Town Hall. See the local and visiting exhibitions in the Gallery, partake in the interactive displays of Ipswich history in the Hall of Time, walk through the indigenous installation in the Return to Kabool section, or try electronic finger-painting in the Children's Gallery. D'Arcy Doyle Pl. Queens Park Nature Centre: native flora, animals and a bird aviary; Goleby Ave; closed Mon. Historical walk: self-guide walk to see the renowned heritage buildings, churches and excellent domestic architecture of Ipswich, including the Uniting Church (1858) and Gooloowan (1864); outstanding colour brochure available from visitor centre.

WHAT'S ON Showground Market: Warwick Rd; each Sun. Ipswich Cup and Race Meeting: July.

NEARBY Queensland Raceway: home to Queensland 500 and host of the V8 Supercar Series. Winternationals Drag-racing Championship runs every June. 15 km W. Wolston House: historic home at Wacol; 16 km E; open weekends and public holidays. Rosewood: heritage town with St Brigid's Church, the largest wooden church in the South Pacific. The Railway Museum, with restored carriages and wagons and displays of area's industrial heritage, runs scenic steam-train rides on the last Sun of each month. 20 km W; museum open every Sun. Recreational reserves: popular picnic and leisure spots to the north-east of Ipswich include College's Crossing (7 km), Mt Crosby (12 km) and Lake Manchester (22 km).

ℹ 14 Queen Victoria Pde; (07) 3281 0555; www.ipswichtourism.com.au

Isisford   Pop. 170

Map ref. 608 A13, 615 P13, 617 O1

Isisford is a small outback community south of Longreach. In the mid-1800s large stations were established in the area. This brought hawkers, keen on trading their goods to the landowners. Two such hawkers were brothers William and James Whitman who, after their axle broke trying to cross the Alice River, decided to stay and established Isisford in 1877. First called Wittown, after the brothers, the town was renamed in 1880 to recall the nearby Barcoo River ford and Isis Downs Station. The town provided inspiration to iconic Australian poet Banjo Paterson, in particular his poems 'Bush Christening' and 'Clancy of the Overflow'.

IN TOWN Whitman's Museum: photographic exhibition documents Isisford's history; St Mary St. Barcoo Weir: excellent spot for fishing and bush camping.

NEARBY Oma Waterhole: popular spot for fishing and watersports, and home to Isisford Fishing Competition and Festival mid-year (subject to rains); 15 km SW. Idalia National Park: 62 km SE; see Blackall.

Wolston House in Wacol, near Ipswich

The Skyrail from Kuranda to Cairns

ⓘ Council offices, St Mary St; (07) 4658 8900; www.isisford.qld.gov.au

Julia Creek   Pop. 513

Map ref. 615 J4

Julia Creek became known as 'The Gateway to the Gulf' after the road to Normanton was sealed in 1964. Pioneer Donald MacIntyre was the first to settle in the north-west when he established Dalgonally Station north of town in 1862. Julia Creek is actually named after his niece and aunt. The town is an important trucking and sale centre for the traditional cattle industry of the region. It is also home to a rare and endangered marsupial, the Julia Creek dunnart, a tiny nocturnal hunter found only within a 100-kilometre radius of town.

IN TOWN *Duncan MacIntyre Museum:* local pioneering and cattle history; Burke St.
WHAT'S ON *Dirt and Dust Triathlon:* April/May. *Campdraft:* May.
NEARBY *WW II bunkers:* remains of concrete bunkers used to assist navigation of allied aircraft; western outskirts. *Punchbowl:* popular swimming, fishing and recreational waterhole on the Flinders River; 40 km N. *Dalgonally Station:* first settlement in north-west Queensland; 75 km NW. *Dalgonally Waterhole:* popular skiing and recreational spot; adjacent to Dalgonally Station.
ⓘ Council offices, 29 Burke St; (07) 4746 7166; www.juliacreek.org

Jundah   Pop. 110

Map ref. 617 M2

Jundah is at the centre of the Channel Country and its name comes from the Aboriginal word for women. Gazetted as a town in 1880, for 20 years the area was important for opal mining, but lack of water caused the mines to close. The waterholes and channels of the Thomson River are filled with yabbies and fish, including yellow-belly and bream. The spectacular rock holes, red sand dunes and beauty of Welford National Park are the natural attractions of this outback town.

IN TOWN *Jundah Museum:* documents area's early pioneer heritage; Perkins St.
WHAT'S ON *Race Carnival:* Oct.
NEARBY **Welford National Park** This large national park protects mulga lands, Channel Country and Mitchell grass downs, three natural vegetations of Queensland. See the rare earth homestead (1882) that is now Heritage trust or go wildlife-watching to see pelicans and whistling kites at the many waterholes of the Barcoo River. There are two self-guide drives that start at the campground: one through the mulga vegetation to the scenic Sawyers Creek; the other a desert drive past the impressive red sand dunes. 4WD is recommended; roads are impassable in wet weather. 20 km S.
Stonehenge: town named not for the ancient English rock formation, but for the old stone hut built for visiting bullock teams. Nearby on the Thomson River are brolgas and wild budgerigars, and there is an excellent view at XXXX Hill. 68 km NE. *Windorah:* holds the International Yabby Race in Sept; 95 km S.
ⓘ Council offices, Dickson St; (07) 4658 6133; www.outbackholidays.tq.com.au

Karumba   Pop. 1329

Map ref. 610 B8, 613 H8

Karumba is at the mouth of the Norman River in the Gulf Savannah. It is the easiest access point for the Gulf of Carpentaria, the key reason the town is centre for the Gulf's booming prawn and barramundi industries. During the 1930s, the town was an important refuelling depot for the airships of the Empire Flying Boats, which travelled from Sydney to England. The fishing enthusiast would enjoy the untouched waters of the Gulf and nearby rivers that offer an abundance of fish.

IN TOWN *Barramundi Discovery Centre:* barramundi display and information with daily feeding at 4.45pm; Riverside Dr. *Ferryman cruises:* tours include birdwatching, Gulf sunset and night crocodile spotting; depart Karumba boat ramp; (07) 4745 9155. *Charters and dinghy hire:* discover the renowned fishing spots in the Gulf or on the Norman River on a charter or hire a dinghy; Karumba Port. *Scenic flights:* air and helicopter flights over the Gulf and region; airport.
WHAT'S ON *Fishing Competition:* follows Easter event at Normanton; April.
NEARBY *Wetland region:* extending 30 km inland from Karumba are the wetlands, habitat of the saltwater crocodile and several species of birds, including brolgas and cranes. *Cemetery:* early-settlement cemetery when Karumba was known as Norman Mouth telegraph station; 2 km N on road to Karumba Point. *Karumba Point:* fish off the golden sands beach; boat hire available; 3 km N. *Sweers Island:* island in the Gulf with beaches, abundant birdlife, excellent fishing and caves. Access is by boat or air; contact visitor centre for details.
ⓘ Council offices, cnr Landsborough and Haig sts, Normanton; (07) 4745 1166; www.gulf-savannah.com.au

Kenilworth   Pop. 390

Map ref. 601 D3, 607 P7

West of the Blackall Range in the Sunshine Coast hinterland is the charming town of Kenilworth. It is known for its handcrafted cheeses and excellent bushwalking in the surrounding national parks and forests. The spectacular gorges, waterfalls, creeks and scenic lookouts make Kenilworth State Forest a popular spot for bushwalking, camping and picnics.

IN TOWN *Kenilworth Cheese Factory:* tastings and sales of local cheeses; Charles St. *Historical Museum:* machinery and dairy display and audiovisual show; Alexandra St; open Sun or by appt (07) 5446 0581. *Lasting Impressions Gallery:* fine-art gallery; Elizabeth St.
NEARBY **Kenilworth State Forest** This diverse park is in the rugged Conondale Ranges. The rainforest, tall open forest and exotic pines are home to birds and wildlife, including the threatened yellow-bellied glider. There are walks signposted, but a highlight is the steep 4 km return hike from Booloumba Creek to the summit of Mt Allan where the forest and gorge views are breathtaking. Visit Booloumba Falls from the Gorge picnic area (3 km return) or picnic in the riverine rainforest at Peters Creek. Turn-off to the park is 6 km SW.

Kenilworth Winery: tastings and sales at boutique winery; 4 km N. *Kenilworth Bluff:* steep walking track to lookout point; 6 km N. *Conondale National Park:* this small forest reserve west of the Mary River is suitable only for experienced walkers. Take the 37 km scenic drive, starting in the adjacent Kenilworth Forest, to experience the rugged delights of the park. *Lake Borumba:* picnics and watersports, and home to a fishing competition each Mar. 32 km NW.
ⓘ 4 Elizabeth St; (07) 5446 0122

Killarney   Pop. 831

Map ref. 515 N1, 607 O11

The attractive small town of Killarney is on the banks of the Condamine River close to the New South Wales border. It is appealingly situated at the foothills of the Great Dividing Range and is surrounded by beautiful mountain scenery.

WHAT'S ON *Rodeo:* Nov.
NEARBY Queen Mary Falls, Main Range National Park The Queen Mary Falls section of this World Heritage-listed park is right on the NSW border. Most of the vegetation is open eucalypt, but in the gorge below the falls is subtropical rainforest. Follow the 2 km Queen Mary Falls circuit to the lookout for a stunning view of the 40 m falls and continue down to the rock pools at the base. If you are lucky, the rare Albert's lyrebird might be seen on the walk or the endangered brush-tailed rock wallaby on the cliffs. 11 km E. *See also Boonah.*
Dagg's and Brown's waterfalls: stand behind Brown's waterfall and see the 38 m Dagg's waterfall; 4 km S. *Cherrabah Homestead Resort:* offers horseriding and fabulous bushwalking; 7 km S.
ⓘ 49 Albion St (New England Hwy), Warwick; (07) 4661 3401

Kingaroy   Pop. 7148

Map ref. 607 N6

Kingaroy is a large and prosperous town in the South Burnett region. The town's name derives from the Aboriginal word 'Kingaroori', meaning red ant. Found in the area, this unique ant has gradually adapted its colour to resemble the red soil plains of Kingaroy. The town is the centre for Queensland's peanut and navy-bean industries, and its giant peanut silos are still landmarks. The region's relatively new wine industry is thriving with an excellent range of boutique wineries close by. Kingaroy is also the home of Sir Johannes (Joh) Bjelke-Petersen, former premier of Queensland.

IN TOWN *Heritage Museum:* history of the region, including videos on peanut and navy-bean industries; Haly St; open Tues–Sat. *Art Gallery:* local and regional artists; Civic Square, Glendon St; open weekdays. *The Peanut Van:* sales of local 'jumbo' peanuts; Kingaroy St. *Apex*

Lookout: panoramic views of town; Carroll Nature Reserve, Fisher St.
WHAT'S ON *Wine and Food in the Park Festival:* Mar. *Peanut Festival:* includes the state duathlon competition; Sept.
NEARBY Bunya Mountains National Park This important park is part of the Great Dividing Range and protects the world's largest natural Bunya-pine forest. It is a significant Aboriginal site as many feasts were held here with the bunya nuts as the main fare. There are many walking trails for beginner and experienced alike. There is the short Bunya Bunya Track or the 8.4 km return Cherry Plain Track. Have a bush picnic and see the many butterflies or go spotlighting to glimpse owls and mountain possums. 58 km SW.
Aboriginal Bora Ring: preserved site; cnr Reagan and Coolabunia rds, just south of Kingaroy. *Taabinga Homestead:* the historic homestead is opened intermittently during the year (check with visitor centre) and holds the Spring Music Festival every Oct. *Mount Wooroolin Lookout:* excellent views over Kingaroy's farmlands; 3 km W. *Bethany:* tour the Bjelke-Petersen's property and taste the famous Bjelke-Petersen scones; open Wed and Sat, bookings essential: (07) 4162 7046; 3 km from the airport off Goodger Rd. *Wooroolin:* quaint town with many heritage buildings including the Grant Hotel (1916). The Gordonbrook Dam is an excellent spot for picnics and birdwatching from the hides. 18 km N. *Scenic aeroplane flights:* over the Burnett region daily; (07) 4162 2629. *Scenic glider flights:* over surrounding area; (07) 4162 2191.
ⓘ 128 Haly St (opposite silos); (07) 4162 3199; www.kingaroy.qld.gov.au

Kuranda   Pop. 1432

Map ref. 604 B7, 611 M6

This small village is set in tropical rainforest on the banks of the Barron River north-west of Cairns. Its beautiful setting attracted a strong hippy culture in the 60s and 70s and, while Kuranda still has a bohemian feel, tourism is now the order of the day. There are many nature parks and eco-tourism experiences on offer around town, along with plenty of art and craft workshops, cafes and a daily market. Even transport to and from the town has been developed into an attraction – the Scenic Railway and Skyrail, both with jaw-dropping views over World Heritage-listed rainforest.

IN TOWN **Scenic Railway and Skyrail** The Scenic Railway is an engineering feat over 100 years old with tunnels, bridges and incredible views of Barron Falls. It begins in Cairns and ends 34 km later in the lush garden setting of Kuranda Station. Travel by rail on the way up and take the Skyrail on the way back (or vice versa), a journey via gondola across the treetops (ends at Caravonica Lakes, 11 km N of Cairns). Bookings (07) 4038 1555.

Butterfly Sanctuary: large enclosure, home to over 1500 tropical butterflies, including the blue Ulysses and the Australian birdwing, the country's largest butterfly; Rod Veivers Dr. *Birdworld:* over 50 species of birds, including the flightless cassowary and some endangered species; close to the heritage markets. *Koala Gardens:* Australian animals in a natural setting; close to the heritage markets. *The Aviary:* birds, frogs, snakes and crocodiles; Thongon St. *Art and craft shops:* including Kuranda Arts Cooperative, next to Butterfly Sanctuary, and Doongal Aboriginal Arts and Crafts on Coondoo St. *River cruises and guided rainforest walks:* depart daily from riverside landing below railway station.
WHAT'S ON *Kuranda Heritage Markets:* Rod Veivers Dr; daily. *Kuranda Original Markets:* behind the Honey House; Wed, Thurs, Fri & Sun (entertainment on Sun). *Folk Festival:* May. *Kuranda Festival:* Aug/Oct.
NEARBY Barron Gorge National Park Most people experience this park via the Scenic Railway or Skyrail, but those who want to get away from the crowds could set out on one of the park's bushwalking tracks leading into pockets of World Heritage wilderness. Perhaps you'll spot a Ulysses butterfly, cassowary or tree kangaroo in its natural habitat. Some trails require overnight bush camping (permit required). And if you haven't already seen Barron Falls from the train or Skyrail, make your way to Wrights Lookout, 7 km SE of Kuranda. The falls are spectacular after rain. Access to the park is via Cairns or Kuranda.
Kuranda Nature Park: wildlife, canoeing, swimming and rainforest tours aboard 4WD Hummers; 2 km W. *Rainforestation Nature Park:* rainforest tours, tropical fruit orchard, Pamagirri Aboriginal Dance troupe, Dreamtime walk, and a koala and wildlife park; 35 km E. *Carrowong Wildlife Eco-tours:* tours to see nocturnal, rare and endangered rainforest creatures; (07) 4093 7287.
ⓘ Therwine St; (07) 4093 9311; www.kuranda.org

Kynuna   Pop. 20

Map ref. 615 J6

Kynuna is a tiny outback town famous for inspiring Banjo Paterson to write his iconic tune, 'Waltzing Matilda'. It is said that Samuel Hoffmeister, at the time of the Shearers' Strike, drank his last drink at the Blue Heeler Hotel and then killed himself at Combo waterhole (south of town). This story stirred Paterson to write the now famous ballad.

IN TOWN *Blue Heeler Hotel:* famous hotel with illuminated blue heeler statue on the roof. *Waltzing Matilda Exhibition:* in barn opposite roadhouse; open during tourist season.
WHAT'S ON *Surf Carnival:* inland ironman contest; Mar. *Rodeo:* Nov.

NEARBY Combo Waterhole Conservation Park The events described in 'Waltzing Matilda' occurred in this conservation park, which comprises waterholes lined with coolibahs. On the Diamantina River, the park is an important dry-weather wildlife refuge. See the Chinese-labour-constructed historic stone causeways from the 1880s or take the 40 min return waterhole walk. Turn-off to park is 13 km s.

McKinlay Although the town is tiny, its famous Walkabout Creek Hotel attracts many visitors. The hotel, originally known as McKinlay Hotel, is featured as the local watering hole in the film *Crocodile Dundee*, which starred famed Australian larrikin Paul Hogan. 74 km NW.
ⓘ Roadhouse and Caravan Park, Matilda Hwy; (07) 4746 8683

Laidley   Pop. 2251

Map ref. 607 O9

Laidley is in the Lockyer Valley in the Brisbane hinterland. The surrounding agricultural farmland produces an abundance of fresh fruit and vegetables, which can be taste-tested at the country market. The quality of Laidley's produce comes from the region's fertile soil, which explains why the town is known as 'Queensland's country garden'.

IN TOWN Das Neumann Haus Restored and refurbished in 1930s style, this 1893 historic home is the oldest in the shire. It was built by a German immigrant, whose carpentry skills can be seen in the excellent details of the building. It houses a local history museum and exhibits local art and craft. William St.
Historical walk: self-guide walk to heritage sites; contact visitor centre for details.

WHAT'S ON *Street market:* Main St; each Fri. *Country market:* Ferrari Park; last Sat each month. *Rodeo:* Mar. *Heritage Day:* April. *Spring Festival:* flower and art show, craft expo, street parade and markets; Sept. *Art Exhibition:* Oct.

NEARBY *Laidley Pioneer Village:* original buildings from old township including blacksmith shop and slab hut; 1 km s. *Narda Lagoon:* flora and fauna sanctuary with picturesque suspension footbridge over lagoon; adjacent to pioneer village. *Lake Dyer:* beautiful spot for fishing, picnics and camping; 1 km w. *Lake Clarendon:* birdwatching area; 17 km NW. *Laidley Valley Scenic Drive:* attractive drive to the south of Laidley through Thornton.
ⓘ Lockyer Valley Tourist Information Centre, Jumbo's Fruit Barn Complex, Warrego Hwy, Hatton Vale (8 km N); (07) 5465 7642; www.laidley.qld.gov.au

Landsborough   Pop. 1383

Map ref. 601 G6, 602 E13, 607 P7

Landsborough is just north of the magnificent Glass House Mountains in the Sunshine Coast hinterland. It was named after the explorer William Landsborough and was originally a logging town for the rich woodlands of the Blackall Ranges.

IN TOWN *Historical Museum:* this excellent local museum documents the history of the shire through memorabilia, photographs and artefacts; Maleny St. *De Maine Pottery:* award-winning clay pottery by Joanna De Maine; Maleny St; open Thurs–Mon.

WHAT'S ON *Market:* in historic Community Hall; every Sat.

NEARBY Glass House Mountains National Park This park protects eight rugged volcanic mountain peaks. The open eucalypt and mountain heath landscape is a haven for many threatened and endangered animals. Three tracks lead to mountain lookouts that provide panoramic views of the Sunshine Coast hinterland. Only experienced walkers should attempt climbing to any of the summits. 13 km SW.

Australia Zoo Once a small park, this zoo is now renowned as the stomping ground of 'The Crocodile Hunter', Steve Irwin. Originally developed by Irwin's parents, the complex is now over 20 ha and home to a wide range of animals. See the otters catching fish, the birds of prey tackling the skies, or the ever-popular crocodile demonstrations. Feed the kangaroos by hand in the Kids' Zoo. The complex also has important breeding programs for threatened and endangered species. 4 km s.
Dularcha National Park: small scenic park with excellent walks. 'Dularcha' is an Aboriginal word describing blackbutt eucalyptus country. 1 km NE. *Big Kart Track:* largest go-kart track in Australia. The outdoor track is open for day and night racing and includes the 'Bungee Bullet'. 5 km N. *Beerburrum State Forest:* short walks and scenic drives to lookouts; access from Beerburrum; 11 km s.
ⓘ Historical Museum, Maleny St; (07) 5494 1755; www.landsborough town.com.au

Laura   Pop. 85

Map ref. 611 K3

Laura is a tiny town in Far North Queensland that boasts only a few buildings, including the quaint old Quinkan Pub nestled in the shade of mango trees. The area to the south-east of town is known as Quinkan country after the Aboriginal spirits depicted at the incredible Split Rock and Gu Gu Yalangi rock-art sites. Every two years Laura hosts possibly the biggest indigenous event on Australia's calendar – the Laura Dance and Cultural Festival.

WHAT'S ON *Laura Dance and Cultural Festival:* around 25 Cape York and Gulf communities gather at a traditional meeting ground by the Laura River. Traditional dance, music, and art and craft feature at the 3-day event; June, odd-numbered years. *Laura Annual Race Meeting:* race meeting on river flat that has run since 1897, and includes dances and rodeo; June.

NEARBY Split Rock and Gu Gu Yalangi rock-art sites These are Queensland's most important Aboriginal art sites. Hidden behind a tangle of trees in the chasms and crevices of the sandstone escarpment, a diorama of Aboriginal lore and culture unfolds. The Quinkan spirits – the reptile-like Imgin and stick-like Timara – can be found hiding in dark places. There are also dingoes, flying foxes, kangaroos, men, women and many hundreds of other things, both obvious and mysterious. More sites exist nearby, though only these two are accessible to the public. 12 km s.

Lakefield National Park This park is Queensland's second largest and a highlight of any visit to the Cape. The large rivers and waterholes of this park are excellent for fishing and boating in the dry season, but become inaccessible wetlands in the wet season. In the south is the Old Laura Homestead, once en route to the Palmer River Goldfields, and in the north are plains dotted with spectacular anthills. See the threatened gold-shouldered parrot and spectacled hare-wallaby in the rainforest fringes of Normanby and Kennedy rivers. 4WD is recommended; access only in dry season (Apr–Nov). Entrance is 27 km N. *Lakeland:* located in a natural basin, this agricultural town offers Laura Valley Coffee as its main fare, which can be taste-tested at the Coffee House; 64 km SE.
ⓘ 101 Charlotte St, Cooktown; 1800 001 770 or (07) 4069 5446

Longreach   Pop. 3646

Map ref. 608 A11, 615 O11

On the Thomson River, Longreach is the largest town in central-west Queensland. It epitomises the outback and features the renowned Australian Stockman's Hall of Fame, devoted to the outback hero. In 1922 Longreach became the operational base for Qantas and remained so until 1934. The world's first Flying Surgeon Service started from Longreach in 1959.

IN TOWN Australian Stockman's Hall of Fame and Outback Heritage Centre This impressive centre was developed as a tribute to the men and women who opened up outback Australia for settlement, industry and agriculture. It deals with everything from Australia's indigenous heritage and the challenges of outback education and communication to the life of the modern-day stockman. Highlights include a photo gallery, an old blacksmith's shop and a 1920s kitchen. Landsborough Hwy.

Qantas Founders Outback Heritage Museum This modern museum details the commercial flight history of the second

Mustering near Longreach

oldest airline in the world. Explore the restored original 1922 hangar with displays on early flights and a replica Avro 504K. Or visit the exhibition hall to see how flying has evolved over the last century. Longreach Airport, Landsborough Hwy.
Powerhouse Museum: displays of old agricultural machinery, power station and local history museum; Swan St; open 2pm–5pm April–Oct. *Botanical Gardens:* walking and cycling trails; Landsborough Hwy. *Banjo's Outback Theatre:* bush poetry, songs and shearing in shearing shed; near airport. *Qantas Park:* replica of original Qantas booking office, it now houses the information centre; Eagle St. *Heritage buildings:* highlights include the courthouse (1892) in Galah St and the railway station (1916) in Sir Hudson Fysh Dr.
WHAT'S ON *Easter in the Outback:* Easter. *Outback Muster and Drovers Reunion:* May.
NEARBY Lochern National Park The Thomson River plays an important role in this national park as its many waterholes are a sanctuary for a variety of birds. Camp beside the billabong in true outback style at Broadwater Hole and watch the brolgas and pelicans. For visitors passing through, drive the 16 km Bluebush Lagoon circuit to see the natural attractions of this park and glimpse Australian favourites – the kangaroo and emu. Visitors must be self-sufficient. Check road conditions before

departing – roads may be impassable in wet weather. Turn-off 100 km s onto Longreach–Jundah Rd; further 40 km. *Thomson River:* fishing, bushwalking and swimming; 4.6 km NW. *Ilfracombe:* once a transport nucleus for the large Wellshot Station to the south, now an interesting outdoor machinery museum runs the length of this town on the highway. Another feature of town is the historic Wellshot Hotel, with a wool press bar and local memorabilia. 27 km E. *Starlight's Lookout:* said to be a resting spot of Captain Starlight. Enjoy the scenic view. 56 km NW. *Sheep and cattle station tours:* visit local stations to try out mustering and shearing; contact visitor centre for details. *Thomson River cruises:* contact visitor centre for details.
ⓘ Qantas Park, Eagle St; (07) 4658 3555; www.longreach.qld.gov.au

Mackay   Pop. 57 321

Map ref. 609 L5

The city of Mackay is an intriguing blend of 1900s and art deco heritage buildings mixed with modern-day architecture. It was first settled in the 1860s by explorer Captain John Mackay, the city's namesake. Sugar was first grown here in 1865. It is now known as Queensland's 'sugar city' as it produces around one-third of Australia's sugar crop and has the world's largest bulk-sugar loading terminal. Tourism is a growth industry in

Mackay with the natural delights of the Great Barrier Reef just off the coast and spectacular inland national parks nearby.
IN TOWN Artspace Mackay This modern art gallery forms part of the Queensland Heritage Trails Network. The museum documents Mackay's history with an interesting permanent exhibition entitled 'Spirit and Place: Mementoes of Mackay'. The gallery section has changing exhibits of both local and international artwork. Gordon St; closed Mon.
Old Town Hall: houses the Heritage Interpretive Centre with displays on Mackay's history and visitor information; Sydney St. *Regional Botanic Gardens:* Follow the picturesque boardwalk over a lagoon and explore specialised gardens of plants of the central coast. Lagoon St. *Queens Park:* includes the Orchid House that displays over 3000 orchids; Goldsmith St. *Heritage walk:* self-guide walk of 22 heritage buildings; brochure available from visitor centre. *City cemetery:* 1.5 km heritage walk; Greenmount Rd. *Horizon Mosaics:* locally constructed mosaics of Mackay region's natural attractions; Victoria St. *Great Barrier Reef tours:* snorkelling, diving, reef fishing and sailing tours; contact visitor centre for details.
WHAT'S ON *Market:* showgrounds, Milton Rd; Sat mornings. *Victoria Street Markets:* Victoria St; Sun mornings. *Walkers Foundry Markets:* Harbour Rd; weekends. *Festival of the Arts:* July. *Troy Dunn International Bull Riding:* July. *Sugartime Festival:* Sept.
NEARBY Eungella National Park This ecologically diverse park is home to some unusual plants and animals including the Eungella gastric brooding frog and the Mackay tulip oak. A highlight of the visit is seeing the platypus in Broken River from the viewing deck. Visit the Finch Hatton Gorge section of the park where the waterfalls, swimming holes and walking tracks are breathtaking. For the more adventurous, try sailing through the rainforest canopy on the eco-tour Forest Flying. Finch Hatton Gorge turn-off is just before Eungella; Broker River is 6 km s of Eungella.
Northern beaches: visit fabulous beaches including Harbour (patrolled, fishing), Town, Blacks (area's longest beach), Bucasia, Illawong, Eimeo, Lamberts (excellent lookout) and Shoal Point. *Farleigh Sugar Mill:* tours during crushing season, July–Oct; 15 km N. *That Sapphire Place:* sapphire display and gem-cutting demonstrations; 20 km N. *Greenmount Homestead:* restored historic home with pioneering history museum; Walkerston; 20 km W; open Mon–Fri mornings. *Homebush:* small town offers art and craft gallery, orchid farms and self-drive tour through historic area; 25 km S. *Melba House:* the home where Dame Nellie Melba spent the first year of her

married life. It is now home to Pioneer Valley Visitor Centre; Marian; 28 km w. *Mirani:* small town in the Pioneer Valley with museum and Illawong Fauna and Flora Sanctuary; 33 km w. *Kinchant Dam:* popular spot for watersports and fishing; 40 km w. *Hibiscus Coast:* comprises the quaint coastal towns of Seaforth, Ball Bay and Cape Hillsborough; 43 km NW. *Cape Hillsborough National Park:* scenic coastal park with sandy beaches, tidal rock pools and walking trails; access from Hibiscus Coast, 44 km NW. *Smith Islands National Park:* the largest island of this group is Goldsmith, with long sandy beaches and snorkelling in surrounding reefs. Access is by private boat or water taxi. 70 km NE via Seaforth. *Cumberland Island National Park:* this group of islands off Mackay coast is popular for boating and also an important rookery for flat back and green turtles. Access is by private boat or water taxi. *Brampton Island:* resort island at southern end of Whitsunday Passage with pristine beaches and coral reef; sea and air access. *Nebo:* historic town of Mackay region, with local artefacts and pioneering history at the Nebo Shire Museum. Nebo holds a Campdraft in July. 93 km SW. ❶ Mackay Tourism, Old Town Hall, 320 Nebo Rd; 1300 130 001 or (07) 4952 2677; www.mackayregion.com

Maleny   Pop. 1104
Map ref. 601 E5, 602 B11, 607 P7

A steep road climbs from the coast to Maleny, at the southern end of the Blackall Range. The surrounding area is lush dairy country, although farmland is increasingly being sold for residential development. The town's peaceful community lifestyle and picturesque position, with views to the coast and Glass House Mountains, makes it popular with artists.
IN TOWN *Art and craft galleries:* excellent quality galleries throughout town.
WHAT'S ON *Handcraft Markets:* Community Centre, Maple St; Sun. *Autumn Flower Show:* Mar. *Chainsaw to Fine Furniture Expo:* May. *Spring Fair and Flower Show:* Sept. *Scarecrow Festival:* Oct. *Festival of Colour:* open gardens; Oct/Nov.
NEARBY Kondalilla National Park The scenic walks, subtropical rainforest and spectacular Kondalilla Falls make this park an inviting place to visit. The 4.6 km return Falls circuit track passes rock pools to the falls, which drop 90 m. 21 km N via Montville. *Mary Cairncross Park:* this beautiful park was donated to the community in 1941 as protected rainforest after the fierce logging days of the early 1900s. Walk through the rainforest to see superb panoramic views. There is Opera in the Rainforest every Oct. Mountain View Rd; 7 km SE. *Baroon Pocket Dam:* popular spot for fishing and boating. Follow the boardwalks through rainforest. North

Maleny Rd; 8 km N. *Montville:* main street lined with cafes, gift shops, potteries and art and craft galleries. There is a growing wine industry and the town holds the Camellia Festival in July. 16 km NE. *Flaxton:* charming tiny village surrounded by avocado orchards. Visit the quality art and craft galleries, Flaxton Winery and miniature English village. 19 km NE. *Flaxton Barn:* model Swiss and German railway with tearooms; 21 km N via Flaxton. *Maleny–Blackall Range Tourist Drive:* this 28 km scenic drive is one of the best in south-east Queensland. Drive north-east from Maleny through to Mapleton, stopping off at museums, antique shops, fruit stalls and tearooms along the way, as well as taking in spectacular views. The drive can be extended to Nambour. ❶ 25 Maple St; (07) 5499 9033; www.tourmaleny.com.au

Mareeba   Pop. 6883
Map ref. 611 M7

Mareeba was the first town settled on the Atherton Tableland. Major tobacco production started in 1928 and continues to flourish today. The area also produces mangoes, coffee and sugarcane, industries that have thrived with the influx of migrants. The morning balloon flights over the tableland are spectacular.
IN TOWN *Heritage Museum:* local history exhibits and information centre; Centenary Park, Byrnes St. *Art Society Gallery:* Centenary Park. *Barron River Walk:* along the banks and to swimming hole. *Bicentennial Lakes:* park with plantings to encourage wildlife. Explore the park on the walking tracks and bridges. Rankine St. *Bunny Seary Lookout:* views over Mareeba; Chewko Rd.
WHAT'S ON *Market:* Centenary Park; 2nd Sat each month. *Mareeba Annual Race Day:* June. *Rodeo:* July. *Multicultural Festival:* Aug. *Country Music Festival:* even-numbered years, Oct.
NEARBY Mareeba Tropical Savanna and Wetland Reserve This not-for-profit conservation reserve of over 2400 ha and 12 lagoons is home to birds, mammals, fish and freshwater crocodiles. The stunning landscape can be seen on self-guide trails by hiring a timber canoe or taking a tour cruise or the guided 'Twilight Reserve Safari' (with cheese and wine afterwards); tour bookings (07) 4093 2514. Turn-off at Biboohra (7 km N); open Wed–Sun, April–Dec (dry season). *The Coffee Works:* see the production of coffee and taste-test the results; Mason St; 2 km S. *The Beck Museum:* aviation and military collection; Kennedy Hwy; 5 km S. *Mango Winery:* produces white wine from 'Kensington Red' mangoes; Bilwon Rd, Biboohra; 7 km N. *Granite Gorge:* impressive boulder and rock formation; 12 km SW off Chewko Rd. *Davies Creek National Park:* walk the 1.1 km Davies Creek Falls circuit to see the falls crashing

over boulders; 22 km E. *Dimbulah:* small town with museum in restored railway station; 47 km w. *Tyrconnell:* historic mining town with tours of goldmine; 68 km NW via Dimbulah. *Scenic balloon flights:* over Atherton Tableland; contact visitor centre for details. ❶ Heritage Museum, Centenary Park, 345 Byrnes St; (07) 4092 5674; www.athertontableland.com

Maroochydore   Pop. 17 579
Map ref. 601 H4, 602 H9, 607 Q7

A popular beach resort, Maroochydore is also the business centre of the Sunshine Coast. The parklands and birdlife on the Maroochy River and the excellent surf beaches began to attract a growing tourist interest in the 1960s, which has only increased since. An incredible range of watersports is available.
IN TOWN *Maroochy River:* enjoy diverse birdlife and parklands on the southern bank with safe swimming. *Endeavour Replica:* replica of Captain Cook's ship; David Low Way.
NEARBY Mount Coolum National Park Located above the surrounding sugarcane fields, the mountain offers spectacular cascading waterfalls after rain. The park is generally undeveloped, but take the rough 800 m trail to the summit to be rewarded with panoramic views of the coast. 13 km N via Marcoola. *Nostalgia Town:* emphasises humour in history on a train ride through fantasy settings; Pacific Paradise; 7 km NW. *Bli Bli:* attractions include medieval Bli Bli Castle, with dungeon, torture chamber and doll museum, the 'Ski 'n' Surf' waterski park and the Aussie Fishing Park. Take a cruise through Maroochy River wetlands. 9 km NW. *Marcoola:* coastal town with quiet beach; 11 km N. *Coolum Beach:* coastal resort town with long sandy beach; 17 km N. *Eco-Cruise Maroochy:* cruises to Dunethin Rock through sugarcane fields; contact visitor centre for details. ❶ Cnr Sixth Ave and Aerodrome Rd; 1800 882 032 or (07) 5479 1566; www.maroochytourism.com

Maryborough   Pop. 21 123
Map ref. 607 P4

Maryborough is an attractive city on the banks of the Mary River. Its fine heritage buildings and famous timber Queenslander architecture date back to the early years of settlement, when Maryborough was a village and port. Maryborough Port was an important destination in the mid-1800s as over 22 000 immigrants arrived from Europe. The Mary River is a popular spot for relaxed boating and some good fishing.
IN TOWN *Bond Store Museum:* located in the historic Wharf Street Precinct, this museum documents the history of the region from a river port to the present

day; Wharf St. *Customs House Museum:* important cultural heritage museum, with special interest on area's industries and early immigration and Kanaka history; Wharf St. *Central Railway Station, Mary Ann:* replica of Queensland's first steam engine with rides in Queens Park every Thurs and last Sun each month; Lennox St. *Queens Park:* unusual domed fernery and waterfall; cnr Lennox and Bazaar sts. *Elizabeth Park:* extensive rose gardens; Kent St. *Anzac Park:* includes Ululah Lagoon, a scenic waterbird sanctuary where black swans, wild geese, ducks and waterhens may be handfed; cnr Cheapside and Alice sts. *Heritage walk:* self-guide walk past 22 historic buildings, including the impressive City Hall, St Paul's bell tower (with pealing bells) and National Trust-listed Brennan and Geraghty's Store. The walk starts at City Hall, Kent St; brochure available from visitor centre. Take a guided tour, weekdays at 9am. *Heritage drive:* a highlight of this historical drive is the original site of Maryborough (until 1885) where a series of plaques document its changing history. Drive starts at City Hall; brochure available from visitor centre. **WHAT'S ON** *Heritage markets:* Adelaide and Ellena sts; Thurs. *Technology Challenge:* Sept. *Maryborough Masters Games:* Oct. **NEARBY** *Teddington Weir:* popular for watersports; 15 km s. *Tiaro:* town with excellent fishing for Mary River cod in surrounding waterways. The historic Dickabram Bridge over the river, and nearby Mount Bauple National Park; 24 km sw. *Tuan Forest:* bushwalking; 24 km se. *Fraser Island:* World Heritage-listed sand island to the east of town; *see feature on p. 413.* ⓘ Maryborough South Visitors Travel Stop, Bruce Hwy; (07) 4121 4111; www.maryborough.qld.gov.au

Miles · Pop. 1194

Map ref. 607 K7

Miles is in the Western Downs. Ludwig Leichhardt passed through this district on three expeditions and named the place Dogwood Crossing. The town was later renamed Miles after a local member of parliament. After spring rains, this pocket of the Darling Downs is ablaze with wildflowers. **IN TOWN** **Dogwood Crossing @ Miles** This modern cultural centre combines history and art in an innovative space. The excellent Wall of Water displays imagery and stories of the local people – a novel way of discovering the personal history of Miles. The art gallery is a dynamic display with continually changing exhibitions from local and regional artists. Murilla St. *Historical Village:* a 'pioneer settlement' with all types of early buildings, a war museum, shell display and lapidary exhibition; Murilla St.

WHAT'S ON *Back to the Bush:* includes the Wildflower Festival; Sept. *Miles Country Music Spectacular:* Sept. **NEARBY** *Condamine:* small town known for inventing the Condamine Bell, a bullfrog bell that, hung around bullocks, can be heard up to 4 km away. A replica and history display are in Bell Park. There is excellent fishing on the Condamine River, and the town holds a famous rodeo in Oct. 33 km s. *The Gums:* tiny settlement with historic church and nature reserve; 79 km s. *Glenmorgan:* the Myall Park Botanical Gardens; 134 km sw. ⓘ Historical Village, Murilla St; (07) 4627 1492; www.murilla.qld.gov.au

Millaa Millaa · Pop. 289

Map ref. 603 B2, 611 M8

Millaa Millaa is at the southern edge of the Atherton Tableland, and is central to a thriving dairy industry. The 17-kilometre Waterfall Circuit and rainforest-clad Wooroonooran National Park are just two of the natural attractions that bring visitors to the mild climate of this town. **IN TOWN** *Eacham Historical Society Museum:* documents history of local area, with special interest in dairy and timber industries; Main St. **NEARBY** **Wooroonooran National Park, Palmerston section** More than 500 different types of rainforest trees means the landscape in this park is both diverse and breathtaking. Tracks include a 5 km return track leading to spectacular gorge views at Crawford's Lookout and a short 800 m track to glimpse the Tchupala Falls. A popular activity in the park is whitewater rafting on the North Johnstone River (permits required). Access via Palmerston Hwy; 25 km sw. **Waterfall Circuit** This 17 km circuit road includes the Zillie, Ellinjaa and Mungalli falls, as well as the popular Millaa Millaa Falls, a great spot for swimming, with

walks leading to other waterfalls. The circuit road is mostly sealed and the route leaves and rejoins Palmerston Hwy east of town. Nearby are also the Souita and Papina falls. *Millaa Millaa Lookout:* panoramic views of tablelands and national parks; just west of town. *Misty Mountains walking trails:* short- and long-distance tracks through World Heritage-listed Wet Tropics, many of which follow traditional Aboriginal paths of the Jirrbal and Mamu people; contact visitor centre for details. ⓘ Millaa Millaa Tourist Park, Millaa Millaa–Malanda Rd; (07) 4097 2290; www.eachamshire.qld.gov.au

Miriam Vale · Pop. 384

Map ref. 607 M1, 609 Q13

Miriam Vale is centre of the 'Discovery Coast', north-west of Bundaberg. The town is renowned for its charming hospitality, its historic fig trees in the main street and its mud-crab sandwiches. The hinterland and coastal national parks are ideal places for bushwalking, four-wheel driving and horseriding. **NEARBY** **Deepwater National Park** A diverse vegetation litters this coastal park, including paperbark forests, swamp mahogany, Moreton Bay ash and subtropical rainforest. Walk along the sandy beaches or enjoy the birdlife of the freshwater stream, Deepwater Creek. Bush camp at Wreck Rock, and explore the rock pools. 4WD access only; 63 km ne via Agnes Water. *Eurimbula National Park:* rugged coastal park with walks along the beach, canoeing on Eurimbula Creek, fishing, and scenic views from Ganoonga Noonga Lookout. 4WD recommended; access between Miriam Vale and Agnes Water, 50 km ne. *Agnes Water:* this coastal town has the most northerly surfing beach in Queensland. A local history museum includes documents of Cook's voyage

Brennan and Geraghty's Store, Maryborough

in 1770. The town holds the surfing competition 1770 Longboard Classic each March. 57 km NE. *Seventeen Seventy:* Captain Cook, while on his discovery voyage, made his second landing on Australian soil at the town site. This seaside village has the Joseph Banks Environmental Park and is the departure point for daytrips and fishing charters to the Great Barrier Reef and Lady Musgrave Island. 63 km NE.
ⓘ Discovery Coast Information Centre, Roe St (Bruce Hwy); (07) 4974 5428

Mission Beach   Pop. 933

Map ref. 603 D3, 611 N9

Mission Beach is named for the Aboriginal mission established in the area in 1914. The beach that features in the town's name is a 14-kilometre-long strip of golden sand fringed by coconut palms and World Heritage-listed wet tropical rainforest. Artists, potters, sculptors and jewellers have settled in the area, now reliant on the strong tourism industry of the coast.

IN TOWN *Porters Promenade:* woodcarving exhibition and rainforest arboretum; next to visitor centre. *Ulysses Link Walking Trail:* this 1.2 km pathway along the foreshore features local history, sculptures and mosaics. *Great Barrier Reef tours:* cruises and day tours to islands and reefs depart from Clump Point Jetty daily. *Boat, catamaran and jetski hire:* contact visitor centre for details.

WHAT'S ON *Market:* Porters Promenade; 1st Sat and 3rd Sun each month. *Monster Markets:* Recreation Centre, Cassowary Dr; last Sun each month (Easter–Nov). *Banana Festival:* Aug. *Aquatic Festival:* Oct.

NEARBY Family Islands Off the coast of Mission Beach and Tully is this 14 km stretch of islands protected by the Family Islands National Park. The most northerly island, Dunk Island, is a popular holiday destination with spectacular forest, rainforest, and 14 km of walking tracks. The resort is private, however camping is available. The less-developed islands of Wheeler and Coombe are perfect for bush camping (visitors must be self-sufficient). There is air service to Dunk Island from Cairns and Townsville or ferry from Clump Point. Islands are accessible by water taxi from Wongaling Beach.
Clump Mountain National Park: this scenic park boasts remnant lowland rainforest, an important habitat for the southern cassowary. A highlight is the 4 km Bicton Hill Track to the summit lookout over Mission Beach and coast. Just north of Mission Beach on Bingil Bay Rd. *Historic cairn:* commemorates the ill-fated 1848 Cape York expedition of Edmund Kennedy; South Mission Beach Esplanade. *Aboriginal Midju:* display of Aboriginal culture; adjacent to

Mission Beach

cairn. *Wet Tropics walking trails:* the area around Mission Beach offers spectacular rainforest walks, including the Lacy Creek Forest circuit (1.2 km) in the major cassowary habitat of Tam O'Shanter State Forest, the Kennedy Trail (7 km) past lookouts and along beaches, and the trails in Licuala State Forest; brochure available from visitor centre. *Adventure activities:* include tandem parachuting, guided canoe and kayak trips and whitewater rafting; contact visitor centre for details.
ⓘ Porters Promenade; (07) 4068 7099; www.missionbch.com

Mitchell   Pop. 1008

Map ref. 606 F6

Mitchell, a gateway to the outback, is on the banks of the Maranoa River at the western edge of the Darling Downs. But, located as it is on the Great Artesian Basin, it does not suffer the dry heat or

exhibit the arid landscape typical of the region. The town was named after Sir Thomas Mitchell, explorer and Surveyor-General of New South Wales, who visited the region in 1846. Its long pastoral history is shown in the fine examples of heritage buildings on the main street.

IN TOWN Kenniff Courthouse This courthouse was in use from 1882 to 1965. It held the murder trials for the infamous bushrangers, the Kenniff Brothers, who killed a policeman and station manager in 1902. The courthouse is now a museum with a bushranger exhibition, visual display, and art and craft sales. The landscaped grounds incorporate a community mosaic, an operating artesian windmill and a small billabong. Cambridge St.
Great Artesian Spa: with relaxing natural waters in a garden surrounding, this is Australia's largest open-air spa; Cambridge St. *Graffiti murals:* depict the past, present and future of the Booringa Shire; around town. *Horse-drawn wagon tours:* in season; contact visitor centre for details.

NEARBY Carnarvon National Park, Mount Moffatt section This section of the park is mainly for driving, with short walks to scenic spots. See the sandstone sculptures of Cathedral Rock, Marlong Arch and Lot's Wife, or visit The Tombs for the ancient stencil art of the Nuri and Bidjara people. The high country woodlands and forest are home to a variety of wildlife, and birdwatching for raptors and lorikeets is exceptional. 4WD recommended; 256 km N. Gorge section: *see Roma*. Ka Ka Mundi section: *see Springsure*. Salvator Rosa section: *see Tambo*.
Neil Turner Weir: birdwatching and picnics; 3.5 km NW. *Fisherman's Rest:* popular fishing spot; 6 km W. *Maranoa River Nature Walk:* informative 1.8 km circuit walk starting at Fisherman's Rest. *Kenniff Statues:* depict story of the brothers at site of their last stand; 7 km S. *Major Mitchell Cruises:* cruises down Maranoa River departing from Rotary Park, Neil Turner Weir, 2 pm daily (except Thurs) in season; book at visitor centre. *Aboriginal tours:* guided tours of local area run by Nalingu Aboriginal Corporation; contact visitor centre for details.
ⓘ Great Artesian Spa complex, 6 Cambridge St; (07) 4623 1073; www.booringa.qld.gov.au

Monto   Pop. 1108

Map ref. 607 M2

Monto, one of the most recent towns in the Capricorn region, was settled in 1924. It is the centre of a rich dairy and beef cattle district and is set picturesquely on a plateau surrounded by rolling hills.

IN TOWN *Monto History Centre:* local history displays and videos; cnr Kelvin and Lister sts. *Historical and Cultural Complex:* variety of historic artefacts and mineral display; Flinders St.

WHAT'S ON *Dairy Festival:* even-numbered years, June. *Monto Gold Buckle Campdraft:* Aug. *Monto Garden Expo:* Oct.
NEARBY Cania Gorge National Park Part of Queensland's sandstone belt, this park has cliffs, gorges and caves of spectacular colours. The freehand Aboriginal art around the park is a reminder of its ancient heritage. There are over 10 walks of varying length and difficulty. See the park's goldmining history on the 1.2 km return Shamrock Mine track or experience breathtaking park views from the Giant's Chair Lookout, reached on the longer Fern Tree Pool and Giant's Chair circuit. 25 km NW.
Mungungo: small town with boutique Waratah Winery; 13 km N. *Lake Cania:* excellent spot for watersports, fishing (permit required) and walking to lookout. Annual Lake Cania Fishing Classic is held here every Mar. 11 km N via Cania Gorge Picnic Area. *Kalpower State Forest:* hoop pine and rainforest vegetation. 4WD or walk rugged tracks to scenic lookouts. 40 km NE. *Wuruma Dam:* swimming, sailing and waterskiing; 50 km S.
ⓘ Touch screen in Newton St; or council offices, 51a Newton St; (07) 4166 9999

Mooloolaba   Pop. 12 633

Map ref. 601 H4, 602 H9, 607 Q7

Mooloolaba is a popular holiday destination on the Sunshine Coast. Its fabulous beaches, restaurants, nightlife and resort-style shopping contribute to the constant influx of families and young people eager for the sun. Mooloolaba Harbour is one of the safest anchorages on the east coast and the base for a major prawning and fishing fleet.
IN TOWN UnderWater World This award-winning complex has a fantastic 80 m walkway through seawater 'ocean', with displays of the Great Barrier Reef and underwater creatures. There are daily shows, including the seal show and crocodile feeding. Spend 15 min swimming with a seal or dive in with sharks (bookings essential). The Touch Tank is a less daunting alternative to get up close to the animals of the sea. Wharf Complex, Parkyn Pde.
Mooloolaba Harbour: popular spot for parasailing, scuba diving and cruises; contact visitor centre for tour operators.
WHAT'S ON *Triathlon Festival:* Mar. *Sydney-to-Mooloolaba Yacht Race:* finishes at Mooloolaba Harbour; April.
NEARBY *Alexandra Headland:* popular coastal town with sweeping views to the Maroochy River and Mudjimba Island. Extensive beaches and parklands on the foreshore provide a popular relaxation spot. Surf lessons and board hire are available from Mooloolaba Wharf. Just north of Mooloolaba. *Mooloolah River National Park:* take a canoe down Mooloolah River, ride along the bike trail or walk on the fire trails in this remnant

wallum heath park; straddles Sunshine Motorway; 6 km SW. *Yachting and game fishing:* trips to nearby offshore reefs; contact visitor centre for details.
ⓘ Cnr First Ave and Brisbane Rd; (07) 5478 2233; www.mooloolababeach.com

Moranbah   Pop. 6125

Map ref. 608 I7

Moranbah is a modern mining town south-west of Mackay. It was established in 1969 to support the huge open-cut coalmines of the expanding Bowen Coal Basin. Coking coal is railed to the Hay Point export terminal just south of Mackay.
IN TOWN *Federation Walk:* 1 km scenic walk starts at Grosvenor Park; Peak Downs Hwy. *Historical walk:* self-guide trail past interesting sites and heritage buildings of town; brochure available from visitor centre.
WHAT'S ON *Australia Day Street Party:* Jan. *May Day Union Parade and Fireworks:* May.
NEARBY *Tours to BHP's Peak Downs Mine:* leave town square each Thurs 10am; book at visitor centre. *Isaacs River:* recreational area with historic monuments and a hiking trail in dry weather; 13 km S. *Lake Elphinstone:* camping, recreation activities, waterskiing, boating and fishing; 70 km N.
ⓘ Library, town square; (07) 4941 7221; www.belyando.qld.gov.au

Mossman   Pop. 1901

Map ref. 605 D8, 611 M5

Mossman, in Far North Queensland, is set among green mountains and fields of sugarcane. Originally named after the explorer Hugh Mosman, the town changed the spelling of its name from Mosman to Mossman to avoid being confused with the Sydney suburb.
WHAT'S ON *Market:* Front St; each Sat. *Music Festival:* Nov.
NEARBY *Cooya Beach and Newell:* coastal towns with popular beaches to the north-east. *Daintree National Park:* including the magnificent Mossman Gorge; 5 km W; *see feature on p. 407. Karnak Rainforest Sanctuary:* amphitheatre and rainforest; 8 km N. *High Falls Farm:* tropical fruit orchard, market garden and open-air restaurant in rainforest setting; 9 km N. *Wonga:* small town with an excellent beach and orchid gardens; 18 km N.
ⓘ Port Douglas Daintree Tourism Association, 23 Macrossan St, Port Douglas; (07) 4099 4588; www.pddt.com.au

Mount Isa   Pop. 20 369

Map ref. 614 E4

The city of Mount Isa is the most important industrial, commercial and administrative centre in north-west Queensland, an oasis of civilisation in

outback spinifex and cattle country. But before John Campbell Miles first discovered a rich silver-lead deposit in 1923, it was barren. Today Mount Isa Mines operates one of the world's largest silver-lead mines. Mount Isa is also one of the world leaders in rodeos, holding the third-largest, which attracts rough-riders from all over Queensland and almost doubles the town's population.
IN TOWN Outback at Isa This modern complex introduces the visitor to the splendours of Queensland's outback country. Don a hard hat and take a guided tour of the 1.2 km of underground tunnels in the Hard Times Mine. The indigenous, pioneering and mining history of Mount Isa is explored in the Sir James Foots building, and the Outback Park offers a scenic lagoon and informative walking trail. Marian St.
Riversleigh Fossil Centre This award-winning centre explores the significant discoveries of the Riversleigh Fossil Site (267 km NW; *see Boodjamulla (Lawn Hill) National Park feature on p. 424*). Through colourful displays, the ancient animals and landscapes come alive. The theatrette shows an excellent film on the fossil story so far and a visit to the laboratory with a working palaeontologist brings fossil discovery up close as precious material is extracted from rocks. Adjacent to Outback at Isa.
Kalkadoon Tribal Centre: preserves the heritage and culture of indigenous Kalkadoon people. There are displays of artefacts and guided tours by Kalkadoon descendants. Centenary Park, Marian St; open weekdays. *National Royal Flying Doctor Service Visitor Centre:* informative video, historic and modern memorabilia and photo display; Barkly Hwy; open weekdays. *Trust Tent House:* an example of the housing provided for miners in the 1930s and 1940s that was designed for good ventilation in extreme conditions; Fourth Ave; open 10am–2pm April–Sept. *School of the Air:* discover how distance education works in the outback; Abel Smith Pde; weekday tours 9am and 10am (on schooldays). *City Lookout:* overview of city and mine area; Hilary St. *Underground Hospital:* tours of hospital built in WW II; Deighton St. *Mount Isa Mine:* the mine's lead smelter stack is Australia's tallest free-standing structure (265 m). Informative surface tours are available; contact visitor centre for details. *Donaldson Memorial Lookout:* lookout and walking track; off Marian St.
WHAT'S ON *Markets:* West St, Sat; Camooweal St, Sun. *International Mining Challenge:* April/May. *Isa Rodeo:* Aug.
NEARBY *Lake Moondarra:* artificial lake for picnics and barbecues, swimming, watersports and birdwatching. Home of the Fishing Classic in Oct. 20 km N. *Mt Frosty:* old limestone mine and swimming hole (not recommended for children as hole is 9 m deep with no shallow areas);

Indarri Falls, Lawn Hill Gorge

Boodjamulla (Lawn Hill) National Park

Boodjamulla (Lawn Hill) National Park in north-western Queensland has a long spiritual history. The Waanyi people inhabited this land known to them as Boodjamulla, or Rainbow Serpent country, for more than 17 000 years, as testified by the rock-art sites of Wild Dog Dreaming and Rainbow Dreaming (Lawn Hill Gorge section). The park also has a rich pastoral history – at 11 000 square kilometres, Lawn Hill Station was once one of Queensland's largest cattle properties, before part of it was set aside for national park.

Beyond this evidence of human habitation are the fossilised remains of life that filled the ancient rainforest that once stood on the now dry, limestone-rich plains. The Riversleigh section of the park has been registered as part of the Australian Fossil Mammal Sites World Heritage Area since 1994 and contains some of the most outstanding and important mammalian fossils in the world, some up to 25 million years old.

Lawn Hill Gorge section

If the Riversleigh section of Boodjamulla (Lawn Hill) National Park is ecologically significant, the Lawn Hill Gorge section is spectacular. Lawn Hill Creek is the centrepiece, which has gradually carved out the impressive Lawn Hill Gorge – see it up close by hiring a canoe from the camping area and exploring the waters. Alternatively, take one of the walking tracks. A highlight is the early-morning climb to Island Stack for spectacular views (4 kilometres return).

Riversleigh section

It is estimated that almost half of what we know about the evolution of Australian mammals in the last 30 million years has been found at Riversleigh, most of it since 1983. Thousands of fossils have been unearthed and documented including carnivorous kangaroos, marsupial lions, giant pythons, and the distant relatives of the platypus and thylacine (Tasmanian tiger).

Access to Riversleigh is restricted to the 'D site'. There is an information shelter here and a self-guide interpretive trail. Commercial tours also operate out of Adel's Grove (adjacent to the park), Mount Isa and Burketown.

New fossils are still being discovered, and at Outback at Isa (see *Mount Isa*) you can see the palaeontologists at work and then wander through the simulated rainforest environment of the Miocene period 25 million years ago. Among the trees are reproductions of the bizarre and exotic animals that Riversleigh has revealed.

Boodjamulla (Lawn Hill) National Park is located around 90 kilometres west of Gregory and can be accessed from Burketown, Cloncurry, Mount Isa and Camooweal. Conventional vehicles are best suited to the route from Cloncurry.

53 km E. *Lake Julius:* canoe at the lake or see the Aboriginal cave paintings and old goldmine on the surrounding nature trails; 110 km NE. *Station visits:* feel the outback spirit at one of the stations in the area; contact visitor centre for details. *Safari tours:* to Boodjamulla (Lawn Hill) National Park and Riversleigh Fossil Fields; contact visitor centre for details. *Air-charter flights:* to barramundi fishing spots on Mornington and Sweers islands in the Gulf of Carpentaria; contact visitor centre for details.
ⓘ Outback at Isa, 19 Marian St; 1300 659 660 or (07) 4749 1555; www.outbackatisa.com.au

Mount Morgan   Pop. 2397

Map ref. 609 N11

Located in the Capricorn region south-west of Rockhampton is the quaint historic mining town of Mount Morgan. Said to be the largest single mountain of gold in the world, Mount Morgan's gold supply was discovered and mined from the late 1800s. What was a big mountain is now a big crater – the largest excavation in the Southern Hemisphere. In the mine's heyday, around 1910, the town was home to about 14 000 people.

IN TOWN *Railway Station:* historic station with tearooms, rail museum and a restored 1904 Hunslett Steam Engine that operates regularly; Railway Pde. *Historical Museum:* varied collection of memorabilia traces history of this mining town; Morgan St. *Historic suspension bridge:* built in the 1890s and spans the Dee River. *Historic cemetery:* with the Chinese Heung Lew (prayer oven) and the Linda Memorial to men killed in underground mines (1894–1909); off Coronation Dr. *The Big Stack:* 76 m high 1905 brick chimney used to disperse mining fumes; at the mine site.
WHAT'S ON *Golden Mount Festival:* May.
NEARBY *The Big Dam:* good boating and fishing; 2.7 km N via William St. *Wowan:* town featuring the Scrub Turkey Museum in old butter factory; 40 km SW. *Tours:* tour to the open-cut Mount Morgan Mine and ancient clay caves with dinosaur footprints; contact visitor centre for details.
ⓘ Heritage Railway Station, 1 Railway Pde; (07) 4938 2312; www.mountmorgan.com

Mount Surprise   Pop. 60

Map ref. 611 J10

Mount Surprise is a historic rail town in the Gulf Savannah. Its name comes from the surprise the Aboriginal people felt when they were resting at the base of the mountain and the loud white people of Ezra Firth's pioneer party arrived in 1864. The region has excellent gemfields for fossicking, especially for topaz, quartz and aquamarine. The town is on the edge of the Undara lava field, formed from the craters of the McBride Plateau. The lava caves can be explored in the Undara Volcanic National Park.

IN TOWN Savannahlander This unique train journey allows the passenger to discover the rugged delights and beautiful landscapes between Mount Surprise and Cairns. Departing from Mount Surprise Station each Saturday, the train stops at towns on the journey to explore the historic and natural delights of the Gulf Savannah region. There are also trips between Mount Surprise and Forsayth. Bookings (07) 3235 1122. *Old Post Office Museum:* documents bush history of region in historic 1870 building; opposite railway station. *Mount Surprise Gems:* runs tours to nearby fossicking spots and provides licences; Garland St.

NEARBY Undara Volcanic National Park The cooling molten lava of an erupted volcano formed the 90 km of hollow underground lava tubes, the longest of its kind in the world. You can only explore the tubes by guided tour; bookings: 1800 990 992; day tours also run from Bedrock Village. See the eggcup-shaped crater on the 2.5 km Kalkani Crater circuit or go birdwatching to see the 120 species of bird in the park. 42 km E. *O'Brien's Creek:* renowned for quality topaz; obtain licence before fossicking; 37 km NW. *Tallaroo Hot Springs:* five natural springs created over centuries; open Easter–Sept; 48 km NW. *Forty Mile Scrub National Park:* vine-thicket park on the McBride Plateau with informative short circuit track from day area; 56 km E. *Georgetown:* small town once one of many small goldmining settlements on the Etheridge Goldfields. It is noted for its gemstones, especially agate, and gold nuggets. 82 km W. *Forsayth:* old mining town; 132 km SW. *Cobbold Gorge:* guided boat tours through sandstone gorge; bookings essential (07) 4062 5470. A full-day tour to Forsayth and gorge also runs from Bedrock Village (*see below*). 167 km SW via Forsayth. *Agate Creek:* fossick for gemstones; 187 km SW via Forsayth.
ⓘ Bedrock Village Caravan Park, Garland St (Savannah Way); (07) 4062 3055; or Mount Surprise Gems, Garland St; (07) 4062 3055; www.gulf-savannah.com.au

Mourilyan   Pop. 450
Map ref. 603 D2, 611 N8

Mourilyan is a small town in Far North Queensland. It is the bulk-sugar outlet for the Innisfail area. The history of this thriving industry can be seen at the Australian Sugar Industry Museum.

IN TOWN Australian Sugar Industry Museum This large museum complex was opened in 1977. Its permanent displays include a museum collection of photographs, books, documents and an incredible display of machinery that includes a steam engine, reputedly one of the largest ever built. A theatre provides an audiovisual display of the history of Australia's sugar industry and there is also an art gallery. Cnr Bruce Hwy and Peregrine St.

NEARBY Paronella Park This 5 ha park was the vision of immigrant sugarcane worker José Paronella. After making his fortune, he started building a mansion on the site (1930–1946). Floods and other natural disasters have ruined the grand buildings, despite rebuilding efforts. Now the visitor can walk through the ruins, admire the spectacular rainforest and birdlife, swim near the falls and have Devonshire tea at the cafe. 17 km SW. *Etty Bay:* quiet tropical beach with caravan and camping facilities; 9 km E.
ⓘ Cnr Eslick St and Bruce Hwy, Innisfail; (07) 4061 7422

Mundubbera   Pop. 1232
Map ref. 607 M4

Mundubbera is on the banks of the Burnett River and is the main citrus-growing area in Queensland. Fruit pickers flock to the town in the cooler months. The unusual company 'Bugs for Bugs' produces a group of predatory bugs that reduces the need for pesticides. The rare Neoceratodus, or lungfish, is found in the Burnett and Mary rivers.

IN TOWN *Historical Museum:* local history; Frank McCauley St. *Jones Weir:* popular spot for fishing; Bauer St. *'Meeting Place of the Waters':* 360-degree town mural; cnr Strathdy and Stuart-Russell sts.

NEARBY Auburn River National Park Through this small park flows the Auburn River, travelling through a sheer-sided gorge and over granite boulders in the riverbed. Dry rainforest grows on the upper part of the tough track that leads down the side of the gorge to the river. An easier walk is the 150 m trail to the lookout above Auburn River. Opposite the campsite catch a glimpse of the nesting peregrine falcons. 4WD is recommended in wet weather. 40 km NW. *Enormous Ellendale:* the big mandarin, another addition to the 'big' monuments of Queensland; outskirts of town at the Big Mandarin Caravan Park. *Golden Mile Orchard:* impressive orchard with tours; 5 km S; open April–Sept. *Eidsvold:* town at the centre of beef cattle country featuring the Historical Museum Complex and Tolderodden Environmental Park; 37 km NW.
ⓘ Historical Museum, Dugong St; or call council offices (07) 4165 4101 or (07) 4165 4549

Murgon   Pop. 2144
Map ref. 607 N6

Murgon, known as 'the beef capital of the Burnett', is one of the most attractive towns in southern Queensland. Settlement dates from 1843, but the town did not really develop until 1904 when the large stations of the area were divided up. The town's name comes from an Aboriginal word for lily pond, a pond found on Barambah Station.

IN TOWN *Queensland Dairy Museum:* this unique museum has static and interactive displays illustrating the history of the dairy industry, with special interest in the development of butter; Gayndah Rd.

WHAT'S ON *Dairy Heritage Festival:* June. *Barambah Shakin' Grape Festival:* Oct.

NEARBY Boat Mountain Conservation Park The flat-topped crest in this park looks like an upturned boat, hence the name. The views from the top are panoramic and take in the surrounding agricultural valley. There are 2 lookout walks and an excellent 1.8 km circuit track. Look out for the bandicoot digs along the way. 15 km NE via Boat Mountain Rd.

Jack Smith Conservation Park This park is adjacent to Boat Mountain and comprises valuable remnant dry rainforest that used to cover the entire region before clearing for agriculture began. Have a picnic overlooking the South Burnett Valley before taking the 20 min return track through scrub to see the abundant birdlife of the park. *Cherbourg:* small Aboriginal community featuring Emu Farm with walk-through enclosures, educational displays, Aboriginal artefacts and sales of emu products; 5 km SE. *Wondai:* attractions include Regional Art Gallery, Heritage Museum and South Burnett Timber Industry Museum. Town hosts Garden Festival in April and Arts Festival in Oct. 13 km S. *Bjelke-Petersen Dam:* popular spot for watersports and fishing (boat hire available) with various accommodation styles at Yallakool Tourist Park. The dam is home to the Annual Fishing Competition in Oct. 15 km SE. *Goomeri:* known as 'clock town' for its unique memorial clock in the town centre. It has numerous antique stores and holds the Pumpkin Festival in May. 19 km NE. *Booubyjan Homestead:* historic home (1847) open to public; 43 km N via Goomeri. *Kilkivan:* Queensland's first discovery of gold was here in 1852. Try fossicking for gold or visit the lavender farm and historical museum. The town holds the Great Horse Ride in April. 44 km NE. *Proston:* small community featuring Sidcup Castle and Crafts Museum (open Wed–Mon); 54 km W. *Lake Boondooma:* watersports, fishing and the Fishing Competition in Feb; 74 km NW via Proston. *Barambah Wine Trail:* within 15 km of Murgon, in the Moffatdale and Redgate areas, are seven excellent wineries with tastings and sales; visit by car or bus tour. *Bicentennial National Trail:* a 5000 km trail for walkers, bike riders and horseriders – you can do just a part of the trail. It runs through Kilkivan. *Fossicking:* semi-precious stones in Cloyna and Windera region; contact visitor centre for details.

ⓘ Queen Elizabeth Park; (07) 4168 3864; www.murgon.qld.gov.au

Muttaburra
Pop. 225

Map ref. 608 B9, 615 P9

Despite being a tiny outback community, Muttaburra has much to promote in its history. Famous cattle duffer Harry Redford (Captain Starlight) planned his daring robbery at nearby Bowen Downs Station in 1870. He stole 1000 head of cattle (thinking they wouldn't be missed) and drove them 2400 kilometres into South Australia. He was arrested and tried; the jury acquitted him, probably because his daring was so admired. These events were the basis for Rolf Boldrewood's novel *Robbery Under Arms*. More recently, a skeleton of an unknown dinosaur was found in 1963 in a creek close to the Thomson River. It was named Muttaburrasaurus. A replica can be seen in Bruford Street.

IN TOWN *Dr Arratta Memorial Museum:* housed in the region's original hospital, this museum has medical and hospital displays with original operating theatres and wards; tours by appt; (07) 4658 7287. *Cassimatis General Store and Cottage:* restored store depicts the original family business in early 1900s. The adjacent cottage was home to the Cassimatis family. Tours by appt; (07) 4658 7287.
WHAT'S ON *Rodeo:* May. *Landsborough Flock Ewe Show:* June.
NEARBY *Agate fossicking:* 5 km w. *Pump Hole:* swimming and fishing for golden perch and black bream; 5 km E. *Broadwater:* part of Landsborough River for fishing, birdwatching, bushwalking and camping; 6 km s.
ⓘ Post office, Sword St; (07) 4658 7147; www.muttaburra.com

Nambour
Pop. 12 822

Map ref. 601 F4, 602 E8, 607 P7

Nambour is a large, unpretentious service town in the Sunshine Coast hinterland. Development began in the 1860s and sugar has been the main crop since the 1890s. Small locomotives pull loads of sugarcane across the main street to Moreton Central Mill, a charming sight during the crushing season (July–October). The town's name is derived from the Aboriginal word for the local red-flowered tea tree.
WHAT'S ON *Queensland Home Garden Expo:* July.
NEARBY **Mapleton Falls National Park**
Volcanic columns jut out of Pencil Creek just before the creek's water falls 120 m to the valley floor. Walk to the falls lookout or see panoramic views of the Obi Obi Valley from Peregrine Lookout. Birdwatchers will delight at the early morning and dusk flights of the park's numerous bird species. 3 km sw of Mapleton.

The Big Pineapple Complex and Macadamia Nut Factory The 16 m fibreglass pineapple makes this complex hard to miss. Inside are displays on the tropical fruit industry. The complex has a variety of interesting activities, including the Plantation Train, Harvest Boat Ride, Rainforest Walk, and Nutmobile through macadamia orchards. See Australian favourites like the koala, kangaroo and wallaby at the Australian Wildlife Garden or get up close at the Animal Nursery. 7 km s.
Mapleton: attractive arts and crafts town in the Blackall Range. It holds the Yarn Festival in Oct. 15 km w. *Mapleton Forest Reserve:* with excellent drive through bunya pines and blackbutt forests starting just north of Mapleton. Along the drive walk to the top of the waterfall from Poole's Dam and take the short Piccabeen Palm Groves Walk. The drive ends with spectacular views from Point Glorious.
ⓘ 5 Coronation Ave; (07) 5476 1933

Nanango
Pop. 2615

Map ref. 607 N7

Nanango is one of the oldest towns in Queensland. Gold was mined here from 1850 to 1900 and fossickers still try their luck today. The industrial Tarong Power Station and Meandu Coal Mine are nearby, yet Nanango still retains a welcoming country atmosphere.
IN TOWN *Historic Ringsfield House:* excellent example of colonial architecture of the 1900s. It houses the historical society and period furnishings. Cnr Alfred and Cairns sts; open weekdays, weekends by appt (07) 4163 3345. *Tarong Power Station Display:* models and displays; adjacent to visitor centre. *Belvedere Gallery:* local art, craft and pottery; Drayton St; closed Mon.
WHAT'S ON *Market:* showgrounds; 1st Sat each month. *Nanart:* Art Show; June. *Burning Beat Music Festival:* Sept. *Pioneer Festival:* Oct. *Criterium Bike Race:* Nov.
NEARBY **The Palms National Park**
Located at the Brisbane headwaters is this vine forest and subtropical rainforest park. Have a bush picnic and then take the 20 min Palm circuit track through natural vegetation and along boardwalks. 42 km sw.
Tipperary Flat: tribute park to early pioneers with old goldmining camp, displays and walking track; 2 km E. *Seven-Mile Diggings:* gold- and gem-fossicking; permit from visitor centre; 11 km SE. *Yarraman:* historic timber town with heritage centre and 'mud maps' for region; 21 km s. *Maidenwell:* small town with Astronomical Observatory and Coomba Falls nearby; 28 km sw. *Blackbutt:* picturesque timber town with country markets 3rd Sun each month; 41 km SE.
ⓘ Henry St; (07) 4171 6871; www.nanango.qld.gov.au

Nerang
Pop. 22 023

Map ref. 599 G11, 600 C5, 607 Q10

Nerang is in the Gold Coast hinterland. Today the town is much more similar in character to that dense urban strip of coast than to the small rural centre it started out as in the mid-1800s.
IN TOWN **Nerang Forest Reserve** On the north-west fringe of Nerang is this hilly rainforest and open eucalypt reserve. An excellent way of exploring the landscape is on the 2.8 km return Casuarina Grove Track through rainforest and along the creek. Look out for the black cockatoos. The reserve is a popular spot for horseriders and cyclists (permit required).
WHAT'S ON *Australian Arena Polo Championships:* Aug.
NEARBY **Springbrook National Park** This rainforest park forms part of the Scenic Rim of mountains. The Springbrook section has an information centre, from which a short walk leads to a spectacular lookout over the Gold Coast. The most popular walk is the 4 km Purlingbrook Falls circuit, but walks range from a short 700 m walk to the more substantial 17 km hike. Access is via Springbrook; 39 km sw. The Natural Bridge section features a unique rock arch over Cave Creek. Take the 1 km rainforest walk to see the natural bridge where Cave Creek plunges through an eroded hole to a cavern below. There are tours to see the glow worms or a 3 km night trail through rainforest; bookings (07) 5533 5239. 38 km sw.
Lamington National Park This beautiful park to the south-west of Nerang protects the world's largest subtropical rainforest. It is a popular bushwalking and scenic park with spectacular waterfalls and mountain landscapes. Have a picnic with the rosellas and brush turkeys or test out one of the bushwalks – there are over 20 on offer. The 1.3 km return rainforest circuit from Green Mountains includes the suspension bridge 15 m high in the forest canopy. Access to the Green Mountains section is via Canungra. Binna Burra is accessed via Beechmont. *Carrara:* nearby town offers scenic balloon flights over the Gold Coast, (07) 5578 2244, and holds weekend markets; 5 km SE. *Hinze Dam on Advancetown Lake:* sailing and bass-fishing; 10 km sw. *Historic River Mill:* 1910 arrowroot mill; 10 km w. *Mudgeeraba:* holds the Somerset Celebration of Literature in Mar. Nearby is the Gold Coast War Museum with militia memorabilia and skirmish paintball. 12 km s.
ⓘ Cavill Walk, Surfers Paradise; (07) 5538 4419

Noosa Heads
Pop. 6033

Map ref. 601 H1, 602 H1, 607 Q6

Noosa Heads, commonly known as Noosa, is a coastal resort town on Laguna Bay on the Sunshine Coast. The relaxed lifestyle, the weather and the safe year-round swimming make this a popular holiday destination. The cosmopolitan Hastings Street offers a relaxed cafe lifestyle, and within walking distance are the natural attractions of superb coastal scenery and the protected coves, surfing beaches and seascapes of Noosa National Park.

IN TOWN *Noosa Main Beach:* safe family swimming. *Adventure sports:* on the spectacular coastal waters of the Coral Sea and inland waterways. Activities include kite surfing, high-speed boating, surfing lessons and kayaking. *Camel safaris:* 2 hr beach and bushland safari on Noosa's North Shore; (07) 5442 4402. *Scenic flights:* contact visitor centre for details.

WHAT'S ON *Half Marathon:* Aug. *Jazz Festival:* Sept. *Beach Car Classic:* Oct. *Triathlon Multi-sport Festival:* Oct/Nov.

NEARBY Noosa National Park This largely untouched rocky coastline national park covering 454 ha of seascape is popular with visitors to the area. There are walks of varying length through rainforest and heathland. Escape the summer crowds of Noosa with the 8.4 km return Tanglewood Track in the Noosa headland to Hells Gate, an unusual rock formation. Return via the coast for scenic ocean views. Access the park via Park Rd in Noosa Heads, coastal boardwalk from Hastings St or Sunshine Beach.
Great Sandy National Park, Cooloola section This park has stunning coloured sands, beaches, lakes, forests and sand dunes, all of which are protected. Because of its valuable coastal position, many rare and threatened species call it home. There are walks for all ranges of fitness and stamina from short circuit walks to overnight hikes. For the serious walker, there is the 2–4 day Cooloola Wilderness Trail with bush camping. For less strenuous activity, picnic in the rainforest at Bymien or see the Teewah Coloured Sands (multicoloured sand cliffs). There is also camel riding, horseriding and surfing, as well as commercial tours from Brisbane, Noosa and Rainbow Beach. The park is separated from the Sunshine Coast by Noosa River and is accessed via vehicle ferry from Tewantin. Access from the north is via Rainbow Beach; 4WD recommended. 14 km N.
Laguna Lookout: views of Noosa River and lakes; on Noosa Hill. *Sunshine Beach:* golden beach popular for surfing; 3 km SE. *Noosaville:* family-style resort with Noosa River as focal point; departure point for river cruises; 5 km SW. *Lake Cooroibah:* ideal for boating, sailing and windsurfing; access by car or boat from Noosaville. *Tewantin:* Noosa Harbour Marine Village in Parkyn Court with restaurants, art gallery, boat hire and cruise tours. The Big Shell and House of Bottles are nearby. 7 km W. *Tewantin State Forest:* hilly rainforest and eucalypt forest reserve

Fishing on the Noosa Inlet

with 10 min walk to Mount Tinbeerwah Lookout offering a panoramic view over Noosa River and lakes; 10 km W via Tewantin. *Noosa River and the Everglades:* the river extends over 40 km north into Great Sandy National Park. Take a cruise into the Everglades – waters known for their reflections – and to Harry's Hut, a relic of timber-cutting days; contact visitor centre for details.
ⓘ Hastings St roundabout; or Noosa Harbour Marine Village (Tewantin); 1800 448 833 or (07) 5447 4988; www.tourismnoosa.com.au

Normanton   Pop. 1431

Map ref. 610 C8, 613 I8

Normanton is a charming historic town at the centre of the Gulf Savannah. It is on a high ridge between the savannah grasslands to the south and the wetlands to the north. It thrived as a port town in the late 1800s when the gold rush was on in Croydon. The Normanton-to-Croydon railway line, established at that time, today runs the award-winning *Gulflander* tourist train. More recently, Australia's largest saltwater crocodile, known as Krys the Savannah King, was shot at nearby Archer's Creek in 1957. A life-size replica of his body, over eight metres long, can be seen in the council park.

IN TOWN *Normanton Railway Station:* National Trust-listed Victorian building; Matilda St. *Original Well:* settlers used it for drawing water; Landsborough St. *Giant Barramundi:* big monument to the fish; Landsborough St. *Scenic walk and drive:* self-guide tours to historic buildings including the penitentiary in Haig St and the restored Bank of NSW building in Little Brown St; brochure available from council offices. *Gulflander:* this historical 140 km railway journey from Normanton to Croydon reveals the remote beauty of the Gulf Savannah; departs 8.30am Wed and returns Thurs afternoons. *'Croc Spot' Cruise:* at sunset on the Norman River; departs Norman Boat Ramp 5pm Mon–Sat. *Norman River fishing tours:* fishing trips and boat hire for barramundi and estuary fish; contact council office for details.
WHAT'S ON *Barra Classic:* Easter. *Rodeo:* Queen's Birthday Weekend, June. *Normanton Races:* July.

428 North Tamborine–Port Douglas

NEARBY *Lakes:* attract jabirus, brolgas, herons and other birds; on the outskirts of Normanton. *Shady Lagoon:* bush camping, birdwatching and wildlife; 18 km SE. *Fishing:* catching barramundi is very popular in the area – try the spots at Norman River in Glenore (25 km SE), Walkers Creek (32 km NW) or off the bridges or banks in Normanton. *Burke and Wills Cairn:* last and most northerly camp of Burke and Wills (Camp 119) before their fatal return journey; off the Savannah Hwy; 40 km SW. *Bang Bang Jump Up rock formation:* a solitary hill on the surrounding flat plains with excellent views; Matilda Hwy; 106 km SW. *Dorunda Station:* cattle station offering barramundi and saratoga fishing in lake and rivers. Accommodation is available. 197 km NE. *Kowanyama Aboriginal community:* excellent barramundi fishing, guesthouse and camping; permit to visit required from Kowanyama Community Council; 359 km NE.
ⓘ Council offices, cnr Landsborough and Haig sts; (07) 4745 1166; www.gulf-savannah.com.au

North Tamborine   Pop. 2500
Map ref. 599 E10

North Tamborine is one of the towns on the Tamborine Mountain ridge in the Gold Coast hinterland. Numerous galleries, arts and crafts shops and boutique wineries make North Tamborine and the nearby towns of Tamborine Village, Eagle Heights and Mount Tamborine popular weekend getaways. The Tamborine National Park covers the majority of the mountain – the Witches Falls section was Queensland's first national park, listed in 1908.
IN TOWN *Tamborine Mountain Distillery:* award-winning distillery with a range of liqueurs, schnapps, vodkas and spirits; Beacon Rd. *Mount Tamborine Winery and Cedar Creek Estate:* tastings and sales; Hartley Rd. *Hang-gliding:* off Tamborine Mountain; Main Western Rd; (07) 5543 5631 or contact visitor centre. *Tamborine Trolley Co:* provides tours of mountain, including weekend hop-on hop-off tour to major sights; (07) 5545 2782.
WHAT'S ON *Tamborine Mountain Markets:* showgrounds, Main Western Rd; 2nd Sun each month. *Springtime on the Mountain:* open gardens and mini-markets; Oct.
NEARBY **Tamborine National Park** This picturesque mountain park protects remnant subtropical rainforest. Waterfalls, cliffs and beautiful walks make it a popular spot for visitors. The scenic drive visits the major waterfalls and lookouts and there are 22 km of walks on offer. Walk highlights are the 5.4 km Jenyns Falls circuit track and the 3 km Witches Falls circuit track, both leading to spectacular waterfalls. Park access points are on Tamborine–Oxenford Rd.
Eagle Heights: picturesque village to the

north-east with the Gallery Walk on Long Rd featuring excellent local crafts; Botanical Gardens in Forsythia Dr are set on 9 ha of rainforest with a variety of plants. Historic buildings are on show at the Heritage Centre, Wongawallen Rd. *Thunderbird Park:* wildlife sanctuary, horseriding, and fossicking for 'thunder eggs'; Tamborine Mountain Rd. *Heritage and Mud Brick wineries:* tastings and sales; Mount Tamborine; 5 km S.
ⓘ Doughty Park, Main Western Rd; (07) 5545 3200; www.tamborine mtncc.org.au

Oakey   Pop. 3464
Map ref. 607 N9

Oakey is an agricultural town on the Darling Downs, surrounded by beautiful rolling hills and black-soil plains. It is also the base for the aviation division of the Australian Army.
IN TOWN *Bernborough:* bronze statue of famous local racehorse; Campbell St. *Oakey Historical Museum:* local memorabilia; Warrego Hwy. *Flypast – Museum of Australian Army Flying:* see a large collection of original and replica aircraft (some still in flying condition) dating back to the army's inception in 1912. There is also aviation memorabilia. At army base via Kelvinaugh Rd.
NEARBY **Jondaryan Woolshed** Built in 1859 and still shearing under steam power, this woolshed is a memorial to pioneers of the wool industry. The complex includes the huge woolshed, historic buildings, and machinery and equipment collections. Visitors can see the shearing and sheepdog demonstrations or sit down to some billy tea and damper. Events are held throughout the year, including the Working Draft-horse Expo in June and the Australian Heritage Festival in Aug. Off Warego Hwy; 22 km NW.
Acland Coal Mine Museum: tours of mine can be arranged; 18 km N; open Sat–Wed, closed Feb.
ⓘ Library, 64 Campbell St; (07) 4692 0154

Palm Cove   Pop. 1984
Map ref. 604 D4, 611 M6

Serene Palm Cove, north-west of Cairns, has white sandy beaches and streets lined with palm trees. It is essentially a resort village, with locals and tourists alike soaking up the relaxed Far North atmosphere. The lifestyle is based around the water – fishing off the jetty, horseriding along the beach and swimming in the Coral Sea's crystal-clear blue water.
IN TOWN *Reef tours:* to Green Island and the Great Barrier Reef; depart Palm Cove jetty daily. *Day tours:* to Atherton Tableland and surrounds; contact visitor centre for details.
WHAT'S ON *Palm Cove Fiesta:* Sept.
NEARBY *Clifton Beach:* resort village with

park-lined beach and attractions such as Wild World, an interactive animal zoo, and Outback Opal Mine, with simulated mine and displays of Australia's most famous stone. 3 km S. *Hartley's Crocodile Adventures:* prides itself on the range of habitats that can be seen from extensive boardwalks and river cruises. Presentations include crocodile and snake shows and koala feeding. 15 km N. *Rex Lookout:* stunning coastal views; 17 km N.
ⓘ Paradise Village Shopping Centre, Williams Espl; (07) 4055 3433

Pomona   Pop. 951
Map ref. 601 E1, 602 B1, 607 P6

This small and relaxed farming centre is in the northern hinterland of the Sunshine Coast. Mount Cooroora rises 439 metres above the town. Each July mountain runners from around the world flock to attempt the base–summit and back again race, the winner being crowned King of the Mountain.
IN TOWN *Majestic Theatre:* authentic silent movie theatre with cinema museum and regular screenings. *Noosa Shire Museum:* tribute to shire's past in old council chambers. *Railway Station Gallery:* converted station featuring local art.
WHAT'S ON *King of the Mountain:* July. *Silent Movie Festival:* at the Majestic Theatre; each Aug/Sept. *Country Show:* Sept.
NEARBY **Boreen Point** This sleepy town is on the shores of Lake Cootharba. The town features a 2.4 km walk from Teewah Land to Noosa's north shore beaches, and boardwalks into the surrounding wetlands. There are holiday cottages, and boat hire is available on Lake Cootharba. Try the many watersports on offer, including canoeing and kayaking. Windsurfing and yachting competitions are held here throughout the year. The lake is near where Mrs Eliza Fraser spent time with Aboriginal people after the wreck of *Stirling Castle* on Fraser Island in 1836. 19 km NE.
Cooroy: large residential area with excellent art gallery and cultural centre in the Old Butter Factory. The Noosa Botanical Gardens and Lake Macdonald are nearby. 10 km SE.
ⓘ Hastings St roundabout, Noosa Heads; 1800 448 833 or (07) 5447 4988

Port Douglas   Pop. 3499
Map ref. 605 F9, 611 M5

Port Douglas lies on the serene waters of a natural harbour in tropical North Queensland. Once a small village, it is now an international tourist destination. The town is surrounded by lush vegetation and pristine rainforests and offers a village lifestyle with shops, galleries and restaurants. Its tropical mountain setting, the pristine Four Mile Beach and its proximity to the Great Barrier Reef make Port Douglas an ideal

The view from Rex Lookout on the road from Cairns to Port Douglas

holiday destination. The drive from Cairns to Port Douglas is one of the most scenic coastal drives in Australia.

IN TOWN Rainforest Habitat Wildlife Sanctuary This sanctuary covers an area of 2 ha and is home to over 1600 animals. Walk along the boardwalks through the four habitats of North Queensland – rainforest, wetlands, woodlands and grasslands. There are regular guided tours of the sanctuary, and the special daily events of Breakfast with the Birds and Habitat After Dark (runs July–Oct). Cnr Captain Cook Hwy and Port Douglas Rd. *Flagstaff Hill:* commands excellent views of Four Mile Beach and Low Isles; end of Island Point Rd. *Dive schools:* numerous; contact visitor centre for details. *Great Barrier Reef tours:* over 100 operators offer reef tours to outer Great Barrier Reef and Low Isles; contact visitor centre for details.

WHAT'S ON *Market:* Anzac Park; each Sun. *Village Carnivale:* May.

NEARBY *Tours:* horse trail-riding; sea-kayaking; rainforest tours; Lady Douglas paddlewheel cruises; 4WD safaris; coach tours to Mossman Gorge, Cape Tribulation, Kuranda and Cooktown; contact visitor centre for details.
ⓘ Port Douglas Daintree Tourism Association, 23 Macrossan St; (07) 4099 4588; www.pddt.com.au

Proserpine   Pop. 3243

Map ref. 609 J3

Proserpine is the inland sugar town and service centre of the Whitsunday Shire. It was named after the Roman goddess of fertility, Proserpina, for the rich and fertile surrounding lands.

IN TOWN *Historical Museum:* local history dating back to settlement; Bruce Hwy.

WHAT'S ON *Harvest Festival:* includes the World Championship Cane Cutting event; Oct.

NEARBY *Lake Proserpine at Peter Faust Dam:* boat hire, waterskiing, fishing and swimming. The Cedar Creek Falls are nearby. 20 km NW on Crystalbrook Rd. *Conway National Park:* 28 km E; *see Airlie Beach*. *Midge Point:* coastal community and an ideal spot for bushwalking, fishing, crabbing and swimming; 41 km SE. *Crocodile safaris:* take a nature tour on an open-air tractor and cruise through mangrove river system on Proserpine River; bookings (07) 4946 5111.
ⓘ Whitsunday Information Centre, Bruce Hwy; 1800 801 252 or (07) 4945 3711; www.whitsundaytourism.com

Quilpie   Pop. 644

Map ref. 617 O7

Quilpie is on the banks of the Bullo River in the outback's famous Channel Country. The town was established as a rail centre for the area's large sheep and cattle properties. Today it is better known as an opal town and, in particular, for the 'Boulder Opal'. The world's largest concentration of this opal is found in the area surrounding Quilpie. The town takes its name from the Aboriginal word 'quilpeta', meaning 'stone curlew'.

IN TOWN *Museum and Gallery:* historical and modern exhibitions; visitor centre; Brolga St. *St Finbarr's Catholic Church:* unique altar, font and lectern made from opal-bearing rock; Buln Buln St. *Opal sales:* various town outlets.

WHAT'S ON *Diggers Races:* May. *Kangaranga Doo:* Sept.

NEARBY Mariala National Park The park was formerly used to breed Cobb & Co horses in the early 1900s. It is a remote park with spectacular contrasts – the rich red earth mixed with green vegetation of mulga trees and shrubs. The threatened yellow-footed rock wallaby and pink cockatoo find refuge in this park. There are no formal walking trails. You can bush camp in the park but visitors must be self-sufficient. 4WD is recommended; roads may become impassable in the wet season; 130 km NE.
Lake Houdraman: popular watersports and recreation area; river road to Adavale; 6 km NE. *Baldy Top:* large geological formation with spectacular views; 6 km S. *Opal Fields:* guided tours (no general access); contact visitor centre for details; 75 km W. *Toompine:* historic hotel, cemetery and designated opal-fossicking areas nearby; 76 km S. *Eromanga:* this is reputedly the town in Australia furthest from the sea. It features the Royal Hotel, once a Cobb & Co staging post, and holds a rodeo at Easter. 103 km W.
ⓘ Brolga St; (07) 4656 2166

Ravenshoe   Pop. 820

Map ref. 603 B2, 611 M8

At 930 metres, Ravenshoe is the highest town in Queensland. Situated on the Atherton Tableland, the town had a thriving logging industry in the surrounding rainforest until it was World Heritage-listed in 1987. A new, alternative-lifestyle population has emerged in the town.

IN TOWN *Nganyaji Interpretive Centre:* showcases the lifestyle of local Jirrbal people, including hunting techniques and community life; Moore St. *Scenic train-ride:* heritage steam-train ride to nearby Tumoulin; contact visitor centre for details.

NEARBY Innot Hot Springs These natural thermal springs reputedly have healing powers for weary bodies. The spring water was originally bottled and sent to Europe as a healing remedy until the 1900s. Lie back in the relaxing waters while watching the diverse birdlife fly overhead. The town runs the Australia Day Festival, which includes the mountain ironman and ironwoman competition. 32 km SW. *Millstream Falls National Park:* enjoy the 1 km return walk past falls and rock pools of Millstream River to the Millstream Falls, the widest single-drop waterfall in Australia; 3 km SW. *Tully Falls:* walk 300 m to Tully Falls (in wet season) and the gorge; 25 km S. *Koombooloomba Dam:* popular spot for swimming, watersports, camping, and fishing for barramundi; 34 km S. *Mount Garnet:* old tin-mining town with prospecting sites nearby; 47 km W.
ⓘ 24 Moore St; (07) 4097 7700; www.athertontableland.com

Richmond   Pop. 616

Map ref. 615 M4

This small town on the Flinders River in the Gulf Country serves the surrounding sheep and cattle properties. The town's main street is lined with beautiful bougainvilleas. In recent years Richmond has become the centre of attention as an area rich in marine fossils dating back around 100 million years, when outback Queensland was submerged under an inland sea.

IN TOWN Kronosaurus Korner This marine fossil museum has a renowned collection of vertebrate fossils, all found in the Richmond Shire. The museum and exhibition space holds over 200 exhibits, including the 100 million-year-old armoured dinosaur Minmi, Australia's best-preserved dinosaur. There is also an activity centre, children's discovery area and fossil preparation area where the visitor can watch the palaeontologist at work. Guided museum tours are available, as well as tours to nearby fossicking sites with a palaeontologist (group bookings). Goldring St. *Cobb & Co coach:* beautifully restored coach with informative history display; Lions Park, Goldring St. *Gidgee Wheel Arts and Crafts:* local craft; Harris St. *Lake Tritton:* recreational lake for waterskiing, picnics and walks; eastern outskirts. *Heritage walk:* follow the self-guide trail with informative history at each stop. It includes the historic flagstone and adobe building, Richmond Hotel, St John the Baptist Church and the Pioneer Cemetery; brochure available from visitor centre.

NEARBY *Fossicking sites:* guided tours to nearby areas; contact visitor centre for details.

ⓘ Kronosaurus Korner, 91–93 Goldring St; (07) 4741 3429

Rockhampton   Pop. 58 950

Map ref. 609 N11

Rockhampton is a prosperous city on the banks of the Fitzroy River, straddling the Tropic of Capricorn. It is known as the beef capital of Australia, with some 2.5 million cattle in the region. Many of the original stone buildings and churches remain, set off by flowering bauhinia and brilliant bougainvilleas. Quay Street is Australia's longest National Trust-classified streetscape, with over 20 heritage buildings picturesquely set on the banks of the river. Watch out for the bent-wing bat exodus in summer and the summer solstice light spectacular in early December to mid-January.

IN TOWN Mount Archer National Park On the north-east outskirts of Rockhampton, this park provides a backdrop to the city. Take a scenic drive up the mountain to Frazer Park, where the panoramic views are breathtaking. Explore the open forest and subtropical vegetation of the mountain on the 11 km walk from top to bottom. Be advised that the return trip is quite strenuous. Other shorter walks lead to scenic lookouts over the city and coast. Access to the summit is via Frenchville

Richmond's Cobb & Co coach

Rd; to the base via German St.

Botanic Gardens Set on the Athelstane Range, these heritage-listed gardens are over 130 years old. There are fine tropical displays, an orchid and fern house, a Japanese-style garden and the bird haven of Murray Lagoon. There is also the city zoo, with free entry and koala and lorikeet feedings at 3pm daily. Access via Spencer and Ann sts.

Customs House: this heritage building (1901) houses the visitor centre and 'Rockhampton Discovery Centre' exhibition, which introduces the visitor to the history, culture and lifestyle of Rockhampton; Quay St. *Archer Park Station and Steam Tram Museum:* interactive displays document the history of rail transport in Rockhampton. A fully restored Purrey Steam Tram operates every Sun 10am–1pm. Cnr Denison and Cambridge sts; closed Sat. *Kershaw Gardens:* follow the Australian native flora Braille Trail; Bruce Hwy. *Rockhampton City Art Gallery:* changing exhibitions and chamber recital 2nd Sun each month; Victoria Pde. *Great Western Hotel:* operates weekly rodeos; Stanley St. *Fitzroy River:* a great spot for watersports, rowing and fishing. A barrage in Savage St that separates tidal salt water from upstream fresh water provides opportunities for barramundi fishing. *Capricorn Spire:* marks the line of Tropic of Capricorn; Curtis Park, Gladstone Rd. *Heritage walk:* self-guide trail around city centre; brochure available from visitor centre.

WHAT'S ON *Markets:* Kern Arcade;

Sun. *May Day Regatta:* May. *Rocky Roundup:* June. *Rocky Barra Bounty:* Oct.

NEARBY *Dreamtime Cultural Centre:* displays on Aboriginal and Torres Strait Island culture set on ancient tribal site. Guided tours are available. 7 km N on Bruce Hwy; open weekdays. *Old Glenmore Historic Homestead:* National Trust-classified complex of historic buildings and displays; 8 km N. *Rockhampton Heritage Village:* heritage buildings with unusual Time after Time clock collection and Life before Electricity exhibition; Parkhurst; 9 km N. *St Christopher's Chapel:* open-air chapel built by American servicemen; Emu Park Rd; 20 km E. *Capricorn Caves:* guided tours and wild caving adventures through limestone cave system. Visit in Dec for the Carols in the Caverns. 23 km N. *Mount Hay Gemstone Tourist Park:* thunder-egg fossicking and sales; 38 km W. *Capricorn Scenic Loop tourist drive:* through coast and hinterland. *Great Keppel Island:* resort island with white sandy beaches and great snorkelling and other watersports; air access.

ⓘ Customs House, 208 Quay St; (07) 4922 5339; www.rockhamptoninfo.com

Roma   Pop. 5894

Map ref. 606 H6

Roma is in the western Downs region and was named after the wife of Queensland's first governor. Roma boasts a few historic 'firsts' for Queensland and Australia. In 1863 Samuel Symons Bassett brought vine cuttings to Roma and Queensland's

first wine-making enterprise began –
Romaville Winery is still running today.
In the same year Captain Starlight faced
trial in Roma for cattle stealing. Australia's
first natural gas strike was at Hospital Hill
in 1900. The excellent complex in town,
The Big Rig, documents the oil and gas
industry since this discovery.

IN TOWN The Big Rig This unique
complex is set on an old oil derrick and
features historic oil rigs and machinery
displays. Photographs, memorabilia
and multimedia displays provide a
comprehensive history of oil and gas
discovery and usage in Australia from
1900 to the present day. A highlight is
the sound and light show on summer
nights. Adjacent to the complex is a
historic slab hut, recreational area and
1915 mini steam train that travels on a
1.4 km circuit. Riggers Rd.
Roma–Bungil Cultural Centre: a 3D mural
by local artists depicting Roma's history;
cnr Bungil and Injune rds. *Heroes Avenue:*
heritage-listed street of bottle trees
commemorating local soldiers who died
in WW I. *Romaville Winery:* Injune Rd.
WHAT'S ON *Roma Picnic Races:* Mar.
Easter in the Country: Easter. *Roma Cup:*
Bassett Park; Nov.
NEARBY Carnarvon National Park, Gorge
section This popular park features the
spectacular scenery of Carnarvon Gorge.
The Carnarvon Creek winds through
this steep-sided gorge, flanked by white
sandstone cliffs. There are over 21 km of
walks through rainforest to waterfalls
and caves. A highlight is the incredible
Aboriginal rock art found throughout
the park – see rock engravings, stencils
and paintings at Cathedral Cave and the
Art Gallery. Turn-off to park is 199 km N
on Carnarvon Developmental Rd. Mount
Moffatt section: *see Mitchell.* Ka Ka Mundi
section: *see Springsure.* Salvator Rosa
section: *see Tambo.*
Roma Cattle Sales: largest inland cattle
market in Australia with sales on Tues
and Thurs; 4 km E. *Meadowbank Museum:*
historic vehicle and machinery collection,
and farm animals; 12 km w. *Surat:* large
town featuring the Cobb & Co Changing
Station Complex with museum, art
gallery, aquarium and information
centre. Visit the award-winning
Villacoola Winery or go fishing for
Murray cod on Balonne River. 78 km SE.
❶ Big Rig Visitor Information Centre,
2 Riggers Rd.; (07) 4622 4355;
www.roma.qld.gov.au

St George   Pop. 2779
Map ref. 606 G10

On the banks of the Balonne River is the
Darling Downs town of St George. It is
the last post in southern Queensland
before the heavily populated east coast
finally gives way to the sparseness of
the outback. The river crossing was
discovered by explorer Sir Thomas

Mitchell on St George's Day, 1846, giving
the town its name. St George is often
referred to as the inland fishing capital of
Queensland with lakes and rivers nearby,
which also support the area's agriculture,
a rich cotton, grape and grain industry.
IN TOWN *Heritage Centre:* historic
buildings including the old gaol and
courthouse, and a local history museum
featuring Aboriginal display. Victoria
St. *Emu Collection:* carved, illuminated
emu eggs; Balonne Sports Store; Victoria
St. *Town murals:* around town, depicting
scenes of St George's history. *Riversands
Vineyard:* boutique winery on the banks
of the Balonne River; Whytes Rd. *Jack
Taylor Weir:* Sir Thomas Mitchell cairn
commemorating landmark crossing in
1846; western outskirts.
WHAT'S ON *St George's Day:* 23 April.
Regional Fishing Competition: 1st weekend
in Oct.
NEARBY *Beardmore Dam:* popular
spot for watersports and picnics in
surrounding parklands. It offers excellent
fishing for yellow-belly and Murray cod.
21 km N. *Ancient Rock Well:* hand-hewn
by Aboriginal people, possibly thousands
of years ago; 37 km E. *Nindigully:* historic
1863 hotel, which holds the annual
Bull Ride in June. See the motorbike
riders arrive each June for the Nindigully
5 hour Enduro. 44 km SE. *Boolba:* holds
the impressive Boolba Wool and Craft
Show each May; 50 km w. *Rosehill Aviary:*
one of Australia's largest collections of
native parrots; 64 km w. *Thallon:* small
town with excellent swimming and
fishing at Barney's Beach on the Moonie
River. The nearby Bullamon homestead
(1860), mentioned in Steele Rudd's
Memoirs of Corporal Keeley, has original
shingle roof and canvas ceilings. Tours
by appt (07) 4625 9217. 76 km SE. *Bollon:*
large koala population in river red gums
along Wallan Creek and a heritage and
craft centre in George St; 112 km w.
Thrushton National Park: undeveloped
park of mulga scrub, sand plains and
woodlands. Access in dry weather only
and 4WD recommended. 132 km NW.
Culgoa Floodplain National Park: in the
Murray–Darling basin, this park, with
over 150 species of birds, is excellent
for birdwatchers. There are no formal
walking tracks and visitors must be self-
sufficient. 4WD recommended; access via
Brenda Rd, Goodooga; 200 km SW.
❶ Cnr The Terrace and Roe St; (07) 4620
8877; www.balonne.qld.gov.au

Sarina   Pop. 2966
Map ref. 609 L6

Sarina is in the hinterland of what has
been dubbed the Serenity Coast, at the
base of the Connor Range. It is central
to the Queensland sugar belt. To the east
and south are fine beaches, many of
which are renowned fishing spots.
IN TOWN *Tourist Art and Craft Centre:*

excellent variety of local art and craft as
well as visitor centre; Bruce Hwy. *'Field
of Dreams' Historical Centre:* local industry
history and memorabilia; Railway
Square; open Tues, Wed, Fri.
WHAT'S ON *Market:* showgrounds; last
Sun each month. *Mud Trials:* buggy racing
on a mud track; May. *Scope Visual Arts
Competition:* May.
NEARBY Cape Palmerston National Park
This remote park features rugged coastal
landscapes of headlands, swamps and
sand dunes. Watch for the soaring sea
eagles overhead or the birdlife around
the swamp. There are spots for bush
camping. The park has no official walking
tracks, but the outlook from the cape
is spectacular. 4WD recommended;
46 km SE via Ilbilbie.
Beaches: including Grasstree and Half
Tide beaches to the north-east (Grasstree
hosts annual bike race; date depends
on tidal conditions). Also Sarina Beach
(east), popular for boating, fishing and
swimming, with a lookout over the coast,
and Armstrong Beach (south), great
for swimming, prawning and fishing.
Hay Point Lookout: viewing gallery at Hay
Point and Dalrymple Bay coal terminal
complex – informative video and excellent
views; 12 km N. *Salonika Beach:* attractive
beach with amazing wildlife, including
loggerhead turtles and seasonal whales;
adjacent to Hay Point Lookout. *Lake
Barfield:* picnic area and bird sanctuary;
12 km N. *Carmila:* small town with beach
just to the east. Visit the nearby Flaggy
Rock Exotic Fruit Garden for delicious ice-
cream. 65 km s. *Clairview:* popular spot for
beach fishing and crabbing; 73 km s.
St Lawrence: once a major port, this town
is now a historical tribute to past days
with many historic buildings and the
remains of the wharf; 110 km s.
❶ Sarina Tourist Art and Craft Centre,
Bruce Hwy; (07) 4956 2251

Springsure   Pop. 771
Map ref. 608 I12

Mt Zamia towers over Springsure, a
small picturesque valley town in the
Central Highlands, settled in the 1860s.
Springsure's early history is dominated by
conflicts between local Aboriginal groups
and the intruding European settlers.
The 1861 massacre of 19 Europeans
at Cullin-la-ringo to the north-west is
commemorated at Old Rainworth Fort.
IN TOWN *Aboriginal Yumba-Burin (resting
place):* in Cemetery Reserve, containing
3 bark burials (around 600 years old).
Rich Park Memorials: includes cattleyard
displays and a Dakota engine from a
plane that crashed during WW II. *Historic
Hospital:* Heritage-listed building (1868)
includes museum.
NEARBY Minerva Hills National Park The
park overlooks the town of Springsure,
with the Boorambool and Zamia
mountains dominating the landscape. See

unusual wildlife, such as the fawn-footed melomys, on a 2.2 km walking track to a spectacular lookout, or have a bush picnic at Fred's Gorge. 4 km w of Springsure, part of road unsealed.

Carnarvon National Park, Ka Ka Mundi section This remote section of the park is in Queensland's brigalow belt and features undulating plains and sandstone cliffs. See the king parrots and fig birds around the springs and creeks or the area's pastoral history at the old cattleyards near the springs. West on Springsure–Tambo Rd for 50 km, then south on Buckland Rd. Mount Moffatt section: *see Mitchell*. Gorge section: *see Roma*. Salvator Rosa section: *see Tambo*. *Old Rainworth Historical Complex*: National Trust-listed historic buildings of old storehouse built after 1861 massacre; 10 km s.
ⓘ Information shed, Rolleston Rd; or council offices; (07) 4984 1166

Stanthorpe
Pop. 4166

Map ref. 515 M2, 607 N12

Stanthorpe is the main town in the Granite Belt and mountain ranges along the border between Queensland and New South Wales. The town came into being after the discovery of tin at Quartpot Creek in 1872, but the mineral boom did not last. The climate is cool, said to be the coldest in Queensland, but the numerous wineries in the vicinity would soon warm any visitor up. Visit in spring to see the fruit trees, wattles and wildflowers in bloom.

IN TOWN *Heritage Museum*: displays memorabilia of the region's past in historic buildings, such as a school room, gaol and shepherd's hut; High St; closed Mon and Tues. *Regional Art Gallery*: touring and local exhibitions; Weeroona Park, Marsh St; open Mon–Fri, Sat–Sun afternoons.

WHAT'S ON *Market in the Mountains*: cnr Marsh and Lock sts; 2nd Sun each month. *In-season markets*: 3rd Sat each month. *Food and Wine Festival*: odd-numbered years; Feb. *Apple and Grape Harvest Festival*: even-numbered years, 1st weekend in Mar. *Rodeo*: Mar. *Brass Monkey Season (winter festival)*: winter; June–Aug. *Granite Belt Spring Wine Festival*: Oct. *Australian Small Winemakers Show*: Oct.

NEARBY **Granite Belt Wineries** In the region surrounding Stanthorpe are over 40 boutique wineries, many open for tastings and sales. Just to the north is Old Caves Winery, followed by a number of others until Heritage Wines at Cottonvale; 12 km n. High-quality wineries are near Glen Aplin; 11 km sw. Ballandean, 21 km sw, features Golden Grove, Winewood, Bungawarra and Robinson's Family wineries. The Ballandean Estate holds Opera in the Vineyard in May and Jazz in the Vineyard in Aug/Sept. Brochure available from visitor centre; bus tours available.

Girraween National Park The stunning granite and creek scenery of this park is very popular with bushwalkers. It is unique in Queensland, not only for the cooler weather, but also because it is home to animals that are rarely seen in the tropical state – like the common wombat. There is a variety of walks, from short to overnight hikes (taking in adjacent Bald Rock National Park). Of particular note is the 3 km return track to the Pyramid, at the top of which is a panoramic view across the park and surrounding region. Visit in spring to see the wildflower display. Turn-off 40 km south of Stanthorpe; further 8 km to park.
Mt Marlay: excellent views; 1 km e. *Ballandean*: picturesque small town boasting Sundown Astronomy observatory with astronomy displays (open nightly); 21 km sw. *Storm King Dam*: popular spot for picnics, canoeing, waterskiing, and fishing for Murray cod and silver perch; 26 km se. *Boonoo Boonoo National Park (NSW)*: spectacular waterfall; 60 km se. *Bald Rock National Park (NSW)*: incredible granite rock formation (second biggest monolith in the world); 65 km se. *Sundown National Park*: rugged national park of gorges and high peaks. Go birdwatching to see the herons and azure kingfishers along the river or take the short Red Rock Gorge Lookout Track for spectacular views. 80 km sw. *Heritage trail*: a historical drive tour of surrounding towns; brochure available from visitor centre.
ⓘ 26 Leslie Pde; 1800 060 877 or (07) 4681 2057; www.southern downsholidays.com

Strathpine
Pop. 11 146

Map ref. 598 D5, 599 D3, 601 F11, 607 P8

Strathpine is north of Brisbane in the Pine Rivers region, a district that includes the forested areas and national parks closest to the capital. Taking advantage of this rural setting so close to the city are a number of art and craft industries.

WHAT'S ON *Pine Rivers Heritage Festival*: Mar. *Camp Oven Bush Poets Festival*: Aug.

NEARBY **Brisbane Forest Park** This natural bushland forest park is a welcome retreat from busy city life. Take a scenic drive from the south-east corner to lookouts, mountain towns and attractive landscapes, ending at Lake Wivenhoe. There are many picnic spots for a relaxing lunch – Jollys Lookout is a highlight, with views over Brisbane, the valley, and north to the Glass House Mountains. A guide to the park's walks is available from the park headquarters at 60 Mount Nebo Rd, The Gap. Access via Ferny Hills.
Lake Samsonvale: fishing, watersports and bushwalking; 8 km nw. *Old Petrie Town*: heritage park that holds markets each Sun and the popular Twilight Markets each Fri evening (Nov–Dec). Catch the free bus from Petrie Railway Station. 9 km n. *Alma Park Zoo*: palm garden and subtropical

rainforest zoo with native and exotic animals. Feed the koalas and explore the Friendship Farm for children. Alma Rd, Dakabin; 14 km n. *Australian Woolshed*: demonstrations of shearing, spinning and working sheepdogs; bush dances with bush band; Ferny Hills; 16 km sw. *Osprey House*: environmental centre; Dohles Rocks Rd; 18 km n. *Brisbane's Vineyard*: wine tastings and sales; Mount Nebo Rd, Mount Nebo; 46 km sw.
ⓘ Pine Rivers Tourism Centre, Daisy Cottage, cnr Gympie and South Pine rds; (07) 3205 4793; www.brisbanehinter land.com

Tambo
Pop. 358

Map ref. 606 B2

Tambo is the oldest town in central-western Queensland. It was established in the mid-1860s to service the surrounding pastoral properties, which it continues to do today. This long history can be seen in the heritage buildings on Arthur Street.

IN TOWN *Old Post Office Museum*: historic photographs; Arthur St. *Tambo Teddies Workshop*: produces popular all-wool teddies; Arthur St. *Coolibah Walk*: nature walk along banks of the Barcoo River.

WHAT'S ON *Australia Day Rodeo*: Jan. *Stock Show*: April. *Tambo Races*: April/May.

NEARBY **Carnarvon National Park, Salvator Rosa section** One of the more remote sections of the park, Salvator Rosa is a perfect spot to escape the crowds. The attractive Nogoa River and Louisa Creek flow through the valley. See the spectacular rock formations, Belinda Springs and other natural attractions on the self-guide trail through the park, which starts at Nogoa River camping area. 130 km e. Mount Moffatt section: *see Mitchell*. Gorge section: *see Roma*. Ka Ka Mundi section: *see Springsure*. *Wilderness Way*: a 420 km self-guide drive including Aboriginal rock art, historic European settlement sites and the Salvator Rosa section of the Carnarvon National Park. Check road conditions before departing; brochure available from council office.
ⓘ Council offices, Arthur St; (07) 4654 6133

Taroom
Pop. 689

Map ref. 607 J4

Taroom is on the banks of the Dawson River in the Capricorn region. Since settlers took land in 1845, cattle raising has been the main local industry. The coolibah tree in Taroom's main street was marked 'L. L.' by explorer Ludwig Leichhardt on his 1844 trip from Jimbour House near Dalby to Port Essington, north of Darwin.

IN TOWN *Museum*: old telephone-exchange equipment, farm machinery and items of local history; open Mon and Fri or by appt (07) 4627 3231.

Scenery along the Dawson River, near Taroom

WHAT'S ON *Leichhardt Festival:* Sept.
NEARBY Expedition National Park This remote park features the 14 km Robinson Gorge. The 4 km return track leads to an excellent lookout over the sandstone gorge. Only experienced walkers should attempt the rough track leading down into the gorge. The Cattle Dip Lookout overlooks a permanent gorge waterhole reached via the 8 km return Shepherd's Peak Trail or from the carpark at the lookout. 4WD recommended; some of the road is gravel; 128 km NW.
Lake Palm Tree Creek: rare Livistona palms; 15 km N. *Murphy Conservation Park:* pristine lake with birdlife, and picnic and camping spots. It was the site of Leichhardt's campsite in 1844. 30 km N. *Glebe Weir:* waterskiing and fishing; 40 km NE. *Wandoan:* the local heritage trail in the town visits all the major sights, including the Waterloo Plain Environmental Park; brochure available from visitor centre in Royd St; 59 km S. *Scenic and historical drives:* self-drive tours to nearby sights; brochure available from visitor centre.
ℹ️ The Old Pub, Yaldwyn St; (07) 4628 6113

Texas   Pop. 700

Map ref. 515 K3, 607 M12

Texas lies alongside the Dumaresq River (pronounced Du-meric) and the Queensland–New South Wales border. Its name comes from the similarity between an 1850s land dispute in the area to a dispute between the Republic of Texas and Mexico. The town was originally on the river flat, two kilometres from its current position. Severe floods forced the move. Remains of the original town can be seen on the river off Schwenke St.
IN TOWN *Historical Museum:* local memorabilia in old police station (1893); Fleming St; open Sat or by appt (07) 4653 1410. *Art Gallery:* local and touring art exhibitions; High St; open Tues–Sat.
NEARBY *Beacon Lookout:* regional views; 3 km SE on Stanthorpe Rd. *Cunningham Weir:* site where Allan Cunningham crossed the Dumaresq River in 1827; 31 km W off Texas–Yelarbon Rd. *Glenlyon Dam:* excellent fishing spot; 45 km SE. *Inglewood:* Texas's twin town at the centre of Australia's olive industry. Visit Inglewood Heritage Centre for local memorabilia (open Sat). Tour the local olive groves and follow the scenic drives in area; brochure available. The town holds the Australian Olive Festival each year in Mar/April. 55 km N. *Coolmunda Reservoir:* picnics, boating and fishing; 75 km NE via Inglewood. *Dumaresq River:* winding river popular for canoeing, fishing and hiking through wilderness areas on its banks.
ℹ️ Newsagency, 19 High St; (07) 4653 1384; www.inglewood.qld.gov.au

Theodore   Pop. 448

Map ref. 607 J12

The palm-lined streets and tropical air of Theodore is a contrast to the irrigated farmland surrounding it. The town was named after Edward Theodore, Queensland premier from 1919 to 1925, and was reputedly designed by Walter Burley Griffin before he designed Canberra.
IN TOWN *Theodore Hotel:* only cooperative hotel in Queensland; The Boulevard. *Dawson Folk Museum:* provides local history; Second Ave; open by appt (07) 4993 1677.
WHAT'S ON *Fishing Competition:* Nov.
NEARBY Isla Gorge National Park The gorges and spectacular rock formations make this highland park an attractive spot to visit. The camping area overlooks the gorge and a 2 km return walk leads to the spectacular Isla Gorge Lookout. If staying overnight, be sure to watch the changing colours of the sandstone cliffs as the sun sets. Turn-off 35 km S.
Theodore Weir: popular spot for fishing; southern outskirts of town. *Moura:* major cattle town that holds the annual Coal and Country Festival in Aug; 48 km NW. *Cracow:* where gold was produced from famous Golden Plateau mine 1932–1976; 49 km SE.
ℹ️ The Boulevard; (07) 4993 1900

Tin Can Bay   Pop. 1968

Map ref. 607 P5

Tin Can Bay is a well-known fishing and prawning region north-east of Gympie. It was originally known as Tuncanbar to the local Aboriginal people. The town is a relaxing hamlet offering an abundance of watersports on the quiet waters of Tin Can Bay inlet.
IN TOWN *Environmental Walkway:* a 9.5 km trail for birdwatching on the Tin Can Bay foreshore. *Boat and yacht hire:* cruise the inlet and Sandy Strait; Tin Can Bay Marina. *Canoeing:* eco-tours down estuaries; (07) 5486 4417. *Norman Point boat ramp:* see the dolphins up close before 10am; access point to waterways.
WHAT'S ON *Market:* Gympie Rd; 3rd Sat each month. *Bush to Bay Seafood Fun Day:* Sept.
NEARBY Rainbow Beach This relaxing coastal town to the east across the inlet offers a pristine sandy beach popular with surfers. A fishing classic is held here each July, as is the Robert Pryde Memorial Surf Classic each April. For adventure, try paragliding from the Carlo Sand Blow; bookings (07) 5486 3048. Tours include dolphin ferry cruises, safaris and 4WD tours. The road south (4WD) leads to the coloured sands and beaches of the Cooloola section of Great Sandy National Park; *see Noosa Heads.* Rainbow Beach is 41 km E by road.
Carlo Point: this popular spot is great for fishing and swimming. There is also boat access to the inlet, with houseboats and yachts available for hire. 43 km E via

Rainbow Beach, Great Sandy National Park, east of Tin Can Bay

Rainbow Beach. *Inskip Point:* camp along the point or take the car ferry to Fraser Island; 53 km NE via Rainbow Beach.
ⓘ Cooloola Regional Information Centre, Matilda's Roadhouse Complex, Bruce Hwy, Kybong (15 km S of Gympie); 1800 444 222 or (07) 5483 5554; www.tincanbaytourism.org.au

Toowoomba
Pop. 88 776

Map ref. 607 N9

Toowoomba is a city with a distinctive charm and graciousness in its wide, tree-lined streets, colonial architecture and over 100 parks and gardens. The city is perched 700 metres above sea level on the rim of the Great Dividing Range. It began in 1849 as a small village near an important staging post. It is now the commercial centre for the fertile Darling Downs.

IN TOWN **Cobb & Co Museum** The museum traces the history of horse-drawn vehicles in the Darling Downs region. It has an excellent collection of carriages, from old wagons to Cobb & Co coaches. The museum has expanded to include exhibits depicting the settlement history of the Downs and Aboriginal history. There is also an interactive discovery centre for children. Lindsay St. **Parks and gardens** No trip to the 'Garden City' would be complete without a visit to some of the superb parks and gardens. Lake Annand is a popular recreation spot with boardwalks, bridges and ducks; MacKenzie St. There are imposing European trees in Queen's Park, which also includes the Botanic Gardens; Lindsay and Margaret sts. Laurel Bank Park features the unique Scented Garden, designed for the visually impaired; cnr Herries and West sts. Birdwatchers should visit Waterbird Habitat where native birds can be watched from observation platforms and floating

islands; MacKenzie and Alderley sts. The impressive Japanese Garden, at the University of Southern Queensland, is the largest in Australia; off West St. *Regional Art Gallery:* changing exhibitions in Queensland's oldest gallery; Ruthven St. *Royal Bull's Head Inn:* National Trust-listed building (1859); Brisbane St, Drayton; open weekends. *Empire Theatre:* live theatre in this restored Art Deco building, opened in 1911; Neil St. *Picnic Point:* offers views of Lockyer Valley, mountains and waterfall. Enjoy the recreational facilities and walks through bushland. Tourist Dr, eastern outskirts. *City tour:* self-guide drive to major city attractions, starting at visitor centre; brochure available from visitor centre.

WHAT'S ON *Markets:* Wilsonton Shopping Centre and James St, Sun; Queen's Park, 3rd Sun each month. *Toowoomba Royal Show:* Mar. *Australian Gospel Music Festival:* Easter. *Carnival of Flowers:* Sept.

NEARBY *Highfields:* growing town featuring Orchid Park, Danish Flower Art Centre and Historical Village with vintage machinery and buildings; 12 km N. *Cabarlah:* small community that has the Black Forest Hill Cuckoo Clock Centre and holds excellent country markets on the last Sun each month; 19 km N. *Southbrook:* nearby Prestbury Farm offers accommodation and the experiece of rural life; 34 km SW. *Lake Cooby:* fishing and walking; 35 km N. *Pittsworth:* in town is the Pioneer Historical Village featuring a one-teacher school, early farming machinery and a display commemorating Arthur Postle, or the 'Crimson Flash', once the fastest man in the world. Village open Sun or by appt; (07) 4693 1997. 46 km SW. *Yandilla:* here you'll find the quaint, steeped All Saints Anglican Church (1877), the oldest building in the shire. 77 km SW. *Millmerran:* colourful murals illustrate the history of this industrial town, including

the dairy industry mural at the Old Butter Factory, and the mural on the water reservoir showing the development of transport. The town's historical museum is open on Sun. 87 km SW. *Scenic drives:* take in places such as Spring Bluff, with old railway station and superb gardens (16 km N), Murphys Creek, Heifer Creek and the Valley of the Sun; brochure available from visitor centre.
ⓘ Cnr James and Kitchener sts; 1800 331 155 or (07) 4639 3797; www.toowoombaholidays.info

Townsville
Pop. 85 239

Map ref. 603 G9, 611 P12

Despite Townsville being Australia's largest tropical city, it has retained the relaxed tropical atmosphere of its smaller counterparts. In 1864 sea captain Robert Towns commissioned James Black to establish a settlement on Cleveland Bay to service the new inland cattle industry. The many historic buildings found around Cleveland Bay are a reminder of this heritage. The city's proximity to the Great Barrier Reef has allowed Townsville to be increasingly recognised as a centre for research into marine life. The foreshore also caters for more cosmopolitan tastes with The Strand's blend of cafes and restaurants combined with tropical parks and spectacular views to Magnetic Island.

IN TOWN **Reef HQ** Home to the headquarters for the Great Barrier Reef Marine Park Authority, this underwater observatory is both informative and visually breathtaking. Its living reef is the largest 'captive' reef in the world. Get up close at the touch pools and see marine feeding and dive shows. Flinders St East. *Museum of Tropical Queensland:* featuring artefacts from wreck of HMAS *Pandora*; Flinders St East. *North Queensland Military Museum:* displaying military artefacts; Kissing Point. *Maritime Museum:* maritime items of historical significance; Palmer St. *Rock Pool Baths:* year-round swimming; The Strand. *Perc Tucker Regional Art Gallery:* local and touring exhibitions; Flinders Mall. *Botanic Gardens:* Anderson Park, Kings Rd. *Imax Dome Theatre:* excellent viewing experience in this theatre, the first of its kind in the Southern Hemisphere; Flinders St East. *Town Common Conservation Park:* a coastline park with prolific birdlife, Aboriginal Plant Trail and forest walks; Pallarenda Rd. *Castle Hill Lookout:* off Stanley St. *Jupiters Townsville Hotel and Casino:* Sir Leslie Thiess Dr. *Ferry Terminal:* for Magnetic Island, and daytrips and dive cruises to the Great Barrier Reef as well as extended cruises to the Whitsundays; Flinders St. *Coral Princess:* cruise to Cairns via resort islands and reef on a luxury catamaran; contact visitor centre for details. *Adventure activities:* numerous tour operators offer jetskiing, waterskiing, abseiling, whitewater rafting and more; contact visitor centre for details. *Dive*

schools: contact visitor centre for details.
WHAT'S ON *Cotters Market:* Flinders Mall, each Sun. *Greek Festival:* Mar. *Australian Festival of Chamber Music:* July.
NEARBY Magnetic Island Over half of this beautiful island is covered by the Magnetic Island National Park. The sandy beaches, granite headlands and hoop pine rainforest make this an attractive daytrip, or stay overnight in the private accommodation on offer. See the natural attractions by taking one of the many walks around the island or hire a bike for a different view. Snorkel and swim at Sandy Bay and see spectacular views from the old WW II forts. Access the island from Townsville by Fast Ferry, vehicle barge or passenger ferry; 8 km NE.
Bowling Green Bay National Park This coastal park offers much for the self-sufficient visitor. Granite mountains blend with a variety of landscapes including saltpans and mangrove country. Walk along Alligator Creek to see cascades and waterfalls. Stay overnight at the Alligator Creek campsite and go spotlighting to glimpse brush-tail possums and sugar gliders. Turn-off Bruce Hwy 28 km SE; park is further 6 km. *Billabong Sanctuary:* covering 10 ha of rainforest, eucalypt forest and wetlands. See koala feeding and crocodile shows. Bruce Hwy; 17 km SE. *Giru:* small community with waterfalls, bushwalks and swimming nearby; 50 km SE.
ⓘ Bruce Hwy; 1800 801 902 or (07) 4778 3555; or The Mall Information Centre, Flinders Mall; (07) 4721 3660; www.townsvilleonline.com.au

Tully   Pop. 2537
Map ref. 603 D3, 611 N9

At the foot of Mt Tyson, Tully receives one of the highest annual rainfalls in Australia – around 4200 millimetres. This abundance of rain supports swift rapids on the Tully River – an attraction for any whitewater-rafting enthusiast. The area was settled in the 1870s by a family keen on growing sugarcane, and the town grew when the government decided to build a sugar mill in 1925. Sugarcane remains a major industry.
IN TOWN *Tully Sugar Mill:* informative tours in the crushing season (June–Nov); tickets from the visitor centre.
WHAT'S ON *Market:* 2nd Sat each month. *Rodeo:* July.
NEARBY Tully Gorge Alcock State Forest This picturesque state forest incorporates the Tully Gorge and the raging waters of the Tully River. Visit the Frank Roberts Lookout for views over the gorge, take the Rainforest Butterfly Walk for a colourful display of butterflies and visit the Cardstone Weir boardwalk in the afternoons to watch rafters negotiate the rapids. Head to the top reaches of the river for superb scenery and swimming.

Visit in dry season only (May–Dec). 40 km W.
Alligator's Nest: beautiful rainforest with swimming in stream; 10 km S. *Tully Heads:* estuary and beachside fishing; separated from Hull Heads by Googorra Beach; 22 km SE. *The Echo Creek Walking Trail:* take this guided trail through rainforest, walking a traditional Aboriginal trading route; turn-off after Euramo; 30 km SW. *Murray Upper State Forest:* rainforest walks to cascades, rock pools and Murray Falls; turn-off 38 km S. *Misty Mountains walking trails:* day walks or longer (up to 44 km) in Wet Tropics World Heritage Area; information available at visitor centre. *Whitewater rafting:* operators run from Tully to the renowned rapids of the Tully River; contact visitor centre for details.
ⓘ Bruce Hwy; (07) 4068 2288; www.greatgreenway.com

Warwick   Pop. 11 981
Map ref. 515 M1, 607 N11

Warwick is an attractive city set alongside the willow-shaded Condamine River. It is known as the 'Rose and Rodeo City', as the Warwick Rodeo dates back to the 1850s, and the parks and gardens have an abundance of roses. There is even a red rose cultivated especially for Warwick – the City of Warwick Rose (or Arofuto Rose). The area was explored by Allan Cunningham in 1827, and in 1840 the Leslie brothers established a sheep station at Canning Downs. Warwick was eventually established in 1849 on the site that Patrick Leslie selected. The surrounding pastures support famous horse and cattle studs.
IN TOWN *Pringle Cottage:* historic home (1870) housing large historic photo collection, vehicles and machinery; Dragon St. *Warwick Regional Art Gallery:* local and touring exhibitions; Albion St. *Jubilee Gardens:* see the displays of roses that Warwick is famous for; cnr Palmerin and Fitzroy sts. *Lookout:* viewing platform for regional views; Glen Rd. *Historical walk or drive:* self-guide tour of historic sandstone buildings dating from the 1880s and 1890s; brochure available from visitor centre.
WHAT'S ON *National Rock Swap Festival:* Easter. *Rose and Rodeo Festival:* Oct.
NEARBY *Leslie Dam:* watersports, fishing and swimming; 15 km W. *Main Range National Park:* 61 km NE; *see Boonah and Killarney. Heritage drive:* 80 km cultural drive in region; brochure available from visitor centre.
ⓘ 49 Albion St (New England Hwy); (07) 4661 3401; www.qldsouthern downs.org.au

Weipa   Pop. 2487
Map ref. 612 B7

The town of Weipa, on the west coast of Cape York, was built in 1961 on the

site of a mission station and Aboriginal reserve. It is home to the world's largest bauxite mine, the main reason why the town was established. This coastal part of Cape York was reputedly the first area in Australia to be explored by Europeans. Although the town is remote, it offers a full range of services for travellers.
IN TOWN Western Cape Cultural Centre This centre was established to introduce the visitor to the culture of western Cape York. The range of artefacts and photos bring the area's indigenous and European history alive. A highlight is the ceramic wall mural depicting sacred images of the local Aboriginal people. There is also information about the landscapes and ecosystems of the cape, and sales of local arts and crafts. Evans Landing.
Tours of Bauxite Mine: guided tours provide excellent coverage of the whole mining process at Weipa; contact visitor centre for details. *Fishing tours:* Weipa's fishing spots can be explored on tours; contact visitor centre for details. *Boat and houseboat hire:* contact visitor centre.
NEARBY Jardine River National Park This remote park is on the north-east tip of Cape York Peninsula. It was known to early explorers as the 'wet desert' because of its abundant waterways, but lack of food. These waters attract varied birdlife including the rare palm cockatoo. See the Fruit Bat Falls from the boardwalk or fish off the beaches at Captain Billy Landing and Ussher Point. 4WD access only; visit between May–Oct; off Peninsula Development Rd south of Bamaga.
Fishing and camping: a number of areas developed for the well-equipped visitor. *Mungkan Kandju National Park:* wilderness park of open forests, swamps and dense rainforest. There is excellent birdlife around lagoons and bushwalking along Archer River. 4WD access only; visit between May–Nov; turn-off 29 km N of Coen. *Mapoon:* camping and scenery; permit required; 85 km N. *Iron Range National Park:* this important lowland tropical rainforest park is a haven for wildlife. There is good fishing at Chili Beach, and bush camping for self-sufficient visitors only. 4WD recommended; visit only between April–Sept; 216 km E. *Bamaga and Seisia:* tours to islands of the Torres Strait; around 350 km N; road impassable in the Wet. *Thursday Island and Torres Strait:* north-west of Cape York; *see feature on p. 437.*
Travellers note: *Roads to the Cape may become impassable during the wet season (Nov–April). Motorists are advised to check the RACQ Road Conditions Report on 1300 130 595 (or www.racq.com.au) before departing. Permits for travel over Aboriginal land can be sought in Weipa; contact visitor centre for details.*
ⓘ Evans Landing; (07) 4069 7566

Winton
Pop. 1313

Map ref. 615 M8

The area surrounding Winton is known as Matilda Country, as Australia's most famous song, 'Waltzing Matilda', was written by Banjo Paterson at nearby Dagworth Station in 1895. Combo Waterhole (near Kynuna) was the setting for the ballad and the tune had its first airing in Winton. A less auspicious event in Winton's history is the declaration of martial law in the 1890s following the Shearers' Strike. In 1920 the first office of Qantas was registered here. The town's water supply comes from deep artesian bores at a temperature of 83°C.

IN TOWN **Waltzing Matilda Centre** Created as a tribute to the swagman life, this centre provides an interesting look into Australian history. The centre incorporates the 'Billabong Courtyard' with its light and sound show, the regional art gallery, interactive exhibits of the swagman life in 'Home of the Legend' hall, and the Matilda Museum – harking back to Winton's pioneering days and the first days of Qantas. Elderslie St. *Royal Theatre:* historic open-air movie theatre and museum, one of the oldest still operating in Australia; Elderslie St. *Corfield and Fitzmaurice Store:* charming National Trust-listed store with diorama of Lark Quarry dinosaur stampede; Elderslie St. *Gift and Gem Centre:* displays and sales; the 'Opal Walk' leads to the theatre museum; Elderslie St. *Arno's Wall:* ongoing concrete-wall creation proudly containing 'every item imaginable'; Vindex St.

WHAT'S ON *Back To Winton:* Easter. *Waltzing Matilda Festival:* June. *Outback Festival:* odd-numbered years, Sept.

NEARBY **Lark Quarry Conservation Park** This park features the preserved tracks of a dinosaur stampede from 93 million years ago – the only preserved tracks of this type known in the world. It occurred when a Therapod chased a group of smaller dinosaurs across the mud flats of a lake. The 'trackways' are protected by a shelter and can be visited on a tour (contact visitor centre). The park also offers a short walk past ancient rock formations, known as the Winton Formation, to a lookout over the region. 110 km sw. **Bladensburg National Park** The vast plains and ridges of this park provide an important sanctuary for a variety of wildlife, including kangaroos, dunnarts and emus. Skull Hole (40 km s) has Aboriginal paintings and bora ceremonial grounds and is believed to be the site of a late-1880s Aboriginal massacre. Walking should only be attempted by experienced bushwalkers. 'Route of the River Gums', a self-drive tour, provides an excellent overview of the region's landscapes. Drive starts 8 km s. *Carisbrooke Station:* a working sheep station with Aboriginal cave paintings and scenic

drives in the surrounds; day tours and accommodation available; 85 km sw. *Opalton:* see the remains of the historic town or try fossicking for opals in one of the oldest fields in Queensland; licence available from visitor centre; 115 km s. *Air charters and ground tours:* to major regional sights; contact visitor centre for details.
ⓘ Waltzing Matilda Centre, 90 Elderslie St; (07) 4657 1466; www.matildacentre.com.au

Yandina
Pop. 1019

Map ref. 601 F3, 602 E6, 607 P7

Yandina is in the Sunshine Coast hinterland north of Nambour. The first land claims in the area were made here in 1868. Yandina is now home to The Ginger Factory, the largest such factory in the world, giving Yandina the title of 'Ginger Capital of the World'.

IN TOWN **The Ginger Factory** This award-winning complex is devoted to everything ginger. Visitors can see Gingertown, watch ginger-cooking demonstrations, see ginger being processed and ride on the historic Queensland Cane Train through subtropical rainforest. Bunya Park is a small wildlife sanctuary in the factory grounds – a highlight is the exotic flowering gingers. Pioneer Rd. *Yandina Historic House:* local history display, arts and crafts, art gallery and visitor centre; Pioneer Rd. *Nutworks Macadamia Processes:* see processing of macadamia nuts and taste-test the results; opposite The Ginger Factory. *Fairhill Native Plants and Botanic Gardens:* fabulous nursery and gardens – a must for any native-plant buff; Fairhill Rd. *Heritage trail:* self-guide trail around town sights; brochure available from visitor centre.

WHAT'S ON *Big Cow Market:* parklands on Nambour/Yandina Connection Rd each Sat. *Ginger Flower Festival:* Jan.

NEARBY **Eumundi** This historic town has a variety of excellent galleries to visit, including indigenous Australian art. The impressive country markets are renowned for their size with over 200 stalls. The quality of the fresh produce, art and craft and cut flowers, along with the wonderful atmosphere, brings visitors to the town each Wed and Sat. 10 km N. *Wappa Dam:* popular picnic area; west of Yandina. *Yandina Speedway:* offers a variety of motor races; contact (07) 5446 7552 for details; just west on Wappa Falls Rd.
ⓘ Yandina Historic House, 3 Pioneer Rd (at the roundabout); (07) 5472 7181

Yeppoon
Pop. 10 656

Map ref. 609 O10

The popular coastal resort of Yeppoon lies on the shores of Keppel Bay. Yeppoon and the beaches to its south – Cooee Bay, Rosslyn Bay, Causeway Lake, Emu Park and Keppel Sands – are known as the

Capricorn Coast. Great Keppel Island Resort lies 13 kilometres offshore and is a popular holiday destination offering great swimming, snorkelling and diving.

IN TOWN *The Esplanade:* attractive strip of shops, galleries and cafes overlooking parkland and crystal-clear water. *Doll and Antiquity Museum:* Hidden Valley Rd.

WHAT'S ON *Market:* showgrounds; Sat mornings. *Fig Tree Markets:* 1st Sun each month. *Australia Day Celebrations:* Jan. *Ozfest:* World Cooeeing Competition; July. *Yeppoon Tropical Pinefest:* Sept.

NEARBY **Great Keppel Island** Popular island holiday destination with over 15 beaches to explore, swim and relax on. There is snorkelling and diving offshore and walks exploring the island's centre, including an interesting Aboriginal culture trail. Various styles of accommodation are offered. Access is by ferry from Keppel Bay Marina at Rosslyn Bay Harbour; 7 km s. **Byfield National Park** This attractive coastal park offers uninterrupted views of the ocean from its long beaches. Explore the open woodlands and forest or take in magnificent coastal views from the headlands at Five Rock and Stockyard Point. Fishing and boating are popular at Sandy Point at the south of the park. 4WD only; experience in sand driving is essential; 32 km N. *Boating:* bareboat and fishing charters; sea access to Great Keppel Island and nearby underwater observatory; water taxis to Keppel Bay Islands; all from Keppel Bay Marina; 7 km s. *Wetland Tour:* Australian nature tour at Rydges Capricorn International Resort; 9 km N. *Cooberrie Park:* noted flora and fauna reserve; 15 km N. *Emu Park:* small village community with historical museum and interesting 'singing ship' memorial to Captain Cook – the sea breezes cause hidden organ pipes to make sounds. There is a Service of Remembrance memorial to American troops each July, and Octoberfest is held each Oct. 19 km s. *Byfield State Forest:* the extremely rare Byfield fern is harvested from here. Walks include the 4.3 km Stony Creek circuit track through rainforest and the boardwalk along Waterpark Creek. Adjacent to Byfield National Park. *Keppel Sands:* this popular spot for fishing and crabbing is home to the excellent emerging Joskeleigh South Sea Island Museum, with the Koorana Crocodile Farm nearby. 38 km sw. *Keppel Bay Islands National Park:* this scenic group of islands is popular for walks, snorkelling, reef-walking and swimming; private boat or water taxi from Keppel Bay Marina. *Capricorn Coast Coffee:* Australia's largest coffee plantation; tours available; contact visitor centre for details. *Scenic flights:* over islands and surrounds from Hedlow Airport (between Yeppoon and Rockhampton); contact visitor centre for details.

QUEENSLAND

Capricorn Coast Tourist Information Centre, Scenic Hwy; 1800 675 785 or (07) 4939 4888; www.capricorncoast.com.au

Yungaburra   Pop. 947

Map ref. 603 B1, 611 M7

Yungaburra is a historic town on the edge of the Atherton Tableland. Originally a resting spot for miners, Yungaburra slowly developed into a town. The tourism boom did not hit until the coastal road opened from Cairns in 1926.

IN TOWN *Historical precinct walk:* take this self-guide walk past beautiful heritage buildings including the popular Lake Eacham Hotel in Cedar St with its charming architecture and historic photographs; brochure available from visitor centre. *Platypus viewing platform:* see the elusive animal at sunrise and sunset; Peterson Creek, Gillies Hwy. *Galleries, craft and gem shops:* various in town.

WHAT'S ON *Market:* renowned produce and craft market; Gillies Hwy; 4th Sat each month. *Folk and Frog Festival:* Oct.

NEARBY Crater Lakes National Park The two volcanic lakes, Lake Eacham (8 km E) and Lake Barrine (12 km NE), are surrounded by rainforest and offer watersports, bushwalking and birdwatching. Look for the eastern water dragons along the 3 km track around Lake Barrine or take a wildlife cruise on the lake. There is a children's pool at Lake Eacham, a self-guide trail through the rainforest and a 3 km circuit shore track. Both lakes are popular recreation areas.
Malanda Malanda is a small town in the middle of rich dairy-farming country – it even claims the longest milk run in the world (to Alice Springs). The town boasts the still-operating 19th-century Majestic Theatre, and the Gourmet Food Factory specialising in local produce. On the southern outskirts of town is the Malanda Falls Conservation Park, with signposted rainforest walks, and the Malanda Environmental Centre, which has displays on local history, vulcanology, flora and fauna. The Malanda Falls actually flow into the local swimming pool. 20 km S. *Curtain Fig Tree:* spectacular example of strangler fig with aerial roots in curtain-like formation; 2.5 km SW. *Tinaburra:* an excellent spot for swimming and watersports on Lake Tinaroo; boat ramp provides access. Nearby Seven Sisters are 7 volcanic cinder cones. 3 km N. *Lake Tinaroo:* watersports and fishing; travel around on a houseboat or dinghy – hire available; north of Yungaburra. *Heales Outlook:* spectacular views over Gillies Range; 16 km NE. *Tinaroo Falls Dam outlet:* views over lake; 23 km N.
Allumbah Pocket Cottages, Gillies Hwy; (07) 4095 3023; or Nick's Swiss-Italian Restaurant, Gillies Hwy; (07) 4095 3330; www.athertontableland.com

Poruma (Coconut Island), central Torres Strait

The Torres Strait

The islands of the Torres Strait stretch from the tip of Cape York Peninsula to Papua New Guinea and comprise 17 inhabited islands. The first European to pass through the strait was the Spanish navigator Luis Vaez de Torres in 1606. By the 1880s a pearling industry was established that continues to this day, alongside crayfishing, prawning and trochus industries. The mix of indigenous culture (more Papua New Guinean than Australian Aboriginal) and European settlement has made the Torres Strait Islands an intriguing place to visit.

Thursday Island lies around 35 kilometres north-west of the Cape York tip and is the administrative centre of the islands. Visit the new Torres Strait Cultural Centre – it preserves the unique cultural heritage of the islands and documents their art, culture, geography and history in an excellent interpretive display. Or see the old underground tunnels of Green Hill Fort at the Historical Museum. For the tastebuds, try some of the famous seafood delicacies at the low-key restaurants and cafes.

The surrounding islands include Friday Island, where you can see pearls being cultivated at Kazu – a pearling farm that has been operating for more than 45 years – and Horn Island, which was an important posting for Australian troops in World War II. For the cultural experience, take a day tour to Badu Island, one of the outer islands of the strait. Pass through spectacular island scenery and enjoy a day of traditional dances, arts and crafts and food.

Mabo Day is held each June – it commemorates the momentous High Court decision that overturned the Terra Nullius claim on Australia at colonisation. It was the tireless work of local man Eddie Koiki Mabo that led to this, and gave Mer (Murray Islands) back to the indigenous people. The Coming of the Light festival is also celebrated on the 1st of July each year, the day that the London Missionary Society arrived at Erub Island in 1871.

Getting there

Getting to the Torres Strait involves either a flight from Cairns (Qantas), a trip on a cargo vessel from Cairns or a ferry ride from Cape York (Seisia or Punsand Bay, near the cape itself). Many people head to Thursday Island via Horn Island, which has an airstrip. The main transport and tour operators include:

Peddells: passenger ferry service to Thursday Island from Seisia and Punsand Bay; also offers tours to Horn Island; (07) 4069 1551; www.peddellsferry.com.au

Seaswift: weekly cargo vessel between Cairns and Torres Strait; (07) 4035 1234; www.seaswift.com.au

Torres Strait Tours: tours from Seisia to Thursday Island and from Thursday Island to Horn and Badu islands; 1800 420 666; www.torrestours.com.au

You can arrange tours to other islands from Thursday Island. Scenic helicopter and charter flights also operate from Thursday and Horn islands.

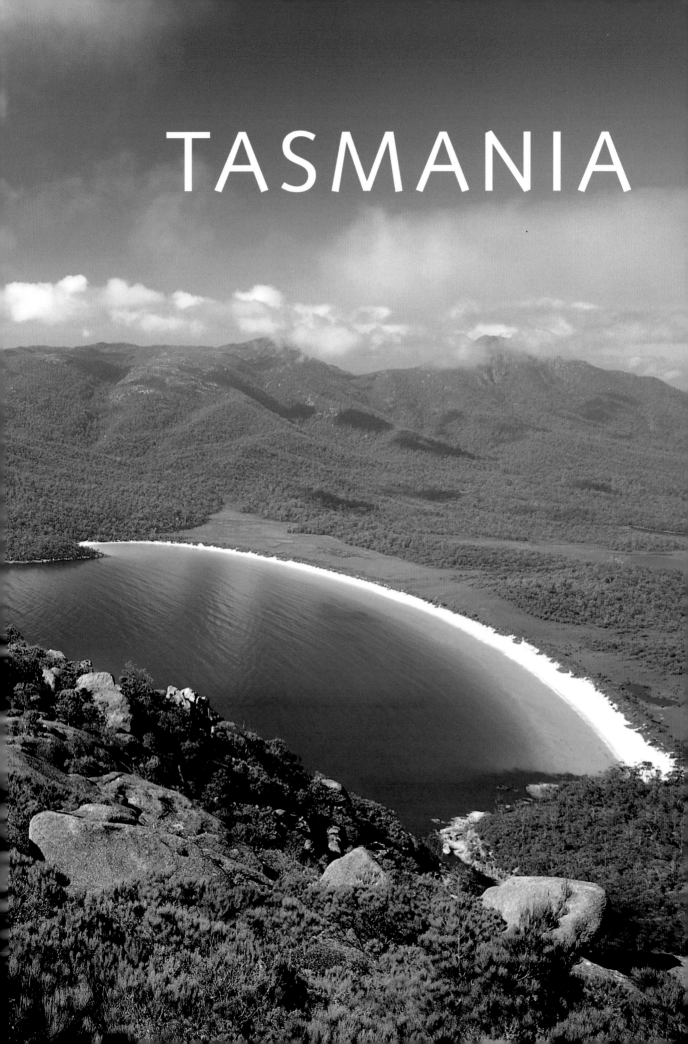

TASMANIA

T asmania has a concentration of delights for travellers. It is edged with uncrowded beaches that include gorgeous Wineglass Bay on the east coast, one of the world's best beaches. In contrast is the wonderfully tempestuous west coast. Places like Marrawah and Strahan's Ocean Beach are pounded by huge swells generated by the roaring forties winds as they blow unhindered all the way from Africa. This provides what might be the world's cleanest air.

A winding country road can suddenly reveal a colonial village, a boutique vineyard or a breathtaking ocean view.

Tasmania is one of the world's most mountainous islands, and this combines with its southern location to add an element of unpredictability to its temperate climate. Dramatic changes in weather conditions often add to the experience of the island's spectacular scenery.

Although it is Australia's smallest state – only 296 kilometres from south to north and 315 kilometres east to west – Tasmania's territory also includes the Bass Strait islands and subantarctic Macquarie Island. A population of just 477 100 is eclipsed by over half a million visitors each year, and Tasmania is famous for its friendly welcome and relaxed pace of life.

The Palawa people have been here for around 35 000 years, and despite the terrible impact that white settlement has had on their culture, they are a large and increasingly influential community today. Middens are common around the coastline, showing where generations of Palawa people cooked shellfish meals. These culturally significant sites can be tens of thousands of years old.

Abel Tasman sighted and named Van Diemen's Land in 1642, closely followed by French and British explorers. The British – never keen to be outdone by the French – acted in 1803 to establish a presence on the River Derwent. With the arrival of the British, white settlement got off to a rollicking and violent start – as a penal colony for the first 50 years. Many of Tasmania's early stories involve escaped convicts like pie-maker Alexander Pearce, who was executed for killing and eating a fellow escapee while trying to get from Macquarie Harbour to Hobart. The Pieman River, beside the tiny west-coast town of Corinna, is named after Pearce.

Tasmania is the home of the world's first Greens party. Local

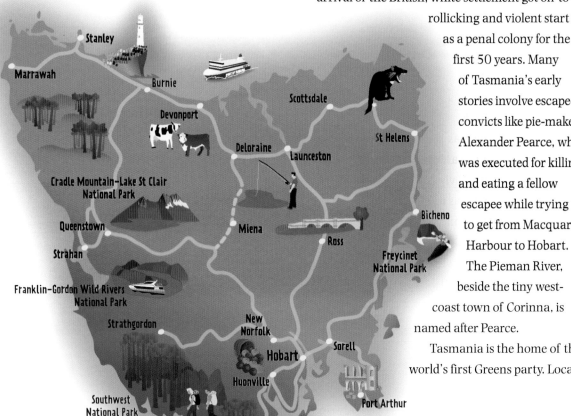

PREVIOUS PAGES *Wineglass Bay, Freycinet National Park*

Walls of Jerusalem National Park

environmental politics captured international attention in the 1980s when the No Dams campaign saved the Franklin River from being flooded for a hydro-electric scheme.

The island's spirited cultural life includes the renowned Tasmanian Symphony Orchestra, award-winning author Richard Flanagan and many arts and literary events. Ten Days On The Island is a biennial festival that attracts island communities from around the world in a celebration of the unique qualities of island life.

Although two-thirds of the land is too harsh for farming, Tasmania has a growing reputation for boutique agriculture and aquaculture. A gastronomic circumnavigation of the island offers as much diversity as the landscape and a chance to discover Tasmania's cool-climate wines, fresh seafood, fruits and fine cheeses.

Tasmania is bursting with wonderful surprises. A winding country road can suddenly reveal a colonial village, a boutique vineyard or a breathtaking ocean view. From landscape and history to food and culture, Australia's island state is a feast for travellers.

FACT FILE

Population 477 100
Total land area 68 102 sq km
People per square kilometre 7
Sheep per square kilometre 49.6
Length of coastline 2833 km
Number of islands 1000
Longest river South Esk River (252 km)
Largest lake Lake Gordon (hydro-electric impoundment), 271 sq km
Highest mountain Mt Ossa (1614 m), Cradle Mountain–Lake St Clair National Park
Coldest place At Liawenee in August the average minimum temperature is -1.8°C
Longest place name Teebelebberrer Mennapeboneyer (Aboriginal name for Little Swanport River)
Best beach Wineglass Bay, Freycinet National Park
Biggest surfable wave Shipstern Bluff near Port Arthur
Oldest pub Hope and Anchor Hotel, Hobart (continuously running since 1807)
Local-born Hollywood star Errol Flynn
Most significant resident Mr Richard Butler, AC, former United Nations Chief Weapons Inspector in Iraq, now Governor of Tasmania
Quirkiest festival National Penny Farthing Championships, Evandale
Most expensive gourmet produce French black truffles are collected in increasing numbers each winter from local farms. Their price can reach $2500 per kilo
Local beers Cascade in the south; Boags in the north

TIMELINE

35 000 years ago

Aborigines walk across the land bridge from what would become Victoria. After this last Ice Age sea levels rise, cutting off Tasmania.

1642

Abel Tasman sails along the west coast and names the island Van Diemen's Land.

1803

Risdon Cove on the eastern shore of the River Derwent is chosen as the first European settlement. Hobart is founded on the other side of the river a year later.

1853

The last shipment of convicts arrives.

1876

Truganini dies. Although a vibrant community survives, she was the last tribal-born Tasmanian Aboriginal.

1877

Port Arthur penal settlement closes.

1983

The High Court of Australia rules against the building of the Gordon-below-Franklin dam. This will become a pivotal event in world green politics.

1986

Archaeologists in the south-west discover Aboriginal rock paintings thought to be 20 000 years old. In 1987 they discover stencils of handprints dating back to the last Ice Age.

1995

The Tasmanian Aboriginal Land Act 1995 is passed. Twelve significant historic and cultural sites are returned to Aboriginal people.

HOBART

HOBART IS . . .

**Browsing Salamanca Market
on Saturdays**

**Fish and chips at
Constitution Dock**

**A drive to the summit
of Mt Wellington**

Exploring Hobart's waterfront

**A visit to the Royal Tasmanian
Botanical Gardens**

**Wandering around historic
Battery Point**

**A visit to the Tasmanian
Museum and Art Gallery**

**A tour of the Cadbury
Schweppes Chocolate Factory**

**A counter meal in a warm
colonial pub**

**Watching beer production at
Cascade Brewery**

**Coffee and a movie at
North Hobart's independent
State Cinema**

Visitor information

Tasmanian Travel and Information
Centre
Cnr Davey and Elizabeth sts, Hobart
(03) 6230 8233
www.discovertasmania.com

The Australian Wooden Boat Festival celebrates Hobart's maritime heritage

Hobart, Australia's most southerly city, began on a rainy and blustery day in 1804 when Lieutenant Governor David Collins took possession of land the Aboriginal inhabitants called 'Nibberloone'. Three hundred convicts, and military and civil servants, set up camp and began building a town in Sullivans Cove; thus, Hobart was the second city in Australia to be established (after Sydney), and its history is well preserved. There are whole areas of 19th-century Georgian sandstone buildings, and inner suburbs boast entire streets of colonial cottages and federation-brick or weatherboard houses.

Hobart's population of about 220 000 is spread along the bays and headlands of the Derwent estuary. The pace of life is relaxed and easygoing. In the city, low-rise buildings line the narrow streets and traffic is unhurried. Stroll through beautiful historic precincts in Macquarie and Davey streets, stop for a coffee in Elizabeth Mall or wander down to the wharves, where you can see Antarctic research vessels and fishing trawlers.

Hobart stands in the shadow of majestic Mt Wellington. The weather visibly moves over its summit, which can be snow-capped at any time of year. The cool and variable climate determines how life is led in Hobart, and the locals make the most of any warm days. With the natural environment featuring so prominently in Hobart, it's no surprise that the world's first 'green' political party was formed here in the 1970s.

Today the fortunes of this small but compact city still centre on the Derwent estuary – one of the world's finest deep-water harbours. The historic buildings and vibrant seafront continue to give the city a strong maritime flavour.

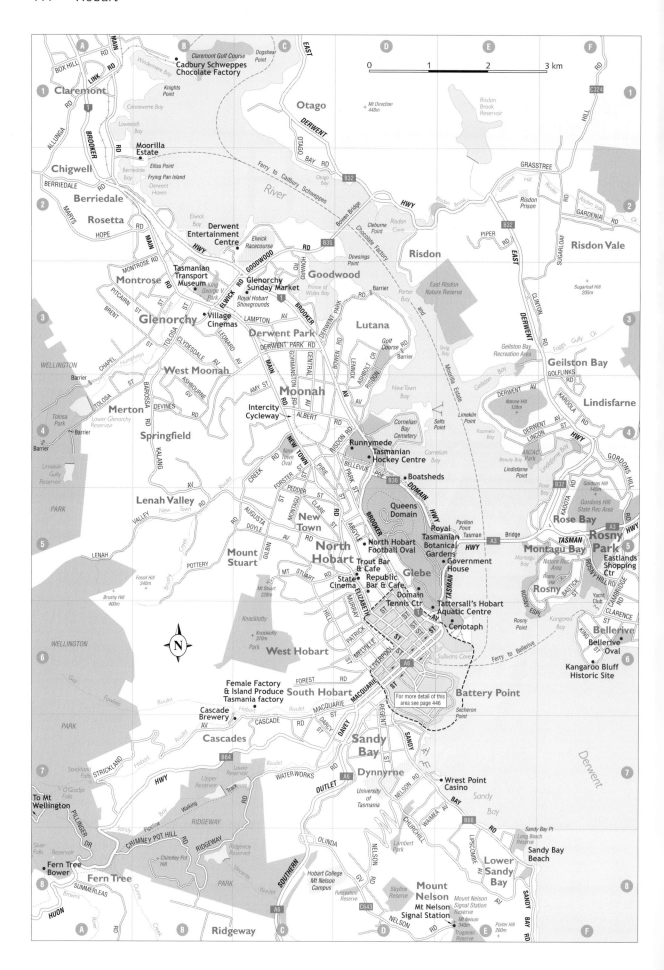

Central Hobart

Hobart city grew north from the waterfront, along Elizabeth Street. The main retail shopping streets are in Liverpool and Collins streets between Elizabeth Mall and Harrington Street. Historic buildings along Macquarie and Davey streets mainly house government and private offices, while there is a growing cultural presence in the dockside area around Argyle and Campbell streets. On the southern side of Sullivans Cove, parks and historic warehouses provide a beautiful setting for galleries, cafes and restaurants along Salamanca Place. The 19th-century village of Battery Point, situated on the hill behind this area, remains almost unchanged and is cherished by those lucky enough to live there.

DOWNTOWN HOBART

Downtown Hobart is centred on Elizabeth Street and extends to the city blocks north of Macquarie Street. There are comparatively few large department stores, fashion and specialty shops, as Hobart is smaller than most mainland capitals. Recently extended shopping hours mean that most stores open on weekends.

Elizabeth Mall

Hobart's only pedestrian mall is a lively and busy place with specialty shops, cafes and places to sit and take a break. An information booth is open on weekdays to help people find their way around the city.

The subterranean **Hobart Rivulet** can be seen below the footpath outside the National Bank. This supply of fresh water was the reason that Collins picked Sullivans Cove for his settlement, but it soon became fouled by sewage and run-off. By the middle of the 19th century it had become a stagnant cesspool and contributed to epidemics of typhoid and diphtheria. Now channelled, the rivulet carries mountain run-off and storm water, and is no longer a health hazard. Visitors can take an underground tour along its course (*see Walks and tours, p. 451*).

Cat and Fiddle Arcade

There are several shopping arcades in the main retail area of Hobart, but the Cat and Fiddle Arcade's nursery rhyme musical clock lends it a certain charm. Much to the delight of children, it plays 'Hey Diddle Diddle' on the hour as moving parts provide accompanying action. The arcade runs between the mall and Murray Street.

Liverpool Street

The stretch of Liverpool Street between Argyle and Harrington streets houses many of the well-known department stores, such as Myer, as well as some interesting arcades and side streets. **Bank Arcade** (between Argyle and Elizabeth streets) will tempt you with breads and spices. **Mathers Lane** and **Criterion Street**, further along towards Murray Street, will interest those with a taste for good coffee and all things retro.

Elizabeth Street

North of the mall, Elizabeth Street continues up the hill towards North Hobart. In the first few blocks there is a cluster of shops selling polar fleece and outdoor equipment – a response to the magnificent wilderness on Hobart's doorstep. Further along there are several antique and second-hand shops that are well worth a look.

NORTHERN WATERFRONT

The northern waterfront of Sullivans Cove covers the area from Hunter Street across to Elizabeth Street and along the lower end of Campbell Street. This is the busiest, smelliest and most fascinating part of the working dock, both on and off the water. Some nearby areas have been redeveloped as apartments, but there are still many 19th-century buildings being recycled for new purposes, especially along Hunter Street. There are also some beautiful views of Hobart, with Mt Wellington as the backdrop, from this part of the harbour.

Constitution and Victoria docks

Constitution Dock and the neighbouring Victoria Dock are the heart of Sullivans Cove, where the smaller fishing and pleasure boats tie up. Constitution Dock is also the temporary home for the yachts participating in the Sydney and Melbourne to Hobart races in January. Punts moored alongside Franklin Wharf sell fish and chips, and there are several seafood restaurants nearby.

Steamers and sailing ships once berthed at **Franklin Wharf**. Every two years it comes alive again with many historic vessels during the Australian Wooden Boat Festival (*see Top events, p. 447*).

Federation Concert Hall

This concert hall is the home of the Tasmanian Symphony Orchestra and was designed to give priority to quality acoustics and the requirements of performers. Described as both intimate and grand, it seats over one thousand people. The outside design has prompted a lot of discussion among locals, who tend to either love it or hate it. *1 Davey St.*

Hotel Grand Chancellor

This hotel was built in 1987 amid controversy between developers and

Getting around

Public transport choices are limited in Hobart as there are no trains or trams, but there are buses, and luckily many places around the city are within easy walking distance (if you don't mind a few hills).

Metro buses service the suburbs, but they are infrequent on weekends and at night. Timetables are on most bus stops and are displayed at the Metro Shop in the Hobart Bus Mall in Elizabeth Street (near the GPO). An all-day ticket allows you to catch any number of buses after 9am.

Hobart's traffic is free-flowing, but there are many one-way streets that can confound the visitor, making it useful to keep a map or street directory handy. There is plenty of parking.

On the river, ferries operate from Brooke Street Pier to Bellerive on the eastern shore twice a day for commuters, and there are also harbour cruises during the day (see Walks and tours, p. 451). Timetable information is available from the pier.

The Intercity Cycleway between Hobart and the northern suburbs is popular on weekends. The most scenic section, linking Hobart to Cornelian Bay and the Royal Tasmanian Botanical Gardens, runs under the approaches to the Tasman Bridge, giving cyclists a spectacular perspective. Bikes can be hired from the Hobart end of the cycleway.

Public transport Bus information line 13 2201

Airport shuttle bus Airporter Bus Service 0419 382 240 or 0419 383 462

Motoring organisation RACT 13 2722, roadside assistance 13 1111

Car rental Ascot 1800 888 725; Autorent Hertz (03) 6237 1111; Avis 13 6333; Budget 1300 362 848; Europcar 1300 131 390; Thrifty 1300 367 227

Taxis Associated Taxis 0500 856 920; Australian Taxi Service 0411 286 780; City Cabs 13 1008; Taxi Combined Services 13 2227; United Taxis 1300 782 244

Ferry services Captain Fells commuter service to Bellerive (03) 6223 5893

Bicycle hire Derwent Bike Hire (weekends and school holidays only) (03) 6234 2910

Climate

The weather in Hobart is notoriously unpredictable. Summer is sunny and mild with temperatures usually in the mid 20s, but it's a known fact that a forecast maximum may be reached for only a short time before an afternoon sea breeze kicks in. The warm, sunny days continue into early autumn, but winter eventually brings short days with temperatures often in the low teens. Because of its waterfront location and proximity to Mt Wellington, rain, low cloud and the mysteriously named 'Bridgewater jerry' river fog occur in any season, but most commonly in winter.

	J	F	M	A	M	J	J	A	S	O	N	D
Max °C	22	22	21	18	15	13	12	13	15	17	19	20
Min °C	12	12	11	9	6	5	4	5	6	7	9	11
Rain mm	37	38	40	49	41	29	49	49	42	48	48	59
Raindays	9	8	10	11	13	11	13	15	14	13	14	13

groups who sought to protect the historical integrity of the waterfront. It provides accommodation, conference facilities and several restaurants featuring Tasmanian produce. *1 Davey St.*

Tasmanian Museum and Art Gallery

The Tasmanian Museum and Art Gallery is the home of Australia's finest collection of colonial art. Further, some of the galleries are, themselves, museum pieces. The museum complex includes Hobart's oldest structure – the 1808 Commissariat building. There are displays of convict and whaling history, as well as a gallery devoted to the continuing presence of Tasmania's Aboriginal people. The zoology galleries get you up close and personal with Tasmania's unique marsupials and extinct mega-fauna, and visitors might even glimpse a thylacine (Tasmanian tiger). *40 Macquarie St; open daily; general admission free.*

Maritime Museum of Tasmania

Located inside the impressive Neoclassical Carnegie Building, this museum brings to life Tasmania's rich maritime history. It displays pictures and equipment from the whaling era, models of various ships, and relics from shipwrecks. *Cnr Davey & Argyle sts; open daily; admission fee applies.*

SOUTHERN WATERFRONT

The docks on the southern side of Sullivans Cove are surrounded by remarkable historic buildings. The work of the docks continues amid cafes, restaurants and pubs, contributing to the area's lively atmosphere.

Salamanca Place

Salamanca Place is undoubtedly Australia's finest row of early merchants' warehouses, with most dating from the 1840s. This area was always a vibrant place that provided services to the whaling fleet, including ships' crews and the 'riff raff' of the port. Two of the original pubs – **Knopwood's Retreat** and **Irish Murphy's** – are still there.

Hobart's famous **Salamanca Market** is held here every Saturday, offering an amazing variety of goods, sidewalk entertainment and the chance to talk with local artisans. Over 300 stalls are spread along Salamanca Place, under the plane trees, and the Tasmanian produce on offer is especially tempting.

The warehouses are now converted into restaurants and quality galleries that specialise in Tasmanian art. Salamanca Square, behind the warehouses, boasts cafes and shops, and the **Salamanca Arts Centre** courtyard is an artists' collective that hosts a free street party with local musicians every Friday evening.

Parliament House

Situated behind the trees in Parliament Square, Hobart's majestic Parliament House faces out to the waterfront. Designed by the colonial architect John Lee Archer, it was built by convicts. Before becoming the home of Tasmania's parliament in 1856 this building was the first Customs House. It was fairly unsuccessful as a bond store – it was reputedly tunnelled into by a gang of convicts who managed to siphon off 28 gallons of brandy. In the vaulted cellars underneath the two parliamentary chambers, broad arrow marks can be seen in the bricks. *Between Salamanca Pl & Murray St; visitors gallery open on sitting days; tours by appointment; 1 300 135 513.*

Castray Esplanade and Princes Wharf

Built in 1870 to provide a promenade for the people of Hobart, Castray Esplanade runs behind Princes Wharf. At the city end of the esplanade are restaurants specialising in Tasmanian seafood. The Taste of Tasmania festival, celebrating everything from soft cheese to salmon, takes place in **Princes Wharf No. 1 Shed** at the beginning of January each year.

For most of the year Princes Wharf is a working dock, berthing Antarctic research and supply vessels. The CSIRO Marine Research Laboratories are situated at the Battery Point end, next to the finish line of the Sydney and Melbourne to Hobart yacht races (*see Top events, on this page*). On the hill are the original **Signal Station** and **Mulgrave Battery**, which was built in 1818 during panic about a rumoured Russian invasion. They are now part of **Princes Park**.

The octagonal **Tide House**, next to the **Ordnance Stores**, is the point from which all distances are measured in Tasmania.

BATTERY POINT

Battery Point, built to house the workers and merchants of the port, is on the hill behind Salamanca Place. Its compact size and village atmosphere make it a perfect place to explore on foot.

Kelly's Steps

Kelly's Steps connect the wharf area to Battery Point via a steep slope. They were built in 1839 by Captain James Kelly, who had a reputation as a fearless sealer, whaler and adventurer. Kelly's good fortune was short-lived – by 1842, seven of his children and his wife had died and he found himself bankrupt, alone and in trouble with the law over another man's wife. He died at the age of 67.

Arthur's Circus

Exploring Arthur's Circus, positioned at the top of Runnymede Street, is like walking into an intact Georgian streetscape. The sixteen cottages were built around a circular village green between 1847 and 1852. The cottages are all private residences.

Hampden Road

Hampden Road is a narrow street winding through the heart of Battery Point (the continuation of Castray Esplanade). Both sides boast handmade-brick workers' cottages as well as grander sandstone houses with optimistic names such as 'Mafeking' and 'Pretoria'. It's still mainly a residential area, but there are excellent fine-dining restaurants near Waterloo Crescent, as well as a busy cosmopolitan bakery and pastry shop, and some antique shops at the Sandy Bay Road end.

One of the earliest houses in Battery Point is **Narryna**. It was built in 1836 by a sea captain who had to sell it a few years later when he went broke. Narryna is now set up as a heritage museum showing the everyday items used by wealthy 19th-century families. Visitors can wander through the rooms of the house and get acquainted with how life used to be. The kitchen is especially worth a look. *Narryna Heritage Museum; 103 Hampden Rd; open 10.30am–5pm Tues–Fri, 2pm–5pm Sat–Sun; admission fee applies.*

Trumpeter Street

At the top end of Trumpeter Street is the **Shipwright's Arms Hotel**, which has traded under this name since 1846. The front bar has a distinctive nautical atmosphere with every inch of wall space covered with photographs of vessels that have sailed on the River Derwent.

A few doors away, across Napoleon Street, are **Mr Watson's Cottages**, a row of simple Georgian brick cottages built by shipbuilder John Watson in 1850. Behind are the boat building and slip yards of the Derwent foreshore that date back to the 1830s.

MACQUARIE AND DAVEY STREETS HISTORIC PRECINCT

These two streets contain magnificent examples of Hobart's early buildings and lead onto two beautiful, classically laid out parks between Molle and Elizabeth streets. The area is now mainly used for government offices, lawyers' premises and consulting rooms. Macquarie Street has always been Hobart's main thoroughfare, adding to its air of sophistication.

Franklin Square

Hobart's first Government House, built of timber and thatch, was built in Franklin

Top events

Hobart Summer Festival *Hobart sparkles with fun activities. December–January.*

Taste of Tasmania *Waterfront gourmet indulgence. December–January.*

Sydney to Hobart and Melbourne to Hobart yacht races *Gruelling races end with a dockside party, and a crowd of people to welcome the yachts no matter what time of the day or night. December.*

King of the Derwent *Maxi yachts battle to capture the crown. January.*

Royal Hobart Regatta *A family regatta and fireworks display since 1838. February.*

Australian Wooden Boat Festival *Biennial dockside celebration of maritime history. February (odd-numbered years).*

Ten Days on the Island *International island culture comes to Tasmania. March–April.*

Targa Tasmania *State-wide classic car rally. April–May.*

Antarctic Tasmania Midwinter Festival *Celebrating all things cold at the winter solstice. June.*

Shopping

Salamanca Place, City *Fine craft and Tasmanian art. See map on p. 446*

Elizabeth Street, City *Gifts, outdoor clothing and antiques. See map on p. 446*

Liverpool Street, City *Fashion and jewellery. See map on p. 446*

Cat and Fiddle Arcade, City *Bargain fashion and sportswear. See map on p. 446*

Bathurst Street, City *Fine furniture and antiques. See map on p. 446*

Sandy Bay Road, Battery Point *Antique furniture, china and art. See map on p. 446*

Sandy Bay Road, Sandy Bay *Classy fashion stores. 444 D7*

Eastlands Shopping Centre, Rosny Park *Hobart's largest undercover suburban mall. 444 F5*

Hunter Island

History is everywhere in Hobart, and there are stories from the past right under your feet in many parts of the city. It's hard to imagine now, but a walk along Hunter Street near Constitution Dock takes you right above a small, once-forested island where ships unloaded people and supplies for the settlement of Hobart. Hunter Island had a colourful and gruesome history, some of which still lies intact below the present dockside buildings.

Just two years after the settlement began at Hobart, gallows were erected on Hunter Island and the first execution was carried out. Ten years later the gallows were removed because there were too many complaints from new arrivals to the colony who were greeted by the nauseating sight of the rotting bodies of felons hanging from the gibbets.

In 1820 a stone causeway was built to join the island to the shore. It runs along the route of Hunter Street in front of the warehouses where the Drunken Admiral restaurant is now located. When excavations uncovered a section of the causeway in 1987, the tracks of men, oxen and carts could still be seen in the muddy surface.

Salamanca Market, a great place to find unique Tasmanian products

Grand old buildings

Lenna *When Alexander McGregor made a fortune from whaling he built this rich, Italianate mansion on a cliff overlooking the cove so that he could keep an eye on shipping movements. Now it's a stylish boutique hotel. 20 Runnymede St, Battery Point.*

Hebrew Synagogue *Australia's first synagogue and a rare example of Egyptian Revival architecture. Small, but it stands out from the crowd. Argyle St (between Liverpool & Bathurst sts), City.*

Theatre Royal *Australia's oldest theatre, with a highly decorated interior and a resident ghost. Laurence Olivier called it 'the best little theatre in the world'. 29 Campbell St, City.*

Town Hall *Classical Revival design by Henry Hunter, it stands where Collins pitched the first tent in Hobart. Macquarie St (between Elizabeth & Argyle sts), City.*

Penitentiary Chapel and Criminal Court *Underground passages, solitary cells and an execution yard. It narrowly escaped demolition in 1966. Cnr Brisbane & Campbell sts, City.*

City Hall *Built from a competition-winning design in 1915, it is perhaps Hobart's most underrated public building. Macquarie St (between Market & Campbell sts), City.*

T & G Building *Built for an insurance company that required its members be tee-totallers. It has an Egyptian inspired clock tower. Cnr Collins & Murray sts, City.*

Hydro-Electric Commission Building *The design brief said that it should represent the new age of electricity, and its Art Deco facade suggests energy and modernity. Cnr Elizabeth & Davey sts, City.*

Colonial Mutual Life Building *Inter-war building with Gothic gargoyles, Moorish balconies, Art Deco chevrons and multicoloured roofing tiles. Cnr Elizabeth & Macquarie sts, City.*

St George's Anglican Church *Built by two noted colonial architects – the body in 1836–38 by John Lee Archer, and the spire in 1847 by James Blackburn – this is Australia's finest Classical Revival church. 28 Cromwell St, Battery Point.*

Square. By 1858 it was almost collapsing and was replaced by this park, situated at the city end of Salamanca Place. A statue of Sir John Franklin, Arctic explorer and Governor of Tasmania (1837–43), stands at the centre of the fountain in the park. At the north-west entrance is a statue of the notorious surgeon and later politician, Sir William Crowther, who was involved in the scandal over the 1869 mutilation of the body of Tasmanian Aboriginal William Lanne.

Corner of Macquarie and Murray streets

This intersection, once the administrative centre of Hobart, has colonial sandstone buildings on each corner. **St David's Cathedral**, on one corner, dates back to 1868 when it was built to replace an earlier cathedral built in 1817. The present cathedral was substantially rebuilt in 1909 and features a parquetry floor of Tasmanian blackwood and stringy-bark laid over Huon pine. Across Macquarie Street are the 1836 **Treasury Buildings**, designed by colonial architect John Lee Archer. These are still used as government offices. Diagonally opposite the cathedral stands the 1875 Henry Hunter-designed **Derwent and Tamar Building**. Stocks used to be erected outside this building, and the gallows of the nearby Hobart Gaol were visible from the street. Across Murray Street, **Hadley's Hotel** stands on a site where there have been hotels since the Golden Anchor opened in 1834. Picturesque views can be seen from this remarkable corner – down Macquarie Street to the **Cenotaph** in the distance, past the Georgian **Ingle Hall**, built in 1814, and the Art Deco *Mercury* newspaper building.

St David's Park

The headstones displayed in the lower section of this park are a reminder that this was the colony's first burial ground. By the turn of the century the burial ground was no longer in use and the land had become a public disgrace. It was made into a park in 1926, and is now one of the city's most attractive classical gardens, with a rotunda and beautiful, mature deciduous trees. *Davey St, between Salamanca Pl & Sandy Bay Rd.*

Royal Tennis Club

These indoor courts in Davey Street, opposite St David's Park, are in Australia's oldest sports building, in use since 1875. Visitors are welcome to watch the curious game of Royal Tennis, an odd mix of squash and modern tennis. *Davey St; open Mon–Fri & Sat mornings; admission fee applies.*

Anglesea Barracks

Situated on the hill at the top of Davey Street, Anglesea Barracks is the oldest military establishment in Australia that is still in use. Its cluster of simple and elegant Georgian buildings date from the 1840s. There is a military museum (open Tuesday only) and some lovely historic grounds, which house a pair of 1770s bronze cannons.

Queens Domain

Queens Domain is a bush reserve on the hill overlooking the Derwent River, to the north-east of the city centre. It has soccer fields, a tennis centre, a cricket oval and the Tattersall's Hobart Aquatic Centre. In **Glebe** ('The Glebe' to locals), there are magnificent weatherboard Federation houses built on some of the steepest streets you will ever find.

Government House 444 E5

Built in 1857 from local timbers and sandstone excavated on-site, Tasmania's Neogothic Government House is one of the finest viceregal residences in the Commonwealth. Surrounded by mature classical gardens, the house dominates the riverside slopes between Hobart and the Tasman Bridge. *Lower Domain Rd; open to the public one Sunday each year, usually in Jan, phone (03) 6234 2611 for the exact date; admission free.*

Royal Tasmanian Botanical Gardens 444 E5
These superb botanical gardens were established in 1818, and today they are one of the best in Australia. There is a restaurant, conservatory, fern house, cactus house, fuchsia house, sub-Antarctic plant house, discovery centre, and the famous Peter Cundall vegie patch. Visitors can also see fireplaces in the convict-built brick wall traversing the garden, designed to provide heating to prevent exotic plants being stunted by the cold weather. *Lower Domain Rd; admission fee applies for conservatory and discovery centre.*

Northern suburbs

Alongside the River Derwent, Hobart's northern suburbs offer visitors a chance to discover some delightful but lesser known attractions. Here you can taste local wines and famous chocolates, or sample life in an 1880s manor. Take a relaxing stroll around Cornelian Bay and breathe in the atmosphere of a bygone era, or kick up your heels at night in cosmopolitan North Hobart. Further north, there are bustling shopping strips at Moonah and Glenorchy, catering for the retail needs of nearby suburban areas.

Elizabeth Street, North Hobart 444 D5
This cosmopolitan strip is busy day and night. At the Federal Street end, the independent **State Cinema** shows art-house and foreign films in Hobart's only old cinema. You can enjoy a glass of wine or an excellent coffee with your film. Further down the street there is a wide choice of casual restaurants, bistros, cafes and takeaway outlets.

On the Burnett Street corner the **Republic Bar & Cafe** is a very popular meeting place for an eclectic mix of musos, artists, writers, activists and students. There is live music every night of the week, complemented by excellent counter meals.

Cornelian Bay 444 D4
Tucked away north of the Botanical Gardens is tranquil Cornelian Bay. A popular swimming beach for families in the 1950s and 1960s, it is now a quiet waterside reserve with barbecue facilities and an all-access playground. There is also a contemporary restaurant and ice-cream kiosk. From here, views of the Tasman Bridge clearly show the

uneven spacing of pylons where repairs were made following the collision of the *Lake Illawarra* in 1975.

Walking around the bay can be an interesting experience, as Aboriginal charcoal and shell middens can be seen from pathways along both sides of the bay. There is also a unique row of boatsheds along the western shore. Cornelian Bay is popular on weekends with cyclists travelling on the Intercity Cycleway.

Runnymede 444 D4
Built in 1836, this Georgian villa has had a number of distinguished owners including a bishop, a captain and the first lawyer to qualify in the colony. It's now in the hands of the National Trust and has been restored and refurbished as an example of an 1860s mansion. Visitors can wander through the gardens and rooms. *61 Bay Rd, New Town; open 10am–4.30pm Mon–Fri, 12pm–4.30pm Sat–Sun (closed July); admission fee applies.*

Tasmanian Transport Museum 444 B3
This museum contains a restored and working collection of steam engines, locomotives and carriages from Tasmania's unique and fascinating railway history. There are also some of the old trams and trolley buses that used to run on Hobart's streets. Visitors can browse through displays in the relocated New Town suburban train station, a relic from a bygone era. In addition to the working engines at the museum, there are also occasional main-line trips scheduled. *Off Anfield St, Glenorchy, behind Northgate Shopping Centre; open 1pm–4.30pm Sat, Sun & public holidays; admission fee applies; bookings for train trips on (03) 6272 7721.*

Moorilla Estate 444 B2
Italian migrant and visionary Claudio Alcorso developed this vineyard in 1955 and put Tasmania's excellent cool-climate wines on the map. Around 12 kilometres north of the city, it has a restaurant open for lunch as well as a Museum of Antiquities displaying artefacts from ancient civilisations of Africa, Central America, Egypt and the Middle East. *655 Main Rd, Berriedale; open daily.*

Cadbury Schweppes Chocolate Factory 444 B1
Among their many other chocolate delights, Cadbury's factory at Claremont makes the 90 million Freddo frogs eaten every year in Australia. Built in 1921, its surrounding sports fields, gardens and housing estate represented an enlightened attitude to workers' welfare. Visitors can tour the factory, taste the products and then indulge themselves in the factory shop. The smell of chocolate here is to die for. *Cadbury Rd, Claremont; open 8am–3.30pm Mon–Fri; admission fee applies; tour bookings essential (03) 6249 0333.*

Eating out

Hampden Road, **Battery Point** *Casual and fine-dining restaurants, and counter meals in nearby pubs. See map on p. 446*

Sullivans Cove waterfront *There are fine-dining restaurants right on the wharves and in the streets close by, many specialising in Tasmanian seafood and local wines. See map on p. 446*

Constitution Dock, City *Excellent fish and chips from the punts or in the busy cafes nearby. These are very popular and you might find you have to wait for a table at peak times. See map on p. 446*

Salamanca Place, City *A choice of restaurants, cafes, bistros and pubs. See map on p. 446*

Downtown Hobart *Elizabeth Mall and Liverpool Street cafes are open during shopping hours. Cheap food courts are in Centrepoint on Murray Street and in the Cat and Fiddle Arcade. See map on p. 446*

Corner Harrington and Collins streets, **City** *Some good cheap takeaways. See map on p. 446*

Elizabeth Street, **North Hobart** *Bistros, takeaways, cafes, pubs and casual restaurants offering Asian, Italian, Indian and contemporary Australian food at affordable prices. 444 D5*

Sport

*The **Sydney to Hobart Yacht Race**, held in December, is Hobart's premier sporting event. Crowds gather to watch the first yacht take line honours, no matter what time of the day or night. Other twilight and weekend sailing events take place on the Derwent throughout the year.*

*As in much of the rest of Australia, cricket and footy are popular in Tasmania. There is a state-wide Australian Rules **football** league, and games are played at the North Hobart Football Oval, with the final in late September. Bellerive Oval is Hobart's premier **cricket** ground, but local games are played throughout Hobart.*

*Tasmania has an international-standard **hockey** centre at New Town, and national and international games attract large crowds. The Domain Tennis Centre is Tasmania's premier **tennis** venue, and Hobart's **horseracing** calendar is dominated by the Hobart Cup, run at Elwick in January.*

*There are more **golf** courses per head of population in Tasmania than in any other state. There are several courses close to Hobart, including the 18-hole Rosny Park, which is open to the public.*

TASMANIA

Entertainment

Cinema

There are multiscreen Village Cinemas at Glenorchy in the northern suburbs, in Bligh Street opposite Eastlands on the eastern shore and in Collins Street in the city. These are ideal for mainstream and latest-release movies. If your taste is for less commercial or foreign films, try the independent State Cinema in Elizabeth Street, North Hobart. See the Mercury for details of films being shown.

Live music

Hobart has a small but thriving live-music scene based around a handful of pub venues. For a night of great blues you can't beat the Republic Bar & Cafe in North Hobart, and for original rock and roots head to the New Sydney Hotel in Bathurst Street, City, or to the Trout Bar and Cafe in Elizabeth Street, North Hobart. Folkies will find bluegrass and acoustic folk music at the Lark Distillery in Davey Street in the city. See Thursday's Mercury for gig guides. Hobart tends to miss out on a lot of tours because of its size, but the Wrest Point Casino in Sandy Bay and the Derwent Entertainment Centre in Glenorchy do attract some touring shows.

Classical music and performing arts

When companies come to Hobart they usually play in the Federation Concert Hall or the Theatre Royal (or the Sandy Bay Conservatorium of Music, for classical music performances). Large-scale popular productions are at the Derwent Entertainment Centre. A livelier theatre scene is supported by smaller venues. The Playhouse Theatre in Bathurst Street is home to an amateur theatrical society and the Peacock Theatre specialises in contemporary works in its tiny Salamanca Place theatre. See the Mercury for details of what's on.

Markets

Glenorchy Showgrounds Market *Trash and treasure, craft, produce and occasionally livestock. Sun. 444 C3*

Kingston Rotary Car Boot Sale *A giant garage sale of bric-a-brac, second-hand clothes, produce, and plants. Coles supermarket carpark, Channel Hwy, Kingston. Sun. 622 H7*

Sorell Market *Produce, craft, and trash and treasure. Sorell Memorial Hall, Cole St. Sun (weekly in summer; fortnightly in winter). 623 K5*

See also Salamanca Market, p. 446

Southern suburbs

The southern suburbs extend from Battery Point south along the river to Taroona and Kingston, and up into the foothills of Mt Wellington. These are some of the more prosperous parts of Hobart. Around the shopping area on Sandy Bay Road there are narrow streets of cottages, many of which accommodate students from the nearby University of Tasmania campus. Along Davey Street and Sandy Bay Road there are rows of impressive mansions, and on the hills above there are whole areas of newer houses with spectacular outlooks.

Wrest Point Casino 444 E7

The iconic Wrest Point Casino, opened in 1973, was Australia's first legal casino. From its rotating top-floor restaurant (open daily for dinner and for lunch on Fridays) there are views across Storm Bay, up the Derwent to the Tasman Bridge, and across to Mt Wellington behind the city. The views are even more spectacular at sunset.

Sandy Bay Beach 444 E8

Sandy Bay Beach has been a popular swimming beach for many decades. Surrounded by some of Hobart's most prestigious addresses, the nearby mature trees, playing fields and a croquet lawn give this area an old-fashioned charm. Open space alongside the beach provides a relaxing place for a family barbecue or enough space to either kick a footy with the kids or take a leisurely stroll. There are also many options for food, with a seafood restaurant at the sailing club, a wood-fired pizza restaurant on the foreshore and a contemporary wine bar in the apartments on Sandy Bay Road.

Female Factory 444 C6

Delicious handmade varieties of fudge, truffles and dessert sauces are now created at this site. The Island Produce Tasmania factory was originally a rum distillery, dating back to 1824. Serving at various times as a contagious diseases' hospital, a home for 'imperial lunatics' and a women's lying-in hospital, it was also a female prison for 50 years. During that time it housed hundreds of convict women and children transported to the colony, many of whom died here. The nearby Remembrance Garden was created in 1995. *16 Degraves St, South Hobart; open 9am–4pm Mon–Fri; admission fee applies; tours of the fudge factory and historic site are available; bookings (03) 6223 1559.*

Cascade Brewery 444 C7

During hard times, men living on Mt Wellington would call in to the brewery and be given free drinks as they walked to and from the city looking for work. Cascade beers have been made here from locally grown hops, barley, and mountain water since 1824, making it Australia's oldest brewery. There are several brewery tours daily – bookings are essential – and samples are included, though visitors are also welcome to purchase a beer in the bar and enjoy it in the cottage gardens. *140 Cascade Rd, South Hobart; open daily; bookings (03) 6224 1117.*

Mt Wellington 622 H6

No trip to Hobart is complete without conquering the summit of Mt Wellington. With stunning views across the Derwent Valley and Storm Bay, Mt Wellington's often-snowy peak is just a twenty-minute drive from the centre of Hobart. Pinnacle Road winds up through tall forest and alpine meadows, passing underneath the sheer cliffs of the Organ Pipes. For explorers on foot, there are many tracks heading into the forest or zigzagging up to the summit. At the pinnacle there is a viewing platform and a visitor's centre offering shelter from the freezing winds. If you enjoy the icy wind in your face, you can arrange with Mt Wellington Descent Cycle Tours to plummet down the road on a mountain bike. On your way back to Hobart the pretty forest suburb of Fern Tree offers refreshments at the local pub, and there are easy forest walks and barbecue facilities at Fern Tree Bower.

Mt Nelson Signal Station 444 E8

In 1811 Governor Macquarie visited Van Dieman's Land and ordered that a signal station be erected on Mt Neslon. He named the station after the brig *Lady Nelson*. There are sweeping views of the Derwent Valley and Storm Bay, and it is spectacular at night – you can enjoy the views from the restaurant at the summit.

Eastern shore

The eastern shore is a residential area spreading along the River Derwent and south to the beachside suburbs of Howrah, Rokeby and Lauderdale. It is reached by travelling over the arching Tasman Bridge. There are small local shopping areas in each suburb, with Hobart's largest undercover mall at Eastlands in Rosny Park.

Bellerive 444 F6

Bellerive was settled in the 1820s. The historic heart of this suburb is the village situated on the hill. There is also a fascinating old fort built in 1885 on the nearby bluff to guard against a feared Russian invasion. Visitors can explore the ruins, including the tunnels. There is a boardwalk along the Kangaroo Bay foreshore.

Cascade Brewery, Australia's oldest brewery

Rokeby 623 J6

Twenty minutes out of Hobart along the South Arm Highway, Rokeby was settled in 1809. It was a productive farming area, which grew Tasmania's first crops of wheat and apples.

St Matthew's Church houses a collection of notable items including its organ, which was the first keyboard brought to Australia. Tasmania's first chaplain, Reverend Robert Knopwood, spent his last days in the Rokeby area and was buried in a plain coffin, with no nameplate, in St Matthew's churchyard. *Cnr King St & North Pde; key required (03) 6247 7527.*

Storm Bay beaches 623 J6

Some of Hobart's calmer beaches are well worth a visit. Take the South Arm Highway to **Lauderdale** or **Cremorne**, or the Tasman Highway to **Seven Mile Beach**.

Fifteen kilometres past Rokeby on the Rokeby Road, **Clifton Beach** is a popular surfing location. A further eight kilometres south, **Goat Bluff**, a cliff-top lookout, offers spectacular views of wild and deserted surf beaches on either side of the bluff.

For a swim in the surf at a safe, patrolled beach, head to **Carlton** (take the turn-off to Dodges Ferry from the Arthur Highway, after Sorell).

Day tours

Richmond *This small settlement just north of Hobart is probably Australia's best-preserved Georgian colonial village and is one of Tasmania's most frequently visited attractions. Highlights include the convict-built Richmond Bridge, Australia's oldest bridge; the gaol, which predates Port Arthur; and galleries and cafes housed in historic shopfronts and cottages. For more details see p. 455*

Tasman Peninsula *The stunning setting of Port Arthur – lawns, gardens, cliffs – and the beauty of the buttery sandstone buildings belie the site's tragic history. Other sites on the peninsula include the spectacular rock formation around Eaglehawk Neck. For more details see p. 455*

Derwent Valley *The Derwent Valley, with its neat agricultural landscape and historic buildings, forms one of the loveliest rural areas of Australia, reminiscent of England. Visit the trout hatchery of Salmon Ponds, the National Trust-classified New Norfolk, and the hop museum at Oast House. For more details see p. 454*

D'Entrecasteaux Channel *The beauty and intricacy of Tasmania's south-eastern coastline can be experienced on a leisurely drive south from Hobart. There are stunning water views, particularly at Tinderbox (via Kingston), and Verona Sands at the Huon River entrance. At Kettering, a car ferry goes to the remote Bruny Island. For more details see p. 454*

Huon Valley *The Huon Valley is the centre of the island's apple-growing industry. The signposted Huon Trail follows the valley between rows of apple trees, with a backdrop of forested mountains. In the far south, at Hastings, visitors can tour a dolomite cave and swim in a thermal pool. For more details see p. 455*

Walks and tours

Hobart Historic Walk *A guided walk to discover more about Hobart's early days and hear some great stories along the way. Bookings (03) 6230 8233.*

Hobart Historic Pub Tour *A pub crawl with colourful tales thrown in. Sample as you listen. Bookings (03) 6230 8233.*

Hobart Historic Maritime Walk *Guided walk around the harbour includes entry to the Maritime Museum of Tasmania. Bookings (03) 6230 8233.*

Sullivans Cove Walk *A self-guided walking tour of the cove with detailed historical content. Brochure available from the visitor centre.*

Art Deco in Hobart *Self-guided tour brings Hobart's collection of Art Deco buildings to life. Brochure available from the visitor centre.*

Hobart Rivulet *Follow a guide into this underground rivulet and see some of Hobart's hidden history. Bookings (03) 6238 2711.*

River Cruises *Combine a river cruise with delicious food and wine; from Brooke Street Pier you can take cruises to the Cadbury Schweppes Chocolate Factory, Moorilla Estate winery and the Peppermint Bay Cheesery, south of Kettering. In summer there are also dinner cruises aboard the grand old Cartela, chugging away on the Derwent since 1913. Go to the Brooke Street Pier for information and bookings, or phone Captain Fells (03) 6223 5893, Derwent River Cruises (03) 6223 1914, or Hobart Cruises 1300 137 919.*

Battery Point Heritage Walk *Walk with National Trust guides around historic Battery Point. Bookings (03) 6223 7570.*

Cornelian Bay Cemetery Tours *Explore the living history of the cemetery. Bookings (03) 6278 1244.*

Ghost Tours of Hobart *Comfy shoes and nerves of steel are needed for this sunset tour of Hobart's spooky past. Bookings (03) 6234 5068.*

Old Rokeby Historic Trail *A self-guided tour of the outer suburb of Rokeby, one of Hobart's earliest rural districts. Brochure available from the visitor centre.*

TASMANIA

TASMANIA'S
REGIONS

⑥ KING ISLAND

FLINDERS ISLAND

⑥

SMITHTON

BURNIE

DEVONPORT

BRIDPORT

④

LAUNCESTON

ST HELENS

⑤

①

QUEENSTOWN

MIENA

SWANSEA

③

② RICHMOND

HOBART

PORT ARTHUR

EAST COAST

The east coast is Tasmania's premier seaside destination, and for good reason. It boasts a mild, sunny climate, some of Australia's most exquisite coastal scenery, historic sites, gourmet produce, and a hinterland of peaks, gorges, waterfalls and forests. Many visitors stay for a week or two in one of the lovely, low-key fishing and holiday villages; others take a leisurely ramble up the coast, stopping off for a night here and there as the mood strikes. There are many activities to enjoy, including diving and fishing in the rich marine environment directly offshore.

The coast south of Swansea

Top events

Jan	St Helens Regatta and Seafood Festival
Mar	Fingal Valley Festival (Fingal)
	Tasmanian Game Fishing Classic (St Helens)
Easter	Jazz in the Vineyard (Freycinet Vineyard, near Bicheno)
June	Suncoast Jazz Festival (St Helens)
	Winter Solstice Festival (St Marys)

Focus on

East Coast Gourmet Trail

Much of this region's appeal has to do with its magnificent seafood. Visitors can taste and buy oysters at Freycinet Marine Farm near Coles Bay, and buy crays, oysters and scallops from Wardlaw's Cray Store at Chain of Lagoons. The area is also known for its dairy produce – try the cheddar at Pyengana Dairy Company in the tiny river town of Pyengana. Kate's Berry Farm near Swansea is a gourmet institution, specialising in fresh berries and berry products. At Swansea Wine and Wool Centre visitors can taste the pinots and chardonnays of the small local industry.

CLIMATE BICHENO

	J	F	M	A	M	J	J	A	S	O	N	D
Max °C	21	21	20	19	16	14	14	15	16	17	18	20
Min °C	13	13	12	10	9	7	6	6	7	8	10	11
Rain mm	52	57	59	60	58	61	53	51	44	56	58	69
Raindays	8	8	8	9	9	9	9	10	9	10	10	10

TASMANIA

Mount William National Park

This fairly remote park, created in 1973, protects Tasmania's forester kangaroo and many bird species. The view from Mt William takes in the sandy beaches and coastal heath of Tasmania's north-east corner and extends north to the Furneaux Islands and south to St Marys.

Fishing

The fishing is excellent along this coast, particularly around St Helens, which is the base for those planning to fish the East Australian Current for tuna, marlin and shark. For land-based and inshore anglers there is the long, narrow estuary of Georges Bay. And for those who prefer the eating to the catching, fish 'n' chip shops like Captain's Catch in St Helens and restaurants like Kabuki by the Sea near Swansea specialise in only the freshest east-coast seafood.

Underwater wonders

The underwater landscape of the east coast is an unsung wonder. Offshore from Bicheno is Governor Island Marine Reserve. Here, beneath clear waters, granite outcrops create cliffs, caves and deep fissures, which provide a home for diverse marine communities. Glass-bottomed boat and diving tours are available.

Freycinet Peninsula

This long, narrow paradise features forests, cliffs, beaches and walking trails. The beautiful Peninsula Walking Track ends at Wineglass Bay, regarded by many as one of the world's best beaches. Coles Bay, which now has an up-market resort, is a peaceful base from which to explore the area.

Experience it!

❶ **Explore** the history of the east coast in St Helens History Room

❷ **See** Aboriginal middens in the Bay of Fires Conservation Area

❸ **Meet** wombats, devils and birds at the East Coast Birdlife and Animal Park near Bicheno

For more detail see maps 625 & 627.
For descriptions of ❼ towns see Towns from A–Z (p. 460).

SOUTH-EAST

Rivers, sea and mountains dominate the landscape of this extraordinarily rich and interesting region, one of Australia's most scenic touring destinations. The coastline fronting the Tasman Sea is a long, ragged and spectacularly beautiful strip of peninsulas, islands, inlets and channels. Imposing mountains shadow the coast in scenes more reminiscent of the seasides of Europe. Two major rivers, the Huon and the Derwent, rise in the high country and meander through luxuriantly pastured valleys. A leisurely pace of development over the last 200 years has kept much of the natural landscape intact. It has also ensured the preservation of many colonial sites, from the arresting sandstone ruins of Port Arthur to the elegant houses, public buildings, pubs and bridges of the small towns that dot the countryside.

Ruins at Port Arthur

Experience it!

1 **Enjoy** *the views in Hartz Mountains National Park, a window onto Tasmania's trackless wildernesses*

2 **Visit** *Devils Kitchen, Tasman Blowhole and Tasmans Arch, dramatic rock formations on the Tasman Peninsula*

3 **Swim** *in the thermal pool and take a cave tour at Hastings Caves*

4 **Stroll** *among the treetops at the Tahune Forest AirWalk, near Geeveston*

5 **Explore** *the historic penal settlement and Painted Cliffs of Maria Island, entirely a national park*

Focus on

The convict system
Reminders of Australia's convict years – long gone in other places – are a feature of Tasmania's south-east. The island was colonised in 1803 as a penal settlement, and over the next 50 years 52 227 males and 12 595 females – 46 percent of the entire Australian convict consignment – were transported to its remote shores. Many prisoners worked on public buildings and infrastructure until the early 1820s, after which most were assigned to free settlers. Reoffending convicts from other prison colonies were sent to Port Arthur from 1830, and in the following years, a penal settlement for re-convicted criminals was built there. Conditions were harsh and escape almost impossible. Some of the state's most emotive and colourful stories stem from its convict past and can be appreciated at the Coal Mines Historic Site (north of Port Arthur) and Eaglehawk Neck, while the fruits of convict labour can be seen in many early structures, such as those in the heritage town of Richmond.

Top events

Jan	Cygnet Folk Festival
Feb–Mar	International Highland Spin-In (wool-spinning competition, odd-numbered years, Bothwell)
Mar	Autumn in the Valley (New Norfolk)
	Taste of Huon (different town each year)
Oct	Village Fair (Richmond)
	Spring in the Valley (including open gardens, New Norfolk)
	Olie Bollen Festival (Dutch community festival, Kingston)
Nov	Huon Agricultural Show (Huonville)
Dec	Boxing Day Woodchop (Port Arthur)

CLIMATE NEW NORFOLK

	J	F	M	A	M	J	J	A	S	O	N	D
Max °C	24	24	21	18	14	11	11	13	15	17	19	21
Min °C	11	11	10	7	5	3	2	3	5	6	8	10
Rain mm	40	35	39	48	45	49	48	47	49	55	47	50
Raindays	8	7	9	10	11	12	13	14	13	14	12	11

Trout fishing

The region's lakes and rivers boast some of Australia's best freshwater fishing. A favourite among trout anglers is the Ouse River, which joins the Derwent north of Hamilton. Other spots include the Clyde, Jordan and Coal rivers east of the Derwent, and the Tyenna, Styx and Plenty rivers west of the Derwent.

Richmond

This charming town is steeped in history. Convict-built Richmond Bridge (1823–25) is Australia's oldest bridge and Old Richmond Gaol (1825) retains its original cells and has displays on the convict system. In Bridge Street, an accurate model of Old Hobart Town offers a wider glimpse of the region's history.

Southern Tasmanian Wine Route

Tasmania's first vineyard was established at New Town (now a suburb of Hobart) in 1821. The modern industry began in 1958 when Claudio Alcorso set up the now acclaimed Moorilla Estate on the Derwent. Today a number of wineries fan out from Hobart, with most offering cellar-door tastings for those who drop in.

Mount Field National Park

Tasmania's oldest national park, 80 km north-west of Hobart, is a wilderness for beginners and daytrippers. The 40 m Russell Falls is a 15-minute walk from the carpark on a wheelchair-friendly track. Other trails wind through moorland and past lakes, offering vistas of mountain and forest.

D'Entrecasteaux Channel

Between the Hartz Mountains and this deep-blue channel lies a world's-end coast of tiny towns in sheltered coves. The famous apple orchards are now complemented by boutique fruit and berry farms, salmon farms and wineries. Peppermint Bay, a new complex at Woodbridge, combines the culinary bounty of the region with superb views.

Port Arthur Historic Site

Port Arthur is Tasmania's most popular tourist attraction and one of Australia's most significant historic sites. Imposing sandstone prison buildings are set in 40 ha of spectacular landscaping. Highlights are the ghost tours and the summer boat trips to the Isle of the Dead, the final resting place for convicts and prison personnel alike.

Tasmanian Devil Park

The feature of this park is undeniably the Tasmanian devils, fierce-looking black creatures the size of small dogs. The park also has interesting displays on the thylacine (Tasmanian tiger), the large marsupial officially regarded as extinct, despite unconfirmed sightings.

For more detail see maps 620, 621, 622–3 & 625.
For descriptions of ❶ towns see Towns from A–Z (p. 460).

Bishop and Clerk peaks, Maria Island

TASMANIA

SOUTH-WEST WILDERNESS

Franklin River

Tasmania's south-west is one of the planet's great wildernesses, an almost uninhabited landscape of fretted mountains, glacial lakes, majestic rivers, waterfalls, gorges, virgin temperate rainforest and 1000-year-old trees. In the valleys and along the coast are rock-art galleries and middens that represent some of the world's best-preserved Ice Age sites. The region attracts nature lovers and adventurers from far afield. The Franklin River is an internationally renowned whitewater-rafting destination, and the network of wilderness tracks challenges the most experienced walkers. A cluster of small towns – two with their history rooted firmly in mining – can be found in the north.

Top events

Jan	Mount Lyell Picnic (Strahan)
Nov	Piners' Festival (Strahan)

Focus on

Preserving the wilderness

The 1972 flooding of Lake Pedder for the Gordon River Hydro-Electric Scheme sparked a campaign to preserve the south-west wilderness from further inroads. Despite the region's 1982 World Heritage listing, the Tasmanian government pressed on. Conservationists blockaded a proposed dam site from December 1982 until the election of a new federal Labor government in March 1983. Arrests and clashes with police made headlines and earned the movement support from mainstream Australia. Finally, federal legislation to stop the project survived a High Court challenge. The historical and ecological significance of the south-west wilderness is imaginatively presented at the Strahan Visitor Centre.

CLIMATE STRATHGORDON

	J	F	M	A	M	J	J	A	S	O	N	D
Max °C	19	20	17	14	12	9	9	10	12	13	16	17
Min °C	10	10	9	7	5	4	3	3	4	5	7	8
Rain mm	150	111	150	208	215	218	270	283	270	253	187	199
Raindays	17	14	18	20	22	22	25	25	24	23	20	20

The ABT Wilderness Railway

One of Tasmania's most recent tourist attractions is a restored 1896 rack-and-pinion railway that travels 34 km across wild rivers and through pristine forests. The journey begins at Queenstown, a mining town huddled beneath some huge and ominous hills, and finishes at Strahan, a charming village on Macquarie Harbour.

South Coast Track

This ten-day walk along the entirely uninhabited south coast has become a mecca for experienced trekkers. The walk starts at Cockle Creek and finishes at Melaleuca, where you can either continue walking north or take a prearranged flight out. The track crosses an unforgettable landscape of mountain ranges, rivers, swampy plains and wild beaches.

Experience it!

1 **Go** *horseriding along Tasmania's longest beach – the 36 km Ocean Beach near Strahan*

2 **Fish** *for brown and rainbow trout at Lake Burbury*

3 **Take** *a walk around National Trust-classified Zeehan, once known as the Silver City of the West*

Franklin–Gordon Wild Rivers National Park

One way to visit this grand wilderness is by boat from Strahan. Cruises run up the Gordon to Heritage Landing, where there is a short walk to a 2000-year-old Huon pine. For a little more adventure, guided whitewater rafting trips begin near the Lyell Highway east of Queenstown and run down the Franklin River.

Strathgordon

Strathgordon is the place to see Tasmania's massive hydro-electricity industry at work. Sights along Gordon River Road include the huge lakes Pedder and Gordon, the Gordon Dam, and the underground Gordon Power Station. Bushwalkers can enter Southwest National Park via the Creepy Crawly Nature Trail.

For more detail see maps 624 & 626.
For descriptions of 🚉 towns see Towns from A–Z (p. 460).

NORTH-WEST

This region is a delight for bushwalkers as well as more traditional holiday-makers. Along the north coast the Bass Highway, intersected by regional centres and holiday villages, offers unparalleled views of Bass Strait. The undulating country near the coast is a patchwork of farms producing vegetables, dairy products, honey and flowers. Further south are the dolomite peaks and still lakes of Cradle Mountain–Lake St Clair National Park. On the west coast, the Arthur and Pieman rivers tumble through gorges and rainforest to a coastline of rolling breakers, dangerous headlands and rich Aboriginal sites.

Table Cape near Wynyard

Top events

Jan	Taste of Ulverstone
	Henley-on-the-Mersey Regatta (Latrobe)
Feb	Tasmazia Lavender Harvest Festival (near Sheffield)
Mar	Taste the Harvest Festival (Devonport)
	Rosebery Folk Festival
	Rip Curl West Coast Classic (near Marrawah)
Oct	Burnie Shines (month-long festival)

Focus on

Overland Track

The 85-kilometre Overland Track, one of Australia's most awe-inspiring treks, takes walkers into the heart of Tasmania's alpine wilderness, past lakes and tarns, buttongrass heath, wildflowers, woodland and rainforest. It runs the length of Cradle Mountain–Lake St Clair National Park and passes Mt Ossa, Tasmania's highest peak. Each year about 5000 people attempt the five to eight day trek. While you can choose to do the walk with a group and a guide, staying in well-appointed private huts along the way, most people do the walk unguided. There are 12 basic, unattended huts for overnight stays, but these quickly fill up, so be prepared to camp. Summer is the best season for walking here, but even then walkers need to prepare for all conditions.

CLIMATE WARATAH

	J	F	M	A	M	J	J	A	S	O	N	D
Max °C	18	18	16	12	10	8	7	8	10	12	14	16
Min °C	6	7	6	4	3	2	1	1	2	3	4	5
Rain mm	110	95	123	174	213	229	251	251	226	204	168	142
Raindays	16	14	18	21	23	23	25	25	24	23	20	18

The Nut
Historic Stanley is dominated by the 152 m high volcanic Circular Head (known as The Nut), Tasmania's version of Uluṟu. A steep stairway and a chairlift go to the cliff-top, where a 40-minute circuit walk offers spectacular views.

Woolnorth
The Van Diemen's Land Company, which was granted tracts of north-west Tasmania in the 1820s, still owns this sheep, cattle and plantation-timber property. Tours from Smithton include a visit to the wind farm and to spectacular Cape Grim, where the air is reputedly the world's cleanest.

Bass Highway
The spectacular scenery on the Ulverstone to Stanley section of this highway recalls Victoria's Great Ocean Road. The route's highlights include the little penguins at the village of Penguin, the Lactos Cheese Tasting Centre in Burnie, the colourful fields of Table Cape Tulip Farm near Wynyard, and the picturesque town of Boat Harbour.

Cradle Mountain–Lake St Clair National Park
This magnificent glaciated landscape is part of the Tasmanian Wilderness World Heritage Area. While the park has become synonymous with the Overland Track, it also includes some fantastic short walks. Take the three-hour circuit around Dove Lake in the north for views of the majestic Cradle Mountain from all angles.

Experience it!

1 **See** rock engravings at Tiagarra Aboriginal Centre on Devonport's Mersey Bluff

2 **Cruise** the Pieman River from Corinna, passing stands of Huon pine before stopping for a wander on the untouched west coast

3 **Taste** Belgian pralines and chocolates at Anvers in Latrobe

For more detail see maps 624, 626–7 & 628.
For descriptions of T towns see Towns from A–Z (p. 460).

TASMANIA

MIDLANDS & THE NORTH

Ross Bridge

The undulating Midland plains run south from Launceston along the island's spine. This fertile region was developed in the 19th century by new arrivals who planted crops and grazed livestock. Colonial gentry built elegant mansions, such as Entally House, Woolmers, Brickendon and Clarendon, in an effort to re-create rural England. These days small-scale wine and gourmet-food production captures something of the style of those early years, as do original buildings in towns like Westbury, Ross and Oatlands. Natural landscapes that have survived development are preserved in national parks and offer walking, skiing and trout fishing.

Focus on

Tasmanian Wine Route
The wineries of northern Tasmania hug the banks of the River Tamar, extending east out to Pipers Brook and Lilydale. Pipers Brook Vineyard, established in 1974, is the largest and best-known producer in the region. Cool-climate varieties ripen well in northern Tasmania, and the superb quality of the wines has much to do with the dry, warm autumn. Local riesling, pinot noir and sparkling wines are gaining international recognition, while cabernet sauvignon, pinot gris, sauvignon blanc, chardonnay and gewurztraminer are also grown. Start a winery tour by picking up a Tasmanian Wine Route brochure at a visitor centre.

Woolmers Estate
Regarded as Australia's most significant colonial property, Woolmers (near Longford) has buildings, antique cars, photographs, art and furniture that reflect the life of six generations of one family, from 1817 to the present day. The Servants Kitchen Restaurant serves morning and afternoon teas.

A stroll through Launceston
Begin at Princes Square, a serene old park surrounded by Georgian churches. Walk north up John Street to one of Australia's oldest synagogues, and then to the town hall and some imposing Victorian bank buildings. Continue past a restored Georgian warehouse to the elegant customs house facing the river.

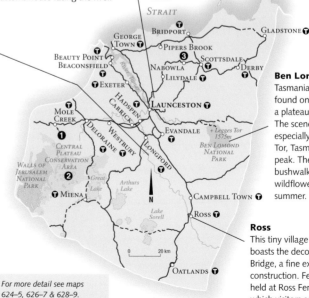

Ben Lomond National Park
Tasmania's best skiing is to be found on Ben Lomond Range, a plateau rising to over 1575 m. The scenery is magnificent, especially the view from Legges Tor, Tasmania's second highest peak. The park also offers easy bushwalking and is ablaze with wildflowers in spring and early summer.

Ross
This tiny village (founded in 1812) boasts the decoratively carved Ross Bridge, a fine example of convict construction. Female convicts were held at Ross Female Factory nearby, which visitors can tour today. The wool centre explains the other focus of this charming town.

CLIMATE LAUNCESTON

	J	F	M	A	M	J	J	A	S	O	N	D
Max °C	23	23	21	17	14	11	11	12	14	16	19	21
Min °C	10	10	9	7	5	3	2	3	4	6	7	9
Rain mm	44	39	38	55	62	62	78	78	64	62	51	51
Raindays	8	7	8	10	12	13	15	16	13	13	11	10

Experience it!

1 **Taste** leatherwood honey, unique to Tasmania, at Stephens Leatherwood Honey Factory in Mole Creek

2 **Go** fishing in one of the best trout-fishing destinations in the world – the lakes around Miena, on Tasmania's Central Plateau

3 **Stroll** through lavender fields at Bridestowe Estate Lavender Farm, near Nabowla (December–January)

For more detail see maps 624–5, 626–7 & 628–9. For descriptions of ⊤ towns see Towns from A–Z (p. 460).

BASS STRAIT ISLANDS

Flinders Island

These islands, known for their produce, fauna and windswept beauty, are the remains of the land bridge between Tasmania and mainland Australia. They offer low-key holidays suited to all energy levels – activities include everything from gentle beach strolls to gamefishing, diving and fossicking. King and Flinders are the main islands. King gets about 13 000 visitors a year, most of whom fly in from Melbourne. Flinders (in the Furneaux Group of 53 islands) welcomes 6000 or so visitors a year, most flying in from Launceston or Melbourne.

Top events

Mar King Island Imperial 20 (marathon from Naracoopa to Currie, King Island)

Easter Three Peaks Race (sailing and hiking event visiting Lady Barron, Flinders Island)

June Flinders Island Annual Golf Tournament (Whitemark)

Oct Flinders Island Show (Whitemark)

Dec/Jan King Island Horseracing Carnival (Currie)

Focus on

Fishing

The Bass Strait islands offer superb coastal fishing. On Flinders Island Australian salmon, flathead, gummy shark, silver trevally, pike and squid can be caught from the rocks and beaches. From Lady Barron, Emita and Killiecrankie several charter boats take anglers offshore for catches of all of the above as well as snapper, yellowtail kingfish, trumpeter and various species of tuna. On King Island there is excellent fishing for Australian salmon, flathead and whiting from the beaches along the east coast. South of Currie is British Admiral Reef, where boat-anglers can try for morwong, warehou, yellowtail kingfish and squid.

CLIMATE CURRIE

	J	F	M	A	M	J	J	A	S	O	N	D
Max °C	20	21	20	17	15	14	13	13	14	16	17	19
Min °C	13	13	13	11	10	9	8	8	8	9	10	11
Rain mm	36	39	48	68	99	102	124	115	84	75	60	52
Raindays	11	10	14	17	21	22	24	24	21	19	15	13

King Island produce

King Island has, in recent years, developed a strong reputation for quality produce, for everything from cheese to beef. The island's name is synonymous with award-winning cheeses and creams made from unpasteurised milk. The peerless double brie and camembert can be sampled at King Island Dairy, north of Currie.

Wybalenna

Wybalenna ('black man's home') was set up on Flinders Island in 1834 to house around 160 Aboriginal people, the few survivors of Tasmania's pre-European population of over 4000. Less than a third of the people held there survived the appalling living conditions. Near Emita, it is one of the most important – albeit tragic – historic sites in Tasmania, and includes a National Trust-restored church and cemetery.

Strzelecki National Park

The granite Strzelecki Range occupies the south-west corner of Flinders Island. On a clear day, the highlight of this largely undeveloped park is a five-hour-return walk to the summit of Strzelecki Peaks, offering spectacular views across Franklin Sound.

Wreck diving

In the storm-lashed waters around King Island lie almost 60 shipwrecks. The best known is the *Cataraqui*, which sank in 1845 off the coast south of Currie with the loss of 399 immigrants and crew, making it Australia's worst peacetime disaster. A number of wrecks around the island are accessible to scuba divers; diving tours are available.

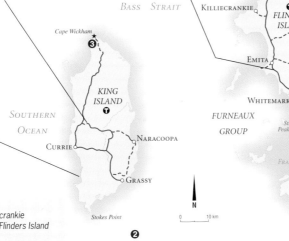

BASS STRAIT

KILLIECRANKIE

FLINDERS ISLAND

Cape Wickham

❸

EMITA

KING ISLAND

WHITEMARK

FURNEAUX GROUP

SOUTHERN OCEAN

Strzelecki Peaks 756m

STRZELECKI NATIONAL PARK

TASMAN SEA

LADY BARRON

CURRIE

NARACOOPA

FRANKLIN SOUND

GRASSY

N

Cape Barren Island

Stokes Point

0   10 km

❷

Reid Rocks

Clarke Island

BANKS STRAIT

Experience it!

❶ **Fossick** for the elusive 'Killiecrankie diamond', a type of topaz, on Flinders Island

❷ **See** Australian fur seals at Reid Rocks, a short boat-ride from Grassy on King Island

❸ **Enjoy** the view from King Island's Wickham Lighthouse (1861), the tallest in the Southern Hemisphere

For more detail see maps 624 (inset), 625 (inset) & 627. For descriptions of ❂ towns see Towns from A–Z (p. 460).

King Is ●   ● Flinders Is

TASMANIA

Sleepy Bay in Freycinet National Park, south of Bicheno

Beaconsfield   Pop. 1000

Map ref. 627 K7, 629 J5

Now a modest apple-growing centre in Tasmania's north, Beaconsfield was once the wealthiest gold town in Tasmania with over 50 companies vying for a slice of its riches. It was also the island's third largest town. Modern-day Beaconsfield is very different, but it has not forsaken its 19th-century heritage. Gold-era relics are its greatest attraction, including two massive Romanesque arches at the old pithead of the Tasmania Gold Mine. The Gold Festival held each December draws a large crowd with street theatre, children's activities, arts and crafts and food and wine.

IN TOWN Grubb Shaft Gold and Heritage Museum This museum was named after W. T. Grubb, director of the Tasmania Gold Mine. The mine constantly struggled with water problems, but still managed to produce 26 tons of gold before it was closed in 1914. Its remains can be seen at the museum complex along with a miner's cottage, the Flowery Gully School and interactive displays. West St. *Van Diemen's Land Gallery:* art and craft; Weld St. *Gem and Stone Creations:* gallery and gift shop; Weld St.

WHAT'S ON *Gold Festival:* Dec.

NEARBY Holwell Gorge This is a fern-covered gorge with beautiful waterfalls in the Dazzler Range to the west of town. There are basic picnic facilities at the eastern entrance and a 3 hr return hiking track. Access is via Holwell or Greens Beach rds; 8 km w.
Auld Kirk: convict-built church (1843) at Sidmouth with views of Batman Bridge, which features a 100 m A-frame across the River Tamar; 13 km se. *Wineries:* cellar-door tastings and sales to the east of town around Rowella, Kayena and Sidmouth. Sidmouth is 13 km e. *Lavender House:* exhibition fields of 70 varieties of lavender, plus tearooms with specialty lavender scones and gift shop with 50 health and beauty products; 15 km e.
ⓘ Tamar Visitor Centre, Main Rd, Exeter; 1800 637 989 or (03) 6394 4454; www.tamarvalley.com.au

Beauty Point   Pop. 1162

Map ref. 627 K6, 629 K5

Beauty Point, near the mouth of the River Tamar about 40 kilometres upstream from Launceston, had the first deepwater port in the area. Today it is the base for the Australian Maritime College and also a good spot for fishing and yachting. Recently the town aligned itself with various webbed, winged and wriggling creatures with the opening of two new attractions, Seahorse World and Platypus House.

IN TOWN Seahorse World Seahorse World began as a farm breeding seahorses for the aquarium and Chinese medicine market, in an attempt to stop these creatures being taken from the wild. Seahorse species and endangered Tasmanian fish are now kept in the aquariums. There is a touch pool, maritime history displays and an expo centre with local wines and craft. Inspection Head Wharf.

Platypus House This centre has three live animal displays, one with platypuses and native beaver rats, another with 38 species of Tasmanian butterfly and the third with many Tasmanian creepy crawlies: leeches, blood-sucking worms and spiders. Like Seahorse World, this centre is doing its best to protect the environment. Scientists here are currently conducting research into a disease attacking the Tasmanian platypus population. Inspection Head Wharf. *Sandy Beach:* safe swimming spot.

WHAT'S ON *Three Peaks Race:* 3-day sailing and mountain-climbing event that begins in town each Easter. It heads north to Flinders Island, then south down the east coast to Hobart.

NEARBY Narawntapu National Park Aboriginal middens and artefact remains lie inland from many of the beautiful sandy beaches of this park. It is a popular spot for horseriding and waterskiing (conditions apply) and has excellent walks such as the 5 hr walk from Badger Head to Bakers Beach. West Head on a clear day has great views across to Ulverstone. Access via Greens Beach or via Badger Head or Bakers Beach rds. *York Town monument:* site marks the first settlement in northern Tasmania (1804); 10 km w. *Kelso and Greens Beach:* popular holiday towns to the north-west.
ⓘ Tamar Visitor Centre, Main Rd, Exeter; 1800 637 989 or (03) 6394 4454; www.tamarvalley.com.au

Bicheno
Pop. 697

Map ref. 625 Q2, 627 Q12

Bicheno (pronounced 'bish-eno') has a chequered history. It was set up as a whaling and sealing centre in 1803, predating the official settlement of Van Diemen's Land by a few months. It became a magnet for men with violent tendencies, which often found expression in the abuse of local Aboriginal women. One of these, Waubedebar, became a heroine after saving two white men from drowning in a storm. Landmarks in town bear her name, and her grave can be seen in Lions Park. After a short stint as a coal port, during which time the population increased considerably, Bicheno relaxed back into what it does best – fishing – and is known today for its abundant seafood. Situated on the east coast, the town has the mildest climate in Tasmania. It is blessed with sandy beaches and popular dive spots, and draws holiday-makers from far afield. Native rock orchids, unique to the east coast, bloom in October and November.

IN TOWN Scuba diving Bicheno has some of the best diving in Tasmania and one of the best temperate dive locations in the world. Its Dive Centre runs diving tours to over 20 locations, including the main site at Governor Island Marine Reserve. In winter, divers have been known to swim among schools of dolphins or migrating whales that pass by Bicheno. Bookings (03) 6375 1138. *Bicentennial Foreshore Walk:* a 3 km track with great views, it starts at Redhill Beach and continues to blowhole. *The Gulch:* natural harbour, with fish for sale from boats; foreshore. *Whalers Lookout:* off Foster St. *National Park Lookout:* off Morrison St. *Bicheno Aquarium:* great for kids; Esplanade. *Scenic boat tours:* glass-bottom boat tours in the Gulch; bookings (03) 6375 1333. *Fishing tours:* rock lobster and premium game fishing in particular; check with visitor centre.

NEARBY East Coast Natureworld This park offers encounters with the region's diverse fauna. The often-misunderstood Tasmanian devil is here, as are Forester kangaroos, Cape Barren geese and Bennett's wallabies. 8 km n.

Douglas–Apsley National Park This national park is Tasmania's last largely undisturbed area of dry eucalypt forest. It encompasses the catchments of the Denison, Douglas and Apsley rivers and has stunning gorges and waterfalls. There is a viewing platform at Apsley Gorge Lookout and Waterhole, and safe swimming spots. 14 km nw. *Freycinet National Park:* begins directly south of town; *see Coles Bay. Sea Life Centre:* aquariums housing local fish including seahorses, eels and crayfish. Produce is for sale. Near East Coast Natureworld. *Bicheno rookery:* where little penguins can be seen. There are guided tours nightly; bookings (03) 6375 1333; 6 km n. *Vineyards:* to the south-west of town, including Springbrook Vineyard and adjacent Freycinet Vineyard, which holds Jazz in the Vineyard festival on Easter Sun. 18 km sw on Tasman Hwy. *Scenic flights:* offered by Freycinet Air over the region; bookings (03) 6375 1694.
ⓘ Foster St; (03) 6375 1500

Bothwell
Pop. 350

Map ref. 625 K5

Bothwell, a peaceful town on the banks of the Clyde River in central Tasmania, is justifiably proud of its heritage. Over 50 buildings date back to the early 1800s and are classified or registered by the National Trust. Golf is also a point of pride in Bothwell. Australia's first golf course was built here in 1837 and there is a museum for golf lovers. There are many craft shops and art galleries, and every second year Bothwell hosts the International Highland Spin-In, a wool-spinning festival that attracts entries from textile enthusiasts around the world.

IN TOWN Heritage Walk Bothwell has 53 colonial cottages, churches, houses and official buildings, which pepper the streetscape around Queens Park. Notable are the Georgian brick Slate Cottage and St Luke's Church. The best way to appreciate the historic buildings is by a self-guide walking tour. Contact visitor centre for pamphlet.
Australasian Golf Museum: displays of golfing memorabilia and history. The museum also sells Tasmanian Highland Cheeses and local tartan. Market Pl. *Bothwell Grange:* guesthouse with tearooms and art gallery; Alexander St. *Ambervale Cottage Craft:* craft shop and treasure trove; Elizabeth St. *Expressions of Interest:* art gallery featuring Tasmanian artists; Patrick St.

WHAT'S ON *International Highland Spin-In:* odd-numbered years, Feb–Mar.

NEARBY Ratho Home to the first game of golf in Australia, Ratho was the elegant 'gentleman's residence' of Alexander Reid in the early 1800s. It is a stone house with wooden Ionic columns. The famous golf course is still intact and in use. Lake Hwy; 3 km w. *Trout fishing:* in nearby lakes, rivers and streams; contact visitor centre for details.
ⓘ Australasian Golf Museum, Market Pl; (03) 6259 4033

Bridport
Pop. 1352

Map ref. 627 N6, 629 R2

On Tasmania's north-east coast, facing Anderson Bay, Bridport is a popular holiday retreat for residents of Launceston and nearby Scottsdale. It has many safe swimming beaches, sand dunes to explore and a healthy fishing culture.

IN TOWN Bridport Wildflower Reserve Best during September and October, this wildflower reserve spans 50 ha of coastal heath and woodland. There is a 2.2 km walking track that covers the length of the reserve and takes in scenic Adams Beach. Access via Main St. *Tom's Turnery:* functional and souvenir wood-turning; 31 Edward St.

WHAT'S ON *Bridport Triathlon:* Jan.

NEARBY *Waterhouse Protected Area:* offers 6700 ha of coastal bush camping, rock pool communities, sand dunes and beautiful beaches. Access via the old goldmining village, Waterhouse; 26 km e. *Wineries:* south-west of town around Pipers Brook and include Delamere, Dalrymple and Pipers Brook; cellar-door tastings and sales.
ⓘ 88 King St, Scottsdale; (03) 6352 6520; www.bridport.tco.asn.au

Bruny Island
Pop. 597

Map ref. 622 H12, 625 M11

Largely undeveloped, Bruny Island has remained a peaceful retreat for many Tasmanians with its striking landscape untainted by excessive tourism. The island is more accurately two islands joined by a narrow isthmus. On one side the coast is pounded by the waves of the Pacific, and on the other it is gently lapped by the waters of the D'Entrecasteaux Channel. After a long Aboriginal occupation, Europeans discovered the islands. Captain Cook's interaction with the Aboriginal people was largely amicable, but the sealers who subsequently came to Bruny decimated the population. Of those who survived, Truganini is the most famous. Memorials dot the island, standing as stark reminders of the grim past amid the spectacular scenery.

Bushwalking Bruny Island is a bushwalker's delight. At the southern tip is South Bruny National Park with stunning scenery and several tracks. Labillardiere State Reserve has a vast range of vegetation including eucalypt woodlands, shrublands, herblands and wildflowers. The rainforest at Mavista Falls is another breathtaking spot, as is Cape Queen Elizabeth. Check with visitor centre for details.

Eco-cruise Arguably one of Tasmania's greatest attractions, this 3 hr cruise takes in the seal colonies, penguins, dolphins, humpback whales and abundant birdlife in the area. It focuses on the ecological and historical nature of the coastline. The tour leaves from Adventure Bay daily; bookings (03) 6293 1465.
Bligh Museum: constructed from handmade convict bricks and housing displays of island history; Adventure Bay. *Morella Island Retreat:* hothouse, cafe and gum tree maze; Adventure Bay. *Truganini memorial:* boardwalk and lookout; on isthmus between islands. *Birdlife:* little penguins and short-tailed shearwaters on Bruny's ocean beaches. *Cape Bruny Lighthouse:* second oldest lighthouse in Australia (1836); South Bruny National Park via Lunawanna. *Beaches:* many good swimming beaches; ask at visitor centre for details. Dennes Point Beach on North Bruny has picnic facilities.
ⓘ Bruny D'Entrecasteaux Visitor Centre, 81 Ferry Rd, Kettering; (03) 6267 4494; www.bruny.tco.asn.au

Burnie   Pop. 18 064

Map ref. 626 G6

From its beginnings as a failed agricultural town, the north-coast centre of Burnie has flourished to become Tasmania's fourth largest city. The first European pioneers believed the Burnie area to be agriculturally rich, but discovered their error after buying 100 000 acres (40 469 hectares) of land. The high rainfall and dense forests covering the surrounding hills made farming virtually impossible. The deep waters in Emu Bay, however, rescued the community by providing an ideal port for the local industries of tin and timber. Today Burnie is a vibrant northern city with beautiful parklands and charming heritage buildings.

IN TOWN Burnie Park The lawns, shaded walkways and diversity of native flora make this park one of Tasmania's

Fishing for trout on the Macquarie River, near Campbell Town

finest. There are also animal enclosures with ducks, swans, wallabies, emus, peacocks and rabbits. Burnie Inn, the city's oldest building, is in the park and has been restored as a tea house. A brochure with details on the trees and history is available from the park information centre. Bass Hwy.
Pioneer Village Museum: re-creation of old Burnie town that houses almost 20 000 items from late 1800s and early 1900s; Civic Centre Plaza. *Creative Paper:* recycled-paper art with demonstrations and activities; tours available 11am and 1pm Mon–Fri; Old Surrey Rd. *Walking track:* 17 km track that skirts the city; start at boardwalk. *Australian Paper:* mill tours held 2pm Mon–Fri; bookings: (03) 6430 7882; Bass Hwy. *Lactos Cheese Tasting Centre:* dairy samples and other Tasmanian specialty produce; Old Surrey Rd. *Burnie Regional Art Gallery:* impressive collection of Australian contemporary prints; Wilmot St; open 1.30pm–4.30pm Sat and Sun.
WHAT'S ON *Burnie Farmers' Market:* Wivenhoe Showgrounds; 1st and 3rd Sat morning each month. *Skilled Burnie Ten:* 10 km road race; Oct. *Burnie Shines:* month-long community festival; Oct.
NEARBY Emu Valley Rhododendron Gardens Considered the city's floral emblem, the rhododendron has pride of place in Burnie. These gardens have over 9000 wild and hybrid rhododendrons on display in a natural 12 ha amphitheatre, and host the floral festival in Oct. Off Cascade Rd; 6 km s; open Aug–Feb.
Fern Glade: tranquil reserve on Emu River with walking tracks and picnic areas; off Old Surrey Rd; 5 km w. *Annsleigh Garden and Tearooms:* voted one of the 10 best gardens in Australia and comprising 2 ha of beautiful gardens and novelty buildings, plus souvenirs and food; Mount

Rd; 9 km s; open Sept–May. *Upper Natone Forest Reserve:* popular picnic spot; Upper Natone Rd; 30 km s. *Lake Kara:* good trout fishing; signposted from Hampshire; 30 km s. *Bushwalks and waterfalls:* many in area, but Guide Falls (near Ridgley, 17 km s) most accessible.
ⓘ Tasmanian Travel and Information Centre, Civic Centre Plaza, off Little Alexander St; (03) 6434 6111

Campbell Town   Pop. 755

Map ref. 625 M2, 627 N12

This small Midlands town, about halfway between the bustling cities of Hobart and Launceston, is best appreciated at a walking pace so that the beauty of the many heritage buildings is not missed. Campbell Town has been prominent in Tasmania's history: the first telephone call in the Southern Hemisphere was made from here to Launceston; the British Commonwealth's first agricultural show was held here in 1839, and the event is still held today; and it is the proud birthplace of Harold Gatty, the first person to fly around the world.

IN TOWN Heritage buildings Of the 35 heritage buildings listed on the National Estate, The Grange, an old manor house built in the centre of town in 1840, is possibly the grandest. Other architectural delights include the Fox Hunter's Return, Campbell Town Inn and Red Bridge, a three-arched structure built over the Elizabeth River by convicts in the 1830s. There is a map in Grange Park at the northern end of High Street that lists the main historic buildings.
Heritage Highway Museum: covers the history of the Midlands, and displays on first round-the-world flight navigation; 103 High St.

WHAT'S ON *Market:* Town Hall; 4th Sun each month. *Festival of Art:* Jan. *Agricultural show:* Australia's oldest; June.
NEARBY *Fishing:* Macquarie River, just west of town, and Lake Leake, 30 km E. are two good trout fishing spots in the area.
ⓘ Heritage Highway Museum and Visitor Centre; 103 High St; (03) 6381 1353

Coles Bay   Pop. 110

Map ref. 625 Q4, 627 Q13

Coles Bay is a dot on the landscape – a few stores and facilities nestled together north-east of Hobart to form a tiny town that is a gateway to the spectacular scenery of The Hazards, Wineglass Bay and Freycinet Peninsula.
WHAT'S ON *Fishing competition:* Southern Game Fishing Club; Mar. *Three Peaks Race:* 3-day sailing and mountain-climbing event; Easter. *Freycinet Challenge:* 2-day event of running, sea-kayaking, road and mountain-bike racing; Freycinet Lodge; Oct.
NEARBY Freycinet National Park
Freycinet is world renowned for its stunning coastal scenery, challenging rock climbs, abundant wildlife, and range of walking tracks and water activities. Wineglass Bay became Tasmania's most famous beach after it hosted an impromptu barbecue for the Queen on a royal visit. The park is covered in wildflowers, including 60 varieties of ground orchid. Visitors can walk to a scenic lookout that takes in the whole bay. There are many safe swimming beaches, and waterskiing, scuba diving, canoeing and sailing facilities. Check with visitor centre for details.
Freycinet Marine Farm: working oyster farm with guided tours and sampling; tour bookings (03) 6257 0140; 9 km NW; open 5pm–6pm Mon–Fri. *Moulting Lagoon Game Reserve:* wetlands of international importance with many bird species; 12 km NW. *Fishing:* Great Oyster Bay is a renowned fishing spot – species include flathead and Australian salmon. Coles Bay is also a base for big-game fishing, particularly southern bluefin tuna in autumn; contact visitor centre for tour details.
ⓘ Freycinet National Park; (03) 6256 7000; www.freycinetcolesbay.com

Cygnet   Pop. 799

Map ref. 622 F10, 625 K10

Despite being one of Huon Valley's main towns, Cygnet is quite small and unassuming. Its principal attraction is the surrounding scenery. It was originally named Port de Cygne Noir by the French admiral Bruni D'Entrecasteaux – after the black swans in the bay. However, in 1915 two local troopers were assaulted in a pub brawl and, in an attempt to avoid eternal infamy, the town name was changed to Cygnet. Now it is a fruit-growing and alternative-lifestyle community, with wood-turning, crafts, vintage car restoration and wholefoods contributing to local industry. In spring, the surrounding area blooms with magnificent wattle, apple and pear blossom.
IN TOWN *Living History Museum:* memorabilia, historic photos; Mary St; open Thurs–Sun. *Trading Post:* antiques, second-hand treasures and collectibles; Mary St. *Town square:* Presbytery, Catholic church (with stained-glass windows dedicated to lost miners) and convent; popular photo spot.
WHAT'S ON *Cygnet Folk Festival:* 3-day music, dance and art festival; Jan.
NEARBY The Deepings A family-run wood-turning company of international repute, Deepings is known primarily for its dolls made from Tasmanian white sassafras. Each doll is unique and can be custom-designed. The owner, Adrian, is usually at his lathe, turning the dolls as well as large bowls and a variety of other wood products. The gallery sells a wide range of merchandise and woodturning tuition is also available. Nicholls Rivulet; 10 km E.
Birdwatching: black swans and other species inhabit Port Cygnet south of town; viewing areas off Channel Hwy. *Wineries:* many around town include Hartzview Wine Centre, known for pinot noir, ports and liqueurs. There are cellar-door tastings and sales; Gardners Bay; 10 km SE. *Beaches:* good boat-launching facilities and beaches at Randalls Bay (14 km S), Egg and Bacon Bay (15 km S) and Verona Sands (18 km S). *Nine Pin Point Marine Nature Reserve:* reef; near Verona Sands; 18 km S. *Fishing:* sea-run trout and brown trout from the Huon River; west and south of town. *Berry orchards:* orchards with pick-your-own sales to the south of town.
ⓘ Esplanade, Huonville; (03) 6264 1838

Deloraine   Pop. 2030

Map ref. 627 J9, 628 I11

Deloraine has become the artistic hub of northern Tasmania since many artists have taken up residence. They are inspired by magnificent scenery of rolling hills, working farms and hedgerows, and the Great Western Tiers nearby. Deloraine, on the Meander River, is Tasmania's largest inland town and a busy regional centre. Although it may not draw as many tourists as some other places, it has been classified by the National Trust as a town of historical significance.
IN TOWN Yarns Artwork in Silk Created by more than 300 people and taking 10 000 hours to complete, Yarns is a 200 m reflection of the Great Western Tiers of Tasmania in 4 large panels – one for each season. Accompanied by an audio presentation and sound and light effects, the Yarns presentation operates every half-hour. 98 Emu Bay Rd.
Jahadi Tours and Art Gallery Jahadi Indigenous Experience runs half- and full-day tours in and around Deloraine that take in the natural landscape and focus on Aboriginal sites such as caves, middens and rock shelters. Tours are organised for a maximum of 8 people to ensure a personal experience. Tour bookings (03) 6363 6172. The Jahadi Art Gallery exhibits artwork from local indigenous artists. 900 Mole Creek Rd. *Deloraine Folk Museum:* showcases the life of a country publican with exhibition gallery, garden, dairy, blacksmith's shop and family history room; 98 Emu Bay Rd. *Galleries:* sales and exhibits of local artwork from paintings to furniture. Venues include Gallery 9 on West Barrack St, Artifakt on Emu Bay Rd and Bowerbank Mill on the Bass Hwy.
WHAT'S ON *Markets:* showgrounds; Lake Hwy; 1st Sat each month. *Grand National Steeplechase:* Easter. *Tasmanian Craft Fair:* largest working craft fair in Australia; Nov.
NEARBY Liffey Falls State Reserve Liffey Falls is one of Tasmania's favourite waterfalls and is surrounded by cool, temperate rainforest species of sassafras, myrtle and leatherwood. Visitors can follow a 45 min return nature walk from the picnic area through lush tree ferns to the falls, taking in smaller falls along the way. 29 km S.
Exton: tiny township full of antique shops and charming old cottages; 5 km E. *Ashgrove Farm Cheeses:* sales and tastings of English-style cheeses; Elizabeth Town; 10 km NW. *Christmas Hills Raspberry Farm:* sales of raspberry products; Elizabeth Town; 10 km NW. *Lobster Falls:* 2 hr return walk from roadside through riverside forest with lookout and wide variety of local birdlife; 11 km W. *Quamby Bluff:* solitary mountain behind town, with 6 hr return walking track to summit starting near Lake Hwy; 20 km S. *Meander Falls:* stunning falls reached by 5–6 hr return trek for experienced walkers that also takes in the Tiers. Shorter walks are outlined at information booth in forest reserve carpark. 28 km S. *Fishing:* excellent trout fishing in Meander River (north and south of town) and Mersey River (around 20 km E). *Scenic drive:* through Central Highlands area via Golden Valley to Great Lake, one of the largest high-water lakes in Australia. Check road conditions with National Parks and Wildlife; (03) 6259 8348.
ⓘ Great Western Tiers Visitor Centre, 98–100 Emu Bay Rd; (03) 6362 3471; www.greatwesterntiers.org.au

Derby   Pop. 133

Map ref. 627 O7

This small north-eastern town was born when tin was discovered in 1874 and seemed assured of a future when the

Cushion plants on the north ridge of Mt Anne

Southwest National Park

Rural Tasmania might seem remote to the mainland or overseas visitor, but this impression pales in comparison with the isolation of Southwest National Park. Tasmania's largest national park is 618 010 hectares of wild and woolly terrain – a true wilderness. Dolerite and quartzite-capped mountains, sharp ridges and steep glacial valleys cut striking profiles across the park. The dense forests bring together eucalypt and myrtle, sassafras and leatherwood, an environment swathed in deep green mosses, ferns and lichens, and tangled with pink-flowered climbing heath and bauera. The weather, too, adopts a wilder slant, unfurling fierce gusts and buffeting the countryside with rain and ice at times. Although visitors should be prepared for such a forecast, they should not be deterred: conditions are surprisingly good for photography and sightseeing.

Walking

The Creepy Crawly Nature Trail is an ideal introduction to the temperate rainforest. It is only 20 minutes return and inexperienced walkers can easily follow the fully boarded track through moss-covered forest, although the walk does have 165 steps. The track is signposted with information about the rainforest as well as its invertebrates and creepy crawlies. The starting point is after Frodshams Pass along Scotts Peak Road, near Strathgordon.

South Cape Bay provides a spectacular setting for a popular walk through lush moorland and wildflower heath. The track leads to an isolated, magnificent beach on the south coast and takes four hours return. It leaves from Cockle Creek in the south-east of the park.

The South Coast Track is one of Australia's finest and most challenging overnight walks. The section from Cockle Creek to Melaleuca takes about six to nine days and includes some river crossings. At Melaleuca is a bird hide built to observe the rare and endangered orange-bellied parrot at its sole breeding ground.

From Melaleuca you can either organise to be flown out from the small airstrip or continue on and walk the Port Davey Track. It takes in the stingray-shaped Bathurst Harbour, then winds north to Lake Pedder. Tasmanian conservationists believe that before it was dammed, Lake Pedder was one of Tasmania's most beautiful and humbling places and they are still fighting to restore it to its original state. The walk takes three to four days.

Contact the Parks and Wildlife office in Huonville, (03) 6264 8460, for up-to-date information on track and weather conditions before commencing any overnight walks.

Scenic drives

For those who prefer the comfort of their vehicles, the park has some beautiful scenic drives. The Gordon River and Scotts Peak roads provide awe-inspiring views of the Western Arthur, Saw Back, Anne and Frankland mountain ranges, with signposted lookouts. Wildflowers line the road in season, and visitors should keep an eye out for the brilliant colours of yellow-throated honeyeaters, green rosellas and black currawongs.

Note: fuel is not available past Maydena. Road conditions may be icy.

Fishing

Southwest National Park is renowned for its fishing. To the north of the park, lakes Pedder and Gordon are popular spots for trout. Fishing is allowed between August and April, but anglers must use artificial lures only and have a current Inland Fisheries Commission licence. Edgar Dam, just before Scotts Peak, is another good fishing area, as is Teds Beach, before the town of Strathgordon.

Note: fishing is not allowed in any river or stream leading into lakes Pedder and Gordon.

'Brothers Mine' opened two years later. The Cascade Dam was built and the mine prospered until 1929, when the dam flooded and swept through the town, killing 14 people. The mine closed and, although it eventually reopened, the town never fully recovered. Today its existence relies on the memory of what it once was. Tourists stroll through the charming streets to view the old buildings and tin mine memorabilia.

IN TOWN Derby Tin Mine Centre The town's major attraction, the centre is a reconstruction of this old mining village. It includes a miner's cottage, general store, butcher's shop, huge sluice and the historic Derby gaol. The old Derby School houses a comprehensive museum with history displays, gemstones, minerals and tin panning. Main St. *Red Door Gallerae*: paintings, carvings and furniture; Main St. *Bankhouse Manor*: arts, crafts and collectibles; Main St.

WHAT'S ON *Derby River Derby*: raft race down Ringarooma River with markets, exhibitions and children's activities; Oct.

NEARBY Ralphs Falls The longest single-drop waterfall in Australia, Ralphs Falls cascades down the cliffs of Mt Victoria. A 20 min return walk under a myrtle rainforest canopy arrives at Norms Lookout at the top of the falls. From here views abound of the Ringarooma Valley, Bass Strait and the Furneaux Islands. Picnic and barbecue facilities are available. 15 km SE of Ringarooma. *Gemstone fossicking*: Weld River in Moorina, where the largest sapphire in Tasmania was discovered; Tasman Hwy; 8 km NE. *Miners' cemetery*: interesting historic cemetery where early tin miners, including some Chinese, were buried; Moorina; 8 km NE. *Fishing*: excellent trout fishing along Ringarooma River north of town.
ⓘ Derby Tin Mine Centre, Main St; (03) 6354 2262

Devonport   Pop. 21 528

Map ref. 626 I6, 628 E5

Devonport is known as the gateway to Tasmania, as it welcomes visitors from the airport and the *Spirit of Tasmania* ferries. Framed by the dramatic headland of Mersey Bluff, beautiful coastal reserves and parklands, and Bass Strait, it offers a glimpse of what the Apple Isle has in store. It was established in 1890 from two small townships on either side of the Mersey River, Formby and Torquay. The early settlers had difficulties with this Tasmanian port, as the river was extremely difficult to cross and there were clashes with the local Aboriginal community. Today Devonport is a thriving city, fuelled by farming, manufacturing and, of course, tourism.

IN TOWN Tiagarra Aboriginal Culture Centre and Museum Meaning 'keep' or 'keeping place', Tiagarra is one of the few sites in Tasmania in which the rock carvings of Aboriginal communities are preserved. A local schoolteacher discovered the carvings in 1929 and the now-protected site has became a popular and important visitor destination. A 1 km circuit walk takes in the carvings. An adjoining art centre exhibits over 2000 artefacts. Dioramas depict the lifestyle of the original inhabitants. Bluff Rd, Mersey Bluff.

Home Hill Now classified by the National Trust, Home Hill was once the abode of two extraordinary Tasmanians, Dame Enid and Joseph Lyons. Joseph Lyons was Tasmania's premier from 1923 to 1928, after which time he moved into federal parliament and, in 1932, became prime minister. He is the only Tasmanian to have achieved this position and the only Australian to have held the positions of both premier and prime minister. Dame Enid became the first female member of the House of Representatives in 1943 and was sworn in as the first female Federal Minister of the Crown in 1949. The Home Hill property comprises a beautiful old building in well-maintained gardens of wisteria and imposing trees. 77 Middle Rd; open 2pm–4pm; closed Mon and Fri. *Devonport Maritime Museum:* comprehensive displays of maritime memorabilia include an amazing model of the four-masted barque *Lawhill.* 6 Gloucester Ave; open 10am–4.30pm (summer), 10am–4pm (winter), closed Mon. *Impressions Gallery:* arts and crafts; Best St. *Devonport Lighthouse:* striking icon of the city completed in 1899 and part of the National Estate; Mersey Bluff. *Anvers Confectionary Tasting Centre:* renowned Belgian chocolatier with truffles, strawberry sweethearts and Turkish-delight mice the specialties; Shop 12, Hub Arcade, The Mall. *Imaginarium Science Centre:* houses over 50 interactive exhibits about everyday science for children and adults; 19–23 MacPhee St. *Scenic flights:* through Tasair from Devonport airport; bookings (03) 6427 9777.

WHAT'S ON *Devonport Cup:* Jan. *Devonport Triathlon:* Feb. *Apex Regatta:* Feb. *Taste the Harvest Festival:* Mar. *Classic Challenge Motorsport Event:* Oct.

NEARBY The Don River Railway Owned and operated by the Van Diemen Light Railway Society, the train offers short rides along Don River to Coles Beach. On-site is a museum housing the largest collection of old steam locomotives and passenger carriages in Tasmania. Train rides hourly, 10am–4pm. Forth Main Rd, Don; 7 km w. *Tasmanian Arboretum:* 47 ha reserve for native trees and animals, with picnic areas and walking tracks; Eugenana; 10 km s. *Braddon's Lookout:* panoramic view of coastline; near Forth; 16 km w. *Tasmanian Trail:* 477 km trail from Devonport to Dover for walkers, mountain-bike riders and horseriders; check with visitor centre for details.

ⓘ Tasmanian Travel and Information Centre, 92 Formby Rd; (03) 6424 8176/ 4466; www.dcc.tas.gov.au

Dover   Pop. 489

Map ref. 622 E12, 625 K11

The picturesque centre of Dover, Tasmania's southernmost town of significance, has an old-world charm. It lies beside the clear waters of Esperance Bay and the D'Entrecasteaux Channel, with the imposing figure of Adamson's Peak in the background. The three islands directly offshore, Faith, Hope and Charity, were named perhaps to inspire the convicts held at the original probation station. The town is a popular destination for yachting enthusiasts.

IN TOWN *Cruises:* along the Huon River and the D'Entrecasteaux Channel on SV *Olive May,* Australia's oldest registered sailing boat, which departs from the jetty; bookings (03) 6298 1062. *Commandant's Office:* well-preserved remnant of Dover's penal history; Beach Rd.

WHAT'S ON *Port Esperance Regatta:* Easter.

NEARBY *Faith Island:* several historic graves; access by boat. *Walks:* epic Tasmanian Trail to Devonport, as well as Dover Coast and Duckhole Lake tracks; details from visitor centre. *Beaches:* safe swimming beaches surround town.

ⓘ Forest and Heritage Centre, Church St, Geeveston; (03) 6297 1836

Dunalley   Pop. 277

Map ref. 623 M6, 625 N9

A quaint fishing village, Dunalley is on the isthmus separating the Forestier and Tasman peninsulas from mainland Tasmania. Nearby is the Denison Canal, which is Australia's only purpose-built sea canal, hand-dug to allow easy access between Dunalley Bay and Blackman Bay. The swing bridge that spans the canal has become quite a spectacle for visitors.

IN TOWN Tasman Monument Erected in 1942 and located near the town jetty, this monument commemorates the landing of Abel Tasman and his crew. The actual landing occurred to the north-east on the Forestier Peninsula, near the fairly inaccessible Cape Paul Lamanon. Imlay St. *Dunalley Fish Market:* offering a huge range of seafood delicacies, the market has sales, samples and a barbecue area; 11 Fulham Rd.

NEARBY Copping Colonial and Convict Exhibition This museum houses a vast array of memorabilia and antiques from the convict era. It has the added highlight of one of only 3 cars manufactured in Australia in the 19th century. Arthur Hwy; 11 km N. *Marian Bay:* popular swimming beach, 14 km NE.

ⓘ Dunalley Hotel, 210 Arthur Hwy; (03) 6253 5101

Eaglehawk Neck   Pop. 233

Map ref. 623 N8, 625 O9

Present-day Eaglehawk Neck is a pleasant fishing destination, speckled with small holiday retreats and striking scenery. The impressive location played a crucial role in the island's convict past. Situated on the narrow isthmus between the Forestier and Tasman peninsulas, Eaglehawk Neck was the perfect natural prison gate for the convict settlement at Port Arthur. Few prisoners escaped by sea, so Eaglehawk Neck was essentially the only viable way out. The isthmus was guarded by soldiers and a line of ferocious tethered dogs. Most convicts knew not to bother, but one of Tasmania's more amusing anecdotes stems from an innovative attempt. William Hunt, convict and former strolling actor, tackled the isthmus in a kangaroo skin. He must have played the role convincingly, as two guards took aim with their muskets, hoping to bag themselves a large specimen of native fauna. Their efforts were cut short by a plaintive shout coming from the kangaroo, 'Don't shoot! It's only me – Billy Hunt!'

IN TOWN Officers' Quarters The one building that remains from the town's penal history, the Officers' Quarters is thought to be the oldest timber military building in Australia. It was built in 1832 and has been restored to house a museum and interpretation centre explaining the area's extraordinary history, including the story of Port Arthur escapee, Martin Cash, who became one of Tasmania's most notorious bushrangers. Off Arthur Hwy.
Bronze dog sculpture: marks the infamous dogline; access by short walking track off Arthur Hwy. *Scuba diving:* the area has a huge diversity of dive sites with the spectacular formations of Sisters Rocks, the 25 m high giant kelp forests, the seal colony at Hippolyte Rock, the wreck of the SS *Nord* and amazing sea-cave systems. Eaglehawk Dive Centre; bookings (03) 6250 3566. *Surfing:* good surf beaches at Eaglehawk Neck and Pirates Bay.

WHAT'S ON *Markets:* community hall; Arthur Hwy; 1st Sat each month.

NEARBY Tasman National Park The major part of Tasman National Park is located on the Tasman Peninsula and has some of the most striking scenery in the state. Tasman Blowhole, Tasmans Arch and Devils Kitchen are the key attractions, occurring in rocks that are Permian in age (about 250 million years old). There are numerous walks throughout the park, the full track reaching from Eaglehawk Neck to Fortescue Bay, and there are fantastic shorter walks to Tasmans Arch, Waterfall

Cape Raoul in Tasman National Park, which surrounds Eaglehawk Neck

Bay and Patersons Arch. Check with visitor centre for details.
Tessellated Pavement Eaglehawk Neck is surrounded by magnificent natural formations, but the Tessellated Pavement is one of the more unusual spectacles. The rocks appear to have been neatly tiled, but the effect is entirely natural. Earth movements have fractured the pavement over the years. 1 km N. *Pirates Bay Lookout:* views across the bay, past the eastern side of Eaglehawk Neck to the massive coastal cliffs of the Tasman Peninsula; 1.5 km N. *Doo Town:* holiday town in which most of the houses bear names with variations of 'doo'; 3 km S. *Tasmanian Devil Park:* animal-rescue centre for native fauna including Tasmanian devils, quolls, eagles, wallabies, owls and wombats. There is a 1.5 km bird trail and free flight bird show, Kings of the Wind. Arthur Hwy, Taranna; 12 km S.
🅘 Officers' Mess, 443 Pirates Bay Dr; (03) 6250 3635

Evandale   Pop. 1057

Map ref. 627 M9, 629 P12

Just south of Launceston is the classified historic town of Evandale, featuring streets lined with beautiful buildings of historical and architectural importance. Remaining true to the days of yore are the annual Penny Farthing Championships, which have placed this small town on the world map. Cyclists come from as far as the Czech Republic to participate in this race, teetering on massive front wheels along the triangular circuit in the centre of the town.

IN TOWN Heritage walk With so many heritage buildings, Evandale is best appreciated with a copy of the brochure 'Let's Talk about Evandale', which lists over 35 historic buildings and sites in the town and many more in the district. Among them are Blenheim (1832), which was once a hotel, St Andrews Uniting Church (1840) with its classic

belltower and Doric columns, and the former Presbyterian Manse (1840). Brochure available from visitor centre. *Miniature railway:* steam railway; adjacent to market, Logan Rd; open Sun. *Penny Farthing tours:* cycling tours, on antique bikes, run through the town ; bookings (03) 6391 9101.

WHAT'S ON *Market:* over 100 stalls; Falls Park, Russell St; open 8am–3pm Sun. *Village Fair and National Penny Farthing Championships:* largest annual event in the world devoted to racing antique bicycles; Feb. *Railex:* model railway exhibition; Nov.

NEARBY Clarendon House Just north of Nile is the stunning National Trust residence, Clarendon House. It was built in 1836 by James Cox, a wealthy grazier and merchant, and has been restored by the National Trust. Clarendon's high-ceilinged rooms, extensive formal gardens and range of connected buildings (dairy, bakehouse, gardener's cottage and stable) make it one of the most impressive Georgian houses in Australia. 8 km S.
Ben Lomond National Park Site of Tasmania's largest alpine area and premier ski resort, this park has both downhill and cross-country skiing, with ski tows and ski hire. The park also offers walking tracks and picnic areas in summer. The view from Jacobs Ladder Lookout takes in Flinders Island, Strickland Gorge and the rock formations of Ben Lomond. Legges Tor, the second highest point in Tasmania, also has spectacular views. The area blooms with alpine wildflowers in summer. 47 km E. *Symmons Plains Raceway:* venue for National and State Touring Car Championships held in March. A track is open for public use; bookings (03) 6249 4683. 10 km S. *John Glover's grave:* burial site of prominent Tasmanian artist beside church designed by Glover; Deddington; 24 km SE. *Trout fishing:* in North Esk and South Esk rivers.
🅘 Tourism and History Centre, 18 High St; (03) 6391 8128

Exeter   Pop. 312

Map ref. 627 L7, 629 L7

Exeter is a small community in Tasmania's north-east best known for its surrounding countryside. It lies just north of Launceston, in the centre of Tamar Valley wine country, which, along with cold-climate wines, has a variety of orchards.

IN TOWN *Crafty Little Devil:* craft and souvenir shop with a wide range; Main Rd.
WHAT'S ON *Showcasing Exeter:* 1-day festival with arts and crafts, children's activities and entertainment; Mar.
NEARBY Brady's Lookout This scenic lookout was once the hideout of bushranger Matthew Brady, who used the high vantage point to find prospective victims on the road below. Today the site is more reputable, but retains its

magnificent view of the Tamar Valley and is an ideal picnic spot. 5 km SE. *Glengarry Bush Maze:* excellent family venue with maze and cafe; Jay Dee Rd, Glengarry; 8 km SW; closed in winter, except Wed. *Paper Beach:* 5 km return walking track to Supply River, where there are ruins of the first water-driven flour mill in Tasmania; 9 km E. *Artisan Gallery and Wine Centre:* displays and sales of Tasmanian arts and crafts and wines from smaller, independent vineyards in area; Robigana; 10 km N. *Chancellor Resort at Grindelwald:* resort in Swiss architectural style with Swiss bakery, chocolatier, crafts, souvenirs and a world-class mini-golf course; 10 km SE. *Notley Fern Gorge:* 11 ha wildlife and rainforest sanctuary with giant man-ferns and moss-covered forest. A 2 hr return walk leads to Gowans Creek. Notley Hills; 11 km SW. *Tasmanian Wine Route:* a string of wineries with cellar-door tastings and sales runs on either side of the Tamar, north and south of town. Closest to Exeter are wineries around Rosevears, 10 km S. Brochure available from visitor centre.
ⓘ Tamar Visitor Centre, Main Rd, Exeter; 1800 637 989 or (03) 6394 4454; www.tamarvalley.com.au

Fingal   Pop. 325

Map ref. 625 P1, 627 P10

Poet James McAuley wrote of Fingal's 'blonding summer grasses', 'mauve thistledown' and the river that 'winds in silence through wide blue hours, days'. Indeed, the overlooking crags of Ben Lomond National Park and the lush greenery of the valley make this small town in Tasmania's east a quiet inspiration for many writers. The town was established in 1827 as a convict station and distinguished itself by becoming the headquarters of the state's coal industry. Just north of Fingal, at Mangana, Tasmania's first payable gold was discovered in 1852.

IN TOWN Historic buildings There are many heritage buildings throughout the township, particularly in Talbot St, including the Holder Brothers General Store (1859), St Peter's Church (1867) and Fingal Hotel (1840s), which claims to stock the largest collection of Scotch whiskies in the Southern Hemisphere.

WHAT'S ON *Fingal Valley Festival:* incorporates the World Coal Shovelling Championships and Roof Bolting Championships; Mar.

NEARBY Evercreech Forest Reserve This reserve is home to the impressive White Knights, the tallest white gums in the world, including one specimen 89 m high. A 20 min circuit walk passes through a man-fern grove and towering blackwoods, then up a hill for a superb view. There is also a 45 min return walk to Evercreech Falls, and many picnic and barbecue spots. On the road to Mathinna; 30 km N.

Avoca: small township with many buildings of historical importance; 27 km SW. *Mathinna Falls:* magnificent four-tier waterfall over a drop of 80 m, with an easy 30 min return walk to the base of the falls; 36 km N. *Ben Lomond National Park: see Evandale.*
ⓘ Old Tasmanian Hotel Community Centre, Main Rd; (03) 6374 2344

Flinders Island   Pop. 915

Map ref. 624 C9, 627 R1

Flinders Island in Bass Strait is the largest of the 52 islands in the Furneaux Group, once part of a land bridge that, before the last Ice Age, joined Tasmania to the mainland. From the spectacular granite peak of Mt Strzelecki, to the Killiecrankie diamonds found along the shoreline, the island is a beautiful and awe-inspiring place, but with a tragic history. In 1831 Tasmania's Aboriginal people, depleted to fewer than 160 (according to official records), were isolated on Flinders Island, first at The Lagoons, then in 1833 at Wybalenna. Lack of good food and water contributed to an appalling death rate so that by 1847, when the settlement was finally abandoned, only 46 Aboriginal people remained. The Wybalenna Historic Site at Settlement Point stands as a reminder of the doomed community. Whitemark is the island's largest town.

NORTH Emita Museum This museum, run by the Historical Society, has a wide range of memorabilia and houses displays on the muttonbird (short-tailed shearwater) industry, the War Service Land Settlement and the nautical and natural histories of Flinders Island. Settlement Point Rd, Emita; open 1pm – 4pm Sat–Sun.
Mt Tanner: lookout with stunning views of the northern end of the island and Marshall Bay; off West End Rd, 5 km south of Killiecrankie. *Port Davies:* from the viewing platform see short-tailed shearwaters fly in to their burrows at dusk. An enormous colony of these birds, spread across local sites including smaller offshore islands, breed here between September and April and then set out on an annual migration to the Northern Hemisphere. West of Emita. *Diving and snorkelling:* tours to shipwreck sites, limestone reefs, and granite-boulder formations including Chalky Island Caves and Port Davies Reef; bookings (03) 6359 8429. *Fishing tours:* from Port Davies to Prime Seal Island for pike and salmon and Wybalenna Island for couta; bookings (03) 6359 8429. *Fossicking:* Killiecrankie diamonds, a form of topaz released from decomposing granite, are found along the beach at Killiecrankie Bay; brochure at visitor centre. *Beachcombing:* rare paper-nautilus shells wash up along the island's western beaches for collecting.

SOUTH Strzelecki National Park The only national park in the Furneaux Group,

Strzelecki is an undeniable highlight. It features the granite mountains of the Peaks of Flinders and the Strzelecki Peaks, and wetlands, heathland and lagoons. A 5 hr return walk to the summit of Mt Strzelecki is steep, but affords excellent views of Franklin Sound and its islands. Trousers Point, featuring magnificent rust-red boulders and clear waters, is located just outside the park.

Flinders Island Ecology Trail The ecology trail includes 5 different locations across the island where visitors can learn about local flora, fauna and landforms. All sites can be visited in a day, but many people choose to take more time. Each site is reached by a gravel road and is well signed. Start from The Bluff, just north of Whitemark, then travel to Walkers Lookout in the Darling Range for a 360-degree panoramic view. North East River at the island's tip is a tidal estuary, and Patriarch Inlet on the east coast has a thriving wetland. Cameron Inlet, on the south-east coast, completes the trail. *Patriarchs Wildlife Sanctuary:* privately owned sanctuary with a diversity of habitats for a vast range of birdlife (including Cape Barren geese) and wallabies, which can be handfed; access via Lees Rd, Memana. *Vinegar Hill Lookout:* 2 areas with views of Franklin Sound, Lady Barron Wharf and the *Farsund* shipwreck; Lady Barron. *Bowman History Room:* displays of memorabilia showing Whitemark since the 1920s; rear of E. M. Bowman & Co, 2 Patrick St, Whitemark. *Logan Lagoon Wildlife Sanctuary:* remarkable wetland housing a great diversity of birdlife in winter including the red-necked stint, common greenshank and eastern curlew; east of Lady Barron.

WHAT'S ON *Three Peaks Race:* annual sailing and hiking challenge from Beauty Point to Flinders Island, then down the east coast to Hobart. It coincides with local produce markets and children's activities at Lady Barron. Easter. *Flinders Island Annual Golf Tournament:* Whitemark; June. *Flinders Island Show:* local and off-shore exhibitors; showgrounds, Whitemark; Oct.
ⓘ The Gem Shop, Interstate Hotel, 6 Patrick St, Whitemark; (03) 6359 2160; www.flindersislandonline.com.au

Geeveston   Pop. 827

Map ref. 622 D10, 625 J10

Geeveston, on the cusp of the enormous Southwest National Park, is driven by thriving timber and forestry industries, and slow-moving timber trucks frequent the roads. Swamp Gum, the trunk of a logged eucalypt 15.8 metres in length and weighing 57 tons, stands on the highway as the town's mascot. The other principal industry, apple farming, is responsible for the magnificent apple blossom in late September.

TASMANIA

Picnic Rocks in Mount William National Park, near Gladstone

IN TOWN Forest and Heritage Centre
Comprising 4 different sections – Forest
Room, Hartz Gallery, craft shop and
tourism information – the centre offers
a comprehensive look at forest practices
with computer games, timber species
exhibits and a wood-turning viewing
area. Church St.
Geeveston Highlands Salmon and Trout Fishery:
world's first catch-and-release Atlantic
salmon fishery with 1.6 ha salmon lake
and 0.4 ha trout lake. Fly-fishing tuition
available; bookings (03) 6297 0030. 172
Kermandie Rd. *The Bears Went Over the
Mountain:* sales of traditional teddy bears
and assorted antiques; 2 Church St.
WHAT'S ON *Tasmanian Timber Festival:*
1-day festival; Mar.
**NEARBY Hartz Mountains National
Park** The Huon Valley used to be wholly
glaciated and this national park displays
some remarkable glacial features and
morainal deposits. Lake Hartz is the
largest of the glacial lakes that surround
the 1255 m high Hartz Mountain.
There are many walking tracks through
forests of Tasmanian waratah, snow
gums, yellow gum and alpine heath and
Waratah Lookout affords fantastic views
over the valley. Self-guide brochure and
park pass are available from the visitor
centre. Off Arve Rd; 23 km sw.
Tahune Forest AirWalk Opened in 2001, the
AirWalk is the longest and highest forest
canopy walk in the world. It stretches
597 m through the treetops of the
Tahune Forest Reserve and, at its highest
point, is 48 m above the forest floor. It
provides a bird's-eye view of wet eucalypt
forest and the Huon and Picton rivers.
Within the forest, visitors can go fishing,
rafting and camping. Tickets from visitor
centre. 28 km w.
Arve Forest Drive: scenic drive following
the Arve River Valley that takes in the
Look-In Lookout (an information booth
and lookout perch), the Big Tree Lookout
(remarkable, large swamp gum), picnic
areas and the Keoghs Creek Walk (a great
short streamside walk); 10 km w. *Southwest
National Park: see feature on p. 464.*

ⓘ Forest and Heritage Centre, Church St;
(03) 6297 1836; www.forestandheritage
centre.com

George Town   Pop. 4123
Map ref. 627 K6, 629 K4

Australia's third oldest settlement, after
Sydney and Hobart, and Tasmania's
oldest town, this is an important
historic site in the north-east. European
settlement can be traced back to 1804
when William Paterson camped here after
running his ship, HMS *Buffalo*, aground
at York Cove. Ignoring the disaster, he ran
up the flag, fired three shots in the air and
played the national anthem. A memorial
stands at Windmill Point to honour
this optimism. Today George Town is
an industrial centre, home to many of
the workers in the Comalco aluminium
smelter in neighbouring Bell Bay.
IN TOWN The Grove Set among formal
gardens, The Grove is one of George
Town's primary historic attractions. The
classic Georgian stone house (c. 1838)
was the home of Mathew Friend, the port
officer and magistrate of the settlement.
The restaurant serves Devonshire tea and
lunch. 25 Cimitiere St.
York Cove: scenic cove where George
Town's centre was built, with mooring and
pontoon facilities, and restaurants. *Self-
guide Discovery Trail:* walking route through
town; brochure from visitor centre.
WHAT'S ON *Tamar Valley Folk Festival:*
Jan. *George Town on Show:* month-long
festival; Nov.
NEARBY Low Head This popular holiday
retreat sits on a sheltered harbour just
north of George Town and has safe
swimming and surf beaches. The
Maritime Museum is housed in Australia's
oldest continuously used pilot station and
has fascinating displays of memorabilia
discovered in nearby shipwrecks. At the
Tamar River's entrance stands a 12 m
high lighthouse, built in 1888, behind
which lies a little penguin colony.
Penguin-watching tours start around
sunset; bookings 0418 361 860. Sailing

trips are offered on *Windeward Bound;*
bookings 1800 008 343. 5 km n.
Mt George Lookout: scenic views of George
Town, the north coast, and south to the
Western Tiers. The lookout has replica
of a Tamar Valley semaphore mast used
to relay messages in the 1800s. 1 km e.
Fishing: excellent fishing at Lake Lauriston
and Curries River Dam; 13 km e. *Lefroy:*
old goldmining settlement, now a ghost
town, with ruins of old buildings;
16 km e. *Hillwood Strawberry Farm:* sales
and pick-your-own patch, along with
sampling of local fruit wines and cheeses;
24 km se. *Seal tours:* cruises to Tenth
Island fur seal colony, a short distance
offshore in Bass Strait; bookings (03)
6382 3452. *Tasmanian Wine Route:* many
wineries to the east of town with cellar-
door sales and tastings; brochure from
visitor centre. *Beaches:* the area has many
beautiful beaches including East Beach,
facing Bass Strait, for walking, swimming
and surfing, and Lagoon Beach on the
Tamar River for family swimming.
ⓘ Cnr Victoria St and Main Rd; (03)
6382 1700; www.georgetown.tas.gov.au

Gladstone   Pop. 90
Map ref. 627 P6

The north-eastern district surrounding
Gladstone was once a thriving mining
area, yielding both tin and gold. Today
many of the once substantial townships
nearby are ghost towns. Gladstone
has survived, but its successful mining
days have long since given way to
tourism. It acts as a tiny service centre
for surrounding dairy, sheep and cattle
farms, as well as for visitors to the Mount
William National Park, and has the
distinction of being Tasmania's most
north-easterly town.
IN TOWN *Gladstone cemetery:* local
graves are a historic reminder of the
miners, including many Chinese, who
were drawn to the area; Carr St.
NEARBY Mount William National Park
The landscape here comprises rolling
hills, rugged headlands and pristine

beaches. Swimming, fishing, diving and bushwalking are popular activities. Georges Rocks and Eddystone Point are favoured diving spots, while Ansons Bay is well known for bream and Australian bass fishing. Walks vary in difficulty and are signposted. A 1.5 hr return walk leads to the top of Mt William for magnificent views. The 1.5–2 hr return Cobler Rocks walk passes through coastal heath to the start of Cod Bay. At Eddystone Point, at the southern end of the park, stands a historic, pink-granite lighthouse. 25 km E.

Bay of Fires Walk This 4-day guided walk takes in the best of Mount William National Park while offering first-class accommodation and catering. It is run by the same company that does the Cradle Mountain Hut Walk along the Overland Track. The highlight of this walk, along with the scenery, is kayaking in Ansons Bay and, of course, bedding down for the night in the architecturally superb Bay of Fires Lodge, surrounded by bush. Contact (03) 6391 9339 for information.

Blue Lake: disused tin mine filled with brilliant blue water (coloured by pyrites) and safe for swimming and waterskiing; South Mount Cameron; 8 km S. *Cube Rock:* large granite monolith on an outcrop, reached by 3 hr return climb; South Mount Cameron; 8 km S. *Beaches:* magnificent beaches to the north, including Petal Point; 25 km N. *Geological formations:* impressive granite formations between Gladstone and South Mount Cameron. *Gem fossicking:* smoky quartz, topaz and amethyst can be found in the district; contact visitor centre for details.
ⓘ Gladstone Hotel, 37 Chaffey St; (03) 6357 2143

Hadspen   Pop. 1845

Map ref. 627 L9, 629 N11

Hadspen is a picturesque historic town outside Launceston, bypassed by the Bass Highway. Many of the town buildings date from the early 19th century, when Hadspen was first settled. The town's best-known resident, Thomas Reibey III, became premier of Tasmania after being fired as archdeacon of Launceston's Church of England. Reibey was prepared to fund construction of Hadspen's Church of the Good Shepherd, but withdrew his offer after a dispute with the bishop, who allegedly discovered Reibey's unorthodox sexual preferences and refused the 'tainted' money. As a result, the church only reached completion in 1961, more than 100 years after its commencement.

IN TOWN *Historic buildings:* Hadspen's Main Rd is lined with heritage buildings, including the Red Feather Inn (c. 1844) and Hadspen Gaol (c. 1840).

NEARBY **Entally House** Thomas Reibey's original abode, Entally House, built in 1819, is one of the most impressive

heritage homes in the state. It was opened to the public in 1948. Entally has sprawling gardens (maintained by National Parks and Wildlife), Regency furniture and other antiques, as well as a stunning riverside location on the South Esk River. 1 km W.

Carrick: neighbouring town with many buildings of historical interest. It hosts Agfest, one of Australia's biggest agricultural field days, in May. 10 km SW. *Tasmanian Copper Gallery:* sales and exhibitions of original artworks made from copper; 1 Church St, Carrick; 10 km SW.
ⓘ Launceston Travel and Information Centre, cnr St John and Cimitiere sts, Launceston; 1800 651 827 or (03) 6336 3133; www.gatewaytas.com.au

Hamilton   Pop. 150

Map ref. 622 D1, 625 J6

Hamilton, an unspoilt National Trust-classified town, has avoided the commercialisation found elsewhere in the state. Its buildings and tranquil lifestyle just outside Hobart conjure up an image of 1830s Tasmania.

IN TOWN **Hamilton Sheep Centre** This centre demonstrates sheepshearing methods and the use of working farm dogs in Tasmanian farming operations. Farm tours can be arranged, with meals provided. Bookings (03) 6286 3332. *Glen Clyde House:* convict-built c. 1840, this place now houses an award-winning craft gallery and tearooms; Grace St. *Hamilton Heritage Museum:* small museum with artefacts and memorabilia of the area; Old Warder's Cottage, Cumberland St. *Jackson's Emporium:* sells local products and wines; Lyell Hwy. *Heritage buildings:* many buildings of historical importance include Old Schoolhouse (1856) and St Peter's Church (1837), which is notable for having just one door to prevent the once largely convict congregation from escaping.

WHAT'S ON *Hamilton Open Garden and Heritage Tour Weekend:* Nov.

NEARBY *Lake Meadowbank:* popular venue for picnics, boating, waterskiing and trout fishing; 10 km NW.
ⓘ Council offices, Tarleton St; (03) 6286 3202

Hastings   Pop. 35

Map ref. 622 D13, 625 J12

Hastings lies in Tasmania's far south and is known for the stunning dolomite caves to the west of town. The caves were discovered in 1917 by a group of timber workers who, among others, flocked to the small town in more prosperous days.

NEARBY **Hastings Caves and thermal springs** The only cave system in Tasmania occurring in dolomite rather than limestone, Newdegate Cave, formed more than 40 million years ago, has stalactites,

stalagmites, columns, shawls, flowstone and the more unusual helictites, making it – and especially Titania's Palace within it – one of Australia's most beautiful caves. Tours run throughout the day, including 3–6 hr adventure tours of King George V Cave (bookings a day in advance at the visitor centre). Near Newdegate Cave is a thermal pool surrounded by native bushland. It remains at 28°C year-round and is an extremely popular swimming and picnic spot. The Sensory Trail, an easy walk through magnificent forest, starts near the pool. 8 km NW.

Ida Bay scenic railway: originally built to carry dolomite, the train now carries passengers to Deep Hole Bay along a scenic section of track. Train times change, so ring for details (03) 6223 5893. Lune River Rd; 5 km S. *Lunaris:* gemstone display and shop; Lune River Rd; 5 km S. *Southport:* seaside resort town and one of the oldest settlements in the area; good fishing, swimming, surfing and bushwalking; 6 km SE. *Cockle Creek:* the southernmost point of Australia that can be reached by car, the town is surrounded by beautiful beaches and mountainous terrain and is the start of the 10-day South Coast walking track; 25 km S. *Hastings Forest Tour:* this self-drive tour begins off Hastings Rd west of town, leads north to the Esperance River and then heads back down to Dover. Short walks and picnic spots en route. Map available from visitor centre. *Adventure caving tours:* tours to Southwest National Park's Entrance Cave, with one of Australia's best glow-worm displays. Tours run every Fri and by appt; bookings through visitor centre.
ⓘ Hastings Caves and Thermal Springs Centre, Hastings Cave Rd; (03) 6298 3209

Huonville   Pop. 1708

Map ref. 622 F8, 625 K9

Nowhere is the title Apple Isle more appropriate than at Huonville, which produces more than half of Tasmania's apples. Indeed, it is the fruit basket of Tasmania, surrounded by blossoming fields of apples, cherries, plums, pears, berries and hops. Although relatively small, it is a prosperous community and the largest town in the Huon Valley.

IN TOWN **Apple Valley Arts and Crafts** Once an apple-packing shed and cool store, this centre now houses a miniature Bavarian village complete with train station, and a scale-model Tudor village. Handmade arts and crafts, pottery, paintings, woodcraft and local produce are on display and for sale. 2273 Huon Hwy. *Huon Jet:* exciting 35 min jet-boat rides along Huon River rapids; bookings (03) 6264 1838. *Huon River Pedal Boats:* aquabikes and pedal boats for hire along river; Esplanade.

WHAT'S ON *Market:* Websters Car Park, Cool Store Rd; 10am–2pm, 2nd

TASMANIA

and 4th Sun each month. *Taste of Huon:* festival venue changes towns yearly so check visitor centre for details; Mar. *Huon Agricultural Show:* biggest 1-day agricultural show in state; Nov.

NEARBY Ranelagh Almost an outer suburb of Huonville, Ranelagh has the atmosphere of a charming English village, complete with an old oast house to process the hops. 5 km NW. *Huon Valley Apple and Heritage Museum:* comprehensive displays on the apple-growing industry and history; Main Rd, Grove; 6 km NE. *Doran's Jam Factory:* tours of the factory with samples, sales and museum displays; Pages Rd, Grove; 6 km NE. *Wooden Boat Discovery Centre:* workshop and interpretive centre; Main St, Franklin; 8 km SW. *Franklin Tea Gardens:* cottage gardens, crafts and curios beside the river; Franklin; 8 km SW. *Apple Heads and Model Village:* features apples carved to resemble heads; Glen Huon; 8 km W; open Sept–June. *Pelverata Falls:* stunning waterfall with medium to difficult walk over scree slope; 14 km SE. *Snowy Range Trout Fishery:* offering trout and salmon fishing in stream-fed waterways. The fishery has barbecue facilities, kiosk and rod hire. Little Denison River; 25 km NW; closed July. *Huon Bushventures:* 4WD tours of the region; bookings (03) 6264 1838. *Fishing:* good trout fishing in Huon River and tributaries.
ⓘ Esplanade; (03) 6264 1838; www.huonjet.com

Kettering   Pop. 307

Map ref. 622 H9, 625 L10

The area around Kettering, in the state's south-east, was first explored in 1792 by Bruni D'Entrecasteaux, after whom the surrounding channel is named. The town was settled in the 1800s by timber cutters, sealers and whalers, and the community was therefore a transient one as settlers often moved on to Hobart Town after difficult times. Kettering is now principally the launching point to Bruny Island, but is charming in its own right with a sheltered harbour full of yachts and fishing vessels.

IN TOWN *Oyster Cove Marina:* well-known marina with boats for hire, skippered cruises and fishing charters; Ferry Rd. *Ocean-kayaking:* guided day tours with Roaring 40s Ocean Kayaking company; bookings (03) 6267 5000. *Herons Rise Vineyard:* picturesque vineyard specialising in cool-climate white and pinot noir wines; sales; 120 Saddle Rd.
NEARBY Peppermint Bay Peppermint Bay is a gastronomic experience of Tasmania on the waterfront. The complex includes restaurants, bars, a farmhouse providores' section specialising in local produce, and a high-speed catamaran and cruise centre, complete with aquaculture industry displays. Woodbridge; 5 km S.

Woodbridge Hill Handweaving Studio: weaving tuition and sales of products woven from silk, cotton, linen, wool, alpaca, mohair and collie-dog hair; Woodbridge Hill Rd; 4 km S. *Channel Historical and Folk Museum:* displays of historical memorabilia of the D'Entrecasteaux Channel region; 2361 Channel Hwy, Lower Snug; 5 km N; closed Wed. *Conningham:* good swimming and boating beaches; 6 km N. *Snug Falls:* pleasant 1.5 hr return walk to falls; 8 km N. *Bruny Island ferry:* trips throughout the day from Ferry Rd Terminal; *for information on the island, see Bruny Island.*
ⓘ Bruny D'Entrecasteaux Visitor Centre, 81 Ferry Rd; (03) 6267 4494; www.tasmaniaholiday.com

King Island   Pop. 1775

Map ref. 625 R10

One of the Bass Strait islands, King Island is known for its clear air, fertile terrain and the sense of isolation that cloaks the hills and beaches. It is also well known for its gourmet produce, including superb soft cheeses and grass-fed beef. The Roaring Forties, the formidable westerlies that cross the strait, are responsible for many of the 57 shipwrecks scattered around the island. Five lighthouses have been erected along the coastline to prevent further disaster – including one at Cape Wickham, which at 48 metres is the tallest lighthouse in the Southern Hemisphere. King Island was officially claimed by Lieutenant Robbins in 1802 in a hurried bid to stave off French occupation. He proudly raised the Union Jack, upside down, while Frenchman Nicholas Baudin was just offshore. Baudin, frustrated at his loss, claimed that the flag looked as if 'it was hanging out to dry' and that he had 'no intention of annexing a country already inhabited by savages'.

NORTH King Island Dairy Internationally recognised for its award-winning cheeses, King Island Dairy has a Fromagerie Tasting Room where visitors can sample the excellent range of brie, camembert, cheddar, washed rind, triple cream and many others. The cows graze year-round, which makes their milk better for cheese production. Loorana. Closed Sat.
Lavinia Nature Reserve: 6400 ha of ocean beaches, heath, dunes, wetland bird habitats, lagoons, and a rare suspended lake formation. Lavinia Point has a popular surfing beach. North-east.
Cape Wickham: lighthouse perched upon rugged cliffs; north of Egg Lagoon. *Fishing:* excellent salmon, flathead and whiting fishing from east-coast beaches.
SOUTH Reid Rocks Nature Reserve King Island's seal community was decimated in the 19th century by the sealing industry, but today visitors can take a boat out to Reid Rocks to see thriving seal and sea elephant colonies. The boat departs from Grassy. Warrana Fishing Charters; bookings (03) 6462 1781.
Currie: main town on King Island, on the west coast (with lighthouse). *King Island Historical Society Museum:* memorabilia of the island; Lighthouse St, Currie; open 2pm–4pm daily in summer, closed in winter. *Penguins:* little penguins return to shore at dusk at Grassy in the south-east. *Seal Rocks State Reserve:* covers 800 ha with the calcified forest and stunning cliffs at Seal Rocks. *King Island Kelp Craft:* specialising in a unique form of handcraft using bull kelp as a medium, with displays and sales; 6 Currie Rd, Grassy. *The Boathouse Gallery:* displays and sales of pottery, sculptures and paintings, plus cafe; Edward St, Currie. *Observatory:* tours when sky is clear; Rifle Range Rd, Currie. *King Island Maritime Trail:* track with interpretive signs takes in sites where

Cattle on King Island

shipwrecks have occurred; details from visitor centre. *Naracoopa:* pleasant seaside town with growing tourist industry; east. *Tours:* full- and half-day tours of the island run by King Island Coaches; bookings (03) 6462 1138. *Diving:* divers can explore wrecks of the *Cataraqui* (1845) and *Neva* (1835), among others; bookings (03) 6461 1133. *Fishing:* morwong, warehou, yellowtail kingfish and squid fishing at British Admiral Reef; south of Currie.

WHAT'S ON *King Island Imperial 20:* marathon from Naracoopa to Currie; Mar. *Queenscliff to Grassy Yacht Race:* Easter. *King Island Horseracing Carnival:* Currie; Dec/Jan.
ⓘ The Trend, Edward St, Currie; 1800 645 014 or (03) 6462 1355; www.kingisland.org.au

Kingston   Pop. 7254

Map ref. 622 H7, 625 L9

Almost an outer suburb of Hobart, the pleasant seaside town of Kingston sits just beyond the city limits. Its literary claim to fame is that Nobel Laureate Patrick White holidayed at Kingston Beach as a child.

IN TOWN Australian Antarctic Headquarters The Australian Antarctic Headquarters houses displays on the dramatic events of Antarctic exploration, including historic photographs, and items such as Sir Douglas Mawson's sledge. Channel Hwy; open Mon–Fri.

WHAT'S ON *Market:* Coles carpark; Sun. *Olie Bollen Festival:* Dutch festival; Oct.

NEARBY Shot Tower This tower, one of the state's most historic industrial buildings (with a National Trust 'A' classification), was completed in 1870. There are wonderful views of the Derwent Estuary from the top of the 66 m structure and at the base there is a museum and a craft shop. Channel Hwy, Taroona; 4 km NE.
Kingston Beach: safe swimming beach at the mouth of the River Derwent; 3 km SE. *Kingston Beach Golf Course:* well-regarded course with specific holes picked by international players as their favourites; Channel Hwy. *Boronia Hill Flora Trail:* 2 km track follows ridge line between Kingston and Blackmans Bay through remnant bush; begins at end of Jindabyne Rd, Kingston. *Blackmans Bay blowhole:* small blowhole at the northern end of the beach that is spectacular in stormy weather; Blowhole Rd; 7 km S. *Alum Cliff walk:* spectacular walk from Browns River area along the coastal cliffs to Taroona. *Train:* 1950s passenger train (non-operational) with tearooms in the buffet car, adjacent antique sales and Sun market; Margate; 9 km S. *Tinderbox Marine Reserve:* follow the underwater snorkel trail; Tinderbox; 11 km S. *Scenic drives:* south through Blackmans Bay, Tinderbox and Howden, with magnificent views of Droughty

Point, South Arm Peninsula, Storm Bay and Bruny Island from Piersons Point. *Fishing:* good fishing at Browns River. Red Tag Trout runs tours from Kingston; bookings (03) 6229 5896. *Horseriding:* trail rides at Cheval Equitation; bookings (03) 6229 4303.
ⓘ Council offices, 15 Channel Hwy; (03) 6211 8200; www.kingborough. tas.gov.au

Latrobe   Pop. 2689

Map ref. 626 I7, 628 E6

Latrobe was once Tasmania's third largest settlement with inns, hotels, a hospital and no less than three newspapers in circulation. It was the best place to cross the Mersey River, which meant that it became the highest profile town on the north coast, ahead of its close neighbour, Devonport. Since the early 19th century, however, Latrobe has ceded its importance as a port town and relaxed into a gentler pace.

IN TOWN Australian Axeman's Hall of Fame This attraction honours the region's renowned axemen and details the role of the town in the creation of woodchop competition. The facility also houses a cafe and gift shop selling local crafts and souvenirs. 1 Bells Pde.
Court House Museum: local folk museum with over 600 prints and photographs in a heritage building; Gilbert St; open 2pm–5pm Fri and Sun. *Sherwood Hall Museum:* original home of pioneering couple Thomas Johnson and Dolly Dalrymple; Bells Parade; open 10am–2pm Tues, Thurs and Sat. *Foster at the Lucas:* exhibition about Dave Foster, multiple world-woodchop champion; 46 Gilbert St. *Anvers Confectionary:* factory of well-known Belgian chocolatier, this outlet has tastings and sales of premium chocolates, fudges and pralines; 9025 Bass Hwy. *Sheean Memorial Walk:* 3 km return walk commemorating local soldiers and WW II hero; Gilbert St. *Bells Parade Reserve:* beautiful picnic ground along riverbank where town's docks were once located; River Rd. *Historical walk:* starts at western end of Gilbert St and turns into Hamilton St; *Let's Talk About Latrobe* brochure from visitor centre.

WHAT'S ON *Markets:* Gilbert St; 7am–3pm Sun. *Henley-on-the-Mersey regatta:* Jan. *Tasmanian Country Music Festival:* Mar. *Latrobe Wheel Race:* prestige cycling event; Dec. *Latrobe Gift footrace:* Dec.

NEARBY Warrawee Forest Reserve Warrawee is an excellent place to view platypuses and a popular spot for swimming, bushwalking and barbecues. A 5 km walking track winds through sclerophyll forest and a boardwalk has been installed around the lake to allow disabled access to trout fishing. Tours are run by LandCare; bookings (03) 6426 2877. 3 km S.

Henry Somerset Orchid Reserve: over 40 native orchids and other rare flora; Railton Rd; 7 km S.
ⓘ Shop 1, 70 Gilbert St; (03) 6426 2693

Launceston   Pop. 68 088

Map ref. 627 L8, 629 O10

Although it is Tasmania's second largest city and a busy tourist centre, Launceston retains a relaxed atmosphere. It lies nestled in hilly country where the Tamar, North Esk and South Esk rivers meet and, reputedly, has the highest concentration of 19th-century buildings in Australia. The magnificent parks and gardens give good cause for its nickname of Tasmania's Garden City.

IN TOWN Cataract Gorge This spectacular gorge is one of Launceston's outstanding natural attractions. Historic Kings Bridge spans the Tamar River at the entrance to the gorge. Above the cliffs on the north side of the gorge is an elegant Victorian park with lawns, European trees, peacocks and a restaurant. The world's longest single-span chairlift and a suspension bridge link this area to first basin lawns on the south side, which has a swimming pool and a kiosk. Walks and self-guide nature trails run on both sides of the gorge.
Penny Royal World The 19th century springs to life in this working replica of a gunpowder mill and surrounding buildings, which include a tavern, museum, watermill, cornmill and windmill. Originally located near Cressy, these structures were moved stone by stone to Launceston. A historic Launceston tram links the watermill and the windmill. Paterson St.
Queen Victoria Museum and Art Gallery This is considered one of the best regional museums in Australia, with permanent exhibits on Aboriginal and convict history, Tasmanian flora and fauna, and many temporary exhibitions. Other features include a strong collection of colonial art, a Chinese joss house, a blacksmith shop and the Launceston Planetarium. Located at two venues – Wellington St and Invermay Rd. *Seaport:* new riverside complex with restaurants, shops and a hotel. *Boags Brewery:* guided or self-guide tours of the brewery; William St. *National Automobile Museum:* displays over 40 fully restored classic vehicles; Cimitiere St. *City Park:* 5 ha park with European deciduous trees, the John Hart conservatory, a kangaroo enclosure and a monkey island; cnr Tamar and Brisbane sts. *Design Centre of Tasmania:* shows contemporary art and craft, specialising in wood design; City Park. *Waverley Woollen Mills:* Australia's oldest woollen mill, with tours and showroom; Waverley Rd; open Mon–Fri. *Historical walk:* takes in 25 places of historical importance in central Launceston including Morton House, Milton Hall and Princes Square,

Historic buildings in Launceston, including the disused gasworks building

where fountain was changed from a half-naked nymph to a pineapple after locals objected; brochure from visitor centre. *Old Umbrella Shop:* unique 1860s shop preserved by the National Trust and housing a gift shop and information centre; George St. *Aquarius Roman Baths:* relaxation centre with Tepidarium (warm bath), Caldarium (hot bath), Spa Alveus (therapeutic spa) and hot rooms; George St; open 9am–9pm. *Ritchies Mill:* contemporary art and craft; Paterson St. *Launceston Federal Country Club Casino:* gambling, golf, and other country club activities; Country Club Ave. *Scenic flights:* Tasmanian Aero Club at Launceston Airport; bookings (03) 6391 8330. *Skydiving:* Tandemanias run skydives from the airport; bookings 0418 550 859. **WHAT'S ON** *Launceston Cup:* state's biggest race day; Feb. *Festivale:* food and wine; Feb. *Launceston Horticultural Society Spring Show:* Sept. *Royal National Show:* Oct. *Tasmanian Poetry Festival:* Oct. *Tamar Valley Classic:* yacht race; Nov. **NEARBY Franklin House** A National Trust-listed Georgian building, Franklin House was built by convicts in 1838 for a Launceston brewer. It is furnished elaborately with period pieces and is a popular historical attraction. 6 km s. *Punchbowl Reserve:* spectacular park with rhododendron plantation, a small gorge and native and European fauna in natural surroundings; 5 km sw. *Trevallyn Dam:* good picnic spot with trail rides, kayaking and walking tracks; 6 km w. *Cable hang-gliding:* Australia's only cable hang-gliding simulator; Reatta Rd; 6 km w; closed weekdays May–Nov. *Launceston Lakes Trout Fishery and Wildlife Park:* Tasmanian devils, emus, wallabies and other native fauna. Good fly-fishing in the lakes with tuition available. 17 km w. *Tasmanian Wine Route:* numerous vineyards to the north-east of town open for tastings and sales; brochure available from visitor centre.

ⓘ Cnr St John and Cimitiere sts; 1800 651 827 or (03) 6336 3133; www.gatewaytas.com.au

Lilydale   Pop. 321
Map ref. 627 M7, 629 P6

Originally called Germantown, the small north-eastern township of Lilydale is better known for the 'Englishness' of its gardens and the almost French quality of its fertile countryside. Yet the bushwalks through surrounding forest reserves and past lush waterfalls are distinctly Australian, with eucalypt and native temperate rainforests lining the trails.
IN TOWN *Painted Poles:* scattered throughout village centre are 15 hydro poles painted by professional and community artists to show the local history.
NEARBY Lilydale Falls Situated within the temperate rainforest of Lilydale Park, the waterfall is at the end of a pleasant 5 min walk through ferns and eucalypts. A picnic area and playground are on-site, as well as 2 oak trees planted in 1937 from acorns picked near Windsor Castle in England to commemorate the coronation of King George VI. 3 km n. *Walker Rhododendron Reserve:* 12 ha park reputed to have the best rhododendron display in Australia. Other species are also on display. Lalla; 4 km w. *Appleshed:* tea house with local art and craft; Lalla; 4 km w. *Tasmanian Wine Route:* numerous vineyards between Lilydale and Pipers Brook include Providence (4 km n), Clover Hill (12 km n) and Brook Eden (15 km n); brochure from visitor centre. *Hollybank Forest Reserve:* 140 ha forest reserve with arboretum, picnic facilities shaded by ash and pine trees, and information centre with details on walking tracks; marked turn-off near Underwood; 5 km s. *Mt Arthur:* 3 hr return scenic walk to summit (1187 m); 20 km se.

ⓘ Launceston Travel and Information Centre, cnr St John and Cimitiere sts, Launceston; 1800 651 827 or (03) 6336 3133; www.gatewaytas.com.au

Longford   Pop. 2818
Map ref. 627 L9, 629 N13

Longford was established when a large number of settlers from Norfolk Island were given land grants in the area in 1813. Fittingly, the district became known as Norfolk Plains, while the settlement itself was called Latour. Today Longford is classified as a historic town and serves the rich agricultural district just south of Launceston.
IN TOWN **Historic buildings** These include the Queen's Arms (1835) in Wellington St, Longford House (1839) in Catherine St and the Racecourse Hotel (1840s) in Wellington St, which was originally built as a railway station, then used as a hospital and later a pub, and in which a patron was murdered after stealing and swallowing two gold sovereigns from local farmhands. The Racecourse Hotel is now a guesthouse and restaurant. Also on Wellington St is Christ Church, a beautiful sandstone building dating back to 1839 with outstanding stained-glass windows, pioneer gravestones and a clock and bell presented by George VI.
Tom Roberts Gallery: old prints, books and information on this Australian artist, who lived here; Marlborough St. *Walk:* track along the South Esk River. *The Village Green:* originally the site of the town market, now a picnic and barbecue spot; cnr Wellington and Archer sts.
WHAT'S ON *Longford Picnic Day Races:* held at the oldest operating racecourse in Australia; Jan. *Blessing of the Harvest Festival:* celebration of the rural tradition with parade and Sheaf Tossing Championships; Mar.

NEARBY Woolmers Estate An excellent example of 19th-century rural settlement in the area, Woolmers was built c. 1817 by the Archer family, who lived there for 6 generations. Tours of the house, the outbuildings, the gardens and the National Rose Garden are conducted daily and the Servants Kitchen restaurant serves morning and afternoon teas. The estate offers a glimpse into the social structure of a colonial pastoral estate. 5 km s. *Brickendon:* historic Georgian homestead built in 1824, now a working farm and historic farm village; 2 km s; open Wed–Sun, June–July; Tues–Sun, Sept–May. *Perth:* small town with historic buildings, including Eskleigh and Jolly Farmer Inn, and market on Sun mornings; 5 km NE. *Tasmanian Honey Company:* tastings and sales of excellent range of honeys including leatherwood and flavoured varieties; 25a Main Rd, Perth; 5 km NE. *Woodstock Lagoon Wildlife Sanctuary:* 150 ha sanctuary for nesting and breeding waterfowl; 9 km w. *Cressy:* good fly-fishing at Brumby's Creek, especially in Nov when mayflies hatch; 10 km s. ⓘ Longford Gallery Cafe, 1 Marlborough St; (03) 6391 1181

Miena   Pop. 70

Map ref. 625 J2, 627 J12

This small settlement on the shores of Great Lake on Tasmania's Central Plateau has been popular with anglers since brown trout were released into the lake in 1870. The Aboriginal name (pronounced 'my-enna') translates to 'lagoon-like'. The surrounding region, known as the Lake Country, can become incredibly cold, with snow and road closures possible, even in summer.
NEARBY Fishing The 22 km Great Lake, which sprawls north of town, is the second largest freshwater lake in Australia and has excellent trout fishing. But Arthurs Lake, 23 km E, is said to be even better. The Highland Dun mayflies that hatch in summer generate an abundance of speckled brown trout, which draws both Australian and international fly-fishing enthusiasts to the area. West of Liawenee (about 7 km N) are many more locations for fly-fishing in the isolated lakes and tarns of the Central Plateau Conservation Area (4WD recommended for several lakes, while some are accessible only to experienced bushwalkers). Lakes are closed over winter.
Bushwalking: along the shores of Great Lake. *Circle of Life:* bronze sculptures by Steven Walker, each representing an aspect of the region's history and character; Steppes; 27 km SE. *Waddamana Power Museum:* housed in the first station built by the Hydro-Electric Corporation, it includes history of hydro-electricity in Tasmania; 33 km s. *Lake St Clair:* a boat service from Cynthia Bay on Lake St Clair provides access to the north of the lake

and to the renowned 85 km Overland Track, which passes through the spectacular Cradle Mountain–Lake St Clair National Park. 63 km w; *for more details see feature on p. 481.*
ⓘ Great Lake Hotel, Great Lake Hwy; (03) 6259 8163

Mole Creek   Pop. 211

Map ref. 626 I9, 628 E12

Mole Creek is named after the nearby creek that 'burrows' underground. Most visitors to the area come to explore the network of limestone caves in Mole Creek Karst National Park. The unique honey from the leatherwood tree, which grows only in the west-coast rainforests of Tasmania, is also a drawcard. Each summer, apiarists transport hives to the nearby leatherwood forests.
IN TOWN Stephens Leatherwood Honey Factory In the home of Tasmania's unique aromatic honey, visitors can see clover and leatherwood honey being extracted and bottled. Tastings and sales are available. 25 Pioneer Dr. Open Mon–Fri. *Mole Creek Tiger Bar:* local hotel with information and memorabilia on Tasmanian tiger; Pioneer Dr. *Mole Creek Bird Park:* aviaries with exotic birds; Caveside Rd.
NEARBY Mole Creek Karst National Park Set in the forests of the Western Tiers, this national park protects the Marakoopa and King Solomons caves, spectacular caverns of calcite formations created by underground streams. Marakoopa Cave has a magnificent glow-worm display, while King Solomons Cave offers coloured stalagmites and stalactites and sparkling calcite crystals. Guided tours daily; details (03) 6363 5182. 13 km w.
Alum Cliffs Gorge: spectacular 30 min return walk; 3 km NE. *Trowunna Wildlife Park:* great opportunity to see Tasmanian devils and other native fauna; 4 km E. *The Honey Farm:* over 50 flavours of honey and an interactive bee display; Chudleigh; 8 km E;

open Sun–Fri. *Devils Gullet State Reserve:* World Heritage Area with natural lookout on a 600 m high cliff, reached by 30 min return walking track; 40 km SE. *Wild Cave Tours:* adventure tours to caves that are closed to general public; bookings (03) 6367 8142. *Cradle Wilderness Tours:* guided 4WD tours; bookings (03) 6363 1173. *Walls of Jerusalem National Park:* the park is accessible on foot only, from the end of the road that turns off around 15 km w of Mole Creek and heads down to Lake Rowallan. This landscape of glacial lakes, pencil pines and dolerite peaks has inspired names such as Herods Gate and Dixons Kingdom and is a wonderland for self-sufficient and experienced bushwalkers.
ⓘ Mole Creek Guest House, 100 Pioneer Dr; (03) 6363 1399; www.greatwestern tiers.org.au

New Norfolk   Pop. 5008

Map ref. 622 F4, 625 K8

Colonial buildings among English trees and oast houses in hop fields give this National Trust-classified town a look similar to that of Kent in England. Located on the River Derwent in Tasmania's south-east, the town was named for the European settlers from the abandoned Norfolk Island penal settlement who were granted land here. The district is also renowned for its hops industry.
IN TOWN Oast House A working oast house from 1867 to 1969, the building has since been converted into a museum that showcases the growing and processing of hops. A cafe and craft market are on-site. Tynwald Park Reserve, Lyell Hwy.
Tynwald House: charming rural residence next to the Oast House, with restaurant; Tynwald Park Reserve. *Old Colony Inn:* heritage house (1835) with folk museum, restaurant and craft shop, and Australia's largest antique doll's house; Montagu St. *Church of St Matthew:* reputedly the oldest church in Tasmania (1823), with striking

Tarn shelf in Mount Field National Park, near New Norfolk

TASMANIA

stained-glass windows; Bathurst St. *Rosedown:* beautiful rose and daffodil gardens along riverbank. Bookings preferred (03) 6261 2030. 134 Hamilton Rd; closed May–Sept. *Jet-boat rides:* on River Derwent rapids. Bookings (03) 6261 3460. *River walk:* from Esplanade to Tynwald Park Wetlands Conservation Area. *Scenic lookouts:* Peppermint Hill, off Blair St; Pulpit Rock and Four Winds Display Gardens, off Rocks Rd. *Self-guide historical walks:* brochure from Historical Centre in Council Chambers; Circle St.
WHAT'S ON *Drill Hall Collectibles Market:* Stephen St; daily. *Autumn in the Valley:* April. *Spring in the Valley:* Oct.
NEARBY Mount Field National Park Tasmania's first national park, Mount Field is best known for the impressive Russell and Lady Barron falls. Most walks pass through lush ferns and rainforests, while the Pandani Grove walk traverses the glaciated landscapes of the mountain country to Lake Dobson. A visitor centre on-site offers interpretive displays. 40 km NW.
Australian Newsprint Mills: the first in the world to manufacture newsprint from hardwoods; tours available; Boyer; 5 km E. *Salmon Ponds:* first rainbow and brown trout farm in Australia, in operation since 1864. There is also a Museum of Trout Fishing and a restaurant. Plenty; 11 km NW. *Possum Shed:* locally made crafts and collectibles; Gordon River Rd, Westerway; 31 km NW. *Styx Tall Tree Reserve:* small reserve with the tallest hardwood trees in the world, the Giant Swamp Gums, which grow to 92 m; 73 km W via Maydena.
ⓘ Circle St; (03) 6261 3700

Oatlands   Pop. 585

Map ref. 625 M5

Approaching Oatlands from the north, the town's welcome is decidedly green. Topiary creations, clipped by former patrolman Jack Cashion, line the Midlands Highway with a gorilla, a kangaroo, a steam train, and a stag so realistic that a motorist once tried to shoot it. The town is on the shores of Lake Dulverton and has the largest collection of pre-1837 buildings in the country – including 87 in town and 138 within the town's environs.
IN TOWN Callington Mill Built in 1836, the old mill is an eye-catching feature of Oatlands that was fully operational until 1892. After being battered by the elements and gutted by fire in the early 1900s, it was finally restored as part of Australia's bicentenary. The view from the top floor takes in beautiful Lake Dulverton. Old Mill La.
Lake Dulverton: the lake is stocked with trout and onshore is a wildlife sanctuary protecting many bird species. Popular picnic spot. Esplanade. *Fielding's Ghost*

Tours: tours run by local historian Peter Fielding; bookings (03) 6254 1135. *Historical walk:* takes in the many Georgian buildings, including the convict-built Court House (1829); *Welcome to Historic Oatlands* brochure from visitor centre. *Scottish, Irish and Welsh Shop:* stocks over 500 tartans, clan crests, badges, pins, and arts and crafts; 64 High St; open Sun–Mon, Thurs–Fri. *Skulduggery:* mystery tour game following true crime clues around town; available from visitor centre.
WHAT'S ON *Oatlands open day:* 1-day festival; Oct.
NEARBY *Convict-built mud walls:* 13 km S on Jericho Rd. *Fishing:* excellent trout fishing in Lake Sorell and adjoining Lake Crescent; 29 km NW.
ⓘ Central Tasmanian Tourism Centre, 85 High St; (03) 6254 1212

Penguin   Pop. 2908

Map ref. 626 H6, 628 A4

This northern seaside town was named after the little penguins that shuffle up the beaches along the coast. The residents of Penguin are notably proud of their namesake and pepper the town with images of the iconic bird. The largest example is the much-photographed Big Penguin, which stands three metres tall on the beachfront and is the town's premier attraction.
IN TOWN Dutch Windmill The windmill was presented to the town during Australia's bicentenary by the Dutch community to commemorate the Dutch explorers and settlers. It is complemented by a colourful tulip display in spring and has play equipment for children on-site. Hiscutt Park, off Crescent St.
Penguins: each evening penguins come ashore; check with visitor centre for tour details; Sept–Mar. *Miniature railway:* runs along foreshore; 2nd and 3rd Sun each month. *Johnsons Beach Reef:* popular walking spot at low tide when reef is exposed. *Penguin Roadside Gardens:* originally a labour of love for two town residents, now a flourishing garden beside the road; Old Coast Rd to Ulverstone.
WHAT'S ON *Old School Market:* there are 150 stalls under cover, and a historic train from Burnie to Ulverstone stops at Penguin on market days. King Edward St; 2nd and 4th Sun each month.
NEARBY Walks Excellent tracks include the walk up Mt Montgomery (5 km S) with magnificent views from the summit, and Ferndene Gorge (6 km S). The Ferndale Bush Walk takes in an old silver-mine shaft, Thorsby's Tunnel. Brochures on walks from visitor centre.
Pioneer Park: beautiful gardens with picnic facilities and walks; Riana; 10 km SW. *Pindari Holiday Farm:* restaurant with scenic lookout; 15 km SW; open Sat–Sun. *Mason's Fuchsia Fantasy:* over 750 varieties of fuchsia on display; Lillico Rd; 20 km E;

open Mon–Fri afternoons. *Scenic drive:* along coast to Ulverstone.
ⓘ Main St; (03) 6437 1421

Pontville   Pop. 1652

Map ref. 622 H3, 625 L7

The area around Pontville (declared a town in 1830) was first explored by Europeans when Hobart, just to the south, experienced severe food shortages in the early 1800s. Soldiers were sent north to kill emus and kangaroos. One of them, Private Hugh Germain, is allegedly responsible for the unusual and often incongruous names found in the region, such as Bagdad, Jericho, Lake Tiberius and Jordan River. Legend has it that Germain carried with him copies of *Arabian Nights* and *The Bible* and found his inspiration within.
IN TOWN Historic buildings Many buildings remain from Pontville's early days, including the Romanesque St Mark's Church (1841), The Sheiling (1819) and The Row, thought to have been built in 1824 as soldiers quarters. On or adjacent to Midland Hwy.
NEARBY *Bonorong Wildlife Park:* popular attraction showing Tasmanian devils, quolls, echidnas, koalas, wombats and Forester kangaroos; Briggs Rd, Brighton; 5 km S. *Historic towns:* Brighton (3 km S); Tea Tree (7 km E); Bagdad (8 km N); Broadmarsh (10 km W); Kempton (19 km N).
ⓘ Council offices, Tivoli Rd, Gagebrook; (03) 6268 7000

Port Arthur   Pop. 205

Map ref. 623 N10, 625 N10

This historic settlement on the scenic Tasman Peninsula was one of Australia's most infamous penal settlements from the 1830s to the 1870s. Over 12 000 convicts from Britain, some of whom did nothing more than steal some food to survive, were shipped to Port Arthur, dubbed 'Hell on Earth'. They lived under threat of the lash and experimental punitive measures that often drove them to madness. This grim past is offset by the stark beauty of the sandstone buildings overlooking the tranquil, often misty, waters of the bay. Port Arthur is Tasmania's number one tourist attraction.
IN TOWN Port Arthur Historic Site Over 30 buildings and restored ruins sit on 40 ha of land, illuminating the life of the convicts and their guards. Day entry tickets include a guided historical walking tour, access to the visitor centre, interpretation gallery and museum, and a harbour cruise in summer. Lantern-lit historical ghost tours depart at dusk and tours of the Isle of the Dead, the cemetery for the colony, unravel emotive stories of the convicts. Details at visitor centre; Arthur Hwy.

Port Arthur Memorial Garden: dedicated to the victims of the 1996 tragedy at the site in which 35 people were killed by a gunman. *Scenic flights:* views of the penal settlement and magnificent Tasman Peninsula; bookings (03) 6250 1114. *Convict Trail drive:* scenic drive; brochure from visitor centre.

WHAT'S ON *Boxing Day Woodchop:* Dec.

NEARBY Remarkable Cave Created by wave erosion, Remarkable Cave affords spectacular views along the coastline to Cape Raoul. It is in Tasman National Park and is the starting point of a 4–5 hr return walk to Crescent Bay. 6 km s. *Bush Mill Steam Railway:* steam-train rides, settlement displays and historic timber mill; 1 km N. *Palmers Lookout:* views of harbour and coastline; 3 km s. *Coal Mines Historic Site:* Tasmania's first operational mine, with self-guide tours; 30 km NW. *Tasman Island Wilderness Cruise:* 2 hr cruise exploring the beautiful coastal scenery of the Tasman National Park; bookings (03) 6224 0033. *Historical nature walk:* to nearby Stewarts Bay; brochure from visitor centre.
ⓘ Port Arthur Historic Site, Arthur Hwy; 1800 659 101 or (03) 6251 2310

Port Sorell   Pop. 1936

Map ref. 627 J6, 628 G5

Sheltered by hills, this holiday town on the Rubicon River estuary enjoys a mild and sunny climate nearly all year round. It was established in the early 1820s and is the oldest township on the north-west coast. Sadly, many of its oldest buildings were destroyed by bushfires.

IN TOWN *The jetty:* popular fishing spot for cocky salmon, mullet, flathead, cod and bream. There are views across the river to Bakers Beach and Narawntapu National Park. Behind caravan park on Meredith St. *Port Sorell Conservation Area:* 70 ha of coastal reserve with an abundance of flora and fauna. Guided tours available; bookings (03) 6428 6072. Park Esplanade. *Estuary:* boating and safe swimming areas.

WHAT'S ON *Port Sorell Regatta:* Jan. *Market:* Memorial Hall; 1st Sat each month, June–Sept; 1st and 3rd Sat each month, Oct–May.

NEARBY *Shearwater:* holiday town with shopping centre and good beach access; 5 km N. *Hawley Beach:* safe swimming, good fishing and historic Hawley House (1878) offering meals; 6 km N. *Walk:* 6 km return track from Port Sorell to Hawley Beach, offering excellent views of Narawntapu National Park and coastline. Starts at beach end of Rice St.
ⓘ 32 Shearwater Blvd; (03) 6428 7920

Queenstown   Pop. 2349

Map ref. 624 E3, 626 E12

The discovery of gold and other mineral resources in the Mt Lyell field in the 1880s led to the rapid emergence of

Queenstown, a west-coast township overshadowed by towering mountains made all the more imposing by their bareness. Continuous mining here from 1893 to 1994 produced over 670 000 tons of copper, 510 000 kg of silver and 20 000 kg of gold. Operations began again in 1995, and are now owned by the Indian company Sterlite Industries. The town has modern facilities, but its wide streets, remaining historic buildings and unique setting give it an old-mining-town flavour. In certain lights, multicoloured boulders – on the hillsides, denuded through a combination of felling, wildfire, erosion and poisonous fumes from the smelter – reflect the sun's rays and turn to amazing shades of pink and gold. However, many Tasmanians view the place as a haunting reminder of the devastating impact humans can have on their environment.

IN TOWN Galley Museum The museum is housed in the Imperial (1898), Queenstown's first brick hotel, and displays over 800 photographs and general memorabilia of the history of the west coast. Cnr Sticht and Driffield sts.
ABT Wilderness Railway This restored 1896 rack-and-pinion railway travels over 34 km of river and forest track to Strahan. It crosses 40 bridges and passes through pristine wilderness areas. Bookings (03) 6471 1700.
Spion Kop Lookout: views of Queenstown and surrounding mountains; off Bowes St. *Historical walk:* takes in 25 locations of historical importance; *The Walkabout Queenstown* brochure from visitor centre.
NEARBY *Mt Lyell Mines:* guided tours of the mines north of town, either surface (1 hr) or underground (3.5 hr); bookings (03) 6471 1472. *Iron Blow:* original open-cut mine where gold was discovered in 1883; Gormanston; 6 km E. *Linda:* ghost town; 7 km E. *Mt Jukes Lookout:* superb panoramic views; 7 km s. *Lake Burbury:* excellent brown and rainbow trout

fishing; picnic areas; 8 km E. *Nelson Falls:* short walk through temperate rainforest leads to falls; 23 km E. *Valley views:* spectacular views from Lyell Hwy as it climbs steeply out of town.
ⓘ Queenstown Galley Museum, cnr Sticht and Driffield sts; (03) 6471 1483

Richmond   Pop. 827

Map ref. 623 J4, 625 M7

Richmond, just north of Hobart, is one of the most important historic towns in Tasmania. The much-photographed Richmond Bridge is the oldest surviving freestone bridge in Australia, built by convicts under appalling conditions in 1823. The situation was so bad that one convict committed suicide by throwing himself off the bridge. Other convicts beat and killed an overseer who was known for his cruelty; legend has it that his ghost still haunts the bridge.

IN TOWN Old Hobart Town Taking 3 years to build, this is an intricate model of Hobart in the 1820s. A remarkable feat, it is also historically accurate. Bridge St.
Richmond Gaol One of Australia's best preserved convict prisons, built in 1825 and once the abode of convict Ikey Solomon, said to be the inspiration for Dickens' Fagin. Self-guide tours. Bathurst St.
Richmond Maze and Tearooms: two-stage maze with surprise ending, puzzle corner, gardens and Devonshire tea; Bridge St. *Historical walk:* many heritage buildings throughout town include Ivy Cottage, Village Store and Richmond Arms; *Let's Talk About Richmond* brochure from visitor centre. *Art Galleries:* local arts and crafts in heritage buildings include Saddlers Court (c. 1848); Bridge St. *Olde Time Portraits:* photographs of people in period costume; Bridge St. *Prospect House:* historic Georgian mansion built in 1830s, supposedly haunted by the ghost of its past owner; restaurant; Richmond Rd.

The ABT Wilderness Railway, which runs between Queenstown and Strahan

T A S M A N I A

WHAT'S ON *Village Fair:* Oct.
NEARBY ZooDoo This Wildlife Park is on a 330 ha farm with native fauna such as Tasmanian devils, galahs, emus and the rare albino Pademelon wallaby. Middle Tea Tree Rd; 6 km w.
Southern Tasmanian Wine Route: vineyards north of town include Stoney (6 km N) and Crosswinds (10 km NW); brochure from visitor centre. *Scenic drive:* north through Campania (8 km) and Colebrook (19 km).
ⓘ Old Hobart Town model village, 21A Bridge St; (03) 6260 2502; www.richmondvillage.com

Rosebery   Pop. 1115

Map ref. 624 E1, 626 E10

Like nearby Queenstown, Strahan and Zeehan, Rosebery found its economic niche in mining. The Pasminco Zinc mine is central to the town's success today, but the region is also known for the ancient rainforests surrounding town, home to unique fauna and rare clusters of the magnificent Huon pine, one of the oldest living things on earth.
IN TOWN *Mine tours:* surface tours of the Pasminco mine; bookings (03) 6473 1247.
WHAT'S ON *Rosebery Folk Festival:* Irish music festival; Mar.
NEARBY Montezuma Falls The highest in Tasmania, the falls plummet 113 m and are accessed from Williamsford in a 3 hr return walk. The track winds through beautiful rainforest and there is a viewing platform at the falls. 11 km SW.
Wee Georgie Wood Steam Train: a 2 km ride along a scenic track on the fully restored steam train runs 1st Sun afternoon each month Sept–April. Tullah; 12 km NE. *Mt Murchison:* difficult but worthwhile 4 hr return walk rising 1275 m through ancient alpine forests; 14 km SE. *Lake Johnson Reserve Tour:* alpine nature tour offering a close-up look at a stand of 10 000-year-old Huon pines; bookings (03) 6473 1247. *Hays Trout Tours:* fishing tours of west-coast lakes and rivers Aug–April; bookings (03) 6473 1247. *Fishing:* good

trout fishing in nearby lakes Rosebery, Mackintosh and Murchison; north and east of town.
ⓘ Hay's Bus Services, 10/12 Esplanade; (03) 6473 1247

Ross   Pop. 266

Map ref. 625 M3, 627 N12

One of the oldest and most beautiful bridges in Australia spans the Macquarie River in Ross. Completed in 1836, the bridge was designed by colonial architect John Lee Archer and constructed by convicts, one of whom, Daniel Herbert, was given a pardon for his efforts. Paid one shilling a day, Herbert was responsible for 186 beautiful stone carvings along the side of the bridge, comprising images of animals, plants, Celtic gods and goddesses and even the governor of the time, George Arthur. Ross Bridge is a point of pride in this Midlands town and it complements the many old sandstone buildings that adorn the main streets. The town's central junction reveals the different aspects of Ross's history and, perhaps, its potential. The four corners are known as Temptation (hotel), Recreation (town hall), Salvation (church) and Damnation (gaol).
IN TOWN Tasmanian Wool Centre Ross has held the world record price for merino wool a number of times and this museum and wool exhibition illustrates the national importance of the wool industry. Church St.
Female Convict Station Historic Site Archaeologically the most intact female convict site in Australia, this operated as a probation station for female convicts and their babies in the 19th century. The women were trained as domestic help and hired out to landowners in the area. The Overseer's Cottage has a historical display and model. Off Bond St.
Heritage walk: takes in 40 historic buildings in town, 22 of which are on Church St, including Uniting Church (1885); booklet from visitor centre. *Old Ross General Store and Tearoom:* local crafts and Devonshire tea; Church St. *Tasmanian*

Scottish Centre: Scottish paraphernalia; Church St. *Ross Memorial Library and Recreation Room:* original headquarters of the Royal Ordnance Corps in the 1830s; Church St. *Skulduggery:* mystery tour game, following true crime clues around town; available from visitor centre.
WHAT'S ON *Ross Rodeo:* Jan.
NEARBY Fishing There is world-class fly-fishing for brown trout in Macquarie River and some of the state's best trout-fishing lakes (Sorell, Crescent, Tooms and Leake) are within an hour's drive of town.
ⓘ Tasmanian Wool Centre, Church St; (03) 6381 5466; www.rosstasmania.com

St Helens   Pop. 1799

Map ref. 627 Q8

This popular resort on the shores of Georges Bay is renowned for its crayfish and scalefish, which help maintain a thriving restaurant industry. The surrounding hills and warm sea breezes create a mild climate year-round, and the nearby beaches have pristine white sand dunes.
IN TOWN *St Helens History Room:* local memorabilia and photos, wooden interactive models and personal narratives given by curators; Cecilia St. *Beaches:* bay beaches ideal for swimming and coastal beaches for surfing. *Fishing:* Scamander River has excellent bream and trout fishing. Charter boats and tours are available for deep-sea fishing and dinghy hire is available for bay fishing. Check with visitor centre for details.
WHAT'S ON *St Helens Regatta and Seafood Festival:* Jan. *Tasmanian Game Fishing Classic:* Mar. *Seafood and Symphony:* Mar. *Suncoast Jazz Festival:* June.
NEARBY Binalong Bay This small holiday town with gorgeous beaches is renowned for its excellent surf and rock-fishing. The Bay of Fires Festival, including the Great Abalone Bakeoff, takes place here in February. 11 km NE. *St Helens Point:* walks with stunning coastal scenery along Maurouard Beach; brochure from visitor centre. 9 km S. *Bay of Fires Conservation Area:* named by

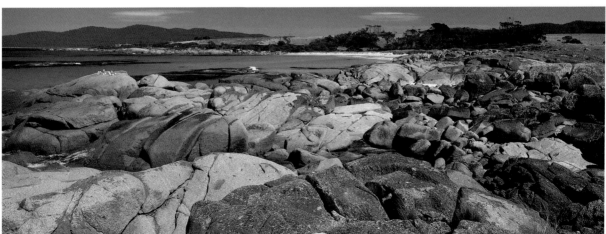

The Gardens, Bay of Fires, north of St Helens

Captain Furneaux for the Aboriginal campfires burning along the shore as he sailed past in 1773, this area features magnificent coastal scenery, good beach fishing and camping. Aboriginal middens are found in area. A guided walk takes in the scenery to the north (*see Gladstone for details*). Begins 9 km N. *Beaumaris*: good beaches and lagoons; 12 km S. *Blue Tier Forest Reserve*: walks with wheelchair access and interpretive sites; 27 km NW. *Pub in the Paddock*: one of Tasmania's oldest country pubs (1880) set in the Pyengana Valley, infamous for its beer-swilling pig; Pyengana; 28 km W. *Healey's Cheese Factory*: restaurant and tastings; Pyengana; 28 km W. *St Columba Falls*: dropping nearly 90 m, the falls flow down a granite cliff-face to the South George River. Walks through sassafras and myrtle lead to a viewing platform. 38 km W.
ⓘ St Helens History Room, 61 Cecilia St; (03) 6376 1744

St Marys
Pop. 538

Map ref. 627 Q10

Despite being the chief centre of the Break O'Day Plains, St Marys is a small town overshadowed by the magnificent St Patrick's Head in the eastern highlands. The roads to and from St Marys venture through picturesque forests or down through the valley.
IN TOWN *Rivulet Park*: platypuses, Tasmanian native hens and picnic and barbecue facilities; Main St.
WHAT'S ON *New Year's Day Races*: Jan. *Winter Solstice Festival*: June. *Spring Festival*: Nov.
NEARBY *St Patricks Head*: challenging 1 hr 40 min return walk to top of rocky outcrop for great 360-degree views of coast and valley; 1.5 km E. *South Sister*: an easier lookout alternative to St Patricks Head, this 10–15 min walk leads through stringybarks and silver wattles to spectacular views of Fingal Valley. 3 km NW. *Jubilee Mine*: 1.5 hr return walk through eucalypt forest to old mine site; 5 km N. *Mount Elephant Pancake Barn*: well-known creperie set in rainforest overlooking Chain of Lagoons; Elephant Pass; 6.5 km SE. *Falmouth*: small coastal township with several convict-built structures, fine beaches and good fishing; 14 km NE. *Scamander*: holiday town with sea- and river-fishing, good swimming, and walks and drives through forest plantations; 17 km N. *Douglas–Apsley National Park*: *see Bicheno*.
ⓘ St Marys Coach House Restaurant, 34 Main St; (03) 6372 2529

Scottsdale
Pop. 1901

Map ref. 627 N7

Scottsdale, the major town in Tasmania's north-east, serves some of the richest agricultural and forestry country on the island. Indeed, as Government Surveyor James Scott observed in 1852, it has 'the best soil in the island'. The town was founded largely by English and Scottish settlers in the mid-19th century and became a prosperous, solid community. A visitor to the town in 1868 noted with some surprise that the town had 'neither police station nor public house, but the people appear to get on harmoniously enough without them'. Present-day Scottsdale, now with both, still retains the sense of harmony.
IN TOWN **Forest EcoCentre** A state-of-the-art centre built to principles of ecological sustainability, this place showcases the story of the forests through greenhouse-style interpretive displays and interactive features. King St. *Anabel's of Scottsdale*: National Trust building now used as a restaurant, set in exquisite gardens; King St.
NEARBY **Bridestowe Estate Lavender Farm** One of the word's largest lavender-oil producers, Bridestowe is renowned for growing lavender that is not contaminated by cross-pollination. Tours are available in the flowering season (Dec–Jan) and there are lavender products for sale. Nabowla; 13 km W. *Mt Stronach*: very popular 45 min climb to magnificent views of the north-east; 4 km S. *Cuckoo Falls*: uphill 2–3 hr return walk to falls; Tonganah; 8 km SE. *Springfield Forest Reserve*: popular, unspoiled picnic spot and 20 min loop walk through arboretum of Californian redwoods, English poplars, pines and native flora; 12 km SW. *Sidling Range Lookout*: views of township and surrounding countryside; 16 km W. *Mount Maurice Forest Reserve*: walks incorporating Ralph Falls; 30 km S. *Winery tours*: tours of wineries in area; bookings (03) 6352 3723.
ⓘ Forest EcoCentre, 88 King St; (03) 6352 6520; www.netasmania.com.au

Sheffield
Pop. 981

Map ref. 626 I8, 628 D9

Sheffield lies in the foothills of Mt Roland, just south of Devonport, in one of the most scenic areas of the state. Once reliant on farming, the town devised a new attraction and now tourism buoys the local economy. Inspired by the Canadian town Chemainus, the people of Sheffield commissioned an artist to cover the town in murals depicting the local history and scenery. Since then, murals have popped up all over – even the rubbish bins have been improved by the local schoolchildren.
IN TOWN **The Tiger's Tale** This theatre uses animatronics to reinvigorate the story of the thylacine, or Tasmanian tiger. The show, complete with life-size tiger and cheeky characters, has become a popular attraction. 38A Main St. *Kentish Museum*: exhibits on local history and hydro-electricity; Main St; open 10am–3pm daily. *Mural House*: unusual interior murals; High St. *Blue Gum Gallery*: arts and crafts; at visitor centre. *Steam train*: Red Water Creek Steam and Heritage Society runs a train 1st weekend each month; cnr Spring and Main sts.
WHAT'S ON *Market*: Claude Road Hall; 3rd Sun each month. *Steam Fest*: Mar. *Mural Fest*: April. *Daffodil Show*: Sept.
NEARBY **Tasmazia** Claiming to be the world's largest maze complex, Tasmazia has a variety of mazes, model village, honey boutique, pancake parlour and lavender farm. A Harvest Festival is held each Feb. Lake Barrington Nature Reserve; 14 km SW. *Stoodley Forest Reserve*: experimental forest planted to assess the best species for tree farms, with a 40 min loop walk through European beech, Douglas fir, radiata pine and Tasmanian blue gum. Picnic areas. 7 km NE. *Lake Barrington Estate Vineyard*: tastings and sales; West Kentish; 10 km W; open Wed–Sun Nov–April. *Mt Roland*: well-marked bushwalks to the summit, which rises to 1234 m, with access from Claude Rd or Gowrie Park; 11 km SW. *Lake Barrington*: internationally recognised rowing course created by Devils Gate Dam. Picnic and barbecue facilities along the shore. 14 km SW.
ⓘ 5 Pioneer Cres; (03) 6491 1036

Smithton
Pop. 3148

Map ref. 626 C4

This substantial town is the administrative centre of Circular Head, renowned for its unique blackwood-swamp forests, and was the first European settlement in the far north-west. Smithton services the most productive dairying and vegetable-growing area in the state and, with several large sawmills, is also the centre of one of Tasmania's most significant forestry areas.
IN TOWN *Circular Head Heritage Centre*: artefacts and memorabilia detailing the area's pioneering history; 8 King St. *Lookout tower*: excellent views from Tier Hill; Massey St. *Western Esplanade Community Park*: popular picnic spot overlooking the mouth of the Duck River, with fishing and walks; Western Esplanade. *Britton Brothers Timber Mill*: tours of the mill by appt, (03) 6452 2522; Brittons Rd, southern outskirts of town.
NEARBY **Allendale Gardens** These beautiful botanic gardens are linked to a rainforest area by 3 easy loop walks that take in the Fairy Glades, a captivating section constructed for children, and towering 500-year-old trees. Peacocks roam the gardens, where Devonshire tea is available. Edith Creek; 13 km S; open Oct–April.
River and Duck Bay: good fishing and boating; 2 km N. *Sumac Lookout*: amazing

TASMANIA

views over Arthur River and surrounding eucalypt forest; 4 km s on Sumac Rd. *Lacrum Dairy:* milking demonstrations, cheese-tastings and sales; Mella; 6 km w. *Milkshake Hills Forest Reserve:* exquisite picnic spot among eucalypts and rainforest. 10 min loop walk or 1 hr return walk to hilltop. 40 km s. *Surfing:* excellent, but turbulent surf beaches near Marrawah where Rip Curl West Coast Classic is held in March; 51 km sw. *Arthur River cruises:* trips into pristine wilderness of Arthur Pieman Protected Area; 70 km sw; run Sept–June. *Gardiner Point:* landmark of The End of the World; 70 km sw. *Woolnorth tours:* coach tours visit spectacular Cape Grim cliffs, wind farm, and Woolnorth sheep, cattle and timber property; bookings (03) 6452 1493.
ⓘ 45 Main Rd, Stanley; (03) 6458 1330

Sorell   Pop. 3604

Map ref. 623 K5, 625 M8

The south-eastern town of Sorell was founded in 1821. It was important in early colonial times for providing most of the state's grain. It was named after Governor Sorell, which is not without irony. Although the governor was known for curbing bushranging in Tasmania, the town was later targeted by bushranger Matthew Brady, who released the prisoners from gaol and left the soldiers imprisoned in their place.
IN TOWN Historic buildings There are 3 churches listed in the National Estate, the most impressive being St George's Anglican Church (1826). Also many heritage buildings include Old Rectory (c. 1826), Old Post Office (c. 1850) and Bluebell Inn (c. 1864).
Orielton Lagoon: important habitat for migratory wading birds on western shore of town. *Pioneer Park:* popular picnic spot with barbecue facilities; Parsonage Pl.
WHAT'S ON *Market:* Cole St; Sun (weekly in summer; fortnightly in winter).
NEARBY Sorell Fruit Farm Specialising in a staggering range of berries, the farm offers pick-your-own patches as well as a ready-picked selection. Other fruits available in season include apricots, cherries, pears, nashi, nectarines and peaches. Visitors can take self-guide tours of the farm and Devonshire tea is available at the cafe. Pawleena Rd; 2 km e; open Oct–May.
Southern Tasmanian Wine Route: many vineyards east of town include Orani (3 km e) and Bream Creek (22 km e); brochure from visitor centre. *Beaches:* popular beach areas around Dodges Ferry and Carlton; 18 km s.
ⓘ Gordon St; (03) 6265 6438

Stanley   Pop. 462

Map ref. 626 D3

This quaint village nestles at the base of an ancient outcrop called The Nut, which

The Nut, Stanley

rises 152 metres with sheer cliffs on three sides. Matthew Flinders, upon seeing The Nut in 1798, commented that it looked like a 'cliffy round lump resembling a Christmas cake'. Today visitors come from far and wide to see this 'lump' and the historic township beside it.
IN TOWN The Nut The remains of volcanic rock, The Nut looms above the surrounding sea and provides spectacular coastal views. Visitors can either walk to the summit along a steep and challenging track or take the chairlift from Browns Rd. There is a 40 min circuit walk along cliffs at the summit.
Historic buildings: many in the wharf area, including the bluestone former Van Diemen's Land (VDL) Company store in Marine Park. *Lyons Cottage:* birthplace of former prime minister J. A. Lyons, with interesting memorabilia; Alexander Tce. *Hearts and Craft:* fine Tasmanian craft; Church St. *Discovery Centre Folk Museum:* displays of local history; Church St. *Touchwood:* quality craft and woodwork; Main St. *Cemetery:* graves of colonial architect John Lee Archer and explorer Henry Hellyer; Browns Rd. *Penguins:* evening tours to small colonies of little penguins near wharf; bookings (03) 6458 1455. *Seal cruises:* daily trips to see offshore seal colonies; bookings 0419 550 134.
WHAT'S ON *Melbourne to Stanley Yacht Race:* Nov.
NEARBY Highfield Historic Site The headquarters of VDL Co, Highfield contains a homestead with 12 rooms, a chapel, convict barracks, a schoolhouse, stables, a barn, workers' cottages and

large gardens. Green Hills Rd; 2 km n. *Dip Falls:* double waterfall surrounded by dense rainforest and enormous eucalypts. There is a picnic area nearby. 40 km se off hwy, via Mawbanna.
ⓘ 45 Main Rd; (03) 6458 1330

Strahan   Pop. 740

Map ref. 624 D3, 626 D12

This pretty little port on Macquarie Harbour, on Tasmania's forbidding west coast, is the last stop before a long stretch of ocean to Patagonia. Sometimes considered the loneliest place on earth, it was dubbed 'The Best Little Town in the World' by the *Chicago Tribune* and continues to attract visitors. Strahan (pronounced 'strawn') came into being as a penal colony operating from the isolated station of Sarah Island. Known as a particularly cruel environment, the station was shut down in 1833, but not before convict Alexander Pearce had managed to escape. Pearce and seven others set off for Hobart but found the terrain too tough an adversary to overcome. Pearce, alone when discovered, was suspected of cannibalism. The following year he again escaped and again killed and ate his cohort. Pearce finally made it to Hobart, where he was executed.
IN TOWN Visitor centre The centre has an impressive historical display on Tasmania's south-west, including Aboriginal history, European settlement, and more recent events such as the fight to save the Franklin River from being dammed in the early 1980s. In the amphitheatre there is an audiovisual slideshow and a nightly performance of

'The Ship That Never Was', about convict escapes. Esplanade.

Morrison's Mill: one of four remaining Huon pine sawmills in Tasmania; tours available; Esplanade. *Strahan Woodworks:* wood-turning, arts and crafts; Esplanade. *Tuts Whittle Wonders:* carvings from forest wood; Reid St. *Ormiston House:* built in 1899 and a fine example of Federation architecture surrounded by magnolia trees and expansive gardens. Morning and afternoon teas are served. Bay St. *Water Tower Hill Lookout:* views of township and harbour; Esk St. *ABT Wilderness Railway: see Queenstown. Gemstone Museum:* mineral and gemstone display; Innes St.

WHAT'S ON *Mount Lyell Picnic:* Jan. *Piners' Festival:* Nov.

NEARBY Franklin–Gordon Wild Rivers National Park This park now has World Heritage listing after an earlier state government tried to dam the Franklin River. Protests were so heated and widespread that the federal government and High Court stepped in and vetoed the proposal, saving the dense temperate rainforest and wild rivers that make up the park. Visitors can go canoeing and whitewater rafting, and there are many bush trails for experienced walkers. A 4-day walk to Frenchmans Cap takes in magnificent alpine scenery. The 40 min return walk to Donaghys Hill is easier and overlooks the Franklin and Collingwood rivers. Gordon River cruises depart from Strahan; bookings 1800 628 288 or (03) 6471 7174. 36 km SE.

Peoples Park: popular picnic spot in botanical gardens setting with a 1 hr return walk to Hogarth Falls through marked rainforest; 2 km E. *Ocean Beach:* Tasmania's longest beach (36 km) offers horseriding, beach fishing and the opportunity to see short-tailed shearwaters in their rookeries from Oct–Mar; 6 km W. *Henty Sand Dunes:* spectacular, vast sand dunes with sandboards and toboggans for hire;

12 km N. *Cape Sorell Lighthouse:* 40 m high lighthouse built in 1899; 23 km SW. *Sarah Island:* ruins of convict station with tours available; check with visitor centre; 29 km SE. *Scenic flights:* bird's-eye views of Gordon River, Sir John Falls and Franklin River valley; bookings (03) 6471 7280. *Platypus Paddle:* view platypuses at twilight in their natural habitat on Henty River north of town; bookings (03) 6257 0500.
ⓘ The Esplanade; (03) 6471 7622

Swansea   Pop. 518

Map ref. 625 P4, 627 P13

Perched on Great Oyster Bay, Swansea looks out across turquoise waters to the Freycinet Peninsula. It is part of the Glamorgan/Spring Bay council, the oldest rural municipality in the country, and many fine old buildings testify to its age. Today it is a popular holiday destination.

IN TOWN Swansea Bark Mill and East Coast Museum The only restored black-wattle bark mill in Australia has machinery that still processes the bark for tanning leather. The museum has comprehensive displays on life in the 1820s, and the adjoining Wine and Wool Centre has wines from over 50 Tasmanian vineyards and textiles from around the state. Tearooms complete the complex. Tasman Hwy.

Historical walk: self-guide tour takes in charming heritage buildings including Morris' General Store (1838), run by the Morris family for over 100 years, and Community Centre (c. 1860), featuring the unusually large slate billiard table made for the 1880 World Exhibition; brochure from visitor centre. *Waterloo Point:* 1 km walking track leads to viewpoint to see short-tailed shearwaters at dusk and Aboriginal middens; Esplanade Rd.

NEARBY Spiky Bridge Built by convicts in 1843, the bridge was pieced together from fieldstones without the aid of mortar or cement. The spikes – vertical

fieldstones – prevented cattle from falling over the sides of the bridge. The beach nearby has a picnic area and good rock-fishing. 7.5 km S.

Coswell Beach: good spot for viewing little penguins at dusk; 1 km S along coast from Waterloo Point. *Kate's Berry Farm:* fresh raspberries and strawberries in season, ice-cream and fruit wines; 2 km S. *Duncombes Lookout:* splendid views; 3 km S. *Kabuki by the Sea:* Japanese restaurant on cliff top with stunning views; 12 km S. *Mayfield Beach:* safe swimming beach with walking track from camping area to Three Arch Bridge. There is also great rock and beach fishing. 14 km S. *Vineyards:* Springvale, Coombend, Freycinet and Craigie Knowe vineyards all have cellar-door sales on weekends and holidays; 15 km N. *Lost and Meetus Falls:* bushwalks past beautiful waterfalls in dry eucalypt forest. Sheltered picnic area is nearby. 50 km NW.
ⓘ Swansea Bark Mill and East Coast Museum, 96 Tasman Hwy; (03) 6257 8382

Triabunna   Pop. 697

Map ref. 623 O1, 625 O6

When Maria (pronounced 'mar-eye-ah') Island was a penal settlement, Triabunna (pronounced 'try-a-bunnah') was a garrison town and whaling base. After an initial boom, this small town on the south-east coast settled into relative obscurity, content with its role as a centre for the scallop and abalone industries.

IN TOWN *Tasmanian Seafarers' Memorial:* commemorates those who lost their lives at sea; Esplanade. *Girraween Gardens and Tearooms:* with large lily pond, day lilies, roses and agapanthus; Henry St.

WHAT'S ON *Spring Bay Festival:* Jan.

NEARBY Maria Island National Park After the convicts were moved to Port Arthur, the island was leased to Italian merchant Diego Bernacchi, who envisaged first a

Franklin–Gordon Wild Rivers National Park under snow, near Strahan

Mediterranean idyll and then a cement works. Both projects were short-lived. Today, bushwalks through the rugged landscape are popular. The extensive fossil deposits of the Painted Cliffs are magnificent and the historic penal settlement of Darlington is also of interest. Daily ferry to the island from town. 7 km s. *Orford:* pleasant walk along Old Convict Rd following Prosser River; 7 km sw. *Thumbs Lookout:* stunning views of Maria Island; 9 km sw. *Church of St John the Baptist:* heritage church (1846) with a stained-glass window (taken from England's Battle Abbey) depicting John the Baptist's life; Buckland; 25 km sw. *Sea-kayaking:* challenging 4-day trip around Maria Island; bookings (03) 6234 2067. *Beaches:* safe swimming beaches around area; contact visitor centre for details. ❶ Cnr Charles St and Esplanade West; (03) 6257 4090

Ulverstone   Pop. 9499

Map ref. 626 H6, 628 C5

At the mouth of the Leven River on the north coast, Ulverstone has some of Tasmania's finest tourist beaches, offering surfing, sailing and powerboating. The laid-back atmosphere permeates the many parks, all with something different to offer the visitor.
IN TOWN *Riverside Anzac Park:* This park has an amazing children's playground, great picnic facilities and a fountain programmed with different variations. It takes its name from a pine tree grown from a seed taken from Gallipoli. Beach Rd. *Fairway Park:* has a giant waterslide; Beach Rd. *Shropshire Park:* has a footpath inscribed with details from 75-year history of the Royal Australian Navy; Dial St. *Legion Park:* magnificent coastal setting; Esplanade. *Tobruk Park:* includes Boer War Memorial; Hobbs Pde. *Ulverstone Local History Museum:* interesting display of old business facades and other memorabilia; Main St. *Shrine of Remembrance:* clock-tower memorial designed and built by European immigrants in 1953; Reibey St. *Ulverstone Lookout:* views over town; Upper Maud St. *Woodcraft Gallery and Workshop:* demonstrations, private tutoring and sales; Reibey St; open Tues, Thurs and Sat.
WHAT'S ON *Market:* Alexandra Rd; Sat. *Taste of Ulverstone:* Jan. *Twilight Rodeo:* Feb. *Christmas Mardi Gras:* Dec.
NEARBY **Gunns Plains Caves** These limestone caves are well-lit for visitors. Tours run hourly, taking in an underground river and glow worms. 24 km sw. *Miniature railway:* 3rd Sun each month; 2 km e. *Goat Island Sanctuary:* cave and good fishing, but walking access to island at low tide only; 5 km w. *Penguins:* view little penguins at dusk; Leith; 12 km e. *Preston Falls:* scenic views; 19 km s. *Leven Canyon:* walking tracks to viewing platform with spectacular views down

the 250 m canyon. Picnic and barbecue facilities are nearby. 41 km s. *Winterbrook Falls:* 5 hr return walk to the falls for fit bushwalkers; 46 km s. *Fishing:* good fishing on beach (especially Turners Beach), river and estuary; contact visitor centre for details. *Beaches:* safe swimming beaches to east and west of town; contact visitor centre for details.
❶ Alexandra Rd; (03) 6425 2839

Waratah   Pop. 246

Map ref. 626 E8

This picturesque little settlement, set in the mountain heathland of the north-west, was the site of the first mining boom in Tasmania. Tin deposits were discovered in 1871 by James 'Philosopher' Smith, and by the late 1800s the Mt Bischoff operation was the richest tin mine in the world. The mine closed in 1947. Waratah lies near the headwaters of the Arthur River, a major waterway in north-west Tasmania.
IN TOWN *Waratah Museum and Gift Shop:* displays early photographs and artefacts of the area and provides brochure for self-drive tour of town; Smith St. *Waratah Waterfall:* in the centre of town; Smith St. *Philosopher Smith's Hut:* replica of late 19th-century miner's hut; Smith St. *St James Anglican Church:* first church in Tasmania to be lit by hydro-power; Smith St. *Lake Waratah:* pleasant picnic and barbecue area with rhododendron garden and walks to Waratah Falls; English St.
WHAT'S ON *Axemen's Carnival:* Feb.
NEARBY **Savage River National Park** The rainforest on the Savage River plateau is the largest contiguous area of cool temperate rainforest surviving in Australia. This park is largely wilderness, with opportunities for self-sufficient bushwalking as well as for fishing, four-wheel driving and kayaking in the adjacent regional reserve. Access tracks lead off the main road out of Waratah, around 20 km w.
Fishing: excellent trout fishing in rivers and lakes in the area, including Talbots Lagoon, 20 km e. *Old mines:* walks and drives to old mining sites; brochure from visitor centre.
❶ Fossey River Information Bay, 8 km s on Murchison Hwy; or council offices, Smith St; (03) 6439 7100

Westbury   Pop. 1241

Map ref. 627 K9, 629 K11

Westbury's village green is said to be unique in Australia. It gives the town a decidedly English air, which is reinforced by hedgerows and old colonial buildings. Just west of Launceston, the town was surveyed in 1823 and laid out in 1828, the assumption being that it would become the main stop between Hobart and the north-west coast. Originally planned as a city, it never grew beyond the charming country town it is today.

IN TOWN **The village green** Used for parades and fairs in the 1830s, the village green is still the focal point and fairground of Westbury – with one small difference: prisoners are no longer put in the stocks for all to see. King St.
White House This collection of buildings, enclosing a courtyard, was built in 1841. Later additions include a coach depot, a bakery and a flour mill. Today the complex is a museum with several collections on display. The house has an excellent collection of 17th- and 18th-century furniture and memorabilia, and a magnificent doll's house. The outbuildings house a toy museum as well as a display of early bicycles, vintage cars and horse-drawn vehicles. The bakery has been restored and serves refreshments. King St; open Tues–Sun Sept–June.
Pearn's Steam World: said to be the largest collection of working steam traction engines in Australia; Bass Hwy. *Westbury Maze and Tearoom:* hedge maze composed of 3000 privet bushes; Bass Hwy; open Oct–June. *Culzean:* historic home with beautifully maintained temperate-climate gardens; William St; open Sept–May. *Westbury Mineral and Tractor Shed:* museum of vintage tractors and farm machinery featuring a scale-model tractor exhibition; Veterans Row.
WHAT'S ON *Market:* St Andrews Church; 2nd Sun each month. *Maypole Festival:* Mar. *St Patrick's Day Festival:* Mar. *Steam Spectacular:* Nov.
NEARBY **Heidi Farm** This is the home of excellent Swiss-style cheeses including the celebrated Heidi gruyère, considered a benchmark cheese and one of the 'big three' of Australian cheeses. Shop on-site with tastings and sales. 7 km w at Exton. *Fishing:* good trout fishing at Four Springs Creek (15 km NE) and Brushy Lagoon (15 km NW).
❶ Clarke's Gingerbread Cottages, 52 William St; (03) 6393 1140; www.greatwesterntiers.org.au

Wynyard   Pop. 4623

Map ref. 626 F5

This small centre at the mouth of the Inglis River on the northern coast has become a well-developed tourist centre. The town has charming timber buildings and is located on a stunning stretch of coastline in an extremely fertile pocket of the state.
IN TOWN *Gutteridge Gardens:* riverside gardens in the heart of town; Goldie St. *Thylacine:* Tasmanian tiger interpretive sculpture at visitor centre. *Nature walks:* include boardwalk along Inglis River; brochure at visitor centre.
WHAT'S ON *Tulip Festival:* Oct.
NEARBY **Boat Harbour** This is a picturesque village with clear water and rocky points ideal for diving and spearfishing. Boat Harbour Beach (4 km NW of town) has safe swimming, marine life in pools at low tide, fishing

and waterskiing. Killynaught Cottage in town offers Devonshire tea and local craft. 10 km NW.

Rocky Cape National Park The park has some of the most well-preserved Aboriginal rock shelters and middens in Tasmania. It incorporates Sisters Beach, an 8 km stretch of pristine white sand and clear water. 29 km NW.

Fossil Bluff: scenic views from an unusual geological structure where the oldest marsupial fossil in Australia was found; 3 km N. *Table Cape Lookout:* brilliant views of the coast from 190 m above sea level. En route to lookout is Table Cape Tulip Farm, with tulips, daffodils and Dutch irises blooming Sept–Oct. From lookout a short walk leads to an old lighthouse. 5 km N. *Flowerdale Freshwater Lobster Haven:* restaurant and artificial lakes stocked with lobster; 6.5 km NW. *Fishing:* Inglis and Flowerdale rivers provide excellent trout fishing; also good sea-fishing around Table Cape. *Scenic flights:* the best way to appreciate the patchwork colours of the fields in the area; bookings at Wynyard Airport (03) 6442 1111. *Scenic walks and drives:* brochure from visitor centre.
ⓘ Cnr Hogg and Goldie sts; (03) 6442 4143

Zeehan
Pop. 891

Map ref. 624 D1, 626 D11

This town on the west coast is inextricably tied to its mining successes. After silver-lead deposits were discovered here in 1882, Zeehan expanded considerably. In its boom period between 1893 and 1908, the mine yielded ore worth eight million dollars, which led to its nickname, the Silver City of the West. However, from 1910 the mine started to slow and Zeehan declined, threatening to become a ghost town. Fortunately the nearby Renison Bell tin mine has drawn workers back to the area.

IN TOWN West Coast Pioneers Memorial Museum The old Zeehan School of Mines building (1894) has been converted into a comprehensive museum outlining the local history with extensive mineral and geological collections. Next door there is a display of well-maintained steam locomotives and rail carriages once used on the west coast. Main St.
Historic buildings: many boom-era buildings lining Main St include Gaiety Theatre, once Australia's largest theatre. *Scenic drives:* self-guide drives in town and environs; brochure from visitor centre.

NEARBY *Fishing:* Trial Harbour (20 km W) and Granville Harbour (35 km NW) are popular fishing spots. *Lake Pieman:* boating and good trout fishing; 42 km NW. *Cruises:* tour the Pieman River, leaving from fascinating former goldmining town, Corinna; bookings (03) 6446 1170; 48 km NW.
ⓘ West Coast Pioneers Memorial Museum, Main St; (03) 6471 62250

Bushwalkers on the Overland Track

Cradle Mountain–Lake St Clair National Park

While much of Tasmania has been tamed by generations of convicts, miners, sealers and settlers, this national park remains one of nature's most formidable and breathtaking stalwarts. Native animals have right of way along the roads and the weather seems to change on a whim. Many explorers have tried to conquer the sprawling, glaciated landscape, but the area has always emerged victorious, which is one of the many reasons why today it is arguably Tasmania's premier attraction.

Covering 124 942 hectares, the national park has over 25 major peaks, including the state's highest, Mt Ossa, and possibly its most spectacular, Cradle Mountain. The terrain is marked by pristine waterfalls, U-shaped valleys, dolerite formations, forests of deciduous beech, Tasmanian myrtle, pandani and King Billy pine, and swathes of wildflowers. At the southern end of the park lies the tranquil Lake St Clair, which occupies a basin gouged out by glaciers over the last 20 000 years. Cruises operate daily.

Visitor centres at both ends of the park are logical starting points for planning walks. There are many tracks for all levels of experience, but conditions change frequently so check with the rangers as they have the most up-to-date information.

The Overland Track

The Overland, covering 85 kilometres, is one of Australia's best-known walks for experienced, well-equipped walkers. The track begins at Cradle Mountain in the north and winds through lush forests and challenging hills to the shores of Lake St Clair (or vice versa). The walk takes five days along the most direct route. Walkers should bring sufficient supplies and be prepared for all weather conditions. Simple wooden huts have been erected at intervals along the track and can provide a basic overnight shelter. However, this on-site accommodation fills up quickly and walkers should also bring tents.

The Overland Track can also be done in style, staying in well-appointed huts and with all meals provided. Contact (03) 6391 9339 or visit www.cradlehuts.com.au for information.

Dove Lake Loop Track

This walk is suitable for everyone. It starts from the eastern side of Dove Lake and passes through beautiful Ballroom Forest, which comprises a canopy of tall trees with a carpet of lush moss underfoot. The walk takes two hours and returns to its starting point. Dove Lake is at the north end of the park near Cradle Mountain.

Summit Walk

This eight hour return walk leads to the top of Cradle Mountain and provides stunning views of the park and north-west Tasmania. It involves scrambling over rock at times, so is by no means an easy walk, but the panorama is well worth the effort.

Contact one of the park's visitor centres for further information: Cradle Mountain (03) 6492 1110; Lake St Clair (03) 6289 1172.

ROAD ATLAS

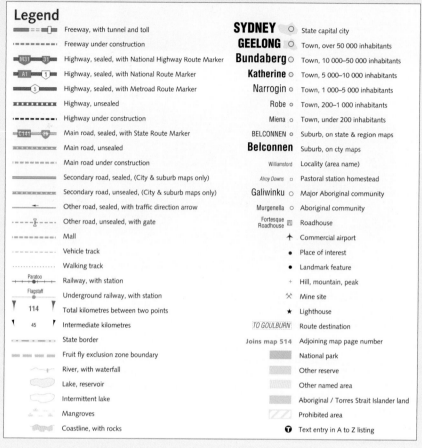

Legend

==== == ☐	Freeway, with tunnel and toll
··········	Freeway under construction
M31 31	Highway, sealed, with National Highway Route Marker
A1 1	Highway, sealed, with National Route Marker
5	Highway, sealed, with Metroad Route Marker
▪▪▪▪▪▪▪▪	Highway, unsealed
▪ ▪ ▪ ▪ ▪	Highway under construction
C141 26	Main road, sealed, with State Route Marker
▪▪▪▪▪▪▪▪	Main road, unsealed
··········	Main road under construction
———	Secondary road, sealed, (City & suburb maps only)
≈≈≈≈≈≈	Secondary road, unsealed, (City & suburb maps only)
—→	Other road, sealed, with traffic direction arrow
- - -⊥- - -	Other road, unsealed, with gate
··········	Mall
··········	Vehicle track
··········	Walking track
Paratoo ┼──┼	Railway, with station
Flagstaff	Underground railway, with station
▼ 114 ▼	Total kilometres between two points
▼ 45 ▼	Intermediate kilometres
———	State border
▪ ▪ ▪ ▪	Fruit fly exclusion zone boundary
～～	River, with waterfall
⬭	Lake, reservoir
⬭	Intermittent lake
⌇⌇	Mangroves
🐾	Coastline, with rocks

SYDNEY ○	State capital city
GEELONG ○	Town, over 50 000 inhabitants
Bundaberg ○	Town, 10 000–50 000 inhabitants
Katherine ○	Town, 5 000–10 000 inhabitants
Narrogin ○	Town, 1 000–5 000 inhabitants
Robe ○	Town, 200–1 000 inhabitants
Miena ○	Town, under 200 inhabitants
BELCONNEN ○	Suburb, on state & region maps
Belconnen	Suburb, on city maps
Williamsford	Locality (area name)
Alroy Downs □	Pastoral station homestead
Galiwinku ○	Major Aboriginal community
Murgenella ○	Aboriginal community
Fortesque Roadhouse ⊞	Roadhouse
✈	Commercial airport
●	Place of interest
●	Landmark feature
+	Hill, mountain, peak
✕	Mine site
★	Lighthouse
TO GOULBURN	Route destination
Joins map 514	Adjoining map page number
▦	National park
▦	Other reserve
▦	Other named area
▦	Aboriginal / Torres Strait Islander land
▨	Prohibited area
❶	Text entry in A to Z listing

Inter-City Route Maps

The following inter-city route maps and distance charts will help you plan your route between major cities. As well, you can use the maps during your journey, since they provide information on distances between towns along the route, roadside rest areas, road conditions and which towns are described in the A-Z listings. The map below provides an overview of the routes mapped.

PAGE	INTER CITY ROUTES		DISTANCE	TIME
486	Sydney–Melbourne via Hume Hwy/Fwy	31 M31	881 km	12 hrs
	Sydney–Melbourne via Princes Hwy/Fwy	1 A1 M1	1037 km	15 hrs
	Sydney–Brisbane via New England Hwy	1 15 A2	1001 km	14 hrs
	Melbourne–Adelaide via Western & Dukes hwys	M8 A8 M1	733 km	8 hrs
	Melbourne–Adelaide via Princes Hwy	M1 A1 B1 M1	906 km	11 hrs
487	Melbourne–Brisbane via Newell Hwy	M31 A39 39 A2	1676 km	20 hrs
	Darwin–Adelaide via Stuart Hwy	A1 A87 87 1	3026 km	31 hrs
	Adelaide–Perth via Eyre & Great Eastern hwys	A1 1 94	2700 km	32 hrs
	Adelaide–Sydney via Sturt & Hume hwys	A20 20 1	1417 km	19 hrs
	Perth–Darwin via Great Northern Hwy	95 1	4032 km	46 hrs
488	Sydney–Brisbane via Pacific Hwy	1 1 M1	966 km	14 hrs
	Brisbane–Darwin via Warrego Hwy	A2 66 87 1	3406 km	39 hrs
	Brisbane–Cairns via Bruce Hwy	1	1703 km	20 hrs
	Hobart–Launceston via Midland Hwy	1	200 km	3 hrs
	Hobart–Devonport via Midland & Bass hwys	1 B52	286 km	4 hrs

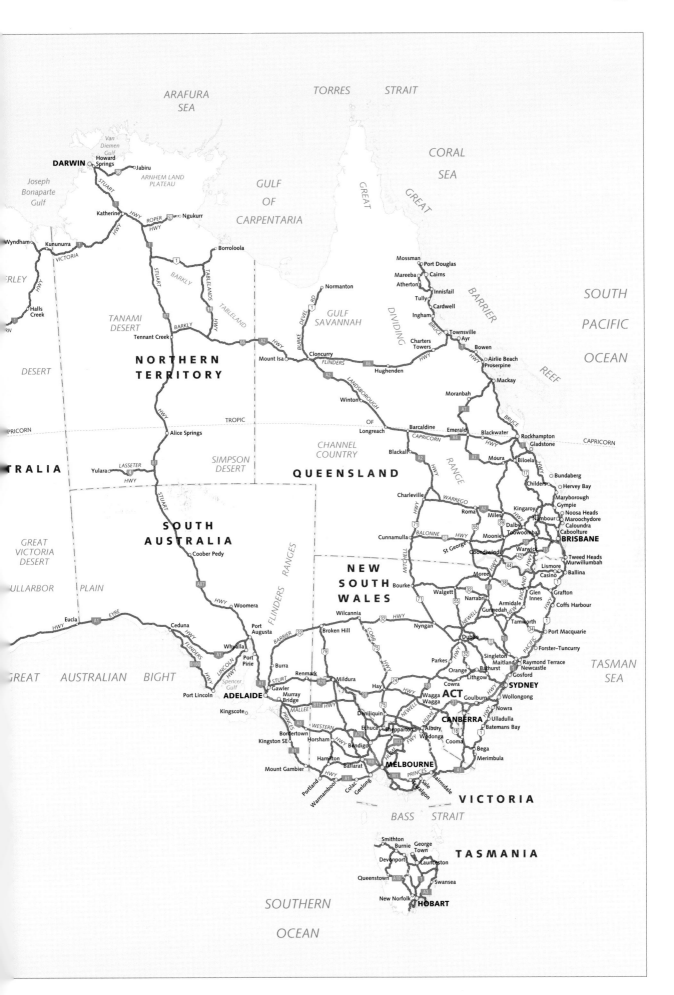

Approximate Distances AUSTRALIA

	Adelaide	Albany	Albury	Alice Springs	Ayers Rock/Yulara	Bairnsdale	Ballarat	Bathurst	Bega	Bendigo	Bordertown	Bourke	Brisbane	Broken Hill	Broome	Bunbury	Cairns	Canberra	Carnarvon	Ceduna	Charleville	Coober Pedy	Darwin	Dubbo	Esperance	Eucla	Geelong
Adelaide		2662	965	1537	1578	1010	625	1198	1338	640	274	1129	2048	514	4268	2887	3207	1197	3568	772	1582	847	3026	1194	2183	1267	711
Albany	2662		3487	3585	3626	3672	3287	3720	4000	3302	2936	3388	4310	2773	2626	335	5466	3719	1300	1890	3841	2895	4428	3526	479	1395	3373
Albury	965	3487		2362	2403	336	412	466	427	313	679	779	1407	865	5093	3712	2764	348	4393	1597	1232	1672	3851	553	3008	2092	382
Alice Springs	1537	3585	2362		443	2547	2162	2595	2875	2177	1811	2263	2979	1648	2731	3810	2376	2594	4114	1695	2320	690	1489	2401	3106	2190	2248
Ayers Rock/Yulara	1578	3626	2403	443		2588	2203	2636	2916	2218	1852	2304	3226	1689	3174	3851	2819	2635	4532	1736	2763	731	1932	2442	3147	2231	2289
Bairnsdale	1010	3672	336	2547	2588		388	802	328	423	736	1115	1743	1119	5278	3897	3100	455	4578	1782	1568	1857	4036	863	3193	2277	349
Ballarat	625	3287	412	2162	2203	388		878	716	124	351	996	1747	754	4893	3512	3104	760	4193	1397	1449	1472	3651	893	2808	1892	86
Bathurst	1198	3720	466	2595	2636	802	878		531	779	1180	569	1000	958	5011	3945	2416	309	4626	1830	1022	1905	3769	205	3241	2325	848
Bega	1338	4000	427	2875	2916	328	716	531		751	1064	994	1399	1447	5436	4225	2910	222	4906	2110	1447	2185	4364	630	3521	2605	677
Bendigo	640	3302	313	2177	2218	423	124	779	751		366	872	1623	696	4908	3527	2980	661	4208	1412	1325	1487	3666	769	2823	1907	210
Bordertown	274	2936	679	1811	1852	736	351	1180	1064	366		1138	1922	788	4542	3161	3257	1071	3842	1046	1591	1121	3300	1068	2457	1541	437
Bourke	1129	3388	779	2263	2304	1115	996	569	994	872	1138		922	615	4442	3613	2078	772	4294	1498	453	1573	3200	364	2909	1993	1082
Brisbane	2048	4310	1407	2979	3226	1743	1747	1000	1399	1623	1922	922		1537	4648	4535	1703	1241	5216	2420	742	2495	3406	854	3831	2915	1745
Broken Hill	514	2773	865	1648	1689	1119	754	958	1447	696	788	615	1537		4379	2998	2693	1097	3679	883	1068	958	3137	753	2294	1378	840
Broome	4268	2626	5093	2731	3174	5278	4893	5011	5436	4908	4542	4442	4648	4379		2417	4045	5214	1451	3750	3989	3421	1870	4806	2745	3255	4979
Bunbury	2887	335	3712	3810	3851	3897	3512	3945	4225	3527	3161	3613	4535	2998	2417		5691	3944	1091	2115	4066	3120	4219	3751	664	1620	3598
Cairns	3207	5466	2764	2376	2819	3100	3104	2416	2910	2980	3257	2078	1703	2693	4045	5691		2619	5428	3576	1625	3066	2803	2211	4987	4071	3102
Canberra	1197	3719	348	2594	2635	455	760	309	222	661	1071	772	1241	1097	5214	3944	2619		4625	1829	1225	1904	3972	408	3240	2324	730
Carnarvon	3568	1300	4393	4114	4532	4578	4193	4626	4906	4208	3842	4294	5216	3679	1451	1091	5428	4625		2796	4747	3801	3253	4432	1628	2301	4279
Ceduna	772	1890	1597	1695	1736	1782	1397	1830	2110	1412	1046	1498	2420	883	3750	2115	3576	1829	2796		1951	1005	3184	1636	1411	495	1483
Charleville	1582	3841	1232	2320	2763	1568	1449	1022	1447	1325	1591	453	742	1068	3989	4066	1625	1225	4747	1951		2026	2747	817	3362	2446	1500
Coober Pedy	847	2895	1672	690	731	1857	1472	1905	2185	1487	1121	1573	2495	958	3421	3120	3066	1904	3801	1005	2026		2179	1711	2416	1500	1558
Darwin	3026	4428	3851	1489	1932	4036	3651	3769	4364	3666	3300	3200	3406	3137	1870	4219	2803	3972	3253	3184	2747	2179		3564	4547	3679	3737
Dubbo	1194	3526	553	2401	2442	863	893	205	630	769	1068	364	854	753	4806	3751	2211	408	4432	1636	817	1711	3564		3047	2131	891
Esperance	2183	479	3008	3106	3147	3193	2808	3241	3521	2823	2457	2909	3831	2294	2745	664	4987	3240	1628	1411	3362	2416	4547	3047		916	2894
Eucla	1267	1395	2092	2190	2231	2277	1892	2325	2605	1907	1541	1993	2915	1378	3255	1620	4071	2324	2301	495	2446	1500	3679	2131	916		1978
Geelong	711	3373	382	2248	2289	349	86	848	677	210	437	1082	1745	840	4979	3598	3102	730	4279	1483	1500	1558	3737	891	2894	1978	
Geraldton	3086	818	3911	4009	4050	4096	3711	4144	4424	3726	3360	3812	4734	3197	1921	609	5890	4143	482	2314	4265	3319	3723	3950	1160	1819	3797
Grafton	1845	4177	1184	3052	3093	1397	1544	825	1069	1420	1719	808	330	1404	4975	4402	2033	911	5083	2287	1069	2362	3733	651	3698	2782	1542
Horsham	433	3095	531	1970	2011	577	192	997	905	218	159	1067	1841	599	4701	3320	3145	879	4001	1205	1520	1280	3459	987	2616	1700	278
Kalgoorlie–Boulder	2184	886	3009	3107	3148	3194	2809	3242	3522	2824	2458	2910	3832	2295	2338	779	4988	3241	1460	1412	3363	2417	4140	3048	407	917	2895
Katherine	2712	4114	3537	1175	1618	3722	3337	3455	3880	3352	2986	2886	3092	2823	1556	3905	2489	3658	2939	2870	2433	1865	314	3250	4233	3365	3423
Kununurra	3224	3602	4049	1687	2130	4234	3849	3967	4392	3864	3498	3398	3604	3335	1044	3393	3001	4170	2427	3382	2945	2377	826	3762	3721	3877	3935
Longreach	2098	4357	1748	1804	2247	2084	1965	1538	1963	1841	2107	969	1175	1584	3473	4582	1109	1741	4856	2467	516	2494	2231	1333	3878	2962	2016
Mackay	2670	4932	2029	2451	2894	2365	2369	1681	2106	2245	2544	1544	968	2159	4120	5157	735	1884	5503	3042	1091	3141	2878	1476	4453	3537	2367
Meekatharra	3055	1159	3880	3978	4019	4065	3680	4113	4393	3695	3329	3781	4703	3166	1467	950	5444	4112	627	2283	4234	3288	3269	3919	1278	1788	3766
Melbourne	733	3395	313	2270	2311	277	111	779	605	146	459	978	1676	842	5001	3620	3033	661	4301	1505	1431	1580	3759	822	2916	2000	72
Mildura	394	2916	571	1791	1832	825	460	804	956	402	417	870	1654	294	4522	3141	2948	803	3822	1026	1323	1101	3280	800	2437	1521	546
Moree	1567	3829	926	2704	2745	1262	1294	578	1003	1141	1482	441	481	1056	4608	4054	1838	781	4735	1939	702	2014	3366	373	3350	2434	1264
Mount Gambier	452	3114	721	1989	2030	697	309	1187	1025	433	186	1324	2098	856	4720	3339	3402	1069	4020	1224	1777	1299	3478	1244	2635	1719	365
Mount Isa	2706	4754	2383	1169	1612	2719	2600	2173	2598	2476	2742	1604	1810	2219	2838	4979	1207	2736	4221	2864	1151	1859	1596	1968	4275	3359	2651
Newcastle	1553	3930	704	2805	2846	917	1116	338	589	1017	1427	768	821	1157	5111	4155	2341	431	4836	2040	1205	2115	3869	404	3451	2535	1086
Perth	2700	410	3525	3623	3664	3710	3325	3758	4038	3340	2974	3426	4348	2811	2230	187	5504	3757	904	1928	3879	2933	4032	3564	738	1433	3411
Port Augusta	307	2355	1132	1230	1271	1317	932	1365	1645	947	581	1033	1955	418	3961	2580	3111	1364	3261	465	1486	540	2719	1171	1876	960	1018
Port Hedland	3921	2025	4746	3264	3707	5100	4546	4979	5259	4561	4195	4647	5181	4032	601	1816	4578	4978	850	3149	4522	3954	2403	4785	2144	2654	4632
Port Lincoln	647	2289	1472	1570	1611	1657	1272	1705	1985	1287	921	1373	2295	758	4149	2514	3451	1704	3195	399	1826	880	3059	1511	1751	894	1358
Port Macquarie	1804	4136	942	3011	3052	1155	1354	565	827	1255	1665	859	584	1363	5150	4361	2287	669	5042	2246	1244	2321	3908	610	3657	2741	1324
Renmark	250	2772	715	1647	1688	969	604	948	1100	546	269	1014	1798	438	4378	2997	3092	947	3678	882	1467	957	3136	944	2293	1377	690
Rockhampton	2336	4598	1695	2486	2929	2031	2035	1347	1772	1911	2210	1210	634	1825	4155	4823	1069	1550	5504	2708	831	3176	2913	1142	4119	3203	2033
Sydney	1414	3936	565	2811	2852	759	977	211	431	878	1288	780	968	1169	5222	4161	2479	292	4842	2046	1233	2121	3980	416	3457	2541	947
Tamworth	1534	3866	893	2741	2782	1186	1233	457	858	1109	1408	589	573	1093	4880	4091	2110	700	4772	1965	974	2051	3638	340	3387	2471	1231
Tennant Creek	2043	4091	2868	531	949	3053	2668	2836	3261	2683	2317	2267	2473	2154	2225	4316	1870	3039	3608	2201	1814	1196	983	2631	3612	2696	2754
Toowoomba	1921	4183	1280	2852	3099	1616	1620	956	1357	1496	1795	795	127	1410	4521	4408	1705	1199	5089	2293	615	2368	3279	727	3704	2788	1618
Townsville	2862	5121	2419	2061	2504	2755	2759	2071	2496	2635	2871	1733	1358	2348	3730	5346	345	2274	5113	3231	1280	2751	2488	1866	4642	3726	2757
Wagga Wagga	948	3470	145	2345	2386	481	550	321	402	426	822	711	1262	848	5076	3695	2619	249	4376	1580	1164	1655	3834	408	2991	2075	527
Warrnambool	649	3311	567	2186	2227	534	174	1052	862	298	383	1170	1933	829	4917	3536	3278	987	4217	1421	1623	1496	3675	1067	2832	1916	185

Distances on this chart have been calculated over main roads and do not necessarily reflect the shortest route between towns.
Refer to page 619 for distance chart of Tasmania.

Approximate Distances AUSTRALIA

	Grafton	Horsham	Kalgoorlie–Boulder	Katherine	Kununurra	Longreach	Mackay	Meekatharra	Melbourne	Mildura	Moree	Mount Gambier	Mount Isa	Newcastle	Perth	Port Augusta	Port Hedland	Port Lincoln	Port Macquarie	Renmark	Rockhampton	Sydney	Tamworth	Tennant Creek	Toowoomba	Townsville	Wagga Wagga	Warrnambool
Adelaide	1845	433	2184	2712	3224	2098	2670	3055	733	394	1567	452	2706	1553	2700	307	3921	647	1804	250	2336	1414	1534	2043	1921	2862	948	649
Albany	4177	3095	886	4114	3602	4357	4932	1159	3395	2916	3829	3114	4754	3930	410	2355	2025	2289	4136	2772	4598	3936	3866	4091	4183	5121	3470	3311
Albury	1184	531	3009	3537	4049	1748	2029	3880	313	571	926	721	2383	704	3525	1132	4746	1472	942	715	1695	565	893	2868	1280	2419	145	567
Alice Springs	3052	1970	3107	1175	1687	1804	2451	3978	2270	1791	2704	1989	1169	2805	3623	1230	3264	1570	3011	1647	2486	2811	2741	531	2852	2061	2345	2186
Ayers Rock/Yulara	3093	2011	3148	1618	2130	2247	2894	4019	2311	1832	2745	2030	1612	2846	3664	1271	3707	1611	3052	1688	2929	2852	2782	949	3099	2504	2386	2227
Bairnsdale	1397	577	3194	3722	4234	2084	2365	4065	277	825	1262	697	2719	917	3710	1317	5100	1657	1155	969	2031	759	1186	3053	1616	2755	481	534
Ballarat	1544	192	2809	3337	3849	1965	2369	3680	111	460	1294	309	2600	1116	3325	932	4546	1272	1354	604	2035	977	1233	2668	1620	2759	550	174
Bathurst	825	997	3242	3455	3967	1538	1681	4113	779	804	578	1187	2173	338	3758	1365	4979	1705	565	948	1347	211	457	2836	956	2071	321	1052
Bega	1069	905	3522	3880	4392	1963	2106	4393	605	956	1003	1025	2598	589	4038	1645	5259	1985	827	1100	1772	431	858	3261	1357	2496	402	862
Bendigo	1420	218	2824	3352	3864	1841	2245	3695	146	402	1141	433	2476	1017	3340	947	4561	1287	1255	546	1911	878	1109	2683	1496	2635	426	298
Bordertown	1719	159	2458	2986	3498	2107	2544	3329	459	417	1482	186	2742	1427	2974	581	4195	921	1665	269	2210	1288	1408	2317	1795	2871	822	383
Bourke	808	1067	2910	2886	3398	969	1544	3781	978	870	441	1324	1604	768	3426	1033	4647	1373	859	1014	1210	780	589	2267	795	1733	711	1170
Brisbane	330	1841	3832	3092	3604	1175	968	4703	1676	1654	481	2098	1810	821	4348	1955	5181	2295	584	1798	634	966	573	2473	127	1358	1262	1933
Broken Hill	1404	599	2295	2823	3335	1584	2159	3166	842	294	1056	856	2219	1157	2811	418	4032	758	1363	438	1825	1169	1093	2154	1410	2348	848	829
Broome	4975	4701	2338	1556	1044	3473	4120	1467	5001	4522	4608	4720	2838	5111	2230	3961	601	4149	5150	4378	4155	5222	4880	2225	4521	3730	5076	4917
Bunbury	4402	3320	779	3905	3393	4582	5157	950	3620	3141	4054	3339	4979	4155	187	2580	1816	2514	4361	2997	4823	4161	4091	4316	4408	5346	3695	3536
Cairns	2033	3145	4988	2489	3001	1109	735	5444	3033	2948	1838	3402	1207	2341	5504	3111	4578	3451	2287	3092	1069	2479	2110	1870	1705	345	2619	3278
Canberra	911	879	3241	3658	4170	1741	1884	4112	661	803	781	1069	2736	431	3757	1364	4978	1704	669	947	1550	292	700	3039	1199	2274	249	987
Carnarvon	5083	4001	1460	2939	2427	4856	5503	627	4301	3822	4735	4020	4221	4836	904	3261	850	3195	5042	3678	5504	4842	4772	3608	5089	5113	4376	4217
Ceduna	2287	1205	1412	2870	3382	2467	3042	2283	1505	1026	1939	1224	2864	2040	1928	465	3149	399	2246	882	2708	2046	1965	2201	2293	3231	1580	1421
Charleville	1069	1520	3363	2433	2945	516	1091	4234	1431	1323	702	1777	1151	1205	3879	1486	4522	1826	1244	1467	831	1233	974	1814	615	1280	1164	1623
Coober Pedy	2362	1280	2417	1865	2377	2494	3141	3288	1580	1101	2014	1299	1859	2115	2933	540	3954	880	2321	957	3176	2121	2051	1196	2368	2751	1655	1496
Darwin	3733	3459	4140	314	826	2231	2878	3269	3759	3280	3366	3478	1596	3869	4032	2719	2403	3059	3908	3136	2913	3980	3638	983	3279	2488	3834	3675
Dubbo	651	987	3048	3250	3762	1333	1476	3919	822	800	373	1244	1968	404	3564	1171	4785	1511	610	944	1142	416	340	2631	727	1866	408	1067
Esperance	3698	2616	407	4233	3721	3878	4453	1278	2916	2437	3350	2635	4275	3451	738	1876	2144	1751	3657	2293	4119	3457	3387	3612	3704	4642	2991	2832
Eucla	2782	1700	917	3365	3877	2962	3537	1788	2000	1521	2434	1719	3359	2535	1433	960	2654	894	2741	1377	3203	2541	2471	2696	2788	3726	2075	1916
Geelong	1542	278	2895	3423	3935	2016	2367	3766	72	546	1264	365	2651	1086	3411	1018	4632	1358	1324	690	2033	947	1231	2754	1618	2757	527	185
Geraldton	4601	3519	978	3409	2897	4781	5356	541	3819	3340	4253	3538	4691	4354	422	2779	1320	2713	4560	3196	5022	4360	4290	4078	4607	5545	3894	3735
Grafton		1638	3699	3419	3931	1502	1298	4570	1473	1451	367	1895	2137	491	4215	1822	5436	2162	254	1595	964	638	311	2800	431	1688	1059	1718
Horsham	1638		2451	3145	3657	2036	2463	3322	300	305	1360	257	2671	1235	3133	740	4188	1080	1462	428	2129	1096	1327	2476	1714	2800	644	230
Kalgoorlie–Boulder	3699	2451		3826	3314	3879	4454	871	2917	2438	3351	2636	4276	3452	582	1877	1737	1811	3658	2294	4120	3458	3388	3613	3705	4643	2992	2833
Katherine	3419	3145	3826		512	1917	2564	2955	3445	2966	3052	3164	1282	3556	3718	2405	2089	2745	3594	2822	2599	3666	3324	669	2965	2174	3520	3361
Kununurra	3931	3657	3314	512		2429	3076	2443	3957	3478	3564	3676	1794	4067	3206	2917	1577	3257	4106	3334	3111	4178	3836	1181	3477	2686	4032	3873
Longreach	1502	2036	3879	1917	2429		791	4750	1947	1839	1135	2293	635	1638	4395	2002	4006	2342	1677	1983	682	1749	1407	1298	1048	764	1680	2139
Mackay	1298	2463	4454	2564	3076	791		5325	2298	2276	1103	2720	1282	1606	4970	2577	4653	2917	1552	2420	334	1744	1375	1945	970	390	1884	2543
Meekatharra	4570	3322	871	2955	2443	4750	5325		3788	3309	4222	3507	4237	4323	763	2748	866	2682	4529	3165	5524	4329	4259	3624	4576	5129	3863	3704
Melbourne	1473	300	2917	3445	3957	1947	2298	3788		548	1195	420	2582	1017	3433	1040	4823	1380	1255	692	1964	878	1162	2776	1549	2688	458	257
Mildura	1451	305	2438	2966	3478	1839	2276	3309	548		1173	562	2474	1159	2954	561	4175	901	1397	144	1942	1020	1140	2297	1527	2603	554	535
Moree	367	1360	3351	3052	3564	1135	1103	4222	1195	1173		1627	1770	503	3867	1474	5088	1814	542	1317	769	641	272	2433	354	1493	781	1449
Mount Gambier	1895	257	2636	3164	3676	2293	2720	3507	420	562	1627		2928	1425	3152	759	4373	1099	1663	455	2386	1286	1584	2495	1971	3057	901	197
Mount Isa	2137	2671	4276	1282	1794	635	1282	4237	2582	2474	1770	2928		2273	4792	2399	3371	2739	2312	2618	1317	2384	2042	663	1683	892	2315	2774
Newcastle	491	1235	3452	3556	4067	1638	1606	4323	1017	1159	503	1425	2273		3968	1575	5189	1915	249	1303	1272	158	289	2936	788	1996	605	1271
Perth	4215	3133	582	3718	3206	4395	4970	763	3433	2954	3867	3152	4792	3968		2393	1629	2327	4174	2810	4636	3974	3904	4129	4221	5159	3508	3349
Port Augusta	1822	740	1877	2405	2917	2002	2577	2748	1040	561	1474	759	2399	1575	2393		3614	340	1781	417	2243	1581	1511	1736	1828	2766	1115	956
Port Hedland	5436	4188	1737	2089	1577	4006	4653	866	4823	4175	5088	4373	3371	5189	1629	3614		3548	5395	4031	4688	5195	5125	2758	5054	4263	4729	4570
Port Lincoln	2162	1080	1811	2745	3257	2342	2917	2682	1380	901	1814	1099	2739	1915	2327	340	3548		2121	757	2583	1921	1851	2076	2168	3106	1455	1296
Port Macquarie	254	1462	3658	3594	4106	1677	1552	4529	1255	1397	542	1663	2312	249	4174	1781	5395	2121		1541	1218	396	270	2975	630	1942	843	1509
Renmark	1595	428	2294	2822	3334	1983	2420	3165	692	144	1317	455	2618	1303	2810	417	4031	757	1541		2086	1164	1284	2153	1671	2747	698	652
Rockhampton	964	2129	4120	2599	3111	682	334	5524	1964	1942	769	2386	1317	1272	4636	2243	4688	2583	1218	2086		1410	1041	1980	636	724	1550	2209
Sydney	638	1096	3458	3666	4178	1749	1744	4329	878	1020	641	1286	2384	158	3974	1581	5195	1921	396	1164	1410		427	3047	926	2134	466	1132
Tamworth	311	1327	3388	3324	3836	1407	1375	4259	1162	1140	272	1584	2042	289	3904	1511	5125	1851	270	1284	1041	427		2705	499	1765	748	1407
Tennant Creek	2800	2476	3613	669	1181	1298	1945	3624	2776	2297	2433	2495	663	2936	4129	1736	2758	2076	2975	2153	1980	3047	2705		2346	1555	2851	2692
Toowoomba	431	1714	3705	2965	3477	1048	970	4576	1549	1527	354	1971	1683	788	4221	1828	5054	2168	630	1671	636	926	499	2346		1360	1135	1794
Townsville	1688	2800	4643	2174	2686	764	390	5129	2688	2603	1493	3057	892	1996	5159	2766	4263	3106	1942	2747	724	2134	1765	1555	1360		2274	2933
Wagga Wagga	1059	644	2992	3520	4032	1680	1884	3863	458	554	781	901	2315	605	3508	1115	4729	1455	843	698	1550	466	748	2851	1135	2274		724
Warrnambool	1718	230	2833	3361	3873	2139	2543	3704	257	535	1449	197	2774	1271	3349	956	4570	1296	1509	652	2209	1132	1407	2692	1794	2933	724	

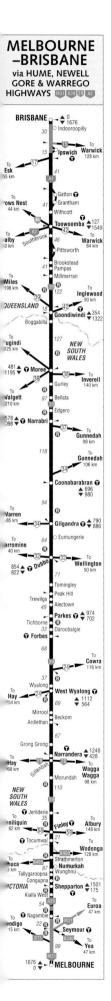

MELBOURNE–BRISBANE
via HUME, NEWELL GORE & WARREGO HIGHWAYS

DARWIN–ADELAIDE
via STUART HIGHWAY

ADELAIDE–PERTH
via PRINCES, EYRE & GREAT EASTERN HIGHWAYS

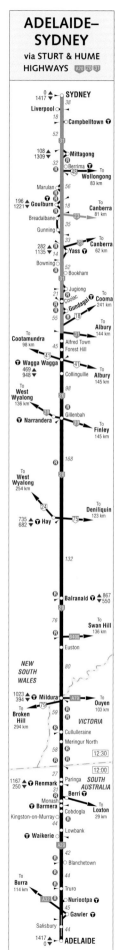

ADELAIDE–SYDNEY
via STURT & HUME HIGHWAYS

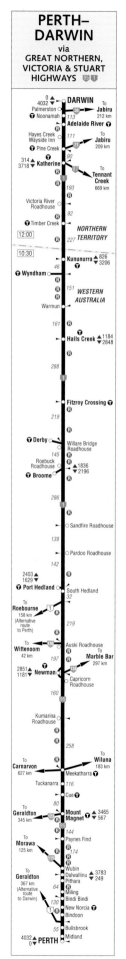

PERTH–DARWIN
via GREAT NORTHERN, VICTORIA & STUART HIGHWAYS

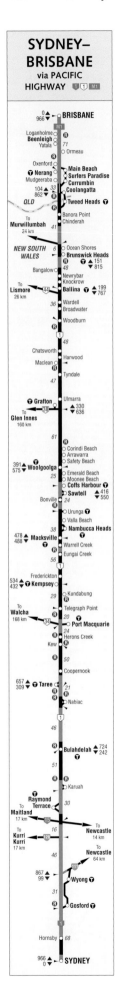

SYDNEY–BRISBANE via PACIFIC HIGHWAY

BRISBANE–DARWIN via WARREGO, LANDSBOROUGH, BARKLY & STUART HIGHWAYS

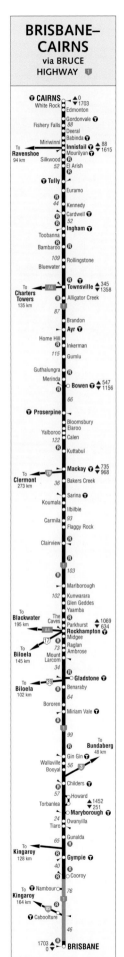

BRISBANE–CAIRNS via BRUCE HIGHWAY

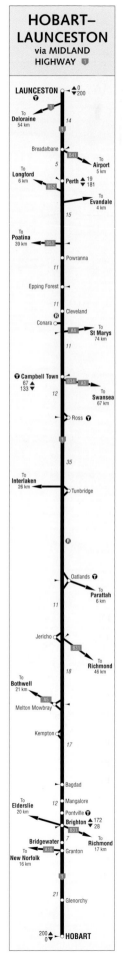

HOBART–LAUNCESTON via MIDLAND HIGHWAY

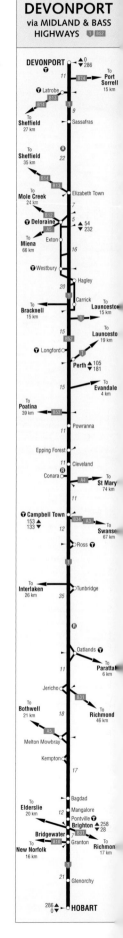

HOBART–DEVONPORT via MIDLAND & BASS HIGHWAYS

NEW SOUTH WALES AND AUSTRALIAN CAPITAL TERRITORY
MAPS

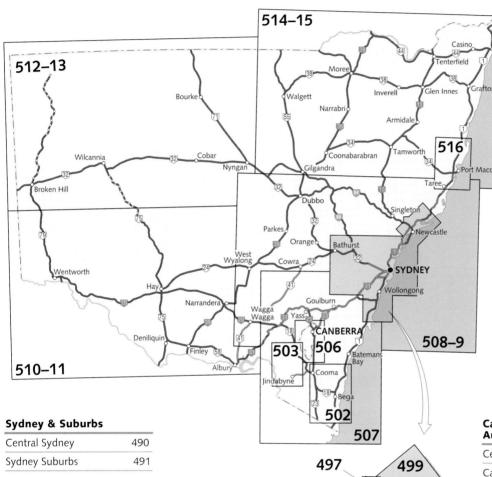

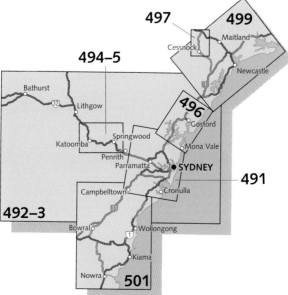

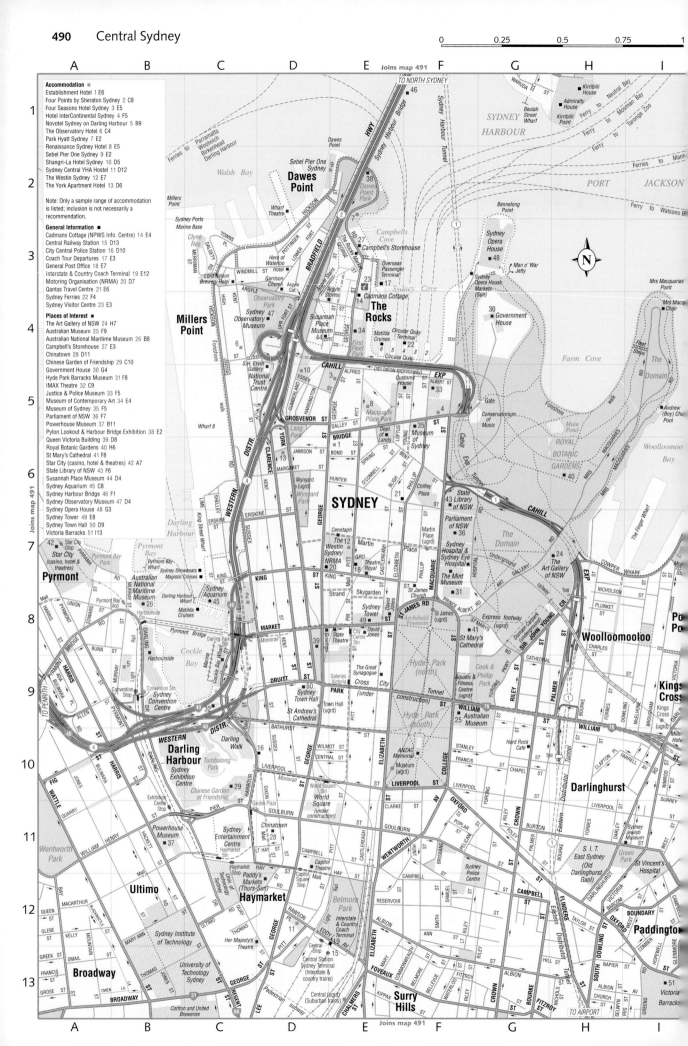

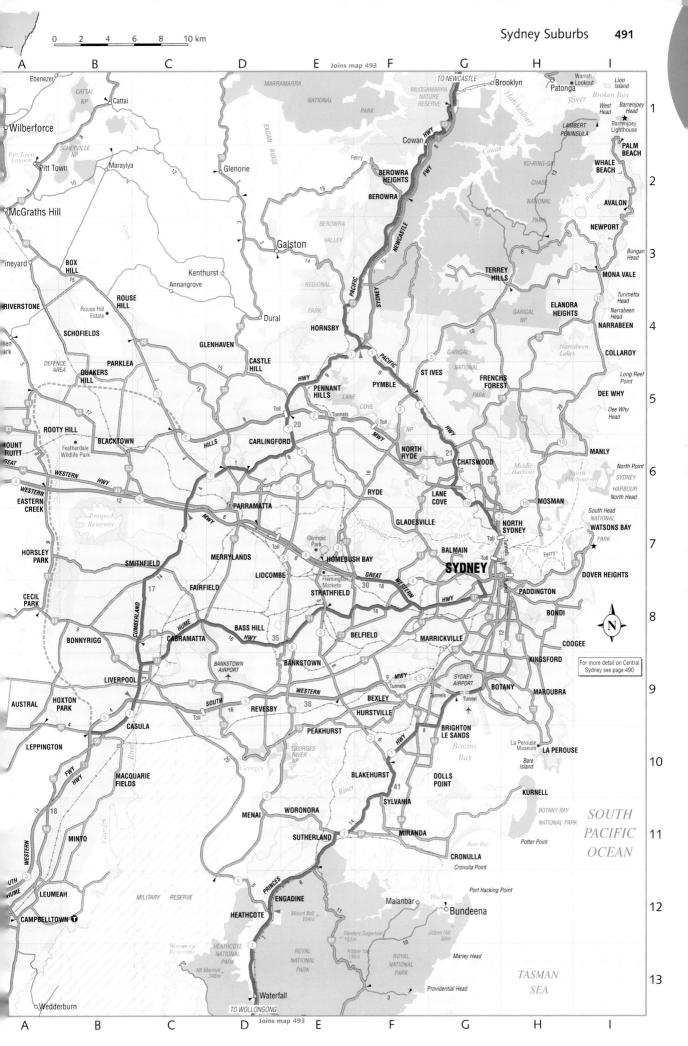

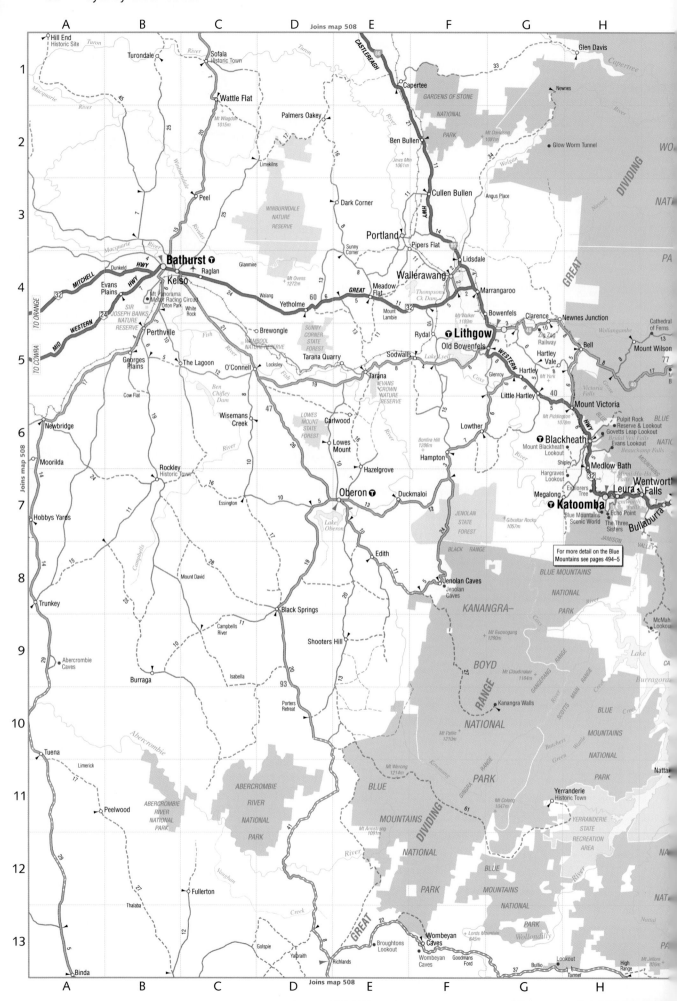

For more detail on the Blue Mountains see pages 494–5

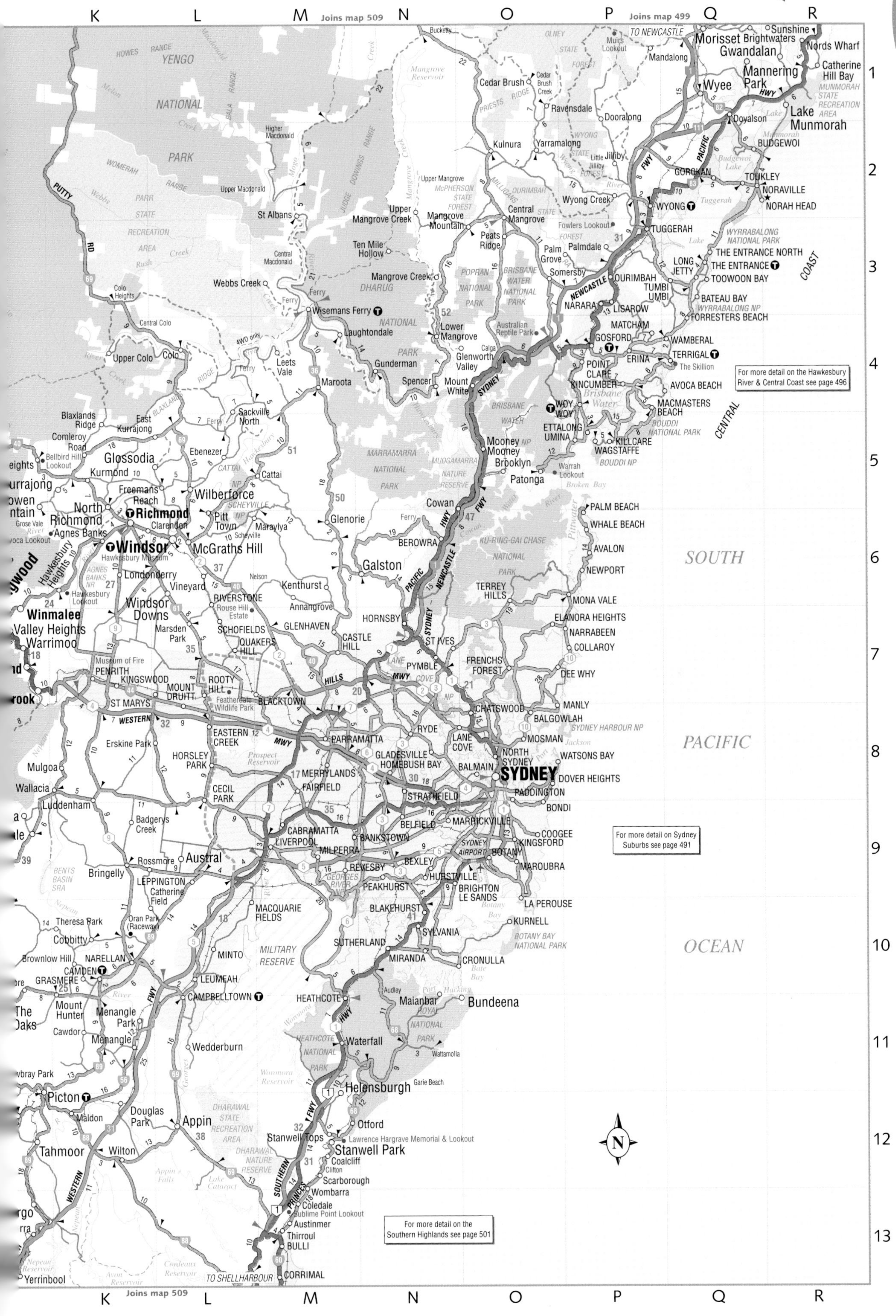

0 5 10 15 20 km
K L M N O P Q R
Joins map 509
Joins map 499
Joins map 509
1 2 3 4 5 6 7 8 9 10 11 12 13
TO NEWCASTLE
TO SHELLHARBOUR
Morisset
Brightwaters
Sunshine
Nords Wharf
Gwandalan
Catherine Hill Bay
Mannering Park
Wyee
Mandalong
Muirs Lookout
OLNEY STATE FOREST
MUNMORAH STATE RECREATION AREA
Lake Munmorah
Doyalson
BUDGEWOI
Budgewoi Lake
TOUKLEY
NORAVILLE
NORAH HEAD
GOROKAN
WYONG
TUGGERAH
Tuggerah Lake
WYRRABALONG NATIONAL PARK
THE ENTRANCE NORTH
THE ENTRANCE
LONG JETTY
TOOWOON BAY
BATEAU BAY
WYRRABALONG NP
FORRESTERS BEACH
CENTRAL COAST
Buckettys
Cedar Brush
Cedar Brush Creek
Ravensdale
Dooralong
Kulnura
Yarramalong
Little Jilliby
Jilliby
WYONG STATE FOREST
OURIMBAH STATE FOREST
Wyong Creek
Fowlers Lookout
Central Mangrove
Peats Ridge
Palm Grove
Palmdale
Somersby
OURIMBAH
TUMBI UMBI
NARARA
LISAROW
MATCHAM
WAMBERAL
GOSFORD
ERINA
TERRIGAL
The Skillion
POINT CLARE
KINCUMBER
AVOCA BEACH
MACMASTERS BEACH
BOUDDI NATIONAL PARK
WOY WOY
ETTALONG
UMINA
KILLCARE
WAGSTAFFE
BOUDDI NP
Brisbane Water
BRISBANE WATER NATIONAL PARK
Australian Reptile Park
Calga
Glenworth Valley
Lower Mangrove
Mount White
Spencer
Gunderman
Laughtondale
Wisemans Ferry
Mangrove Creek
Mangrove Reservoir
Upper Mangrove
McPHERSON STATE FOREST
Upper Mangrove Creek
Mangrove Mountain
Ten Mile Hollow
DHARUG NATIONAL PARK
POPRAN NATIONAL PARK
St Albans
Central Macdonald
Higher Macdonald
Upper Macdonald
Webbs Creek
HOWES RANGE
YENGO NATIONAL PARK
WOMERAH RANGE
PARR STATE RECREATION AREA
PUTTY RD
Colo Heights
Central Colo
Upper Colo
Colo
Leets Vale
Maroota
Sackville North
East Kurrajong
Blaxlands Ridge
Comleroy Road
Bellbird Hill Lookout
Glossodia
Kurmond
Ebenezer
CATTAI NP
Cattai
Freemans Reach
Wilberforce
North Richmond
Richmond
Clarendon
Pitt Town
Maraylya
Agnes Banks
Grose Vale
Windsor
Hawkesbury Museum
McGraths Hill
Londonderry
Vineyard
Hawkesbury Lookout
Hawkesbury Heights
Winmalee
Valley Heights
Warrimoo
Windsor Downs
RIVERSTONE
Rouse Hill Estate
SCHOFIELDS
Marsden Park
QUAKERS HILL
Nelson
Kenthurst
Annangrove
GLENHAVEN
CASTLE HILL
Glenorie
MARRAMARRA NATIONAL PARK
MUOGAMARRA NATURE RESERVE
Mooney Mooney
Brooklyn
Patonga
Warrah Lookout
Broken Bay
Cowan
BEROWRA
Galston
HORNSBY
PALM BEACH
WHALE BEACH
AVALON
NEWPORT
KU-RING-GAI CHASE NATIONAL PARK
TERREY HILLS
MONA VALE
ELANORA HEIGHTS
NARRABEEN
COLLAROY
DEE WHY
FRENCHS FOREST
ST IVES
PYMBLE
LANE COVE NP
HILLS MWY
CHATSWOOD
MANLY
BALGOWLAH
SYDNEY HARBOUR NP
MOSMAN
NORTH SYDNEY
WATSONS BAY
SYDNEY
DOVER HEIGHTS
PADDINGTON
BONDI
COOGEE
KINGSFORD
MAROUBRA
LA PEROUSE
KURNELL
BOTANY BAY NATIONAL PARK
BOTANY
SYDNEY AIRPORT
MARRICKVILLE
STRATHFIELD
BALMAIN
LANE COVE
RYDE
GLADESVILLE
HOMEBUSH BAY
PARRAMATTA
MERRYLANDS
FAIRFIELD
BELFIELD
BANKSTOWN
CABRAMATTA
LIVERPOOL
MILPERRA
REVESBY
BEXLEY
HURSTVILLE
PEAKHURST
BRIGHTON LE SANDS
BLAKEHURST
SYLVANIA
SUTHERLAND
MIRANDA
CRONULLA
Bate Bay
Port Hacking
Bundeena
Maianbar
Audley
ROYAL NATIONAL PARK
HEATHCOTE
Waterfall
HEATHCOTE NATIONAL PARK
Wattamolla
Garie Beach
Helensburgh
Otford
Stanwell Tops
Lawrence Hargrave Memorial & Lookout
Stanwell Park
Coalcliff
Clifton
Scarborough
Wombarra
Coledale
Sublime Point Lookout
Austinmer
Thirroul
BULLI
CORRIMAL
PRINCES HWY
SOUTHERN FWY
Museum of Fire
PENRITH
KINGSWOOD
MOUNT DRUITT
ROOTY HILL
Featherdale Wildlife Park
BLACKTOWN
ST MARYS
WESTERN MWY
EASTERN CREEK
Erskine Park
HORSLEY PARK
Prospect Reservoir
CECIL PARK
Mulgoa
Wallacia
Luddenham
Badgerys Creek
Rossmore
Austral
Bringelly
BENTS BASIN SRA
LEPPINGTON
Catherine Field
MACQUARIE FIELDS
Oran Park (Raceway)
Theresa Park
Cobbitty
NARELLAN
Brownlow Hill
CAMDEN
GRASMERE
MINTO
MILITARY RESERVE
LEUMEAH
CAMPBELLTOWN
The Oaks
Mount Hunter
Menangle Park
Menangle
Cawdor
Wedderburn
Woronora Reservoir
Picton
Maldon
Douglas Park
Appin
DHARAWAL STATE RECREATION AREA
DHARAWAL NATURE RESERVE
Tahmoor
Wilton
Appin Falls
Lake Cataract
Cordeaux Reservoir
Avon Reservoir
Nepean Reservoir
Yerrinbool
SOUTH PACIFIC OCEAN
PACIFIC HWY
NEWCASTLE FWY
SYDNEY NEWCASTLE FWY
WESTERN FWY
For more detail on the Hawkesbury River & Central Coast see page 496
For more detail on Sydney Suburbs see page 491
For more detail on the Southern Highlands see page 501

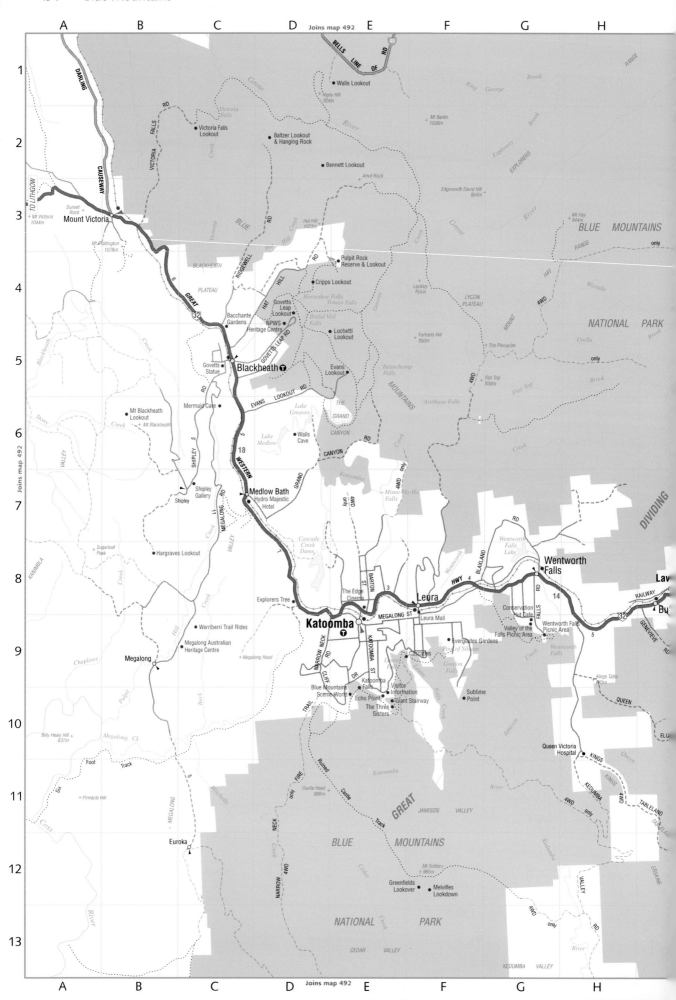

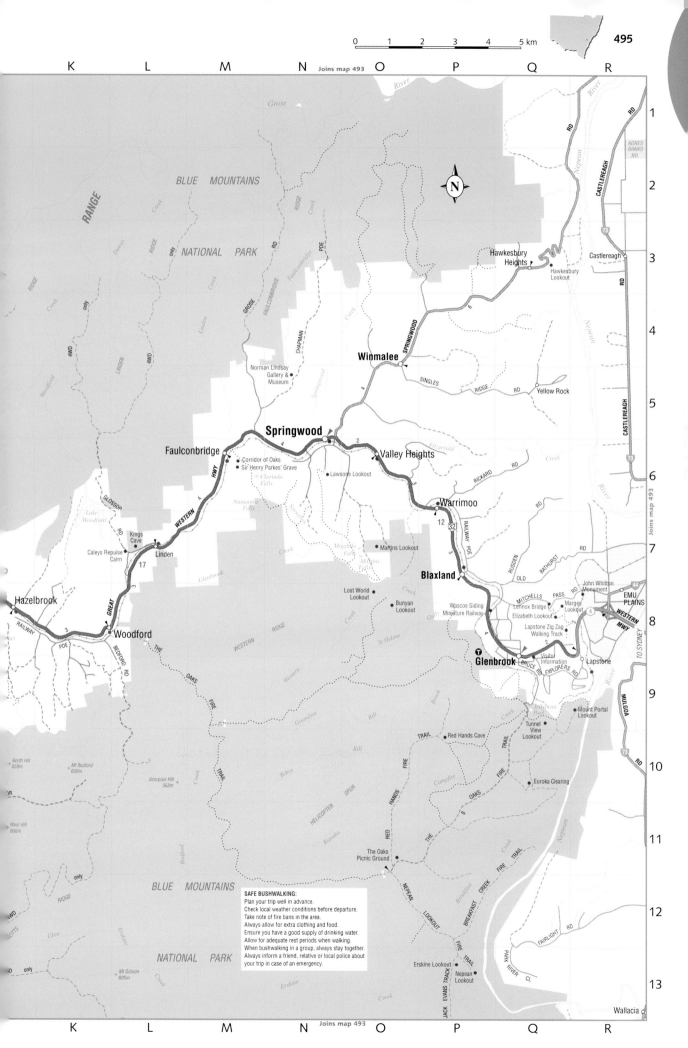

0 1 2 3 4 5 km

K L M N O P Q R

1

BLUE MOUNTAINS

RANGE

2

CASTLEREAGH RD

AGNES BANKS NR

NATIONAL PARK

Grose

River

Nepean

Dewes Creek

RIDGE only

Creek

Linden Creek

RIDGE only

GROSE RD

FAULCONBRIDGE PDE

CHAPMAN

3

Hawkesbury Heights

Castlereagh

Hawkesbury Lookout

SPRINGWOOD

6

RD

4

4WD

4WD

LINDEN

Woodland

Springwood Creek

Norman Lindsay Gallery & Museum

Winmalee

SINGLES

RIDGE RD

Yellow Rock

Nepean

River

5

CASTLEREAGH

RD

73

Springwood

Faulconbridge

2

Valley Heights

Fitzgerald Creek

RICKARD RD

WESTERN HWY

4

Corridor of Oaks
Sir Henry Parkes' Grave

Lawsons Lookout

Clarinda Falls

RD

6

River

Joins map 493

GLOSSOP RD

Lake Woodford

Numantia Falls

Sassafras Creek

Warrimoo

12 32

RAILWAY PDE

RD

7

Kings Cave

Caleys Repulse Cairn

17

Linden

Glenbrook Creek

Creek

Magdala Falls

Martins Lookout

3

Martins Falls

Blaxland

RUSDEN RD

OLD BATHURST RD

MITCHELLS PASS

John Whitton Monument

44

EMU PLAINS

8

Hazelbrook

RAILWAY

3

GREAT

PDE

Woodford

BEDFORD RD

THE OAKS

WESTERN

RIDGE

Lost World Lookout

Bunyan Lookout

Si Helens Gully

Wascoe Siding Miniature Railway

Lennox Bridge
Elizabeth Lookout

Lapstone Zig Zag Walking Track

Marges Lookout

WESTERN MWY

4

Glenbrook

Visitor Information

EXPLORERS RD

Lapstone

BRUCE RD

TO SYDNEY

9

FIRE TRAIL

Groundra Rill

Creek

Brook

Jellybean Pool

Mount Portal Lookout

Tunnel View Lookout

73 RD

10

North Hill 658m

Mt Bedford 639m

Scorpion Hill 563m

Creek

TRAIL

FIRE

Tobys Rill

HELICOPTER SPUR

Kanuka Creek

RED HANDS FIRE TRAIL

THE OAKS FIRE TRAIL

Red Hands Cave

OAKS FIRE TRAIL

Euroka Clearing

Nepean

11

West Hill 666m

RIDGE only

Bedford Creek

The Oaks Picnic Ground

NEPEAN LOOKOUT FIRE TRAIL

THE

Creek

Campfire Creek

BREAKFAST CREEK FIRE TRAIL

12

BLUE MOUNTAINS

4WD only

Glen

Mt Gibson 605m

NATIONAL PARK

Erskine Creek

SAFE BUSHWALKING:
Plan your trip well in advance.
Check local weather conditions before departure.
Take note of fire bans in the area.
Always allow for extra clothing and food.
Ensure you have a good supply of drinking water.
Allow for adequate rest periods when walking.
When bushwalking in a group, always stay together.
Always inform a friend, relative or local police about
your trip in case of an emergency.

Erskine Lookout

Nepean Lookout

JACK EVANS TRACK

PARK RIVER CL

FAIRLIGHT RD

Wallacia

13

K L M N O P Q R

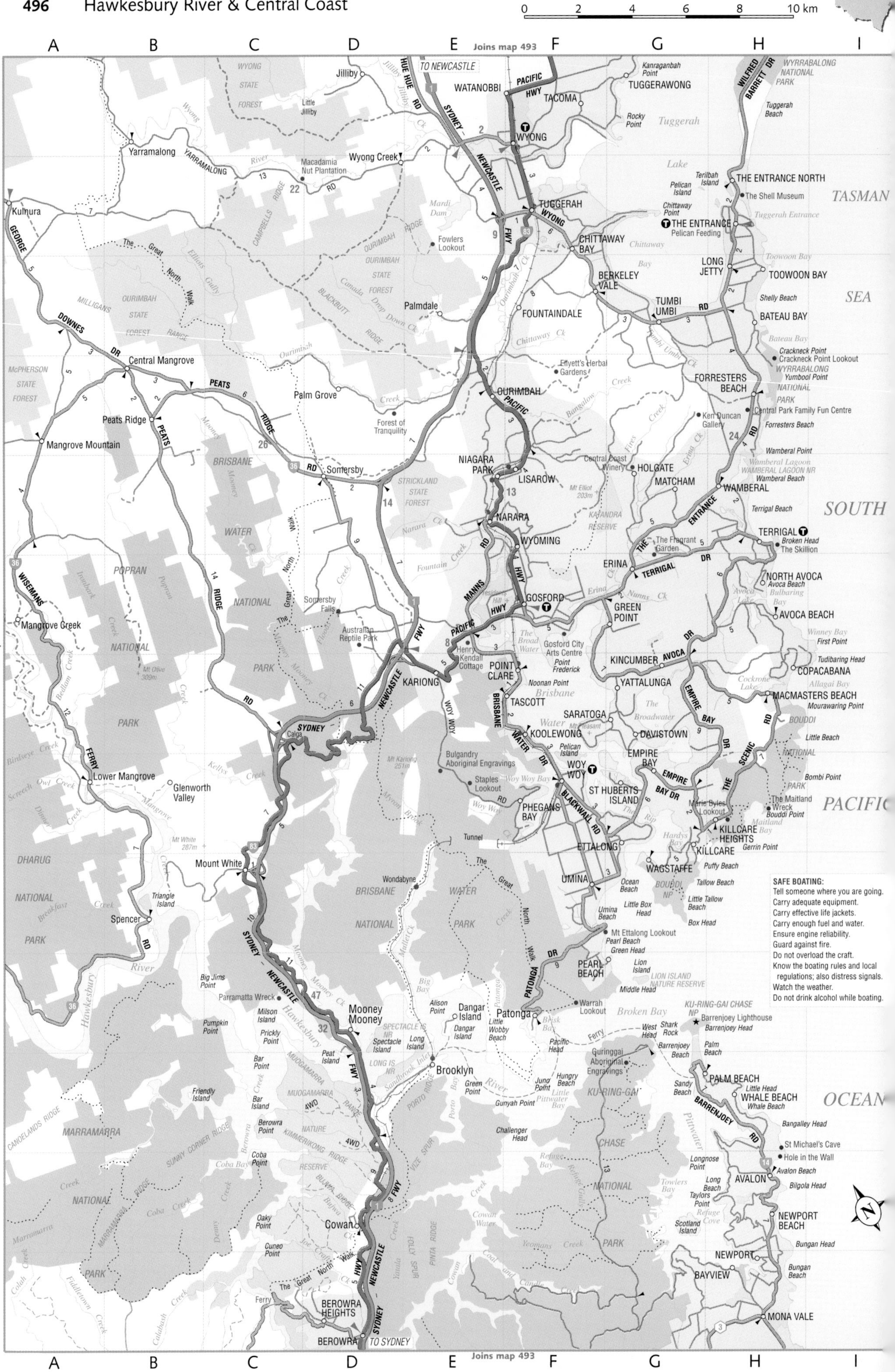
0 2 4 6 8 10 km
A B C D E F G H I
Joins map 493
1 2 3 4 5 6 7 8 9 10 11 12 13
TO NEWCASTLE
TO SYDNEY
Jilliby
Little Jilliby
WYONG STATE FOREST
WATANOBBI
PACIFIC HWY
TACOMA
TUGGERAWONG
Kanraganbah Point
Rocky Point
Tuggerah Lake
WYRRABALONG NATIONAL PARK
WILFRED BARRETT DR
Tuggerah Beach
WYONG
Yarramalong
YARRAMALONG RD
Wyong River
Macadamia Nut Plantation
Wyong Creek
HUE HUE RD
SYDNEY – NEWCASTLE FWY
Kulnura
GEORGE DOWNES DR
The Great North Walk
CAMPBELLS RIDGE
OURIMBAH RIDGE
Mardi Dam
Fowlers Lookout
TUGGERAH
WYONG RD
Pelican Island
Terilbah Island
THE ENTRANCE NORTH
The Shell Museum
TASMAN SEA
Chittaway Point
THE ENTRANCE
Pelican Feeding
Tuggerah Entrance
CHITTAWAY BAY
Chittaway Bay
Toowoon Bay
LONG JETTY
TOOWOON BAY
BERKELEY VALE
MILLIGANS OURIMBAH STATE FOREST RANGE
BLACKBUTT RIDGE
OURIMBAH STATE FOREST
Canada Drop Down Ck
Palmdale
FOUNTAINDALE
Ourimbah Ck
TUMBI UMBI RD
Shelly Beach
BATEAU BAY
Chittaway Ck
Bateau Bay
Crackneck Point
Crackneck Point Lookout
Central Mangrove
McPHERSON STATE FOREST
PEATS RIDGE RD
Ourimbah
Ellyett's Herbal Gardens
WYRRABALONG
Yumbool Point
NATIONAL PARK
FORRESTERS BEACH
Central Park Family Fun Centre
Forresters Beach
Palm Grove
OURIMBAH
Forest of Tranquility
Bangalow Creek
Ken Duncan Gallery
Peats Ridge
Mangrove Mountain
BRISBANE WATER NATIONAL PARK
NIAGARA PARK
LISAROW
Central Coast Winery
HOLGATE
MATCHAM
Wamberal Point
Wamberal Lagoon
WAMBERAL LAGOON NR
Wamberal Beach
Somersby
STRICKLAND STATE FOREST
Mt Elliot 203m
KATANDRA RESERVE
WAMBERAL
Terrigal Beach
SOUTH
NARARA
THE ENTRANCE RD
TERRIGAL
Broken Head
The Skillion
WISEMANS FERRY RD
POPRAN NATIONAL PARK
Narara Ck
Fountain Creek
WYOMING
The Fragrant Garden
ERINA
TERRIGAL DR
NORTH AVOCA
Avoca Beach
Bulbaring Bay
MANNS RD
Somersby Falls
GOSFORD
Erina
Nunns Ck
GREEN POINT
Avoca Lake
AVOCA BEACH
Mangrove Creek
Australian Reptile Park
Henry Kendall Cottage
The Broad Water
Gosford City Arts Centre
Point Frederick
Winney Bay
First Point
Mt Olive 309m
KARIONG
POINT CLARE
Noonan Point
KINCUMBER
AVOCA DR
Tudibaring Head
COPACABANA
Allagai Bay
Cockrone Lake
MACMASTERS BEACH
Mourawaring Point
TASCOTT
YATTALUNGA
The Broadwater
BRISBANE WATER DR
SARATOGA
EMPIRE BAY DR
Mt Pleasant
DAVISTOWN
BOUDDI
Calga
KOOLEWONG
Pelican Island
Bulgandry Aboriginal Engravings
Mt Kariong 251m
EMPIRE BAY
Little Beach
THE SCENIC RD
NATIONAL PARK
Bombi Point
Lower Mangrove
Glenworth Valley
Staples Lookout
Woy Woy Bay
WOY WOY
ST HUBERTS ISLAND
Marie Byles Lookout
The Maitland Wreck
Bouddi Point
PACIFIC
Woy Woy
PHEGANS BAY
BLACKWALL RD
The Rip
KILLCARE HEIGHTS
Maitland Bay
DHARUG NATIONAL PARK
Mt White 287m
Tunnel
Hardys Bay
KILLCARE
Gerrin Point
Mount White
ETTALONG
Puffy Beach
WAGSTAFFE
Tallow Beach
Wondabyne
UMINA
Ocean Beach
BOUDDI NP
Triangle Island
Little Box Head
Little Tallow Beach
Spencer
Umina Beach
Box Head
Mt Ettalong Lookout
Pearl Beach
Green Head
SAFE BOATING:
Tell someone where you are going.
Carry adequate equipment.
Carry effective life jackets.
Carry enough fuel and water.
Ensure engine reliability.
Guard against fire.
Do not overload the craft.
Know the boating rules and local regulations; also distress signals.
Watch the weather.
Do not drink alcohol while boating.
PATONGA DR
PEARL BEACH
Lion Island
LION ISLAND NATURE RESERVE
Middle Head
Hawkesbury River
Big Jims Point
Parramatta Wreck
Big Bay
Warrah Lookout
Broken Bay
KU-RING-GAI CHASE NP
Barrenjoey Lighthouse
Barrenjoey Head
Milson Island
Mooney Mooney
Alison Point
Dangar Island
Patonga
Brisk Bay
West Head
Shark Rock
Pumpkin Point
Prickly Point
SPECTACLE IS NR
Spectacle Island
Long Island
Little Wobby Beach
Pacific Head
Ferry
Barrenjoey Beach
Palm Beach
Peat Island
LONG IS NR
Bar Point
Sandbrook Inlet
Brooklyn
Green Point
Guringgai Aboriginal Engravings
Juno Point
Hungry Beach
Little Pittwater Beach
Gunyah Point
PALM BEACH
Sandy Beach
Little Head
WHALE BEACH
Whale Beach
OCEAN
Friendly Island
Bar Island
MUOGAMARRA NATURE RESERVE
PORTO RIDGE
Porto Bay
KU-RING-GAI CHASE NATIONAL PARK
BARRENJOEY RD
CANOELANDS RIDGE
MARRAMARRA NATIONAL PARK
SUNNY CORNER RIDGE
Berowra Point
Berowra Creek
KIMMERIKONG RIDGE
4WD
Challenger Head
Bangalley Head
St Michael's Cave
Hole in the Wall
Coba Bay
Coba Point
Refuge Bay
Pittwater
Longnose Point
Avalon Beach
AVALON
Bilgola Head
Long Beach
Taylors Point
Refuge Cove
Towlers Bay
Scotland Island
Oaky Point
Cowan
Cowan Water
HOLLY SPUR
PINTA RIDGE
VIZE SPUR
NEWPORT BEACH
Bungan Head
Cuneo Point
Joe Crafts Ck
Yeomans Creek
Coal and Candle Creek
NEWPORT
BAYVIEW
Bungan Beach
BEROWRA HEIGHTS
BEROWRA
MONA VALE
Marramarra Creek
Colah Creek
Fiddletown Creek
Calabash Creek

Joins map 509

Lower Hunter Valley

TO SINGLETON

Belford

NEW ENGLAND HWY

Branxton

TO MAITLAND

Pothana

North Rothbury

RAILWAY

NORTHERN

Hot-air Ballooning

TUCKERS LA

Rothbury

Talga

Wilderness

Butterflies Gallery

Broke

Peppers Guest House

Gillards

German Tourist & Holiday Estate

CESSNOCK AERODROME

LOWER HUNTER NP

Rusa Park Zoo

Pokolbin

Debeyers

Loverdale

Nulkaba

Oakey Creek

O'Connors

Marrowbone

Cessnock

Mt Bright 483m

Bimbadeen Lookout

Bellbird

WOLLOMBI

ABERDARE RD

Aberdare

ABERDARE STATE FOREST

KITCHENER

TO KURRI KURRI

Joins map 499

Upper Hunter Valley

MANOBALAI NATURE RESERVE

Manobalai

Halls Mtn 338m

Black Jack Mtn 499m

YARRAMAN RD

RIDGELANDS

Wybong

Castle Rock

WYBONG

Roxburgh

Mangoola

TO MERRIWA

Sandy Hollow

Hollydeen

GOLDEN HWY

TO MUSWELLBROOK

Myambat

Rosemount

Denman

DENMAN RD

GOLDEN (JERRYS PLAINS) HWY

To Arrowfield Wines

TO SINGLETON

WOLLEMI NATIONAL PARK

Esdai

Martindale

BUREEN RD

WOLLEMI NATIONAL PARK

WINERIES:

LOWER HUNTER VALLEY

Allandale Winery	1 E8
Allanmere Wines	2 E7
Audrey Wilkinson Vineyard	3 A8
Bimbadgen Estate Winery	4 C6
Blueberry Vineyard	5 C5
The Boutique Wine Centre	6 C8
Briar Ridge Vineyard	7 B11
Brokenwood	8 B8
Calais Estate	9 D7
Capercaillie Wine Co.	10 E8
Carindale Wines	11 D7
Chateau Francois	12 A7
Constable & Hershon Vineyards	13 B7
Drayton's Family Wines	15 B10
Farrell's Limestone Ck Vineyard	16 B11
Golden Grape Estate	17 C10
Hardys Hunter Ridge	18 A5
Hermitage Rd Cellars & Winery	19 A5
Honeytree Estate Wines	20 B7
Hungerford Hill Wines	22 A9
Hunter Cellars	23 B7
Hunter Valley Wine Society	24 D8
Ivanhoe Wines	25 A9
Jackson's Hill Vineyard	26 B11
JYT Wine Co.	28 B8
Kevin Sobels Wines	29 C8
Lake's Folly Vineyard	30 D8
Lindemans Ben Ean	31 B9
Little's Winery	32 C6
McGuigan Cellars	33 B8
McLeish Estate	34 C9
McWilliam's Mount Pleasant Estate	35 B10
Maling Family Estate	36 C7
Marsh Estate	37 A5
Mistletoe Wines	38 A4
Molly Morgan Vineyard	39 E5
Montagne View Estate	40 A3
Moorebank Vineyard	41 D7
Mount View Estate	42 C11
Murray Robson Winery	43 D4
Oakvale Winery	44 A6
Peacock Hill Vineyard	45 D7
Pendarves Estate	46 A3
Pepper Tree Wines	47 C8
Peppers Creek Winery	48 B7
Petersons House	49 D8
Petersons Wines	50 B11
Piggs Peake Winery	51 A4
Pokolbin Estate Vineyard	52 B8
Reg Drayton Wines	53 A9
Rothbury Estate	56 C7
Rothvale Wines	57 B5
Saddler's Creek Wines	58 C11
Sandalyn Estate	59 E6
Scarborough Wine Co.	60 B7
Sutherland Wines	61 C5
Tamburlaine Wines	62 B8
Terrace Vale Wines	63 B5
Thalgara Estate	64 B9
Tinkler's Vineyard	65 A9
Tintilla Vineyard	66 A4
Tulloch Wines	67 B9
Tyrrell's Wines	68 A7
Van De Scheur Wines	69 C10
Vinden Estate Wines	70 B7
Warrarong Estate	71 E6
Wilderness Estate Wines	72 D8
Windarra Winery	73 C8

UPPER HUNTER VALLEY

Cruikshank Callatoota Estate	14 G4
Horseshoe Vineyard	21 F9
James Estate	27 F7
Reynold's Yarraman	54 H3
Rosemount Estate	55 G6

0   0.25   0.50   0.75   1

A   B   C   Joins map 499   D   E   F   G   H   I

INDUSTRIAL
GROSS ST
GEORGE ST
KINGS RD
DR
Tighes Hill
ELIZABETH
Throsby Creek
ELIZABETH ST
HANNELL ST
Maryville
HARRISON
DOWNIE
ROBERT ST
ALBERT ST
Wickham Park
HANNELL ST
Wickham
THROSBY ST
RAILWAY
HUNTER ST
School
PARRY
111
ST
TUDOR ST
AV
DENISON ST
HEBURN ST
TAFE
School
EVERTON ST
CORONA ST
Hamilton East
DUMARESQ ST
KEMP ST
ALEXANDER ST
JENNER ST
PDE
PARKWAY
KEMP ST
JENNER
School
PARK
The Junction
STEWART ST
STANLEY ST
TURNBULL ST
CRAM ST
NATIONAL ST
SMITH ST
FARQUHAR ST
GLEBE RD
1
RAILWAY
LINGARD ST
BERNER ST
LLEWELYN ST
SELWYN ST
MORGAN ST
CALDWELL ST
RIDGE ST
Mitchell Park
School
PATRICK ST
BUCHANAN ST
HELEN ST
Bar Beach
OCEAN ST
Dixon Park
WATKINS ST
FREDERICK ST
JANET ST
CURRY ST
Merewether
MEREWETHER ST
MITCHELL ST
PELL ST
Gibbs Bros Park
SCENIC DR
HICKSON ST
Lookout
North Rocks
Lookout
Reserve
The Great
Merewether Baths
29
Merewether Beach
Walk

GIPPS ST
YOUNG ST
BOURKE ST
BOOTH ST
DARLING ST
HARGRAVE ST
Carrington
ROBERTSON ST
HOWDEN ST
Pat Jordan Oval
Connolly Park
COWPER ST
FITZROY ST
DENISON ST
NORTH ST
LEE ST
WHARF
Floating Dock
Wickham
HUNTER ST
KING ST
7
Birdwood Park
Newcastle West
PARRY ST
STEEL ST
RAVENSWORTH ST
BULL ST
School
Newcastle Workers Club
30
Newcastle High School
National Park
TOOKE ST
Centennial Park
DARBY ST
DAWSON ST
BROOKS ST
LIGHT ST
WRIGHTSON ST
Cooks Hill Gallery 22
Cooks Hill
COUNCIL ST
LAMAN ST
38
39 33
School
City Park
8
Civic Park
10 NRMA
4
16
17
Water Police
WHARF
MERE WETHER ST
Civic
WHARF
STEAMSHIP
William IV
40
State Dockyard
The Basin
Floating Dock
HUNTER
Throsby Creek
RIVER
Port Hunter
Dyke Point
Sydney Harbour Seaplanes
37
Queens Wharf
32
9
Ferry
Newcastle Harbour
Lee Wharf

HEREFORD ST
MONMOUTH ST
Stockton
FULLERTON ST
School
ROXBURGH ST
DOUGLAS ST
DUNBAR ST
MITCHELL ST
CLYDE ST
KING ST
QUEEN ST
MITCHELL ST
CHURCH ST
NEWCASTLE ST
PITT ST
WHARF CR
Griffith Park
Rawson Park
Stockton
Caravan Park
Northern Breakwater
Pirate Point
Stony Point
Nobbys Beach
Horseshoe Beach
Harbourside Park (The Foreshore)
Frog Pond
STEVENSON PL
24 Fort Scratchley
28 Maritime & Military Museums
6
2
5 SHORTLAND
35 Soldiers Ba (swimming
ESP
NOBBYS RD
ALFRED ST
Newcastle 11
23
21
SCOTT ST
HUNTER ST
26 Mall
13
14
KING ST
15 Royal Newcastle Hospital
12
BOLTON ST
NEWCOMEN ST
Court House
WATT ST
Pacific ST
NEWCASTLE
Newcastle Beach
CHURCH ST
Christ Church Cathedral
20
Cathedral Park
School
HUNTER ST
BROWN ST
KING ST
Historical Navigation Tower 25
TYRRELL ST
SWAN ST
WOLFE ST
The Hill
NBN3 TV Studio
Obelisk 31
RESERVE RD
HIGH ST
ANZAC PDE
NESCA
GREENSLOPES
Nesca Park
PDE
AV
18 York
27
King Edward Park
Shepherds Hill Lookout
Hill Rocks
Lookout
Bogey Hole (swimming pool)
19
Susan Gilmore Beach
Empire Park
Bar Beach
MEMORIAL DR
Lookout
Dixon Park Beach

N

TASMAN

SEA

A   B   C   D   E   F   G   H   I

0   5   10   15   20 km

Joins map 509

A   B   C   D   E   F   G   H   I

1
2
3
4
5
6
7
8
9
10
11
12
13

SOUTH

PACIFIC

OCEAN

TASMAN

SEA

TO TAREE

TEA GARDENS RD

Tea Gardens

Hawks
Nest

Providence
Bay

Fort Tomaree Lookout

Shoal Bay

Fingal Bay

Nelson
Bay

Corlette

Soldiers
Point

Salamander
Bay

Anna Bay

Boat Harbour

TOMAREE
NATIONAL
PARK

North Arm
Cove

Lemon Tree
Passage

Koala
Reserve

Tilligerry
Habitat

Tanilba
House

Tanilba
Bay

Port Stephens
Winery

Stockton
Beach

Oakvale Farm &
Fauna World

Salt Ash

Stockton Sand
Dunes

Newcastle
Bight

Medowie

Fighter
World

NEWCASTLE
AIRPORT

Williamtown

Fullerton
Cove

Stockton
Bridge

STOCKTON

NEWCASTLE

Karuah

KARUAH
NATURE
RESERVE

WORIMI
NATURE
RESERVE

WALLAROO
NATURE
RESERVE

Limeburners
Creek

Clarence Town

Dungog

Marshdale

Flat Tops

Alison

Glen William

Brookfield

Wiragulla

Wallaroba

Hilldale

Glen
Martin

Glen Oak

Seaham

Wallalong

Woodville

Hinton

Morpeth
Historic Village

Raymond
Terrace

Duckenfield

Hunter
Region Botanic
Gardens

KOORAGANG
NR

Thornton

Hexham

Beresfield

HEXHAM
SWAMP
NR

Shortland
Wetlands

MEREWETHER

GLENROCK
STATE
RECREATION
AREA

NEW
LAMBTON

ELERMORE
VALE

CHARLESTOWN

CARDIFF

WALLSEND

Minmi

Seahampton

West
Wallsend

Boolaroo

WARNERS
BAY

REDHEAD

Killingworth

Toronto

Awaba

Rathmines

Wangi
Wangi

BLACKSMITHS

BELMONT

Swansea

Dobell
House

Silverwater

Nords Wharf

Catherine Hill
Bay

Sunshine

Mirrabooka

Gwandalan

Chain Valley
Bay

MUNMORAH
STATE
RECREATION
AREA

Mannering
Park

Lake Munmorah

Yarrawonga
Park

Eraring

Bonnells
Bay

Brightwaters

Windermere
Park

Dora
Creek

Morisset

Wyee
Point

Avondale

Cooranbong

Martinsville

WATAGAN
NATIONAL
PARK

Wishing
Well

Muirs
Lookout

Mandalong

Wyee

Doyalson

BUDGEWOI

NORAVILLE

NORAH HEAD

TOUKLEY

GOROKAN

TO WYONG

Maclean's
Lookout

Heaton
Lookout

Freemans
Waterhole

Brunkerville

Quorrobolong

Millfield

Paxton

Ellalong

Bellbird

Kitchener

Abernethy

Aberdare

Kearsley

Cessnock

Neath

Lovedale

Pokolbin

Abermain

Weston

Kurri Kurri

Pelaw Main

Richmond Vale
Mining Museum

Heddon Greta

Lochinvar

Greta

Mount Vincent

Mulbring

LOWER
HUNTER
NATIONAL
PARK

BROKEN BACK RANGE

Wollombi
Historic Village

MAITLAND

Bolwarra

Walka
Waterworks

Paterson

Vacy

Tocal
Agricultural
College

Martins
Creek

ROSEBROOK RIDGE

Rosebrook

th Rothbury

Flat Rock
Lookout

Mt Warrawolong
640m

For more detail on the
Hunter Valley see page 497

For more detail on
Newcastle see page 498

Joins map 509
Joins map 493

Joins map 501

TASMAN

SEA

Accommodation ■
Belmore All Suite Hotel 1 G9
Boat Harbour Motel 2 G9
Downtown Motel 3 F10
Novotel Northbeach 4 G8
Park Street Apartments 5 F8
Quality Hotel City Pacific 6 E10
Surfside 22 Motel 7 G10

Note: Only a sample range of
accommodation is listed; inclusion is
not necessarily a recommendation.

General Information ■
Coach Terminal 8 F9
Motoring Organisation (NRMA) 9 F10
Police Headquarters 10 F9
Post Office 11 F10
Wollongong Entertainment Centre 12 G10
Wollongong Railway Station 13 E10
Wollongong Visitor Centre 14 F10

Places of Interest ■
City Gallery 15 F10
Illawarra Historical Society Museum 16 G
Illawarra Performing Arts Centre 17 F10
International Centre 18 F10
Wollongong Botanic Gardens 19 C7

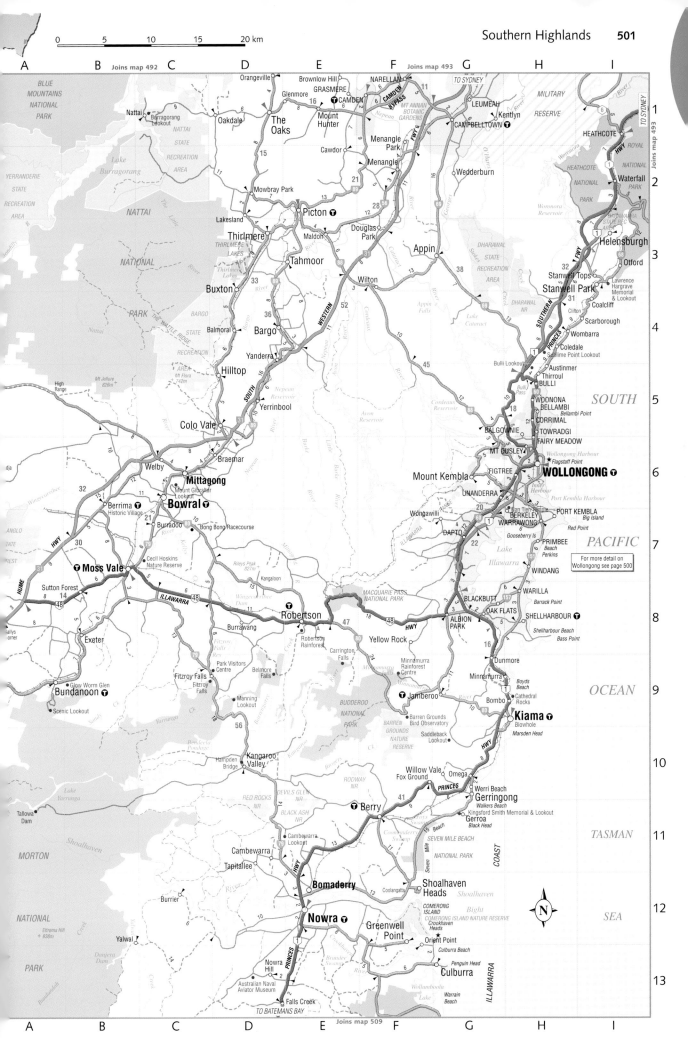

0 5 10 15 20 km

A   B   C   D   E   Joins map 507   F   G   H   I

TO CANBERRA
23
Bunyan
TO BATEMANS BAY
Tuross Head
Bodalla
Nerrigundah
9
Eurobodalla
EUROBODA
Numeralla
Big
Badje
River
12
Countegany
22
Tuross
Lake Bu
Pc
Pc
Dalme
Cooma
30
Tuross Falls
Belowra
Wagonga
Kianga
BODALLA
STATE
Naroo
Wagonga Inlet
MONARO
11
42
Kybeyan
51
Yowrie
Wandella
Peak Alone
954m
Mt Dromedary
FOREST
Tilba Valley
Vineyard
Central Tilba
Historic Village
Corunna
Corunna
Lake
HWY
Cape Drome
Tilba Tilba
18
54
Tilba
Tilba
23
DANGELONG
NATURE
RESERVE
Coonerang
Kydra
Mt Kydra
1298m
WADBILLIGA
NATIONAL
PARK
Cobargo
PRINCES
Narira
WALLAGA
LAKE
NP
Umbarra
Cultural
Centre
EUROBODALLA
NATIONAL PARK
MONTAG
NATUR
RESER
Nimmitabel
Brogo
Dam
11
Quaama
18
Creek
Bermagui
Bermagui South
Baragoot Point
SOUTH
Bobundara
River
6
River
Maclaughlin
SNOWY
Brown Mtn
1260m
18
22
MOUNTAINS
HWY
SOUTH EAST FOREST
NATIONAL PARK
(Bemboka Section)
HWY
41
Brogo
BIAMANGA
NATIONAL
PARK
Cuttagee
Lake
Murrah
Lagoon
Goalen Point
Bunga
Wapengo
MIMOSA ROCKS
NATIONAL
Wapengo
Lake
PARK
PACIFIC
Mt Cooper
1018m
20
66
Bemboka
2
Bega
10
Numbugga
Morans
Crossing
17
18
Grevillea Estate
Winery
Bega Cheese
Heritage Centre
Bega
Tanja
16
MIMOSA
ROCKS
NATIONAL
PARK
Baronda Head
12
OCEAN
Joins map 507
MONARO
41
Ando
1
18
SOUTH EAST
FOREST
NATIONAL PARK
(Tantawangalo Section)
Bimbaya
Kameruka
18
13
8
13
Jellat
Jellat
Kalaru
Tathra
Bukalong
Bibbenluke
12
Black
Lake
Cathcart
4
9
Mount Darrah
36
Candelo
Historic
Village
4
10
11
PRINCES
12
35
Wolumla
Magic Mountain
Family
Recreation
Park
BOURNDA
NATURE
RESERVE
SAPPHIRE COAST WAY
15
BOURNDA
NATIONAL
PARK
Wallagoot Lake
Bombala
13
COOLUMBOOKA
NATURE
RESERVE
Coolumbooka
River
Towamba
River
22
79
SOUTH EAST
FOREST
NATIONAL
PARK
(Yurmmie
Section)
2
Tura Beach
Merimbula
Aquarium
Merimbula Point
Merimbula
Bay
10
Maharatta
23
Rocky Hall
10
Wyndham
21
Lochiel
Pambula
4
5
Pambula Beach
Haycock Point
42
HWY
Genoa
River
Platts
White Rock Mtn
1090m
5
8
River
Burragate
SOUTH EAST
FOREST
NATIONAL
PARK
(Coolangubra
Section)
Greigs Flat
6
Pambula
Lake
17
19
BEN BOYD
NATIONAL
PARK
The Pinnacles
Nethercote
BONDI GULF
NATURE
RESERVE
Wog Wog Mtn
1139m
Pericoe
20
Eden
Worang Point
Killer Whale Museum
Bay- & whale-
watching cruises
TASMAN
SEA
24
33
Towamba
25
HWY
East Boyd
Boydtown
Boyd's Tower
Twofold Bay
Seahorse
Inn
Davidson Whaling
Station Historic Site
Mowarry Point
MONARO
13
SOUTH EAST
FOREST
NATIONAL
PARK
(Genoa
Section)
Nungatta Mtn
SOUTH EAST
FOREST
NATIONAL
PARK
(Waalimma
Section)
Waalimma Mtn
722m
MT IMLAY
NATIONAL
PARK
Mt Imlay
886m
1
6
5
Kiah
BEN BOYD
NATIONAL
PARK
Cooracombra
958m
COOPRACAMBRA
NATIONAL PARK
NEW SOUTH WALES
VICTORIA
Wog
River
Wallagaraugh
Imlay
River
Genoa
River
Wonboyn
River
4
Narrabarba
2
12
Wonboyn
Lake
Wonboyn
21
Green Cape
Disaster
Bay
PRINCES
TO CANN RIVER
TO CANN RIVER
Joins map 507

1 2 3 4 5 6 7 8 9 10 11 12 13

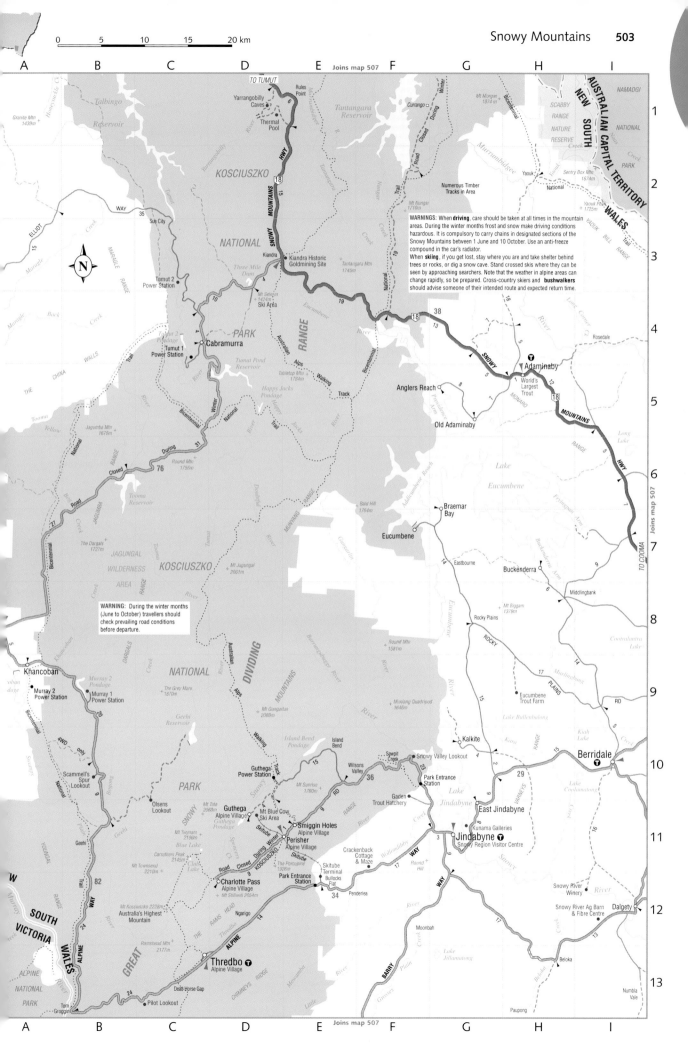

Joins map 507

WARNINGS: When **driving**, care should be taken at all times in the mountain areas. During the winter months frost and snow make driving conditions hazardous. It is compulsory to carry chains in designated sections of the Snowy Mountains between 1 June and 10 October. Use an anti-freeze compound in the car's radiator.

When **skiing**, if you get lost, stay where you are and take shelter behind trees or rocks, or dig a snow cave. Stand crossed skis where they can be seen by approaching searchers. Note that the weather in alpine areas can change rapidly, so be prepared. Cross-country skiers and **bushwalkers** should advise someone of their intended route and expected return time.

WARNING: During the winter months (June to October) travellers should check prevailing road conditions before departure.

Joins map 507

Joins map 507

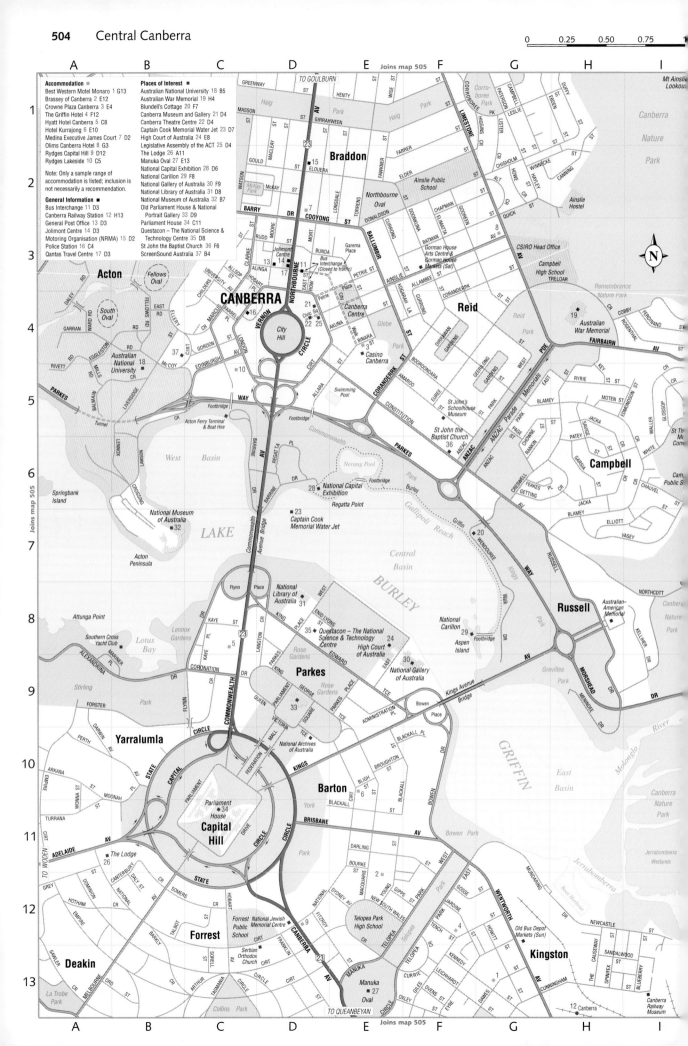

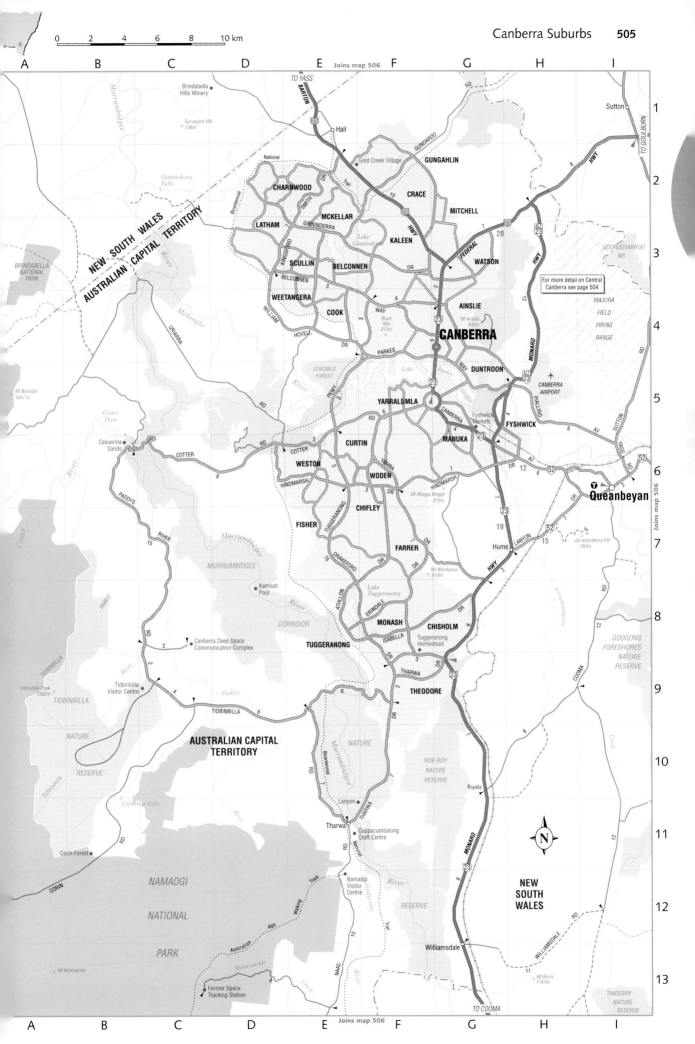

Joins map 506

TO YASS

BARTON

Hall

Brindabella
Hills Winery

Surveyors Hill
736m

Murrumbidgee

Ginninderra
Falls

National

Gold Creek Village

GUNGAHLIN

CHARNWOOD

CRACE

MCKELLAR

MITCHELL

LATHAM

KALEEN

Lake
Ginninderra

SCULLIN

BELCONNEN

FEDERAL

WATSON

BELCONNEN

WEETANGERA

AINSLIE

For more detail on Central
Canberra see page 504

COOK

Black
Mtn
812m

CANBERRA

Mt Ainslie
843m

MONARO

MAJURA
FIELD
FIRING
RANGE

GOOROOYARROO
NR

PARKES

Lake
Burley

DUNTROON

Stromlo
Forest

YARRALUMLA

Canberra
Airport

Canberra Deep Space
Communication Complex

CURTIN

Griffin

Canberra

Manuka

Fyshwick
Markets

FYSHWICK

PIALLIGO

SUTTON

YASS

WESTON

HINDMARSH

WODEN

Mt Mugga Mugga
813m

HINDMARSH

Queanbeyan

CHIFLEY

FISHER

Mt Wanniassa
810m

FARRER

Hume

Jerrabomberra Hill
782m

Kambah
Pool

Lake
Tuggeranong

MONASH

Tuggeranong
Homestead

CHISHOLM

GOOGONG
FORESHORES
NATURE
RESERVE

TUGGERANONG

ERINDALE

Isabella

TIDBINBILLA
NATURE
RESERVE

Tidbinbilla
Visitor Centre

TIDBINBILLA

Tharwa

THEODORE

AUSTRALIAN CAPITAL
TERRITORY

NATURE

Gibraltar Falls

Murrumbidgee

ROB ROY
NATURE
RESERVE

Royalla

Corin Forest

Lanyon

Cuppacumbalong
Craft Centre

Tharwa

N

NEW
SOUTH
WALES

NAMADGI

NATIONAL

Namadgi
Visitor Centre

River

RESERVE

WILLIAMSDALE

Mt Burra
1147m

PARK

Mt McKnailnie

Australian

Alps

Walking

Trail

Honeysuckle

Former Space
Tracking Station

Williamsdale

TO COOMA

TINDERRY
NATURE
RESERVE

Joins map 506

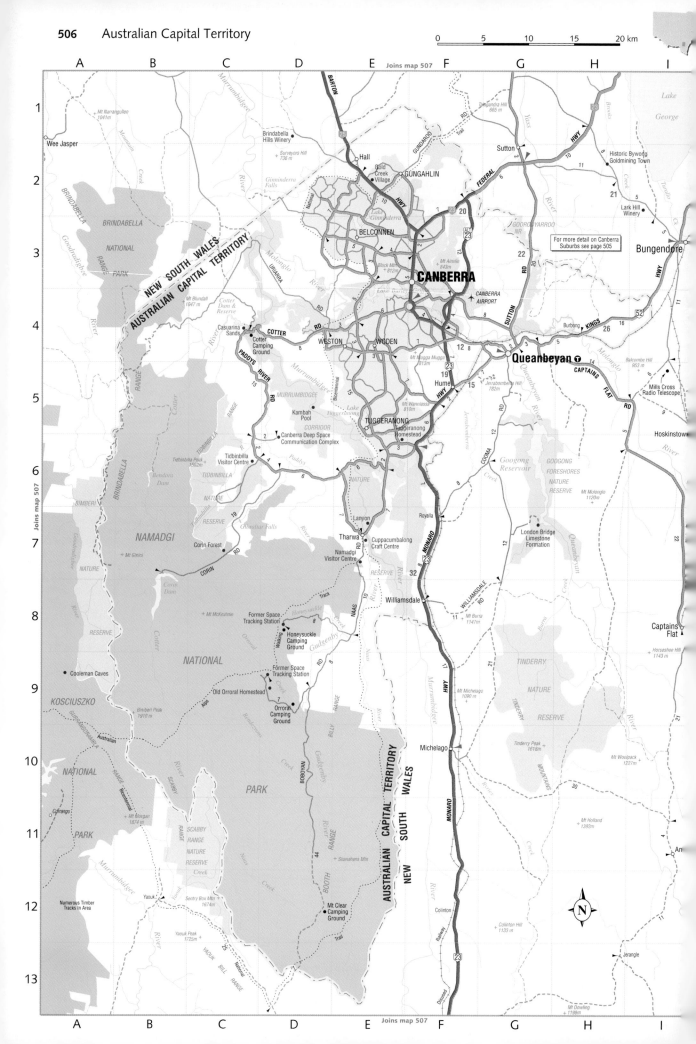

0 5 10 15 20 km

A B C D E F G H I

1

Mt Narrangullen
+ 1041m

Tangandra Hill
665 m

Brooks

Lake
George

2

Wee Jasper

Mountain

Creek

Murrumbidgee

Ginninderra
Falls

Surveyors Hill
+ 736 m

Brindabella
Hills Winery

Hall

Gold
Creek
Village

GUNGAHLIN

GUNGAROO

RD

FEDERAL

HWY

Sutton

2

10

11

HWY

Historic Byworg
Goldmining Town

21

5

Lark Hill
Winery

BRINDABELLA

NATIONAL

Ginninderra

River

Goodradigbee

RANGE

PARK

NEW SOUTH WALES

AUSTRALIAN CAPITAL TERRITORY

Molonglo

URIARRA

River

RD

BELCONNEN

Lake
Ginninderra

Black Mtn
+ 812m

5

Mt Ainslie
+ 843m

CANBERRA

20

22

20

RD

SUTTON

GOOROOYARROO
NR

For more detail on Canberra
Suburbs see page 505

Bungendore

3

4

River

RANGE

Mt Blundall
1047 m

Cotter
Dam &
Reserve

Casuarina
Sands

COTTER

Cotter
Camping
Ground

RD

WESTON

WODEN

Lake Burley Griffin

Mt Mugga Mugga
813m

Canberra
AIRPORT

8

12

Queanbeyan

Burbong

KINGS

26

16

52

HWY

Balcombe Hill
953 m

Mills Cross
Radio Telescope

5

PADDYS RIVER

15

RD

MURRUMBIDGEE

Murrumbidgee

Bicentennial

15

Kambah
Pool

Canberra Deep Space
Communication Complex

Mt Wanniassa
810m

Hume

HWY

19

23

15

Jerrabomberra Hill
782m

CODOMA

RD

12

Queanbeyan

River

CAPTAINS FLAT

RD

5

9

Hoskinstown

6

Joins map 507

BIMBERI

RANGE

Bendora
Dam

Tidbinbilla Peak
1562m

TIDBINBILLA

NATURE

RESERVE

Tidbinbilla
Visitor Centre

2

4

Paddys

6

Abratlar Falls

NATURE

TUGGERANONG

Tuggeranong
Homestead

3

12

Googong
Reservoir

GOOGONG
FORESHORES
NATURE
RESERVE

Mt Molonglo
1120m
+

River

7

NAMADGI

NATURE

Mt Ginini
+

Corin Forest

CORIN

RD

Tibinbilla

R.

19

River

RESERVE

Lanyon

Tharwa

Namadgi
Visitor Centre

Cuppacumbalong
Craft Centre

NAAS

RD

Royalla

MONARO

32

23

London Bridge
Limestone
Formation

12

Queanbeyan

8

Cooleman Caves

NATIONAL

+ Mt McKeahnie

Former Space
Tracking Station

Honeysuckle
Camping
Ground

Walking

Track

Honeysuckle

Gudgenby

8

Williamsdale

WILLIAMSDALE

RD

11

Mt Burra
1147m

21

TINDERRY

NATURE

Captains
Flat

Horseshoe Hill
1143 m

9

KOSCIUSZKO

River

RESERVE

Bimberi Peak
1910m

Alps

Old Orroral Homestead

Former Space
Tracking Station

7

Orroral
Camping
Ground

Ormoral

River

Naas

Gudgenby

RANGE

BILLY

Mt Michelago
1090 m

TINDERRY

RESERVE

Tinderry Peak
1618m

MOUNTAINS

Mt Woolpack
1227m

River

21

10

NATIONAL

Cotter

River

Australian

Bicentennial

+ Mt Morgan
1874 ttl

SCABBY

RANGE

PARK

BOBOYAN

RD

Gudgenby

GUDGENBY

Creek

Michelago

RIVER

30

Mt Holland
1392m

4

11

PARK

Cotango

Murrumbidgee

RANGE

SCABBY

RANGE

NATURE

RESERVE

Naas

Creek

Slananahans Mtn

BOOTH

RANGE

44

Creek

AUSTRALIAN CAPITAL TERRITORY

NEW SOUTH WALES

An

12

Numerous Timber
Tracks In Area

Yaouk

Sentry Box Mtn
1674m

Mt Clear
Camping
Ground

Colinton

River

Railway

MONARO

HWY

17

Colinton Hill
1133 m

N

11

13

Yaouk Peak
1725m

YADUK

BILL

RANGE

26

National

Trail

Disused

23

Mt Dowling
+ 1198m

Jerangle

A B C D E F G H I

0 20 40 60 80 100 km

Joins map 508

Joins map 509

A B C D E F G H I

1 2 3 4 5 6 7 8 9 10 11 12 13

SOUTH PACIFIC OCEAN

TASMAN SEA

NEW SOUTH WALES

VICTORIA

EAST GIPPSLAND

CANBERRA
Queanbeyan
ACT

Goulburn
Young
Cootamundra
Grenfell
Boorowa
Crookwell
Nowra
Bomaderry
Bowral
Mittagong
Moss Vale
Robertson
Berry
Kangaroo Valley
Bundanoon
Nowra Hill
Callala Bay
Huskisson
Vincentia
Jervis Bay
St Georges Basin
Sanctuary Pt
Sussex Inlet JBT
Milton
Ulladulla
Burrill Lake
Tabourie Lake
Bawley Point
Kiola
Pebbly Beach
Durras
Long Beach
Batemans Bay
Malua Bay
Mossy Point
Broulee
Moruya
Moruya Heads
Congo
Tuross Head
Bodalla
Dalmeny
Narooma
Central Tilba
Tilba Tilba
Bermagui
Bermagui South
Cobargo
Quaama
Bega
Tathra
Kalaru
Wolumla
Candelo
Merimbula
Tura Beach
Pambula
Pambula Beach
Wyndham
Eden
East Boyd
Boydtown
Kiah
Wonboyn
Green Cape
Gabo Island
Mallacoota
Gipsy Point
Fairhaven
Cape Howe
Genoa
Cann River

Gundagai
Tumut
Adelong
Batlow
Tumbarumba
Talbingo
Cabramurra
Corryong
Khancoban
Thredbo
Jindabyne
Berridale
Dalgety
Adaminaby
Cooma
Cooma West
Bredbo
Bunyan
Numeralla
Nimmitabel
Bombala
Delegate
Bibbenluke
Cathcart
Bombala
Bemboka
Nerrigundah
Eurobodalla
Braidwood
Bungendore
Captains Flat
Michelago
Williamsdale
Tharwa

Yass
Murrumbateman
Gunning
Binda
Taralga
Marulan
Bungonia
Tallong
Wingello
Penrose
Berrima
Sutton
Collector
Tarago
Bungendore

Harden
Murrumburrah
Cunningar
Galong
Binalong
Bookham
Bowning
Jerrawa
Dalton

Camden
Picton
Thirlmere
Buxton
Bargo
Hilltop
Wilton
Yanderra
Yerrinbool
Colo Vale
Silverdale
Warragamba
Cobbitty
Oakdale
The Oaks
Nattai

Shooters Hill
Abercrombie Caves
Burraga
Peelwood
Tuena
Fullerton
Roslyn
Kialla
Woodhouselee
Gurrundah

KOSCIUSZKO NATIONAL PARK
MORTON NATIONAL PARK
DEUA NATIONAL PARK
WADBILLIGA NATIONAL PARK
SOUTH EAST FOREST NP
BEN BOYD NATIONAL PARK
NADGEE NATURE RESERVE
CROAJINGOLONG NATIONAL PARK
GREAT DIVIDING RANGE
SNOWY MOUNTAINS
BUDAWANG NP
EUROBODALLA NATIONAL PARK
MIMOSA ROCKS NATIONAL PARK
WALLAGA LAKE NP
BOURNDA NATIONAL PARK
ILLAWARRA COAST
SOUTH COAST

For more detail on the Snowy Mountains see page 503
For more detail on the ACT see page 506
For more detail on the South Coast see page 502

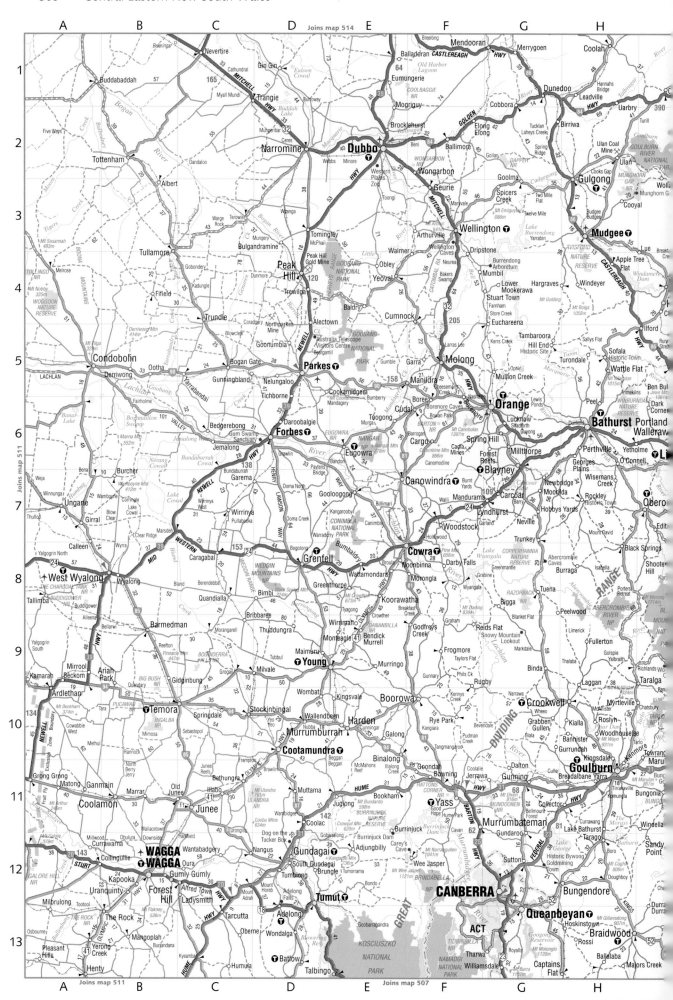

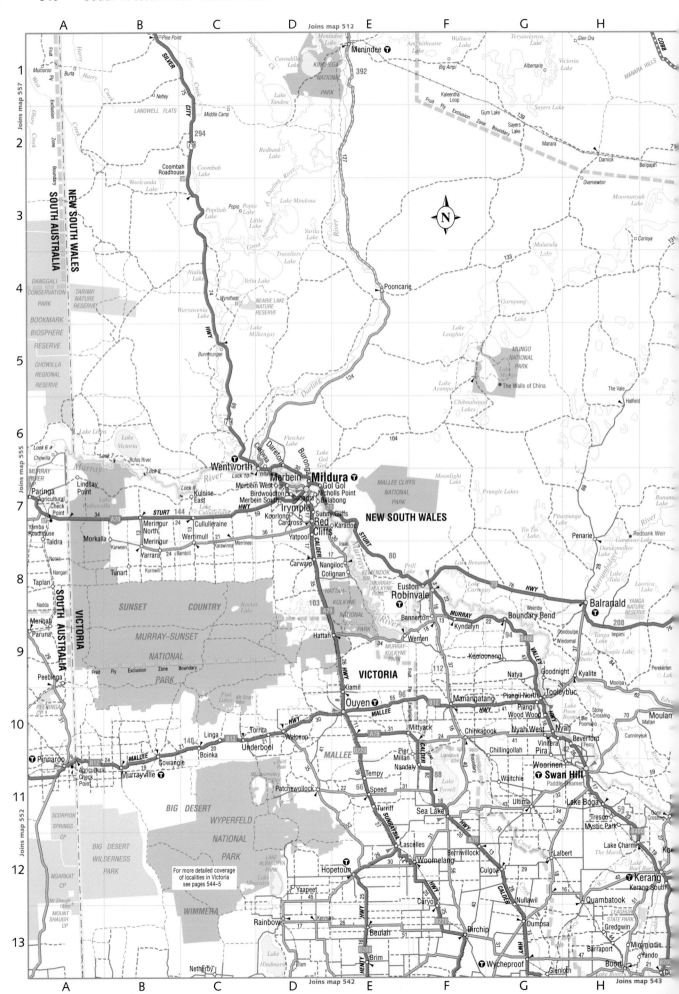

Joins map 512
Joins map 557
Joins map 555
Joins map 552
Joins map 542
Joins map 543

For more detailed coverage of localities in Victoria see pages 544–5

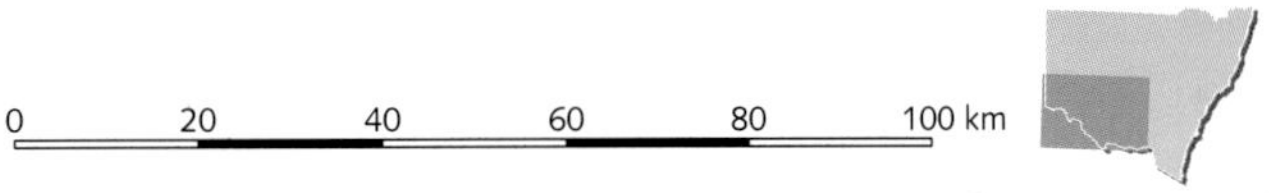

Joins map 513

0 20 40 60 80 100 km

K L M N O P Q R

1 2 3 4 5 6 7 8 9 10 11 12 13

Albert
Tullamore
Condobolin
Derriwong
Oootha
Fifield
Melrose
Fairholme
Mt Tilga 329m
Gunebang
Euabalong West
Euabalong
Burcher
Burgooney
Tullibigeal
Ungarie
Weja
Bena
Winnunga
Clear Ridge
Wyrra
Calleen
Yalgogrin North
Naradhan
Gubbata
Kikoira
Thullo
Gibsonvale
Girral
Corinella
Lake Cowal
Marsden
Lake Cargelligo
Wallanthery
Hannan
West Wyalong
Wyalong
Bland
Tallimba
Barmedman
Reefton
Gidginbung
Quandary
Bellarwi
Mt Ariah 424m
Yalgogrin South
Rankins Springs
Erigolia
Eurabba
Weethalle
Mudidigower
Mt Buddigower
Alleena
Hillston
Langtree
Goorawin
Merriwagga
Allawah
Goolgowi
Gunbar
Tabbita
Beelbangera
Yenda
Bilbul
Yoogali
Binya
Barellan
Moombooldool
Mirrool
Ariah Park
Kamarah
Beckom
Ardlethan
Temora
Mimosa
Sebastopol
Griffith
Hanwood
Murrami
De Bortoli Wines
Miranda Wines
Murrumbidgee Irrigation Area
McWilliams Winery
Carrathool
Bringagee
Willbriggie
Wamoon
Colinroobie
Tara
Mt Beckham 374m
Hay
Darlington Point
Whitton
Leeton
Yanco
Grong Grong
Matong
Ganmain
Marrar
Old Junee
Junee
Waddi
Narrandera
Gillenbah
Coolamon
Coleambally
Coleambally Irrigation Area
Corobimilla
Sandigo
Kywong
Morundah
Widgiewa
Birrego
Collingullie
Wagga Wagga
Gumly Gumly
Oura
Booroorban
Boree Creek
Lockhart
Kapooka
Uranquinty
Forest Hill
Alfred Town
Ladysmith
Wanganella
Milbrulong
The Rock
Tootool
Osbourne
Mangoplah
Burrandana
Conargo
Coree South
Urana
Yerong Creek
Henty
Cogkardinia
Kyeamba
Jerilderie
Logie Brae
Mayrung
Myall Plains
Oaklands
Rand
Pleasant Hills
Urangeline East
Ferndale
Morven
Woolloona
Little Billabong
Deniliquin
Blighty
Finley
Ellerslie
Berrigan
Daysdale
Buraja
Coreen
Walbundrie
Rennie
Culcairn
Holbrook
Woomargama
Mullengandra Village
Talmalmo
Mathoura
Bunnaloo
Wombboota
Tocumwal
Savernake
Sanger
Lowesdale
Brooklesby
Walla Walla
Gerogery
Gerogery West
Bandiana
Echuca
Moama
Nathalia
Numurkah
Katamatite
Cobram
Barooga
Mulwala
Corowa
Wahgunyah
Rutherglen
Howlong
Jindera
Albury
Yarrawonga
Bundalong
Brimin
Chiltern
Barnawartha
Wodonga
Belbridge
Talgarno
Bethanga

NEW SOUTH WALES
VICTORIA

Joins map 538   Joins map 539

Joins map 508
Joins map 507

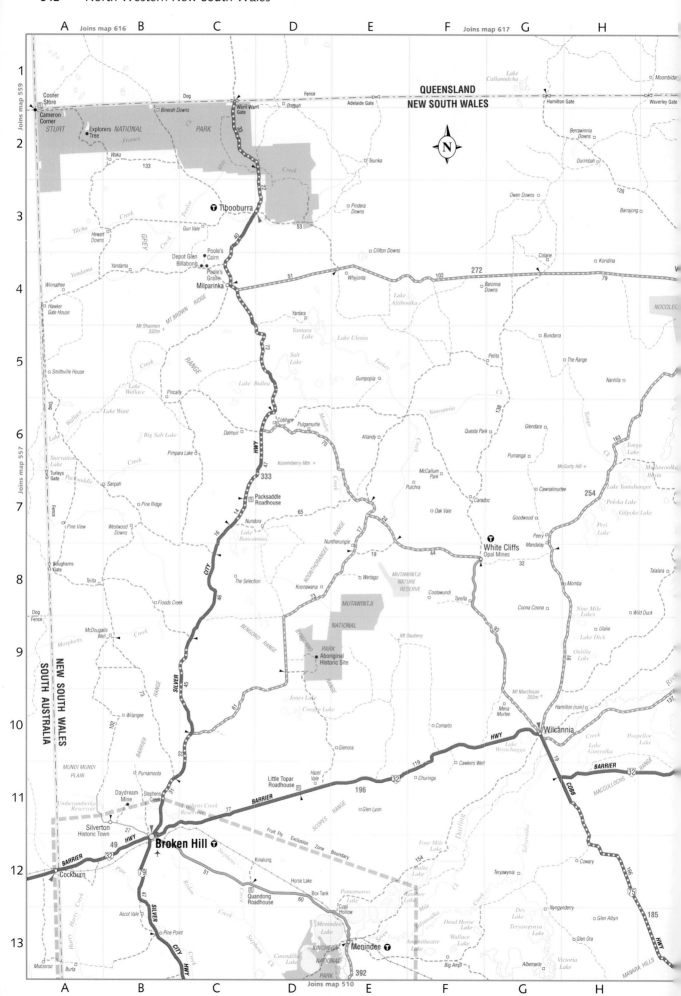

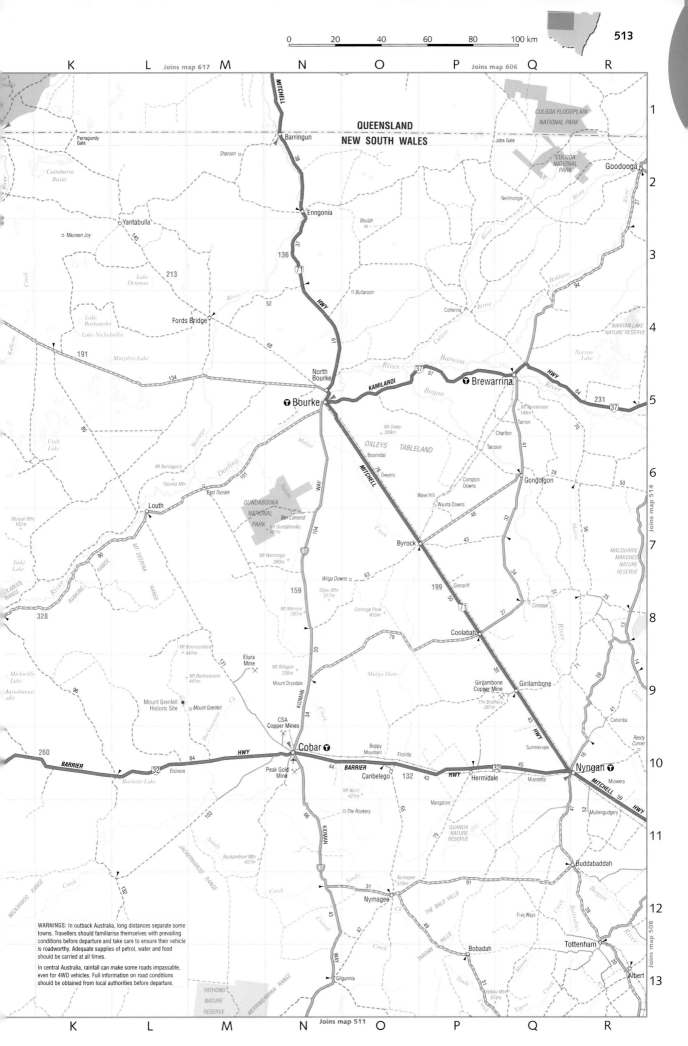

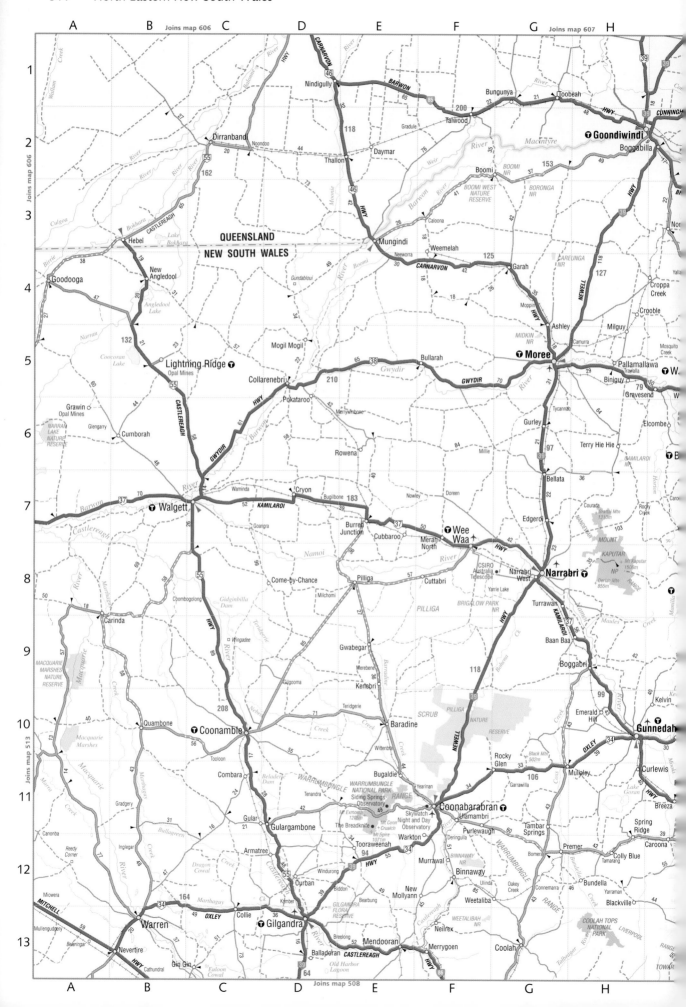

Joins map 607

0 20 40 60 80 100 km

K L M N O P Q R

GREAT

Inglewood
42
Karara
Coolmunda Reservoir
200 HWY
Warwick
Truck 'n' Travel Roadhouse
Yangan
Tannymorel
MAIN RANGE NATIONAL PARK
Maroon
Rathdowney
LAMINGTON NP
MT BARNEY NP
Springbrook
COOLANGATTA
TWEED HEADS
Fingal
Banora Point
Chinderah
Kingscliff
Bogangar

Killarney
Queen Mary Falls
Legume
Woodenbong
Chillingham
Tumbulgum
Terranora
Condong
Murwillumbah
Uki
Burringbar
Mooball
Pottsville
Hastings Point

Texas
QUEENSLAND
Stanthorpe
Dalveen
Cottonvale
The Summit
Applethorpe
Liston
Amosfield
Mulli Mulli
Urbenville
Grevillia
Rukenvale
Toonumbar
Kyogle
Nimbin
Mullumbimby
New Brighton
Ocean Shores
Brunswick Heads
Tyagarah
Cape Byron
Byron Bay

NEW SOUTH WALES
Ashford
Mingoola
Bonshaw
Tenterfield
Drake
Tabulam
Mallanganee
Casino
Lismore
Alstonville
Wollongbar
Ballina
Suffolk Park
Lennox Head

DIVIDING

Emmaville
Deepwater
Dundee
Copmanhurst
Eatonsville
Junction Hill
Grafton
Lawrence
Maclean
Iluka
Yamba
Angourie
Brooms Head

Inverell
Glen Innes
Red Range
Nymboida
Coutts Crossing
Glenreagh
Corindi
Red Rock
Arrawarra
Woolgoolga
Sandy Beach
Emerald Beach

Guyra
Ebor
Dorrigo
Boambee
Coffs Harbour
Sawtell
Bellingen
Urunga

Armidale
Wollomombi
Point Lookout
Darkwood
Raleigh
Mylestom
Valla Beach
Hyland Park
Nambucca Heads

Uralla
Hillgrove
Dangarsleigh
Bowraville
Macksville
Scotts Head
Warrell Creek
Stuarts Point

Walcha
Lower Creek
Bellbrook
Eungai Creek
South West Rocks
Jerseyville
Trial Bay Gaol

Kootingal
Nemingha
Woolbrook
Willawarrin
Frederickton
Green Hill
Gladstone
Kempsey
Hat Head
Smithtown

Niangala
Brackendale
Mount Seaview
Telegraph Point
Pembroke
Beechwood
Crescent Head
Kundabung

Nundle
Ellenborough
Long Flat
Wauchope
Port Macquarie
Lake Cathie
Bonny Hills
North Haven
Dunbogan

Combyne
Byabarra
Kendall
Kew
Laurieton

Wingham
Marlee
Coopernook
Moorland
Crowdy Head
Taree
Harrington
Purfleet

Joins map 509

SOUTH

PACIFIC

OCEAN

For more detail on Port Macquarie & Surrounds see page 516

1
2
3
4
5
6
7
8
9
10
11
12
13

0   5   10   15   20 km

Joins map 515

A B C D E F G H I

TO ARMIDALE

TO MACKSVILLE

GARRAI NATIONAL PARK

FIFES KNOB NR

THE CASTLES NATURE RESERVE

BOONANGHI NATURE RESERVE

Willawarrin

ARMIDALE RD

17

Shark Is

Trial Bay Gaol

ARAKOON STA REC AREA

South West Rocks

Everglades Aquarium

Jerseyville

Smoky Cape Lighthouse

HAT HEAD NATIONAL PARK

Clybucca

Kinchela

Upper Kinchela

WEST ROCKS

SOUTH

Bellimbopinni

Smithtown

Gladstone

Hat Head

Macleay

NGAMBAA NATURE RESERVE

SKILLION NATURE RESERVE

Collombatti Rail

Turners Flat

Fredrickton

Green Hill

Kempsey

OXLEY WILD RIVERS NATIONAL PARK

Kookaburra

WILLI WILLI

36

37

15

River

Macleay

+ Double Head

Parrabel Ck

+ Mt Motherabah

ABBOTSMITH RANGE

Kemps Pinnacle

Spokes Hill

WERRIKIMBE NATIONAL PARK

Brister Mtn 1182m

Mt Banda Banda 1258m

Mt Boss

NATIONAL PARK Wilson

STEAMS RANGE

KUMBATINE NATIONAL PARK

Wittitrin

Dungay Ck

BELLBIRD WILDLIFE SANCTUARY

Rodeo Arena

Kundabung

49

PACIFIC

14

15

MARIA NATIONAL PARK

Crescent Head

Killick Beach

Little Nobby

Big Nobby

Goolawah Beach

Racecourse Head

Big Hill Point

TASMAN

SEA

Maria River

Pipers Creek

Rollands Plains

Upper Pappinbarra

River

20

21

22

KOOREBANG NATURE RESERVE

MOUNT SEAVIEW NR

JASPER NATURE RESERVE

Birdwood

Hastings River

Telegraph Point

Pembroke

RD

Torrens Island

LIMEBURNERS CREEK NATURE RESERVE

Saltwater Lake

Point Plomer

Ferry

Pelican Island

Rawdon Island Nth

Rawdon Island

Cassegrain Winery

Ferry

Port Macquarie

TO WALCHA

34

OXLEY HWY

13

Yarras

Ellenborough

Long Flat

42

Bagnoo

Byabarra

Beechwood

PEMBROKE

Wauchope

Timbertown

OXLEY HWY

34

HWY

Flynns Beach

Shelly Beach

Sea Acres Rainforest Centre

Miners Beach

Tacking Point

BIRIWAL BULGA NATIONAL PARK

BAGO RANGE

Old Bottlebutt

BAGO BLUFF NATIONAL PARK

LAKE INNES NATURE RESERVE

Lake Innes

Camel Rides

LAKE INNES NATURE RESERVE

OCEAN DR

BROKEN

Mt Comboyne 668m

Combyne

Herons Creek

Lighthouse Beach

Lake Cathie

Middle Rock Head

Rainbow Beach

Bonny Hills

Grants Head

Ellenborough Falls

BOORGANNA NATURE RESERVE

Bulga

Elands

TAPIN TOPS NATIONAL PARK

KILLABAKH NATURE RESERVE

COMBOYNE

Lorne

Camden Haven

Kendall

Kew

QUEENS LAKE NATURE RESERVE

Queens Lake

DOORAGAN NP

North Brother

North Haven

Dunbogan

Laurieton

KATTANG NATURE RESERVE

SOUTH

Bobin

Caparra

Killabakh

BULGA RD

Marlee

Cedar Party Creek

KENDALL STATE FOREST

Big Fella Gum Tree

COORABAKH NATIONAL PARK

Middle Brother

YOORIGAN NP

Wilson Taylor Lake

Diamond Head

CROWDY BAY NATIONAL PARK

PACIFIC

Lansdowne

Moorland

Coopernook

PACIFIC

Coralville

South Brother

Johns River

51

Crowdy Bay

Mamboo Island

OCEAN

Wingham

Wingham Brush

GLOUCESTER RD

Kimbriki

Taree

Tinonee

TO NEWCASTLE

Cundletown

Dumaresq Is

Oxley Island

Mitchells Island

Manning River

Jones Island

Crowdy Head

Harrington

Harrington Inlet

Manning Point

Joins map 509

VICTORIA
MAPS

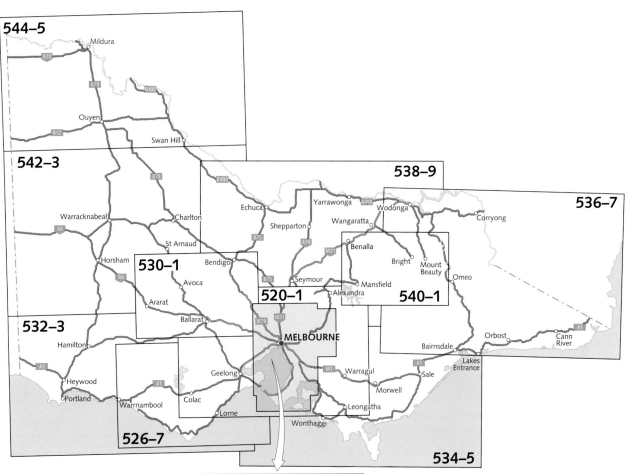

544–5
Mildura
A20
A79
B400
Ouyen
B12
Swan Hill

542–3
A79
Warracknabeal
A8
Charlton
B400
St Arnaud
530–1
Bendigo
Horsham
A8
Avoca
Ararat
Ballarat
532–3
Hamilton
A1
Heywood
Portland
526–7
Warrnambool
Colac
Lorne
Geelong

Echuca
Yarrawonga
Shepparton
B75
A39
M31
Seymour
B75
520–1
Alexandra
M79 M31
MELBOURNE
Warragul
M1
Morwell
Leongatha
Wonthaggi
534–5

538–9
Wodonga
Wangaratta
Benalla
Bright
Mount Beauty
Mansfield
540–1
Omeo
B400

536–7
Corryong
A1
Orbost
Cann River
Bairnsdale
Lakes Entrance
A1
Sale

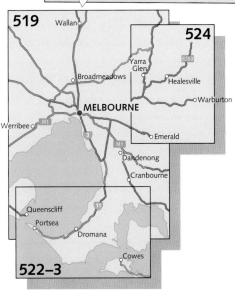

519
Wallan
Broadmeadows
MELBOURNE
Werribee M1
3
M1
Dandenong
Cranbourne
Queenscliff
Portsea
11
Dromana
Cowes
522–3

524
Yarra Glen
B360
Healesville
Warburton
Emerald

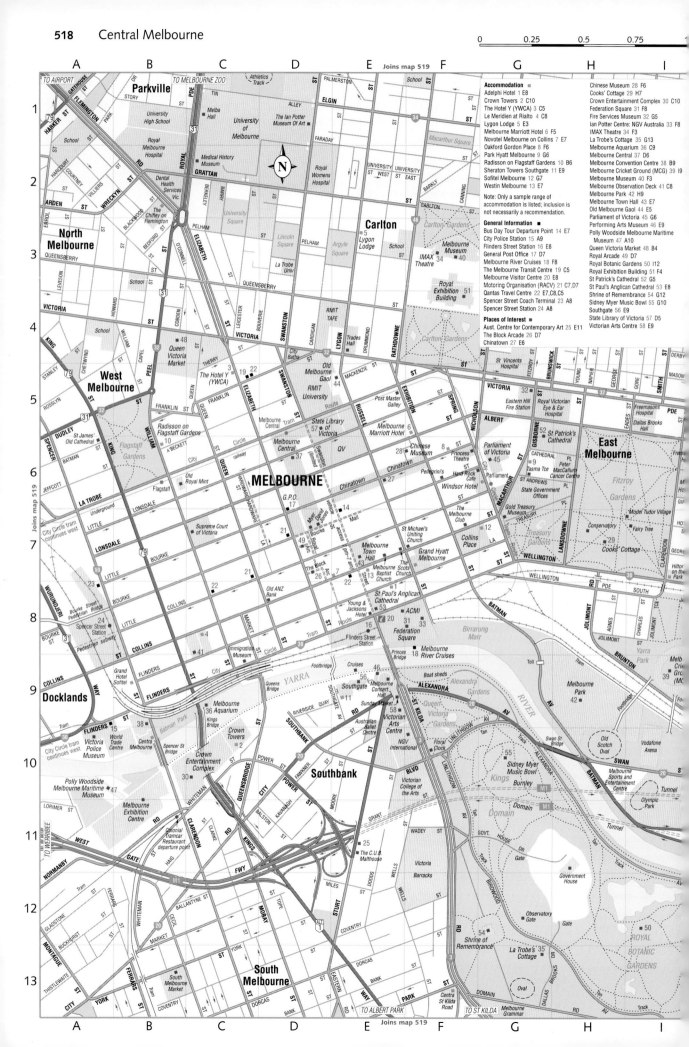

Accommodation ■
Adelphi Hotel 1 E8
Crown Towers 2 C10
The Hotel Y (YWCA) 3 C5
Le Meridien at Rialto 4 C8
Lygon Lodge 5 E3
Melbourne Marriott Hotel 6 F5
Novotel Melbourne on Collins 7 E7
Oakford Gordon Place 8 F6
Park Hyatt Melbourne 9 G6
Radisson on Flagstaff Gardens 10 B6
Sheraton Towers Southgate 11 E9
Sofitel Melbourne 12 G7
Westin Melbourne 13 E7

Note: Only a sample range of accommodation is listed; inclusion is not necessarily a recommendation.

General Information
Bus Day Tour Departure Point 14 E7
City Police Station 15 A9
Flinders Street Station 16 E8
General Post Office 17 D7
Melbourne River Cruises 18 F8
The Melbourne Transit Centre 19 C5
Melbourne Visitor Centre 20 E8
Motoring Organisation (RACV) 21 C7,D7
Qantas Travel Centre 22 E7,C8,C5
Spencer Street Coach Terminal 23 A8
Spencer Street Station 24 A8

Places of Interest
Aust. Centre for Contemporary Art 25 E11
The Block Arcade 26 D7
Chinatown 27 E6

Chinese Museum 28 F6
Cooks' Cottage 29 H7
Crown Entertainment Complex 30 C10
Federation Square 31 F8
Fire Services Museum 32 G5
Ian Potter Centre: NGV Australia 33 F8
IMAX Theatre 34 F3
La Trobe's Cottage 35 G13
Melbourne Aquarium 36 C9
Melbourne Central 37 D6
Melbourne Convention Centre 38 B9
Melbourne Cricket Ground (MCG) 39 H9
Melbourne Museum 40 F3
Melbourne Observation Deck 41 C8
Melbourne Park 42 H9
Melbourne Town Hall 43 E7
Old Melbourne Gaol 44 E5
Parliament of Victoria 45 G6
Performing Arts Museum 46 E9
Polly Woodside Melbourne Maritime Museum 47 A10
Queen Victoria Market 48 B4
Royal Arcade 49 D7
Royal Botanic Gardens 50 I12
Royal Exhibition Building 51 F4
St Patrick's Cathedral 52 G5
St Paul's Anglican Cathedral 53 E8
Shrine of Remembrance 54 G12
Sidney Myer Music Bowl 55 G10
Southgate 56 E9
State Library of Victoria 57 D5
Victorian Arts Centre 58 E9

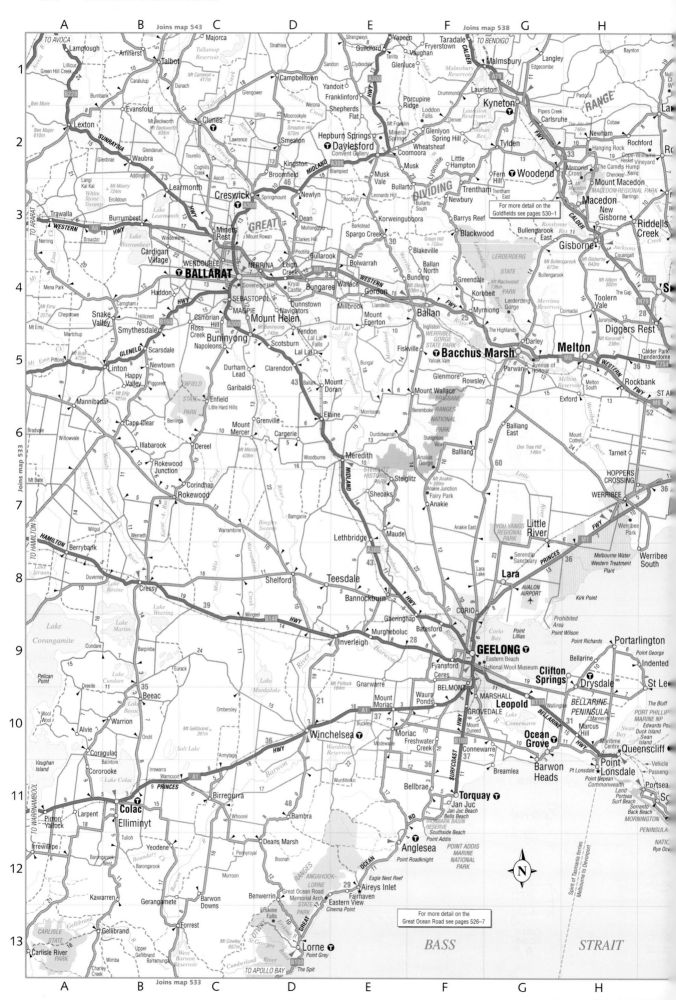

For more detail on the
Goldfields see pages 530–1

For more detail on the
Great Ocean Road see pages 526–7

BASS   STRAIT

Joins map 538 | Joins map 539

0 10 20 30 km

K L M N O P Q R

Map of Victoria — Melbourne, Yarra Valley and Gippsland region

Selected place names (top to bottom, left to right):

Broadford, TO SEYMOUR, GOULBURN VALLEY HWY, Yea, Molesworth, Yarck, Alexandra, LAKE EILDON NATIONAL PARK, Eildon, Goughs Bay, Macs Cove, Piries, Howqua

Whittlesea, Kinglake, Marysville, Jamieson, Kevington, Gaffneys Creek, A1 Mine Settlement, Wood's Point

Hurstbridge, Yarra Glen, Healesville, YARRA RANGES NATIONAL PARK

MELBOURNE, Lilydale, Coldstream, Seville, Warburton, Yarra Junction, Mt Baw Baw

Dandenong, Belgrave, Emerald, Cockatoo, Gembrook, Powelltown, Noojee, Neerim South, Hill End

Cranbourne, Pakenham, Bunyip, Drouin, Warragul, Moe, Trafalgar, Newborough

Mt Eliza, Mornington, Somerville, Hastings, Crib Point, Koo-wee-rup, Lang Lang, Poowong, Korumburra, Mirboo North, Thorpdale

Flinders, Cowes, PHILLIP ISLAND, Newhaven, San Remo, Bass, Grantville, Leongatha, Mirboo, Boolarra

FRENCH ISLAND, WESTERN PORT

(Dense road map of central/eastern Victoria, Australia; numerous towns, roads, national parks and rivers labelled.)

1 2 3 4 5 6 7 8 9 10 11 12 13

K L M N O P Q R

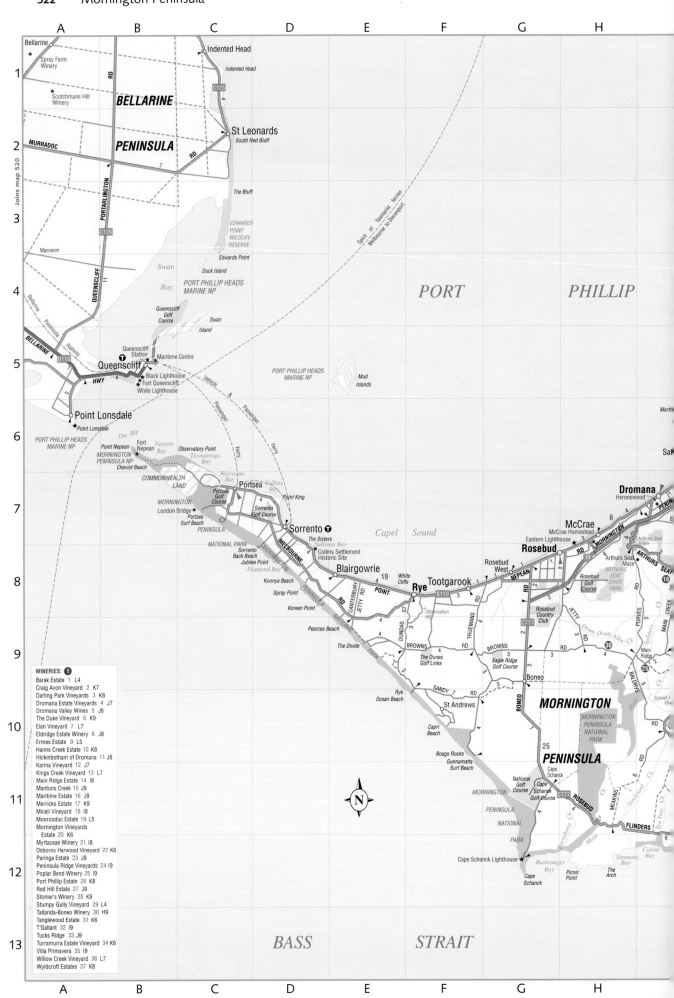

Joins map 520

BELLARINE

PENINSULA

Bellarine
Spray Farm Winery
Scotchmans Hill Winery

MURRADOC RD

Indented Head
Indented Head

St Leonards
South Red Bluff

The Bluff

EDWARDS POINT WILDLIFE RESERVE

PORTARLINGTON RD

C126

Mannerim

C125

Swan Bay

Duck Island
Edwards Point

PORT PHILLIP HEADS MARINE NP

Spirit of Tasmania ferries
Melbourne to Devonport

PORT   PHILLIP

Queenscliff Golf Course

Swan Island

Queenscliff Station
Maritime Centre

BELLARINE HWY
Queenscliff
Black Lighthouse
Fort Queenscliff
White Lighthouse

B110

PORT PHILLIP HEADS MARINE NP

Mud Islands

PORT PHILLIP HEADS MARINE NP

Point Lonsdale
Point Lonsdale

The Rip

Point Nepean
Fort Nepean
MORNINGTON PENINSULA NP
Cheviot Beach

Nepean Bay

Observatory Point
Ticonderoga Bay

Weeroona Bay

Collins Bay

Portsea

Point King

COMMONWEALTH LAND

MORNINGTON
London Bridge
Portsea Surf Beach
PENINSULA

Portsea Golf Course

Sorrento Golf Course

Sorrento

The Sisters
Sullivan Bay
Collins Settlement Historic Site

Capel   Sound

Martha

Sar

Dromana
Heronswood

McCrae
McCrae Homestead
Eastern Lighthouse

MORNINGTON RD

Arthurs Seat
Arthurs Seat Maze

ARTHURS SEAT

NATIONAL PARK
Sorrento Back Beach
Jubilee Point
Diamond Bay

Blairgowrie

White Cliffs

Rosebud West

Rosebud

Rosebud Golf Course

18

ARTHURS SEAT STATE PARK

Koonya Beach

Spray Point

Koreen Point

Tootgarook
Rye

B110

Observation Hill

CANTERBURY JETTY RD

POINT

DUNDAS RD

NEPEAN RD

Rosebud Country Club

Rosebud
Country Club

JETTY RD

PURVES RD

Drum Drum Alloc Ck

BALDRYS RD

School

Pearces Beach

The Divide

NATIONAL PARK

BROWNS RD

BROWNS RD

The Dunes Golf Links

Eagle Ridge Golf Course

Main Ridge

30

25

Rye Ocean Beach

SANDY RD

BONEO RD

Boneo

St Andrews

MORNINGTON

MORNINGTON PENINSULA NATIONAL PARK

RD

Capri Beach

Boags Rocks
Gunnamatta Surf Beach

25

PENINSULA

Cape Schanck

MEAKINS RD

Stockyard RD

Tea Tree Ck

National Golf Course

Cape Schanck Golf Course

ROSEBUD RD

C777

FLINDERS

6

MORNINGTON

PENINSULA

NATIONAL

PARK

Burrabong Ck

Main

Cairns Bay

Simmons Bay

Cape Schanck Lighthouse

Bushranger Bay

Picnic Point

The Arch

Cape Schanck

N

BASS   STRAIT

0   2   4   6   8   10 km

Joins map 521

K L M N O P Q R

FRANKSTON
TO MELBOURNE
CRANBOURNE
Cranbourne South
BROWNS
TO DANDENONG
Five Ways
LANGWARRIN
Ballam Park Homestead
Daveys Bay
Pelican Point
Canadian Bay
Langwarrin Flora & Fauna Reserve
ROBINSONS
Devon Meadows
MANKS
SOUTH
GIPPSLAND

Mt Eliza
Sunnyside Beach
Mornington Golf Course
Schnapper Point
Mt Eliza 160m
Baxter
Baxter Park
WARRANDYTE
BAXTER – TOORADIN
Pearcedale
BAXTER – TOORADIN
Cannons Creek
Warneet
Blind Bight
Tooradin
TO KORUMBURRA

Mornington
Studio City Pop & Media Museum
Somerville
ERAMOSA
Eramosa Ck
Bembridge 9 Hole Golf Course
Watson Inlet
Warneet
Quail Island
YARINGA MARINE NP

Craft Market
Mornington Racecourse
TYABB
Moorooduc
DERRIL
BUNGOWER
COOLART
JONES
TYABB
Tyabb
Western Port Airfield
BHP Steel Western Port Works
WESTERN   PORT
Scrub Point

The Briars Homestead
Devilbend Golf Course & Rec Res
GRAYDENS
Devilbend Reservoir
HODGINS
BOES
BAYVIEW
Long Point
Long Island
FRENCH ISLAND MARINE NATIONAL PARK

Bittern Reservoir
Warringine Ck
Hastings
Hastings Bight
Sandstone Island
FRENCH ISLAND
NATIONAL   PARK

Bulldog Ck
Tubbarubba
COOLART
HENDERSONS
Bittern
WOOLLEYS
Crib Point
Fairhaven
Mt Wellington 98m

DROMANA
Tubbarubba
Balnarring Racecourse
Emu Plains Market
MYERS
STUMPY
FLINDERS
DISNEY
Crib Point
The Pinnacles 66m
FRENCH
ISLAND

BITTERN – DROMANA
FRANKSTON
Balnarring
SOUTH BEACH
SANDY POINT
Coolart Reserve
Coolart Homestead
Crib Point
Stony Point
Passenger
Tankerton
Tankerton Jetty

RED HILL
STANLEYS
Merricks North
Balnarring Beach
Somers Beach
South Beach
Somers
HMAS CERBERUS NAVAL BASE
Western Park Beach
Tortoise Head

Red Hill South
Ashcombe Maze
Merricks
Merricks Beach
Point Summer
Sandy Point
Long Point

FLINDERS
Point Leo
Point Leo
Shoreham
Shoreham Beach

Seal Rocks
Penguin Rock
Cowes
CHURCH ST
Cowes Golf Course
Observation Point
Rhyll Inlet
Rhyll
Fishermans Point

WESTERN   PORT
McHaffie Point
VENTNOR
COWES
RHYLL
Bird Sanctuary

West Head
Ventnor
VENTNOR
Phillip Island Wildlife Park
PHILLIP ISLAND
Koala Res
Koala Conservation Centre
Five Ways
A Maze 'N Things
NEWHAVEN

PHILLIP   ISLAND
BACK BEACH
Phillip Island Vineyard & Winery
THE GAP RD
Grand Prix Circuit & Visitor Centre
CHURCHILL ISLAND MARINE NP
Churchill Island
Swan Bay

Point Grant
The Nobbies
The Blowhole
Seal Rocks
Phillip Is Penguin Reserve
Penguin Parade
Summerland Beach
PHILLIP ISLAND NATURE PARK
BERRYS BEACH RD
Cat Bay
Swan Lake
PYRAMID ROCK
Cunningham Bay
Berrys Beach
Storm Bay
Pyramid Rock
Australian Dairy Centre
Wooby Point
Newhaven
Cape Woolamai
San Remo
Phillip Is Airfield
The Narrows

Joins map 521

K L M N O P Q R

0 2 4 6 8 10 km

A | B | C | D | E | F | G | H | I

Joins map 521

Pheasant Creek

KINGLAKE NATIONAL PARK

C724

TO YEA
Glenburn
B300

TOOLANGI–BLACK RANGE

STATE FOREST

Mt Despair
684m

Mt Mitchell
957m

RD

TO ALEXANDRA

CATHED. RANGE STATE PARK

Buxton
Buxton Trout Farm

MARYSVILLE

Kinglake East
Kinglake Central

HEALESVILLE
RD
C724

Mount Slide

Castella

Mt Slide

Toolangi

MELBA

GREAT

Yea

DIVIDING

Mt Klondyke
869m

RANGE

B360

Marysville

Steavenson Falls

C51

Mittons Bridge

KINGLAKE NATIONAL PARK

C746

Mt Beggary
432m

Mt Everard
472m

Kinglake Mountain
411m

Mt Jerusalem

RD

Steels Creek

B300

Dixons Creek

21

7

1 10

15

29

20

26

KINGLAKE

RD

C724

Mt Blue

St Fillans

MAROONDAH

C512

MARYSVILLE

Narbethong 40

Granton

Bicentennial

Mt Gordon

National

Trail

Mt Strickland
1219m

Mt Kitchener
960m

ELTHAM

YARRA GLEN
RD

Christmas Hills

Sugarloaf Reservoir Park

Yarra Glen

25

Yarra Glen Racecourse

27

Gulf Station
OLD

HEALESVILLE

14

HEALESVILLE
RD

Donnelly's Weir Park

B360

Black Spur

Maroondah Reservoir Park

Mt Juliet
1105m

White Hill

Mt Vinegar

YARRA

RANGES

NATIONAL

C507

WAY

POLEY

RANGE

Sugarloaf Reservoir Park

Yering Station

LILYDALE AIRFIELD

B300

MELBA

19

22

Yarra Valley Dairy

8

15

22

17 2 9

B360

YARRA GLEN
RD

Railway Tunnel

Healesville

Hedgend Maze

Healesville Sanctuary

BADGER CREEK RD

DON RD

Mt Riddell

Badger Weir Park

YARRA

NATIONAL

PARK

RANGES

Maroondah
Reservoir

Coldstream

3

Coldstream Airfield

Gruyere

23

6

HEALESVILLE
RD

17

DONNA
BUANG

Mallesons Lookout

Mt Toole-Be-Wong
792m

DONNA BUANG

Ben Cairn
1071m

Mt Donna Buang
1250m

Mt Boobyalla

C505

Cement Creek

Mt Victoria

ACHERON WAY

RD

Smith Hill

Warburton East

G511

Chirnside Park Golf Course

LILYDALE

MAROONDAH HWY

WARBURTON HWY

Lilydale Lake

C404

C401

Wandin North

Seville

16

HWY
B380

16

Wandin Yallock

11

Woori Yallock

17

HEALESVILLE RD

Don Valley

Launching Place

Yarra Junction

24

19

5

Millgrove

Tommy Finn's Trout Farm

Wesburn

Warburton

Big Pats Creek

4

Brahams Creek

MT DANDENONG

Croydon Golf Course

O'Shannassy Pipeline

Mt Evelyn

C415

Dorset Golf Club

Eastwood Golf Course

CANTERBURY

22 RD

32

KALORAMA

Mt Dandenong
633m

William Ricketts Sanctuary

DANDENONG RANGES NP

MONBULK

C404

Silvan

Olinda Falls

Olinda

Silvan Reservoir

DANDENONG RANGES NATIONAL PARK

Yellingbo

Hoddles Creek

Gladysdale

JUNCTION

C425

Mt Tugwell

Groom Hill

BLUE RANGE

Three Bridges

NOOJEE RD

Lookout Tower

DANDENONG RANGES NATIONAL PARK

SHERBROOKE

Sherbrooke Falls

Monbulk

THE PATCH

Macclesfield

Mt Thule

C411

Nangana

Spies Hill

Mt Beenak
743m

McCrae

Barber Hill

BURWOOD

C415

UPPER FERNTREE GULLY

BELGRAVE

C412 HWY

Puffing Billy

SELBY

C404

Menzies Creek

Puffing Billy Steam Museum

Clematis

C412

Emerald

Avonsleigh

Cockatoo

18

Cardinia Reservoir

Gembrook

GEMBROOK

C424

LAUNCHING PLACE RD

Kennedy Creek

Cockatoo Ck

Beenak Creek

Tomahawk Creek

BUNYIP STATE PARK

Shepherd Ck

Black Snake Ck

WELLINGTON RD

HALLAM

C413

LYSTERFIELD LAKE PARK

C413
RD
BELGRAVE

WELLINGTON

Birds Land Reserve

Rainy Hill

Clark Ck

Joins map 521

WINERIES: ❶

Allinda Winery 1 C5
Badgers Brook Winery 2 D7
Bianchet Winery 3 A7
Brahams Creek Winery 4 H8
Britannia Falls Winery 5 G9
Coldstream Hills 6 D8
De Bortoli Wines 7 C4
Domaine Chandon 8 C6
Eyton on Yarra 9 D7
Fergusson Winery & Restaurant 10 C5
Five Oaks Vineyard 11 C10
Kellybrook Winery & Restaurant 12 A7
Lirralirra Estate 13 A8
Long Gully Estate 14 D5
Lovey's Estate 15 C5
McWilliams Lillydale Vineyards 16 D9
Oakridge Estate 17 C7
Paternoster 18 D13
St Huberts Vineyard 19 C7
Shantell Vineyard 20 C4
Steels Creek Estate 21 B4
Tarrawarra Estate 22 D6
Warramate Vineyard 23 D7
Yarra Burn Winery & Restaurant 24 F9
Yarra Ridge 25 B6
Yarra Track Vineyard 26 C6
Yering Station-Yarrabank Vineyards 27 B6

A   B   C   D   E   F   G   H

Joins map 533

TO ARARAT

Lake Bolac

TO SKIPTON

TO HAMILTON

Moffat

Chatsworth

Woorndoo

Mt Hamilton 319m

Pura Pura

Nerrin Nerrin

Vite Vite North

Mingay

Bradvale

Willowvale

Mt Bute

Mt Kintore 270m

Wallinc

Lake Gellies

Lake Eyang

Lake Logan

Deep Lake

Vite Vite

Derrinallum

Lismore

HAMILTON HWY

Berryban

Caramut

HAMILTON HWY

Hexham

MORTLAKE RD

ARARAT RD

Lake Barnie Bolac

Darlington

DARLINGTON

Mt Elephant 394m

Lake Tooliorook

Gnarpurt

Lake Struan

C164

Lake Gnarpurt

Foxbow

C148

C165

Woolsthorpe

Mortlake

Mt Shadwell 292m

HAMILTON HWY

52

40

Cloven Hills

LISMORE RD

56 RD

Bald Hill

Leslie Manor

Lake

Ellerslie

B120

Kolora

Glenormiston North

Mt Meningoort 220m

Lake Booka

Lake Milangil

CAMPERDOWN RD

FOXHOW RD

Lake Terangpom

Pelican Point

Corangamite

C174

Joins map 532

Framlingham East

Glenormiston

Noorat

28

Mt Njorat 245m

Lake Kellambete

Lake Colongulac

Kariah

Lake Koreetnung

Mt Myrtoon

Lake Weeranganuk

Wool Wool

Alvie

Red Rock Lookout

Ballangeich

The Sisters

Boorcan

PRINCES HWY

Camperdown

Lake Gnotuk

Gnotuk

Weerite

Pomborneit North

Herring Point

50

Framlingham

Terang

21

Naroghid

Lake Bullen Merri

Mt Leura 311m

10

Lake Purrumbete

Pomborneit

Pomborneit East

Vaughan Island

Nalangil

Winslow

Hopkins River

45

Garvoc

Dixie

Cobrico

C156

Bostock Creek

C164

Tesbury

Köallah

Mt Porndon 289m

46

Stoneyford

HWY

A1

Mailors Flat

Grassmere

Purnim

C168

Mumblin

Tandarook

Purrumbete South

C149

12

Larper

Woodford

Purnim West

Wangoom

Panmure

Laang

Lake Elingamite

C157

Jancourt

C155

Carpendeit

Bungador

Swan Marsh

Pirron Yallock

E

Bushfield

Grassmere Junction

Cudgee

Naringal

C167

Ecklin South

Glenfyne

Elingamite

Jancourt East

Carpendeit

C163

Irrewillipe

RD

C161

Dennington

TO PORTLAND

PRINCES HWY

Warrnambool

Logans Beach

Allansford

B100

Ayrford

12

22

Deep Creek

Scotts Creek

51

C164

19

15

TIMBOON

C163

85

COLAC

14

Tomahawk Creek

C163

Barongaro Wer

Mepunga West

Mepunga East

The Cove

Nullawarre

C163

Brucknell

Timboon

PORT CAMPBELL RD

Cowleys Creek

Scotts

Simpson

Cooramingul

COLAC

Mt Murray

CARLISLE STATE PARK

Buttress Point

Nirranda

Curdie Vale

66

Nirranda South

Lower Heytesbury

Paaratte

Newfield

Waarre

21

Crayfish Ck

LAVERS HILL

Tomahawk Ck

Bryant

CARLISLE

Carlisle River

LAV

Peterborough

GREAT OCEAN RD

B100

Curdies Inlet

London Bridge

The Arch

Port Campbell

PORT CAMPBELL

Mutton Bird Island

Loch Ard Gorge

The Twelve Apostles

Gibson Steps

C164

Ferguson Hill

Kennedys Creek

COBDEN RD

Gellibrand R

Chapple Vale

Pile Siding

Weeaprofna

COLAC RD

C159

SOUTHERN

TWELVE APOSTLES MARINE NP

NATIONAL PARK

PRINCETOWN RD

Devondale

17 RD

Wangerrip

COLAC RD

Kincaid

Wyelangta

MELBA GULLY STATE PARK

Mt Chapple 550m

Lavers Hill

B100

49

Princetown

Yuulong

Lower Gellibrand

Johanna Falls

5

Moonlight Beach

Moonlight Head

Wattle Hill

Point Reginald

Cape Volnay

Lion Headland

Johanna

OTWAY

OCEAN

Glenaire

Hordern Vale

Lake Craven

Eagle Nest Rock

Sentinel Rock

NATIONAL

PARK

Point Flinders

Lighthouse

Cape Otway

Sea Poin

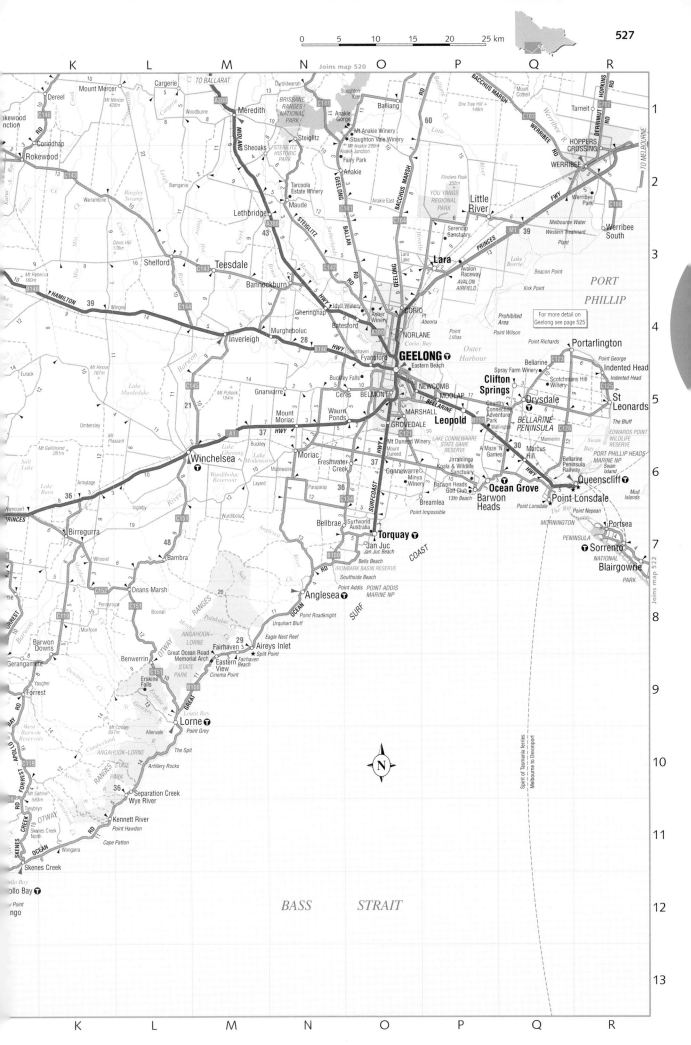

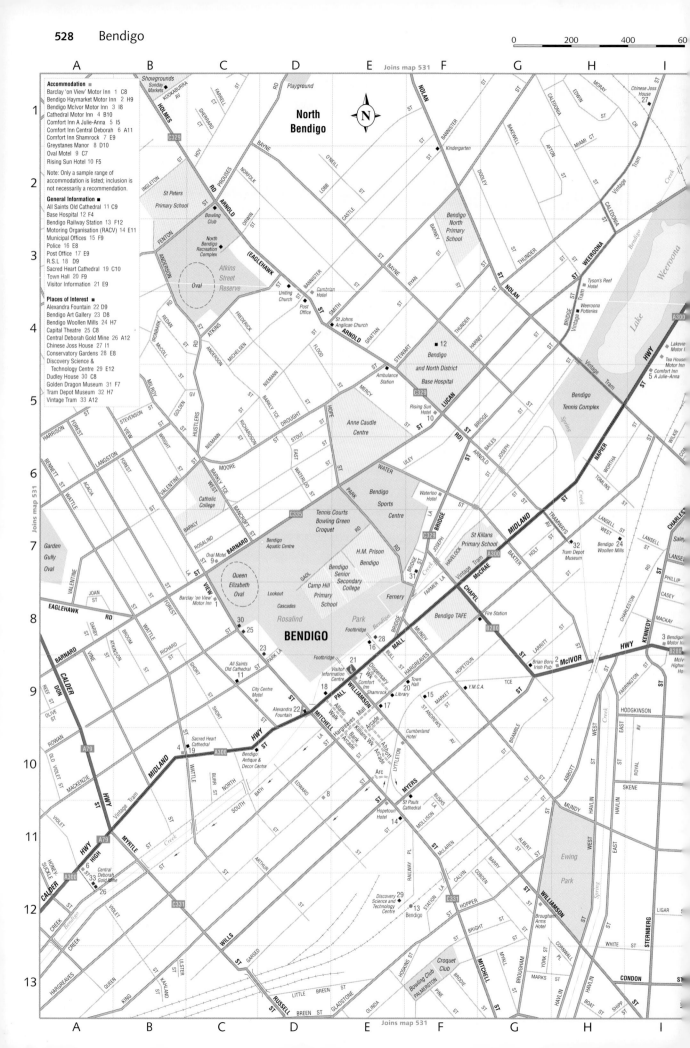

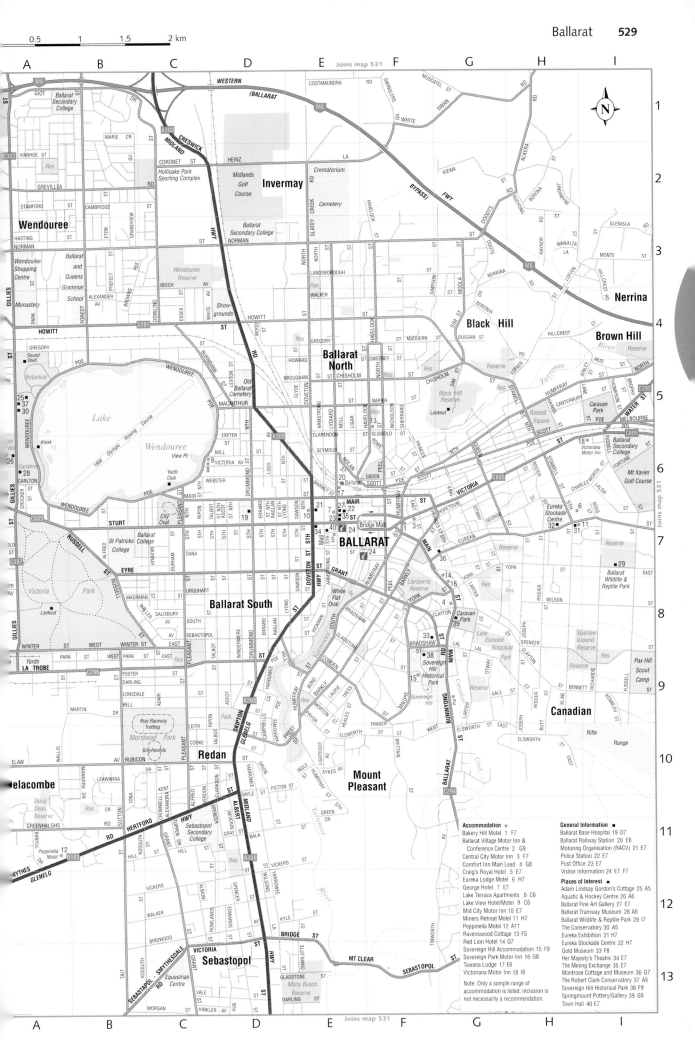

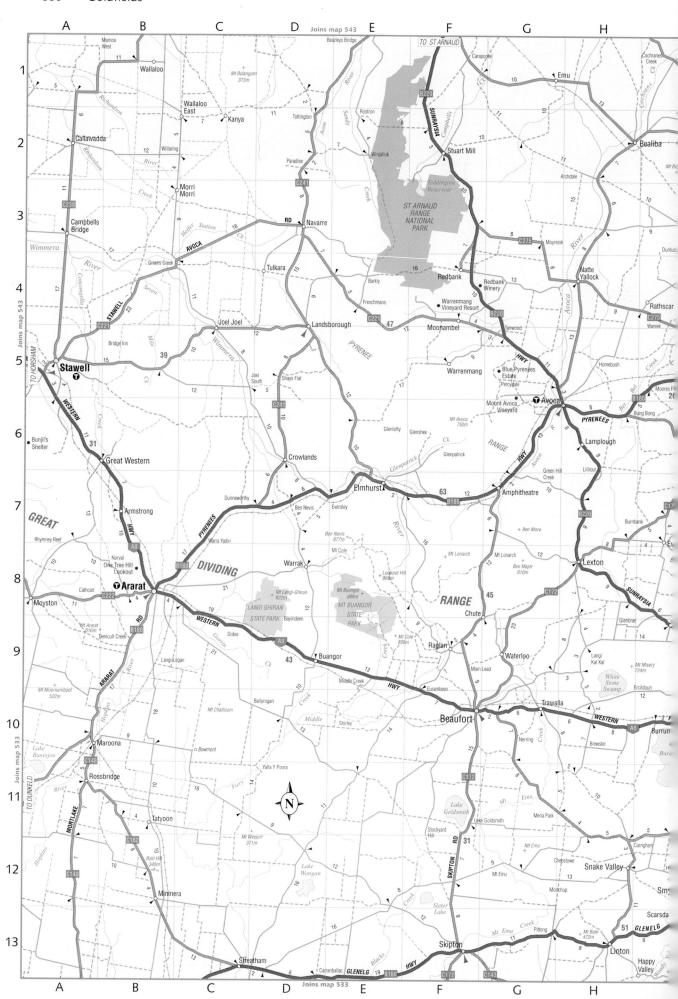

0 5 10 15 20 25 km

Joins map 543

K L M N O P Q R

Top / northern area

TO INGLEWOOD
TO KERANG
GREATER BENDIGO NP
Woodvale
TO ECHUCA
HWY
Huntly
Bagshot
A300
Epsom
Leichardt
B260
For more detail on Bendigo see page 528
Myers Flat
EAGLEHAWK
MIDLAND
Arnold West
Arnold
Murphys Creek
Llanelly
Newbridge
B240
ST. ARNAUD RD
Marong
Maiden Gully
Bullock Creek
HWY
Golden Dragon Museum
WHITE HILLS
B280
McIVOR
Longlea
Junortoun
Fosterville
Tarnagulla
KANGAROO FLAT
BENDIGO
Central Deborah Gold Mine
Strathfieldsaye
HWY
Axedale
TO HEATHCOTE
Laanecoorie
MARYBOROUGH RD
Woodstock
Lockwood
Goldfields Mohair Farm
Lockwood South
Mandurang
Emu Creek
Sedgwick
Dunolly
Bromley
Eddington
Laanecoorie Reservoir
Eastville
Shelbourne
Bradford
CALDER
A790
Ravenswood
Mandurang South
GREATER BENDIGO NP
Sedgwick's Camel Farm
Pilchers Bridge
Eppalock
Bet Bet
Betley
Havelock
C277
C288
BENDIGO
Baringhup
Nuggetty
Porcupine Flat
Walmer
Ravenswood South
A300
Myrtle Creek
Sutton Grange
Lyal
Mia Mia
C327
Lake Eppalock
Joins map 538

Central area

Maryborough
Old Railway Station
Carisbrook
PYRENEES
Moolort
Joyces Creek
Lookout
Mt Tarrengower 570m
Perkins Reef
Maldon Historic Town
Gower
C282
Welshmans Reef
B180
Harcourt North
Harcourt
Mt Alexander 741m
C326
Redesdale
Craigie
Majorca
Tullaroop Reservoir
Strathlea
Newstead
Mackidd Ck
Barkers Creek
Castlemaine
MIDLAND HWY
Market Building Buda Historic Home and Garden
Faraday
Golden Point
35
Metcalfe
Barfold
Glenhope
C283
Dingo Farm
Chewton
34
B180
Elphinstone
Caliban
Campbelltown
C238
Glengower
Strathlea
Sandon
Clydesdale
Campbells Creek
Yapeen
Fryerstown
Taradale
A79 HWY
Malmsbury
C326
Langley
Sidonia
Mt Cameron 417m
Jim
Guildford
Loddon
Vaughan
Irishtown
Malmsbury Reservoir
Edgecombe
Yandoit
40
A300 HWY
Tarilta
Glenluce
CALDER
Lauriston
Pastoria
Franklinford
Werona
Porcupine Ridge
Mt Franklin
Loddon Falls
Drummond
Lauriston Reservoir
C316
Clunes
C291
BALLARAT
Shepherds Flat
Lavandula Lavender Farm
Mineral Springs
Mt Franklin
Denver
Kyneton
Pipers Creek
Carlsruhe
The Jim Jim 746m
Newham
Lawrence
Smeaton
Hepburn Springs
Glenlyon
Upper Coliban Res
C317
Coghills Creek
Broomfield
Allendale
Kingston
Daylesford
Convent Gallery
Coomoora
Wheatsheaf
Spring Hill
Tylden
33
FWY
Hanging Rock
Ascot
MIDLAND A300
Springmount
Newlyn
Eganstown
Blampied
Musk
Lyonville Mineral Springs
Little Hampton
Trentham Falls
Fern Hill
C317
Memorial Cross
The Camel Hump
Creswick
46
Sailors Falls
Musk Vale
Lyonville
Bullarto
RANGE
Woodend
Mt Macedon 1013m
MACEDON RP
Mount Macedon
Dean
Rocklyn
Leonards Hill
Newbury
Trentham
Bullarto South
Macedon
Miners Rest
GREAT
Mount Rowan
White Swan Res
Mollongghip
Barkstead
30
Korweinguboora
DIVIDING
Barrys Reef
Mineral Springs Reserve
Blue Mountain
Rosslynne Reservoir
M79
New Gisborne
FWY
Clarkes Hill
Spargo Creek
Blackwood
Garden of St Erth
Green Hill 705m
Bullengarook East
Gisborne
C287
WENDOUREE
Moorabool Reservoir
Korweinguboora Reservoir
Mt Hops 779m
Blakeville
LERDERDERG STATE PARK
Bullengarook
Mt Bullengarook 673m
Mt Gisborne 643m
BALLARAT
Eureka Stockade Centre
Sovereign Hill
Ballarat Exhibition & Entertainment Centre
NERRINA
Leigh Creek
M8
Bullarook
Bolwarrah
Wallace
Ballan North
Bunding
Werribee
Greendale
32
Bullengarook
C704
Merrimu Reservoir
Toolern Vale
C705
SEBASTOPOL
MAGPIE
MOUNT CLEAR
Kryal Castle
Bungaree
WESTERN
Gordon
C141
Mt Steiglitz 638m
Pykes Ck Res
Lerderderg Gorge
Coimadai
Cambrian Hill
Mount Helen
Buninyong Flora & Bird Park
Dunnstown
Millbrook
Ballan
M8
Myrniong
Korobeit
Merrimu Reservoir
A300 MIDLAND
Buninyong
Yendon
Yuulong Lavender Estate
Mt Egerton
Llandello Bostock Res
Mt Egerton
Ingliston
25
The Highlands
Napoleons
Scotsburn
HWY
Lal Lal Falls
Lal Lal
Bungal
Fiskville
WERRIBEE GORGE STATE PARK
Jurunjung
TO MELBOURNE
C146
Durham Lead
Clarendon
Lal Lal Reservoir
TO GEELONG
Yaloak Vale
Bacchus Marsh
Darley
FWY
Melton
Avenue of Honour
Parwan
M8
TO MELBOURNE

Joins map 520

K L M N O P Q R

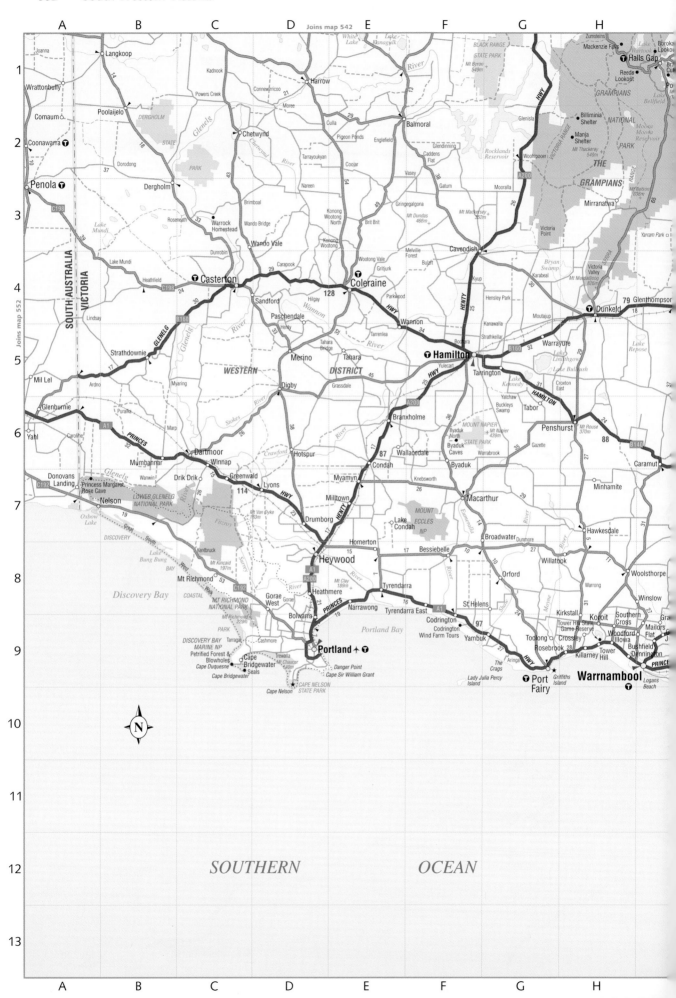

0 10 20 30 40 50 km

Joins map 543

K L M N O P Q R

Joins map 538

Glenlofty
For more detail on the Goldfields see pages 530–1
Lamplough
Daisy Hill
PADDYS RANGES SP
Tullaroop Reservoir
Strathlea
Loddon
Yapeen
Taradale
Barfold
Langley
Great Western
Crowlands
Elmhurst
Majorca
Sandon
Guildford
Vaughan
CALDER
Malmsbury
Amphitheatre
Amherst
Talbot
Glenluce
Glengower
Campbelltown
Yandoit
A300
Drummond
Porcupine Ridge
Lauriston
Armstrong
Dunneworthy
63
Eversley
14
B180
Lexton
Evansford
Dunach
Mt Cameron + 417m
Loddon Falls
Denver
Upper Coliban Res
Kyneton
PYRENEES
HWY
Warrak
Ben Nevis 966m
Mt Lonarch
23
Clunes
Glengower
Ullina
Lawrence
Smeaton
Hepburn Springs
Glenlyon
Little Hampton
Carlsruhe
Tylden
Ararat
Mt Ararat + 616m
Buangor
20
Chute
Raglan
Langi Kal Kal
Mt Misery + 724m
Learmonth
Waubra
Broomfield
Kingston
Allendale
MIDLAND
86
Daylesford
Bullarto
Trentham
Newbury
Woodend
WESTERN
Waterloo
Trawalla
Brewster
Burrumbeet
Lake Barrumbeet
Creswick
Miners Rest
Cardigan Village
Newlyn
Rocklyn
HWY
Blackwood
Bullengarook East
LERDERDERG STATE PARK
Maroona
Beaufort
97
HWY
25
Nerring
Spargo Creek
Blakeville
Bunding
Greendale
Rossbridge
Bowmont
Yalla Y Poora
Lake Goldsmith
Haddon
BALLARAT
Sovereign Hill
Nerrina
Leigh Creek
34
Bullarook
Bolwarrah
WESTERN
Myrniong
Lerderderg Gorge
Mininera
Bald Hill 340m
Stockyard Hill
Snake Valley
Ross Creek
Dunnstown
Mt Helen
Millbrook
Gordon
Wallace
FWY
M8
Ballan
49
Slater Lake
Smythesdale
Buninyong
Napoleons
Scotsburn
Yendon
Mt Egerton
Fiskville
WERRIBEE GORGE STATE PARK
Bacchus Marsh
Westmere
Streatham
GLENELG
Skipton
102
28
Linton
Newtown
Happy Valley
Durham Lead
Clarendon
Lal Lal Res
Lal Lal
Bungal
38
Glenmore
Mount Wallace
Rowsley
Brisbane Ranges National Park
Parwan
Lake Bolac
HWY
25
Lake McLaren
Nerrin Nerrin
B160
Mt Widderin 360m
Bradvale
Cape Clear
Berringa
Pitfield
Piggoreit
ENFIELD STATE PARK
Enfield
Garibaldi
Grenville
Mount Doran
Elaine
Durdidwarrah
Mount Wallace
BALLIANG EAST
Balliang
Mt Hamilton 319m
Lake Gellies
Pura Pura
Vite Vite North
Mt Bute
Mingay
Willowvale
Illabarook
Dereel
Mount Mercer
Cargerie
86
Meredith
Woodburne
STEIGLITZ HISTORIC PARK
Steiglitz
Anakie Gorge
Anakie
Woorndoo
Derrinallum
149 12
HAMILTON
Lismore
Berrybank
Wilgul
Rokewood Junction
Corindhap
Rokewood
Warrambine
Bamganie
Sheoaks
Maude
Anakie East
Little River
Darlington
Mt Elephant 394m
Tooliorook
Gnarpurt
Duverney
Cressy
Lake Weering
Wingeel
Shelford
Teesdale
Lethbridge
A300
Lara
MI
FWY
PRINCES
Mt Shadwell 292m
HWY
Cloven Hills
Lake Gnarpurt
Lake Martin
Barpinba
HWY
39
Inverleigh
Bannockburn
Murgheboluc
CORIO
Batesford
Geelong
Bookar
Glenormiston North
Kariah
Lake Corangamite
Lake Bookar
Dreeite
Eurack
Ombersley
Lake Murdeduke
Gnarwarre
Mount Moriac
Waurn Ponds
Ceres
MARSHALL
Leopold
Lake Connewarre
B110
Kolora
Glenormiston
Gnotuk
112
Camperdown
Wool Wool
Alvie
Warrion
Beeac
Lake Beeac
Moriac
37
A1
Ocean Grove
Noorat
Mt Noorat 313m
Boorcan
Coragulac
Salt Lake
Winchelsea
HWY 73
Freshwater Creek
B100
Barwon Heads
Terang
PRINCES
A1
Pomborneit
Cororooke
Lake Colac
Warncoort
Modewarre
Bellbrae
Torquay
Garvoc
Cobden
Dixie
Tandarook
Koallah
Stoneyford
Colac
Birregurra
Bambra
Breamlea
Ecklin South
Mumbilla
Swan Marsh
Pirron Yallock
Larpent
Elliminyt
Yeodene
Deans Marsh
POINT ADDIS MARINE NP
Laang
Glenfyne
Carpendeit
Irrewillipe
Barongarook West
Boonah
Anglesea
Ayrford
Scotts Creek
Brucknell
Cowleys Creek
Kawarren
Barwon Downs
Gerangamete
Benwerrin
ANGAHOOK-LORNE STATE PARK
Fairhaven
Aireys Inlet
Eastern View
Timboon
Simpson
Gellibrand
Forrest
Mt Cowley 657m
Lorne
Peterborough
Newfield
Kennedys Creek
CARLISLE STATE PARK
Carlisle River
Wimba
Murroon
B100
London Bridge
The Arch
Port Campbell
PORT CAMPBELL NATIONAL PARK
Chapple Vale
Dinmont
Beech Forest
Mt Sabine 583m
OTWAY RANGES
Separation Creek
Wye River
Kennett River
Loch Ard Gorge
The Twelve Apostles
Gibson Steps
Princetown
Weeaproinah
Lavers Hill
Tanybryn
Skenes Creek
Cape Patton
TWELVE APOSTLES MARINE NP
Moonlight Head
Point Reginald
Johanna
141
OTWAY NATIONAL PARK
Glenaire
Hordern Vale
Paradise
Apollo Bay
Marengo
Cape Otway
Blanket Bay

For more detail on the Great Ocean Road see pages 526–7

BASS STRAIT

1 2 3 4 5 6 7 8 9 10 11 12 13

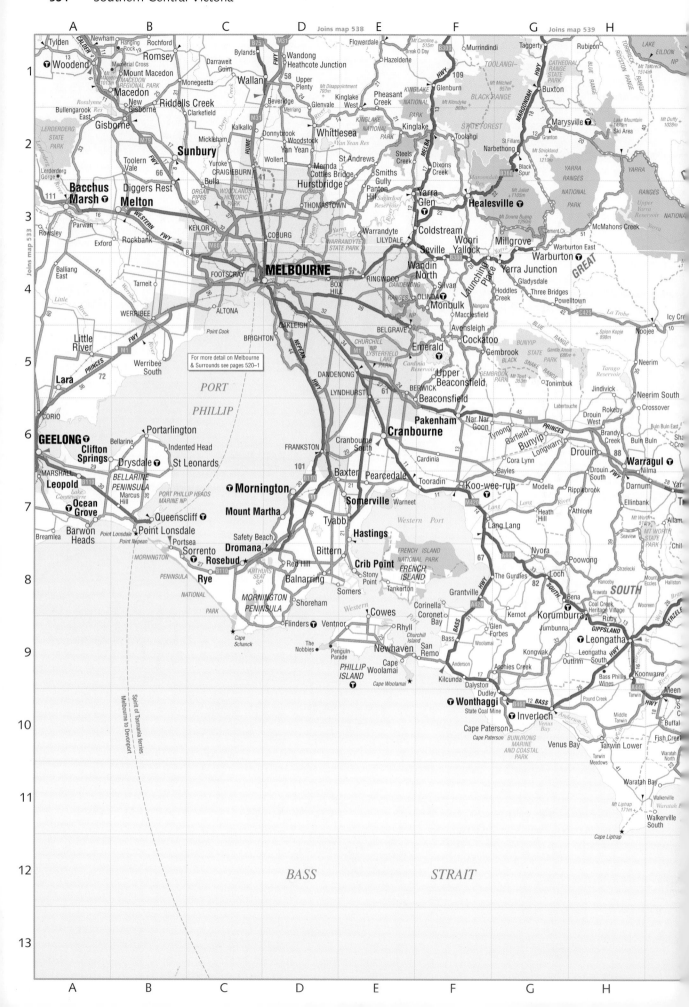

0 10 20 30 40 50 km

Joins map 539
Joins map 536
Joins map 536

K L M N O P Q R

RANGE

Mt McDonald 1625m

Mt Skene 1571m

ALPINE

NATIONAL

Swifts Creek

Doctors Flat

Big Hill 675m

Ensay North

Brookville

Mt Delusion 1399m

Ensay

Reedy Flat

Mt Baldhead 1377m

Ensay South

121

Mt Settlement

Burkly River

Mt Tainboritha 1640m

PARK

Crooked River

Mt Kent 1563m

Mt Dow +1000m

Stirling

22

RD

Tambo Crossing

Mt Elizabeth 942m

Wongungarra River

Dargo

Mt Djoandah 610m

B500

31

Wonnangatta

Mt Useful 1432m

Licola

Lake Tali Karng River

AVON

WILDERNESS

Castleburn

Waterford

Mt Sugarloaf 890m

EAST

GIPPSLAND

Aberfeldy

Red Jacket

Jericho

Gable End 1570m

Mt Selma 1457m

PARK

Mt Wellington 1635m

Castle Hill 1418m

Morris Peak 789m

Tabberabbera

Deptford

Little Dick 320m

Aberfeldy River Picnic and Camping Area

Beardmore

Ben Cruachan 839m

Cobbannah

Mt Alfred 503m

ALPINE

Bruthen

1st Gunnear Area

Mt Talbot Peak 1519m

Bullumwaal

Clifton Creek

Wiseleigh

Mt Taylor 475m

Messiface

Colquhoun

Baw Baw National Park

Lake Glenmaggie

Valencia Creek

Briagolong

Den of Nargun

Glenaladale

Iguana Ck

Wuk Wuk

Mount Taylor

Sarsfield

GREAT

24

16

Tambo Upper

Swan Reach

BAW BAW NATIONAL PARK

Walhalla

Walhalla Goldfields Railway

Coongulla

Boisdale

Stockdale

Woodglen

30

Calulu

Lucknow

East Bairnsdale

Nicholson

A1

14

Johnsonville

Nungurner

Kalimna

Corner

Rawson

Erica

Glenmaggie

Newry

Maffra West Upper

Bushy Park

Munro

Walpa

Lindenow

Wy Yung

PRINCES

22

Bairnsdale

Metung

Lakes Entrance

Moondarra

Heyfield

Maffra

Tinamba

Llowalong

Fernbank

Lindenow South

HWY

20

Aboriginal Museum

Eagle Point

Raymond Island

Paynesville

Gippsland Lakes Coastal Park

Thomson

Cowwarr

Denison

Stratford

PRINCES

69

Delvine

32

Forge Creek

GIPPSLAND LAKES

Moondarra Reservoir

Toongabbie

Dawson

Swing Bridge

Airly

34

Goon Nure

The Lakes National Park

Tyers Park

Glengarry

Seaton

Winnindoo

Nambrok

Kilmany

Montgomery

Perry Bridge

Bengworden

Clydebank

Victoria

Loch Sport

Yallourn North

Tyers

La Trobe River

HWY

26

Fulham

Sale

The Heart

Lake Coleman

Lake Wellington

GIPPSLAND LAKES COASTAL PARK

Newborough

Morwell

Traralgon

PRINCES

23

65

Rosedale

Kilmany South

Wurruk

Longford

Marlay Point

Seacombe

Reeve

Beach

Open Cut Mine

Flynn

Susan St

HOLEY PLAINS

28

Dutson

Paradise Beach

Open Cut Mine

Traralgon South

Loy Yang

Loy Yang Power Station

HYLAND

20

Flynns Creek

STATE

PARK

Golden Beach

Churchill

Callignee North

Gormandale

Hiamdale

Willung

35

Stradbroke West

Stradbroke

24

Mile

Flamingo Beach

MORWELL NATIONAL PARK

Jeeralang North

Callignee

Le Roy

Willung South

Carrajung South

A440

31

Seaspray

Budgeree

Jumbuk

Budgeree East

Balook

Blackwarry

Carrajung

GIPPSLAND

HWY

Gilfard

Ninety Mile Beach

NINETY MILE BEACH MARINE NP

TARRA-BULGA NATIONAL PARK

Madalya

Macks Creek

Won Wron

Darriman

Ryton

Hiawatha

Devon North

Jack River

Greenmount

19

Woodside

C482

Woodside Beach

GIPPSLAND

Gunyah

Binginwarri

Wonyip

Yarram

Hunterston

McLoughlins Beach

Mt Best

Whoorra

Alberton West

Gelliondale

163

Alberton

Tarraville

Manns Beach

Hazel Park

Agnes

SOUTH

28

Hedley

Langsborough

Port Albert

Toora

Welshpool

Port Welshpool

TASMAN

Corner Inlet

Entrance Point

CORNER INLET MARINE NP

NOORAMUNGA MARINE AND COASTAL PARK

WILSONS PROMONTORY MARINE PARK

Mt Hunter 348m

SEA

Mt Roundback 314m

WILSONS PROMONTORY NATIONAL PARK

Mt Vereker 637m

N

Mt La Trobe 759m

Mt Oberon 700m

South East Point

WILSONS PROMONTORY MARINE NP

1 2 3 4 5 6 7 8 9 10 11 12 13

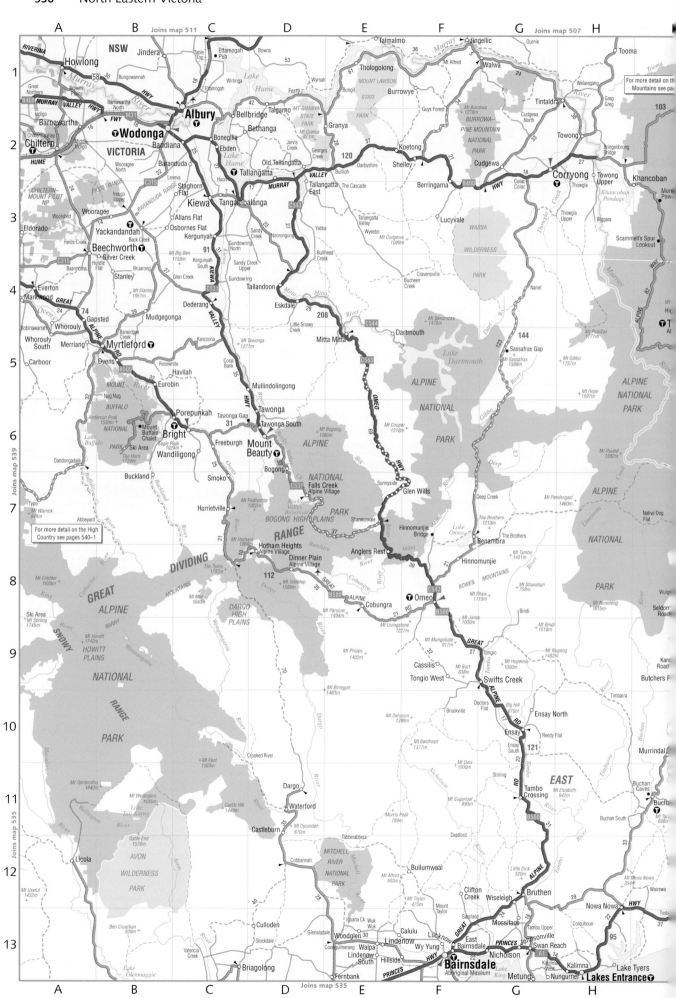

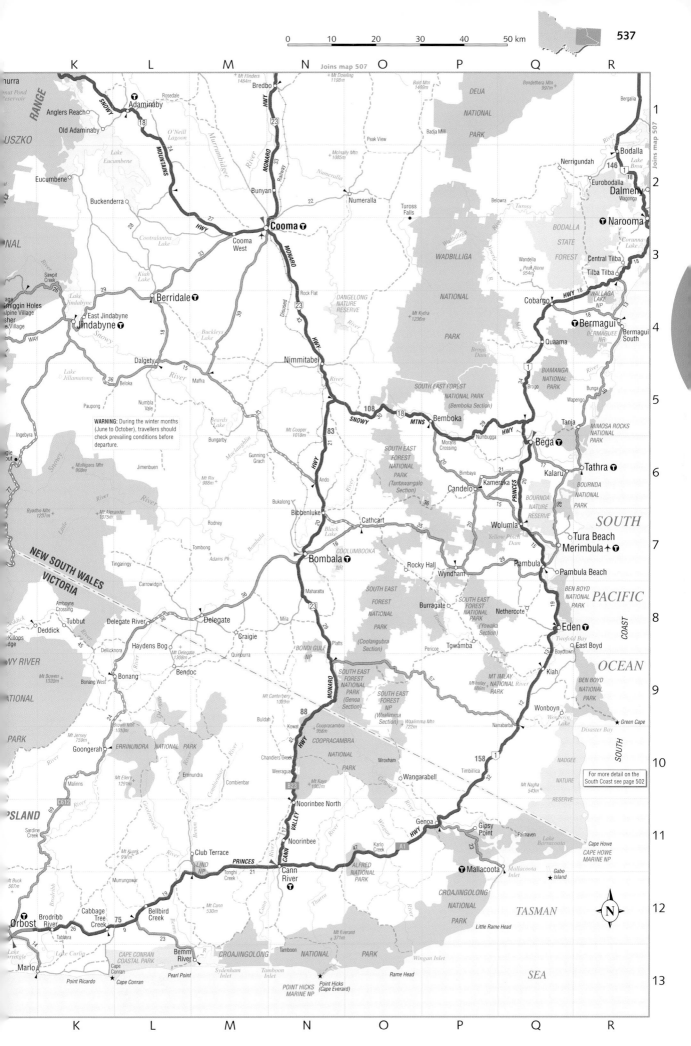

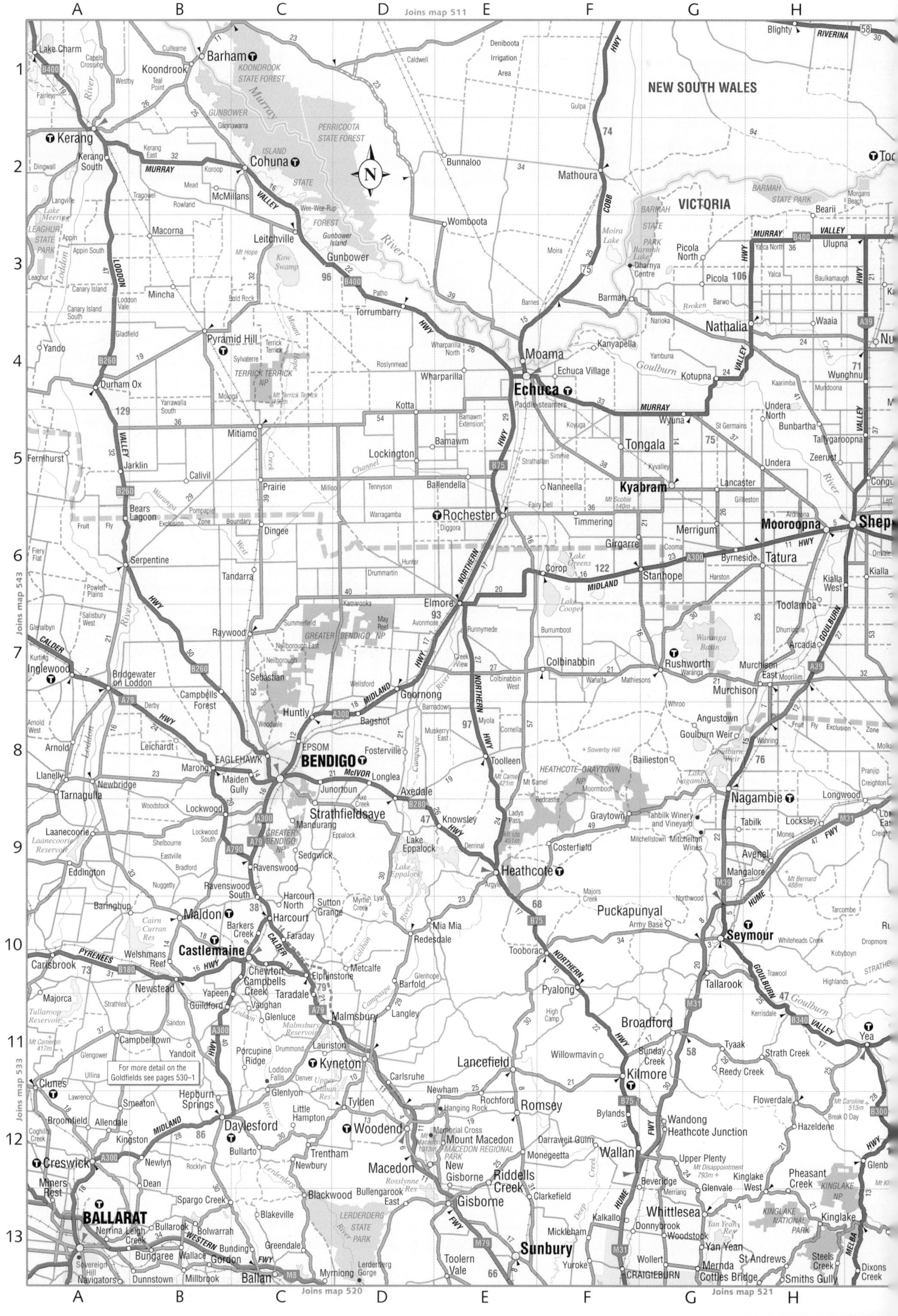

Joins map 511

NEW SOUTH WALES

VICTORIA

RIVERINA

BARMAH STATE PARK

KOONDROOK STATE FOREST

GUNBOWER STATE FOREST

PERRICOOTA STATE FOREST

GUNBOWER ISLAND STATE FOREST

TERRICK TERRICK NP

GREATER BENDIGO NP

HEATHCOTE-GRAYTOWN NP

MACEDON REGIONAL PARK

LERDERDERG STATE PARK

KINGLAKE NATIONAL PARK

LEAGHUR STATE PARK

Lake Charm, Kerang, Kerang South, Koondrook, Barham, Cohuna, Leitchville, Gunbower, Pyramid Hill, Mitiamo, Durham Ox, Mincha, Macorna, Torrumbarry, Wharparilla, Moama, Echuca, Echuca Village, Kotta, Bamawm, Lockington, Ballendella, Rochester, Elmore, Goornong, Bagshot, Huntly, Epsom, Eaglehawk, Maiden Gully, Marong, Lockwood, Strathfieldsaye, Junortoun, Axedale, Knowsley, Heathcote, Colbinabbin, Rushworth, Murchison, Murchison East, Tatura, Mooroopna, Kyabram, Tongala, Stanhope, Merrigum, Byrneside, Nagambie, Avenel, Seymour, Puckapunyal, Tabilk, Locksley, Longwood, Mangalore, Nathalia, Picola, Barmah, Moira, Toolamba, Arcadia, Angustown, Costerfield, Graytown, Redcastle, Toolleen, Fosterville, Longlea, McIvor, Mandurang, Sedgwick, Ravenswood, Ravenswood South, Harcourt, Harcourt North, Faraday, Maldon, Barkers Creek, Castlemaine, Chewton, Elphinstone, Metcalfe, Redesdale, Mia Mia, Tooborac, Pyalong, Broadford, Kilmore, Tallarook, Welshmans Reef, Newstead, Guildford, Vaughan, Glenluce, Taradale, Malmsbury, Lauriston, Kyneton, Carlsruhe, Lancefield, Romsey, Wandong, Heathcote Junction, Flowerdale, Hazeldene, Daylesford, Hepburn Springs, Trentham, Woodend, Tylden, Little Hampton, Macedon, Mount Macedon, New Gisborne, Gisborne, Riddells Creek, Bullengarook, Blackwood, Sunbury, Wallan, Beveridge, Upper Plenty, Whittlesea, Kinglake West, Kinglake, St Andrews, Creswick, Ballarat, Bungaree, Gordon, Ballan, Myrniong, Toolern Vale, Kalkallo, Craigieburn, Mernda, Cottles Bridge, Smiths Gully

Joins map 520

Joins map 521

Joins map 543

Joins map 533

BALLARAT
BENDIGO
Echuca
Kyabram
Mooroopna

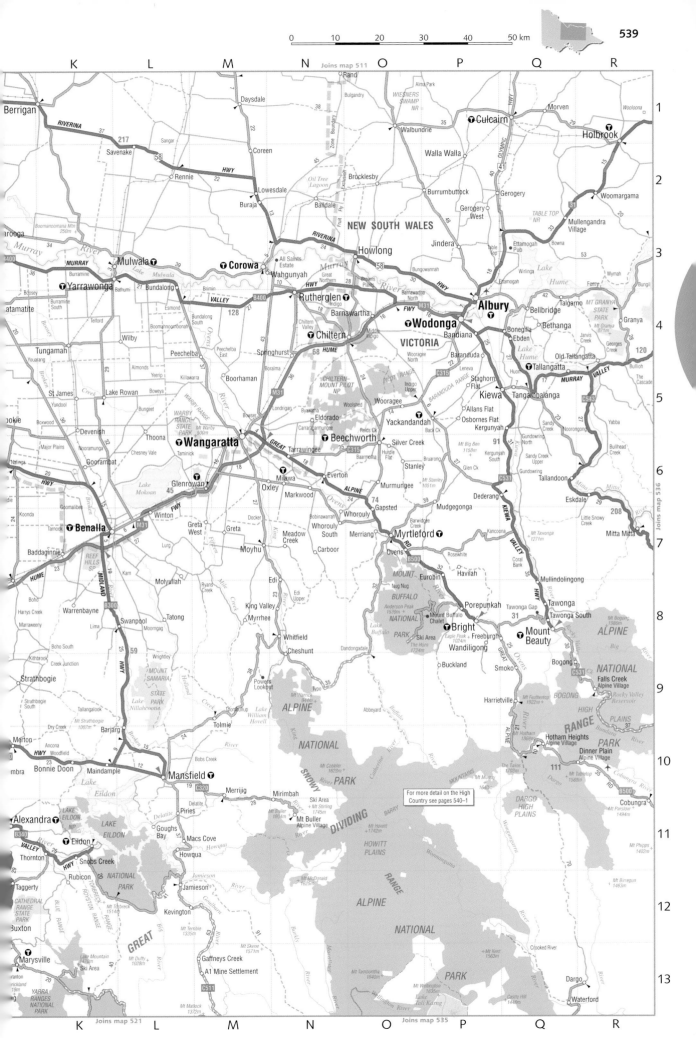

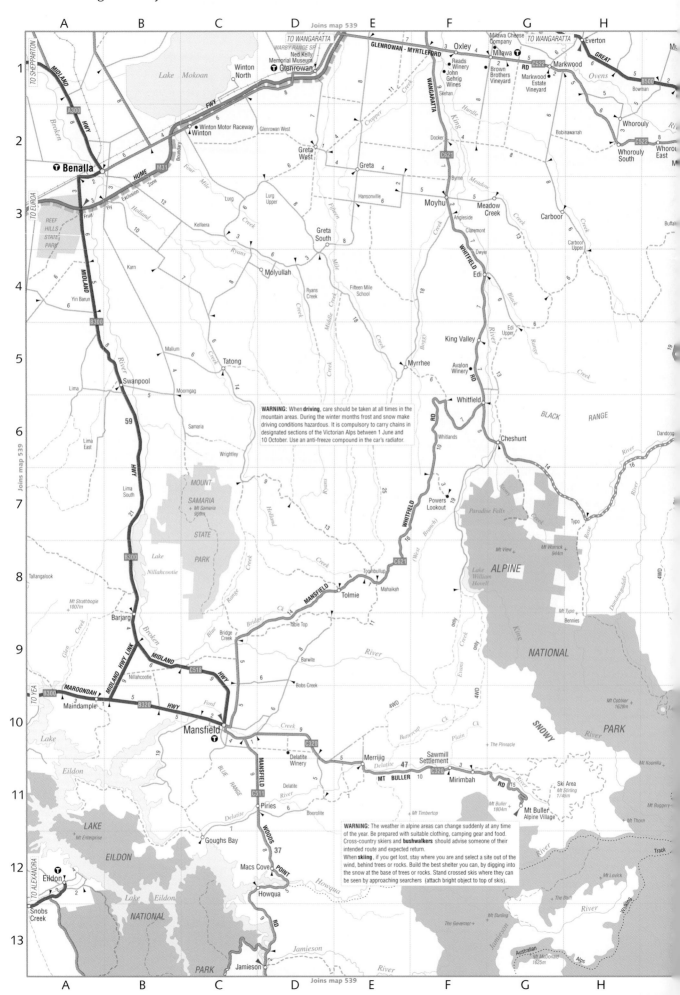

WARNING: When **driving**, care should be taken at all times in the mountain areas. During the winter months frost and snow make driving conditions hazardous. It is compulsory to carry chains in designated sections of the Victorian Alps between 1 June and 10 October. Use an anti-freeze compound in the car's radiator.

WARNING: The weather in alpine areas can change suddenly at any time of the year. Be prepared with suitable clothing, camping gear and food. Cross-country skiers and **bushwalkers** should advise someone of their intended route and expected return.

When **skiing**, if you get lost, stay where you are and select a site out of the wind, behind trees or rocks. Build the best shelter you can, by digging into the snow at the base of trees or rocks. Stand crossed skis where they can be seen by approaching searchers (attach bright object to top of skis).

Joins map 539

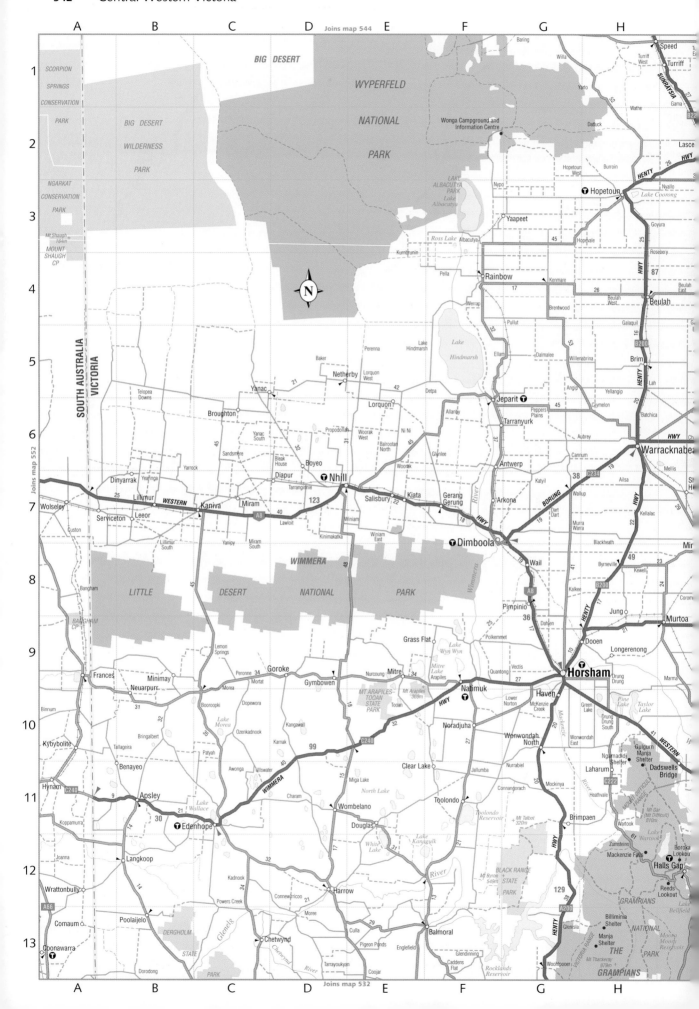

Joins map 544
Joins map 552
Joins map 532

VICTORIA

NEW SOUTH WALES

Scale: 0 10 20 30 40 50 km

Joins map 545 (top)
Joins map 533 (bottom)
Joins map 538 (right)

Grid columns: K L M N O P Q R
Grid rows: 1 2 3 4 5 6 7 8 9 10 11 12 13

Selected place names:

Sea Lake, Lake Tyrrell, Ultima, Lake Boga, Fish Point, Burraboi, Wakool, Berriwillock, Goschen, Tresco, Mystic Park, Murrabit, Ballbank, Culgoa, Lake Charm, Koondrook, Barham, KOONDROOK STATE FOREST, GUNBOWER STATE FOREST, PERRICOOTA STATE FOREST, Nullawil, Quambatook, Kerang, Kerang South, Cohuna, ISLAND STATE, McMillans, Macorna, Leitchville, Gunbower, Birchip, Dumosa, Gredgwin, Mincha, Wee-Wee-Rup FOREST, Gunbower Island, Watchem, Wycheproof, Barraport, Mimmindie, Yando, Pyramid Hill, TERRICK TERRICK NP, Mt Terrick Terrick, Corack East, Corack, Glenloth, Boort, Durham Ox, Mitiamo, Litchfield, Wooroonook, Charlton, Barrakee, Buckrabanyule, Wychitella, Fernihurst, Jarklin, Calivil, Prairie, Dingee, Donald, Korong Vale, Borung, Bears Lagoon, Tandarra, Cope Cope, Swanwater West, Wedderburn, Wedderburn Junction, Mt Korong, Serpentine, Raywood, Summerfield, GREATER BENDIGO NP, St Arnaud, Logan, KOOYOORA SP, Melville Caves, Kingower, Inglewood, Bridgewater on Loddon, Campbells Forest, Sebastian, Neilborough, Huntly, Bagshot, Marnoo, Emu, Moliagul, Murphys Creek, Llanelly, Rheola, Arnold, Newbridge, Leichardt, Marong, EAGLEHAWK, EPSOM, Fosterville, BENDIGO, Longlea, Wallaloo, Kanya, Bealiba, Tarnagulla, Laanecoorie, Lockwood, Maiden Gully, Strathfieldsaye, Mandurang, Sedgwick, Junortoun, Navarre, Stuart Mill, Goldsborough, Dunolly, Eddington, Ravenswood, Harcourt North, Sutton Grange, Redbank, Landsborough, Moonambel, Moyreisk, Bet Bet, Havelock, Baringhup, Maldon, Barkers Creek, Harcourt, Faraday, Maryborough, Carisbrook, Welshmans Reef, Castlemaine, Chewton, Taradale, Elphinstone, Stawell, Avoca, Lamplough, Amherst, Talbot, Campbelltown, Newstead, Guildford, Vaughan, Glenluce, Malmsbury, Great Western, Crowlands, Elmhurst, Amphitheatre, Evansford, Clunes, Yandoit, Porcupine Ridge, Lauriston, Kyneton, Ararat, Armstrong, Buangor, Raglan, Waterloo, Lexton, Learmonth, Creswick, Smeaton, Allendale, Hepburn Springs, Daylesford, Glenlyon, Tylden, Carlsrube, Trentham

Highways: CALDER HWY (A79, B260), SUNRAYSIA HWY, MIDLAND HWY, PYRENEES HWY, WESTERN HWY, LODDON VALLEY HWY, MURRAY VALLEY HWY

For more detail on the Goldfields see pages 530–1

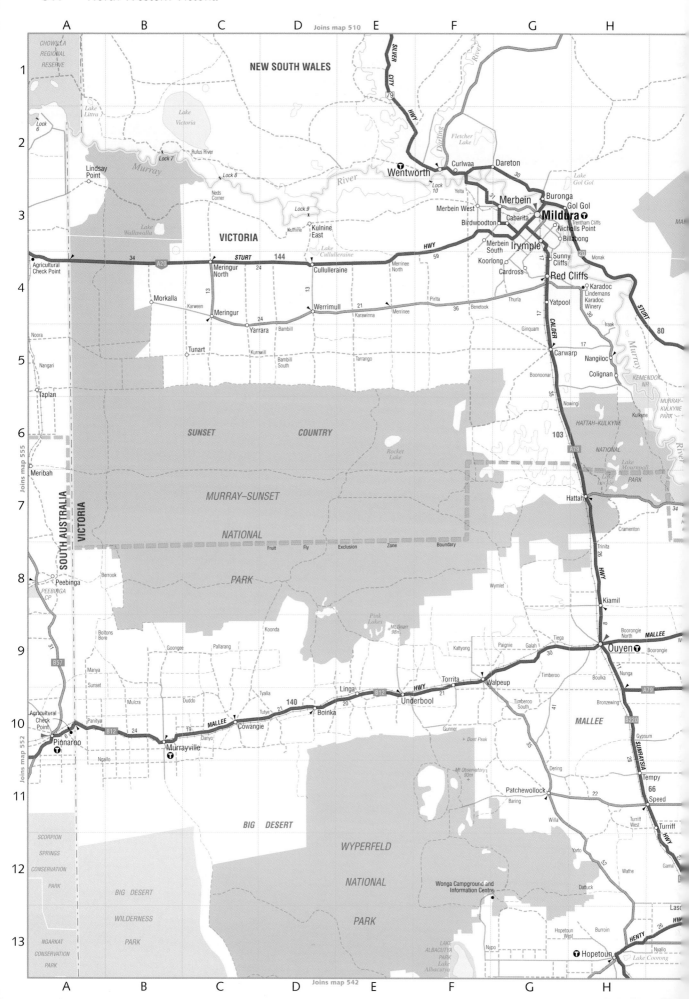

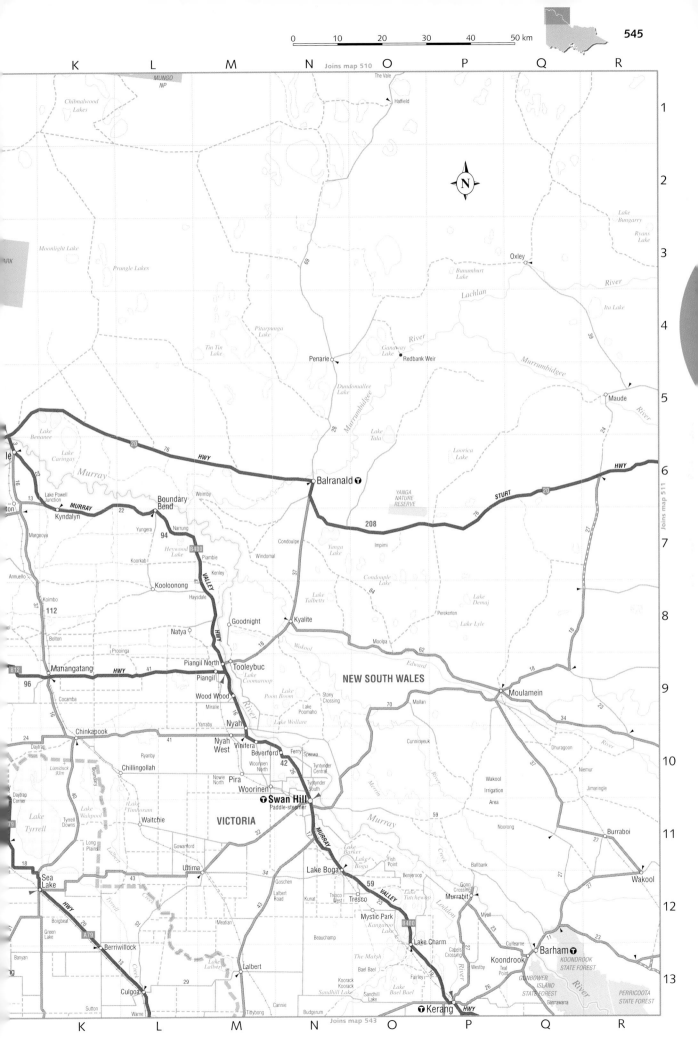

0 10 20 30 40 50 km

K   L   M   N   O   P   Q   R

1
2
3
4
5
6
7
8
9
10
11
12
13

Chibnalwood Lakes

MUNGO NP

The Vale

Hatfield

Moonlight Lake

Prungle Lakes

Oxley

Lake Bungarry

Ryans Lake

Lachlan   *River*

Pitarpunga Lake

Bunumburt Lake

Ita Lake

Tin Tin Lake

Penarie

Ganaway Lake

Redbank Weir

River

Murrumbidgee

39

Maude

Lake Benanee

20   76   HWY

3

Lake Caringay

16   23

Murray

Lake Powell Junction

13

Kyndalyn   MURRAY   22

Boundary Bend

94

Weimby

Dundomallee Lake

Lake Tala

Balranald

YANGA NATURE RESERVE

STURT   20   HWY

6

Loorica Lake

River

24

Margooya

Yungera   Narrung

Koorkab

Condoulpe

208

76

27

Annuello

B400   Piambie

VALLEY

Kenley

Heywood Lake

Kooloonong

Haysdale

Windomal

37

Yanga Lake

Condouple Lake

Impimi

84

Lake Talbetts

Perekerten

Lake Demaj

Lake Lyle

18

Koimbo

112

Natya

Goodnight

HWY

Kyalite

Moolpa

62

Edward

Wakool

37

Bolton

Prooinga

18

River

Lake Coomaroop

NEW SOUTH WALES

B12   Manangatang   HWY   41

96

Cocamba

Piangil North

Piangil

Tooleybuc

Wood Wood

Miralie

Lake Poom Boom

Stony Crossing

Mallan

Moulamein

34

23

Chinkapook

24   Daytrap

41

Ryanby

Yarraby

Nyah

River

16

Lake Poomaho

Lake Wollare

70

Cunninyeuk

Dhuragoon

Niemur

18

River

Lianidock 93m

Chillingollah

Nyah West

Vinifera

Beverford

42

Ferry

Speewa

Woorinen North

Tyntynder Central

Jimaringle

Merran

Wakool Irrigation Area

Daytrap Corner

Boundary

Lake Timboram

Pira

Nowie North

Woorinen

Swan Hill

Paddle-steamer

Tyntynder South

Murray

Nootong

59

Burraboi

27

A79

Lake Tyrrell

Tyrrell Downs

Waitchie

VICTORIA

32

17

MURRAY

Lake Barker

Lake Boga

Fish Point

Ballbank

Wakool

Long Plains

Gowanford

Ultima

34

Goschen

Lake Boga

Benjeroop

Gonn Crossing

Murrabit

27

18

Sea Lake

43

Lalbert Road

Kunat

Tresco West

59   VALLEY

Tresco

Lake Tutchewop

Myall

23

HWY

20

Boigbeat

Tyrrell Creek

Meatian

43

Mystic Park

B400

Kangaroo Lake

Cuttearne

11

Barham

KOONDROOK STATE FOREST

A79

Green Lake

Berriwillock

13

Lalbert

Creek

29

Beauchamp

Lake Charm

Capels Crossing

27

Koondrook

23

River

Loddon

Banyan

Culgoa

Sutton

Warne

Tittybong

Cannie

The Marsh

Bael Bael

Budgerum

Koorack   Koorack

Sandhill Lake

Lake Bael Bael

Sandhill Bael

Fairley

19

Westby

Teal Point

GUNBOWER ISLAND STATE FOREST

26

Gannawarra

PERRICOOTA STATE FOREST

River

Kerang   HWY

K   L   M   N   O   P   Q   R

SOUTH AUSTRALIA
MAPS

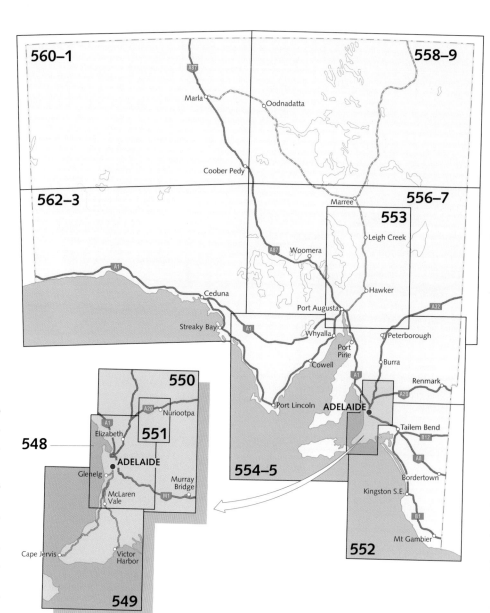

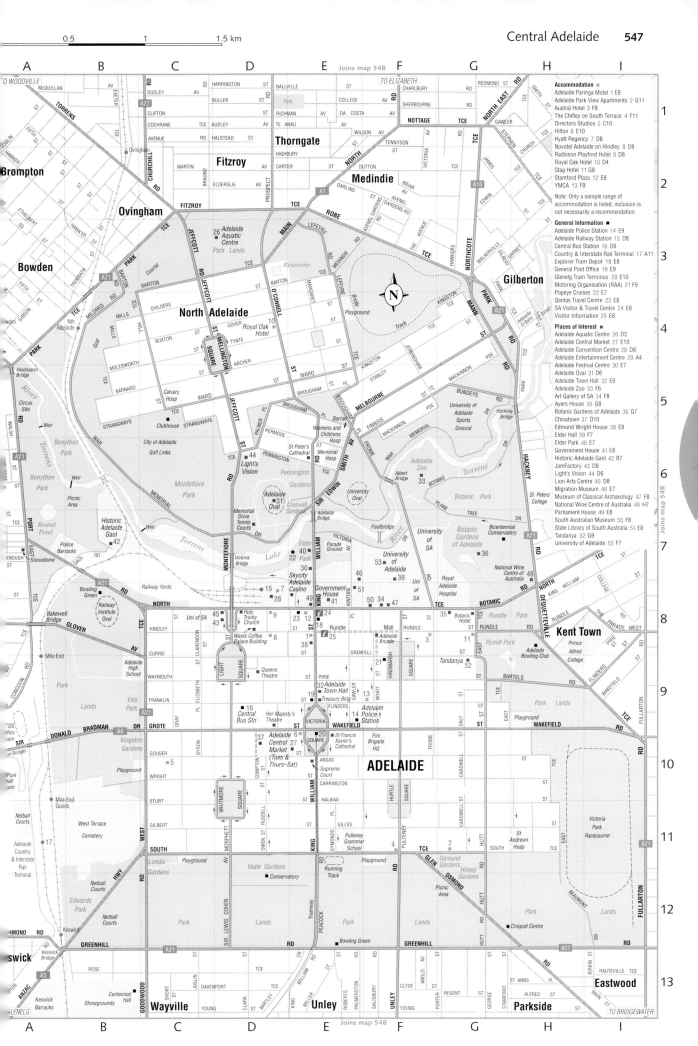

0 5 10 15 km

A B C D E F G H I

Joins map 550

Light *River*
TO PORT WAKEFIELD
PRINCES
Kangaroo Flat
TO BURRA TO NURIOOTPA
STURT HWY
A20
Two Wells
24
Rosedale
Gawler
WAKEFIELD
B19 Sandy Creek
Rowland Flat
B19
Middle Beach
9
BAROS HISTO MUSE
22
Angle Vale
Lyndoch
BAROS WIN REGIC
Cockatoo Valley
Kies Hill
Port Gawler
A1
Virginia
17
MAIN NORTH RD
Whispering Wall
Pewsey Vale Peak 629m
PORT GAWLER CONSERVATION PARK
Gawler
6
PENFIELD
SMITHFIELD
A20
16
PARA WIRRA RECREATION PARK
Barossa Reservoir
Williamstown
HALE CP
B34 Warren Reservoir

Waterloo Corner
39
Elizabeth
44
South Para Reservoir
WARREN CP
Mt Crawford 562
MOUNT CRAWFORD FOREST
St Kilda
HWY
Little Para Reservoir
Bare Hill 344m
15
9

BOLIVAR
Para River
SALISBURY
A18
Heysen
OUTER HARBOR
Barker Inlet
A13
GOLDEN GROVE
Kersbrook
Mt Gould 530m
Forreston
B31
NORTH HAVEN
Torrens Island
A20
PARA HILLS
A18
REDWOOD PARK
Chain of Ponds
B10
13
OSBORNE
Garden Is
12
Inglewood
8
Gumeracha
The Toy Factory
Birdw NATIONAL MOTOR MUSE
A16
Largs Bay
MODBURY
Houghton
11
Millbrook Reservoir
7
B31
Cudlee Creek
SEMAPHORE PARK
PORT ADELAIDE
A13
3
A16
ENFIELD
6 A16
17
MT CRAWFORD FOREST
MT CRAWFORD FOREST
Mt Torrens 583m
Mo Torr
South Australian Maritime Museum
7
Junction Market
A11
A10
14
Torrens River
Kangaroo Creek Reservoir
13
B34
Investigator Science & Technology Centre
Windsor Gardens
15
BLACK HILL CP
Castambul
MONTACUTE CP
14
WEST LAKES
A7
KIDMAN PARK
A13
R.M. Williams Outback Heritage Museum
7
MORIALTA CP
MOUNT CRAWFORD FOREST
Lobethal
A22
WALKERVILLE
18
Norton Summit
13
Charleston
GULF
13
A15
River
A21
HACKNEY
A11
MAGILL
Penfolds Magill Estate
Lenswood
HENLEY BEACH
A6
A17
Ashton
14
Forest Range
Woodside
14
WEST BEACH
ADELAIDE AIRPORT
A14
ADELAIDE
A21
13
3
Uraidla
KENNETH STIRLING CP
A5
A1
CLELAND CP
Summertown
ADELAIDE HILLS
Brukunga
GLENELG
A3
12
Mt Lofty 727m
5
Oakbank
15
B34
For more detail on Central Adelaide see page 547
MITCHAM
16
Crafers
35
Petaluma's Bridgewater Mill Winery
Balhannah
Shephards Hill 450m
MARION
A15
BELAIR
BELAIR NP
Stirling
Verdun
11
ST VINCENT
BRIGHTON
Bridgewater
Hahndorf
BEDFORD PARK
Sturt
DARLINGTON
STURT GORGE RECREATION PARK
10
Mylor
Nairne
A14
7
SOUTH
EASTERN
HALLETT COVE
2
Happy Valley Reservoir
Littlehampton
5
HALLETT COVE CONSERVATION PARK
11
9
Mount Barker
Mt Barker
M2
SCOTT CREEK CP
B33
M1 FWY
WOODCROFT
Clarendon
Mt Bold
Echunga
10
Wistow
CHRISTIES BEACH
21
MORPHETT VALE
A15
Jupiter Creek Gold Fields
A13
River
Mt Bold Reservoir
Walking
PORT NOARLUNGA
14
HACKHAM
LOFTY
11
Flaxley
13
ONKAPARINGA RIVER REC PARK
ONKAPARINGA RIVER NP
Kangarilla
Mt Panorama 359m
Heysen
B34
Macclesfield
Old Noarlunga
16
RANGES
MOUNT
11
MOANA
B23
Onkaparinga River
McLaren Flat
Meadows
Paris Creek
B33
B37
Maslin Beach
A13
McLaren Vale
Wineries
Mt Wilson 408m
SOUTH
Prospect Hill
Bull Creek
Woodchester
TO VICTOR HARBOR
KUITPO FOREST
B34
Joins map 549

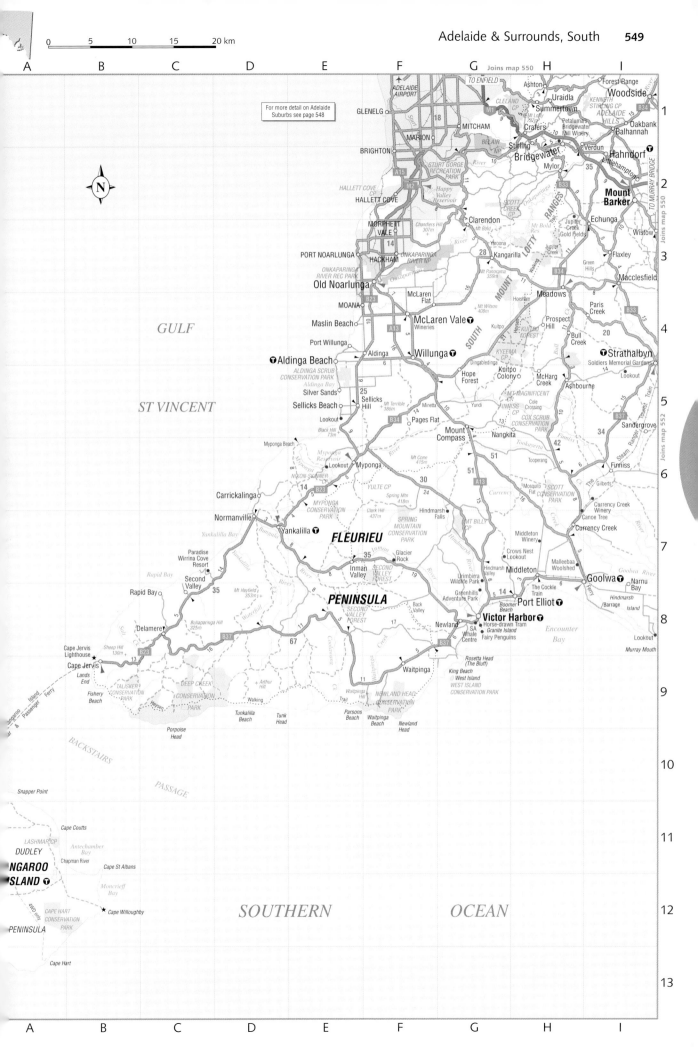

For more detail on Adelaide
Suburbs see page 548

Map labels

GULF ST VINCENT

SOUTHERN OCEAN

BACKSTAIRS PASSAGE

FLEURIEU PENINSULA

MOUNT LOFTY RANGES

SOUTH

TO ENFIELD

ADELAIDE AIRPORT

GLENELG
MITCHAM
MARION
BRIGHTON
HALLETT COVE
MORPHETT VALE
PORT NOARLUNGA
HACKHAM
Old Noarlunga
MOANA
Maslin Beach
Port Willunga
Aldinga Beach
Silver Sands
Sellicks Beach
Sellicks Hill
Lookout
Pages Flat

Ashton
Uraidla
Woodside
Forest Range
Summertown
Crafers
Oakbank
Balhannah
Stirling
Bridgewater
Verdun
Hahndorf
Mylor
Littlehampton
Mount Barker
Echunga
Wistow
Clarendon
Kangarilla
Flaxley
Green Hills
Macclesfield
McLaren Flat
McLaren Vale
Wineries
Meadows
Paris Creek
Prospect Hill
Bull Creek
Willunga
Hope Forest
Kuitpo Colony
McHarg Creek
Ashbourne
Strathalbyn
Soldiers Memorial Gardens
Lookout
Mount Compass
Nangkita
Sandergrove
Finniss
Myponga Beach
Lookout
Myponga
Hindmarsh Falls
Tooperang
The Gilberts
Currency Creek Winery
Canoe Tree
Currency Creek
Carrickalinga
Normanville
Yankalilla
Glacier Rock
Inman Valley
Middleton Winery
Crows Nest Lookout
Malleebaa Woolshed
Goolwa
Narnu Bay
Paradise Wirrina Cove Resort
Second Valley
Urimbirra Wildlife Park
Greenhills Adventure Park
Middleton
Port Elliot
The Cockle Train
Rapid Bay
Delamere
Newland
Victor Harbor
SA Whale Centre
Horse-drawn Tram
Granite Island
Fairy Penguins
Boomer Beach
Hindmarsh Barrage
Hindmarsh Island
Cape Jervis Lighthouse
Cape Jervis
Lands End
Fishery Beach
Waitpinga
Rosetta Head (The Bluff)
King Beach
West Island
Lookout
Murray Mouth

Encounter Bay

Snapper Point
Cape Coutts
DUDLEY PENINSULA
KANGAROO ISLAND
Chapman River
Cape St Albans
Antechamber Bay
Cape Willoughby
Cape Hart
CAPE HART CONSERVATION PARK
Moncrieff Bay

DEEP CREEK CONSERVATION PARK
TALISKER CONSERVATION PARK
SECOND VALLEY FOREST
MYPONGA CONSERVATION PARK
YULTE CP
SPRING MOUNTAIN CONSERVATION PARK
NEWLAND HEAD CONSERVATION PARK
WEST ISLAND CONSERVATION PARK
SCOTT CONSERVATION PARK
COX SCRUB CONSERVATION PARK
KYEEMA CP
KUITPO FOREST
FINNISS CP
MT MAGNIFICENT CP
MT BILLY CP
CLELAND CP
BELAIR NP
STURT GORGE RECREATION PARK
ONKAPARINGA RIVER NP
ONKAPARINGA RIVER REC PARK
ALDINGA SCRUB CONSERVATION PARK
SCOTT CREEK CP
KENNETH STIRLING CP
ADELAIDE HILLS

Porpoise Head
Tunkalilla Beach
Tunk Head
Parsons Beach
Waitpinga Beach
Newland Head
Arthur Hill
Sheep Hill 130m
Bullaparinga Hill 325m
Mt Hayfield 353m
Black Hill 73m
Spring Mtn 418m
Clark Hill 437m
Mt Cone 415m
Mt Terrible 386m
Mt Wilson 408m
Mt Panorama 359m
Chandlers Hill 307m
Mt Bold
Mt Lofty

Happy Valley Reservoir
Myponga Reservoir
Mt Bold Res
Jupiter Creek Gold Fields

Rapid Bay
Yankalilla Bay
Aldinga Bay
Back Valley

Joins map 550
Joins map 552

0 5 10 15 20 km

TO BURRA

Giles Corner
Alma
Owen
Pinery
Barabba
Hamley Bridge
Stockport
Linwood
Bethel
Fords
Tarlee
NORTH
BARRIER
MOUNT LOFTY RANGES
HWY
RD
MAIN NORTH
Kapunda
Kapunda Museum
Hamilton
Allendale North
Bagot Well
Koonunderie
Neales Flat
Brownlow
Frankton
Hansborough
Mt Rufus 547m
St Kitts
Bald Hill
Dutton
Stonefield
Koonunga
Belvidere 391m
Hawker Hill 442m
HWY
A20
Truro
Freeling
Wasleys
Templers
Greenock
Daveyston
Seppeltsfield
Nuriootpa
Stockwell
Moculta
Mt Karinya 444m
Mallala
Red Banks
Roseworthy
Shea-Oak Log
Paterson Hill 300m
BAROSSA VALLEY WINERIES
Tanunda
Barossa Historical Museum
Mengler Hill
Angaston
Towitta
TO PORT WAKEFIELD
PORT WAKEFIELD RD
A1
Two Wells
Lewiston
Kangaroo Flat
Rosedale
Concordia
Gawler
BAROSSA VALLEY WAY
Rowland Flat
Bethany
Kaiserstuhl 599m
BAROSSA WINE REGION
KAISERSTUHL CONSERVATION PARK
Keyneton
Sed
Port Gawler
PORT GAWLER CONSERVATION PARK
Virginia
Angle Vale
Sandy Creek
SANDY CREEK CP
Lyndoch
Cockatoo Valley
Kies Hill
Whispering Wall
Barossa Reservoir
Pewsey Vale Peak 629m
Peggys Hill 491m
Mons Hill 471m
Eden Valley
Cambra
SMITHFIELD
Waterloo Corner
Elizabeth
St Kilda
A1
SALISBURY
Williamstown
PARA WIRRA RECREATION PARK
HALE CP
Warren Reservoir
WARREN CP
Mt Crawford 562m
Karl Seppelt Grand Cru Estate
Springton
Mt Colin
Burns 502m
Cookes Hill 309m
Sanderston
OUTER HARBOR
Barker Inlet
Little Para Reservoir
Bare Hill 344m
South Para Reservoir
B31
MOUNT CRAWFORD FOREST
Mt Pleasant 542m
Mount Pleasant
Scotts Hill 473m
Millendella
Largs Bay
PORT ADELAIDE
MODBURY
ENFIELD
GOLDEN GROVE
Kersbrook
Chain of Ponds
Inglewood
Houghton
Mt Gould 530m
Forreston
Gumeracha
The Toy Factory
Birdwood
National Motor Museum
Tungkillo
Palmer
Apamurra
Punthari
WEST LAKES
MAGILL
Norton Summit
Cudlee Creek
Castambul
BLACK HILL CP
MONTACUTE
Mt Crawford 453m
Kangaroo Ck Reservoir
Mt Torrens 593m
Mount Torrens
Fendlers Hill 473m
Harrison Creek
Mannum
HENLEY BEACH
ADELAIDE
ADELAIDE AIRPORT
A17
HORSNELL GULLY CP
Ashton
MORIALTA CP
Uraidla
Summertown
MOUNT CRAWFORD FOREST
Lobethal
Lenswood
Charleston
Forest Range
KENNETH STIRLING CP
ADELAIDE HILLS
Woodside
Harrogate
Brukunga
Rockleigh
Whalleys Hill 357m
Mt Beevor 503m
Murrays Hill 415m
Caloote
GLENELG
MITCHAM
MARION
CLELAND CP
Mt Lofty 732m
Crafers
Stirling
Petaluma's Bridgewater Mill Winery
Oakbank
Balhannah
Kanmantoo
Tepko
Pompo
Po
BRIGHTON
BELAIR NP
Bridgewater
Mylor
Verdun
Hahndorf
Nairne
Littlehampton
Shephards Hill 450m
Monarto
HALLETT COVE
M2
STURT GORGE RECREATION PARK
Happy Valley Reservoir
Mount Barker
Mt Barker
Kanmantoo
Monarto South
Avoca Dell
HALLETT COVE CONSERVATION PARK
MORPHETT VALE
Clarendon
Mt Bold
SCOTT CREEK CP
Jupiter Creek Gold Fields
Echunga
Wistow
Callington
SOUTH EASTERN FWY
M1
Murray Bridge
PORT NOARLUNGA
HACKHAM
Kangarilla
Yaroona
Mt Panorama 359m
Flaxley
Green Hills
Macclesfield
MONARTO CONSERVATION PARK
Hartley
Swanport
MOANA
Old Noarlunga
McLaren Flat
ONKAPARINGA RIVER NP
MOUNT LOFTY RANGES
KYEEMA CF
Meadows
B34
Paris Creek
B33
B37
Woodchester
Bletchley
FERRIES MCDONALD CONSERVATION PARK
Brinkley
Port Willunga
Maslin Beach
Aldinga
McLaren Vale
Wineries
SOUTH
Kuitpo
Prospect Hill
Bull Creek
Strathalbyn
Soldiers Memorial Gardens

Joins map 555
Joins map 549
Joins map 552

For more detail on the Barossa Valley see page 551

For more detail on Adelaide Suburbs see page 548

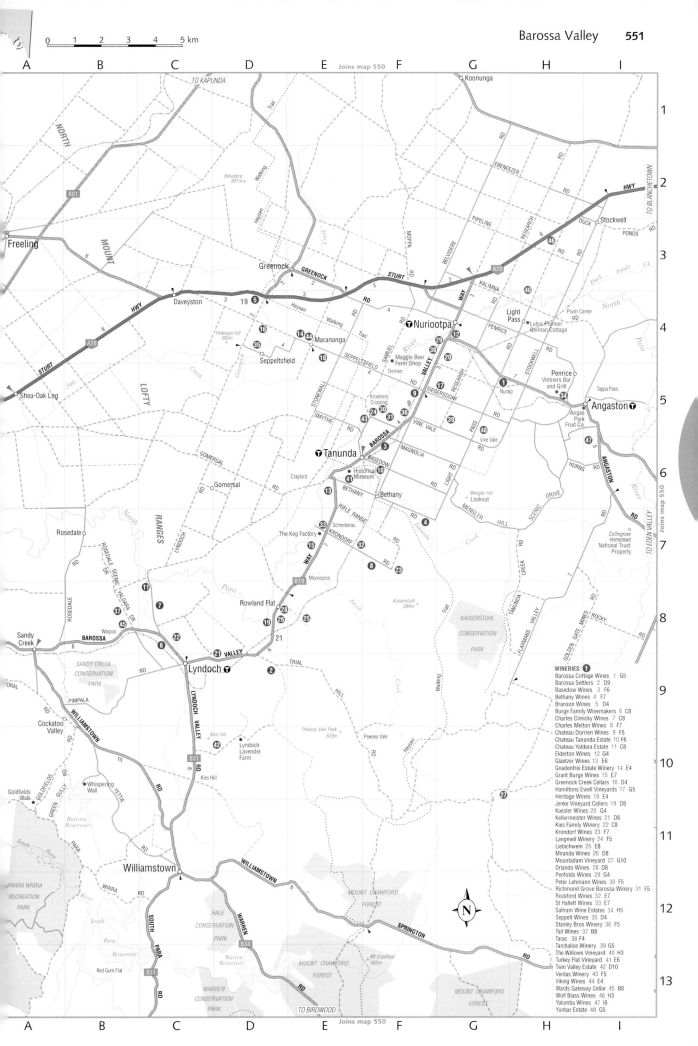

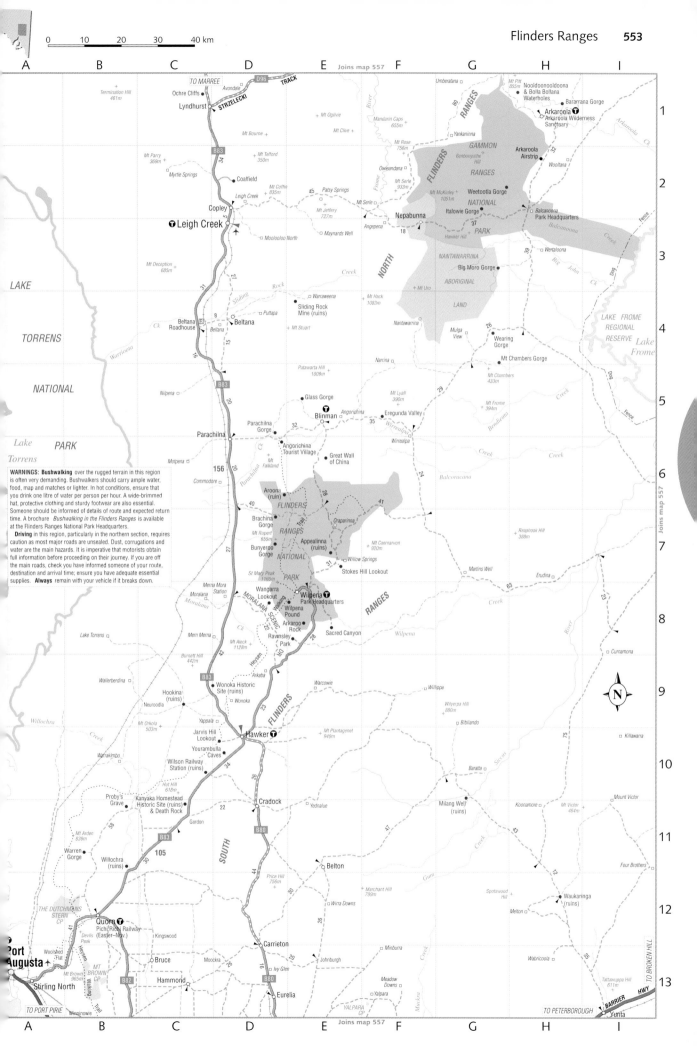

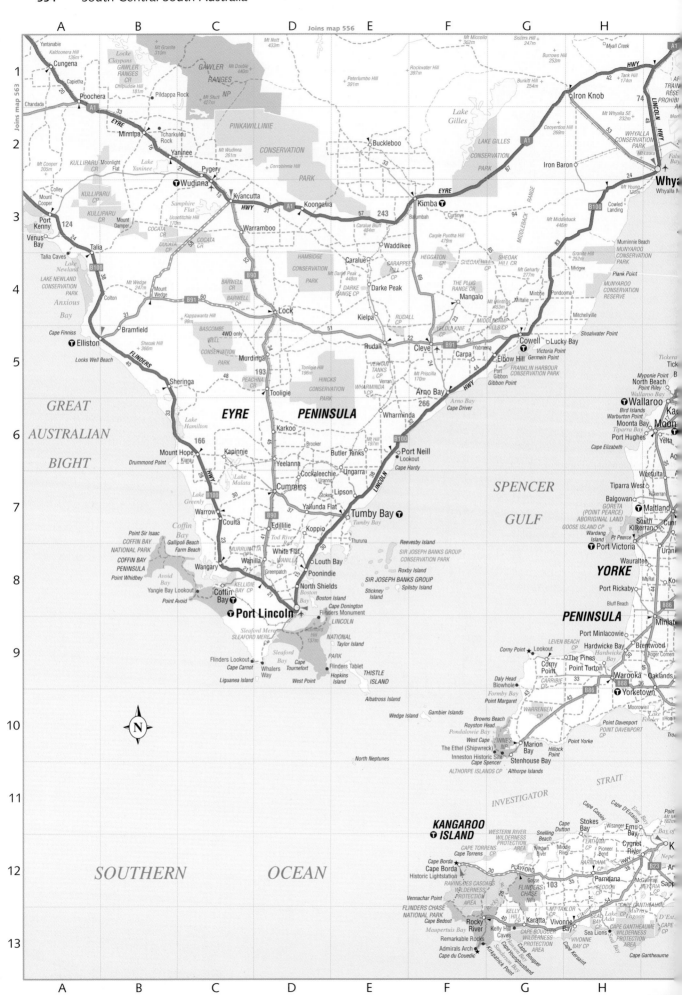

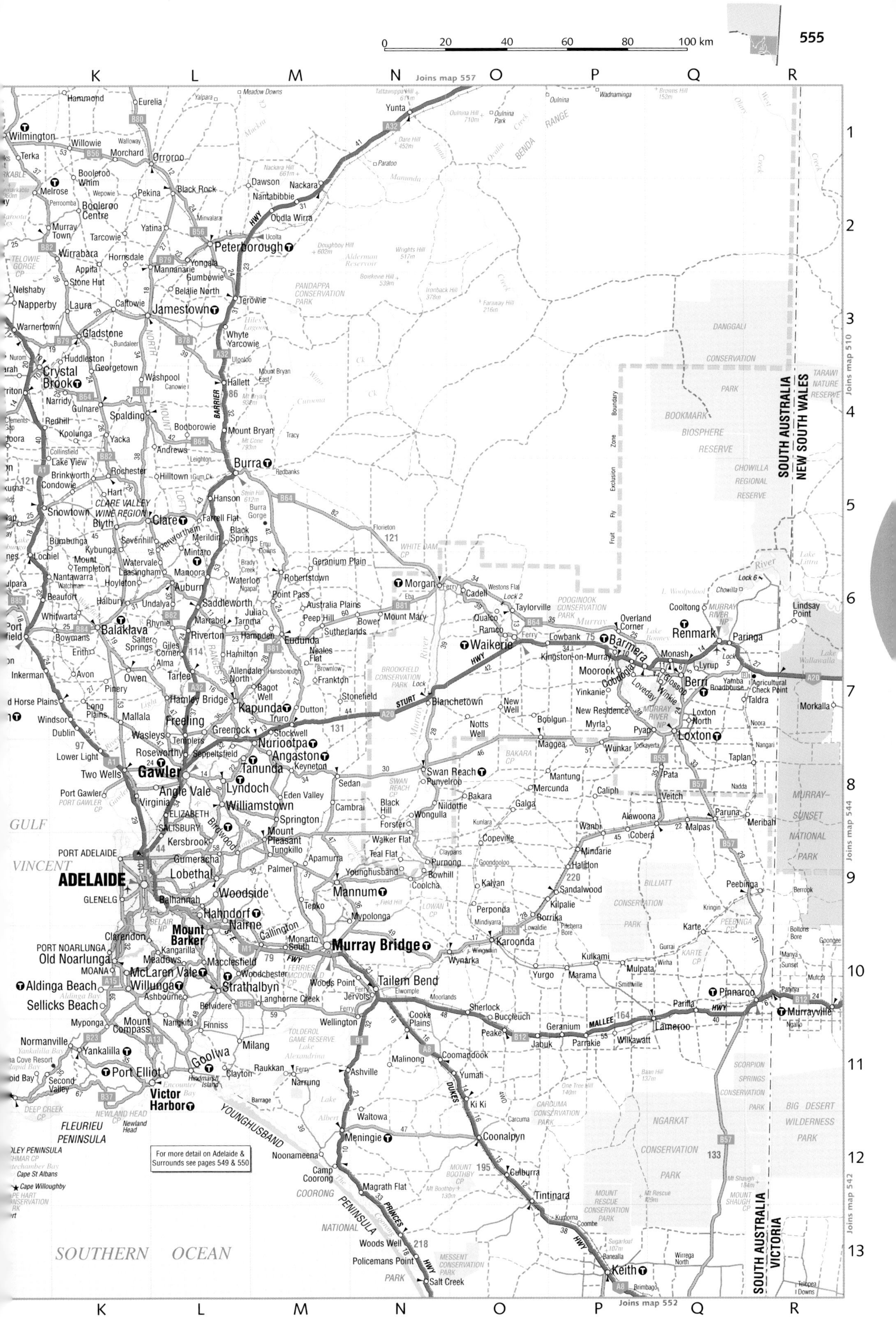

0 20 40 60 80 100 km
K L M N O P Q R
Joins map 557
Joins map 510
Joins map 544
Joins map 542
Joins map 552
1 2 3 4 5 6 7 8 9 10 11 12 13
Hammond
Eurelia
Yalpara
Meadow Downs
Yunta
Oulnina
Wadnaminga
Wilmington
Willowie
Walloway
Morchard
Orroroo
Terka
Booleroo Whim
Melrose
Wepowie
Pekina
Black Rock
Booleroo Centre
Dawson
Nantabibbie
Nackara
Oodla Wirra
Murray Town
Yatina
Tarcowie
Peterborough
Ucolta
Wirrabara
Hornsdale
Yongala
Mannanarie
Appila
Gumbowie
Stone Hut
Belalie North
Nelshaby
Terowie
Napperby
Laura
Caltowie
Jamestown
Warnertown
Gladstone
Whyte Yarcowie
Huddleston
Georgetown
Crystal Brook
Washpool
Canowie
Hallett
Narridy
Gulnare
Spalding
Redhill
Koolunga
Yacka
Bodborowie
Mount Bryan
Andrews
Tracy
Lake View
Rochester
Brinkworth
Condowie
Burra
Hilltown
Redbanks
Hanson
Hart
Snowtown
CLARE VALLEY WINE REGION
Clare
Farrell Flat
Blyth
Burra Gorge
Bumbunga
Sevenhill
Penwortham
Black Springs
Florieton
Kybunga
Mintaro
Lochiel
Mount Templeton
Watervale
Leasingham
Manoora
Geranium Plain
Nantawarra
Hoyleton
Waterloo
Robertstown
Beaufort
Auburn
Morgan
Cadell
Point Pass
Halbury
Undalya
Saddleworth
Australia Plains
Taylorville
Whitwarta
Marrabel
Julia
Tarnma
Peep Hill
Bower
Mount Mary
Qualco
Ramco
Overland Corner
Renmark
Paringa
Lindsay Point
Cooltong
Chowilla
Balaklava
Rhynie
Riverton
Hampden
Eudunda
Sutherlands
Waikerie
Lowbank
Barmera
Bowmans
Salter Springs
Giles Corner
Hamilton
Neales Flat
Kingston-on-Murray
Monash
Lyrup
Erith
Alma
Moorook
Cobdogla
Berri
Inkerman
Avon
Owen
Tarlee
Allendale North
Bagot Well
Frankton
Loveday
Glossop
Winkie
Yamba
Agricultural Check Point
Yinkanie
Pinery
Stonefield
Blanchetown
Taldra
Long Plains
Hamley Bridge
Kapunda
Dutton
New Well
New Residence
Loxton North
Morkalla
Windsor
Mallala
Freeling
Truro
Notts Well
Boolgun
Myrla
Pyap
Loxton
Dublin
Wasleys
Templers
Greenock
Stockwell
Nuriootpa
Maggea
Wunkar
Noora
Lower Light
Roseworthy
Seppeltsfield
Angaston
Keyneton
Taplan
Two Wells
Gawler
Tanunda
Swan Reach
Pata
Port Gawler
Angle Vale
Lyndoch
Sedan
Punyelroo
Mantung
Mercunda
Caliph
Nadda
Virginia
Eden Valley
Bakara
Veitch
Williamstown
Cambrai
Black Hill
Nildottie
Galga
GULF
ELIZABETH
Springton
Wongulla
Alawoona
Paruna
Meribah
SALISBURY
Mount Pleasant
Forster
Wanbi
Cobera
Malpas
Kersbrook
Birdwood
Tungkillo
Walker Flat
Copeville
MURRAY-SUNSET NATIONAL PARK
PORT ADELAIDE
Apamurra
Teal Flat
Mindarie
VINCENT
Gumeracha
Palmer
Purnong
Halidon
ADELAIDE
Lobethal
Younghusband
Bowhill
GLENELG
Woodside
Mannum
Coolcha
Kalyan
Sandalwood
Peebinga
Balhannah
Tepko
Kilpalie
Hahndorf
Perponda
Borrika
Mount Barker
Nairne
Mypolonga
Karte
Clarendon
Callington
PORT NOARLUNGA
Kangarilla
Monarto South
Murray Bridge
Karoonda
Old Noarlunga
Meadows
Macclesfield
Wynarka
Kulkami
MOANA
McLaren Vale
Woodchester
Yurgo
Marama
Mulpata
Aldinga Beach
Willunga
Strathalbyn
Woods Point
Tailem Bend
Pinnaroo
Sellicks Beach
Ashbourne
Langhorne Creek
Jervois
Murrayville
Myponga
Belvidere
Sherlock
Parilla
Mount Compass
Nangkita
Finniss
Wellington
Cooke Plains
Buccleuch
Lameroo
Normanville
Milang
Peake
Geranium
Jabuk
Parrakie
Wilkawatt
Yankalilla
Goolwa
Coomandook
Port Elliot
Clayton
Raukkan
Malinong
Second Valley
Victor Harbor
Narrung
Ashville
Yumali
Ki Ki
FLEURIEU PENINSULA
Waltowa
Meningie
Coonalpyn
Noonameena
Camp Coorong
Culburra
Magrath Flat
Tintinara
COORONG NATIONAL PARK
SOUTHERN OCEAN
Woods Well
Policemans Point
Salt Creek
Keith
Wirrega North
SOUTH AUSTRALIA
NEW SOUTH WALES
VICTORIA
DANGGALI CONSERVATION PARK
BOOKMARK BIOSPHERE RESERVE
CHOWILLA REGIONAL RESERVE
TARAWI NATURE RESERVE
PANDAPPA CONSERVATION PARK
BILLIATT CONSERVATION PARK
NGARKAT CONSERVATION PARK
MOUNT RESCUE CONSERVATION PARK
SCORPION SPRINGS CONSERVATION PARK
BIG DESERT WILDERNESS PARK
For more detail on Adelaide & Surrounds see pages 549 & 550

Joins map 558

WARNING: While visitors are permitted in the township of Woomera, entry to the Woomera Prohibited Area is by permit only, except in the immediate corridors of the Stuart Highway and the road from Coober Pedy to William Creek. Camping is not permitted in the area.

WOOMERA

PROHIBITED

AREA

OODNADATTA

Mt Sandy 223m
Mt Soward 224m
McDouall Peak
White Hill 223m
Yarraboolla Hill 180m
Hume Hill 226m
Harrison Hill 213m
Hatthorn Hill 213m
Danse Hill 205m
Mt Hawker 187m
Mt Morgan 175m
New Twin Hill 110m
Stuart Creek
Mt Alford 82m
Hermit Hill 121m
Mt Norwest 313m
Finniss Springs
Mulgaria

The Twins
Snow Hill 215m
Sloane Hill 191m
Mt Paisley 250m
Hogarth Hill 198m
Billa Kalina
Tent Hill 110m

Bulgunnia
Haggard Hill 216m
122
Mount Eba
Jacks Hill 180m
Bamboo Swamp
Black Swan Swamp
Mattaweara Lagoon

STUART
90
367
Mt Sabine 227m
Curdlawidny Lagoon
Reedy Lagoon
Parakylia
Dog Fence

Bon Bon
Orwell Well
Rawlinson Hill 168m
Gambier Hill 136m
Chermside Hill 129m
Olympic Dam Village
Roxby Downs
Andamooka
Opal Fields

Lake Labyrinth
35
Hickson Hill 199m
Mount Vivien
Locks Well
Beddome Hill 117m
Roxby Downs
Andamooka

Mt Eba 231m
53
Parakylia Hill 159m
Lake Younghusband
Roxby Hill 149m
Heaton Hill 144m
Purple Downs
LAKE TORRENS NATIONAL PARK

HWY
Kingoonya
Glendambo
Lake Patricia
Jims Hill 168m
Open Hill 167m
Lake Hanson
Hanson Hill 169m
Knoll
Whitefield Hill 187m
Ashton Hill 130m
64
Arcoona
Bosworth
ANDAMOOKA RANGES

80
Renton Hill 161m
Kingoonya Hill 176m
43
Mulga Hill 174m
Relief Hill 184m
113
A87
Lake Hart
Woomera
Pimba
Lake Richardson
Intercept Hill 217m
Marsella Hill 185m
Lake Windabout

Lake Harris
Meerklebee Hill 152m
Last Resort Hill 164m
Yeltacowie
Pernatty Ck
Lucas Hill 187m
Mt Gonson 259m
Pernatty Lagoon
Pernatty

Chitanilga Hill 315m
Clucas Hill 198m
Island Lagoon
94
South Gap
Whittata Hill 262m

LAKE GAIRDNER NATIONAL PARK
Lake Everard
Waulalumbo Hill 227m
Lake Gairdner
South Oakden Hill 262m
Oakden Hills
Lake Finniss
Lake Dutton
STUART
40
Beda Hill 200m

Glyde Hill 252m
Blue Dam
Dingo Hill 213m
Mt Harper 259m
LAKE GAIRDNER NATIONAL PARK
Mahanewo
Lake Macfarlane
Belo Hill 148m
173

Nuckulla Hill 264m
Lake Everard
Bomb Hill 336m
Belt Hill 332m
Moonarie Hill 322m
Moonaree
28
Hesso

96
Waverley Hill 399m
Lake Acraman
Mt St Mungo 364m
Jumpuppy Hill 347m
117

Mt Hiltaba 465m
Barber Hill 412m
52
Kolaynmeeka Hill 396m
GAWLER
38
Mt Gairdner 336m
Mt St Granite 310m
Mt Kolendo 487m
Unalla Hill 301m
Mt Nonning 307m
North Tent Hill 298m
51
A87
HWY

Kaldoonera Hill 136m
Locke Claypans
GAWLER RANGES CR
Chilpeddie Hill 181m
Mt Double 440m
Mt Sturt 427m
Mt Centre 393m
Mt Ive
Mt Nott 433m
Mt Miccolo 382m
Sisters Hill 247m
Port Augusta
Myall Creek
Burrows Hill 253m
Stirling North
A1
Tassie Hill 268m
PRINCES

Poochera
A1
33
Pildappa Rock
GAWLER RANGES NP
RANGES
Rockwater Hill 397m
Peterhumbo Hill 391m
LAKE GILLES CONSERVATION RESERVE
Burkitt Hill 254m
Iron Knob
42
Tank Hill 174m
ARMY TRAINING RESERVE PROHIBITED AREA
WINNINNOWIE Blanche CP
Monument Hill 196m
Mamt Point Douglas

Minnipa
EYRE
16
Tcharkuldu Rock
Yaninee
Mt Wudinna 261m
Corrobinnie Hill
Buckleboo
Lake Gilles
LAKE GILLES CONSERVATION PARK
Cooyerdoo Hill 269m
74
Mt Whyalla SE 232m
WHYALLA CONSERVATION PARK
53
48
LINCOLN HWY
Backy Point
Port Lowly
False Bay
Point Lowly

KULLIPARU CR
Moonlight Flat
Lake Yaninee
27
Pygery
Wudinna
Kyancutta
13
31
Koongawa
A1
57
243
Balumbah
Curtinye
EYRE
Iron Baron
87
94
MIDDLEBACK RANGE
Mt Laura
Whyalla
Whyalla Maritime Museum
Ge
24
Mt Young 136m

KULLIPARU CP
KULLIPARU CR
Mount Damper
Samphire Flat
Ucontitchie Hill 170m
Warramboo
HWY
33
Kimba
EYRE
Mt Middleback 446m
B100
Cowled Landing
Port P
Jarrold Point
Port Da

Joins map 563

Joins map 554

0   20   40   60   80   100 km

Joins map 559

K   L   M   N   O   P   Q   R

Marquee Hill
111m
Wilpoorinna
Lake Pinnarie
adna
arina
(ruins)
Mount Hopeless
Lake Callabonna
Winnathee Creek
Hawker Gate House

1

rst
Avondale
Mt Lyndhurst
286m
STRZELECKI
D096
195
TRACK
Trent Hill
247m
Dog
Mount Freeling
Fence
Mt Gardiner
374m
Mt Babbage
369m
Moolawatana
Mt Livingston
616m
Mt Fitton
Mt Neil
549m
Hamilton
Bootkaree Creek
Yandama
Lake Yannerpi
Smithville House
Fence
Dog

2

Mount Lyndhurst
Mt Ogilvie
Mt Bourne
Mt Telford
350m
Mt Thomas
689m
Mandarin Caps
655m
Mt Pitt
855m
Mt Painter
790m
Nooldoonooldoona
& Bolla Bollana
Waterholes
Arkaroola
Arkaroola
Wilderness
Sanctuary
FLINDERS
GAMMON
RANGES
Woottola
Arkaroola Creek
Wallace
Lake Want
Lake
Starvation Lake
Turleys Gate
Puckapuddle Ck
Sanpah
WARNINGS: In outback Australia, long distances separate some
towns. Travellers should familiarise themselves with prevailing
conditions before departure and take care to ensure their vehicle
is roadworthy. Adequate supplies of petrol, water and food
should be carried at all times.

In central Australia, rainfall can make some roads impassable,
even with a 4WD vehicle. Full information on road conditions
should be obtained from local authorities before departure.

If visitors intend diverting off public roads within Aboriginal Land
areas, a permit is required from the relevant Aboriginal authority.

3

B83
Copley
Leigh Creek
34
Mt Coffin
835m
Mt Jeffery
727m
Leigh Creek
45
Mt Rose
933m
Mt Serle
933m
Mt McKinley
1051m
Weetootla Gorge
NATIONAL
RANGES
Balcanoona
Park Headquarters
55
Wertaloona
Pine View
Bagghams Gate
Teilta
Lake
Want

4

Maynards Well
NORTH
Nepabunna
PARK
NANTAWARRINA
ABORIGINAL
LAND
Sliding Rock Ck
Warraweena
Mt Hack
1083m
Nantawarrina
Big John Ck
39
26
Mt Chambers
Gorge
Mt Chambers
433m
Alt Frome
394m
Lake
Frome
LAKE FROME
REGIONAL
RESERVE
Lake
Maljanapa
Lake
Culberta
Lake
Carnanto
Bagghams
Gate

5

47
18
Beltana
Sliding Rock
Mine (ruins)
Mt Stuart
Patawarta Hill
1005m
Narrina
29
Mt Lyall
390m
Wirrealpa
Lake
Millyera
Lake
Moko
Lake
Karpi
Dog
Fence
Creek
McDougalls Well

6

Parachilna
20
156
Blinman
35
Great Wall
of China
28
Balcoracana
Wirrealpa
Creek
Frome Downs
Eurinilla
Lake
Tarkaroloo
Lake
Namba
Lake
Yentaanwena
Morphetts Creek
Mulyungarie

7

commodore
Aroona (ruin)
FLINDERS
RANGES
Mt Rupert
655m
NATIONAL
Orapariinna
Reapllook Hill
388m
For more detail on the Flinders
Ranges see page 553
Benagerie
Wilangee
102

8

89
ana
St Mary Peak
1165m
Wangarra
Lookout
Wilpena
Wilpena Pound
Arkaroo
Rock
PARK
RANGES
51
Martins Well
Erudina
Wilpena Creek
River
Curnamona
Mooleulooloo
MUNDI MUNDI
PLAIN

8

Mt Ainch
1128m
att Hill
2m
Arkaba
B83
Wonoka Historic
Site (ruins)
FLINDERS
Willippa
Wilyerpa Hill
380m
Bibliando
Killawarra
Old Telechie
Umberumberka
Reservoir
Silverton
Historic Town

9

ourambulla
Caves
ailway
(ruins)
34
Hawker
Mt Plantagenet
949m
Baratta
Siccus River
Mount Victor
Mt Victor
464m
Plumbago
Bimbowrie
Outalpa Hill
496m
Donatia Ck
Wompinie
49
BARRIER
HWY
32
Cockburn

9

105
22
26
Cradock
B80
Yednalue
Four Brothers
Spotswood
Hill
Waukaringa
(ruins)
37
Weekeroo
Weekeroo Hill
568m
Outalpa
A32
HWY
Olary
44
Mingary
24
Tepco
Mingary Ck
Aroona
SOUTH
AUSTRALIA
NEW SOUTH
WALES

10

44
Belton
Marchant Hill
799m
Wira Downs
Gum Creek
Mannahill
221
Olary Creek
Wiawera
Olary
Ballara
Mutooroo
Boundary
Zone

10

Moockra
Carrieton
Johnburgh
Ivy Glen
Meadow Downs
Yalpara
Dataurupa Hill
611m
44
Quinina Hill
710m
Quinina
Park
Wadnaminga
Quinina
Maldusky Hill
428m
Bronsis Hill
132m
Burta

11

Hammond
156
Eurelia
B80
Wira Downs
Muckra Creek
Yunta
41
BARRIER
Dare Hill
452m
Yunta Creek
Oxalia Creek
BENDA
RANGE

11

Willowie
B56
Walloway
Morchard
Orroroo
Black Rock
Dawson
A32
Nackara
Paratoo
Manunda
Exclusion

12

Booleroo
Whim
Pekina
12
Nackara Hill
667m
Narntabibbie
Oodla Wirra
37
Doughboy Hill
602m

12

Boolleroo
Centre
Tarcowie
Yatina
B56
Minvalara
14
Agricultural
Check
Point
Ucolta
Peterborough
Alderman
Reservoir
Wrights Hill
517m
Ironback Hill
378m
Faraway Hill
216m
Fly
Fruit
DANGGALI
CONSERVATION
PARK

13

Virrabara
Appila
Stone Hut
Hornsdale
Mannanarie
Yongala
Gumbowie
Belalie North
22
23
PANDAPPA
CONSERVATION
PARK
Hack Lagoon
Boiekekevie Hill
539m

ray
Laura
82
Gladstone
B79
Jamestown
Caltowie
24
Terowie
Whyte
Yarcowie

13

K   L   M   N   O   P   Q   R

Joins map 555

Joins map 512
Joins map 510

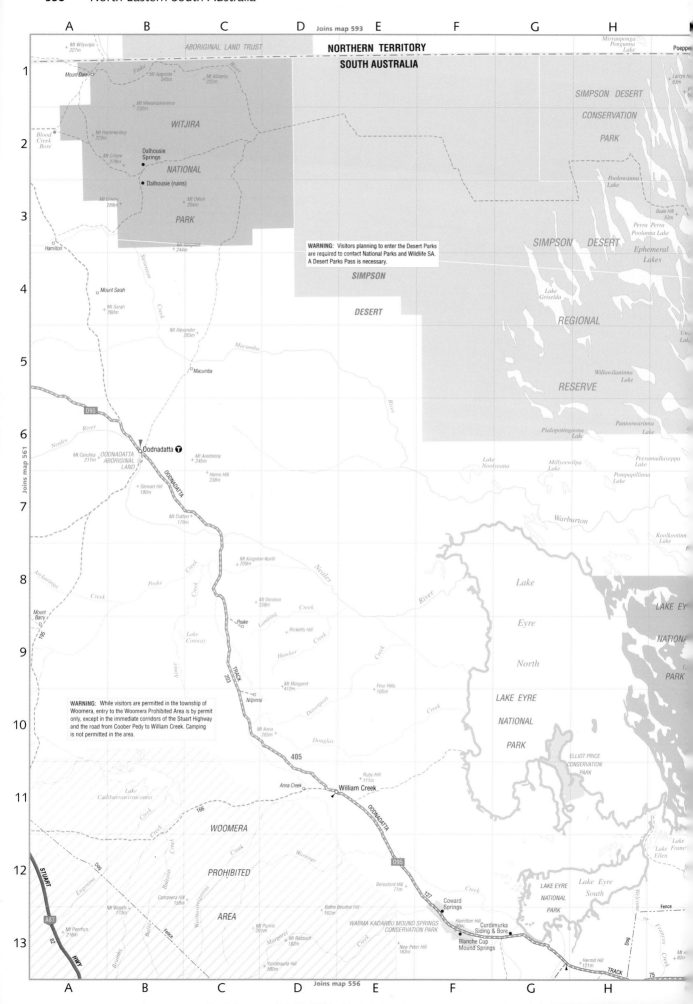

Joins map 593

NORTHERN TERRITORY

SOUTH AUSTRALIA

Joins map 561

ABORIGINAL LAND TRUST

Mt Wilyunpa +227m

Mount Dare

Mt Anperda +245m

Mt Alnaarta +222m

Mt Weearlakitenna +292m

WITJIRA

Mt Hummersley +229m

Blood Creek Bore

Mt Crispe +279m

Dalhousie Springs

NATIONAL

Dalhousie (ruins)

Mt Emere +289m

Mt Dillon +234m

PARK

Hamilton

Stevenson

Creek

Mt Tongolani +244m

Mount Sarah

Mt Sarah +260m

Mt Alexander +285m

Macumba

Macumba

SIMPSON DESERT

CONSERVATION

PARK

Poolowanna Lake

Beale Hill +53m

Perra Perra Poolanna Lake

SIMPSON DESERT

Ephemeral Lakes

Lake Griselda

SIMPSON

DESERT

Finke

River

River

WARNING: Visitors planning to enter the Desert Parks are required to contact National Parks and Wildlife SA. A Desert Parks Pass is necessary.

REGIONAL

Willawilaninna Lake

RESERVE

Pialopotingoona Lake

Pantoowarinna Lake

Mt Carolina +211m

OODNADATTA ABORIGINAL LAND

D95

Oodnadatta

Neales

River

Mt Areebinna +245m

Hanns Hill +238m

Stewart Hill +180m

OODNADATTA

Mt Dutton +178m

Lake Noolyeana

Millyeewilpa Lake

Peeramudlayeppa Lake

Pompapillinna Lake

Warburton

Koolkootinn Lake

An'karinga

Creek

Peake Creek

Creek

Mt Kingston North +209m

Mt Denison +238m

Neales

Ricketts Hill

River

Lake

Eyre

LAKE EY

NATIONA

PAR

Mount Barry

195

Peake

TRACK 203

Lake Conway

Aimer

Creek

Lambing

Creek

Hawker

Creek

Mt Margaret +412m

Davenport

Creek

Four Hills +105m

Creek

North

LAKE EYRE

NATIONAL

PARK

ELLIOT PRICE CONSERVATION PARK

Nilpinna

405

Mt Anna +265m

Douglas

Ruby Hill +111m

WARNING: While visitors are permitted in the township of Woomera, entry to the Woomera Prohibited Area is by permit only, except in the immediate corridors of the Stuart Highway and the road from Coober Pedy to William Creek. Camping is not permitted in the area.

Anna Creek

William Creek

OODNADATTA

Lake Cadibarrawirracanna

166

WOOMERA

Creek

Creek

Baluni Creek

Walumbaregkuna

Warriner

Creek

PROHIBITED

D95

Lake Eyre South

Lake Franc

Lake Ellen

STUART

Engenina

Dog

Baltut

Fence

Campeera Hill +158m

Mr Woods +170m

AREA

Mt Purvis +201m

Margaret

Bidna Boudna Hill +162m

Mt Riddoch +182m

WABMA KADARBU MOUND SPRINGS CONSERVATION PARK

Beresford Hill +71m

127

Coward Springs

Creek

LAKE EYRE NATIONAL PARK

Lake Eyre South

Fence

A87

82

HWY

Mt Penrhyn +216m

Varrabouna Hill +180m

New Peter Hill +163m

Hamilton Hill +80m

Blanche Cup Mound Springs

Curdimurka Siding & Bore

Dog

Hermit Hill +121m

TRACK

Mt +82m

75

Joins map 556

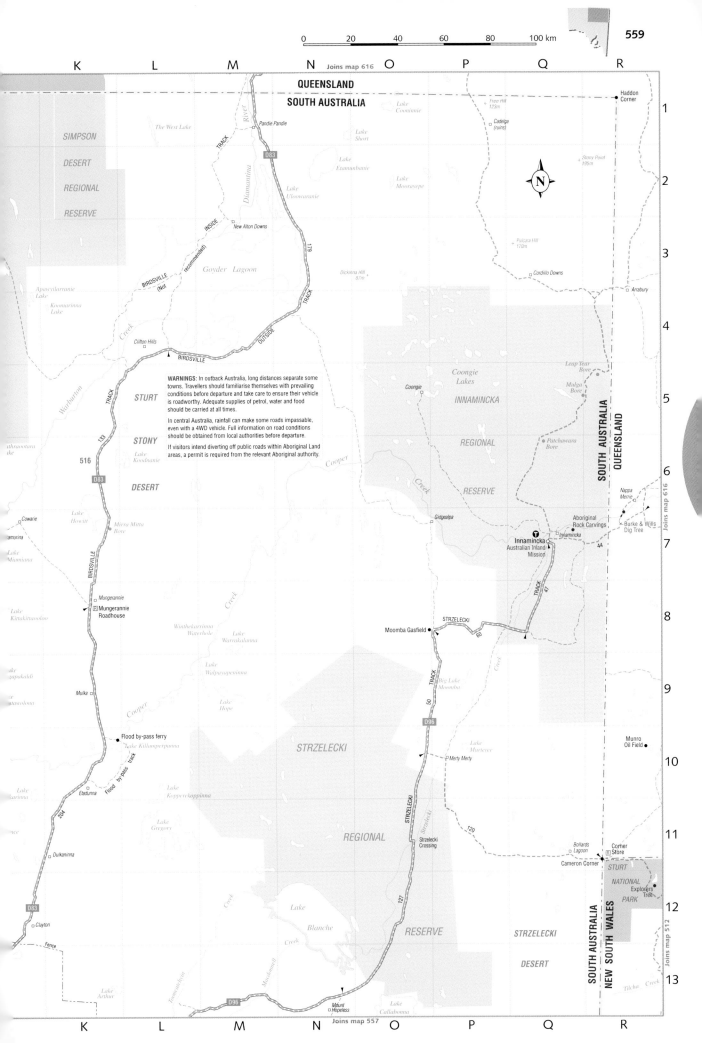

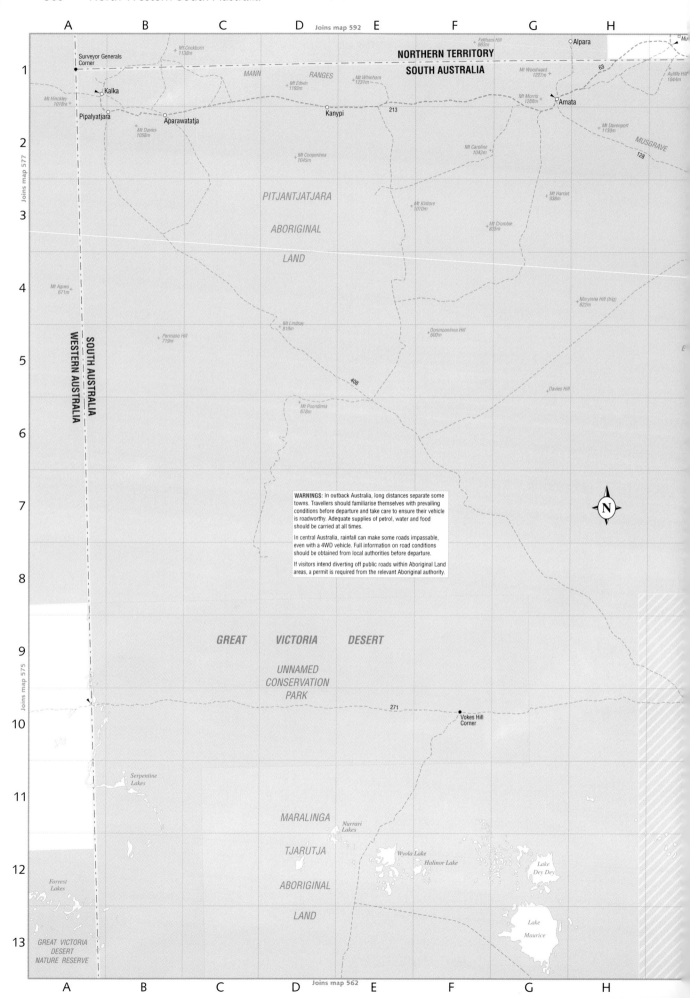

Joins map 592
Joins map 577
Joins map 575

NORTHERN TERRITORY
SOUTH AUSTRALIA

SOUTH AUSTRALIA
WESTERN AUSTRALIA

MANN RANGES

PITJANTJATJARA

ABORIGINAL

LAND

MUSGRAVE

Surveyor Generals Corner

Mt Hinckley 1018m

Kalka

Pipalyatjara

Aparawatatja

Mt Davies 1058m

Mt Cockburn 1138m

Mt Edwin 1193m

Mt Cooperinna 1045m

Mt Whinham 1231m

Kanypi

213

Felthanks Hill 863m

Alpara

Mt Woodward 1227m

63

Ayliffe Hill 1044m

Mt Morris 1288m

Amata

Mt Davenport 1139m

128

Mt Caroline 1042m

Mt Kintore 1070m

Mt Crombie 835m

Mt Harriet 938m

Mt Agnes 671m

Mt Lindsay 819m

Permano Hill 719m

Oonmooninna Hill 600m

Maryinna Hill (trig) 622m

409

Mt Poondinna 678m

Davies Hill

WARNINGS: In outback Australia, long distances separate some towns. Travellers should familiarise themselves with prevailing conditions before departure and take care to ensure their vehicle is roadworthy. Adequate supplies of petrol, water and food should be carried at all times.

In central Australia, rainfall can make some roads impassable, even with a 4WD vehicle. Full information on road conditions should be obtained from local authorities before departure.

If visitors intend diverting off public roads within Aboriginal Land areas, a permit is required from the relevant Aboriginal authority.

GREAT VICTORIA DESERT

UNNAMED CONSERVATION PARK

271

Vokes Hill Corner

Serpentine Lakes

MARALINGA

TJARUTJA

ABORIGINAL

LAND

Nurrari Lakes

Wyola Lake

Halinor Lake

Lake Dey Dey

Forrest Lakes

Lake Maurice

GREAT VICTORIA DESERT NATURE RESERVE

N

0 20 40 60 80 100 km

K   Joins map 592   L   M   N   O   P   Joins map 593   Q   R

NORTHERN TERRITORY
SOUTH AUSTRALIA

1

Mount
Cavenagh

Victory Downs

Mt Cecil
551m +

Mt Grundy
397m +

Sentinel Hill
910m +

A87

Mt Darling
544m +

Mt Parlee
478m +

Mt Mead
376m +

Mt Hisme
308m +

2

180

Tieyon

Eringa

Mt Barr
222m +

Mt Warrabilloma
1125m +

PITJANTJATJARA

Mt Howe
519m +

117

3

ABORIGINAL

Echo Hill
804m +

Mt Britton
334m +

STUART

LAND

(trig)

Hamilton

n

Marble Hill
523m +

4

Alberga

Lambina (ruins)

Mimili

143

Iwantja (Indulkana)

Chandler

River

Todmorden

Mt Iilbillee
917m +

RANGE

Mt Chandler
551m

44

5

OODNADATTA

D95

212

TRACK

Mintabie

33

Marla

Welbourn Hill

6

A87

HWY

Neales

River

Ammaroodinna Hill
389m +

CENTRAL

83

7

Wintinna

Arckaringa

AUSTRALIA

Arckaringa Hills
(The Painted
Desert)

Mt Arckaringa
243m +

140

Cadney
Homestead

Mount
Willoughby

Arckaringa

8

MARALINGA

235

32

Copper
Hills

Evelyn

Creek

TJARUTJA

Mount
Barry

196

RAILWAY

Evelyn Downs

Lora

Creek

ABORIGINAL

STUART

9

LAND

Pootnoura

Pootnoura

Creek

Algebullcullia

129

mu Junction

10

TALLARINGA

Woorong

Giddi-Giddinna

Creek

Dog

Fence

CONSERVATION

BREAKAWAYS
RESERVE

Oolgelima

Creek

11

284

Manguri

23

Coober Pedy

PARK

Creek

WOOMERA

A87

12

PROHIBITED

WARNING: While visitors are permitted in the township of
Woomera, entry to the Woomera Prohibited Area is by permit
only, except in the immediate corridors of the Stuart Highway
and the road from Coober Pedy to William Creek. Camping
is not permitted in the area. Note the overlap with Aboriginal
Lands where you need additional separate permits.

Mabel

HWY

AREA

Mt Penrhyn
216m +

82

13

Lake
Phillipson

Wirrida

Dog

Wilkinson
Lakes

Fence

Joins map 563

K   L   M   N   O   P   Q   R

Joins map 558

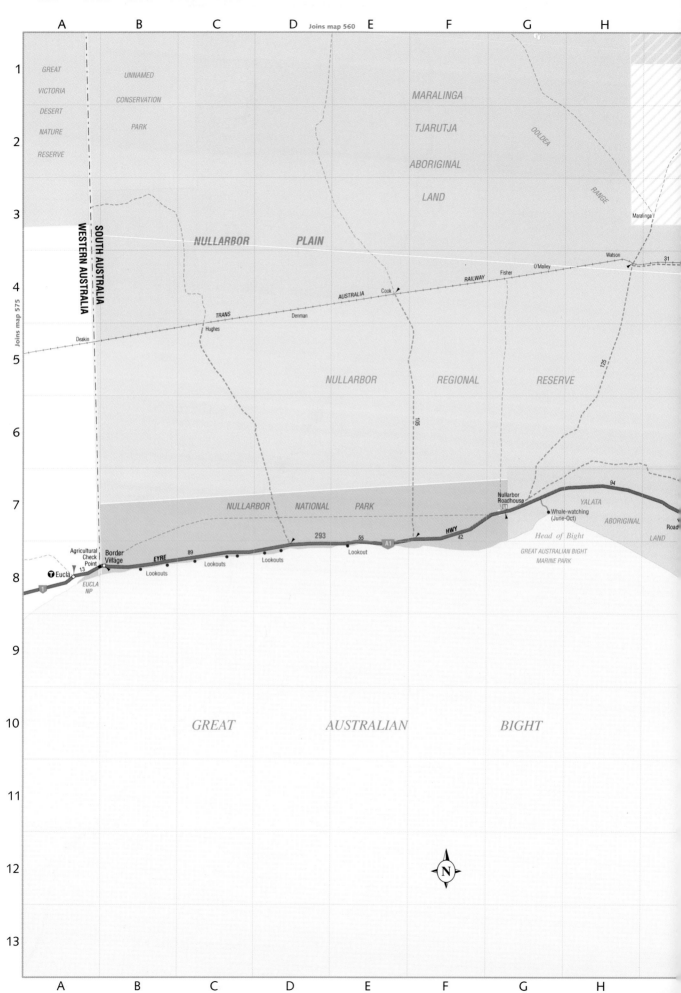

GREAT
VICTORIA
DESERT
NATURE
RESERVE

UNNAMED
CONSERVATION
PARK

SOUTH AUSTRALIA
WESTERN AUSTRALIA

Joins map 560

Joins map 575

MARALINGA
TJARUTJA
ABORIGINAL
LAND

OOLDEA

RANGE

Maralinga

NULLARBOR   PLAIN

Watson

31

O'Malley

Fisher

RAILWAY

AUSTRALIA   Cook

Denman

TRANS

Hughes

Deakin

125

NULLARBOR   REGIONAL   RESERVE

105

Nullarbor
Roadhouse

94

YALATA

ABORIGINAL

LAND

Road

NULLARBOR   NATIONAL   PARK

Whale-watching
(June-Oct)

Head of Bight

GREAT AUSTRALIAN BIGHT
MARINE PARK

Agricultural
Check
Point

Border
Village

EYRE

293

55

A1

HWY

42

Lookout

89

Lookouts

Lookouts

Lookouts

Eucla

13

EUCLA
NP

1

GREAT   AUSTRALIAN   BIGHT

N

0   20   40   60   80   100 km

K   L   M   N   O   P   Q   R

1

WARNING: While visitors are permitted in the township of
Woomera, entry to the Woomera Prohibited Area is by permit
only, except in the immediate corridors of the Stuart Highway
and the road from Coober Pedy to William Creek. Camping
is not permitted in the area. Note the overlap with Aboriginal
Lands where you need additional separate permits.

MARALINGA

Ingomar

Mt Soward
224m

Dog   Fence

West Point Hill
230m

McDouall Peak

RAILWAY

TJARUTJA

2

Dog

Lake
Anthony

Half Moon
Lake

WOOMERA

Bulgunnia

ABORIGINAL

Muckanippie

Carnes

AUSTRALIA

3

LAND

Mulgathing

PROHIBITED

Mt Christie
233m

Gibraltar Rocks

CENTRAL

PARTRIDGE RANGE

TRANS

AREA

Bates

Barton

Warrior

Whigena Hill
253m

Lake
Labyrinth

4

AUSTRALIA

Mungala

Mount
Christie

Wynbring

RAILWAY

Malbooma

Lake
Moolkra

Tarcoola

80

YELLABINNA

ould Lake

Mt Finke
361m

TRACK

Bulpara Hill
237m

Renton Hill
161m

5

REGIONAL

Dog

LAKE GAIRDNER
NATIONAL PARK

6

RESERVE

Lake Everard

Glyde Hill
252m

7

Colona

YUMBARRA
CONSERVATION
RESERVE

Dog   Fence

YUMBARRA
CONSERVATION
PARK

GOODS

Fence

Nuckulla Hill
264m

Lake Everard

8

Nundroo
Roadhouse

39   EYRE   202

Bookabie

35

Telstra Earth
Station

Koomba Hill
169m

Koonibba

PUREBA
CONSERVATION
PARK

Yarlbrinda Hill
348m

Waverley Hill
399m

9

Coorabie

25

Talala Hill
84m

31

Bookabie Hill
149m

Cooper Hill
126m

Penong

CHADINGA
CR

Gundilippy

KOONIBA
ABORIGINAL
LAND

A1   73   HWY

Woolshed Hill
134m

Coppelturba Hill
147m

PUREBA
CR

Nurka Hill
130m

Mt Hitabo
485m

Barber Hill
412m

10

FOWLERS
BAY CR

Fowlers Bay

Fowlers Bay

Point Fowler

Cactus Beach

Point Sinclair

Lake
MacDonnell

McKenzie (ruins)

Agricultural
Check
Point

Ceduna

Thevenard

EYRE

Mudamuckla

40

Chinbingina

92

Nunjikompila

NUNNIYAH
CONSERVATION
RESERVE

Oak Hill
117m

KOOLGERA
CONSERVATION
RESERVE

Wallula Hill
166m

67

GAWLER
RANGES
NP

11

Point Bell

POINT
BELL CR

St Peter
Island

WITTELBEE CP
LAURA BAY CP

Dental
Bay

FLINDERS

Smoky Bay

Eyre Island

Pimbaacla Hill
121m

Carawa

222

Wirrulla

A1

Yantanabie

Kaldoonera Hill
136m

Locke
Claypans
GAWLER
RANGES
CR

Chilpuddie Hill
181m

NUYTS
ARCHIPELAGO
CONSERVATION
PARK

Smoky Bay

30

109

Petina

27

Cungena

Point de Mole

ACRAMAN CREEK
CONSERVATION
PARK

Haslam

ISLES OF
ST FRANCIS
CONSERVATION
PARK

Isles of
St Francis

Point Brown

Streaky
Bay

B100

Chilpanunda

Capiethar

20

Poochera

12

Cape Bauer

Olive Islands

Eba Island

39

Piednippie

Chandada

HWY

33

Minnipa

Streaky Bay

Corvisart
Bay

62

13

Point Westall

Yanerbie Beach

Sceale Bay

SCEALE BAY CR

Sceale Bay

CALPATANNA
WATERHOLE
CP

Murphy's Haystacks

Calca

65

Mt Cooper
205m

KULLIPARU
CR

Moonlight
Flat

Lake
Yaninee

Searcy Bay

POINT LABATT CP

Sea lion Colony

Point Labatt

Cape Radstock

Baird
Bay

VENUS BAY CR

Port Kenny

VENUS BAY CP

Venus Bay

124

Mt Hall
208m

Colley

Mount
Cooper

KULLIPARU
CP

Mount
Damper

KULLIPARU
CR

K   L   M   N   O   P   Q   R

WESTERN AUSTRALIA
MAPS

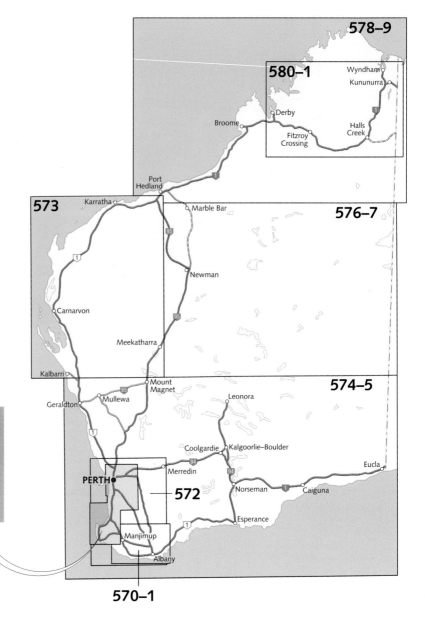

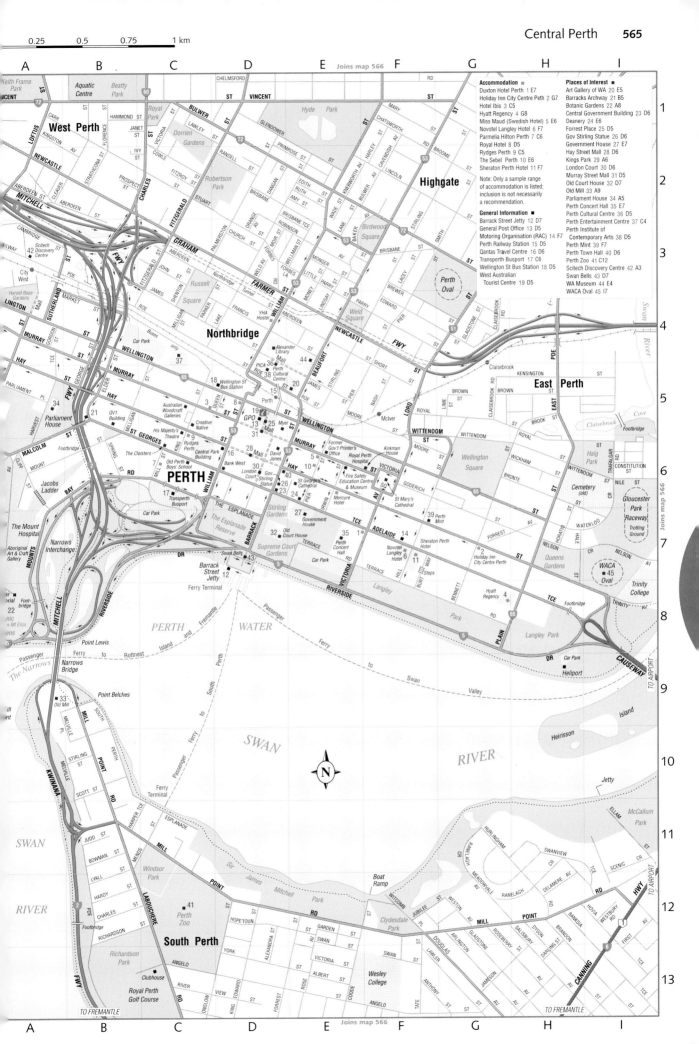

0   5   10   15   20 km

A   B   C   D   E   F   G   H   I

1

Yanchep
Yanchep Beach
YANCHEP NATIONAL PARK
Crystal & Yonderup Caves
60
6
WANNEROO
13

TO GERALDTON   TO MOUNT MAGNET
Joins map 567
BRAND HWY
GREAT
95
Muchea
2
11
MOONDYNE NATURE RESERVE
AVON VALLEY NATIONAL PARK
River

2
NEERABUP
60
NATIONAL
86
29
Bullsbrook
NORTHERN
13
Avon
River
MORANGU NATURE RESERVE
50
12

3
QUINNS ROCKS
77
5
8
86
3
PARK
RD
6
65
BURNS BEACH
JOONDALUP
WANNEROO
GNANGARA
PINE
95
54
WALYUNGA NP
River
Swan
Gidgegannup
12

4
MARMION MARINE PARK
MULLALOO
HILLARYS
53
84
60
2
83
18
KINGSLEY
Wanneroo Markets
LANDSDALE
PLANTATION
Whiteman Park
HENLEY BROOK
WEST SWAN
83
UPPER SWAN
52
95
13
HWY
SWAN VALLEY
50
23
50
Woorploo
94
Chidlow

5
Hillarys Boat Harbour
Sorrento Beach
SORRENTO
71
MITCHELL
REID
FWY
76
GWELUP
MIRRABOOKA
18
HWY
CAVERSHAM
MIDLAND
1
51
GUILDFORD
GREENMOUNT
EASTERN DARLINGTON
JOHN FORREST NP
50
94
16
Stoneville
Mount Helena
Mundaring
Sawyers Valley
HWY
16
Parkerville

6
SCARBOROUGH
Passenger Ferry to Rottnest Island
CITY BEACH
SUBIACO
72
54
72
75
53
56
65
61
71
PERTH
River
94
GREAT
TOMLIN
55
PERTH AIRPORT
REDCLIFFE
HIGH WYCOMBE
HILLS FOREST
Mahogany Creek
C.Y. O'Connor Museum
Mundaring Weir
11
KALAMUNDA NP
Helena River Reservoir
KALAMUNDA
41

For more detail on Central Perth see page 565

7
Rottnest Island
Thomson Bay
Passenger Ferry to Rottnest Island
COTTESLOE
19
Swan
5
HWY
12
1
6
2
26
9
LEACH
1
CANNING
FREMANTLE
4
30
34
HWY
QUEENS PARK
13
CANNINGTON
27
ROE
31
25
19
MADDINGTON
FORRESTFIELD
35
ORANGE GROVE
41
30
HWY
New Victoria Dam
RANGE
41
Darling
River

8
SOUTH FREMANTLE
13
12
FWY
Adventure World
Stock Road Markets
JANDAKOT
9
Swan Brewery
Canning Vale Markets
KELMSCOTT
ROLEYSTONE
40
Araluen Botanic Park
BROOKTON
10
Mt Dale 548m
DALE CONSERVATIC PARK

9
INDIAN
OCEAN
COOGEE
Cables Water Ski Park
23
Woodman Point
MUNSTER
WATTLEUP
14
14
FORRESTDALE
16
ARMADALE
20
30
10
8
Canning Dam
Wungong Dam
ALBANY
16
HWY

10
Garden Island
HMAS STIRLING NAVAL BASE
NAVAL BASE
12
40
WANDI
CASUARINA
21
Byford
40
Tumbulgum Farm
19
DARLING
15
Mt Randall 525m
KWINANA
KWINANA BEACH
1
21
8
2
17
22
21
Mundijong
10
10

11
Cockburn Sound
SHOALWATER ISLANDS MARINE PARK
ROCKINGHAM
SAFETY BAY
18
WAIKIKI
3
5
6
8
2
3
KWINANA
Baldivis
River
15
8
Serpentine
WESTERN
20
6
Jarrahdale
SERPENTINE NATIONAL PARK
15
Canning
River
23
HWY

12
Warnbro Beach
Becher Point
9
Karnup
Golden Bay
Singleton
Madora
26
10
16
Serpentine
3
11
Keysbrook
SOUTH
8
20
Mt Solus 574m
Serpentine Dam

13
Mandurah
Halls Head
Miami
TO BUNBURY
4
Furnissdale
17
1
North Dandalup
TO BUNBURY
Joins map 567

A   B   C   D   E   F   G   H   I

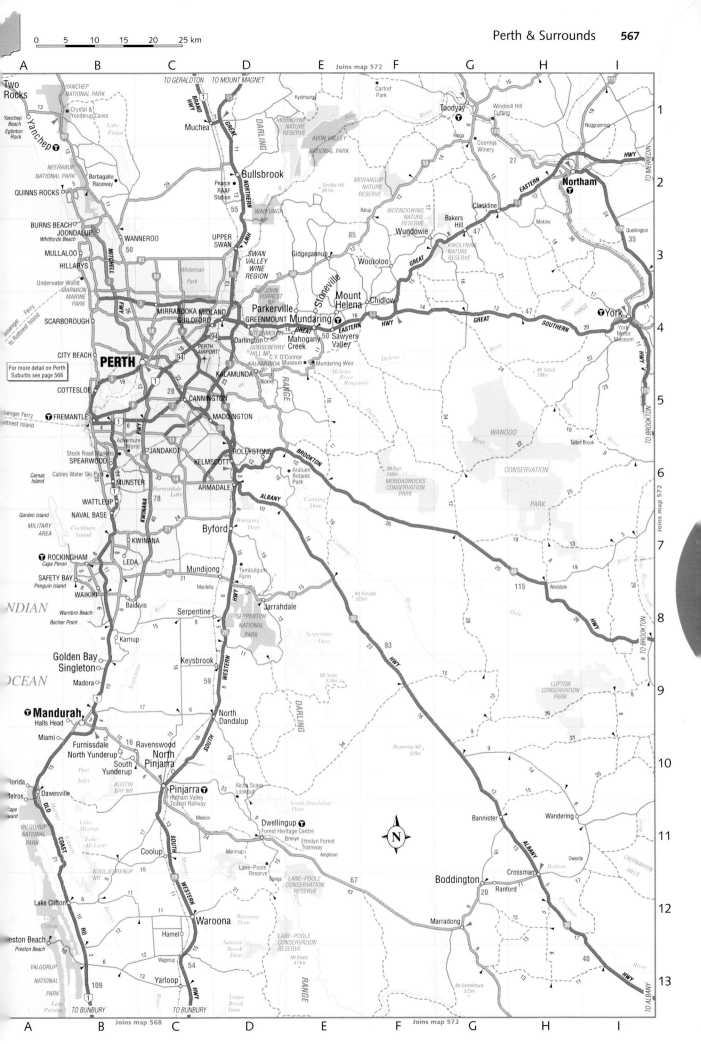

Joins map 567

0 5 10 15 20 25 km

A B C D E F G H I

INDIAN OCEAN

TO PERTH

YALGORUP NATIONAL PARK

OLD COAST RD

Lake Preston

Wagerup

Yarloop

Logue Brook Dam

Harvey Weir

Myalup Beach

Warawarrup

🛈 Harvey

Wokalup

Binningup Beach

Benger

SOUTH WESTERN HWY

Worsley Aluminium Refinery

Beela

Leschenault

Brunswick Junction

Leschenault Inlet

🛈 Australind

Roelands

Burekup

Koombana Bay

★ Eaton

WELLINGTON NATIONAL PARK

🛈 Bunbury

Waterloo

Picton

Gelorup

Bunbury Speedway

Dardanup

Dalyellup

Stratham

Boyanup

TUART FOREST NP

Peppermint Grove Beach

Lowden

TUART FOREST NP

Capel

🛈 Donnybrook

Cape Naturaliste

Lighthouse & Museum

Eagle Bay

Point Piquet

Geographe Bay

Wonnerup

Ludlow

TUART FOREST NP

Capel River

SOUTH WESTERN HWY

Sugarloaf Rock

Meelup

Dunsborough

Wonnerup Beach

Ludlow

Newlands

Grimwa

🛈 Yallingup

Quindalup

🛈 Busselton

BUSSELL

Abba

Kirup

Mullalyup

Canal Rocks

Cape Clairault

Vasse

Yunderup

Marybrook

VASSE

Ruabon

Tutunup

🛈 Balin

LEEUWIN-NATURALISTE NATIONAL PARK

Carbunup River

Jindong

Acton Park

Yoongarillup

Jarrahwood

Quinnup

Yelverton

Metricup

RANGE

Blackwood River

Willyabrup

Chapman Hill

WHICHER

VASSE HWY

Cowaramup Point

Gracetown

Cowaramup

Treeton

Margaret River

WHINSTON HILLS

Bramley

Osmington

🛈 Nannup

Cape Mentelle

Margaret River

Mowen

Mt Yates

Prevelly

Eagles Heritage

Rosa Glen

Pioneer Settlers Memorial

Heritage Trail

Witchcliffe

BUSSELL HWY

Sues Bridge

BROCKMAN HWY

Cape Freycinet

LEEUWIN-NATURALISTE NATIONAL PARK

Warner Glen Bridge

The Four Aces

North Point

Boranup

Alexandra Bridge

Nillup

HWY

One Tree Bridge

Boranup Lookout

BROCKMAN

Hamelin Bay

Karridale

SCOTT NATIONAL PARK

VASSE HWY

Hamelin Island

Foul Bay

Kudardup

Hardy Inlet

Cape Hamelin

Hillview Lookout & Golf Course

LEEUWIN-NATURALISTE NATIONAL PARK

Scott River

GINGILUP SWAMPS NATURE RESERVE

Gingilup Swamps

D'ENTRECASTEAUX NATIONAL PARK

🛈 Augusta

Flinders Bay

Matthew Flinders Memorial

Seal Island

Lake Jasper

Lake Quitjup

Flinders Bay Lighthouse

Cape Leeuwin

TO PEMBERTON

BEEDELUP NP

Joins map 572

0 5 10 15 20 km

Joins map 568

WINERIES: ❶

bbey Vale Vineyard 1 C3
mberley Estate 2 C3
lewood Estate 3 C5
shbrook Estate 4 C5
eckett's Flat 5 D4
he Berry Farm 6 E8
rookland Valley Vineyard 7 B5
ape Clairault Wines 8 C4
ape Mentelle 9 C7
hapman's Creek 10 C4
hateau Xanadu 11 C7
ullen Wines 12 C5
eep Woods Estate 13 C3
iftwood Estate 14 B4
vans & Tate 15 C5
rmoy Estate 16 C5
alyn Cellars 17 C5
een Valley Vineyard 18 C9
amelin Bay 19 D10
app's Vineyard 20 C3
ay Shed Hill 21 C5
nt's Foxhaven Estate 22 B3
and Brook Estate 23 D4
eeuwin Estate 24 C8
nton Brae Wines 25 C5
arybrook 26 D3
oss Brothers 27 C4
oss Wood 28 C5
erro Margaret River
  Vineyards 29 C5
dgate Wines 30 C8
bbon Vale Estate 31 C5
vendell Gardens 32 C3
sabrook Estate 33 C7
ndalford Wines 34 C5
rventy Organic Wines 35 D9
ellar Ridge Estate 36 C5
eeton Estate 37 D5
sse Felix 38 C5
sse River Wines 39 D4
yager Estate 40 C8
dwood Winery 41 C3
llespie 42 C5
se Winery 43 C2
oody Nook 44 C5
ights Wines 45 C5

GEOGRAPHE BAY

Cape Naturaliste

Lighthouse & Museum

Bunker Bay

Rocky Point

Sugarloaf Rock

Eagle Bay

Point Piquet
Gannet Rock
Sail Rock
Castle Point
Castle Rock

Meelup

Peppermint Grove Beach

TUART FOREST NATIONAL PARK

Capel

TO BUNBURY

Bird Rock

Bannamah Wildlife Park

Dunsborough

Dunn Bay

Dunsborough Beach

Wonnerup Beach

Wonnerup

Ludlow

Yallingup

Ngilgi Caves

Quindalup

Toby Inlet

Molly Ditch

Busselton Jetty Interpretive Centre,
Train & Underwater Observatory

Old Railway Jetty

Wonnerup House

Gunyulgup Galleries

CAVES RD

Busselton

St Mary's Church

Old Butter Factory Museum

Wonnerup Estuary

Tutunup

Canal Rocks

Marybrook

The Broadwater

Oceanarium

Ballarat Engine

Vasse Estuary

Abba

Ruabon

Cape Clairault

Carbunup River

Vasse

Yunderup

Four Mile Hill

CAPE NATURALISTE RD

North Jindong

Jindong

Boallia

Walsali

Acton Park

Yoongarillup

Whistle Stop (miniature railway)

LEEUWIN–NATURALISTE NATIONAL PARK

Quinnup

Bootleg Brewery

Yelverton

Metricup

Bunyup

Kaloorup

Chapman Hill

Chapman Hill

RANGE

Willyabrup

WHICHER

Cowaramup Point

Gracetown

Cowaramup

Margaret River Regional Wine Centre

Treeton

Cowaramup Bk

Bramley

Margaret River

Osmington

Heritage Trail

Joins map 568

Ellensbrook Homestead

Kilcarnup

Margaret River

Mowen

Cape Mentelle

Eagles Heritage

Rosa Glen

Pioneer Settlers Memorial

Mt Yates

INDIAN

Prevelly

BUSSELL HWY

Boodjidup Brook

Margaret River Marron Farm

Witchcliffe

Busselton

Blackwood

Sues Bridge

Cape Freycinet

Mammoth Cave

Bobs Hollow

Lake Cave

Forest Grove

Warner Glen Bridge

OCEAN

North Point Boranup Beach

LEEUWIN–NATURALISTE NATIONAL PARK

Boranup Gallery

Boranup Hill

Warner Glen

Alexandra Bridge

Nillup

BROCKMAN HWY

Alexandra Bridge

STEWART RD

Boranup Lookout

Boranup Maze

BROCKMAN

CAVES RD

Hamelin Bay

Hamelin Island

Karridale

Hamelin Bay

Foul Bay

BUSSELL HWY

Kudardup

Molly Island River Cruises

SCOTT NATIONAL PARK

TO NANNUP

Cape Hamelin

CAVES RD

Moondyne Cave

Jewel Cave

Hillview Lookout & Golf Course

Hardy Inlet

GINGILUP SWAMPS NATURE RESERVE

Gingilup Swamps

LEEUWIN–NATURALISTE NATIONAL PARK

Augusta

Historical Museum

Flinders Bay

D'ENTRECASTEAUX NATIONAL PARK

From the cape it is

Waterwheel

Flinders Bay

Whale Rescue Memorial

Matthew Flinders Memorial

SOUTHERN OCEAN

Lighthouse

Cape Leeuwin

Seal Island

Lake Quitjap

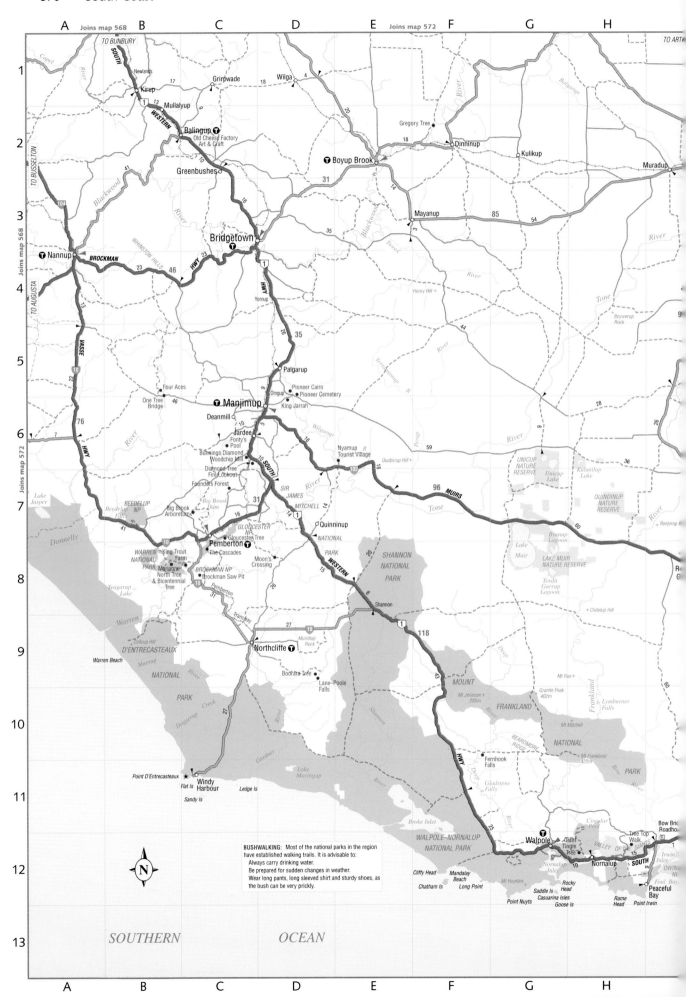

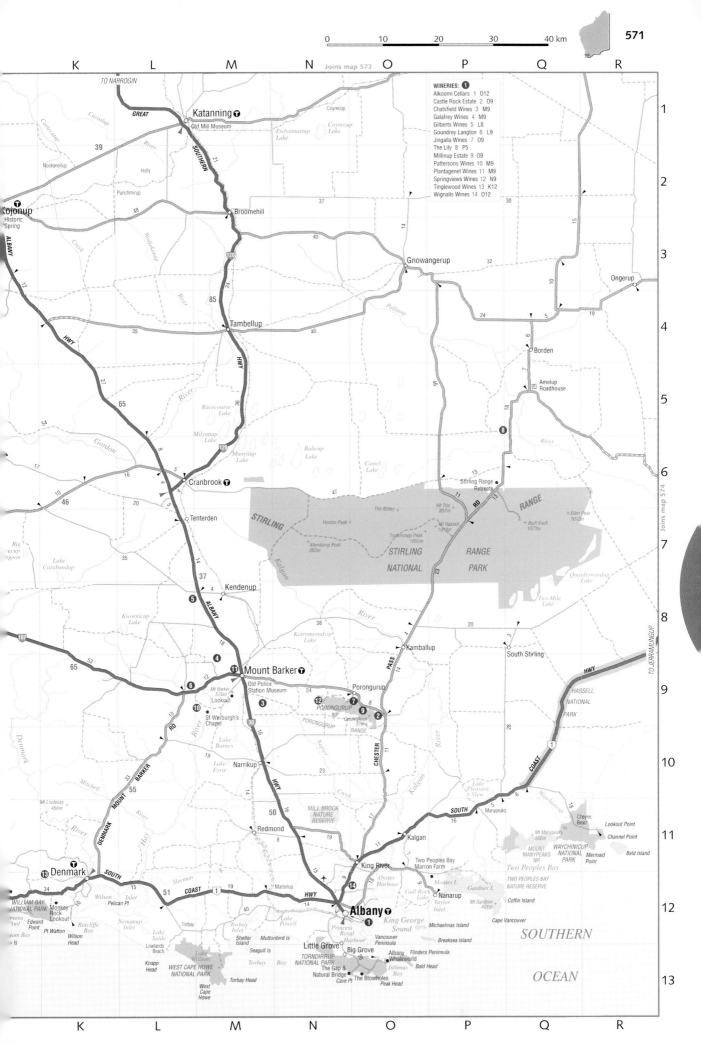

0   10   20   30   40 km

Joins map 572

WINERIES: ❶
Alkoomi Cellars 1 O12
Castle Rock Estate 2 O9
Chatsfield Wines 3 M9
Galafrey Wines 4 M9
Gilberts Wines 5 L8
Goundrey Langton 6 L9
Jingalla Wines 7 O9
The Lily 8 P5
Millinup Estate 9 O9
Pattersons Wines 10 M9
Plantagenet Wines 11 M9
Springviews Wines 12 N9
Tinglewood Wines 13 K12
Wignalls Wines 14 O12

Joins map 574

TO NARROGIN

GREAT

Katanning
Old Mill Museum

Coyrecup

Coyrecup
Lake

Ewlyamartup
Lake

Carrolup

Carrolup

Nookanellup

Holly

Punchimrup

Broomehill

Kojonup
Historic
Spring

Gnowangerup

Widdikundup

Creek

SOUTHERN

HWY

ALBANY

Tambellup

Borden

Amelup
Roadhouse

Ongerup

River

Racecourse
Lake

Milyunup
Lake

Munrilup
Lake

Balicup
Lake

Camel
Lake

STIRLING RANGE

Stirling Range
Retreats

Ellen Peak
1012m

Cranbrook

Gordon

Tenterden

STIRLING

The Abbey

Mt Trio
857m

Bluff Knoll
1073m

RANGE

Quanderwardup
Lake

Big
Grecup
Lagoon

Lake
Carabundup

Henton Peak

Mondurup Peak
863m

Toolbrunup Peak
1052m

Mt Hassell
1018m

STIRLING

RANGE

NATIONAL

PARK

Two Mile
Lake

Kendenup

River

ALBANY

Kwornicup
Lake

Kairnmerndyip
Lake

Kamballup

South Stirling

HWY

HASSELL

NATIONAL

PARK

Mount Barker
Old Police
Station Museum

Porongurup

PORONGURUP
NP

PORONGURUP
RANGE

Castle Rock
576m

Mt Barker
576m
Lookout

St Werburgh's
Chapel

Denmark

Mitchell

Mt Lindesay
456m

DENMARK

MOUNT BARKER

RD

River

Lake
Barnes

Lake
Eyrie

Narrikup

CHESTER

PASS

Kalgan

Mt Manypeaks
562m

Cheyne
Beach

Lookout Point

Channel Point

MOUNT
MANYPEAKS
NR

WAYCHINICUP
NATIONAL
PARK

Bald Island

Mermaid
Point

RD

HWY

MILL BROOK
NATURE
RESERVE

Lake
Pleasant
View

SOUTH

Manypeaks

COAST

Redmond

Kalgan

King River

Two Peoples Bay
Marron Farm

Moates L

TWO PEOPLES BAY
NATURE RESERVE

Denmark

WILLIAM BAY
NATIONAL PARK

SOUTH

COAST

HWY

Marbelup

Oyster
Harbour

Gull Rock
Lake

Nanarup

Taylor
Inlet

Mt Gardner
401m

Coffin Island

Cape Vancouver

Wilson
Inlet

Monkey
Rock
Lookout

Edward
Point

Pt Walton

Wilson
Head

Pelican Pt

Nenamup
Inlet

Lake
Saide

Torbay

Lake
Powell

Albany

King George
Sound

Michaelmas Island

Breaksea Island

SOUTHERN

Ratcliffe
Bay

ffam Bay

vens
ool

am Is

Knapp
Head

WEST CAPE HOWE
NATIONAL PARK

West
Cape
Howe

Torbay Head

Lowlands
Beach

Seagull Is

Muttonbird I

Shelter
Island

Torbay
Inlet

Little Grove

Big Grove

Albany
Whaleworld

TORNDIRRUP
NATIONAL PARK

The Gap &
Natural Bridge
Cave Pt

The Blowholes

Peak Head

Princess
Royal
Harbour

Vancouver
Peninsula

Flinders Peninsula

Bald Head

Isthmus
Bay

OCEAN

0   20   40   60   80 km

A   B   C   D   E   F   G   H   I

Joins map 574

1

2

3

4

5

6

7

8

9

10

11

12

13

N

Lancelin
Ledge Point
Regans Ford
Mogumber
New Norcia
Calingiri
Konnongorring
Ejanding
Minnivale
Trayning
Kununoppin
Nungarin
Edna May
Goldmin
MOORE RIVER NP
BOONANARRING NR
Wyalkatchem
BRAND HWY
NORTHERN HWY
249
Seabird
Guilderton
Gingin
YEAL NR
MOORE RIVER NR
Bindoon
Wyening
Bolgart
Goomalling
Dowerin
36
179
Mekering
Meredin
Two Rocks
Yanchep
Muchea
South Bindoon Chittering
Cartref Park
Lower Chittering
Dewars Pool
Jennacubbine
Tarramon
Yarramony
Cunderdin
94
Hines Hill
Ulva
GREAT HWY
NEERABUP NP
YANCHEP NP
Lake Pinjar
AVON VALLEY NP
Toodyay
Ringa
Noggojerring
Meenar
Waeel 23
Kellerberrin Hill Lookout
Doodlakine
Baandee
Nangeenan
QUINNS ROCKS
WANNEROO
Bullsbrook
Northam
Clackline
Moklne
Quellington
Meckering 162 Tammin
Kellerberrin
Bungulla
Korbel
Belka
Jura
GREAT EASTERN HWY
DARENG HILLS
SCARBOROUGH
Mount Helena
Chidlow
York
Greenhills
Belmunging
Youndegin
Kokerbin Rock
Kwolyin
Eriklin
Euphin
Yarding
Shackleton
Bruce Rock
PERTH
Darlington
Mundaring
47
101
Beverley East
Jacobs Well
Balkuling
Mawson
Quairading
Pantapin
Babakin
Ardath
116
FREMANTLE
Helena Reservoir
Mt Talbot
Beverley
Dubbling
Dangin
Caroling
Sth Kummir
For more detail on Perth & Surrounds see page 567
ARMADALE
BROOKTON
MONDADNOCKS CP
WANDOO CONSERVATION PARK
Talbot Brook
Avondale Discovery Farm
County Peak Lookout
YENYENING LAKES
Bilbarin
Lake Kurrenkutten
KWINANA
ROCKINGHAM
Mundijong
Byford
Jarrahdale
143
DARLING RANGE
Westdale
Brookton
Aldersyde
Nalya
Kweda
Bulyee
Dubuck
Kunip
Corrigin
Gorge Rock
Kondinin Lake
Waikiki
Baldivis
Serpentine
Keysbrook
North Dandalup
SERPENTINE NP
Mt Solus 574m
199
Boyagin Rock
BOYAGIN NR
Kulyaling
OUTARNING RANGE
Bullaring
Kondinin
Golden Bay
Singleton
Mandurah
North Yunderup
South Yunderup
Dawesville
North Pinjarra
Pinjarra
Dwellingup
South Dandalup Dam
Boonering Hill 529m
Bannister
Pingelly
Moorumbine
Popanyinning
Malyalling Rock
Yealering
Kulin
Jilakin Roc
INDIAN OCEAN
Lake Clifton
Coolup
Hamel
Nanga
LANE-POOLE
Boddington
Crossman
Dwarda
CARNARVON HILLS
Dryandra Woodland
Minnigin
121
Malyalling
Walters Hill 382m
Streton
Preston Beach
YALGORUP NATIONAL PARK
181
Waroona
Marradong
Wandering
Yornaning
Cuballing
Boundain
Yillimining Rock
Wickepin
Jitarning
OCEAN
Binningup
Myalup
Yarloop
109
Harvey
Benger
Logue Brook Dam
Warawarrup
Mt Saddleback 575m
61
Quindanning
Williams
Narrogin
Geealying
Toolibin
Harrismith
Tincurrin
Australind
Brunswick Junction
Beela
Wild Horse Hill 395m
Boraning
Culbin
Josbury
ALBANY HWY
Piesseville
Highbury
YOCKRINE RANGE
120
Kukerin
Moulyinning
Bunbury
Eaton
Burekup
Waterloo
Boelands
Allanson
Collie
Shotts
Buckingham
Darkan
Hillman
Warup
Dardadine
Arthur River
Wagin
Nippering
Wbstn
Dumbleyung
GELORUP
Dalyellup
Stratham
Boyanup
WELLINGTON
Dardanup
Collie Burn
Collie Cardiff
146
Bowelling
Duranillin
Cordering
Boscabel
Woodanilling
Nyabing
Capel
Donnybrook
Lowden
Mumballup
129
Norring Lake
Beaufort
Cartmeticup
Katanning
Cape Naturaliste
Eagle Bay
Dunsborough
Geographe Bay
Wonnerup
Tutunup
Newlands
Grimwade
Wilga
McAlinden
Nookanellup
Holly
Punchmirup
Coyrecup
Yallingup
Vasse
Busselton
89
Kirup
Mullalyup
Balingup
Dinninup
Kulikup
Muradup
Kojonup
Broomehill
LEEUWIN-NATURALISTE NATIONAL PARK
104
Jarrahwood
Greenbushes
Boyup Brook
Mayanup
Jingalup
Historic Spring
Gnowangerup
Cowaramup
Gracetown
Treeton
Osmington
Nannup
Bridgetown
Palgarup
Dingup
74
Tambellup
Borden
Margaret River
Rosa Glen
Blackwood River
BROCKMAN
135
Deanmill
Jardee
Manjimup
Nyamup Tourist Village
95
Frankland
Cranbrook
Tenterden
STIRLING Mt Hassell 1018m
LEEUWIN-NATURALISTE NATIONAL PARK
Karridale
GINGILUP SWAMPS NATURE RESERVE
Lake Jasper
BEEDELUP NP
46
Quinninup
UNICUP NR
Rocky Gully
102
Kendenup
STIRLING RANGE NATIONAL PA
Augusta
Cape Leeuwin
SCOTT NATIONAL PARK
Cape Beaufort
WARREN NP
Pemberton
SHANNON NP
Lake Muir
Mt Barker
Kalgan
Kambalup
Stir
HASSELL NATIONAL PARK
D'ENTRECASTEAUX
BROCKMAN
Shannon
Frankland River
Narrikup
Porongurup
PORONGURUP NP
NATIONAL PARK
Northcliffe
Mt Frankland
Mt Lindesay 456m
Redmond
King River
Nanarup
Manypea
Point D'Entrecasteaux
Sandy Is
Windy Harbour
Lake Maringup
270
Fernhook Falls
MOUNT FRANKLAND NP
Bow Bridge Roadhouse
Denmark
Albany
Little Grove
Big Grove
TWO PEOPLES NATURE RES
Broke Inlet
Cliffy Head
Walpole
Point Nuyts
Nornalup
Peaceful Bay
Point Hillier
WILLIAM BAY NP
Wilson Head
WEST CAPE HOWE NATIONAL PARK
West Cape Howe
The Blowholes
TORNDIRRUP NATIONAL PARK
WALPOLE-NORNALUP NATIONAL PARK
SOUTH COAST HWY
Torbay
SOUTHERN OCEAN

For more detail on the South-West see page 568

For more detail on the South Coast see pages 570–1

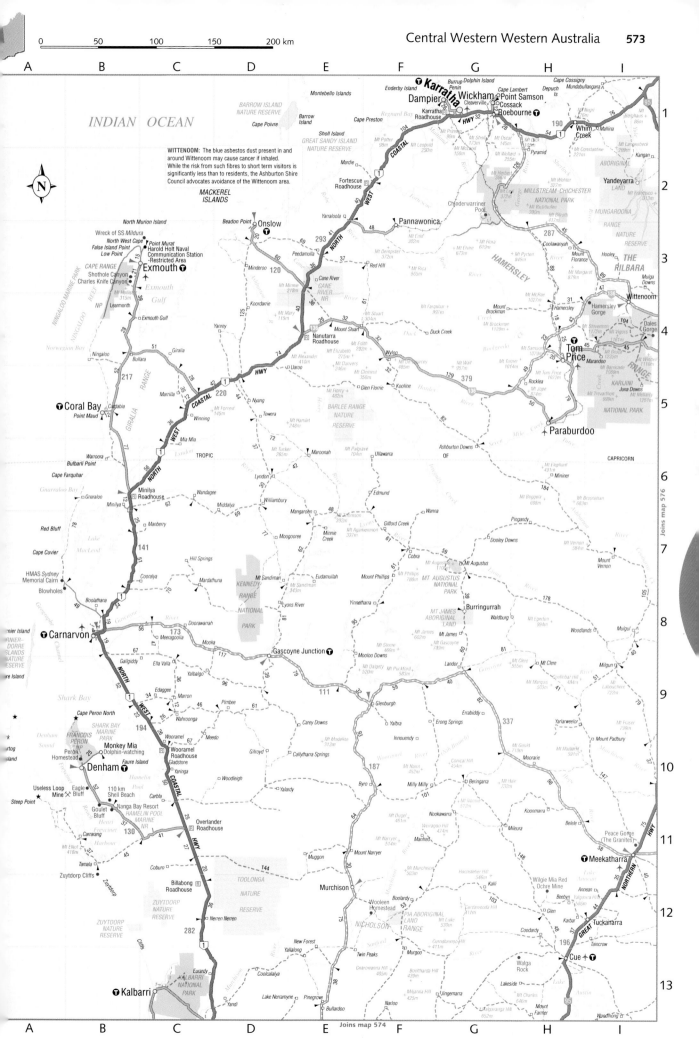

INDIAN OCEAN

0   50   100   150   200 km

WITTENOOM: The blue asbestos dust present in and
around Wittenoom may cause cancer if inhaled.
While the risk from such fibres to short term visitors is
significantly less than to residents, the Ashburton Shire
Council advocates avoidance of the Wittenoom area.

MACKEREL
ISLANDS

N

BARROW ISLAND
NATURE RESERVE

GREAT SANDY ISLAND
NATURE RESERVE

Montebello Islands

Cape Poivre

Barrow
Island

Karratha
Dampier
Wickham
Point Samson
Cossack
Roebourne
Whim
Creek

THE PILBARA

ABORIGINAL
LAND

Yandeyarra

MUNGAROONA
RANGE
NATURE
RESERVE

MILLSTREAM-CHICHESTER
NATIONAL PARK

HAMERSLEY

Wittenoom
Hamersley
Gorge
Dales
Gorge

KARIJINI

NATIONAL PARK

Tom
Price

Paraburdoo

RANGE

Fortescue
Roadhouse

Pannawonica

Chinderwarriner
Pool

Onslow
Beadon Point

CAPE RANGE
NP

Exmouth
Gulf

Exmouth
Exmouth Gulf

Learmonth

NINGALOO MARINE PARK

Norwegian Bay

Ningaloo

CANE
RIVER
NR

Nanutarra
Roadhouse

Mount Stuart

Duck Creek

Coral Bay
Point Maud

GIRALIA
RANGE

Cardabia

Marrilla

Bullara
Giralia

Winning

Mia Mia

BARLEE RANGE
NATURE
RESERVE

TROPIC

Cape Farquhar

Warroora

Bulbarli Point

Gnaraloo

Minilya
Roadhouse

Minilya

Towera

Maroonah

Nyang

Lyndon

Ullawarra

Ashburton Downs

OF

CAPRICORN

Gnaraloo Bay

Red Bluff

Cape Cuvier

Manberry

Wandagee

Williambury

Middalya

Edmund

Joins map 576

Lake
MacLeod

HMAS Sydney
Memorial Cairn
Blowholes

Boolathana

Hill Springs

Mangaroon

Minnie
Creek

Moogooree

Gifford Creek

Wanna

Cobra

Mount Augustus

Mount
Vernon

Carnarvon

Galligiddy

Meeragoolia

Mooka

Dooawarrah

Coorialya

Mardathuna

Lyons River

KENNEDY
RANGE
NATIONAL
PARK

Mt Sandiman

Eudamullah

Yinnetharra

Mount Phillips

MT AUGUSTUS
NATIONAL
PARK

Burringurrah

MT JAMES
ABORIGINAL
LAND

Waldburg

Woodlands

Mulga

Shark Bay

Cape Peron North

SHARK BAY
MARINE
PARK

FRANCOIS
PERON
NP

Monkey Mia
Dolphin-watching

Peron
Homestead

Denham

Ella Valla

Yalbalgo

Marron

Pimbee

Wahroonga

Carey Downs

Yalbra

Erong Springs

Errabiddy

Gascoyne Junction

Glenburgh

Landor

Innouendy

Mt Clere

Milgun

Useless Loop
Mine

Eagle
Bluff

110 km
Shell Beach

Nanga Bay Resort

Goulet
Bluff

HAMELIN POOL
MARINE
NR

Edaggee

Wooramel

Meedo

Gilroyd

Callytharra Springs

Byro

Milly Milly

Beringarra

Mooriary

Mt Padbury

Belele

Peace Gorge
(The Granites)

Meekatharra

Steep Point

Denham
Sound

Cararrang

Henri
Freycinet
Harbour

Mt Elliot

Tamala

Zuytdorp Cliffs

ZUYTDORP
NATURE
RESERVE

Wooramel
Roadhouse

Gladstone

Yaringa

Woodleigh

Overlander
Roadhouse

Yalardy

Carla

Coburn

Billabong
Roadhouse

TOOLONGA
NATURE
RESERVE

Nerren Nerren

Muggon

Mount Narryer

Murchison

Woolleen
Homestead

Boolardy

PIA ABORIGINAL
LAND

NICHOLSON RANGE

Glen

Coodardy

Tuckanarra

Kalbarri

KALBARRI
NATIONAL
PARK

Eurardy

Coolcalalya

Lake Nerramyne

Pinegrove

Bullardoo

New Forest

Yallalong

Twin Peaks

Murgoo

Nookawarra

Mileura

Koonmarra

Annean

Beebyn

Wilgie Mia Red
Ochre Mine

Kalli

Walga
Rock

Lakeside

Cue

GREAT
NORTHERN
HWY

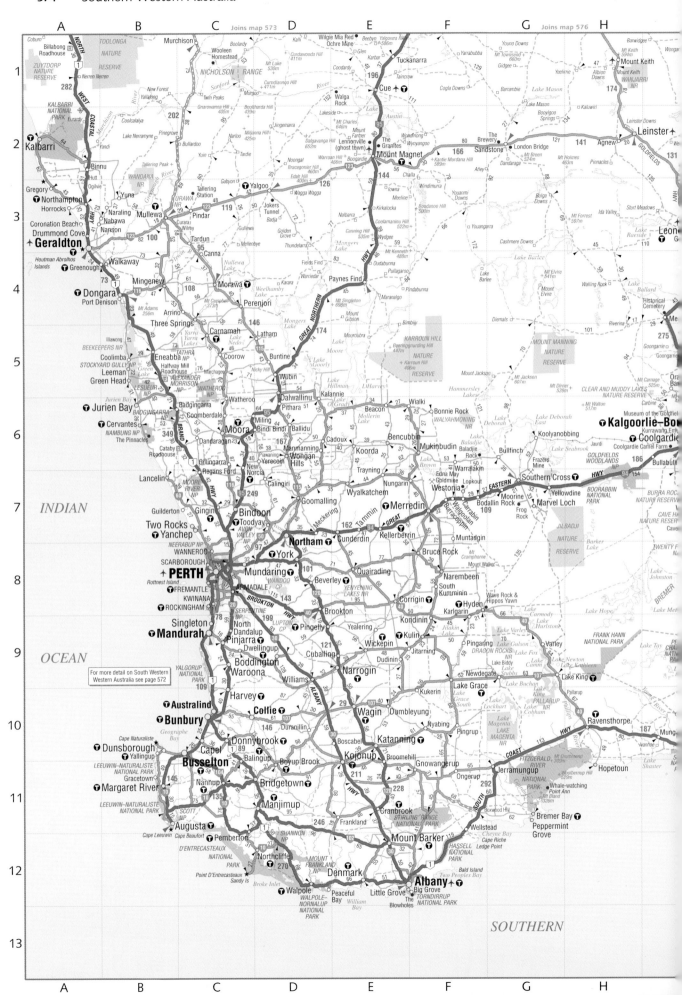

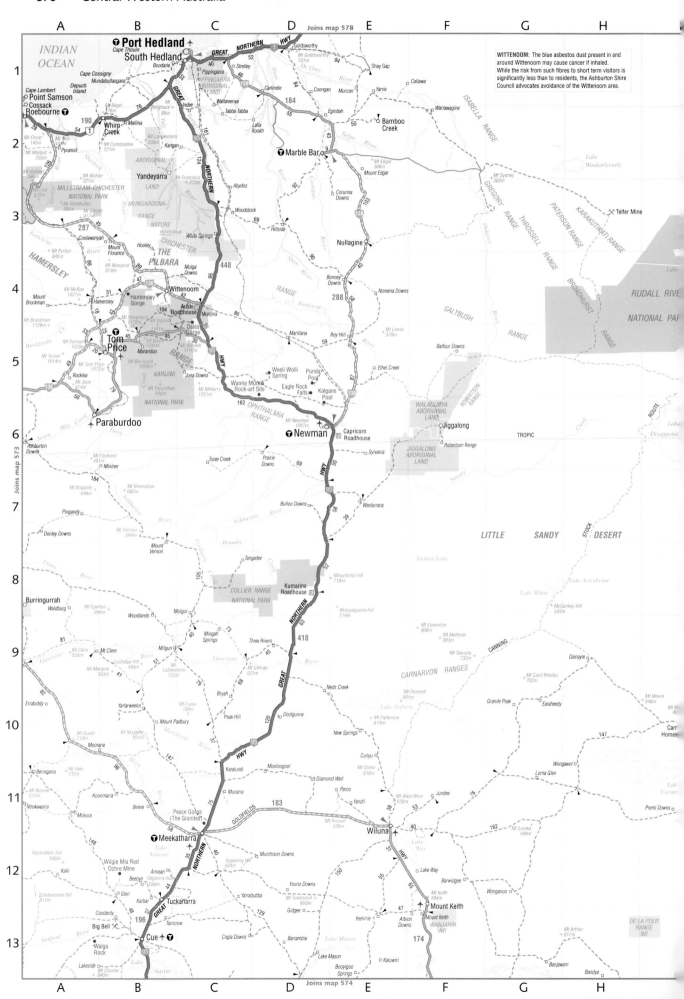

A   B   C   D   E   F   G   H

INDIAN
OCEAN

Port Hedland
South Hedland

Joins map 578

WITTENOOM: The blue asbestos dust present in and
around Wittenoom may cause cancer if inhaled.
While the risk from such fibres to short term visitors is
significantly less than to residents, the Ashburton Shire
Council advocates avoidance of the Wittenoom area.

Cape Lambert
Point Samson
Cossack
Roebourne

Whim
Creek

Marble Bar

Bamboo
Creek

Yandeyarra

THE PILBARA

Wittenoom
Auski
Roadhouse
Dales
Gorge

Nullagine

Hamersley
Gorge

Tom
Price

RUDALL RIVE
NATIONAL PAR

Marandoo

KARIJINI

NATIONAL PARK

Paraburdoo

Wanna Munna
Rock-art Site

Weeli Wolli
Spring
Eagle Rock
Falls
Punda
Pool
Kalgans
Pool

OPHTHALMIA
RANGE

Newman
Capricorn
Roadhouse

Jiggalong

WALAGUNYA
ABORIGINAL
LAND

TROPIC

JIGGALONG
ABORIGINAL
LAND

Joins map 573

Prairie
Downs

Sylvania

Weelarrana

LITTLE   SANDY   DESERT

Bulloo Downs

CARNARVON   RANGES

Burringurrah

Kumarina
Roadhouse

COLLIER RANGE
NATIONAL PARK

Three Rivers

Neds Creek

CANNING

Granite Peak

Earaheedy

Carr
Homes

Peak Hill

Doolgunna

New Springs

Carr

GOLDFIELDS

Karalundi

Cunyu

Moologool

Wiluna

Paroo

Meekatharra

Peace Gorge
(The Granites)

Wilgie Mia Red
Ochre Mine

Mount Keith

Tuckanarra

Cue

DE LA POER
RANGE
NR

Joins map 574

A   B   C   D   E   F   G   H

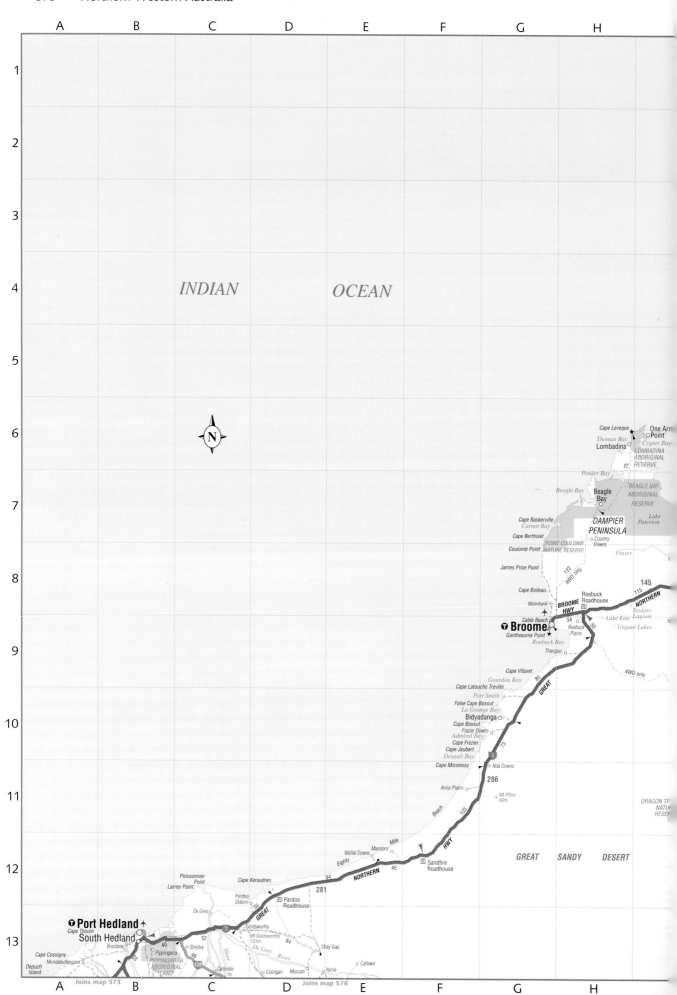

INDIAN OCEAN

GREAT SANDY DESERT

Cape Leveque
One Arm Point
Thomas Bay
Cygnet Bay
Lombadina
LOMBADINA ABORIGINAL RESERVE
Pender Bay
Beagle Bay
BEAGLE BAY ABORIGINAL RESERVE
Lake Paterson
Cape Baskerville
Carnot Bay
DAMPIER PENINSULA
Cape Bertholet
POINT COULOMB NATURE RESERVE
Country Downs
Coulomb Point
Fraser
James Price Point
4WD only
145
Cape Boileau
115
NORTHERN
Waterbank
BROOME HWY
Roebuck Roadhouse
Taylors Lagoon
Cable Beach
34
Lake Eda
Broome
Roebuck Plains
Ungani Lakes
Gantheaume Point
Roebuck Bay
Thangoo
4WD only
Cape Villaret
Gourdon Bay
GREAT
Cape Latouche Treville
Port Smith
False Cape Bossut
La Grange Bay
Bidyadanga
Cape Bossut
Frazier Downs
Admiral Bay
Cape Frezier
Cape Jaubert
Desault Bay
Cape Missiessy
Nita Downs
286
Anna Plains
Mt Phire 90m
Beach
103
Mile
Wallal Downs
Mandora
Eighty
45
NORTHERN
Sandfire Roadhouse
94
HWY
DRAGON TR NATU RESE
Poissonnier Point
Cape Keraudren
281
Larrey Point
GREAT
Pardoo Station
Pardoo Roadhouse
De Grey
Port Hedland
Goldsworthy
Cape Thouin
South Hedland
52
Mt Goldsworthy 131m
84
Shay Gap
40
Boodarie
De Grey River
Cape Cossigny
Pippingarra
46
Coongan
Muccan
Yarrie
Callawa
Mundabullangara
130
PIPPINGARRA ABORIGINAL LAND
Carlindie
Depuch Island
Show R

Joins map 573
Joins map 576

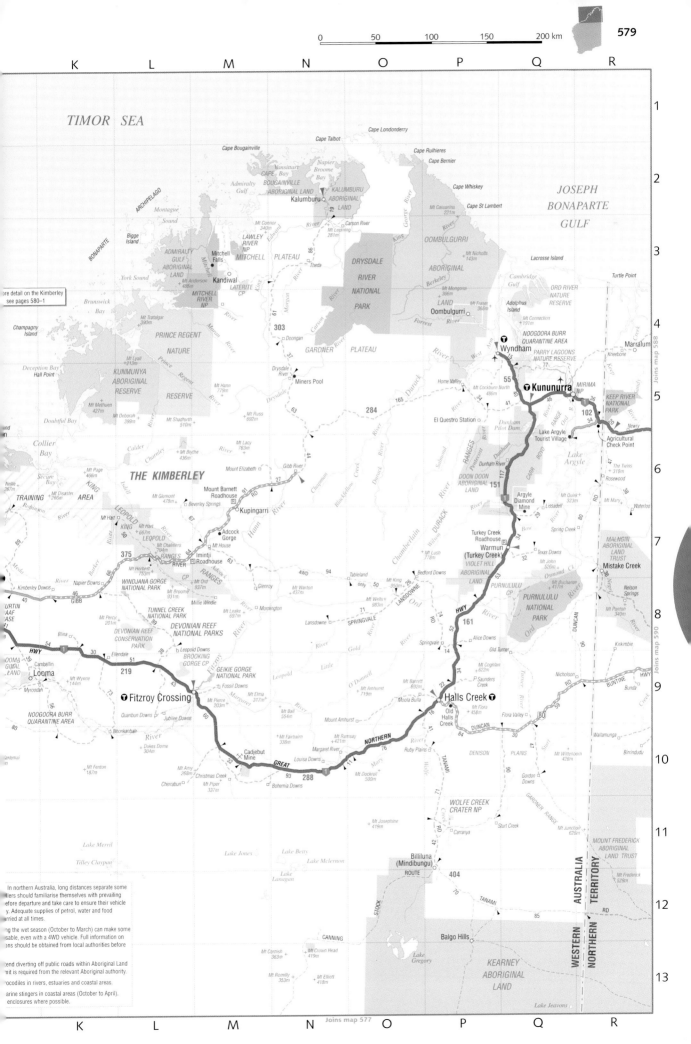

0   50   100   150   200 km

K   L   M   N   O   P   Q   R

1

TIMOR SEA

Cape Talbot

Cape Londonderry

2

Cape Bougainville

*Vansittart
Bay*

Cape Ruihieres

*Napier
Broome
Bay*

Cape Bernier

*CAPE
BOUGAINVILLE
ABORIGINAL LAND*

Cape Whiskey

Cape St Lambert

*JOSEPH
BONAPARTE
GULF*

*Admiralty
Gulf*

*KALUMBURU
ABORIGINAL
LAND*

Kalumburu

Mt Casuarina
221m

3

BONAPARTE ARCHIPELAGO

*Montague
Sound*

*Bigge
Island*

Lacrosse Island

*LAWLEY
RIVER
NP*

Mitchell Falls

Mt Connor
340m

Carson River

*MITCHELL
PLATEAU*

Theda

*DRYSDALE
RIVER
NATIONAL
PARK*

Mt Leipning
281m

*OOMBULGURRI
ABORIGINAL*

Mt Nicholls
143m

*Cambridge
Gulf*

*ORD RIVER
NATURE
RESERVE*

Turtle Point

more detail on the Kimberley
see pages 580–1

York Sound

Kandiwal

*MITCHELL
RIVER
NP*

*LATERITE
CP*

Mt Anderson
488m

303

GARDNER

PLATEAU

LAND

Mt Mongona
306m

Mt Fraser
368m

*Adolphus
Island*

Mt Connection
191m

Oombulgurri

4

*Brunswick
Bay*

Mt Trafalgar
390m

*PRINCE REGENT
NATURE*

Mt Lyall
213m

Miners Pool

Drysdale River

*NOOGOORA BURR
QUARANTINE AREA*

Wyndham

Marralum

Kneeboone

*Champagny
Island*

Mt Deborah
399m

*KUNMUNYA
ABORIGINAL
RESERVE*

Mt Hann
779m

Mt Russ
692m

63

284

165

Home Valley

Mt Cockburn North
496m

*PARRY LAGOONS
NATURE RESERVE*

77

15

55

Kununurra

*MIRIMA
NP*

36

*KEEP RIVER
NATIONAL
PARK*

5

Deception Bay
Hall Point

Mt Methuen
427m

Mt Shadforth
510m

Doubtful Bay

RESERVE

El Questro Station

46

102

34

20

Newry

*Collier
Bay*

Mt Page
466m

Calder

Charnley

Mt Lacy
763m

Mt Blythe
436m

Mount Elizabeth

*Dunham
Pilot Dam*

*Lake Argyle
Tourist Village*

*Lake
Argyle*

*Agricultural
Check Point*

47

The Twins
318m

Rosewood

38

*Secure
Bay*

Nellie
267m

Mt Disaster
266m

THE KIMBERLEY

44

27

Gibb River

151

Argyle
Diamond
Mine

Lissadell

Mt Quirk
323m

80

Mt Mary

Waterloo

6

TRAINING

Mt Hart
667m

Mt Giemont
478m

Mount Barnett
Roadhouse

RD

GIBB

117

Beverley Springs

51

Kupingarri

29

Spring Creek

*MALNGIN
ABORIGINAL
LAND
TRUST*

AREA

KING

89

LEOPOLD

50

Adcock
Gorge

Mt House

67

HANN

Turkey Creek
Roadhouse

Warmun
(Turkey Creek)

32

Texas Downs

Mt John
526m

Mistake Creek

7

Robinson

Mt Herbert
753m

Mt Ord
937m

375

LEOPOLD
KING

Mt Chalmers
794m

Imintji
Roadhouse

83

Mt Lush
778m

Tableland

Mt King
950m

26

*VIOLET HILL
ABORIGINAL
LAND*

Mt Buchanan
417m

Nelson
Springs

Meda

66

RANGES

RIVER

CP

Mt Broome
931m

RANGES

Millie Windie

4WD
only

94

50

71

Bedford Downs

34

*PURNULULU
CP*

Mt Panton
340m

DURACK

Kimberley Downs

Napier Downs

46

GIBB

Glenroy

Mt Warton
437m

Mt Wells
983m

*PURNULULU
NATIONAL
PARK*

Chamberlain

LANSDOWNE

74

HWY

161

52

8

40

*CURTIN
RAAF
ASE*

Blina

Mt Percy
201m

*TUNNEL CREEK
NATIONAL PARK*

*DEVONIAN REEF
CONSERVATION
PARK*

Mt Leake
697m

Lansdowne

SPRINGVALE

Springvale

14

Alice Downs

Old Turner

Kirkimbie

Ord

96

DUNCAN

54

Ellendale

30

*DEVONIAN REEF
NATIONAL PARKS*

Mornington

Gold

34

Mt Coghlan
622m

P Saunders
Creek

Nicholson

RD

Burda

BUNTINE

HWY

9

*OOMA
GINAL
AND*

Looma

Mt Wynne
144m

Camballin

51

38

219

43

Leopold

LEOPOLD DOWNS

*BROOKING
GORGE CP*

*GEIKIE GORGE
NATIONAL PARK*

Fossil Downs

Mt Pierre
203m

Little

O'Donnell

Mt Anhurst
719m

Mt Barnett
692m

22

Moola Bulla

Halls Creek

DUNCAN

84

Mt Flora
458m

Flora Valley

30

80

Wallamunga

Myroodah

Fitzroy Crossing

Quanbun Downs

Jubilee Downs

60

Margaret

Mt Elma
317m

Mt Ball
554m

Mount Amhurst

Old
Halls
Creek

16

41

Birrindudu

Noonkanbah

80

Dukes Dome
304m

River

Cadjebut
Mine

32

Louisa Downs

Margaret River

Mt Fairbairn
338m

Mt Ramsay
421m

NORTHERN

76

Ruby Plains

TANAMI

DENISON

Mary

River

PLAINS

Mt Wittenoom
428m

10

arlemul

Mt Fenton
187m

Mt Amy
268m

Christmas Creek

GREAT

93

288

Mt Dockrell
500m

Walle

Gordon
Downs

Sturt

Cherrabun

Mt Piper
337m

Bohemia Downs

Stuart

Mt Junction
628m

11

Lake Merril

Tilleys Claypan

Lake Jones

Lake Betty

Lake McLernon

Mt Josephine
419m

42

RD

Cananya

Sturt Creek

*WOLFE CREEK
CRATER NP*

96

GARDNER RANGE

*MOUNT FREDERICK
ABORIGINAL
LAND TRUST*

Mt Frederick
529m

In northern Australia, long distances separate some
llers should familiarise themselves with prevailing
fore departure and take care to ensure their vehicle
y. Adequate supplies of petrol, water and food
rried at all times.

g the wet season (October to March) can make some
able, even with a 4WD vehicle. Full information on
ns should be obtained from local authorities before

nd diverting off public roads within Aboriginal Land
it is required from the relevant Aboriginal authority.

ocodiles in rivers, estuaries and coastal areas.

rine stingers in coastal areas (October to April).
enclosures where possible.

Billiluna
(Mindibungu)

ROUTE

404

70

TANAMI

STOCK

85

12

WESTERN AUSTRALIA

NORTHERN TERRITORY

RD

CANNING

13

Balgo Hills

Mt Carnish
363m

Mt Crown Head
419m

*Lake
Gregory*

*KEARNEY
ABORIGINAL
LAND*

Mt Romilly
353m

Mt Elliott
418m

Lake Jeavons

K   L   M   N   O   P   Q   R

Joins map 577

Joins map 588

Joins map 590

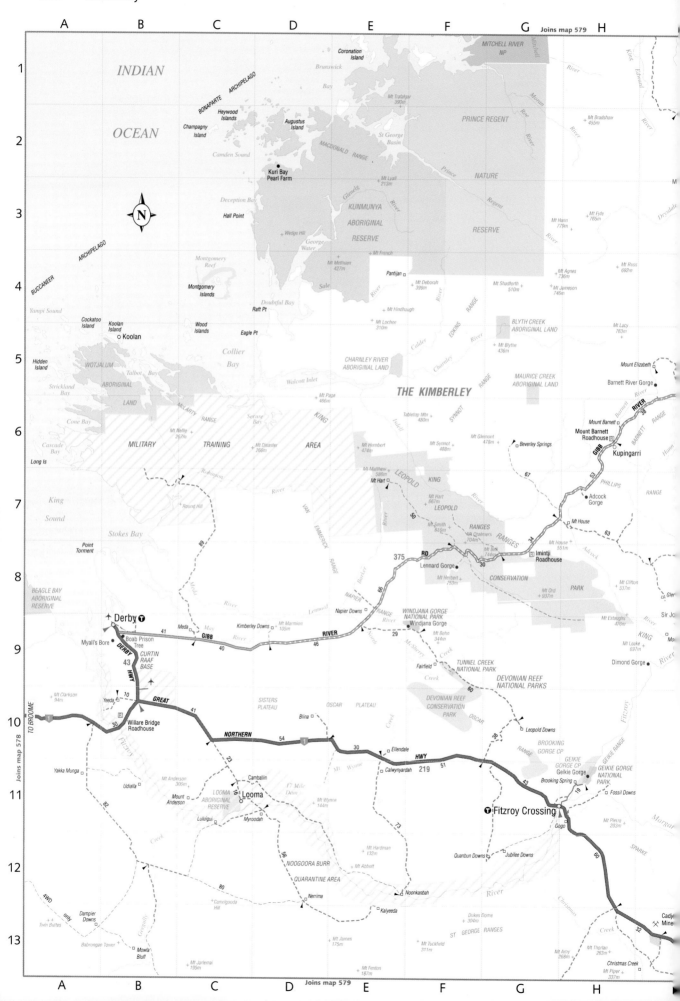

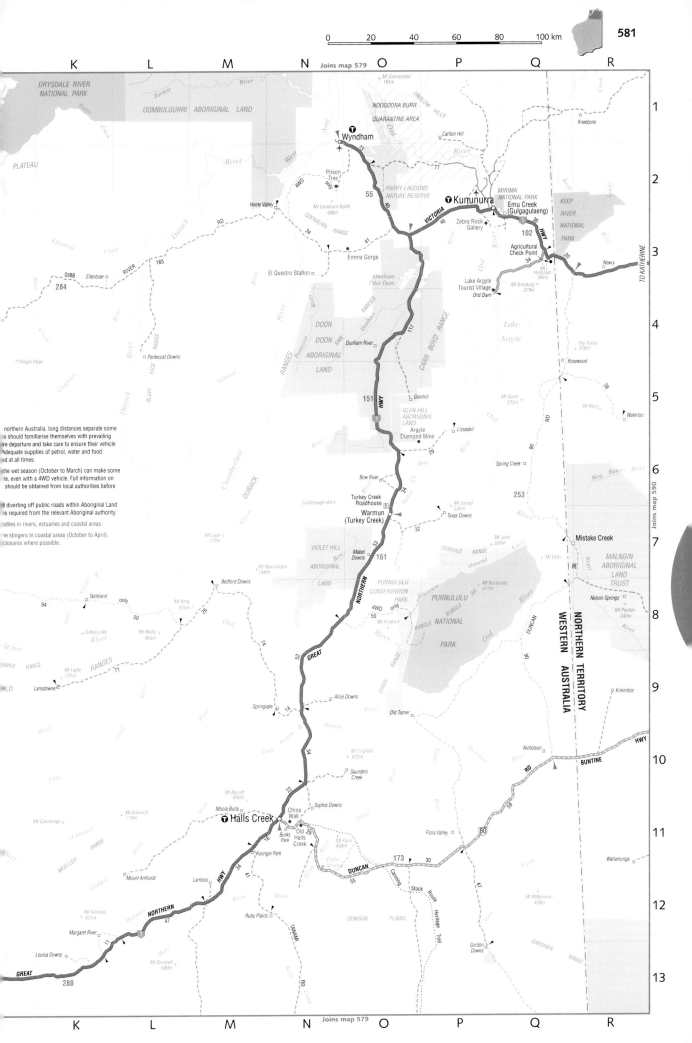

NORTHERN TERRITORY
MAPS

584

Nightcliff · Casuarina
Berrimah

583

DARWIN

Palmerston · Howard Springs

Noonamah

588–9

DARWIN · Jabiru

Adelaide River

586–7

Katherine

Mataranka · Ngukurr

Timber Creek

96

Daly Waters · Borroloola

590–1

Top Springs
80

Kalkarindji · Elliott

96
87

Tennant Creek
65

592–3

Barrow Creek

87

594–5

Alice Springs

Yulara
Uluru
(Ayers Rock)
87

0.25 0.5 0.75 1 km

A   B   C   D   E   F   G   H   I

TO FANNIE BAY

Joins map 584

TO AIRPORT

TO WINNELLIE

1

Mindil Beach Sunset Market (Thurs & Sun, dry season) ■ 35

Beach

Mindil Beach Reserve

■ 30

GEORGE BROWN DARWIN BOTANIC GARDENS

St Johns College

CHARLES

WESTRALIA

Mangroves

Chinese Cemetery ■

Boat ramp

2

GERANIUM

Gardens Oval NTFL

Amphitheatre

MGM Grand ■ 5
34 ■
MGM Grand Casino

Tennis Courts

Palmerston Park Oval

Gardens Cemetery

The Gardens

BLAKE

Dinah Oval

Stuart Park

Dinah Beach ■ Sailing Club

3

■ 36
Myilly Point Heritage Precinct

Gardens Park Golf Course

BEACH

Lock

FRANCES BAY

4

Small Boat Harbour

Palms Motel

Frontier Darwin

Daly Bridge

5

Larrakeyah Primary School

Asti Motel

Metro Inn

Ti Tree Holiday Apartments

Fishermans Wharf

6

Greek Orthodox Church
City Gardens Apartments

Elkes Backpackers

Frogshollow Backpackers

Frogshollow Park

7

Banyan View Lodge ■ 1

YMCA of Darwin 10 ■

Marrakai Apartments

St Marys Cathedral ◆

Mirambeena Resort Darwin 6

DARWIN

Top End Hotel 9 ■

22 ■ Aquascene
Ramp

Doctors Gully
Lookout

Poinciana Inn 8 ■
Darwin Performing Arts Centre 28 ■
Holiday Inn Darwin

18 ■ AANT

GPO 16 ■

8

Bicentennial Park

Holiday Inn Esplanade Darwin 4 ■

Darwin Cinema Centre

17 ■ 13 ◆ Darwin Memorial Uniting Church

Luma Luma Holiday Apts

Boat Ramp

Cherry Blossom Motel

Novotel Atrium Darwin 7 ■
YHA 3

Saville Park Suites

Melaleuca Lodge

46 ◆ Raintree Park

RSL Club

Don Hotel ■

26

9

24 ■

Darwin Tourist Precinct 14

Lyons Cottage 33 ◆

2 ◆ Crowne Plaza Darwin

15

20

47 ◆ Tree of Knowledge
12 Darwin Civic Centre & Library

Magistrates Court & Registrar General ◆

Mavie

Stokes Hill

10

Old Admiralty House ◆

Lameroo Beach

19 ◆
Law Court

State Square

Supreme Court
44 ◆

25 ◆
Christ Church Cathedral
27 ◆

Civic Square

Parliament House & NT Library 41 ◆

Old Police Station & Courthouse 38 ◆

Survivors Lookout 45 ◆

Indo Pacific Marine 32 ■

23 ◆ Australian Pearling Exhibition

11

Cenotaph ■

Deckchair Cinema (Apr–Nov) 29

31 ◆ Government House

WWII Oil Storage Tunnels 49 ◆

Darwin Harbour

Overland Telegraph Memorial 39 ◆

PORT DARWIN

Fort Hill

Wharf Precinct
Cruise Ship Passenger Terminal ■

Old Fort Hill Wharf

43 ◆ Stokes Hill Wharf

12

Fort Hill Wharf

Iron Ore Wharf

13

A   B   C   D   E   F   G   H   I

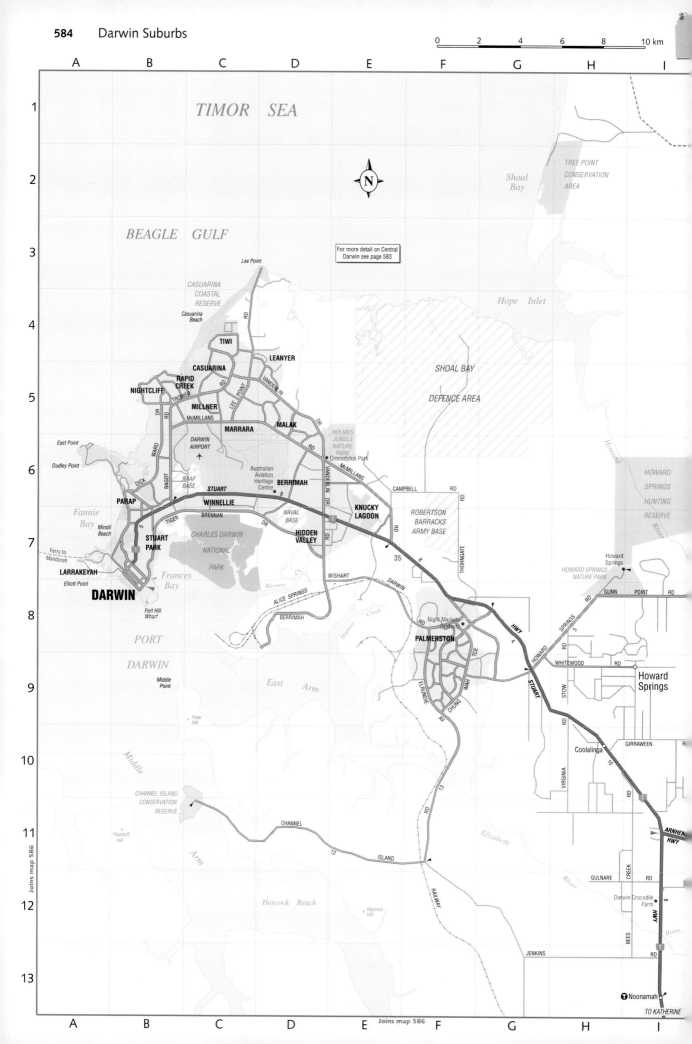

For more detail on Central Darwin see page 583

TIMOR SEA

Shoal
Bay

TREE POINT
CONSERVATION
AREA

BEAGLE   GULF

Hope   Inlet

Lee Point

CASUARINA
COASTAL
RESERVE

Casuarina
Beach

SHOAL BAY

DEFENCE AREA

TIWI

LEANYER

CASUARINA

RAPID
CREEK

NIGHTCLIFF

MILLNER

McMillans

MARRARA

MALAK

East Point

DARWIN
AIRPORT

HOLMES
JUNGLE
NATURE
PARK

Dudley Point

Crocodylus Park

McMILLANS

HOWARD
SPRINGS
HUNTING
RESERVE

RAAF
BASE

Australian
Aviation
Heritage
Centre

BERRIMAH

CAMPBELL   RD

Fannie
Bay

PARAP

WINNELLIE

BRENNAN

NAVAL
BASE

KNUCKY
LAGOON

ROBERTSTON
BARRACKS
ARMY BASE

Howard

River

Mindil
Beach

STUART

TIGER

35

Howard Springs

HOWARD SPRINGS
NATURE PARK

Ferry to
Mandorah

STUART
PARK

CHARLES DARWIN

HIDDEN
VALLEY

8

THORNGATE

GUNN   POINT   RD

LARRAKEYAH

NATIONAL

WISHART

Elliott Point

Frances
Bay

PARK

ALICE SPRINGS

DARWIN

HWY

SPRINGS

Howard
Springs

DARWIN

Fort Hill
Wharf

BERRIMAH

Bleesers

Hudson

Creek

Night Markets
(Fridays)

HOWARD

WHITEWOOD   RD

PORT

Middle
Point

East   Arm

PALMERSTON

STUART

STOW

GIRRAWEEN   R

DARWIN

Peak
Hill

ELRUNDIE

CHUNG

WAH

TCE

Coolalinga

10

VIRGINIA

Middle

CHANNEL ISLAND
CONSERVATION
RESERVE

Flagstaff
Hill

13

RD

ARNHEM   HWY

Arm

CHANNEL

12

ISLAND

Elizabeth

River

GULNARE

CREEK   RD

RAILWAY

Darwin Crocodile
Farm

8

Haycock   Reach

Haycock
Hill

HWY

BEES

JENKINS   RD

Noonamah

TO KATHERINE

Joins map 586

Joins map 586

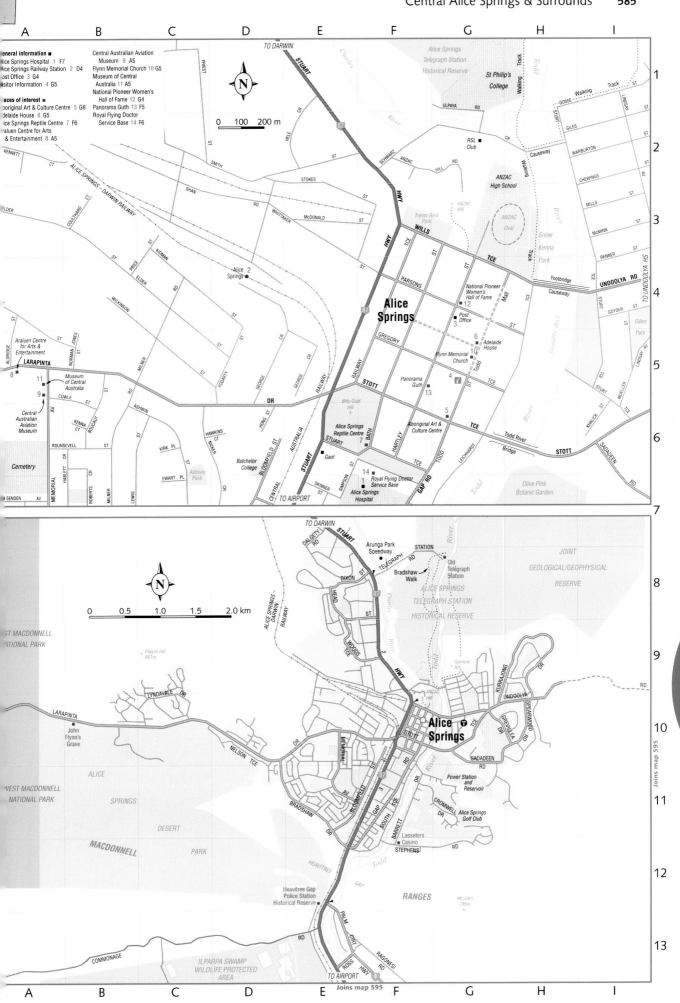

Joins map 595

Joins map 595

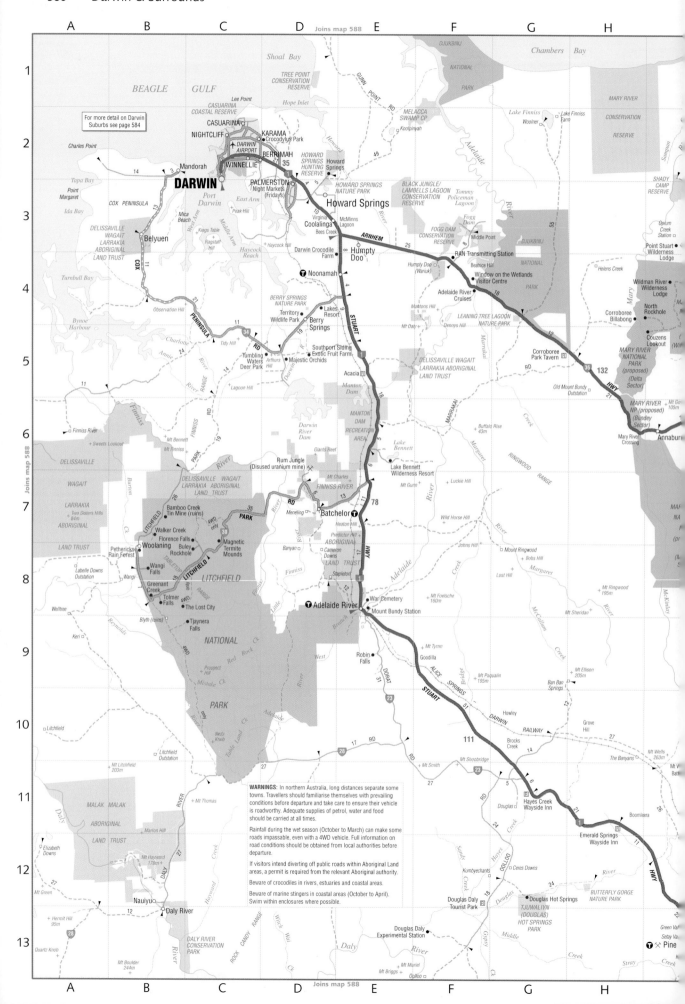

WARNINGS: In northern Australia, long distances separate some towns. Travellers should familiarise themselves with prevailing conditions before departure and take care to ensure their vehicle is roadworthy. Adequate supplies of petrol, water and food should be carried at all times.

Rainfall during the wet season (October to March) can make some roads impassable, even with a 4WD vehicle. Full information on road conditions should be obtained from local authorities before departure.

If visitors intend diverting off public roads within Aboriginal Land areas, a permit is required from the relevant Aboriginal authority.

Beware of crocodiles in rivers, estuaries and coastal areas.

Beware of marine stingers in coastal areas (October to April). Swim within enclosures where possible.

For more detail on Darwin Suburbs see page 584

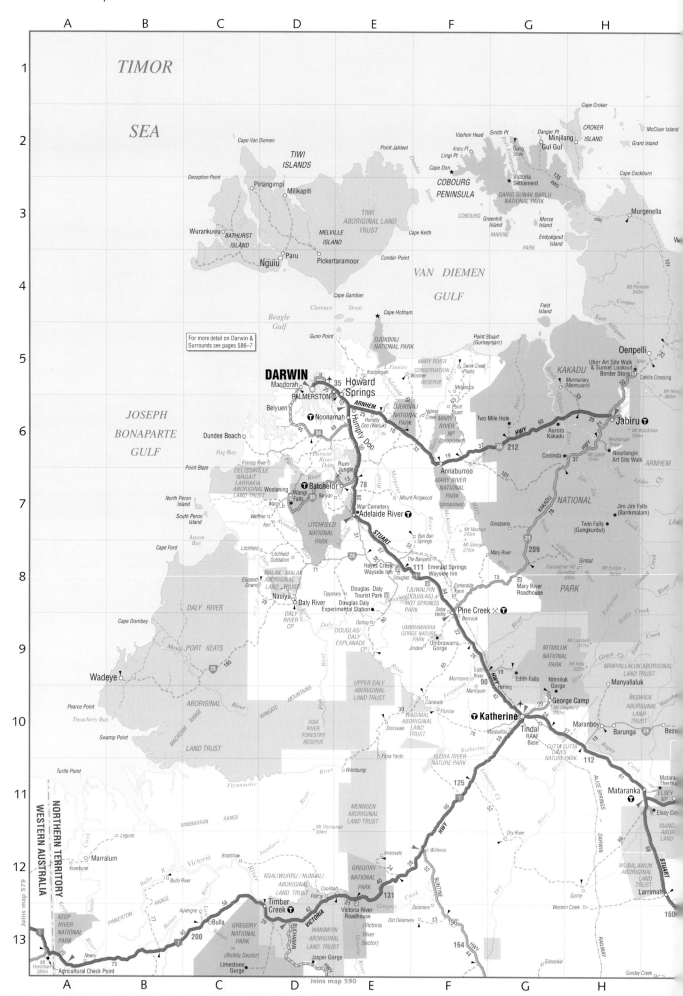

TIMOR

SEA

JOSEPH
BONAPARTE
GULF

VAN DIEMEN
GULF

Cape Van Diemen

TIWI
ISLANDS

Deception Point

Pirlangimpi
Milikapiti

Wurankuwu
BATHURST
ISLAND

TIWI
ABORIGINAL LAND
TRUST

MELVILLE
ISLAND

Nguiu
Paru
Pickertaramoor

Cape Gambier

Cape Keith

Conder Point

Beagle
Gulf

Clarence   Strait

Cape Hotham

Gunn Point

Point Jahleel

Vashon Head   Smith Pt
Araru Pt
Lingi Pt
Cape Don

COBOURG
PENINSULA

Danger Pt
Guriq
Gurig
Victoria
Settlement

COBOURG

GARIG GUNAK BARLU
NATIONAL PARK

Greenhill
Island

Morse
Island

Minjilang
Gul Gul

CROKER
ISLAND

MARINE

Endyalgout
Island

Field
Island

PARK

Cape Croker

McCluer Island

Grant Island

Cape Cockburn

Murgenella

Mt Permain
240m

Cooper

W

DARWIN
Mandorah
PALMERSTON
Belyuen

Howard
Springs

35

ARNHEM

Noonamah

Dundee Beach

Fog Bay

Point Blaze

Finniss River

DELISSAVILLE
WAGAIT
LARRAKIA
ABORIGINAL
LAND TRUST   Woolaning

North Peron
Island

South Peron
Island

Anson
Bay

Cape Ford

Keri

Welltree

Litchfield
Outstation

Wangi
Falls
Wangi

Batchelor
Banyan

LITCHFIELD
NATIONAL
PARK

Litchfield

28

Darwin
River Dam

Rum
Jungle

13
78

HWY

Humpty Doo

Humpty
Doo (Wariuk)

25
34
49

45

55

50

18
33

War Cemetery
Adelaide River

STUART

31

DJUKBINJ
NATIONAL
PARK

Koolpinyah

L Finniss

MARY
RIVER
CONSERVATION
RESERVE

Melaleuca

Helens
Creek

Mount Ringwood

Ban Ban
Springs

Point Stuart
(Gurnaynjarr)

DJUKBINJ
NATIONAL PARK

Swim Creek
Plains
Woolner

MARY
RIVER
NP
(proposed)

Point
Stuart

63

19

Annaburroo

MARY RIVER
NATIONAL PARK
(proposed)

Mt Masson
243m
Mt George
275m

3T

60

UBIRR Art Site Walk
& Sunset Lookout
Border Store

Munmarlary
(Munmularn)

Aurora
Kakadu

Nourlangie
Rock

KAKADU

36   212

Cahills Crossing

20   21

Jabiru

Mt Brockman
209m

Nourlangie
Art Site Walk

101

Cooinda

37

Mt Cahill
154m

ARNHEM

KAKADU

78

NATIONAL

Jim Jim Falls
(Barrkmalam)

Twin Falls
(Gungkurdul)

209

Mt Evelyn
349m

Coronation Hill
(Guratba)
300m

Gimbat

LA

PARK

Oenpelli

Ubirr

23

Mt Howe
368m

Cape Fourcroy

For more detail on Darwin &
Surrounds see pages 586-7

Reynolds

FINNISS

Daly

Marrakai

McKinlay

Mary River

Goodparla

21

Mt Lambell
212m

Mt Fell
330m

Gimbat

Katherine

Cape Dombey

DALY RIVER

Movie

PORT KEATS

Litchfield
Outstation

Nauiyu
Daly River

Douglas Daly
Experimental Station

Tipperary

Hayes Creek
Wayside Inn

Douglas Daly
Tourist Park

MALAK MALAK
ABORIGINAL
LAND TRUST

Elizabeth
Downs

DALY
RIVER
CP

DOUGLAS/
DALY
ESPLANADE
CP

39

Oolloo

Daly

71

38

Douglas

111

Emerald Springs
Wayside Inn

TJUWALIYN
(DOUGLAS)
HOT SPRINGS
PARK

The Banyans

UMBRAWARRA
GORGE NATURE
PARK

Jindare

Setay
Valley

Mary River
Roadhouse

73

Esmeralda
Farm

54

Pine Creek

Bonrook

Umbrawarra
Gorge

Mt Felix
330m

NITMILUK
NATIONAL
PARK

Edith
River

Claravale

Florina

Morrisons

Mariliyum

Katherine

DALY   RIVER

MACADAM   RANGE

LAND   TRUST

ABORIGINAL

River

WINGATE   MOUNTAINS

FISH
RIVER
FORESTRY
RESERVE

UPPER DALY
ABORIGINAL
LAND TRUST

WAGIMAL
ABORIGINAL
LAND
TRUST

Dorisvale

26

30

Florina

Flora Yards

Flora River

Wombungi

Innesvale

24

Manbulloo

FLORA RIVER
NATURE PARK

76

28

Edith Falls

Nitmiluk
Gorge

Helling

George Camp

Maranboy

Barunga

19

Nitmiluk
Gorge

90

HWY

42

24

23

27

Tindal
RAAF
Base

CUTTA GUTTA
CAVES
NATURE PARK

112

Manyalluluk

MANYALLALUK ABORIGINAL
LAND TRUST

BESWICK
ABORIGINAL
LAND TRUST

Manyalluluk

Roper

Grace

Cr

Waterhouse

Bes

Wadeye

Pearce Point

Treachery Bay

Swamp Point

Turtle Point

NORTHERN TERRITORY
WESTERN AUSTRALIA

Joins map 579

Kneebone

Marralum

Legune

YAMBARRAN   RANGE

KEEP
RIVER
NATIONAL
PARK

Mt Hensman
384m

20

Newry

Agricultural Check Point

73

40

200

Bulla

Auvergne

77

Bradshaw

Victoria

Angalarri

River

Bullo River

Bullo

Fitzmaurice

Baines

58

Mt Thynnan
304m

MENNGEN
ABORIGINAL
LAND
TRUST

NGALIWURRU / NUNGALI
ABORIGINAL
LAND TRUST

GREGORY
NATIONAL
PARK

Coolibah

Fitzry

Timber
Creek

42

Victoria River
Roadhouse

VICTORIA

131

WANIMIYN
ABORIGINAL
LAND
TRUST
(Victoria
River
Sector)

Victoria

Gregory

Creek

BUNTINE

Willeroo

Dry River

52

Katherine

King

River

Dry

52

Roper

125

66

HWY

Larrimah

STUART

WUBALAWUN
ABORIGINAL
LAND
TRUST

MANG
ABOR
LAND

DARWIN

Mataranka

ELSEY
NP

Elsey Ce

Matara
Therma

160

Marandoo

Barunga

74

Limestone   Ck

GREGORY
NATIONAL
PARK
(Bullita Sector)

Limestone
Gorge

Jasper Gorge

Old Delamere

Delamere

23

164

HWY

96

44

Western Creek

Gorrie

RAILWAY

Sunday Creek

Gilnockie

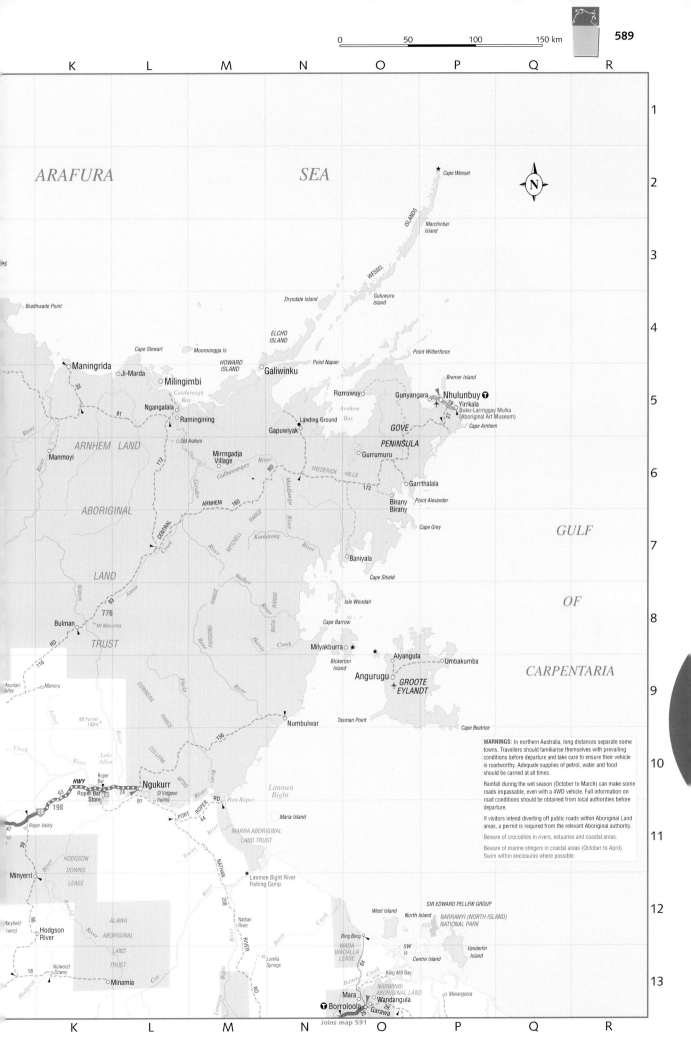

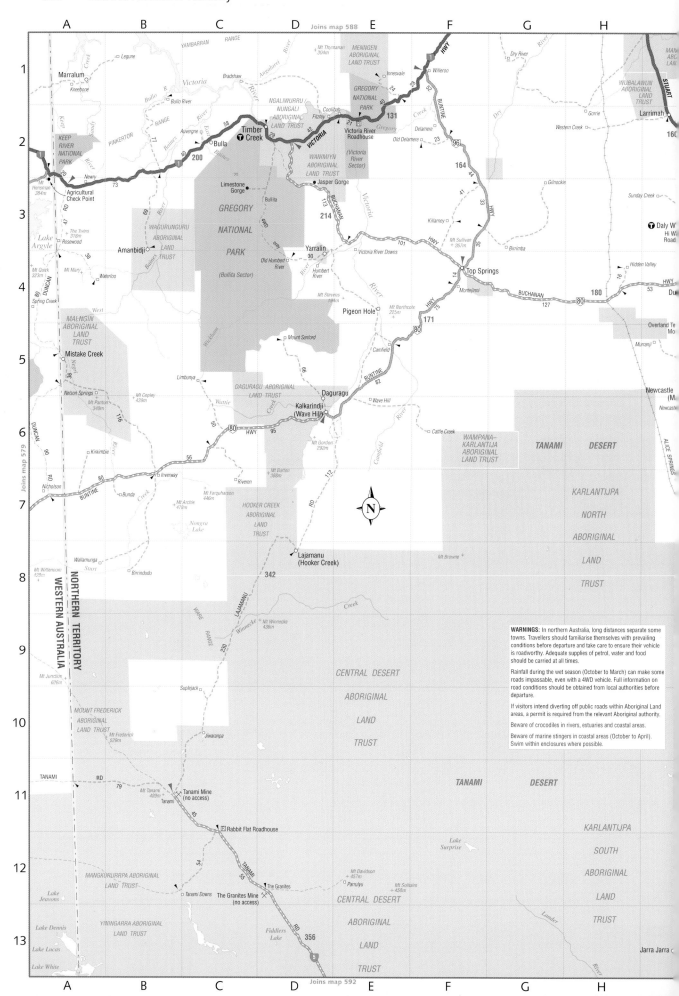

Joins map 588

Joins map 579

Joins map 592

WARNINGS: In northern Australia, long distances separate some towns. Travellers should familiarise themselves with prevailing conditions before departure and take care to ensure their vehicle is roadworthy. Adequate supplies of petrol, water and food should be carried at all times.

Rainfall during the wet season (October to March) can make some roads impassable, even with a 4WD vehicle. Full information on road conditions should be obtained from local authorities before departure.

If visitors intend diverting off public roads within Aboriginal Land areas, a permit is required from the relevant Aboriginal authority.

Beware of crocodiles in rivers, estuaries and coastal areas.

Beware of marine stingers in coastal areas (October to April). Swim within enclosures where possible.

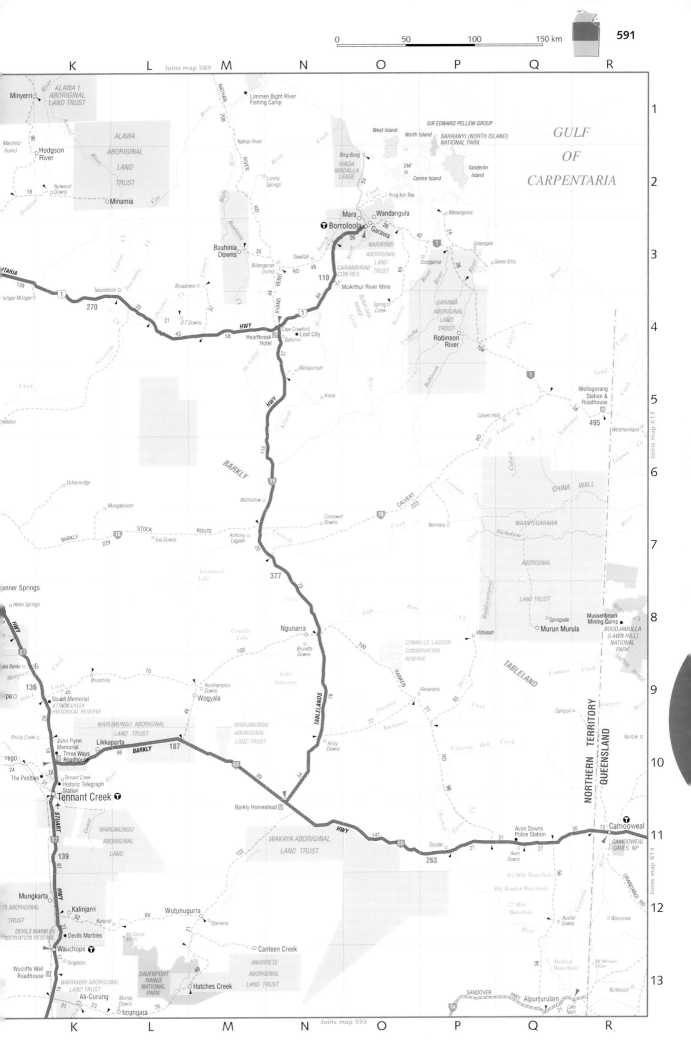

Joins map 590

A B C D E F G H

KARLANTIJPA
SOUTH
ABORIGINAL
LAND
TRUST

Rabbit Flat Roadhouse

MANGKURURRPA ABORIGINAL
LAND TRUST

Lake Jeavons

Lake Surprise

TANAMI DESERT

54

Tanami Downs

The Granites
The Granites Mine
(no access)

356

Mt Davidson
457m

Parrulyu

Mt Solitaire
458m

CENTRAL DESERT
ABORIGINAL
LAND
TRUST

Jarra Jarra

YININGARRA ABORIGINAL
LAND TRUST

Lake Dennis

Lake Lucas

Lake White

125

Fiddlers Lake

WIRLIYAJARRAYI
ABORIGINAL
LAND
TRUST

Lake Hazlett

LAKE MACKAY
ABORIGINAL
LAND
TRUST

Ranahan

MALA
ABORIGINAL
LAND
TRUST

Mt Theo
582m

Mt Theo

Willowra

Mt Patricia
577m

Chilla Well

RD

68

Mt Campbell
811m

Mt Leichhardt
1139m

Mount Barkly

Mt Psake
568m
Old Mount Peake

40

Anningie

Lake Mackay

Mt Farewell
603m

Mt Singleton
807m

Mt Hardy
840m

Mount Doreen

31

28

YUENDUMU
ABORIGINAL
LAND
TRUST

Mt Stafford
1047m

MOUNT DENISON

Mount Denison

Coniston

Coniston (ruins)

Mt Gardiner
998m

178

RD

Mt Finniss
979m

Nturiya

Pmara Ju

38

Vaughan Springs

77

Yuelamu

Yuendumu

30

Mt Nicker
832m

YUNKANJINI
ABORIGINAL
LAND
TRUST

YALPIRAKINU
ABORIGINAL
LAND
TRUST

Laramba

72

Aileron

RYANS WE
HISTORIC RESER

Nyirripi

Gurner

Newhaven

Mt Cockburn
846m

Lake Bennett

118

72

Central
Mount Wedge

27

Mt Hammond
750m

TANAMI

5

Tilmouth Well
Roadhouse

98

NATIVE
CONS

Lake Lewis

50

289

RD

Mt Harris
721m

Mt Tietkens
546m

Ininti

Pinpirnga

Kintore

Mt Leisler
901m

Tinki

273

Warren Creek Bore

Mount Liebig

Mt Liebig
1267m

Papunya

Ulambaura

51

31

Derwent

Narwietooma

Mt Chapple
1206m

Milton Park

39

Ambrula

44

Mt Hay
1252m

Hamilton Downs

Ulpilla

Lake Macdonald

TROPIC OF CAPRICORN

Ualki

HAASTS BLUFF

Haasts Bluff

Haasts Bluff
1105m

45

Mt Sonder
1380m

Redbank
Gorge

Ormiston
Gorge &
Pound

WEST MACDONNEL
NATIONAL PARK

Serpentine
Gorge

131 DR N

ABORIGINAL

LAND

TRUST

Mt Forbes
762m

WARNING: Visitors planning to travel along the Larapinta Drive through Aboriginal Land require a permit. Check road conditions before departing; 4WD vehicle may be required.

Glen Helen
Resort

NAMATJIRA

84

TNORALA
(GOSSE BLUFF)
CON RES

Tnorala (Gosse Bluff)

ROULPMAULPMA
ABORIGINAL LAND
TRUST

DR

LARAPINTA

LARAPINTA
124

27

(MEREENIE)

LOOP

41

RD)

Hermannsburg

6

D

6

19

Ipolera

Areyonga

Palm
Valley

Wallace
Rockhole

WATARRKA
NATIONAL
PARK

Lake Neale

Mt Murray

Kings
Canyon

MIDDLE RANGE

FINKE
GORGE
NATIONAL
PARK

Stuar

Kings Canyon
Resort

Ulpanyali

LURITJA

Mt Lewis
808m

ILLAMURTA SPRINGS
CONSERVATION RES

35

Lake Hopkins

Mt Harris
1067m

PETERMANN

ABORIGINAL

Kings Creek Station
(Camping ground)

358

63

RD

Tempe Downs

47

GILES

51

Henbury
Meteorite
Craters

30

Mt Taylor
1001m

Kaltukatjara
(Docker River)

LAND

TRUST

ERNEST

51

RD

Palme

LIDDLE

RD

Desert Oak Hill
624m

TJUKARURU
(OUTBACK

78

183

231

RD
HWY)

68

HILLS

3

PETERMANN

RANGES

KATITI ABORIGINAL
LAND TRUST

Mt Olga
1069m

Yulara

Ayers Rock Resort

LASSETER

136

84

(OUTBACK

LURITJA

KERNOT

RANGE

BASEDOW

RANGE

Imanpa

HWY)

51

106

HWY

Erld

(OUTBACK

68

Kata Tjuta
(The Olgas)

41

ULURU-KATA TJUTA
NATIONAL PARK

Uluru
(Ayers Rock)
863m

Curtin
Springs

11

Mygoora
Lake

Mt Ebenezer
Roadhouse

4

55

STUART

74

WARNING: Visitors planning to travel along Tjukaruru Road through Aboriginal Land require a permit. A second permit is required for those venturing over the WA border.

Stevensons Pk
1319m

Butlers Dome
1111m

Mt Connor
863m

Mt Connor (ruins)

68

Lyndavale

87

Mt Gosse
885m

Surveyor Generals
Corner

Mt Cockburn
1138m

Feltham Hill
863m

Alpara

Mulga Park

63

165

Kulgera

Mount
Cavenagh

105

Mt Aloysius
1085m

Mt Hinckley
1018m

55

MANN

Mt Whinham
1231m

Mt Edwin
1193m

NORTHERN TERRITORY
SOUTH AUSTRALIA

Mt Woodward
1227m

Mt Cuthbert
1035m

Sentinel Hill
910m

Victory Downs

A87

Kalka

Pipalyatjara

Aparawatatja

Kanypi

213

RANGES

Mt Morris
1288m

Amata

Ayfitte Hill (trg)
1044m

Mt Davenport
1139m

Marryat Ck

180

Joins map 560 Joins map 561

Joins map 577

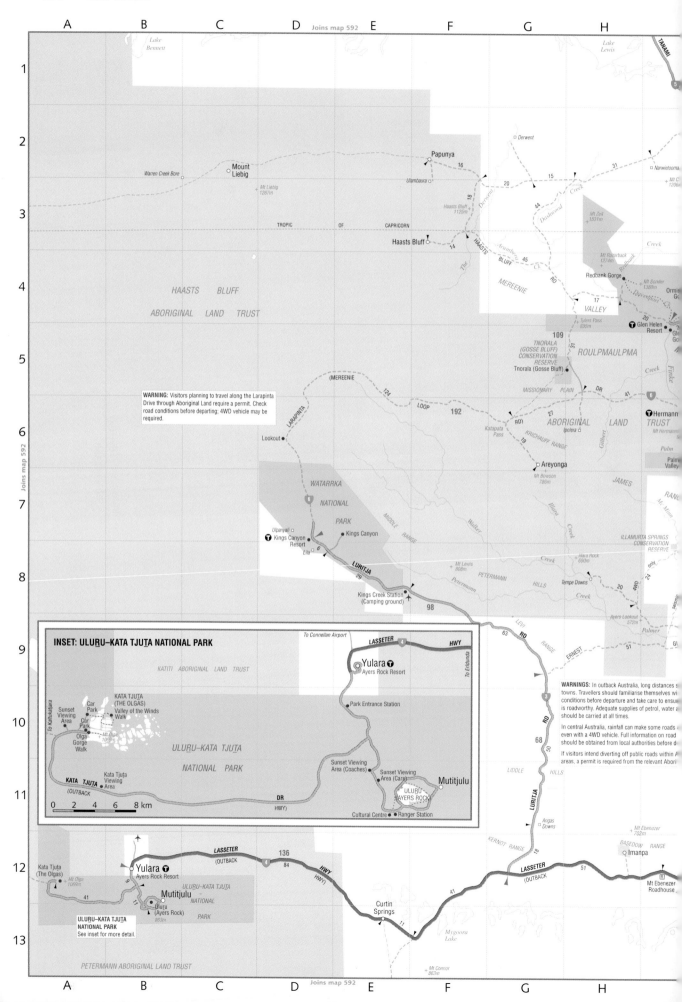

Map: Red Centre, Northern Territory

Joins map 592

WARNING: Visitors planning to travel along the Larapinta Drive through Aboriginal Land require a permit. Check road conditions before departing; 4WD vehicle may be required.

INSET: ULURU–KATA TJUTA NATIONAL PARK

WARNINGS: In outback Australia, long distances s[...] towns. Travellers should familiarise themselves wi[...] conditions before departure and take care to ensu[...] is roadworthy. Adequate supplies of petrol, water a[...] should be carried at all times.

In central Australia, rainfall can make some roads [...] even with a 4WD vehicle. Full information on road [...] should be obtained from local authorities before d[...]

If visitors intend diverting off public roads within A[...] areas, a permit is required from the relevant Abori[...]

ULURU–KATA TJUTA NATIONAL PARK See inset for more detail.

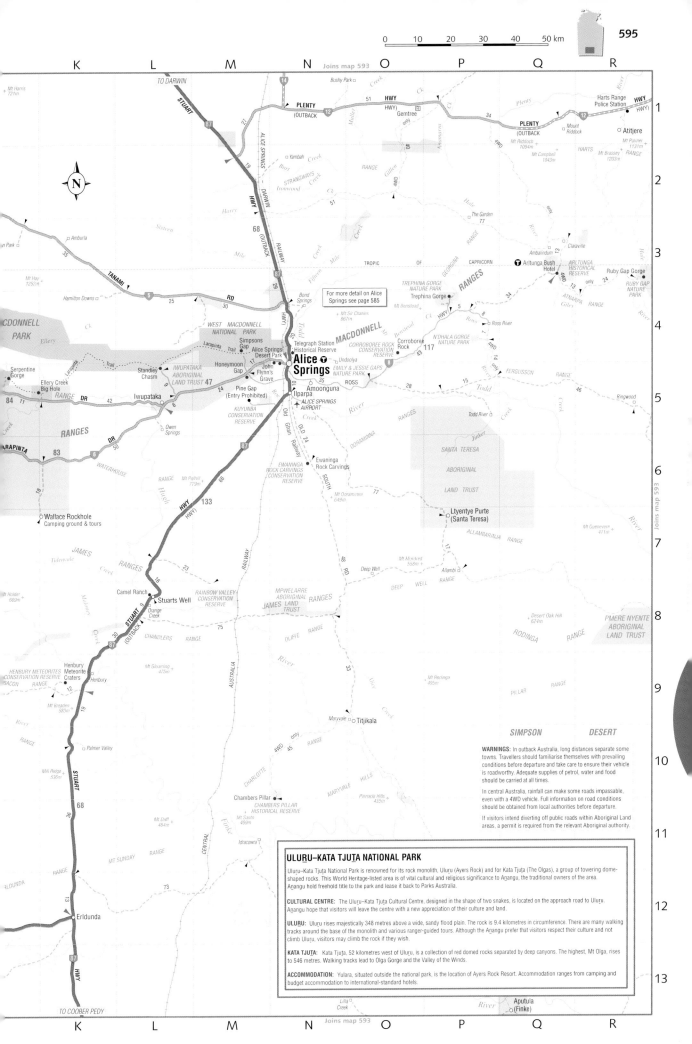

0 10 20 30 40 50 km

For more detail on Alice Springs see page 585

Joins map 593

WARNINGS: In outback Australia, long distances separate some towns. Travellers should familiarise themselves with prevailing conditions before departure and take care to ensure their vehicle is roadworthy. Adequate supplies of petrol, water and food should be carried at all times.

In central Australia, rainfall can make some roads impassable, even with a 4WD vehicle. Full information on road conditions should be obtained from local authorities before departure.

If visitors intend diverting off public roads within Aboriginal Land areas, a permit is required from the relevant Aboriginal authority.

ULURU–KATA TJUTA NATIONAL PARK

Uluru–Kata Tjuta National Park is renowned for its rock monolith, Uluru (Ayers Rock) and for Kata Tjuta (The Olgas), a group of towering dome-shaped rocks. This World Heritage-listed area is of vital cultural and religious significance to Anangu, the traditional owners of the area. Anangu hold freehold title to the park and lease it back to Parks Australia.

CULTURAL CENTRE: The Uluru–Kata Tjuta Cultural Centre, designed in the shape of two snakes, is located on the approach road to Uluru. Anangu hope that visitors will leave the centre with a new appreciation of their culture and land.

ULURU: Uluru rises majestically 348 metres above a wide, sandy flood plain. The rock is 9.4 kilometres in circumference. There are many walking tracks around the base of the monolith and various ranger-guided tours. Although the Anangu prefer that visitors respect their culture and not climb Uluru, visitors may climb the rock if they wish.

KATA TJUTA: Kata Tjuta, 52 kilometres west of Uluru, is a collection of red domed rocks separated by deep canyons. The highest, Mt Olga, rises to 546 metres. Walking tracks lead to Olga Gorge and the Valley of the Winds.

ACCOMMODATION: Yulara, situated outside the national park, is the location of Ayers Rock Resort. Accommodation ranges from camping and budget accommodation to international-standard hotels.

QUEENSLAND
MAPS

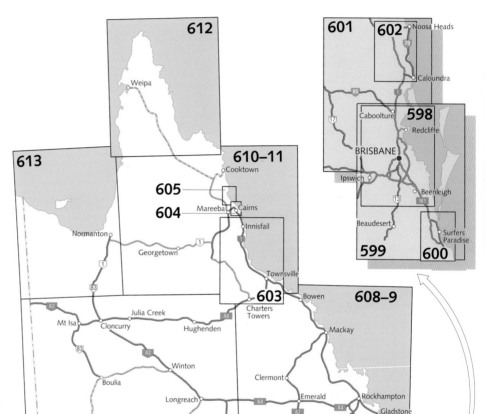

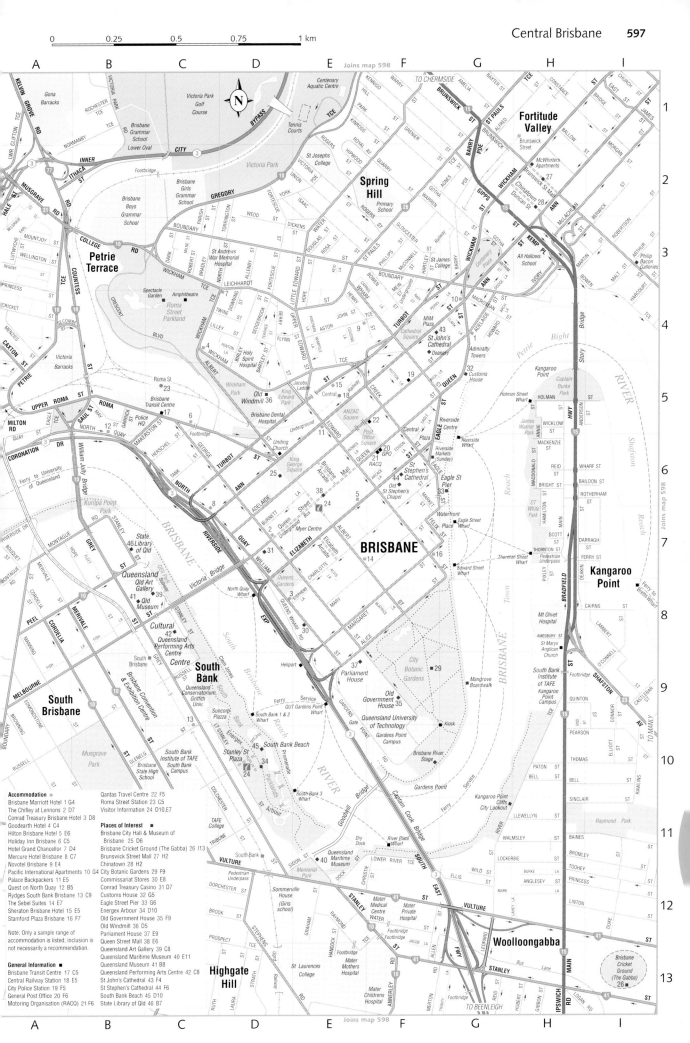

Accommodation ■
Brisbane Marriott Hotel 1 G4
The Chifley at Lennons 2 D7
Conrad Treasury Brisbane Hotel 3 D8
Goodearth Hotel 4 C4
Hilton Brisbane Hotel 5 E6
Holiday Inn Brisbane 6 C5
Hotel Grand Chancellor 7 D4
Mercure Hotel Brisbane 8 C7
Novotel Brisbane 9 E4
Pacific International Apartments 10 G4
Palace Backpackers 11 E5
Quest on North Quay 12 B5
Rydges South Bank Brisbane 13 C9
The Sebel Suites 14 E7
Sheraton Brisbane Hotel 15 E5
Stamford Plaza Brisbane 16 F7

Note: Only a sample range of accommodation is listed; inclusion is not necessarily a recommendation.

General Information ■
Brisbane Transit Centre 17 C5
Central Railway Station 18 E5
City Police Station 19 F5
General Post Office 20 F6
Motoring Organisation (RACQ) 21 F6

Qantas Travel Centre 22 F5
Roma Street Station 23 C5
Visitor Information 24 D10,E7

Places of Interest ■
Brisbane City Hall & Museum of Brisbane 25 D6
Brisbane Cricket Ground (The Gabba) 26 I13
Brunswick Street Mall 27 H2
Chinatown 28 H2
City Botanic Gardens 29 F9
Commissariat Stores 30 E8
Conrad Treasury Casino 31 D7
Customs House 32 G5
Eagle Street Pier 33 G6
Energex Arbour 34 D10
Old Government House 35 F9
Old Windmill 36 D5
Parliament House 37 E9
Queen Street Mall 38 E6
Queensland Art Gallery 39 C8
Queensland Maritime Museum 40 E11
Queensland Museum 41 B8
Queensland Performing Arts Centre 42 C8
St John's Cathedral 43 F4
St Stephen's Cathedral 44 F6
South Bank Beach 45 D10
State Library of Qld 46 B7

0   5   10   15   20 km

Joins map 601

A   B   C   D   E   F   G   H   I

1
WARARBY CK CP
Wamuran   TO WOODFORD
Wamuran Basin
Mount Mee   Mt Mee 495m   Caboolture Historical Village
Campbells Pocket   Moodlu
46   BYRON CK CP   Mt Pleasant 524m   Rocksberg
Toorbul   White Patch
BRIBIE ISLAND
BRIBIE ISLAND NATIONAL PARK
Bellara   Woorim
Caboolture
Godwin Beach   **Bongaree**
BUCKLEYS HOLE CONSERVATION PARK

2
Mount Pleasant
SHEEP STATION CK CP
Morayfield
Beachmere
Ferry   Pearl   Channel

3
D'AGUILAR RANGE
Dayboro
Upper Laceys Creek
FRESHWATER NP
BURPENGARY
NARANGBA   DABABIN   Alma Park Zoo
DECEPTION BAY
26   25
Deception Bay
ROTHWELL
SCARBOROUGH   Scarborough Point
Vehicle

4
Wivenhoe Lookout
D'AGUILAR NATIONAL PARK
STATE FOREST
Mount Samson
Lake Samsonvale
KALLANGUR
PETRIE
CLONTARF   REDCLIFFE   Redcliffe Point
WOODY POINT
MORETON
Bramble
BRIGHTON
Main   Vehicle

5
Mount Glorious   Mt Glorious
Upper Cedar Creek
Yugar   Closeburn
45
BRAY PARK   STRATHPINE
ALBANY CREEK   CARSELDINE   SANDGATE
SHORNCLIFFE
BOONDALL   Nudgee Beach
Mud Island
BAY
Juno Point
Fisherman Islands
St Helena Island

6
Highvale   Samford
D'AGUILAR NP
Australian Woolshed
BRISBANE FOREST PARK
BUNYAVILLE STATE FOREST PARK
EVERTON HILLS   GEEBUNG   VIRGINIA
FERNY HILLS   CHERMSIDE   NUNDAH
Mount Nebo   Jolly's Lookout
STAFFORD   KEDRON
NEWMARKET   HENDRA
BRISBANE AIRPORT
ST HELENA ISLAND NP
Green Island

7
D'AGUILAR RANGE
McAfees Lookout
THE GAP
Enoggera Military Camp
ASCOT
ASHGROVE   PADDINGTON
FORTITUDE VALLEY
BRISBANE
HEMMANT   WYNNUM
Darling Point
MANLY
Waterloo Bay   Wellington Point

8
Borallon
Mt Crosby
KARANA DOWNS
BROOKFIELD
INDOOROOPILLY   KENMORE
TOOWONG
WOOLLOONGABBA
CAMP HILL   CARINDALE
TINGALPA   BIRKDALE   WELLINGTON POINT
ANSTEAD
MOUNT OMMANEY
ANNERLEY
MOUNT GRAVATT
CHANDLER   Ormiston House   ORMISTON
MACKENZIE   CAPALABA   Old Court House   CLEVELAND
Peel Island
Raby Bay

9
TO TOOWOOMBA   TO ESK
WARREGO
CHUWAR
KARALEE
RIVERVIEW
MOGGILL   DARRA   OXLEY
SALISBURY
ROBERTSON
Archerfield Airport
DURACK   INALA
SUNNYBANK
BURBANK
ROCHEDALE
SHELDON
THORNLANDS
Point Halloran   Coochiemudlo Island
VICTORIA POINT

10
TIVOLI   BUNDAMBA
WACOL   RICHLANDS   WILLAWONG
UNDERWOOD
LEICHHARDT   Amberley RAAF Base   Amberley
REDBANK   GOODNA   PALLARA
FOREST LAKE
WOODRIDGE   LOGAN   SPRINGWOOD
LOGAN CENTRAL
SHAILER PARK
REDLAND BAY
POINT TALBURPIN
CHURCHILL   CAMIRA
YAMANTO   SPRINGFIELD
REDBANK PLAINS
FORESTDALE
MARSDEN
VENMAN BUSHLAND NP
CARBROOK WETLANDS CP
MacLel Isla

11
Loamside
Ripley
WHITE ROCK CP
GREENBANK MILITARY CAMP
BRONS PLAINS
PARK RIDGE
BORONIA HEIGHTS
Greenbank
WATERFORD   LOGANHOLME
EAGLEBY
BEENLEIGH   Rum Distillery   Alberton
Lagoon Island
Cabbag Tree Point

12
Flinders   Peak Crossing
Mt Goolman 454m
MT PERRY CP
Mt Blaine 457m
North Maclean
Chambers Flat
Parkridge South
Buccan
Windaroo
YATALA   STAPYLTON
Wolfdene
Ormeau
Woongoolba
Norwell   Steigli
Jacob Well

13
Limestone Ridge
Flinders Peak 679m
FLINDERS PEAK
Mt Welcome 332m   Mt Elliot 436m
Jimboomba
TO BEAUDESERT
Joins map 599
TO NERANG
Sanctuary Cove

For more detail on Central Brisbane see page 597

0 10 20 30 40 km

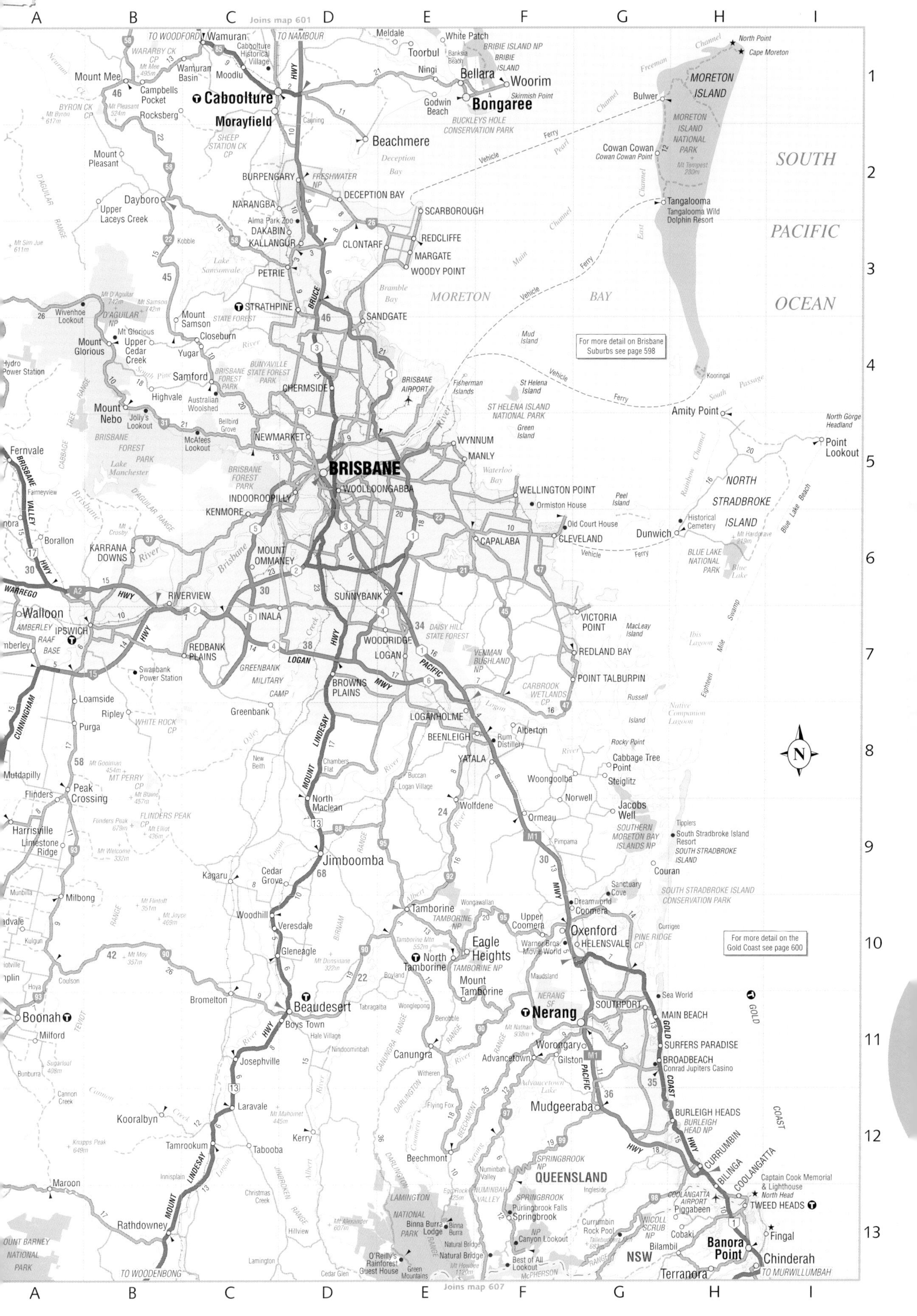

A B C D E F G H I
1 2 3 4 5 6 7 8 9 10 11 12 13
Joins map 601
Joins map 607
TO WOODFORD
Wamuran
TO NAMBOUR
Meldale
White Patch
BRIBIE ISLAND NP
BRIBIE ISLAND
North Point
Cape Moreton
WARARBY CK CP
Mt Mee 495m
Wamuran Basin
Caboolture Historical Village
Toorbul
Banksia Beach
Mount Mee
Moodlu
Ningi
Bellara
Woorim
Skirmish Point
Bongaree
Godwin Beach
Campbells Pocket
Caboolture
BYRON CK CP
Mt Byron 617m
Mt Pleasant 524m
Rocksberg
Morayfield
Caboolture
BUCKLEYS HOLE CONSERVATION PARK
Freeman
Channel
Bulwer
MORETON ISLAND
MORETON ISLAND NATIONAL PARK
Mt Tempest 280m
SHEEP STATION CK CP
Caboolture
Beachmere
Deception Bay
Ferry
Vehicle
Pearl
Cowan Cowan
Cowan Cowan Point
Mount Pleasant
D'AGUILAR RANGE
BURPENGARY
FRESHWATER NP
DECEPTION BAY
SOUTH PACIFIC OCEAN
Dayboro
Upper Laceys Creek
NARANGBA
Alma Park Zoo
DAKABIN
KALLANGUR
SCARBOROUGH
Tangalooma
Tangalooma Wild Dolphin Resort
Mt Sim Jue 611m
Kobble
REDCLIFFE
MARGATE
WOODY POINT
CLONTARF
Lake Samsonvale
PETRIE
Main Channel
East Channel
Bramble Bay
MORETON BAY
Mt D'Aguilar 742m
Mt Samson 742m
D'AGUILAR NP
Wivenhoe Lookout
STRATHPINE
BRUCE HWY
SANDGATE
Mount Samson
STATE FOREST
Mount Glorious
Mt Glorious
Upper Cedar Creek
Closeburn
Yugar
Mud Island
For more detail on Brisbane Suburbs see page 598
Hydro Power Station
Samford
BRISBANE FOREST PARK
BUNYAVILLE STATE FOREST PARK
South Pine River
CHERMSIDE
BRISBANE AIRPORT
Fisherman Islands
St Helena Island
ST HELENA ISLAND NATIONAL PARK
Kooringal
South Passage
Highvale
Australian Woolshed
Mount Nebo
Jolly's Lookout
BRISBANE FOREST PARK
Bellbird Grove
McAfees Lookout
NEWMARKET
Green Island
Amity Point
North Gorge Headland
Point Lookout
Fernvale
BRISBANE VALLEY HWY
Lake Manchester
BRISBANE
WYNNUM
MANLY
Waterloo Bay
Rainbow Channel
NORTH STRADBROKE ISLAND
Fairneyview
BRISBANE FOREST PARK
INDOOROOPILLY
WOOLLOONGABBA
WELLINGTON POINT
Ormiston House
Peel Island
Blue Lake Beach
KENMORE
Old Court House
CLEVELAND
Historical Cemetery
Dunwich
Mt Hardgrave 219m
Borallon
KARRANA DOWNS
MOUNT OMMANEY
CAPALABA
Vehicle
Ferry
BLUE LAKE NATIONAL PARK
Blue Lake
WARREGO HWY
RIVERVIEW
SUNNYBANK
VICTORIA POINT
MacLeay Island
Walloon
AMBERLEY RAAF BASE
IPSWICH
INALA
DAISY HILL STATE FOREST
Ibis Lagoon
Eighteen Mile Swamp
REDBANK PLAINS
LOGAN
WOODRIDGE
LOGAN
VENMAN BUSHLAND NP
REDLAND BAY
POINT TALBURPIN
Swanbank Power Station
GREENBANK MILITARY CAMP
BROWNS PLAINS
PACIFIC MWY
CARBROOK WETLANDS CP
Russell Island
Native Companion Lagoon
CUNNINGHAM
Loamside
Ripley
WHITE ROCK CP
Greenbank
LOGANHOLME
Alberton
Purga
BEENLEIGH
Rum Distillery
Rocky Point
Cabbage Tree Point
Steiglitz
Mt Goolman 454m
MT PERRY CP
Mt Blaine 457m
New Beith
Chambers Flat
YATALA
Buccan
Logan Village
Woongoolba
Norwell
Mutdapilly
Flinders
Peak Crossing
MOUNT LINDESAY
North Maclean
Wolfdene
Ormeau
Jacobs Well
SOUTHERN MORETON BAY ISLANDS NP
Tipplers
South Stradbroke Island Resort
SOUTH STRADBROKE ISLAND
FLINDERS PEAK CP
Flinders Peak 679m
Mt Elliot 436m
Harrisville
Limestone Ridge
Mt Welcome 332m
Jimboomba
Pimpama
Couran
Kagaru
Cedar Grove
Sanctuary Cove
SOUTH STRADBROKE ISLAND CONSERVATION PARK
Munbilla
Milbong
Mt Flintoff 351m
Mt Joyce 469m
Woodhill
Tamborine
Wongawallan
Dreamworld
Coomera
Veresdale
TAMBORINE NP
Upper Coomera
Oxenford
HELENSVALE
Currigee
PINE RIDGE CP
Kulgun
Gleneagle
Mt Dorrsinane 322m
Tamborine Mtn 552m
North Tamborine
Eagle Heights
Warner Bros Movie World
For more detail on the Gold Coast see page 600
Mt Moy 357m
TAMBORINE NP
Boyland
Maudsland
Coulson
Bromelton
Beaudesert
Mount Tamborine
NERANG SF
Nerang
SOUTHPORT
Sea World
MAIN BEACH
GOLD
Hoya
Boonah
Tabragalba
Wonglepong
Boys Town
Hale Village
Benobble
Mt Nathan 938m
Milford
Nindooinbah
SURFERS PARADISE
Worongary
Advancetown
Gilston
BROADBEACH
Conrad Jupiters Casino
Josephville
Canungra
Sugarloaf 408m
Bunburra
Witheren
Advancetown Lake
PACIFIC M1
GOLD COAST HWY
Cannon Creek
Laravale
Flying Fox
Mudgeeraba
BURLEIGH HEADS
BURLEIGH HEAD NP
Mt Mahomet 445m
Kooralbyn
Knapps Peak 649m
Tamrookum
Kerry
Beechmont
CURRUMBIN
COAST
Tabooba
BEECHMONT
Numinbah Valley
SPRINGBROOK NP
QUEENSLAND
BILINGA
COOLANGATTA
Captain Cook Memorial & Lighthouse
North Head
Innisplain
Ingleside
Maroon
Christmas Creek
Egg Rock 425m
NUMINBAH VALLEY
LAMINGTON NATIONAL PARK
SPRINGBROOK
Purlingbrook Falls
Springbrook
COOLANGATTA AIRPORT
Piggabeen
TWEED HEADS
Rathdowney
Mt Alexander 607m
Hillview
Binna Burra Lodge
Binna Burra
Currumbin Rock Pool
NICOLL SCRUB NP
Cobaki
Fingal
MOUNT BARNEY NATIONAL PARK
Canyon Lookout
Bilambil
Banora Point
Chinderah
Natural Bridge
O'Reilly's Rainforest Guest House
Green Mountains
Mt Howbree 1120m
Best of All Lookout
McPHERSON RANGE
NSW
Terranora
TO MURWILLUMBAH
Lamington
Cedar Glen
TO WOODENBONG

0 2 4 6 8 10 km

A B C D E F G H I

Joins map 599

1

TO BRISBANE
PACIFIC
Oakey
Creek
River
SANCTUARY COVE
Houseboat Hire and Cruises
COOMERA ISLAND
Sanctuary Cove
SANTA BARBARA
The Palms Golf Course
Dreamworld
HOPE ISLAND
The Pines Golf Course
Coomera
Wongawallan Mtn 376m
SOUTHERN MORETON BAY ISLANDS NP
Sovereign Island
Brown Island
SOUTH STRADBROKE ISLAND CONSERVATION PARK
SOUTH STRADBROKE ISLAND
Currigee

2

TAMBORINE
OXENFORD
95
RD
Upper Coomera
Oxenford
M1
OXENFORD RD
Saltwater Creek
Coomera River
BOYKAMBIL
SOUTHPORT
COOMBABAH
PARADISE POINT
HOLLYWELL
Ephraim Island
RD
DR
PINE RIDGE CP
Crab Is
Broadwater
The Spit
Ferry

3

MAUDSLAND
BEAUDESERT
NERANG
RD
RD
90
Maudsland
Mount Nathan
Coomera River
HELENSVALE
Warner Bros. Movie World
Wet 'n' Wild Water World
Coombabah Lake
COOMBABAH LAKE CONSERVATION PARK
PACIFIC
GOLD
COAST
HWY
Gaven
5
RUNAWAY BAY
BIGGERA WATERS
Lands End
Wave Break Is
Porpoise Point
Nerang Head
OXLEY
SOUTH

4

Coomera RD
River
NERANG
Nerang State Forest
Coombabah
GAVEN WAY
18
Parkwood International Golf Course
SMITH
ERNEST
OLSEN
Griffith University
Showgrounds
SOUTHPORT
LABRADOR
AV
ST
10
THE SPIT
Sea World
Marina Mirage
Mariners Cove
Southport Yacht Club
PACIFIC

5

BEAUDESERT
Mt Nathan 938m
NERANG
RD
90
Nerang
M1
SOUTHPORT
MOLENDINAR
20
NERANG
ASHMORE
24
Nerang River
Carrara Sports Complex
Royal Pines Resort
Gold Coast Arts Centre
Southport Golf Course
Mt Widgee
6
9
BUNDALL
SURFERS PARADISE
27
Ripleys Believe It or Not Museum
Macintosh Island Park
Narrow Neck
MAIN BEACH
PACIFIC

6

BEECHMONT
RD
97
Latimers Crossing
NERANG
Gilston
Advancetown
Worongary
GILSTON
CARRARA
BROADBEACH
Tigermoth Joy Flights
Palm Meadows Golf Course
BENOWA
Gold Coast Turf Club
BROADBEACH WATERS
Conrad Jupiters Casino
Cascade Park & Gardens
GOLD
OCEAN

7

MURWILLUMBAH
NERANG
RD
Cedar Lake Country Club
Hinze Dam
GILSTON
GILSTON – MUDGEERABA (WORONGARY RD)
PACIFIC
GOLDCOAST
SPRINGBROOK
MERRIMAC
CLEAR ISLAND WATERS
MERMAID WATERS
Worongary Creek
Mudgeeraba Creek
M1
MERMAID BEACH
Oasis Shopping Resort & Monorail
BROADBEACH
Pacific Fair Shopping Resort
ST
HWY

8

12
Advancetown Lake
Mudgeeraba
Balloon Down Under
SPRINGBROOK
99
Wallaby Ck
Robina
Bond University
STEPHENS
REEDY
BERMUDA
CREEK
BURLEIGH KNOLL CP
MIAMI
Nobbys Beach
North Burleigh Beach
BURLEIGH WATERS
BURLEIGH HEADS
Burleigh Head
BURLEIGH HEAD NATIONAL PARK
COAST
COAST
3
8

9

97
NERANG
Boomerang Farm Golf Course
Reedy Creek
Springbrook Creek
3
WEST BURLEIGH
Reedy Creek
ANDREWS
M1
MWY
10
22
David Fleay Wildlife Park
Tallebudgera Beach
PALM BEACH
Palm Beach
Currumbin Point
Currumbin Beach
CURRUMBIN
World of Bees
Currumbin Wildlife Sanctuary
HWY
GOLD

10

Mt Wunburra 572m
17
COAST
30
GOLD
RANGE
19
Neranwood
SPRINGBROOK NP
Wunburra Lookout
Little Nerang Dam
Tallebudgera Creek
Tallebudgera
Tallebudgera Valley
Tallebudgera
ELANORA
CURRUMBIN WATERS
TUGUN
BILINGA
Kirra Beach
Point Danger
COOLANGATTA
Captain Cook Memorial Lighthouse
North Hill
COAST

11

WOMBURRA
RD
99
Horseshoe Falls
Purlingbrook Falls
SPRINGBROOK
Ingleside
Baily Mtn 488m
Tallebudgera Dam
Tallebudgera
CREEK
CURRUMBIN
Olson's Bird Gardens
98
CREEK
RD
NICOLL SCRUB NP
QUEENSLAND
NEW SOUTH WALES
Piggabeen
Cobaki
Cobaki Broadwater
The New Seagulls
Sullivan's Pioneer Park
COOLANGATTA AIRPORT
TWEED HEADS
Twin Towns Services Club
Minjungbal Aboriginal Cultural Centre
TWEED HEADS

12

SPRINGBROOK
RD
Springbrook
Hardy's Lookout
NATIONAL
Mt Gannon 632m
Information Centre
Canyon Lookout
PARK
(Springbrook Section)
Schuster's Lookout
Currumbin Rock Pool
CREEK
TOMEWIN
CURRUMBIN
Cobaki
Terranora
Terranora Golf Resort
BILAMBIL
Club Banora
BYPASS
10
Banora Point
A1
HEADS

13

SPRINGBROOK NATIONAL PARK
Natural Bridge
(Natural Bridge Section)
Mt Springbrook 946m
Goomoolahra Falls
SPRINGBROOK NATIONAL PARK
(Mt Cougal Section)
NUMINBAH NATURE RESERVE
Camp Eden Health Resort
Mt Cougal
Best of All Lookout
McPHERSON
TOMEWIN CP
Tomewin
Arthur Freeman Lookout
RANGE
Tallebudgera Mtn 683m
Mt Sommerville 352m
John Hogan Rainforest
Urliup
Bilambil
NICOLL SCRUB NP
Cobaki
Bilambil
TERRANORA
Terranora
Broadwater
PACIFIC
Tweed
Chinderah
1
TO MURWILLUMBAH

A B C D E F G H I

N

SOUTH

PACIFIC

OCEAN

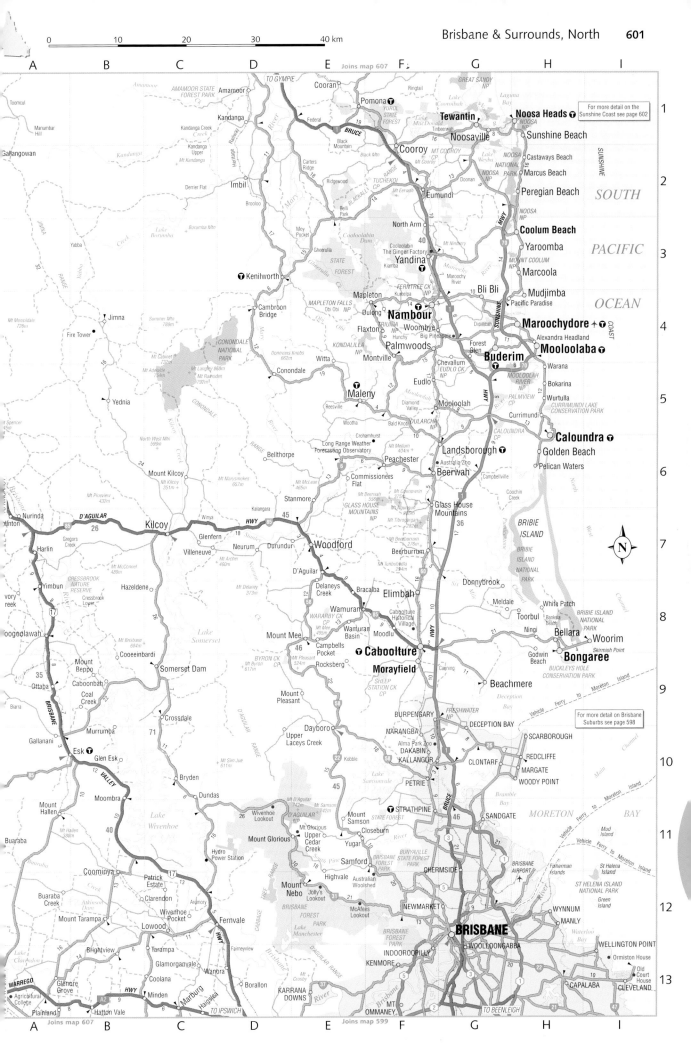

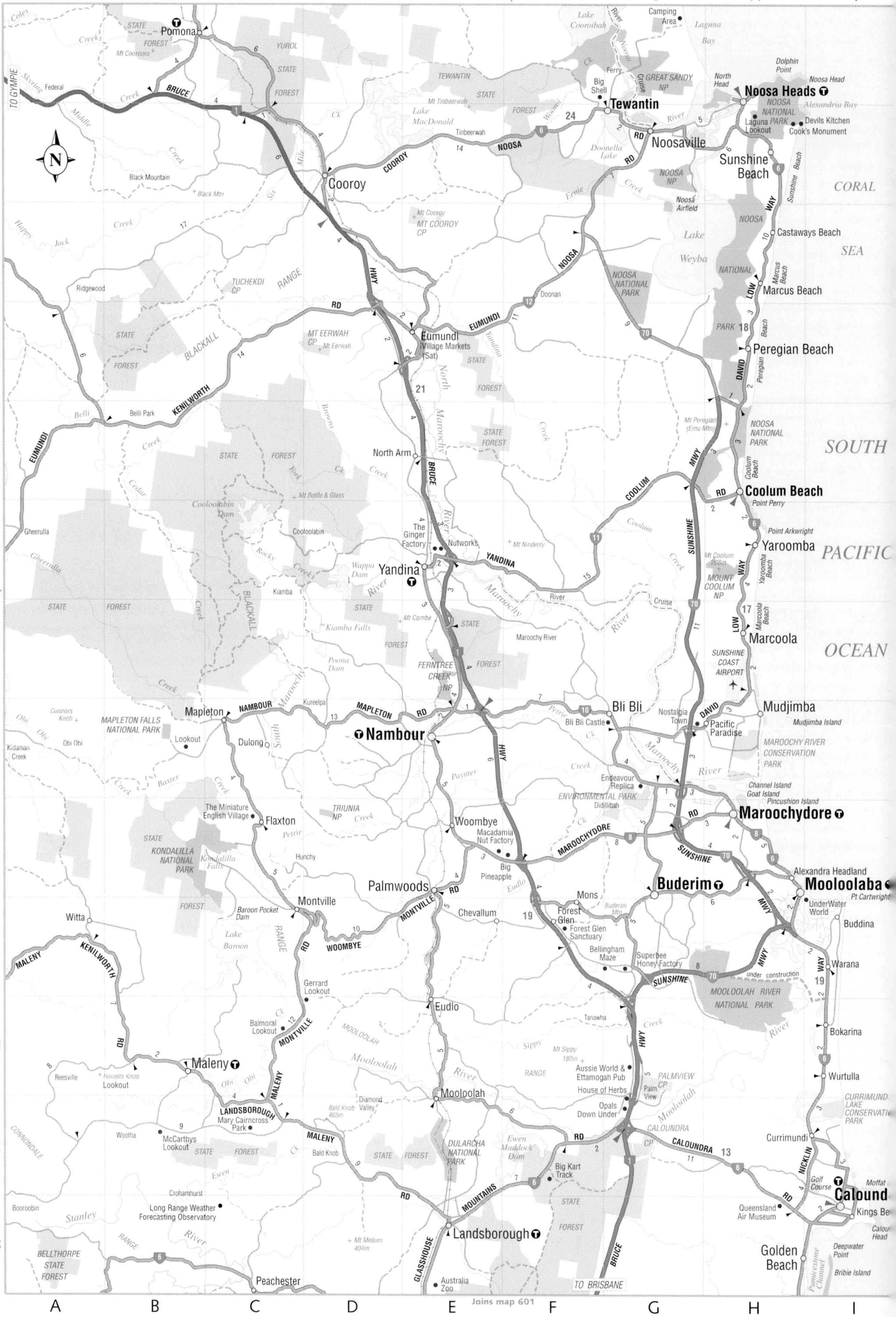

0   2   4   6   8   10 km

A   B   C   D   E Joins map 607 **F   G   H   I**

1

Pomona

TO GYMPIE

BRUCE

Tewantin

Camping Area

Laguna Bay

Dolphin Point

Noosa Heads

Noosa Head

Alexandria Bay

2

Noosaville

Sunshine Beach

Cooroy

CORAL

3

CP

Doonan

Marcus Beach

SEA

4

Eumundi
Village Markets

EUMUNDI

Peregian Beach

5

North Arm

BRUCE

Coolum Beach

Point Perry

SOUTH

6

The Ginger Factory

Nutworks

Yandina

Yandina

Point Arkwright

Yaroomba

PACIFIC

7

Marcoola

OCEAN

8

Mapleton

NAMBOUR

MAPLETON RD

Nambour

Bli Bli

SUNSHINE COAST AIRPORT

Pacific Paradise

Mudjimba

Mudjimba Island

9

Flaxton

Woombye

MAROOCHYDORE

Maroochydore

Alexandra Headland

Mooloolaba

Buddina

Palmwoods

Montville

Buderim

Mons

Forest Glen

Warana

10

MALENY

KENILWORTH

Witta

WOOMBYE

MONTVILLE

Eudlo

Bokarina

11

Maleny

Mooloolah

Wurtulla

12

LANDSBOROUGH

MALENY

Big Kart Track

CALOUNDRA

Currimundi

Calound

13

BELLTHORPE STATE FOREST

Peachester

Landsborough

GLASSHOUSE MOUNTAINS

Australia Zoo

TO BRISBANE

Golden Beach

Bribie Island

A   B   C   D   E Joins map 601 **F   G   H   I**

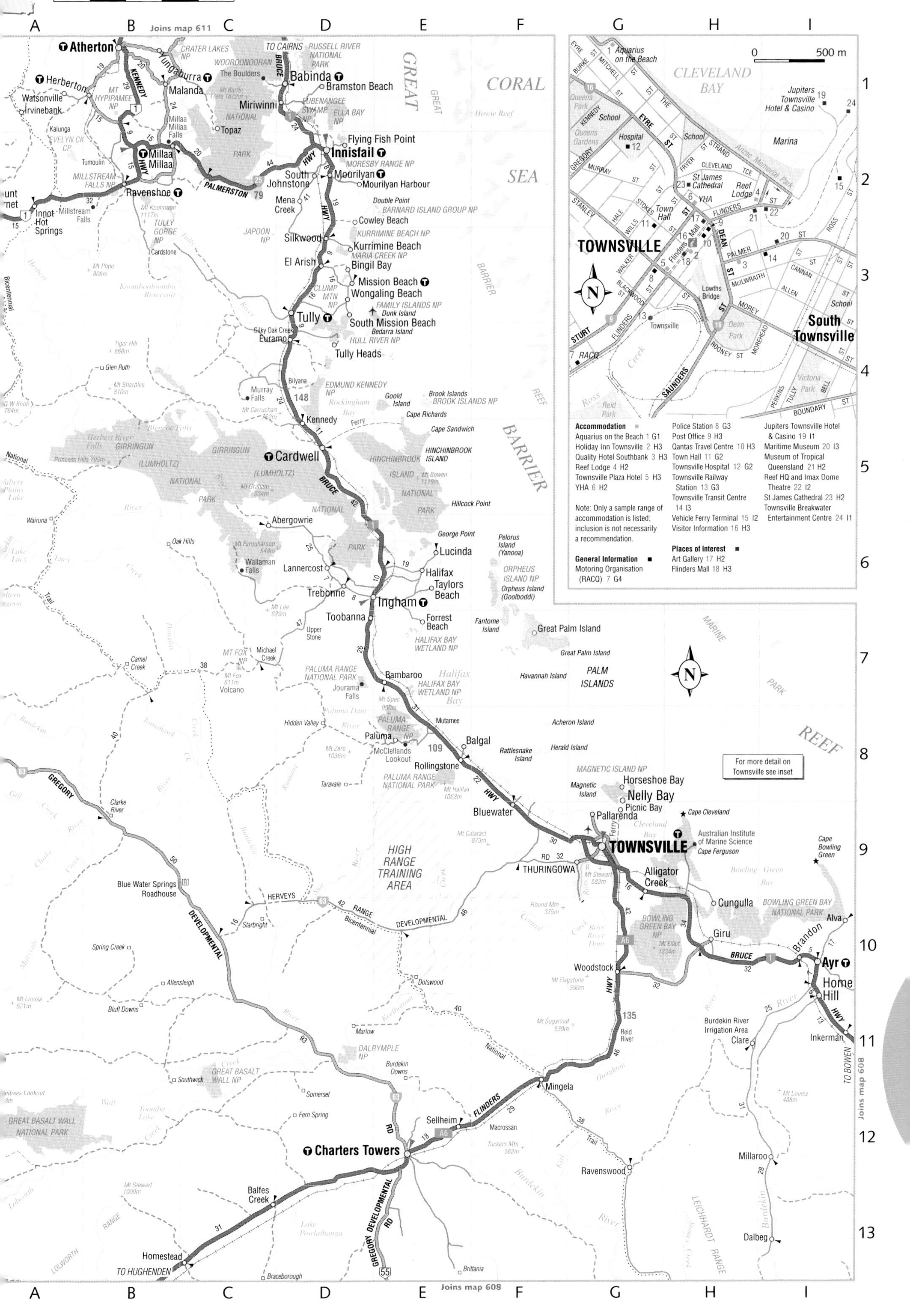

0 10 20 30 40 50 km

Map labels (main map)

Atherton, Herberton, Watsonville, Irvinebank, Kalunga, Tumoulin, Malanda, Yungaburra, The Boulders, Topaz, Millaa Millaa, Ravenshoe, Innot Hot Springs, Millstream Falls NP, Cardstone, Babinda, Bramston Beach, Miriwinni, Flying Fish Point, Innisfail, South Johnstone, Mourilyan, Mourilyan Harbour, Mena Creek, Cowley Beach, Double Point, Silkwood, Kurrimine Beach, El Arish, Bingil Bay, Mission Beach, Wongaling Beach, Tully, South Mission Beach, Euramo, Tully Heads, Murray Falls, Bilyana, Kennedy, Gould Island, Brook Islands, Cape Richards, Cape Sandwich, Abergowrie, George Point, Pelorus Island (Yanooa), Lucinda, Oak Hills, Wallaman Falls, Lannercost, Halifax, Taylors Beach, Trebonne, Ingham, Orpheus Island (Goolboddi), Toobanna, Forrest Beach, Fantome Island, Great Palm Island, Upper Stone, Bambaroo, Halifax Bay Wetland NP, Havannah Island, Palm Islands, Michael Creek, Jourama Falls, Mt Spec, Paluma, Mutarnee, Acheron Island, Herald Island, Hidden Valley, McClellans Lookout, Rollingstone, Balgal, Rattlesnake Island, Taravale, Bluewater, Magnetic Island NP, Horseshoe Bay, Nelly Bay, Picnic Bay, Pallarenda, Magnetic Island, Cape Cleveland, Blue Water Springs Roadhouse, Starbright, Townsville, Thuringowa, Australian Institute of Marine Science, Cape Ferguson, Alligator Creek, Cungulla, Cape Bowling Green, Spring Creek, Giru, Alva, Allensleigh, Woodstock, Bluff Downs, Ayr, Home Hill, Burdekin River Irrigation Area, Clare, Inkerman, Dotswood, Marlow, Reid River, Somerset, Southwick, Mingela, Ravenswood, Millaroo, Sellheim, Macrossan, Charters Towers, Balfes Creek, Brittania, Homestead, Braceborough, Dalbeg

GREAT BARRIER REEF, CORAL SEA

Inset: Townsville

TOWNSVILLE, South Townsville, Cleveland Bay, Aquarius on the Beach, Jupiters Townsville Hotel & Casino, Marina, Queens Gardens, Hospital, St James Cathedral, Reef Lodge, Town Hall, Lowths Bridge, Townsville, Dean Park, Victoria Park

Legend

Accommodation
- Aquarius on the Beach 1 G1
- Holiday Inn Townsville 2 H3
- Quality Hotel Southbank 3 H3
- Reef Lodge 4 H2
- Townsville Plaza Hotel 5 H3
- YHA 6 H2

Note: Only a sample range of accommodation is listed; inclusion is not necessarily a recommendation.

General Information
- Motoring Organisation (RACQ) 7 G4

- Police Station 8 G3
- Post Office 9 H3
- Qantas Travel Centre 10 H3
- Town Hall 11 G2
- Townsville Hospital 12 G2
- Townsville Railway Station 13 G3
- Townsville Transit Centre 14 I3
- Vehicle Ferry Terminal 15 I2
- Visitor Information 16 H3

- Jupiters Townsville Hotel & Casino 19 I1
- Maritime Museum 20 I3
- Museum of Tropical Queensland 21 H2
- Reef HQ and Imax Dome Theatre 22 I2
- St James Cathedral 23 H2
- Townsville Breakwater Entertainment Centre 24 I1

Places of Interest
- Art Gallery 17 H2
- Flinders Mall 18 H3

For more detail on Townsville see inset

Joins map 611
Joins map 608
Joins map 608

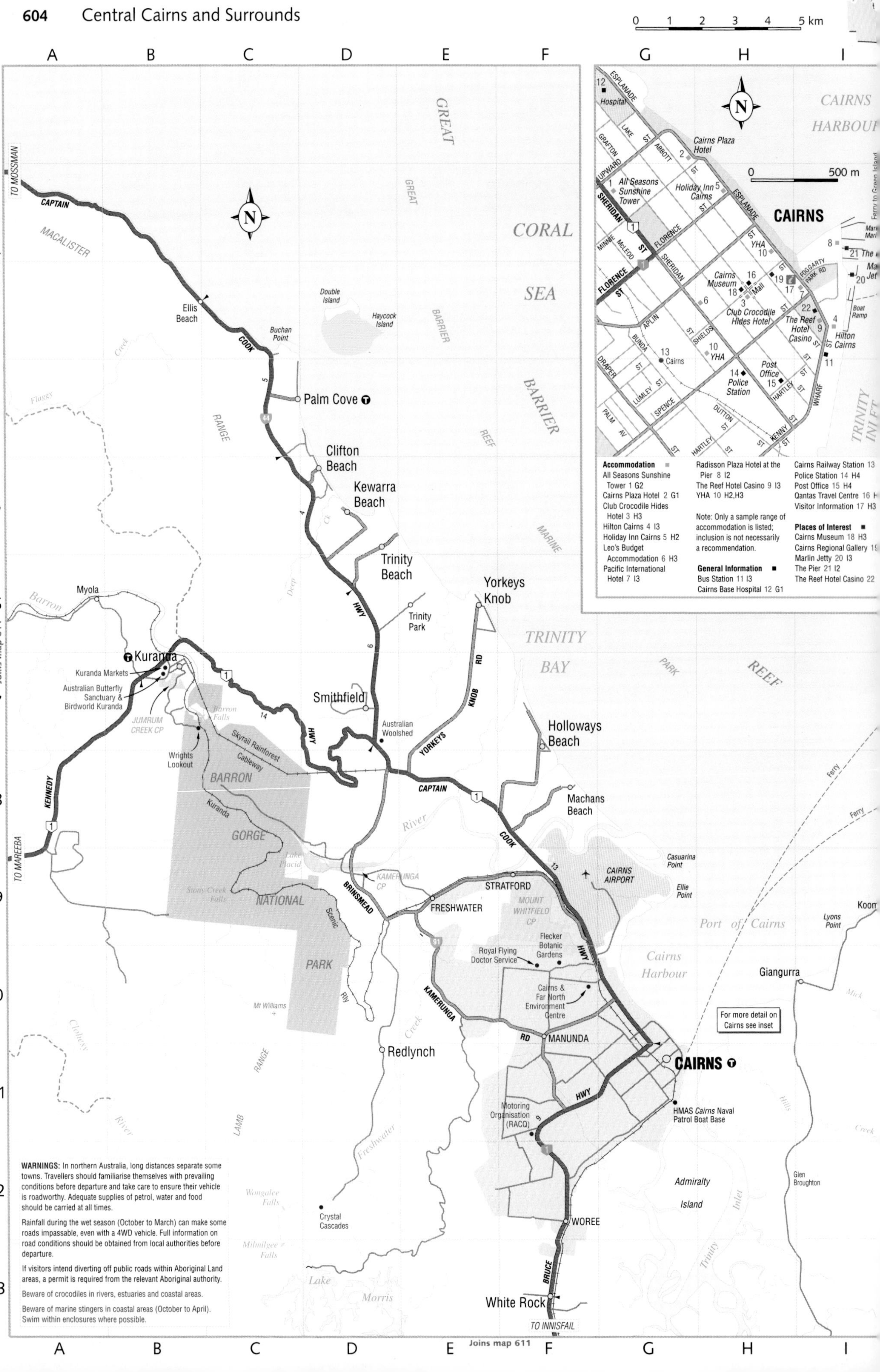
0 1 2 3 4 5 km
A B C D E F G H I
1 2 3 4 5 6 7 8 9 10 11 12 13
TO MOSSMAN
Joins map 605
Joins map 611
CAPTAIN COOK HWY
MACALISTER RANGE
GREAT CORAL SEA
GREAT BARRIER REEF MARINE PARK
Ellis Beach
Double Island
Haycock Island
Buchan Point
Palm Cove
Clifton Beach
Kewarra Beach
Trinity Beach
Trinity Park
Yorkeys Knob
YORKEYS KNOB RD
TRINITY BAY
Holloways Beach
Machans Beach
Smithfield
Australian Woolshed
Myola
Barron
Kuranda
Kuranda Markets
Australian Butterfly Sanctuary & Birdworld Kuranda
JUMRUM CREEK CP
Barron Falls
Wrights Lookout
Skyrail Rainforest Cableway
BARRON GORGE NATIONAL PARK
Kuranda Scenic Rly
Lake Placid
Stony Creek Falls
KENNEDY HWY
TO MAREEBA
KAMERUNGA CP
BRINSMEAD
FRESHWATER
STRATFORD
MOUNT WHITFIELD CP
CAIRNS AIRPORT
Casuarina Point
Ellie Point
Port of Cairns
Cairns Harbour
Royal Flying Doctor Service
Flecker Botanic Gardens
Cairns & Far North Environment Centre
KAMERUNGA RD
MANUNDA
CAIRNS
Redlynch
Mt Williams
LAMB RANGE
Freshwater Creek
Motoring Organisation (RACQ)
HMAS Cairns Naval Patrol Boat Base
Admiralty Island
Trinity Inlet
Glen Broughton
Giangurra
Lyons Point
Koombal
For more detail on Cairns see inset
Crystal Cascades
Wongalee Falls
Milmilgee Falls
Lake Morris
WOREE
BRUCE HWY
White Rock
TO INNISFAIL
Joins map 611
Ferry
CAIRNS
CAIRNS HARBOUR
TRINITY INLET
0 500 m
ESPLANADE
Hospital
Cairns Plaza Hotel
All Seasons Sunshine Tower
Holiday Inn Cairns
SHERIDAN ST
FLORENCE ST
YHA
Cairns Museum
Mall
Club Crocodile Hides Hotel
The Reef Hotel Casino
Hilton Cairns
Post Office
Police Station
Boat Ramp
Marlin Jetty
The Pier
Ferry to Green Island
WHARF ST
Accommodation
All Seasons Sunshine Tower 1 G2
Cairns Plaza Hotel 2 G1
Club Crocodile Hides Hotel 3 H3
Hilton Cairns 4 I3
Holiday Inn Cairns 5 H2
Leo's Budget Accommodation 6 H3
Pacific International Hotel 7 I3
Radisson Plaza Hotel at the Pier 8 I2
The Reef Hotel Casino 9 I3
YHA 10 H2,H3
Note: Only a sample range of accommodation is listed; inclusion is not necessarily a recommendation.
General Information
Bus Station 11 I3
Cairns Base Hospital 12 G1
Cairns Railway Station 13
Police Station 14 H4
Post Office 15 H4
Qantas Travel Centre 16 H
Visitor Information 17 H3
Places of Interest
Cairns Museum 18 H3
Cairns Regional Gallery 19
Marlin Jetty 20 I3
The Pier 21 I2
The Reef Hotel Casino 22

WARNINGS: In northern Australia, long distances separate some towns. Travellers should familiarise themselves with prevailing conditions before departure and take care to ensure their vehicle is roadworthy. Adequate supplies of petrol, water and food should be carried at all times.

Rainfall during the wet season (October to March) can make some roads impassable, even with a 4WD vehicle. Full information on road conditions should be obtained from local authorities before departure.

If visitors intend diverting off public roads within Aboriginal Land areas, a permit is required from the relevant Aboriginal authority.

Beware of crocodiles in rivers, estuaries and coastal areas.

Beware of marine stingers in coastal areas (October to April). Swim within enclosures where possible.

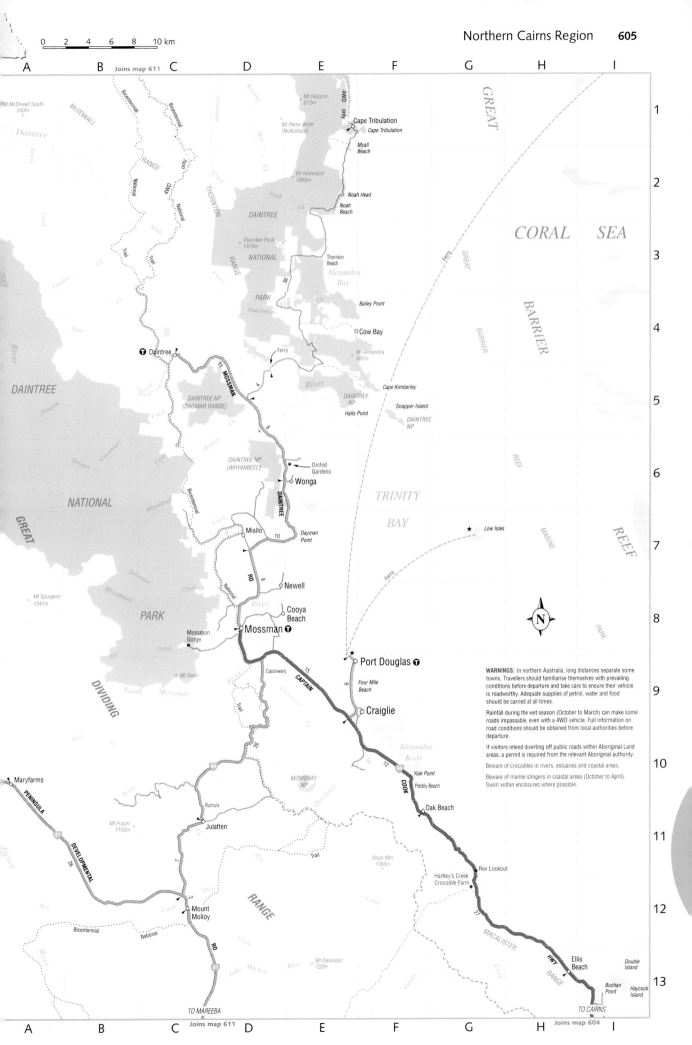

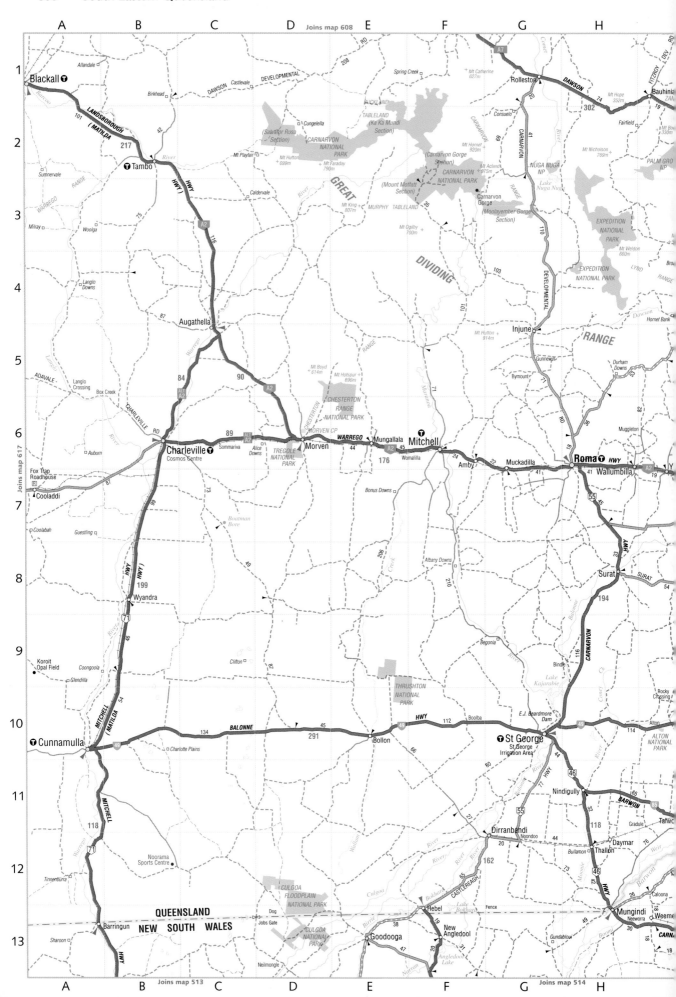

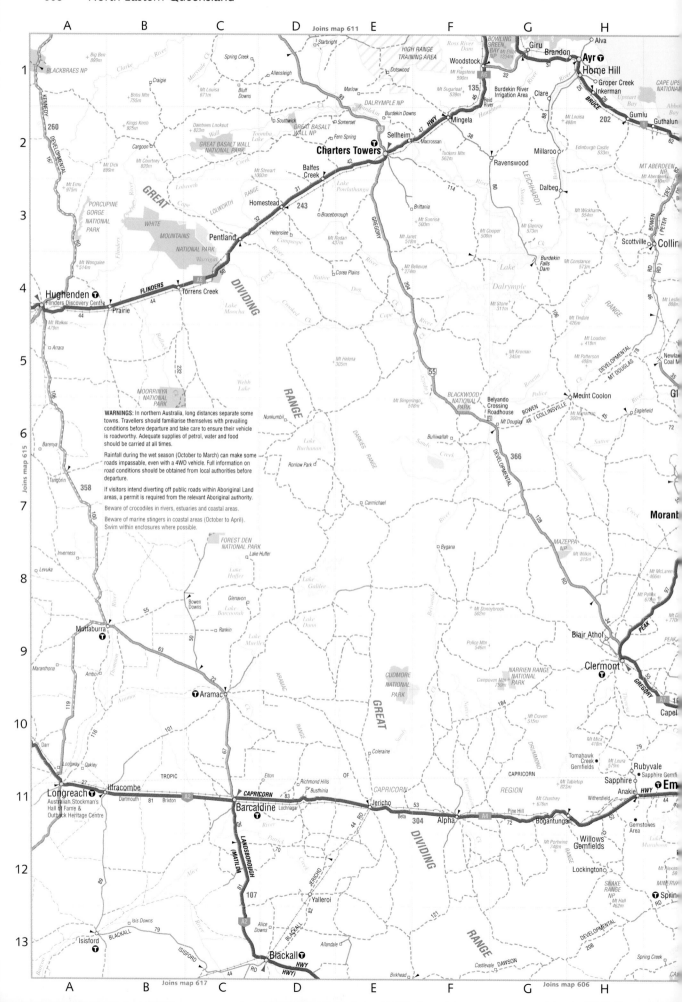

WARNINGS: In northern Australia, long distances separate some towns. Travellers should familiarise themselves with prevailing conditions before departure and take care to ensure their vehicle is roadworthy. Adequate supplies of petrol, water and food should be carried at all times.

Rainfall during the wet season (October to March) can make some roads impassable, even with a 4WD vehicle. Full information on road conditions should be obtained from local authorities before departure.

If visitors intend diverting off public roads within Aboriginal Land areas, a permit is required from the relevant Aboriginal authority.

Beware of crocodiles in rivers, estuaries and coastal areas.

Beware of marine stingers in coastal areas (October to April). Swim within enclosures where possible.

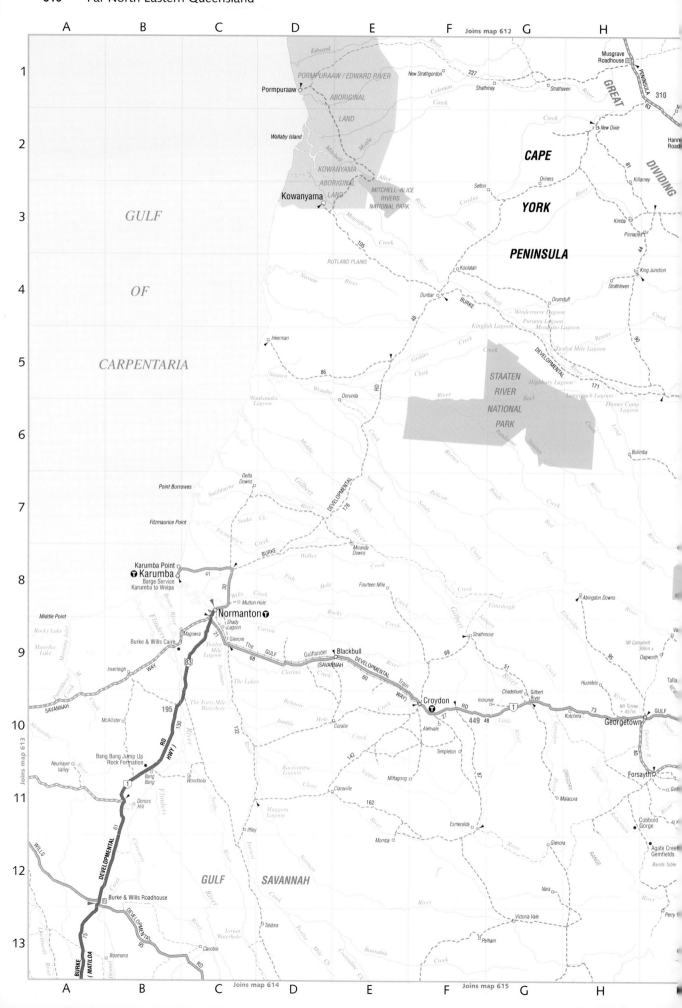

Joins map 612

Joins map 613

Joins map 614

Joins map 615

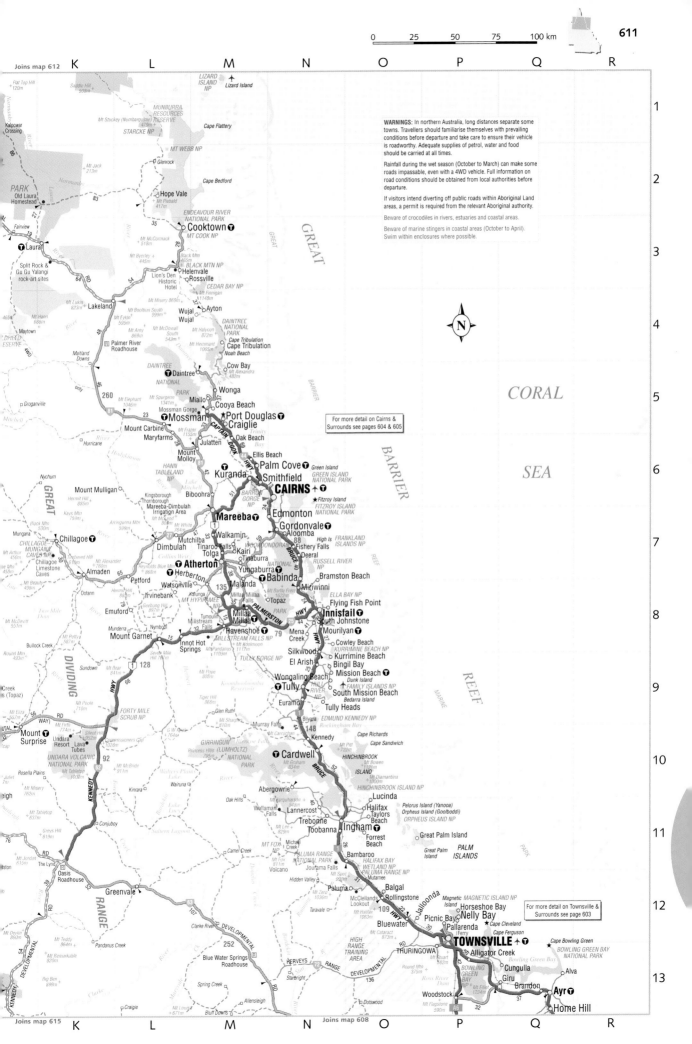

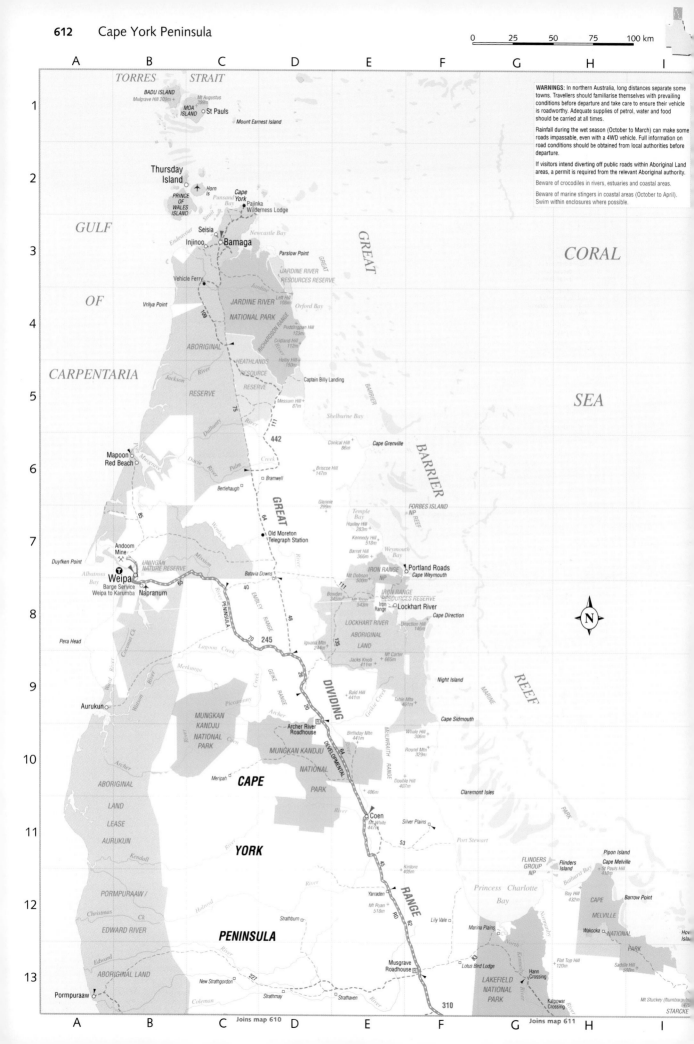

WARNINGS: In northern Australia, long distances separate some towns. Travellers should familiarise themselves with prevailing conditions before departure and take care to ensure their vehicle is roadworthy. Adequate supplies of petrol, water and food should be carried at all times.

Rainfall during the wet season (October to March) can make some roads impassable, even with a 4WD vehicle. Full information on road conditions should be obtained from local authorities before departure.

If visitors intend diverting off public roads within Aboriginal Land areas, a permit is required from the relevant Aboriginal authority.

Beware of crocodiles in rivers, estuaries and coastal areas.

Beware of marine stingers in coastal areas (October to April). Swim within enclosures where possible.

Joins map 610
Joins map 611

0   25   50   75   100 km

A   B   C   D   E   F   G   H   I

1

GULF OF

2

CARPENTARIA

3

WARNINGS: In northern Australia, long distances separate some towns. Travellers should familiarise themselves with prevailing conditions before departure and take care to ensure their vehicle is roadworthy. Adequate supplies of petrol, water and food should be carried at all times.

Rainfall during the wet season (October to March) can make some roads impassable, even with a 4WD vehicle. Full information on road conditions should be obtained from local authorities before departure.

4

If visitors intend diverting off public roads within Aboriginal Land areas, a permit is required from the relevant Aboriginal authority.

Beware of crocodiles in rivers, estuaries and coastal areas.

Beware of marine stingers in coastal areas (October to April). Swim within enclosures where possible.

N

5

Birri Fishing Resort
MORNINGTON ISLAND
WELLESLEY ISLANDS
Gununa   *ABORIGINAL LAND*
Bountiful Islands

6

FORSYTH ISLANDS
Bentinck Island
SOUTH WELLESLEY ISLANDS
Allen Island
Sweers Island Resort
Sweers Island

Point Burrowes
Delta Downs

7

Wollogorang Station & Roadhouse
495
59
Westmoreland
Hells Gate Roadhouse
Buck Hill 258m

Tarrant Point
Pascoe Inlet
Kangaroo Point

Fitzmaurice Point

Karumba Point
Karumba
Barge Service Karumba to Weipa
41
30

8

CHINA WALL
WAANYI/GARAWA
Nicholson
ABORIGINAL
LAND TRUST

QUEENSLAND
NORTHERN TERRITORY

SAVANNAH (GREAT
80
TOP
72

DOOMADGEE ABORIGINAL LAND

Escott Barramundi Lodge
Burketown
26
Doomadgee
74
NARDOO

Middle Point
Timor Lagoon Rocky Lake
Dingo Dam Marilda Lake

Inverleigh
Burke & Wills Cairn
Magowra
SAVANNAH
155   TOP
Wernadinga

Normanton
Shady Lagoon
Glenore
26
Forty Mile Lagoon

9

WILLS
113
87
Mt Oscar 115m
Almora

DEVELOPMENTAL
BURKETOWN
34

Floraville
Leichhardt Falls
(GREAT   229
McAllister

195
134
The Forty Mile Waterhole
132

10

BOODJAMULLA (LAWN HILL) NATIONAL PARK
Mussellbrook Mining Camp
Lawn Hill
Adels Grove

CONSTANCE RANGE
4WD only
Springvale

74   Gregory Downs
126

Gregory
WILLS
64
Nardoo
141

DEVELOPMENTAL
35
73
Augustus Downs

Neumayer Valley
Bang Bang Jump Up Rock Formation
1
Bang Bang
Donors Hill
Wondoola

GULF   SAVANNAH
Iffley
Maggiera Lagoon

11

SMITHS RANGE
Riversleigh Fossil Site
4WD only

CAMOOWEAL
RD
GREGORY
DOWNS

WILLS
77
DEVELOPMENTAL
61
DEVELOPMENTAL

12

Gallipoli
Norfolk
Thorntonia

Burke & Wills Roadhouse
75

BURKE (MATILDA
95
Boomarra
Canoble
Taldora
Lynham Waterhole

13

Mammoth Mines

Joins map 614
Joins map 610

A   B   C   D   E   F   G   H   I

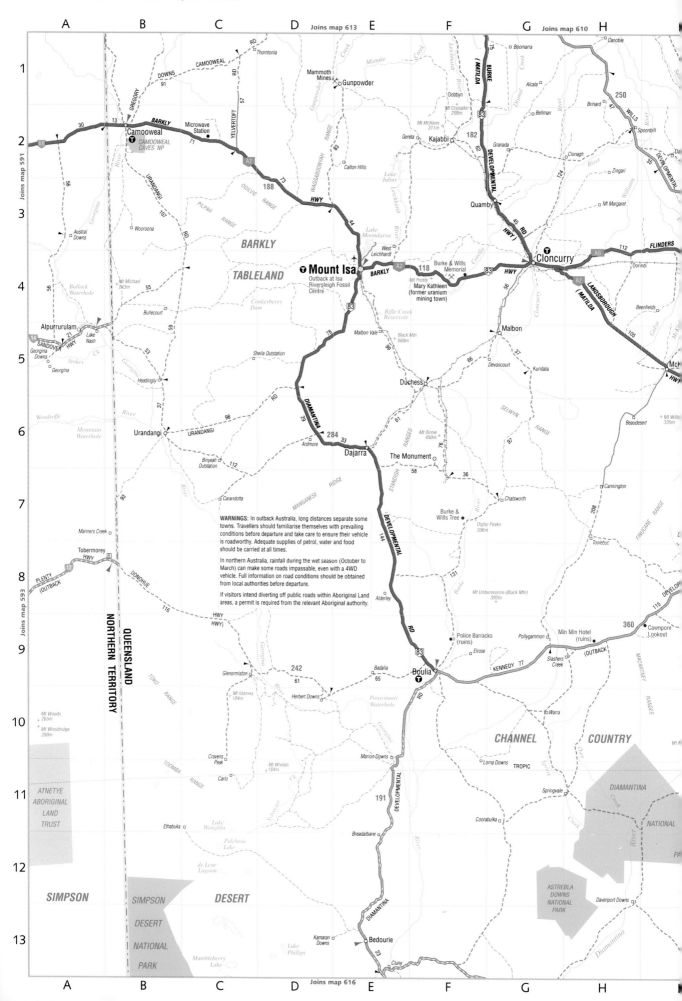

WARNINGS: In outback Australia, long distances separate some towns. Travellers should familiarise themselves with prevailing conditions before departure and take care to ensure their vehicle is roadworthy. Adequate supplies of petrol, water and food should be carried at all times.

In northern Australia, rainfall during the wet season (October to March) can make some roads impassable, even with a 4WD vehicle. Full information on road conditions should be obtained from local authorities before departure.

If visitors intend diverting off public roads within Aboriginal Land areas, a permit is required from the relevant Aboriginal authority.

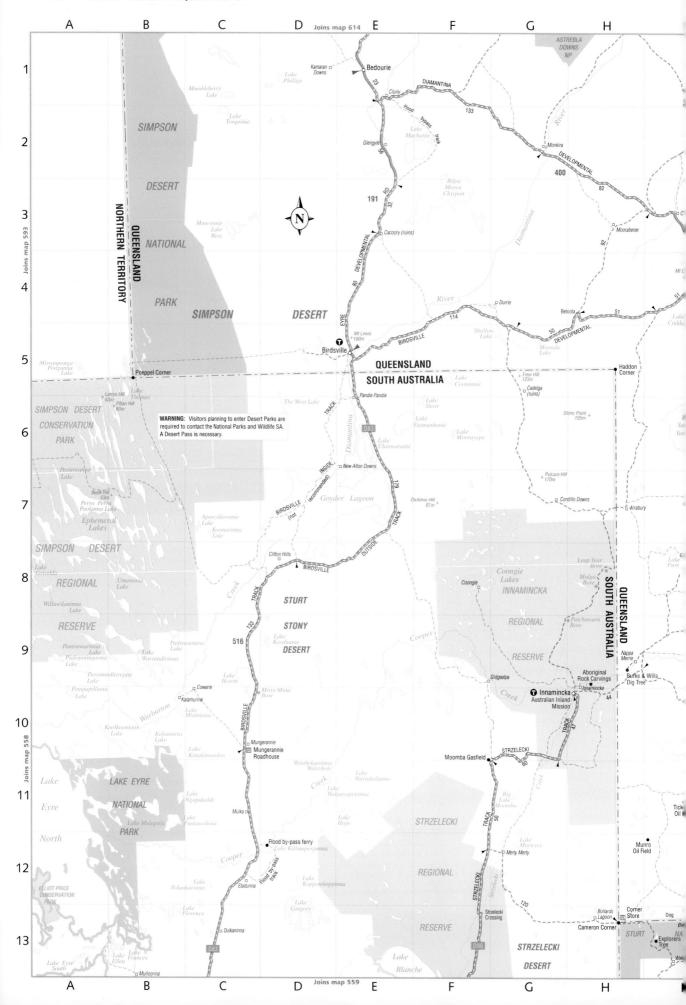

Joins map 614

Joins map 593

Joins map 558

Joins map 559

WARNING: Visitors planning to enter Desert Parks are required to contact the National Parks and Wildlife SA. A Desert Pass is necessary.

0 25 50 75 100 km

K L M N O P Q R

Connemara

Warbreccan

Flodden Hills

Trewalla

Mutti

Bimerah

Stonehenge

79

RD

56

Swan Vale

Arno

Isisford

BLACKALL

79

Isis Downs

Blackall

LANDSBOROUGH
(MATILDA
HWY)

A2

HWY

HWY

Benlidi

44

RD

70

Alice
Downs

1

South Galway

Tanbar

Windorah

Hammond Downs

Jundah

Budgerygar

WELFORD
NATIONAL
PARK

Retreat

Emmet

Aibilbah

Highlands

Yaraka

MACEDON RANGE

Emmet Downs

Mount
Harden

Mt Grey
533m

IDALIA

NATIONAL

PARK

Lorne

Sumnervale

Milray

Langlo
Downs

2

3

DEVELOPMENTAL

WINTON

THOMSON

QUILPIE

JUNDAH

RD

DIAMANTINA

109

95

74

68

50

79

57

38

50

Thomson

Kyabra

Cooper

Clifton

CHEVIOT

RANGE

Bulgroo
Outstation

134

Canaway Downs

GREY

RANGE

HELL HOLE GORGE
NATIONAL
PARK

Wakes Lagoon

Bulloo

Gilmore
Gas Field

Adavale

MARIALA
NATIONAL
PARK

ADAVALE

CHARLEVILLE

179

Varna

Lake
Dartmouth

Ambathala

RD

Langlo
Crossing

Box
Creek

GOWAN

RANGE

BLACKALL

220

Bronte

WARREGO

RANGE

4

5

Keeroongooloo

Malagarga

Mount Howitt

COLEMAN

RANGE

Plevna
Downs

Kyabra

Permanent water
at Kyabra Creek

Earlstoun

DEVELOPMENTAL

103

Bull Creek
Opal Field

427

91

Grenfield

Dungiven

Moble Springs

Boothulla

Auburn

6

Numerous
Opal Fields

Cooma

Mt Bellalie
216m

Oil Fields

67

Eromanga

Quilpie

RD

36

68

Cheepie

45

Cooladdi

Fox Trap
Roadhouse

7

Karmoha

Naccowlah Oil Field

151

MCGREGOR RANGE

Oil Fields

Mount
Margaret

167

Congie

Moble

GREY

RANGE

Tobermory

Tinderry

NOBLEY RANGE

76

Bulloo

RD

35

THARGOMINDAH

Toompine
Roadhouse

Opal Mines

Wareo

Mt Prara
309m

Coolabah

Humeburn

Guestling

8

Bundeena

151

122

Noccundra

Wilson

Lake
Bullawarra

Microwave
Station

QUILPIE

82

127

Koroit
Opal Field

Coongoola

Glendilla

MITCHELL

MATILDA HWY

71

9

Tennappera

Watson
Oil Field

151

Bransby

Orient

Thargomindah

BULLOO

River

LAKE BINDEGOLLY
NATIONAL PARK

Lake
Bindegolly

130

DEVELOPMENTAL

Yowah
Opal Field

Blackgate Opal Field

198

Mud Springs

Eulo

RD

68

Cunnamulla

18

10

11

WARNINGS: In outback Australia, long distances separate some
towns. Travellers should familiarise themselves with prevailing
conditions before departure and take care to ensure their vehicle
is roadworthy. Adequate supplies of petrol, water and food
should be carried at all times.

In central Australia, rainfall can make some roads impassable,
even with a 4WD vehicle. Full information on road conditions
should be obtained from local authorities before departure.

If visitors intend diverting off public roads within Aboriginal Land
areas, a permit is required from the relevant Aboriginal authority.

146

Zenonie

Lake
Wyara

Boorara

122

Calwarro (ruins)

Lake
Numalla

Tinnenburra

MITCHELL

118

71

Dunno

Bulloo

Balloo
Lake

Lake
Callamulcha

Moombidary

CURRAWINYA
NATIONAL
PARK

Lake
Numalla

12

34

Warri Warri
Gate

33

Onepah

Adelaide Gate

Teurika

Berrawinnia
Downs

Ourimbah

Hamilton Gate

QUEENSLAND

NEW SOUTH WALES

Fence

Waverley
Gate

Hungerford

Cattaharra
Basin

Parragundy
Gate

Dog

Fence

Sharoon

Barringun

HWY

13

TASMANIA
MAPS

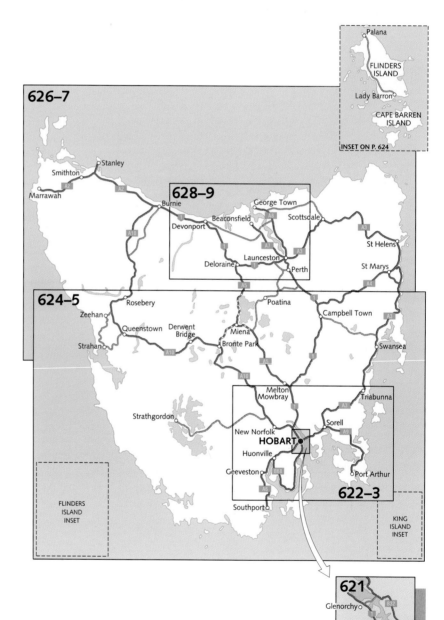

Approximate Distances TASMANIA	Burnie	Campbell Town	Deloraine	Devonport	Geeveston	George Town	Hobart	Launceston	New Norfolk	Oatlands	Port Arthur	Queenstown	Richmond	Rosebery	St Helens	St Marys	Scottsdale	Smithton	Sorell	Strahan	Swansea	Ulverstone
Burnie		200	101	50	391	204	333	152	328	247	432	163	304	110	300	263	222	88	318	185	267	28
Campbell Town	200		99	150	191	119	133	67	128	47	232	304	104	357	122	85	137	288	118	344	67	172
Deloraine	101	99		51	290	103	232	51	227	146	331	207	203	211	199	162	121	189	217	247	166	73
Devonport	50	150	51		341	154	283	102	278	197	382	213	254	160	250	213	172	138	268	235	217	22
Geeveston	391	191	290	341		310	58	258	95	144	157	308	85	361	313	276	328	479	84	348	197	363
George Town	204	119	103	154	310		252	52	247	166	351	310	223	314	182	182	83	292	237	350	186	176
Hobart	333	133	232	283	58	252		200	37	86	99	250	27	303	265	228	270	421	26	290	139	305
Launceston	152	67	51	102	258	52	200		195	114	299	258	171	262	167	130	70	240	185	298	134	124
New Norfolk	328	128	227	278	95	247	37	195		81	136	213	64	266	250	213	265	416	63	253	176	300
Oatlands	247	47	146	197	144	166	86	114	81		175	257	57	310	169	132	184	335	71	297	125	219
Port Arthur	432	232	331	382	157	351	99	299	136	175		349	87	402	312	275	369	520	73	389	186	404
Queenstown	163	304	207	213	308	310	250	258	213	257	349		277	53	426	389	328	253	276	40	389	191
Richmond	304	104	203	254	85	223	27	171	64	57	87	277		330	226	189	241	392	14	317	123	276
Rosebery	110	357	211	160	361	314	303	262	266	310	402	53	330		410	373	332	222	329	75	442	138
St Helens	300	122	199	250	313	182	265	167	250	169	312	426	226	410		37	99	388	240	466	126	272
St Marys	263	85	162	213	276	182	228	130	213	132	275	389	189	373	37		136	351	203	429	89	235
Scottsdale	222	137	121	172	328	83	270	70	265	184	369	328	241	332	99	136		310	255	368	204	194
Smithton	88	288	189	138	479	292	421	240	416	335	520	253	392	222	388	351	310		406	275	355	116
Sorell	318	118	217	268	84	237	26	185	63	71	73	276	14	329	240	203	255	406		316	113	290
Strahan	185	344	247	235	348	350	290	298	253	297	389	40	317	75	466	429	368	275	316		429	213
Swansea	267	67	166	217	197	186	139	134	176	125	186	389	123	442	126	89	204	355	113	429		239
Ulverstone	28	172	73	22	363	176	305	124	300	219	404	191	276	138	272	235	194	116	290	213	239	

Distances on this chart have been calculated over main roads and do not necessarily reflect the shortest route between towns.

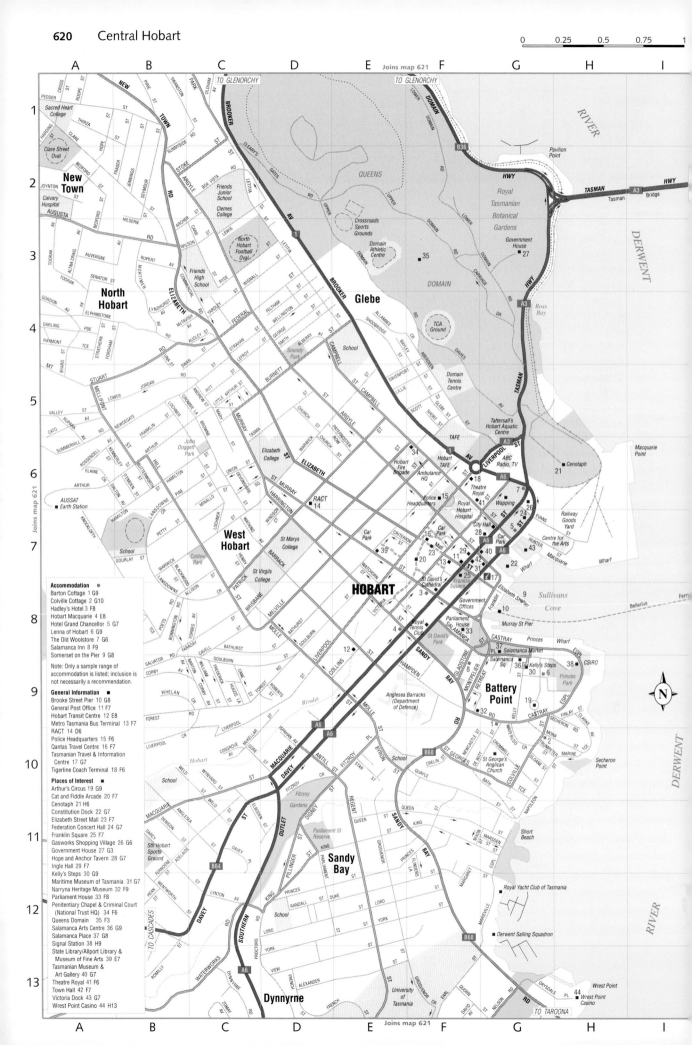

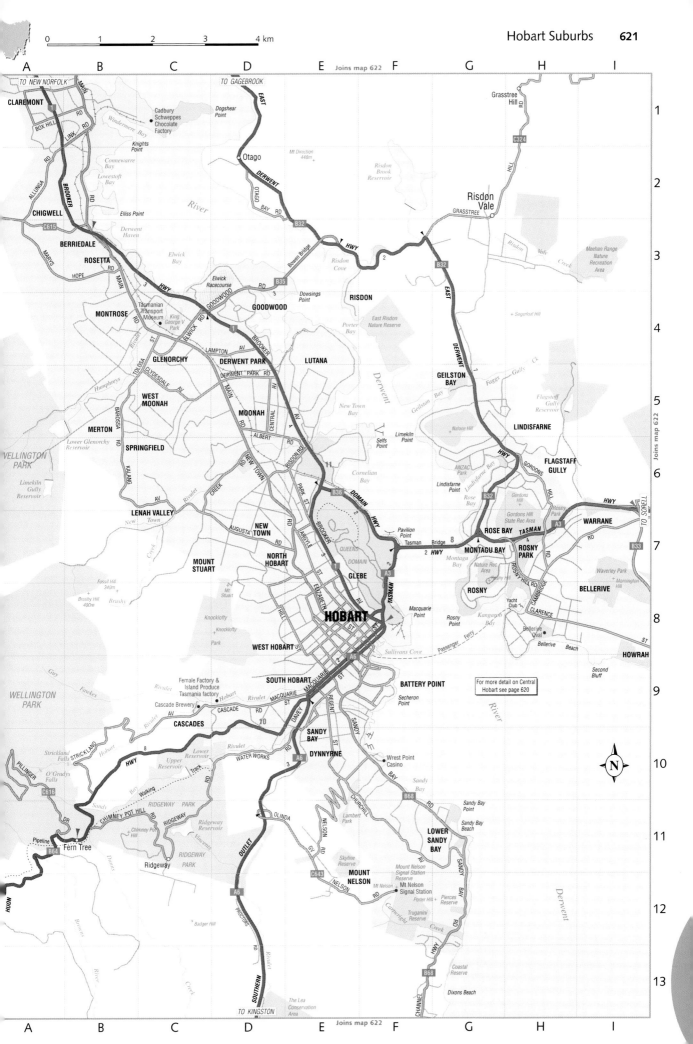

0   1   2   3   4 km

TO NEW NORFOLK

CLAREMONT

BOX HILL

CHIGWELL

BERRIEDALE

ROSETTA

MONTROSE

Cadbury
Schweppes
Chocolate
Factory

Dogshear
Point

TO GAGEBROOK

Otago

DERWENT

Bowen Bridge

River

Elwick
Bay

Knights
Point

Conneware
Bay

Lowestoft
Bay

Elliss Point

Derwent Haven

Elwick
Racecourse

Tasmanian
Transport
Museum

King
George V
Park

GLENORCHY

DERWENT PARK

LAMPTON

GOODWOOD

Dowsings
Point

RISDON

East Risdon
Nature Reserve

Porter
Bay

LUTANA

Mt Direction
448m

Risdon
Brook
Reservoir

Grasstree
Hill

Risdon
Vale

Grasstree

Risdon
Vale
Creek

Meehan Range
Nature
Recreation
Area

Sugarloaf Hill

WEST
MOONAH

MOONAH

ALBERT

MERTON

Lower Glenorchy
Reservoir

SPRINGFIELD

VELLINGTON
PARK

Limekiln
Gully
Reservoir

LENAH VALLEY

New
Town

NEW
TOWN

MOUNT
STUART

Fossil Hill
340m

Brushy Hill
400m

Knocklofty

Knocklofty
Park

Mt Stuart

NORTH
HOBART

GLEBE

HOBART

WEST HOBART

New Town
Bay

Cornelian
Bay

QUEENS
DOMAIN

DOMAIN

Pavilion
Point

Tasman

Selfs
Point

Limekiln
Point

Derwent

Geilston
Bay

GEILSTON
BAY

Natone Hill

Lindisfarne
Point

Rose
Bay

LINDISFARNE

ANZAC
Park

FLAGSTAFF
GULLY

Flagstaff
Gully
Reservoir

Foggs
Gully

Gordons
Hill

Gordons Hill
State Rec Area

ROSE BAY

MONTAGU BAY

WARRANE

TO SORELL

ROSNY
PARK

Waverley Park

Mornington
Hill

BELLERIVE

Montagu
Bay

Nature Rec
Area

ROSNY

Rosny
Point

Yacht
Club

Bellerive
Oval

Bellerive
Beach

HOWRAH

Second
Bluff

Macquarie
Point

Sullivans Cove

Passenger Ferry

Kangaroo
Bay

Rosny Hill
Park

Rosny
Point

Female Factory &
Island Produce
Tasmania factory

Cascade Brewery

CASCADES

SOUTH HOBART

BATTERY POINT

Secheron
Point

For more detail on Central
Hobart see page 620

River

WELLINGTON
PARK

Guy
Fawkes

Strickland
Falls

O'Gradys
Falls

STRICKLAND

Lower
Reservoir

Upper
Reservoir

WATER WORKS

SANDY
BAY

DYNNYRNE

Wrest Point
Casino

Sandy
Bay

CHIMNEY POT HILL

Chimney Pot
Hill

Ridgeway
Reservoir

RIDGEWAY
PARK

Fern Tree

Pipeline

Ridgeway

OLINDA

Lambert
Park

Skyline
Reserve

Mount Nelson
Signal Station
Reserve

MOUNT
NELSON

Mt Nelson
Signal Station

LOWER
SANDY
BAY

Sandy Bay
Point

Sandy Bay
Beach

Derwent

Porter Hill

Pierces
Reserve

Truganini
Reserve

Cartwright
Creek

Dunn

Badger Hill

The Lea
Conservation
Area

TO KINGSTON

SOUTHERN

Coastal
Reserve

Dixons Beach

CHANNEL

Joins map 622

Joins map 622

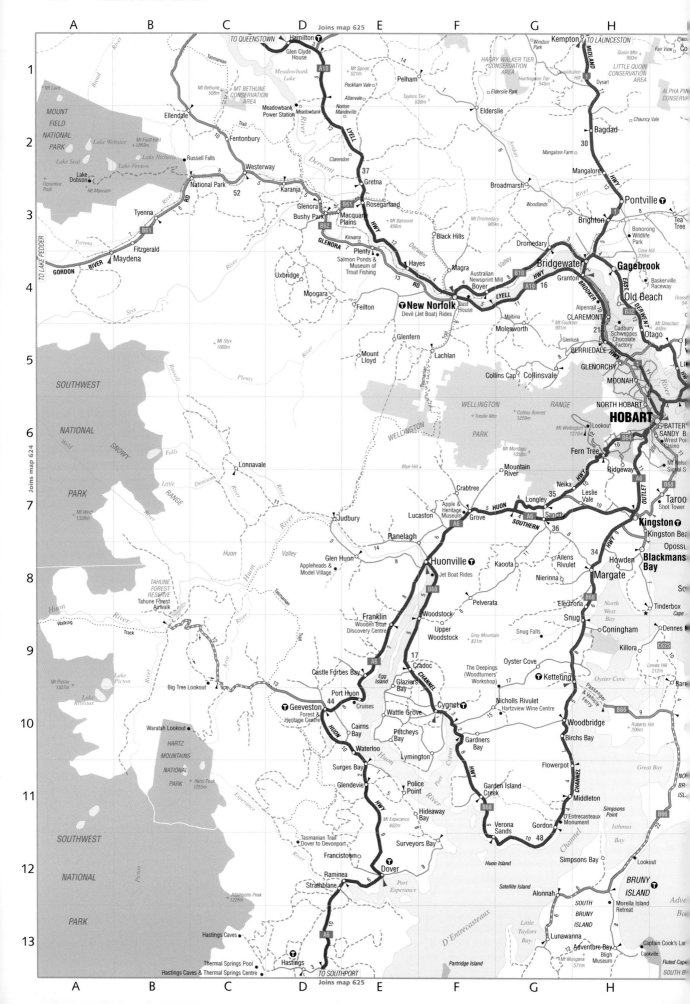

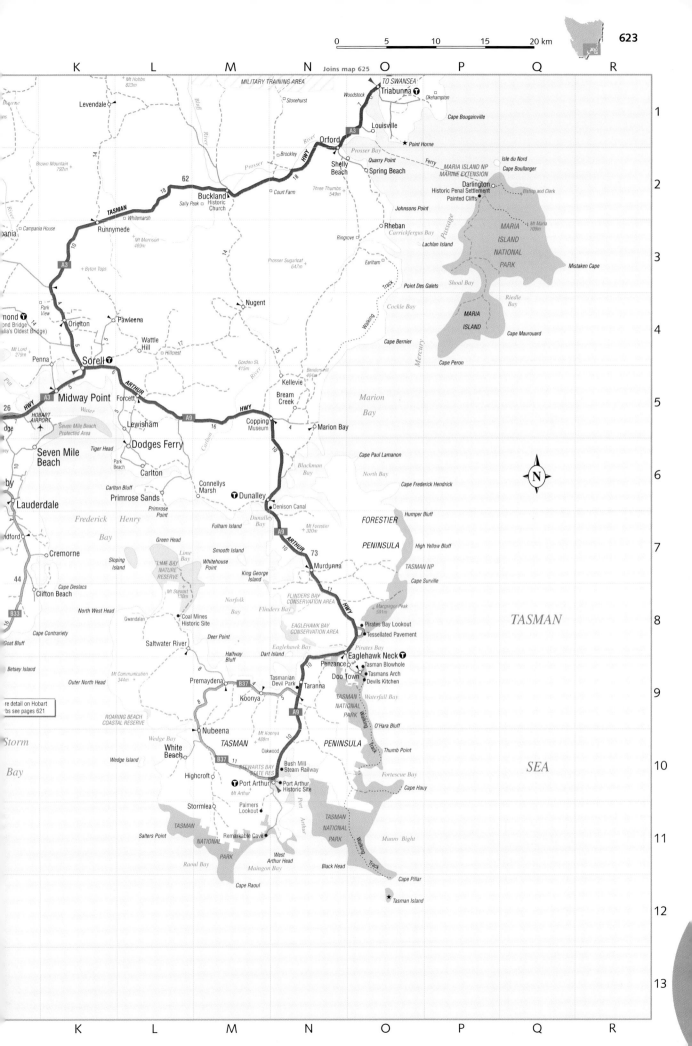

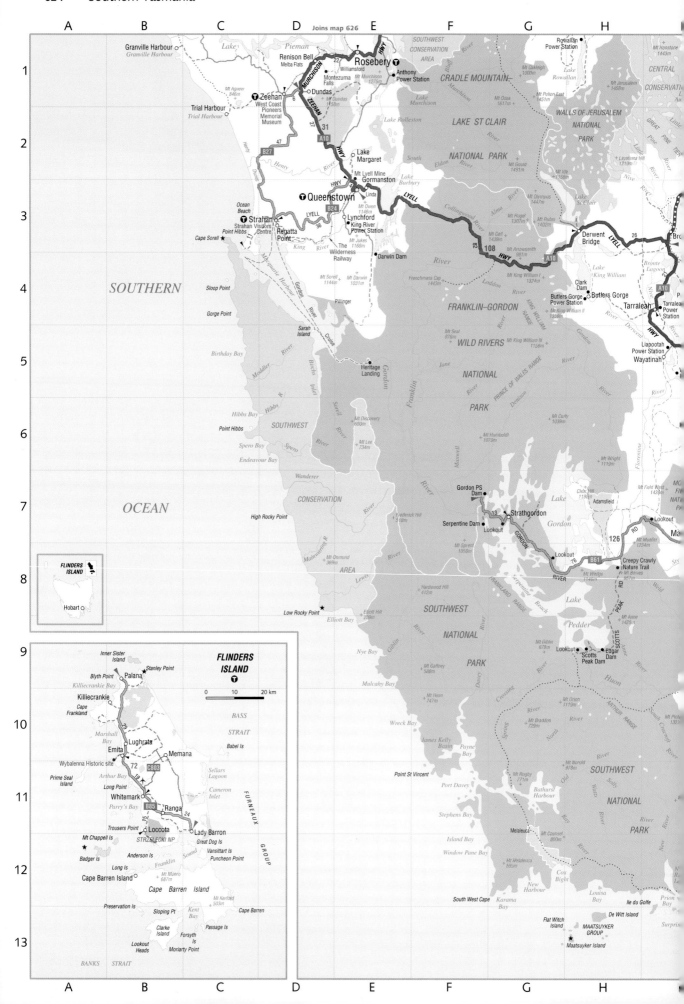

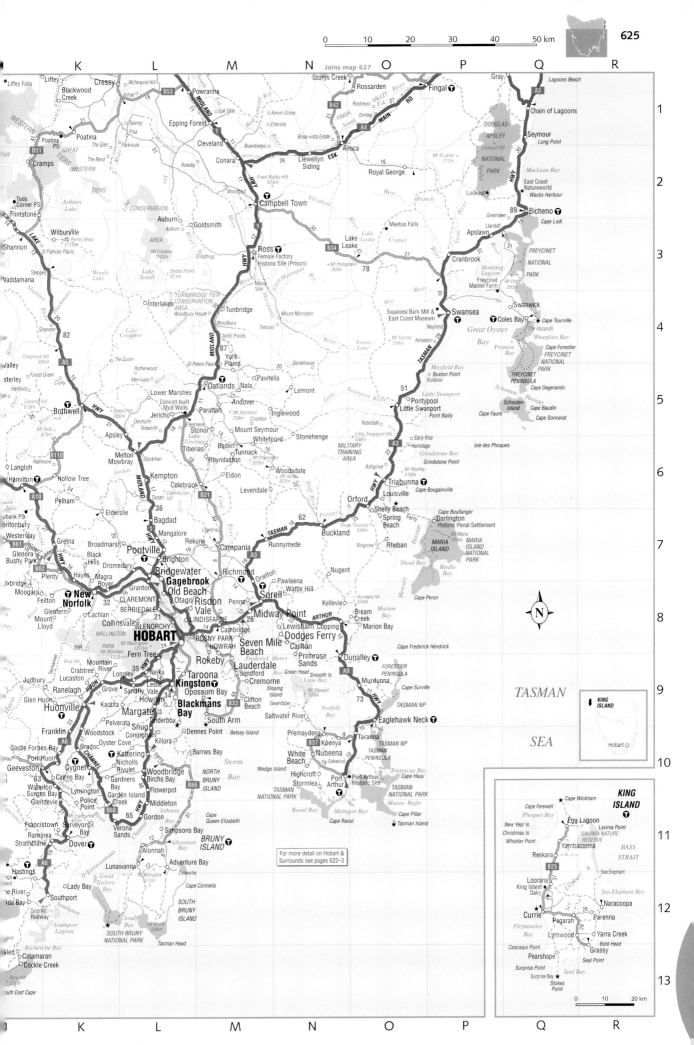

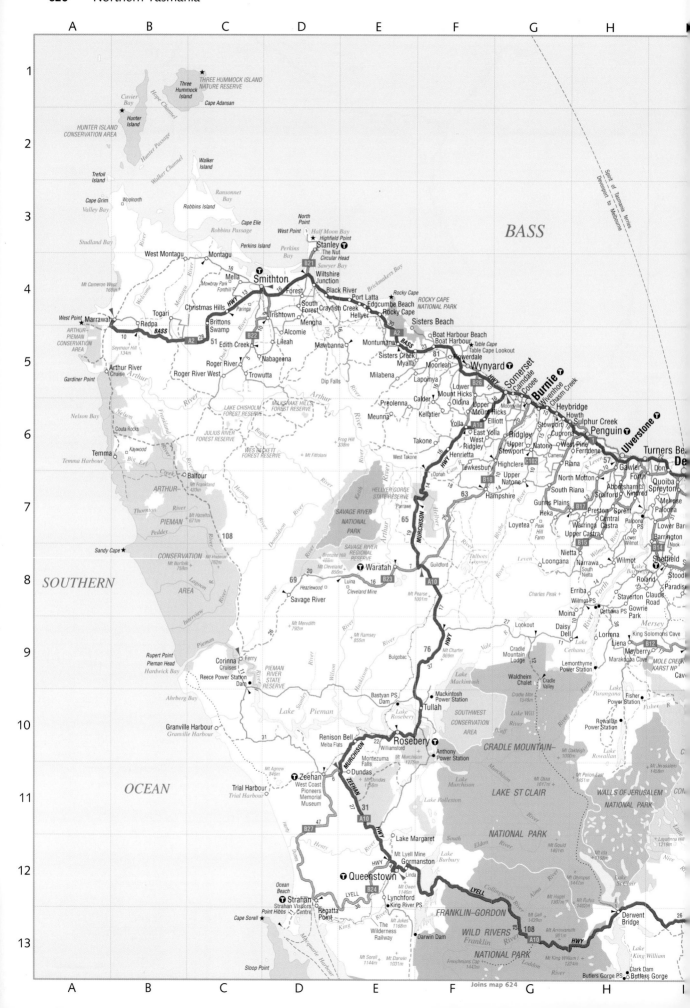

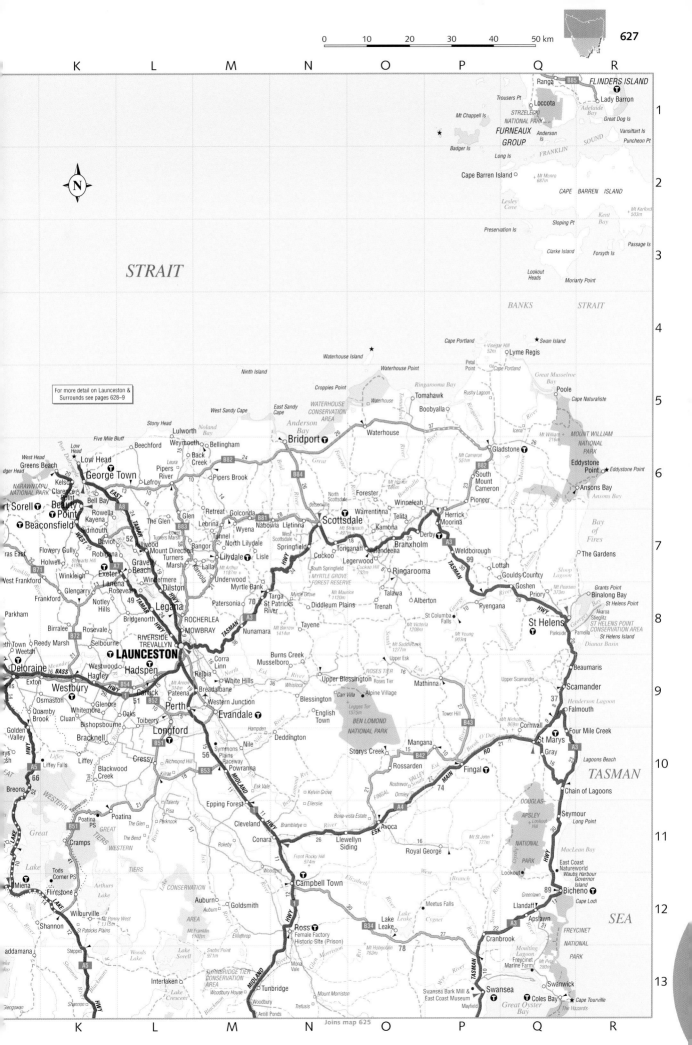

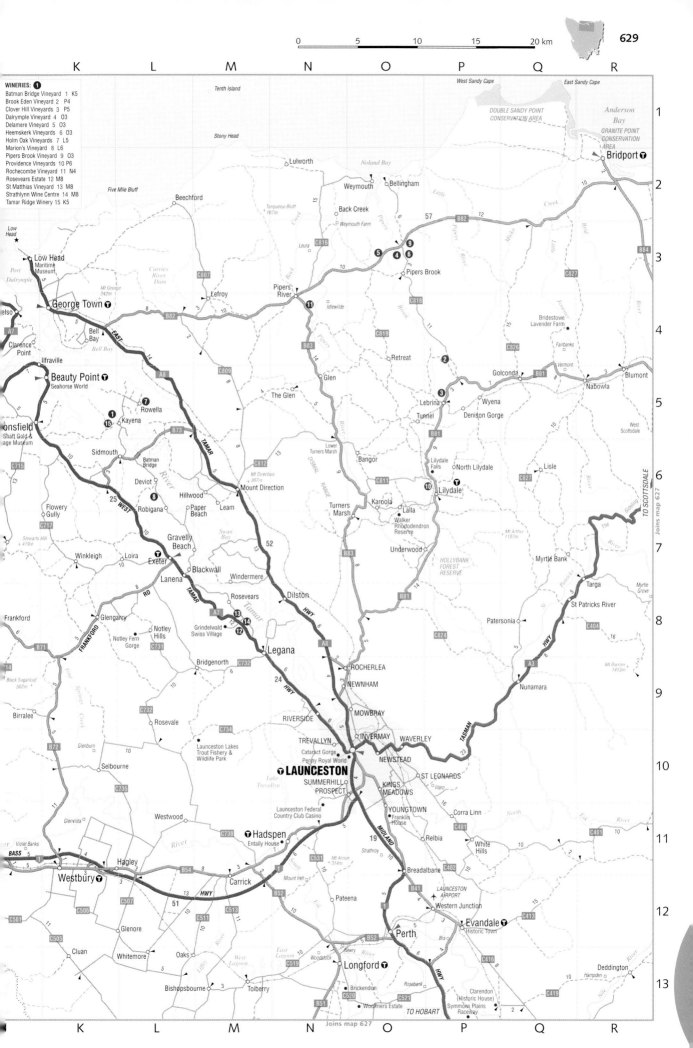

INDEX OF PLACE NAMES

This index includes all towns, localities, roadhouses and national parks shown on the maps and mentioned in the text. In addition, it includes major places of interest, landforms and water features.

Place names are followed by a map page number and grid reference, and/or the text page number on which that place is mentioned. A page number set in **bold** type indicates the main text entry for that place. For example:

Gundagai NSW 507 B5, 508 D12, 49, **76**

Gundagai	– Place Name
NSW	– State
507 B5, 508 D12	– Gundagai appears on these map pages
49	– Gundagai is mentioned on this page
76	– Main entry for Gundagai

The alphabetical order followed in the index is that of 'word-by-word' – a space is considered to come before 'A' in the alphabet, and the index has been ordered accordingly. For example:

Green Lake
Green Mountains
Green Point
Greenacre
Greenacres
Greenbank

Names beginning with Mc are indexed as Mac and those beginning with St as Saint.

The following abbreviations and contractions are used in the index:

ACT	–	Australian Capital Territory
JBT	–	Jervis Bay Territory
NSW	–	New South Wales
NT	–	Northern Territory
Qld	–	Queensland
SA	–	South Australia
Tas.	–	Tasmania
Vic.	–	Victoria
WA	–	Western Australia

A

A1 Mine Settlement Vic. 521 R4, 535 J2, 539 M13
Abbeyard Vic. 536 A7, 539 O9, 540 I8
Abbotsham Tas. 626 H7, 628 C6
Abercorn Qld 607 M3
Abercrombie River National Park NSW 492 C11, 507 F1, 508 H8, 92
Aberdare NSW 497 E12, 499 C10
Aberdeen NSW 509 K2, **88**
Aberfeldy Vic. 535 J3
Abergowrie Qld 603 C6, 611 N10
Abermain NSW 499 C9, 509 M4
Abernethy NSW 499 C10
ABT Wilderness Railway Tas. 624 D3, 626 E13, 456, **475**
Acacia NT 586 E5
Acheron Vic. 521 O2, 539 J11
Acland Qld 607 N8
Acton ACT 504 A3
Acton Park WA 568 E8, 569 G4
Adaminaby NSW 503 H5, 507 D8, 537 L1, 48, **53**
Adamsfield Tas. 624 H7
Adavale Qld 617 P5
Addington Vic. 520 B2, 530 I9
Adelaide SA 547, 550 B10, 552 B1, 555 K9, **208–18**, 239
Adelaide Festival Centre SA 547 E7, 215
Adelaide Hills SA 548 G9, 550 D10, 218, **222**, 228, 233
Adelaide Lead Vic. 530 I5
Adelaide River NT 586 E8, 588 E7, 342, 346, **350**, 357
Adelong NSW 507 B5, 508 D13, **53–4**

Adjungbilly NSW 507 C4, 508 E12
Advancetown Qld 599 F11, 600 B6
Adventure Bay Tas. 622 H13, 625 L11, 462
Agery SA 554 I6
Agnes Vic. 535 J10
Agnes Banks NSW 493 K6
Agnes Water Qld 609 Q13, 388, 421–2
Agnew WA 574 H2
Aileron NT 592 I6, **351**
Ailsa Vic. 542 H7
Ainslie ACT 505 G4
Aireys Inlet Vic. 520 E12, 527 M8, 533 P10, **160**
Airlie Beach Qld 609 K3, **395**, 400
Airly Vic. 535 N5
Akaroa Tas. 627 R8
Alawoona SA 552 H1, 555 Q8
Albacutya Vic. 542 F3
Albany WA 571 N12, 572 H13, 574 E12, 265, 285, **292–3**, 323
Albany Creek Qld 598 D5
Albert NSW 508 B3, 511 R1, 513 R13
Alberton Qld 598 H11, 599 F8
Alberton Tas. 627 O8
Alberton Vic. 535 L9
Alberton West Vic. 535 K9
Albion Park NSW 501 G8
Albury NSW 511 Q13, 536 C1, 539 P4, 50, **54**, 201
Alcomie Tas. 626 D5
Aldersyde WA 572 G5
Aldinga SA 549 F4, 550 A13
Aldinga Beach SA 549 E4, 552 B3, 555 K10, 220, **230**
Alectown NSW 508 D4
Alexander Morrison National Park WA 574 B5

Alexandra Vic. 521 O1, 539 J11, **159**
Alexandra Bridge WA 569 E10
Alexandra Headland Qld 601 H4, 602 H9, 423
Alford SA 554 I5
Alfred National Park Vic. 507 F13, 537 O11
Alfred Town NSW 507 A5, 508 C12, 511 R10
Alice NSW 515 O4, 607 P13
Alice Springs NT 585, 593 J8, 595 N5, 333, 348, **351–3**
Alice Springs Desert Park NT 595 N4
Ali-Curung NT 591 K13, 593 K2
Alison NSW 499 B2
Allambee Vic. 521 Q11, 534 I7
Allambee South Vic. 521 Q12, 534 I8
Allanby Vic. 542 F6
Allans Flat Vic. 536 B3, 539 P5, 203
Allansford Vic. 526 B8, 532 I9
Allanson WA 572 D8
Allawah NSW 511 M6
Alleena NSW 508 A9, 511 Q6
Allendale Vic. 531 L9, 533 P2, 543 P13
Allendale East SA 552 H12
Allendale North SA 550 E2, 555 L7
Allens Rivulet Tas. 622 G8
Allenvale Vic. 527 L10
Allies Creek Qld 607 M5
Alligator Creek Qld 603 G9, 611 P13
Allora Qld 607 N10, 382, **395–6**
Alma SA 550 B1, 555 L7
Alma Vic. 530 I5

Alma Park NSW 511 P12, 539 O1
Almaden Qld 611 K7, 405
Almonds Vic. 539 L5
Alonnah Tas. 622 G12, 625 L11
Aloomba Qld 611 N7
Alpara NT 560 G1, 592 E13
Alpha Qld 608 F11
Alphadale NSW 515 Q3
Alpine National Park Vic. 503 A13, 507 A10, 535 L1, 536 D6, 539 O12, 540 G8, 541 P5, 156, 165, 182, 183, **186**, 187
Alpurrurulam NT 591 Q13, 593 Q2, 614 A5
Alstonville NSW 515 Q3, 607 Q12, 54
Alton Qld 606 I10
Alton National Park Qld 606 I10
Altona Vic. 519 C7, 520 I7, 534 C4
Alva Qld 603 I10, 608 H1, 611 Q13
Alvie Vic. 520 A10, 526 I6, 533 N8
Alyangula NT 589 O9
Amamoor Qld 601 D1
Amamoor State Forest Qld 412
Amanbidji NT 590 B3
Amata SA 560 G1, 592 E13
Amberley Qld 598 A10, 599 A7
Amboyne Crossing Vic. 507 D11, 537 K8
Ambrose Qld 609 O12
Amby Qld 606 F6
Amelup Roadhouse WA 571 Q5
American Beach SA 554 I12
American River SA 554 I12, 242
Amherst Vic. 520 B1, 530 I6, 533 N1, 543 N12
Amiens Qld 515 M2, 607 N12
Amity Point Qld 599 H5
Amoonguna NT 593 J8, 595 N5
Amosfield NSW 515 M2, 607 O12

Fentonbury Tas. 622 C2, 625 J7
Fentons Creek Vic. 543 N8
Ferguson Vic. 526 I10
Fern Hill Vic. 520 G2, 531 P9
Fern Tree Tas. 621 B11, 622 H6,
625 L9
Fernbank Vic. 535 O5, 536 E13
Ferndale NSW 511 P11
Ferndene Tas. 626 H6, 628 A5
Fernhill NSW 500 E2
Fernihurst Vic. 538 A5, 543 O6
Fernlees Qld 608 I12
Ferntree Gully Vic. 519 G7,
521 L7, 188
Fernvale Qld 599 A5, 601 C12,
607 P9
Ferny Hills Qld 598 D6
Fields Find WA 574 D4
Fiery Flat Vic. 538 A6, 543 O7
Fifield NSW 508 B4, 511 R2
Fifteen Mile School Vic. 540 E4
Figtree NSW 500 A11, 501 H6
Finch Hatton Qld 609 J5
Fine Flower Creek NSW 515 O5
Fingal NSW 515 Q1, 599 I13
Fingal Tas. 625 P1, 627 P10, 453,
467
Fingal Bay NSW 499 I2
Finke NT 593 K12, 595 Q13
Finke Gorge National Park NT
592 H9, 594 I7, 349, **354**
Finley NSW 511 M12, 538 I11, **71**
Finniss SA 549 I6, 552 C3, 555 L11
Fish Creek Vic. 534 I10, 175
Fish Point Vic. 543 O1, 545 O11
Fisher ACT 505 E7
Fisher SA 562 G4
Fishery Falls Qld 611 N7
Fiskville Vic. 520 F5, 531 O13,
533 Q4
Fitzgerald Tas. 622 B3, 624 I7
Fitzgerald River National Park
WA 574 G11, **295**, 324
Fitzroy SA 547 D2
Fitzroy Crossing WA 579 M9,
580 G11, 290, 291, **304**
Fitzroy Falls NSW 501 D9
Fitzroy Island Qld 611 N6, 385,
386, 402
Fitzroy Island National Park Qld
611 N7
Fitzroy River WA 579 M9,
580 B10
Five Ways NSW 508 A2, 513 Q12
Five Ways Vic. 523 O12
Five Ways Vic. 523 Q1
Flaggy Rock Qld 609 L7
Flagstaff Gully Tas. 621 H6
Flamingo Beach Vic. 535 O7
Flat Tops NSW 499 C2
Flaxley SA 548 G12, 549 I3,
550 D12
Flaxton Qld 601 F4, 602 C9, 383,
420
Flemington Vic. 519 D6
Fletcher Qld 515 L3, 607 N12
Fleurieu Peninsula SA 549 E7,
552 A4, 555 K12, 216, 217, 218,
220, 221, 228
Flinders Qld 598 A12, 599 A8
Flinders Vic. 521 J12, 523 J11,
534 D9, **174–5**
Flinders Bay WA 568 C13,
569 D13

Flinders Chase National Park SA
554 F1
Flinders Group National Park Qld
612 G11, 406
Flinders Island Tas. 624 C9,
627 R1, 459, **467**
Flinders Ranges SA 553, 557 K8,
228, 231, 234, 238, 240, 243,
246, 254
Flinders Ranges National Park SA
553 D6, 557 K7, 228, **260**
Flinton Qld 606 I10
Flintstone Tas. 625 J2, 627 K12
Flora River Nature Park NT
588 F10
Florida NSW 513 O10
Florida WA 567 A10
Florieton SA 555 N5
Flowerdale Tas. 626 F5
Flowerdale Vic. 521 L2, 534 E1,
538 H12
Flowerpot Tas. 622 H11, 625 L10
Flowery Gully Tas. 627 K7,
629 K7
Flying Fish Point Qld 603 D2,
611 N8
Flying Fox Qld 599 E12
Flynn Vic. 535 L7
Flynns Creek Vic. 535 K7
Fogg Dam NT 586 F3, 346, 357
Foleyvale Aboriginal Community
Qld 609 M11
Footscray Vic. 519 C6, 521 J6,
534 C4
Forbes NSW 508 D6, **71–2**
Forcett Tas. 623 L5
Fords SA 550 E3
Fords Bridge NSW 513 M4
Fordwich NSW 509 L4
Forest Tas. 626 D4
Forest Den National Park Qld
608 C7, 615 Q7, **396**
Forest Glen Qld 601 G4, 602 F9
Forest Grove WA 569 D9
Forest Hill NSW 507 A5, 508 B12,
511 R10
Forest Lake Qld 598 D10
Forest Range SA 548 G8, 549 I1,
550 D10
Forest Reefs NSW 508 G6
Forestdale Qld 598 D10
Forester Tas. 627 O6
Forestier Peninsula Tas. 623 O7,
625 O9, 465
Forge Creek Vic. 535 P5
Forrest ACT 504 C12
Forrest Vic. 520 B13, 527 J9,
533 O10, 169
Forrest WA 575 Q6
Forrest Beach Qld 603 E7,
611 O11, 414
Forrestdale WA 566 E8
Forresters Beach NSW 493 Q4,
496 H4
Forrestfield WA 566 F6
Forreston SA 548 H5, 550 E8
Forsayth Qld 610 I11, 425
Forster SA 552 E1, 555 N8
Forster–Tuncurry NSW 508 P2,
509 P2, 42, **72**
Fortescue Roadhouse WA 573 F2
Forth Tas. 626 I7, 628 D5
Fortis Creek National Park NSW
515 O5

Fortitude Valley Qld 597 H1,
598 E7
Forty Mile Scrub National Park
Qld 611 L9, 425
Foster Vic. 535 J10, 145, **175**
Fosterville Vic. 531 R2, 538 D8,
543 R9
Fountaindale NSW 496 F3
Four Mile Creek Tas. 627 Q10
Fowlers Bay SA 563 K9, 235
Fox Ground NSW 501 F10,
509 K11
Fox Studios NSW **33**
Fox Trap Roadhouse Qld 606 A7,
617 Q7
Foxhow Vic. 526 H3
Framlingham Vic. 526 C6, 533 J8
Framlingham East Vic. 526 C5,
533 J8
Frampton NSW 507 B3, 508 C11
Frances SA 542 A9, 552 I8, 249
Francistown Tas. 622 E12,
625 K11
Francois Peron National Park WA
573 B9, 301
Frank Hann National Park WA
574 H9, 313
Frankford Tas. 627 K8, 629 J8
Frankland WA 570 I7, 572 F11,
574 E11
Frankland Islands National Park
Qld 611 N7
Franklin Tas. 622 E9, 625 K10, 470
Franklin–Gordon Wild Rivers
National Park Tas. 624 F4,
626 F13, 456, **479**
Franklin River Tas. 624 E6,
626 F13, 456, 478
Franklinford Vic. 520 E1, 531 O7
Frankston Vic. 519 E10, 521 K9,
523 L1, 534 D6
Frankton SA 550 H2, 555 M7
Fraser Island Qld 607 Q3, 384,
413, 414, 421
Fredrickton NSW 515 O10,
516 G3, 81
Freeburgh Vic. 536 C6, 539 Q8,
541 M6
Freeling SA 550 D4, 551 A3,
555 L7, 239
Freemans Reach NSW 493 L5,
509 K7
Freemans Waterhole NSW
499 E10, 509 M5
Fregon SA 561 J3
Fremantle WA 566 C7, 567 B5,
572 C4, 574 C8, 265, 269, **275–8**
French Island Vic. 519 H13,
521 L11, 523 Q8, 534 E8
French Island Marine National
Park Vic. 519 H13, 521 M11,
523 Q6
French Island National Park
Vic. 519 H13, 521 M11, 523 Q7,
534 E8, **175**
Frenchmans Vic. 530 E4
Frenchmans Cap Tas. 624 F4,
626 F13
Frenchs Forest NSW 491 G5,
493 O7
Freshwater Qld 604 E9
Freshwater Creek Vic. 520 F10,
527 O6, 533 Q8
Freshwater National Park Qld
598 E3

Freycinet National Park Tas.
625 Q4, 627 Q12, 441, 461, **463**
Freycinet Peninsula Tas. 625 Q5,
453, 463
Frogmore NSW 507 D2, 508 F9
Fryerstown Vic. 520 F1, 531 O6,
167
Fulham Vic. 535 M6
Fullerton NSW 492 C12, 507 F2,
508 H9
Fumina Vic. 521 Q7
Furneaux Group Tas. 624 C11,
467
Furner SA 552 G10
Furnissdale WA 566 D13, 567 B10
Furracabad NSW 515 L6
Fyansford Vic. 520 F9, 527 O5,
533 Q7, 176
Fyshwick ACT 505 H5

G

Gaffneys Creek Vic. 521 R4,
535 J2, 539 M13
Gagebrook Tas. 622 H4, 625 L7
Gagudju Crocodile Holiday Inn
NT 587 P4, **355**
Galah Vic. 544 G9
Galaquil Vic. 542 H4
Galaquil East Vic. 542 I4
Galga SA 552 F1, 555 O8
Galiwinku NT 589 M5
Gallanani Qld 601 A10
Gallangowan Qld 601 A2, 607 O6
Gallipoli Beach SA 554 B7, 236
Galong NSW 507 D3, 508 E10
Galston NSW 491 D3, 493 N6,
509 L7
Gama Vic. 542 I1, 544 I12
Gammon Ranges National Park
SA 553 G2, 557 L4, **231**, 234, 243
Ganmain NSW 508 A11, 511 Q9
Gannawarra Vic. 538 B2, 543 Q3,
545 Q13
Gantheaume Point WA 578 G9,
290, **296**
Gapsted Vic. 536 A4, 539 O7,
540 I2, 187
Gapuwiyak NT 589 N5
Garah NSW 514 G4, 606 I13
Garawa NT 589 O13, 591 O2
Garden Island WA 567 A7
Garden Island Creek Tas.
622 F11, 625 K11
Gardens of Stone National Park
NSW 492 F1, 508 I5, 84
Gardners Bay Tas. 622 F10,
625 K10
Garema NSW 508 D7
Garfield Vic. 521 O9, 534 G6
Garfield North Vic. 521 O8
Garibaldi Vic. 520 C5, 533 O4
Garig Gunak Barlu National Park
NT 588 G3, 345
Garigal National Park NSW
491 H4
Garland NSW 508 F7
Garra NSW 508 F5
Garrawilla NSW 514 G11
Garrthalala NT 589 O6
Garvoc Vic. 526 C7, 533 J9
Gary Junction WA 577 M4
Gascoyne Junction WA 573 D8,
304–5

Kennedy Range National Park WA 573 D8, **305**

Kennedys Creek Vic. 526 G10, 533 L11

Kennett River Vic. 527 K11, 533 O11

Kennys Creek NSW 507 D2, 508 F10

Kent Town SA 547 H8

Kentbruck Vic. 532 C8

Kenthurst NSW 491 D3, 493 M6

Kentlyn NSW 501 G1

Kentucky NSW 515 L9

Keppel Bay Islands National Park Qld 609 P10, 436

Keppel Sands Qld 609 O11, 388, 389, 436

Keppoch SA 552 H8

Kerang Vic. 510 I12, 538 A2, 543 P3, 545 P13, 155, **179–80**

Kerang East Vic. 538 B2, 543 P3

Kerang South Vic. 510 I12, 538 A2, 543 P3

Kergunyah Vic. 536 C3, 539 Q5

Kergunyah South Vic. 536 C4, 539 P6

Kernot Vic. 521 N12, 534 G8

Kerrabee NSW 509 J3

Kerrie Vic. 520 H2

Kerrisdale Vic. 521 L1, 538 H11

Kerrs Creek NSW 508 G5

Kerry Qld 599 D12

Kersbrook SA 548 H5, 550 E8, 552 C1, 555 L9, 233

Keswick SA 547 A13

Kettering Tas. 622 H9, 625 L10, **470**

Kevington Vic. 521 R3, 534 I1, 539 L12

Kew NSW 515 O12, 516 E10

Kew Vic. 519 E6, 521 K6

Kewarra Beach Qld 604 D5

Kewell Vic. 542 H8

Keyneton SA 550 H5, 555 M8

Keysbrook WA 566 F12, 567 D9, 572 D5

Khancoban NSW 503 A9, 507 B9, 536 H3, **169**

Ki Ki SA 552 F4, 555 O11

Kiah NSW 502 F12, 507 G12, 537 Q9

Kialla NSW 507 F3, 508 H10

Kialla Vic. 538 I6, 195

Kialla West Vic. 538 H6

Kiama NSW 501 H9, 509 K10, 39, **81**

Kiamba Qld 601 F3, 602 C6

Kiamil Vic. 510 E10, 544 H8

Kiana SA 554 C6

Kiandra NSW 503 D3, 507 C7

Kianga NSW 502 I2

Kiata Vic. 542 E7

Kidaman Creek Qld 602 A8

Kidman Park SA 548 C7

Kidston Qld 611 J11

Kielpa SA 554 E4

Kies Hill SA 551 C10

Kiewa Vic. 536 C3, 539 Q5

Kikoira NSW 511 P5

Kilcarnup WA 569 B7

Kilcoy Qld 601 C7, 607 P7

Kilcunda Vic. 521 M13, 534 F9, 201

Kilkerran SA 554 I7

Kilkivan Qld 607 O5, 378, 425

Killabakh NSW 515 N13, 516 B11

Killarney Qld 515 N1, 607 O11, **417**

Killarney Vic. 532 H9

Killawarra Vic. 539 L5

Killcare NSW 493 P5, 496 G8

Killcare Heights NSW 496 H8

Killiecrankie Tas. 624 A10

Killingworth NSW 499 E9

Killora Tas. 622 H9, 625 L10

Kilmany Vic. 535 M6

Kilmany South Vic. 535 M6

Kilmore Vic. 521 J2, 538 F11, **180**

Kilpalie SA 552 G2, 555 O9

Kimba SA 554 F3, 556 E13, 229, **243**

Kimberley, The WA 579 L6, 580 E5, 265, **290–1**, 301, 304, 312, 328

Kimbriki NSW 509 O1, 515 N13, 516 A13

Kinalung NSW 512 D12

Kincaid Vic. 526 H11

Kinchega National Park NSW 510 D1, 512 D13, **85**

Kinchela NSW 515 P10, 516 H2

Kincumber NSW 493 P4, 496 G7, 509 M6

Kindred Tas. 626 H7, 628 C6

King Ash Bay NT 589 O13, 591 O2, 353

King Island Tas. 625 R10, 459, **470–1**

King River WA 571 O11, 572 H13

King Valley Vic. 539 N8, 540 F5, 184

Kingaroy Qld 607 N6, 378, **417**

Kinglake Vic. 519 H3, 521 M4, 524 B3, 534 E2, 538 H13

Kinglake Central Vic. 521 L3, 524 A2

Kinglake East Vic. 519 H2, 521 M4, 524 B2

Kinglake National Park Vic. 519 G3, 521 M3, 524 B1, 534 E1, 538 H13, **203**

Kinglake West Vic. 519 G2, 521 L3, 534 E2, 538 H13

Kingoonya SA 556 B5

Kingower Vic. 543 O9, 179

Kings Beach Qld 602 I13

Kings Camp SA 552 E9

Kings Canyon NT 592 F9, 594 E7, 349, 356

Kings Canyon Resort NT 592 F9, 594 D7, 356

Kings Cross NSW 490 I9

Kings Meadows Tas. 629 O10

Kings Plains National Park NSW 515 K5

Kings Point NSW 507 I6, 509 J13

Kingsborough Qld 611 L6

Kingscliff NSW 515 Q1, 607 R11

Kingscote SA 554 I12, 221, **242**

Kingsdale NSW 507 G3, 508 H10

Kingsford NSW 491 H9, 493 O9

Kingsley WA 566 D4

Kingsthorpe Qld 607 N9

Kingston ACT 504 G13

Kingston Tas. 622 H7, 625 I9, 450, 454, **471**

Kingston Vic. 520 D2, 531 L9, 533 P2, 538 B12, 543 P13

Kingston Beach Tas. 622 H7, 471

Kingston-on-Murray SA 555 P7, 226

Kingston S.E. SA 552 F8, 227, **243**

Kingstown NSW 515 K8

Kingsvale NSW 507 C2, 508 E10

Kingswood NSW 493 K7

Kingswood SA 553 C12, 557 J10

Kinimakatka Vic. 542 D7

Kinka Beach Qld 609 O10

Kinnabulla Vic. 543 J4

Kintore NT 577 R6, 592 B7, 333

Kioloa NSW 507 H6, 509 J13

Kioa Vic. 526 D5, 533 K8

Kirkstall Vic. 532 H9

Kirup WA 568 H7, 570 B1, 572 C9

Kitchener NSW 499 C10

Kitchener WA 575 L6

Kithbrook Vic. 539 J9

Kiwirrkurra WA 577 P5

Knebsworth Vic. 532 F7

Knockrow NSW 515 Q3, 607 Q12

Knockwood Vic. 521 R3

Knorrit Flat NSW 509 O1, 515 M13

Knowsley Vic. 538 E9

Knucky Lagoon NT 584 E7

Koallah Vic. 526 F7, 533 L9

Kobble Qld 599 B3, 601 E10

Kobyboyn Vic. 538 H10

Koetong Vic. 507 A8, 536 E2

Kogan Qld 607 L8

Koimbo Vic. 545 K8

Kojonup WA 571 J2, 572 G9, 574 E11, 285, **311**

Koloona NSW 515 J6

Kolora Vic. 526 D5, 533 K8

Komungla NSW 507 G4, 508 H11

Konagaderra Vic. 520 I4

Kondalilla National Park Qld 601 E4, 602 C9, **420**

Kondinin WA 572 I5, 574 F9

Kongal SA 552 H6

Kongorong SA 552 H12

Kongwak Vic. 521 O13, 534 G9

Konnongorring WA 572 F1

Konong Wootong Vic. 532 D3

Konong Wootong North Vic. 532 D3

Kookaburra NSW 515 N10, 516 B3

Kookynie WA 574 I4, 287, 314

Koolan WA 579 J5, 580 B5

Koolan Island WA 580 B5

Koolewong NSW 496 F7

Kooloonong Vic. 510 G9, 545 L8

Koolunga SA 555 K4, 238

Koolyanobbing WA 574 G6

Koolywurtie SA 554 I8

Koombal Qld 604 I9

Koonalda Cave WA 286, 304

Koonda Vic. 539 J7, 544 D9

Koondrook Vic. 510 I12, 538 B1, 543 Q2, 545 Q13

Koondrook State Forest NSW 538 C1, **56**

Koongawa SA 554 D3, 556 C13, 261

Koonibba SA 563 N9

Kooninderie SA 550 G1

Koonoomoo Vic. 538 I2

Koonunga SA 550 F3, 551 G1

Koonwarra Vic. 521 P13, 534 H9, **181**

Koonya Tas. 623 M9, 625 N10

Koorack Koorack Vic. 543 N3, 545 N13

Kooralbyn Qld 599 B12

Koorawatha NSW 507 C1, 508 E8

Koorda WA 574 E6, 316

Kooreh Vic. 543 M9

Kooringal Qld 599 H4

Koorkab Vic. 545 L7

Koorlong Vic. 510 D7, 544 G4

Kootingal NSW 515 K10

Koo-wee-rup Vic. 519 I11, 521 M10, 534 F7, 144, **180**

Kooyoora State Park Vic. 543 N8, **179**

Koppamurra SA 542 A11, 552 I9

Koppio SA 554 D7

Korbel WA 572 I3

Koriella Vic. 521 O1

Korobeit Vic. 520 F4, 531 P12

Koroit Vic. 532 H9

Korong Vale Vic. 543 O7

Koroop Vic. 538 B2, 543 Q3

Korora NSW 515 P8, 66

Korumburra Vic. 521 O12, 534 H8, 144, **180–1**

Korweinguboora Vic. 520 E3, 531 N10

Kosciuszko National Park NSW 503 D2, 506 A9, 507 C8, 508 E13, 537 J1, 48, 57, **92**, 100, 101, 169, 186

Kotta Vic. 538 D5

Kotupna Vic. 511 L13, 538 G4

Koumala Qld 609 L6

Kow Swamp Vic. 511 J13, 538 C3, 543 Q4, 168

Kowanyama Qld 610 D3

Kowat Vic. 507 E12, 537 N10

Koyuga Vic. 538 F5

Krambach NSW 509 O1

Kringin SA 552 H2, 555 Q9

Kroemers Crossing SA 551 F5

Krongart SA 552 H11

Kroombit Tops National Park Qld 607 L1, 609 O13, 411

Krowera Vic. 521 O12

Kudardup WA 568 C12, 569 D12

Kuitpo SA 549 G4, 550 C13

Kuitpo Colony SA 549 H5

Kukerin WA 572 I7, 574 F10

Kulgera NT 592 I13

Kulgun Qld 599 A10

Kulikup WA 570 G2, 572 E9, 295

Kulin WA 572 I6, 574 F9, **311–12**

Kulkami SA 552 G2, 555 P10

Kulkyne Vic. 544 H6

Kulnine Vic. 544 D3

Kulnine East Vic. 510 C7, 544 D3

Kulnura NSW 493 O2, 496 A2, 509 L5

Kulpara SA 555 J6

Kulpi Qld 607 N8

Kulwin Vic. 544 I9

Kulyalling WA 572 F5

Kumarina Roadhouse WA 576 D8

Kumarl WA 575 J9

Kumbarilla Qld 607 L8

Kumbatine National Park NSW 515 O11

Kumbia Qld 607 N7

Kumorna SA 552 G5, 555 P13

Kunama NSW 507 B6

Kunat Vic. 543 N1, 545 N12

Tallaroo Hot Springs Qld 610 I9, 425

Tallarook Vic. 538 G10

Tallarook State Forest Vic. 195

Tallebudgera Qld 600 F10, 380, 411

Tallebudgera Valley Qld 600 D10

Tallebung NSW 511 P2

Tallimba NSW 508 A8, 511 Q6

Tallong NSW 507 H3, 508 I11

Tallygaroopna Vic. 538 I5

Talmalmo NSW 507 A8, 511 R13, 536 E1

Talwood Qld 514 F2, 606 I11

Tamar River Tas. 627 L7, 629 L6

Tamarang NSW 514 H12

Tambar Springs NSW 514 G11

Tambaroora NSW 508 G5

Tambellup WA 571 M4, 572 H10

Tambo Crossing Vic. 507 B13, 535 Q2, 536 G11

Tambo Qld 606 B2, **432**

Tambo Upper Vic. 535 R4, 536 G13

Tamboon Vic. 537 N13, 183

Tamborine Qld 599 E10, 607 Q10

Tamborine Mountain Qld 599 E10

Tamborine National Park Qld 599 E10, 381, **428**

Tamboy NSW 509 O3

Taminick Vic. 539 L6

Tamleugh Vic. 539 J7

Tamleugh North Vic. 539 J7

Tamleugh West Vic. 538 I7

Tammin WA 572 G3, 574 E7

Tamrookum Qld 599 C12

Tamworth NSW 515 J11, 44, **97–8**

Tanami NT 590 B11

Tanawha Qld 602 F11

Tandarook Vic. 526 F7, 533 L9

Tandarra Vic. 538 C6, 543 Q7

Tangalooma Qld 599 G2

Tangambalanga Vic. 536 C3, 539 Q5

Tangmangaroo NSW 507 D3, 508 F10

Tangorin Qld 608 A7, 615 O6

Tanilba Bay NSW 499 G3

Tanja NSW 502 G7, 507 G10, 537 R5

Tanjil Bren Vic. 521 R7, 535 J4

Tanjil South Vic. 521 R9, 535 J6

Tankerton Vic. 521 L12, 523 P9, 534 E8

Tannum Sands Qld 609 P12, 410

Tannymorel Qld 515 N1, 607 O11

Tansey Qld 607 N5

Tantanoola SA 552 G11, 246–7

Tanunda SA 550 F5, 551 E6, 555 L8, 223, **257**

Tanwood Vic. 530 G5, 543 M11

Tanybryn Vic. 527 J11, 533 O11

Tapin Tops National Park NSW 515 M12

Tapitallee NSW 501 D11

Taplan SA 510 A8, 544 A5, 555 R8

Tappa Pass SA 551 I5

Tara NSW 508 A10, 511 Q8

Tara NT 593 J4

Tara Qld 607 K8

Taradale Vic. 520 F1, 531 P6, 533 R1, 538 C11, 543 R12

Tarago NSW 507 F4, 508 H12

Tarago Vic. 521 P9

Taralga NSW 507 G2, 508 I9

Tarampa Qld 601 C13

Tarana NSW 492 E5

Tarana Quarry NSW 492 E5

Taranna Tas. 623 N9, 625 O10, 466

Tarcombe Vic. 538 H10

Tarcoola SA 563 Q5

Tarcoon NSW 513 P6

Tarcowie SA 555 K2, 557 K12

Tarcutta NSW 507 A5, 508 C13

Tardun WA 574 C3

Taree NSW 509 O1, 515 N13, 516 C13, 42, **98**

Targa Tas. 627 M8, 629 R7

Tarilta Vic. 520 E1, 531 N7

Tarlee SA 550 D1, 555 L7, 243

Tarlo NSW 507 G3, 508 H10

Tarlo River National Park NSW 507 G3, 508 I10

Tarnagulla Vic. 531 K2, 538 A8, 543 O10, 172

Tarneit Vic. 519 B6, 520 H6, 527 R1, 534 B4

Tarnma SA 555 L6

Tarnook Vic. 539 K7

Taroom Qld 607 J4, **432–3**

Taroona Tas. 622 I7, 625 L9, 471

Tarpeena SA 552 H11

Tarra–Bulga National Park Vic. 535 K8, 199, **203**

Tarragal Vic. 532 C9

Tarraleah Tas. 624 I4

Tarranginnie Vic. 542 D7

Tarrango Vic. 544 E5

Tarranyurk Vic. 542 F6

Tarraville Vic. 535 L10, 191

Tarrawanna NSW 500 D1

Tarrawingee Vic. 539 N6

Tarrayoukyan Vic. 532 D2, 542 D13

Tarrenlea Vic. 532 E5

Tarrington Vic. 532 G5

Tarrion NSW 513 Q5

Tarwin Vic. 534 H10

Tarwin Lower Vic. 534 H10

Tarwin Meadows Vic. 534 H10

Tarwonga WA 572 F7

Tascott NSW 496 F7

Tasman Blowhole Tas. 623 O9

Tasman National Park Tas. 525 O10, 623 N9, **465–6**, 475

Tasman Peninsula Tas. 623 M10, 625 O10, 451, 454

Tasman Sea NSW 509 N11, 535 O10

Tasmans Arch Tas. 623 O9

Tasmazia Tas. 477

Tatham NSW 515 P3

Tathra NSW 502 G8, 507 G10, 537 R6, **98**

Tathra National Park WA 574 B5, **297**

Tatong Vic. 539 L8, 540 C5

Tatura Vic. 538 H6, 195

Tatyoon Vic. 530 B11, 533 K3

Tawonga Vic. 536 D6, 539 Q8, 541 N4

Tawonga South Vic. 536 D6, 539 Q8, 541 N5

Tayene Tas. 627 N8

Taylors Arm NSW 515 O9

Taylors Beach Qld 603 E6, 611 O11, 414

Taylors Flat NSW 507 E2, 508 F9

Taylorville SA 555 O6

Tea Gardens NSW 499 H1, 509 O4

Tea Tree Tas. 622 I3, 474

Teal Flat SA 552 E1, 555 N9

Teal Point Vic. 538 B1, 543 P2, 545 P13

Teddywaddy Vic. 543 M6

Teesdale Vic. 520 D8, 527 M3, 533 P7

Teewah Coloured Sands Qld 383, 427

Telegraph Point NSW 515 O11, 516 F6

Telford Vic. 539 K4

Telita Tas. 627 O7

Telopea Downs Vic. 542 B5, 552 I6, 555 R13

Temma Tas. 626 B6

Temora NSW 507 A2, 508 C10, 511 R8, 49, 67, **98**

Templers SA 550 D4, 555 L7

Templestowe Vic. 519 F6, 521 K6

Templin Qld 599 A10, 399

Tempy Vic. 510 E11, 544 H11

Ten Mile Vic. 521 R3

Ten Mile Hollow NSW 493 N3

Tenandra NSW 514 D11

Tennant Creek NT 591 K10, 348, **358–9**

Tennyson Vic. 538 D5, 543 R7

Tenterden WA 571 L7, 572 H11

Tenterfield NSW 515 M4, 607 N13, 44, **98–9**

Tenth Island Tas. 629 M1, 468

Tepko SA 550 H10, 552 D2, 555 M9

Terang Vic. 526 D6, 533 K8, 148, **197**

Teridgerie NSW 514 E10

Terip Terip Vic. 538 I10

Terka SA 555 J1, 557 J12

Termeil NSW 507 H6, 509 J13

Terowie NSW 508 C3

Terowie SA 555 L3, 557 L13, 250

Terranora NSW 515 Q1, 599 H13, 600 H13

Terrey Hills NSW 491 G3, 493 O6

Terrick Terrick Vic. 538 C4, 543 Q5

Terrick Terrick National Park Vic. 538 C4, 543 Q5, **192–3**

Terrigal NSW 493 Q4, 496 H5, 509 M6, 40, **99**

Territory Wildlife Park NT 586 D4, 346, **357**

Terry Hie Hie NSW 514 H6

Tesbury Vic. 526 F7

Tessellated Pavement Tas. 623 O8, **466**

Teviotville Qld 599 A10

Tewantin Qld 601 G1, 602 G2, 607 Q6, 427

Tewinga NSW 515 O9

Tewkesbury Tas. 626 F6

Texas Qld 515 K3, 607 M12, **433**

Thalaba NSW 492 B13, 507 F2, 508 H9

Thalia Vic. 543 L5

Thallon Qld 514 E2, 606 H12, 431

Thangool Qld 607 K1, 609 N13, 397

Tharbogang NSW 511 N7

Thargomindah Qld 617 N10

Tharwa ACT 505 E11, 506 E7, 507 E6, 508 G13

The Basin WA 572 B4

The Brothers Vic. 507 A11, 536 G7

The Cascade Vic. 536 E3, 539 R5

The Caves Qld 609 N10

The Channon NSW 515 Q2, 90

The Coorong SA 552 D5, 555 M12, 226, 239, 246

The Cove Vic. 526 C9, 533 J10

The Entrance NSW 493 Q3, 496 H2, 509 M6, 40, **99–100**

The Entrance North NSW 493 Q3, 496 H2

The Gap Qld 598 D7

The Gap Vic. 520 H4

The Gardens NT 583 D3

The Gardens Tas. 627 R7

The Glen Tas. 627 L7, 629 N5

The Granites NT 590 D12, 592 D1

The Gulf NSW 515 L4, 607 M13

The Gums Qld 607 K8, 421

The Gurdies Vic. 521 N12, 534 F8

The Heart Vic. 535 N6

The Highlands Vic. 520 G5, 531 P13

The Hill NSW 498 F7

The Junction NSW 498 B8

The Lagoon NSW 492 B5

The Lakes National Park Vic. 535 Q5, 158

The Lynd Qld 611 K11

The Monument Qld 614 F6

The Nobbies Vic. 521 K13, 523 L13, 534 D9, **190**

The Nut Tas. 626 D3, 457, **478**

The Oaks NSW 493 J11, 501 D1, 507 I1, 509 J8, 64

The Palms National Park Qld 607 N7, **426**

The Patch Vic. 519 H7, 521 M7, 524 B12

The Pines SA 554 H9

The Risk NSW 515 P2, 607 P11

The Rock NSW 508 B13, 511 Q11, 103

The Rocks NSW 490 E4, 28, 29, 30

The Sisters Vic. 526 C6, 533 J8

The Summit Qld 515 M2, 607 N12

The Vale NSW 510 H5, 545 O1

Theodore ACT 505 F9

Theodore Qld 607 J2, **433**

Theresa Park NSW 493 K10

Thevenard SA 563 N10, 235

Thirlmere NSW 493 J12, 501 D3, 507 I2, 509 J9, **94**

Thirlmere Lakes National Park NSW 493 J12, 501 D3, 94

Thirlstane Tas. 627 J7, 628 G6

Thirroul NSW 493 M13, 501 H5, 509 K9

Thistle Island SA 554 E9

Thologolong Vic. 511 R13, 536 E1

Thomas Plains SA 555 J6

Thomastown Vic. 519 E4, 521 K5, 534 D3

Thomson Vic. 525 H10

Thomson Bay WA 566 A7

Thoona Vic. 539 L5

Thora NSW 515 O8

Thornborough Qld 611 L6

Thorngate SA 547 D1

Thornlands Qld 598 H9
Thornton NSW 499 D7
Thornton Qld 605 E3, 607 O10
Thornton Vic. 521 P2, 539 K11
Thorpdale Vic. 521 R11, 534 I7,
185
Thowgla Vic. 536 H3
Thowgla Upper Vic. 507 B9,
536 H3
Thredbo NSW 503 C13, 507 C10,
536 I5, 48, 92, **100**
Three Bridges Vic. 521 O7,
524 G11, 534 G4
Three Mile Valley WA **328**
Three Sisters, The NSW 492 H7,
494 E10, 38, 80, 81
Three Springs WA 574 C4
Three Ways Roadhouse NT
591 K10
Thrington SA 554 I6
Thrushton National Park Qld
606 E9, 431
Thuddungra NSW 507 B1, 508 D9
Thulimbah Qld 515 M2, 607 N12
Thulloo NSW 508 A7, 511 P5
Thuringowa Qld 603 G9, 611 P13
Thurla Vic. 544 G4
Thursday Island Qld 612 B2, 353,
392, 437
Thuruna SA 554 E7
Ti Tree NT 592 I5, **359**
Tia NSW 515 M11
Tiaro Qld 607 P4, 421
Tibbuc NSW 509 N1, 515 M13
Tiberias Tas. 625 M6
Tibooburra NSW 512 D3, 19, 51,
100–1
Tichborne NSW 508 D5
Tickera SA 554 I5
Tidal River Vic. 535 J12, 145, 174
Tidbinbilla Nature Reserve ACT
505 A9, 506 C6
Tiega Vic. 544 G9
Tieri Qld 609 J10
Tighes Hill NSW 498 A1
Tilba Tilba NSW 502 H3, 507 H9,
537 R3, 89
Tilmouth Well Roadhouse NT
592 H6
Tilpa NSW 513 J8
Timbarra Vic. 507 B12, 536 H10
Timber Creek NT 588 D13,
590 D2, 347, **359**
Timberoo Vic. 544 G9
Timberoo South Vic. 544 G10
Timbillica NSW 507 F12, 537 P10
Timboon Vic. 526 E9, 533 K10, 191
Timmering Vic. 538 F6
Timor Vic. 531 J4, 543 O11
Timor Sea Vic. 588 B1
Timor West Vic. 531 J4, 543 N11
Tin Can Bay Qld 607 P5, 383,
433–4
Tinaburra Qld 611 M7, 437
Tinamba Vic. 535 M5
Tinaroo Falls Qld 611 M7
Tinbeerwah Qld 601 F1, 602 E2
Tincurrin WA 572 H7
Tindal NT 588 G10
Tinderbox Tas. 622 I8, 625 L9, 471
Tingalpa Qld 598 F7
Tingaringy NSW 507 D11, 537 K7
Tingha NSW 515 K7
Tingoora Qld 607 N6

Tinonee NSW 509 O1, 515 N13,
516 B13
Tintaldra Vic. 507 B8, 536 H1
Tintinara SA 552 F5, 555 O12, 243
Tiona NSW 509 P2, 72
Tiparra West SA 554 I7
Tipplers Qld 599 H9
Tipton Qld 607 M9
Tirranaville NSW 507 G4,
508 H11
Titjikala NT 593 J10, 595 O9
Tittybong Vic. 543 M3, 545 M13
Tivoli Qld 598 B9
Tiwi NT 584 C4
Tiwi (Bathurst and Melville)
Islands NT 588 D2, 346, **358**
Tjukayirla Roadhouse WA
575 M1, 577 L12
Tjuwaliyn (Douglas) Hot Springs
NT 586 G12, 588 E8, 358
Tnorala (Gosse Bluff)
Conservation Reserve NT
592 G8, 594 G5, 354
Tobermorey NT 593 Q5, 614 B8
Tocal Qld 615 N12
Tocumwal NSW 511 M12, 538 I2,
50, **101**
Todd River NT 585 G7, 593 L9,
595 N4, 333, 351
Togari Tas. 626 B4
Togganoggera NSW 507 F6
Toiberry Tas. 627 L9, 629 M13
Tolga Qld 611 M7, 396
Tolmie Vic. 539 M9, 540 E8
Tom Groggin NSW 503 A13
Tom Price WA 573 H4, 576 B5,
265, 289, **326**
Tomahawk Tas. 627 O5
Tomahawk Creek Vic. 526 H8
Tomalla NSW 509 M1, 515 L13
Tomaree National Park NSW
499 H2, 509 O4, 89, **90**
Tombong NSW 507 E11, 537 M7
Tomboye NSW 507 G5, 508 I12
Tomewin Qld 600 D13
Tomingley NSW 508 D3
Tongala Vic. 538 F5
Tonganah Tas. 627 N7, 477
Tonghi Creek Vic. 507 E13,
537 M12
Tongio Vic. 507 A12, 536 G9
Tongio West Vic. 507 A12, 536 F9
Tonimbuk Vic. 521 O8, 534 G5
Tooan Vic. 542 E10
Toobanna Qld 603 D7, 611 N11
Toobeah Qld 514 G1, 607 J11, 412
Tooborac Vic. 538 F10
Toodyay WA 567 G1, 572 E2,
574 D7, 284, **326**
Toogong NSW 508 E6
Toogoolawah Qld 601 A8, 607 O8
Toogoom Qld 607 P3, 414
Tookayerta SA 555 P8
Toolamba Vic. 538 H7
Toolangi Vic. 519 I3, 521 M4,
524 D3, 534 F2, 538 I13, 177–8
Toolern Vale NSW 519 A4, 520 H4,
531 R12, 534 B2, 538 E13
Tooleybuc NSW 510 G10, 545 M9,
196
Toolibin WA 572 H6
Tooligie SA 554 D5
Toolleen Vic. 538 E8
Toolondo Vic. 542 F11

Toolong Vic. 532 G9
Tooloom NSW 515 N2, 607 O12
Tooloom National Park NSW
515 N2
Tooloon NSW 514 C10
Tooma NSW 507 B8, 536 H1, 101
Toombullup Vic. 539 M9, 540 E8
Toomcul Qld 601 A1
Toompine Roadhouse Qld 617 O8,
429
Toongabbie Vic. 535 L6, 197
Toongi NSW 508 E3
Toonumbar NSW 515 O2, 607 P12
Toonumbar National Park NSW
515 O2, 82
Tooperang SA 549 H6
Toora Vic. 535 J10
Tooradin Vic. 519 H11, 521 M10,
523 R3, 534 F7, 180
Tooraweenah NSW 514 E12
Toorbul Qld 598 F1, 599 E1,
601 H8, 401
Toorongo Vic. 521 Q6
Tootgarook Vic. 519 C13, 520 I11,
522 F8
Tootool NSW 508 A13, 511 Q10
Toowong Qld 598 D7
Toowoomba Qld 607 N9, 382, **434**
Toowoon Bay NSW 493 Q3,
496 H3
Top Springs NT 590 F4
Topaz Qld 603 C1, 611 M8
Torbanlea Qld 607 P3
Torndirrup National Park WA
571 N13, 572 I13, 574 F12, 285,
293
Toronto NSW 499 F10, 509 M5
Torquay Vic. 520 F11, 527 O7,
533 Q9, 125, 148, 149, 166, **197**
Torrens Creek Qld 608 B4,
615 Q4, 414
Torres Strait Qld 612 B1, 392, **437**
Torrington NSW 515 L4, 607 N13,
73
Torrita Vic. 510 D10, 544 F9
Torrumbarry Vic. 511 J13, 538 D3
Tostaree Vic. 536 I13
Tottenham NSW 508 B2, 513 R12
Tottington Vic. 530 D2
Toukley NSW 493 Q2, 499 H13,
509 M6, 100
Tourello Vic. 520 C2, 531 J9
Towallum NSW 515 O7
Towamba NSW 502 D11, 507 F12,
537 P8
Towan Vic. 545 L9
Towaninny Vic. 543 M3
Tower Hill Tas. 627 P9
Tower Hill Vic. 532 H9
Tower Hill State Game Reserve
Vic. 532 H9
Towitta SA 550 I5
Townsville Qld 603, 611 P12, 363,
390, **434–5**
Towong Vic. 507 B8, 536 H2
Towong Upper Vic. 507 B8,
536 H2
Towradgi NSW 500 G3, 501 H5
Towrang NSW 507 G3, 508 I10
Tracy SA 555 M4
Trafalgar Vic. 521 R10, 534 I7,
185
Tragowel Vic. 538 B2, 543 P4
Trangie NSW 508 C1

Traralgon Vic. 535 K7, 144, **197**
Traralgon South Vic. 535 K7
Trawalla NSW 514 H5
Trawalla Vic. 520 A3, 530 G10,
533 M3
Trawool Vic. 538 H10
Trayning WA 572 H1, 574 E7
Traynors Lagoon Vic. 543 K8
Treasures Homestead Vic.
541 O11
Trebonne Qld 603 D6, 611 N11
Treeton WA 568 C9, 569 D6,
572 B9
Tregole National Park Qld
606 D6, **404**
Trenah Tas. 627 O8
Trentham Vic. 520 F3, 531 P9,
533 R2, 538 C12, 543 R13, **181**
Trentham Cliffs NSW 544 H3
Trentham East Vic. 520 G3,
531 P10
Tresco Vic. 510 H11, 543 O1,
545 O12
Tresco West Vic. 543 N1, 545 N12
Trevallyn NSW 509 M3
Trevallyn Tas. 627 L8, 629 N10
Trewalla Vic. 532 D9
Trewilga NSW 508 D4
Triabunna Tas. 623 O1, 625 O6,
479–80
Trial Harbour Tas. 624 C2,
626 D11, 481
Trida NSW 511 L3
Trida Vic. 521 P11
Trinita Vic. 544 H8
Trinity Beach Qld 604 D5
Trinity Park Qld 604 E6
Tropical North Islands Qld 385,
386
Troubridge Island SA 554 I10,
225, 238
Trowutta Tas. 626 C5
Truck 'n' Travel Roadhouse Qld
515 M1
Trundle NSW 508 C4
Trunkey NSW 492 A8, 508 G7, 57
Truro SA 550 H3, 555 M7
Tuan Qld 607 P4
Tuart Forest National Park WA
568 F6, 569 H1, **297**
Tubbul NSW 507 B2, 508 D9
Tubbut Vic. 507 D11, 537 K8
Tucabia NSW 515 P6
Tuckanarra WA 574 E1, 576 B12,
578 I12
Tucklan NSW 508 G2
Tuena NSW 492 A10, 507 F1,
508 G8, 69
Tuggerah NSW 493 P3, 496 F2,
40, 108
Tuggeranong ACT 505 E8, 506 E5
Tuggerawong NSW 496 G1
Tugun Qld 600 G10
Tulendeena Tas. 627 O7
Tulkara Vic. 530 D4, 543 K11
Tullah Tas. 626 F10
Tullamore NSW 508 B3, 511 R1
Tullibigeal NSW 511 P4
Tulloh Vic. 520 B12, 526 I8
Tully Qld 603 D3, 611 N9, 363,
435
Tully Gorge National Park Qld
603 B2, **435**
Tully Heads Qld 603 D4, 611 N9

Publications manager
Astrid Browne

Editor
Rachel Pitts

Design
Internal pages by Peter Dyson –
P.A.G.E. Pty Ltd; cover by KPD

Layout
P.A.G.E. Pty Ltd

Illustrated maps
Katherine Haynes

Cartographers
Paul de Leur, Claire Johnston, Mike
Archer, Bruce McGurty

Copyeditors
Brigid James, Alexandra Payne,
Helen Duffy, Rachel Pitts, Astrid
Browne

Editorial assistant
Karina Biggs

Proofreader
Bettina Stevenson

Indexer
Fay Donlevy

Photo selection
Rachel Pitts

Pre-press
Digital Imaging Group Pty Ltd

Writers
NEW SOUTH WALES *Introduction*
Carolyn Tate *Sydney* Ruth Ward
Towns Carolyn Tate ACT *Canberra*
Alexandra Payne VICTORIA
Introduction Rachel Pitts *Melbourne*
Rachel Pitts *Towns* Karina Biggs,
Antonia Semler SOUTH AUSTRALIA
Introduction Sue Medlock *Adelaide*
Terry Plane, Rachel Pitts *Towns*
Karina Biggs, Rachel Pitts WESTERN
AUSTRALIA *Introduction, Perth and
Towns* Heather Pearson NORTHERN
TERRITORY *Introduction and
Darwin* David Hancock *Towns*
Carolyn Tate, Helen Duffy
QUEENSLAND *Introduction* Sue
Medlock *Brisbane* Alexandra Payne
Towns Karina Biggs TASMANIA
Introduction and Hobart Sue
Medlock *Towns* Emma Schwarcz

Journey through Australia and state
regions originally written by Ingrid
Ohlsson with assistance from Tony
Ohlsson

Assistance with research

The publisher would like to thank the following
organisations for assistance with information:

Australian Bureau of Statistics
Bureau of Meteorology
National Road Transport Commission
St John Ambulance

New South Wales
Roads and Traffic Authority
New South Wales National Parks & Wildlife Service
Tourism New South Wales

ACT
Australian Capital Territory Land Information Centre
Australian Capital Tourism Corporation

Victoria
VicRoads
Parks Victoria
Tourism Victoria

South Australia
Transport SA
Primary Industries and Resources South Australia
National Parks & Wildlife South Australia,
 Department of Environment & Heritage
South Australian Tourist Commission

Western Australia
Main Roads Western Australia
Aboriginal Affairs Department Western Australia
Aboriginal Lands Trust
Department of Conservation & Land Management
 Western Australia
Western Australia Tourism Commission

Northern Territory
Department of Transport and Infrastructure
Northern and Central land councils
Northern Territory Department of Lands, Planning
 and the Environment
Parks Australia
Nothern Territory Tourist Commission

Queensland
Department of Main Roads
Queensland Department of Natural Resources &
 Mines
Queensland Parks & Wildlife Service
Tourism Queensland

Tasmania
Department of Infrastructure, Energy & Resources
Parks and Wildlife Service
Tourism Tasmania

Photography credits

Cover
Camels on Cable Beach, Broome *Wildlight (Hugh
Brown)*; Shark Bay *Ted Mead*

Back cover
Boardwalk through rainforest *Getty Images (Glen
Allison)*

Half-title page
Lake Gairdner, South Australia *Jeff Drewitz
Photography*

Title page
Magela Creek, Kakadu National Park *Auscape
International (Jaime Plaza Van Roon)*

Contents
Gantheaume Point, near Broome *Andrew Gregory*

Journey through Australia opening page
Vegetation on Mt Rufus, Cradle Mountain–Lake St
Clair National Park *Auscape International (Dennis
Harding)*

Pages 2–3 *(main photo)* Anangu Tours *(left to right)* (a) NR (b) AUS (JF) (c) Stock Photos (Rogge Otto) (d) Tourism New South Wales (e) BB (f) Tandanya – National Aboriginal Cultural Institute; 4–5 *(main photo)* Sovereign Hill Museums Association *(left to right)* (a) AUS (JLR) *(left to right)* (a) SFP (JS) (b) AUS (GL) (c) Chris Groenhout (d) EAP (JB) (e) AUS (TA) (f) AUS (David Messent) (g) AUS (David Messent); 8–9 *(main photo)* AUS (JF) *(left to right)* (a) TQ (Susan Wright) (b) JM (c) EAP (Gary Lewis) (d) Tourism Tasmania (GM) (e) AUS (JF) (f) TQ; 10–11 *(main photo)* AUS (JF) *(left to right)* (a) JM (b) JD (c) BB (d) Tourism Tasmania (George Apostolidis) (e) Christo Reid (f) AUS (JF); 12–13 *(main photo)* AUS (JF) *(left to right)* (a) AUS (JF) (b) LT (JL) (c) AUS (JF) (d) AUS (John Cancalosi) (e) EAP (Gary Lewis) (f) LT (Nick Gales) *(flowers top to bottom)* (a) ANGB (b) ANBG (c) AUS (Mark Newton) (d) ANGB (e) SATC (f) ANGB (g) ANGB (h) ANGB (i) ANBG; 14–15 *(main photo)* Grant Dixon *(left to right)* (a) Stock Photos (Kelvin Aitken) (b) Alex Julius (c) BB (d) AUS (Mark Spencer) (e) AUS (Glenn Tempest) (f) JD; 16–17 AUS (JF); 19 AUS (TA); 20–1 AUS (TA); 26 AUS (JLR); 29 AUS (JF); 30 AUS (JF); 32 AUS (JF); 38 AUS (Tom Till); 39 EAP; 40 JM; 41 AUS (JF); 42 AUS (JP); 43 AG; 44 NR; 45 BB; 46 EAP (JB); 47 JM; 48 AUS (TA); 49 GM; 50 AUS (JLR); 51 GM; 52 AUS (JF); 53 JM; 55 JD; 56 AUS (JF); 59 GM; 60 BB; 63 AUS (JF); 65 AUS (Karen Gowlett-Holmes–Oxford Scientific Films); 66 GM; 69 AC; 70 JD; 73 JD; 74 AUS (JF); 77 AC; 78 AUS (Marianne F. Porteners); 80 AUS (BG); 83 JD; 84 JD; 87 JM; 89 EAP; 91 AUS (BA); 92 JD; 94 EAP; 96 AUS (BG); 99 AUS (BG); 100 Boris Hlavaca; 103 AUS (WL); 104 EAP; 106 JM; 109 JB; 110–11 AUS (Michael Jensen); 112–13 Chris Groenhout; 118 JB; 120 JB; 121 JB; 122–3 AG; 125 JM; 126–7 AC; 133 Chris Groenhout; 135 AC; 136 AC; 139 AC; 142 AC; 143 BB; 144 AUS (MLE); 145 AUS (Davo Blair); 146 JM; 147 AC; 148 AUS (JF); 149 JM; 150 AUS (MLE); 151 AUS (JLR); 152 JD; 153 LT (Marie Lochman); 154 JM; 155 JM; 156 (EAP) NR; 157 JB; 158 JM; 159 AC; 161 AC; 162 AUS (JLR); 166 JM; 168 AUS (JLR); 171 JD; 173 AC; 174 AUS (JF); 177 National Library of Australia; 178 AUS (MLE); 180 AUS (JLR); 183 AUS (JLR); 184 AUS (JLR); 186 AUS (JLR); 188 AC; 190 Paul Sinclair; 192 JM; 194 JD; 197 AUS (JLR); 198 GM; 201 BD; 202 AUS (MLE); 204–5 JD; 207 TM; 208–9 NR; 214 SATC; 216 EAP; 220 JM; 221 JM; 222 Christo Reid; 223 JD; 224 JM; 225 SATC; 226 BB; 227 SATC; 228 Boris Hlavaca; 229 TM; 230 Christo Reid; 233 EAP; 235 JD; 237 AUS (JLR); 238 SATC; 241 BB; 242 LT (Nick Gales); 245 AUS (David Messent); 247 AUS (JLR); 249 AUS (JLR); 251 NR; 252 AG; 255 JM; 256 JD; 259 AUS (JF); 260 JD; 262–3 AUS (JF); 265 JD; 266–7 LT (Peter & Margy Nicholas); 271 LT (LS); 272 JD; 273 AG; 275 LT (DS); 277 AG; 278 AUS (JF); 280 AUS (JF); 281 LT (LS); 282 AG; 283 LT (JL); 284 JD; 285 JD; 286 AUS (JLR); 287 LT (JL); 288 LT (JL); 289 BB; 290 AG; 291 BB; 292 AUS (JLR); 294 JD; 296 AG; 298 JD; 301 AUS (BLC); 303 LT (JL); 305 AUS (Greg Harold); 307 AG; 308 LT (DS); 311 EAP; 313 LT (DS); 314 LT (BD); 317 BB; 319 BB; 321 LT (DS); 323 LT (JL); 325 BB; 327 AG; 329 LT (LS); 330–1 TM; 333 AG; 334–5 AG; 339 SS (DH); 340 Wildlight (Hugh Brown); 344 TM; 345 SS (DH); 346 SS (DH); 347 SS (DH); 348 BB; 349 DH; 350 NR; 352 TM; 355 AUS (JF); 356 SS (DH); 358 SS (DH); 360–1 AUS (BLC); 363 JB; 364–5 JD; 370 TQ; 372 TQ; 374 TQ; 376 TQ; 378 JD; 379 AG; 380 NR; 381 AUS (JF); 382 TQ; 383 NR; 384 AUS (JF); 385 AUS (JF); 386 AG; 387 NR; 388 AUS (JP); 389 NR; 390 JM; 391 AUS (ML); 392 AUS (BA); 393 GM; 394 NR; 395 JD; 396 EAP; 398 JD; 401 AUS (JF); 403 AG; 405 NR; 407 AUS (Ferrero-Labat); 408 AUS (WL); 410 NR; 413 AUS (JF); 415 JM; 416 TQ; 419 NR; 421 JM; 422 AG; 424 JD; 427 AUS (JF); 429 JB; 430 AUS (WL); 433 AUS (WL); 434 AUS (JF); 437 AUS (JF); 438–9 SFP (JS); 441 GM; 442–3 GM; 448 AUS (Graham Robinson); 451 TM; 453 AUS (GR); 454 AUS (GL); 455 SFP (JS); 456 TM; 457 BB; 458 AUS (Dennis Harding); 459 JM; 460 JM; 462 BB; 464 AUS (Dennis Harding); 466 JM; 468 AUS (BA); 470 SFP (JS); 472 AUS (GR); 473 JD; 475 SFP (JS); 476 BB; 478 SFP (JS); 479 AUS (GR); 481 AUS (JP)

Abbreviations

AC Andrew Chapman
 Photography
AG Andrew Gregory
ANBG Australian
 National Botanic
 Gardens
AUS Auscape
 International
BA Barry Ashenhurst
BB Bill Bachman
BD Brett Dennis

BG Brett Gregory
BLC Ben & Lynn Cropp
DH David Hancock
DS Dennis Sarson
EAP Explore Australia
 Publishing
GL Geoffrey Lea
GM Geoff Murray
JD Jeff Drewitz
 Photography
JB J. P. & E. S. Baker

JF Jean-Paul Ferrero
JL Jiri Lochman
JM John Meier
JLR Jean-Marc La Roque
JP Jaime Plaza Van Roon
JS Joe Shemesh
LS Len Stewart
LT Lochman
 Transparencies
ML Mike Langford
MLE Mike Leonard

NR Nick Rains
 Photography
SATC South Australian
 Tourism Commission
SFP Storm Front
 Productions
SS Skyscans
TA Tim Acker
TM Ted Mead
TQ Tourism Queensland
WL Wayne Lawler

Explore Australia Publishing Pty Ltd
85–97A High Street
Prahran 3181

This twenty-third edition published by
Explore Australia Publishing Pty Ltd,
2004

First published by George Phillip &
O'Neil Pty Ltd, 1980

Second edition 1981

Third edition 1983

Reprinted 1984

Fourth edition 1985

Fifth edition 1986

Sixth edition published by Penguin
Books Australia Ltd, 1987

Seventh edition 1988

Eighth edition 1989

Ninth edition 1990

Tenth edition 1991

Eleventh edition 1992

Twelfth edition 1993

Thirteenth edition 1994

Fourteenth edition 1995

Fifteenth edition 1996

Sixteenth edition 1997

Seventeenth edition 1998

Eighteenth edition 1999

Nineteenth edition 2000

Twentieth edition 2001

Twenty-first edition 2002

Twenty-second edition 2003

Copyright © Explore Australia
Publishing Pty Ltd, 2004

ISBN 1 74117 086 9

Printed and bound in China by
Midas Printing (Asia) Ltd

Publisher's Note: Every effort has been
made to ensure that the information in
this book is accurate at the time of
going to press. The publisher
welcomes information and suggestions
for correction or improvement. Write
to the Publications Manager, Explore
Australia Publishing, 85–97A High
Street, Prahran 3181, Australia, or
email explore@hardiegrant.com.au

Disclaimers: The publisher cannot
accept responsibility for any errors or
omissions. The representation on the
maps of any road or track is not
necessarily evidence of public right
of way.

SUGGESTION FORM

This 23rd edition of Explore Australia is updated from information supplied by consultants, tourist organisations and the general public. We would welcome suggestions from you.

SUGGESTED AMENDMENT OR ADDITION

TEXT

Page no	Amendment/Addition

MAPS

Page no	Grid	Amendment/Addition

GENERAL COMMENTS

_____

_____

_____

_____

OPTIONAL

Name: _____

Address: _____

_____

Phone no.: _____ email address: _____

Place of purchase (shop name and suburb/town): _____

Date of purchase: _____

Age group:

20 and under ☐	20–29 ☐	30–39 ☐
40–49 ☐	50–59 ☐	60 and over ☐

I would like to receive information on new and updated guides, maps and atlases in the _Explore Australia_ range:
YES/NO (please indicate)

Please cut out and send to: Publications Manager, Explore Australia Publishing, Private bag 1600, South Yarra, Victoria 3141. Alternatively, email your comments to explore@hardiegrant.com.au

USEFUL INFORMATION

STATE TOURIST BUREAUS

New South Wales
Sydney Visitor Centres
106 George St, The Rocks
(02) 9240 8788

Palm Grove, Darling Harbour
(02) 9240 8788
www.visitnsw.com.au

New South Wales Visitor
Information Line
13 2077

Canberra
Canberra Visitor Centre
333 Northbourne Ave, Dickson
(02) 6205 0044; 1300 554 114
www.visitcanberra.com.au

Victoria
Melbourne Visitor Information
Centre
Federation Square
Cnr Flinders St and St Kilda Rd
Melbourne
(03) 9658 9658
www.visitvictoria.com

Victorian Tourism Information
Service
13 2842

South Australia
South Australia Visitor and Travel
Centre
18 King William St, Adelaide
(08) 8303 2220; 1300 655 276
www.southaustralia.com

Western Australia
Western Australia Visitor Centre
Albert Facey House
Cnr Forrest Pl and Wellington St
Perth
(08) 9483 1111; 1300 361 351
www.westernaustralia.net

Northern Territory
Tourism Top End
Cnr Mitchell and Knuckey sts
Darwin
(08) 8936 2499; 1300 138 886
www.tourismtopend.com.au

Central Australian Tourism Industry
Association
60 Gregory Tce, Alice Springs
(08) 8952 5800; 1800 645 199
www.centralaustraliantourism.com

Queensland
Brisbane Visitor Information Centre
Cnr Albert and Queen sts
Queen Street Mall, Brisbane
(07) 3006 6290
www.queenslandholidays.com.au

Queensland Visitor Information
Line
13 8833

Tasmania
Tasmania Travel and Information
Centre
Cnr Davey and Elizabeth sts, Hobart
(03) 6230 8233
www.discovertasmania.com.au

MOTORING ORGANISATIONS

Roadside assistance is one of the
most valued services of Australia's
state-based motoring organisations.
The country-wide network of these
organisations gives members access
to virtually the same services in
every state and territory.

Roadside assistance (country-wide)
13 1111

New South Wales
National Roads and Motorists'
Association (NRMA)
74–76 King St, Sydney
13 1122
www.nrma.com.au

Australian Capital Territory
National Roads and Motorists'
Association (NRMA)
333 Northbourne Ave, Braddon
13 1122
www.nrma.com.au

Victoria
Royal Automobile Club of Victoria
(RACV)
422 Little Collins St, Melbourne
13 1955
www.racv.com.au

South Australia
Royal Automobile Association (RAA)
55 Hindmarsh Sq, Adelaide
(08) 8202 4600
www.raa.net

Western Australia
Royal Automobile Club of Western
Australia (RAC)
228 Adelaide Tce, Perth
13 1704
www.rac.com.au

Northern Territory
Automobile Association of Northern
Territory (AANT)
AANT Building
81 Smith St, Darwin
(08) 8981 3837
www.aant.com.au

Queensland
Royal Automobile Club of
Queensland (RACQ)
GPO Building
261 Queen St, Brisbane
13 1905
www.racq.com.au

Tasmania
Royal Automobile Club of Tasmania
(RACT)
Cnr Patrick and Murray sts, Hobart
13 2722; (03) 6232 6300
www.ract.com.au

For Motorcyclists
Motorcycle Riders Association
Australia
22 Ross St, South Melbourne
(03) 9699 1811
www.mraa.org.au

ROADS AND TRAFFIC AUTHORITIES

For licensing and registration,
information on vehicle standards,
and road condition reports.

New South Wales
Roads and Traffic Authority
Centennial Plaza
260 Elizabeth St, Surry Hills
13 2213
www.rta.nsw.gov.au

Australian Capital Territory
Road User Services
Department of Urban Services
13–15 Challis St, Dickson
(02) 6207 7000
www.urbanservices.act.gov.au

Victoria
VicRoads
459 Lygon St, Carlton
13 1171
www.vicroads.vic.gov.au

South Australia
Transport SA
EDS Centre
108 North Tce, Adelaide
13 1084
www.transport.sa.gov.au

Western Australia
Department for Planning and
Infrastructure
Cnr Troode St and Plaistowe Mews,
West Perth
13 1156; (08) 9427 6404
www.dpi.wa.gov.au
www.mainroads.wa.gov.au

Northern Territory
Transport and Infrastructure
Division
Department of Infrastructure,
Planning and Environment
Energy House
20 Cavenagh St, Darwin
(08) 8999 3111
www.nt.gov.au/dtw

Queensland
Queensland Transport
229 Elizabeth St, Brisbane
13 2380
www.transport.qld.gov.au

Tasmania
Transport Division
Department of Infrastructure,
Energy and Resources
10 Murray St, Hobart
1300 135 513
www.transport.tas.gov.au

ACCOMMODATION

General
State-based motoring organisations
are a good point of contact for
information on accommodation in
motels, apartments and caravan
parks. All share a comprehensive
accommodation database that can
be accessed from their websites.

Caravan Parks
Top Tourist Parks
(08) 8363 1901
www.toptouristparks.com.au

Big4 Parks
1800 632 444
www.big4.com.au

Family Parks of Australia
1800 682 492
www.familyparks.com.au

Bed and Breakfasts
Bed and Breakfast Australia
(02) 9763 5833
www.bedandbreakfast.com.au

Backpackers
VIP Backpackers Resorts of Australia
(07) 3395 6111
www.vipbackpackers.com

YHA Australia
(02) 9261 1111
www.yha.com.au

Farmstays
Australia-wide/New South Wales
Australian Farm Host Holidays
(02) 9810 0800
www.australiafarmhost.com

Victoria
Farm and Country Tourism Victoria
(03) 9614 0892
www.factv.com

South Australia
SA Farm and Country Holidays
(08) 8296 3617

EMERGENCY

**DIAL 000 FOR POLICE,
AMBULANCE & FIRE BRIGADE**

Accident Action – Feel Confident with St John First Aid

It is reassuring to know that you have the simple skills to preserve life if, at any moment, you are confronted with an emergency.

Priorities at an Accident Site

In dealing with the casualties of an accident, the St John DRABC Action Plan remains the first priority. However, an accident brings in other factors that have to be considered. The following guidelines will help:

Hazards:

- Make sure everyone at accident site is protected, by safely parking your car and putting hazard lights on
- Light up a night accident scene with headlights
- Assess scene for other dangers and remove if possible
- Move casualty from danger if this is more appropriate (e.g. if there is a fire)

Assessment:

Make a rapid assessment of:
- Number of casualties
- Severity of injuries
- Any dangerous circumstances to report
- Whether anyone is trapped

Ensure all occupants of cars are accounted for.

Help:

- Call 000 for an ambulance and police
- Consider need to call other services (e.g. fire brigade, electricity authority)

Follow the remainder of the St John DRABC Action Plan to manage casualties.

St John DRABC Action Plan

This Action Plan is a vital aid to the first aider in assessing whether the casualty has any life-threatening conditions and if any immediate first aid is necessary.

D - check for Danger
- to you
- to others
- to casualty

R - check Response
- is casualty conscious?
- is casualty unconscious?
  If not responsive, turn casualty into the recovery position and **ring 000 for an ambulance.**

A - check Airway
- is airway clear of objects?
- is airway open?

B - check for Breathing
- is chest rising and falling?
- can you hear casualty's breathing?
- can you feel the breath on your cheek?

C - check for signs of Circulation
- can you see any movement including swallowing or breathing?
- can you see any obvious signs of life?
- can you feel a pulse?

In any life-threatening situation, ring 000 for an ambulance. If possible, ask someone to do this for you so that you can stay with the casualty.

Learn St John First Aid